Israel
and the
Palestinian Territories

THE ROUGH GUIDE

There are more than one hundred Rough Guide titles
covering destinations from Amsterdam to Zimbabwe

Forthcoming titles include
Bangkok • Central America • Chile • Japan

Rough Guide Reference Series
Classical Music • European Football • The Internet • Jazz
Opera • Reggae • Rock Music • World Music

Rough Guide Phrasebooks
Czech • Egyptian Arabic • French • German • Greek
Hindi & Urdu • Hungarian • Indonesian • Italian • Japanese
Mandarin Chinese • Mexican Spanish • Polish• Portuguese
Russian • Spanish • Swahili • Thai • Turkish • Vietnamese

Rough Guides on the Internet
www.roughguides.com

ROUGH GUIDE CREDITS

Text editors: Caroline Osborne and Vivienne Heller
Series editor: Mark Ellingham
Editorial: Martin Dunford, Jonathan Buckley, Samantha
Cook, Jo Mead, Kate Berens, Amanda Tomlin,
Ann-Marie Shaw, Paul Gray, Chris Schüler, Judith Bamber,
Kieran Falconer, Orla Duane, Olivia Eccleshall, Ruth
Blackmore, Sophie Martin, Jennifer Dempsey, Sue Jackson,
Geoff Howard (UK); Andrew Rosenberg, Andrew Taber (US)
Production: Susanne Hillen, Andy Hilliard, Judy Pang,
Link Hall, Helen Ostick, James Morris, Julia Bovis

Cartography: Melissa Flack, Maxine Burke, Nichola
Goodliffe
Picture research: Eleanor Hill
Online editors: Alan Spicer, Kate Hands (UK); Geronimo
Madrid (US)
Finance: John Fisher, Celia Crowley, Neeta Mistry
Marketing & Publicity: Richard Trillo, Simon Carloss,
Niki Smith (UK); Jean-Marie Kelly, SoRelle Braun (US)
Administration: Tania Hummel, Alexander Mark Rogers

ACKNOWLEDGEMENTS

The author and contributors were aided in their research
for this book by a number of people and organizations of
very different persuasions, who do not necessarily
endorse any of the views or attitudes expressed in the
guide. Among those we would like to thank are:

In Israel: Haimke and Anna Margolin; Nick Day of *The
Traveller* magazine; Uncle Ted at the *Petra Hostel*
(Jerusalem); Hannan Shlomsky; Aya Tse'elim; Yossi
Mautner; Ilan Ronnell of Krembo Records; Matta Abdo of
Bet HaGefen (Haifa); Hassan Ghafari; Shlomo Zelkine;
Kovi and Debbie Sokol; Desert Shade in Mitzpe Ramon;
the SPNI in Tel Aviv; the municipality of Ramle; the IGTO
in Tel Aviv and Haifa, and the municipal tourist offices of
Ashdod and Ashqelon.

In the Palestinian Territories: Fahmi Nashabahibi of
the *Pilgrims Palace Hotel* in Jerusalem; Hani Abu-Dayyeh
of NET Tours; Sa'ad Abdul Hadi; Yasir at the *al-Ahram
Hostel* in Jerusalem; Yousef Shahin at the *Hebron Hotel*;
Osama Rached of the PNA Tourist Ministry in Gaza;
Mr Jamal and Mr Kamal at the PNA Tourist Ministry in
Nablus; the staff of the PNA tourist office in Bethlehem

and the Christian Information Centre in Jerusalem; and
the town planning departments of the municipalities of
Nablus and Gaza.

In London: Matthew Teller; Noam and Louise Margolin;
Percy and Cynthia Jacobs; Rev. Bernard Koshland; Hedia
Bakal; Virginia Myers; the staff of the IGTO; Meisoon
Shorafa of the Palestinian General Delegation; and the
Council for the Advancement of Arab–British
Understanding, in particular John Gee.

Thanks also to Jack Holland for getting the ball rolling
and to Martin Dunford and Sam Cook for keeping it
rolling, to Caroline Osborne and Vivienne Heller for
patient and sympathetic editing, to Narrell Leffman in
Australia, and Melanie Ross in the USA for additional
Basics research, Maxine Burke and Kingston
Presentation Graphics for their cartographic art and pre-
cision, to James Morris and Judy Pang for masterful
typesetting, to Carole Mansur for hawk-eyed proofread-
ing, to Eleanor Hill for sorting, selecting and arranging
the photos, and to Jessica Goldberg and Judy Margolin
for their sound appraisal and advice.

PUBLISHING INFORMATION

This second edition published September 1998 by
  Rough Guides Ltd, 62–70 Shorts Gardens,
  London WC2H 9AB. Previous edition by Shirley Eber
  and Kevin O'Sullivan, 1989.
  Distributed by the Penguin Group:
Penguin Books Ltd, 27 Wrights Lane, London W8 5TZ.
Penguin Books USA Inc., 375 Hudson Street, New York
  10014, USA.
Penguin Books Australia Ltd, 487 Maroondah Highway,
  PO Box 257, Ringwood, Victoria 3134, Australia.
Penguin Books Canada Ltd, 10 Alcorn Avenue, Toronto,
  Ontario, Canada M4V 1E4.
Penguin Books (NZ) Ltd, 182–190 Wairau Road,
  Auckland 10, New Zealand.
Typeset in Linotron Univers and Century Old Style to an
  original design by Andrew Oliver.
Printed in England by Clays Ltd, St Ives PLC.
Illustrations in Part One and Part Three by Edward Briant.

© Daniel Jacobs 1998
No part of this book may be reproduced in any form
  without permission from the publisher except for the
  quotation of brief passages in reviews.
560pp – Includes index.
A catalogue record for this book is available from the
  British Library.
ISBN 1-85828-248-9

The publishers and authors have done their best to
  ensure the accuracy and currency of all the information
  in *The Rough Guide to Israel and the Palestinian
  Territories*; however, they can accept no responsibility
  for any loss, injury, or inconvenience sustained by any
  traveller as a result of information or advice contained
  in the guide.

Israel
and the
Palestinian Territories

THE ROUGH GUIDE

written and researched by
Daniel Jacobs

with additional contributions from
Shirley Eber (author of first edition)
and Francesca Silvani

THE ROUGH GUIDES

THE ROUGH GUIDES

TRAVEL GUIDES • PHRASEBOOKS • MUSIC AND REFERENCE GUIDES

 We set out to do something different when the first Rough Guide was published in 1982. Mark Ellingham, just out of university, was travelling in Greece. He brought along the popular guides of the day, but found they were all lacking in some way. They were either strong on ruins and museums but went on for pages without mentioning a beach or taverna. Or they were so conscious of the need to save money that they lost sight of Greece's cultural and historical significance. Also, none of the books told him anything about Greece's contemporary life – its politics, its culture, its people, and how they lived.

So with no job in prospect, Mark decided to write his own guidebook, one that aimed to provide practical information that was second to none, detailing the best beaches and the hottest clubs and restaurants, while also giving hard-hitting accounts of every sight, both famous and obscure, and providing up-to-the-minute information on contemporary culture. It was a guide that encouraged independent travellers to find the best of Greece, and was a great success, getting shortlisted for the Thomas Cook travel guide award,

and encouraging Mark, along with three friends, to expand the series.

The Rough Guide list grew rapidly and the letters flooded in, indicating a much broader readership than had been anticipated, but one which uniformly appreciated the Rough Guide mix of practical detail and humour, irreverence and enthusiasm. Things haven't changed. The same four friends who began the series are still the caretakers of the Rough Guide mission today: to provide the most reliable, up-to-date and entertaining information to independent-minded travellers of all ages, on all budgets.

We now publish a hundred titles and have offices in London and New York. The travel guides are written and researched by a dedicated team of more than a hundred authors, based in Britain, Europe, the USA and Australia. We have also created a unique series of phrasebooks to accompany the travel series, along with an acclaimed series of music guides, and a best-selling pocket guide to the Internet and World Wide Web. We also publish comprehensive travel information on our Web site:

www.roughguides.com

HELP US UPDATE

We've gone to a lot of effort to ensure that this edition of The Rough Guide to Israel and the Palestinian Territories is accurate and up-to-date. However, places get "discovered"; telephone numbers change; restaurants, hotels and other tourist facilities raise prices or lower standards; archeological sites close and reopen after excavations; and, here especially, political developments and disturbances can influence accessibility and advisability of visiting certain towns and sites of interest. If you feel we've got it wrong or left something out, we'd like to know, and if you can remember the address, price, the time, the phone number, so much the better.

We'll credit all contributions, and send a copy of the next edition (or any other Rough Guide if you prefer) for the best letters. Please mark letters: "Rough Guide Israel and the Palestinian Territories Update" and send to:
Rough Guides Ltd, 62–70 Shorts Gardens, London WC2H 9AB, or Rough Guides, 375 Hudson St, 9th Floor, New York, NY 10014.
Or send email to: *mail@roughguides.co.uk*
Online updates about this book can be found on Rough Guides' Web site at *www.roughguides.com*

THE AUTHOR

Daniel Jacobs has contributed to numerous Rough Guides, including West Africa, Morocco, Egypt and India, and is co-author of *The Rough Guide to Tunisia*. He lives in South London, and is a non-practising Jew.

CONTENTS

Introduction xi

PART THREE CONTEXTS   479

LIST OF MAPS

MAP SYMBOLS

Railway		Cave	
Major road		Airport	
Road		Bus stop	
Path		Parking	
Waterway		Tourist office	
Chapter division boundary		Post office	
Undisputed international border		Building	
Other border		Church	
Wall		Christian cemetery	
Accommodation		Muslim cemetery	
Eating Places		Jewish cemetery	
Hill		Park	
Peak		Beach	
Viewpoint			

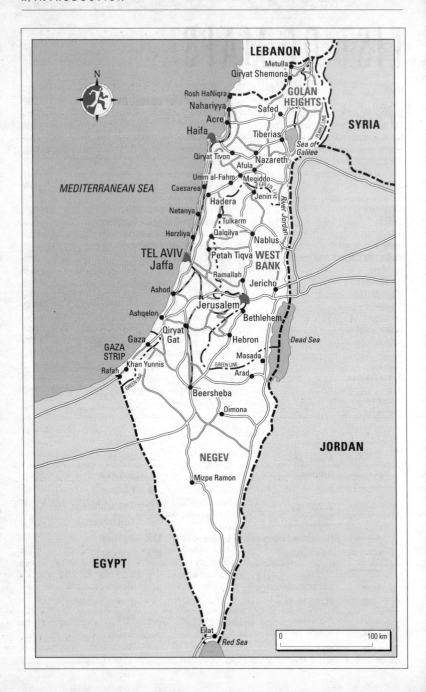

INTRODUCTION

P ositioned uniquely between Europe, Africa and the Middle East, and at the centre of three major monotheistic religions – Judaism, Christianity and Islam – the Holy Land has been fought over since biblical times. Given its extraordinary significance, it often comes as a surprise, therefore, to learn that what is now Israel and the Palestinian Territories of the West Bank and the Gaza Strip together take up an area only one and a half times the size of Wales or slightly larger than the state of Maryland, and contain a tiny, yet fractious, population of just 5.5 million.

Packed into this small region is an astonishing range of **scenery**: from the sandy beaches of the Mediterranean coastal strip, inland to the green valleys of the Galilee and goat-tracked, olive-groved hills of the West Bank – largely unchanged backdrops to many biblical events; from the towering, snowcapped peak of Mount Hermon northeast in the Golan Heights, south to the Dead Sea – the lowest point on earth – and the lunar landscapes of the Negev desert, at whose southernmost tip lie the spectacular coral reefs of the Red Sea. It's home too, to some of the world's **holiest sites**; visiting them and the abundant **historic monuments** to its troubled past, you'll be walking in the footsteps of David and Solomon, of Jesus and Mohammed, and of the numerous armies – Roman, Crusader and otherwise – who have conquered the region. Add to the pot a handful of vibrant **cities** – primarily cosmopolitan Tel Aviv and the holy city of Jerusalem – and you have an unrivalled density and variety of things to see, often only a couple of hours apart.

Sooner or later, however, even on the most hedonistic beach vacation, you're going to come face to face with the **complexities** and contrasts of a region that eludes easy definitions – whether geographical, political or cultural. It's here that East meets West head on, with all the bizarre juxtapositions that brings – religion and secularism, tradition and innovation, Jewish-Arab synthesis and Jewish-Arab conflict. The political situation, in particular, hits you as soon as you arrive. For all the millennia of **religious and political strife**, the question that has dominated the area since the State of Israel came into being just over fifty years ago is: one country or two? Though increasingly seen as the latter – Israel and Palestine – there are still those on both sides who deny the other's right to exist. But for all the fits and starts that the peace process has been through, attitudes have mellowed, and most Israeli Jews and Palestinian Arabs, however reluctantly, now accept each other's claim to nationhood, and even each other's right to self-determination. Even so, it's not always clear where one ends and the other begins: Israeli settlements dot the West Bank and Gaza Strip, while in Israel itself, nearly one in five of the population are Arabs, most of whom regard themselves as Palestinians. As a visitor you are unlikely to encounter trouble, but conflict still simmers.

Inhabiting this complicated yet intoxicating melting pot is a multicultural **population** equally difficult to classify. Though it belongs, for the most part, to one of two ethnic groups – Israeli Jews and Palestinian Arabs – there are a plethora of subdivisions within both. Israeli Jews can be religious or secular, and ethnically Sephardi or Ashkenazi, while further diversity arises from each Jewish immigrant community retaining something of the culture of its country of origin, be they Yemeni, Russian or Ethiopian, Cochinese Jews from Kerala (south India), the Shinlung of Manipur (northeast India), or Jews from the English-speaking countries of the West. Among Palestinian Arabs, too, there is a religious-secular divide, and further separation into Muslim and Christian. Smaller ethnic communities that have found a home here include the Samaritans of Nablus and Holon, the Druze of the Carmel, the Galilee and the Golan Heights, and the Armenians of Jerusalem, who have one of the Old City's quarters virtually to themselves.

Where to go

Unsurprisingly, the biggest concentration of **religious sites** is in **Jerusalem**. The same (hectic) day could see you visiting the Wailing Wall, Judaism's holiest shrine; the Dome of the Rock, the third holiest site in Islam; and, in an approximation of the footsteps of Christ, walking along the Via Dolorosa to the Church of the Holy Sepulchre, holiest site in Christendom. There are literally hundreds of other sites, too numerous to mention, that resonate with biblical associations, though inevitably only a famous handful of those find their way on to the majority of pilgrims' or tourists' itineraries: **Bethlehem**, where, in the grotto beneath the Church of the Nativity, you'll be standing on the site of Christ's birth; **Hebron**, home to the Haram al-Khalil, built over the Cave of Makhpela, where the Old Testament patriarchs Abraham, Isaac and Jacob are buried; **Jericho**, famous for its tumbling walls and unrivalled age; **Megiddo** (Armageddon), equally well-known as the scene of past battles and the final battle to come; the **Sea of Galilee** (Lake Kinneret), on whose waters Jesus walked, and on whose shores He preached and recruited His disciples; and **Nazareth**, His home town, which has just about enough churches for all the pilgrims who make their way up there. In addition to places of importance to Jews, Christians and Muslims, the Holy Land also houses the world centre of the Bahai faith, the beautiful Shrine of the Bab in **Haifa**.

There's an abundance of **historical sites**, too, many dating back to the time of the Crusaders, the Romans and beyond. Outstanding among them are **Caesarea**, capital of the Roman province of Judea, administrative centre of Pontius Pilate and later Crusader stronghold, and the incredible natural fortress of **Masada**, where the Jewish rebels of the First Revolt resisted the might of Rome until the bitter end. Not far away in **Qumran**, the authors of the Dead Sea Scrolls lived a monastic existence echoed by Christian orders who later established **monasteries** in the Judean desert, many of which can be seen and visited today. Further evidence of the strong Roman presence lies at **Bet She'an**, with its magnificent amphitheatre; **Sepphoris**, Roman capital of the Galilee, and **Hammat Gader** (al-Hamma), a Roman spa resort. Other unmissable highlights include **Bet She'arim**, with its Jewish catacombs dating from Roman times, and **Bet Guvrin**, whose amazing natural and artificial caves saw use from the third century BC to the seventh century AD. Crusader sites are also well represented; in addition to Caesarea, there is the impressive subterranean Crusader City at **Acre** and the fortresses at **Belvoir** and **Castle Nimrod**. Glimpses of a lesser-known people – the ancient Nabateans, pioneers of desert irrigation – can be seen in the Negev at **Avdat** and **Mamshit**.

But for thousands every year, it's not the history but the option of a one- or two-week fix of sun, sand and sea that draws them to Israel. The most famous resort is **Eilat**; set on the limpid, coral-fringed waters of the Red Sea – one of the country's amazing natural wonders – it's a magnet for snorkellers, divers and water-sports fanatics. Other resorts, including **Herzliya Pituah**, playground of the rich, and **Nahariyya**, the country's premier honeymoon destination, are concentrated along the Mediterranean. **Tiberias** is a resort with a difference: the "sea" here is the freshwater Sea of Galilee, and, when you've had enough of sunbathing, you can visit an ancient spa and the tombs of some of Judaism's greatest sages.

Vying with the Red Sea and its reefs for the number-one spot in the list of **natural wonders** is the **Dead Sea**, a unique lake of thick, mineral-rich saltwater situated in the Great Rift, 395m below sea level, where you can enjoy mudbaths and a variety of natural treatments. Southward, either independently or on organized jeep tours, you can explore the Negev desert, visiting the massive **Makhtesh Ramon**, the largest of five naturally formed craters unique to this part of the world. More breathtaking desert scenery can be taken in at the springs of **Ein Avdat** and the site of King Solomon's mines at **Timna**. The wooded **Carmel mountains** offer spectacular landscapes of a different sort, as do the plateaux, covered with flowers in springtime, of the **Golan Heights**, where, on the slopes of Mount Hermon, the ski resort of **Neve Atif** lies just a stone's throw from the Mediterranean.

Naturally, of the region's **cities**, it's **Jerusalem** that steals the show. On the pilgrimage trail for centuries, it's now just as firmly on the tourist track; beyond its religious sites, the bustling streets and souqs of the Old City and the wealth of museums and historical sites provide ample incentive for further exploration. It's a remarkable place. **Tel Aviv**, built from scratch this century, is Israel's most vibrant city in terms of fashion, nightlife and streetlife, though even here, historical interest is on hand in **Jaffa**, nowadays a suburb of the bigger city. Ranging up the slopes of the Mount Carmel, **Haifa** is a cooler, more laid-back place, geared up for work rather than play, while in the Palestinian Territories it's the historic towns of **Bethlehem** and **Hebron** that are the obvious draws – though you could find that **Nablus**, with its unspoiled and atmospheric souq, provides one of the unexpected highlights of your visit. And even the Gaza Strip, more commonly thought of by outsiders as being a no-go area of refugee camps and settlements, has the ancient Philistine city of **Gaza**, with its markets and old quarter to recommend it.

When to go

The wonderful **climate** in Israel and the Palestinian Territories means that at any time of year you'll find the sun shining somewhere. In **winter**, Eilat and Tiberias are favourite resorts, and even though Jerusalem, up in the hills, often sees snow, it can be quite warm during the day. The coastal plain (including Tel Aviv and Haifa) is cool but never freezing, so your major problem there will be the rain – wet weather here can be pretty miserable, as the architecture and facilities are not generally geared up for it. In **summer**, it's a case of how to cool off, though a respite from the sauna-like humidity of the coast and the roasting desert can be found in the hills of the Galilee and the Golan. **Spring** is definitely the best time to come, with the country a blaze of flowers and greenery, and the weather temperate enough to make touring enjoyable just about everywhere.

CLIMATE CHART

Average minimum and maximum temperatures in degrees Celsius/Fahrenheit.

	J	F	M	A	M	J	J	A	S	O	N	D
Jerusalem												
min	6/43	7/44	8/47	12/53	15/60	17/63	19/66	19/66	19/66	16/61	12/54	8/47
max	11/53	14/57	16/61	21/69	25/77	27/81	29/84	30/86	28/82	26/78	19/67	14/56
Tel Aviv												
min	9/49	9/48	10/51	12/54	17/63	19/67	21/70	22/72	20/69	15/59	12/54	9/47
max	18/65	19/66	20/69	22/72	25/77	28/83	30/86	30/86	31/89	28/83	25/76	19/66
Haifa												
min	8/46	9/47	8/47	13/55	15/58	18/64	20/68	21/70	20/68	16/60	13/56	9/48
max	17/63	18/64	21/70	26/78	25/76	28/82	30/86	30/86	30/85	27/81	23/74	18/65
Tiberias												
min	9/48	9/49	11/51	13/56	17/62	20/68	23/73	24/75	22/71	19/65	15/59	11/53
max	18/65	20/67	22/72	27/80	32/89	35/95	37/98	37/99	35/95	32/89	26/78	20/68
Dead Sea												
min	11/53	13/56	16/61	20/68	24/75	27/80	28/83	29/83	27/81	24/75	18/65	13/56
max	20/68	22/72	25/78	29/85	34/93	37/99	39/102	38/101	36/96	32/90	27/80	22/71
Eilat												
min	10/49	11/51	13/56	17/63	21/69	24/75	25/77	26/79	24/75	20/69	16/61	11/51
max	21/70	23/73	26/79	31/87	35/95	37/99	40/103	40/104	36/98	33/92	28/83	23/74

WHAT'S IN A NAME?

Use of names such as Israel and Palestine is a matter of contention. Israel usually means the Jewish state within its pre-1967 borders, but the state itself defines Israel to include East Jerusalem, Latrun and the Golan Heights. "Palestine" can be used to mean the entire area of the pre-1948 British Mandate, especially in a historical context, or when referring to the whole of that area in an Arab context, since most Israeli Arabs consider themselves to be Palestinian. However, Palestine is increasingly used to refer particularly to those parts of the former Mandate which are not within the State of Israel, namely the West Bank and the Gaza Strip, also referred to as the Palestinian Territories (the term used in this book), and may also mean in particular those areas which are autonomous under the Palestinian National Authority (PNA).

You may meet people whose definitions of Israel and/or Palestine differ from these: some Israelis, for example, consider that Israel is the whole of the former Mandate plus the Golan Heights, or that Palestine means or includes Jordan, while those who dispute the legitimate existence of the State of Israel or of a country called Palestine may object to the use of one or other of those terms altogether. In this book, "Israel" usually means the country within its pre-1967 borders, while "Palestine", where used, refers to the whole pre-1948 Mandate in a historical context or to the Arab inhabitants of the whole country in a cultural context.

PART ONE

THE

BASICS

GETTING THERE FROM BRITAIN

The easiest, quickest and cheapest way to get to Israel from Britain is to fly direct, with both scheduled and charter flights available at very reasonable prices. Flying time from Britain to Israel is around four to five hours. For the more intrepid, it is also possible to travel overland to Greece and take a ferry from there to the port of Haifa, or even to go round the long way through Turkey, Syria and Jordan, though the land route is only really worthwhile if you want to spend time in some of the countries en route.

Airport departure tax is charged from both the UK (£20) and Israel (about £8), but should be included in the price of your ticket, and is included in the fares quoted below.

BY AIR

Direct scheduled flights from London to Tel Aviv's Ben Gurion Airport (see box on p.73 for details on arrival and departure at Ben Gurion) are operated by British Airways (BA) and Israel's national airline El Al. British Airways flies at least once daily from both Heathrow and Gatwick; El Al flies from Heathrow once or twice daily except Friday. From regional airports, El Al flies four times weekly from Stansted and twice weekly from Manchester to Ben Gurion. They also operate one to two flights a week from Heathrow to Eilat's Ovda Airport.

Fares vary according to the season: high season for Tel Aviv is summer; to Eilat fares are gen-

erally higher in winter. If you intend to travel during the main Jewish holidays (Passover or Jewish New Year) or Christian holidays (Christmas or Easter), you'll need to book well in advance. Official scheduled return fares to Ben Gurion start at around £250 from London or £310 from Manchester (£90 more in both cases in high season) for a ticket booked and paid for in advance with no change of dates allowed, but special offers for less than £230 are sometimes available from BA, and you should be able to get a cheaper deal from one of the specialist travel agents listed in the box on pp.4–5.

Flying indirect, which rarely costs any less than going direct, KLM (with their British subsidiary KLM UK) offers the widest choice of departures from British airports, with daily flights to Ben Gurion. Lufthansa also flies daily to Ben Gurion from Heathrow, Birmingham and Manchester, connecting at Frankfurt or Munich. Other possibilities are Olympic via Athens, and East European airlines, such as TAROM via

AIRPORT PROCEDURE AND SECURITY

Security is very tight in Israel, and your first experience of it will probably be at your airport of departure, especially if you are travelling with an Israeli airline. In addition to the standard check-in questions, you may also be asked whether you are carrying any weapons (for self-defence or otherwise), why you're going to Israel, whether you've been before, if you know anyone there, where you intend to go and so on. Their reasons for asking the questions are obvious enough (see box on p.000), and Israeli security officials are generally polite, though Jewish people (in particular those with family in the country) will probably be asked fewer questions than non-Jews (especially young backpackers and kibbutz volunteers). They are also likely to be suspicious if you are of Arab (especially Palestinian) origin, or if your passport has stamps in it from countries hostile to Israel, such as Iran, Libya, Syria and Iraq. Once you've received security clearance and are on the plane, arriving in Israel is usually no problem. You will receive similar questioning if arriving by land from Egypt or Jordan, or at Haifa port by boat from Greece or Cyprus.

See box on p.73 for details and advice on departure from Israel by air.

AIRLINES, AGENTS AND TOUR OPERATORS

AIRLINES

British Airways 156 Regent St, London W1R
6LB; 146 New St, Birmingham B2 4HN; 19–21 St
Mary's Gate, Market St, Manchester M1 1PU; 64
Gordon St, Glasgow G1 3RS; 30–32 Frederick St,
Edinburgh EH2 2JR, and branches nationwide (all
enquiries ☎0345/222111; www.britishairways.
com).

El Al UK House, 180 Oxford St, London W1N 0EL
(☎0171/957 4100); 231 Royal Exchange,
Manchester M27 7DD (☎0645/125725).

KLM Reservations ☎0990/750900; ticket office
at Terminal 4, Heathrow.

KLM UK Stansted House, Stansted Airport,
Essex CM24 1AE (☎0990/074074; Web site:
www.klmuk.com).

Lufthansa 7–8 Conduit St, London W1R 9TG;
Phoenix House, 78 St Vincent St, Glasgow G2
5UB (☎0345/737747).

Olympic Airways 11 Conduit St, London W1R
0LP (☎0171/409 3400).

TAROM 27 New Cavendish St, London W1M
7RL (☎0171/224 3693; flight consolidators
Magnum ☎0181/360 5353).

DISCOUNT FLIGHT AGENTS

Campus Travel 52 Grosvenor Gardens, London
SW1W 0AG (☎0171/730 3402); 541 Bristol Rd,
Selly Oak, Birmingham B29 6AU (☎0121/414
1848); 61 Ditchling Rd, Brighton BN1 4SD
(☎01273/570226); 39 Queen's Rd, Clifton, Bristol
BS8 1QE (☎0117/929 2494); 5 Emmanuel St,
Cambridge CB1 1NE (☎01223/324283); 53 Forrest
Rd, Edinburgh EH1 2QP (☎0131/668 3308);
105–106 St Aldates, Oxford OX1 1BU
(☎01865/484730). *Student/youth travel specialists,
with branches also in YHA shops and on university
campuses all over Britain. Publishes some "from"
fares on their Web site (www.campustravel. co.uk/
europe.htm).*

Council Travel 28a Poland St, London W1V 3DB
(☎0171/437 7767). *Flights and student discounts.*

North South Travel Moulsham Mill Centre,
Parkway, Chelmsford, Essex CM2 7PX
(☎01245/492882). *Friendly, competitive travel
agency, offering discounted fares worldwide –
profits are used to support projects in the developing world (including Jeel al-Amal, a
Palestinian organization for the welfare of
orphans and other boys in need in the Jerusalem
area), and the promotion of sustainable tourism.*

STA Travel 86 Old Brompton Rd, London SW7
3LH; 117 Euston Rd, London NW1 2SX; 38 Store St
London WC1E 7BZ (☎0171/361 6161); 25 Queens
Rd, Bristol BS8 1QE (☎0117/929 4399); 38 Sidney
St, Cambridge CB2 3HX (☎01223/366966); 75

Deansgate, Manchester M3 2BW (☎0161/834
0668); 88 Vicar Lane, Leeds LS1 7JH (☎0113/244
9212); 36 George St, Oxford OX1 2OJ (☎01865/
792800); and branches in Aberdeen, Birmingham,
Canterbury, Cardiff, Coventry, Durham, Glasgow,
Loughborough, Nottingham, Warwick and
Sheffield. *Worldwide specialists in low-cost flights
and tours for students and under-26s. Current fares
published on their Web site: www.futurenet.co.uk/
STA/Guide/Europe/GetThere.htm).*

Trailfinders 42–50 Earls Court Rd, London W8
6FT (☎0171/937 5400); 194 Kensington High St,
London, W8 7RG (☎0171/938 3939); 58
Deansgate, Manchester M3 2FF (☎0161/839
6969); 254–284 Sauchiehall St, Glasgow G2 3EH
(☎0141/353 2224); 22–24 The Priory,
Queensway, Birmingham B4 6BS (☎0121/236
1234); 48 Corn St, Bristol BS1 1HQ (☎0117/929
9000). *One of the best informed and most efficient agents.*

Travel Bug 597 Cheetham Hill Rd, Manchester
M8 5EJ (☎0161/721 4000); 125a Gloucester
Road, London SW7 4SF (☎0171/835 2000). *Large
range of discounted tickets.*

Travel CUTS 295a Regent St, London W1R 7YA
(☎0171/255 1944); 33 Prince's Sq, London W2
4NG (☎0171/792 3770). *British branch of
Canada's main youth and student travel specialist. Current fares published on their Web site:
www.travelcuts.co.uk.*

CHARTER FLIGHTS AND ISRAEL SPECIALISTS

All Abroad 26 Temple Fortune Parade, London
NW11 0QS (☎0181/458 2666); 394 Harrogate Rd,
Leeds LS17 6PY (☎0113/269 3117). *Cheap flights
and package holidays.*

AMG Travel 70 Edgware Way, Edgware,
Middlesex HA8 8JS (☎0181/958 5636). *Small
firm with a good reputation for reliability, and
often the best flight-only deals.*

Blue Line 17 Hendon Lane, London N3 1RT (☎0181/346 5955). *Travel agent specializing in Israel and worth trying for cheap flight deals.*

Britannia Thomson Travel Group, Greater London House, Hampstead Rd, London NW1 7SD (☎0990/329300). *Charter flights from Gatwick and Manchester to Ovda (Eilat).*

Broadway Holidays 76 The Broadway, Stanmore, Middlesex HA7 4DU (☎0181/420 7000). *Travel agent specializing in Israel.*

Expert Travel 782 Finchley Rd, London NW11 7TH (☎0181/458 9166). *Sometimes has particularly good deals on Israel package holidays.*

Ipale 92 West End Lane, London NW6 2LU (☎0171/328 8431). *Especially good for flights and occasional last-minute deals.*

Israel Travel Service 546–550 Royal Exchange, Old Bank St, Manchester M2 7EN (☎0161/839 1111). *Wide range of tours including tailor-made.*

Longwood 3 Bourne Ct, Southend Rd, Woodford Green, Essex IG8 8HG (☎0181/551 4494). *Flights and a range of packages.*

Peltours 11 Ballards Lane, London N3 1UX (☎0181/343 0590); 14a Cross St, London EC1N 8XA (☎0171/430 2230); 240 Station Rd, Edgware, Middlesex HA8 7AU (☎0181/958 1144); 27 Church St, Manchester M4 1QA (☎0161/834 3721). *The main Israel package specialists, with a wide array of tours, breaks and fly-drive options.*

Pullman 31 Belgrave Rd, London SW1V 1RB (☎0171/931 7016). *Charter flights and a variety of package deals, including some of the lowest-priced ones.*

Superstar UK House, 180 Oxford St, London W1N 0EL (☎0645/125847). *El Al subsidiary offering an impressive range of tours, city breaks and beach holidays.*

Travellink 50 Vivian Ave, London NW4 3XH (☎0181/931 8000). *Travel agent specializing in Israel.*

Unijet Sandrocks, Rocky Lane, Haywards Heath, West Sussex RH16 4RH (☎0990/114114). *Winter charters from Luton, Gatwick and Manchester to Ovda.*

West End Travel Barratt Hse, 341 Oxford St, London W1R 2LE (☎0171/409 0630). *More upmarket package holidays using scheduled flights and high-class hotels.*

WST Holidays 65 Wigmore St, London W1H 9LG (☎0171/224 0504; email: wstchar@demon.co.uk). *British agents for Israeli student travel specialists ISSTA, and a good source for low-priced air tickets.*

PILGRIMAGE TOUR OPERATORS

C-L Bible Tours Oakdale, High Ongar Rd, Ongar, Essex CM5 9LZ (☎01277/366137). *Staunchly Christian tour operators. Runs an eight-day "Easy Riders" tour for physically restricted people who require a leisurely pace and less demanding itinerary.*

Fairlink Christian Travel 12–14 Glendower Pl, London SW7 3DP (☎0171/225 0555). *Choice of three- or four-star accommodation on an eight-day "Steps of Jesus" tour in the Holy Land (£559–975), or a nine-day "Joshua to Jesus" tour including Jordan (£663–995).*

Interchurch Travel Saga Building, Middleburg Sq, Folkestone, Kent CT20 1AZ (☎0800/300444). *Interdenominational pilgrimage tours, ranging from £699 to £899 for ten days to £1089 for eleven days including Jordan.*

Jasmin 53–55 Balham Hill, London SW12 9DR (☎0181/675 6828; email: info@jasmin-tours. co.uk). Eleven-day pilgrimage and ancient sites tour including Jordan (£1125–1435).*

Rosary Pilgrimage Apostolate 12 Farleigh Crescent, The Lawns, Swindon, Wilts SN3 1JY (☎01793/422714). *Tours for Roman Catholic pilgrims with a wide range of Holy Land options starting at £529, plus a special senior citizens' tour in November for £419.*

Saga Holidays Saga Building, Middleburg Sq, Folkestone, Kent CT20 1AZ (☎0800/318225). *Tours for senior (over-50) members of all denominations or none, with nine days in the Holy Land for £749–889, eleven days combination with Jordan for £1029–1099, or a ten-day Christmas tour for £869.*

Star Tours 93 Church Rd, Hove BN3 2BA (☎01273/329080). *Pilgrimages including combined trips to Israel and Jordan.*

Bucharest, whose prices may compensate for low standards of service and reliability.

Charter flights from London and Manchester tend to serve Ben Gurion in summer and Eilat in winter. Fares range from around £185 to £375 depending on the airline, destination and time of year. Most charters are for a limited period only, usually two or three weeks, and your return date cannot be changed (see "Charter Flights" in the box on pp.4–5).

The best place to look for **flight deals**, including scheduled seats for considerably less than the official fares, is the weekly *Jewish Chronicle*, published on Fridays and most easily found wherever there is a reasonably large Jewish community. It's also worth shopping around the agents specializing in Israel, since one or other may well have a special deal on at any particular time. Also worth checking out are the youth/student specialists Campus Travel or STA (see box on p.4 for addresses), and adverts in London's *Time Out* and *Evening Standard*, Manchester's *City Life*, the Australasian freebie *TNT* (on stands outside many Underground stations), and the Sunday broadsheets. If you are a student or under 26, it's worth investigating special fares offered by the airlines and by the discount agents and Israel specialists listed on pp.4–5.

PACKAGE TOURS AND PILGRIMAGES

Almost any High Street travel agent can sell you a **package holiday** in Israel, usually of the two weeks on the beach variety, although most of them also offer a see-the-sights option, too, sometimes including Jordan or Egypt. These can work out cheaper than going it alone, especially if you want to stay in hotels at the higher end of the market. In addition, there are a number of specialist operators (see box above) offering activities ranging from diving to bird-watching, though the largest group are those running **pilgrimages** and biblical interest tours. Almost all of the latter are Christian to a greater or lesser degree, though most are ecumenical (suitable for members of all Christian denominations); Interchurch and Saga claim to cater for anyone with an interest in religion, whether Christian or not.

Most packages offer all-in deals, with return flight, hotel accommodation and, where appropriate, tours. The cheapest deals are midweek off-season, starting from around £300 b&b for a one-week stay (though Peltours offers "Supersavers" with prices from £229 for a week in Eilat if you agree to let them allocate you a hotel on arrival; see p.5 for address). The **Israeli Government Tourist Office** (IGTO; see box on p.26 for offices abroad) stocks a range of brochures from travel firms offering a variety of holidays: kibbutz accommodation, self-drive, holiday apartments, nature trips and combined itineraries including one or more of Jordan, Egypt and Turkey.

TRAVELLING OVERLAND TO ISRAEL

Travelling **overland** from Britain to Israel generally involves going **to Greece** and taking a ferry from there. It is also possible to go by land through **Turkey, Syria and Jordan**, but that is something of an expedition. The simplest surface route is by train to Athens and then by ferry from Piraeus to Haifa.

BRITAIN TO GREECE

The fastest and easiest **rail route** from London to Athens is **via Italy**, taking a ferry from Brindisi to Patrás. The fare for this journey (including the ferry) is around £240 one-way/£420 return (£175/£315 if you're under 26), and the minimum journey time is around 56 hours. You can save five or six hours (for an extra £50) by taking the Eurostar from London Waterloo to Paris, and buying an onward ticket there.

If you want to see a bit of Europe on your way, consider buying an **InterRail pass**, available from most major stations in Britain. The pass is valid for a month's unlimited train travel in up to eight zones covering most of Europe (half-price in the country of purchase) and are available to residents of the participating countries (if not a national, you are supposed to prove residence over the previous six months). A pass covering **two zones** gets you from France to Greece via Italy, allowing you to travel in the Benelux countries, Slovenia and Turkey too (£209 under-26/£279 over-26). A **three-zone** pass allows you to travel via Yugoslavia, and also covers Bulgaria, Romania and the Republic of Macedonia (£229/£309). You still have to pay the fare to France (or add another zone to your pass and pay half), and although the InterRail remains a bargain, more and more trains carry supplements that are not covered: invariably these are the most convenient ones. **Over-60s** can save up to thirty percent on rail and ferry fares across Europe with a Rail Europe Senior Card costing £5.

North Americans, Australians and New Zealanders can use a **Eurail Pass** (purchased in the home country, or from Rail Europe in London; see box below), which gives unlimited first-class train travel in seventeen European countries. The pass costs US$522/A$695/NZ$829 for 15 days, US$678/A$905/NZ$1077 for 21 days, US$838/A$1115/NZ$1331 for one month, and $1188/A$1585/NZ$1795 for two months. The **Eurail Youthpass** (for under-26s) is valid for second-class travel and costs US$365/A$485/NZ$580 for 15 days, US$475/A$635/NZ$856 for 21 days, US$587/A$785/NZ$932 for one month, and US$832/A$1110/NZ$1259 for two months. Alternatively, the **Eurail Flexipass** is good for a certain number of travel days in a two-month period. This, too, comes in first-class and under-26/second-class versions: 10 days cost $616/$431; 15 days, $812/$568. Australasian prices are: 10 days A$575/NZ$685 for under-26s, A$820/NZ$978 first-class; 15 days A$755/NZ$902 or A$1085/NZ$1289 first-class.

RAIL CONTACTS

UK

British Rail International Rail Centre, Victoria Station, London SW1V 1JY (European information line ☎0990/848 848).

Eurostar EPS House, Waterloo Station, London SE1 8SE (reservations ☎0345/303030; Web site: www.eurostar.com/eurostar/).

Eurotrain Campus Travel, 52 Grosvenor Gardens, London SW1W 0AG (☎0171/730 3402).

Le Shuttle Customer Services Centre ☎0990/353535.

Rail Europe 179 Piccadilly, London W1V 0BA (☎0990/300003).

Wasteels Victoria Station (by platform 2), London SW1V 1JY (☎0171/834 7066).

NORTH AMERICA

Rail Europe 226 Westchester Ave, White Plains, NY 10604 (☎1-800/438 7245). *The official Eurail agent in North America.*

ScanTours 1535 6th St, Suite 205, Santa Monica, CA 90401 (☎1-800/223 7226).

AUSTRALASIA

CIT 263 Clarence St, Sydney 2000 (☎02/9299 4754; other branches in Melbourne, Brisbane, Adelaide and Perth).

Thomas Cook Rail Direct Level 8, 130 Pitt St, Sydney 2000 (☎1300/361 941) or 96 Anzac Ave, Auckland 1 (☎09/263 7260).

The cheapest, if most gruelling, way to get to Greece is by **bus**, a three- to four-day journey. The main operator is Eurolines (52 Grosvenor Gardens, London SW1W 0AU; ☎0990/808080; Web site: *www.eurolines.co.uk*), which does a one-way fare from London to Athens for £128.

Driving doesn't make much sense unless you leave your car in Greece. If you intend driving in Israel, it would be far cheaper to rent a car there (see p.32) than to take your own – cycling or taking a motorbike would be a little more feasible. Again, there are two basic routes: one is **via Italy**, with Adriatic ferry crossings from Ancona, Bari and Brindisi to Igoumenítsa and/or Patrás, and longer and less frequent crossings from Venice and Trieste; the other route is **via Yugoslavia**. Both are around 3000km, or at least two days' non-stop driving. An international driving licence is not compulsory in most European countries, but certainly a good idea; in Italy, holders of non-EC licences must carry an Italian translation of them.

The cheapest but most unreliable option of all is to **hitchhike**. It is actually possible to get from London to Athens or Istanbul in one lift, though you'd need a very lucky thumb to do that, and you should allow at least a week to reach Athens. The best route is to cross on the ferry to Ostend or the Hook of Holland, plugging directly into the major European through-routes and avoiding Calais and Paris, two of Europe's most notorious hitching black spots. Hitching through Italy and taking a ferry across the Adriatic is again a safer and easier bet than going via Croatia and Yugoslavia.

Finally, if travelling at all through Croatia, Bosnia, Yugoslavia, Albania or the Republic of Macedonia, remember that the political situation in the Balkans can be almost as volatile as in the Middle East: keep your ear to the ground and steer clear of trouble spots.

GREECE TO ISRAEL

Two boats a week sail between **Piraeus and Haifa**, calling at Rhodes and Limassol (the journey time is 2.5 days from Piraeus, 33 hours from Rhodes and 10 hours from Limassol). Ferries are operated by Salamis Lines and Poseidon Lines (see box on this page for addresses). **Fares** vary according to season, but the cheapest cabin will set you back £89–100 per person from Piraeus, £90–110 from Rhodes, or £47–50 from Limassol; you can save £12–23 (depending on the time of year) by travelling steerage. Prices quoted are

---

SHIPPING COMPANIES

Poseidon Lines Alkyonídhon 32, 16673 Kavoúri Voúlas (near Athens), Greece (☎01/965 8300); c/o Amathus Navigation, Sindágmatos 2 (entrance to Old Harbour), Limassol, Cyprus (☎05/341043); c/o Jacob Caspi, 1 Nathan, Haifa, Israel (☎04/867 4444).

Salamis Lines Filellinon 9, 18536 Piraeus, Greece (☎01/429 4325); 28th October Ave, PO Box 531, Limassol, Cyprus (☎05/355555); c/o Allalouf Shipping, 40 HaNamal, Haifa, Israel (☎04/867 1743).

Viamare Travel 2 Sumatra Rd, London NW6 1PU (☎0171/431 4560; email: *ferries@viamare.com*). *British agents for both Poseidon and Salamis.*

---

inclusive of embarkation tax of £14 and port tax (Rhodes only) of £14. Students and under-26s get a twenty percent discount on the basic fare (ie, excluding embarkation charge and port tax).

BY LAND VIA TURKEY AND SYRIA

Alternatively, you can travel **by bus or train to Istanbul** (the shortest train journey takes 60 hours via the Channel Tunnel, Paris, Munich, Budapest and Bucharest), then on to Syria, either direct to Damascus (2 buses daily; 30hr), or by stages via Antakya and Aleppo using a combination of bus, shared minibuses (known in Turkish as *dolmuş*), service taxis and even train (one weekly from Istanbul to Aleppo, taking up to two days). From Damascus, there are buses, service taxis or another very slow train to Amman in Jordan. For details on getting from Jordan to Israel and the West Bank, see p.17.

Visas for **Romania** are required by citizens of the UK, Ireland, Canada, Australia and New Zealand (but not the US), and Canadians, Australians and New Zealanders also need them for **Bulgaria**. Australians, Canadians, New Zealanders and South Africans do not need a visa to pass through **Turkey**, but Americans, British and Irish have to buy one (this can be done at the border). Most nationalities need a visa for **Syria** (best obtained at home, but otherwise try the Syrian embassy at Abdullah Cevdet Sok 7, Çankaya, Ankara, ☎0312/138 8704, or the consulate at Sîlâhhane Cad 59/9, Ralli Apt, Teşvikiye, Şişli, Istanbul, ☎0212/148 3284). You do not of course want the Syrian authorities to know where you are heading.

GETTING THERE FROM IRELAND

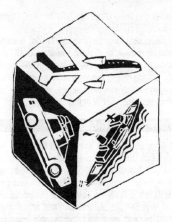

There are no direct flights from Ireland to Israel so you will have to fly via London or a European city, or travel overland by rail and boat.

Scheduled flights from Dublin and Belfast to Tel Aviv's Ben Gurion Airport are offered by British Airways (via London; ☎1800/626747), Air France (via Paris; ☎01/844 5633), KLM (via Amsterdam; ☎01/608 0090) and Lufthansa (via Frankfurt; ☎01/844 5544); see the box on p.4 for addresses. Return **fares** start at around IR£370–400. **Charter flights** out of London Gatwick (see p.4), with through fares from Ireland, start at around IR£250.

Taking a **package holiday** is another option and there are also a couple of operators running **pilgrimage tours** from Ireland. Travelling by **surface routes**, you will probably want to go via Britain, taking from there one of the routes covered on p.7. If you decide to get an **InterRail pass**, you will need to add an extra zone to get you across Britain. InterRail passes and international rail tickets are available from the Continental Rail Desk at Iarnod Eireann, 35 Lower Abbey St, Dublin 1 (☎01/677 1871), from Northern Ireland Railways at Great Victoria Station, Belfast BT2 7UB (☎01232/230671), and at most major stations.

See the box on p.3 for airport procedure and security when departing from your home country and the box on p.73 for details on arrival and departure at Ben Gurion.

TRAVEL AGENTS AND TOUR OPERATORS IN IRELAND

Budget Travel 134 Lower Baggot St, Dublin 2 (☎01/661 1866); other branches citywide. *Discounted flights.*

Explore c/o Maxwells Travel, D'Olier Chambers, 1 Hawkins St, Dublin 2 (☎01/677 9479). *Bus tours for the more adventurous, including a "Holy Land Tour" of Israel, and one of Israel and Jordan.*

Joe Walsh Tours 8–11 Lower Baggot St, Dublin 2 (☎01/676 3053); 31 Castle St, Belfast BT1 1GH (☎01232/241144); 117 Patrick St, Cork (☎021/277959). *General budget fares agent, also offering pilgrimage tours.*

Sadlier 32 Nassau St, Dublin 2 (☎01/670 4880). *Pilgrimage tours.*

Student & Group Travel 71 Dame St, Dublin 2 (☎01/677 7834). *Student specialists.*

Thomas Cook 11 Donegal Place, Belfast BT1 5AA (☎01232/242341); 118 Grafton St, Dublin 2 (☎01/677 1721). *Package holiday and flight agent with occasional discount offers.*

Trailfinders 4–5 Dawson St, Dublin 2 (☎01/677 7888). *Competitive fares out of all Irish airports, as well as deals on hotels, insurance, tours and car rental worldwide.*

USIT O'Connell Bridge, 19–21 Aston Quay, Dublin 2 (☎01/679 8833); Fountain Centre, College St, Belfast BT1 6ET (☎01232/324073); 10–11 Market Parade, Patrick St, Cork (☎021/270900); 33 Ferryquay St, Derry (☎01504/371888); Victoria Place, Eyre Square, Galway (☎091/565177); Central Buildings, O'Connell St, Limerick (☎061/415064); 36–37 Georges St, Waterford (☎051/872601). *Ireland's main student and youth travel specialists.*

GETTING THERE FROM NORTH AMERICA

You can fly direct to Tel Aviv's Ben Gurion Airport from the USA and Canada. Alternatively, a number of airlines fly via Europe, with a stopoff in their respective hub cities. A more intrepid option is to fly to a European city and continue overland using a combination of rail and boat (see p.7 for details of routes and rail passes).

See the box on p.3 for airport procedure and security when departing from your home country and the box on p.73 for details on arrival and departure at Ben Gurion.

SHOPPING FOR TICKETS

You can normally cut the costs of buying tickets direct from the airline by going through a **specialist flight agent** – either a **consolidator**, who buys up blocks of tickets from the airlines and sells them at a discount, or a **discount agent** (see box opposite). Some agents specialize in **charter flights**, which may be cheaper than anything available on a scheduled flight, but again departure dates are fixed and withdrawal penalties are high (check the refund policy).

Regardless of where you buy your ticket, **fares** will depend on the season: **high season** is May to September; "shoulder" seasons April and October; and low season, when you'll get the best prices, is from November to March (excluding Christmas and New Year when prices are hiked up and seats are at a premium). Travelling on the

weekend to Israel is not, typically, more expensive then travelling during the week. If Israel is only one stop on a longer journey, you might want to consider buying a **Round-the-World (RTW) ticket**. There are no "off-the-shelf" RTW tickets that include Israel; agents have to assemble one for you, which can be tailored to your needs. **Fares** start from $2780 in low season.

FLIGHTS FROM THE US

El Al operates **direct scheduled flights** to Tel Aviv's Ben Gurion Airport from Newark and New York JFK (daily) and LA (5 weekly), as well as Chicago, Baltimore, Miami, Orlando (all less frequent), while **TWA** and **Tower Air** fly direct daily from New York JFK. All three airlines' return fares from New York are roughly comparable – around $1030 (low season) to $1280 (high season) – though TWA's tend to be the lowest. From Miami, Chicago or LA, on TWA or El Al, add around $150, $200 and $300, respectively (Tower flies only from LA and Miami, stopping in New York). Keep an eye out for specials which are plentiful; at the time of writing, TWA had one for $800 from New York.

Air France, Alitalia, British Airways, Iberia and Lufthansa all operate **indirect scheduled flights** via their home bases at similar fares to those of El Al, TWA and Tower. For example, a British Airways flight from New York is around $1000 (low season) to $1350 (high season). From Miami, Chicago or LA add $300, $350 and $400, respectively.

If a **stop in Amman** appeals, **Royal Jordanian** flies from New York (daily except Mon and Thurs) to Amman for $1020 (low season), $1370 (high season), from where it's a further $125 (all year) return to Ben Gurion. You'd pay considerably more for a **stop in Egypt: Egyptair**'s flights from New York to Cairo are $1600 (low season), $1785 (high season); flights from Cairo to Ben Gurion are around $370 return, year round.

FLIGHTS FROM CANADA

Air Canada flies direct from Toronto and Montréal to Tel Aviv's Ben Gurion Airport (see p.73) five times a week (three times a week in low season). Flights **from Toronto** are CAN$1500 (low season), CAN$1925 (high season), those

USEFUL ADDRESSES IN NORTH AMERICA

AIRLINES

Air Canada ☎1-800/776 3000 in US; ☎1-800/663 3721 in BC; ☎1-800/542 8940 in Alberta, Saskatchewan and Manitoba; ☎1-800/ 268 7240 in eastern Canada. *Non-stop flights from Toronto and Montréal. Flights from Vancouver and standard US cities stopping in Toronto.*

Air France ☎1-800/237 2747 in US; ☎1-800/667 2747 in Canada; *www.airfrance.fr/. From NY, Miami, Chicago, Washington DC, Houston, San Francisco and LA via Paris.*

Alitalia ☎1-800/223 5730 in US; ☎1-800/361 8336 in Canada. *NY, Boston, Miami, Chicago and LA via Rome.*

Balkan Airlines ☎1-800/852 0944 or ☎212/371 2047. *Flights from NY stopping in Budapest.*

British Airways ☎1-800/247 9297 in US; ☎1-800/668 1059 in Canada; *www.british-airways.com. From standard US cities and Canada via London.*

CSA Czech Airlines ☎1-800/223 2365; *www.csa.cz. Flights from NY (erratic departure dates) via Prague. Includes a full-day stopover in Prague.*

Egyptair ☎1-800/334 6787. *NY and LA to Cairo. Connections to Tel Aviv.*

El Al ☎1-800/223 6700; *www.elal.co.il/. Non-stop flights from NY/JFK, Newark, LA, Chicago, Baltimore, Miami and Orlando. Toronto flights stop at JFK.*

Iberia ☎1-800/772 4642 in US; ☎1-800/423 7421 in Canada; *www.iberiausa.com/. Flights from NY, Miami and LA via Madrid.*

KLM ☎1-800/374 7747 in US; ☎1-800/361 5073 in Canada; *www.klm.nl/. Flights from standard US cities via Amsterdam.*

Lufthansa ☎1-800/645 3880 in US; ☎1-800/563 5954 in Canada; *www.lufthansa-usa.com/. Flights from standard US cities and Canada via Frankfurt.*

Olympic Airways ☎1-800/223 1226; *agn.hol.gr/info/olympic1.htm. Flights from NY and Boston via Athens.*

Royal Jordanian Airlines ☎1-800/223 0470; *www.sita.int/rj/info/rj.html. Non-stop flights from NY and Chicago to Amman. Connections to Tel Aviv.*

Tower Air ☎1-800/221 2500. *Non-stop flights from NY. Flights from Miami and LA stop in NY.*

TWA ☎1-800/892 4141; *www.twa.com/. Non-stop flights from NY. Flights from all standard US cities and Toronto (via JFK).*

CONSOLIDATORS AND DISCOUNT TRAVEL AGENTS

Air Brokers International 323 Geary St, Suite 411, San Francisco, CA 94102 (☎1-800/883 3273 or ☎415/397 1383; *www.aimnet.com/~airbrokr/*). *Consolidator and specialist in RTW and Circle Pacific tickets.*

Airtech 584 Broadway, Suite 1007, New York, NY 10012 (☎1-800/575-TECH or ☎212/219 7000). *Standby seat broker; also deals in consolidator fares and courier flights.*

Council Travel 205 E 42nd St, New York, NY 10017 (☎1-800/226 8624; *www.ciee.org/*), and branches in many other US cities. *Student/budget travel agency.*

Educational Travel Centre 438 N Frances St, Madison, WI 53703 (☎1-800/747 5551 or ☎608/256 5551; *www.edtrav.com/*). *Student/ youth and consolidator fares. Flights from Chicago.*

Now Voyager 74 Varick St, Suite 307, New York, NY 10013 (☎212/431 1616; *www.nowvoyagertravel.com*). *Courier flight broker and consolidator. A two-week courier flight to Tel Aviv is $600 return, high season. Now Voyager also offers flights on TWA for 25 percent off.*

Skylink 265 Madison Ave, 5th Floor, New York, NY 10016 (☎1-800/AIR-ONLY or ☎212/573 8980) with branches in Chicago, Los Angeles, Montréal, Toronto and Washington DC. *Consolidator.*

STA Travel 10 Downing St, New York, NY 10014 (☎1-800/777 0112 or ☎212/627 3111; *www.sta-travel.com/*), and other branches in the Los Angeles, San Francisco and Boston areas. *Worldwide discount travel firm specializing in student/youth fares; also student IDs, travel insurance, car rental, rail passes, etc.*

TFI Tours International 34 W 32nd St, New York, NY 10001 (☎1-800/745 8000 or ☎212/736 1140), and other offices in Las Vegas and Miami. *Consolidator.*

Travac Tours, 989 6th Ave, New York, NY 10018 (☎1-800/872 8800 or ☎212/563 3303; *www.travac.com/*). *Consolidator and charter broker.*

Worldtek Travel 111 Water St, New Haven, CT 06511 (☎1-800/243 1723 or ☎203/772 0470). *Discount travel agency.*

USEFUL ADDRESSES IN NORTH AMERICA

TOUR OPERATORS

Abercrombie & Kent 1520 Kensington Road, Oak Brook, IL 60523 (☎1-800/323 7308). *Offers an eight-day "Ancient Voices" tour of Israel and Egypt or a tour of Israel and Jordan.*

American Express Vacations PO Box 1525, Fort Lauderdale, FA 33301 (☎1-800/241 1700; www.americanexpress.com/travel/). *Fifteen-day tour of the highlights of Israel including the Dead Sea, Bethlehem, Jerusalem and Tel Aviv. Also offers tours with a Christian or Jewish emphasis.*

Contiki Holidays 300 Plaza Alicante, Suite 900, Garden Grove, CA 92640 (☎1-800/CONTIKI). *Nine-day tour of Jerusalem, Galilee and Tel Aviv for 18- to 35-year olds.*

El Al Milk & Honey Vacations 120 W 45th St, 18th floor, New York, NY 10036 (☎1-800/ELAL-SUN). *Packages of varying prices which feature tours of Jerusalem, Haifa and Tel Aviv, a stay on a kibbutz and bus travel.*

Isram World of Travel 630 Third Avenue, New York, NY 10017-6780 (☎1-800/223 7460, or ☎212/661 1193). *Tours of all types: pilgrimage, religious, adventure, chauffeur-driven car.*

Tower Air Smart Vacations PO Box 578, Valley Stream, NY 11582-0578 (☎1-800/34-TOWER). *Wide array of tours such as the "Best of Israel" tour (10 days/7nights in Tel Aviv, Tiberias and Jerusalem) that ranges from $1495 to $2295. You can "add on" extensions inside Israel itself or outside, to Jordan and Egypt.*

ADVENTURE AND SPECIALIST OPERATORS

International Diving Expeditions 18380 Avenida Caleta, Suite 3201, Murrieta, CA 92562 (☎1-800/544 3483 or ☎714/897 3770). *Offers adventure tours hiking and touring the Negev in a four-wheel drive for about $110 per day. Boat-stays for up to a week for scuba diving in the Red Sea.*

Adventure Centre 1311 63rd Street, Ste 200, Emeryville, CA 94608 (☎1-800/227 8747). *Exploratory adventure trips from nine days to a month (from $1395). Tours of Caesaria, Akko and Qumran. Also offers a Nile cruise.*

Religious Tours PO Box 0042, Danforth 04424 (☎1-800/752 8090). *Specializes in Christian tours and pilgrimages to the "lands of the Bible."*

Israel Nature Trails 89 5th Avenue, Suite 800, New York, NY 10003 (☎1-800/323 0035 or ☎212/645 8732). *All profits from tours are used for the protection of nature in Israel. Biking, hiking, adventure and coach tours. Twelve days in Galilee, Golan, Jerusalem and the Negev; regional travel packages; day tours.*

from Montréal are around CAN$60 less. **From Vancouver**, through fares are CAN$1845 (low season), CAN$2265 (high season).

    Indirect flights on **British Airways** from Montréal, via London, and on Air France, via Paris, start at around CAN$1405 (low season) to CAN$1635 (high season). From Toronto you'll pay about CAN$50 more. Alternatively, **Lufthansa** flies from Vancouver via Frankfurt for CAN$1825 (low season), CAN$2055 (high season).

PACKAGE TOURS TO ISRAEL

Package tours to Israel are offered by various companies and include both beach holidays and sightseeing tours. Among other options available are fly-drive deals, kibbutz stays and additional tours to Egypt and Jordan. Specialist operators have diving, hiking and religious interest tours. See box above for a selection of tour operators.

GETTING THERE FROM AUSTRALIA AND NEW ZEALAND

There are no direct flights from Australasia to Israel. The cheapest and most direct routes are via Asia and either the Middle East or Europe, though some of the European routings can result in a longer flight time, with either a transfer or stopover in the air-

line's home city. Flying time is long – between 20 and 30 hours – so a stopover may be the better option. If you're planning to see Israel as part of a longer trip, round-the-world (RTW) tickets (see p.15) are worth considering, and are generally better value than a simple return flight. Finally, there's the option of flying to a European city and continuing overland (see p.7 for details of routes and rail passes).

Airline fares are structured according to seasons: **low season** is mid-January to the end of February, and October to the end of November; **high season** mid-May to the end of August, and December to mid-January; **shoulder season** covers the rest of the year. There is no price variation during the week. Predictably, prices for flights (and everything else) tend to soar around Easter and Christmas time.

Whatever kind of ticket you're after, first call should be one of the **travel agents** listed in the box on p.14, which can fill you in on all the latest fares and any special offers. If you're a **student** or **under 26**, you may be able to undercut some of the prices given here; STA is a good place to start.

AIRLINES IN AUSTRALIA AND NEW ZEALAND

Air New Zealand 5 Elizabeth St, Sydney, NSW 2000 (☎13 2476); 139 Queen St, Auckland 1 (☎09/357 3000). *Teams up with Lufthansa and Alitalia to offer a connecting service from Auckland through to Ben Gurion via a transfer in Kuala Lumpur.*

Alitalia 32 Bridge St, Sydney, NSW 2000 (☎02/9247 1308); 6/229 Queen St, Auckland 1 (☎09/379 4457). *Three times a week to Ben Gurion from Sydney and Auckland via a transfer in Rome (codeshares with Qantas and Cathay Pacific from Auckland).*

British Airways 26/201 Kent St, Sydney, NSW 2000 (☎02/9258 3300); 154 Queen St, Auckland 1 (☎09/356 8690).

Egyptair 630 George St, Sydney, NSW 2000 (☎02/9267 6979). *Twice weekly to Ben Gurion from Sydney via a transfer in Cairo.*

El Al 261 George St, Sydney, NSW 2000 (☎02/9221 8011). *Teams up with Thai Airways and Cathay Pacific to offer a connecting service from Australasia.*

KLM 5 Elizabeth St, Sydney, NSW 2000 (☎02/9231 6333 or ☎1800/505 747). *Twice a week to Ben Gurion from Sydney via a transfer in Amsterdam: codeshares with Korean Airlines.*

Korean Airlines 36 Carrington St, Sydney, NSW 2000 (☎02/9262 6000); 7 Falcon St, Auckland 1 (☎09/307 3687). *Twice weekly to Ben Gurion from Sydney via a transfer in Seoul.*

Olympic Airways 3/37 Pitt St, Sydney, NSW 2000 (☎02/9251 2044). *Twice a week from Sydney, Melbourne and Auckland to Tel Aviv via a transfer in Athens (teams up with Air New Zealand from Auckland to Sydney).*

Qantas 70 Hunter St, Sydney, NSW 2000 (☎13 1211); 154 Queen St, Auckland 1 (☎09/357 8900 or ☎ 0800/808 767).

Thai Airways 75 Pitt St, Sydney, NSW 2000 (☎13 1960); 22 Fanshawe St, Auckland 1 (☎09/377 3886).

USEFUL ADDRESSES IN AUSTRALIA AND NEW ZEALAND

DISCOUNT TRAVEL AGENTS

Anywhere Travel 345 Anzac Parade, Kingsford, Sydney NSW 2000 (☎02/9663 0411).

Brisbane Discount Travel 260 Queen St, Brisbane, Queensland 4000 (☎07/3229 9211).

Budget Travel 16 Fort St, Auckland 1, plus branches around the city (☎09/366 0061 or ☎0800/808 040).

Destinations Unlimited 3 Milford Rd, Auckland 1 (☎09/373 4033).

Flight Centres Australia: 82 Elizabeth St, Sydney, NSW 2000 plus branches nationwide (☎13 1600). New Zealand: 205 Queen St, Auckland 1 (☎09/309 6171), plus branches nationwide.

Northern Gateway 22 Cavenagh St, Darwin, NT 0800 (☎08/8941 1394).

STA Travel Australia: 702 Harris St, Ultimo, Sydney; NSW 2007; 256 Flinders St, Melbourne, Vic 3000; other offices in state capitals and major universities (nearest branch ☎13 1776, fastfare telesales ☎1300/360 960). New Zealand: 10 High St, Auckland 1 (☎09/309 0458, fastfare telesales ☎09/366 6673), plus branches in Wellington, Christchurch, Dunedin, Palmerston North, Hamilton and at major universities. (email: traveller@statravelaus.com.au, www.statravelaus.com.au).

Thomas Cook Australia: 175 Pitt St, Sydney, NSW 2000; 257 Collins St, Melbourne, Vic 3000; plus branches in other state capitals (local branch ☎13 1771, Thomas Cook Direct telesales ☎1800/063 913); New Zealand: 96 Anzac Ave, Auckland 1 (☎09/379 3920).

Tymtro Travel Level 8, 130 Pitt St, Sydney, NSW 2000 (☎02/9223 2211 or ☎1300 652 969).

SPECIALIST AGENTS AND TOUR OPERATORS

Adventure World 73 Walker St, North Sydney, NSW 2000 (☎02/9956 7766 or ☎1800/221 931), plus branches in Brisbane and Perth; 101 Great South Rd, Remuera, Auckland 1 (☎09/524 5118). *Agents for Explore Worldwide and many other international adventure travel companies.*

Explore Holidays 55 Blaxland Rd, Ryde, Sydney, NSW 2000 (☎02/9857 6200; book through travel agents). *Sightseeing tours, plus car rental and hotel bookings for independent travellers.*

Insight 39–41 Chandos St, St Leonards, Sydney, NSW 2000 (☎02/9901 0444; book through travel agents). *A wide range of city stopovers and fully escorted tours, including eight-day bus tours for A$825–1280, (flight not included); other alternatives add Petra or Mount Sinai.*

Peregrine Adventures 258 Lonsdale St, Melbourne, Vic 3000 (☎03/9663 8611), plus offices in Brisbane, Sydney, Adelaide and Perth. *Agent for walking and cycling tours run by* The Imaginative Traveller.

Sonya's Bon Voyage Shop 6, Royal Parade, 175 Oxford St, Bondi Junction, Sydney, NSW 2020 (☎02/9387 1333). *Flights and holiday packages to Israel.*

Sun Island Tours 92 Goulburn St, Sydney, NSW 2000 (☎02/9283 2144). *All Middle Eastern travel arrangements.*

Ya'lla Tours 1st floor, West Tower, 608 St Kilda Rd, Melbourne, Vic 3000 (☎03/9510 2844). *Holidays to Israel, Egypt, Jordan and Syria.*

Seat **availability** on most international flights out of Australia and New Zealand is often limited so it's best to book several weeks ahead.

See the box on p.3 for airport procedure and security when departing from your home country and the box on p.73 for details on arrival and departure at Tel Aviv's Ben Gurion Airport.

FROM AUSTRALIA

From **Australia** most flights are out of Sydney. Currently the cheapest **scheduled flight** to Tel Aviv's Ben Gurion Airport is with **Alitalia** via Rome and ranges from A$1670 (low season) to A$2200 (high season). The next best prices are offered by Olympic and Egyptair, flying via Singapore and then Athens or Cairo, respectively, for around A$1750–1950. Of the Asian carriers, Korean flies via Seoul from A$1800–1950, while El Al teams up with Thai Airways (via Bangkok) and Cathay Pacific (via Hong Kong), both for around A$2100–2400. With airlines such as British Airways, KLM and Qantas you'll be looking at low-season fares in excess of A$2000. Most airlines have a set fare from major eastern

Australian cities (this includes a shuttle service to their main point of departure), while fares from Perth and Darwin are between $100–200 cheaper.

FROM NEW ZEALAND

From **New Zealand** the choice of airlines flying to Ben Gurion is quite limited and fares are all around NZ$2399–2799. Air New Zealand teams up with Alitalia via Rome and Lufthansa via Kuala Lumpur and Frankfurt, while El Al, along with either Thai Airways or Cathay Pacific, can take you via Bangkok or Hong Kong respectively.

RTW TICKETS

Round-the-world tickets that take in **the Middle East** are worth considering, especially if you have the time to make the most of some stopovers. There are any number of airline combinations to choose from, and although few itineraries take in Tel Aviv, several offer a stop in Cairo, Istanbul or Rome, from where you can take a side-trip to Israel. The most flexible are Cathay Pacific–UA's "Globetrotter", Air New Zealand–KLM–Northwest's "World Navigator" and Qantas–BA's "Global Explorer" with six stopovers worldwide, limited backtracking, and additional stopovers (at extra cost), from A$2600/NZ$3300–A$3189/NZ$3700.

PACKAGES AND TOURS

Package deals from Australia and New Zealand are pretty flexible, and most specialist agents (see box opposite) can do anything from booking a few nights' accommodation in Tel Aviv or Jerusalem for when you first arrive, to arranging a fully escorted tour. Explore Holidays, for example, offers hotels for around A$60–80 per person, and short sightseeing tours in Jerusalem or Tel Aviv for A$400–600.

Most tour companies offer a range of itineraries that take in the major sights, many with the option of spending a few days in Egypt, Jordan or Syria as well. Most of the more **adventure-orientated** operators such as Explore Worldwide offer small-group tours, visiting Jerusalem, the Dead Sea and Galilee, and including an overnight stay on a kibbutz (8–9 days; A$950–1080, airfares extra); other itineraries tag on Jordan (10 days, A$1390; 16 days A$1895) or Egypt (10 days, A$1030; 17 days, A$1780), again excluding flights.

For **New Zealand travellers**, an eight-day tour of the major sights will set you back around NZ$1150, while a ten-day tour starting in Jerusalem, visiting Petra and finishing in Cairo will cost NZ$1200, plus international flights.

GETTING THERE FROM EGYPT

Getting from Egypt to Israel or Gaza by land is easy enough, either direct from Cairo or in stages via Suez or the Sinai, but note that Egyptian border stamps may be a problem if you intend using the same passport for other Arab countries (see p.19).

BY AIR FROM CAIRO

It is possible to **fly from Cairo** to Tel Aviv's Ben Gurion Airport, six times weekly with both **Air Sinai** (Nile Hilton arcade off Midan Tahrir; ☎02/760948) and **El Al** (1st floor, 5 Sharia el-Makrizi, just south of Zamalek Bridge, Zamalek; ☎02/341 1620). One-way tickets cost E£660 (£115/$190) in Egypt, or around £85/$140 if purchased abroad (the date does not have to be fixed at time of purchase), plus departure tax of around £30/$50.

For details of airport procedure prior to departure see box on p.3; for arrival and departure details at Ben Gurion see box on p.73.

BY BUS FROM CAIRO

Coming from Cairo, most travellers opt for one of the **tourist bus services** to Tel Aviv or Jerusalem (all of them offer the choice), a journey of some eleven to twelve hours. **Travco**, at 13 Sharia Mahmoud Azmi, near the *Marriott Hotel* in Zamalek (☎02/342 0488), runs a service departing from the *Cairo Sheraton Hotel* in Dokki (daily except Sat, 5.30am). Tickets are available downtown from Spring Tours, 11 Sharia Talaat Harb, and Misr Travel, 7 Sharia Talaat Harb, which also sells tickets for an overnight service via Eilat, leaving on Mondays and Thursdays at 5.30pm.

OTHER ROUTES FROM EGYPT

If you prefer to use ordinary public transport, you can use one of two **border crossings**. The main one is at **Rafah** between northern Sinai and the Gaza Strip, the other is at **Taba**, near Eilat in the far south of Israel and handy if coming from Dahab or the other southern Sinai beach resorts and heading specifically to Eilat, the southern Negev, or to Petra in Jordan. **Onward transport** connections into Israel are available at both crossings, though bus connections are better from Taba.

CAIRO, QANTARA AND EL ARISH TO RAFAH

Service taxis **to Rafah** run from Cairo (by Koulali bus terminal on Sharia Orabi near Ramses Station; 5hr), Qantara (by the café on the east bank of the Canal; 3hr), and El Arish (where you may have to change anyway if you do not find a direct vehicle; 30min). At the border (daily 9am to 5pm) you go through Egyptian and Israeli controls (although the Gaza Strip is autonomous under the Palestinian National Authority, Israel still controls border formalities), before entering autonomous Palestine. There are direct bus connections **into Israel** serving Tel Aviv (#362; 1 daily; 2hr) via Ashqelon (1hr), and Beersheba (#35; 1 daily; 2hr 20min).

If travelling **into the Gaza Strip**, you may well find that service taxis (2NIS) into Rafah Town are unavailable and you will have to walk or take a special (25NIS). From Rafah Town, there are service taxis to Gaza City (4NIS), and also buses (every 30min; 1hr). A "special" taxi all the way from the border into Gaza City would cost around 50NIS, depending on your bargaining skills. There is no accommodation in Rafah, so try to time your journey to arrive during the day when onward transport is available. If coming straight from Cairo, set out very early.

CAIRO, SUEZ AND SINAI TO TABA

Buses from Cairo **to Taba** leave from the Sinai bus terminal (3 daily; 10hr). There are also various services from the Sinai terminal to Sharm el-Sheikh, Dahab and Nuweiba. The cheapest way to get to Sinai from Cairo, however, is to take a service taxi from Midan Ramses or the nearby Koulali terminal to Suez (1hr 30min), from where there is one daily bus to Taba (6hr 30min), with others to Nuweiba, Dahab, St Catherine's Monastery and Sharm el-Sheikh, and also occasional service taxis. If you are not planning to stay in Suez, you should try to arrive there by noon to be sure of getting a bus out.

Within **Sinai**, there are **buses to Taba** from Sharm el-Sheikh and Na'ama Bay (2 daily; 4hr 30min), Dahab (2 daily; 3hr), Nuweiba (4 daily; 2hr) and St Catherine's monastery (1 daily; 4hr), but these can get very crowded, and you may have to stand all the way. Service taxis run from all of these places except St Catherine's, but can be few and far between, so you may have to take a string of them where there is none direct, especially if coming from Sharm or Na'ama. From St Catherine's, you should be able to share a taxi to Dahab with a few others (prices rise sharply once the last bus has left), and to get transport on from there. Note that transport from Dahab leaves from Dahab City, not the beach resort; if staying at the latter, it's best to arrange transport into town in advance rather than have to negotiate a price when in a hurry for a bus connection.

The border is open 24 hours, though it is best to avoid crossing during the Sabbath, when you will find no transport on the Israeli side. Otherwise, there are regular **buses into Eilat** (#15 and #16; every 15–20min), from where there are connections nationwide (see p.298).

See the *Rough Guide to Egypt* for more detailed coverage of transport routes within Egypt.

GETTING THERE FROM JORDAN

You can fly direct to Tel Aviv from Jordan. Alternatively, travelling overland, there are three border crossings from Jordan into Israel and the West Bank, all of which charge a departure tax of JD4.

BY AIR

You can **fly from Amman to Tel Aviv**'s Ben Gurion Airport five times weekly with **El Al** (☎06/562 2526), or seven times weekly with **Royal Wings** (☎06/875201), three of whose flights start at the more convenient Marka Airport (the others all leave from Queen Alia Airport). One-way tickets cost JD54.1 (£47/$78). Pending the opening of Gaza Airport, Palestinan Airways flies from Amman to El Arish in northern Sinai, from where passengers are bussed to Sinai. British, American and Canadian nationals do not need a visa for this journey, but others must apply in advance to the Egyptian embassy in Amman.

For details of airport procedure prior to departure see box on p.3; for arrival and departure details at Ben Gurion see box on p.73.

OVERLAND

The most obvious border crossing to use if coming from Amman is **Allenby Bridge** (see also p.428), always referred to in Jordan as King Hussein Bridge – Jisr al-Malik Hussein (Sun–Thurs 8am–midnight, Fri & Sat 8am–3pm; enquiries on the Israeli-held side ☎02/994 2302). As this crossing is into the West Bank rather than Israel itself, you can leave and re-enter Jordan here and only here, if your Jordanian visa is still valid, without officially having left the country (even though Jordan no longer claims sovereignty over the West Bank). This is handy if you are going on to Syria or Sudan afterwards, so long as you make sure that neither Jordanians nor Israelis stamp your passport (see p.19). Note that at all three border crossings from Jordan, the Jordanians will stamp you in or out on a separate piece of paper if you ask. At the border you pay your tax, get an exit stamp in return, and then take a bus (which can take anything from ten minutes to a couple of hours to leave) across the Jordan River to the Israeli checkpoint.

There are several ways **to get to Allenby Bridge**. A JETT bus (JD6) leaving from the JETT office in Sharia al-Malik Hussein in Amman, 500m uphill from Abdali bus station, at 6.30am (45min) takes you direct to the Israeli terminal – the driver collects passports to give to the border officials leaving Jordan, but insist on taking yours to them in person if you don't want that stamp in your passport. Alternatively, service taxis (JD2) run from the southern end of Abdali bus station to the foreigners' terminal next to the bridge. A cheaper option is to take one of the buses that run to the local people's terminal, but you'll still have to get to the foreigners' terminal and take a bus from there across the bridge (JD1.5).

On the Israeli side, be sure to make it very clear indeed if you don't want a stamp (see p.19), as the Israeli border officials have been known to forget. Once through customs and immigration, you'll find money-changing facilities (though you can in fact use Jordanian dinars on the West Bank), and service taxis to Jericho, Jerusalem and Ramallah.

Direct buses run by Trust International (☎06/581 3427 in Amman; ☎02/251878 in Irbid) and Nazareth Tours from Amman and Irbid to Tel Aviv, Nazareth and Haifa (Sun–Thurs 2 daily for Tel Aviv; Mon–Fri & Sun 2 daily, Sat 1 daily to Haifa via Nazareth) use the northernmost border crossing at **Sheikh Hussein Bridge** (Sun–Thurs 6.30am–10pm, Fri & Sat 8am–8pm; enquiries on the Israeli side ☎06/658 6442 or 4). Buses leave from Trust's Amman office next to the Royal

Jordanian building off the airport highway near 7th circle, best reached by taxi (JD1.5 from downtown). It is also possible to travel by bus from Amman or from the Syrian border at Ramtha to Irbid, from where there are minibuses to Sheikh Hussein. **On the Israeli side**, there are sheruts (Israeli service taxis) and buses (5 daily) to Bet She'an (Baysan in Arabic), and service taxis to East Jerusalem.

The southernmost crossing from Jordan to Israel is at **'Araba** ('Arava in Hebrew; Sun–Thurs 6.30am–10pm, Fri & Sat 8am–8pm; enquiries on the Israeli side ☎07/633 6811 or 5), 5km north of Aqaba and very convenient if you've been visiting Petra. You can get there by *servees* (JD1) from Aqaba's bus station. Once on the Israeli side, you are 2km from downtown Eilat – a short walk or bus ride. Israelis will refrain from stamping your passport on request when leaving or entering Israel at 'Araba and Sheikh Hussein.

For further details on travelling around Jordan see the *Rough Guide to Jordan*.

RED TAPE AND VISAS

Citizens of the UK, Ireland, the USA, Canada, Australia, New Zealand, South Africa and most EU countries (except Germans born before 1928) need only a valid passport to visit Israel and the Palestinian Territories: a visa will be issued free of charge on entry. Visitors are usually allowed to stay in the country for three months from the date of arrival, though sometimes, especially at the Taba crossing from Egypt, you may be given less time unless you ask. Note that if you enter Israel on a one-way ticket you will either have to demonstrate your intention to leave again (a ticket home from Egypt, for example) or show evidence of plenty of money to support yourself and buy a ticket home.

On **arrival** in Israel, you will be asked to fill in an **entry card** which you hand over with your passport. Half of it will be torn off and the rest returned to you. You must keep this returned portion safe to hand back when you leave; losing it will make the departure procedure even longer and more tiresome than it already is (see box on p.73). Israeli airport **departure tax** (£8/$13) is now included in the price of the airline ticket, which should have a stamp confirming payment; check that yours has one. The same applies to boat tickets out of Haifa. Departure tax of around £18/$30 is also payable when leaving Israel by land at Rafah and Taba, along with a £2/$3 entry tax into Egypt. Crossing by land into Jordan, you pay £12/$18, at Sheikh Hussein and 'Arava, and a massive £20/$32 (split between Israel and the PNA) at Allenby.

EXTENDING YOUR VISA

Visa extensions can be obtained at government offices in Afula, Acre, Ashqelon, Beersheba, Eilat, Hadera, Haifa, Herzliya, Holon, Jerusalem, Nazareth, Netanya, Petah Tiqva, Ramat Gan, Ramle, Rehovot, Safed, Tel Aviv and Tiberias. You can extend your visa only in the town where you are staying, and queues can be long so you should try to arrive early. A visa extension costs 100NIS, plus one passport photo, and you will have to demonstrate that you have sufficient means to remain in the country without seeking employment.

Remember that, though many travellers do it, it is illegal to work on a tourist visa (see p.61 for further details on working in Israel and the Palestinian Territories).

CUSTOMS AND ALLOWANCES

Duty-free allowances for entry into Israel are one litre of spirits, plus two litres of wine, 250 cigarettes or 250g of tobacco for over-17-year-olds, a quarter of a litre of perfumes containing alcohol (such as cologne), and gifts worth up to US$150. Videos, camcorders, laptop PCs and diving equipment should be declared on arrival, since you have to pay a deposit on them, refunded when you leave the country with them.

ISRAELI STAMPS AND ARAB COUNTRIES

At one time, any evidence that you had been to Israel would mean no entry to most Arab countries, and to some other Islamic countries too. Of late, the list of countries refusing entry to bearers of passports containing **Israeli stamps** has gone down slightly, but those taking a hard line against Israel (Libya, Sudan and Iran head the list) still deny entry to anyone whose passport has not only stamps issued by Israel itself, but even those issued by Egypt or Jordan at their borders with Israel and the Palestinian Territories, or any visa for anywhere issued in

Israel. If you intend travelling to these countries, you will have to think of ways to ensure that there is no evidence of your having been in Israel.

The more likely destinations of **Syria or Lebanon** also refuse entry to anyone who has been to Israel ("Disneyland" as travellers in Syria used to call it to avoid discovery by eavesdropping members of the secret police). Syrian practice has become more ambiguous recently, and the strictness with which the policy is applied depends on the latest political situation and the particular bureaucrat who scans your papers. Even so, at the time of writing, Israeli stamps as well as Egyptian stamps from Rafah or Taba, and Jordanian ones from Allenby, Sheikh Hussein or 'Arava, are likely to exclude you from both Syria and Lebanon.

When **entering Israel**, you can ask the immigration official to **stamp your visa** onto the entry card rather than in your passport. Israeli officials should be prepared to do this, but make sure you ask when you hand over your passport. More problematic is the fact that Egyptian officials will almost always insist on stamping your passport at border crossings into and out of Israel and the Palestinian Territories. A few travellers avoid these when leaving (but not entering) Egypt by

ISRAELI EMBASSIES AND CONSULATES ABROAD

Australia 6 Turrana St, Yarralumla, Canberra (☎02/6273 1309); 37 York St, Sydney (☎02/9264 7933).

Canada 50 O'Connor St, Suite 1005, Ottawa, ON K1P 6L2 (☎613/567 6450); 180 Bloor St W, Suite 700, Toronto, ON M5S 2V6; 1115 Bd René Levesque Oueste, Suite 2620, Montréal, PQ H3B 4S5 (☎514/393 9372).

Cyprus 1 Gryparis St, Nicosia (☎02/445195).

Denmark Lundevangsvej 4, 2900 Hellerup (☎3962 6288).

Egypt 6 Sharia Ibn al-Malik, Giza (☎02/361 0545).

Greece Odos Marathonodromou 1, Palaio Psychiko, 15410 Athens (☎01/671 9530).

Ireland 122 Pembroke Rd, Dublin 4 (☎01/668 0303).

Jordan 47 Sharia Mayasaloun, Rabiya, PO Box 950866, Amman 11195 (☎06/552 4680).

Netherlands Buitenhof 47, 2513 AH, Den Haag (☎070/376 0500).

New Zealand DB Towers, 111 The Terrace, PO Box 2171, Wellington (☎04/472 2362).

Norway Drammensven 82C, 0244 Oslo (☎2244 7924).

South Africa Dashing Centre, 3rd floor, 339 Hilda St, Hatfield, Pretoria 0083 (☎012/342 2693).

Sweden Tortenssonsgt 4, 10440 Stockholm (☎08/663 0435).

UK 2 Palace Green, London W8 4QB (☎0171/957 9500).

USA 800 2nd Avenue 15th floor, New York, NY 10017. (☎212/499 5400); 24 Greenway, Suite 1500, Houston, TX 77046 (☎972/627 3780); 6380 Wilshire Blvd, Suite 1700, LA, CA 90048 (☎215/651 5700); 100 North Biscayne Blvd, Suite 1800, Miami, FL 33132 (☎305/358 8111); 1100 Spring St ☎440, Atlanta, GA 30309 (☎404/075 7851); 1020 Statler Office Building, Boston, MA 02116 (☎617/542 0041); 111 E. Wacker Drive, Suite 1308, Chicago, IL 60601 (☎312/565-3300); 456 Montgomery Street, Suite 2100, San Francisco, CA, 94104 (☎415/398 8885); 230 South 15th St, 8th floor, Philadelphia, PA 19102 (☎215/546 5556).

persuasion, and even bribery, though the latter is of course a risky business. At Allenby Bridge, 'Araba and Sheikh Hussein Bridge, the Jordanians will stamp you out and in on a separate piece of paper if you ask.

Many Western countries will issue **second passports** to citizens visiting both Israel and Arab countries, especially if those visits are fre-

quent, but even with the incriminating stamps in a different passport, you still have the problem of explaining how you came to be asking for a Sudanese visa in Cairo, for example, without apparently having any evidence in your passport of entry into Egypt. A new passport issued in Egypt or Jordan is doubly suspect, so "losing" your old one there will not help you.

COSTS, MONEY AND BANKS

Israel is an expensive country to visit, with accommodation and food at prices comparable to those found in Europe and North America, rather than its Middle Eastern neighbours. The Palestinian Territories, with the exception of East Jerusalem, are cheaper as far as food is concerned, but this does not extend to its rather limited range of hotels.

The Israeli economy is closely linked to the US dollar; it's dependent on huge American subsidies, and the US is by far the country's biggest trade partner. In the mid-1980s, the Israeli government even considered abandoning the shekel and adopting the dollar as the national currency. They didn't, but even so, prices, particularly for more expensive goods or upmarket hotel accommodation, are often quoted in dollars. In tourist areas, many shopkeepers will be just as happy (if not more) to accept dollars as shekels.

COSTS

In terms of a **daily budget**, if you stay in hostels, eat at street stalls or the cheapest restaurants, and don't travel around too much, you'll get by on

a minimum of around £15/$20 a day (excluding entrance to museums and sites). Cooking for yourself, hitching and staying with people (both Israelis and Palestinians are extremely hospitable, so this isn't unlikely) may reduce that figure but only by a little. On a more comfortable budget, staying in a mid-range hotel and eating out in standard restaurants will set you back around £50/$70 a day. An **ISIC card** entitles you to discounts on museum entrance fees and train fares.

As a visitor, your biggest outgoing is likely to be **accommodation**. In Tel Aviv, Jerusalem and Eilat, as well as other main cities and tourist resorts, you can stay in a hostel dorm for as little as £5/$7 a night, but you'll be hard put to find anything in that price range anywhere else. Hotels start at £25/$40 a night for a double room, more in high season, but in some places you won't find anything below £40/$60. At the top end of the scale, the sky's the limit, with some deluxe hotels charging well over £150/$200 a night for a double room in low season.

As for **food**, if you're prepared to survive on street food like falafel and hummus, you can stay alive for very little: a pitta-full of falafel is likely to set you back about £2/$3 or less. Even in the cheapest restaurants, you probably won't get much for under £4/$7, and in many restaurants you'll pay around £20/$30 per head for a three-course meal excluding wine. Buying food at supermarkets and cooking it yourself (some hostels provide cooking facilities) costs much the same as at home. Food in the West Bank or Gaza is rather less expensive; you can get a very decent meal for around £5/$8, while a top-whack dinner in most Palestinian towns will set you back £15/$20.

Finally, although **transport** is not outrageously expensive by British or American standards, it costs a lot more than you would pay in neighbouring countries. As a guideline, the bus or train fare from Tel Aviv to Jerusalem (62km) or Haifa (95km) is around £4/$6; from Jerusalem or Tel Aviv to Eilat (312–354km), it's £11/$18. Travelling around the Palestinian Territories is cheaper, with a fare of £2.50/$4 from Jerusalem to Nablus (61km) by bus or service taxi.

MONEY

Israel's **currency** is the **New Israeli Shekel (NIS)**. At present there are roughly 3.70NIS to the US dollar, or six to the pound sterling. The shekel tends to fall against both of these, but the government's intention to abolish exchange controls and make it fully convertible testifies to the currency's stability.

The **shekel** is divided into one hundred **agorot**. Coins exist in denominations of ten and fifty agorot, and one, five and ten shekels. Notes come in denominations of twenty, fifty, one hundred and two hundred shekels. Ten-shekel notes are gradually being phased out, and although coins of one and five agorot exist, they're totally useless in practice.

As yet, Palestine does not have its own currency, though it is the PNA's intention to introduce one. It will probably be called a dinar, and divided into a thousand fils (PNA stamps are priced in fils). In the meantime, Israeli shekels are the main currency throughout the Palestinian Territories, with Jordanian dinars also in use, especially on the West Bank.

However, it's worth noting that American dollars are widely accepted in all areas of Israel and the Palestinian Territories, and along with other hard currencies can be used to pay bills not only in hotels (rates are usually quoted in dollars anyway), but also in restaurants and shops. The advantage of paying for hotels, car rental or air tickets in hard currency is that it avoids payment of VAT (currently seventeen percent).

BANKS AND EXCHANGE

In many towns, the only place you can change money is a **bank**. It's a laborious process; you have to queue at one desk, show ID, wait while the clerk types out a form, take it to another desk, then stand in line again to get your shekels. Banks usually charge commission, and don't offer particularly good rates of exchange either – for the correct daily **exchange rate** look in the *Jerusalem Post*. Banks in Israel accept most major hard currencies including Euros, but not usually New Zealand dollars, Irish pounds, South African rand, Cyprus pounds or Greek drachmas, and definitely not Egyptian pounds, Jordanian dinars, or Scottish or Northern Irish sterling notes. Some banks in large cities or tourist resorts have **24-hour exchange machines** which accept US dollars, pounds sterling, and major European currencies, though their rates are even poorer than the banks'. In autonomous Palestine, moneychangers are ubiquitous and you may never need to see the inside of a bank, but if you do have to use one, you'll find procedures equally cumbersome, and you may find in some that cash US dollars and Jordanian dinars are the only currencies accepted.

Opening hours for banks in Israel are usually Sunday, Tuesday and Thursday 8.30am to 12.30pm and 4 to 5.30pm, Monday, Wednesday and Friday 8.30am to 12.30pm only. In autonomous Palestine, they are open Saturday to Thursday 8.30am to 12.30pm.

Moneychangers are the obvious alternative to a bank. Long-established throughout the Palestinian Territories, they offer a quick service, better rates than the banks and usually no commission. Unlike banks, they also accept Egyptian, Jordanian and Cypriot currency, but not always travellers' cheques. In Israel itself, moneychangers are new, and so far confined to major tourist centres, although there is not yet one in Haifa. Like their Palestinian counterparts they're quick and easy, and offer good rates of exchange; they don't charge commission for changing cash, but some of them do charge it on travellers' cheques. They are also likely to accept Egyptian, Jordanian, Cypriot, Greek and South African currency (though not Irish or New Zealand). **Hours** vary: Palestinian moneychangers tend to be open daily from around 8am to 4pm, while in Israel they are usually open Sunday to Thursday from 8.30 or 9am until any time between six and nine in the evening; on Fridays they close at 2 or 3pm. One or two may also open for a couple of hours after sunset on Saturdays. In Tel Aviv, Jerusalem and Haifa, there are also branches of **American Express** (see "Listings" of each town for addresses), who will change their own travellers' cheques without commission.

Large branches of Israeli **post offices** (see p.45) have exchange facilities. They're efficient, offer decent rates, accept travellers' cheques, and don't charge commission. They accept major hard currencies, except Irish pounds, New Zealand dollars, or Egyptian, Jordanian or Cypriot money. Large **hotels** will change money for their guests, but are loath to do so for anyone else; their rates will be the worst of all.

It's still illegal to change money on the street and the **black market** should only really be used as a last resort when everything else is closed (eg on Shabbat). In Israel, it exists mainly in Tel Aviv. Rates are no better than at banks and it's easy to be ripped off, so never hand over your hard currency until you have counted the shekels in your own hand. In autonomous Palestine, the black market is far more open, and can be found on the streets of Gaza and Ramallah. Rates are much the same as those offered by moneychangers with premises, though the latter are of course a safer bet.

Arriving in Israel, you'll find 24-hour exchange facilities at borders, airports and ports, though rates are not always as good as inside the country. **Leaving Israel**, you can change shekels back into hard currency (if it's more than $500, you'll need to show exchange receipts), but expect to lose around ten per cent of the value.

CASH, TRAVELLERS' CHEQUES AND PLASTIC

As far as **cash** is concerned, US dollars are definitely the best currency to bring as they fetch the best rates and are accepted as payment in most tourist places, including hotels, shops and restaurants. Pounds sterling and other major European currencies can also be used to pay hotel bills (except in the cheapest places). Canadian and Australian dollars may be accepted in hotels, but you're unlikely to be able to pay in Irish pounds, New Zealand dollars or South African rand.

Travellers' cheques are widely accepted by banks, moneychangers and hotels in Israel, slightly less so in the West Bank and Gaza, and have the advantage over cash that they can be replaced if lost or stolen. It's best to go for Thomas Cook/Mastercard, American Express, or Visa, as less well-known varieties may be difficult to change. US dollars are the best currency to use. **Eurocheques** can also be used in Israel with a Eurocheque card.

Most hotels, shops and restaurants in Israel accept the major **credit cards**. Your card will also enable you to get **cash advances** from certain **ATMs**, as will **debit cards** on the Cirrus and Plus systems. ATMs can be found in most towns, but remember that cash advances on credit cards accrue interest daily from the date of withdrawal; there may be a transaction fee on top of this, and there will invariably be a minimum amount you can withdraw.

WIRING MONEY

Funds can be sent via **Western Union** or **MoneyGram**; the former is more covenient as money can be wired through them to most major post offices in Israel. Fees depend on the amount being transferred, but as a guide, wiring £700/$1000 will cost around £40/$60. Funds should be available for collection (usually in shekels) from the company's local agent within minutes of being sent (this can be done in person at the company's nearest office, or over the phone using a credit card with Western Union). It's also possible to have money wired directly from a bank in your home country to a bank in Israel or the Palestinian Territories, although this is somewhat less reliable because it involves two separate institutions, but you may be able to draw it in dollars rather than shekels if desired.

HEALTH AND INSURANCE

Israel and the Palestinian Territories do not present any major health hazards and no vaccinations are required to enter. You may experience the odd bout of diarrhoea, and it's worth being fussy when it comes to eating street food, but apart from that, the main source of health problems is the climate, especially in desert areas where the sun can be very fierce. Hospitals vary in standard, but healthcare in general is good and comparable to that in the West, while pharmacies offer medical advice as well as remedies.

HEALTH PROBLEMS AND HAZARDS

It's wise to check that you're up to date with **polio** and **tetanus** boosters and, if you're planning to spend a long time in the Middle East, protection against **hepatitis A** is also a good idea. Although it exists here, rabies is not a serious problem; a vaccination is available (if expensive), but in the unlikely case that you are bitten by an infected animal, you will still need to seek immediate treatment to back up the initial vaccination. The best precaution is not to touch any animals.

However, the worst you're likely to encounter is an attack of **diarrhoea** (*shilshul* in Hebrew, *is-haal* in Arabic). This may simply be due to a change in diet, but could also be caused by eating street food that's been left out uncovered for too long. Be choosy and wash all fruit and vegetables and you should avoid an outbreak. If symptoms persist, and especially in the case of children, ensure that fluid levels are kept up: dissolving rehydration salts in water helps your body absorb

it. Failing that, half a teaspoon of table salt with four of sugar in a litre of water a day should see you all right. For the duration of the bout avoid greasy or spicy food, caffeine and most fruit or dairy products (although some say that bananas, pawpaws and prickly pears can help, while plain yoghurt provides a form of protein that can be easily absorbed by your body). Drugs such as Lomotil or Immodium plug you up and undermine your body's efforts to rid itself of infection, but can be a temporary stop-gap if you have to travel.

Despite the odd scare, **tap water** is generally safe to drink throughout the country, and in any case you should always be able to get locally produced mineral water. It is inadvisable, however, to drink from streams and wells unless they are clearly supplies of drinking water.

Never underestimate the **heat**, especially in desert areas; it's surprisingly easy to get sunstroke while sightseeing during the summer months. A hat is an essential precaution – the classic kibbutznik hat is ideal, and can be soaked in water for an extra cooling effect. Even a hazy Middle Eastern sun can burn fiercely so a high-factor sunscreen (available in Israel, but much more expensive than at home), is another essential item. Remember also to drink plenty of fluids to avoid dehydration. A potentially fatal hazard to be aware of is heatstroke. Signs are a very high body temperature without a feeling of fever, accompanied by headaches and disorientation/irrational behaviour. Lowering body temperature, with a tepid shower or bath for example, is the first step in treatment, but you should always seek further medical advice.

Mosquitoes can be a problem during the summer; to avoid getting bitten, take a mosquito repellent with you and apply it to all exposed parts of your body, especially around dusk, when the mozzies are most active. Remember that feet and ankles are their favourite target.

MEDICAL ATTENTION

For **minor complaints** you should go to a **pharmacy** (*mirkahat* in Hebrew, *saydaliya* in Arabic), where you will almost certainly find someone who speaks English. Pharmacists are well-trained and usually helpful. For more **serious complaints**, go to a doctor (*rofei* in Hebrew, *tabeeb* or *doktur* in Arabic); they virtually all speak English.

There is some form of hospital or clinic in even the smallest of places to which you can go in an **emergency**, and the standard of care is generally very good, though expensive if you are not insured, and generally better in Israel than in autonomous Palestine, where resources are scarcer. If you are taken seriously ill or involved in an accident in Israel, dial ☎101 for an ambulance.

INSURANCE

Wherever you're travelling from, it's a very good idea to have some kind of **travel insurance** to cover you for loss of possessions and money as well as the cost of medical and dental treatment. But before buying a policy, check to see what you are already covered for: **credit and charge cards** (particularly American Express) often include some degree of medical or other insurance, and travel insurance may also be included if you use a major credit or charge card to pay for your trip. Some package tours may include insurance, but more commonly offer an insurance deal as an extra.

Premiums vary, though maximum payouts tend to be meagre, so shop around. Activities such as scuba **diving** are usually specifically excluded, but can be added for a supplement, usually 20–50 percent. The best deals are usually offered by student/youth travel agencies, such as STA, Campus or USIT (see pp.4, 9, 11 and 14 for addresses). A 24-hour medical emergency contact number is a must, and one of the rare policies that pays your medical bills directly is better than one that reimburses you on your return home. The per-article limit for loss or theft should cover your most valuable possession (a camcorder for example).

Finally, and with the greatest hope that it will not come to this, remember that **war zones** are not covered by insurance policies, and that wars are not unknown in this part of the world. Make sure that your insurance policy covers all the places you intend to visit.

INSURANCE IN THE UK AND IRELAND

Travellers from the UK can obtain travel insurance from any bank or travel agent. Most travel agents and tour operators will offer you insurance when you book your flight or holiday, and some will insist you take it – their policies are usually reasonable value. Alternatively, you can buy a policy from a specialist travel firm like Campus Travel or STA (see p.4 for addresses), or from the

low-cost **insurers** Endsleigh Insurance and Columbus Travel Insurance. Two weeks' cover starts at around £27; one month costs from £34. Good-value policies for long-term (or multiple trip) travellers can be had from Marcus Hearn & Co: a year's cover (with no single journey exceeding 120 days) will cost around £100. Note that some insurance companies refuse to cover travellers over 65, or stop at 69 or 74 years of age, and most that do charge hefty premiums. The best policies for **older travellers**, with no upper age limit, are offered by Age Concern (☎01883/346964).

If you have a good "all risks" home insurance policy it may cover your possessions against loss or theft even when overseas, or you can extend cover through your household contents insurer. Many private medical schemes also cover you when abroad.

In **Ireland**, travel insurance is best obtained through a travel specialist such as USIT (see p.9 for addresses). Their policies cost £21 for six to ten days, £31 for one month. Discounts are offered to students and anyone under 35.

INSURANCE IN NORTH AMERICA

For **travellers from North America**, an important thing to bear in mind is that most policies do not insure against **theft** of anything while overseas, but apply only to items lost from, or damaged in, the custody of an identifiable, responsible third party (hotel porter, airline, baggage deposit, etc). Even in these cases you will have to contact the local police to have a complete **report** made out so that your insurer can process the claim.

Canadian provincial health plans typically provide some overseas medical coverage, although they are unlikely to pick up the full tab. Holders of official **student/teacher/youth cards** are also entitled to accident coverage and hospital in-patient benefits (annual membership is far less than the cost of comparable insurance), while university students will often find that their student health coverage extends during the vacations and for one term beyond the date of last enrolment. Finally, homeowners' or renters' insurance often covers theft or loss of documents, money and valuables while overseas, though conditions and maximum amounts vary from company to company.

In the **US**, the best **premiums** are usually to be had through student/youth travel agencies – for example, ISIS policies (including medical insurance) cost $60 for fifteen days, $110 for a

TRAVEL INSURANCE COMPANIES AND AGENTS

BRITAIN AND IRELAND

Columbus Travel Insurance 17 Devonshire Square, London EC2M 4SQ (☎0171/375 0011).

Endsleigh Insurance 97–107 Southampton Row, London WC1B 4AG (☎0171/436 4451).

Marcus Hearn & Co 65–66 Shoreditch High St, London E1 6JL (☎0171/739 3444).

USIT (see p.9 for full list of addresses) Dublin ☎01/679 8333; Belfast ☎01232/324073.

Worldcover PO Box 555, Cardiff CF5 6XH (☎0800/365121).

NORTH AMERICA

Access America PO Box 90310, Richmond, VA 23230 (☎1-800/284 8300).

Carefree Travel Insurance PO Box 310, 120 Mineola Blvd, Mineola, NY 11501 (☎1-800/323 3149).

Desjardins Travel Insurance 200 Ave des Commandeurs, Lévis, PQ G6V 6R2 (☎1-800/463 7830).

International Student Insurance Service (ISIS) – sold by STA Travel (see p.11; ☎1-800/777 0112).

Travel Guard 1145 Clark St, Stevens Point, WI 54481 (☎1-800/826 1300; www.noelgroup.com).

Travel Insurance Services 2930 Camino Diablo, Suite 300, Walnut Creek, CA 94596 (☎1-800/937 1387).

AUSTRALASIA

AFTA (Australian Federation of Travel Agents), 144 Pacific Highway, North Sydney, NSW (☎02/9264 3299).

Cover More Level 9, 32 Walker St, North Sydney, NSW (☎02/9202 8000, toll-free ☎1800/251 881).

Ready Plan 141–147 Walker St, Dandenong, Vic (toll-free ☎1800/337 462); 10th floor, 63 Albert Street, Auckland (☎09/379 3208).

UTAG (United Travel Agents Group), 347 Kent St, Sydney, NSW (toll-free ☎1800/809 462).

month, $165 for two months, $665 for a year. Insurance covers up to $50,000 of medical fees.

INSURANCE IN AUSTRALIA AND NZ

In **Australia and New Zealand**, travel insurance is put together by the airlines and travel agent groups such as UTAG, AFTA, Cover More and Ready Plan in conjunction with insurance companies. They are all similar in premium and coverage but Ready Plan gives the best value for money. **Adventure sports** are usually covered, but not unassisted diving without an Open Water licence, so check your policy if you plan on doing that. A typical policy will cost A$190/NZ$220 for one month, A$270/NZ$320 for two months and A$330/NZ$400 for three months.

INFORMATION AND MAPS

There's no shortage of information on tourist sights and resorts in Israel although any reference to political controversy is, as you might expect, subtly avoided. Leaflets, pamphlets and a large number of maps and town plans are easy to get hold of both inside the country and from Israeli Government Tourist Offices abroad.

Information on the **Palestinian Territories** is much harder to come by, and is usually best obtained from independent sources rather than official ones, since the Palestinian Ministry of Tourism is not tremendously efficient and produces little in the way of literature, the exception to this rule being Bethlehem. East Jerusalem and Latrun, along with the Golan Heights, are considered by the Israeli government to be part of Israel, and are therefore covered by official Israeli tourist offices.

INFORMATION ON ISRAEL

The **Israeli Government Tourist Office (IGTO)** produces a vast collection of leaflets, maps and brochures in English and several European languages, including glossy pamphlets on the main towns and resorts, lists of hotels and kibbutzim, guides to archeological sites, and details of study programmes. As all of them are available in Israel, there's not much point lugging them with you, though you might want to have a look at some before you leave.

Within the Green Line, there are IGTO offices or municipal tourist offices in virtually every major town (locations are given in the Guide). These dis-

IGTOs ABROAD

AUSTRALIA 395 New South Head Rd, Double Bay, Sydney (☎02/9326 1700).

CANADA 180 Bloor St West, Suite 700, Toronto, Ontario M5S 2V6 (☎1-800/669 2369 or 416/964 3784).

NETHERLANDS Wijde Kapelsteeg 2 (Hoek Rokin), 1012 NS Amsterdam (☎02/624 9642).

SOUTH AFRICA 5th floor, Nedbank Gds, 33 Bath Ave, Rosebank, PO Box 52560, Saxonwold 2132, Johannesburg (☎011/788 1700).

UK UK House, 180 Oxford St, London W1N 0EL (☎0171/299 1111).

USA 800 Second Ave, New York, NY 10017. (☎212/499 5650); 5 South Wabash Av, Chicago, IL 60603 3073 (☎1-800/782 4306 or ☎312/782 4306); 5151 Belt Line Rd, Suite 1280, Dallas, Texas 75240 (☎1-800/472 6364 or ☎214/991 9097 or 8); 6380 Wilshire Blvd ☎1718, Los Angeles, CA 90048 (☎213/658 7462 or 3).

pense more detailed **local information**, usually a free town plan, cards for hotels, restaurants and places of interest, and free Israeli listings magazines such as *Hello Israel*, *This Week in Israel* and *This Week in Jerusalem.* Sometimes, tourist offices can arrange "Zimmer" b&b accommodation, and they will also help recommend restaurants or accommodation and have information about free tours and events. There are also independent organizations able to offer information on Israel that will be of interest to the visitor (see box on p.28).

An alternative source of information within Israel itself is the (roughly) monthly free **The Traveller** – a travellers' newspaper available at hostels and traveller-oriented bars in Tel Aviv, Jerusalem, Eilat and Tiberias. As well as regular features on sites and cities of tourist interest, and reviews of bars, restaurants and hostels, it also has information on working in Israel and the latest developments on the local travel front.

INFORMATION ON THE PALESTINIAN TERRITORIES

Sources of tourist information on the Palestinian Territories are somewhat limited. The **PNA's**

USEFUL WEB SITES

There are thousands of **Web sites** specializing in Israeli and Palestinian issues. They cover many subjects, but most are concerned with politics and many are extremely partisan, a fact you should bear in mind when reading them. Listed below is a small selection of the most comprehensive and useful ones.

SITES SPECIFIC TO ISRAEL AND THE PALESTINIAN TERRITORIES

Alternative Information Centre
www.aic.netgate.net/index.htm
Information from ground level on the latest situation from a Jerusalem-based research organization and pressure group.

Ariga www.ariga.co.il/gentoc.htm
A good source of information and resources both Israeli and Palestinian.

Bir Zeit University www.birzeit.edu
A vast quantity of authoritative information on Palestinian affairs put out by the West Bank's main university.

B'Tselem www.btselem.org
The latest from a very active Israeli human rights organization.

Euroweb www.euroweb.co.uk/middleeast/
ISRAEL.HTM or WESTBANK.HTM or GAZA.HTM
Solid data on Israel and the Palestinian Territories, covering geography, politics and the economy.

Guide to the Peace Process
www.israel-mfa.gov.il/peace/guide.html
The Israeli Foreign Ministry's comprehensive guide to the peace process.

Islamic Association for Palestine
www.iap.org *Human rights updates and links to other sites.*

Israeli Foreign Ministry www.israel.org
Official Israeli angle on latest Middle East news.

Israel Tourist Ministry www.infotour.co.il
A well-organized and comprehensive site covering accommodation, restaurants, sites, museums, tours, events and transport.

Jerusalem Post www.jpost.com
The latest Israeli news from Israel's right-wing English-language daily newspaper.

Jerusalem Report www.jreport.virtual.co.il
Samples from Israel's equivalent of Time, Newsweek *or* The Economist.

Jewish/Israel Links www.maven.co.il
Enormous search engine covering everything related to Israel and Judaism. Over 4500 links to all manner of subjects.

Palestine Information Centre www.alquds.org
Mainly for Palestinians abroad, but still a useful source of information covering both sides of the Green Line.

Palestine Links
www.birzeit.edu/links/index.html
Huge and authoritative list of links for anything Palestinian.

Palestine National Authority www.pna.org
Official site with regularly updated information.

Palestine Times www.ptimes.com
Monthly English-language Palestinian newspaper.

Peace Now www.peace-now.org
Left-wing Israeli pro-peace pressure group.

RELEVANT MIDDLE EAST SITES

Amnesty International Library
www.amnesty/org/ailib
Coverage of human rights infringements and prisoners of conscience, critical of all sides without fear or favour.

Arab Net www.arab.net

The Arab World www.1001sites.com

Arab World Online www.awo.net
Three sites with background and statistics on most Arab countries.

Human Rights Watch Middle East
www.hrw.org/about/divisions/mideast.htm *The latest human rights situation from a highly respected Washington-based research institution.*

MENIC www.menic.utexas.edu/mes.html *Huge and authoritative site run by the University of Texas's Middle East and North Africa Information Centre.*

Middle East Links
www.129.177.211.69:80/smi/links.html and www.isn.ethz.ch
Two sites for links on all subjects of Middle East relevance.

PeaceNet Middle East
www.igc.org/igc/issues/me
International peace organization with links to other sites.

Ministry of Tourism has offices in Gaza, Jericho and Bethlehem but is a good deal less efficient than its Israeli counterpart. Independent tourist information organizations do exist but they tend to specialize in information for pilgrims, though they're happy to supply other tourist information if they have it – the main example being the Christian Information Centre in Jerusalem (see below). Information and maps are also sometimes available from municipalities (town halls) – Gaza's municipality, for example, puts out a particularly good map.

If you have an interest in the political situation, organizations primarily concerned with political issues (generally critical of Israel, and often of the PNA too) may be able to offer advice, provide or suggest background reading material and recommend people and places to visit. There are also numerous **Palestine solidarity and support groups** whose members often have first-hand experience to share with prospective visitors, and who will be able to provide details on summer workcamps and visiting refugee camps. Within Israel and the Palestinian Territories, various Palestinian (and some Israeli) institutions will be able to offer advice on the advisability or otherwise of visiting certain areas. It's best to phone before going along to see them, as they are pri-

ALTERNATIVE SOURCES OF INFORMATION

IN ISRAEL AND THE PALESTINIAN TERRITORIES

Alternative Information Centre 6 Koresh, PO Box 31417, West Jerusalem (☎02/624 1159, fax 625 3151, email: *aicmail@trendline.co.il*). Publishes the monthly News from Within, *a commentary on the latest situation by a peace-orientated group of Israelis and Palestinians. See also p.000.*

Christian Information Centre PO Box 14308, Omar Ibn al-Khattab Square, Jaffa Gate, Jerusalem (☎02/627 2692, fax 628 6417, email: *cicbarat@netmedia.net.il*). *Information for pilgrims and anyone else visiting religious or other sites in the Holy Land.*

PNA Ministry of Tourism and Antiquities Sharia Tarek ben Ziad, Gaza City (☎07/829461 or 2); Manger Square, PO Box 534, Bethlehem (☎02/741581, fax 743753). *The PNA's tourist office.*

Palestine Human Rights Information Centre top floor, 12 Mas'udi, East Jerusalem (☎02/628 7076 or 7, email: *phric@baraka.org*). *Briefings on the latest human rights situation.*

Palestinian Centre for Human Rights Qadada Building, PO Box 1204, Sharia Omar al-Mukhtar, Gaza City (☎07/825893, fax 824776, email: *pchr@trendline.co.il*). *Publishes regular bulletins and occasional reports.*

Jerusalem Media and Communication Centre PO Box 25047, Nablus Rd, East Jerusalem (☎02/581 9776 or 7, fax 582 9534, email: *jmcc@baraka.org*). *Publishes the weekly* Palestine Report, *and daily press briefings.*

Arab Studies Society 10 Abu Obeida, PO Box 20479, East Jerusalem (☎02/626 4070). *Publishes an excellent political and historical map of twentieth-century Palestine.*

ABROAD

Al Saqi Bookshop 26 Westbourne Grove, London W2 5RH (☎0171/229 8543). *Britain's main specialist bookshop on the Arab world.*

The Centre for the Advancement of Arab-British Understanding (CAABU) 21 Collingham Rd, London SW5 0NU (☎0171/373 8414). *Also the Friends of Bir Zeit University at the same address.*

Islamic Information and Support Centre of Australia (IISCA), 18a Lygon St, Brunwick East, Vic 3057 (☎03/9387 4722).

Jerusalem Times 200 Rhine Drive, Alpharetta, GA 30202 (☎770/640 8360; email *tjt@palnet.* com). *The US office of the Palestinian English-language weekly.*

Palestine General Delegation Unit 3, Galena Rd, London W6 0LT (☎0181/563 0008); 818 18th St, NW 620, Washington, DC 20006 (☎202/785 8394); 170 Laurier Ave, W 600, Ottawa, ON K1P 5V5 (☎613/238 2523); 27 State Circle, Deakin, Canberra, ACT 2600 (☎02/6360 9171). *The official representative of the PNA and the PLO.*

Palestine Times PO Box 10355, London NW2 3WH (email: *paltimes@ptimes.com*). *Publishers of a monthly English-language newspaper.*

marily concerned with issues more pressing than those of tourism; but their staff are usually helpful.

Many of these organizations are detailed in the relevant chapters, above all in Jerusalem where most are concentrated, but the main ones are listed in the box on p.28. East Jerusalem travel agents, too numerous to list, will also be knowledgeable about travel to the Palestinian Territories. **Abroad**, you may be able to obtain information about visiting the Palestinian Territories from the local Palestine General Delegation (representing the PLO and the PNA).

MAPS

Good **touring maps** are easily available in Israel, and free ones are available from IGTO offices nationwide. However, one of the best maps is supplied by the **National Parks Authority** (NPA,

---

MAP OUTLETS AROUND THE WORLD

UK AND IRELAND

London Daunt Books, 83 Marylebone High St, W1M 3DE (☎0171/224 2295); 193 Haverstock Hill, NW3 4QL (☎0171/794 4006); National Map Centre, 22–24 Caxton St, SW1H 0QU (☎0171/ 222 2466); Stanfords, 12–14 Long Acre, WC2E 9LP (☎0171/836 1321); The Travel Bookshop, 13–15 Blenheim Crescent, W11 2EE (☎0171/229 5260).

Dublin Eason's, 40 O'Connell St, Dublin 1 (☎01/873 3811).

Aberdeen Aberdeen Map Shop, 74 Skene St, AB10 1QE (☎01224/637999).

Belfast Waterstone's, Queens Bldg, 8 Royal Ave, BT1 1DA (☎01232/247 355).

Cardiff Blackwell's, 13–17 Royal Arcade, CF1 2PR (☎01222/395036).

Glasgow John Smith and Sons, 57–61 St Vincent St, G2 5TB (☎0141/221 7472).

*NB: Maps by **mail or phone order** are available from Stanfords (☎0171/836 1321) and several of the other listed suppliers.*

USA

Chicago Rand McNally, 444 N Michigan Ave, IL 60611 (☎312/321 1751).

Maryland Travel Books & Language Centre, 4931 Cordell Ave, Bethesda, MD 20814 (☎1-800/220 2665).

New York The Complete Traveler Bookstore, 199 Madison Ave, New York, NY 10016 (☎212/685 9007); Rand McNally, 150 E 52nd St, New York, NY 10022 (☎212/758 7488); Traveler's Bookstore, 22 W 52nd St, New York, NY 10019 (☎212/664 0995).

San Francisco Rand McNally, 595 Market St, San Francisco, CA 94105 (☎415/777 3131); Sierra Club Bookstore, 6014 College Ave, Oakland, CA 94618 (☎510/658 7470).

Washington DC The Map Store Inc, 1636 1st St, Washington DC 20006 (☎202/628 2608).

Vermont Adventurous Traveler Bookstore, PO Box 1468, Williston, VT 05495 (☎1-800/282 3963).

*NB: For other locations of **Rand McNally** across the US, or for direct-mail maps, phone ☎1-800/333 0136, ext 2111.*

CANADA

Montréal Ulysses Travel Bookshop, 4176 St-Denis, Montréal, PQ H2W 2M5 (☎514/843 9447).
Toronto Open Air Books and Maps, 25 Toronto St, Toronto, ON M5R 2C1 (☎416/363 0719).

Vancouver World Wide Books and Maps, 552 Seymour St, Vancouver, BC V6B 3J5 (☎604/687 3320).

AUSTRALIA AND NEW ZEALAND

Adelaide The Map Shop, 16a Peel St, SA 5000 (☎08/8231 2033).
Auckland Specialty Maps, 58 Albert St (☎09/307 2217).
Brisbane Worldwide Maps and Guides, 187 George St, Qld 4000 (☎07/3221 4330).

Melbourne Bowyangs, 372 Little Bourke St, Vic 3000 (☎03/9670 4383).
Perth Perth Map Centre, 891 Hay St, WA 6000 (☎09/9322 5733).
Sydney Travel Bookshop, Shop 3, 175 Liverpool St, NSW 2000 (☎02/9261 8200).

scale 1:400,000); available at IGTO offices abroad (see p.26 for addresses), though not in Israel itself. The Israeli firm MAP produces good 1:350,000 road maps, and very detailed road atlases of the country too on scales of 1:50,000 and 1:100,000. The Survey of Israel also produces a two-sheet 1:250,000 touring map.

What you won't find on Israeli-produced maps, however, is the **Green Line** between Israel and the West Bank and Gaza Strip, or the border between Israel and the Golan Heights, as this is prohibited by Israeli law (though recent maps do show the areas under the jurisdiction of the PNA). You'll need to bring a map from abroad if you want to know what side of the line you are on, something which may be important during times of political tension.The maps at the beginning of each chapter of this book show the political divisions clearly, and those for the chapters on Jerusalem, the West Bank, Gaza Strip and Golan Heights show them in some detail, for both historical and practical reasons.

Of road **maps produced abroad**, one of the best, and certainly the best-value is Hildebrand's 1:350,000, although it doesn't cover all of the Golan Heights. Freytag & Berndt's 1:400,000 is a good second. Of the rest: Hallwag's 1:500,000 isn't brilliantly accurate; Kummerly & Frey's 1:750,000 isn't detailed enough for navigation off main routes, though it does cover the main parts of Jordan and Egypt; Baedecker's 1:600,000 is reasonable, but still not as good as the free NPA map; while IGN's is basically the same as the NPA's, but you pay for it.

An excellent map more of historical than practical interest is published by the **Arab Studies Society** (see box on p.28 for address). It shows the present international borders, the armistice lines, the borders according to the 1947 Partition Plan, the distribution of Palestinian towns and villages in 1945, and the Jewish settlements that have since been established.

CITY AND TOWN MAPS

Town plans are available for most major tourist destinations in Israel, from tourist offices in the towns themselves and very often from IGTO offices elsewhere. In other towns, detailed maps with a street index are posted in the town centre and by the bus station; the problem with these is that they are usually in Hebrew only. Municipalities may also be able to provide you with a map, but again they are likely to be in Hebrew. Maps of Tel Aviv, Jerusalem and Haifa are available in bookshops: particularly recommended are those published by MAP.

Outside the Green Line, in the West Bank and Gaza, the Palestinian Ministry of Tourism produces maps of Bethlehem and Jericho; maps of Gaza are available from the municipality there.

HIKING MAPS AND MAPS OF ARCHEOLOGICAL SITES

The Survey of Israel produces an excellent set of **hiking maps** (£10/$16 each), available from their offices in Tel Aviv (1 Lincoln, near the corner of Ibn Gvirol – take ID if visiting) and Jerusalem (Heleni HaMalka at the corner of Jaffa Road), and from camping shops such as Lamtayel and those run by the SPNI.

The National Parks Authority gives out free maps of virtually all the **archeological sites** it maintains, which are usually very good and contain quite detailed explanations. Their "map" of Caesarea is in fact an aerial photograph. Plans of many other sites can be found in Jerome Murphy-O'Connor's excellent book, *The Holy Land: an Archaeological Guide from Earliest Times to 1700*, published by OUP in Britain (see p.508), but also available (at a higher price) in Israel.

GETTING AROUND

By far the most common means of public transport in Israel is the bus, with almost the entire country covered by an efficient, regular and comfortable service. In the Palestinian Territories, buses are privately run and a bit more ramshackle, with the result that many people prefer to use a shared "service taxi". These are similar in price and connect all the major towns, setting out as soon as enough people have gathered to fill one up. There's a railway along the coast and inland to Jerusalem, with talk of extending the network along lines currently used only for freight. Renting a car may be worthwhile in the remoter parts, and hitching is still popular, if risky. Internal flights connect the major centres but distances are so short that they are rarely worthwhile.

BUSES

The **bus system in Israel**, run by the national **Egged** cooperative, is well-developed, efficient and frequent. Buses are modern and fast, with air conditioning on most major routes, and often a choice between direct and stopping services. If you want a bus to stop en route, ring the bell before the stop. Likewise, if waiting at a bus stop, you should hail the bus or it may sail on past.

Tickets can be bought on board but, especially for less frequent inter-city routes (Eilat to Jerusalem, for instance), it's worth buying your ticket from the kiosk at the bus station before departure to ensure you get on. **Fares**, subsidized by the government, are pretty reasonable (£11/$18

from Eilat to Jerusalem, for example). On presentation of an ISIC card, students can obtain a ten percent discount on most inter-city routes. You can also buy **Israbus passes** that allow unlimited travel on Egged services anywhere in Israel. A 7-day ticket costs 185NIS, 14 days 290NIS, 21 days 360NIS and 30 days 400NIS. These are available from all main bus stations and Egged offices, but you'd have to be travelling more or less permanently to make the saving worthwhile.

Although some Egged routes do cross the Green Line, they serve only Jewish settlements, and, for the most part, buses **outside the Green Line** are operated by a multiplicity of small companies. Some of the vehicles are battered old veterans that rattle along the road, stopping frequently, not least at army roadblocks. The seats aren't especially comfortable, and the services aren't very fast, but they're just as frequent as Israeli buses and the fares are rather cheaper. Services usually stop at sunset.

Hours of operation for most Egged services are Sunday to Thursday 5am to 11.30pm. There are usually no buses on Friday evenings, the evenings before holidays, or most of Saturday (services may run after nightfall on Saturday, especially long-distance ones). The exceptions are Haifa and Nazareth, where a partial bus service operates on the Sabbath and holidays. In the West Bank (including East Jerusalem) and the Gaza Strip, buses run every day.

Bus tours, ranging from visits to archeological and biblical sites to desert tours and scenic trips, are another way of getting around. The **main operators** are Egged Tours, Galilee Tours and United Tours. All have offices in Tel Aviv, Jerusalem and Eilat, while Galilee Tours also has an office in Tiberias, and Egged Tours has an office in Haifa, and at the bus stations in Ashdod, Beersheba, Nahariyya, Netanya, Rishon Le Zion and Tiberias. Addresses are given under "Travel agents" in the "Listings" sections of major towns in this book. You can also pick up the companies' brochures at IGTOs, and United Tours has a website at *www.intournet.co.il/unitedtours/index. html*.

Egged **city buses** run on a nationwide flat fare (currently 4.10NIS). Like inter-city buses, they do not operate on Shabbat, except in Haifa and Nazareth.

TAXIS

The main rival to the buses are **service taxis** or **sheruts** (*sherut* is Hebrew for "service"; in Arabic they say *servees*). Generally seven-seater Mercedes, but sometimes minibuses, they operate along set inter-urban routes. Individual **fares** are similar to those on buses or slightly higher, but the taxis are faster, more comfortable, and more convenient; the driver will drop you off where you want along the way and may agree to take you on to your destination in town for an extra charge. They may also run on the Sabbath and festivals, when there are no inter-city buses in Israel.

The driver will not set off until the car is full, so you may be in for a long wait on some routes (especially on Shabbat and festivals), though on the main inter-city routes, such as Jerusalem–Tel Aviv, you'll rarely have to hang around for more than a few minutes. Sheruts run throughout the night on some routes but can take some time to fill up. You can sometimes hail a service taxi on the road, particularly in remoter areas; if there is room, the driver will stop to pick you up and charge you a fare according to the distance.

Sherut or *servees* stands in town are usually located near the Central Bus Station (but see relevant town accounts). In Tel Aviv, there are also minibus sheruts running along two city bus routes at a slightly higher price than the bus. In the Gaza Strip, many private cars function as unofficial service taxis both within Gaza City and around the Strip.

Regular **private ("special") taxis** are not cheap; drivers must by law operate the taxi meters, but many object to this and will try to get you to accept a set fare – invariably higher than the meter rate. You could threaten to report them (to the IGTO or the police) but don't expect them to quake in fear and, at peak times in particular, they will often just drive off if you don't accept their price. For inter-city journeys, be sure to agree a price beforehand. They are also supposed to give you a receipt on demand which will have their cab number on it.

TRAINS

Israeli trains are modern, efficient and clean. Routes are concentrated along the coast, with regular services from Tel Aviv north to Netanya, Haifa, Acre and Nahariyya, and south to Lydda and Ashdod (with talk of extension to Ashqelon). There is also one daily train between Tel Aviv and Jerusalem – a particularly picturesque journey – and currently an experimental twice-weekly service to Beersheba. A line to Eilat is under construction, and there is also talk of rebuilding the lines into neighbouring countries that were cut during various wars. One reason why the rail system has not been developed much so far is the fear that it would be a prime target for Palestinian paramilitaries, as it was for Jewish paramilitaries under the British Mandate, but buses have shown themselves to be equally vulnerable to attack, a fact that may have been partly responsible for the rethink.

Fares are not expensive (Tel Aviv to Jerusalem or Haifa costs just over £3/$5), and students get a 25 percent discount on production of an ISIC card. As with buses, however, there is no service on the Sabbath or on Jewish holidays. One disadvantage of trains is that the stations are often some way out of the towns they serve, and you may even need to take a city bus into town from them. A full **timetable** is usually available from major stations, and a copy will be posted up at all stations. For **enquiries**, call ☎03/693 7515.

DRIVING AND CAR RENTAL

Israeli driving is notorious, but in fact it has improved markedly in recent years. Roads in Israel are good, and car rental is a good way to see the country. However, it is not advisable to take rented vehicles into the West Bank or Gaza. Driver's licences from most Western countries are valid in Israel and the Palestinian Territories.

CAR RENTAL

Car rental is well worth considering, the only problem being that you cannot really **cross the Green Line** in a rented vehicle. Cars rented in Israel (or East Jerusalem) will easily be recognizable by their yellow **number plates** (those in the rest of the West Bank are blue, green or white), and may be the target of stone-throwers in the West Bank and Gaza; while cars rented in the West Bank or Gaza will be the object of much unwelcome attention from security forces in Israel. And all this is assuming that the rental firm will allow you to take their vehicle either way across the Green Line in the first place.

To rent a car, you must have a valid driver's licence and be over 21, or sometimes (depending on the company) over 23. Rental **charges** for unlimited distance start at around £20/$35 per day basic with supplements for collision waiver, insurance, high season and under-23-year-old drivers adding an extra £8–18/$10–25. Payment in hard currency avoids VAT. Local firms are sometimes cheaper than the big international companies, but their vehicles may not be in such good condition, and they may not have as many branches. A selection of car rental offices in major towns is given in the relevant "Listings" sections in this book (see also Orabi car hire, p.391)

Car rental in Eilat, a duty-free zone, is about ten percent cheaper than anywhere else in the country, the only drawback being that you usually have to return the car to Eilat.

BRINGING YOUR OWN VEHICLE

It is possible, but hardly convenient, **to import a vehicle** (a car of up to 4.25m can be carried on the ferry from Piraeus for around £90–110/$150–180 depending on the season, a motorbike for around £40–55/$65–90). Land borders with Egypt and now also Jordan are open to private vehicles too. To import a vehicle, you must have a driver's licence, ownership documents and a green card for international insurance covering Israel, and you must re-export it within a year (unless you want to pay massive duty).

ROAD CONDITIONS AND RULES OF THE ROAD

In general, **roads** in Israel are good and well maintained. Those in the West Bank and Gaza are much less so, following years of neglect, although the PNA is now trying to improve those under its jurisdiction. You **drive on the right**, and at unmarked junctions, priority is from the right. **Speed limits**, seldom observed, are 50km/hr (31mph) in built-up areas, 80km/hr (50mph) in open country, and 90km/hr (56mph) on the motorway, unless otherwise indicated. **Seat belts** are only compulsory outside city limits.

Although driving standards are gradually improving, **road fatalities** are still alarmingly high – a commonly quoted statistic is that more people have died in traffic accidents than in all the Arab-Israeli conflicts put together. In general, people drive with chutzpah, and will try to get away with anything they can: they overtake on both sides (legally you must pass on the left), come up close behind vehicles they wish to overtake and flash or honk, speed up when being overtaken, drive slowly in the overtaking lane encouraging others to pass on the right, and turn or change lanes without indicating. To stay out of trouble, it's best to drive defensively, keep your distance, and give way to aggressive drivers.

Traffic jams are now a big problem in central Israel and the roads are increasingly clogged up in the entire Tel Aviv region and beyond during the rush hour (7–9am coming into Tel Aviv, 4–6pm leaving). Routes 1, 2, 4, 42 and 481 are especially badly hit, and even Route 40 is not immune. If at all possible, avoid driving in the area at those times, and especially in those directions.

CYCLING

Because of their compact size, Israel and Palestine – and in particular central Israel – are well suited for exploration **by bicycle**. Major roads generally have a hard shoulder suitable for cyclists, and Egged buses will take them for half-fare. Some areas are rather hilly, notably the Galilee, the Carmel and the northern part of the West Bank, but cycling down into the Jordan Valley is a breeze, though the heat and gradient will probably conspire to get you on a bus for the return journey. Most people intending to tour extensively by bike bring their own (you can usually check in a bicycle as baggage on a plane but confirm this with your airline – you may have to pack it first); it's a good idea to bring with you as full as possible a set of **spares**. You can **rent cycles** in Tiberias, Eilat and Jericho, but these are mainly intended for local visits. An alternative is to **buy a bike** and sell it before leaving.

For further **information** on cycling in Israel, contact the Jerusalem Cycling Club (☎02/561 9416).

HITCHING

Hitching ("*tremping*") is not as common as it once was in Israel, and is increasingly dangerous with several cases of hitchhikers being attacked, molested, robbed or worse: in August 1997, two British hitchhikers were shot, one fatally, by a motorist who had picked them up in the Negev, and whose motives remain obscure. **Women** should definitely not hitch alone.

If, in spite of the dangers, you still want to hitch, hold out your arm with your forefinger pointing down: thumbs up is a rude sign. There are specific hitching spots, called "*trempim*", usually next to bus stops. It's best to hitch from a bus stop anyway so that cars can pull in and it also gives you the option of the bus if you don't get a lift. Priority is still generally given to soldiers (even though they have been given free bus travel and are now actively discouraged from hitching), though many drivers will also stop for tourists and other civilians. Always ask drivers where they are going before you reveal your destination; this not only ensures that they really are going to the same place as you, but also gives you a brief time to get an impression of them. Avoid hitching at night and try not to get dropped in the middle of nowhere.

The same guidelines apply to **hitching in the West Bank and Gaza Strip**, though the hazards are if anything even greater given the political situation. Remember on the West Bank especially that where you can go depends on who picks you up: no Palestinian will be happy to take you into Jewish settlements like Qiryat Arba for example, while Jewish settlers are equally unlikely to drive you into Palestinian towns such as Nablus or Jenin. **Number plates** (see p.32) will give you a clue as to whether the car has a Jewish or Palestinian driver. Many vehicles plying the roads of the West Bank and, more especially, Gaza also function as taxis and may expect a fare, something it is wise to establish before getting in.

FLIGHTS

The Israeli airline **Arkia** operates a number of **internal flights** between Eilat, Jerusalem, Tel Aviv (Sede Dov Airport), Haifa, Rosh Pinna, Qiryat Shemona and Yotvata, although the country is so small that they're only worthwhile to or from Eilat, and then only if you're short of time. A one-way ticket from Eilat to Tel Aviv or Jerusalem costs $80. Arkia has a toll-free central reservations number at ☎1800/444888. From abroad, flights can be booked with Arkia's local General Sales Agent or through their Tel Aviv office (☎972-3/690 3333). If you're flying into Israel with El Al you can also book through them. For the latest fares, check the Web site at *www.arkia.co.il*.

ACCOMMODATION

Accommodation in Israel and the Palestinian Territories is rather expensive in comparison to most of their Mediterranean neighbours. In autonomous Palestine, accommodation can be thin on the ground, and almost all the hotels that exist are in the mid-range. In Israel, while the big cities offer cheaper alternatives, hotels and hostels in more out-of-the-way places can charge a small fortune. During the main Jewish holidays (Passover and New Year), accommodation is scarce in resorts such as Tel Aviv, Tiberias and Eilat; unsurprisingly, Jerusalem and Bethlehem are booked out at Christmas and Easter. At these times, therefore, it's advisable to book well in advance, though you can usually find a bed somewhere less popular.

HOTELS

Israeli **hotels** vary widely in price, typically from £35/$50 for a double in a basic guesthouse to well over £190/$300 in a super deluxe establishment. Where **breakfast** is included, which it usually is in low-priced and mid-range establishments, it is often a massive buffet, which goes some way to offsetting the price. Cheaper hotels tend to gather around the bus station or the local red-light district, which are often in the same place. They vary from clean and homely to grubby and tatty, but rooms are nearly always small,

ACCOMMODATION PRICE CODES

Throughout this guide, **hotel accommodation** is graded on a scale from ① to ⑥. The numbers represent the cost per night of the **cheapest double room in high season**, though remember that many of the cheap places will have more expensive rooms with en-suite facilities. For **hotels**, the code represents the price of **two dorm beds** and is followed by the code for a double room where applicable, eg ①/②. Hostels are listed in ascending price order.

① less than $20	③ $40–60	⑤ $80–100
② $20–40	④ $60–80	⑥ over $100

though usually with their own bathroom. Pricier hotels will be along the seafront or wherever the best views are to be had.

Prices can vary quite widely with the **season**, particularly in the more expensive establishments. High season is concentrated on the Jewish festivals of Passover (usually around April), the Jewish New Year (usually around September), and the summer months of July and August. The exception is Eilat, whose high season is at the end of December. Low season is from October to May, excluding the main Christian and Jewish holidays. At slack times a little **bargaining** over the price rarely goes amiss. Students may be entitled to a discount, so it's always worth asking. Note that the cheaper places tend to use solar heaters, so if visiting in winter, it's worth testing the **hot water** when checking out a room.

In the **Palestinian Territories**, hotels can be sparse, and cheap accommodation non-existent (the main exception to this rule is Bethlehem). For this reason, many travellers opt to stay in Jerusalem and visit the West Bank towns on day trips. Luxury hotels, too, are thin on the ground, though there is a good one in Nablus, and others in the pipeline for Jericho and the Gaza coast. Mid-range hotels, on the other hand, are much better value than they are in Israel and, though choice is limited, Gaza City, Jericho and Hebron have some very pleasant places to stay in the £20–30/$30–50 a night range.

HOSTELS AND OTHER ALTERNATIVES

Hostels with dormitory accommodation are usually the cheapest places to stay. In addition to the 31 **official hostels** run or recognized by the Israeli Youth Hostel Association (**IYHA**), there are a large number of **privately run hostels**, mostly in Tel Aviv, Jerusalem and Eilat, but with a few scattered around the main tourist destinations countrywide.

PRIVATE HOSTELS

Private hostels vary widely in terms of facilities and atmosphere: the best are considerably better than cheap hotels, the worst can be awful. Although a selection is listed in this book, they open, close, change prices, improve and degenerate very fast, and your most up-to-date information will come from other travellers. Most are informal, and good places to meet other travellers and exchange information. They usually offer some sort of communal cooking and eating facilities as well as a laundry service, TV room and tours, but others are very basic and one or two are notorious for thefts and harassment of women, so it's a good idea to take a walk around and suss out the atmosphere before you book in.

Other things worth finding out about in advance are: **curfews and lock-outs** (most private hostels are open 24hr, but some have a night-time curfew or lock you out for cleaning around midday); checkout time; availability of lockers or safe-rooms for your baggage or valuables; cooking facilities; breakfast (generally not included in the price); and whether there are women-only dorms if you prefer not to share with men. Many of the cheapest and most basic places are favoured by long-stay travellers, who are often working in Israel.

Prices vary according to location, time of year and demand, but in general expect to pay £5–8/$8–12 for a bed in dormitory accommodation, £20/$30 for a private room. Some hostels offer mattresses "under the stars", usually on the roof, from about £3/$5. If it's hot, mosquitoes, muezzins and early dawns apart, this alternative can make for a better night's sleep than a stuffy room indoors.

IYHA HOSTELS

Official hostels tend to be much cleaner and generally better run than private hostels, and are not usually as regimented as in other countries (they are often open all night, for example). Expect to pay around £10/$16 a night in a dorm, with a saving of £3/$5 or so if you are a member of Hostelling International. A **list of IYHA hostels** can be obtained from their office at the International Conference Centre, Binyaney Ha'Ooma, PO Box 6001, Jerusalem 91060 (☎02/655 8400, fax 655 8432, email: *iyha@netvision.net.il*), or from IGTO offices. The IYHA also has a Web site at *www.youthhostels.org.il*.

The IYHA runs **tours** called "Israel on the Youth Hostel Trail". These 7-, 14- or 21-day tour packages (at $340, $650 and $910 respectively) include accommodation, breakfast and dinner, unlimited Egged bus travel, a phonecard, an information pack and free entrance to National Parks Authority sites throughout the country.

HOSPICES

Christian **hospices** generally offer facilities much the same as those of the better hostels and at similar prices. They're geared primarily to Christian pilgrims and therefore usually located in areas of particular interest to them, such as Jerusalem, Bethlehem, Nazareth, Tiberias and Haifa. Bear in mind, though, that a few won't accept lone visitors, and at others you'll need to reserve in advance during peak times (Christmas and Easter). Many hospices have quite austere regimes – very early curfews, for example – but they can also be wonderfully peaceful and relaxing. Accommodation is in single, double, three-, four-, or six-bed **rooms**, offering breakfast, half-board or full-board.

A **list of hospices** can be obtained from the Christian Information Centre (see p.28 for address). Among the best are the *Church of Scotland Hospice* in Tiberias and *St George's Hostel* in Jerusalem; both are in beautiful old buildings with a relatively informal atmosphere.

KIBBUTZ INNS

Kibbutz inns, guesthouses maintained by kibbutzim, have mushroomed in recent years as kibbutzim look for alternative ways of bringing in income. A few still offer basic, hostel-style accommodation, but many are much more upmarket, with a range of attractions from mountain climbing, water sports and horse-back riding to hot springs for health cures and ultra-kosher accommodation for the most orthodox Jewish holidaymakers.

Most kibbutz inns are in the countryside, with a few very near tourist sights (Megiddo, for example), and are therefore far more useful to those who have their own transport. Details of kibbutz inns are given in the relevant sections of the Guide. Some of them are affiliated to the **Israel Kibbutz Hotels** chain, who can supply a list and also take reservations. Their office is at 1 Smolanskin, PO Box 3139, Tel Aviv 61031 (☎03/524 6161, fax 527 8088, email: *info@kibbutz.co.il*; Web site at *www.kibbutz.co.il*).

In a similar vein to kibbutz inns, there is also the guesthouse of the bi-ethnic peace village of Neve Shalom/Wahat al-Salam (see p.125), offering the chance to see and contribute to a unique community.

APARTMENTS AND HOMESTAYS

If you're planning a **long stay**, and especially if you can find people to share with, **renting an apartment** can be an economical option. Purpose-built holiday and time-share apartments, ranging from modest to luxurious, are available in all the tourist areas and can be booked in advance through companies such as Homtel at 31 HaBarzel, Tel Aviv 69710 (☎03/647 4140, fax 647 1109). In Israel you could also try looking through the ads in the weekend edition of the *Jerusalem Post*, though these are likely to stipulate a stay of at least one month.

Short-term stays – one night at a time if you want – can be arranged through the many local IGTO offices who run a **homestay** accommodation service, sometimes referred to as a "**zimmer**" scheme (*zimmer* being German for room). The idea is to give travellers the chance to meet Israelis and experience Israeli home life, but of course it's pot luck who you'll end up with. You should always give the place a once-over and be clear exactly what's included before taking the room. You can also set up this kind of accommodation privately through firms such as Israel Bed and Breakfast, PO Box 24119, Jerusalem 91240 (☎02-581 7001). Prices start at around £25/$40 a night for two people sharing a room.

CAMPING

There are **campsites** throughout the country and in the summer camping can be a really tempting alternative. It also allows you to stay in remoter places where there are no hostels or hotels, although most are still accessible by bus. Many sites offer tents for hire, or cabin or caravan accommodation, though inevitably this is more expensive. Basic prices start at £2/$3, depending on the facilities offered: washing, electricity, restaurant and stores, telephone, picnic and campfire areas, swimming pool (on site or close by) and 24-hour guards. Some of the better sites have a safe in which you can keep your valuables.

Camping or **sleeping rough** outside the official sites in Israel is a cheap alternative and fairly common. The authorities usually turn a blind eye as long as tents are not in full view of paying hotel guests, and campers don't cause too much trouble by being noisy, untidy, stoned or drunk. However, you do need to be vigilant with your valuables and careful of your own **safety**: don't camp alone or miles away from civilization. Freelance camping is also not a good idea in the West Bank or the Gaza Strip. Mosquitoes and other assorted nippers can be a pest, but, for women, it's the males of the human species that are often more of a nuisance (see p.57). On the **beaches** of big cities and major tourist spots, notably Tel Aviv, Caesarea, Haifa and Eilat, gangs of thieves and lone opportunists prey on campers and those sleeping out.

EATING AND DRINKING

In a land of two often warring peoples, food is one area where the cultures have markedly converged. Much of the food considered typically Israeli, such as the national dish, falafel, is actually Arab in origin. Likewise, hummus (whose name is simply Arabic for chickpeas or garbanzo beans), *tehina* (sesame paste), shashlik, kebab, and many of the other foods you'll come across on your travels, are as Palestinian as they are Israeli (and vice versa), and part of a cuisine common to the whole of the Middle East.

In Israel, eating can be pretty pricey, though it is possible to dine cheaply if you stick to basic staples and avoid the incredible range of often very good international food available. In the Palestinian Territories, on the other hand, international cuisine barely has a look-in, but you'll pay far less for high-quality Middle Eastern cooking.

BREAKFASTS, STREET FOOD AND SNACKS

Typical **breakfasts**, provided in most hotels and kibbutzim, are hearty affairs which may take a bit of getting used to. Usually buffets, they serve a cornucopia of food, including salads, eggs, cheese, yoghurts, olives and pickles, fresh bread, fruit juices, tea and coffee. Working people will often breakfast at a hummus bar and these are excellent places to fill up of a morning. Many cafés offer good-value set breakfasts, and travellers' bars in big cities may even have bacon and eggs on the menu. Other options include fruit, of which there is always a plentiful supply, or a shop-bought selection of bread, cheese, yoghurt and hummus.

Unsurprisingly, **street food** represents the cheapest eating option; stalls and markets everywhere dish out a wide variety of delicious **snacks**. Most common, and arguably the best, is the staple **falafel**, spicy balls of ground chickpeas (though often padded out with breadcrumbs), usually served stuffed into a flat round pitta bread and available from practically every street corner and bus station. At most stalls or kiosks, you can help yourself to a variety of salads and dressings of *tehina* or chilli sauce. One whole pitta with six to eight balls costs around £1.50/$2 and you can usually keep refilling your bread with salad until you're full. Or you can just have a sandwich of hummus and salad in pitta bread. In restaurants, a bowl of hummus and/or tehina is dressed with fresh green olive oil and served with pitta bread to dip, and often a helping of brown *fuul* beans, chickpeas or *snobar* (roasted pine kernels). It should be accompanied by a side plate of pickles, including green chilli peppers (to be treated with caution).

Burekas are the second most popular finger food – puff-pastry triangles usually stuffed with cheese, potatoes, or spinach. Though sometimes they can be soft and greasy, the best ones are freshly made, crisp and delicious. Another tasty and filling snack is **ka'ak**, a freshly baked ring of hot sesame bread, traditionally eaten with *za'atar* (a combination of thyme and other herbs) and olive oil, or with a large onion-stuffed falafel ball or hard-boiled egg. **Bagels** are also increasingly popular, though not up to the standards of those in North America or Britain.

Of **kebabs**, the most popular is **shawarma**, slices of marinated lamb (sometimes chicken or other meat) cooked on a vertical spit like a doner kebab, carved and stuffed into pitta with salad. **Shashlik** is more like what would in the West be called a shish kebab, pieces of lamb with vegetables on a skewer grilled over charcoal; it can be served in pitta, but is more commonly eaten on a plate in a restaurant. If you just ask for a "kebab", you'll get one made of *kofta*, minced lamb, usually mixed with coriander and onion, and again served in a pitta with salad.

Other street food includes, in season, charcoal-grilled or boiled **corn on the cob**, sold out of huge vats in the streets, yellow turmus beans boiled and sold in plastic bags, and, especially in Gaza, sweet potatoes (red yams) roasted in the vendor's oven-on-wheels. If you're only after a light nibble, you can choose from a wonderful variety of **nuts, seeds and pulses** – peanuts, pistachios, almonds, sunflower and melon seeds, roasted chickpeas, broad beans – which you can buy from stalls and shops by the hundred grams, or the kilo even, and which also serve to replace the valuable salt lost in the summer heat. All of these are collectively known in Hebrew as *bitzuhim*, or in Arabic as *bizr*.

One final thing to look out for are the various **specialities** produced for **religious holidays**, which may compensate for shortages of other foods, or even of food in general, at such times. During the eight days of Passover (*Pesah*) for example, bread is virtually unobtainable in Israel, particularly in the more Orthodox areas (though

you will find it in Arab shops), **matza** being eaten instead, while flourless cakes and biscuits – cinnamon balls, coconut pyramids and almond macaroons being the favourites – are also on sale. **Doughnuts** (*sofganiot* in Hebrew) are traditionally eaten in quantities around Succot, while during the fast of Yom Kippur, the Day of Atonement, you may find it hard to find anything to eat at all. Likewise, during Ramadan, the month of fasting for Muslims, Arab-run restaurants are shut until sunset, when they open up in festive mood. Don't miss one food with which this fast is traditionally broken in the evenings: **atayef**, pancakes stuffed with pistachio nuts or sweet cheese and covered in syrup.

FRUIT, VEGETABLES AND DAIRY PRODUCTS

In the outdoor markets, you'll find a huge range of fresh produce. **Fruit** is especially good and you can find almost anything here (depending on the season), from the famous **Jaffa oranges** to watermelons. Those traditional fruits that often crop up in the Bible, such as figs, dates, pomegranates and grapes, are still in abundance, but are accompanied now by the more exotic fruits – mangoEs, pawpaws (papayas), lychees, custard apples (sweetsops) and starfruits – that Israel has gone into growing since the Jaffa export market was undercut by cheap Spanish oranges.

Apart from oranges, other fruits with a special Israeli connection include prickly pears, known in Hebrew as **sabra** – a name also applied to the native-born Israeli who, like the fruit, is said to be tough and prickly on the outside, but soft and sweet inside. Resist the temptation to pick a prickly pear yourself off a nearby cactus, unless you want to spend the next week pulling spines out of your hand. **Persimmons** come in several varieties ranging from the soft and very sweet "sharon fruit" to harder, more apple-like versions. Local apples, on the other hand, are soft and tasteless, best used for flavouring *argila* tobacco. Fresh **vegetables** are also plentiful in season and, like fruit, are cheapest and freshest from the open-air markets.

There's also a whole range of deli items, including several that you won't find at home. There are multifarious varieties of smoked fish, a massive variety of **olives**, all sorts of **pickled vegetables**, and a whole host of things to spread on bread such as hummus with *za'atar* or paprika, *tehina*, mashed aubergine, various preparations of herring, and all manner of dips or spreads, sold by weight or in tubs.

From supermarkets or local grocery stores, you can buy a variety of delicious yoghurts and similar **dairy products**, such as *gil* (low-fat yoghurt), *eshel* (thick live yoghurt), or *shamenet* (sour cream). *Rivion* is soured milk, a refreshing drink that's a lot tastier than it sounds, as is *labaneh*, a delicious, salty, sourish cream cheese that, eaten with olive oil and a side dish of pickles, lemon, garlic, olives, chilli peppers and onions (or some of these), can be a meal in itself.

SWEETS

The big Israeli **sweet** experience is *halva*, a bar of crushed sesame seeds, often with pistachios or covered with chocolate, and crunchier than the Greek version. Some like it best on a chunk of *halla*, the yeast-and-egg bread traditionally eaten on Shabbat. Not to be missed either are the wonderful range of East European-type cakes stuffed with cheese, apple or poppy seed. Palestinian sweets, generally stickier and sicklier, include *kanafeh*, sweet cheese on a layer of crumbly pastry and drenched in syrup, *burma*, made with pistachios, and *baklawa*, usually stuffed with hazelnut (filberts), though cheaper versions use peanuts. Candied pecans, sold on street nut stalls, are one of the best treats of all.

American **ice cream** is widely available in Israel – Ben and Jerry's and Häagen Dazs both have several outlets – but home-grown brands such as Dr Lek can also be good, cost half as much, and offer some interesting flavours, too, including poppy seed and cheesecake.

RESTAURANTS

For such a small country, Israel has an amazing number of **restaurants** offering an extraordinary variety of different types of food: from the typical cuisine of the Middle East or the traditional dishes of Jewish communities around the world, to European, North and South American, Chinese, Thai, Indian, North African, Ethiopian or Yemeni.

In general, Jewish and Middle Eastern food is the least expensive; the more exotic food can be quite pricey, with French-style cooking the most expensive of all. The **price of a meal** ranges from £4/$7 in the cheapest places, to £30/$50 plus (not including wine) per head in a fancy restaurant. In the Palestinian Territories, eating

out is usually much cheaper, ranging from £3/$5 to £15/$25 for a meal. However, your choice of cuisine is usually limited to Middle Eastern dishes, and the number of restaurants is much smaller, partly due to the fact that eating out is less of a pastime among Palestinians, who generally prefer to eat at home with their families.

Lunch is traditionally the main meal of the day, while **supper** is a light affair. **Menus** usually have an English translation, and the bill includes tax but not usually service; tips are expected in most places (ten to fifteen percent is a typical amount).

WHAT TO EAT

Israeli restaurants at the cheaper end of the range will serve the basics, starting with hummus, falafel, *tehina* and aubergine dips, and followed by simple meat and vegetable meals such as schnitzel, kebabs, and chicken and chips.

The fare at other restaurants reflects their ethnic basis: Hungarian locales will serve such traditional dishes as goulash or *blintzes*; at Eastern European restaurants, you can get gefilte fish (usually served with a beetroot and horseradish relish called *khreyn*), borscht or chicken soup with *knaidels* (dumplings) and other specialities of the type considered traditionally Jewish in North America or the British Isles. If you fancy something a bit different and altogether spicier, Yemeni and North African restaurants are the places to try.

Smaller **Palestinian restaurants**, on either side of the Green Line, often specialize in one dish, or type of dish only. You'll find places that

IS IT KOSHER?

Most, but not all, Israeli restaurants serve **kosher** food (see p.502–3), supervised by a religious religious authority such as the Beth Din. Places that are kosher will have a sign to that effect in the window or on the menu. It means, amongst other things, that meat and dairy dishes are not served in the same establishment, and that the restaurant is closed on the Sabbath. Kosher establishments will also not serve pork, of course, nor shellfish, squid or octopus, eel, shark or rabbit. There are degrees of kosher; **Glatt** or **Badatz** are stricter forms, and restaurants or food manufacturers adhering to those must, for example, have only religious Jews preparing the food.

COMMON FOODS AND RESTAURANT TERMS

English/*Hebrew*/*Arabic*

USEFUL WORDS

Bill, check	*HaKheshbon/al-Hissab*	Knife	*sakeen/sikina*
Bottle	*bakbuk/anina*	Spoon	*kapeet/mala'a*
Fork	*mazleg/shawka*	Table	*shulkhan/tawla*
Glass or cup	*kos/kas*		

BASICS

Beer	*bira/bira*	Honey	*dvash/'asal*	Salt	*melakh /melah*
Butter	*khem'a/zibda*	Liver	*kaved/kibda*	Sugar	*sukar/sukar*
Cheese	*givna/jibna*	Meat	*bassar/lahma*	Tea	*tay/shai*
Chicken	*'off/djaj*	Milk	*halav/haleeb*	Water	*mayim/mai*
Coffee	*cafay/qahwa*	Oil	*shemen/zeit*	Wine	*yayin/sharab*
Eggs	*beitzim/beid*	Olives	*zeitim/zeitoun*	Yoghurt	*eshel/rayeb*
Fish	*dag/samak*	Pepper	*pilpil/filfil*		

BREAD/*LEKHEM*/*KHUBZ*

Bagel	Bread ring, boiled briefly before baking to give a chewy texture	*Mana'ish*	Flat bread baked with *za'atar*
Halla	Traditionally plaited loaf eaten on Shabbat and festivals, made with eggs	*Matza*	Unleavened bread, eaten during Passover
Ka'ak	Bread ring covered with sesame seeds	*Pitta*	Round, flat, hollow bread, for dipping or stuffing (with salad, falafel, etc)

SALADS AND STARTERS/*MEZZE*/*MEZZE*

Ba'adunis	Tehina mixed with fresh coriander	*Muttabal*	Baked aubergines mashed with tehina
Hummus	Chickpea (garbanzo) paste, mixed with tahini, olive oil, lemon juice and garlic	*Tabbouleh*	Cracked wheat mixed with finely chopped tomatoes, lemon and fresh herbs (mint, coriander and parsley)
Labaneh	Sour white cream cheese served with green olive oil	*Tehina*	Tahini (sesame seed paste) mixed with lemon juice and garlic
Masabaha	Whole cooked chickpeas (garbanzos) in tehina		

MIDDLE EASTERN SPECIALITIES

Bureka	Puff pastry triangle stuffed with cheese, spinach or potatoes	*Maqluba*	Layers of meat or chicken, vegetables and rice, served "upside down"
Djaj mahshi	Chicken stuffed with rice and pine nuts, almonds or meat	*Melukhia*	Jew's mallow, a green leaf vegetable with a slimy texture when stewed
Falafel	Deep-fried chickpea (garbanzo bean) balls, Israel's national dish	*Mujadara*	Rice cooked with lentils, pasta, cumin and pepper, served with fried onions, yoghurt and salad
Ftireh	Three-cornered pie stuffed with meat or spinach	*Musakhan*	Chicken soaked in olive oil, baked with onions and *sumak* on a bed of pitta
Fuul	Egyptian brown fava bean stew	*Ruz Falastini*	Rice cooked with fine pasta, fried pine nuts and saffron
Kofta	Lamb minced with coriander, usually served as a kebab (if you just ask for "a kebab", this is what you'll get)	*Sfiha*	Palestinian "pizza", baked with minced meat, tomatoes and onion
Kubbeh	Minced meat enclosed in a case of *burghul* (cracked wheat) and deep fried		

Shawarma	Marinated meat kebab (usually lamb) on a vertical spit, carved and usually served in a pitta: Looks like a doner kebab, but is insulted by the comparison		and ground to make a lemony-flavoured red spice
		Waraq dawali	Stuffed vine leaves (like Greek *dolmades*)
Shashlik	Lamb and vegetable kebab grilled on a skewer over charcoal	*Za'atar*	Thyme pounded with *sumak*, salt and sesame for use as a condiment, sometimes made into a paste with oil
Sumak	The berries of a local herb (elm-leafed sumac) dried, de-seeded		

JEWISH SPECIALITIES

Blintzes	Pancakes, usually stuffed with sweet cheese	*Khreyn*	Beetroot and horseradish relish, served especially with gefilte fish
Borscht	Beetroot soup served hot or cold, often with potatoes	*Kneidels*	Matza-meal dumplings, eaten in chicken soup
Cholent	Sabbath stew of beef, beans, barley, potatoes, dumplings and vegetables, cooked slowly overnight	*Kreplakh*	Ravioli-type envelopes of pasta stuffed with minced meat and eaten in chicken soup
Gefilte fish	Sweet minced fish balls, boiled or fried (originally the stuffing for a carp)	*Kugel*	Savoury potato and onion mix, or sweet noodles and raisins, baked in the oven
Goulash	Meat, usually beef, stew cooked with sweet paprika and pepper (but no sour cream in the Jewish version)	*Latkes*	Fried patties of grated potato
Kasha	Cracked buckwheat usually served to accompany meat instead of rice or potatoes	*Schnitzel*	Veal, chicken or turkey steaks covered with matza meal (the Jewish equivalent of breadcrumbs) and fried

VEGETABLES/*YERAKOT/KHUDAAR*

Aubergine (eggplant)	*hatzil/ beitinjan*	Haricot beans	*she'u'it/fasulia*
Carrots	*gezer/jezer*	Okra	*bamya/bamya*
Chickpeas (garbanzo beans)	*humus/humus*	Onion	*betzal/basal*
Corn	*tiras/doura*	Peas	*afuna/basella*
Courgette (zucchini)	*kishu/cusa*	Potatoes	*tapuhey 'adama/batata*
		Rice	*orez/ruz*

FRUIT/*PRIYOT/FAWAKA*

Apple	*tapuah/tufah*	Melon	*milon/shamam*
Apricot	*mishmish/mismish*	Orange	*tapuz/burtuqal*
Banana	*banana/mooz*	Persimmon	*afarsimon/afarsimon*
Custard apple (sweetsop)	*ancona/kenya*	Pomegranate	*rimon/ruman*
Dates	*tamar/tamar*	Prickly pear	*sabra/teen shawki*
Fig	*tena/teen*	Starfruit	*carambola/carambola*
Grapes	*anavim/'anib*	Strawberries	*tutim/farawla*
Lemon	*limon/limoun*	Watermelon	*avatiah/battikh*

NUTS AND DRY SNACKS/*BITZUHIM/BIZR*

Almonds	*shkadim/loz*	Pistachios	*pistachio/fozdok*
Peanuts	*botnim/fuul sudani*	Sunflower seeds	*garinim/bizr*
Pecans	*pekanim/goz*	Watermelon seeds	*garinei avatiah/lib battikh*

COMMON FOODS AND RESTAURANT TERMS *(cont.)*

SWEETS (Palestinian)/*HALAWIYAT*

Atayef	Pancakes stuffed with walnuts, pistachio nuts, raisins or cheese, eaten in the evenings during Ramadan	*Kanafeh*	Soft cheese covered with a layer of orange-coloured shredded or crumbled pastry, served hot with very sweet syrup
Baklawa	Layers of pastry stuffed with nuts and covered in syrup	*Luqum*	Turkish delight
		Sahlab	Sweet hot milk, thickened with arrowroot and served with coconut and raisins
Burma	Sweet shredded wheat stuffed with pistachios		

SWEETS (Israeli)/*METUQIM*

Halva	Crunchy crushed sesame seed bar, sometimes chocolate-covered	*Hamentashen*	Three-cornered pastries stuffed with poppy seeds, eaten at Purim	*Sofganiot*	Doughnuts eaten especially around Hannukah

DRINKS/*SHTIYA*/*MASHRUB*

Mitz/'Asir	Juice	*Shai bi-maramiya*	Tea with sage
Tamar hindi	Tamarind cordial	*Qahwa bi-hel*	Turkish coffee with cardamom
Shai bi-na'ana	Tea with mint	*Botz*	Turkish coffee made like instant

have little else other than hummus or grilled chicken, for example, served with side salads and pitta bread. Larger Palestinian restaurants serve the sort of cooked food traditionally eaten at home, usually consisting of a selection of starters or **mezze** (mixed hors d'oeuvres), a dessert of Middle Eastern sweets or fruit, followed by tea or coffee.

Pork is prohibited by both Jewish and Muslim dietary law, but is available in some non-kosher Israeli restaurants (as is seafood), and Palestinian ones owned by Christian Arabs.

For fresh **fish**, the best places are by the sea (or at least the Sea of Galilee, where the local speciality is St Peter's fish, a rather bony species

of tilapia), with a big choice in Tiberias, Eilat, Gaza and Jaffa. Many kosher restaurants (see box on p.39) serve fish and dairy products, but not meat.

Vegetarians can eat well in Israel and the Palestinian Territories. The staples of the local diet – hummus, falafel and so on – are based on beans and pulses, and all manner of salads, olives and other non-animal-based delicatessen is widely available. Dairy produce and eggs are also served in abundance; indeed, some kosher restaurants specialize in dairy products and will not therefore serve meat. If you stretch to fish, you have a massive choice of restaurants (admittedly mainly upmarket) that specialize in that alone. And, although there are few specifically vegetarian restaurants outside the largest cities, most establishments serving Middle Eastern food will have a range of vegetarian mezze if nothing else. **Vegans** might like to try out the restaurants (one in Tel Aviv, see p.280, one in Dimona see p.93) run by the Black Hebrews, who are strictly vegan.

RESTAURANT PRICES

Throughout the text, except where it is obvious, we have stated whether **restaurants** are **cheap**, **moderate** or **expensive**. Obviously, these terms are subjective, and prices will depend on what you eat, but roughly speaking, a typical meal (excluding wine) in a restaurant described as "cheap" will cost less than US$10; you can expect to eat for $10–20 per head in restaurants described as "moderate"; $20+ in those described as "expensive".

DRINK

Israelis are not big drinkers, so even in bars, coffee and soft drinks are served. Cafés, on the other hand, often keep a small stock of liquor (handy if you fancy a slug of brandy in your coffee), which means that the distinction between a café and a bar can get blurred in Israel. In the Palestinian Territories, cafés (usually male-only) serve usually rather better tea and coffee, accompanied by hookah pipes of tobacco, but no alcohol.

TEA, COFFEE AND SOFT DRINKS

Tea can be a bit touch and go. It's usually served black, often with a sprig of mint (in which case it is known in Arabic as *shai bi-nana* and in Hebrew as *tay binana*) or a slice of lemon, but either way in Israel it usually consists of a meagre bag dunked in a cup of hot water. Traditional Arab coffee houses or **qahwas** (which also means "coffee"; see box on this page for more on *qahwas*) are more likely, but by no means certain, to make it properly with loose-leaf tea and boiling water, and may also serve it with other herbs such as sage (*shai bi-maramiya*).

Israeli cafés, on the other hand, do generally serve very good espresso **coffee**. A "cappuccino" is usually topped with a large amount of whipped cream and chocolate; to avoid these, ask for an "*afukh*" instead. Instant coffee (known universally as Nescafé, or just "Nes") is also usually available; it comes with milk unless you specify "no milk" (*bliy halav*). Arab *qahwas* (see box on this page) invariably serve Turkish coffee, which in the Palestinian Territories usually comes spiced with cardamom (*bi-hel*). It can be ordered very sweet (*ziyyada*), medium (*mazbout*), with a little sugar (*ariha*), or plain (*saada*). As bitter, unsweetened coffee is commonly served to guests at funerals, it is considered a little strange to order one, though as a foreigner, you're likely to be excused such strangeness. Israelis most often serve Turkish coffee as "*botz*" (literally "mud"), which means that instead of bringing it to the boil in a little metal pot in the traditional fashion, it is just put into a cup and hot water is added. Purists may recoil in shock, but unless you are a connoisseur, it really doesn't make that much difference.

By far the best thirst-quenching, non-alcoholic drinks are freshly squeezed **fruit juices**: orange and grapefruit are the obvious ones, but fruit-juice stalls in Israel frequently sell more exotic varieties too; some are straight juice, while others, such as lemon, are mixed with sugar and water. In the Palestinian Territories, you'll also find the less exotic juices, at rather lower prices, as well as

less expected tastes such as almond milk (*'asir loz*) or highly sweetened, brown tamarind cordial (*tamar hindi*), which is said to have aphrodisiac properties. The usual fizzy **soft drinks** like Coca-Cola and 7-Up are also widely available, as well as "black" or "malt beer" (see below).

BEER, WINE AND SPIRITS

Alcohol is easily available in Israel. In the Palestinian Territories, however, it may be frowned upon in areas where Islamic fundamentalism is strong; in Gaza, for example, it's almost impossible to get hold of, and you won't find any in Jerusalem's Muslim Quarter either. Duty-free Eilat is the best place to stock up on booze.

The most common alcoholic drink in Israel is locally produced **beer**, of which there are two main brands: the light **Maccabi**, and the darker, more flavoursome **Goldstar**. Harder to come by are Nesher, a weaker, cheaper version of

Maccabi, usually sold only in supermarkets or grocery stores, and **Taybeh**, produced by the microbrewery at Ramallah. The latter, by far the best beer in the country, is made in accordance with the famous German beer law from only four ingredients (barley, hops, yeast and water), but is hard to find inside the Green Line and not much easier to find outside it (Ramallah, Bethlehem and East Jerusalem are the best places to look; specialist liquor stores in Israel proper may have it if you're lucky).

Foreign brands such as Carlsberg, Tuborg and Amstel are brewed in Israel under licence but don't taste much like the real thing (they're usually made with maize as well as barley, for one thing). In Israel, draught beer is sold in glasses of a half a litre (*hetzi*) or a third (*shleesh*). Olives, pickles, pretzels or sunflower seeds are often served with beer in bars. Note that "**black beer**" or "malt beer" is not beer at all, but a malt-flavoured soft fizzy drink.

Israeli **wines** vary in quality from mediocre to eminently drinkable. The best brands are **Carmel**, **Yarden** and **Bathan**. Carmel's better wines are labelled as "selected", and their best as "private collection". Wine is also produced in the Golan Heights, including Golan Cabernet Blanc, a refreshing white wine with the appearance of a rosé. The right-wing Jewish settlers in Hebron also produce a cheap and nasty plonk.

Israeli versions of brandy, vodka, gin, rum and other **spirits** are usually awful, and best avoided. The quality can be disguised with fruit juice or mixers, but over-indulgence will result in a severe hangover the next day: even deaths from drinking too much low-grade spirit are not unknown. Ramallah in the West Bank produces the country's best *araq*, an aniseed drink similar to Turkish raki or Greek ouzo, and usually drunk diluted with water and ice, though many travellers prefer to take it straight. *Arak Extra Fine*, with a green and gold label, is the best brand.

COMMUNICATIONS, POST AND PHONES

The phone system in Israel leaves much to be desired but postal services are easily up to international standards, and the latest forms of telecommunications and information technology are also available here. Autonomous Palestine has its own stamps and postal services, generally pretty good, but its phones depend on the Israeli system and are in an even worse state than those in Israel. Israel does not have mail or tele-phone links with several Arab countries, although you can write to them from autonomous Palestine.

THE POST

The postal service to and from Israel is pretty efficient, with **letters** and postcards to Europe taking from three days to a week by airmail – a couple of days longer to North America or Australasia. An **Express Mail Service** (EMS) is also available for letters to most countries, and claims to guarantee delivery within 72 hours. **Stamps** are sold at all post offices, as well as at some newsagents, hotels and tourist souvenir shops; at the time of writing a letter from Israel costs 1.70NIS to the British Isles, 2NIS to North America, and 2.50NIS to Australia.

The **PNA** runs mail services in areas of the West Bank and Gaza under its jurisdiction, and has its own post offices and stamps, but letters posted in East Jerusalem or other areas outside PNA control still go through the Israeli postal network. Letters to and from autonomous Palestine are likely to take a little longer than to or from Israel. Note that some Arab and Muslim countries who do not recognize the State of Israel will not accept letters posted from there, but will accept mail sent from the Palestinian Territories via the Palestinian postal system.

Parcels can be sent a number of ways: by sea, airmail or by the more expensive airmail express (although this doesn't seem to be any quicker than regular airmail). Packages should be submitted for security checks before sealing. You must also take your passport for identification when you post a parcel.

To receive mail in Israel, there is **Poste Restante** (general delivery) in most main post offices. Letters should be addressed to you (preferably with surname in capitals), c/o "Poste Restante, [city name], Israel". It's best to use Israeli post offices rather than ones in the West Bank or Gaza. You'll need your passport or some other identification when collecting your mail. **American Express** in Tel Aviv, Jerusalem and Haifa (addresses given in the "Listings" sections for those towns) will keep mail for holders of their cards and travellers' cheques. **Telegrams** can be sent from post offices and hotels, or by dialling ☎171.

Main **post offices** in Israel are usually open Sunday to Thursday 8am to 6pm and Friday 8am to 2pm, though certain major offices in big cities may be open longer hours. Branch offices, and post offices in smaller towns are open Sunday, Monday, Tuesday and Thursday 8am to 12.30pm and 3.30 to 6pm, Wednesday 8am to 1.30pm, Friday and evenings before holidays 8am to noon; all post offices in Israel are closed on Saturdays and holidays. Palestinian post offices are open Saturday to Thursday 8am to 2pm.

PHONES

Public telephones in Israel are run by the phone company Bezeq (though they do not have a monopoly on lines) and operate on **phonecards**, available from newsstands and shops throughout the country and valid for both national and international calls. Cards are available in denominations of 20, 50 and 120 units, currently costing 13NIS, 24NIS and 54NIS respectively. Cheap-rate **international calling cards** with a toll-free access number and their own PIN numbers are also available, give substantially lower rates, and can be "recharged" by credit card when finished. Another way to get slightly cheaper rates on international calls is to go through private compa-

nies, such as **Solan Communications** (offices open 24hr) in Tel Aviv, Jerusalem, Netanya and Tiberias (addresses under "Telecommunications" in the "Listings" sections for each of those towns), and in the arrivals area at Ben Gurion Airport. **Calls from hotels** are likely to be rather more expensive than from private phones or phone booths.

Overseas rates go down by 25 percent after 10pm and all day Saturday and Sunday, and by fifty percent from 1am to 8am – particularly handy for calling North America. There is now a choice of companies offering international connections from any phone, of which Bezeq are usually the most expensive. Their international access code is ☎00 but for most destinations at most times, it is better to use international access codes ☎012, ☎013 or ☎014.

One thing you will see (and hear) everywhere in Israel are **mobile phones** – thanks to its compact size the country is fully covered and has the world's highest rate of ownership and it's easy enough to join the crowd and rent one for the duration of your stay.

Calling within Israel is a different matter, with lines frequently out of order, especially those to the Palestinian Territories (see below). However, Bezeq is upgrading their system, and all phones in the country should now have **new 7-digit numbers**, not including the area code. In the Guide, we have noted how the old six-digit numbers have changed for each major town, generally by prefixing the old number with a single digit. For places not detailed, dial the old number and you should receive a message from Bezeq (in Hebrew and English) explaining how the number has changed. "Golden Pages" **phone directories** in English do exist, and major post offices should keep a copy, with numbers of services deemed useful for tourists. The complete phone directory is published in Hebrew only, but **directory information** (☎144) will answer queries in English.

Bezeq is still responsible for phone lines **in the Palestinian Territories**, but these are the most neglected part of the network, still using six-digit numbers in most of the West Bank and Gaza, and with lines even more frequently out of order. "Public" phones in those places tend to be private phones in shops or cafés, and are mainly for local calls. You may also find one or two which are operated by coins, or by Israel's old *assimonim*, special telephone tokens, which will be sold on the premises where the phone is located.

DIALLING CODES AND USEFUL NUMBERS

TO PHONE ISRAEL/THE PALESTINIAN TERRITORIES FROM ABROAD

To call **a number in Israel or the Palestinian Territories from overseas**, dial your country's international access code, then 972 (country code), the area code minus the initial zero (see below), and then the number.

Israel/Palestinian Territories area codes:

02 Jerusalem, the Jerusalem Corridor and the south and central West Bank
03 Tel Aviv, the Dan Conurbation and around
04 Haifa and the Carmel

06 The Galilee and the Golan Heights
07 Ashqelon, the Negev and the Gaza Strip
08 Ashdod, Ramle, Lydda and around
09 The Sharon and northern West Bank
050, 052, 062 etc Mobile phones

TO PHONE ABROAD FROM ISRAEL/THE PALESTINIAN TERRITORIES

Dial the international access code (013 is usually the cheapest, but 00, 012 and 014 may cost less to certain destinations at certain times of day), followed by the international dialling code (see below), area code (without initial zero), and number.

International dialling codes:

Australia 61
Canada 1
Ireland 353
New Zealand 64
South Africa 27
UK 44
USA 1

Home Country Direct (toll-free access)

UK (BT) ☎177-440 2727
USA (AT&T) ☎177-100 2727
USA (MCI) ☎177-150 2727
USA (SPRINT) ☎177-102 2727

USEFUL TELEPHONE NUMBERS

Information (directory enquiries) ☎144   International operator ☎188   Telegrams ☎171

International calls are best made from post offices or private phone centres, or, more expensively, from your hotel. Bezeq directory information does not give numbers for areas under PNA jurisdiction.

FAX AND EMAIL

You can send and receive **faxes** from main post offices (see p.45 for opening hours) and offices of Solan Communications in Israel, and at other private international phone centres in Israel and the Palestinian Territories. Post offices will call to let you know a fax has arrived, so long as your name

and phone number are clearly displayed at the top. **American Express** in Tel Aviv, Jerusalem and Haifa (addresses and fax numbers given in "Listings" for those towns) will also receive and keep faxes for their customers; make sure that your name is displayed prominently at the top, preferably in the form: "To American Express customer John DOE, please keep." Most hotels will also receive and keep faxes for their guests.

Email can be sent and received at the growing number of cyber-cafés and computer communications centres in large cities (see "Telecommunications" in main city "Listings" sections for local details).

THE MEDIA

The media in Hebrew is extremely diverse, but much more limited in Arabic, as both the Israelis and the PNA keep strict tabs on what is published in their respective territories. English-language publications are similarly thin on the ground, with only one Israeli daily newspaper in English and one Palestinian weekly, though there are a few magazines. On television, however, many programmes are in English with Hebrew and/or Arabic subtitles.

NEWSPAPERS AND MAGAZINES

The **press** in Israel is, in principle, as free as in any Western country, with the gamut of views from left to right represented, and attacks on the government often extremely outspoken. As in the West, however, there is a political consensus to which all press-owners subscribe, and publications outside that consensus – those which advocate the overthrow of the Israeli state, for example – are uncommon (though not illegal), and boycotted by all the main distributors. Those which are published, mainly in Arabic, face a certain amount of unofficial pressure. The most popular Hebrew daily papers in Israel are the tabloid-style *Ma'ariv* and *Yediot Ahronot*, followed by the more left-wing and intellectual *Ha'Aretz*. The most widely read Palestinian paper is *Al-Quds*.

Military censorship and "reasons of security" are also used to restrict reporting on the activities of the IDF, especially in the West Bank and Gaza. In the Palestinian Territories under PNA jurisdiction, there is no freedom of the press at all, and editors who publish articles critical of the PNA, and of Yasser Arafat in particular, face arrest and imprisonment or much worse. Publications critical of such human rights abuses can be obtained from human rights groups such as the Palestinian Centre for Human Rights (see box on p.28), but even these groups must be careful. In areas of the Territories under Israeli jurisdiction, freedom of the press is slightly less restricted, but not so greatly, and methods of control are usually more subtle (military censorship and bureaucratic restrictions on the movement of Palestinian journalists, for example), though Palestinian journalists have on occasion been assaulted by soldiers or Jewish settlers, and it is not unknown for Israeli soldiers to fire baton rounds at reporters covering West Bank demonstrations.

There are only two **English-language newspapers**: the very right-wing Israeli daily (except Sat) *Jerusalem Post*, and the Palestinian weekly *Jerusalem Times*. The former contains mainly Israeli news, although it does have some international coverage, plus a rundown of TV and radio programmes, cinema listings, night pharmacies, exchange rates, weather and handy phone numbers. The Friday edition is particularly helpful, with a supplement giving more detailed "what's on" information (see also p.27 for Web site address). The *Jerusalem Times* is mainly useful for giving the other side of the Israel/Palestine story. It has interesting articles on Palestine and Palestinian culture, but no international news except of specific Palestinian interest.

Other English-language publications covering news and politics include: the *Jerusalem Report*, a glossy news magazine similar in style to *Time* or *Newsweek*; *News from Within*, put out monthly by the Alternative Information Centre, a left-wing group of Israelis and Palestinians working together to provide a non-nationalist analysis of the local situation; and the *Palestine Report*, a pro-Palestinian critique of the latest news, published weekly by the Jerusalem Media and Communication Centre. On subjects other than politics and current affairs, the most interesting English-language publication is *Eretz*, a glossy quarterly that focuses on the history, culture and wildlife of the country and often has articles which offer interesting alternatives to the usual tourist trail.

Of the **foreign newspapers**, most British national daily papers are available in Israel the day after publication (newsstands in large cities and tourist resorts will have them, as will Steimatzky's bookshops), as is the *Herald Tribune*, and sometimes *USA Today*, the *New York Times* and the *Wall Street Journal*. Magazines such as *Newsweek*, *Time* and *The Economist*, can be found at newsstands and bookshops on both sides of the Green Line. *Middle East International*, published in the UK, is occasionally available too.

TELEVISION AND RADIO

Israelis are major-league newshounds, with an ear always cocked for the latest bulletin – hardly surprising in a country where bombs go off with alarming frequency (and in a population of only five million, the victims could easily include a friend or relative) and where war has been known to break out unannounced (in 1973, for example). If you are in a bus or taxi, chances are the driver will turn up the volume for the hourly news broadcasts, particularly if there has been an incident in the area. If staying in an Israeli home, expect bulletins to be listened to in an earnest hush. **The news** is always given from an Israeli angle, which may seem outrageously biased to an outsider, and sometimes tantamount to sheer propaganda. On the other hand, Israelis often have the impression that all foreign media are biased against Israel, and are even anti-Semitic, while Palestinians seem to believe all foreign media are pro-Israel.

Israel has two government-run television channels. More time is devoted to politics in comparison to British or American TV, with lots of political discussion shows, but there's also the usual diet of quiz shows, dramas, soaps and sitcoms and also English-language films and programmes from the UK and US, subtitled in Hebrew and sometimes Arabic, or even Russian. **Channel 1** is financed by TV licence fees and carries no advertising, **Channel 2** is financed by commercials and caters more to popular taste. The Israeli **news in English** is broadcast on

Channel 1 at 6.15pm Sunday to Thursday, and 5pm on Saturday. Many Israeli homes, and most larger hotels, also have **cable TV**, with a host of channels in English, including the BBC World Service, CNN, MTV, Eurosport, Discovery, and Rupert Murdoch's Star TV and Sky News.

In most of the country, it's possible to pick up the Christian **Middle East TV**, transmitted from southern Lebanon, and in and around the Golan Heights, Syrian TV can also be viewed. **Jordan Television** has a foreign-language channel, showing programmes in English and French. Its news bulletin, which always begins with the latest on the Jordanian royal family, is broadcast in English at 10pm.

Israeli **radio** stations include **Radio 1** on 576KHz and 1458KHz MW, or 88.2MHz and 100.7MHz FM, with the news in English at 7am and 5pm daily, and a new English-language station, **Radio West**, broadcasts on 90.6MHz and 102.8MHz FM. Otherwise, there is the Israeli Forces Radio, which puts out foreign and Israeli pop music, and the Voice of Music playing classical music; both are on various MW and FM frequencies, depending on where you are (details are in the *Jerusalem Post*'s Friday entertainment supplement). Pop music is also played by **Radio 3** (*Reshet Gimel*) on 531KHz MW and 97.8MHz FM from 6am to 1am daily.

The **BBC World Service** can be picked up on 1323KHz and (at some times of the day) 1413KHz MW. The **Voice of America** can be received on 792KHz and 1197KHz MW.

OPENING HOURS AND PUBLIC HOLIDAYS

Given that there are three major religions here (and numerous subdivisions within them), it's no surprise to find that opening times vary widely and are regularly thrown out by a bewildering array of public and religious holidays. While this is all very confusing, it does mean that in mixed cities such as Jerusalem you are bound to find something open on any day, although it pays to check before traipsing off miles to see a site that may be closed.

OPENING HOURS

While most **shops and businesses** are open 8am to 1pm and 4pm to 7pm, more and more are now staying open right through the day and on into the late evening, especially in tourist areas. Jewish-owned shops close early (around 2pm) on Friday, the start of the Jewish Sabbath, and stay closed all Saturday. They also close for religious holidays (see overleaf) and on the eve preceding them. Muslim-owned shops and offices may be closed on Friday and on Muslim religious holidays, and Christian-owned ones on Sunday and Christian festivals. Both Muslim and Christian shops may also close for Palestinian national holidays, particularly in the Palestinian Territories, and will certainly do so in areas under the jurisdiction of the PNA.

Sites run by the **National Parks Authority** are usually open seven days a week (Sat–Thurs 8am–4pm & Fri 8am–3pm), closing an hour later in summer. **Museums** have varying hours: most close early on Friday, but some are open on Saturday. See p.21 for opening hours of **banks** and p.45 for **post office** hours.

VISITING PLACES OF WORSHIP

Times of Sunday and holiday **church services** for all denominations can be obtained from the Christian Information Centre in Jerusalem (see p.28 for address). Obviously, if you just want to look around, it's best to visit outside these times, but remember that **public opening times** for churches of special tourist interest are sometimes limited, for example to mornings only (in such cases, opening hours have been specified in the Guide).

Unless otherwise stated, **mosques** are open to the public at all times except during the five daily prayer periods and on Fridays and holidays (except, that is, for Muslims who wish to pray). **Synagogue prayer times** are morning and evening daily, with Sabbath services beginning at sunset on Friday and throughout Saturday. At all places of worship, **modest behaviour and dress** are expected (and usually enforced), particularly for women, for whom head covering in all of them is recommended, as well as long sleeves and skirts. Men should remove head covering in church, but definitely put it on in a synagogue (and sites such as the Wailing Wall in Jerusalem). Shorts and short skirts should not be worn. Shoes should be taken off when entering a mosque: canvas slippers or coverings are often provided at the door.

HOLIDAYS

The sheer number of holidays is further complicated by the fact that **Jewish and Muslim holidays** are dated according to **lunar calendars**, in which each month begins and ends at the new moon. To make up the difference between a year of twelve lunar months and a solar year of 365–366 days, the **Jewish calendar** adds an extra month every three or four years. The **Muslim calendar** does not have such leap years, and consequently regresses against the Western (Gregorian) calendar by approximately eleven days a year.

What this means in practice is that Jewish and Muslim festivals fall on different days of the Gregorian calendar every year. To help you plan ahead, the box on p.51 details the dates of Jewish and Muslim holidays for the years 1998–2002; but be warned that dates of Muslim holidays are fixed according to actual sightings of the new moon, so predicted dates are only approximate.

Christian holidays don't escape complication either, being celebrated on different dates by different denominations: Roman Catholics and most Protestants follow the Gregorian calendar, but the Eastern Orthodox churches use the Julian calendar (13 days later than the Gregorian), while the Armenian Church operates a further 12 days on. There are also several **Palestinian secular holidays**.

YEARS: AM, AD or AH?

Muslim and Jewish years are numbered differently from ordinary Gregorian ones. **Jewish years** (AM or Anno Mundi) start from the creation of the world – 3761 BC according to calculations made from the text of the Old Testament – so, if you subtract 3761 from a year AM, you'll discover which year AD (usually in September) it began. **Muslim years** (AH or Anno Hegirae) date from the Hegira, Mohammed's flight to Medina (see p.504) in 622 AD; to find the equivalent AD year, add 622 and then subtract the original AH year divided by 3/100 to compensate for the eleven-day gap. Many writers, especially Jewish ones, prefer to substitute for the Christian-derived terms "BC" and "AD", the more interdenominational "**BCE**" (Before the Common Era) and "**CE**" (in the Common Era) respectively, so you will often see those terms used for historical dates in Israel.

JEWISH HOLIDAYS

Jewish holidays are of two sorts: serious religious festivals (*yom tov*) specified by the Torah and subject to the same kind of strictures as the Sabbath, with all forms of work forbidden; and other celebrations, which may be religious in origin, but which allow work to continue. The former, which involve major shutdowns of shops and public services such as transport, are: **New Year** (Rosh HaShannah), usually in September; **Yom Kippur** (the Day of Atonement) ten days later, the most serious and solemn day of the Jewish year, observed with a 25-hour fast, during which the whole of Israel more or less shuts down; **Succot** (Tabernacles), five days after that, followed by **Simhat Torah** a week later; **Passover** (Pesah), around Easter time, when no leavened bread may be eaten for a week, though only the first and last days are holidays as such; and **Shevuot** (Pentecost), seven weeks after that. For an explanation of the religious significance of these, see p.502.

Festivals which do not involve major shutdown are: **Hannukah**, a winter solstice festival of lights which celebrates the Maccabees' 164 BC rededication of the Temple in Jerusalem after its profanation by the Seleucids, and during which Jewish homes light candles for eight days, starting with a single one on the first day, and building up to eight on the last; **Purim** in early spring, honouring the events of the biblical book of Esther, when a Jewish Queen of Persia saved her people from the empire's racist prime minister Haman; and **Tu Bishvat**, a tree festival in autumn, in which there is much planting of trees.

Religious Jews also celebrate a number of minor fast days such as **Tisha Be'Av**, in the summer, which berates the destruction of the First and Second Temples, held to have occurred on the same day. The seven-week period between Passover and Shevuot is a Lent-like period called the **Omer**, when celebration is generally discouraged and various calamities that befell the Jewish people are remembered. It is punctuated by a number of commemorative days: **Yom HaShoah** (Holocaust Day), on the 22nd day, mourns the victims of the Holocaust with a two-minute silence at 11am and the closure of cinemas, theatres, nightclubs and concert halls; a week later, **Yom HaZikaron** (Remembrance Day) honours Israel's war dead with prayers and another two-minute silence, and leads into **Independence Day** (Yom Ha'Atzma'ut), which begins at nightfall and celebrates Israel's 1948 independence from British rule. **Lag Be'Omer**, on the 33rd day of the Omer, is another, much older lull in the period of restraint, and a popular day for marriages.

MUSLIM HOLIDAYS

Muslim holy days start with **al-Hijra**, the Islamic New Year, commemorating the flight of the Prophet Mohammed from Mecca to Medina. The feast of **Moulid al-Nabi**, celebrates the Prophet's birthday and **Leilat al-Miraj** is the night on which the Koran was first revealed to the Prophet. However, **Ramadan** is the most important event in the Muslim calendar with fasting from dawn to dusk and much celebration at night. Shops stay open as usual but close before sunset so that people can eat; cafés and restaurants are shut sunrise to sunset but may open after dark. Its end, and therefore the breaking of the fast, is marked by **Eid al-Fitr**. The holiday **Eid al-Adha** (also called Eid al-Kabir) recalls Abraham's attempted sacrifice of his son Isma'il, and the end of the haj (pilgrimage to Mecca) season. The two Eids are public holidays in autonomous Palestine.

PALESTINIAN HOLIDAYS

Of the main **secular Palestinian holidays** and commemorations (see box on p.51 for dates), all of which follow the Gregorian calendar, only two are official public holidays: **Fatah Day**, marking the founding, in 1965, of Fatah, the largest

JEWISH AND ISRAELI HOLIDAYS

(begin evening before)

Festival (first day)

	Purim	Passover	Independ-ence Day	Shevuot	New Year	Yom Kippur	Succot	Hannukah
1998	12 Mar	11 Apr	30 Apr	31 May	21 Sept	30 Sept	5 Oct	14 Dec
1999	2 Mar	1 Apr	20 Apr	21 May	11 Sept	20 Sept	25 Sept	4 Dec
2000	21 Mar	20 Apr	9 May	9 June	30 Sept	9 Oct	14 Oct	22 Dec
2001	9 Mar	8 Apr	27 Apr	28 May	18 Sept	27 Sept	2 Oct	10 Dec
2002	26 Feb	28 Mar	16 Apr	17 May	7 Sept	16 Sept	21 Sept	30 Nov

MUSLIM HOLIDAYS

*(approximate dates, subject to new moon sightings. * = official public holidays in autonomous Palestine)*

Festival (first day)

	Eid al-Adha*	Al-Hijra (New Year)	Moulid al-Nabi	1st of Ramadan	Eid al-Fitr*
1998	8 Apr	28 Apr	7 July	20 Dec	30 Jan
1999	29 Mar	17 Apr	26 June	9 Dec	19 Jan
2000	17 Mar	5 Apr	14 June	27 Nov	8 Jan & 27 Dec
2001	6 Mar	24 Mar	3 June	16 Nov	16 Dec
2002	23 Feb	13 Mar	23 May	5 Nov	5 Dec

PALESTINIAN NATIONAL DAYS

(= official public holidays)*

Fatah Day	1 Jan*	Black September	18 Sept
Jerusalem Day	22 Feb	Balfour Day	2 Nov
Land Day	30 March	Independence Day	15 Nov*
Deir Yassin Day	19 April	UN Palestine Day	29 Nov

grouping in the PLO, and **Independence Day**, celebrating the declaration of a State of Palestine by the Palestine National Council in 1988. Of other anniversaries and commemorations, **Jerusalem Day** is marked throughout the Muslim world to commemorate the Israeli occupation of the third holiest Muslim city. **Land Day** recalls the death of six Israeli Arabs defending their land in 1976; the 1948 massacre of the inhabitants of Deir Yassin (see p.378) is similarly recalled by **Deir Yassin Day**. Next, **Black September** marks the attack on Palestinians by Jordanian forces in 1970 as well as that by the Phalangists in Lebanon during the Israeli invasion of 1982, while **Balfour Day** recalls the 1917 Balfour Declaration, in which the British Foreign Secretary promised the Jewish people a homeland in Palestine. **Palestine Day** was declared by the UN as a "day of solidarity with the Palestinian people". May 14, the anniversary of Israel's independence, is marked by Palestinians as **al-Nakba** ("the catastrophe").

CHRISTIAN HOLIDAYS

Here in the Holy Land, **Christian holidays** are far more religious affairs than their counterparts in most Western countries. They are also rather spread out because of their celebration on different dates by different churches, each working according to a different calendar (see p.49). As an example, **Christmas** is celebrated by the Western churches on December 25, by the Eastern on January 7, and by the Armenians on January 19. The Roman Catholic/Protestant Christmas on December 25 is biggest in Bethlehem, of course, with visitors from around the world coming to cel-

THE MILLENNIUM

If the **millennium** represents roughly the two-thousandth anniversary of the birth of Jesus, then where better to celebrate it than in the land where it all happened? Indeed, Israel and the Palestinian Territories are expecting four to seven million visitors for the millennium, making them the second biggest pilgrimage destination after Rome.

For obvious reasons, Bethlehem will be the main centre of millennium activity; the PNA-sponsored project – **Bethlehem 2000** – is geared to renovating important sites for celebrations that are expected to span two years from January 1, 1999 to December 31, 2000. Not to be outdone, the Israeli government has a **Nazareth 2000** project underway, and expects to attract around 1.2 million visitors to the town. Jerusalem is likely to see a similar influx of pilgrims. Assuming predic-

tions are false and the world doesn't come to an end there, the other main millennium site will be **Megiddo** (Armageddon; see p.152). Nothing less than "virtual Armageddon" is planned for this site; though, despite its name, this combination of light shows and holograms actually aims to transport visitors back into the Holy Land's ancient and biblical history rather than forward to the world's destruction.

Sadly, the mood of celebration has already been marred by **political disputes**, with Palestinians accusing Israel of building the controversial Jewish settlement at Har Homa in East Jerusalem partly with the aim of enticing pilgrims visiting Bethlehem to stay and spend their money in Israeli-controlled Jerusalem rather than PNA-controlled Bethlehem. Whether the party mood can overcome such conflict remains to be seen.

ebrate the birth of Christ. **Easter** is marked particularly in Jerusalem, with pilgrims arriving en masse to follow the footsteps of Jesus along the Via Dolorosa. Lesser Christian festivals are also celebrated here, notably **Palm Sunday**, when Jesus entered Jerusalem a week before Easter, **Ascension**, marking Jesus's departure from the

earth five and a half weeks after Easter (on a Thursday), and **Epiphany** (Twelfth Night), twelve days after Christmas Day, when the three kings came to visit the infant Jesus in Bethlehem. Also, in a land walked by so many saints, each has their day of celebration, notably St George in Lydda on April 23 (see p.106).

ENTERTAINMENT

As you might expect in such a multicultural country, there's a wide variety of entertainment, most of it in Hebrew or Arabic. The

Israeli film industry's product is mixed in quality, and may or may not be subtitled, but the cinema is arguably worth visiting for the experience alone. Regular theatre productions pose more of a problem for non-Hebrew or Arabic speakers, but there's often something on in English and, again, you may find it interesting to spend an evening at the theatre even if you barely understand a word. The best place to look for entertainment listings in English is the Friday entertainment supplement of the *Jerusalem Post*.

MUSIC

The **Israeli music** scene has diversified greatly in recent years. In the early days, it consisted mainly of folk songs that reflected the "pioneering" spirit of the country or celebrated the beauty of the land,

and which reached a climax with Israel's victory in 1967. Thereafter, it gave way to more mellow music, such as that of the old Dylanesque master, **Arik Einstein**, or the gentle tones of **Yudit Ravitz**. The influence of American and British rock was then reflected by home-grown punk and heavy metal bands. Protest songs also became popular, notably those of **Si Hyman** who shocked Israeli society with her condemnation of the army's actions in the Palestinian Territories in *Shooting and Crying*. More recently, **Aviv Geffen** provoked attacks from Jewish fundamentalists and other elements of the extreme right with his passionate advocacy of Jewish-Palestinian reconciliation, withdrawal from the Palestinian Territories, and equal rights for women and gay people. *I Cry For You*, which he performed at a peace rally where he was embraced by Yitzhak Rabin ten minutes before the latter's assassination, became an anthem for Israel's youth.

A significant development in Israeli music that occurred in the 1980s was the "coming out" of **Sephardi musicians**, no longer embarrassed by their Arab heritage but singing it loud and clear. Among their number **Ofra Haza** is the best known internationally for her updated traditional Yemeni tunes. Others include Haim Moshe, whose music is also very much Arabic in style though sung in Hebrew, and HaBreira HaTivit (Natural Choice), a band who blend oriental and Western traditions to create an "Israeli sound". Taking it a stage further in the 1990s, an Arab-Jewish band called Bustan Abraham point out that just as Israeli music in the 1980s, previously Ashkenazi-dominated, began to accept Sephardic influences, so it should now expand further to take in Israeli Arabs as well as Jews.

Meanwhile, there has also been a revival in Ashkenazi **kletzmer** folk music, Yiddish melodies traditionally played by itinerant musicians on instruments such as violins, flutes and trumpets that could be carried around, and at one time the staple entertainment at East European Jewish weddings. There is a 3- to 5-day summer Kletzmer festival in Safed (see p.241).

In the late 1990s an unlikely Israeli pop superstar emerged in the form of transsexual singer **Dana International**, winner of the 1998 Eurovision Song Contest. Dana's success has been hailed as a victory for secularism over the religious lobby, who bitterly attacked her. Israel has a **rave scene**, but it's a clandestine affair, advertised by word of mouth and put on secretly in hidden locations. Clubs in Tel Aviv, more easily accessible for most travellers, also play a variety of dance sounds. One of the best legitimate dance venues, if you can get to it, is the Vertigo Club at Kibbutz Ramat David on Route 73, 10km west of Nazareth (☎06/654 9901).

Palestinian talent abounds with such groups as Sabreen, In A'id Rifaqi, Yo'ad and the ever-popular **Marcel Khalifeh** reflecting Palestinian resistance and aspirations for independence. Occasionally (but these days rarely), you may be lucky to catch a live concert and join in with the hand-clapping and spontaneous dancing. Music is an intrinsic part of Palestinian culture and played at joyful events such as weddings rather than at concerts.

Music from other Arab countries is also available everywhere, and you'll probably get as much as you want on any service taxi journey. Most is Egyptian – the great and eternal Umm Kalthoum, Mohammed Abd al-Wahab or Farid al-Attrash – but also popular are the sweet tones of the Lebanese singer, Fairuz.

Western popular music too can be heard everywhere, though it tends to be rather out of date by the time it gets here, so don't be surprised to find young Israelis listening to music recorded before they were born. International **rock and jazz groups** are increasingly including Israel on world tours, though this trend may depend on the progress of the peace process. Major **venues** for rock and folk music include the Sultan's Pool in Jerusalem (see p.369), and Tzavta and Maxim in Tel Aviv (see p.96). Jazz is best sought in small clubs such as Tel Aviv's Camelot (see p.96).

CLASSICAL MUSIC

As for **classical music**, there is a wide choice of concerts and festivals at which top-rate international and Israeli orchestras (such as the reputable Israel Philharmonic) and soloists perform. Classical music reaches its crescendo during the **Israel Festival**, held annually in May and early June, when a number of major international orchestras and musicians perform in the festival's four main centres: Tel Aviv, Jerusalem, and the restored Roman theatres in Beit She'an and Caesarea. The three major cities – Tel Aviv, Jerusalem and Haifa – all have major concert halls (see the relevant sections) as well as chamber music venues. Information can be found in the Friday edition of the *Jerusalem Post*, in listings magazines or from any IGTO.

FILM

Cinemas can be pretty full and noisy – movie-going is a popular form of entertainment, and Israelis and Palestinians go in for quite a bit of audience participation, which adds greatly to the sense of occasion. **Foreign films**, especially those in English, are usually shown in their original language, subtitled in Hebrew and/or Arabic. Arabic or Israeli films, on the other hand, are unlikely to be subtitled in English. The *Jerusalem Post* Friday supplement has the fullest and most up-to-date cinema listings for Israel. A cinema ticket costs around 25NIS.

Israel has a small but interesting **film industry**, which began with Natan Axelrod's *Oded the Wanderer* (1933), pre-independence Palestine's first Hebrew-language feature film. Although Golan Globus's *Lemon Popsicle* (1977) and its sequels gave the country something of a reputation for trashy movies, modern Israeli films are often far more thought-provoking, analyzing the dynamics of human relationships as well as the inevitable questions of Middle Eastern politics. Films such as Uri Barbash's *Beyond the Walls* (1984), Shimon Dotan's *The Smile of the Lamb* (1986), Rafi Bukaee's *Avanti Poppolo* (1986) and Assi Dayan's *Life According to Agfa* (1992) and *An Electric Blanket* (1994) deal with issues such as prison conditions, Palestinian-Israeli relations, the 1973 war, the Intifada and army conscription. Also worth looking out for is Dan Wolman's acclaimed 1975 film version of Amos Oz's novel *My Michael*.

There is no Palestinian film industry as such, but there is a whole range of excellent films, mostly documentary, produced by both Palestinian and foreign film-makers. There's more chance of seeing these at home, but the **Jerusalem Cinematheque**, for example, does have a fairly broad repertoire. Michel Kleifi, a Palestinian currently living and working in Belgium, has made several notable films about Palestinian life under occupation, including *Fertile Memory* and *Wedding in Galilee*. Others include Antonia Caccia's excellent *On Our Land* (about Umm al-Fahm) and the more recent *Voices from Gaza*.

THEATRE

There are four main **Israeli theatres**: the national Habimah and Cameri theatres in Tel Aviv, the Khan in Jerusalem and the Municipal Theatre in Haifa, with a few smaller ones, mainly in the same three cities. Almost all productions will be in Hebrew, but a few are performed **in English** (see the *Jerusalem Post* Friday entertainment supplement for details), and the Cameri has simultaneous translation into English on Tuesday evenings. If you think you can handle **Hebrew theatre**, try for a performance of more controversial playwrights such as Hanoch Levin, or Joshua Sobol, whose *Soul of a Jew* and *Ghetto* caused a stir in Israel's theatre world in the 1980s. Israeli theatre had a tradition of radicalism that went into abeyance somewhat during the Intifada, but which has recently resurfaced in the form of the **Gesher Theatre Company**, currently based in Jaffa (see p.97 for details), which has scored a massive hit with Tel Aviv audiences.

Naturally enough, Israel is one of the best places (along with New York) to see the sort of **Yiddish theatre** that was once performed by the Jewish communities in the ghettoes of Europe. Again, if you don't know the language, you'll miss the subtle, linguistic jokes, but you can still pick up on the more slapstick humour and, above all, the great **kletzmer music and songs** (see p.53).

Palestinian theatre is also worth going to see; another lively occasion in which audience participation is positively encouraged. There is only one fixed venue in the Palestinian Territories: Nuzha al-Hakawati in East Jerusalem (see p.386), but plays, folklore festivals and dance are often performed in the Palestinian universities of Bir Zeit, Bethlehem or Najah (in Nablus). The most famous Palestinian theatre group is **al-Hakawati**, who have presented such pieces as *Mahjoub Mahjoub*, *Slaves Go West* and *The Story of the Eye and the Tooth* in many European cities, but there are many other lesser-known groups who play wherever and whenever they are not prevented from doing so by the censor or the military authorities. Inside the Green Line (in Nazareth or Haifa, for example), you may be lucky to catch a performance of *Return to Haifa*, a play adapted from the novel of the same name by Palestinian writer Ghassan Kanafani (who died in a car-bombing in Beirut).

DANCE AND PERFORMANCE

One further form of entertainment, which you may be offered as part of an Israeli tour, or get thrown in with a package deal, is an "authentic **folklore evening**" – rather staid versions are held regularly at many of the larger hotels, but those put on occasionally for local consumption in city parks or cultural centres are more genuine, fun, and involve lots of audience participation. Generally a mixture of song and dance originating from various traditions, with elements of East European (Polish, Hungarian, Russian), Greek and Arabic cultures, the shows may also contain belly dancing, usually adapted for Western tastes. Traditional song and dance is much more alive in Palestinian culture, being an essential element of local weddings and festivities.

THE POLICE, TROUBLE AND SECURITY

You'll already have experienced Israeli security at your point of arrival, and it's no less noticeable once inside the country. Keep your personal belongings with you at all times, since parcels, packages and baggage left unattended may be reported to the police as suspicious, and either confiscated or detonated. Similarly, if you notice an unguarded package, you should report it to the bus driver, storeowner, hotel staff or whoever else seems relevant, since bomb attacks on civilian targets by a whole plethora of Palestinian nationalist and Islamic fundamentalist groups are not uncommon. At present, suicide bombings by young Hamas, Hizbollah or Islamic Jihad militants are in vogue, and often incur fatalities amongst innocent bystanders. For all these reasons, expect to have your bags checked frequently, especially at entrances to museums, large stores, supermarkets, cinemas and post offices.

If you travel in the Palestinian Territories (see p.56) there is a slight but real possibility of being caught up in disturbances. Confine your visit to areas within the Green Line, however, and it's unlikely that you will even notice, let alone encounter, any clashes other than the odd bout of fisticuffs between taxi drivers on a sweltering summer's day. Before you leave, you may want to contact your government for their official advice on visiting the region. At present, the US State Department is advising American nationals not to travel at all in the Palestinian Territories.

POLICE AND THE ARMY

Day-to-day authority inside Israel (and in the Golan Heights and East Jerusalem) rests with the regular **police**, recognizable by their navy-blue uniforms and flat caps. Like most police forces, they're helpful if you are a tourist, reasonably co-operative if you've been robbed, and decidedly unfriendly if you're breaking the law. If you need **to report a crime** – a robbery, mugging or attack – go to the nearest police station, where hopefully someone will be sympathetic. In the event of rape or sexual assault, several major towns have rape crisis centres (see "Sexual Harassment" below), whose staff will offer advice and accompany you to a police station to file a report.

Operating mostly in the Israeli-controlled areas of the West Bank, the so-called **border guards**, with their military-style uniform and green berets, are officially part of the police force. Their role is often interchangeable with that of the army, but they have something of a reputation for brutality towards Palestinians. The PNA has its own police force, as well as a number of security forces in a variety of uniforms from whatever sources were available to kit them out. Other security forces, directly responsible to President Arafat, already have a bad record for brutality and human rights abuses, but all are likely to be friendly and helpful towards tourists.

The **Israeli army** (IDF or *Tzahal*) is everywhere and the sight of fully-armed khaki-clad soldiers at bus stations, hitching along the highways or walking through the streets is a common and, until you get used to it, slightly shocking one. Do remember, however, that pretty well everyone in Israel does military service: the army therefore consists of ordinary Israeli youth. The soldiers that you see out and about will in any case probably be off-duty and making their way home or to base.

"THE CONFLICT": AVOIDING TROUBLE

On the beach in Tel Aviv or Eilat, the **Israeli-Palestinian conflict** can seem as far away as it would if you were sunning yourself on the Costa Brava. Even in Jerusalem, geographically and politically at the heart of the problem, it's possible to avoid it completely if you stay in the western half of the city. However, a quick stroll **across the Green Line** to the Old City, reveals Israeli soldiers stationed at strategic points (particularly when tension is high), stopping and checking Palestinian residents. As a tourist, you are unlikely to be bothered by them unless mistaken for a local resident (in which case making your status clear should take a matter of seconds) but **riots** do break out, the ammunition used to quell them is often real, and you could easily be mistaken by either side for an adversary. In general therefore, the best advice is to keep your eyes and ears open, steer clear of trouble, and make it as clear as possible that you are a tourist. If you do get caught up in a confrontation, it is unlikely to be a foreigner that you will be deliberately targeted by either side.

The same applies in general when **visiting the Palestinian Territories**. Israeli police or soldiers may ask you to produce ID when entering or leaving PNA-controlled areas, and legally you should **carry a passport** (or state-issued identity card) at all times. It is not unknown for Israeli soldiers to break or confiscate the cameras of journalists, Palestinian, Israeli or foreign, who photograph things the army does not want on film, and journalists are even occasionally shot at or beaten up, so you take your chances if you want to stick around and point your camera at the wrong thing. In the unlikely event that you are detained for political reasons, you may initially be denied access to your consul, but try to contact them or a lawyer as soon as you can (or pass word to someone else to do so).

Another problem in visiting the Palestinian Territories, particularly during times of trouble, is that you may be mistaken for an Israeli spy, especially in areas where tourists don't normally venture, and even stoned at times of tension. Such cases are unusual, but they do occur. Again, your passport as proof of identity and nationality may help, but your best bet is to make it abundantly clear that you are a foreign tourist, avoid hot spots and, if necessary, seek advice from Palestinian or neutral sources (such as the Christian Information Centre, see p.309) before setting out (Israeli sources will generally tell you that it is unsafe to visit Palestinian areas, especially those under PNA jurisdiction, in any case).

At the time of writing, the main flashpoint is Hebron (see p.407), but even there you shouldn't encounter any trouble from either side. The announcement of any new Jewish settlement, especially in East Jerusalem, also tends to mean trouble.

AVOIDING OFFENCE: DRESS AND BEHAVIOUR

Generally speaking this is an extremely conservative society, and anything that might be interpreted as immodest or disrespectful behaviour could bring trouble from the authorities or from local people. **Dress**, for women in particular, is the obvious cause of trouble: while sunbathing topless may be normal on the more cosmopolitan beaches around Tel Aviv, it's not a good idea to show any sort of flesh at all in ultra-orthodox areas of Jerusalem, such as Mea She'arim where wall notices warn women not to display bare arms and legs. Therefore, modest attire – loose-fitting dresses, or long skirts and long-sleeved baggy tops – is advisable at all times and a must at **religious sites** and in religious Arab areas of Israel and throughout the Palestinian Territories – keep yourself well covered, with no shorts or bare shoulders. Ignoring this advice may make you the target of hostility from religious Jews and Arabs alike – usually in the form of verbal abuse but violence such as stone-throwing has been known to occur. In any case, keeping bare flesh to a minimum will also help reduce the amount of sexual harassment you're likely to encounter (see p.57). Public displays of affection are frowned on by religious Jews and Muslims alike, and people who drive through ultra-orthodox areas on Shabbat will find their car being stoned by residents.

Photography can also be contentious. Before you start snapping away at people (especially Orthodox Jews, who object to taking photographs on the basis that it constitutes "making a graven image"), inside synagogues, churches or mosques, or taking pictures of anything which could be regarded as a security installation (airports etc), try to ask permission.

SEXUAL HARASSMENT

Sexual harassment is, alas, all too common in both Israel and the Palestinian Territories. In part, this is a symptom of sexual repression in a society dominated by religious mores, but it's also a result of the macho culture endemic to the Mediterranean. Women tourists, especially those travelling alone, are all too often assumed to be "up for it", and likely to suffer unwanted advances, verbal abuse and sometimes groping. This is particularly true in Palestinian areas, where the Islamic tendency towards sexual segregation means a lot of very frustrated young men, but you'll also find plenty of it in Israel.

Although most sexual harassment is of the low-key variety – wolf-whistling, staring and propositioning – it's more or less constant, and extremely annoying and frustrating. Sadly, what this in fact means is that it's difficult for any woman to be alone and enjoy a stroll, a coffee or a sunbathe (verbal pestering is particularly heavy on the beach) and while dressing modestly will go some way to avoiding trouble, there are no hard and fast rules for dealing with unwanted admirers. Taxi drivers are also notorious – taking what you intend to be friendly conversation as an open invitation, although this is unlikely to get too heavy as they have their job to protect. One way of keeping this to a minimum is to sit in the back of the cab rather than beside the driver.

DRUGS

Mainstream Israeli and Palestinian society remains extremely conservative in their attitudes towards all **illegal drugs**, which include cannabis, commonly smoked but very illegal. Legal penalties on cannabis in Israel remain harsh, with high fines and suspended prison sentences the norm for possession of even a small amount (though a foreigner would probably just be slung in a cell for a day or two, and deported thereafter). Anything over 15g is considered a dealing quantity, for which a prison term can be expected.

One thing that is completely legal and socially acceptable however is **qat**, a mildly narcotic stimulant from Yemen and the Horn of Africa, brought to Israel by Yemeni Jews. Something of an acquired taste, qat consists of the leaves, or young bark from the shoots, of a shrub frequently grown in the gardens of Yemeni-Jewish homes, and has to be chewed continuously for some time before any effect is felt. It is widely available in markets anywhere with a large Yemenite population, but beware of taking any home, since it is a controlled drug in many countries, including the United States and Ireland, though it is legal in the UK.

The guidelines for avoiding rape and indecent assault are basically the same as those you'd follow at home: stay away from dark, lonely streets; don't hitch (especially at night and alone or even with another woman); and don't sleep on isolated beaches. In the worst event, there are several 24-hour rape crisis numbers that you can call for counselling and advice and for someone to accompany you to the police to file a complaint (see "Listings" section of relevant cities).

TRAVELLERS WITH DISABILITIES

Israel is now beginning to cater to the needs of those with disabilities, including a number of its war veterans previously unacknowledged in shame, and ramps for wheelchairs are becoming more common in public buildings (and at Ben Gurion Airport). On the other hand, buses do not cater in any way for the wheelchair-bound, and the possibilities of travelling in a rented car are rather limited by the political situation, which makes it hard to cross from Israel to the Palestinian Territories or vice versa (see "Getting Around" p.32).

Information on suitable hotel accommodation and accessibility to museums, nature reserves and archeological sites is readily available in Israel from JDC-Israel or MILBAT (addresses in the box below), as are details of places catering for those with impaired sight or hearing. Hotels claiming to cater for disabled visitors include the *Holiday Inn* and *Ramada Continental* in Tel Aviv, the *Holiday Inn*, *Jerusalem Tower*, *Laromme*, *Renaissance* and *Sheraton* in Jerusalem, the

Holiday Inns in Tiberias and Eilat, and IYHA youth hostels in Jerusalem, Tel Aviv and Beersheba, but you should always call ahead to check that your particular disability is covered. The most useful publication for disabled travellers visiting Israel remains *Access Israel* (1988) published by the Access Project, 39 Bradley Gardens, London W13 8HE, and obtainable by post (no price but donation requested: cheques payable to Access Project). Though a little out of date it is still unsurpassed for its list of wheelchair-accessible hotels, lavatories and public buildings, as well as a map of Jerusalem's Old City showing a wheelchair route that covers the main sights while avoiding the steps.

The conventional package holiday industry in Israel makes some attempt to cater for people with various disabilities, especially if wheelchair-bound. In addition, there are **organized tours and holidays** specifically for people with disabilities – the contacts in the box will be able to put you touch with any covering Israel and the Palestinian Territories.

CONTACTS FOR TRAVELLERS WITH DISABILITIES

NORTH AMERICA

Directions Unlimited, 720 N Bedford Rd, Bedford Hills, NY 10507 (☎914/241 1700). *Travel agency specializing in custom tours for people with disabilities.*

Flying Wheels Travel Service, PO Box 382, 143 West Bridge, Owatonna, MN 55060 (☎1-800/535 6790). *Operates tours for disabled travellers.*

Jewish Rehabilitation Hospital, 3205 Place Alton Goldbloom, Chomedy Laval, PQ H7V 1R2 (☎514/688 9550 ext. 226). *Guidebooks and travel information.*

Mobility International USA, PO Box 10767, Eugene, OR 97440 (Voice and TDD: ☎541/343 1284). *Information and referral services, access guides, tours and exchange programmes.*

Society for the Advancement of Travel for the Handicapped (SATH), 347 5th Ave, Suite 610, New York, NY 10016 (☎212/447 7284; Web site: http://www.sittravel.com/). *Non-profit travel-industry referral service that passes queries on to its members as appropriate. Extremely helpful for telephone queries. Does not recommend El Al as carrier for people with disabilities.*

Travel Information Service (☎215/456 9600). *Telephone information and referral service.*

Twin Peaks Press, Box 129, Vancouver, WA 98666 (☎360/694 2462 or ☎1-800/637 2256). *Publisher of the* Directory of Travel Agencies for the Disabled ($19.95), *listing more than 370 agencies worldwide;* Travel for the Disabled ($19.95); *the* Directory of Accessible Van Rentals ($9.95) *and* Wheelchair Vagabond ($14.95), *loaded with personal tips.*

UK & IRELAND

Across Trust for Disabled, Bridge House, 70–72 Bridge Rd, East Molesey, Surrey KT8 9HF (☎0181/783 1355). *Runs an annual end-of-season biblical sites tour for people with disabilities.*

Holiday Care Service, 2nd floor, Imperial Building, Victoria Rd, Horley, Surrey RH6 7PZ (☎01293/774535; Minicom ☎01293/776943). *Provides free lists of accessible accommodation. Information on financial help for holidays available.*

Tripscope, The Courtyard, Evelyn Rd, London W4 5JL (☎0181/994 9294). *A national telephone information service offering free transport and travel advice for those with mobility problems.*

RADAR, 12 City Forum, 250 City Rd, London EC1V 8AF (☎0171/250 3222; Minicom ☎0171/250 4119). *A good source of advice on holidays and travel abroad; they also publish their own guides for travellers with disabilities (Israel and the Palestinian Territories are in their* Long Haul *book; £5).*

Disability Action Group, 2 Annadale Ave, Belfast BT7 3JH (☎01232/491011).

Irish Wheelchair Association, Blackheath Drive, Clontarf, Dublin 3 (☎01/833 8241; email: iwa@iol.ie). *National voluntary organization for people with disabilities, including services for holidaymakers.*

AUSTRALASIA

ACROD, PO Box 60, Curtin, Canberra, ACT 2605 (☎06/6282 4333). *Can offer advice and keeps a list of travel specialists.*

Disabled Persons Assembly, 173-175 Victoria St, Wellington (☎04/811 9100).

ISRAEL AND THE PALESTINIAN TERRITORIES

Yad Sarah, Main office, 43 HaNevi'im, PO Box 6992, Jerusalem 91609 (☎02/624 4242). *Free loan of wheelchairs and mobility aids from branches Israel-wide.*

MILBAT, Sheba Medical Centre, Tel HaShomer, Ramat Gan (☎03/530 3739). *Advisory centre for disabled people; can provide information on accessibility to tourist sites.*

MATAM, 130 Dizengoff, Tel Aviv 64397 (☎03/523 7571). *Home-care organization which can provide care services for disabled visitors, and check on accessibility of sites and hotels.*

Amir Tours, 11 Shlomzion HaMalka, Jerusalem 94182 (☎02/623 1261). *Travel firm specializing in tours and holidays for mobility-, sight- and hearing-impaired visitors.*

Roof, Eliahu House, 2 Ibn Gvirol, Tel Aviv 64077 (☎03/696 6212 or 3). *Umbrella group for Israeli associations for people with disabilities; runs an information centre at the above address.*

Lotam, 13b Balfour, Jerusalem 92102. *Can organize nature hikes for disabled, including wheelchair-bound.*

JDC-Israel Information Centre, PO Box 3489, Jerusalem 91043 (☎02/678 7454, fax 678 8458). *Can supply information on accommodation catering for people with different disabilities, and on accessibility of tourist sites.*

GAY TRAVELLERS

Male homosexuality only ceased to be illegal in Israel in 1988 – after years of pressure from the Citizens' Rights Movement – and attitudes still tend to be puritanical, especially given the country's vociferous and influential religious lobby. The Torah (Leviticus 20:13) advocates death to male homosexuals, and neither are gays helped by societal values, Arab and Jewish alike, which place heavy emphasis on marriage, family life and children. Legal reforms have however continued, with protection from employment discrimination introduced in 1991, and a court ruling extending equal rights to gay and heterosexual partners of companies' employees in 1994.

Lesbians find themselves in a slightly different situation. Sexual relations between women are not mentioned by the Bible, and nor have they ever been proscribed by law, since the law on homosexuality, like so many others, is a product of the Mandate's British legal system, which fails to countenance the existence of lesbianism. However, the pressure on women to conform, to marry and have children, is even greater than on men; and attitudes towards lesbians even more outdated than towards male homosexuality.

AIDS has affected gay life here as it has everywhere else, helping to reinforce reactionary attitudes. A volunteer AIDS task force has been set up which, in concert with the Ministry of Health, runs an information hotline and AIDS centres around the country. But since positive tests must be reported to the Ministry, many gays are afraid to take advantage.

Gay travellers will find the coastal cities and resorts, Tel Aviv and Eilat especially, infinitely more tolerant than smaller places or the interior. *Aguda*, formerly the Society for the Protection of Personal Rights (PO Box 37604, Tel Aviv 61375; ☎03/629 3681; email: *sppr@netvision.net.il*), Israel's only significant gay organization, runs a gay and lesbian switchboard, **The White Line**, in Tel Aviv (☎03/629 2797; Tues, Thurs & Sun 7.30–11.30pm), and Haifa (☎04/852 5352; Mon 7.30–11pm). They also run a Web site at *http://www.geocities.com/WestHollywood/hights/8197*, and publish a twice-yearly English-language bulletin called *Israel Update*.

More specific advice for gay male visitors to Israel and the Palestinian Territories can also be found in *Spartacus Gay Guide*, published by Bruno Gmünder Verlag, Leuschnerdamm 31, 10999 Berlin, Germany (☎030/615 0030); c/o *Bookazine Co*, 75 Hook Rd, Bayonne, NJ 07002 (☎201/339 7777); c/o Prowler Press, 3 Broadbent Close, 20–22 Highgate High St, London N6 5GG (☎0181/340 7667); c/o *Edition Habit Press*, 72–80 Bourke Rd, Alexandria, NSW 2015 (☎02/9310 2098).

WORK

Although working in Israel on a tourist visa is illegal, many visitors do it and the authorities often seem to turn a blind eye, though the occasional raid does take place, and you'll be deported if caught. Most unofficial work is in bars, nightclubs and cafés in the big coastal resorts: Tel Aviv, the Sea of Galilee, and especially Eilat; you may also find work in travellers' hostels, at least enough to cover food and board and, particularly in Tel Aviv, there is casual work for travellers in the building trade.

Working legally is limited to kibbutzim and moshavim, and less commonly archeological digs and workcamps. Au pair work is also possible: check the adverts in *The Traveller* (the free monthly paper available at travellers' hostels in Tel Aviv, Jerusalem, Eilat and Tiberias).

Apart from the possibility of being caught and deported and the low rates of pay, the big disadvantage of **working illegally** is that you have no legal rights whatsoever, and even if your employer withholds payment (something that is all too common, especially in Eilat), you won't legally have any comeback. If, despite all this, you are still interested, the best way to find this kind of work is by word of mouth in the travellers' hostels in Tel Aviv, Eilat and, to a lesser extent, Jerusalem. Otherwise, try turning up around 5–6am at the *Peace Café* in Eilat, or on Rehov Nes Ziona in Tel Aviv.

KIBBUTZ AND MOSHAV VOLUNTEERS

Working on a kibbutz is a unique experience that enables you to stay in Israel at very little cost. Bear in mind, though, that your regime may be fairly strict and you won't be able to take time off as and when you choose, so sightseeing will have to wait. Many kibbutzim make up for this with occasional day trips for their volunteers; others provide *ulpanim* – Hebrew-language courses – on half-days.

Living conditions in the first kibbutzim were pretty basic but nowadays many are well equipped with the latest technology, entertainment facilities and swimming pools. The normal deal is that in return for eight hours' work a day, six days a week, you get food, accommodation (the latter in separate volunteers' quarters), and a small payment of around £50/$70 per month. The type of work you're given depends on the economic base of your particular kibbutz. In general, the **tasks** are divided into three main groups: service work (kitchens, laundry and children's homes); farm work (citrus fields, banana and date plantations, vineyards, poultry and livestock); and factory work – usually involving packing or making components. Volunteers with special skills may get more interesting opportunities. It's best to avoid coming in the summer months (June–Aug), as the higher number of volunteers means there's less work available.

Relations between kibbutzniks and volunteers aren't always what they might be. Kibbutzniks may regard volunteers as drunken debauchees and a bad influence on their youth, a stereotype that volunteers all too often do their best to live up to. Sleeping or smoking dope with their offspring (even if that's who you bought it from) is unlikely to get you in their good books either. All said and done, you don't have to be on your absolute best behaviour, but a little discretion is always advisable.

Volunteers on a **moshav** either live in separate accommodation (two or four to a cabin) or are placed with a family and expected to join in their social and cultural life. In return for your labour, you will get board, lodging and a small wage of around £200/$300 per month.

A few **conditions** apply to both kibbutzim and moshav volunteers. The minimum period of com-

KIBBUTZIM AND MOSHAVIM

The **kibbutz** is probably the world's most famous communal society, based on ideals of absolute socialism, mixed with the Zionist ideal of building a Jewish homeland in Palestine. The first kibbutz, **Deganya**, was founded in 1910 and there are now some 250 in Israel, the Palestinian Territories and the Golan. Nowadays, the number of foreign volunteers on kibbutzim has fallen dramatically from the heyday in the 1970s when they numbered some fifty thousand a year; the figure stands today at below ten thousand.

Conceived as **collective agricultural settlements**, kibbutzim were owned and administered communally by their members. Children were raised together in a children's home, and the whole kibbutz ate together in the canteen. Money was jointly administered, with members' needs being met from a kitty. In the end, however, this proved too communal for most people, and few kibbutzim survive with their original ways of life and ideals intact. Most have also abandoned reliance on agriculture, diversifying into industrial enterprises such as plastics and computer factories or processing plants to supplement their dwindling resources. More significantly, however, many kibbutzim now depend on hiring cheap **outside labour** for their survival. Palestinians from the Palestinian Territories were the first outsiders to be drafted in (only Jews can be members of a kibbutz, so Palestinians were unable to join), only to be replaced, following the Intifada, by "guest workers" from Eastern Europe or Southeast Asia.

Many, not unreasonably, see this kind of exploitation as a betrayal of the kibbutz movement's original socialist ideals.

A **moshav** is an agricultural smallholders' co-operative village on state-owned land leased by the moshav itself and centred around the **family unit**. Moshavim developed as an alternative for those who wanted to work the land but weren't too keen on the total collectivism of a kibbutz: in particular, they appealed to the immigrants of the third aliyah in the early 1920s, the first moshav being founded at Nahalal in 1921. There are now around four hundred moshavim. Although each family is a separate economic unit, produce is marketed cooperatively, and supplies are bought by the moshav and sold to its members through its store. Originally, everybody had to supply their own labour, but that principle has been relaxed, and outside labour is now common, again often Palestinian or "guest worker"; again, non-Jews are unable to join a moshav.

A compromise between the kibbutz and the straight moshav is the **moshav shitufi**, of which there are around fifty. Families live separately and run their own financial affairs, but work and ownership of land and production are communal.

All kibbutzim and moshavim in Israel and the Territories are affiliated to one of several movements with differing political ideologies or levels of religious belief. Some of these are in turn affiliated to political parties.

mitment is eight weeks, and you have to be 18–32 years old for a kibbutz, 18–35 for a moshav.

APPLICATION AND INFORMATION

There are several ways to go about finding work on a kibbutz or moshav, the most common being to **apply from home** to a kibbutz or moshav representative in your own country (see box on p.63), who will arrange you a place before you leave. In general, they assign you a place, though you can always turn it down. Write to the relevant office with a stamped addressed envelope, asking for an application form. You will need two letters of reference and a medical certificate to prove that you are fit for work, and you will also have to pay a registration fee of £32/$52. Some private companies such as Project 67 offer a package which includes kibbutz placement, return airfare and insurance

cover. If you do it this way, though, you can't choose the kibbutz you want – they pick you.

You can also **apply in Israel** to the central kibbutz or moshav offices in Tel Aviv, or through private agencies there (though you pay a little more that way). This should give you more say in where you end up, although you may find that the kibbutz you want to go to is booked, particularly in the busy summer months between June and August. If there are vacancies, you will be interviewed and, if offered a place, will be expected to make your own way there. At the interview, you must produce a valid passport, an insurance certificate covering medical expenses, personal accidents and loss of possessions, a medical fitness certificate, two letters of reference and an onward air ticket. If you entered Israel as a tourist, you will also have to change your immigration status, which will cost around £11/$17.

Finally, it is possible to **apply directly** to a kibbutz or moshav. It's pretty unlikely that you'll be accepted on this basis, but there is always a chance, so no harm in trying if you run across a kibbutz on your travels that particularly appeals.

Some kibbutzim treat volunteers very well indeed; others treat you like dirt. If at all possible, go for one that has been personally recommended. As kibbutzim are generally aligned to political movements, you also may want to find out the persuasion of the one you're going to work in. Full details about all the kibbutzim in the country and much valuable information besides are available in *Kibbutz Volunteer* by Victoria Pybus (Vacation Work; UK, 1996; £7.99).

PALESTINIAN WORKCAMPS

A number of Palestinian towns and villages, both in Israel and in the Palestinian Territories, run **workcamps** in which volunteers are invited to participate, performing many basic manual tasks, such as road laying, rock and rubbish clearing, painting and building that need to be done.

Most of the workcamps are held in the summer, particularly during July and August. Volunteers are supplied with food and accommodation, either with families or in communal quarters such as a school or campsite. You have to pay your own travel and insurance and provide your own spending money. In some cases, you

KIBBUTZ/MOSHAV VOLUNTEER INFORMATION OFFICES

ABROAD

Australia

Kibbutz Program Centre 104 Darlinghurst Rd, Darlinghurst, NSW 2010 (☎02/9360 6300); 306 Hawthorn Rd, South Caulfield, Vic 3162 (☎03/9272 5531); Perth, c/o Israel Information Centre, 61 Woodrow Av, Yokine, WA 6060 (☎08/9276 8730).

Canada

Israel Program Centre 151 Chapel, Ottawa, ON K1N 7Y2 (☎613/789 5010).

Israel Aliya Centre 950 W 41st Ave, Vancouver, BC V5Z 2N7 (☎604/ 257 5141).

Kibbutz Program Centre Lipagreen Building, 4600 Bathurst, Suite 315, ON M2R 3V0 (☎416/633 6373).

New Zealand

Kibbutz Programme Desk Wellington Jewish Community Centre, Kensington St, PO Box 27–156, Wellington (☎04/384 4229).

South Africa

Peltours PO Box 6988, Johannesburg 2000 (☎011/880 8241).

UK

Kibbutz Representatives 1A Accommodation Rd, London NW1 8ED (☎0181/458 9235); c/o Peltours, 27 Church St, Manchester M4 1QA (☎061/236 0006); 222 Fenwick Rd, Glasgow G46 6UE (☎0141/620 2194).

Project 67 10 Hatton Garden, London EC1N 8AH (☎0171/831 7626).

USA

Kibbutz Aliya Centre 110 E 59th St, 4th floor, New York, NY 10022 (☎1-800/247 7852 or ☎318 6130); other offices around the country change addresses frequently – for latest details of your nearest office call ☎1-800/247 7852.

IN ISRAEL

HaKibbutz HaDati, 7 Dubnov St, Tel Aviv (☎03/525 7231). *Office of the religious kibbutz movement, accepting Orthodox Jewish volunteers only.*

Kibbutz Program Centre 18 Frishman (cnr Ben Yehuda), Tel Aviv 61030 (☎03/527 8874). *The official representative of the kibbutz movement.*

Meira's 73 Ben Yehuda, 1st floor, Tel Aviv 63435 (☎03/523 7369). *A private firm placing volunteers with kibbutzim and moshavim.*

Moshav Movement, 19 Leonardo da Vinci, Tel Aviv 64733 (☎03/695 8473). *The official representative of the moshav movement.*

Project 67 94 Ben Yehuda, Tel Aviv (☎03/523 0140). *A private firm placing volunteers with kibbutzim and moshavim.*

also have to pay a registration fee of around £15/$20.

Work is usually allotted to small groups of participants on a daily basis and, depending on what needs to be done, you can have a choice in the matter. After a hard day's work, there's often a full programme of entertainment – either laid on or provided by participants.

The best-known workcamp in the West Bank is the one run by **Bir Zeit University**. Other work-camps are regularly held in Nazareth, Jaffa, Umm al-Fahm, Deir al-Assad, Shafr Amr, Majd al-Shams, Kufr Kana and Acre. You are advised to apply from home before you leave if you wish to volunteer. The box below lists some organizations you can contact for further information and/or application forms; they will also be able to help in arranging or advising on other sorts of volunteer and non-volunteer longer-term work, such as teaching, medical aid, research or field work.

ARCHEOLOGICAL DIGS

At any one time there are dozens of **archeo-logical excavations** going on at sites all over Israel, and many of them accept volunteers during the summer to do the donkey work (digging, shov-elling, lugging baskets, cleaning pottery and the like). Volunteers must normally be over 18 and commit themselves for a minimum period, usually one or two weeks. Accommodation can be any-thing from bedding down on the site to staying in a three-star hotel. Note that some digs have reg-istration fees, which can be as much as £65/$100.

A list of **contact addresses and conditions** for digs accepting volunteers can be obtained from any IGTO or the Department of Antiquities and Museums, Ministry of Education and Culture, PO Box 586, Jerusalem 91004 (☎02/629 2607, fax 629 2628; email: *harriet@israntique.org.il*). Apply early in the year to be certain of a place, though

WORKCAMPS AND OTHER VOLUNTEER WORK

APPLYING FROM ABROAD

Friends of Bir Zeit University (FoBZU), 21 Collingham Rd, London SW5 0NU (☎0171/373 8414). *Support group associated with the West Bank's largest university, placing volunteers on workcamps run by the university.*

Medical Aid for Palestinians (MAP), 33A Islington Park St, London N1 1QB (☎0171/226 4114). *Places volunteers with medical training in Palestinian hospitals and clinics.*

United Nations Association International Service (UNAIS), Suite 3A, Hunter House, 57 Goodramgate, York YO1 2LS (☎01904/657799). *Places volunteers with special skills with Palestinian development organizations and projects.*

Universities Fund for Palestinian Refugees (UNIPAL), 63 Holbrook Rd, Cambridge CB1 4SX (☎01223/211864). *Places volunteer EFL teachers.*

Volunteers for Peace, 43 Tiffany Rd, Belmont, VT 05730 (☎802/259-2759; Web site: http:// www.vfp.org/). *Non-profit organization with links to a huge international network of "workcamps", two- to four-week programmes to carry out need-ed community projects. Most workcamps are in summer, with registration in April–May. Annual directory $10.*

APPLYING IN THE PALESTINIAN TERRITORIES AND ISRAEL

League of Arab Jaffa (al-Raabita) 73 Yefet, Jaffa (☎03/681 2290).

Association for the Support and Defence of Bedouin Rights in Israel 37 Hativat HaNegev, PO Box 5212, Beersheba (☎07/623 1687).

Nazareth Municipality 606 Street, Nazareth (☎06/645 9200).

Umm al-Fahm Municipality Umm al-Fahm, The Triangle (☎06/631 2040).

Deir al-Assad Progressive Front Deir al-Assad, Galilee (☎04/987078).

Association of University Graduates in the Golan Heights Majd al-Shams, Golan Heights (☎06/598 1624).

Al-Nahda Centre PO Box 92, Taibe, The Triangle (☎052/993035).

you may be lucky to get on a dig once you're in Israel. If you don't feel like spending the best part of your holiday digging, you can get your hands dirty for just a morning with the **Dig For A Day** programme run by Archaeological Seminars, 34 Habad, PO Box 14002, Jerusalem 91140 (☎02/627 3515). It will cost you around £15/$25 to work on a site.

DIRECTORY

BAGGAGE DEPOSIT (LEFT LUGGAGE) Because of the security risk, there are very few left-luggage offices anywhere in Israel (large bus stations may have them, but they are expensive). For the same reason, you must keep your bags with you at all times – any unattended baggage is likely to be cordoned off by the army and detonated.

BARGAINING is the name of the game in Palestinian souqs (markets), and particularly when shopping for souvenirs, but it's not common practice in shops, stores or restaurants, nor so much in Israeli markets. Bargaining should always be good-humoured; never haggle for something you don't really want, nor mention a price you're not prepared to pay. It helps to start off with an upper limit in mind but, contrary to popular belief, there's no magic figure to aim for, such as half or a third of the asking price: you could end up paying as little as a tenth or almost as much as the starting price. You can also bargain for accommodation in some hotels and hostels, depending on how business is at the time.

CHILDREN Palestinians and Israelis alike dote on children and travelling with them is fine. Baby needs – food, disposable nappies, medication, etc – are widely available in supermarkets and shops, and many hotels and hostels either have family rooms or will put in an extra bed. Baby food should be no problem: Gerber produces a range that is widely available in Israeli shops. Child seats should be available if renting a car, but are best booked well in advance.

CLOTHES The main thing to bear in mind is the heat. Wear loose-fitting cotton clothes and a sun-hat (traditional kibbutz hats are ideal) to protect you from sunstroke. In winter, you'll need warm clothes, too, especially in the Galilee, the West Bank and the desert (which gets wickedly cold at night). You'll also need long-sleeved tops, trousers and/or a skirt, since local people in Palestinian villages and ultra-orthodox Jewish districts of cities don't take kindly to miniskirts or shorts, and even frown on trousers or short sleeves for women; in any case you must dress "modestly" to visit a mosque, synagogue or church.

ELECTRICITY 220v 50Hz with triple-round-pin plugs and sockets. British, Irish and Australasian plugs will need an adapter (double-round-pin electric shavers will be all right, though, and double-round-pin European plugs should fit most sockets). American and Canadian appliances will need a transformer, too, unless multi-voltage.

EMBASSIES AND CONSULATES Although Jerusalem is the seat of Israel's government, most foreign countries do not recognize it as Israel's capital (the United States is the biggest exception), and their embassies remain in Tel Aviv. However, most have consulates in West Jerusalem and occasionally Haifa or Eilat (Egypt, helpfully, has an Eilat consulate, handy if you're crossing the border there and need a visa). Gaza is the acting Palestinian capital, but as Palestine is not a state, there are no embassies here. Most of the countries that do have consulates serving Palestine have located them in East Jerusalem.

Addresses are given in the "Listings" sections for the relevant towns.

EMERGENCIES Ambulance ☎101; Police ☎100; Fire ☎102; Emergency services in English ☎911; medical help for tourists ☎177/022 9110. For local police, medical services and rape crisis centres, see the "Listings" sections for the relevant towns.

LAUNDRY The larger towns all have a couple of self-service laundromats, but they're not all that common. You can get washing done at most hotels and some hostels have washing machines for residents.

NATIONAL PARKS A 14-day Green Card (£25/$40) is available which gives free access to all the major archeological sites and parks: contact the National Parks Authority, 4 Makleff, HaKirya, Tel Aviv 61070 (☎03/695 2281).

SPELLING Hebrew and Arabic of course use different alphabets from English, and spellings of Hebrew and Arabic words in English vary. Certain sounds in Arabic, and in Hebrew if pronounced strictly correctly (usually by Sephradic speakers), do not exist in English. Some of these are often represented by putting a dot under letters like "h" and "t", though that has not been done in this book. "Ch" is often used in Israel to represent its sound in "loch" rather than in "cheese", though that is going out of fashion in favour of an "h" for the Hebrew letter *het*, and "kh" for the soft *kaf*, a trend followed in this book, though both are in practice pronounced the same in Modern Hebrew. A "q" is generally used for both the Hebrew *quf* and the Arabic *qa*, correctly pronounced as a guttural "k" at the back of the throat, though *quf* is usually pronounced just like an ordinary "k" in Modern Hebrew. An apostrophe is used in this book to represent the Arabic *'ayn* and Hebrew *'ayin*, which make a guttural sound not found in any Western language (though the *'ayin* is in practice often just silent in Modern Hebrew), as well as the Arabic *hamza* (glottal stop). Spelling in this book tries to be consistent, but if there is already an established English spelling for something, that has been used, even if it does not conform to the latest transliteration standards.

TIME Israel is on GMT+2, which means that in principle it is two hours ahead of the British Isles, seven hours ahead of the US East Coast (EST), eleven hours ahead of the North American West Coast (PST), six hours behind West Australia, eight hours behind eastern Australia, and ten hours behind New Zealand, but daylight saving time in those places and in Israel may vary that difference by one or two hours. Clocks in Israel go forward for daylight saving in March, and back again before the New Year (usually in September). The Palestinian Territories are also on GMT+2, but may change over to DST and back at different dates, though just to confuse things still further, many Palestinians ignore the PNA's dictates on this, and follow the Israeli time regardless.

VAT Value Added Tax (17%) for items (other than tobacco and electrical or photographic goods) bought at stores recommended by the Tourism Ministry is refundable at the airport, border or Haifa port when you leave, provided the goods are in a sealed transparent bag, and that you have an invoice stating the amount of VAT paid. You are also exempt from VAT on hotel bills, car rental or air tickets, so long as you pay in hard currency. Eilat is VAT- and duty-free but you will not notice the difference in prices except of booze.

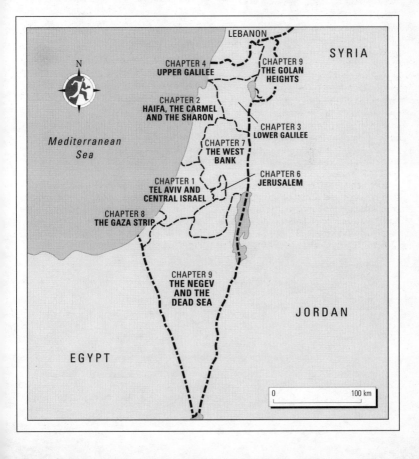

- CHAPTER 4 **UPPER GALILEE**
- CHAPTER 9 **THE GOLAN HEIGHTS**
- CHAPTER 2 **HAIFA, THE CARMEL AND THE SHARON**
- CHAPTER 3 **LOWER GALILEE**
- CHAPTER 7 **THE WEST BANK**
- CHAPTER 1 **TEL AVIV AND CENTRAL ISRAEL**
- CHAPTER 6 **JERUSALEM**
- CHAPTER 8 **THE GAZA STRIP**
- CHAPTER 9 **THE NEGEV AND THE DEAD SEA**

LEBANON
SYRIA
Mediterranean Sea
JORDAN
EGYPT

0   100 km

CHAPTER ONE

TEL AVIV AND CENTRAL ISRAEL

el Aviv and its suburbs, known collectively as the **Dan conurbation** (after the Israelite tribe of Dan, who ruled the territory in biblical times), are home to almost a third of Israel's population. Israel's heart may lie in Jerusalem, but this is the centre of the country in terms of economy and infrastructure. At its core is **Tel Aviv**, a frenetic modern city – brash, tacky and expensive, but also hip, cosmopolitan and exciting. Behind its sandy beaches, high-rise buildings jostle each other for air, and, in the numerous hotels, bars and nightclubs, residents out on the razzle rub shoulders with tourists, out-of-town Israelis, and the growing number of expatriate and "guest" workers.

The ancient town of **Jaffa**, less than 2km to the south, still manages to hold on to something of its historic past despite the ever-increasing encroachment of the big city. Although officially within the municipal boundaries of Tel Aviv, it remains largely a Palestinian Arab town, with its own history, architecture and culture – there's a small working port, some attractive churches and mosques, a popular if somewhat touristy market and some great restaurants. Nevertheless, the area is fighting a losing battle against development into boutiques, galleries and expensive studio apartments.

There's little of interest to the tourist in the settlements surrounding Tel Aviv: mostly soulless dormitories for commuters, of whom up to a million travel through Tel Aviv's Central Bus Station every day. **Ramat Gan**, **Petah Tiqva** and **Rehovot**, established by European settlers in the late nineteenth and early twentieth centuries, are now virtually indistinguishable from each other due to the ubiquitous *shikunim* (communally run apartment blocks) thrown up since the 1950s. **Ramle**, on the other hand, is one of Israel's best-kept secrets – a handsome city with bags of character, whose centre has escaped the unpleasant history and neglect that mars its neighbour, **Lydda** (Lod).

Although the **coastline** to the south of Tel Aviv is attractive and for the most part undeveloped, the absence of important biblical or historic sites keeps the area off

ACCOMMODATION PRICE CODES

Throughout this guide, **hotel accommodation** is graded on a scale from ① to ⑥. The numbers represent the cost per night of the **cheapest double room in high season**, though remember that many of the cheap places will have more expensive rooms with en-suite facilities. For **hostels**, the code represents the price of **two dorm beds** and is followed by the code for a double room where applicable, ie ①/②. Hostels are listed in ascending price order.

① = less than $20	② = $20–40	③ = $40–60
④ = $60–80	⑤ = $80–100	⑥ = over $100

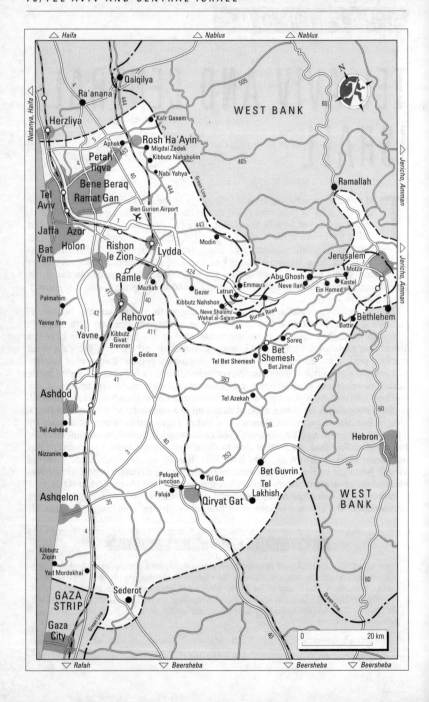

most travellers' itineraries. Virtually all pre-1948 habitation has been cleared to make way for a smattering of moshavim and kibbutzim, while the next city down the coast, **Ashdod**, is a modern, working port and naval base with little of tourist interest other than its beaches. Beyond it, **Ashqelon**, birthplace of Herod, retains traces of its long history and has some fine beaches, but its attractions are still somewhat overhyped by its tourist office.

Inland from Ashqelon, the main highlight is **Bet Guvrin National Park** (Bet Jibrin), whose ancient ruins and hundreds of caves are undeservedly some of the least-visited tourist sights in the country. But, there's little else in the region and the few small development towns such as **Qiryat Gat** exude an air of stagnation, with nowhere to stay and little to do. To the northeast, the **Jerusalem corridor**, which carries the Tel Aviv–Jerusalem highway, saw many an Old Testament battle, but less halcyon history was made here in the war of 1948 when it was one of the most bitterly fought-over parts of the country. Great feats of heroism were performed here by both sides, most famously around the police post at **Latrun**. Now a museum, this can be combined with a visit to the nearby Trappist monastery and supposed site of biblical **Emmaus**.

If you're heading for Tel Aviv or the coastal plain in July or August, be warned that the **weather** can be extremely wearing. With upwards of 75 percent humidity, the sticky climate can turn even the simplest tasks into an ordeal, make the dust and dirt seem grimier than usual, and cause tempers to fray. Unless you enjoy this sort of climate – or can afford to stay in an air-conditioned hotel – it might be best to avoid Tel Aviv during the summer. Those extra five degrees of warmth can, however, make the city seem a lot more attractive when viewed from the freezing heights of Jerusalem in the middle of winter.

Tel Aviv and Jaffa

TEL AVIV is a city with chutzpah – a loud, gesticulating expression of urban Jewish culture. Straight-talking and brash, its streets teem with Jews of every conceivable origin, and its restaurants serve the food that they brought with them from around the globe. Though its connections have always been international rather than local, Tel Aviv's cosmopolitanism has in some ways been limited by its Jewishness, but an influx of "guest workers" from West Africa, Eastern Europe and Southeast Asia has of late given the city some new blood, helped along by a growing awareness among Israeli Jews of their own diversity.

Few people like Tel Aviv when they first arrive, but it's a city that grows on you. What it lacks in finesse, it makes up for in sass, giving the finger to the parochialism of the rest of Israel, particularly Jerusalem. While others sit around on Fridays lighting candles, Tel Avivians head for the beach, the bar or the movies, happy to drink and dance all night, even (in fact especially) on the Sabbath. If the city seems on the surface less sophisticated than the capitals of Europe, it is often more streetwise, less pretentious, and certainly just as cultured. As the financial, business, sporting and entertainment centre of the country, it is endlessly on the move, and you'll find people here into everything from classical music and modern literature to the Internet and dance music.

With its pavement cafés and sun worshippers, Tel Aviv is unmistakably Mediterranean, though being only a century old it lacks the architectural grandeur of its older Mediterranean counterparts, though it is beginning to take pride in its heritage of 1930s International Style buildings. Neither does it exhibit the planning of other Mediterranean cities; its streets, laid out parallel to the coast, block off the cooling sea breezes (a problem compounded by the barrier of high-rise hotels along the seafront), making Tel Aviv in summer a bit like a live-in sauna.

Attached to Tel Aviv, and now really a part of it, is the ancient walled city of **JAFFA** (see p.86). Though thoroughly sanitized nowadays for the benefit of tourists, it is virtually the only part of town with a history that predates the twentieth century and still well worth taking the time to explore.

Some history

The reason behind **Tel Aviv**'s layout lies in its history as the first Zionist city. By the 1880s it had become clear to the settlers in Jaffa – Palestine's main port and pre-eminent town – that expansion was necessary if it was going to absorb new Jewish immigrants. With land to the east and south under cultivation, the city had no choice but to colonize the dunes to the north. Neve Zedek, now part of Tel Aviv, was founded in 1887 as a Jewish quarter of Jaffa, but Tel Aviv as such wasn't **officially inaugurated** until April 11, 1909. Conceived as the world's first all-Jewish city, it was soon the centre of the Yishuv, housing the offices of the Jewish Agency and Jewish National Fund. But security was by no means certain, and in March 1917 all Jews were expelled from Tel Aviv and Jaffa by the Ottomans: their exile ended eight months later when British forces took the city. The British garrison set up camp here and Tel Aviv finally had its future assured, receiving its own town council in 1921, the same year in which ethnic riots in Jaffa drove most of its Jewish population up to Tel Aviv, expanding and consolidating the city further. Meanwhile, incoming Europeans opened up new businesses, and the political, intellectual and artistic elites argued the toss in the cafés and restaurants. By 1948, the population had grown to around 230,000, the vast majority of them new immigrants.

When the **State of Israel** was proclaimed on May 14, 1948 from Independence House on Sederot Rothschild, Tel Aviv became its first capital and even after the government's move to Jerusalem in 1949, it remained the diplomatic centre. Few countries today recognize Jerusalem as Israel's capital and virtually every embassy remains here, along with the defence ministry and the main representatives of Israel's fashion, commercial, culture and entertainment industries.

However, the official version of Tel Aviv's past – that the city was built entirely on "uninhabited sand dunes" – doesn't tell the whole story. Following the 1948 war, the city expanded over and almost completely destroyed the Palestinian villages of Abu Kabir, Sumayyil, Jamasin and Sheikh Mu'annis, whose inhabitants had been forced out during the fighting: the *Hilton Hotel* and neighbouring Gan Ha'Atzma'ut park stand on the site of a Muslim cemetery; the headquarters of the Histadrut (Israeli Workers' Company and Trade Union Federation) in Rehov Arlozorov are built on the lands of Sumayyil; and Tel Aviv University was constructed over the land of Sheikh Mu'annis – some of the original homes can be seen behind the campus and the event is remembered in the name of the Palestinian student newspaper, *The Voice of Sheikh Mu'annis*.

Arrival, orientation and information

Tel Aviv is the hub of a vast urban sprawl stretching for 30km from Herzliya (north along the coast) to Rehovot (south inland). Like any big city it is initially intimidating, but most of what you'll want to see falls within a small area bounded on the west by the Mediterranean, the east by **Rehov Ibn Gvirol**, the north by the **Yarkon River**, and the south by the **Central Bus Station** and the Old City of **Jaffa**.

The majority of hostels, hotels, restaurants, airline offices and other everyday needs can be found on four streets just inland from the beach – **Allenby**, **Ben Yehuda**, **HaYarkon** and **Dizengoff**. The "old" and increasingly trendy districts of **Kerem HaTaymanim** (also known as the Yemenite Quarter), **Neve Zedek** and **Florentin** lie to the south between here and Jaffa, while sandy **beaches** front the whole city centre, from Jaffa in the south to the marina and old port in the north.

Points of arrival

From **Ben Gurion Airport** (see box below), there are regular buses to Tel Aviv; alternatively, you could take one of the waiting taxis. Tel Aviv's own **Sede Dov Airport**, for internal flights, is connected to town by bus #26.

BEN GURION AIRPORT

The vast majority of international flights in Israel use Ben Gurion Airport, located 18km east of Tel Aviv, near the town of Lydda (see p.105), and named after Israel's first prime minister. Ben Gurion has the tightest security of any airport in the world, an upshot of the fact that during the 1970s – the heyday of air hijacking – it became the setting for two particularly horrific guerrilla incidents. In May 1972, four members of Black September (an unofficial Fatah group) hijacked a Belgian plane and forced it to land here, demanding the release of political prisoners; Israeli commandos stormed the plane and, in the ensuing battle, two hijackers were killed and six passengers wounded, one fatally. Later that month, a Japanese Red Army suicide squad working with the PFLP fired at random and threw grenades in the customs hall, killing 25 people, largely Puerto Rican Christian pilgrims. The massacre is commemorated with a memorial by baggage carousel #4.

Arrival

Leaving the customs hall, you'll find **car rental** desks of the major firms, including Avis (☎03/971 1080, fax 522 3649), Budget (☎03/971 1504 or 5, fax 971 1522), Eldan (☎03/972 1027 or 8) and Thrifty (☎03/971 1780 or 1, fax 971 1752), in addition to a Solan Communications office, where you can make calls or buy phonecards. Outside, taxi drivers will be waiting to pounce.

  Bus stops are well over to the left as you exit. **For Tel Aviv**, Egged bus #475 (daily except Fri evening & Sat; every 10–30min from 5.30am until 11pm; 20min), runs to the Central Bus Station, while United Tours bus #222 (Sun–Thurs hourly 4am–midnight; till 8pm Fri & from 1pm Sat; 45min) passes the Central Train Station, coming into town at the northern end on Nordau, crossing Dizengoff and Ben Yehuda, and descending along the seafront to the *Dan Panorama*. Egged also serves **Jerusalem** (every 30–40min; 45min) and **Haifa** (every 30–40min; 1hr 45min), with less frequent connections to other places. Last buses for both are usually around 9pm. To Jerusalem there is also a 24-hour sherut service operated by Nesher Taxis, 21 King George St, Jerusalem (☎02/625 2223 or 6).

Departure

When **leaving Israel**, be sure to confirm your flight with the airline concerned at least 72 hours in advance and arrive in good time to **check in** (officially 3 hours before take-off, but see below). There are two terminals to check in, connected by regular shuttle bus: buses to the airport from elsewhere serve both. Expect heavy questioning about your movements in Israel (where you stayed, who you met, etc), especially regarding any time spent in the Palestinian Territories, and major security searches. Young non-Jewish travellers get the heaviest treatment which can occasionally mean up to an hour's questioning, a complete and thorough baggage check, and even a strip-search. Anti-Zionist political literature or publications, even if legal in the country, may be confiscated, or at least taken away and photocopied, and it is not unknown (though rare) for people to be held up so long that they miss their flights.

  If flying with El Al you can check in your **luggage** the day before at their offices in Tel Aviv (El Al Town Terminal in Rehov Arlozorov by the Central Train Station), Jerusalem (7 Kanfei Nesharim, Givat Sha'ul), Haifa (the Conference Centre, 2 Kedoshei Yasi), or Beersheba (Bet Noam, 21 Shazar), and it will be taken directly to the plane. You get your seat allocation and boarding card and need only turn up at the airport an hour and a quarter before departure.

For airport information call ☎03/973 1122.

Travelling by bus or sherut you arrive at the **Central Bus Station** (☎03/694 8888), a rather disorientating hub for Egged inter-city buses and Dan local buses located southeast of the city centre on Rehov Levinsky. To get into town from here, take city bus #4 or #5 from the fourth floor (platform 417 & 418 respectively), or the sherut minibuses on the same routes from the other side of the floor, opposite platforms 410–414. For Jaffa, take bus #46 from the first floor (platform 106). Alternatively, it's a thirty-minute walk into town; leave by the Levinsky exit on the third floor, turn left down Levinsky and then right up HaAliya which leads into Allenby. **Buses from Cairo** may leave you on Ibn Gvirol near the Egyptian embassy, from where your best route into town is on foot down Rehov Basel to Dizengoff.

The **Central Train Station** (also called Merkaz or Savidor) is 2km out of town at the eastern end of Rehov Arlozorov, which is also the way into town if you're walking. The bus stand is to your right as you exit the station: #10 runs to Rehov Ben Yehuda and Jaffa; #18 to Rehov Allenby; #32 to Allenby via Ben Yehuda; and #22 to the Central Bus Station. Trains also stop at **HaShalom Station**, 1km to the south, but as there are no bus connections into town you'll have to walk the 1500m west along Rehov Kaplan and Rehov Dizengoff. For details of moving on from Tel Aviv, see pp.98–99.

Information

The IGTO **information office**, on the sixth floor of the new Central Bus Station, opposite platform 630 (Sun–Thurs 9am–5pm, Fri 9am–1pm; ☎03/639 5660, fax 639 5659), stocks free maps of Tel Aviv and Old Jaffa, plus various free booklets such as the weekly *Hello Israel* (a mix of information, maps and vouchers covering mainly Tel Aviv, Jerusalem and Haifa), the tackier *Tel Aviv Non-Stop*, and the more solid *This Week in Tel Aviv*, which also covers the surrounding resorts (particularly Netanya). However, *The Traveller*, a free newspaper found in hostels and travellers' bars, often proves the most useful for up-to-date information on budget eating and accommodation, bars and services.

City transport

Although the centre of Tel Aviv is best negotiated on foot, the reliable and well-developed **bus** network, operated by the **Dan** transport cooperative, provides the easiest means of crossing from one end of the city to the other. Services run frequently

---

USEFUL CITY BUS ROUTES

#1 & **#2** Reading Terminal (just north of Yarkon River), Little Tel Aviv, Dizengoff (southbound) or Reines and Sokolov (northbound), Pinsker, Allenby, HaAliya, Abu Kabir, Holon. *Every 8–15min.*

#4 Central Bus Station, Allenby, Ben Yehuda, Little Tel Aviv, Reading Terminal. *Every 3–10min, supplemented by sheruts on Fri & Sat.*

#5 Central Bus Station, Allenby, Rothschild, Dizengoff, Nordau, Yehuda HaMaccabi (for the HI Hostel). *Every 3–8min, supplemented by sheruts on Fri & Sat.*

#10 Central Train Station, Arlozorov, Ben Gurion, Ben Yehuda, Jaffa (Rehov Yefet), Bat Yam. *Every 10–25min.*

#18 Central Train Station, Shaul HaMelekh, HaMelekh George, Allenby, Salame, Jaffa (Derekh Yerushalayim), Bat Yam. *Every 4–12min.*

#25 Bat Yam, Jaffa (Sederot Yerushalayim), Neve Zedek, HaMelekh George, Ibn Gvirol, Eretz Yisra'el Museum, Tel Aviv University, Bet Hatefutsot (Diaspora Museum). *Every 5–10min.*

#27 Central Bus Station, Derekh Petah Tiqva, Derekh Namir, Eretz Yisra'el Museum, Tel Aviv University. *Every 8–20min.*

#46 Central Bus Station, Derekh Yafo, Jaffa (Rehov Yefet), Bat Yam. *Every 5–15min.*

from approximately 6am to midnight, except Friday evenings and during the day on Saturday. Within the city there's a flat **fare** of 4.10NIS, or a one-day travelcard will cost you 8NIS (both can be purchased on board). Route **maps** are displayed on bus stops, or a good map in Hebrew is available infrequently from the **Dan information kiosk** (☎03/639 4444) inside the Central Bus Station.

Taxis patrol the city day and night – always insist on the meter, as you'll certainly be overcharged if it's not switched on (for call-outs see p.100 for a list of companies).

Accommodation

Downtown Tel Aviv has dozens of hotels and hostels to suit all budgets and tastes and you shouldn't have any problems finding a bed, except during July and August. Most of the cheaper options are clustered around the junction of Allenby and Ben Yehuda, and along HaYarkon Street, but as the main red-light district it's also pretty seedy (albeit low-key by international standards).

Spread along the beach and a couple of blocks inland, Tel Aviv's **hotels** run the whole gamut from pleasant, family-run places and tacky tourist traps to the truly deluxe. With the exception of *HaGalil*, however, you won't find a double room for less than $40. **Jaffa** offers a more attractive setting but has a limited choice of accommodation – though both its hostels are excellent.

In addition to dormitory accommodation, many of the **hostels** offer private rooms; deals for stays of a week or longer are often available and the cheaper places in particular tend to have a semi-permanent community of long-termers. Curfews are the exception rather than the rule, though a few places will turf you out around midday for cleaning. **Sleeping on the beach** in Tel Aviv is not recommended, as muggings, thefts and harassment are alarmingly common.

Hostels
Casa Nostra, 1 Shefer, Kerem HaTaymanim (☎03/510 8348). New, clean and friendly, but won't hold baggage after checkout. ①.

The Office, 57 Allenby (☎03/528 9984). Situated in the raviest part of town, this good-value option is friendly and has a popular bar. Open 24hr. ①/②.

Seaside Hostel, 20a Trumpeldor (☎03/620 0513). A small, basic place with dorms only but nevertheless popular with long-stay travellers. ①.

Hotel Josef, 15 Bograshov (☎ & fax 03/525 7070). An old favourite, aka *The Hostel*, offering dorms and private rooms, though you might be tempted by the option of sleeping on the roof. Open round the clock. ①/②.

Old Jaffa Hostel, 8 Olei Tziyon, Jaffa (☎03/682 2370, fax 682 2316). Excellent, well-run travellers' hostel in an old house in Jaffa, with clean dorms, private rooms and a roof terrace, plus cooking and laundry facilities. Open 24hr. ①/②.

Travellers' Hostel, 47 Ben Yehuda (☎03/524 3083) and 122 Allenby (☎03/566 0812, fax 523 7218). The Allenby branch is the cheaper and grubbier of the two, but refurbishment is under way. Both have dorms and private rooms, with discounts for long-termers. ①/②.

The Home, 20 Alsheikh, Kerem HaTaymanim (☎03/517 6736). Long-established travellers' hostel of the old school; private rooms are full long-term. Friendly if not exactly spotless. ①.

Momo's, 28 Ben Yehuda (☎03/528 7471). Basic and not very clean, but popular and central. ①/②.

Gordon Hostel, 2 Gordon (☎03/522 9870, fax 523 7419). One of Tel Aviv's oldest and best hostels, clean and well run. Discounts are offered for weekly stays. Closed 1–2pm, but no night curfew. ①.

The Wandering Dog, 3 Yordei HaSira (☎03/546 6333). Up in Little Tel Aviv (see p.80), all dorms but very clean, with its own sauna. ①.

HI Tel Aviv Youth Hostel, 36 Bnei Dan (☎03/544 1748, fax 544 1030). A bit out of the way in a quiet location opposite a park. As you'd expect of the official hostel, it's clean and well run. Open round the clock. Take bus #5, #24 or #25. ①.

No. 1 Hostel, 4th floor, 84 Ben Yehuda (☎03/523 7807, fax 523 7419). Run by the same firm as the *Gordon*, and pretty similar. Closed 11am–2pm, but no night curfew. ①/②.

Beit Immanuel, 8 Auerbach, Jaffa (☎03/682 1459, fax 682 9817). Spotless, Anglican-run hostel with a choice of dorms or private rooms. Serves meals in the garden for six months of the year. Curfew at 11pm. ①/②.

Dizengoff Square Hostel, 11 Kikar Dizengoff (☎03/522 5184, fax 522 5181). Dorms and private rooms are spotless but rather institutionalized, with a locker-room atmosphere. ①/③.

Mid-range hotels

Adiv, 5 Mendele (☎03/522 9141, fax 522 9144). Small but cosy and well-maintained rooms. ⑤.

Ami, 152 HaYarkon, but in fact on Rehov Am Yisra'el Hay (☎03/524 9141 or 5, fax 523 1151). Small, comfortable en-suite rooms, some with balconies and sea views. ⑤.

Armon HaYarkon, 288 HaYarkon (☎03/605 5271 or 3, fax 605 8485). Reasonable hotel in Little Tel Aviv (see p.80), with a/c, cable TV and the usual mod cons. ④.

Aviv, 287 HaYarkon (☎03/510 2784 or 5, fax 523 9450). Popular place by the beach; rooms are not great value, but the restaurant is good. ③.

Bell, 12 Allenby (☎03/517 4291 or 2). Clean and carpeted, with pleasant and efficient staff. ③.

Center, 2 Zamenhoff (☎03/546 8126, fax 546 7687). Right next to Kikar Dizengoff and one of a group of hotels in the *Atlas* chain, with modern decor and small but comfortable rooms. ④.

Gordon Inn, 17 Gordon (☎03/523 8239, fax 523 7419). Guesthouse run by the same company as the hostel and offering a choice of dorms or plusher private rooms. ①/③.

HaGalil, 23 Bet Yosef, Kerem HaTaymanim (☎03/517 5036). Basic but clean alternative to the hostels. ②.

Moss, 6 Ness Tziyona (☎ & fax 03/517 1655). Homely, friendly little hotel with mainly European clientele and all home comforts. ④.

Ness Ziona, 10 Ness Tziyona (☎03/510 6084, fax 510 3404). A bit shabby, with smallish, carpeted rooms, some with balcony. ③.

Shalom, 216 HaYarkon (☎03/524 3277, fax 523 5895). A range of rooms with sea views and prices to match the facilities offered. ④.

Tal, 287 HaYarkon (☎03/544 2281, fax 546 8697). One of the more upmarket hotels in the *Atlas* chain, and handy for the best stretch of city beach. ⑤.

Expensive hotels

Dan Panorama, Retsif Herbert Samuel (☎03/519 0190, fax 517 1777). Down towards Jaffa and slightly less plush than its sister on HaYarkon but all rooms have sea views. ⑥.

Dan Tel Aviv, 99 HaYarkon (☎03/520 2525, fax 524 9755). Swish and classy, with deluxe furnishings, hand-and-foot service, three restaurants and a swimming pool. ⑥.

Holiday Inn, 145 HaYarkon (☎03/520 1111, fax 520 1122). Modern and efficient, American-style hotel with direct beach access and two pools. ⑥.

Regency Suites, 80 HaYarkon (☎03/517 3939, fax 516 3276). Suite-only deluxe accommodation, without all the hotel paraphernalia. ⑥.

Sheraton Tel Aviv, 115 HaYarkon (☎03/521 1111, fax 523 3322). A fine hotel with the comfort and sharp service you'd expect, together with a pool and excellent restaurant; prices rise at Easter, when you'll pay $333 for bed only. ⑥.

Tel Aviv Hilton, Gan Ha'Atzma'ut, off HaYarkon (☎03/520 2111, fax 527 2711). Tel Aviv's top executive address has its own beach, five restaurants, a pool and all the other trappings and services. ⑥.

The City

Tel Aviv's age increases the further south you go: from the modern downtown area around **Dizengoff** and **Ben Yehuda**, through the neighbourhoods of **Kerem HaTaymanim** (the Yemenite Quarter), **Neve Zedek** and **Florentin**, which date from the turn of the century, to the ancient port of **Jaffa** (see p.86) – the only area with a his-

NORTH DOWNTOWN TEL AVIV

0   500m

N

Yarkon River

Yarkon Park

Old Port

LITTLE TEL AVIV

Jana Wiener Park

SEDEROT NORDAU

REHOV YORDEI HASIRA

REHOV HAYARKON

REHOV BEN YEHUDA

REHOV DIZENGOFF

REHOV BASEL

REHOV IBN GVIROL

REHOV JABOTINSKY

Egyptian Embassy

Gan Ha'Atzma'ut

Marina

REHOV PERI

KIKAR NAMIR

Pool

Ben Gurion's House

SEDEROT BEN GURION

REHOV ARLOZOROV

REHOV SHLOMO HAMELEKH

City Hall

KIKAR RABIN

REHOV GORDON

REHOV REINES

REHOV FRISHMANN

KIKAR DIZENGOFF

REHOV BEN YEHUDA

RETSIF HERBERT SAMUEL

Dizengoff Centre

Old Cemetery

REHOV PINSKER

REHOV TRUMPELDOR

Gan Meir

REHOV HAMELEKH GEORGE

REHOV BOGRASHOV

REHOV HANEVIIM

SEDEROT SHA'UL HAMELEKH

Habima Theatre

Jabotinsky Institute

Helena Rubenstein Pavillion

Mann Auditorium

KIKAR HABIMA

Cinematique

SEDEROT ROTHSCHILD

REHOV KAPLAN

City History Museum

Bet Bialik

Bet Reuven

REHOV ALLENBY

SIMTA POLONIT

Central Railway Station

HaShalom Railway Station

ACCOMMODATION

Adiv	1
Ami	2
Armon HaYarkon	3
Aviv	4
Bell	5
Center	6
Dan Tel Aviv	7
Dizengoff Square Hostel	8
Gordon Hostel	9
Gordon Inn	10
HI Hostel	11
Hilton	12
Holiday Inn	13
Momo's Hostel	14
Moss	15
Ness Ziona	16
No.1 Hostel	17
Regency Suites	18
Seaside Hostel	19
Shalom	20
Sheraton	21
Tal	22
The Hostel	23
Travellers' Hostel	24
Wandering Dog	25

EATING PLACES

Batya	A
Ben and Jerry's	B
Ben and Jerry's	C
Ben and Jerry's	D
Cactus	E
Dolci Melodie	F
Dr Lek	G
LeHayyim	H
Mamaia	I
Manolitos	J
Red Chinese	K
Shoshanna & Uris	L
Tandoori	M
Vienna	N

CAFÉS

Café de la Paix	a
Tola'at Sefarim	b

BARS

Beers	c
MASH	d
White Gallery	e
Zanzibar	f
Rose	g
Café Nordau	h
Kassit	i

BREAKFAST

Marese	j
Presto	k

tory in any way venerable, and a great deal quainter and more charm-laden than the rest of the city. Should you be tempted by the **beaches**, be warned that although popular with Tel Avivians, they can be pretty grubby, overcrowded (particularly on Saturdays) and, with the craze for smashing balls around in the game of *matkot*, downright hazardous (see p.91 for a rundown of the beaches).

Along Rehov Dizengoff

The backbone of downtown Tel Aviv and named after the city's first mayor, **Rehov Dizengoff** is lined with cafés and restaurants, all striving to be chic. It's an obvious choice for an afternoon's bar-hopping or café-crawling but for many people just strolling up and down is an entertainment in itself. There's no shortage of shops either; the northern part of the street has the most fashionable offerings and for Tel Avivians is the place to shop and be seen shopping. Halfway along, at the tackier southern end, **Kikar Dizengoff** offers a respite from Tel Aviv traffic in the form of an open pedestrianized plaza raised above the road. Its avant-garde, hi-tech water sculpture was designed by Yaacov Agam, a leading Israeli artist – don't be surprised if it suddenly spurts into action as there's a twenty-minute music and light show on the hour every hour (except 2 & 3pm). On Saturdays, the whole area from Kikar Dizengoff north up to Sederot Ben Gurion is closed to traffic until sunset. This section of the street became the unwanted focus of international attention in October 1994, when in one of a spate of bus bombings aimed at derailing the peace process, a #5 bus was blown up by a Palestinian suicide bomber, killing 22 people. The route was well-chosen, being one used by almost all Tel Avivians and most tourists too.

Apart from the consumer delights of the **Dizengoff Centre**, a vast and flashy shopping mall 100m to the south of Kikar Dizengoff, the main reason to venture any further along the street is to visit the arts centre on **Kikar HaBima**, 300m east at the junction with Dizengoff and Sederot Tarsat. The complex houses the **HaBima Theatre**, the **Mann Auditorium** (see p.97) and the **Helena Rubinstein Pavilion** – the latter, at 6 Tarsat (☎03/528 7196), hosts temporary exhibitions of painting, sculpture and photography, and is an annexe of the **Tel Aviv Museum of Art**, whose main building is a fifteen-minute walk beyond the easternmost end of Dizengoff at 27 Shaul HaMelekh (Sun, Mon, Wed & Thurs 10am–6pm, Tues 10am–10pm, Fri & Sat 10am–2pm; 20NIS, covering both the main museum and the Helena Rubinstein Pavilion; ☎03/696 1297). The museum is home to an impressive collection of Impressionist and post-Impressionist artworks with a roll call of famous names including Picasso, Dalí, Monet, Cézanne, Chagall (look out for his *Wailing Wall*), Lichtenstein, Munch, Rodin and Moore. Permanent and temporary exhibitions of Israeli and Jewish artists and sculptors are also held here; its diary of events lists exhibitions, concerts, films, plays and dance programmes, which are among the best-value in town.

Kikar Rabin

Renamed to reflect the dramatic event that occurred here, **Kikar Yitzhak Rabin** – formerly known as Kikar Malkhei Yisra'el (Kings of Israel Square) – is located 500m north along Rehov HaMelekh George from its junction with Dizengoff. A vast expanse of concrete, it's the natural stage for most of the city's political demonstrations: in 1982 over 400,000 people – ten percent of Israel's population – gathered here to protest against Israeli complicity in the Phalangist massacre of Palestinians in the Sabra and Shatilla refugee camps in Lebanon, and it was during the 150,000-strong rally held here in November 1995 in support of the Oslo Peace Accord that Prime Minister Yitzhak Rabin was shot by Yigal Amir, a young right-wing extremist who objected to the deal Rabin had negotiated with the PLO.

THE AFTERMATH OF RABIN'S ASSASSINATION

It is difficult to imagine the severe dent that **Rabin's assassination** made in Israel's national psyche. True, not all Israelis supported the peace process, a fact made plain when Rabin's Labour Party lost power at the polls less than a year later, but his status as a veteran of the wars of 1948 and 1956, and as the army's chief of staff during the Six Day War, meant that most Israelis respected him as a man who knew when to be tough and when to talk peace. What shocked them more than anything was that he was killed not by an Islamic fundamentalist or Palestinian hardliner, but by one of their own – an Israeli Jew. From the early days of the Yishuv, Israelis had always felt in some way "one big family", united against a common enemy. Rabin's murder shattered that illusion, and gave Israel a jolt from which it will never recover. Comparisons with Sadat's murder are obvious, and it has also been compared to those of Gandhi and Kennedy, but it failed to do for the Oslo Accord what Kennedy's murder did for the Civil Rights Bill: within a year, Israel had elected a hardline, right-wing government and the peace process was on the rocks yet again.

The square is dominated by the large concrete mass of **City Hall**. Behind it, at the spot where Rabin fell, the **monument** to his memory consists of a section of pavement seeming to rise up in revolt against the murder committed on it. The concrete walls around bear the testimonies of ordinary people, among them portraits, poems, stickers bearing Bill Clinton's words "Shalom, haver" (which he translated as "Goodbye, friend", though *shalom* of course also means "peace"), and messages in Hebrew, English, Spanish, Russian and French. Arabic is conspicuous by its absence – to most Palestinians, Rabin was not the apostle of peace he was to Israelis, but the defence minister who took a tough line during the Intifada (see p.498).

Ben Yehuda and around

Midway between Dizengoff and the sea and running parallel to both, **Rehov Ben Yehuda** (named after the inventor of Modern Hebrew) is more workaday than Dizengoff. Here you'll find many of the cheap hostels and restaurants, major airline offices and travel agents specializing in charter tickets or cut-price excursions to Egypt and Jordan (see "Listings", p.100). For those in search of art, a turn halfway along its length, on to Rehov Gordon in the direction of Dizengoff, reveals a number of private **galleries**.

Just off the southern end of Ben Yehuda and east along Rehov Trumpeldor, the **Old Cemetery** (Sun–Thurs 9.30am–2pm, Fri 9.30am–noon), opened in 1903, is the final resting place of several famous Israelis and many early Zionist settlers, some of whom died alone and unidentified and were recorded simply as *galmud* (unattached). The monument to the left of the main entrance is to the victims of anti-Jewish riots by Jaffa Arabs in 1921 and 1929, and settlers who died in the 1948 war. If you follow the main path to the end and take the one which leads off to the right you come to a little space with a bench, behind which lies the cubic mausoleum of early Zionist leader **Max Nordau**. To its right are the tombs of mayor **Meir Dizengoff**, Tel Aviv's first mayor, and the poet **Shaul Tchernikovsky**; to the left lies Ahad Ha'Am, aka Asher Ginzberg, advocate of a "spiritual" Zionism rooted more deeply in Jewish culture than Herzl's purely political version. The poet **Haim Bialik** is also buried here, along with **Haim Arlosoroff**, the Socialist Zionist who advocated co-operation with Palestinian Arabs and for whose murder in June 1933, still unsolved, three supporters of Jabotinsky's Revisionist movement were tried and acquitted.

Rehov HaYarkon to Little Tel Aviv

Given its prime location one street back from the beach it's no surprise to find **Rehov HaYarkon** dominated by flashy hotels, with new ones constantly under construction.

Even if you don't stay at any of them, you may well find yourself down here in search of bars, restaurants or travel agents. Most of the sights on and off HaYarkon are found at its northern end, beyond **Kikar Namir** (also known as Kikar Atarim), a dual-level plaza of shops and restaurants which is now considerably run down. Back at sea level, Tel Aviv's **marina** is the usual tangle of expensive boats, mostly off-limits to the inquisitive tourist, though there is a popular **swimming pool** next door (daily 5am–6pm; Sun–Thurs 33NIS, Fri & Sat 38NIS).

Just off HaYarkon to the east of Kikar Namir, **Ben Gurion House**, 17 Sederot Ben Gurion (Sun, Tues, Wed & Thurs 8am–3pm, Mon 8am–5pm, Fri 8am–1pm, Sat 11am–2pm; free), was home to Israel's first prime minister, David Ben Gurion, and displays some of his possessions; most impressively, his 20,000-volume library. Back on HaYarkon at **no. 181**, 100m north of Kikar Namir, you'll find the street's most architecturally interesting building; its striking Gaudiesque facade is on Rehov Eliezer Peri but the HaYarkon side features a mosaic of flamingoes, swans and peacocks topped by an angel and studded with trees.

Around 500m further north, HaYarkon, Ben Yehuda and Dizengoff meet at the misnamed and shabby **Old Port**. Opened by Tel Aviv's Jewish City Council in 1936 in response to the closure of Jaffa's port by Palestinian Arabs during their uprising against the British, it has long been abandoned by shipping, virtually all of which now uses the port of Ashdod further south (see p.112). Behind the Old Port, the area known as **Little Tel Aviv** was once the home of the city's "alternative" scene, with the requisite complement of artists and hangers-on. Nowadays it's wealthy and conventional, but the scores of bars and restaurants crammed into this small area still manage to give it a truly laid-back Mediterranean atmosphere.

Ramat Aviv: The Eretz Yisra'el Museum and the Diaspora Museum

Tel Aviv's two most exciting museums lie to the north of the city centre, across the Yarkon River in Ramat Aviv – a quiet suburb that's also home to the university. The sprawling site of the **Eretz Yisra'el Museum**, or HaAretz Museum, at 2 Levanon (Sun, Mon & Thurs 9am–2pm; Tues & Wed 9am–7pm; Sat 10am–2pm; 18NIS; free guided tour in English Sat at 11am; buses #7, #7a, #13, #24, #25, #27, #74, #86 and #274), encompasses an immensely varied collection displayed in a number of small specialist exhibitions. Most important among them is the **Glass Museum** housed in the green circular building at the top of the hill, which relates the history of glass-making from its origins to the present day and contains one of the finest collections of ancient glassware in the world. Relics from the copper mines at Timna – known by their more famous name of King Solomon's Mines (see p.300) – are housed in the **Nehustan Pavilion**, with other buildings devoted to stamps, coins, folklore and ethnography, ceramics and the alphabet. The complex also boasts **Tel Qasila** – one of the few archeological sites to have been preserved in Tel Aviv. Excavations here have revealed evidence of occupation in the area for the past 3000 years, although the only substantial remains are the outlines of two **Philistine temples** from the twelfth century BC. Some scholars believe it could be the site of ancient Jaffa, or at least its port in the pre-Christian era.

Further north, on the Tel Aviv University campus, the **Diaspora Museum**, or Bet Hatefutsot (Sun–Tues & Thurs 10am–4pm, Wed 10am–6pm, Fri 9am–1pm; 22NIS; buses #6, #25, #27, #45 and #49), features a well-presented assortment of maps, models, videos and displays exploring the history of the Jews, their traditions, religion and settlement throughout the world. There's plenty to keep you interested, from an introduction to the Hassidic way of life to models of synagogues, exhibits on Jewish communities and a section on Jewish music. There's also a massive library of films on different Jewish communities available for viewing (5NIS), and Jewish visitors can trace their ancestry by computer (6NIS for 15min). It's clear that the museum has a message: the Jews are a nation whose homeland is Israel, and whose destiny it is to return here.

Rehov Allenby and around

Tel Aviv's biggest shopping street, **Rehov Allenby**, runs north for 1km from a point just southeast of the Shalom Tower to the junction with Ben Yehuda. Old photographs show a stylish, tree-lined boulevard but now it's rather drab and somewhat overshadowed by the glitz of Dizengoff and Ben Yehuda. The street bears the name of the British general whose 1918 victory over the Ottoman Turks ushered in the Mandate

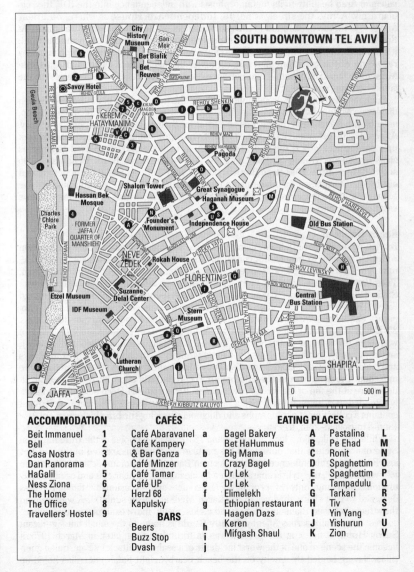

ACCOMMODATION		CAFÉS		EATING PLACES			
Beit Immanuel	1	Café Abaravanel	a	Bagel Bakery	A	Pastalina	L
Bell	2	Café Kampery		Bet HaHummus	B	Pe Ehad	M
Casa Nostra	3	& Bar Ganza	b	Big Mama	C	Ronit	N
Dan Panorama	4	Café Minzer	c	Crazy Bagel	D	Spaghettim	O
HaGalil	5	Café Tamar	d	Dr Lek	E	Spaghettim	P
Ness Ziona	6	Café UP	e	Dr Lek	F	Tampadulu	Q
The Home	7	Herzl 68	f	Elimelekh	G	Tarkari	R
The Office	8	Kapulsky	g	Ethiopian restaurant	H	Tiv	S
Travellers' Hostel	9			Haagen Dazs	I	Yin Yang	T
		BARS		Keren	J	Yishurun	U
		Beers	h	Mifgash Shaul	K	Zion	V
		Buzz Stop	i				
		Dvash	j				

– which is ironic given its later role as the location of various incidents in the Zionist movement's **struggle for independence** from the British. At its southern end, a short detour east along Sederot Rothschild reveals two places which together offer useful background to the events that took place on Allenby. At no. 23, the **Haganah Museum** (Sun–Thurs 9am–4pm, Fri 8am–12.30pm; 6NIS) traces the development of the pre-state Zionist militia from its early origins through its struggle against British rule and Arab hostility to its metamorphosis with independence into the IDF, the regular army. Across the street, at no. 16, **Independence House** is where, on Friday May 14, 1948, the declaration of the establishment of the state of Israel was made. At that time the building served as the headquarters of Voice of Israel radio and the Mint: it's now a memorial to the event (Sun–Thurs 9am–2pm; 10NIS) where you can hear a recording of the ceremony and buy copies of the declaration. There's also a **Bible Museum** (Sun–Thurs 9am–1pm; entrance fee included) inside, with exhibits on the Good Book in print and art.

Back on Allenby, the decrepit building above the ground-floor bar at **no. 54** (which displays a Middle Eastern style rare in Tel Aviv) was formerly the Philco Radio Shop, used by the Haganah in the Forties as a front for their wireless equipment laboratory. At no. 117, the cellar and attic of the **Great Synagogue**, built in 1926 (men should pick up a cardboard *kippa* at the door if they want to look around), were used as an arms stash by the Stern Gang (see box on p.85). Across the street, **Bank Pekao** at no. 95 and the **Mercantile Discount Bank** at no. 103 were both scenes of robberies carried out by the Stern Gang for fund-raising purposes; and, in 1944, the Irgun bombed the Mandate's immigration office at **no. 138** to protest at British restrictions on Jews entering Palestine.

Rehov Bialik

Branching off to the right from Allenby, a couple of hundred metres before the junction with Ben Yehuda, **Rehov Bialik** is a small street that nevertheless boasts three museums. The first of these, **Bet Reuven**, at no. 14 (Sun, Mon, Wed & Thurs 10am–2pm, Tues 10am–1pm & 4–8pm, Sat 11am–2pm; 9NIS), was the home of the painter Reuven Rubin (1893–1974), whose favoured subjects were scenes of Tel Aviv, Jerusalem and Safed. The permanent exhibition of his work here is occasionally accompanied by temporary exhibitions, mainly of modern Israeli art. A couple of doors further down at no. 22, **Bet Bialik** (Sun–Thurs 9am–5pm, Sat 10am–2pm; free) remains more or less as it was when it was home to Israel's best-known poet, Haim Nahman Bialik (1873–1934), and contains an exhibition of his books and writings – which also extended to essays and children's stories – as well as a display on his life and interests. The last of the three museums, the **Museum of the History of Tel Aviv–Jaffa** at no. 27, dominates the little square at the top of the street. A wonderful 1925 proto-Art Deco structure originally intended as a hotel, it overlooks a pretty mosaic **fountain** by Nathan Gutman and contains a collection of photographs and documents tracing the brief history of Tel Aviv (Sun–Thurs 9am–2pm; free).

While on Bialik, take a look at nos. 16 and 18 – classic examples of the **International Style** of architecture that dominates the parts of Tel Aviv constructed in the Thirties and Forties. Highly influenced by the German Bauhaus school under the motto "form follows function", the style is characterized by clean lines, right angles and minimal decoration consisting only of protruding balconies and occasionally flanged edges designed to cast sharp shadows in the harsh Mediterranean sunlight. A walk around the streets between Bialik and Rothschild yields plenty more examples of the style.

West from Bialik across Allenby, **Rehov Geula** is home to the small but significant **Savoy Hotel**, at no. 5. In the 1940s it was an Irgun hang-out; later, in March 1975, it became the scene of one of the worst incidents of a seaborne attack by Palestinian guerrillas. Having landed by dinghy on the beach nearby, eight Fatah guerrillas holed up here, taking ten guests hostage and demanding the release of thirteen political prisoners. As Israeli troops stormed the hotel, the guerrillas set off an explosion, which killed five tourists. Three Israeli guests, three soldiers and seven guerrillas also died in the fighting.

Off Kikar Magen David

Allenby meets HaMelekh George at **Kikar Magen David** (Star of David Square) – so-called because of its six points. The main reason to venture northeast up **Rehov HaMelekh George** (King George Street) is to visit the **Jabotinsky Institute** and **Etzel Museum** at no. 38 (Sun–Thurs 8am–4pm; 6NIS), where a combination of photographs, documents, relics, ammunition and models illustrates the history of the pre-independence, right-wing Zionist paramilitary, the Irgun, and the Revisionist movement of which it was part. En route, look out for the two curiously named alleys situated about 100m along on your right: **Simta Almonit** (Unnamed Alley) and **Simta Polonit** (Unspecified Alley). The latter, entered between stylized obelisks, has something of an old-fashioned air for Tel Aviv; the fearsome stucco lion guarding the end house must have been even more alarming in the days when its eyes lit up.

East off Kikar Magen David, **Rehov Shenkin**, once the haunt of ultra-orthodox "dossim" and lefties, is now Tel Aviv's trendiest street. By day the young and beautiful hang out in its cafés or wander round the shops containing Indian and African art, rave clothes, candles, incense and Art Nouveau antiques. At night, the same groovy crowd meets up here before moving on to the nightclubs and dance events advertised on posters in its shops. *Café Tamar* at no. 57 is Tel Aviv's answer to *Les Deux Magots* on the Left Bank – a long-time hang-out of Israeli Labour Party hacks and assorted intellectuals, leftists and journos, and one of the most atmospheric cafés in the city. With time to spare, continue along Shenkin and turn on to **Sederot Rothschild** for a rare glimpse of Thirties' charm. An air of dignity pervades its tree-lined pavements and a wander along its length reveals several International Style buildings – nos. 63, 67, 79 and 140, in particular, are classic examples.

Shuq HaCarmel, west across Allenby from Shenkin, is Tel Aviv's main market (Sun–Thurs sunrise to sunset, Fri till late afternoon) – a vibrant mix of colour and culture where you'll find anything from Eastern European delicatessen, household goods, T-shirts and cheap cassettes, to an abundance of fruit and vegetables (including *qat*, see p.57), live fish and chickens. As many of the stalls are run by Palestinians from Jaffa, the market can unfortunately be a focus for anti-Arab violence in the wake of bombings by Palestinian paramilitaries.

After the bustle of Shuq HaCarmel, pedestrianized **Nahalat Binyamin**, next to the market's entrance, is an enjoyable place to stroll and take time out for a drink at one of the open-air cafés. On Tuesdays and Fridays in particular, street stalls display a variety of handicrafts and buskers ply their trade. At no. 8, the ornate balconies, wooden shutters and leaded and stained-glass windows are in a sad state of neglect and bear witness to Tel Aviv's previous lack of awareness of its early architectural heritage. Things are changing, however: one building now undergoing belated renovation is the **Pagoda** on Kikar HaMelekh Albert, so-called because of its 1925 pseudo-Japanese facade. To get there, walk east to the end of Montefiore from Nahalat Binyamin.

Kerem HaTaymanim (the Yemenite Quarter) and the former Manshieh Quarter

To the west of Shuq HaCarmel, **Kerem HaTaymanim** – or the Yemenite Quarter – is a characterful maze of narrow lanes and alleys and cramped buildings, with a collection of good cafés and popular restaurants. Like the other older areas of Tel Aviv, it's now back in fashion after a long period as a run-down neighbourhood. Just southwest of here, the elegant sandstone **Hassan Bek Mosque** is one of only two surviving buildings of Jaffa's former Manshieh Quarter. Of strategic importance in the 1948 war when its minaret was used by Palestinians for sniping, the mosque was the last building in the quarter to be taken by the Irgun (see p.89). The buildings around it were destroyed in the mid-1970s to make way for office blocks and hotels, and the mosque narrowly avoided the same fate when the brother of Israeli Labour Party leader Shimon Peres received permission to convert it into a nightspot, though he was later prevented from doing so by a law enforcing respect for religious buildings. In 1981, Arab residents of Jaffa initiated the restoration of Hassan Bek with finance from Palestinian sources, but shortly after work began, an explosive charge demolished the minaret and restoration ground to a halt amid a welter of court orders, arrests and recriminations. Restoration began again in 1985 under Jaffa's Arab League and its completion will be a tribute to their tenacity.

South along the promenade towards Jaffa, the **Etzel Museum** (Sun–Thurs 8.30am–4pm; 6NIS) is, like its namesake in Rehov HaMelekh George (see p.83), dedicated to the history of the Irgun, this time specializing in the years 1947–48. The hi-tech structure that houses it lies within the ruin of the only other of Manshieh's buildings to have survived in any form, and a lot more interesting than the museum itself.

Neve Zedek

The neighbourhood of **Neve Zedek**, situated to the south of the Yemenite Quarter, dates from 1887 when it became the first area to be settled by former Jewish residents of Jaffa. Now one of Tel Aviv's trendiest quarters, its Arab-style houses, built almost on top of each other, are highly sought after, and many have been renovated by artists and Israeli yuppies. The oldest house here is **Rokah House**, at 36 Rokah (Sat only 10am–2pm; 2.50NIS). Built by Shimon Rokah, it has now been restored by his granddaughter, the sculptor Lea Majaro-Mintz, and houses a collection of her works: chiefly human figures with flattened-out limbs. Around the corner at 6 Yehieli, the **Suzanne Dellal Centre** (☎03/510 5656; also, see p.97), formerly the Neve Zedek Theatre, is one of Tel Aviv's main centres for cultural and theatrical events, with an excellent and well-deserved reputation for experimental and avant-garde performance. Built in 1908 as a girls' school, it served as a training base and arms stash for the Haganah from 1942 to 1948, and was later the first Israeli theatre to host a radical Palestinian production.

South towards Jaffa, off Rehov Eilat, the **IDF** (Israeli Defence Force) or **Tzahal Museum** at 33 Rehov Elifelet (Sun–Thurs 8.30am–3pm; 6NIS) traces the history of Israel's army with the help of a display of military hardware and armoured vehicles. The "terrorism" section in hall 9 is, perhaps unsurprisingly, a little politically biased, but the ingenuity of the armed forces in the War of Independence, shown in halls 1–5, is quite astounding and no doubt an inspiration to the groups of soldiers who get shown around the museum as part of their training.

The Shalom Tower and Florentin

Situated at the northern end of Rehov Herzl – Tel Aviv's original main street – the **Shalom Tower** is the tallest building in Israel and said to be top of Islamic Jihad's list of ideal bomb targets. If this doesn't put you off, you can take the lift to the **observatory** on the 34th floor, where a café, interactive multi-media exhibition on the city's history, and the best view in Tel Aviv await (Sun–Thurs 10am–6.30pm, Fri 10am–1.30pm, Sat 11am–4pm; 12NIS; entrance in the east wing). Equally worth checking out are the colourful **mosaics** in the lobby of the west wing, one by Nathan Gutman illustrating the history of Tel Aviv, and a sequel by David Sharir entitled "Tel Aviv, the Second Generation". The tower stands on the site of the Herzliya Gymnasium (High School), demolished in 1959 to make way for it but still commemorated on the 1949 **Founders' Monument** nearby at the junction of Herzl with Rothschild. The monument depicts three stages in the city's growth, from its foundation in the first decade of this century, to the modern city of the Forties complete with art museum, national theatre and port; the gymnasium is depicted in the centre.

Rehov Herzl continues south through **Florentin**, a district dating back to the 1920s and yet another one to have undergone something of a renaissance. Its dilapidated International Style buildings (1 Frenkel is a fine example) are gradually undergoing redecoration (if not restoration) and though its streets are still lined with shops and small businesses – aromatic spice shops on Rehov Levinsky, furniture on Rehov Florentin – property prices are on the rise, and new bars and cafés are opening up by

---

THE STERN GANG

Although best known for the assassinations of Lord Moyne and Count Bernadotte (see p.495) and their part in the Deir Yassin massacre (see p.378), the **Stern Gang** were more than just the crazed Fascists they appear to be at first glance, for although that element was dominant, they also exhibited an anti-imperialist tendency that at times identified them as much with the extreme left as extreme right.

Officially named Lohamey Herut Yisra'el, meaning "Fighters for the Freedom of Israel", and known by the acronym **Lehi**, the group was set up in 1939 after the Irgun, the main Revisionist paramilitary (see p.493), decided to cooperate with Britain against Nazism. Several Irgun members broke away to continue their fight against the British on the grounds that "the enemy is the one who rules your country", and that the British were a more immediate foe than the Nazis, or indeed the Arabs. Led by **Avraham Stern**, a Polish Jew fired up by Jabotinsky's ideas who had emigrated to Palestine and joined the Irgun, the gang was small and close knit, its methods (robbery, assassination, bombings) as extreme as its political views (mystical nationalism). It was loathed by most Palestinian Jews, and its members were regularly turned in to the British by the Haganah and even the Irgun.

Eventually the British set Stern up: an *agent provocateur* posing as an Italian agent offered him rule over a Jewish state in return for help against Britain. While Stern considered this (he had already in fact attempted to negotiate an anti-British alliance with Nazi Germany's agent in Vichy-controlled Syria), intelligence sources leaked the story to the press. In December 1942, the CID raided the house where he was hiding out, shot him in the head, and planted evidence to brand him a Fascist quisling. "Good riddance," thought most, but Lehi carried on without Stern. Under Israel Scheib, Yitzhak Shamir and Natan Yalin-Mor, they chalked up some of their most infamous crimes, including the shooting in 1944 of Lord Moyne (Britain's Minister for the Middle East). On trial in Cairo for his murder, one of the defendants made a speech that appeared to propose an Arab–Jewish anti-British front, an idea that gained quite a body of support among Sternists. Following the 1948 assassination of Count Bernadotte (the UN envoy who wanted to internationalize Jerusalem), the Israeli government disbanded the group and imprisoned most of its members.

Scheib continued to preach totalitarianism, racism, expansionism and Jewish fundamentalism in a monthly magazine called *Sulam*. **Shamir** put his experience to good use for many years in Shin Bet (Israeli intelligence) before returning to politics to head two governments (1983–84 and 1986–92) whose right-wing views did not go quite as far as Scheib's. **Yalin-Mor**, always a maverick within the group, was elected for the Sternist "Fighters' Party" to the first Knesset, where he preached a pan-Semitic anti-imperialism aiming to unite Jewish and Palestinian nations in a federal Middle East, and proposed a two-state solution to the Israel–Palestine problem long before it gained currency on the conventional left. Writer Maxim Ghilan, a follower of his, has even portrayed the Stern Gang as essentially a left-wing, anti-imperialist organization, but his silence on the subject of Deir Yassin is so deafening it all but drowns out the message. Meanwhile, the Sternists have now been rehabilitated to respectability in Israel, but across the ethnic divide, Hamas and Islamic Jihad are arguably their true heirs.

the week. In the heart of Florentin, the house at 8 Rehov Stern (formerly Rehov Mizrahi B) is where British CID officers shot Avraham Stern. Now the **Lehi Museum** (Sun–Thurs 8.30am–4pm; 6NIS), it's home to an exhibition on the Stern Gang, the ultra-right paramilitary organization that he founded (see box on p.85), and contains a collection of photographs, cuttings and manuscripts relating to Stern's life and activities.

Southeast of Florentin, the run-down district of **Shapira** has become Tel Aviv's African quarter, populated by West African "guest workers", largely from Ghana and Nigeria. The community is new and limited in its scope by immigration rules that severely restrict right of abode; as yet, there are no West African restaurants or clubs here.

Jaffa

In a reversal of fortune, **JAFFA**, once Palestine's main port and second largest city, is now little more than an appendage of Tel Aviv, its former suburb. The town's rapid decline – so rapid that it occurred almost overnight – was a direct consequence of the 1948 war, when most of the population fled before Israeli forces. Its port, the main entry point into Palestine for pilgrims for centuries, was immobilized, while the orange groves that had made its property-owning classes so wealthy were neglected and finally appropriated.

Nowadays, there is an empty heart to this once grand city. Tourists are shepherded to a sanitized **Old Jaffa**, where many of the beautiful old buildings have been converted into galleries, studios, exorbitant nightclubs and restaurants. However, with a little effort, further exploration will reward you with a wealth of interesting historical nooks and crannies that make a pleasant change from the concrete and tarmac of Tel Aviv. **Walking tours** of Old Jaffa, organized by the IGTO (see p.74 for address), depart once a week from the clock tower (Wed at 9.30am; free). Free, detailed **maps** of Old Jaffa are available from the excavations in Kikar Kedumin, at its centre, where there is an information desk run by the Jaffa Development Corporation.

The district of Manshieh, to the north of Old Jaffa, no longer exists, but the centre of **modern Jaffa**, to the south, is still largely Palestinian and gives some idea of what the city was like before 1948. Sanctuary from the hustle and bustle can be found at the former village of Abu Kabir, set in a green space to the east, whose additional attractions include a *sabil* (old fountain), zoo and Russian Church.

Some history

If history repeats itself, then maybe **Jaffa**, which has been conquered no fewer than 22 times, is a prime example. Stone Age artefacts (from around 5000 BC) have been excavated in and around Jaffa, and the early **Canaanite** settlement was conquered perhaps as early as 1468 BC by Thuti, a general serving Pharaoh Thutmose III. From Thuti to the State of Israel, Jaffa's list of rulers could be a complete catalogue of Middle Eastern and European powers: Egyptians, Philistines, Israelites, Assyrians, Persians, Greeks, Romans, Crusaders, Mongols, Mamluks, Ottomans, French, British and more.

With its strategic location, natural harbour and abundance of fresh water from nearby wells, Jaffa has been a major prize, fought over from the earliest times. Possibly the oldest port in the world, it was from here that the biblical Jonah set sail on his ill-fated voyage (Jonah 1: 3). **Judas Maccabeus** burnt down the harbour after Greek residents had taken its Jewish community out to sea and drowned them (II Maccabees 12: 3–7), and his brother Simon later seized the city and used it as a military base (I Maccabees 13: 11). Simon's son, John Hyrcanus, held it with the help of the Romans, but when Herod built Caesarea he diverted much of Palestine's trade there, and with the growth of Lydda in the ninth century and the subsequent building of Ramle, it was several hundred years before Jaffa recovered the ground it had lost. The **Crusaders** held the town

JAFFA

MANSHIEH

Lutheran Church

Andromeda's Rock

Mahmudiyya Mosque

Clock Tower

OLD CITY

Minaret

St Joseph's Convent

SHUQ HAPISHPESHIM

ex-Hostel

Tabeetha School

Collegé des Frères

Port

Jewish Cemetery

ABU KABIR

St Peter's Russian Church

Zoo

Sabil of Abu Nabut

Gan HaHaganah

Anglican Church

San Antonio Church

Maronite Church

Coptic Church

Gan HaShnayim

AJAMI

Ajami Mosque

Arab Cultural Centre

REHOV NES HAGOYIM

Gaza vehicles

DAKAR

ACCOMMODATION

Beit Immanuel 1
Old Jaffa Hostel 2

EATING PLACES

Abu Elafia	A
Bet HaHummus	B
Dr Lek	C
Dr Shakshuka	D
Eli's Caravan	E
Keren	F
Le Relais	G
Misu	H
Taboon	I
Turquoise	J

N

0   500 m

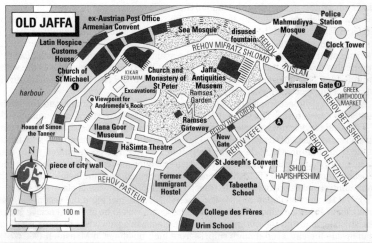

OLD JAFFA

ex-Austrian Post Office
Armenian Convent

Sea Mosque

disused fountain

Police Station

Mahmudiyya Mosque

Clock Tower

Latin Hospice Customs House

REHOV MIFRATZ SHLOMO

RUSLAN

Church of St Michael

KIKAR KEDUMIM

Church and Monastery of St Peter

Jaffa Antiquities Museum

Ramses Garden

Jerusalem Gate

GREEK ORTHODOX MARKET

harbour

Viewpoint for Andromeda's Rock

Excavations

Ramses Gateway

House of Simon the Tanner

Ilana Goor Museum

HaSimta Theatre

New Gate

A

SHUQ HAPISHPESHIM

N

piece of city wall

REHOV PASTEUR

Former Immigrant Hostel

St Joseph's Convent

Tabeetha School

College des Frères

Urim School

0   100 m

three times in all – Saladin's brother al-'Adil sold the entire population of the city into slavery in 1187 and Richard the Lionheart stormed it by sea to relieve its besieged Christian community while on his way home from Acre. In 1260, Jaffa fell to the Mongols, but was retaken by Baybars eight years later, only to be razed by his Mamluk successors in 1345, when they filled in the port because of the renewed threat of European invasion.

Under the Ottomans the port was re-opened, and Jaffa's bloodiest times came when it was captured from them by **Napoleon Bonaparte** in March 1799. After thirty hours of pillage and plunder the Arab garrison inside the city surrendered and over four thousand prisoners were brought to the French camp, where Napoleon ordered them shot before the march on Acre. The city was left in ruins, its population decimated, its streets so full of corpses that the resulting outbreak of plague spread even to the French camp. Much of the city's rebuilding took place under the new Ottoman governor Mohammed Aja, known as **Abu Nabut** (Father Cudgel) from his habit of wandering the streets armed with a large club.

By the middle of the nineteenth century, the town had once again entered a period of rapid expansion, fuelled by trade with western Europe. Local landowners had planted mulberry bushes some years earlier and by the end of the 1850s tons of raw **silk** were passing through Jaffa. The increased prosperity of villages in the hinterland rejuvenated commercial activity, and as the century continued growth was further boosted by the export of **Jaffa oranges** – in 1886 over one thousand vessels passed through the port and over one hundred thousand boxes of Jaffa oranges were exported – and by the beginning of large-scale European tourism and pilgrimage to the Holy Land. Jaffa expanded southward after 1888, when its walls were mostly demolished, while the Manshieh Quarter to the north was founded following the 1892 opening of the **Jaffa–Jerusalem railway**, Palestine's first.

Up to the mid-nineteenth century Jaffa had been almost exclusively a Muslim-Christian town. Jerusalem rabbis, seeking to increase the Jewish population of their own city, had issued a *herem* (rabbinical interdict) which forbade Jews from settling in Jaffa but this was lifted in 1841, and, as the century progressed, Jaffa saw an increasing flood of European **Jewish immigrants**. The town prospered, but political friction between Jews and Palestinians was never far from the surface – Arab opposition to Zionism was already felt in Jaffa by 1911 when a group of Arab notables set up an association to protest against Jewish land purchases. Tensions came to a head in 1921, as two rival Jewish marches came to blows in the centre, and crowds gathered to watch; Arabs in Manshieh then began smashing Jewish shop windows, starting three days of **race riots** that left 320 dead. The British Commission of Enquiry which followed noted the role of Arab constables in leading mobs against Jewish targets, in particular the immigrants' hostel on the Gaza Road (now Rehov Yefet), and the upshot was the withdrawal of Jews and their organizations and businesses to Tel Aviv. The two cities, divided by race, now glared menacingly at each other.

Meanwhile, the economic transformation of Palestine under Britain and the introduction of new industries had stimulated the formation and growth of trade unions, radical political parties, progressive newspapers and a host of other social, artistic and cultural groups. Many of these were based in Jaffa, which became a centre of resistance to the British during the **Palestinian Revolt** of 1936–39. The port's limited space and rocky shore had already begun to prove inadequate for modern shipping so when the rebellion brought it to a standstill for months the British, with the help of the Jewish community, used the opportunity to transfer trade to Tel Aviv and Haifa.

By **1948**, the population of Jaffa had risen to 100,000, making it the second largest Arab city in Palestine. Under the UN partition plan, it was to be an Arab enclave in the Jewish state, and with the outbreak of war the Haganah's policy was to contain rather than invade the city, even though snipers from high buildings in Manshieh (see p.84) were able to fire on central Tel Aviv. However, they were forced to intervene when the Irgun, without informing them, attacked on April 25 before the British had left, and turned to them for help when the going got tough. British forces responded by threatening to shell Tel Aviv if the invasion continued, but when the Mandate officially ended two weeks later, the British left and Israeli forces moved into Jaffa. One side of the town was left open and all but four thousand Palestinians fled. The Irgun went on a spree of looting, later described by Prime Minister David Ben Gurion as a "shameful and distressing spectacle". Homes and businesses were taken over by opportunist Tel Avivians and later, in a more systematic way, the new Israeli government settled Jewish immigrants in Palestinian homes whose owners were unable to reclaim them due to the Absentee Property Act (see p. 495).

The port's decline continued (it was finally closed in 1965) and the once impressive buildings fell into ruin, creating the atmosphere of shabbiness you see in the untouristed parts of Jaffa today. In 1960, however, the Israeli government and the municipality set up the **Old Jaffa Development Corporation**, which has restored the old city and turned it into a fashionable "artists' quarter". The Palestinian areas were meanwhile allowed to fall into ruin: boarded-up houses of Palestinian refugees were designated state property and no one was allowed to move into them, and planning regulations were used to prevent Palestinian residents from improving or extending their homes and to close down a small industrial area they had tried to establish. Only recently have some of these regulations been eased. Many streets have been renamed, though the signs bearing their names are in Hebrew and English only: Palestinian residents, especially older folk, will often use the original names, which may lead to some confusion.

Old Jaffa

From central Tel Aviv, it's less than thirty minutes' walk along the seafront, or down Derekh Yafo (Jaffa Road), to the impressive 1906 **clock tower** on Rehov Yefet, which marks the heart of tourist Jaffa. To its west lies the formerly walled city of **Old Jaffa**. Directly opposite the clock tower, on Rehov Ruslan, the **Mahmudiyya Mosque**, with its elegantly slender minaret, was built, like much of Old Jaffa, in the early nineteenth century following the destruction wrought by Napoleon. The open interior is decorated with Classical stonework brought from Roman sites up the coast, but unfortunately it's closed to non-Muslims. Before moving on, take a look at the beautiful (but disused) **Ottoman fountain** built into the wall of the mosque. It once dispensed water from taps that sprouted out of three small archways surmounted by inscriptions and contained within a larger rounded arch. A little further north up Ruslan, a marble hexagonal base decorated with arches and columns is all that remains of another street fountain dating from the same period.

Across Ruslan from the mosque, a small alley leads to the unassuming **Jerusalem Gate** at the beginning of Rehov Hatsorfim – until 1869 this was the only entrance into Jaffa. In the neighbouring coffee shops, Jewish men from Arab countries sit around drinking mint tea or Turkish coffee and playing backgammon – on the surface at least, not so different from their Palestinian neighbours. Back on Ruslan, Rehov Mifratz Shlomo branches off to the west, offering fine views of the seafront as it approaches the **Museum of Jaffa Antiquities** (Sun, Mon & Thurs 9am–2pm, Tues & Wed 9am–7pm, Sat 10am–2pm; 10NIS), housed in an eighteenth-century Ottoman administration building whose foundations date back to the Crusades, and displaying Jaffa's archeological finds – clay pots for the most part. The museum's highlight is a skeleton from the fourth millennium BC, set in a foetal position according to the burial custom of the time. The bathhouse adjoining the museum has been converted into a restaurant.

Beyond the museum, **Kikar Kedumin**, Old Jaffa's main square, is dominated by the Italian-style Roman Catholic **Church and Monastery of St Peter** (March–Sept daily 8–11.45am & 3–6pm, rest of year till 5pm) with its attractive bell tower. In the middle of the square a staircase (there's a ramp for wheelchairs) leads down to a well-labelled **excavation** of remains dating from the third century BC to the third century AD (Sun–Thurs 9am–10pm, Fri 9am–2pm, Sat 10am–10pm; free). Opposite the entrance, a terrace by *Ella* restaurant offers a good view of **Andromeda's Rock**, just out to sea. According to Greek legend, Perseus, son of Zeus, rescued Andromeda from the rock as she was being sacrificed to a sea monster – the grooves in the rock are said to have been made by the chains that tied Andromeda down. Off Kikar Kedumin, at 8 Simtat Shimon HaBurski, the **House of Simon the Tanner** is where, according to legend, St Peter stayed after being summoned to raise Tabitha, aka Dorcas, "a woman full of good works and almsdeeds", from the dead (Acts 9: 36–43) and where he subsequently had a vision on the roof in which animals descended from heaven accompanied by a voice telling him to kill and eat them (Acts 10: 9–19). Once a mosque, it is now an attractive private house, but dates from the nineteenth century and not biblical times at all.

Opposite the steps leading down to Simon the Tanner's House, the **Ilana Goor Museum** (Sun, Mon, Wed & Sat 10am–10pm, Tues & Thurs 10am–2pm, Fri 10am–4pm; 15NIS), once an eighteenth-century khan for Jewish pilgrims, is now the home of artist Ilana Goor and displays a collection of her artwork, including furniture, jewellery and (rather impractical) brassieres. Across the alley to its right, a small part of Jaffa's **city wall** still stands alongside Rehov Louis Pasteur. Behind all of these, a patch of grass grandly called the **Ramses Garden** takes its name from a gateway, reconstructed from meagre remains found here, bearing the cartouche of the nineteenth-dynasty pharaoh Ramses II, long thought to be the pharaoh of the Exodus.

The harbour

The **harbour**, on the shore of Old Jaffa, was one of the more interesting sections of town until the Palestinian fishermen, who still provide fare for local restaurants, were edged out into the southern part to make way for a **marina** for Tel Aviv's yachting crowd. But the shadows of Jaffa's illustrious maritime history still linger in the form of deserted berths and decaying warehouses. The **Sea Mosque** on the quayside was built in 1820 to serve local fishermen, and the now derelict building to its right once served as the **Austrian post office**, one of several run by foreign governments in the last century for international mail. To the right of that, the **Armenian Convent** and **Latin Hospice** date back to the seventeenth century. Behind them lies the mid-nineteenth-century Greek Orthodox **Church of St Michael**.

The souqs and further east

Across Rehov Yefet from Old Jaffa is the flea market, **Shuq HaPishpeshim**, run primarily by Sephardi Jews and reached from any of the streets to the left of the clocktower. Festooned with rugs and baubles, this is arguably Israel's most colourful street market, thronging with locals in search of bargains and tourists looking for antiques; genuine, high-quality antiques do turn up here, but with prices to match. Venturing further down the back streets you'll discover a wonderful selection of junk, anything from electric guitars to obsolete Palestinian passports, rugs and orientalia, second-hand clothes and old books and papers. Just north of the modern-day flea market, the largely derelict area now belongs to the Greek Orthodox Church, whose symbol can still be seen above gateways leading into it. At the end of Rehov Bet Eshel, which runs alongside, a minaret is all that remains of a mosque once used by shoppers patronizing the markets that extended over the whole of this area until 1948.

Five hundred metres east of Old Jaffa, along Derekh Ben Tzvi and a little before the corner of Herzl, you'll find the attractive domed **Sabil of Abu Nabut** – a public fountain put up by the early nineteenth-century Ottoman governor as part of his programme of public works following Jaffa's decimation by Napoleon, and which also serves as his last resting place. **Gan HaHaganah**, beyond, is one of the more central of Tel Aviv's green spaces and contains a **zoo** (Sun–Fri 9am–4pm, Sat 9.30am–4pm; 12NIS) and botanical garden. Behind the zoo, **St Peter's Russian Church** (closed to the public) with its landmark pink-and-white tower, is where Tabitha, the godly woman resurrected by St Peter (see opposite), was buried after she finally died.

Palestinian Jaffa

The Jaffa that most tourists see is but a small section at its northern end; for the Jaffa that people actually live in, you need to head further south down **Rehov Yefet**. On the way you pass several remnants of Jaffa's Christian community and the building spree undertaken by the European powers in the final years of the Ottoman Empire. You come first to the Roman Catholic **St Joseph's Convent** and the Presbyterian Church of Scotland's **Täbeetha School** facing it, behind which there's a small Protestant cemetery that is the resting place of, among others, Thomas Hodgkin, discoverer of the disease named after him. The dingy gateway in the passage by 30 Yefet is the **New Gate**, opened in 1869 because the Jerusalem Gate had become inadequate for traffic entering the Old City. **No. 34** served as a hostel for new Jewish immigrants until a rioting mob led by Palestinian Arab constables broke in and murdered thirteen of them in 1921.

A couple of hundred metres further down Rehov Yefet, across Rehov Yehuda HaYamit, the **Franciscan Church of San Antonio**, built in the 1930s, is one of the few churches to have survived with its building and congregation intact after 1948. The small, tree-lined park a few hundred metres further along Yefet is known in Hebrew as "Gan HaShnayim" and marks the centre of Palestinian Jaffa, though you'd never guess it from the lack of activity. Just south of here, the **Arab Cultural Centre** at 73 Yefet, founded by al-Raabita al-Yafawi al-Arabi (the League of Arab Jaffa), is a local community organization which, among other things, runs regular summer voluntary workcamps (see p.63).

Lying between Rehov Yefet and the sea, the **Ajami Quarter** is Jaffa's main residential district. After taking the city in 1948, the Israelis moved the remaining Palestinian inhabitants into this area, declaring many of them absentee owners (see p.495) of their homes. The municipality's subsequent demolition of these absentee homes and its prohibition for many years of home improvements have further scarred the area. Nevertheless, a wander around the streets reveals some architecture that points to a grander past. The curious combination of luxury and derelict housing also apparent is a result of Ajami's now very mixed (though far from integrated) population, with Arab residents being increasingly replaced by Jewish newcomers prepared to pay high prices for properties. As Ajami becomes more and more Jewish, however, Jaffa's Palestinian community (currently 20,000 out of 55,000) continues to be squeezed ever smaller. The down-at-heel district of **Dakar** to the east across Sederot Yerushalayim, is more genuinely mixed – one of the few places in the country where Jewish and Palestinian families of similar (low) income live on cordial terms as neighbours, renting flats in the same buildings and buying food at the same shops.

Beaches

The **strand** runs parallel to Rehov HaYarkon for almost all of the city's four-kilometre seafront, with little to differentiate any one spot on the main drag from another besides the presence of a lifeguard. Much of this stretch has breakwaters a few hundred metres out to sea. The least frenetic beach in Tel Aviv lies just east of the junction of Ben Yehuda and Dizengoff, behind the *Tal Hotel*. Alternatively, head south to the resort of **Bat Yam** (see p.103), whose white sandy beaches are basically an extension of Tel Aviv's; north to Herzliya (see p.154); or just beyond to an even better beach at Kefar Shmaryanu, a half-hour bus ride away.

Eating

Tel Aviv's **restaurants** offer the widest range of cuisine in the country with new places opening up all the time. As you might expect, Jewish, East European and Middle Eastern cuisine tend to be the best, though you can also get Chinese (variable), Indian (surprisingly good), Thai (a reasonable attempt), Mexican (inauthentic), French (expensive but good), Italian (reasonable pasta, but generally awful pizzas) and North African (good but not classic). Fish restaurants are particularly popular but vary in quality, so it pays to be choosy. Most restaurants in Tel Aviv are not kosher.

Dizengoff boasts some good, well-established restaurants: the chic ones can be found at its northern end, those more geared to tourists are around Kikar Dizengoff. Slightly cheaper options can be found nearby on **Ben Yehuda** and **HaYarkon**. At the northern end of these three streets, **Little Tel Aviv** is popular with Tel Avivians, and boasts a number of rather upmarket restaurants serving a variety of innovative cuisine. Budget restaurants serving Middle Eastern and traditional Jewish food can be found on and around **Allenby**, while the **Yemenite Quarter** is the place to go for inexpensive, and especially Yemeni Jewish, home-style cooking. **Florentin** is an up-and-coming restaurant area, with trendy places opening up all the time and offering a cosmopolitan selection of different cuisines, though you'll find some older, traditional places here too. **Neve Zedek** lags behind Florentin in terms of numbers of restaurants, but what it does have tends to be more upmarket. In **Jaffa**, you should avoid places aimed at tourists and go for either the cheap places frequented by locals, or the swanky, expensive ones patronized by well-heeled Tel Avivians. The restaurants listed below have been described as cheap, moderate or expensive; see p.42 for details of the price ranges that these terms cover.

Of Tel Aviv's **supermarkets**, *Supersol*, 79 Ben Yehuda, is open late; others are at 55 Arlosorov at the corner of Shlomo HaMelekh, and 157 Ibn Gvirol at the corner of Nordau. In Jaffa, there's *Super Shekem*, 1 Ben Shatah, at the corner of Yerushalayim near the post office.

BREAKFAST, SNACKS AND ICE CREAMS °

Breakfast is usually no problem in Tel Aviv, though you may have trouble finding somewhere that serves food before 8am. Many cafés and restaurants offer an Israeli spread of eggs and salad – try *Kassit* at 117 Dizengoff; *Marese* at 98 Ben Yehuda; or *Presto* at 81 Ben Yehuda – while any café can supply a breakfast of coffee with a croissant or pastry. Alternatively, travellers' bars often serve English breakfasts all day for $5–10 (see "Cafés" and "Bars", pp.94–95).

There are hundreds of **falafel** stalls all over the city, but most are concentrated in three main areas centred on the old bus station, the intersection of Allenby and Ben Yehuda, and Kikar Dizengoff. Those at the latter are pricier but stay open until at least 2am; *shawarmas* or *burekas* and the like are also available from stalls here. A number of **24-hour bakeries and cafés** cater for late-night hunger pangs. The most famous is *Abu Elafia*, 5 Yefet in Jaffa near the clock tower, though nowadays it falls somewhat short of its reputation. Popular with young Israelis after a night out is the bakery at 11 Pines in Neve Zedek, which sells fresh **bagels** (10pm–8am except Fri night/Sat morning). *Crazy Bagel*, 1 Shenkin (sign in Hebrew only), also has reasonable bagels plus massive *burekas* round the clock.

Ice-cream outlets exist on almost every corner. Try: *Dr Lek*, in Jaffa at 8 Goldmann and downtown at 234 Ben Yehuda and 30 Shenkin; *Blue Moon*, in the Dizengoff Center; *Manolitos*, 21 Ibn Gvirol; *Dolci Melodie*, 122 Ben Yehuda; and *LeHayyim*, 60 Ben Yehuda, whose vegan ice cream is pleasantly light.

Dizengoff, Ben Yehuda and around

Batya, 197 Dizengoff. Chopped liver, gefilte fish and similar Jewish fare, with a good, home-cooked Shabbat lunch. Daily 11am–9pm. Moderate.

Cactus, 66 HaYarkon. Trendy downtown Tex-Mex open 24hr. Moderate.

LeHayyim, 60 Ben Yehuda. Tel Aviv's only vegan eatery, run by a group of Black Hebrews; salads and tofu dishes dominate the menu, with vegan ice cream for afters or to take away. Sun–Thurs 9am–11pm, Fri 9am–2pm, Sat nightfall–11pm. Moderate.

Mamaia, 192 Ben Yehuda (☎03/523 9621). Swanky Romanian eatery that just has the edge over its competitor *Mon Jardin*, at no. 186 (☎03/523 1792). Daily noon–midnight. Expensive.

Red Chinese, 324 Dizengoff (☎03/546 6347). Upmarket Chinese with some Thai dishes. Daily 1pm–midnight. Expensive.

Shoshanna & Uri's, 35 Yirmiyahu. Serves sweet and savoury Hungarian blintzes. Sun–Thurs noon–4pm & 7pm–1am, Fri noon–4pm only, Sat nightfall–1am. Moderate.

Tandoori, 2 Zamenhof, below Kikar Dizengoff (☎03/629 6185). Tel Aviv's top Indian restaurant, specializing in North Indian meat dishes. Daily 12.30–3.30pm & 7pm–1am. Expensive.

Vienna, 48A Ben Yehuda. Ashkenazi nosh at decent prices, including a traditional Shabbat lunch of kishke and cholent. Daily 11.30am–3.30pm. Moderate.

Around Allenby and Kerem HaTaymanim

Big Mama, 12 Rabbi Akiva, Kerem HaTaymanim. An oasis of real pizzas in a desert of plastic ones. Sat–Thurs 8pm–4am. Moderate.

Mifgash Shaul, 73 Nahalat Binyamin. A choice of different – and excellent – *shawarmas* to eat in or take away. Sun–Thurs 6am–7.30pm. Cheap to moderate.

Nameless Ethiopian restaurant, 42 Neve Sha'anan. The city's only Ethiopian food outlet, a hole in the wall with only a couple of dishes daily. Sat–Thurs 9am–10pm, Fri 3–10pm. Cheap.

Pe Ehad, 26 Mikve Israel. Cheap and cheerful Middle Eastern diner near the post office, with a sign in Hebrew only. Sun–Thurs 10am–6pm.

Spaghettim, 18 Yavne (☎03/566 4479) and 7 Rival (☎03/687 6097 or 9). Pasta with a massive choice of traditional and new-fangled sauces. Daily noon–1am. Expensive.

Tiv, 130 Allenby, on the corner of Yehuda HaLevi. Great-value Jewish East European self-service eatery, with a sign in Hebrew only. Sun–Fri 7am–3pm. Cheap.

Yin Yang, 64 Rothschild (☎03/560 4121). Tel Aviv's poshest Chinese. Sun–Fri noon–11pm, Sat 1–11pm. Expensive.

Yishurun, 4 Maze. Orthodox Yiddische cooking; the gefilte fish with home-made beetroot and horseradish sauce is excellent. Sun–Thurs 11am–6pm. Cheap to moderate.

Zion, 28 Peduyim, Kerem HaTaymanim. Popular Yemeni restaurant, whose dishes include heart, brain and sweetbreads, as well as more conventional meats. Sun–Thurs noon–midnight, Fri noon–3pm, Sat nightfall–midnight. Moderate.

Florentin and Neve Zedek

Elimelekh, 35 Wolfson, Florentin. Well-established and much loved by its devoted clientele for its old-school Jewish home cooking. Daily 10am–3am. Moderate.

Pastalina, 16 Elifelet, Florentin (☎03/683 6401). Trendy pasta place. Sun–Thurs 7pm–midnight, Fri noon–midnight. Expensive.

Ronit, 10 Yehoshua HaTalmi, Neve Zedek. A popular place for grills, schnitzels, steak and kebabs. Sun–Thurs 9.30am–7pm. Moderate.

Tampadulu, 1 Florentin, Florentin (☎03/518 0012). Indonesian eatery offering a "rice table" (*rijstaffel*, or *nasi Padang*): rice served with a large range of spicy dishes. Daily noon–4pm & 7pm–midnight. Expensive.

Tarkari, 68 HaKishon, Florentin. Indian vegetarian restaurant serving pukka veg curries and *thalis*. Sun–Thurs 11.30am–3pm & 7pm–midnight, Fri noon–3.30pm, Sat nightfall–midnight. Moderate to expensive.

Jaffa

Bet HaHummus, 6 Goldman, Jaffa. An excellent hummus bar. The *masabaha* is particularly good, and they do a mean falafel too. Sun–Fri 9am–5pm. Cheap.

Dr Shakshuka, 3 Bet Eshel, Jaffa. Couscous and *shakshuka* head the cast of North African dishes served here in the old Greek Orthodox market. Daily 10am–1am. Moderate.

Eli's Caravan, 1 HaDolphin, Jaffa. Sign in Hebrew only. Hummus joint of such renown that it spills onto the surrounding streets at lunchtime. Sun–Fri 8am–2pm. Cheap.

Keren, 12 Eilat, Jaffa (☎03/681 6565). High-class French food served in stylish surroundings. Mon–Sat noon–2.30pm & 7–10.30pm, Sun 7–10.30pm only. Expensive.

Le Relais, 13 HaDolphin, Jaffa (☎03/681 0637). Swanky French restaurant known for its haute cuisine and classy atmosphere. Daily 7–11.30pm. Expensive.

Misu, 7 Raziel, Jaffa. Excellent-value East European lunchtime canteen. Sun–Fri noon–3pm. Cheap.

Taboon, Jaffa Port (☎03/681 6011). Excellent Mediterranean-style fish restaurant by the harbour. Daily 12.30pm–midnight. Expensive.

Turquoise, Bat Galim, Jaffa (☎03/658 8320). Pronounced "Toor-keeze", this renowned seafood restaurant is in a delightful beachside setting at the southern end of Ajami. Daily 11.30am–midnight. Expensive.

Drinking

In common with their counterparts in other Mediterranean cities, natives of Tel Aviv enjoy sitting in cafés during the day and don't visit bars until late. Though Dizengoff is well known for its **cafés**, the cognoscenti prefer the likes of Shenkin and Nahalat Binyamin (off Allenby), Rehov Basel (between Dizengoff and Ibn Gvirol in north downtown), and the Florentin district. Most cafés serve espresso rather than Turkish coffee, and it's usually pretty decent. Arab *qahwas* are few in number and confined to the southern end of Jaffa (nos. 77 and 88 Yefet, for example); they tend to be patronized by old-timers who do not really expect tourists to drop in for a tug on a *sheesha* – and certainly not female tourists.

You'll find **bars** all over town, particularly in the downtown area around Allenby, Dizengoff and Ben Yehuda, as well as further afield along Ibn Gvirol. All bars are open late and most serve food. The trendiest place for bar-hopping is Florentin, where the hippest bar changes from month to month; don't expect to see many drinkers before midnight. Travellers' bars (many of them attached to hostels) tend to be boozier than those frequented by Israelis, and to have an early-evening happy hour.

Cafés

Abaravanel, 64 Abaravanel, Florentin. A café-bar attracting a very mixed young crowd. Daily 8pm–2am.

C.C@fé, 84 Ben Yehuda. The first Internet café in town. Sip your cyber-coffee while you surf (10NIS per half-hour on the Net). Mon–Sat 11am–3am, Sun 7pm–3am.

Café de la Paix, 292 Dizengoff. Pleasant, quiet place for coffee and cakes at the upmarket end of Dizengoff. Daily 9am–midnight.

Herzl 68, 68 Herzl, Florentin. A daytime favourite with Florentin's young crowd. Sun–Thurs 8am–2am, Fri 8am–2pm, Sat 5pm–2am.

Café Kampery, 20 Shenkin. Coolest of three cafés looking onto the little open space in the middle of Shenkin. Daily 9am–1am.

Kapulsky, 10 Nahalat Binyamin. Part of a chain known for their delicious deluxe cakes (anyone on a diet or a budget look elsewhere). Sun–Thurs 7am–7pm, Sat nightfall–10pm.

Café Minzer, 28 Gedera. Easy-going, congenial coffee bar with a crowd that varies from the progressive thirty-somethings who hang out here of an evening to the wide-eyed ravers who stagger out of neighbouring clubs around dawn. Open 24hr.

Café Tamar, 57 Shenkin. Atmospheric hang-out of lefty intellectuals and journalists (see p.83), and the only place in Tel Aviv that really feels like a local. Sun–Thurs 7am–8pm, Fri 7am–7pm.

Tola'at Sefarim, 30 Basel. Café attached to a bookshop, and a good place for Israeli or Continental breakfasts. Sun–Thurs 8am–11pm, Fri 8am–4pm, Sat nightfall–11pm.

Café UP, 56 Shenkin. Café, deli and takeaway with seating outside or upstairs. Sun–Thurs 8.30am–1am, Fri 8.30am–3pm, Sat 8pm–1am.

Bars

Bar Ganza, 26 Shenkin. Meeting place for the rave crowd, with music to match but no room to dance. Daily from noon till the last person leaves.

Beers, 16 Allenby. Wooden decor, a congenial atmosphere and, as its name suggests, a big selection of different beers. Daily from noon till the last person leaves.

Buzz Stop, 86 Herbert Samuel. "Opened and run by travellers", with a good mix-and-match English breakfast. Open round the clock for booze, 9am–3am for food.

Dvash, 44 Salma, Florentin. Friendly bar with kitsch vampire decor, an ultra-violet loo and a hip crowd. Daily from 10pm until the last person leaves.

Embassy, 22 Ben Yehuda. Friendly place with good music and good food (jacket potatoes, pies, egg and bacon breakfasts). Daily 8.30am–2am.

Gordon Inn, 17 Gordon. Quiet bar with great buffet breakfasts. Daily 8am–2am.

MASH (More Alcohol Served Here), 275 Dizengoff. Boozy approximation of a British pub, complete with draught Guinness and dartboard. Happy hour 5–8pm. Daily 10am–3am.

The Office, 57 Allenby. Hostel bar popular with travellers and Israelis alike, with food by day and music Thursday and Friday nights. Open round the clock.

Shankar, 40 Shalom Shabazi, Neve Zedek. Popular meeting place for a younger local crowd. Sun–Thurs 9am–midnight, Fri 9am–4pm, Sat 6pm–midnight.

The White Gallery, 4 Kikar HaBima. Suave, upmarket bar patronized by culture vultures (the Mann Auditorium and Habima Theatre are just across the street). Daily noon–midnight.

Zanzibar, 19 Ibn Gvirol. Watering hole for yuppies from the Cinemateque, often full (in which case, try the nearby and similar *Rose*, at 147 Yehuda HaLevi). Daily noon–3am.

GAY BARS

Gay bars in Tel Aviv open, close and change at a dizzying pace, so keep your ear to the ground: *Café Nordau*, 145 Ben Yehuda on the corner of Arlozorov, is a long-standing meeting place, though by no means exclusively gay. For somewhere louder and more exclusive, current favourites include *HeShe*, in Rehov Rambam, and *Abbie's*, at 40 Geula.

Nightlife and entertainment

Tel Aviv takes its nocturnal activities seriously. Much of the **nightlife** revolves around bars and restaurants, but there are some good nightclubs, and a few live music venues too. For most of the big **concerts** a section of HaYarkon Park is cordoned off and the bands play under the stars; there's some kind of performance in the park every week or two during the summer (details in the *Jerusalem Post*). **Tickets** for all events in Tel Aviv (and around the country) can be bought from *LeAn*, in the arcade at 101 Dizengoff (☎03/524 7373); *Kastel*, the kiosk at 153 Ibn Gvirol (☎03/604 4725); or *Hadran*, 90 Ibn Gvirol (☎03/527 9797).

Tel Aviv's **nightclubs** come and go so fast it's hard to keep up, though chart-sound discos tend to be more permanent than serious music clubs. Tel Aviv has its share of the dance-techno clubs found in most Western capitals, along with the more party-style, singalong nightclubs favoured by middle-aged Israelis, especially those of Sephardic origin, that play golden oldies and Israeli folk hits – great fun if you get into the spirit.

Several clubs have a **gay night**, which changes frequently; currently, it's Friday at the *58*, Saturday at *Shehitut*, and every other Monday at the *Lemon Club*. For the latest on dance music events, *Musica Plus* in the Old Port, the only dance-record shop in town, has flyers for clubs, and the staff should be able to provide up-to-date information.

Live music venues

Bet Leissin, 34 Weizmann (☎03/694 1111). Regular events include new rock bands in the Upper Cellar on Thursday evenings, as well as jazz and folk.

Camelot, 16 Sholom Aleikhem (☎03/528 5222 or 3). The best jazz club in town. Enthusiasts might also want to move on to the after-hours jam session at 14 Ibn Gvirol.

Cossit, 5 Kikar Rabin (☎03/522 3244). Live jazz and funk on Tuesdays and Thursdays.

Lolu, 54 Allenby. Downtown bar with occasional live rock or jazz bands.

Maxim, 44 HaMelekh George (☎03/525 7766). A well-established venue for rock and folk concerts.

Roxanne, 10 HaBarzel, Ramat Aviv (☎03/648 4222). Large rock venue with regular local and foreign bands.

Theatre Moadon, 10 Yerushalayim, Jaffa (☎03/527 7205). Primarily a theatre but stages the odd jazz concert.

Tzavta, 30 Ibn Gvirol (☎03/695 0156 or 7). One of Tel Aviv's better venues, owned by the kibbutz movement and featuring Israeli pop and folk.

Zen, 21 Eilat (☎03/510-3243). Small jazz and blues club – basically a bar with a band.

Clubs and discos

Coliseum, Kikar Namir. Disco playing chart sounds to which women get free entry. Daily 11.30pm till dawn.

58 Club, 58 Allenby. A three dance-floor venue in a converted theatre with different serious dance sounds on different nights. Dress to impress or you may not get in. Usually midnight till 6am.

Golem, 7 Hillel HaZaken, Kerem HaTaymanim. Behind the *58*, playing the latest beats from Britain and the US; this was the first club in Tel Aviv to play drum 'n' bass and jungle. Usually open till 4 or 5am.

Hamishba'a (the Happy Casserole), 344 Dizengoff. The place for a Mediterranean-style knees-up. Let your hair down and leave your pretensions at home. Plays Israeli folk and Sixties' hits.

Ku, 117 Salma. House music club named after Ibiza's famous venue. Fridays are the main night.

Lemon Club, 17 HaNagarim, Florentin. Intimate club currently specializing in New York garage and house, popular with a crew of Tel Aviv regulars – others may not get in, especially if they don't look sufficiently cool. Friday is the main night (1am–7am).

Porto Loco, Yordei HaSira, Tel Aviv Port. Brazilian club with salsa, samba and sometimes live bands.

Shehitut, 146 Herzl. A club with a young, mostly student crowd and a gay night on Saturdays.

Soweto, 6 Frishman. Tel Aviv's top reggae spot (revival, dance hall and dub). Nightly from 10pm.

Theatre, dance and classical music

In cultural terms, Tel Aviv remains the capital of Israel, enjoying a surprisingly diverse selection of events, though ticket prices can be high. For the best idea of what's on, see the Friday edition of the *Jerusalem Post*, or *Israel Today*, put out by the IGTO and available free in their offices and in the lobbies of some hotels.

Theatre is mostly performed in the modern HaBima Theatre, Kikar HaBima (☎03/629 2793). Other venues include Tzavta, 30 Ibn Gvirol (☎03/695 0156 or 0157); HaSimta, 8 Mazal Dagim, Old Jaffa (☎03/682 1459); and Bet Leissin, 34 Weizmann (☎03/694 1111). Most plays are performed in Hebrew, with the occasional production in English, though for the best of both worlds, the Cameri Theatre, 101 Dizengoff

(☎03/523 3335), has Hebrew plays with simultaneous English translation on Tuesday evenings. If you understand Hebrew (or Russian), you could try to catch one of the internationally acclaimed productions by the most innovative theatre in the country – Gesher at 4 Nahmani (☎03/566 4888), founded in 1991 by a company of Russian Jewish immigrant actors, under Moscow director Yevgeny Ariye.

Classical music reaches a crescendo during the **Israel Festival** (see p.53), held annually in May and early June, when a number of major international orchestras and musicians perform in Tel Aviv. The Israel Philharmonic plays regularly in Tel Aviv throughout the year, and its sponsors are able to bring in virtuosi from all over the world. Their home is Tel Aviv's main **concert hall**, the Mann Auditorium, 1 Huberman, by Kikar HaBima (☎03/525 1502). Other venues include ZOA (Zionist Organization of America) House, 1 Frisch (☎03/695 9341 or 3), and the Tel Aviv Museum of Art, 27 Sha'ul HaMelekh (☎03/696 1297). The new **Opera House** at the Performing Arts Centre, 19 Shaul HaMelekh (☎03/692 7777), has two to three weekly performances, all in the original language.

There should be some kind of contemporary dance or **ballet** performance in Tel Aviv on just about any night during the summer months. The main venue is the Suzanne Dellal Centre, at 6 Yehieli, Neve Zedek (☎03/510 5656), with regular performances in the main hall as well as the Inbal Dance Theatre (☎03/517 3711). The Israel Ballet Company, which appears regularly at the HaBimah Theatre (see p.78), has a good reputation; the Bat Dor Dance Company puts on regular performances at the Bat Dor Auditorium, 30 Ibn Gvirol (☎03/696 3175); and there are also occasional performances at the Tel Aviv Performing Arts Centre, 19 Shaul HaMelekh (☎03/692 7777).

Israeli **folk dancing** (accompanied by Sixties' pop hits) can be seen at *Ben & Jerry's* on the promenade by the *Ramada Continental* hotel (Sat 11am–3pm). If you're really keen, lessons are available at Bicurei HaEtim, 6 Heftman (☎03/691 9510).

Cinemas

Most **cinemas** show the latest Hollywood offerings in English with subtitles, opening late on Fridays with the last screenings often around midnight. See the Friday edition of the *Jerusalem Post* for a rundown of what's on. Venues include Cinemateque, 1 HaArka'a (☎03/521 0028); Dizengoff, Dizengoff Centre (☎03/620 0485); and a drive-in called, appropriately, the Drive-In, off Sederot Rokah behind the Israel Trade Fairs and Convention Centre, near HaYarkon Park (☎03/642 8030).

Listings

Airlines Air Canada, 59 Ben Yehuda (☎03/527 3781); Air Sinai, 13th floor, 1 Ben Yehuda (☎03/510 2481–3); American Airlines, 1 Ben Yehuda (☎03/510 4322); Arkia, 11 Frishman (☎03/524 0220); British Airways, 13th floor, 1 Ben Yehuda (☎03/510 1581–5); Canadian Airlines, 1 Ben Yehuda (☎03/517 2163); CSA, 3 Bograshov (☎03/523 8834); Cyprus Airways, 71 Ben Yehuda (☎03/527 8065); Delta, 29 Allenby (☎03/620 1101); Egyptair, c/o Air Sinai; El Al, 32 Ben Yehuda (☎03/526 1222); KLM, 124 Ibn Gvirol (☎03/527 2722); Lufthansa, 9th floor, 1 Ben Yehuda (☎03/514 2350); Olympic, 13 Idelson (☎03/629 4381); Royal Jordanian, 5 Shalom Aleikhem (☎03/528 8333); Qantas, 1 Ben Yehuda (☎03/517 2163); SAA, 11th floor, 1 Ben Yehuda (☎03/510 2828); SAS, 1 Ben Yehuda (☎03/510 1177); Tower Air, 78 HaYarkon (☎03/517 9421); TWA, 74 HaYarkon (☎03/517 1212); United, 41 Ben Yehuda (☎03/527 9551).

American Express 112 HaYarkon (☎03/524 2211, fax 522 9166).

Banks and exchange Banks are concentrated along Allenby, Dizengoff and Ben Yehuda (Sun, Tues & Thurs 8.30am–12.30pm & 4–5.30pm; Mon & Wed 8.30am–12.30pm only), with 24-hour change machines operated by Bank HaPoalim at 104 HaYarkon, Bank HaPoalim and Bank Leumi on Dizengoff at the Dizengoff Centre. Cheque services are available at Thomas Cook c/o Bank HaPoalim, 50 Rothschild (☎03/567 3333, or toll-free on ☎177-440 8424), or at American Express, 112

HaYarkon (see above). Offices at 22 Gordon, 13, 64 & 70 Ben Yehuda, 140 Dizengoff, 94 HaYarkon, and branches of ISSTA travel agency are among those that do not charge commission on travellers' cheques (typical hours Sun–Thurs 8am–8pm, Fri 8am–4pm), along with post offices (see below).

Books Steimatzky at 103 Allenby, plus 101 & 109 Dizengoff, are the largest stockers of English-language books. The area around the junction of Allenby with Yona HaNavi has several second-hand bookshops including White Raven at 48 Allenby, and others at nos. 35 and 44. Nun Bet at 45 Ben Yehuda, and Pollack at 31 and 42 HaMelekh George, specialize in antiquarian books.

Camping gear Just about everything you could want can be got from the SPNI shop in the basement at 3 Hashfela, by the old bus station (entrance in HaSharon; ☎03/537 4884), or from Lamtayel, in the Dizengoff Centre (top level, above gate #5; ☎03/528 8418). Maslool at 36 Ben Yehuda (☎03/528 8418) and 23 Bograshov (☎03/620 3508) also buy and sell second-hand equipment.

Car rental Several companies have branches in the arrivals hall at Ben Gurion Airport (see p.73). The main firms in Tel Aviv are: Avis, 113 HaYarkon (☎03/527 2346, 7 or 8, fax 522 3649); Budget, 99 HaYarkon (☎03/524 5233, fax 524 5234); Eldan, 112 HaYarkon (☎03/527 1166 or 7); Eurodollar, 2 Mapu/112 HaYarkon (☎03/527 1122, fax 527 1124); Europcar, 126 HaYarkon (☎03/524 8181, fax 522 6292); Hertz, 144 HaYarkon (☎03/522 3332, fax 562 1818), also at *Hilton* and *Dan Panorama* hotels; Thrifty, 8 HaMelakha/43 HaMasgar (☎03/561 2050, fax 561 7774).

MOVING ON FROM TEL AVIV

BY BUS
You can get **buses** to pretty well anywhere in Israel (though not the West Bank or Gaza Strip) from Tel Aviv. Most of them (exceptions are private services to Jordan and Egypt, and bus #222 to the airport as specified below) leave from the new Central Bus Station (take city bus #4 from Ben Yehuda or #5 from Dizengoff, or sheruts along the same routes). Most Egged services leave from the sixth floor, one or two from the fourth. Services to the local region may call additionally at the old bus station on HaShomron.

Egged **destinations** include: Afula (2–3 per hour; 1hr 45min); Arad (3 daily; 2hr); Ashdod (roughly every 15min; 50min); Ashqelon (roughly every 15min; 1hr); Beersheba (3–4 per hour; 2hr); Eilat (10 daily; 5hr); Ein Boqeq (1 daily; 3hr 15min); Hadera (for Caesarea; 3–4 per hour; 1hr); Haifa (2–3 per hour; 1hr 45min); Jerusalem (3 per hour; 1hr 15min); Lydda (roughly every 15min; 20min); Nazareth (1–2 per hour; 2hr); Netanya (roughly every 15min; 45min); Qiryat Shemona (2 per hour; 3hr 30min); Rafah border post (1 daily; 2hr); Ramle (roughly every 15min; 20min); Rehovot (roughly every 10min; 25min); Rishon Le Zion (at least five per hour; roughly 30min); Safed (3 daily; 3hr); Tiberias (1–3 per hour; 2hr 30min); Yad Mordekhai junction (for Erez checkpoint; 7 daily; 1hr 15min).

To Jordan
The Jordanian company Trust International (☎03/638 8838) runs services **to Amman** (2 daily Sun–Thurs; 4–5hr), which depart from the Central Bus Station (platform 417). You cannot get a visa at the border if you take this bus so you must obtain one in advance. The current fare is $8, excluding border tax.

To Egypt
Bus services **to Cairo**, with a change of vehicle at Rafah, are run by: Mazda Tours, 141 Ibn Gvirol (☎03/544 4454, fax 546 1928; morning departures daily except Sat, evening departures 3 times weekly); Nizza Tours opposite the Egyptian embassy (75 HaYarkon; ☎03/510 2832, fax 510 2842), leaving from Ibn Gvirol with Basel; and by Galilee Tours, 42 Ben Yehuda (☎03/525 2888, fax 525 1239). The current fare is around $35 one-way, excluding border tax. Visas must be obtained in advance as they are not available at the border.

BY SHERUT
Sheruts from the Central Bus Station leave from opposite platforms 410–414 and serve Jerusalem, Haifa, Ramle, Lydda, Rehovot, Ashdod, Ashqelon, Qiryat Gat, Beersheba,

Cultural centres The British Council, 140 HaYarkon, has a public library with British newspapers (Mon–Thurs 10am–1pm & 4–7pm, Fri 10am–1pm only). The American Cultural Centre is on the 5th floor at 1 Ben Yehuda (☎03/510 6935).

Embassies and consulates Australia, 37 Shaul HaMelekh (☎03/695 0451); Canada, 220 HaYarkon (☎03/527 2929); Cyprus, Top Tower, 50 Dizengoff (☎03/691 8282 or 3); Egypt, 54 Basel (☎03/546 4151); Sun–Thurs 9–11am; visas cost $20 plus two passport photos and can be collected same day noon–2pm); Greece, 35 Shaul HaMelekh (☎03/695 9704); Ireland, 10 Miriam, Herzliya (☎09/950 9055); Jordan, 10th floor, 14 Abba Hillel, Ramat Gan (☎03/751 7722; Sun–Thurs 9am–1pm; visas cost around 80NIS plus two passport photos and take around 10 days to issue; also available at the Arava and Sheikh Hussein border crossings, but not at Allenby Bridge); Netherlands, 4 Weizmann (☎03/695 7377); New Zealand c/o UK; Turkey, 34 Amos (☎03/605 4155); UK (consular section), 6th floor, 1 Ben Yehuda (☎03/510 0166); USA, 71 HaYarkon (☎03/519 7575).

Emergencies Police ☎100; ambulance (Magen David Adom, equivalent of Red Cross) ☎101 or ☎03/546 0111; Fire ☎102 or ☎03/699 4111. Private ambulance ☎177/022 4224 or 1818 (toll-free). Rape crisis line on ☎03/685 0041 for confidential help and counselling round the clock. See also "Medical services", below.

Netanya, Hadera, Afula and Nazareth. They take less time than buses, and currently cost a little less. Some routes also have the considerable advantage of operating at night (though they can take all night to fill up) and on Shabbat.

BY TRAIN

Trains leave from the Central Train Station (bus #10 from Ben Yehuda or Jaffa, or bus #18 from Allenby). HaShalom Station further south is generally less convenient as there are no bus connections from the town. **Destinations** include: Acre (14 daily; 1hr 45min–2hr); Ashdod (2 daily; 1hr 40min); Bet Shemesh (1 daily; 1hr); Hadera (1–2 hourly; 35min); Haifa (1–2 hourly 6am to 10pm; 1hr–1hr 40min); Herzliya (1–2 hourly; 10min); Jerusalem, (1 daily; 1hr 52min); Lydda (12 daily; 25min); Nahariyya (7 daily; 2hr–2hr 20min); Netanya (1–2 hourly; 25min); Ramle (1 daily; 30min); Rehovot (11 daily; 30min). There is also a new experimental service to Beersheba (2 weekly, Sunday am & Thurs pm; 2hr). There are no trains Friday evenings or daytime Saturdays. For rail enquiries call ☎03/693 7515.

BY AIR

International: For Ben Gurion Airport, take Egged bus #475 from the Central Bus Station (daily except Fri evening & Sat; every 10–30min from 5.30am until 11pm), or United Tours bus #222 from the *Dan Panorama* hotel (Sun–Thurs hourly 4am–midnight, Fri until 8pm, Sat from 1pm; 45min), which calls at various places up the seafront en route. There is no regular shared taxi from Tel Aviv to the airport, but a private taxi should take you for around $25–30. For departure information call ☎03/973 1122.

Domestic: Tel Aviv's own Sede Dov Airport can be reached by bus #26 from the old bus station on HaShomron. There are 17–18 flights most days to Eilat (1hr), 6–7 daily to Rosh Pinna (25min), 5 daily to Qiryat Shemona (35min) and 3 weekly to Neve Zohar, or sometimes Masada, by the Dead Sea (30min).

HITCHING

For routes **north** and **east** there are specific hitching points known as *trempim*, both of which are next to railway stations. For Haifa and points north, head for Arlozorov Interchange by the Central Train Station; for Jerusalem, go to the Shalom Interchange next to HaShalom Station. For routes **south** there are no specific hitching points; try Derekh Yigal Allon east of Jaffa, or Derekh Kheil HaShiryon near the Kibbutz Galuyot interchange.

Gay information Aguda runs a community centre in the basement of 28 Nahmani, on the corner of Ahad Ha'Am (Sun–Thurs 9am–5pm; ☎03/629 3681). For gay bars and clubs, see pp.95 & 96.

Kibbutz and Moshav Volunteer Offices The official ones, which are the best ones to use, are the Kibbutz Program Centre at 18 Frishman (☎03/527 8874, fax 523 9966) for kibbutzim, and the Moshav Volunteers Office in the basement at 19 Leonardo da Vinci (☎03/695 8473, fax 695 6437) for moshavim. Private offices are operated by Project 67 at 94 Ben Yehuda (☎03/523 0140/5) and Meira at 73 Ben Yehuda (☎03/523 7369, fax 524 1604). For further details see p.61.

Laundry The best-value laundromat (4NIS for 13kg) is at 15 Bograshov, but others (usually 8NIS for 7kg) can be found all over town, with a fair few on Ben Yehuda.

Left luggage On the sixth floor of the Central Bus Station (Sun–Thurs 7am–7pm, Fri 7am–3pm). 8NIS per item per day.

Medical services Emergency medical help call toll-free ☎177/022 9110; emergency doctor toll-free ☎177/022 5005; Magen David Adom (equivalent of Red Cross) ☎101 or ☎03/546 0111; emergency dental treatment at the Israel Dental Association, 49 Bar Kokhba (☎03/528 0507) or 24hr at the Medical Centre, Suite 305, 18 Reines (☎03/528 5584). Pharmacies can be found on Allenby, Ben Yehuda and Dizengoff; Mohenson's, 83 Ben Yehuda, sells homeopathic remedies. The night-time and Shabbat service rota is posted outside each pharmacy, but in Hebrew only.

Newspapers The best ranges of British and American newspapers and magazines are sold either at Steimatzky (103 Allenby) or at newsstands on Allenby and Dizengoff.

Police Police station at 221A Dizengoff, 14 HaRakevet, and in Jaffa at 20 Raziel (☎100 or ☎03/546 1133 for local stations).

Post office The GPO at 7 Mikve Yisra'el (Sun–Thurs 8am–6pm, Fri 8am–2pm) is the place to pick up poste restante mail; they also keep faxes (☎03/564 3645; 4NIS) and will even call you if your name and phone number are displayed at the top. This branch and the one at 132 Allenby (Sun–Thurs 7am–9pm, Fri 7am–2pm) accept Western Union cash transfers, and both, theoretically, change foreign currency and travellers' cheques. Jaffa's post office is in Sederot Yerushalayim at the corner of Rehov HaDoar.

Taxis Bograshov, 1 Bograshov (☎03/522 0220); Balfour, 59 Balfour (☎03/560 4545); Gordon, 22 Gordon (☎03/527 2999); HaBima, 4 Tarsat (☎03/528 3131 or 2); HaShekhem, 69 Gordon (☎03/527 0404); Nordau, 16 Nordau (☎03/546 6222); Shenkin, 66 Shenkin (☎03/560 7444).

Telecommunications Various places around the new and old bus stations (such as Discountel at 74 Levinsky) offer discount rates for international phone calls. Solan at 13 Frishman is open around the clock to make calls or buy phonecards. You can send and receive faxes at the post office at 7 Mikve Yisra'el (☎03/564 3645) as well as Solan (☎03/522 9449) and Discountel (☎03/639 7158). Solan is open round the clock, but Discountel and similar firms nearby have better prices. Make sure your name and if possible phone number are displayed clearly at the top of any faxes sent for you to these places. Email and Internet access is available at *C.c@fé*, 85 Ben Yehuda (*ccafel@netvision.net.il*) or Internet InBar, 2 Schlomo HaMelekh (*barak@isralink.co.il/inbar 999*).

Thomas Cook c/o Bank HaPoalim, 50 Rothschild, or call toll-free on ☎177/440 8424.

Travel agents ISSTA, 128 Ben Yehuda (☎03/641 5941), is the best for cheap flights and youth or student fares. Other agents, especially in Ben Yehuda, sometimes have one-offs or last-minute one-way tickets, especially to London; try Mona Tours, 45 Ben Yehuda (☎03/523 7103), the Travel Centre, 69 Ben Yehuda (☎03/527 5514), or Golan, 124 Ben Yehuda (☎03/527 3113). Gordon and some of the other hostels do cheap air tickets too. For boat tickets out of Haifa, go to Caspi, 1 Ben Yehuda (☎03/517 5749, fax 516 0989), or Mano, at 97 Ben Yehuda (☎03/522 4611). The leading operators for tours in Israel are Egged Tours, at 15 Frishman (☎03/527 1222 or 5, fax 527 2020), 59 Ben Yehuda (☎03/527 1212 or 5, fax 527 1229), Kikar Namir (☎03/527 1818, fax 527 1812), and in the Central Bus Station; and United Tours, 113 HaYarkon (☎03/693 3412, fax 522 1270).

Visa renewal Shalom Tower, East Wing, 14th floor (Sun–Thurs); numbers in the queue given out from 7am, the last at around 10am, so arrive early. The price is currently 100NIS plus one passport photo; you must be staying in Tel Aviv or Jaffa to extend your visa here.

Work Finding work in Tel Aviv is rarely a problem. Bar work, hotels and construction are your most likely bets, though in the summer it's even occasionally possible to find work as a film extra. Hostels such as *Momo's* and *The Office* are often approached by local employers for temporary workers so it's worth asking around there and directly in bars, restaurants and on building sites. Au pair agencies can be contacted at ☎03/965 9937 and ☎03/634 0604.

East of Tel Aviv: Ramat Gan, Petah Tiqva and Rosh Ha'Ayin

The suburbs and satellite towns to the **east of Tel Aviv** are, for the most part, an unending procession of bland apartment buildings, saved from obscurity by a few worthwhile sights: the museums and parks in and around **Ramat Gan**; the old-fashioned orthodox quarter of **Bene Beraq**; and a scattering of historic sites near the towns of **Petah Tiqva** and **Rosh Ha'Ayin**. Dan city buses to Ramat Gan and Petah Tiqva leave every 10 to 15 minutes from the first floor of the Central Bus Station.

Ramat Gan

Sprawling northeast of Tel Aviv, the genteel suburb of **RAMAT GAN** ("Garden Heights") is home to Bar Ilan University and a small clutch of sights varied enough to justify a visit, especially if you have a keen interest in art. Here you'll find the **Museum of Israeli Art**, 146 Abba Hillel (Sun, Mon & Wed 8am–5pm, Tues & Thurs 8am–8pm, Fri 8am–2pm, Sat 10am–4pm; 10NIS), displaying modern works by Israeli artists; the **Museum of Jewish Art**, Bet Yad Lebanim in Rehov Ma'ale HaBanim (Sun–Thurs 10am–1pm & 6–7pm, Sat 10am–1pm only), with pieces by Jewish artists from Eastern Europe; and the **Russian and Far Eastern Art Museum**, 18 Hibbat Zion (Sat–Thurs 10am–1pm & 4–7pm; 5NIS), housing a collection (mainly from China and Japan) of paintings, prints, sculpture, ceramics and furniture. In addition, the **Harry Oppenheimer Diamond Museum** at 1 Jabotinsky (Sun–Thurs 10am–4pm, Fri 10am–noon; 10NIS) offers guided tours of what is basically a diamond-cutting factory.

Ramat Gan lies between two parks. **Park HaLe'umi**, to the southeast, contains a one-hundred-hectare **Safari Park** (Sun–Thurs 9am–2.30pm, Fri 9am–1pm, Sat 9am–3pm; 27NIS), which counts several African species among its inmates; while the **National Stadium**, also in the park, is the venue for most of the country's major sporting events including the Maccabiades, a mini Olympic Games for Jewish athletes from around the world. The peaceful and pleasant **HaYarkon Park**, to the north, hosts regular open-air concerts in summer (details from the IGTO or *Jerusalem Post*) and has a small lake. An extension to this park stretches westward along the Yarkon River, reaching the northern end of Rehov Ibn Gvirol.

Bene Beraq, Petah Tiqva and the site of Aphek

BENE BERAQ, Tel Aviv's ultra-orthodox quarter, lies northeast of Ramat Gan. Something of an architectural oasis among the urban sprawl, its beautiful East European-style houses are grouped around cobbled squares, while its culture and pace of life seem centuries removed from the rest of Tel Aviv. If you decide to visit, dress modestly and note that the quarter is closed to traffic on the Sabbath. Beyond Bene Beraq, the urban sprawl extends almost continuously to **PETAH TIQVA**, one of the first agricultural settlements to be established in Palestine by Jews from Europe and now a major town. Set up and abandoned in 1878 after being ravaged by malaria and boycotted by the orthodox (who were hostile to the settlers' secularism), it was revived in 1882 by the Russian Jewish emigration society Bilu (see p.490). Its history as a focus of the Yishuv and home to several of its leaders is explored in its only real attraction, the **Yad Lebanim Museum**, 30 Arlozorov (Tues, Thurs & Sun 4.30–7.30pm, Sat 10am–1pm & 4–7pm; free), which also houses art exhibitions.

Two kilometres northeast of Petah Tiqva, on a hill to the north of Route 483, the impressive ruin of a sixteenth-century Ottoman fortress stands on the site of excavations of the biblical city of **Aphek**, later renamed Antipatris by Herod in memory of his

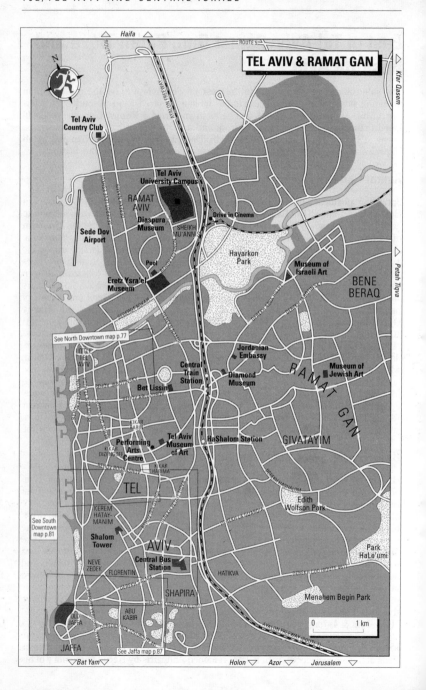

TEL AVIV & RAMAT GAN

Haifa

ROUTE 2

AYALON FREEWAY

ROUTE 5

Kfar Qasem

Petah Tiqva

Tel Aviv
Country Club

Tel Aviv
University Campus

RAMAT
AVIV

Drive in Cinema

Diaspura
Museum

SHEIKH
MU'ANNIS

Sede Dov
Airport

Hayarkon
Park

Pool

Museum of
Israeli Art

BENE
BERAQ

Eretz Ysra'el
Museum

See North Downtown map p.77

TEL
AVIV

Jordanian
Embassy

RAMAT
GAN

Central
Train
Station

Museum of
Jewish Art

Bet Lissin

Diamond
Museum

KIKAR
RABIN

Tel Aviv
Museum
of Art

HaShalom Station

GIVATAYIM

KIKAR
DIZENGOFF

Performing
Arts
Centre

KIKAR
HABIMA

TEL

See South
Downtown
map p.81

KEREM
HATAY-
MANIM

Edith
Wolfson Park

Shalom
Tower

AVIV

Park
HaLe'umi

NEVE
ZEDEK

Central Bus
Station

FLORENTIN

HATIKVA

SHAPIRA

Menahem Begin Park

ABU
KABIR

OLD
JAFFA

0   1 km

JAFFA

See Jaffa map p.87

Bat Yam

Holon   Azor   Jerusalem

father. The entrance to the site is by an unsignposted turn-off half a kilometre west of the junction with Route 444. In its northwestern part, remains of a Bronze Age city wall have been exposed, as well as elements of Canaanite, Herodian and Byzantine settlement, while a piece of a Roman street and house are visible to the south. The site is owned by the National Parks Authority but as it's currently unmanned it can be visited at any time; to get there from Petah Tiqva take Dan bus #7, #17, #27 or #83.

Sites around Rosh Ha'Ayin

Four kilometres east of Petah Tiqva, the town of **ROSH HA'AYIN** is nondescript in itself but its immediate environs contain a few sites of historical significance. On the southeastern edge of town, the ruin of a white Ottoman building, **Migdal Zedek**, marks the site of a fortress used by the Jewish rebels against the Romans during the Jewish War of 66–70 AD. It was built on Byzantine and Crusader remains, of which a Byzantine doorway topped by a Greek inscription still survives. The building is closed to the public at present, but the hilltop offers a good view of the area. The way up, marked by a small 1948 war memorial, is just to the north of Route 444 off the Rosh Ha'Ayin east turn-off (Rehov Yehuda HaLevi). Dan bus #93 from Petah Tiqva stops nearby.

All that remains of the pre-1948 Palestinian village of Mzera'a, 4km to the south, is the **Mosque of Nabi Yahya** (John the Baptist), by the east side of Route 444 at a turn-off for Karei Tzo'n. A small square structure, it is in fact a second-century Roman mausoleum, with a small mihrab added in a corner of the room that once held the sarcophagus.

Four kilometres northeast of Rosh Ha'Ayin, by the border of the West Bank, the village of **KAFR QASEM** is known among Palestinians for the events of October 29, 1956, just prior to Israel's invasion of Sinai in the Suez crisis. Along with other villages by the border, it was put under curfew, but the mayor was told of this only half an hour before it came into effect. Villagers coming home from work knew nothing of the curfew, and 47 were shot dead by troops on their way home that evening. Eleven soldiers were eventually tried for the massacre; the brigadier who ordered the killings was reprimanded and two of his officers were jailed, though they were released within the year.

South of Tel Aviv

You'll find little in the suburbs **south of Tel Aviv** to prevent you from pressing on further down the coast or inland, except maybe the beaches of **Bat Yam** – a less crowded alternative to those in the city itself. The coastal road (Route 4) is a fast if dull route south to the Gaza Strip with few attractions between Tel Aviv and Ashdod (see p.112) bar a surfing scene and small archeological museum at **PALMAHIM** (☎03/968 1281; open by appointment only), and the ruins of the ancient port of Jabneh, now **Yavne-Yam**, just to the south, where the Sorek River meanders into the sea. Its beach is used mostly by locals and is generally quiet; camping out here seems to be tolerated, though better in the safety of a group.

Inland, a number of larger towns are worth a visit in their own right, notably the wine-producing centre of **Rishon Le Zion**, and the two historic and formerly entirely Palestinian cities of **Lydda** (Lod) and **Ramle**, though the lack of accommodation in all three makes them accessible only on day trips (all can be reached by bus from Tel Aviv, see box on p.98). There's also the ancient Canaanite site of **Tel Gezer** and Israel's largest kibbutz, **Givat Bremner**, near the suburban enclave of **Rehovot**.

Bat Yam, Holon and Azor

South of Jaffa, the suburb of **BAT YAM** (Daughter of the Sea) tries to portray itself as a new and exciting beach resort but is really no more than an extension of Tel Aviv's beaches. All the hotels are on Sederot Ben Gurion, as is the **tourist office**, 43 Ben Gurion (☎03/507 2777). Neighbouring **HOLON**'s one claim to fame is that it is home to the only sizeable **Samaritan** population outside Nablus (see p.440), totalling around fifty families.

Next door, **AZOR** is built over the Arab village of Yazur, whose inhabitants fled in 1948. Scant remains of a **Crusader fort** called the Casal des Plaines, built for Richard the Lionheart, still survive in the old village, where there's a multi-domed seventeenth-century mosque and a tomb from the fourth millennium BC.

Rishon Le Zion

Although on Tel Aviv's doorstep (only 8km south), the town of **RISHON LE ZION** has retained some individuality because of its central role in Israeli wine production. Rishon Le Zion ("First in Zion") was founded in 1882 by ten pioneers from a Russian Jewish emigration society called Bilu, seeking self-sufficiency and a new life in the promised land. Being rather more idealistic than practical – they had no farming experience and little capital – their attempt soon failed, and in desperation they turned to the French philanthropist **Baron Edmond de Rothschild**, sponsor of several agricultural settlements around the world. He hit upon the idea that they should produce wine like the northern settlement of Zikhron Ya'acov (see p.166), and sent vines, experts and cash to build cellars, leading to the inauguration of the Société Cooperative Vigneronne des Grandes Caves, later known as **Carmel**. The cooperative now has over eight hundred members who supply 85 percent of Israel's wine grape crop.

The Town

Rishon Le Zion preserves its heritage from those early days of pioneer Zionism while managing to avoid the blandness of Zikhron Ya'acov. Its older parts have a lived-in feel and sport a sunny slap of Mediterranean whitewash. The town centre lies at the junction of Herzl and Sederot Rothschild – the main thoroughfare, pedestrianized uphill from here, with a pleasant selection of cafés and falafel joints. You'll also find most of Rishon's historical buildings on Rothschild. The **town hall**, at no. 24, dates from 1888, and it was the collapse of the **old well** at no. 19 (admission with museum ticket, see below) that precipitated the villagers' appeal to Rothschild for funds. **Ya'acov Kanner**, a local farmer-made-good lived at no. 7 (his Hebrew initials decorate the front wall), and gave his home over to public use: a first-aid post for Magen David Adom (the Jewish version of the Red Cross) and then a base for the Haganah in the days before independence. At no. 1, the old post office is now the town's **museum** (Sun & Tues–Thurs 9am–2pm, Mon & Fri 9am–1pm, Mon 4–8pm; 8NIS; also open first Sat of each month 10am–2pm; free), with a well-presented history of Rishon, featuring several reconstructions of pioneer life – among them a mocked-up settlers' house. At the head of Rehov Herzl, on Rehov Ahad Ha'Am, the **old synagogue** was constructed on a permit obtained from the Ottoman authorities under false pretences (and with a little baksheesh) to build a warehouse for local farmers.

MOVING ON FROM RISHON LE ZION

From the bus station, there are Egged services to Tel Aviv (at least 5 per hour; 30min or more depending on traffic), Jerusalem (1–2 per hour; 1hr 10min), Lydda (1–2 per hour; 1hr) via Ramle (40min), and Rehovot (hourly; 20min). Dan buses also serve Rishon, with #83 and #85 running from the bus station to Tel Aviv's Central Bus Station, #19 from Herzl with Rothschild to Allenby, Rothschild and Derekh Yafo in Tel Aviv, and #174 from the bus station along Rehov Ha'am to Tel Aviv's Sederot Ben Gurion.

The original **winery**, on the corner of Herzl and HaCarmel, just across the park from Rothschild (Sun–Thurs usually at 9am, 11am, 1pm & 3pm; 12NIS; ☎03/967 3404), is still working and offers tours with the usual "tasting" and souvenir bottle (call ahead for a tour in English). In the Forties, the winery was put to different purposes by the Haganah as a place to stash arms. Across the street, in what was originally a house for the firm's management, and later the staff canteen, you can buy the wine, though you won't get a better deal here than anywhere else.

Practicalities

The **bus** station is on Rehov Herzl, a couple of blocks north of Rothschild. For **food**, *The Well*, by the old well at 19 Rothschild (daily 9am–midnight; expensive; ☎03/966 8103), is a good choice, or you could go for a selection of *shawarmas* at *Mifgash Shaul*, 62 Herzl, near the bus station.

Lydda (Lod) and around

To the visitor, the town of **LYDDA** (**Lod** in Hebrew, and often left untranslated in English), twenty kilometres southeast of Tel Aviv, is best known as the location of Ben Gurion Airport. However, beyond the characterless *shikunim* of the new town, its old city, despite being sadly neglected, contains traces of its long history, not least the church containing the tomb of St George; the town so charmed Richard the Lionheart that he was inspired to adopt the saint as England's patron.

Lydda's **history**, according to the Bible (I Chronicles 8: 12), begins with its founder Shamed, son of Elpaal from the tribe of Benjamin, and, like Jaffa and Ashqelon, the city also appears in records of the eighteenth-dynasty pharaoh Thutmose III. After the destruction of the Second Temple it became the seat of a small sanhedrin (Jewish legal and administrative body) and a prominent religious seminary. After it was turned into a district administrative centre and junction for the Middle Eastern railway network under the British, its economic importance provided fertile conditions for the development of radical political movements and the growth of an active **trade unionism**

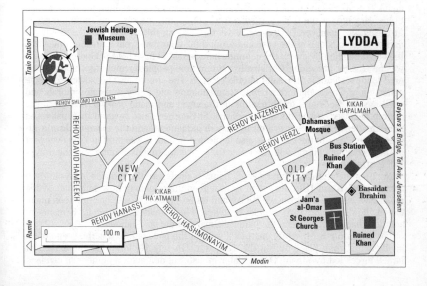

among its workers. A campaign against the discriminatory wage policy applied by the British during a public works programme, in which Jews in the workforce were paid higher rates than Arabs, gave the Arab trade unionists experience that they later put to good use in the revolt of 1936–39. The British army's brutal repression of the revolt did little to pacify the population and when Jewish strikebreakers were brought in to keep the trains running, tensions reached an all-time high. Little love was lost between the Jews and their Arab neighbours – the city's original Jewish community having been driven out by ethnic rioting in 1921.

Nevertheless, Lydda continued to grow and was one of the most prosperous Arab towns in the country until most of its Arab population was driven out in the 1948 war, following events at the Dahamash Mosque (see below). Today its population is one of the most cosmopolitan in Israel; over twenty percent of the town's residents are Palestinian, among them Bedouins driven here by the poverty of their reservations in the Negev, while its Jewish residents are of Middle Eastern, Georgian and Indian origin.

The best day to visit is on Tuesday when there's a **market** in the old city; otherwise, it's on **St George's Day** (April 23) that Lydda really comes alive, with a procession through the town and a Mass at the church attended by Palestinian Christians from all over the country. The saint's burial date (Nov 15) is also a local festival.

The Town

An important Crusader centre, Lydda was embellished with many churches and other new buildings during their period of control, though it also retains traces from its Byzantine and Arab periods. A couple of hundred metres south of the bus station, the **Church of St George**, whose spire can be seen from the centre of the new town, boasts an impressive mixture of all three: Byzantine apses, Crusader arches and Islamic columns. The first church on this site was built around the sixth century to house the tomb of St George (identified in Islam with a spirit known as al-Kader, see box on p.468), who, legend has it, was born in Lydda, and whose remains were brought here following his martyrdom. Destroyed when the Crusaders conquered the town, the church was rebuilt in the second half of the twelfth century, and later ruined again; the Greek Orthodox church that stands here today was built just over a hundred years ago for the large Christian Arab community. As you enter, note the sculpture over the doorway, portraying St George slaying the Dragon. To the right, the darker areas of stone in the apse and around the altar date from Crusader times and the chain hanging by one of the columns here is said to have held St George when he was on trial for preaching Christianity; at one time people deemed insane were tethered to it overnight for the saint to effect a cure. The church also boasts an extensive collection of Greek Orthodox icons, candleholders and richly decorated murals and paintings. **St George's tomb** itself is in the crypt and made of white marble. If the church is closed, ask at the door opposite. St George is also revered by Muslims as the defender of good over evil on the day of judgement, and the mosque, **Jamia al-Omar**, next door to the chuch, is also dedicated to him. It was built in 1268 over part of the Byzantine church; you can enter the courtyard to look around, but the prayer hall is off limits.

North of the church, behind a small housing estate, are the remains of an old Arab caravanserai, **Khan Hilu**. Its extent gives a good impression of how important Lydda must have been as a pilgrimage centre and trading post. The site has not been maintained, however, and care should be taken when walking around it. Remains of another khan stand between the Jamia al-Omar and the bus station.

The **Dahamash Mosque**, one block west of the bus station, was the scene of an incident that took place during the 1948 war. On July 10, following the arrival of Israeli forces led by Moshe Dayan (later minister of defence), a number of civilians

MOVING ON FROM LYDDA

There are **buses** to Tel Aviv (roughly every 15 mins; 45min), Ramle (roughly every 30min; 15min) and Rehovot (2–4 per hour; 45min). For Jerusalem change at Ramle. **Sheruts** for Tel Aviv leave very nearby, in front of the Dahamash Mosque. The **train** station, west of town, is rather less handy, but has departures for Rehovot (10 daily; 10min), Tel Aviv (10 daily; 25min), Netanya (8 daily; 50min), Haifa (3 daily; 1hr 45min), Acre (1 daily; 2hr 20min), Nahariyya (1 daily; 2hr 35min), Jerusalem (1 daily; 1hr 30min) and Ashdod (2 daily; 35min).

took shelter in the mosque. What happened there two days later is disputed, but it seems that a Jordanian patrol entered the city, found itself trapped by Israeli forces, and fired its way out causing many casualties. An Israeli soldier, angered by this and the active support for the Jordanians from the townspeople including, according to Israeli sources, some of those within the mosque, fired a mortar into the building, killing around a hundred people. Of Lydda's Arab population only vital workers on the railway were allowed to remain; among the refugees was a 21-year-old medical student, **George Habash**, who went on to co-found the Arab National Movement in 1952, the merger of which in 1967 with the Palestine Liberation Front formed the PFLP, which he still leads today. The mosque re-opened on July 12, 1996, exactly 48 years after the tragedy.

Two kilometres north of the old city, on the road connecting it to Route 40, just past a Sonol petrol station and visible from the main road, an old **stone bridge** over a small river bears an Arabic inscription commemorating Sultan Baybars, who had it built in 1278. On either side of the inscription is a leopard crushing a rat: the leopard represents Baybars' Arab army, and the rat, the Crusaders. It was Baybars whose campaigns finally put an end to European Christian plans for Palestine.

The only sight as such in the new city is the **Museum of Jewish Heritage**, 20 David HaMelekh (Sun–Thurs 9am–4pm; 10NIS; ☎08/924 9569), worth a visit if you're in the vicinity. Mostly concentrating on Jewish life in North Africa, its labels are in Hebrew only, although English speakers may be able to arrange a guided tour if they call ahead.

Practicalities

The **bus** station is in the old town, close to most of the sights. Lydda makes little attempt to cater for visitors but for **food**, *Basaidat Ibrahim* (sign in Hebrew only, though Arab-run; daily 9am–1pm; cheap), opposite the mosque, is a pleasant café popular with local residents and which also serves kebabs. For more upmarket dining, try the *Abu Michel* at 29 Tzahal (Mon–Sat 9am–10pm, Sat 9am–8.30pm; expensive), offering a variety of Middle Eastern dishes.

The Tombs of the Maccabees

Six kilometres west of Lydda, just south of Route 443 on the site of the ancient town of Modin and above the settlement of Mevo Modi'im, eighteen rock-cut tombs are purported to be the **Tombs of the Maccabees**. The Maccabees, heroes of two books in the biblical Apocrypha, were the five sons of Modin's priest, Mattathias. When the Seleucid king Antiochus IV Epiphanes (175–163 BC), claiming to be an incarnation of Zeus, insisted on worship of the god throughout his empire, Mattathias refused to comply. He murdered the first Jew who sacrificed at the town altar to Zeus, as well as the king's local commissioner, and pulled down the altar. He and his sons then took to the hills and began a guerrilla war against the Seleucid empire, with startling success. On

Mattathias's death in 166 BC, leadership went to his son Judas, nicknamed "Maccabeus" (the Hammer) – a name taken up by the whole family – and Jerusalem fell to them two years later. Judas died in battle in 160 BC, and was succeeded by his brother Jonathan. On Jonathan's death in 143 BC the leadership fell to brother Simon, who had both of them buried with their father and two other brothers at Modin, and was eventually laid to rest there himself. Whether these tombs are really theirs, however, is far from certain. The site is undeveloped and not accessible by public transport.

Ramle

RAMLE, a friendly town just a few kilometres southwest of Lydda, has an equally rich history but rather more to show for it. One of Israel's best-kept secrets, the town has all sorts of unexpected treats, from Indian sweet shops to the chance to visit an eighth-century underground water cistern by boat. Unlike in so many other towns in Israel, its old centre has escaped dereliction or sanitization and remains a lively, working place with one of the best souqs in the country. Unfortunately, there's no accommodation but you can easily pop over for the day from Tel Aviv or Jerusalem, or stay at Kibbutz Gezer (see p.110), 7km away.

The town's **history** is relatively short by Palestinian standards: founded in 716 AD by Caliph Abd al-Malik, it claims to be the only town to have been born in Palestine under Arab rule. Deliberately promoted as a new regional capital, Ramle grew rapidly in the early years and visitors in the ninth century remarked on its size and beauty and the importance of its markets and mosques. The dyeing industry was organized early on to ensure its prosperity continued to flourish and its products were sold to many of the finest cloth and carpet manufacturers in the Arab world.

Earthquakes in 1033 and 1067 destroyed many of Ramle's finer buildings, and it suffered further damage by a fire in 1177 and in a battle ten years later between Saladin and the Crusaders. In 1191, when **Richard the Lionheart** briefly held the city, its fortifications were destroyed by the retreating Arab forces. Retaken by the Muslims under **Sultan Baybars**, Ramle again flourished, and in the Middle Ages it became an important commercial centre on the road from Jaffa to Jerusalem.

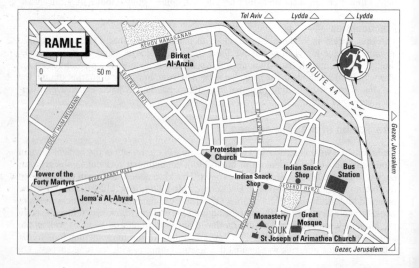

Apart from a brief stay by Napoleon in the eighteenth century, Ramle spent the succeeding centuries in the relative peace of gradual decline, halted only in 1948, when many of its Palestinian residents fled before the Israelis' **Operation Dani**. Their houses were given to Jewish immigrants, mostly from Yemen, North Africa and Iraq. Today Ramle is one of the most integrated towns in Israel, with about 10,000 Arabs and 52,000 Jews; both communities are pretty mixed – in the case of Palestinians between Christians and Muslims, and, in the case of the Jews, between Russians, Yemenis, Indians and Ethiopians, among others.

The Town

Ramle's town centre still boasts much of its pre-1948 architecture, almost all of which lies on or off its main street, **Sederot Herzl**. Grandest of the town's buildings is the **Great Mosque** (al-Jama'a al-Kabir), almost opposite the Central Bus Station. Originally built by the Crusaders in 1150 as St John's Cathedral, its basic structure is a fine example of early Christian architecture. It was converted into a mosque following the Muslim recapture of the city, and its walls are adorned with superb Arabic calligraphy. Its minaret is among the most beautiful in the country.

The mosque stands on the edge of a large, rambling **souq**, the busiest part of town and the best place to go for a café snack or meal. This is also one of the most enjoyable markets in Israel, its life and atmosphere uncorrupted by twee restoration or crude tourist traps. On the far side of the souq, beneath a tall white tower, is the Franciscan **Church of St Joseph of Arimathea** (Mon–Fri 9–11.30am; the monks ask for silence and "modest dress" during your visit). Christian tradition associates Ramle with biblical Rama (Arimathea in its Hellenized form), and the church commemorates one of Christ's earliest disciples, the owner of the tomb in which Jesus was laid after the crucifixion. The first church on the site was built in 1296 but the current structure, as its architecture suggests, dates from the beginning of this century. The adjacent **monastery** was built in 1750 but has been deserted since 1948; there's not much to see, but a wander through the narrow passageways and up spiralling stairs is an experience in itself, and you can visit the room where **Napoleon Bonaparte** stayed on his way to conquer Jaffa in 1799, although this too is nothing special, a dusty white chamber with an old bed and a few pictures of Napoleon.

A few hundred metres west of the monastery, at the end of Rehov Danny Mass, the **Tower of the Forty Martyrs** (Sun–Thurs 8am–3pm, Fri 8am–noon, Sat 8am–4pm; 5NIS) is named after the companions of the Prophet Mohammed, who, according to Islamic tradition, are buried on the site. Built in 1328, the six-storey, thirty-metre-high tower is a beautiful example of fourteenth-century Arab architecture, with an unusual square shape. Napoleon is said to have directed the siege of Jaffa from the top, which gives you an idea of the views you'll get if you're willing to make the climb. The tower originally served as a minaret for **al-Jama'a al-Abyad** (the White Mosque), believed to date from the eighth century. The mosque covered a massive 10,000 square metres in it heyday, but was destroyed by an earthquake in 1546; the remains can be seen here and there.

A turn to the east off Herzl on to Rehov HaHaganah brings you to a park, opposite which is the **Birket al-Anzia**, also known as the Pool of St Helena (Sun–Thurs 8am–3pm, Fri 8am–noon, Sat 8am–4pm; 5NIS), an underground cistern built in the eighth century under Caliph Haroun al-Rashid of *Arabian Nights* fame, and one of three such Abassid constructions in Ramle (another is under the White Mosque, and a third underneath what is now a synagogue). It is thought that the original water was brought in by aqueduct. Boats are available inside and you can row around the eerie vaults, whose stone arches are in fact the earliest pointed ones in Islamic architecture. The style was later adopted by the Crusaders to become a classic feature of European Gothic.

MATSLIAH AND THE KARA'ITES

On the surface, the settlement of **Matsliah**, 2km south of Ramle, off Route 40, seems no different from any Israeli moshav. However, its inhabitants belong to a sect, the **Kara'ites**, who once caused a major schism in the Jewish religion and threatened to split the faith asunder.

Founded in mid-eighth-century Babylon by **Anan ben David**, the sect revived the ideas of the Roman Sadducean party, rejecting the Talmud and Rabbinical teachings in favour of a literal interpretation of the Torah. They were, in effect, rather like Jewish Protestants. The movement spread through the Jewish communities of Mesopotamia and Palestine, reaching as far as Spain, and for a time seemed likely to divide or even take over Judaism altogether. However, internal divisions weakened it fatally and decline soon set in.

Today, the Kara'ites are a tiny sect of around 7000 people in Israel, most of whom moved here from Arab countries following Israeli independence. Matsliah, founded by immigrants from Egypt in 1950, is the largest community, with others in Ashdod and in Ofaqim and Ranen near Beersheba.

Practicalities

You can get falafel, *shawarmas* and other street **food** in the souq or along the same stretch of Herzl, which also features a couple of Indian places, notably the *Maharaja*, opposite Rehov Nordau (Sun, Mon, Wed & Thurs 8.30am–8.30pm, Tues & Fri 8.30am–4pm; cheap), where you can sit in for *puris, masala dosa* or a *lassi*.

Services from Ramle's **bus station**, on Sederot Herzl near the Great Mosque, run to Tel Aviv (every 15min; 1hr), Jerusalem (every 20–30min; 1hr 30min) and nearby towns at similar intervals. **Sheruts** leave a little further up Sederot Herzl towards Rehov Nordau, and serve Tel Aviv, Lydda and Petah Tiqva.

Tel Gezer

Tel Gezer, 7km east of Ramle along Route 424 (the Latrun road), is the site of an ancient Canaanite city – letters on clay tablets from its kings to Egypt's heretical eighteenth-dynasty pharaoh Akhenaton are among the **Amarna Letters** (see p.482). Gezer managed to retain its independence from the Israelites until it was attacked and destroyed by an Egyptian pharaoh, usually identified as Siamun of the 21st dynasty, but thought by David Rohl (see p.424) to have been Horemheb, who ruled not long after Akhenaton. He gave it as a dowry to his daughter on her marriage to King Solomon, who rebuilt and fortified it (I Kings 9: 15–17); a Solomonic inscription known as the Gezer Calendar was found here in 1908, one of very few known examples of Classical Hebrew outside the Old Testament. It is now in the Museum of the Ancient Orient in Istanbul; other finds are on display in Skirball Museum in Jerusalem (see p.368).

The site itself isn't particularly well maintained and there's not a great deal left to see except a row of monoliths, a massive ancient wall and a well, but the view over the coastal plains from the top is impressive. To get there, follow the track up from Kibbutz Gezer (see below), keeping the tel to your left, past a copse of trees at the end of which is a concrete water tank. Turn left here and onto the path that runs across the top. Should you want to stay in the area, **accommodation** is available at **Kibbutz Gezer** (☎08/927 0646; ④), which prides itself in keeping up the original ideals of the kibbutz movement (see p.62). Although the largely English-speaking residents now supplement their income with a glue factory and tourism, agriculture is still the kibbutzniks' mainstay, and communal living the order of the day. If you are staying here, you may be able to arrange for somebody to show you around the tel. The turn-off on the main road, 1km away, is served by **buses** #404, #433, #435 and #439 from Jerusalem, and #16 and #18 from Ramle.

Rehovot

REHOVOT, founded in 1890 by settlers from Poland, lies 8km southeast of Ramle, in an area once known for the citrus-growing prowess of its Arab farmers during the Mandate. Now thoroughly suburbanized by overflow from Tel Aviv, its main claims to fame are that it was the town where the Sephardic pronunciation used in Modern Hebrew (which differs from the pronunciation used for prayer by Ashkenazim) was first officially taught, and that it is home to the **Weizmann Institute** (Sun–Thurs 8am–4pm; ☎08/934 3852 or 8), a prestigious scientific research establishment twenty minutes' walk from the bus station through town along Rehov Herzl. Established in 1934 as the Daniel Sieff Research Institute with cash put up by the Marks & Spencer dynasty, it was renamed in 1949 in honour of **Haim Weizmann** – organic chemist and first president of the State of Israel. Weizmann, who worked there from 1936, was one of Zionism's early giants, and the main lobbyist behind the 1917 Balfour Declaration (see p.491), issued partly in appreciation of his invention of the industrial manufacture of acetone, which played a vital part in the mass production of explosives during World War I.

Nowadays the institute has ongoing projects in the fields of cancer research, astrophysics, immunology, solar energy and computer sciences, all of which are summarized in a free film shown in English at 11am and 2.45pm in the **Wix Auditorium**, the large building on your left as you walk through the main gates. You can also take a look at the massive atomic particle accelerator, wander through the beautiful gardens and visit **Weizmann's House** (guided tours by appointment daily except Fri & Sat), an excellent example of 1930s International Style (see p.82). It has a library, an impressive art collection and what is said to have been Palestine's first private swimming pool. Weizmann himself is buried just outside.

Practicalities

There are several reasonably priced **restaurants** along Rehov Herzl, and in the covered **Levkovitz Market** on the corner of Rehov Bilu, which leads to the main shopping mall and **bus station**. Rehovot's only **accommodation** is at the *Margoa Hotel*, 11 Maskovitz Street (☎08/945 1303, fax 945 1236; ③).

South of Rehovot

The largest kibbutz in Israel, **Kibbutz Givat Brenner** (☎07/635 7777), is a short bus ride out of Rehovot and one of the best to wander round if you're keen to see a slice of kibbutz life. Founded in 1928 in memory of the writer Yosef Haim Brenner, it has now grown to over 2000 inhabitants; their high standard of living reflects the success of the agrobusiness and three factories that have taken Givat Brenner a long way from the pioneering socialism of its early days.

GEDERA, a few kilometres further south on Route 40, was founded, like Rishon Le Zion (see p.104), by pioneering Russian immigrants in 1884. As at Rishon, their attempts at self-sufficiency failed and they had to be bailed out. A **museum** (Sun–Fri 8.30am–1.30pm, Mon & Wed 4–6pm; 6NIS) illustrates their story but is worth a visit only if you have a special interest in the history of Zionism.

Six kilometres southeast of Gedera, beyond Kibbutz Revadim, which is off Route 3, **Tel Miqne** is all that remains of the once great Philistine city of **Ekron**, one of the five city states of the Philistine Pentapolis. It was to Ekron's gates that the Israelites chased the Philistines after David's slaying of Goliath (I Samuel 17: 52). Cursed by Old Testament prophets such as Amos (Amos 1: 2), and taken by the Assyrians in the eighth century BC, it was destroyed by the Babylonians under Nebuchadnezzar in 603 BC, though a village remained on the site for around twelve hundred years after that.

Excavations on the tel have revealed Ekron's ancient importance as a producer of olive oil, and a reconstructed oil press can be seen at nearby Kibbutz Revadim's small **museum**, but, unless you're an archeologist or have a particular interest in the Philistines, there's little to tempt you here.

Yavne

Six kilometres southwest of Rehovot, **YAVNE**, site of the ancient city of Jabneh, is somewhat off the beaten tourist track, but it's an important ancient town with a few sights worth a look if you're passing. Yavne also enjoys a certain notoriety as the site of Israel's first atomic research reactor built in 1960, 4km northwest of town.

The town has been settled for at least two thousand years, and was an important centre of Jewish religious learning during the Hasmonean period and after the destruction of the Second Temple. Later it became a Roman and Crusader stronghold and an important town during the early period of Arab rule. Not much is left of this rich heritage today, but such sites as do remain are pretty close together in the southeast of town, and easily seen in an hour's stroll. A block south of Sederot Ha'Atzma'ut, a pretty little multi-domed building in a small park is said to be the **tomb of Rabbi Gamliel of Yavne**, a great Jewish scholar who lived here in the first century AD. Originally built as a shrine to a Muslim saint, Abu Hureira, one of the Prophet Mohammed's companions, it is now a synagogue and the possibility of it being Rabbi Gamliel's tomb has achieved the status of fact, as tends to happen when religion is a weapon in a war of two nationalisms. On the other side of the tomb, a couple of blocks north, the **market** on the corner of Sederot Duani and Rehov Giborei HaHayil is not the most folkloric in Israel, but worth a brief wander.

Three hundred metres from its junction with Sederot Ha'Atzma'ut, the Rehovot road crosses a creek on a bridge known as **Gesher HaKofetz** (the "Jumping Bridge"), so-called because of the tendency of cars to jump over the sharp bump in the middle when they're going too fast – the fault of its thirteenth-century Mamluk builders, who carelessly forgot to plan for modern traffic. Looking down the creek from here, you'll spot a 1948-vintage **pillbox** guarding the railway line; if you turn right there and head southwest, parallel with the track, you come to a tower on your right known as **Tel Yavne**. Once the minaret of a mosque, it was previously the tower of a Crusader church.

Buses from Tel Aviv, Rehovot and Ashdod will drop you on Sederot Ha'Atzma'ut (Route 42) at its junction with the Rehovot road (Route 410), which is near to all the main sights.

Ashdod

Settled since the late Iron Age and frequently mentioned in the Bible, **ASHDOD** was one of the five cities of the Philistine Pentapolis (see p.482), becoming a Greek colony called Azotus in the third century BC. In 712 BC, the city revolted against the Assyrians but the withdrawal, at the last minute, of Egyptian support, enabled Sargon II's troops to march in, sack the city and annexe Philistia as an Assyrian province. Later it grew into the Palestinian town of Isdud. The modern Israeli city was established only in 1957 and today it's one of Israel's most agreeable new towns – a commercial port with good

---

ASHDOD TELEPHONE NUMBERS

Ashdod **telephone numbers** are now all seven-digit; if you have an old six-digit one, try adding an eight at the beginning.

MOVING ON FROM ASHDOD

From the **bus** station there are departures to Tel Aviv (roughly every 15min; 1hr), Jerusalem (roughly every hour; 1hr 20min), Ashqelon (roughly every hour; 25min) and Beersheba (2 daily; 1hr 40min), as well as local services; **sheruts** to Tel Aviv and Ashqelon leave nearby. Two **trains** a day serve (experimentally) the station; both leave early morning, returning mid-evening, and call at Rehovot (25min), Lydda (35min), Tel Aviv (1hr) and Netanya (1hr 30min), one continuing to Haifa (2hr 20min), Acre (3hr) and Nahariyya (3hr 10min).

---

beaches and areas divided by boulevards and named rather functionally after letters of the Hebrew alphabet.

The town has little to show for its past except for a small **museum** of archeological finds at 15 HaSheyatim, in Area Dalet (Sun–Wed 9am–noon & 5–7pm, Thurs & Fri 9am–noon, Sat 10.30am–1.30pm; 8NIS, Sat free), and the desultory remains of a tenth-century Fatimid castle, **Qala'at al-Mina** (Ashdod Yam in Hebrew), on the beach at the southern edge of town at the end of Sederot Yitzhak Rabin (bus #6a or #10), where you'll have only the odd lizard for company. More recent history is represented on the eastern edge of town at **Ad Halom**, not far from the railway station near the end of Sederot Yerushayim and Sederot Menahem Begin, where a red granite **obelisk** stands as a monument to Egypt's fallen in the 1948 Battle of Ashdod. A product of the Camp David Peace Accord, it is inscribed in Arabic, Hebrew, English and hieroglyphics, and bears the symbol of Aton, God as the sun, worshipped under the regime of the eighteenth-dynasty pharaoh Akhenaton.

Ashdod's **beaches** are fine in themselves, soft sand and generally quiet during the week, but if that's what you're after, it's probably better to push on to Ashqelon (see below). Things liven up a bit on Wednesdays with a small flea **market** at the central Lido Beach, but it's during August that you'll see Ashdod at its liveliest, when the whole strand hosts a **Mediterranean Folklore Festival**.

Practicalities

Ashdod's **bus station** is 1km south of town, on Haim Massa Shapira by the junction with Rogozin; the **train station** is east of town, just by the turn-off from the Tel Aviv–Ashqelon road (Route 4) and is connected to town by bus #6. The **tourist information office**, run by the municipality, is in the Kanyon Ashdod shopping mall on Rehov Nordau in Area Aleph (Sun–Thurs 9.30am–9.30pm, Fri 9.30am–1.30pm, Sat nightfall–11pm; ☎08/852 1203), opposite Ashdod's only two **hotels**, the *Orly* (☎08/856 5380, fax 856 5382; ③) and the *Miami* (☎08/852 2085, fax 856 0563; ③). Sleeping on the beach should be no problem, for men or for a group at any rate. The main shopping area, complete with cafés, pubs and post office, is around the corner from the hotels, on Rehov Rogozin.

Ashdod to Ashqelon

The road south of Ashdod, with the sand dunes of Ashdod on your right, is fast, flat and featureless. Four kilometres out of town and just west of Route 4, **Tel Ashdod** was the centre of the village of Isdud – ancient Ashdod – and site of the Philistine port. Get off the bus if you like old mounds, derelict Palestinian homes, fragments of pottery or archeologists.

Six kilometres further south is the kibbutz of **Nizzanim** (☎07/672 1464 or 675 2726; ④), offering accommodation in six-bed bungalows with shared showers. Just west of here are the unmarked remains of a settlement from the Persian Period (451–640 BC) and remnants of a **Byzantine church** complete with mosaic and tomb, a pleasant walk if it's not too hot. The beach at Nizzanim was the scene of some drama in May 1990 when a Libyan ship in the Mediterranean let down six motorboats bearing PLF guerrillas, aiming to attack beaches up and down the coast that were packed out for the Shevuot holiday. Although several broke down at sea, and one was intercepted offshore by the Israeli navy, they actually managed to land at Nizzanim. Luckily, Israeli security forces reached the beach in time to prevent civilian casualties; four of the guerrillas were shot dead and seven more surrendered.

Ashqelon

Despite the presence of 12km of beautiful beaches (see p.117) and enthused promotion by its tourist board, **ASHQELON**, the most southerly town on Israel's Mediterranean coast, is still far from being Israel's finest beach resort, with few facilities to speak of so far. Aside from the obvious attractions of sand and sea, the town possesses a few remnants of its long history, though they're pretty far apart from each other and the only really impressive one was closed at the time of writing. The Thursday **market** is quite lively, but the former Arab part of town in which it takes place is a sanitized version of its former self.

One of the five great cities of the **Philistine Pentapolis** and birthplace of Herod, Ashqelon was taken in the eighth century by the Assyrians, and later by the Egyptians, Babylonians and Persians. During a period of Judaean expansion, the city put itself under Roman protection, though it was nominally independent from 104 BC onward. Ashqelon's strong defences enabled it to hold out against the **First Crusade**, even when 10,000 soldiers and civilians were slaughtered in front of its gates in 1099, and when the city finally fell in 1153, it was the last Muslim bastion in Palestine. **Saladin** retook it 34 years later and destroyed it to prevent the Crusaders' return, though **Richard the Lionheart** did manage to hold the area long enough to build a fortress to replace the destroyed defences, only for it to be flattened when he was forced out of Palestine in 1192 by Saladin. It was razed yet again in 1270 by **Baybars** to neutralize it in the face of another European threat, and the Arab town of **Majdal** (now the district of Migdal) was constructed on the ruins.

Ashqelon was given to the Palestinian Arabs by the 1947 UN partition plan and opposed Israel in the **1948 war**. In 1950, those inhabitants who hadn't already left were driven in army trucks to the Gaza frontier; Ashqelon was quickly settled with new immigrants (necessary in the face of mounting international pressure to allow its Palestinian population to return), and considerable resources, largely donated by Zionists abroad, were devoted to its development. Nowadays, many who commute from Gaza daily to work here are descendants of those deported.

Arrival, information and accommodation

Most people arrive at the **Central Bus Station**, in the town centre on Sederot Ben Gurion. From here, buses run to the various districts of the city: #1, #2, #4, #4a and #10 go to Migdal; #2, #4, #4a, #5 and #6 to Afridar; #2 and #5 to Barnea; #1 and #8 to Giv'at Zion; and #4 and #10 to Shimshon. Bus #3 along with #2 connects Migdal and Barnea. The **tourist office**, run by the municipality, is on Sederot HaNassi in Afridar opposite

<table>
<tr><td>ASHQELON TELEPHONE NUMBERS</td></tr>
</table>

Ashqelon **telephone numbers** are all now seven-digit; if you have an old six-digit one, try adding a six at the beginning.

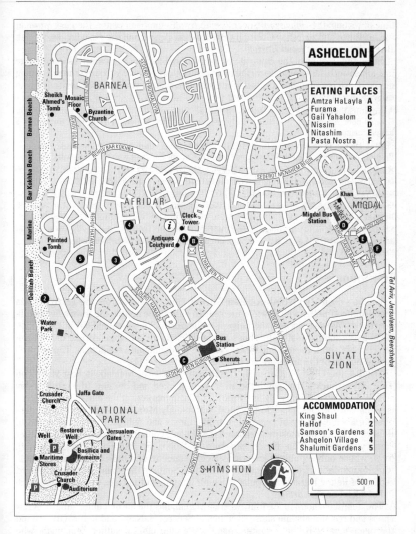

the clock tower in Kikar Tzefania, Afridar's main square (Sun–Thurs 8am–7pm, Fri 8am–noon; ☎07/673 2412). The helpful staff should be able to provide a detailed city map and help with accommodation.

Accommodation

Most of Ashqelon's **hotels** cater for mid-market Israeli customers. As far as budget accommodation goes, your best bet is the **zimmer scheme** run by the tourist office, where they'll fix you up in a small guesthouse or private house approved by them (around ②). The *Shulamit Gardens* hotel is the only high-class establishment in the town at present, though three others were under construction along the beach at the time of writing: the *Holiday Inn*, near Sheikh Awad's tomb in Barnea; the *Park Plaza*, at the northern end of Rehov Golani by Bar Kokhba Beach; and the *Paradise*, on Delilah Beach, just south of *Hotel HaHof*.

Since the closure of the campsite at the National Park, many **campers** congregate just to its south, far enough from the town centre to be relatively free of crime. Sleeping on the beach is commonplace during the summer, though you'd be well advised only to do so as part of a group.

Ashqelon Village (aka *Hotel Dagon*), 2 Moshe Dorot (☎07/673 6111 or 3, fax 673 0666). Ground-floor rooms in a "vacation village" which is serviceable enough but with the feel of a holiday camp. ④.

HaHof, Delilah Beach (☎ & fax 07/673 5111). Slightly faded beach hotel with the usual mod cons. Friendly and homely, though a Jewish mother-in-law might find fault with the housework. ⑤.

King Shaul (aka *King's Club Hotel*), 28 Harakefet, Afridar (☎07/673 4124 or 8, fax 673 4129). Strictly orthodox – no smoking or driving here on the Sabbath, when it's full-board only. ⑥.

Samson's Gardens, 38 HaTamar, Afridar (☎07/673 4666, fax 673 9615). Well-kept, pleasant hotel in a quiet location. All rooms at ground-floor level with outside front door. The cheapest and also the best-value hotel in town. ④.

Shulamit Gardens, 11 HaTayasim (☎07/671 1261, fax 671 0066). Ashqelon's only upmarket address at present, and not too bad, though not up to the standards of the deluxe hotels further up the coast. ⑥.

The Town

Ashqelon's main artery, **Sederot Ben Gurion**, runs east–west from the Tel Aviv–Gaza road (Route 4) pretty well down to the sea. To either side of it lie the town's five neighbourhoods: Afridar, Barnea and Migdal to the north; Shimshon and Giv'at Zion (Zion Hills) to the south. Most of the shops and businesses are in Migdal, Afridar or the town centre; Shimshon, Barnea and Giv'at Zion are predominantly residential. Though well spread out, all of the areas are accessible by bus (see p.114).

Migdal, the Old City (formerly the Palestinian city of Majdal), is best visited on Thursdays, **market** day, when the streets are packed and buzzing (though Monday and Wednesday are generally lively too). The main market, at the end of Rehov Herzl, is by far the cheapest place to buy food, with mainly Moroccan and Iraqi stallholders offering a wide variety of vegetables, fruits, meats and fish. At the northern end of Rehov Herzl, the old mosque, renamed the "khan", contains a few shops and a rather cursory **museum** (Sun–Thurs 9am–1pm & 4–6pm, Fri 9am–1pm, Sat 10am–1pm; free), whose only exhibit of interest is a cute statuette of a bull-calf with an earthenware house, dating from the second century BC. South of the khan, the pedestrianized section of Rehov Herzl is a popular place for hanging out in cafés or grabbing a pitta-full of falafel or *shawarma*.

The neighbourhood of **Afridar**, west of Migdal, has the air of a quiet suburb. A few shops and restaurants line short stretches of Sederot HaNassi and Rehov Orit around the main square, **Kikar Tzefania**, named after the biblical author Zephaniah, who prophesied that Ashqelon would be "a desolation" (Zephaniah 2: 4). In the corner of the green by the square's clock tower on HaNassi, you can pop into the **antiquities courtyard** (Sun–Thurs 8.30am–4pm, Fri 8.30am–1.30pm; free) to have a look at two beautiful Hellenic sarcophagi. The carvings on one depict the abduction of Persephone, daughter of Demeter, Goddess of Fertility; the other portrays a battle scene between Greeks and Barbarians. Afridar also contains the only truly impressive archeological site in Ashqelon – a third-century AD **painted Roman tomb**, situated above the beach behind the *Shulamit Gardens* hotel, but closed to the public for the time being. The end wall of the tomb is decorated with a fresco of two nymphs resting by a stream, while the ceiling features the god Pan playing his pipes, a naked boy gathering grapes, plus birds, stags, antelopes, dogs and, possibly to ward off the evil eye, a Gorgon's head. Discovered in a remarkably good state of preservation in 1936, the tomb is believed to have belonged to a wealthy local family.

To the north of Afridar, on Rehov Zvi Segal in the **Barnea** district, are the scant remains of a sixth-century **Byzantine church**, and, off Sederot Yerushalayim, a **mosaic floor** from the last decade of the sixth century AD. On the shore nearby, the little, domed, thirteenth-century **tomb of Sheikh Awad** commemorates a local saint, and was once used for prayer (note the mihrab in the wall). The side rooms are later additions.

The beaches

There are some 12km of beach around Ashqelon, with little to distinguish any one part, just sand and kiosks selling soft drinks. **North Beach**, just inside the municipal boundaries, is the most secluded – popular for topless bathing but not covered by the lifeguards who patrol everywhere else. South of here, there's **Barnea Beach**, **Bar Kokhba Beach** at the end of Rehov Bar Kochba, and a separate beach for religious bathers near the Roman Tomb. The most popular beach, **Delilah Beach**, is just past the marina and has three small islands a few hundred metres offshore – a good, long swim if you're up to it. Just by here is a small **water park**, with water slides, pools and a few fairground rides. Beyond, the beaches continue into the National Park, the crowds dwindling the further you go. If all of them prove too crowded, as they can be at weekends, the beach at **Kibbutz Ziqim**, about 8km south, is a pleasant alternative.

The National Park

The remains of the once great Philistine city of Ashqelon are located in the pleasant beachside **National Park** at the southern end of town (officially Sat–Thurs 8am–4pm, Fri 8am–3pm; 15NIS, but in practice freely accessible from the beach; bus #6 hourly). However, you don't have to be a philistine to find this motley collection of fallen pillars and bits of old wall rather a disappointment.

The early ramparts of the **Philistine port**, with their great columns, are down by the beach. Nearer the centre of the park, a collection of **Roman** memorabilia from all over the area is exhibited in two displays. Under Herod the town was spectacularly endowed with baths, fountains and colonnaded quadrangles; remnants of one such quadrangle can be seen in the field near the cafeteria, along with hundreds of standing columns. There are also remains of Crusader and Byzantine churches, collapsed towers, esplanades and pillars scattered throughout the park. Next to the Crusader remains at the southern end of the park, an open-air **auditorium** hosts theatre and musical programmes; details of events are available from the tourist office.

Eating and drinking

You can **eat** cheaply and well at basic stalls and cafés all over Ashqelon, particularly in Migdal where you'll find numerous falafel bars on Rehovot Herzl and David Remez, and plenty of good food stalls in the market. The better restaurants are concentrated in Afridar and the city centre, with more tourist-oriented places centred on Delilah Beach. The restaurant in the National Park serves reasonable kebabs. For a **drink**, try *Signon*, a pub opposite the tourist office in Sederot HaNassi, Afridar, which also offers music.

Amtza HaLayla, between the clock tower and petrol station on Kikar Tzefania, Afridar; sign in Hebrew only. Sit-down *shawarma* or falafel with a side dish of hummus or tehina, washed down with a cold beer. Daily 5pm–1am. Cheap.

MOVING ON FROM ASHQELON

From the Central Bus Station, there are **buses** to Tel Aviv (roughly every 15min; 1hr), Jerusalem (roughly hourly; 1hr 15min), Beersheba (roughly hourly; 1hr 30min), Haifa (every 1–2hr; 2hr 45min), Erez checkpoint (for Gaza; 3 daily; 30min), and the Egyptian border at Rafah (1 daily; 1hr). **Sheruts** run by Muniyot HaMerkazit, in Sederot Ben Gurion opposite the bus station, serve Tel Aviv and Ashdod around the clock. It is possible that passenger train services will be extended to Ashqelon in the future.

Furama, by the post office, Orit, Afridar (☎07/673 8497). For those who can't do without a Chinese, this is the only one in town. Sun–Fri noon–3pm & 7pm–midnight, Sat 12.30pm–midnight. Expensive.

Gail Yahalom, 101 HaNassi, just north of Ben Gurion in the town centre; sign in Hebrew only. Delicious grilled fish and meat. Sun–Thurs noon–midnight or later (usually 2am in summer), Sat from nightfall. Moderate to expensive.

Nissim, 19 HaAvodah, Migdal. A good steak, kebab and salad joint on the corner of David Remez. Sat–Thurs 8am–11pm. Cheap to moderate.

Nitashon, Herzl pedestrian zone, near the corner of Zahal, Migdal. Great Middle Eastern cooking, from stuffed cabbage to chicken hearts. Sat–Thurs 7am–11pm. Moderate.

Pasta Nostra, Herzl pedestrian zone, near the corner of HaPalmah, Migdal. Unpretentious pasta house. Sun–Thurs 11am–11pm, Sat nightfall–11pm. Moderate.

Listings

Banks and exchange Banks are your only currency exchange option. You'll find branches by the tourist office in Afridar, in the pedestrianized area of Rehov Herzl and on Rehov Zahal in Migdal, and on Rehov HaGibora in the town centre.

Car rental Eldan, corner of Ben Gurion and Herzl (☎07/672 2724); Amado, 97 HaNassi (☎07/673 5777).

Medical services Magen David Adom (☎07/672 3333); Brazilai Hospital, 3 HaHistadrut (☎07/674 5555). Pharmacies include R&M, 97 HaNassi (☎07/673 5542), Super-Pharm, Kanyon Giron Mall, Sederot Ben Gurion (☎07/671 1431) and Ashqelon, Afridar Centre, Afridar (☎07/673 5542).

Police Rehov HaNassi (☎07/677 1444).

Post office Rehov HaGiborah behind the bus station; Rehov Orit, off Kikar Tzefania in Afridar; and on the corner of Herzl and HaPalmah in Migdal.

Taxis HaMerkaz (☎07/673 3077); HaShekhem (☎07/672 8555); Shimshon (☎07/675 1333).

Travel agents Ashqelon Tours, Civic Centre, Rehov HaGiborah, behind the bus station (☎07/675 1055); Nirashqelon Tours, 36 Herzl, Migdal (☎07/675 1205).

South of Ashqelon

The road running south from Ashqelon **into the Gaza strip** follows the railway line that once linked Aswan in southern Egypt with Turkey. Ten kilometres south of Ashqelon is **Kibbutz Yad Mordekhai**, named after Mordekhai Anwilewitz, the leader of the Warsaw Ghetto uprising (see p.228). A **museum** here (daily 9am–4pm; 7NIS) displays photos and some information about Jewish resistance in the Warsaw Ghetto, the establishment of settlements in the Negev on Yom Kippur in 1946, and local kibbutzim in the 1948 war, but coverage is cursory. More interesting is a **reconstruction** (same hours and ticket as the museum), on the actual battlefield, of the 1948 Egyptian army assault on the kibbutz, whose members held out for six days before making their escape – the metal figures representing the soldiers manage to give a realistic impression of how the battle must have looked to the defenders. If you want to read more about it, *The Six Days of Yad Mordekhai* by Margaret Larkin is on sale. Finally, the kibbutz also has a small **zoo** of mainly edible birds and animals (in theory Sun–Fri 8am–4pm, Sat 10am–4pm; 5NIS). Various **buses** from Yad Mordekhai junction, by the kibbutz, serve Ashqelon, Tel Aviv and Beersheba, but only one #36 and three #37s daily reach the checkpoint at Erez, 4km south.

If you turn away from the coast at Yad Mordekhai junction, down Route 34, you'll embark on a rather laborious route **south into the Negev** – a land of green fields and tiny settlements. A dozen or so kilometres south of the junction you pass **SEDEROT**, named after the avenues of trees (*sederot* means "avenues" in Hebrew) planted by the Jewish National Fund (JNF), and eminently missable. It is possible to follow the road south, skirting the Gaza Strip, to the Egyptian border at **Rafah** (see p.459). To get to **Beersheba**, follow the road east at the **Magen junction**. If you intend to hitch south make sure you have plenty of water, food for a day or so and warm clothes for the cold nights. There's little traffic on the roads and it's very easy to get stuck in the middle of nowhere.

Inland from Ashqelon

Inland of Ashqelon there are a few sparsely populated towns, kibbutzim and moshavim, with virtually nothing in between and little to detain you at any of them other than a cold drink as you press on towards Beersheba or Eilat. The area's main town and transport hub is **Qiryat Gat**, but the only real interest lies in three isolated archeological sites to its east – **Tel Lakhish**, **Tel Maresha** and **Bet Jibrin**, the latter two within **Bet Guvrin National Park**, one of the most interesting sites in the country. However, **public transport** around the area is sparse at best, rendering these and the other archeological and biblical sites effectively off limits without a car. The other main hindrance is the lack of **accommodation** – the nearest is several kilometres northeast at kibbutzim Gal'on (☎07/687 2410; ④) and Gat (☎07/687 1215 or 6, fax 687 1400; ④), both off Route 353 – though there are plenty of opportunities for freelance camping if you have a tent.

Qiryat Gat

The industrial town of **QIRYAT GAT**, 18km east of Ashqelon, is the capital of the **Lakhish region**, a network of thirty Israeli settlements established in 1954. Although it's the only

---

FALUJA

The road south from Tel Aviv (Route 40) meets the Ashqelon–Hebron road (Route 35) at **Pelugot (literally "troops") Junction**, just outside Qiryat Gat, with ruins of the Arab village of **Faluja** southwest of the crossroads. This junction was a pivotal point in a swathe of land from Ashqelon to Hebron held by the Egyptian army from May 1948, cutting off Israeli forces from Jewish settlements in the Negev. The Israelis, however, had managed to smuggle troops and arms into Negev settlements with the supplies allowed under the war's two truces. On October 14, under the second truce, they sent an unarmed convoy to the settlements under UN supervision, and blew it up at the crossroads to make it appear that the Egyptians had shelled it, using this as an excuse to attack from all sides, cutting off the Egyptian Fourth Brigade at Faluja. The brigade's Sudanese commander, Taha Bey, though surrounded, refused to surrender. Among his soldiers was **Gamal Abd al-Nasser**, later President of Egypt. Israeli forces went on to take Lakhish and Beersheba, while the Egyptian troops were eventually allowed to leave following negotiations; Faluja's Palestinian villagers ended up as refugees. The main road to Beersheba and Eilat still runs through here, traversed frequently by buses and bypassing virtually everything along the way.

place of any size in the region, and useful as a transport hub, there's no accommodation, few bars or cafés, and limited bus connections to surrounding sites. Tel Gat (to the northeast, off Route 353) was thought to be the site of biblical **Gath**, one of the five Philistine cities, but numerous excavations have failed to turn up any Philistine artefacts, though there was apparently a Judean town here during the post-Solomonic divided kingdom.

Buses connect Qiryat Gat with Ashqelon (every 1–2hr; 25min), Tel Aviv (3–5 per hour; 1hr 15min), Jerusalem (1–2 per hour; 1hr 30min) and Beersheba (3–4 per hour; 1hr). For **sites** east of Qiryat Gat (on Routes 35 and 38), covered in the sections that follow, buses are scarce, with just two a day to Tel Lakhish (15min) and Bet Guvrin (25min). Failing that, hitchhiking is your only option, but traffic is sparse so you may have more than one long wait.

Tel Lakhish

The first site east of Qiryat Gat, on Route 35, is **Tel Lakhish**, an ancient Canaanite city which, while not the most visually stimulating, is perhaps the most archeologically important of the sites in this area. A Canaanite civilization thrived here for almost 2000 years until Joshua and the Israelites "smote it with the edge of the sword, and all the souls that were therein" (Joshua 10: 32). After this conquest the city lay in ruins until it was fortified between 928 and 911 BC by Rehoboam and grew to become the second most important city in Judah after Jerusalem.

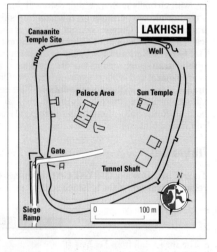

Among archeologists, the site is known primarily as the source of the **Lakhish Letters**, which describe life in the city under Nebuchadnezzar, King of Babylon, who captured it in 588 BC. Most of the artefacts from the site now rest in museums around the world and only the foundations remain. They won't mean much to the untrained eye, but should you decide to go, the main things to look out for are the three-chambered **inner gate** as you enter the site, the largest in Israel and the Palestinian Territories; the **palace area**, distinguishable by a large platform; and the **sacred area**, which is believed to be the first Israelite sanctuary and features a slightly raised altar dating from the time of Rehoboam.

The site lies 2.5km south of the road 7km east of Qiryat Gat. Take the turn-off for Amatzya and Hazan Cave, and it's the big mound on your right just after the turn-off to the moshav of Lakhish: a track 200m further on leads up the side of it.

Bet Guvrin National Park: Tel Maresha and Bet Jibrin

Six kilometres east of the Lakhish turn-off on Route 35, and just west of its junction with Route 38, the road passes the entrance to **Bet Guvrin National Park** (Sat–Thurs 8am–4pm, Fri 8am–3pm; 15NIS; ☎07/681 1020), which encompasses the sites of **Tel Maresha** and **Bet Jibrin**. In addition to the remains of ancient buildings, there are over 4000 artificial and natural caves here, first used – and expanded – by a colony of

Sidonians established by the Ptolemies in the third century BC. Most were robbed of everything of importance centuries ago, but there is still plenty worth exploring, with more being discovered all the time. Among the vast array of caves you'll see burial chambers, olive presses, water cisterns, storage areas, dwellings and shrines.

When **visiting the caves**, it's advisable to equip yourself with a flashlight and wear non-slip shoes and old clothes: you tend to emerge covered in white dust from the soft chalk out of which the caves are carved. The sites are pretty spread out and could easily take five hours to see on foot; if you are walking, stick to the paths, as the ground is pitted with hidden holes. By car it will take around three hours; there are five car parks in the park.

Tel Maresha

Tel Maresha, a kilometre and a half south of the site entrance, was already an established city in the time of Joshua (thirteenth century BC). Like Tel Lakhish, it was fortified by Rehoboam and, though never as important, it became quite prosperous. It was a profitable centre of the Palestine–Egypt slave trade during the third century BC, was taken from the Greeks by the Hasmonean king John Hyrcanus I at the end of the sec-

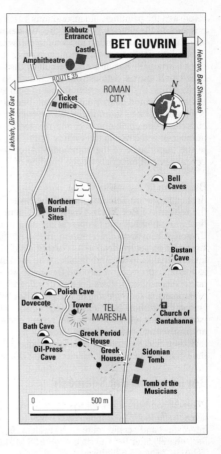

ond, and destroyed by Parthian invaders in 40 BC. At the northwestern corner of its summit are the remains of a massive defensive **tower**, dating from the third century BC, and to the south those of a **Greek-period house**, probably destroyed by Hyrcanus's forces in 112 BC, along with adjoining water cisterns.

Some of the most exciting **caves** are to the west of the tel; one of them, 200m away, is thought to have been a giant underground **dovecote**. After crawling through the small opening you descend into a large cross-shaped chamber, its walls pitted with thousands of small holes arranged neatly in rows in which doves were bred to be sacrificed to the goddess Aphrodite. To the southeast is one of the many caves used for bathing, and another housing an olive press. To the east of the tel is the most impressive of all the caves: a small **Sidonian tomb** quarried from brilliant white rock and housing 41 burial compartments. Located at the far end, the most important-looking tomb is thought to be that of the chamber's creator, Apollophanes, and his family. Apollophanes was ruler of the Sidonian colony for 33 years during the third century BC, and the tomb continued in use through to the first century BC. It's empty now, but some of the intricate rock carvings that adorned it during Apollophanes' reign have survived, and the paintings and inscriptions have recently been restored. To its south is the entrance to the smaller **Tomb of the Musicians**, also dating from the Sidonian period and named after a painting inside of a man with a flute and a woman playing a harp.

Heading north towards the main road, you pass the **Church of Santahanna** (St Anne), originally Byzantine but rebuilt by the Crusaders, before reaching a group of so-called **bell caves** dating from the fourth to the seventh century AD. Their name derives from their shape: miners had to chip away a small round hole in the hard rock before they could quarry out the chalk beneath, leaving behind large, bell-shaped caverns with spacious interiors (some are over 300m high), that have the air of abandoned churches. The chalk dug here was roasted to produce mortar and plaster, and the vast number of bell caves in the vicinity (there are said to be over a thousand) bear witness to the importance of the commodity. After the Arab conquest of Eleutheropolis, the caves provided materials for the building of Ramle.

Bet Jibrin

At the junction to Tel Maresha and the caves, below the Kibbutz Bet Guvrin, you'll see the remains of **Bet Jibrin Castle** (Bet Guvrin in Hebrew), closed to the public at the time of writing but due to open in the near future. Built for Fulk of Anjou, ruler of the Crusader Kingdom of Jerusalem in the twelfth century, the castle is recognizably a Crusader structure despite its current state of dilapidation. That it survives relatively intact is thanks to the Arab families who lived in it for generations, adding features such as the olive press. Signs around the castle warn of "falling stones" and "danger of tick-borne disease" so visitors need to tread carefully and wear trousers and long sleeves.

Remains of the Palestinian village of **Bet Jibrin** can be seen all around, especially among the kibbutz buildings: the old village school now serves as the kibbutz's administration block. Behind the castle, recent excavations have uncovered a small **Roman amphitheatre**, but the better finds, all from the original site of ancient Bet Guvrin, including fine Roman and Byzantine mosaic floors, have been ripped up and taken to the Israel Museum in Jerusalem (see p.373), leaving behind little more than dust.

Bet Guvrin to Bet Shemesh

Route 35 winds its way **east from Bet Guvrin** through forests, Bedouin camps and villages in the foothills of Judea on the way to Hebron (see p.407). This is much the most interesting and scenic route to Jerusalem, but if you're in a hurry, a left turn almost immediately after Bet Guvrin on Route 38 will take you up to Bet Shemesh and the main Tel Aviv–Jerusalem highway.

Three places of interest lie off the road between Bet Guvrin and Bet Shemesh, none accessible by public transport. The first lies just to the south of Route 383, which branches off to the west 11km north of Bet Guvrin. Here, a mound topped by an excavated fort marks the site of **Tel Azekah**, a city conquered by the invading Israelites under Joshua, with the help of some divine hailstones (Joshua 10: 10–11). Around its northern side winds the Elah, whose valley was the scene of the famous battle between David and Goliath (I Samuel 17). Second, east of the road 4km north of here (3km south of Bet Shemesh), at **Bet Jimal Monastery** (☎02/991 3195), is the originally Byzantine church of St Stefanos. This claims to be the burial site of St Stephen, the first Christian martyr (Acts 6–7), and also of the great Jewish scholar and head of the Sanhedrin, Rabbi Gamliel the Elder, who taught St Paul and defended Jesus's apostles before the Sanhedrin (Acts 5: 34–40). The monks sell crafts, olive oil and wine, and host classical **concerts** on Saturdays. Finally, right by the road just west of Bet Shemesh, **Tel Bet Shemesh** is more noteworthy for its location and view than for the interest of its Hyksos, Israelite and Byzantine period excavations. This is Samson country: the valley you see to the north, that of the Sorek, was the home of his lover and betrayer, Delilah (Judges 16: 4).

Re-founded in 1951 on the site of a Jewish settlement dating back to 1895, the modern town of **BET SHEMESH** has little to offer beyond good transport connections (roughly hourly buses to Jerusalem and Tel Aviv, plus occasional sheruts). In the town centre, about 1km from the main road, you'll find cafés, falafel stands and shops; otherwise there's no reason to leave the bus stop. However, a worthwhile detour lies 10km northeast of Bet Shemesh in the **Absalom Nature Reserve** (Sat–Thurs 8.30am–3.45pm, Fri 8.30am–12.45pm; 13NIS), where the **Soreq Cave** is a local beauty spot popular with Israeli day trippers, especially on Saturdays. Over 90m long, and 80m high in places, the cave is packed with astoundingly beautiful stalactites, stalagmites and other rock formations. You'll need your own transport or you could walk here from town; it's mostly uphill but offers superb views.

The road to Jerusalem

The all-new **Ayalon freeway** (Route 1) from Tel Aviv to Jerusalem passes only 8km north of Bet Shemesh, replacing what is now Route 424. In the 1948 war, the old road was Arab-held at Ramle, forcing the Jews to use the road through Rehovot (now routes 412, 411 and 3) to get supplies to West Jerusalem, under siege by Arab forces. The Arabs dominated the road at three points: Kastel, which fell to the Haganah in April 1948; Bab al-Wad, over which Israel managed to gain control by May 8; and Latrun. Despite four assaults, the Israelis failed to take Latrun, which remained on the West Bank, forcing them after the war to build a new road (Route 44).

A much greater feat, however, was their construction during the war itself of the **Burma Road**, now just a dirt track, but in 1948 a vital lifeline that enabled Israel to hold onto West Jerusalem. Work began after the Israelis' second abortive assault on Latrun on May 30 and had to be completed ahead of the June 11 "First Truce", which would fix the status quo as it stood on that day. Continuing a track that already existed as far as the now-destroyed Arab village of Bet Susin, this road, stretching east of what is now Route 38, was built by Histadrut-recruited volunteers working under fire from Arab positions. Up and running in five days, it was able to take a group of American correspondents through to Jerusalem on June 10, and was named the Burma Road after the supply route built by the Allies through Burma to China in World War II. Today it is a popular **hike**, beginning on the site of Bet Susin, just north of Route 44, 4km west of its junction with Route 3, where a watchtower, complete with warning not to climb it, gives a view across to Latrun. The road crosses Route 38 just south of the Sha'ar HaGay interchange with Route 1, 5km east of Latrun. If you want to stay in the area, there is a **guesthouse** at Harel (☎02/991 8958; ④), and another at Neve Shalom/Wahat al-Salam (see p.125).

Latrun

The strategic road junction at **LATRUN**, on the southern fringe of the Ayalon Valley, has always been crucial to the conquest and control of Jerusalem. A list of those who have fought over it reads like a who's who of the country's history. Here Judas Maccabeus defeated the Syrians in 161 BC, the Roman Fifth Legion camped for two years before their attack on Jerusalem in 70 AD, Arab armies established a large military camp in the seventh century, and the Crusaders built a fortress to guard the road to Jerusalem.

In World War I the British took Latrun, and in World War II they set up prisoner-of-war camps here for captured Germans and Italians, later using the same camps to detain members of Jewish paramilitaries (twenty members of the Stern Gang escaped from it in November 1943 by digging a 71-metre tunnel). With the fall of Kastel (see

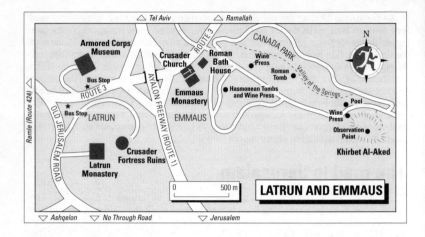

p.126) in April **1948**, Latrun became the key to control of the supply route to West Jerusalem, the fortified British Police Post having command over the road. At first the post was held by ALA volunteer "irregulars" (see p.494) who abandoned it when Transjordan's Arab Legion moved into Palestine on May 15, leaving it unoccupied for two days before the Legion arrived to replace them, though the Israelis failed to notice this (luckily, since taking it would have opened up the road to Ramallah for them too). Israeli forces attacked on May 25 and again on May 30, managing on the second occasion to get into the courtyard of the police post before being repulsed. Supporters of the cock-up theory of history may care to note that its Arab defenders, rushing up to the roof to fire on them, neglected to lock the front door, a fact that escaped the notice of the Israeli soldiers attempting under fire to set charges and blow it open. Israel again attacked Latrun on June 9, this time just a diversion to protect the Burma Road, which they had all but completed (see above), and one last time on July 15. In the 1967 **Six Day War**, however, the police fort and the Latrun corridor were captured by the Israelis on the first night of fighting. Determined never to lose control again, Israel unilaterally annexed it along with East Jerusalem, and does not consider it to be part of the West Bank.

The police post, just south of the Latrun interchange on Route 1, is now an **Armored Corps Museum** (Sun–Thurs 8.30am–4.30pm, Fri 8.30am–12.30pm, Sat 9am–4pm; 10NIS). Entering the site, you are greeted by an array of tanks, one cut in half to reveal its interior. Those of 1948 vintage are over to the left, while to the right, a tank perched on a concrete tower points the way to Jerusalem. Shell-holes from 1967 puncture the walls of the police station, whose door is still surmounted by a battered sign dating from Mandate days. The exhibits themselves are not very exciting (the stamps and coins are not even real), but you can climb to the roof to see how strategic the position really is, dominating the valley of the Ayalon creek (which runs north–south across the highway named after it), with a view as far as Tel Aviv.

On the hillside opposite is **Latrun Monastery** (Mon–Sat summer 7.30–11.30am & 2.30–4.30pm, winter 8–11am & 2.30–4.30pm), established in 1891 as an inn for Christian pilgrims travelling the rough road to Jerusalem. When the road was paved and there was no longer any need to stay, it was sold to French Trappist monks, who built the present monastery in 1926. Set within beautifully tended gardens, olive groves and vineyards, the monastery is home to 25 monks who are famous for their liqueurs, wines and honey. On the summit of the hill above the monastery is a twelfth-century **Crusader fortress**, built by Flemish knights to guard the road from Jaffa to Jerusalem. The name Latrun is a corruption of the name of this fortress: Le Toron des Chevaliers ("Tower of the Knights"). However, since the sixteenth century, Christian tradition has identified this as the birthplace of the thief who was crucified alongside Jesus, on the supposition that Latrun comes from the Latin *boni latronis* ("good thief"). The remains of the castle's arches, huge columns, underground passages and outer walls can still be seen, along with trenchworks of 1948 vintage.

Latrun is connected to Jerusalem by **buses** #403, #433, #434, #435 and #439. In the other direction, buses #434 and #435 go to Ramle and Rehovot; Ramle is also served by bus #432 which, along with #433, goes to Rishon le Zion.

Emmaus and Canada Park

On the other side of the junction from Latrun Monastery, on the Ramallah road, is the site of **Emmaus**, where the resurrected Jesus appeared to and had supper with two of his disciples (Luke 24: 13–32). The **monastery** here is now used as the French Centre for Prehistorical Research; below it are the remains of a twelfth-century Crusader **church**, built over a fifth-century Byzantine basilica. The delicate-coloured mosaics, one featuring a panther, are the site's main attraction, and formed the floor of an earlier Roman villa that may have been a meeting place for Emmaus's early Christian community.

A little further along the road you come to **Canada Park**, a wooded recreation centre owned by the Jewish National Fund. It's undeniably beautiful, with a preserved **Roman bathhouse** (off the road 300m south of the park entrance) and an **observation point** in the centre overlooking the central and western Ayalon Valley, Ramle and the coastal plain and the foothills of Judea. The **Valley of Springs**, which runs through the park, once supplied agricultural and drinking water to the residents of Amwas; along its course are Hasmonean and Roman graves, and Byzantine winepresses.

Neve Shalom/Wahat al-Salam

A little to the west of Latrun on Route 3, just before Kibbutz Nahshon, a road leads off to **NEVE SHALOM** or **WAHAT AL-SALAM**, meaning "Oasis of Peace". Founded in 1972 by Father Bruno Husar, a Jewish-born Benedictine monk, it is a cooperative village of fifty percent Palestinian Arabs and fifty percent Israeli Jews, determined not only to live together in harmony, but to encourage peace and mutual understanding between their two peoples. The village has had great success, attracting visitors from far and wide, educating children from the surrounding region (populated by both Jews and Arabs) bilingually and biculturally, and having to expand massively to allow in others who want to move here. It is supported by a network of "Friends of Neve Shalom/Wahat al-Salam" in Britain, North America and Europe. The villagers, not surprisingly perhaps, are a friendly lot, happy to see outsiders and show them around.

The **guesthouse** here (☎02/991 7160, fax 991 7412; ⑤), but special deals for four people sharing), offering full- and half-board, has pleasant, airy rooms and great views – on a clear day, you can see Tel Aviv and the sea. It is also possible to stay in the village as a volunteer (☎02/991 2222, fax 991 2098 for details). A new **restaurant**, the *White Dove*, serves expensive French and Israeli cuisine (Mon–Thurs 6.30pm–midnight, Fri 3pm–midnight, Sat noon–midnight; reservation required; ☎02/999 3030). **Bus** #24 runs to the village three times daily from Ramle and Rehovot, or bus #434 from Ramle or Jerusalem will leave you at the turn-off, 3km short.

Bab al-Wad, Abu Ghosh and Neve Ilan

The next interchange on Route 1, 5km southeast of Latrun, is called **Sha'ar HaGay** (Gate of the Valley), the Hebrew name for the gorge that begins here, known in Arabic as **Bab al-Wad**. This was the scene of fierce battles in the 1948 war, when its control was vital for Israeli forces trying to hold onto West Jerusalem. Remains of Haganah vehicles ambushed by Arab forces have been left by the roadside as memorials, sprayed with anti-rust paint to preserve them; the first wrecks can be seen on the southern side of the road, 2km east of the interchange, but the main convoys are north of the road a few kilometres further, just west of the Shoresh interchange. Westbound in your own transport, you can pull off the highway here for a closer look, and there's even a picnic site. On 8 May 1948, Israeli forces took the village of Bet Makhsir, south of the gorge, giving them control over it and ending the ambushes of their convoys which had been a regular occurrence here during the previous three months.

East of the Shoresh interchange is the turn-off for **ABU GHOSH**, a Christian Arab village once thought to be the site of Emmaus (see p.125), and named after an early nineteenth-century bandit chieftain licensed by the Ottomans to extract "taxes" from passing travellers. In **1948**, Abu Ghosh took the side of the Israelis, as a result of which its inhabitants have been labelled "collaborators" by other Palestinians. At the top of the village, the 1924 **Church of Notre Dame de l'Arche de l'Alliance** ("Our Lady of the Ark of the Covenant") is said to occupy the site of the house of Abinadab where the Ark rested for twenty years (I Samuel 7: 1–2) until taken by David to Jerusalem. It is built on the site of a fifth-century Byzantine church, whose floor mosaics are still visible. At the bottom of the village are a khan and a **Crusader church** put up by the Knights Hospitallers in the twelfth century, the latter restored by Benedictine monks at the end of the nineteenth century, who also added a small monastery. Abu Ghosh is popular with gourmets, who come to sample the excellent Palestinian cooking of the *Caravan Inn* **restaurant**, founded in 1947 (☎02/534 2744; daily 11am–11pm; expensive), and the several imitators that have sprung up alongside it. Abu Ghosh can be reached from Jerusalem on buses #185 and #186.

Coming off Route 1 into Abu Ghosh you pass **Neve Ilan**, home of Israel's movie industry, where Golan Globus productions came up with such classics as *Lemon Popsicle* and *Raid on Entebbe*. Next to the production site, an Elvis-themed *Elvis Inn* (daily 7.30am–8pm; moderate) has opened, and serves Middle Eastern nosh to the sounds of "the king" – look for the statue of him out front.

Ein Hemed and Kastel

South of Route 1 at the Qiryat Anavim junction, **Ein Hemed** (Aqua Bella) is the site of a Crusader monastery, maintained by the National Parks Authority (Sat–Thurs 8am–4pm, Fri 8am–3pm; 11NIS). Its interest nowadays is more as a pleasant picnic spot than a historical site, since the ruins themselves are rather minimal.

Kastel, another site maintained by the NPA, is a Roman fortress atop a large hill south of the highway at the next junction west, just before Jerusalem (Sat–Thurs 8am–4pm, Fri 8am–3pm; 7NIS), from which it's accessible on bus #183. Again, the scant ancient remains are of minimal interest; the site's main significance is the **battle** fought here at the beginning of April 1948. Israeli forces took Kastel on April 2, and held it against a Palestinian assault over the next two days. Volunteers under Abd al-Qader al-Husseini (a cousin of the Grand Mufti of Jerusalem, Haj Amin al-Husseini), managed to regain the position on April 8, but Abd al-Qader's death in the fighting led to a collapse of the Palestinian assault force and the Israelis were able to retake it. Kastel's fall made it easier for the Haganah to send supplies through to Jewish West Jerusalem, though for another month Arab forces were still able to ambush them further west at Bab al-Wad. Signs and models illustrating the battle are posted around the site in commemoration of the event.

Betar

Approaching Jerusalem by train rather than road, you'll pass the Arab village of **BATTIR**, 3km north of Route 375. On the hill northwest of here, scant remains known in Arabic as Khirbet al-Yahud ("Ruins of the Jews") mark the site of **Betar**, where Simon Bar Kokhba, leader of the **Second Jewish Revolt** against the Romans, made his last stand in 135 AD. Though not very impressive nowadays, the site has faint echoes of Masada (see p.265), with a central **fort** surrounded by a **siege wall**. There was also a siege ramp and two Roman encampments to the southwest, though these are visible only from the air. Little is known about the Second Revolt, though the rebels seem to have taken Jerusalem at one point and to have held out for over three years before their final defeat and massacre. Rabbi Akiva was so impressed with Bar Kokhba that he hailed him as "Messiah".

CHAPTER TWO

HAIFA, THE CARMEL AND THE SHARON

Haifa, protruding thumb-like into the sea at the northern end of the Carmel mountain range, is Israel's third city, and the industrial and economic centre of the north. Climbing steeply from a bustling port to the peaks of Mount Carmel behind, it offers an ideal middle way between the buzz of Tel Aviv and the conservatism of Jerusalem. Haifa also bears the stamp of the British Mandate more than any other Israeli town, and enjoys a freer mix of Jews and Arabs than the two other main cities, a fact that adds substantially to its easy-going feel.

Stretching some 40km to the south and east of Haifa, the tree-clad slopes of the **Carmel mountain range** provide one of the country's most agreeable regions, where the cooler climate seems somehow to temper the frenetic pace of Israeli life. The picturesque plateaux are largely given over to the dramatic and undeveloped **Carmel National Park**, which can nevertheless be easily explored on a series of trails. Other popular excursions in the Carmel include the two large Druze villages of **Daliat al-Karmel** and **Isfiya**, which, though commercialized, retain a distinct atmosphere of their own. A few kilometres to the west, the former Palestinian village of **Ein Hod** has become an "artists' colony", its beautiful setting now a little too touched by tourism.

East of the Carmel range, the monastery at **Al-Muhraqa** sits on the edge of the highly scenic Jezreel Valley, famous for its biblical connections (see p.188); the views it offers over the valley are among the most breathtaking in the country. The road from Haifa to Nazareth (see p.184) takes you past the catacombs of **Bet She'arim**, an important Jewish burial site during the first few centuries AD; while to the south lies **Megiddo** – or **Armageddon** – whose ancient remains give little indication of the conflagration to come. Further south of here, hugging the Green Line border with the West Bank, is the area known as **the Triangle**, whose villages house the heaviest concentration of Palestinians in Israel proper.

Hedged between the West Bank and the Mediterranean and extending from Tel Aviv to Haifa, the coastal plain of **Sharon** is a land of orchards and groves that pro-

---

ACCOMMODATION PRICE CODES

Throughout this guide, **hotel accommodation** is graded on a scale from ① to ⑥. The numbers represent the cost per night of the **cheapest double room in high season**, though remember that many of the cheap places will have more expensive rooms with en-suite facilities. For **hostels**, the code represents the price of **two dorm beds** and is followed by the code for a double room where applicable, ie ①/②. Hostels are listed in ascending price order.

① = less than $20	② = $20–40	③ = $40–60
④ = $60–80	⑤ = $80–100	⑥ = over $100

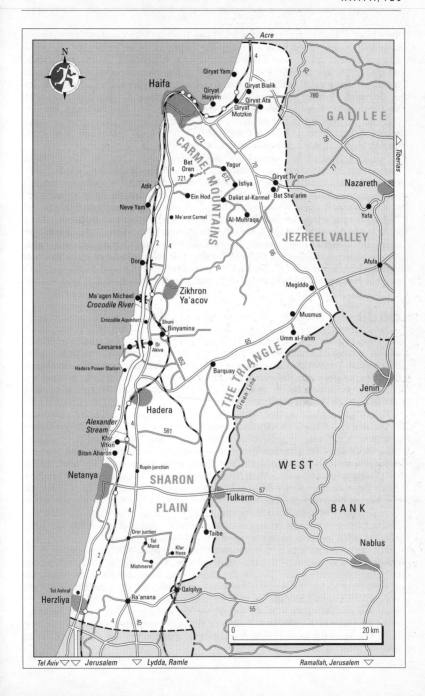

N

Acre

Qiryat Yam

Haifa

Qiryat Bialik

Qiryat Hayyim

Qiryat Ata

Qiryat Motzkin

GALILEE

CARMEL MOUNTAINS

Bet Oren

Yagur

Qiryat Tiv'on

Nazareth

Atlit

Isfiya

Ein Hod

Daliat al-Karmel

Bet She'arim

Neve Yam

Me'arot Carmel

Al-Muhraqa

Yafa

JEZREEL VALLEY

Dor

Afula

Zikhron Ya'acov

Megiddo

Ma'agen Michael
Crocodile River

Crocodile Aqueduct

Shuni

Musmus

Binyamina

Caesarea

Or Akiva

Umm al-Fahm

THE TRIANGLE

Hadera Power Station

Barquay

Jenin

Hadera

Alexander Stream

Kfar Vitkin

Bitan Aharon

Rupin junction

WEST

Netanya

SHARON

PLAIN

Tulkarm

BANK

Dror juction

Taibe

Tel Mond

Kfar Hess

Nablus

Mishmeret

Tel Ashraf

Ra'anana

Qalqiliya

Herzliya

0   20 km

Tel Aviv ▽ ▽ *Jerusalem*   ▽ *Lydda, Ramle*   *Ramallah, Jerusalem* ▽

Tiberias

duce most of Israel's famous citrus fruit. The 100-kilometre coastline itself is punctuated by occasional enclaves of luxury, the odd downmarket resort and the archeological sites of Tel Dor and Crocodile Aqueduct. In between, the extensive, undeveloped stretches of free, empty shoreline are perfect for swimming and sunbathing, though you'll really need your own transport to get to them. **Herzliya**, one of the country's main beach resorts, lies on the fringes of Tel Aviv's sprawl, probably the nearest thing to South-of-France chic you'll find in Israel. **Netanya**, the next place of any size up the coast, has aspirations to being the same sort of classy resort, but its diamond industry and status as a regional centre and agricultural market town balance out the hedonism.

North of Netanya and around an hour's drive from either Tel Aviv or Haifa, **Caesarea** is one of the most outstanding archeological sites in the country. In the midst of the excavated remains of Herod's Roman city – amphitheatre, hippodrome, temples, port and, as ever, an impressive ancient sewage system – are the extensive ruins of a smaller Crusader town, whose magnificent fortifications are solidly threatening still. Beyond here is a little-developed stretch of shore, interrupted only by the occasional kibbutz, moshav or minor historical site. The one real blight on the landscape around here is the **Hadera power station**, towering above the plains. Just inland, the late nineteenth-century settlements of **Zikhron Ya'acov** and **Binyamina**, set up by Baron de Rothschild, rate a visit only if you have a special interest in that period of Zionist history or, in the case of Zikhron Ya'acov, an insatiable appetite for mediocre wine.

Haifa

The third largest city in Israel, **HAIFA** dominates the north of the country politically, socially and commercially. It's a working city (the Israeli aphorism goes "In Jerusalem they pray, in Tel Aviv they dance, but in Haifa they work") and a very attractive one at that, ranging steeply up the side of Mount Carmel from the sea. It's also home to two important institutes of higher learning – Haifa University and the Technion – to which it owes its large student population.

Haifa is a stronghold of the Zionist labour movement and its Israeli citizens are proud of the "Red Haifa" label. The city also claims a reputation for liberalism: three religious groups with a history of persecution – the Bahais, the Ahmadis and the Carmelite order of monks – have found a haven here; buses run on the Sabbath; and Jews and Arabs mix more here than elsewhere in the country. There's also a relative lack of racial segregation in housing: Wadi Nisnas and Kababir, for example, though predominantly Palestinian areas, are far from being exclusively so. Sadly, the spirit of integration has not been carried far enough to prevent several Palestinian areas, especially in the outer parts of town, from being run down, or knocked down and replaced with Jewish homes, nor has it prevented friction between Sephardi and Ashkenazi Jews, which erupted into riots on one occasion (see p.134).

The city's working area is based around the thriving **port**, which is supported by the railway and heavy industry; its main industrial base, which includes an oil refinery and the largest grain-processing plant in the Middle East, lies to the north, mercifully out of sight from all but the peaks of the mountains. From the port, the city climbs the slopes of the **Carmel Mountains**, its residential areas getting more exclusive the higher up you go. The views from the top are terrific, and the cooling breezes sweeping along the range help make Haifa's **climate** pleasantly temperate. In its **architecture**, Haifa still bears the mark of British occupation, with much of the city centre having been built during the Mandate.

Jerusalem: inside the Church of the Holy Sepulchre

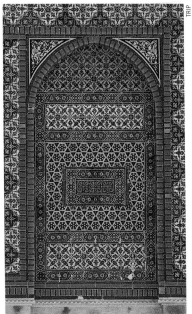

Jerusalem: the Dome of the Rock

Jerusalem post boxes, a legacy of the Mandate

Jerusalem: the Dome of the Rock

Jerusalem: the Wailing Wall

Jerusalem: crosses for rent at the Church of the Holy Sepulchre

Jerusalem: the Citadel (Tower of David)

Caesarea: Hadrian's aqueduct

TRIP

Haifa: the Bahai Shrine

TRIP

Fishing in the harbour at Jaffa

TRIP

The Druze village of Daliat al-Karmel

TRIP

Jerusalem: the Via Dolorosa

Jaffa's Sea Mosque and Tel Aviv's skyline

Tel Aviv street life: a bar on Shenkin

Some history

Archeological remains indicate that the area around Haifa has been inhabited since the Paleolithic period. A **port** was founded in the fourteenth century BC at a site east of the present city now known as Tel Abu Haram, and in the early Christian era the area was a fishing centre, known particularly for the production of purple dye extracted from the murex, a small, spiny shellfish. By the eleventh century a local shipbuilding industry had also developed, but its progress was interrupted by the **Crusader** invasion of 1099. Having all but destroyed the town and its population, the Crusaders proceeded to fortify and enlarge what was left: a small town very much overshadowed by Acre.

The following century saw Haifa fought over in the manner of its more important neighbours: Saladin recaptured the city in 1187 and destroyed the ramparts; Louis IX grabbed it back for the Crusaders; and in 1291 Sultan Baybars marched in, putting an end to the problem by destroying the place altogether. At the time of the **Ottoman conquest** in 1517, Haifa was little more than an impoverished village, but its fortunes picked up with the expansion of trade between Europe and the Orient, and the port thrived once more. However, disaster struck again in 1751 when the city was conquered by **Daher al-Omar** (see p.487) and destroyed during the battle; this time, however, instead of rebuilding on the same site (today Bet Galim), al-Omar ordered the construction of a walled city in the area today known as Old Haifa, a better site strategically since it controlled the narrow corridor between the mountains and the sea. Above the city he built a huge fortress.

Enjoying relative stability at last, Haifa developed quickly. Its importance was assured in 1904 with the building of a **railway** from Haifa to Damascus and Mecca; and under the **British Mandate**, Haifa became the only significant working port in northern Palestine (a situation encouraged by the British, as it allowed greater control of the area). In the 1922 census, the population of the city stood at 25,000 – 17,000 Arabs and 8000 Jews. However, economic growth, coupled with growing Jewish immigration, brought new tensions. It was from Haifa in 1935 that the elderly Syrian **Sheikh Izzedin Qasim** set out for the hills of the West Bank with 800 men in an attempt to overthrow the British and secure Palestine for the Palestinians. It didn't take long for the British, with the aid of a few reconnaissance planes, to track him down and force him into a hopeless battle. But although the fighting lasted only a few hours, its boost to Arab morale, along with Qasim's martyrdom, far outweighed its military significance. For the first time armed rebellion had been used by Palestinian Arabs, and the 1936–39 Arab Revolt, though not a consequence of it, clearly owed it a large measure of inspiration.

After the revolt, it was the turn of the **Zionists** to take up arms, following the publication of the May 1939 White Paper which restricted the numbers of Jewish **immigrants** to Palestine in order to maintain a 2:1 ratio of Arabs to Jews. With Haifa the main port of entry for both legal and illegal immigrants, the city became an obvious focus for Zionist protest; their first act was the bombing of police patrol boat *Sinbad II* in the port on August 8, 1939, but their next ended in disaster. The British, deciding to deport illegal immigrants rather than detain them at Atlit (see p.168), had put 1900 aboard an ageing boat called the *Patria*, ready for transport to Cyprus. To prevent its departure, the Haganah bombed the vessel with the intention of disabling it, but the *Patria* was weaker than they thought, and sank with the loss of 252 lives. The British stuck by their policies, with further loss of life: in February 1942 the *Struma*, carrying over seven hundred Romanian Jews, was refused entry to the port and eventually sank off Istanbul with only one survivor. The most famous of the immigrant ships, however, was the *Exodus*, which in 1947 headed for Haifa crammed with 4500 Jewish survivors from European death camps. British troops boarded by force before it entered

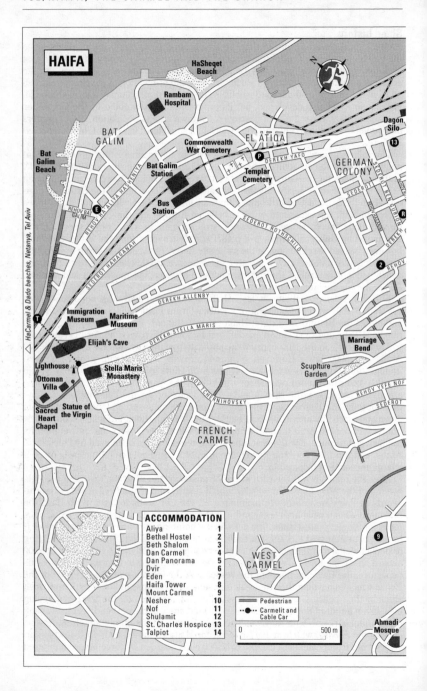

HAIFA

HaSheqet Beach

Rambam Hospital

BAT GALIM

Bat Galim Beach

EL ATIQA

Dagon Silo

13

Commonwealth War Cemetery

GERMAN COLONY

P

DEREKH YAFO

Templar Cemetery

SEDEROT BEN GURION

Bat Galim Station

REHOV IM ALIYA HA-SHNIYA

R

E

REHOV BAT GALIM

SEDEROT HE-HALUTZ

Bus Station

SEDEROT HAHAGANAH

SEDEROT ROTHSCHILD

2

REHOV

HaCarmel & Dado beaches, Netanya, Tel Aviv

DEREKH ALLENBY

Immigration Museum

Maritime Museum

T

DEREKH STELLA MARIS

Elijah's Cave

Marriage Bend

Lighthouse

Stella Maris Monastery

REHOV TCHERNIHOVSKY

Sculpture Garden

Ottoman Villa

REHOV YEFE NOF

Sacred Heart Chapel

Statue of the Virgin

SEDEROT

FRENCH CARMEL

DEREKH TZFA

WEST CARMEL

9

ACCOMMODATION

Aliya	1
Bethel Hostel	2
Beth Shalom	3
Dan Carmel	4
Dan Panorama	5
Dvir	6
Eden	7
Haifa Tower	8
Mount Carmel	9
Nesher	10
Nof	11
Shulamit	12
St. Charles Hospice	13
Talpiot	14

Pedestrian

Carmelit and Cable Car

0   500 m

Ahmadi Mosque

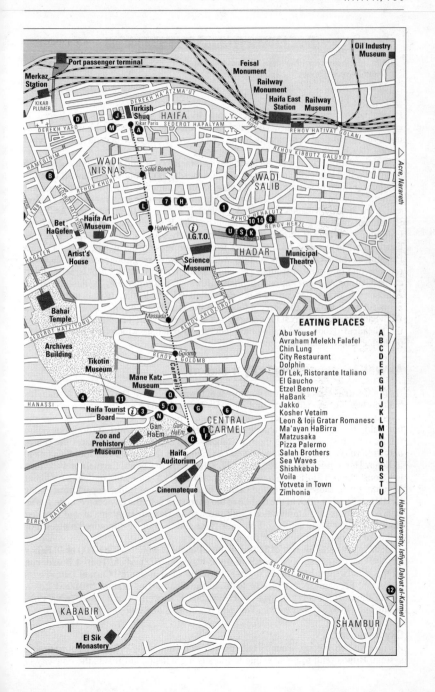

Oil Industry Museum

Port passenger terminal

Feisal Monument

Railway Monument

Merkaz Station

DEREKH HA'ATZMA'UT

Haifa East Station

Railway Museum

KIKAR PLUMER

Turkish Shuq

OLD HAIFA

REHOV HATIVAT GOLANI

DEREKH YAFO

Kikar Paris

SEDEROT HAPALYAM

REHOV KIBBUTZ GALUYOT

HAMEGINIM

WADI NISNAS

Solel Boneh

WADI SALIB

REHOV KHURI

ALLENBY

SEDEROT HATZIYONU

REHOV HEHALUTZ

REHOV HAZIYON

Bet HaGefen

Haifa Art Museum

HaNevi'im

I.G.T.O.

REHOV HERZL

Artist's House

Science Museum

HADAR

Municipal Theatre

Bahai Temple

SEDEROT HATZIYONU

REHOV ARLOZOROFF

Archives Building

REHOV GOLOMB

Golomb

Tikotin Museum

Massada

Mane Katz Museum

Carmel

HANASSI

Haifa Tourist Board

Gan HaEm

Gan HaEm

CENTRAL CARMEL

Zoo and Prehistory Museum

Haifa Auditorium

Cinemateque

DEREKH HAYAM

SEDEROT MORIYA

KABABIR

SHAMBUR

El Sik Monastery

△ Acre, Nazareth

△ Haifa University, Isfiya, Dalyat al-Karmel △

EATING PLACES

Abu Yousef	A
Avraham Melekh Falafel	B
Chin Lung	C
City Restaurant	D
Dolphin	E
Dr Lek, Ristorante Italiano	F
El Gaucho	G
Etzel Benny	H
HaBank	I
Jakko	J
Kosher Vetaim	K
Leon & Ioji Gratar Romanesc	L
Ma'ayan HaBirra	M
Matzusaka	N
Pizza Palermo	O
Salah Brothers	P
Sea Waves	Q
Shishkebab	R
Voila	S
Yotveta in Town	T
Zimhonia	U

Palestinian waters, leaving three dead and 146 injured in the process, and forced its eventual return to Germany. The whole sorry episode, detailed in the world's press, brought a great deal of sympathy to the Zionist cause and later became the subject of a book (see p.512) and film.

With **partition**, Haifa was quickly taken by Israeli forces, and the majority of its Arab population fled into exile in Lebanon, despite messages put out by the Jewish community urging them to remain. Most of today's Arab community, some five to ten percent of the population, were (or are descended from) refugees from rural parts of Galilee, and from nearby villages destroyed by Israeli forces in their advance. As far as Palestinian politics go, Haifa has established itself as an important centre of the Communist Party – *Al-Ittihad*, the Communist Party's Arabic daily newspaper, is published here. In general, though, apart from some tension during the Intifada, Haifa Palestinians have coexisted peacefully with their Jewish neighbours since 1948 and it remains one of the most trouble-free cities in the country. In fact it is Israel's undercurrent of resentment among Sephardi Jews at discrimination against them by Ashkenazi Jews that has caused more disruption in Haifa; leading to riots in 1959 when Sephardi Jews took to the streets following the fatal shooting of a Moroccan Jew in Wadi Salib during his arrest for being drunk and disorderly. The rioters' first target was the Histadrut (labour and trade union federation) building, which they burnt down in protest at employment discrimination.

Arrival, information and city transport

Haifa's **Central Bus Station** is northwest of town on Sederot Derekh HaHaganah. It's built on two levels – suburban and inter-city buses depart from the back of the lower level, while local services leave from the front of the upper level. Behind the bus station, and connected to it by a pedestrian tunnel, is the main **train station**, Bat Galim (all trains also stop at Haifa's Central Station – also called Merkaz – nearer the centre of town). To reach the town centre, you can take a bus (#15, #15a, #19, #36, #36a or #40 to Rehov Herzl in Hadar; #5, #21, #22, #27, #28 or #37a to Central Carmel) or walk: turn left along Derekh HaHaganah, which becomes Derekh Yafo and continues for about 1km into town. Buses back to the Central Bus Station from Hadar depart from Rehov HeHalutz. **Ferries** dock in the middle of the port, very near the city centre: once you've cleared customs and immigration, walk through to Derekh HaAtzma'ut and turn left along it – Kikar Paris will be off on your right after a couple of hundred metres. For details of moving on from Haifa, see p.145.

Haifa has several **tourist offices**, the most helpful of which is the IGTO at 18 Rehov Herzl (Sun–Thurs 9am–5pm, Fri 9am–1pm; ☎04/866 6522). Haifa Tourist Board, run by the municipality, has offices at 106 Sederot HaNassi in Central Carmel (Sun–Thurs 8am–7pm, Fri 8am–1pm; ☎04/837 4010), in the Central Bus Station (☎04/851 2208), and in the port for ferry arrivals (☎04/864 5692), as well as a 24-hour "what's on" phone line (☎04/837 4253) and a Web site (*www.insite.co.il/tour/haifa/haifa.htm*).

City transport

It's no problem getting around Haifa thanks to its unusually efficient local transport system. **Buses** tend to be slow due to the steep gradients, but this is the only city in

Israel where they run on Saturdays (before sunset on Sat they start from Rehov Herzl, not the Central Bus Station); information on local services is available from the Egged booth (☎04/854 9131) in the central section of the Central Bus Station.

A much speedier alternative than the bus is the **Carmelit Subway Line** – Israel's only underground railway. Built in 1959 and recently refurbished, it's basically a funicular that shuttles up and down the mountainside between Kikar Paris and Central Carmel with a few stops en route (Sun–Thurs 6am–10pm, Fri 6am–3pm, Sat 7pm/later in summer till midnight; 3.70NIS per journey); look out for the yellow station entrances.

Accommodation

Although Haifa doesn't have a vast choice of accommodation, there are decent places in all price brackets. You'll find a few cheap and mid-range **hotels** in Hadar, but, if you're prepared to pay for it, the best accommodation is located in Carmel. Both of the **hostels** in town are Christian and quite strictly run, so most budget travellers head out to the excellent but hardly central *Carmel Youth Hostel* (see below). Another option is the *Stella Carmel Hospice* in Isfiya (see p.146), reached by sherut from Rehov Eliyahu or by bus #192.

Downtown
Hotel Aliya, 35 HaHalutz (☎04/862 3918). Basic and bare hotel with shared bathrooms. ②.

Bethel Hostel, 40 HaGefen (☎04/852 1110). Clean and friendly, Christian-run hostel usually limited to 18–35-year-olds. 11pm curfew, dorms closed 9am–5pm. Take bus #22 from the Central Bus Station. ①.

Eden Hotel, 8 Shmarjahu Levin (☎04/866 8593). Large rooms with balconies but a shared bathroom. Natives of Berlin get a ten percent discount. ③.

Haifa Tower, 63 Herzl (☎04/867 7111, fax 862 1863). Modern hotel with good-sized rooms in the centre of Hadar. ⑥.

Nesher Hotel, 53 Herzl (☎04/862 0644). Clean and tidy, but with a rather moribund atmosphere. ②.

St Charles Hospice, 105 Yafo (☎04/855 3705). Run by Roman Catholic nuns, but accepts pilgrims and tourists of all denominations. Airy rooms and a well-kept garden. 10pm curfew. ②.

Talpiot Hotel, 61 Herzl (☎04/867 3753 or 4). Pleasant if not exactly cosy, with a shower (but no toilet) in each room. ③.

Carmel
Beth Shalom, 110 HaNassi (☎04/837 7481 or 2, fax 837 2443). Good-value, Christian-run guesthouse that's friendly, comfortable and often full. Guests must stay for a minimum of three nights; all bookings by post or fax quoting credit card number. ④.

Dan Carmel, 85–87 HaNassi (☎04/830 6306, fax 838 7504). Haifa's most luxurious establishment, with tastefully furnished spacious rooms, as well as nineteen suites and two penthouses. ⑥.

Dan Panorama, 107 HaNassi (☎04/835 2222, fax 835 2235). Top-whack hotel at the top of the town, with views to match its name. ⑥.

Hotel Dvir, 124 Yefe Nof (☎04/838 9131, fax 838 1068). Great views and excellent service, at rather less than the price of the neighbouring deluxe hotels (many of whose facilities, such as the *Dan Panorama*'s pool, guests can use). ⑤.

Nof Hotel, 101 HaNassi (☎04/835 4311, fax 838 8810). Small and friendly hotel offering great views, especially from the top floors; you'll pay more for those rooms. Reservations can be made in the UK on ☎0181/995 8211, fax 995 2474. ⑥.

Out of the city centre
Carmel Youth Hostel, 4km south of Haifa off the main Tel Aviv road (☎04/853 1944). A free, uncrowded beach nearby, combined with the sea views, landscaped lawns, excellent food and nearby tennis courts and fitness centres, make this a very pleasant place to stay. A choice of dorms or double rooms. Bus #43 from the Central Bus Station will drop you off at the door. ①/②.

Marom Hotel, 15 HaPalmah, Romema (☎04/825 4355, fax 825 4358). Three kilometres out of Haifa, this mid-market place has few special advantages unless you particularly want to stay in Romema. ④.

Mount Carmel, 103 HaYam (☎04/838 1413 or 5, fax 838 1763). Bright, pleasant new hotel up where the air is clear. ④.

Shulamit Hotel, 15 Qiryat Sefer, Shambur (☎04/834 2811, fax 825 5206). Sedate hotel in a quiet area, but again rather too far out of town (3km) if you don't have a special reason for staying in Shambur. ④.

The City

Haifa is not a city of great architectural delights, but it's an enjoyable enough place to wander around; the houses aren't ancient, but they're old enough to have a bit of character, and the streets are infused with cool breezes and the scent of pine and fig. The city is built on three levels with many of its streets running horizontally across the hillside, joined by flights of steps. The busy **Port area** at the bottom offers little of specific interest, but is the most atmospheric part of town (albeit slightly seedy in parts) and houses most of the older buildings. Around it lie the town's other old quarters, including Wadi Nisnas and the German Colony. **Hadar**, just up the hill, is the business, shopping and entertainment centre, and by far the most crowded and vibrant section of the city, its labyrinthine streets dominated by good, cheap restaurants and shops. At the top is **Carmel**, the most attractive area, characterized by small parks and marvellous vistas. It's also where Haifa's large student population hangs out, and its parks, theatres and art cinemas are generally packed out.

The two-hour **city tour** (Sat at 10am; free), run by the Haifa Tourist Board and starting from the corner of Yefe Nof and Sha'ar HaLevanon, is an excellent way to gain an overview of the city.

The Port and Old Haifa

The area around the **Port** is known locally as the **black-market area**, though there's no sign of anything more illicit than the odd red-light bar. At its heart is **Kikar Paris**, named in honour of the French firm that built the Carmelit Subway, which has its terminus here; just to the west lies the **Turkish Shuq**, a small fruit and vegetable market where you can stock up for a picnic. **Sha'ar Plumer**, opposite, is the seediest part of the port area, and the city's red-light district, though hardly lurid compared to ports at the western end of the Mediterranean. Northwest along Derekh Ha'Atzma'ut, Kikar Palmer is bounded on three sides by the passenger port entrance for boats to Cyprus and Greece, the Central (Merkaz) Train Station, and, on the shorefront, the enormous fortress-like **Dagon Grain Silo** – the largest granary in the Middle East and used to stock subsidized US wheat imports. There are free tours available of its **Archeological Museum of Grain Handling in Ancient Israel and the Near East** (Sun–Fri 10.30am or by appointment; free; ☎04/866 4221), with artefacts from 12,000 BC to the present day, but nothing on the country's Arab history.

Sederot HaPalyam and Derekh Ha'Atzma'ut, running southeast from Kikar Paris, are the two main thoroughfares of **Old Haifa**, whose mosques are all in a state of disrepair or renovation, amid a plethora of roadworks and construction sites. The two streets converge at Kikar Feisal, named after the Iraqi king known for his enlightened views, who died in France in 1933 while undergoing medical treatment. His body landed at Haifa on its way home for burial and a **broken column** inscribed with one of the king's quotes – "Freedom is not given; it must be taken" – was erected here to commemorate his passing. Now by the roadside, it originally stood in the centre of the intersection. Just beyond, by Haifa East train station, a monument decorated with a stone steam locomotive commemorates the completion of the **Hegaz Railway** in 1904, which ran to Damascus and Mecca. Rail buffs might be interested in visiting the small **Railway Museum** (Sun, Tues & Thurs 9am–noon; 3NIS), next to the station, which pays tribute to the role of the railway in the development of Haifa with some dusty exhibits, among them some of the old British-built steam trains that plied the now defunct Hejaz Railway.

A little further out, in the industrial zone on the other side of the railway, there's yet another museum to Haifa's industriousness: the **Israel Oil Industry Museum** at 2 Tuvim (Sun–Thurs 9am–noon; 5NIS), run by the Shemen edible oil company and illustrating the history of local oil production, mostly from olives.

Around Wadi Nisnas and the German Colony

Just north of the port area, **Wadi Nisnas** is a crowded quarter with a population of around six thousand and liberally dotted with mosques, churches and crumblingly impressive Arab architecture. At its heart is a market; another – the so-called melon market – lies at the southern end of the wadi. Here, during the Arab Revolt, two bombs (generally thought to have been the work of Revisionist Zionists) exploded three weeks apart in July 1938, killing a total of 72 people.

A little to the north of Wadi Nisnas, the admirable **Bet HaGefen Arab-Jewish Cultural Centre**, at no. 2 Rehov HaGefen (Sun–Fri 10am–1pm & 4–8pm, Sat 10am–1pm; free; ☎04/852 5251/2), was established in 1963 by members of both communities in an effort to overcome the ethnic barrier between them and provides activities in which Jews and Arabs can participate together. The main feature of interest for visitors is the art gallery upstairs, with regular exhibitions, but, attractions aside, it's just good to know that such a place exists. Just around the corner at 21 HaTziyonut, the **Artist's House** (Sun–Thurs 9am–1pm & 4–7pm, Sat 10am–1pm; free) is a small gallery hosting regular exhibitions of modern art by Israeli artists.

Across Sederot HaTziyonut, at 26 Shabtai Levi, the **Haifa Museum of Art**, (Sun–Fri 10am–1pm, Sat 10am–3pm, and Tues, Thurs & Sat 5–8pm; 12NIS – ticket also valid for the Tikotin and Maritime museums over three days; ☎04/852 3255), is the largest of the city's museums, but in many ways the most disappointing. It is housed in the drab British Mandate headquarters and laid out with an extraordinary lack of imagination; the best display is probably that of **ancient art** on the top floor, with a substantial collection of Greco-Roman sculpture, some of it very fine. Up here too is a magnificent **mosaic floor** from the ancient city of Shiqmona, a forerunner of Haifa. Other collections cover Jewish ethnology (clothing, writings, and the minutiae of daily life) and modern Israeli art.

Lying west of Wadi Nisnas, around Sederot Ben Gurion, the **German Colony** was established in 1868 by the Tempel Gemeinde or "Templars", a German Christian sect who saw themselves as the chosen people, with a mission to build the Kingdom of God in the Holy Land. The colony, bounded by Rehov HaGanim and Rehov Ruthery and surrounded by fields, was modelled on a German village, with a single main street (now Sederot Ben Gurion) – the Germanic influence can still be seen in the odd Gothic spire or stairwell, and German inscriptions above some doorways. The Templars, many of whom were Nazi sympathizers, were rounded up and deported by the British during World War II. Their cemetery lies just off Derekh Yafo alongside a rather better-kept **Commonwealth War Cemetery**, resting place mainly for victims of World War I.

Hadar

Sitting above Old Haifa, **Hadar** is the commercial centre of modern Haifa, bustling with streetlife, shops and traffic, a breather from which is offered by the pedestrianized **Rehov Nordau**, where you can relax with a coffee and sticky pastry. At its southern end, you can eschew the concrete altogether in the pine-shaded **Binyamin Garden**, which houses the city's Municipal Theatre (see p.143). At the other end of Nordau, just up Rehov Balfour, the **National Museum of Science and Technology** (Mon, Wed & Thurs – also Sun in July & Aug – 9am–5pm, Tues 9am–7pm, Fri 9am–1pm, Sat 10am–2pm; 15NIS), housed in the old campus of the Technion, is the sort of museum beloved of young would-be scientists (and older ones), with plenty of hands-on working models among its exhibits.

Carmel

Mount Carmel dominates every view in Haifa and is as spectacular an observation point as you could wish for. It also makes a good starting point for exploration of the city. Uptown in all senses of the term, Carmel has the most expensive houses, shops, hotels and restaurants as well as a collection of worthwhile sights for the visitor. It's most easily reached using the Carmelit Subway which drops you at the top at Central Carmel.

From the Carmelit stop it's a short walk northwest along Sederot HaNassi to the **Tikotin Japanese Art Museum** at no. 89 (Sun, Mon, Wed & Thurs 10am–5pm, Tues 4–8pm, Fri 10am–1pm, Sat 10am–4pm; 12NIS, valid also for the Haifa Art and Maritime museums over three days; ☎04/838 3554), arguably the most rewarding and interesting museum in Haifa. The collection of nineteenth-century prints and etchings occupies a replica of a traditional **Japanese house**: a single room divided by rice-paper screens and narrow troughs, which, in its intimate relation between art and environment, is a living example of the Japanese concept of art. In the museum's excellent poster shop you can buy reproductions of many of the prints on display at reasonable prices.

Just opposite the museum, the lovingly tended lawns and refreshingly peaceful air of **Gan HaEm** ("Mothers' Park") make it a popular place for a stroll. Within the park you'll also find a playground, an open-air theatre and several cafés and bars. In its northern section there's a small **Zoo** and **Prehistory Museum** (both Sun–Thurs 8am–3pm, Fri 8am–1pm, Sat 10am–2pm, open until 6pm in July & Aug; 20NIS; ☎04/837 1833); the former concentrates on the plant and animal life of northern Israel, particularly the Carmel mountains, while the latter uses mini-dioramas to illustrate the life of prehistoric man in the area.

Behind the Tikotin Museum, the aptly named **Rehov Yefe Nof** (Panorama Road) offers stunning views of the port and downtown areas. At no. 89, the **Mane Katz Museum** (Sun, Mon, Wed & Thurs 10am–4pm, Tues 2–6pm, Fri 10am–1pm, Sat 10am–2pm; free) was once the home of the Expressionist painter Mane Katz, who studied and painted with Marc Chagall and Modigliani, and worked in Paris, Vienna and the US before retiring to Haifa in 1958. The house contains displays of his paintings and sculptures, as well as his collection of oriental rugs and religious artefacts from Jewish communities throughout the world. Yefe Nof leads down onto Sederot HaZiyyonut, where a **Sculpture Garden** (dubbed "peace point" by local people), tucked away unassumingly on the north side of the road, features works by one of Haifa's leading contemporary artists, Ursula Malkin. Across the road from the lower left-hand exit of the park is the **Marriage Bend**, so named because of the constant flow of newlyweds who use the place as a backdrop to wedding photos.

THE BAHAI SHRINE

The shining golden dome of the **Bahai Shrine** (more correctly the Shrine of the Bab; temple daily 9am–noon, closed three weeks in Aug; garden daily 8am–5pm; free; bus #22 or #26 from the Central Bus Station, #22 from Central Carmel), just east of the Sculpture Garden on Sederot HaZiyyonut, is visible from all over town. The shrine is the world centre of the Bahai religion (see box opposite) and, together with the adjoining archives building, forms by far the most impressive and imposing complex of buildings in Haifa. It was built in 1953 to house the remains of the prophet **Al-Bab**, brought

BAHAISM

The **Bahai faith** was founded in Iran in the mid-nineteenth century by **Mizra Hussein Ali (Baha'Ullah)**, son of a noble family who became a follower of the prophet **Al-Bab (Sayyid Ali Muhammad)**. Sayyid Ali was born a Shi'ite Muslim but, at the age of 25, declared: "I am the Bab, the Gate to a new age of Peace and Universal Brotherhood." The growing number of his followers alarmed the authorities, who tried to clamp down on them, but persecution served only to make them more militant, and attacks on them led to fighting. The Bab himself was arrested and executed in 1850.

On the death of the Bab, his movement split between the militants, led by Subh-i-Azad, and the pacifist Bahais, led by Mizra, Azad's half-brother. Mizra had taken the title Baha'Ullah ("Glory of God") after experiencing visions while in prison in Tehran in 1852 telling him that he was a new prophet of God. On his release, he was exiled to Iraq, where he continued to attract followers. Baha'Ullah wrote letters to world leaders urging them to turn to God and establish universal peace; Queen Victoria replied to the effect that if he was a god (or prophet) then this was good; and if not, at least he was harmless. The Ottoman authorities, however, disagreed. In 1863, they exiled him to Edirne (European Turkey) and five years later imprisoned him in Acre, where he wrote his most important work, the **Kitabi Aktar**, a book of law determining marriage, divorce, inheritance and lifestyle. He died in Acre under house arrest in 1892.

Today, the Bahai faith has around five million followers worldwide; they regard the Baha'Ullah as the latest in the line of teachers that also includes Moses, Jesus, Zoroaster, Buddha and Mohammed. Like Muslims, they do not worship their messenger as divine but regard him as a manifestation or reflection of God who is too distant and too awesome for human beings to know directly. The basic **Bahai philosophy** teaches that all peoples should unite, lay down their arms, and form a universal government in which all people – men and women alike – enjoy equal rights. They eschew alcohol and other intoxicants, along with gambling, extramarital sex, violence and racism, and stress the value of individual morality, obedience to the law, work, education and cleanliness.

to Haifa in 1909 by **Abd al-Baha** (son of Baha'Ullah, founder of the faith), whose own remains now lie alongside those of the Bab. The Baha'Ullah himself is buried in the Bahai Gardens near Acre (see p.228), and all three are revered by Bahais as prophets on whose teachings the faith was founded.

The temple is huge: its Chiampo stone walls were cut and carved in Italy and the supporting columns are made from Rose Baveno granite. With its classical, golden **dome** supported on Arabic arches and columns, the building is an interesting mix of Europe and the Middle East, a fitting combination for a faith whose central message is the unity of all religions. The **interior** is lavishly furnished and decorated, housing an impressive collection of ancient Persian rugs laid out beneath a grotesque French chandelier. Dress respectfully and remove your shoes before entering.

The **Persian Gardens** surrounding the temple merit a visit in themselves. Towering eucalyptus and delicate date palms rise from lush vegetation; the views and the beauty of the buildings are a joy. Across the road from the temple, the **archives building** is modelled on the Parthenon. Built in 1957, it looks a lot sturdier than the original, and you have to admire both the beauty of Greek architecture and the audacity of the designer who dared reproduce it. The building is the administrative headquarters of the religion and is closed to the public.

The Stella Maris Monastery and Elijah's Cave

On the northwestern side of town, the nineteenth-century **Stella Maris Monastery** is current home of the Carmelite order of Roman Catholic monks (Mon–Sat 8.30am–1.30pm & 3–6pm; free). The monastery can be reached by bus #27 from

Central Carmel, or #26 and #27 from the Central Bus Station. Alternatively you could come up in the egg-shaped **cable car** (Sat–Thurs 10am–6pm, Fri 9am–2pm; one-way 12NIS, return trip 16NIS) which starts at the beach, past the bus station, and makes a stop right next to the monastery: the views are great but the running commentary is uninformative and for the most part unintelligible.

Since their order was founded in 1150, the monks have been forced to move several times due to centuries of harassment by various authorities; given their Crusader origins and their collaboration with Napoleon during his 1799 siege (the monastery was used as a hospital for his troops, a fact that did not endear the Carmelites to the Ottoman regime), their unpopularity is perhaps understandable. Remains of earlier Carmelite centres are preserved in the monastery's tiny **museum**, along with a bizarre jumble of miscellaneous items that seem to have little to do with the order. The **church** is a beautiful neo-Gothic structure whose stained-glass windows depict Elijah's ascension to heaven in a chariot of fire. Entrance to the museum and church is at the whim of the monks; if possible try and attach yourself to a group of visiting pilgrims, and dress conservatively.

Across the street from the monastery, the **Stella Maris Lighthouse**, built in 1928 on top of a villa belonging to a nineteenth-century Ottoman pasha, is still in use today; its name (Latin for "Star of the Sea") is now used for the monastery too. The statue of the Virgin Mary nearby was sent from Chile in 1894 and rests on an iron column said to be cast from the metal of cannons used by the Chileans in their struggle for independence from Spain. It stands at the entrance to a naval base whose main building was once a villa built for the Ottoman governor in 1821 out of stones from the monastery which he had had blown up on the excuse that Greek rebels fighting for independence might use it as a bridgehead to invade.

Legend has it that just below the present site of the Carmelite monastery is **Elijah's Cave** (Sun–Thurs 8am–5pm, Fri 8am–12.30pm; free) where the prophet Elijah lived and meditated before the contest between monotheism and paganism in which he is said to have challenged and destroyed the "False Prophets of Baal" (I Kings 18: 16–45). Mount Carmel is one of two possible sites of this challenge; the other is at al-Muhraqa (see p.148). Inside the cave, a small altar has become a shrine for Jews, Christians, Muslims and Druze alike. On a path from the cave up to the monastery, the tiny white **Chapel of the Sacred Heart** commemorates a supposed visit to Elijah's cave by the holy family on their return from Egypt. The cave is clearly visible from the main Tel Aviv–Haifa road and is surrounded by smaller caves, which can also be explored.

Across the street, and just a ten-minute walk from the Central Bus Station, is the **Clandestine Immigration and Navy Museum**, 204 Allenby (Sun–Thurs 9am–4pm, Fri 9am–1pm; 6NIS). The museum is divided into two parts; the first and most interesting explores clandestine Jewish immigration into Palestine during the British Mandate. There are details of all the sailings (over 100,000 illegal immigrants arrived in 118 ships), a map showing the routes they took from Europe, the nameplate of the ill-fated *Patria* (see p.13), and articles from the Cyprus internment camps where would-be immigrants caught by the British ended up. The centrepiece is the *Ef Al Pi Khen*, a ship actually used to run in illegal immigrants. The other half of the museum is devoted to the history of the Israeli navy.

Continuing the naval theme, the **National Maritime Museum** (Sun, Mon, Wed & Thurs 10am–4pm, Tues 4–8pm, Sat 10am–1pm; 12NIS – ticket also valid for Haifa Art and Tikotin museums over three days), close by at 198 Allenby, is largely devoted to models of ships built according to plans and paintings discovered in ancient tombs and palaces throughout the Middle East. These include the first sea-going vessel from the reign of Pharaoh Sahure (2500 BC), a Canaanite merchant ship (1400 BC), the

Tarshish ships mentioned in the Bible, and a series of Byzantine and Greco-Roman vessels. An excellent collection on maritime archeology includes three wooden Egyptian funerary boats dating from about 2000 BC.

Outlying Areas

Situated high on the slopes behind Central Carmel, the spacious suburb of **Kababir** with its large houses and well-kept gardens was established in 1836, and is so separate from its surroundings that it feels almost like a village. It is also home to a community of adherents to **Ahmadism**, a Sufi sect of Islam founded in the nineteenth century by Mirza Ghulam Ahmad and widely persecuted for its belief in Ahmad as a prophet – a heresy to Sunni Muslims, for whom Mohammed was the "seal of the prophets". Pakistan, which has the world's largest Ahmadi community, has declared them non-Muslims, whose religious services are blasphemous and therefore punishable by death. Kababir's large, richly decorated **Ahmadi Mosque** (Sat–Thurs 9am–noon; free), completed in 1984, takes pride of place among the fine buildings, most of which date back to the nineteenth century, having escaped the ravages of subsequent wars. If you don't fancy the short and pleasant walk from Central Carmel, you can get to Kababir from there on bus #34 (no direct bus from the Central Bus Station). It is also possible to reach Kababir on foot from the *Carmel Youth Hostel*, though it's a steep climb.

   Haifa University sits on the summit of a mountain near the beginning of the Carmel National Park; from its impressive 25-storey **Eshkol Tower** you can see as far as the Golan Heights, Rosh Haniqra and, on a clear day, the snow-covered top of Jabal al-Sheikh (Mount Hermon). The tower houses the student union, and normally has some kind of exhibition in its foyer. The other attraction here is the **Reuben and Edith Hecht Museum** (Sun, Mon, Wed & Thurs 10am–4pm, Tues 10am–7pm, Fri & Sat 10am–2pm; free), one half of which is occupied by archeological artefacts illustrating ancient Jewish life in Israel, the other half with paintings by French Impressionists, including works by Monet, Pissarro and Soutine. To get to the campus take **bus** #36 or #36a from Rehov Herzl, or #24, #36 or #192 from the Central Bus Station, or #192 from Central Carmel. Campus tours can usually be arranged by appointment (call ☎04/824 0097–9 for details).

The beaches

Situated on the northwestern side of town, the city's **beaches** abut Bat Galim – Haifa's original site, demolished by Daher al-Omar in 1761 – but being small and rocky they're not really worth a visit. **HaShaqet** (Quiet) Beach, reached from Derekh Yafo by walking down Rehov Hel HaYam, is for religious bathers (summer only; closed Fri pm & Sat), with separate days for men and women. From rocky **Bat Galim Beach**, nearby, a pleasant promenade leads to the lower station of the cable car (see above).

   Better beaches lie further southwest alongside the main Tel Aviv–Haifa road (bus #44a, #45 or #45a from Derekh Allenby). **HaCarmel Beach** is the most commercialized and favoured by the bronzed beach set, **Dado Beach** is much less so, though a yachting marina is in the pipeline. The open beaches south of Dado are subject to treacherous currents, so you should avoid swimming there. North of town, there is another, less crowded, beach at **Qiryat Hayyim**.

Eating

Haifa boasts some of the best **falafel** and **street food** in the country (see box on p.142). As for actual **restaurants**, those in and around Kikar Paris are aimed primarily at working people, good if you're after a reasonably priced, filling meal, though the Jewish ones in particular tend to open for lunch only. In Hadar, Rehovot Herzl and HeHalutz are

SNACKS, ICE CREAM AND PASTRIES

Haifa has two main concentrations of **shawarma**, **falafel** and **bureka** stands: one at 130–144 Derekh Yafo, by El Atiqa, a couple of hundred metres east of the Central Bus Station (a couple of these are open 24hr); the other on Rehov HeHalutz, near the junction with HaNeviim, right in the centre of Hadar. For the sweet-toothed, there are mouth-watering (but pricey) **pastries** at *Kapulsky's*, 11 Nordau, and *Dr Lek* has an **ice-cream** outlet by Gan HaEm Carmelit station. A wide choice of **fruit juices** can be had from stalls at 5 Herzl and 11 HaNeviim.

where you'll find the lower-priced eating places, while swankier joints are generally in and around the pedestrianized Rehov Nordau, also the place for **café** terrace-sitting. Central Carmel is the place for more expensive dining and international cuisine, with restaurants ranging from East Asian to South American and offering anything from light sushi to hefty T-bones.

Port Area and German Colony

Abu Yousef, 1 Kikar Paris. Sign in Arabic and Hebrew only. Renowned Palestinian restaurant serving grills, mezze and kebabs, with a second branch in El Atiqa in a small street by 144 Derekh Yafo. Daily 9am–midnight. Moderate.

Avraham Melekh Falafel, 34 Allenby. The sign (in Hebrew only) means "Abraham King of Falafel". Old-established and well-known falafel stall, considered by many to be the best in town. Sun–Thurs 9am–10.30pm, Fri 9am–1pm, Sat nightfall–10.30pm. Cheap.

City Restaurant, 7 HaBankim. Ashkenazi food in a pleasant little restaurant. The set menu is especially good value. Sun–Fri noon–4pm. Moderate.

Dolphin, 13 Bet Galim (☎04/852 3837). Upmarket seafood restaurant in Bat Galim. Daily noon–4pm & 7pm–midnight. Expensive.

Jakko, 12 HaDekalim. Sign in Hebrew only. Excellent and very good-value seafood restaurant by the Turkish shuq. Sun–Thurs noon–11pm, Fri noon–5pm, Sat noon–6pm. Moderate.

Ma'ayan HaBirra, 4 Natanson. Sign in Hebrew only. The speciality is Romanian *pastrama*, reasonably similar to American-Jewish pastrami, but with a choice of beef or pork. Also has a choice of beers on tap, including Guinness. Sun–Fri 8am–5pm. Moderate.

Salah Brothers, 7 Kikar Paris. Excellent Palestinian cuisine with mezze to start and *sahlab* for afters. Daily 8am–1am. Moderate.

Shishkebab, 59 Ben Gurion. Iraqi restaurant specializing in, as its name suggests, kebabs. Sun–Thurs 12.30–11.30pm. Moderate.

Yotveta in Town, Bat Galim Promenade by lower cable-car station (☎04/852 6853). Part of a chain serving dishes based on dairy products from a kibbutz famous for them. The decor is plastic and the prices high, but the food is good and the portions large. Daily 8am–4am. Expensive.

Hadar

Etzel Benny, 23 HeHalutz. Sign in Hebrew only. Unpretentious hummus and kebab joint. Sun–Fri 10am–9pm. Cheap to moderate.

Kosher Vetaim, 40 Herzl. Sign in Hebrew only. Long-established self-service Ashkenazi restaurant. Sun–Thurs 10.30am–6pm. Cheap to moderate.

Leon & Ioji Gratar Romanesc, 31 HaNeviim. Popular Romanian restaurant with pork on the menu. Daily 10am–midnight. Moderate.

Voilà, 21 Nordau (☎04/866 4529). French haute cuisine at serious prices, tempered by a good lunchtime set menu. Daily 1pm–midnight. Expensive.

Zimhonia, 130 Herzl. Semi-vegetarian (serves fish), with great Ashkenazi food. Sun–Fri 9.30am–7pm. Cheap to moderate.

Carmel

Chin Lung, 126 HaNassi (☎04/838 1305). Tasty Szechuan cuisine. Daily noon–3pm & 6.30pm–midnight. Expensive.

El Gaucho, 120 Yefe Nof (☎04/837 0997). Big hunks of grilled beef are the mainstay of this Argentinian steakhouse chain. Mon–Thurs 12.30pm–midnight, Fri & Sat 12.30pm–12.30am, Sun 6pm–midnight. Expensive.

HaBank, 119 HaNassi. Popular café for light snacks, dairy dishes and salads, opposite Gan HaEm Carmelit station. Daily 8am–1am. Moderate.

Matsuzaka, 130 HaTishbi (☎04/838 2401). Japanese sushi bar and café serving sashimi, tempura, and noodle soup; eat indoors or in the garden. Daily noon–1.30am. Expensive.

Pizza Palermo, Panorama Centre, 107 HaNassi. Pukka pizza – whole or by the slice – and other Italian dishes in the mall by the *Dan Panorama* hotel. Sun–Thurs 11am–midnight, Fri 11am–3pm, Sat noon–midnight. Moderate to expensive.

Sea Waves, 99 Yefe Nof (☎04/838 3025). High-class Cantonese cuisine with a view. Daily noon–3.30pm & 7–11.30pm. Expensive.

Bars and nightlife

Haifa is not known for its **nightlife** but when there's a captive audience – sailors from the US Sixth Fleet for example – the **port area** becomes a seething mass of drunkenness and insistent pimps, and even when the docks are relatively empty the atmosphere down here is pretty sleazy. If you want to sample it, head for Derekh HaAtzma'ut, where the *London Pride* (in an alley by no. 84 and distinguished by its lack of anything remotely resembling London) and a few other plastic cafés and clubs form the centre of the scene. Rehov Hammam Pasha in **Old Haifa** has a rather better selection of drinking holes: try the *Muse*, the *Klafte* or the *Hay Bar*.

Hadar at night is much more respectable, but rather quiet. The busiest area is around Rehovot Herzl and Arlozorov, where crowds gather to stroll between the outdoor cafés. Among these, *Rodeo*, 23 Balfour, is reasonably animated. An alternative area is **Bat Galim** Promenade, which has the added attraction of being near the beach. **Carmel** offers a wider choice, with numerous pubs in and around Gan HaEm Park and Sederot HaNassi. Try *Little Haifa*, at 4 HaLevanon, just off HaNassi near the *Dan Panorama* hotel.

Busier than any of these in summer, however, are the **parks**, where locals spend the warm evenings hanging out and sometimes enjoying organized entertainment. The Sculpture Garden in particular is popular for a drink sunk to the strains of a guitar. On most summer nights you'll also find some kind of entertainment at the **beach** – discos, musical performances or rock videos. Dado Beach, for example, has a free, open-air disco Tuesday evenings in summer. Zamir and Qiryat Hayyim beaches also host summer happenings. For further details of the beach discos contact the IGTO, or if you're staying at the youth hostel ask the staff, who often lead night-time sorties themselves.

Film and theatre

Two venues, both in Carmel, dominate Haifa's cultural scene: the **Cinemateque** at 142 HaNassi (☎04/838 3424), and the **Haifa Auditorium** (☎04/838 0013) next door. For movie fans, the Cinemateque often shows **films** in English (and even, occasionally, the latest Hindi hits from Bollywood), while the Haifa Auditorium offers a largely musical programme, with **classical concerts** throughout the year. There is also a small outdoor theatre in Gan HaEm Park which runs classical music evenings, usually on Monday and Wednesday.

Theatre is often a forum for dissent in Israel and the **Haifa Municipal Theatre**, 50 Pevsner, Hadar (☎04/862 0670), though not so radical now, was one of the most controversial playhouses in the country during the 1980s, its programme of modern works regularly bringing it into conflict with the municipality and the government. Most of the plays are of course in Hebrew, but it's worth scanning the *Jerusalem Post* for the latest political furore, and perhaps finding someone to go with you and translate. The Haifa Art Museum (see p.137; ☎04/852 3255) also has an evening programme of entertainment and concerts, which is detailed in leaflets available at the museum (also at the Maritime and Tikotin museums) or at the IGTO and Haifa Tourist Board offices.

For **information** on all these events contact the IGTO, whose quarterly events guide advertises a range of activities, or take a look at the *Jerusalem Post* weekend supplement.

Listings

Airlines Arkia, Haifa Airport (☎04/872 2220) and 84 HaAtzma'ut (☎04/864 3371); El Al, 5 Palyam (☎04/861 2612); British Airways, 84 HaAtzma'ut (☎04/867 0756 or 7); Lufthansa, 5 Palyam (☎04/867 9258); Olympic, 104 Ha'Atzma'ut (☎04/851 0221 or 2); Tower, 76 Ha'Atzma'ut (☎04/867 4485); TWA, 104 Ha'Atzma'ut (☎04/852 8266).

American Express c/o Meditrad Rehov 'Azza (☎04/864 5609, fax 864 2267), in an alley by 80 Ha'Atzma'ut.

Banks and exchange You'll find bank branches throughout the city, but the main ones are down by the port along Derekh Ha'Atzma'ut and in the centre of Hadar. So far there are no licensed moneychangers, but Bank Leumi in Central Carmel has a 24-hour change machine, and larger post offices change cash and travellers' cheques without commission. A black market exists around the port but rip-offs are common, and rates no better than in a bank.

Books Steimatzky's has three outlets in Haifa – at the Central Bus Station, 130 HaNassi and 82 HaAtzma'ut. You'll find a wide choice of second-hand books in English at 31 HeHalutz. Studio 5, at 5 HaYam, has second-hand English books, but nothing very intellectually stimulating.

Car rental Avis, 7 Ben Gurion (☎04/851 3050); Budget, 46 HaHistadrut (☎04/842 4004); Europcar, 90 HaMaginim (☎04/851 7842); Eurodollar, 31 HaHistadrut (☎04/842 1422); Hertz, 19 Yafo (☎04/853 9786 or 8); Thrifty, 10 HaHistadrut (☎04/872 5525).

Consulates USA 12 Yerushalayim (☎04/867 0616).

Emergencies Police ☎100; ambulance ☎101; rape crisis helpline ☎04/853 0533; see also "Medical services" below.

Gay information The Haifa branch of AGUDA runs a gay information hotline Tuesday evenings 7–11pm (☎04/852 5352).

Medical services Magen David Adom (first aid), 10 Sedei Yitzhak (☎101 or ☎04/851 2233); Carmel Hospital, 7 Mikhal (☎04/825 0211); Rambam Hospital, Bat Galim (☎04/854 3111). There is a homeopathic pharmacy at the corner of Daniel with HaNeviim.

Police 28 Jaffa Road (☎100).

Post office The branch for poste restante is in the port area at 19 HaPalyam (Sun–Thurs 7am–6pm, Fri 7am–noon). There's another large post office at Kikar Masaryk (the junction of HaNeviim and Shabtai Levi in Hadar; Sun–Thurs 8am–7pm, Fri 8am–noon).

Taxis Hamonitax, 4 HaNeviim (☎04/866 4343); Muniot, at the Central Bus Station (☎04/866 8383); Ora Afor, 42 Herzl (☎04/866 2020); HaNitzahon, 4 Sha'ar Palmer (☎04/866 3555); Amal, 6 HeHalutz (☎04/866 2324); Aviv Ya'el Droma, 21 HeHalutz (☎04/867 1868).

Telecommunications International phone calls can be made from Lima B Gold, 1st floor, 3 Sha'ar Palmer (Sun–Thurs 8am–4pm, Fri 8am–1pm). Internet access and email service is available at Active Communications, in the entrance to the *Haifa Tower* hotel (☎04/867 6115, email: *info@actcom.co.il*).

Travel agents ISSTA, 2 Balfour (☎04/867 0222), the Israeli student and budget travel specialist, is the best place to start looking for cheap flights. Egged Tours has offices at 4 Nordau (☎04/862 3132) and in the Central Bus Station (☎04/854 9486). Mazda Tours has a branch at 4 Kyat, also just off HaAtzma'ut near Kikar Paris (☎04/862 4440), for bus tickets from Tel Aviv or Jerusalem to Cairo, as do Nizza Tours at 4 Nordau (☎04/862 4433 or 4).

Visa extensions Apply at 11 Hassan Shukri (☎04/866 7781), if staying in Haifa.

MOVING ON FROM HAIFA

BUSES
Almost all buses leave from the **Central Bus Station**. However, #192 to Isfiya and Daliat al-Karmel can also be picked up in Central Carmel.

Inter-city destinations include: Acre (every 15min; 30min); Afula (every 20–30min; 1hr); Beersheba (hourly; 4hr); Ben Gurion Airport (every 30–40min; 1hr 45min); Eilat (3 daily; 7hr); Hadera (1–2 per hour; 1hr); Herzliya (3–4 hourly; 1hr 30min); Jerusalem (every 30min; 3hr); Tel Aviv (every 20–30min; 1hr 45min); Nahariyya (every 15min; 1hr); Nazareth (every 30min; 45min); Netanya (every 30–60min; 1hr 20min); Qiryat Shemona (hourly; 2hr 30min); Safed (every 20–30min; 2hr); Tiberias (every 30–40min; 1hr 30min); Zikhron Ya'acov (hourly; 45min). Note that there are no inter-city services on Friday afternoons or Saturday. For enquiries about Egged inter-city services, call ☎04/854 9555.

To Jordan
Buses **to Amman** are operated by Nazareth Tours in Kikar Plumer (☎04/862 4871), running twice a day (once on Sat; 5hr), and currently costing only around $7.50.

SHERUTS
For many destinations, **sheruts** are not only faster than buses, but also cheaper, and prepared to risk incurring divine wrath by travelling on the Sabbath. To Tel Aviv, they run all day and night from 6 HeHalutz (☎04/866 2324); for Acre and Nahariyya, they leave from 16 HaNeviim (☎04/866 4422); for Isfiya and Daliat al-Karmel, from Rehov Eliyahu by Kikar Paris till 5pm, then from Shemerayahu Levin with Herzl till 8pm (☎04/866 4640); and for Nazareth, they leave from Kikar Paris itself, next to *Salah Brothers* restaurant (☎04/866 9927). There are no sheruts to Jerusalem or Tiberias.

TRAINS
The main **train** station is Bat Galim, behind the Central Bus Station, but all trains also stop at Merkaz (Central) Station, which is usually more convenient. Like inter-city buses, they don't run Friday evenings or most of Saturday.

Destinations include: Acre (14 daily; 30–40min); Ashdod (1 daily; 2hr 20min); Beersheba (2 weekly; 3hr 30min); Hadera (1–2 hourly; 40min); Herzliya (1–2 hourly; 1hr 15min); Jerusalem (1 daily; 3hr 20min); Nahariyya (8 daily; 40–50min); Netanya (1–2 hourly; 55min); Rehovot (6 daily; 1hr 40min–2hr); Tel Aviv (1–2 hourly; 1hr 10min–1hr 40min). For enquiries, call ☎04/856 4564.

FERRIES
The passenger terminal (☎04/851 8111) for **ferries to Greece and Cyprus** is off Kikar Plumer – arrive in plenty of time. Tickets are best bought in advance from agents around the port such as Caspi, 1 Nathan St, (☎04/867 4444) and Mano, 2 Sha'ar Palmer (☎04/853 1631); see also "Listings" opposite. Ferries to Greece and Cyprus run weekly (more often in summer), and there are sometimes services to Egypt and Italy too.

Current one-way **fares** are (low season/high season): to Limassol (11hr) steerage $47/58, cabins from $90/105; to Rhodes (37hr) steerage $90/100, cabins from $172/201; to Piraeus (59hr) steerage $96/105, cabins from $176/205. It's a Greek boat, so neither shekels nor Cyprus pounds are accepted on board, only drachmas (but there's an exchange kiosk), and remember not to ask for "Turkish" coffee!

PLANES
Haifa's airport (☎04/872 2220) is east of town, reached by bus #58 or #58a from the Central Bus Station. There are flights to **Eilat** (Sun–Thurs 3 daily; Fri & Sat 1 daily; 1hr 10min); Jerusalem (4 weekly; 30min), and Tel Aviv (5 weekly; 30min), though a sherut is easier and a lot cheaper.

Around Haifa

If you want to escape the city for a day, there are several options all accessible by public transport, but the only real choice if you want something more stimulating than lazing on the beach is to head inland. Though the coast **to the north** of the city is heavily polluted by the industrial belt that spreads up to Acre, you don't have to stray too far from the sea before you reach much prettier surroundings, particularly around **the Qrayot** – the collective name for a group of towns whose names all begin with "Qiryat". The towns themselves, however, hold little of interest.

South of Haifa, a detour inland has much to recommend it: there are the mountains of the **Carmel**, much of whose picturesque splendour lies within the **Carmel National Park**; the Carmel's two much-visited Druze villages, **Isfiya** and **Daliat al-Karmel**, together offering a glimpse into the culture and way of life of the Middle East's most enigmatic religious group; and the monastery at **Al-Muhraqa**, which boasts one of the best views in Israel from its roof. Archeological sites include the catacombs at **Bet She'arim**, with their finely carved tombs, and the excavations at **Megiddo** (Armageddon), the prophesied site of the end of the world whose past is almost as violent as its future. Nearby, **the Triangle** has the largest concentration of Arab villages in Israel, of which the easiest and most rewarding to visit is **Umm-al-Fahm**.

The Carmel Mountains

The Carmel range forms a triangular plateau spreading south from its apex at Haifa, bounded by a narrow coastal plain on its western side, and a wider one around the Qrayot to its northeast. Further down its eastern side, the plateau overlooks the Jezreel Valley, beyond which rise the hills of Galilee. The Carmel's gentle undulations, natural forest and exquisite wild flowers (especially plentiful in the spring) lend it a special beauty, and one which is relatively easy to explore as much of the area is given over to the **Carmel National Park** with trails and picnic tables laid on for the visitor. Information is available at the main entrance.

Bus #192 from Haifa's Central Bus Station passes through the park on the way to the Druze villages of Isfiya and Daliat al-Karmel. The route is also plied by **sheruts**, which leave from Rehov Eliyahu HaNavi during the day (6am–5pm), and from the corner of Shmeriyahu Levin and Herzl in the evening (5pm–8pm). There is no onward transport from Daliat al-Karmel to al-Muhraqa, but hitching is easy and taxis affordable.

The Druze villages: Isfiya and Daliat al-Karmel

The people of Isfiya and Daliat al-Karmel arrived at the beginning of the seventeenth century when the Druze warlord, Fakir al-Din, carved out a fiefdom in Lebanon and the Galilee. **ISFIYA** is much the quieter of the two villages: lacking the market or abundant commercialism of Daliat al-Karmel, its attraction lies in the fact that it remains largely a living, working village. Not that its inhabitants are unaware of the money to be made from the hordes of tourists – over recent years a few souvenir shops and a number of fine restaurants have opened. There's also a good place to **stay**: the *Stella Carmel Guest House* (☎04/839 1692, fax 839 0233; ①/②) at the northern end of the village, on your right if coming from Haifa. An Anglican hospice run by volunteers, it offers dormitory accommodation and neat, clean private rooms. There are also some good, moderately priced **restaurants** in the village (rather better value than those in Daliat al-Karmel), notably the *Druze Restaurant*, opposite the guesthouse (daily 8.30am–midnight), and the pricier *Nof Carmel*, 100m towards Haifa (daily noon–8.30pm), both of which serve good *shashlik*. Druze specialities you might like to try include the Druze pitta – bigger and softer than the standard version – *labaneh* sour cheese, and *za'atar*.

THE DRUZE

Druzism grew out of the following of Egypt's sixth Fatimid Caliph, al-Hakim, who ruled from 996 AD until his disappearance in 1021. Known as Egypt's Caligula for excesses such as massacres of Jews and Christians, and the destruction of Jerusalem's Church of the Holy Sepulchre (see p.333), al-Hakim declared himself a manifestation of God, implying his superiority over Mohammed, who was merely a prophet. The idea was preached by Hamza ibn 'Ali, an Afghani who became the first and greatest of the five Druze *huddud* (founding fathers). However, the new religion took its name from his disciple, **Mohammed al-Darazi**, who spread the message to Palestine, Lebanon and Syria, before later being declared a heretic and assassinated in 1019. Al-Hakim's successor, al-Zahir, suppressed Druzism, driving it out of Egypt and the Syrian cities into the mountainous regions where it is still based today. Another of Hamza's disciples, Baha al-Din al-Muqtana, put together the six secret books of **Druze scripture** from the teachings of the *huddud*, encrypting them lest they should fall into the wrong hands. In 1043, proselytization ended and in theory no further converts to Druzism were allowed: to be a Druze now, you must be born one (Druze rarely marry out, but religion is inherited from the father).

Though historically rebellious, the Druze did not regard Israel as being worse than the Ottomans or the British and although a Druze battalion supported a Palestinian assault in Galilee at the beginning of the 1948 war, they committed themselves to the State of Israel during the war and have proved extremely loyal. This is despite their position as Arabs (albeit non-Muslim), and the tensions created by Israel's annexation of the Golan Heights in 1981 which drew staunch opposition from Golani Druze (see p.472), not to mention the occasional conflict of interests between Lebanese Druze and Israeli forces in Lebanon. **Druze loyalty** has been repaid with full citizenship privileges, alongside duties such as military service, but many Palestinians regard Israeli Druze as traitors. Although Israel tries not to discriminate against them, there does seem to be a glass ceiling preventing Druze from reaching the very highest echelons of politics, industry and the army.

Today, there are around a million Druze in the world, including about 400,000 each in Syria and Lebanon, 60,000 in Israel and 17,000 in the disputed Golan Heights. Their symbol is a five-pointed star divided into five segments for the five *huddud*, and their flag has five different-coloured stripes (or four stripes with a triangle at the side). Only around a fifth of Druze men and women, the initiates or *'uqqal*, know all the tenets of the faith. The remaining 80 percent, the *juhhal*, learn only the religion's basic teachings and moral code, but their scrupulous adherence to it explains the integrity and honesty for which the Druze are known, as well as their famed hospitality – outstanding even by Middle Eastern standards. Unlike Muslims, Druze believe in reincarnation. Al-Hakim is revered as something like the Messiah, while Abraham, Moses, Jethro (Moses's father-in-law), Jesus and Mohammed are accepted as prophets. Circumcision is not compulsory and has no religious significance. Druze meet at the village *majlis*, the nearest equivalent to a mosque, particularly on Thursday evenings, when communal affairs are discussed, and then the *juhhal* leave and the *'uqqal* pray.

On entering the village of **DALIAT AL-KARMEL**, 5km south of Isfiya, you can't help but be struck by the profusion of colour. From Persian to Bedouin rugs, brass coffeepots to large hookah pipes, the place seems on first impression to be one giant market for oriental goods. Its tourist trade aside, however, villagers do still farm much of the local area; tractors speed through the village, almost oblivious to ambling tourists, and in the backstreets the atmosphere is surprisingly calm and rural. It's this ordinary working side – and the friendliness of the villagers, especially if you try out some Arabic – which stops the place from being just another tourist centre. Saturdays are the busiest for the **market**, so you'll probably find it more relaxing to visit during the week, though it's closed on Fridays.

At the T- junction in the centre of the village, there's a café and (rather good) confectioner – *Shafik* (sign in Hebrew only). Twenty metres before the junction on your left (coming from Isfiya), stuck incongruously in the back room of the *Mifqash Ha'Akhim* restaurant, the **House of Druze Heritage** is a museum of sorts where, by calling in advance (☎04/839 3169), preferably in a group, you can look around the collection of memorabilia and listen to a talk (in English if the group is large enough) on the Druze, their religion and way of life. The road heading right at the T junction forks after 20m, converging again after 500m at a small square with a prettily painted *majlis* (Druze mosque), beyond which lies **Bet Oliphant**, a house named after its former occupant, the nineteenth-century Christian Zionist Sir Lawrence Oliphant. It was Oliphant's aide and secretary, Naftali Imber, who composed "HaTikva", the song about the Jews' ancient hope of return to their homeland which became Israel's national anthem. In front of the house is a memorial to Druze soldiers who have died fighting for Israel.

Al-Muhraqa

If you turn left at the T-junction in Daliat al-Karmel and take a small road off to the left after about a kilometre, a scenic three-kilometre walk from here will eventually bring you to **AL-MUHRAQA**, one of two sites claiming to be the location of Elijah's battle with the Priests of Baal (I Kings 18), the other being Mount Carmel in Haifa (see p.140). Whatever the truth, Al-Muhraqa is a delightful spot, with a church commemorating Elijah's victory, a popular picnic area and spectacular views.

The **church** you see today is relatively new (Mon–Sat 8am–1.30pm & 2.30–5pm, Sun 8am–1.30pm only). Carmelite monks began construction of a large monastery here in 1867, but in the face of obstruction from the Ottoman authorities only the chapel was completed. The site then received considerable damage during World War I and wasn't fully restored until 1964. Nowadays, despite an estimated 150,000 visitors a year, the church and its surroundings have remained surprisingly tranquil, a popular site of veneration with Palestinian Christians. If you want to get into the spirit of things, come on July 20, the Feast of St Elias (Elijah), when local families camp out here in their hundreds: there's a small picnic and barbecue area, open all year round. The fee of 1NIS to ascend to the **terrace** of the church is money well spent: Al-Muhraqa is on the edge of the Jezreel Valley, and the view over it from the terrace is absolutely stunning.

An interesting alternative to heading back the way you came is to **walk** down into the valley below. It's only about 3km (starting from the corner of the nearby car park) along a path marked by red- and black-striped rocks. The path is hard to follow in places but make sure you stick to it or you'll be ensnared by brambles on the lower reaches of the hill. At the bottom is Route 70, the Haifa–Megiddo road, served by regular **buses**. Nearby is the junction with Route 722 to Bet She'arim and Qiryat Tivon.

Bet She'arim

The main road southeast out of Haifa splits after 12km at the head of the Jezreel Valley. Four kilometres down the Nazareth road (Route 75), which runs along the valley's northern edge, it's well worth stopping off at **QIRYAT TIVON** to visit the remains of the ancient city of Bet She'arim, located 2km to the south.

Bet She'arim (House of the Gates; Sat–Thurs 8am–4pm, Fri 8am–3pm; 11NIS) is famous as one of the many seats of the Sanhedrin, the 71-member Jewish supreme judicial, ecclesiastical and administrative council of New Testament times. After the failure of the Bar Kokhba revolt in the second century AD, the Sanhedrin fled from Jerusalem to Bet She'arim: having re-established themselves here, they were recognized by the Romans as the supreme Jewish authority. At Bet She'arim their most famous leader, Rabbi Yehuda HaNassi, undertook the task of setting down the *Mishnah*, codifying the laws that governed the day-to-day lives of the Jews, previously passed down orally (see p.501).

Rabbi Yehuda's internment here turned Bet She'arim into a popular burial site and its vast complex of **catacombs** is the main attraction, varying in style from caves with simple inscriptions to ornate mausoleums. An extraordinary number of tombs belong to wealthy Jews from all over the Roman world, and the range of languages represented in the inscriptions gives some idea of the diversity of the people who chose this as their final resting place until the Romans destroyed the city in 352 AD, following yet another Jewish revolt. After Bet She'arim was destroyed, the town's Jewish population was virtually extinguished. Later, an Arab village, **Sheikh Abreik**, grew up in its place, named after a local sufi who performed a miracle by making bubbling water gush from a broken jug. The water, which formed a swamp, was said to possess healing powers. For this miracle the sheikh was proclaimed a saint; his tomb stands 100m southeast of the basilica.

Buses from Haifa, Nazareth and Afula, as well as the #826 from Tel Aviv and the #431 from Tiberias, can drop you at convenient places on the main road. If coming from Haifa, you'll probably be dropped at the Qiryat Tivon roundabout (where there's a bank, post office, café and falafel); from there, take the road to the southern part of town, not to the centre – follow the signpost down Rehov Hanna Senesh, turn right down Rehov Yizre'el and take the first right after 1km, down Rehov HaShomrim. The main tombs are well lit, but it's worth bringing along a flashlight to explore further.

The site

The first part of the ancient town you come to is a partly excavated second-century **synagogue** on your left, of which one lone arch still stands. Although not terribly impressive today, this was once the biggest synagogue in Palestine. The doors oriented the building towards Jerusalem, and a *bema* (raised platform from which the Torah is read) was framed by pillars in the centre. Just beyond the synagogue there's an **oil press**, and further (left off the road and up the hill), a large **basilica** comprising a collection of pillars and stone slabs thought to have been a traders' meeting place.

Continuing around the bend, you come to the **necropolis**, where more than 26 burial chambers have been excavated, not all of them open to the public. Among the most interesting are **tomb #14** – the family grave of Rabbi Yehuda HaNassi – with its partly restored triple-arched facade, and **tomb #20**, the most elaborate of all the chambers, with its glorious restored facade and numerous richly decorated sar-

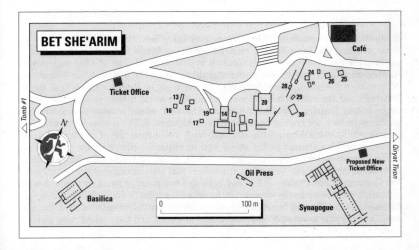

MOVING ON FROM QIRYAT TIVON

From Qiryat Tivon there are frequent buses to Haifa and Nazareth, the latter via the scenic Route 75 through the **Balfour Forest** (a popular picnic site) and the Palestinian village of **Yafa**, which has a mixed (Muslim and Christian) population of over 6000 and contains within it the tel of Japhia, mentioned in the Bible (Joshua 19: 13) and in the Amarna letters (see p.482).

cophagi. Entering tomb #20, the first passage on the left leads to some of the most interesting sarcophagi: look out for the **Hunt Sarcophagus**, most of the way down on the left, which features a lion hunting a gazelle, and the **Lion Sarcophagus** almost at the end on the right, depicting two lions apparently in the act of licking a vase. Back in the main passage, the second chamber on the left contains the **Mask Sarcophagus**; the face carved into one end may be that of its occupant. In the next chamber (also on the left), the **Shell Sarcophagus** is so called for the large cockle-like shell carved in its lid.

Tomb #28 has been turned into a small and very informative **museum**, featuring explanations (in Hebrew and English) and finds from the site, notably a massive slab of glass from around the fifth century AD. **Tomb #1**, a labyrinthine complex with 55 burial chambers and over 400 graves, is not open to the public, one reason being objections from the ultra-orthodox to excavation of a Jewish burial site.

Megiddo (Armageddon)

The spirits of devils… go forth unto the the kings of the earth and of the whole world, to gather them to the battle of that great day of God Almighty… And he gathered them together into a place called in the Hebrew tongue Armageddon. And the seventh angel poured out his vial [of God's wrath] into the air, and there came a great voice out of the temple of heaven, from the throne, saying, "It is done." And there were voices and thunderings and lightnings, and there was a great earthquake, such as was not since men were upon the earth, so mighty an earthquake and so great. And the great city was divided into three parts, and the cities of the nations fell.

(Revelation 16: 14–19)

Route 66, along the southern side of the Jezreel Valley, leads to the West Bank town of Jenin, meeting the Afula–Hadera road (Route 65) at Megiddo Junction. A kilometre north of the junction, conveniently shielded by a small wooded area, is the ancient site of **Megiddo**, otherwise known as **Armageddon** (from the Hebrew *Har Megiddo* – Mountain of Megiddo). Here, according to the book of Revelation, the final battle between good and evil will take place at the end of the world, though you get little sense of impending disaster at the dusty site now. However, as the location of innumerable battles in history, the choice wasn't completely unfounded. The reason for its troubled past lies in its domination of the strategic trade route from Egypt to Mesopotamia, known under the Romans as Via Maris, and an important thoroughfare (now traced partly by route 65) virtually throughout Palestine's history. **Battles for Megiddo** feature frequently in the Old Testament: it was here that Deborah sang of her victory over the Canaanite kings (Judges 5: 19), and here also two kings of Judah met their deaths – Ahaziah after being fatally wounded by Israel's King Jehu (II Kings 9: 27), and Josiah in battle against Pharaoh Neco (II Chronicles 35: 20–24). As recently as 1918, the site saw further battle between British and Ottoman forces, and General Allenby, given a peerage, took the title Viscount Allenby of Megiddo. During the 1967 Six Day War, the junction was the focal point for supplies for Israeli army depots in the north and west of the country, less than 1km from what was then the Jordanian border.

The excavations and museum

The earliest traces of habitation found on the **archeological site** (Sat–Thurs 8am–4pm, Fri 8am–3pm; 15NIS) go back some 6000 years – archeologists have unearthed the remains of at least twenty cities built here (or rebuilt after destruction). The position of **Tel Megiddo** was strategic, enjoying a vantage point over the main transport artery, and also supplied by a good spring at the foot of the hill. Yet this heavily fortified city had one major flaw: as the spring was outside the city walls, water was likely to be cut off in times of siege. Around 900 BC the inhabitants overcame this crucial weakness by engineering a 66-metre-long **tunnel** under the walls to allow safe access to the spring. This architectural masterpiece is one of the central features of the site, accessible by negotiating a steep spiral staircase.

Another worthy feature is the ancient **temple mound**, which the guides gleefully claim was the site of ritual sacrifice and public executions during the early Canaanite period (third and second millennia BC). Of the two **palaces**, the southern one may have been the governor's residence, while the northern one (later replaced by stables) could have housed the king himself when he came here. Both are thought to date from Solomonic times, as is the **four-chambered gate** at the northern end of the site, whose more ancient predecessors lie nearby. After Solomon, under the kings of Israel, Megiddo became a garrison city with **stables** holding perhaps as many as 450 horses

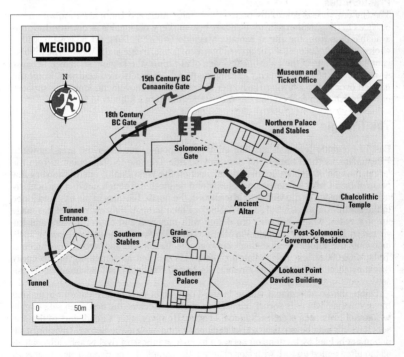

MOVING ON FROM MEGIDDO

There are **buses** from the site to Haifa (hourly; 50min), Afula (5 daily; 20min) and Umm al-Fahm (3 daily; 20min). From Megiddo Junction, 1km away, there are more buses to Afula (2–3 per hour; 15min), Nazareth (every 30–90min; 40min), Tiberias (2–3 per hour; 1hr 15min), Hadera (2–3 per hour; 50min) and Tel Aviv (every 30min; 1hr 45min).

---

at its peak during the reign of King Ahab (around 869–850 BC). Artefacts and pottery discovered during the excavation of the mound are displayed in a **museum** at the entrance to the site, though a famous ivory plaque found here and thought by archeologist David Rohl to portray King Solomon is now in the Rockefeller Museum in Jerusalem. Inside, you'll find a model of the city as it may have been during the periods of Solomon and Ahab, circa 1000–600 BC (though Rohl and others challenge the dating of archeological strata on which this is based, see p.424). There's also a small restaurant and a shop selling jewellery made of Roman glass.

Given the site's significance, it's no surprise that plans are under way to make the most of the **millennium**. Visitors will be awed by a multi-media "virtual Armageddon" using IBM's "magic window" technology. Hailed as the next step on from virtual reality, it will bring the area's turbulent past to life in fourteen visitor centres. The project has already been dubbed "Apocalypso".

Practicalities

The site entrance is served by **buses** from Haifa, Afula and Umm al-Fahm, with more services to the junction nearby (see box below). Very reasonable **accommodation** is available 2km from the site at Kibbutz Megiddo (☎06/652 5011, fax 652 5945), with a choice of cheap dorms (①), or private rooms with a/c, fridge and TV (③). The kibbutz is built on the site of the Palestinian village of **al-Lajun** (the Legion, so named because it was the site of a Roman army encampment), whose confiscated land was, ironically, handed over to the left-wing Hashomer Hatza'ir Zionist movement, long-time supporters of Jewish-Arab cooperation, for the establishment of a kibbutz in 1949.

The Triangle

East of Megiddo Junction, past the military compound, you enter the area known to Palestinians as **the Triangle** (or sometimes Little Triangle to distinguish it from the larger triangle of Nablus, Jenin and Tulkarm on the West Bank), one of the very few parts of Israel with a Palestinian majority and delineated (though not in a particularly triangular shape) by the village of **Musmus** in the north, Barquay in the east and Taibe to the south. Known as Wadi Ara in Arabic or Emeq Irron in Hebrew, most of it is made up of a valley, whose hillsides are dotted with minarets and church towers and traversed by Route 65 (the ancient Via Maris). The Triangle became part of Israel in 1949, following the Rhodes negotiations between the Israeli and Jordanian governments. Today's 60,000-strong Palestinian population is regarded as something of a security threat by some Israelis and, as a result, the Jewish National Fund has financed Jewish settlements in the region.

Taibe, the southernmost village in the Triangle, is worthy of mention for making history in 1996 when its soccer team, Hapo'el Taibe, became the first Arab side to gain promotion to Israel's premier National League. However, after a good start to the season, it wasn't long before they were facing relegation back to the Second Division, a situation not helped by the tension between its fans and those of rival Israeli clubs, which all too often ended up with with fans chanting the names of sectarian murderers at each other across the pitch. Nonetheless, Taibe broke the mould: although there are no Arab teams currently in the National League, three now play in the Second Division.

Musmus and Umm al-Fahm

Heading southwest from Megiddo on Route 65, the first village you'll pass through is **MUSMUS** whose houses, built on columns in the local style, straggle along either side of the road – the older ones looking perilously close to falling down. More interesting is **UMM AL-FAHM**, signposted from the junction a few kilometres to the east. Tightly packed over the side of a mountain that marked the Jordanian border until 1967, the town has a population of over 25,000, and is known as one of the most politically active places in the country; many of its residents are key campaigners for Palestinian rights. Bear in mind that Umm al-Fahm is in some ways rather conservative, so it's advisable to dress modestly to avoid offending some of the inhabitants. The centre of town is at the top of the hill. **Buses** along the Hadera–Afula road (Route 65) leave you at the bottom – only bus #248 from Haifa actually runs into town. **Service taxis** make regular journeys to the centre from the restaurant (see below) at the beginning of the road into town; wave down any that pass and eventually one will stop. You could also walk into town, 25 minutes or so, but uphill all the way.

The town centre (*al-markaz*) is basically a taxi rank surrounded by restaurants, bakeries and coffee houses offering spiced Turkish coffee and delicious Arabic pastries; sitting in one of these cafés is as good a way as any to take in the place. Wandering around the incredibly steep streets, you'll encounter old men in their white *keffiyas*, stooped almost double and contrasting sharply with the swarms of young children milling about. For a place its size Umm al-Fahm has a suprising number of **mosques**, their minarets poking up into the skyline from every part of town. A couple of hundred metres to the west of the centre, the impressive domed mosque crowning the hill doubles as a clinic for the sick, while a mosque boasting an almost equally impressive golden dome, and a minaret, stands a short way beyond. To appreciate them better, you can make the half-hour climb up to the top of **Jabal Iskander**, the highest point in town (to the east of the centre). Stay a few hours, or arrive at prayer time, and you'll be able to listen to the mesmerizing chorus of the muezzins echoing their call to prayer across the hills.

Al-Hilmi **restaurant** (daily 7am–7pm; cheap to moderate), at the beginning of the road up into town, by the Dalek gas station, serves good Arabic coffee and steak, *kofta* or *shashlik* on a pleasant outdoor terrace. Should you wish to **stay** longer here, check out the summer **workcamp** (see p.63), which tackles a few of the town's many urgent problems (building sewage channels or resurfacing roads) for completion in a few weeks. For details call Hassan Ghafari (☎06/631 5040), or contact the Municipality (☎06/631 2040) between the two mosques at the top of the town. **Moving on**, Route 65 is served by frequent **buses**, so you shouldn't have to wait long whichever direction you decide to head in.

The Sharon Plain and the coast

Extending beyond the northern tentacles of Tel Aviv, the broad agricultural stretches of the **Sharon Plain** are carpeted with orange groves and persimmon trees (one variety of persimmon is the "Sharon fruit"). However, most of the region's sights are found along the coast, including the ancient site of **Caesarea** – the country's capital in Roman times and later an important Crusader port – and lesser remains at **Dor** and around **Kibbutz Ma'agen Michael**. Naturally enough, this is also where you'll find a number of beach resorts. Heading north from Tel Aviv, the first town you come to is the rather chic resort of **Herzliya**, just outside the city limits, while further up the shore there are the new developments at Caesarea and **Netanya**, which should be able to cater to all your needs. Unless you're heading into the West Bank (roads cut across from Herzliya and Netanya to the now autonomous towns of Qalqilya and Tulkarm), there's no real need to stray inland, except perhaps to visit the modern towns of **Hadera** and **Zikhron Ya'acov**, which have come a long way since their foundation by early Zionist pioneers at the end of the nineteenth century.

Transport across the plain is fast and efficient, with two main roads and a railway hugging the coastline, though rarely in view of the sea, all the way to Haifa. Towns are linked by frequent bus and sherut services, and even at smaller places you will rarely wait more than an hour. Since it takes less than two hours to get from Tel Aviv to Haifa, virtually anywhere on the coast is an easy day trip from either city. For a rundown of travel details from Haifa to the following destinations, see the box on p.145.

Herzliya

Built in 1924 and named after Zionism's founder, Theodore Herzl, the town of **HERZLIYA** is now totally eclipsed by its more opulent suburb, the resort of **HERZLIYA PITUAH**, on whose beaches you'll probably end up spending most of your time given that there's little in the way of sights. As Israel's premier upmarket resort, its pay beaches, shorefront ice cream parlours, cafés, restaurants and hotels are patronized by wealthy Israelis, diplomats (many of whom have their residences around here) and the top end of the package tour market, with not a cheap bed or youth hostel in sight. But Herzliya's comfortable opulence hasn't always been secure: this is the narrowest part of Israel and the West Bank lies only 16km to the east, a fact that, as Israelis will often argue, rendered it – and the country – rather vulnerable between 1948 and 1967.

From Tel Aviv, **buses** serving Herzliya include United Tours #90 from the *Dan Panorama* hotel and Rehov Dizengoff (every 30–60min 7am–midnight; 40min), and the less frequent Dan bus #91, which also leaves from the *Dan Panorama*. **Trains** to Netanya (see p.159) stop at Herzliya.

The Town

Such places of interest as there are in Herzliya lie in the main town and to the north along the beach road. However, most visitors never make it that far, and head straight for the soft sandy **beaches** of Herzliya Pituah. Officially you have to pay to use the **main beach**, off Kikar de Shalit by the *Sharon*, though you may simply be able to walk in; alternatively, take the #90 bus (or walk) a couple of kilometres north along the beach road to **Nof Yam**, which has free access and has the added advantage of being cleaner and less crowded. Occupying a striking clifftop location here, the **Sidna Ali Mosque** (no public access) was originally a thirteenth-century Mamluk construction in honour of one of Saladin's lieutenants, famed for his acts of bravery in battle against the Crusaders, and was rebuilt around the turn of the century as a caravanserai. It now serves both as a mosque and a religious school. Steps just beyond it lead down to the sands, which throng with campers in the summer. A little beyond Sidna Ali, an enterprising beach lover has carved an imaginatively decorated house out of the sandstone cliffs, and in the summer runs the *Caveman Café*, which stays open late. It's not hard to track down – just follow the music.

Less than 1km north of the mosque the ancient site of **Tel Arshaf** lies on a rocky promontory. Originally the Canaanite setttlement of Rishpon, dedicated to the Semitic god Reshef, it was later established as a port by the Greeks and renamed **Apollonia**, since Apollo was Reshef's Greek equivalent, only to fall in 95 BC to the Hasmonean king Alexander Jannai. The Arabs called it Arsuf, and the Crusaders built a fortress here, which was taken by Saladin in 1187, but which four years later became the scene of his only defeat by a Christian monarch, Richard the Lionheart. Like many coastal

---

ports, it was destroyed by Sultan Baybars in 1265 to dissuade the European invaders from returning, and not a great deal is left of it. Most of the port has been overwhelmed by the sea, but parts of the city walls and some buildings are still clearly visible, as are a few scanty remains of the fortress.

Herzliya proper lies just inland from the beach, across the Haifa coast road (Route 2). On the way, you pass the **Yad Lema'apil**, a small fishing boat used to bring in illegal immigrants in the Forties, which has been installed next to the main Tel Aviv road (Route 2) at the Hassira Interchange, one block south of the junction with Medinat HaYehudim. It stands as a monument to those intrepid souls who braved the British blockade to reach the Promised Land. If you make it as far as the town itself, you'll find a couple of museums to reward your efforts: the **Herzliya Museum of Art**, on Rehov Wolfson (☎09/955 1011; Sun–Thurs 5–8pm, Fri & Sat 10am–2pm; free), displays a wide range of contemporary art, and has a "sculpture garden" featuring works by local modern sculptors; while the **Founders' Museum**, at 8 HaNadiv (Mon–Thurs 9am–1pm, Fri 8.30am–12.30pm; free) covers the pre-independence history of the settlement.

Practicalities

Buses from Tel Aviv drop you at the main square, Kikar de Shalit, from Haifa you'll be let off at the Accadia junction on Route 2. The **train station** is across Route 2 in Herzliya proper. The main **hotels**, almost all of them pretty upmarket, are in Herzliya Pituah by the beach along Rehov Ramat Yam. The southernmost is the *Dan Accadia* (☎09/959 7070, fax 959 7090 or 1; ⑤), a low-rise, almost country-clubbish establishment set around a swimming pool with medium-sized rooms, and all the amenities you could want. Next up is the *Holiday Inn* (☎09/954 4444, fax 954 4675; ⑤), newly built, with the smartly efficient service typical of the chain. The marginally less slick *Sharon* at the northern end of Rehov Ramat Yam (☎09/957 5777, toll-free in Israel ☎177/02 4131, fax 09/957 2448; ⑤) overlooks Kikar de Shalit, opposite the (by comparison), rather down-at-heel *Hotel Eshel* (☎09/957 0208, fax 957 0797; ④). **Camping** is permitted on the sands just north of the Sidna Ali Mosque at Nof Yam (see above), but during the summer the beach is overrun by school children, local scout and paramilitary youth groups and sometimes, it seems, virtually everyone in the country who owns a sleeping bag.

Restaurants and cafés of various descriptions can be found on Rehov Maskit in the new industrial zone, off Rehov Medinat HeYehudim east of the *Dan Accadia*. The best budget option is the *Barbecue*, at no. 15, providing good, solid grub for the locals (Sun–Thurs 8am–5pm; cheap). Alternatively, the *Whitehall Steak House* at no. 1 (☎09/958 0402; daily noon–midnight; expensive) specializes in giant-size T-bones, while *Churrascaria Brasileira* at no. 29 (☎09/951 2313 or 4; daily noon–2am; expensive) has delicious Brazilian dishes, both fish and meat, as well as a salad bar, with the added attraction of live entertainment nightly except Tuesday and Sunday; both of these also offer a reasonably priced lunchtime menu.

From Kikar de Shalit, there are Dan and United Tours **buses** to Tel Aviv (1–2 per hour; 40min), and Egged services to Netanya (every 15–30min; 20min) and Jerusalem (1 daily; 1hr 45min). Most buses along Route 2 stop at Herzliya and serve Tel Aviv, Netanya, Haifa and Jerusalem.

Netanya

With its beaches backed by garish restaurants and package-tour hotels, **NETANYA** lacks the upmarket chic of Herzliya Pituah, some 20km to the south. Yet alongside the commercialism, an older and more interesting town survives, thriving on a diamond industry and its continuing role as an agricultural market centre.

Founded by European settlers in 1928 as a farming village, Netanya very soon became a small market town selling the harvest from the nearby fruit orchards. However, with the collapse of the citrus industry in World War II, it turned to diamond cutting and polishing, a traditional Jewish industry, and finally to tourism. The mix has been remarkably successful: diamonds are still processed here in their thousands, and there's a thriving tourist industry, along with retirement and holiday homes for Jewish people from Western countries – particularly French and Quebecois Jews.

Arrival, information and accommodation

From the **bus station** on Sederot Binyamin (☎09/833 7052) it's a short walk west along Herzl into town. The **train station** (☎09/882 3470) lies further out, 1500m southeast of the centre, but is linked to it by bus #5. There's an IGTO **tourist office** (Sun–Thurs 8.30am–6pm, Fri 9am–noon; ☎09/882 7286; Web site: *www.insite.co.il/netanya/netanya. htm*), in the southwest corner of Kikar Ha'Atzma'ut (Independence Square), which dishes out the usual array of maps and leaflets.

ACCOMMODATION

Netanya has plenty of **hotels** catering to the beach tourist trade, but not much in the way of low-priced or characterful accommodation. Nonetheless, you should find something to your taste in the following selection. Sleeping on the beach is not recommended.

Atzmauth Hostel, 2 Ussishkin (☎09/862 1315, fax 882 2562). Right in the centre, this hostel is the budget travellers' number one choice in Netanya. The spotless four- or six-bed dorms each have a/c, bathroom and fridge, plus many enjoy views over Kikar Ha'Atzma'ut. Open around the clock, with no curfews or lock-outs. Private rooms also available. ①/②.

The Motel, 32 Jabotinsky (☎09/882 2634). Budget hostel; rather tatty and, in summer at any rate, pricier than the *Atzmauth*. ①.

Hotel Orit, 21 Sederot Hen (☎ & fax 09/861 6818). Small and friendly Scandinavian-run place with Swedish food and a barbecue on Fridays. Only seven rooms, so book ahead. ③.

Hotel Mizpe Yam, 4 Karlebakh (☎ & fax 09/862 3730). A homely little place with comfortable, medium-sized rooms. ③.

Ginot Yam Hotel, 9 David HaMelekh (☎09/834 1007, fax 861 5722). Packed out with French tourists in summer, but very reasonable off season. ⑤.

Metropol Grand, 17 Gad Machnes (☎09/862 4777, fax 861 1556). An alternative to the *Ginot Yam*, cheaper in summer, pricier off season. ⑤.

The Seasons, 1 Sederot Nitza (☎09/860 1555, fax 862 3022). The lap of luxury, for those who can afford it, with large, tastefully decorated rooms, a pool, tennis courts, gym, sauna and massage parlour. ⑥.

NETANYA TELEPHONE NUMBERS

Telephone numbers in Netanya are now seven-digit; if you have an old six-digit number, try adding an eight in front of it.

The Town

Netanya's main street, **Rehov Herzl**, runs east to west through the town centre, the main part of which lies between Herzl's junction with Sederot Weizmann and Binyamin by the central bus station, and Rehov Dizengoff a couple of hundred metres west. Beyond Dizengoff, Herzl is pedestrianized up to the large square of **Kikar Ha'Atzma'ut** (Independence Square), which overlooks the main beach and is surrounded by restaurants catering mostly to tourists. The **beaches** are free though often crowded – walk down the steps by the tourist office to get to them – but note that the area around Gan HaMelekh park, just above the main beach, has something of a reputation for harassment and muggings.

There's not much else of interest to the tourist in the town centre: the Yemeni community run a small museum in the **Yemenite Folklore Centre**, on the fifth floor of 11 Kikar Ha'Atzma'ut (in the passage by *Ben & Jerry's* at the eastern end of the square; Sun–Thurs 9–11am; 3NIS), and next to the Cultural Centre on Rehov Raziel (see p.159) there are a couple of private art galleries which may contain something of interest to those of an artistic bent – more of their kind can be found on HaMa'apilim promenade, together with a sculpture garden. However, the main **market** on Rehov Shoham, just north of the bus station, is definitely worth a wander for its excellent selection of local

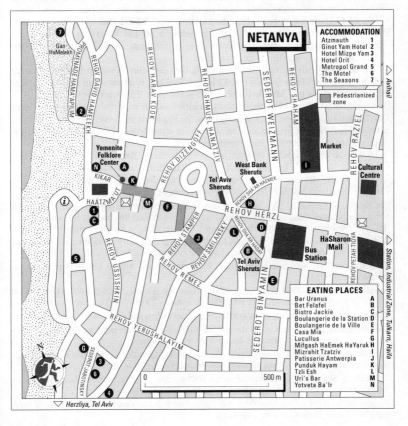

NETANYA

ACCOMMODATION

Atzmauth	1
Ginot Yam Hotel	2
Hotel Mizpe Yam	3
Hotel Orit	4
Metropol Grand	5
The Motel	6
The Seasons	7

Pedestrianized zone

EATING PLACES

Bar Uranus	A
Bet Felafel	B
Bistro Jackie	C
Boulangerie de la Station	D
Boulangerie de la Ville	E
Casa Mia	F
Lucullus	G
Mifgash HaEmek HaYaruk	H
Mizrahit Tzatziv	I
Patisserie Antwerpia	J
Punduk Hayam	K
Tzli Esh	L
Uri's Bar	M
Yotveta Ba'Ir	N

fruit, as well as stalls selling clothes, kitchenware and delicatessen, all eagerly sought by a veritable army of shoppers from the town and its surrounds.

East of the junction with Weizmann and Binyamin, Herzl continues for nearly a kilometre, past the main post office and HaSharon shopping mall and on to the **National Diamond Centre** at 90 Herzl (Sun–Thurs 8am–7pm, Fri 8am–2pm; free) where you can see a short video on the diamond industry and have a free guided tour of the factory before being ushered into the showroom. For those who prefer a more affordable and consumable commodity, the **Tempo Brewery** – makers of Goldstar and Maccabi – can be found on Rehov HaMalekha in the Poleg industrial zone, east of town across the Haifa Coast Road. They offer free guided tours (by appointment only; ☎09/863 0630) and the chance to sample their brews. A burning interest in military history might tempt you to venture to the suburb of Avihail, in the north of town, to visit **Bet HaGedudim** (Sun–Thurs 8am–4pm; 6NIS; bus #1a hourly), a museum illustrating the exploits of the Jewish Legion, who fought for the British Army in Palestine during the First World War. The display features a range of military memorabilia: photographs, maps, weapons, uniforms and medals.

Eating and drinking

Good-value **eating** is thin on the ground in Netanya, especially at the cheaper end of the scale. Low-priced eateries, many of them open lunchtime only, can be found along Rehov Ahad Ha'Am, just behind the bus station, with **falafel** stalls and the like along Rehov Sha'ar HaGay. **Fast-food** joints, including a *Dr Lek* ice-cream parlour and a branch of the *Original Pancake House* (see p.160), can be found upstairs in the HaSharon mall opposite the main post office.

The **market** (daily except Fri afternoon & Sat) on Rehov Shoham is a good source of picnic fare, and *Haim Bukobza*, at 13 Rehov Shaham, is an excellent deli for smoked fish, olives, pickles and Middle Eastern salads and dips. There are supermarkets at 13 Smilansky, 8 Nitza and 14 Stamper, and a **health-food store** in the passage at 12 Herzl. Two **bakeries** on Sederot Binyamin right by the bus station – *Boulangerie de la Station*, at no. 11, and *Boulangerie de la Ville*, across the street at no. 4 – are open around the clock except Friday evening to Saturday evening.

To sit out with a **coffee** or fruit juice, try *Patisserie Antwerpia*, 1 Rehov Eliyahu Krause. Of the town's **bars**, *Uranus*, 7 Kikar Ha'Atzma'ut (in the passage by *Ben & Jerry's* at the eastern end of the square), has the most congenial atmosphere, while *Uri's*, 26 Dizengoff just off Herzl, caters to a younger crowd.

Bet Falafel, Sha'ar HaGay. Sign in Hebrew only (next to *Pulcino*); you pay for a pitta, then stuff it with as much falafel, salad, hummus and pickles as you can, making this the best deal among Sha'ar HaGay's falafel stands. Sun–Thurs 9am–midnight, Fri 9am–2pm, Sat nightfall–midnight. Cheap.

Bistro Jackie, 2 Ussishkin, next to *Hostel Ha'Atzma'ut*. A popular place for sandwiches, snacks and beer; handy for breakfast. Daily 7am–1am. Cheap to moderate.

Casa Mia, 10 Herzl. Your best bet for Italian food in town. Noon–3.30pm & 6.30–11pm. Moderate to expensive.

Lucullus, 2 Jabotinsky (☎09/861 9502 or 4). One of the best in town, a refined, French-style seafood restaurant which also does a cheaper set menu. Daily noon–3.30pm & 7–11.30pm. Expensive.

Mifagash HaEmek HaYaruk, 2 Sha'ar HaEmek. Netanya's best *fuul* joint. Daily 10am–2pm. Cheap.

Mizrahit Tzatziv, Rehov Shaham, by the market. Middle Eastern diner popular with market traders and their customers. Sun–Thurs 8am–8pm, Fri 8am–3pm. Cheap.

Pundak Hayam, 1 Harav Kook. Middle Eastern eatery renowned for its kebabs. Sun–Thurs noon–12.30am, Fri noon–4.30pm. Moderate to expensive.

Tzli Esh, 6 Sha'ar HaGay. A popular street stall serving everything from gizzards to steak. Sun–Thurs 9am–11.30pm, Fri 9am–2pm, Sat nightfall–11.30pm. Cheap.

Yotveta Ba'Ir, Kikar Ha'Atzma'ut (☎09/862 7576). Garish plastic decor, but big portions of good, dairy-based food. Daily 8am–4am. Expensive.

Entertainment and sports

The **Cultural Centre** at 4 Raziel, behind the main post office (☎09/860 3392), puts on regular concerts and plays, while the **Herzliya Chamber Orchestra** (☎09/950 0761) performs regularly at Bet Ya'ari auditorium in Bitan Aharon, 5km north of Netanya, along with guest conductors and soloists from Israel and abroad. **Sports** enthusiasts are rather more spoilt for choice: the Elizur Sports Centre, at the end of Rehov Rambam, off Derekh Petah Tikva 1km south of Rehov Herzl (☎09/865 2931), has tennis courts, a fitness centre and a heated swimming pool. Other local activities include windsurfing on Herzl Beach, paragliding from Ariba (☎09/884 0010), and horseback riding along the seashore at the Cactus Ranch, Sederot Ben Ali, off Sederot Jabotinsky 1km south of Kikar Ha'Atzma'ut (☎09/865 1239). Large-piece chess games are played in the pedestrianized area of Rehov Herzl during the summer.

Listings

Banks and exchange Most of the banks are along Herzl but there are also commission-free exchanges (even for travellers' cheques) at: Changepoint, Kikar Ha'Atzma'ut, and Changespot, 5 Herzl on the corner of Dizengoff. Both open Sun–Thurs 8.30am–8pm, Fri 8.30am–1pm, Sat nightfall–10pm. For 24hr change machines try Bank Leumi next door, or Bank HaPoalim, and the Israel Discount Bank, facing each other at the eastern end of Kikar Ha'Atzma'ut.

Car rental Avis, 1 Ussishkin (☎09/833 1619); Budget, 2 Gad Makhnes (☎09/862 0454); Eldan, 12 Kikar Ha'Atzma'ut (☎09/861 6982); Hertz, 8 Kikar Ha'Atzma'ut (☎09/882 8890).

Medical Services Magen David Adom ☎101 or ☎09/862 2333 or 5. Pharmacies are at 2, 11, 24 & 36 Herzl, with a homeopathic pharmacy at 24 Weitzmann.

Post office The main post office is at the junction of Herzl and Raziel, 200m east of the bus station (Sun, Mon, Tues & Thurs 8am–12.30pm & 3.30–6pm, Wed 8am–1.30pm, Fri & holiday eve 8am–noon). There's another branch off the pedestrianized zone of Rehov Herzl opposite Rehov Harav Kook (same hours).

Telecommunications Solan Communications, 8 Kikar Ha'Atzma'ut, is open 24hr for international calls and sending and receiving faxes.

Travel agents ISSTA, 2 Herzl (☎09/832 0002).

Visa extensions 13 Remez is the place to apply if you are staying in Netanya.

Around Netanya

Netanya is well placed for a number of day trips into the surrounding area, either north or south along the coast or further inland to the Sharon Plain. **To the south**, the **Poleg**

MOVING ON FROM NETANYA

From the **bus** station there are regular departures to Tel Aviv direct or via Herzliya (about every 15min; 45min), Jerusalem (every 20–30min; 1hr 45min) via Ben Gurion Airport (1hr), Haifa (every 20–30min; 1hr 20min), Hadera (about every 30min; 30min), Herzliya (every 15–30min; 20min), Beersheba (4 daily; 2hr 30min) and Eilat (1 daily; 5hr 30min). For Caesarea, change buses at Hadera.

Sheruts to Tel Aviv leave from just across the street on the other side of Sederot Binyamin, and also from Rehov Shmuel HaNatziv by the junction with Rehov Herzl. For Tulkarm and other nearby West Bank towns, they leave from the square in Rehov Sha'ar HaEmek, mostly mid-afternoons when the workers are returning home.

The **train station** is hardly convenient, but if you want to go by rail there are 1–3 trains every hour to Tel Aviv (25min), most calling at Herzliya (15min), with five a day continuing to Rehovot (1hr), one to Ashdod (1hr 30min), one in the morning to Jerusalem (2hr 30min), and 2 weekly to Beersheba. Going north, fourteen trains a day run to Haifa (1hr–1hr 15min), via Hadera (15min), of which six continue to Acre (1hr 15min–1hr 45min) and Nahariyya (1hr 30min–2hr).

Nature Reserve, which begins 8km beyond Netanya at the point where the Poleg River meets the sea, is a pleasant wooded area, especially beautiful in spring when full of blossom; it's approached from the Kibbutz Yakum turn-off from Route 2. With your own transport you can take up some of the more eclectic outings on offer from local communities keen to attract tourists, such as a tour of the beehives at **MISHMERET**, 12km southeast of Netanya (☎09/796 1260; appointment only), or a visit to a parrot farm in nearby **KFAR HESS** (☎09/796 1773; appointment only). Both can be reached from Dror Junction south of Netanya on the Old Haifa Road (Route 4). On the way, you could stop off at **Tel Mond**, to see the local history museum (Sun–Thurs 8.30am–12.30pm, Tues also 4.30–6.30pm; free).

Spread over limestone hills just **north of Netanya**, the **Bitan Aharon Reserve** (☎09/866 3750) is another area of natural beauty, with an observation point for views over the Sharon, some Byzantine caves and an early settlers' museum to supplement the natural attractions. Several kilometres further north of Netanya, by **Kfar Vitkin**, the Emeq Hefer **Youth Hostel** (☎ & fax 09/866 6032; ①) is beautifully located in rural surroundings, a ten-minute walk from a quiet sandy beach. Reached from Netanya by bus #29, and by various bus lines from Tel Aviv and Haifa, it lies just south of the Paz petrol station on the Haifa Coast Road (Route 2). Next to the petrol station, the *Original Pancake House* (daily 24hr), is a Formica fast-food joint famous for its pancakes. The road east from Kfar Vitkin to Route 4 crosses **Alexander Stream**, a reserve inhabited by large turtles, which you may be lucky enough to see.

Hadera

The town of **HADERA** lies roughly halfway between Netanya and Caesarea, and is one of the main citrus-growing centres in the Sharon Plain. It's a largely residential place of very little interest to visitors, though you may well find yourself changing buses here. Egyptian labourers hired by Baron de Rothschild reclaimed the land from swamps for the group of Russian Zionists who started the settlement in 1891; in the process, scores of the labourers and most of the settlers fell victim to the malaria they eventually helped eradicate. The house where the settlers lived, known as **the Khan**, next to the main synagogue at 74 Rehov HaGiborim, is now open to the public as a museum (Sun–Thurs 8am–1pm & 4–6pm; 12NIS), and gives a rather romanticized version of the settlers' history, showing where they slept and exhibiting some of their farming implements, but failing to mention the Egyptian labourers who did most of the work or the rather worse conditions under which they lived. To get there from the bus station, head up Rehov Ahad Ha'Am to where it ends at a water tower perched on a decorated concrete wall, then turn left up HaGiborim for two blocks and it's on your right.

A **coffee shop and bakery** called *Burekas* (sign in Hebrew only; 24hr), at the main Hadera junction on the Old Haifa Road – on the corner of the "Hadera West" exit – is renowned for its excellent *burekas*, and particularly popular with young Israelis on their way home from clubs in the small hours.

MOVING ON FROM HADERA

Hadera's **bus station** is a couple of blocks off the Haifa–Tel Aviv road, with regular departures to Tel Aviv (various; 3–4 per hour; 1hr); Haifa (1–2 per hour; 1hr); Netanya (1–2 per hour; 30min); Caesarea (7 daily; 30min); Or Akiva (2–4 per hour; 15min); Afula (approximately hourly; 1hr); Nazareth (14 daily; 1hr 40min); Bet She'an (2 daily; 2hr) and Tiberias (10 daily; 2hr). There is also a **train station**, rather inconveniently located across the main road in West Hadera, and served by the same trains as Netanya (see p.159).

A little to the north of Hadera, the landmark Hadera power station towers above the plain and stands on the site of **Arab al-Mifger**, a Bedouin settlement which in 1981 became the last Palestinian village in Israel to be destroyed. One of the villagers, Ali al-Kaisi, became a national celebrity when, despite having no formal education, he personally fought each demolition order on his house (which he rebuilt each time he lost) in court. Having finally failed, he moved into a tent that he erected in the grounds of the Knesset in protest.

Caesarea

Caesarea (Qeysaria in Hebrew), 8km northwest of Hadera and midway between Netanya and Haifa, is probably the finest and largest archeological site in Israel. Although a few excellently preserved Roman buildings and sculptures remain, much of the Roman masonry was borrowed by successive rulers to adorn buildings up and down the country so what you see today is largely a monument to the Crusaders, and it is their buildings that provide the real highlights. The site has undergone rampant commercialization, in the form of souvenir stores, cafés and a disco, and is relatively difficult to reach on public transport, but even this cannot diminish its significance. As well as the cordoned-off **archeological site** run by the National Parks Authority, there are a few remains in the surrounding area, most notably a Roman hippodrome and two aqueducts that brought water to the city. Be warned that crime is a problem around the site: keep valuables with you all the time, as car locks are no obstacle to local entrepreneurs.

Modern **CAESAREA**, inland of the archeological site and beach, has a number of residential developments and a bevy of luxury hotels springing up, but has few shops or other facilities to recommend it.

Some history

Around 22 BC, Herod ordered the construction of **Caesarea** to honour Augustus Caesar. A fine career move for Herod, it was also a magnificent city – the second largest in his kingdom. Every contemporary account lauds the grandeur of its palaces, hippodrome and amphitheatre, and the two large aqueducts that kept Caesarea supplied with water were masterpieces of engineering. But by far the most spectacular part of the city was the **harbour**, in its day the finest in the eastern Mediterranean. Constructed on the site of a Phoenician anchorage called Strato's Tower (which had existed since at least 259 BC), Caesarea took twelve years to build, and its magnificent inaugural celebration in 10 BC became a four-yearly festival in honour of Augustus Caesar. After Herod's death, Caesarea became capital of the Roman province of Judea for five centuries, and the seat of the province's Roman Procurators, most famously Pontius Pilate.

Judaism and Caesarea always had an uneasy relationship. It was here that the Roman policy of enforced Hellenization of the country was devised, sparking off the **Jewish Revolt** of 66 AD, which culminated in the Roman seizure of Jerusalem and the destruction of the Temple. It began with rioting in the city during which, according to the Roman historian Josephus, "the people of Caesarea massacred the Jewish colony, slaughtering more than 20,000 and emptying Caesarea of the last Jew in less than an hour". As if to rub salt in the wound, Caesarea witnessed the execution, in 132 AD, of the leaders of the Bar Kokhba revolt, among them Rabbi Akiva, whose teachings are widely quoted in the *Mishnah* (see p.501). Nonetheless, Caesarea was at this time and later an important Jewish and **Christian** centre: here Peter baptized the centurion Cornelius (Acts 10: 24–48), and Paul was tried for his heretical teachings (Acts 24–26). In 640 AD Caesarea was captured by the **Arabs**, and under their guidance continued to prosper, as they developed both the harbour and the surrounding lands.

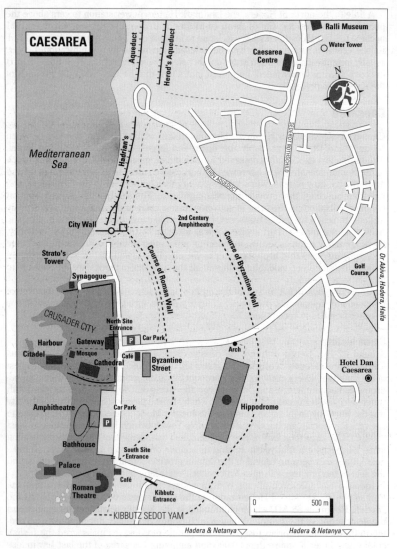

CAESAREA

Ralli Museum
Water Tower
Caesarea Centre
Aqueduct
Herod's Aqueduct
Mediterranean Sea
Hadrian's
REHOV AQUEDUCT
SDEROT ROTHSCHILD
N
Or Akiva, Hadera, Haifa
City Wall
2nd Century Amphitheatre
Golf Course
Strato's Tower
Synagogue
Course of Roman Wall
Course of Byzantine Wall
CRUSADER CITY
North Site Entrance
P Car Park
Café
Arch
Harbour
Gateway
Citadel
Mosque
Cathedral
Byzantine Street
Hotel Dan Caesarea
Amphitheatre
Car Park
P
Hippodrome
Bathhouse
South Site Entrance
Palace
Café
Roman Theatre
Kibbutz Entrance
KIBBUTZ SEDOT YAM
0   500 m
Hadera & Netanya ▽   *Hadera & Netanya* ▽

The **Crusader** era began in 1107, the year when most of Palestine fell under their dominion. In 1187, after the Battle of Hittin, Saladin ousted the Crusaders, destroying much of the city, which then changed hands no fewer than five times before being reconquered by the Crusaders in 1251 under Louis IX of France. In a fourteen-year occupation, Louis managed to construct one of the most spectacular fortified cities in the Middle East, much of it still visible. A final conquest by Sultan Baybars in 1275 reduced all his work to nothing, however, as the city was largely destroyed and lay unoccupied for six centuries.

In 1878, the Ottoman rulers settled Muslim refugees from Bosnia nearby, establishing a farming and fishing village. Part of their land was bought up during the 1930s by the Palestine Jewish Colonisation Association – a land society founded by Baron Edmund de Rothschild to promote Jewish settlement – and the nearby kibbutz Sedot Yam was established on it. All that remains of the Muslim village that existed here until 1948 is a mosque beside the port.

The Crusader City

The main entrance to the site (Sat–Thurs 8am–5pm, Fri 8am–4pm; 15NIS) leads through the impressive main gateway of the **Crusader City**, commissioned by Louis IX and flanked by two enormous Gothic towers overlooking the moat. While revamping the city's fortifications, Louis also had the moat (now dry) constructed, strengthened the wall with an embankment, and added a large passageway at right angles to the old gate with an opening at its northern end. This served to break the approach of invaders, slowing them down and forcing them to pass beneath the defenders of the gate: to the same end, the bridge over the moat, supported by four pointed arches, passed in the shadow of the nine-metre-high tower. As you cross the bridge and proceed under the **gateway**, notice the hewn grooves for the portcullis, and the sockets for the hinges of the iron doors. Within, the gateway is a beautifully proportioned structure with high vaulted interior supports made from smooth limestone.

Once inside, you're confronted by a large collection of Roman, Arab and Crusader ruins. It's all a bit of a jumble, but everything is well marked and it's easy enough to identify the various periods. Just inside the gateway a massive foot is all that remains of a lost Roman statue. Next to it is a replica of an inscription found here, now in the Israel Museum in Jerusalem (see p.373), whose words "[PON]TIVS PILATVS [PRÆF]ECTVS IVDA[EÆ]" (Pontius Pilate, prefect of Judea), were the first extra-biblical evidence of Pilate's existence.

Perhaps the easiest place to start exploring is the **Crusader Cathedral** dedicated to St Paul: it's in the main square; turn left just beyond the gate and follow the walls around for about 200m. Built originally as a mosque in the early Arab period, the cathedral was taken over and substantially remodelled by the Crusaders, although the work was abandoned before completion when the vaults underneath started to crack. Excavations have revealed a finely proportioned building with a triple apse at the eastern end and a row of eight Corinthian columns bearing the cross of Richard the Lionheart (who recaptured the city from Saladin's forces during the third Crusade). Adjacent is a second Crusader building, of which you can see the foundations and a small part of the upper structure.

As you make your way up the broad road by the side of the cathedral, it is possible to get a sense of how each successive period reused, reworked and redesigned previous architectural styles. Statues taken from Roman temples were smashed and used for stone by the Byzantines; floors of early Arab houses were used as the bases of later Crusader buildings; massive pillars of porphyry rock were hewn into rounded slabs for use as millstones; and, most interesting of all, Roman columns were split in two and put to use as wall supports or door frames. Examples of this architectural reclamation can be seen as far afield as Acre, where purloined Roman masonry from Caesarea is commonplace.

East of the small gate, past the rows of souvenir shops, the area around the **Crusader Citadel** is the most heavily commercialized on the site: the citadel itself has even had a restaurant built into it (see below) – tastefully done, but a pity nonetheless. From here there's a fine view of the Crusader City – only a fraction of the area of Roman Caesarea – and the surrounding coast.

North of the Crusader City, by the ancient harbour from the original Phoenician settlement of Strato's Tower, lie the partially excavated remains of a fourth-century synagogue discovered by an expedition in 1956 and basically consisting of the shell of the building and a mosaic floor. This area was probably occupied by the Jewish community throughout the city's history.

The Roman Theatre

Leaving the Crusader City to the south and walking along the old Byzantine road through the remains of the Roman and Byzantine city, you'll pass the site of Herod's main amphitheatre (used for sporting events), and the Roman bathhouse, reaching the **Roman Theatre** in around five minutes. Built into the side of a hill overlooking the sea, it has been heavily refurbished and is now used for ballets, concerts and operas, especially during the **Israel Festival** (see p.53). Semi-circular and multi-tiered, and still scattered with ruined marble columns and capitals, the theatre is vast, as befitted a Roman city of Caesarea's size and importance. Here the entire community would meet, not just for theatrical performances but for trials, executions and other civic matters. Excavations at the site began in the late 1950s, and when fully restored in 1961, the theatre was opened with a concert by the renowned Spanish cellist Pablo Casals. There is an entrance to the site here at the southern end, too, open the same hours as the main entrance.

Outside the site

By the main entrance to the Crusader City, a small excavated area by the main car park reveals a marble-paved Byzantine street flanked by two headless but impressive statues (the red one may be the emperor Hadrian). Half a kilometre east along the road is a stone arch on the right; going through it and round the fruit grove on the other side, you come to the **Roman Hippodrome**, now just a large field, but once a chariot race-track with room for as many as 20,000 spectators. Lying on the ground in the centre of the field is an obelisk and three granite turning posts. Known by early Christians as "The Table of Christ" and "Our Lord's Candlesticks", a reference to the furniture at the last supper, they stood in the middle of the track and the chariots had to turn outside rather than inside them.

To the north of the site, a portion of the original **city wall** has been excavated, with the remains of a round tower clearly visible (if the gate is open, you can leave and re-enter the site here by a bridge across the moat from the ancient synagogue – keep hold of your ticket if you do this). North of the wall, but best reached via Rehov Aqueduct, the two **aqueducts** stretching northward are the work of two great Roman rulers, Herod and Hadrian. The western water channel, facing the sea, was commissioned by Hadrian and built in the second century AD; the eastern side dates from the first century BC. Although the brick arches are half buried in sand, their presence remains majestic and will no doubt be familiar from photographs in dozens of travel agents' brochures. As you explore, you may be approached by local youths selling "genuine Roman coins" – fake, naturally, but good, cheap souvenirs all the same.

Finally, two **museums** exist outside the site. You have to pay for the one on Kibbutz Sedot Yam, just south of the site (theoretically Sat–Thurs 10am–4pm, Fri 10am–2pm; 7NIS) but its random and not very enlightening collection of pillars, sarcophagi and bits of sculpture and mosaic found on the site is hardly worth the money or effort. Much more worthwhile is the **Ralli Museum**, northeast of the site, 1500m up Sederot Rothschild (Mon, Tues, Thurs, Fri & Sat 10.30am–3pm; Fri & Sat only in Jan; free). Housed in an Andalusian-style villa and founded by one of the members of the Ralli family, who own the Israel Discount Bank, most of the museum is dedicated to modern painting and sculpture, mainly from Hispanic countries – look out for the sculpture by Salvador Dalí of a long-legged elephant. Even more interesting, though, and certainly more pertinent, is the section on archeology, which gives clear explanations, with maps and charts as well as artefacts, of the history of Caesarea and its excavation.

Practicalities

Bus #76 runs from Hadera to the site and back seven times daily (30min). Other buses stop 3km east at Or Akiva, where you'll get at least two buses hourly into Hadera, with others to Haifa and Tel Aviv.

If you want to **stay** at the site, your choice is basically between nearby Kibbutz Sedot Yam (☎06/636 4453, fax 636 2211), at its southern entrance, in hostel-style dorms (②) or private rooms (④); or the deluxe *Hotel Dan Caesarea*, 1km east (☎06/626 9111, fax 626 9122; ⑥). Further luxury hotels are opening up to the south of modern Caesarea. Camping on the beach is permitted, but definitely not recommended, as you're highly vulnerable to theft.

Should traipsing round the ruins give you an appetite, you have the choice of three places **to eat** on the site. By the main entrance, the *Statues Coffee Restaurant* (daily 9am–7pm; moderate) is not tremendously appetizing, with Israeli fare at prices befitting its tourist location. The snack bar by the southern entrance, run by Kibbutz Sedot Yam, is preferable (daily 9am–7pm; moderate). Inside the site itself, down by the citadel, the *Harbour Citadel Restaurant* (daily noon–5pm in winter, until midnight or later in summer; expensive; ☎06/636 1988 or 9) offers a wider and rather classier choice of international cuisine, specializing in seafood, with the option of outdoor dining and a fine view of the Roman port.

The small, rather stony **beach** is accessible from the Crusader citadel, though there's a steep entry fee (around $6 in summer, when there's a lifeguard and bathing is allowed); you can swim down by the Roman theatre for free, but bathing is not allowed at the beaches immediately south of the Crusader City due to a dangerous undertow. The 18-hole **golf course** (☎06/626 1174), 1km east of the site by the *Hotel Dan Caesarea*, is Israel's only course so far, with temporary membership available to tourists who wish to use it.

Caesarea to Haifa

In the 30km **between Caesarea and Haifa**, the scenery becomes rather more inspiring, as the wooded and flower-decked Carmel Mountains (see p.146) rise on the landward side. There's plenty of interest along the route: several fine beaches, the minor archeological sites at **Tel Dor** and **Crocodile Aqueduct**, a reconstructed prison camp at **Atlit**, an artists' colony at **Ein Hod**, and the wine-making town of **Zikhron Ya'acov**. All of these are best accessed from the inland Old Haifa Road (Route 4), plied by numerous bus services, since the coastal road (Route 2) is now a freeway with few exits and no stopping bus services.

Binyamina and Shuni

Two kilometres north of Or Akiva, a turning on the right heads inland to the village of **BINYAMINA**, named after France's Zionist aristocrat, Baron Edmond de Rothschild, who established several settlements in the area (practising Jews, of whatever nationality, use a Hebrew name for religious purposes: Rothschild's was Binyamin).

On the other side of town, Route 652 leads north, passing after 1km the springs of **Shuni**, from which Caesarea drew its water. The JNF have opened up a site here called Jabotinsky Park after Ze'ev Jabotinsky, the founder of Zionism's right-wing "Revisionist" tendency. Set amidst landscaped gardens, the site's main feature is a reconstructed **Roman theatre** (Sat–Thurs 9am–5pm, Fri 9am–noon; 6NIS), probably constructed to celebrate the water festival of Mayumas. The fortified granary built on top of it in the last century was used in the Thirties and Forties by Jabotinsky's disciples in the Irgun, who planned a number of their operations here, notably the 1947 breakout from Acre jail.

The site is served by **buses** to Hadera, Netanya, Haifa, Zikhron Ya'akov (north on Route 652) and Tel Aviv.

Crocodile Aqueduct and Ma'agan Mikhael

The aqueduct from Caesarea crosses the main road 2km north of the Binyamina turn-off, with the best-preserved section on the coastward side, accessible via the turning to the Palestinian village of Bet Hanaya. This section is called **Crocodile Aqueduct** after the nearby Crocodile River, which contained said reptiles until the end of the nineteenth century and which was also tapped for Caesarea's water supply.

Three kilometres further along the main road is the turn-off for **Kibbutz Ma'agan Mikhael**. One of the wealthiest kibbutzim in the country, it funds its own **wildlife sanctuary**, located about 1500m south of the kibbutz (turn left in front of the main gate, following the sign to Bet Gail). Set along the banks of Crocodile River, this is a good site for spotting migratory birdlife and the occasional turtle. The lightly wooded sanctuary is not very extensive, but large enough for a pleasant stroll, and there is a picnic area by the car park, where a dam and bridge over the river date from Roman times.

Accommodation is available at the *Hof HaCarmel Field School*, next to the sanctuary (☎06/399654 or 5, fax 391618; ⑤). The rather institutional rooms should be booked in advance, and although they sleep six, each party has to take a separate one.

Zikhron Ya'acov

Route 652, the next turn-off (after just 1km), heads north to the town of **ZIKHRON YA'ACOV**. Perched on a hill overlooking the coast, it was founded in 1882 with financial backing from Baron Edmond de Rothschild, who is buried in a memorial garden here. In among the red-roofed, whitewashed bungalows of the town centre, you'll find several buildings from the settlement's early days preserved in a manner too tasteful to be authentic. Among them are the unpretentious little stone synagogue on Rehov HaMeyasdim, the largely pedestrianized main street, with the founders' plaque next door, and, around the corner on Rehov Herzl, the 1893 Town Hall.

However, the town would be eminently missable were it not for the opportunity to visit the **Carmel-Oriental Wine Co**, established by Rothschild in 1888, and one of the best vineyards in Israel and the Palestinian Territories; a walking tour (in Hebrew: hourly Sun–Thurs 9am–3pm, Fri 9am–1pm; in English: Tues 11am; 12NIS) introduces both the wine and the production techniques employed, and samples of the product are on offer at the end. To reach the winery, get off at the Central Bus Station, walk north along Rehov HaMeyasdim and turn right down Rehov HaNadiv. The memorial garden containing the Rothschild family tomb lies close by.

En route from the bus station to the winery, on the corner of HaMeyasdim and Rehov Nili, you pass **Bet Aaronson**, the home of the agronomist Aaron Aaronson (1876–1919), who discovered the strain from which all modern wheat is descended. The house is now a museum (Sun–Thurs 8.30am–2pm, Fri 9am–noon; 7NIS), and worth a browse if you're passing. It contains some of his original furniture and among the exhibits are Aaronson's catalogue of Palestinian plants, and his diaries and letters. During World War I, Aaronson ran a spy-ring called NILI for the British, tipping them off with information as to Turkish troop movements aimed at the Suez Canal which he observed while travelling around the country organizing defence measures against locusts. The British became increasingly reliant on NILI information, but in September 1917 a NILI carrier pigeon fell into Ottoman hands and the group's members were rounded up, tortured and executed. Aaronson himself was in Cairo and escaped but he later died in a plane crash on the way from London to the Versailles Peace Conference. Some photographs of NILI personnel – chief among them were Aaronson's sisters Sarah and Rebecca, and his aide Avshalom Feinberg – are on display in the museum.

There's a **tourist office** by the founders' memorial next to the bus station (Sat–Thurs 8.30am–1pm, Fri 8.30am–noon; ☎06/398892), but most tourists here are Israeli so there may not be anyone who can speak English. Should you need to stay in town, there are several **hotels**, none of them cheap but all come with a pool. The least expensive is the *Maimon*, 4 Zahal (☎06/390212 or 4, fax 396547; ④), which has a sun terrace but its views aren't as good as those you'll get from the *Radisson Moriah*, 1 Etzion (☎06/300111, fax 397030; ⑤) or its deluxe neighbour, the *Havat HaBaron* (☎06/300333, fax 300313; ⑥), both of which have a bar and restaurant.

Buses from the bus station in the centre of town (☎06/399777) serve Tel Aviv (hourly; 1hr 30min), Hadera (2–3 per hour; 30min), Haifa (hourly; 45 min) and Netanya (hourly; 1hr).

Dor and around

Four kilometres north of the Zikhron Ya'acov junction on Route 4, a turn-off leads to the excellent beach and temples at **Dor**. The **beach** is sheltered by four small, rocky islands that join at low tide and provide a nesting place for terns and plovers; you can wade out to the islands when the tide is out.

Moshav Dor, at the southern end of the beach, was built on the site of the destroyed Palestinian village of **Tantura**, which was famous for its murex – shellfish whose purple colouring was used as raw material by the Haifa dye works. Two hundred metres to the north, **Kibbutz Nahsholim** maintains a small **museum** of marine archeology (Sun–Thurs 8.30am–2pm, Fri 8.30am–1pm, Sat 10am–3pm; 8NIS) in a building once used by Baron de Rothschild's company to make the bottles for their wine. There's not much to see; it's mostly photographs of discoveries with few actual artefacts on show.

A path from the museum leads to the archeological site of **Tel Dor** at the northern end of the beach. Settled from the Bronze Age, Dor was described in Egyptian papyrus texts as "a site of magnificence", and in the fifth century BC was the base of King Ashmanezer, a Canaanite from Sidon. Its zenith, however, came in the Hellenic period, when it was capital of an Assyrian province. **Temples** dedicated to Zeus and Astarte have been found at Tel Dor along with the remains of an early Byzantine church. The Crusaders built a fortress here, Castle Merle, whose sea-washed remains can still be seen. There is a large archeological dig at Tel Dor through most of the summer, and one of its members will usually be happy to show you the key points. Otherwise, all you'll see is plenty of excavation but no explanation. For details on volunteering on the dig, see "Work" in Basics (p.64).

If you want **to stay**, Moshav Dor (☎ & fax 06/397180; ⑤) runs a "holiday village" by the beach featuring comfortable igloo-shaped chalets, and also a very reasonably priced campsite (12NIS per person). It can be crowded in summer, but it's a very pleasant place to stay. Alternatively, you could try next door at Kibbutz Nahsholim's hotel (☎06/399533, fax 397614; ⑥). **Buses** serving the Dor junction on Route 4 are the #202 to Zikhron Ya'akov and Binyamina, and the #921 and #922 to Petah Tikva and Tel Aviv. All run the other way to Haifa.

Nahal Me'arot Nature Reserve, 8km north of Dor Junction and 1km inland from the main road (Sat–Thurs 8am–4pm, Fri 8am–1pm; admission to caves 13NIS), is served by the same buses (though the bus stop is a little way past the junction). It features three caves built into the limestone cliffs, of which two were inhabited twenty thousand years ago. The two-hour guided tour takes in all three: the **Tabun Cave** has archeological workings exposing several different strata; the **Gamal Cave** features a homely reconstruction of a caveman family scene, somewhat ironic since this cave was probably never inhabited; while the **Nahal Cave**, occupied from 40,000 BC to 20,000 BC, has remains of a support wall and niches cut into the stone by its ancient occupants. From an observation point on the way, you can see the "finger", a large rock made of fossilized coral, as indeed are the cliffs. Signposted walks from the entrance enable you to appreciate the local wild flowers, spot birds of prey such as falcons, kestrels and eagle owls, or spy on sunbathing rock hyraxes.

Ein Hod

EIN HOD, 2km off the Old Haifa Road and 3km north of Me'arot Karmel (the turn-off is connected to Haifa by buses #121, #122, #202, #921 and #922), crowns a small hill overlooking the Mediterranean. In the early 1950s the village was settled by Israeli artists drawn by the classical simplicity of its Arab architecture, undamaged in 1948, and the muted greens of its nearby olive trees. Today, it's one of Israel's leading artistic centres, boasting more than two hundred galleries and studios, and hosting courses in everything from sculpture to needlework. The village is packed with artists of every imaginable genre, from traditional landscape painters and contemporary impressionists to glassblowers, potters, weavers, jewellers and sculptors; some of them producing works aimed squarely at the tourists who flock here, especially in the summer.

Two galleries, facing each other across the main square, deserve special mention as their collections are more permanent and not geared to sale: the **Artists' Gallery** (Sat–Thurs 9.30am–5pm, Fri 9.30am–4pm; 2NIS) is a showcase for the village's resident artists; while the **Janco Dada Museum** (same hours; 8NIS) is dedicated to Marcel Janco – one of the colony's founding members – and the Dadaist movement, of which he was a leading light. You could spend hours browsing around the village's other galleries (most of which are free), or simply absorbing the atmosphere as you sit at one of the many cafés or dine at the **restaurant** in the main square (☎04/984 2016; daily 10am–1am; expensive).

In the small **Roman theatre** off the main square, concerts (rock or classical) are held most Friday evenings in summer: you'll need your own transport as there'll be no public transport running by the time it's over. More intimate classical performances are held every week or two at **Yad Gertrude Kraus**, a private house just off the main square (☎04/984 1058).

Outside Ein Hod, an encampment of its former Palestinian residents has been there since 1948, petitioning the government to let them return to the homes they fled in the face of war. Denied permission to return under the Absentee Property Act (see p.495), they made their encampment semi-permanent, with small concrete houses, and Yitzhak Rabin's Labour government eventually gave it recognition as a village in its own right.

Atlit and Neve Yam

Just 1km north of Ein Hod, a left-hand turn-off leads south to the coastal village of **ATLIT**. Just before the turning, you'll see on your right a **reconstructed camp** (Sun–Thurs 8am–4pm, Fri 9am–1pm, Sat 9am–4pm; 12NIS) used by the British in the Forties to detain illegal immigrants, many of them concentration camp survivors and refugees from Nazism. The camp also held members of various Zionist paramilitaries, who organized a number of escapes, the biggest of which was in October 1945 when Palmah commandos infiltrated the camp posing as Hebrew teachers, disarmed the guards, quietly took over the camp and released 208 inmates. The released prisoners headed for nearby kibbutzim Bet Oren and Yagur, which were then besieged by British troops. But, in a display of solidarity, thousands of unarmed Jewish residents from nearby towns placed themselves in front of the troops, forcing them to back down. After independence, the camp housed legal immigrants in transit, but part of it has now been restored to an approximation of its original state – little more than a wooden, barrack-like building fenced in with barbed wire, though the bunks, models of inmates, and old photographs attempt to inject some sense of what it was actually like when in use. To the south, the Crusader castle on a small outcrop at the end to the beach is used by the army and does not welcome visitors.

Further south, beyond Atlit village, **Neve Yam** was for many years a tranquil beachside **campsite** with superb sands and a pleasant, laid-back atmosphere. The beach is still there, but is nowadays a favourite spot for weekend day trippers, while the campsite is now used to house "guest workers" from Turkey, Thailand and Eastern Europe, though it may also have room for tourists.

CHAPTER THREE

LOWER GALILEE

Wherever sycamores do not grow from Kfar Hananya and above is Upper Galilee.
Wherever sycamores grow from Kfar Hananya and below is Lower Galilee.

Ancient saying

I t is a pity that so many tourists miss out on visiting the **Lower Galilee** as even a short trip reveals a glorious countryside of mountain peaks and lush, fertile valleys, particularly attractive in springtime. The tempo here is altogether slower and calmer than in the coastal or historic towns that most overseas visitors stick to, while the growth of domestic tourism provides the option of spending a night or two in a pleasant rural setting.

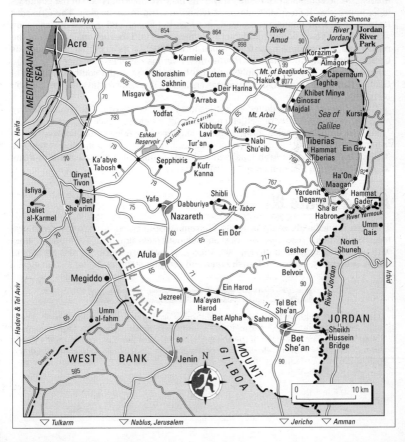

There is no hard and fast dividing line between Upper and Lower Galilee, but the east–west **Route 85** acts as a convenient demarcator, with the Lower Galilee to its south characterized by a number of **valleys**. At the eastern edge of Bet Kerem Basin (Bik'at Bet HaKerem), which straddles the centre of Route 85, the Jewish development town of **Karmiel** provides an interesting contrast with Palestinian **Sakhnin** to its south. Forming the Lower Galilee's southwestern edge is the massive and fertile **Jezreel Valley** (Emek Yizre'el), skirted by Routes 70 and 66 (from Haifa to Jenin on the West Bank), while at the region's eastern extremity and part of the Great Rift itself are **Bet She'an Valley** (Emek Bet She'an) in the south and, to its north, the Kinneret Valley (Emek Kinneret), filled by the waters of the **Sea of Galilee**, famed as the place where **Jesus** gathered many of his disciples, and where he walked on water. Naturally, it's now a much-visited tourist site with Israelis and foreigners alike, popular as much for its year-round warm climate as for its natural beauty and historic sites.

The region's most famous town and the largest Arab city in Israel, **Nazareth**, where Jesus grew up, is staunchly Christian of course, and vies with Bethlehem and Jerusalem for the pilgrimage trade. Rising to the west of Nazareth **Mount Tabor**, the accepted site of the transfiguration of Christ, is another major Christian pilgrimage destination, while southeast, **Bet She'an** with its massive theatre, is one of the country's most impressive Roman sites – a must-see on any trip to the region. The Crusader fortress of **Belvoir** dominates the lands between Bet She'an and the Sea of Galilee, on whose shores you'll find one of Israel's premier resorts, **Tiberias**, major town of the region and an excellent base from which to explore. To its north, at sites such as **Capernaum** and the **Mount of Beatitudes**, pilgrims can follow further in the footsteps of Christ. Last but certainly not least, tucked away to the south of the Sea of Galilee, **Hammat Gader (Al-Hamma)** is an ancient spa resort, whose waters can still be taken today

Today, Lower Galilee is dotted with Palestinian villages, many of them overlooked by *mitzpim*, Jewish *yishuvim* or settlements, built after independence as part of Israel's "Judaicization of the Galilee" project aiming to entice Israeli Jews from the main population centres to shift the demographic balance in a region that nonetheless remains largely Arab. Among its Arab inhabitants, the **Bedouins** maintain a culture in many ways distinct from that of their fellow Palestinians.

Along Route 85

The area immediately south of Route 85 from Acre to Safed is packed with natural forests and wildlife reserves, historical and religious sites aiming also to attract visitors with a range of organized outdoor activities and adventure tours. It's also an area of mixed settlement – modern Jewish cities and *mitzpim* stand on hilltops strategically

---

ACCOMMODATION PRICE CODES

Throughout this guide, **hotel accommodation** is graded on a scale from ① to ⑥. The numbers represent the cost per night of the **cheapest double room in high season**, though remember that many of the cheap places will have more expensive rooms with en-suite facilities. For **hostels**, the code represents the price of **two dorm beds** and is followed by the code for a double room where applicable, ie ①/②. Hostels are listed in ascending price order.

① = less than $20	② = $20–40	③ = $40–60
④ = $60–80	⑤ = $80–100	⑥ = over $100

placed to overlook Arab villages and towns. Two places in particular exemplify the contrast between Jewish and Arab Galilee: the modern Jewish city of **Karmiel** immediately south of the Acre–Safed road, built in the settlement style seen also on the West Bank; and the town of **Sakhnin**, about 6km south, a long-established and major centre of Palestinian life in Lower Galilee.

Karmiel and around

KARMIEL was established in 1964 on land that provided a livelihood for hundreds of Palestinians from its high-quality marble quarries. Today it has a Jewish population of over 30,000 – a sizeable proportion of whom are new immigrants from the former Soviet Union and Eastern Europe. The city's bunches of incongruous concrete houses with red-tiled roofs are encircled by a spaghetti-like maze of streets, with road signs in Hebrew only. A relatively affluent, modern development town, Karmiel offers little of interest other than its annual **Dance Festival**, usually held in July, when a variety of international and local folk dance is presented; the **Karmiel Information Bureau** (☎04/998 3010 or 1433) can provide details of this and other events.

The **town centre**, just a few hundred metres south of the main road, is marked by a large **mural** depicting the history of the Jewish people in Israel; around it are cafés, bars, and falafel stalls. A shopping centre, post office and banks provide other useful services. Should you need to **stay** in Karmiel, the *Kalanit Hotel* at 10 Nesei Yisrael Boulevard (☎ & fax 04/998 3878; ③) is the only place in town, and if you feel like a sit-down meal, a range of **restaurants** offer food as varied as Russian, Romanian and Chinese. The **bus station** – little more than a collection of bus stops around a large patch of grass – has frequent services to Acre, Haifa and on towards Safed, or there are **sheruts** to the same destinations.

Shorashim and Misgav

Another option for staying in the area is at **SHORASHIM**, about 5km southwest of Karmiel, off Route 784 towards Misgav Junction. Here you can find **accommodation** in holiday apartments called *Makom BaGalil* (A Place in the Galilee) (☎04/990 2431, fax 990 2476; ④), complete with kosher restaurant. They also run **tours**, including a trip to Sepphoris (see p.184).

Shorashim is just one of numerous kibbutzim and moshavim Galilee-wide which have had to change under the pressure of modernization and the collapse of socialist ideology, and are now known as "communal villages". These include **Yodfat** and **Lotem** (see p.174) in the heart.of the Misgav region, whose administrative centre is the settlement of **MISGAV**, 8km south of Karmiel along Route 784. The information centre here, called Galileria (☎04/980 0161, fax 980 0503) has details on tours and accommodation in the area, such as the holiday apartments at **Rakefet Holiday Village**, about 1km south of Misgav (☎04/980 0403, fax 980 0317; ⑤).

Sakhnin

Surrounded by the fertile hills of Galilee and, less picturesquely, by strategic *yishuvim*, the sprawling Palestinian city of **SAKHNIN** lies 5km south of Karmiel. Although the population of each place is roughly the same, they couldn't be more different: Sakhnin, like other Palestinian towns inside the Green Line, suffers visibly from lack of funding, infrastructure and amenities. Many of its population work as wage labour in Israeli industry and construction since their agricultural base has been whittled away by the construction of the Jewish settlements.

Recently, however, some locals are turning their attention to the economic possibilities offered by tourism. These include the **Museum of Palestinian Folk Heritage** and a couple of **guesthouses** which make it possible to spend more than just a few hours here and benefit from the town's wonderful mountain air. Ambitious plans include the development of the village spring and museum, the construction of more hotels and even a holiday village, some of which may be in place by the time this book goes to press.

An interesting time to visit Sakhnin is during the **Olive Oil Festival,** held in October/November at the time of the olive harvest. The festival, partly organized by the Jewish settlement of Misgav (see p.171), is growing in popularity and hosts over 6000 daily visitors. Another significant date in the local calendar is March 30, *Yom al-'Ard* or **Land Day**, commemorating protests against local land confiscations which, in 1976, erupted into a pitched battle between the Israeli army and the villagers that spread across the Galilee and left six dead, three of them in Sakhnin.

The Town
Although Sakhnin dates back to around 1500 BC, when it was settled by the Canaanites, there is little to see of this ancient period. Indeed, the place is simply an overgrown village with one main road running through the centre. Apart from the **museum**, sites of interest yet to be developed include a tomb attributed to one Rabbi Yehoshua of Sakhnin, and an oft-rebuilt church.

Sakhnin's only notable landmark, the **Omari Mosque**, named after Omar Ibn Khattab, has a green dome visible from the main road that runs through the middle of town. Most sights are within walking distance of here.

THE MUSEUM OF PALESTINIAN FOLK HERITAGE
The **Museum of Palestinian Folk Heritage**, uphill from the Omari Mosque (daily 8am–4.30pm; 10NIS) takes very seriously its remit to attempt to maintain the identity of the 750,000 Palestinian citizens of Israel. It provides an enjoyable and rare insight into a changing world; curator and founder, Amin Abu Ra'ya, is a mine of information and is more than happy to take you on a guided tour of the place.

The museum consists of six rooms around the central *hohsh*, the courtyard of a traditional Palestinian house, which holds stone seating, a well, a *taboun* for baking bread, a pigeon coop and beehives. Most interesting of the exhibits is the *madafa* (also called the *majlis* or *diwan*) or **sitting room,** which illustrates the male social structure of traditional Palestinian society. Mattresses on the floor around the walls provide seating for papier-mâché characters, each dressed in attire appropriate to his profession and standing: here is the grand-looking *mukhtar* (village leader) with his guest reclining on cushions; here the storyteller. Beside him is the barber, who also served as local dentist and doctor, while the musician keeps the party entertained, and the servant, sitting apart from the company, brews coffee for the guests. The **living room** is the traditional women's space, with mats on the floor for sleeping, a wooden dowry box that contained the linen and clothes that a woman brought to her marriage and, in the centre, suspended from the domed ceiling, a pulley platform covered by gauze where food could be kept cool and safe from flies and insects.

On the upper floor you can see **handicrafts** still made today: ceramics from Jerusalem, glassware from Hebron, wood from Bethlehem, and mother-of-pearl from Bet Sahur. Embroidered Palestinian dresses from the various regions of the country, each with its own distinctive motifs, threads, colours and cloth, immediately identify the origins of the wearer, and strike an incredible contrast with the ubiquitous jeans and T-shirts worn by Palestinians nowadays.

Practicalities

With tourism in its early days, a visit to Sakhnin acquires the dimensions of an exploration. There are no signs, so once in town, you have to depend on locals for directions. Although not everyone speaks English – which is where a little Arabic or Hebrew comes in handy – most are more than willing to guide you. Visitors can also get help in finding accommodation or directions by calling Trees – a Dutch woman living in Sakhnin with her husband Ali (☎06/674 5821). They are happy to help on an unofficial basis and can tell you about other activities – such as walking – in the surrounding area.

Of Sakhnin's **guesthouses**, *Ali Baba* (☎06/674 3156; ②), perched high on the hill on the outskirts of town, benefits from spectacular views from its terrace and wonderful cool, clean air from the surrounding mountains. It's a seven-room family-run place, with double rooms that can also accommodate two extra adults or children; rates include a Palestinian breakfast of *labaneh*, *za'atar*, *fuul* and hummus. *Al-Mal* provides a similar service (☎06/674 2664; fax 674 2438; ②), as does a small third guesthouse, *Shadi* (no phone; ②).

The handful of **restaurants** in Sakhnin dish up authentic, plentiful and reasonably priced Palestinian food. Try the little place near the Arab Mercantile Bank on the main street, south of the mosque and the museum.

Sakhnin is connected by **bus** to Nazareth (hourly; 25min); Haifa (10 daily; 40min), and Acre (10 daily; 20min), and by **sherut** to Haifa and Acre.

Around Sakhnin: 'Arraba and the Bedouin villages

The countryside around Sakhnin is a great place to walk or cycle, with several Palestinian villages to visit on the way. These include **'ARRABA**, a 300-year-old village in the Sakhnin Valley which boasts tombs from the Canaanite period, a twelfth-century mosque, ancient olive presses and the tomb of a Jewish sage, Hananya Ben Dosa. 'Arraba lies 5km east of Sakhnin on Route 805.

The latest tourism enterprise in 'Arraba is a Bedouin-style **tent**, erected on a hillside overlooking the village by a local resident, Omar Ayyada. His place, first called the

---

BEDOUIN OF THE GALILEE

It comes as a suprise to most foreign visitors – and perhaps even to urban Israelis – to learn that there are some 22 **Bedouin tribes** in the Galilee, and sixteen Bedouin villages numbering about 45,000 inhabitants. The once-nomadic Bedouins are said to have migrated into the Galilee from Syria, Iraq, Jordan and Lebanon in the early sixteenth century.

Traditionally, each tribe in the Galilee had its own grazing and living area. Some groups, such as the Tzaker tribe of the **Bet She'an** region, and the Tza'bieh – the ancestors of the present-day Shibli (see p.187) – tended to dominate in disputes over land and water sources. Today, however, with ownership of livestock diminishing in importance, grazing land limited by agricultural activity and confiscations, and total nomadism a thing of the past, a rapid and dramatic transformation in lifestyle is taking place. Houses have replaced tents and the Bedouins are increasingly integrated into modern economic and social patterns. Political changes are also in evidence: the once-powerful role of the traditional leader or *sheikh* has been progressively weakened, and the Bedouins of the Galilee are today represented by local councils, three of which are Bedouin-run.

All these changes have thrown up issues for the Bedouins about their place, status and identity in modern Israeli society; Bedouin cultural centres, museums and organizations, set up by local people to reaffirm Bedouin heritage in the Galilee, testify to this dynamic and ongoing process.

"People's Tent", changed to "Peace Tent" following the assassination of Yitzhak Rabin. Inside, amidst photos of himself shaking hands with VIPs such as the Israeli minister of tourism, Omar plays host to predominantly Israeli guests, including soldiers brought here on "familiarization" visits. A stonemason by trade, Omar has left a more aesthetic and lasting legacy in the form of a **sculpture garden** on the edge of town which also offers great views over the surrounding countryside.

'Arraba has a total of six b&b **rooms** (②). You can also sleep in Omar's tent (①); showers and toilets are nearby. Volunteers willing to help out in the tent (light construction, cleaning, hosting and the like) get free board and lodging. Lodging is also available at **Deir Hanna**, 3km east on Route 805 (☎06/678 2039, fax 678 2013; ②)

In the mountains between these villages and Karmiel are a number of small, isolated **Bedouin villages**. Collections of tin huts, breeze-block houses and the occasional tent, they have few of the services enjoyed by their immediate neighbours. As in the Negev (see box on p.278), the Bedouins here are engaged in a complex dispute over land rights and demands for compensation for land already confiscated. The Israelis maintain that most of these Bedouin settlements are illegal, and hence refuse them permission to build: from time to time the police come and demolish houses to underline the point. The Bedouins, meanwhile, claim to have lived in the area for at least as long as the State of Israel has existed (and in many cases have land deeds to prove it).

Lotem and Yodfat

The Jewish settlement of **LOTEM**, on a hilltop north of the valley from 'Arraba, started out as a kibbutz in 1979 but, in line with moves towards privatization in general, has pretty much abandoned notions of collectivism. Of the fifty or so original families, only sixteen remain, and the *mitzpe* is now turning to tourism as a way of earning a living. **Accommodation** is available in the *Lotem Guest House* (☎06/678 7293, fax 678 7277; ⑤), which has 24 rooms and family apartments in modernized kibbutz-style buildings set in tended vegetation. Bicycle rental is free for guests; mountain biking in the area is especially good because of the well-defined agricultural tracks and paths.

Delicious kosher home-cooking is served in a terrace **restaurant** overlooking the spectacular hills and valleys of the Galilee. But the main addition is a variety of organized activities in the area: **cycling** and **kayaking** on the Jordan, and a series of innovative **jeep tours**. These include frequent **day trips** to the tombs of renowned rabbis, and the ruins of an ancient priestly town set in the midst of olive groves. Other tours have herbal medicine or artisans as their theme and take in a number of Palestinian villages. The tours are proving so popular that plans are afoot to bring the SPNI (Society for the Protection of Nature in Israel) and Arkia airline on board. Arkia is due to fly groups from Tel Aviv or Jerusalem to **Mahanayim Airport** (30–40min) near Rosh Pinna (see p.249) where a bus and tour guide will be waiting. The whole package is expected to cost $90–100. For information, contact *Lotem Guest House*.

The Jewish settlement of **YODFAT**, 3km southeast of Sakhnin, has also joined the tourism bandwagon, and runs a programme entitled "Tourism in the Spirit of Galilee". This includes trips to a nearby **monkey forest** (daily 9am–3pm) where you can see a host of animals including squirrels and makak monkeys living in a natural habitat. **Guided tours** to and **accommodation** in Arab villages can be booked through Ruth Avidor or her son Yuval (☎04/980 0033).

East of the settlement are the sparse remains of **Jotapata**, where during the First Revolt in 67 AD Jewish rebels held out for nearly two months under siege by Roman forces led by Vespasian (later emperor) in person. On its fall, the Jewish commander and rebel governor of the Galilee, Yosef ben Matitzyahu, hid out in a cave with forty of the most prominent defenders before making a suicide pact with them on which he reneged when he was one of only two remaining. He then surrendered to the Romans and changed sides. Known to us by his Latin name, Flavius Josephus, he later wrote the definitive account of the First Revolt (the *Jewish War*), as well as a major history of the Jews (the *Antiquities*).

Nazareth

Philip findeth Nathanael, and saith unto him, "We have found Him of whom Moses in the Law and the prophets did write, Jesus of Nazareth, the son of Joseph." And Nathanael said unto him, "Can there any good thing come out of Nazareth?" Philip saith unto him, "Come and see."

(John 1: 45–46)

Located in the mountains between the open plain of the Jezreel Valley to the south and the Bet Netofa Basin to the north, **NAZARETH** (al-Naasira in Arabic, Natzeret in Hebrew) resounds with New Testament associations. According to St Luke, this was the home of Mary and Joseph, where the Annunciation of Jesus's birth to Mary by the archangel Gabriel took place (Luke 1: 26–38), and the town is acknowledged as Jesus's home by all four Gospels (Matthew has the Holy Family moving here from Bethlehem following Jesus's birth and the flight to Egypt). It is here that the child Jesus "grew and waxed strong in spirit, filled with wisdom" (Luke 2: 40) and here, too, stood the synagogue in which Jesus preached (Luke 4: 16–30).

The city today is actually divided into two. **Nazareth** proper is the bustling old town containing all the major tourist and pilgrimage sites – a sprawling place bulging at the seams with a population of some 60,000 Christian and Muslim Palestinians. **Upper Nazareth** (*Natzeret Illit*), built in 1957 to settle Jews in the Galilee, overlooks the old town from hills to the northeast. One of the Jewish cities built as part of Ben Gurion's "Judaicization of the Galilee" project, it houses 45,000 people in a modern development of high-rise blocks and government departments, receiving all the benefits of government funding and preferential status as a development town.

Although an estimated one million visitors pass through the city each year, few stay overnight; most simply pile out of **tour buses**, pay homage at the holy sites and are shepherded into designated restaurants and souvenir shops. This deprives smaller local businesses of income and is the source of some resentment, though it does make locals rather more receptive to independent travellers. In fact, the still existing sense of community and hospitality in Nazareth seems to extend itself to anyone who's open to it: just changing money at the bank, buying a postcard or stamp in a backstreet shop, or eating a falafel at a roadside snack bar can become an occasion for striking up conversation.

Some history

Nazareth was **settled** between 600 and 900 BC, but the small agricultural village was too insignificant to be included in the 45 cities of the Galilee mentioned by Josephus; neither is it one of the 63 towns referred to in the Talmud. Although **Luke** is clear that Nazareth is the home town of the Virgin Mary (Luke 1: 26), Matthew implies that Mary and her carpenter husband Joseph always lived in Bethlehem. This hardly matters, though, since Nazareth is not about to relinquish its claim, and all scholars agree that it was here that the Holy Family settled when they returned after their flight to Egypt to escape Herod's massacre of Bethlehem's newborns (Matthew 2: 23).

As a predominantly Jewish village, Nazareth was destroyed during the Roman suppression of the **Jewish Revolt** in 67 AD. Even after Emperor Constantine legitimized **Christianity**, the new religion failed to gain a foothold here, and only in the sixth century was the first church built over the cave that is the traditional site of the

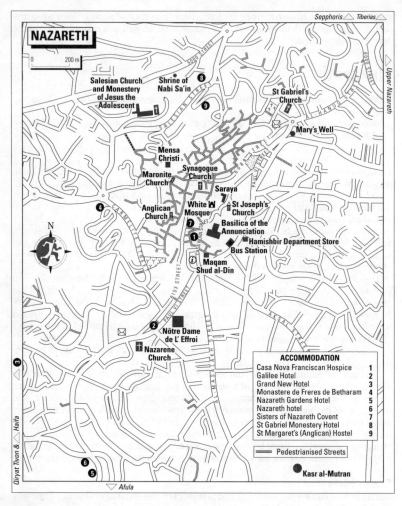

Sepphoris △ Tiberias △

NAZARETH

0   200 m

Salesian Church and Monestery of Jesus the Adolescent

Shrine of Nabi Sa'in

St Gabriel's Church

Mary's Well

Upper Nazareth

Mensa Christi

Maronite Church

Synagogue Church

Saraya

White Mosque

St Joseph's Church

Anglican Church

Basilica of the Annunciation

Hamishbir Department Store

Bus Station

Maqam Shud al-Din

Nôtre Dame de L' Effroi

Nazarene Church

Qiryat Tivon & △ Haifa

ACCOMMODATION

Casa Nova Franciscan Hospice	1
Galilee Hotel	2
Grand New Hotel	3
Monastere de Freres de Betharam	4
Nazareth Gardens Hotel	5
Nazareth hotel	6
Sisters of Nazareth Covent	7
St Gabriel Monestery Hotel	8
St Margaret's (Anglican) Hostel	9

Pedestrianised Streets

● Kasr al-Mutran

▽ Afula

Annunciation. An Italian pilgrim visiting the Holy Land in 570 AD does not mention the church, referring only to "the synagogue and the book with which the Lord was taught the alphabet"; he seems to have been rather more impressed by "the beauty of the Hebrew women" of the town which they claimed to have inherited from their kinswoman Mary.

The capture of Nazareth by the **Crusader** Tancred in 1099 marked the start of its transformation from insignificant village to famous town. The Archbishopric of All Galilee was moved here from Bet She'an in the early twelfth century, and construction began of a new church on the ruins of the old Byzantine one. Although not completed, many Christians made, and still make, annual pilgrimage to the church on August 15 to celebrate the **Feast of the Annunciation**.

When Nazareth fell under **Muslim** rule in 1291, Christians were afraid to venture here. The Franciscan fathers established a church and monastery in 1300 to accommodate pilgrims; they were expelled in 1362, returned in 1468, got the boot again in 1542, and were finally allowed back in 1620 by the Druze chieftain **Fakr al-Din**, who sold the Basilica of the Annunciation to them, and set the town on the path to redemption.

The **nineteenth century** saw a flourishing of Western "scientific" interest in the Bible lands. Travellers, artists and scholars flocked to the country, creating between them the romantic Orientalist image of Nazareth as a timeless, picturesque village which persists until the present. But modernization was on its way: the construction by the German Templars of a road from Haifa docks to Nazareth, then of a road to Kufr Kanna and Tiberias, boosted the pilgrimage trade. Hotels and hospices were built and during Ottoman times the town became important enough to have its own mayor.

During **World War I**, Nazareth was the headquarters of the Ottoman army in Palestine under German command. Seized by the British in 1918, it became the district capital of the Galilee during the Mandate period and was an important trading centre for the Lower Galilee. Barracks and offices, schools, hospices and churches were built, encouraging the growth of the Muslim and Christian population.

With the outbreak of hostilities in **1948**, many residents of surrounding villages sought refuge in Nazareth. On July 16, 1948, the Israeli Seventh Brigade attacked and captured the city, which was the headquarters of Fawzi al-Kaukji's Arab Liberation Army. That there was no forced exodus of its Arab inhabitants is due to the commander of the Seventh Brigade, Ben Dunkelman, who refused to carry out the evacuation order, which was rescinded after he and his forces were replaced, "because of [the town's] importance to the Christian world" and the bad publicity which doing so would attract to the new state.

However, although Ben Gurion realized the importance of Nazareth as a "city sacred to millions", the Arab population was placed under military rule and little was done to develop the town. When the Israeli Ministry of Tourism was established in the 1950s, pilgrimage to Nazareth was little encouraged; then, as now, most pilgrims and tourists were accommodated around the Sea of Galilee, in Tiberias and in local kib-

NAZARETH 2000

The face of the city today may be changing in light of the grand plans for **Nazareth 2000** in celebration of two millennia of Christianity. A conglomerate of interests – the Israel Government Tourist Corporation, the Ministry of Tourism, and the Arab-run municipality – are intending to turn Nazareth into one of Israel's central millennium sites, with around 1.2 million pilgrims expected to visit during the year 2000. Plans set in motion in 1994 involve the investment of over $100,000,000, to be spent on refurbishing the older parts of town, building hotels, giving the souq a face-lift, constructing a scenic walkway between the Basilica of the Annunciation and Mary's Well, and resurfacing the streets with ancient-style paving. The project will undoubtedly encourage tourism and bring economic benefits to the town, but not everyone is thrilled: the renovation of the souq, for example, is turning the once chaotic but exciting area into a sterile and pale echo of its former self. The Labour Party's former Tourism Minister, Uzi Baram, saluted Nazareth 2000 as a way of furthering peaceful relations by creating "a situation in which the Arabs of Israel will feel they are equal citizens of Israel"; but actually the project was part of the payoff on a 1992 deal in which two Arab political parties (Hadash and the Arab Democratic Party) agreed to support Labour in government in return for an unwritten commitment to put more money into Arab areas of Israel, a little bit of horse-trading from which Nazareth seems to have benefitted vastly.

butzim. Nazareth sees mainly day trippers, whose buses add to the town's traffic jams and air pollution.

The resounding victory of the Nazareth Democratic Front in the 1975 municipal elections, and the election of **Tawfiq Zayyad** as mayor of Nazareth, were significant events in the town's modern history. Zayyad was a remarkable figure in Israeli politics: besides being the Muslim mayor of a predominantly Christian town, he was also an Arab nationalist, a prominent figure in the Israeli Communist Party (Rakah) and an outspoken member of the Knesset. He was also a poet of considerable repute not only in Israel and Palestine, but in the Arab world as a whole. His death in a car accident in 1994 – on his way back from a historic meeting with Yasser Arafat shortly after the latter's installation in Gaza – undoubtedly deprived the region of one of its foremost advocates for peace and reconciliation.

Arrival, orientation and information

Nazareth is the destination of a number of **day trips** run from Tel Aviv, Jerusalem and Haifa by firms such as Egged and United Tours. These often include time in Tiberias and Capernaum. It is also perfectly easy to get here on public transport: **buses** and **sheruts** drop off at the **bus station** (✆06/654 9555), little more than a couple of shop fronts containing information and left-luggage offices, on Paul VI Street about 100m north of the intersection with Casa Nova.

It's easy to get lost in the narrow winding backstreets of Nazareth, but equally easy to reorient yourself by making your way to one of two main streets: **Paul VI** and **Casa Nova**. Most of the major sites are off one or other of these. Paul VI Street runs from the junction with the Haifa–Afula highway right through the heart of town. Heading north along it towards the great dome which sits atop the Basilica of the Annunciation, you will come to the other main artery, Casa Nova Street, on your left. Here the **tourist information office** (Mon–Fri 8.30am–5pm; Sat 8.30am–2pm; ✆06/657 0555 or 3003, fax 657 5279) provides free maps and advice; it also has a **database** which you can use to check out events in the region.

Accommodation

At busy times – from August through to the end of October and on major Christian holidays – **rooms** in Nazareth are at a premium so it's as well to phone ahead or check with the tourist office before trekking around. Construction under way for the year 2000 may mean that some extra accommodation will be available in the near future.

There is no youth or travellers' hostel in Nazareth, but a number of Christian **hospices** and **hostels** may offer a bed; these cater to pilgrim groups (mainly from Italy, Eastern Europe, Britain and North America) but will accept lone travellers, depending on room availability. Most of them provide modest but impeccably clean accommodation, a peaceful atmosphere and surroundings.

Nazareth's **hotels** are generally more expensive than the hospices but still relatively cheap. As elsewhere in the country, you may be able to bargain at slack times. Most of the better places are on Paul VI Street.

Nazareth **telephone numbers** are now all seven-digit; if you have a six-digit number, try adding a six at the beginning.

Hospices and hostels

Sisters of Nazareth Convent, Casa Nova St (☎06/655 4304, fax 646 0741). A beautiful, cloistered establishment generally restricted to pre-booked pilgrim groups, but lone women stand more chance than others of getting in. Single-sex dorms, and double and single rooms; 9pm curfew. ①/②.

Monastère des Frères de Betharam, Schneller Rd (☎06/657 0046). Usually reserved for pilgrims, but you may find accommodation within its peaceful garden setting. ③.

Casa Nova Franciscan Hospice, Casa Nova St opposite the Basilica of the Annunciation (☎06/657 1367, fax 657 9630). Popular and comfortable, with a tended garden, dining room serving Italian cuisine, and coffee bar – one of the few places in town to spend the evening. 10.30pm curfew. ③.

St Margaret's (Anglican) Hostel, Salesian St on the hill to the north (☎06/657 3507, fax 656 7166). This former orphanage, with 33 high-ceilinged rooms, is one of the best hostels in town. Wonderful views of the city, a relaxed atmosphere and a garden cafeteria planned. ④.

Hotels

Galilee Hotel, Paul VI St, south of the Basilica (☎06/657 1311, fax 655 6627). Renovated place with a new wing, posh modern lobby and massive dining room. ⑤.

Grand New Hotel, St Joseph St, up the hill from the Greek Catholic Seminary of St Joseph (☎06/657 3020, fax 657 6281). Ninety-room hotel overlooking the old town, with central heating, bar and games room. ⑤.

Nazareth Gardens Hotel, Paul VI St on the southern edge of town (☎06/656 6007, fax 656 6008). A luxury 120-room hotel with its own pool, gardens, a/c, satellite TV and in-house movies. ⑥.

Nazareth Hotel, Paul VI St (☎06/657 7777, fax 657 8511). Centrally located, modest affair near the *Nazareth Gardens*. ④.

St Gabriel Monastery Hotel, Salesian St (☎06/656 7349, fax 655 4071). This former monastery converted to a splendid 60-room hotel occupies a prime site high above the city; it has an excellent restaurant, 24hr bar and coffee shop. ⑤.

The Town

Today's Nazareth, for all its biblical importance, is very much a living town, with attendant overcrowding and frustrating traffic jams. As a Christian centre, it is one of the few towns in Israel open on Saturday – when Israelis come to do their shopping – and closed on Sunday. The chief sights in Nazareth are in the **Old Town** which contains the souq and the churches. A walk off the beaten track through the narrow, steep streets reveals some fine views and traditional architecture.

But for the best views of the town's red rooftops and spires, you have to get out to the surrounding hills: Jabal en-Nabi Sain to the north, Upper Nazareth to the northeast, and the **Mount of Precipice**, 2km southeast (which is up for development and may have accommodation to offer by the time this book goes to press). The mount is said to be the one from which the citizens of Nazareth, "filled with wrath" at Jesus's teachings, attempted to "cast him down headlong" (Luke 4: 26–29). On Paul VI Street, opposite the *Galilee Hotel*, the **Convent of Notre Dame de l'Effroi** marks the spot where Mary is supposed to have watched these proceedings in terror for for her son. A new road is being built from the Mount of Precipice into the town centre and will eventually be the main access from the Jezreel Valley. Swiss Mountain nearby is also due for tourism development, with a cable car planned to the Mount of Precipice.

Unless stated otherwise, **church opening hours** in Nazareth tend to be: April–Sept Mon–Sat 8.30–11.45am & 2–5.45pm, Sun & holidays 2–4.45pm; Oct–March Mon–Sat 9–11.45am & 2–4.45pm, Sun & hols 2–3.45pm.

The souq

At the top of Casa Nova Street, the **souq** is one of Nazareth's few secular attractions. The Nazareth 2000 plans (see p.177) are rapidly changing the nature of the place: where once it was all too easy to get lost in its labyrinth of narrow streets, today new signs (in Hebrew, Arabic and English) help you find your way around, and a new pedestrian walkway, complete with shops and tourist facilities, is planned to open up space between the Basilica of the Annunciation and Mary's Well Church. Despite being touristy, naturally, it's still a great place to wander around; it is also a working market where you can buy almost anything from fruit and veg to souvenirs and clothing. Thursday is the main market day, but it is open daily (except Sunday), between 8.30am and 5pm.

Basilica of the Annunciation

Said to be the largest church in the Middle East, the Roman Catholic **Basilica of the Annunciation** (Mon–Sat 8.30–11.45am & 2–5pm; open Sun for Mass only) is the most important and impressive of Nazareth's churches. Right in the heart of town, the bulky stone structure seems far too large and too modern for its setting – it was completed in 1969 – and dominates everything in the vicinity.

Its massive cupola, which can be seen from most parts of town, is topped by a lantern symbolizing the Light of the World. Inside the entrance to the church compound, a statue of Jesus stands above a relief showing the Archangel Gabriel announcing the all-important birth, and the four Evangelists – Matthew, Mark, Luke and John. The entrance to the church itself is a massive triple door with bronze reliefs: the central one depicts six events in the life of Jesus, the left portrays the Fall of Man, and on the right one are engraved Old Testament prophesies of redemption. Colourful mosaics along the walls of the cloisters are gifts from Roman Catholic communities around the world; Pope Paul VI's 1964 visit is commemorated by the mosaic nearest the entrance gate.

The church itself, the fifth to stand on this spot, is a two-storey structure standing over the sunken **Grotto of the Annunciation**, the site, it is claimed, where Gabriel told Mary that she was to be the mother of Jesus (Luke 1: 26–38). Inside, along with the remains of earlier Byzantine and Crusader constructions, it is adorned with murals, stained-glass windows and a collection of artworks from around the world. That said, it's so vast and modern that it seems to have been built more for visiting than for praying. Like many holy sites that are also tourist sights, the mix of secular and religious in the same space is an uneasy one, as pilgrims pray while sightseers film the priests proffering communion in the central basin atrium, and the building itself, with its overuse of grey concrete, is hardly what you would expect from one of the most venerated sites in Christendom.

St Joseph's Church

From the upper floor of the Basilica, beyond the Baptistry, a side exit leads towards **St Joseph's**, otherwise known as the **Church of the Carpenter's Shop**. Between the two churches, a small green park contains the remains of four churches from the Byzantine and Crusader periods, set amongst a collection of religious sculptures. The peaceful atmosphere (when there are no tour groups) is enhanced by the elegant facade of the Terra Sancta Franciscan Monastery alongside, which is not open to the public.

By contrast to the Basilica, St Joseph's is a human-size church well-suited to meditation and prayer, a stone building with pretty mosaic windows letting in a soft light. It was constructed in 1914 on the remains of a Crusader church that mark the supposed home and workshop of Mary's husband, Joseph. Although the exact location of either is in doubt, the venerated site was probably used as a dwelling. The crypt below is believed to have been Joseph's carpenter's shop; at the back of it there's a pit with a mosaic floor, thought to be a baptismal pool dating from the first to third century AD. Eight stone courses of the Crusader church are visible here, as are the caverns below, which were probably used as grain silos.

A small booth outside the church sells an array of religious souvenirs, including a wonderful collection of kitsch 3-D postcards.

Other religious sites

Opposite the Basilica, a short street leads down to the very English-looking **Anglican Church**, the home of the Church of England in Nazareth. Completed in 1871, this cruciform church was only the second Anglican church to be built in the country. Its most famous vicar, Canon Riyah Abu al-Asal, a major Palestinian political figure and outspoken peacenik, is now Anglican Bishop of Jerusalem.

Located in the centre of the souq is the Greek Catholic **Synagogue Church** (daily 8.30am–5pm), accepted site of the synagogue where Jesus worshipped and preached (Luke 4: 16–30) before being ignominiously thrown out of town by the congregants. This sturdy stone structure has little to show except some wooden seating around the walls and a plain altar at the end. There is no sign of the old synagogue, and one can only assume that the Crusaders who built the church here had good reason to do so.

West of the Synagogue Church is the plain Franciscan chapel of **Mensa Christi** or Table of Christ, built around a large block of limestone said to be the table at which Jesus and the disciples sat after the Resurrection (John 21: 12–13). Note the graffiti engraved by generations of pilgrims. The nearby **Maronite Church of St Anthony** dates from the eighteenth century.

To the east of the Synagogue Church, the **White Mosque** (Jama'a al-Abyad), is the oldest mosque in Nazareth, constructed in 1812. The **Saraya** was the summer palace of the Bedouin warlord, Daher al-Omar, who had it built in 1730. Plans are afoot to convert it to a museum.

Mary's Well and the Church of St Gabriel

Another important site for Christian pilgrims is **Mary's Well**, a rather disappointing solid stone structure by the roadside in al-Hanuq Street. This is where the Greek Orthodox church locates the annunciation rather than in the Catholic site marked by the Basilica, since in Greek Orthodox tradition Gabriel appeared to Mary while she was drawing water, not sitting at home.

Behind the well, to the left, is **St Gabriel's Greek Orthodox Church**, or the **Church of Mary's Well** (daily 8.30–11.45am & 2–6pm). Amidst a glorious profusion of religious relics and objects, the walls are elaborately frescoed, the floor done out in intricately patterned marble and the altar hidden from view by a screen – the "iconostasis" – decorated with icons and holy pictures. In a low vaulted cavern built by Crusaders in the twelfth century is the source of Mary's Well, a **spring** connected to the well by an underground aqueduct. To get to the spring, walk down the steps directly in front of the main entrance of the church. Behind an iron balustrade you can view the trickle of water; a jug on a rope lets you draw some of the cool, fresh water and test its miraculous properties.

Jabal al-Nabi Sa'in

If you continue from Mary's Well and the church along al-Hanuq Street, you'll pass a *hammam* – Turkish baths built in 1887 under Nazareth's first mayor, Tanous Qa'awar. At the end of the street, steps lead up to the main through road, Route 754, also confusingly known as 6000 Street. To your left, just up the hill, you'll come to a fork in the road: 6000 Street, to the right, leads to Tiberias and Upper Nazareth, worth the walk if only to see how the other half lives; the first left off the left fork, 5000 Street, brings you after a kilometre to the mountain of **Jabal al-Nabi Sa'in**. A scenic walkway, appropriately called **Heaven's Promenade**, is under construction along the mountainside and will no doubt come complete with refreshment stops. Living up to its name, the view northward from the walkway will take in Sepphoris, Haifa, Safed and the mountains of Upper Galilee and, on a clear day, even Jabal al-Sheikh (Mount Hermon) way up north. To the left of 5000 Street is the former monastery and now fine hotel of **St Gabriel's** (see p.179), definitely worth the climb, if only for a coffee or a meal in the tended gardens that provide a fine view of the town and its skyline of spires. This prime spot was home to Franciscan monks until 1993 when it was acquired by a local family who developed it into a hotel. However, they have maintained some of its religious flavour by preserving the original building and keeping the church as a place of prayer, albeit a non-consecrated one. You can climb the church bell tower for an even better view of the surroundings.

Below St Gabriel's on the way back into town is the **Salesian Church and Monastery of Jesus the Adolescent** (which you can also reach from the Synagogue Church by walking up Salesian Street). The church, which belongs to the Salesian Order of French Monks, is housed in a secondary school named Dom Bosco; visitors are welcome to walk through the school into the massive, high-arched church built in 1929 in modern Gothic style. With its white stone interior and brilliant yellow and gold stained-glass windows, it's a rather splendid structure. Behind and above the high altar is a statue of the **adolescent Jesus** standing on a rock, illuminated by natural light filtered through blue glass windows. Outside, a large terrace overlooks the whole town, with spectacular views of Precipice Mountain in the southeast and Mount Tabor due east. The school and the church are used as the main venue for the **Festival of Liturgical Music** (see below), when the terrace turns into a cafeteria.

On 5000 Street, north of the Salesian and St Gabriel's is the *maqam* or **Tomb of Nabi Sa'in**, a holy man revered by both Christians and Muslims, and a nephew of Saladin.

If you don't fancy the climb up the hill from town to Jabal al-Nabi Sa'in – not the best idea in summer or if you have any luggage – a good alternative is to do the whole thing in reverse: catch bus #9 from any of the bus stops along Paul VI Street or take a taxi (around 12NIS) to St Gabriel's. From there, you can walk down to the Salesian Church: a **stepped walkway** opposite winds down through residential areas into the centre, past the Mensa Christi and the Synagogue Church and back to the souq and the old town.

Eating and drinking

Nazareth has dozens of **street kiosks** and restaurants vying for tourist custom along Paul VI and Casa Nova streets. **Falafel**, generally good, is available almost everywhere; try the row of places around the bus station. For **snacks** on the move, try the self-service *Tourist Restaurant* on Paul VI (near the Basilica) for hot baguettes, "fride" chicken, *shawarma*, falafel and pizza. *Mahroum Bakery* opposite makes delicious **bread** (*man'oush*) baked with *za'atar* or cheese (*man'oush bi jibna*) and pizza; they also sell great little pastries stuffed with figs, dates or other fillings. Nazareth's most renowned **sweet shop** is *Abu Diab Mahroum's*, with several namesake·imitators around town. The original, on Casa Nova Street by the Casa Nova Hospice and nearly opposite the Basilica, is particularly known for its *baklava* and *burma*.

For sit-down meals, there are many options on **Paul VI Street**. *Al-Amal* and *Al-Salam* offer the usual range of small dishes: hummus, falafel, salads and the like. *Diana (Abu al-Dukhul)*, the *Riveira*, and the *Holy Step* all offer typical Palestinian menus, as does the *YMCA* self-service restaurant on Wadi al-Juwani off the southern end of Paul VI, and opposite the French Hospital. More **upmarket** restaurants along Paul VI include *Al-Jeneenah* near Mary's Well, a large place, popular for local celebrations and lively in the evening, serving excellent food on its verandah. Another splendid place, behind Mary's

---

MOVING ON FROM NAZARETH

The **bus station** has stops on both side of the street: buses from the east side serve Tiberias (every 30min; 45min) and Acre (hourly; 45min); from the west side of the street, they run to Haifa (every 30min; 45min), Afula (1–2 per hour; 20min), Hadera (14 daily; 1hr 40min), Megiddo Junction (1–2 per hour; 40min), Qiryat Tivon (for Bet She'arim; every 30min; 25min) and Tel Aviv (1–2 per hour; 2hr). Buses to Kufr Kanna leave from St Mary's Well (hourly; 15min).

Sheruts to Haifa, Tel Aviv and Tiberias leave from in front of HaMashbir department store on Paul VI by the bus station, and the side street by the petrol station nearby (☎06/657 1140 and 655 4412).

Well, *is La Fontana di Maria*, a restaurant and coffee shop, with an extensive menu and excellent food and surroundings. Whether you're staying there or not, the restaurant at *St Gabriel's* (see p.179) has delicious food combined with wonderful views and mountainside gardens, and the choice of a moderately priced set menu or slightly pricier à la carte. On **Casa Nova Street**, *Al-Fahoum* dishes up good Palestinian food.

If and when you tire of Middle Eastern food, there are also three **pizza** joints in town: *Pizza Inn*, near the Nazareth Community Centre; *Pizza Panorama* at the Nazareth-Tiberias junction; and *Pizza St Paulus* on Paul VI. And if you need to do some **self-catering**, groceries can be bought from stores along Paul VI Street. For fresh fruit or vegetables, the market is the place to go.

Events in Nazareth

Christmas in Nazareth is an event to rival the festivities in Bethlehem: on the afternoon of Christmas Eve (3pm), there's a large, lively and colourful **parade** along Paul VI and through the streets. Later that day, at 7.30pm, traditional **Mass** is celebrated in six churches in town – first and foremost the Basilica of the Annunciation. Tickets are available from the tourist information office (☎06/657 0555 or 3003) which remains open until midnight on Christmas Eve. On December 26, a festival of international choirs takes place in the Orthodox Youth Club, and concerts of liturgical music are held from December 27 to 28 at the Salesian Church (see p.182).

Nazareth celebrates **Easter** with another series of **Musica Sacra concerts**; the town also holds a **summer festival** between August and September which presents a programme of good modern Arab music, theatre, art exhibitions, and movies. As part of these events, tourists are also offered guided off-the-beaten-track tours around the old town (☎06/655 4696 or 645 2450 for information).

Listings

Banks and moneychangers Two stores on Paul VI carry large change signs: a jewellery shop downhill from the Central Bus Station and another across the street (Mon–Sat 8.30am–8.15pm). Banks include the Arab Bank, Bank HaPoalim and Bank Leumi, all on Paul VI, and the Discount Bank on Casa Nova.

Car rental Europcar, Garage HaZafon (☎06/657 2046); Idan HaShalom, Paul VI St (☎06/657 5313).

Laundromat Mouslam Naif, 6089 St, next to the police station.

Left luggage (baggage deposit) Next door to the Egged information office, at the bus station 100m north of Paul VI with Casa Nova (Sun–Thurs 7.30am–5pm, Fri 7.30am–1pm).

Medical services Hospitals include Nazareth Hospital, 5112 St (☎06/657 1501); French Hospital, 6184 St (☎06/657 4530); and Holy Family Hospital (☎06/657 4535). A number of pharmacies are to be found along Paul VI St.

Police 6089 St near Mary's Well (☎100 or ☎06/657 4444).

Post office A couple of blocks west of Mary's Well, next to the Municipality, with a branch office on Paul VI with 3030 St.

Taxis Abu el-Asal, Paul VI with Casa Nova (☎06/657 5464); Diana, French Hospital (☎06/655 5554); Fountain, Paul VI at Mary's Well (☎06/655 5105); Jalil, Paul VI at Mary's Well (☎06/655 5536); Saiegh, al-Hanuk Rd (☎06/657 1176).

Around Nazareth

The region around Nazareth, on the ridge of hills between the valleys of Jezreel to the south and Bet Kerem to the north, has several spots worth visiting, perhaps as day trips out of Nazareth. To the northwest lies **Sepphoris**, one of the most attractive Roman sites in the country, and **Ka'abiye Tabash** with its Bedouin Tradition Centre. To the northeast of Nazareth, you'll find **Kufr Kanna**, biblical Cana, where Jesus turned water into wine, and to the east, **Mount Tabor**, scene of the transfiguration of Christ, **Shibli**, with its Bedouin Heritage Centre, and **Ein Dor**, whose resident witch summoned up a ghost for the Bible's King Saul.

Sepphoris

A real delight, even for those without a penchant for archeology, lies about 3km northwest of Nazareth, off Route 79 towards Acre. This is **Sepphoris** (Zippori in Hebrew), the site of the Roman capital of Galilee, which was a separate Roman province from Judea. According to the Babylonian Talmud, Zippori was so called because it is perched on the top of a mountain like a bird (*zippor* in Hebrew). It became the Roman capital of the Galilee in 55 BC, retaining that status until the end of the Herodian period in 4 BC. Christian tradition says that the Virgin Mary's parents, St Anne and St Joachim, were from here, though there is nothing in the New Testament to support that. During the First Revolt (66–70 AD), the Jewish population of Zippori signed a peace with the Roman army, and, the "Ornament of All Galilee", it remained a mixed Jewish-Hellenistic town with fashionable houses and a Roman theatre until its Jewish leadership was ousted at the time of the Second Revolt under Bar Kokhba (132–135 AD).

Zippori's place in Jewish scholarship was resumed in the third century when the Sanhedrin (High Court) was moved here from Bet She'arim (see p.148) under Rabbi Yehudah HaNassi; some say it was here that he compiled and edited the *Mishnah*. At this period, the town is said to have had eighteen synagogues and several *yeshivot*. Christian presence in the town during the Byzantine period saw the construction of a church and assured its continued growth. The Crusaders called the place Le Saphorie and, as usual, built a citadel; from here they marched to the Battle of Hittin (see p.207) against Saladin. It became one of Daher al-Omar's strongholds during the eighteenth century and its strategic position was put to use during the 1936–39 Palestinian Revolt, when it was a major rebel base.

One **bus** a day (#16) connects Sepphoris with Nazareth; in addition, bus #343 to Nazareth (10min) and Acre (50min) passes the turn-off on Route 79, about 3km south of the site, approximately every hour.

The site

Excavations at **Zippori National Park** (daily 8am–4pm; 15NIS; guided 3hr walking tours to be booked in advance; ☎06/656 8272, fax 656 8273) have so far revealed only about one-fifth of the treasures of ancient Sepphoris, the "Ornament of All Galilee", but that's plenty to make a visit really worthwhile. A map of the park, sold at the entrance

(10NIS) is invaluable for visiting some of the many sites: these include a **Byzantine house** with a lovely geometrical mosaic floor; a massive first-century **Roman theatre** that contained 4500 stone seats (a symbol of paganism which aroused the disapproval of the rabbis); the impressive remains of the **Church of St Anne** built by the Crusaders on the site of the home of Mary's parents Anne and Joachim; and the remains of **houses** from the Second Temple, Roman and Byzantine periods (1 BC–6 AD) fronting onto a paved street. But the *pièce de résistance* comes in the shape of a delicate mosaic of a blushing young woman named the **"Mona Lisa of the Galilee"**. She is set in the carefully preserved and intricate mosaics of a stone floor of a luxurious third-century Roman residence, in the company of Dionysos, the Greek god of wine.

More recent finds include a network of second-century **Roman streets**, including a Cardo with the grooves of wagon wheels, the stumps of colonnades and the verges of coloured mosaic clearly visible. Most intriguing is the **"Nile Mosaic"** in the remains of a building to the east of the Cardo: this colourful and detailed tableau depicts Egyptian festivals celebrating the annual Nile floods, the Alexandria lighthouse and extravagant hunting scenes with a plethora of wild animals – including lions, bulls and donkeys.

About ten minutes' walk west of the main sites is another extraordinary find – an **ancient reservoir** dating from the second and fourth centuries, and two **aqueducts** which supplied it with water from springs in the Nazareth Hills. Descending into the now empty and cavernous interior carved into the bedrock is an eerie experience and you can still make out the sophisticated construction of the place.

There is also a **visitors' centre** complete with video presentations and computer terminals on which you can try creating your own mosaic. This is housed in **Sepphoris Fortress** (*Metzudat Tzipori*), the Crusader citadel renovated by Daher al-Omar in the eighteenth century as a schoolhouse and again during the British Mandate period. From the top of the citadel, there's a splendid view of the surrounding fertile valleys and of the **Eshkol Reservoir** (named after former prime minister, Levi Eshkol) to the north, and the open part of the **national water carrier** – *HaMovil HaArtzi* – which brings fresh water from the Sea of Galilee to the Israeli heartland. This disappears underground at **Hamovil Junction**, another 3km along Route 79 towards Acre.

After the site closes, on July and August evenings there's a **reconstruction** of life in Roman times, complete with peddlers, scholars, actresses and musicians who will show you how to make ancient crafts, and Roman waiters who will serve you a kosher Roman meal outdoors by torchlight. The four-hour presentation (5–9pm) runs for five weeks; tickets (70NIS including craft workshop and dinner) are available from from the park office or from Makom BaGalil at Kibbutz Shorashim (☎04/990 2431, fax 990 2476; see p.171).

Ka'abiye Tabash

Southwest of Hamovil Juction, left along Route 77 in the direction of Bet She'arim, is the village of **KA'ABIYE TABASH**. Of major interest here is the **Bedouin Tradition Centre** (☎04/983 4874) which contains the obligatory Bedouin tent, complete with anthropological explanation, and tea and coffee for visitors. The restaurant at the centre serves vegetarian meals, as well as meats, in a "traditional Bedouin atmosphere". You can watch bread being baked in the traditional way and then buy silver jewellery and other handicrafts. Horseback and camel rides are also available from the centre, along with organized trips to the nearby Tzipori Stream and the so-called "Horse Spring".

The views from here are splendid since the village is situated above Tzipori Stream, overlooking Sepphoris to the east, Mount Atzmon in the north, the Mediterranean and the suburbs of Haifa to the west.

Kufr Kanna

Just 6km northeast of Nazareth on Route 754, the lively Palestinian village of **KUFR KANNA** is said to be **Cana of Galilee** where, at a wedding feast, Jesus performed the miracle of turning water into wine (John 2: 1–11). To commemorate the miracle, the **Franciscans** built a church in 1879 – the **Church of the Wedding Feast** – over the remains of a house said to be where the event happened. Today, thousands of Christian pilgrims and tourists visit the village in order to ". . . adore the place upon which His feet trod", according to the inscription on the red-domed church. A remnant of a mosaic pavement with an Aramaic dedication is visible here. The dedication is to "the memory of Yosef . . .", who may have been Joseph of Tiberias who converted to Christianity and founded many churches in the Galilee. In the crypt is a commemorative water pot containing neither water nor, unfortunately, wine. The village also has a **Greek Orthodox church** competing for holy connections; it too contains water jugs said to be the very ones involved in the miracle. You're unlikely to get lost since both churches are clearly visible as you enter the village; but if you do need directions, the villagers are used to hosting tourists and pilgrims in their midst.

Kufr Kanna's mixed Christian and Muslim population of over 10,000 inhabitants also includes a small Circassian community (see p.249) whose distinctive **mosque** is also worth a look.

Local **buses** run approximately hourly to St Mary's Well in Nazareth, and Kufr Kanna is also served roughly every half-hour by Egged bus #431 to Nazareth (15min) and Tiberias (30min).

Tur'an and Golani Junction

Another Palestinian village launching out into the virgin territory of tourism, **TUR'AN** lies just off Route 77, 5km north of Kufr Kanna, in a splendid setting at the foothills of Mount Tiran. The village, which today has a mixed Muslim and Christian population of around 8000, dates back to Roman times, and is named after a Roman general called Turino (who came from Turin). **Accommodation** is provided by Ali Sabbah (☎06/651 8508, fax 641 1657; ③).

Five kilometres east of Tur'an, Route 77 crosses Route 65 which runs northward from Mount Tabor. This crossing, known as **Golani Junction**, is named after the Golani Brigade of the Israeli army. Here, on a hill overlooking a spectacular pine forest, is a memorial site to soldiers who fell during the wars of 1948, 1967 and 1973. The **Golani Brigade Museum** (Sun–Thurs 9am–4pm, Fri 9am–1pm, Sat 9am–5pm; ☎06/676 7215, fax 676 7219) tells the story of these battles and displays the files of the 1143 casualties. Guided tours (in English, Spanish and Russian) should be arranged in advance. The museum is run by the nearby **Kibbutz Lavi**, which has a 124-room *glatt-kosher* **hotel** (☎06/679 9450, fax 679 9399) for Orthodox Jewish visitors.

Mount Tabor

Nine kilometres east of Nazareth, the distinctive breast-shaped summit of **Mount Tabor** dominates the ancient coastal road – the **Via Maris** – and, as the highest peak in the region at 588m, has been coveted territory throughout history. Today, its major claim to fame is as the site of the **Transfiguration of Christ**. Though over the centuries the exact location of the transfiguration has been disputed and placed also on Mount Hermon and the Mount of Olives, it is now generally accepted that this site, established in 348 AD, is where Jesus came with Peter, James and his brother John and "was transfigured before them: and his face did shine as the sun, and his raiment was white as the light. And behold, there appeared unto them Moses and Elias [Elijah] talking with him." (Matthew 17: 2–3; parallel versions appear in Mark 9: 2–13 and Luke 9: 28–36).

Although Mount Tabor's main association is with the New Testament, it is first mentioned in the **Old Testament** as the site of a battle between forces of the Canaanite King Jabin under his captain Sisera, and those of the Israelite leader Barak under the guidance of the judge Deborah (Judges 4: 13–16). In 67 AD, during their revolt against Rome, the Jews built a wall around the summit but were enticed out by the Romans who feigned retreat to draw the Jews down onto the plain where they were cut off from the mount and easily defeated. A Byzantine church was replaced by a Crusader building in 1099, destroyed in turn by a Turkish attack in 1113. A new, well-defended church, built by Benedictine monks, capitulated with the Crusaders' defeat at the hand of **Saladin** in 1187. Melek al-Adel, governor of Damascus, further fortified it at the beginning of the thirteenth century, enabling it to withstand a seventeen-day siege during the Fifth Crusade in 1217. Christians were allowed to return to the site in 1631, when Fakr al-Din gave it to the Franciscan fathers.

It's a pleasant but reasonably strenuous eight-kilometre walk up the mountain; many people time it to catch the **sunrise** from the top. Pilgrims have been coming here since the fourth century to worship at the churches on the summit and dominating them all is the **Franciscan Basilica** (Sun–Fri 8am–noon & 2pm–5pm, except during services), built in the 1920s on the site of earlier Byzantine and Crusader churches. Inside are artworks and frescoes depicting the transfiguration and a splendid mosaic of the nativity. Older remains include what is said to be a Canaanite shrine to Baal, and there are chapels dedicated to Moses and Elijah. North of the Franciscan Basilica is a 1911 **Greek Orthodox church** dedicated to St Elias (Elijah), while to the west lies a cave named the Cave of Melchizedek, after the King of Salem (Jerusalem) who was "the priest of the most high God" and gave Abraham bread and wine (Genesis 14: 18). The summit is surrounded by the scant remains of Melek al-Adel's walls, with older walls surrounding them.

Outside the Basilica, to the right of its two protruding front towers, you can climb onto the roof of the **observation post** to catch the unparalleled view. On a clear day, beyond the patchwork splendour of the Jezreel Valley to the southwest and the Bet She'an Valley in the southeast, you can see the distant mountains of Lebanon, Syria and Jordan, and even the pinkish hills of Saudi Arabia.

Practicalities

Getting to Mount Tabor can be tedious without a car: there are three buses a day from Afula, and Tel Aviv–Tiberias services can drop you at the signpost for **Dabburiya**, where you walk along the tree-lined lane towards the village. A turning, marked with the distinctive orange sign indicating a tourist site, leads up to the mountain. You can either try and catch a **taxi** from here or walk a little way up to the **snack bar** where, if you don't want to walk up, you can haggle for a taxi to take you to the summit and wait to bring you down again for around 60NIS. A **campsite** on the summit offers spectacular sunrises and sunsets but no other facilities – bring food and drink if you plan to stay.

Descending the mountain, you might want to rest at the **snack bar** and enjoy a tea, coffee, or cold drink under the shade of olive trees and breathe in the clear mountain air; here there's also an essential **public toilet**.

Shibli

SHIBLI, on Mount Tabor's northern slopes, can be reached from the snack bar, by continuing through pine, cypress and olive trees along the northeastern slope of the mountain. One of sixteen Bedouin villages in the Galilee, it has a population of about 2500 – all of whom are said to be members of one extended family or tribe that migrated from Iraq about 400 years ago and settled here. Although they traditionally married from within the *'ashira*, they now increasingly marry out, as much to avoid the risk of inbreeding as under the influence of modernization.

The **Galilee Bedouin Heritage Centre** (Sat–Thurs 9am–4pm; 10NIS), attracts Israeli schoolchildren and adults interested in the lives of the ethnic group living in their midst and also serves as an education centre for Bedouin children for whom some aspects of their tradition are fast becoming irrelevant. It's a pleasantly informal place, with fifteen open-air sections, including family and guest tents; charcoal production, agricultural and threshing areas; baking, weaving and livestock corners; a herbal and medicinal garden; an exhibition gallery, and a gift shop. Local Bedouins are on hand to provide tea, coffee, freshly baked pitta bread and explanations of the site.

As well-presented and interesting as the centre is, it is the story of the **oak tree** at the entrance to the Heritage Centre which reveals more about the changes facing today's Bedouins. The 350-year-old tree, it is said, once had the power of healing; it thus became a place of pilgrimage where offerings were made and where elders would meet and take important decisions. However, according to one local, as the Bedouins' nomadic lifestyle changed and they started to live in houses, the tree has progressively lost its power to heal. Modernization, it seems, affects not just people.

As yet, there is no hotel or hostel in Shibli, but if you want to **stay** in the village to enjoy the wonderful clean mountain air and experience something a little different, it is possible to get a room: ask at the Heritage Centre.

Four kilometres southeast of Mount Tabor, **Kibbutz Ein Dor** stands on the site of biblical **Endor**, where King Saul went in disguise to consult a witch, and persuade her to conjure up for him the spirit of the dead prophet Samuel (I Samuel 28: 7–20). Samuel's wraith duly appeared and foretold Saul's defeat and death at the hands of the Philistines. Little remains today of the town where these spooky events took place, but the kibbutz does maintain a small archeological **museum** (Sun–Thurs 8am–3pm, Fri 8am–1pm, Sat noon–2pm; 8.50NIS), mainly visited by schoolchildren.

The Jezreel Valley

The main road south of Nazareth, **Route 60**, is one of the most beautiful in the country. The descent from Nazareth into the **Jezreel Valley**, a steep and winding road, is an especially memorable journey whatever the time of year. The valley itself has its own place in history, being the epic battleground where the Israelite judge Gideon, with only 300 men, defeated the Midianites and the Amalekites who "lay along in the valley like grasshoppers for multitude" and whose camels were "without number, as the sand by the sea side". (Judges 7: 12). Today the valley is far calmer, with the intensive agriculture of a dozen moshavim and Palestinian smallholdings glistening in the sunlight.

Afula

A stark contrast with the splendour of the valley, drab **AFULA**, the first major town through which Route 60 passes, stands about 9km south of Nazareth. The administrative and commercial centre of the region, it dates from the 1920s and its current population is predominantly Sephardi in origin.

There is little reason to stop here, but it is an interchange point for **bus** services, which run from here to Bet She'an (2–3 per hour; 30min), Hadera (approximately hourly; 1hr), Haifa (every 20–30min; 1hr), Megiddo Junction (5 daily; 20min), Mount Tabor (3 daily; 30min), Nazareth (1–2 per hour; 20min), Qiryat Shemona (1–2 per hour; 2hr), Qiryat Tivon (for Bet She'arim; 11 daily; 40min), Tel Aviv (2–3 per hour; 1hr 45min) and Tiberias (hourly; 1hr). **Sheruts** to Nazareth, Haifa, Tel Aviv and places en route leave from just behind the bus station. If you're driving or hitching through Afula, be warned that there are no signposts to help get you out of town. If you need to stay, the **youth hostel** at Ma'ayan Harod (see below) is the best option; bus #411 from the station will get you there.

From Afula, Route 65 heads through the Jezreel Valley towards **Megiddo Junction**, 10km southwest (see p.150). Here, the contrast in land use is striking: the large open fields are mostly farmed by kibbutzim and moshavim employing advanced farm machinery. The smaller fields, often no more than patchworks of garden-size strips, are Palestinian farmlands.

Jezreel

Directly south of Afula, Route 60 heads towards the West Bank, with Jenin 12km distant, but no public transport to take you there. Before it crosses the Green Line, however, the road passes the kibbutz and junction of **Yizre'el (Jezreel)**, and nearby the Arab village of **Zar'in**, which stands on the site of biblical Jezreel, the town after which the valley was named. Jezreel was the summer capital of the northern kingdom of Israel under the nefarious King Ahab (c869–850 BC) and his wife, the "wicked" Queen Jezebel, whose set-tos with the prophets Elijah and Elisha are recounted in the biblical books of Kings and Chronicles. In one famous episode (I Kings 21), Ahab coveted the vineyard of his Jezreel neighbour Naboth, who refused to sell it, putting the king in a sulk. Jezebel thereupon had Naboth framed for blasphemy and stoned to death, giving Ahab his seized land. Elijah then prophesied death upon both of them, adding that their corpses would be eaten by dogs; sure enough, they both met their comeuppance, Ahab after being wounded in battle (I Kings 22: 37–39), and Jezebel following Jehu's coup d'état (II Kings 9: 30–37), giving Jezreel's stray pooches a royal dinner. Nothing now remains of ancient Jezreel, and the lesson on land seizure is apparently forgotten too.

Southeast of Afula: Route 71

Route 71 is a busy road running southeast of Afula towards Bet She'an and the junction with Route 90 – the main road up through the Jordan Valley that links the West Bank with Tiberias. Buses and sheruts run frequently along this route.

About 10km along the road, the HI **Ma'ayan Harod Youth Hostel** (☎06/653 1660; ②/③) and **campsite** are set back from the main road in beautiful rural surroundings, complete with a huge natural swimming pool popular with local families in summer. **Kibbutz Ein Harod** is along Route 717, which branches off Route 71. The kibbutz has a museum but its prime association is with Amos Kenan's prize-winning political thriller, *The Road to Ein Harod* (see p.511), in which the kibbutz is the centre of resistance following a military takeover.

Belvoir

About 17km from Ein Harod, Route 717 leads to the Crusader castle of **Belvoir** (Sat–Thurs 8am–4pm, Fri 8am–3pm; 9NIS). As its French name indicates, the castle commands stunning views: the Jezreel Valley to the west, the Jordan River and the mountains of Jordan to the east, and the Sea of Galilee to the north. It is set in the **Kokhav HaYarden** (Star of Jordan) **Reserve**, the name deriving from the poetic description of the castle by one of Saladin's commanders who tried to capture it from the Crusaders in 1182: he depicted Belvoir as "joining the stars, an eagle's nest, and the habitation of the moon". In the eighteenth century, Bedouins settling near the fortress continued the tradition by naming their village *"Kawkab al-Hawa"* – Star of the Wind.

The Knights Hospitallers built Belvoir Fortress in 1168 surrounded by a deep moat to prevent the walls being destroyed by battering rams. The formidable outer fortifications enclose a courtyard containing a **citadel** with a two-storey, four-turret tower, as well as a dining hall and kitchen. A water cistern under the arches ensured that the castle was prepared for siege conditions. Several decorated stones on the fortress's walls include one of a seven-branched candelabrum that apparently belonged to an ancient synagogue from a nearby hill, also named Kokhav.

Most of the stories about the castle relate to its stand against Saladin's army. After the Crusaders' defeat in 1187 at the Horns of Hittin (see p.207), it was one of only two citadels left in their hands, the other being at Tyre in modern Lebanon. Saladin sent a force of 12,000 mounted archers to Belvoir, and the siege lasted four years until his army dug a trench under the southeastern tower and brought down part of it. The terms of surrender allowed the Crusaders to march out to Tyre. The castle was destroyed in the thirteenth century to prevent the Crusaders from retaking it, which they did (briefly) in 1241.

Belvoir also played a part in the conflicts of 1948, when an Iraqi militia force crossed the Jordan River and attacked **Kibbutz Gesher**, about seven kilometres north. Another Iraqi unit, on its way towards the castle intent on capturing this strategic vantage point, was stopped by waiting Israeli forces who shelled them with two 65mm cannons – one of which is on display in Tiberias (see p.202).

Sahne

South of the Afula–Bet She'an road (Route 71), **SAHNE** features numerous natural lakes and underwater caves, with water at an all-year temperature of 28°C (its name in Arabic means "warm"). The landscaped park (Sat–Thurs 8am–6pm, Fri 8am–5pm; 18NIS), has been renamed **Gan HaShlosha** (Garden of the Three) in remembrance of three settlers killed here by a landmine in 1938. It is also a good site for **bird-watching** and is particularly popular with locals at weekends (Fri & Sat). The ticket for the park also gives admission to the small but interesting archeological **museum** at nearby Nir David (Sun–Thurs 8am–2pm, Fri 8am–1pm, Sat 10am–1pm).

Bet Alpha

Kibbutz Hefzibah, 1km west of Sahne, preserves the site of **Bet Alpha Synagogue** (Sat–Thurs 8am–4pm, Fri 8am–3pm; 7NIS), best-known for its superb mosaic floor. Fragments of the wall show that the building was oriented towards Jerusalem, as tradition demands, while Aramaic inscriptions on the floor show that it dates from between 518 and 527 AD.

The three-panelled mosaics are astonishingly vivid and well-preserved: the top panel reveals an assortment of Jewish symbols, including a double *menora*, the Ark of the Torah overhung by an ornate lamp, two *shofars* (ram's horns) and four animals. All are framed by a mosaic curtain as if on a stage. The bottom panel depicts Abraham on the point of sacrificing Isaac in obedience to divine command (Genesis 22: 1–19); beside him is the sacrificial lamb caught in the brambles and, observing the whole scene, a donkey driver with tethered donkey. But it is the central panel that is the most remarkable, showing, in the middle of a detailed **zodiac**, Helios the Greek sun god riding a four-horse chariot across the sky. The zodiac wheel is divided into the twelve signs that we recognize today, and is itself framed by four winged women representing the seasons. This combination of traditional Jewish with Greek and pagan, of sacred and profane, provides an intriguing glimpse of the way that cultures and civilizations have influenced each other in the Middle East.

Mount Gilboa

Rising behind Bet Alpha are the slopes of **Mount Gilboa**, where Israel's first king, Saul, and his son Jonathan both died in battle as the victorious Philistines inflicted their most serious defeat upon the Israelites. David, on hearing the news, cried, "How are the mighty fallen!" (II Samuel 1: 19) and declared, "Ye mountains of Gilboa, let there be no dew, neither let there be rain upon you!" (II Samuel 1: 21). Politically, he was to benefit from the defeat, and at this time was under Philistine protection, but Jonathan was his closest friend (his lover, some claim), and he could hardly remain sanguine in the face of such a disaster for his compatriots. David Rohl (see p.424) believes that Saul's defeat was due to the treachery of the people of Jenin, on the other side of the mountain, who he says must have betrayed the Israelites by allowing Philistine archers around to their flank. This would fit with his belief that Saul is the same man as Lebayu, one of Pharaoh Akhenaton's Amarna Letter correspondents (see p.482), whose death was also apparently caused by the Jeninites.

Bet She'an and around

At first glance, the modern town of **BET SHE'AN** seems to be another of those nondescript places which are just a stopover on the way elsewhere. The town's saving grace, however, is one of the country's largest archeological sites, at **Tel Bet She'an**, containing its best-preserved Roman theatre.

All the main sites are well signed from the **Central Bus Station** – a motley collection of bus stops overlooked by a 1930s-style terminal and café –and none is more than fifteen minutes' walk away. There are plenty of falafel stands and snack bars around if you get peckish. Buses from the town serve Afula (2–3 per hour; 30min), Tiberias (2–3 per hour; 50min) and Sheikh Hussein Bridge (5 daily; 15min).

Some history

Bet She'an does have a significant place in history: since it is at an important crossroads, with access to water from nearby springs, a hot climate and fertile land, it has been under continuous occupation since the late Stone Age. It was a **Canaanite** city state, but the earliest historical reference dates from the nineteenth century BC when it appears in Egyptian records as a centre of their rule over Palestine. Bet She'an subsequently fell to the Philistines who lived here in the eleventh century BC. After defeating the Israelites at Mount Gilboa, where they found the bodies of Saul and his three sons, the Philistines took the dead leader and "fastened his body to the wall of Bethshan" (I Samuel 31: 10).

After conquest by Alexander the Great, its name changed to **Scythopolis**. Judas Maccabaeus marched against it, but was dissuaded from slaughtering its Greek population by the local Jewish community, who "testified that the Scythopolitans dealt lovingly with them, and entreated them kindly in the time of their adversity" (II Maccabees 12: 30). Under the Romans, the city gained autonomy as part of the Decapolis, a federation of ten city states in Syria, Jordan and Palestine. With the advent of Christianity, the city became an important Christian religious centre. All this was put paid to by a tremendous earthquake in 749 AD when the major part of the ancient town was devastated and buried under a thick layer of debris which has been excavated only this century.

During Arab rule, the much reduced town revived and was renamed **Beisan**, an Arabized version of its original name. The small Jewish community that lived here and survived the Crusaders produced a famous geographer, Eshtori Haparchi, who wrote a detailed account of Palestine of that period, entitled *Button and Flower*, in 1322 AD. Of Bet She'an, he said: "I chose to sit here, on this place of many waters, still waters and a blessed land of beauty and full of joy like the garden of the Lord . . . and near the Gate of Paradise."

In early May **1948**, Beisan, with a prewar population of around 6000 Palestinians, was besieged by the Golani Brigade. The fall of Tiberias two weeks earlier and the evacuation of its inhabitants troubled the people of Beisan, and those that could left for

Transjordan. On the night of May 11, the town came under heavy shelling; it surrendered the following day and most of its remaining inhabitants were taken to the Jordan crossing. On May 28, about 300 mainly Christian Palestinians were transported to Nazareth. The fate of Beisan was repeated throughout the area, enabling Golani Brigade historian David Yizhar to write, "For the first time . . . the Bet She'an Valley had become a purely Jewish valley."

The museum and the Monastery of the Lady Mary

Situated on the edge of town, past the municipal park, the small **museum** (Sun–Thurs 8.30am–3.30pm, Fri 8.30am–1.30pm; free) has a good collection of archeological finds illustrating day-to-day life in the Roman city, as well as some interesting mosaic floors.

The Byzantine **Monastery of the Lady Mary** (daily except Sat 8.30am–3pm; free) is stranded in the industrial part of town in modern Bet She'an. The building is generally locked but the keys can be obtained from the museum if you leave your passport as security. The monastery, built around 567 AD, has some beautifully ornate **mosaic floors**, including, in the main hall, an intricately designed calendar mosaic showing the

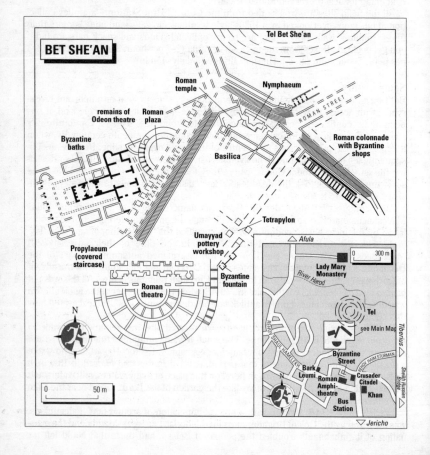

twelve months of the year around the sun and moon. Though the style is very different, it recalls that of Bet Alpha 7km to the west (see p.190), which may well have inspired it. Other mosaics on the floor of the chapel, at the far end of the entrance hall, show animals, including lions, giraffes and donkeys, and birds and peacocks set within circular medallions.

Tel Bet She'an

Much the most rewarding site is **Tel Bet She'an** (Sun–Thurs & Sat 8am–5pm, Fri 8am–3pm; 15NIS) and its **Roman theatre**, an exceptionally well-preserved example of Roman architecture, dating from around 200 AD. Above the stage, rows of stone benches climb up for at least 30m, providing seating for an audience of around 5000. You enter through one of the eight original tunnels, all still in immaculate condition. The only part of the theatre not to have survived is the wooden roof which provided necessary shade for the terraces, although the niches for the supporting joists are still clearly visible. A grand **Roman street** running down to the theatre, and buildings including a basilica and a temple, have been recently excavated. The large sixth-century **Byzantine baths**, decked out in marble and mosaics, add to the impressiveness of the place and show how important a town this must once have been. Its former prosperity is epitomized by the mosaic of the goddess of good fortune, Tyche, at the baths.

If you can, arrange your visit for either early morning or late afternoon to avoid both the blazing heat and the bus parties which descend on the place around midday.

Crossing into Jordan

The **border crossing** into Jordan at **Sheikh Hussein Bridge** (☎06/658 6444) is 6km east of Bet She'an, and reached from there by sherut or #16 bus (5 daily; 15min). It can also be reached by service taxi from East Jerusalem (though Allenby Bridge would be a more obvious crossing-point from there). The border is open from Sunday to Thursday (6.30am–10pm, Fri & Sat 8am–8pm), and it will cost you 56NIS in exit tax to leave Israel. Shuttles run from the Israeli side to the Jordanian terminal, and Jordanian visas are available for nationals of Western countries at the border. On the other side, there are minibuses and taxis to Irbid, and onward transport from there to Amman. For advice on coming the other way, see p.17.

The Sea of Galilee (Lake Kinneret)

There are few sights in Israel to parallel the first views of the **Sea of Galilee**. As part of the Great Rift Valley and attached by the Jordan River to the Dead Sea in the south, it is 200m below sea level, and the approach from any direction always entails a dramatic descent. Indeed, this freshwater lake is one of Israel's major tourist sites and, for all its religious associations, a thoroughly secular paradise, too, with beaches and water sports all around the shore and a backdrop of hills that are a challenge to any walker.

Confusingly, the Sea of Galilee is known by several different names. Road signs point towards Lake Kinneret, an approximate translation of the Hebrew – *Yam Kinneret* (Sea of Kinneret) – derived from *kinor* or "harp". The Gospel St Luke (5: 1) calls it "the Lake of Gennesaret", while St John (6: 1) refers to it as the "Sea of Tiberias", and it is sometimes called "Lake Tiberias" even today. Whatever its name, the sea is replete with New Testament associations – particularly as the water on which Jesus walked (Matthew 14: 25–26; Mark 6: 48; John 6: 19). Christian pilgrimage sites are situated mainly in the north and include **Magdala**, traditionally the birthplace of Mary Magdalene; **Tabgha,** the site of the "Feeding of the Multitudes"; the **Mount of Beatitudes**, where the "Sermon on the Mount" was delivered; and **Capernaum**, the adopted home town of Jesus. The Sea of Galilee is also closely associated with **St Peter** who fished its waters – the fish most commonly served around the lake is a species of tilapia known as St Peter's fish.

The capital of the Sea of Galilee, **Tiberias**, attracts not only holidaymakers but also Orthodox Jewish pilgrims. Though not as revered as its northern sister Safed, Tiberias was once home to the historical Talmudic Academy and was the centre of Judaic scholarship. Many prominent rabbis and sages are buried in the town and their tombs have become the focus of annual pilgrimage and celebrations, mainly during the festival of Lag Ba'Omer, which attracts thousands of religious Jews from Israel and abroad.

The Sea of Galilee is also renowned for its curative powers; there are no fewer than seventeen **spas** in the area. The pungent and distinctive smell of sulphur, particularly around such places as **Hammat Tiberias** and **Hammat Gader**, may be unpleasant to the nose, but does wonders for the body.

On an even more material level, the Sea of Galilee is the lifeline of much of the Israeli heartland, including the Negev, since its waters are pumped through the **National Water Carrier** (HaMovil HaArtzi), a channel and pipeline to cities throughout the country, supplying around sixty percent of Israel's needs. The project has, however, been criticized by environmentalists who point to the drastic lowering of the Dead Sea (which it feeds via the Jordan River) as one consequence. Another is the rising salinity of the Sea of Galilee itself, and of the surrounding water table, which threatens agriculture across the area. A more benign result of the drop in level of the Sea of Galilee was the exposure, in 1986, of a first-century fishing boat, now on display at Kibbutz Nof Ginossar on the western shore.

Ginossar is just one of the many **kibbutzim** providing accommodation around the Sea of Galilee, in addition to a number of hotels, campsites and hostels all within travelling distance of Tiberias. The western and northern shores of the lake are busy with tourists throughout the year, while the eastern side remains somewhat more rural: here, under the shadow of the Golan Heights, are the kibbutzim of Ha'On and Ein Gev.

Public **transport** to Tiberias from all the main towns in Israel is good, although getting around the lake itself – a distance of some 53km – is more difficult. There is, in effect, one road around the sea, made up of **Route 90**, which comes north up the Jordan Valley and skirts the western shore, and **Route 92** along the east side, the two linked at the northern tip of the sea by **Route 87**, which continues into the Golan Heights. However, there are only intermittent local **buses** along the road, and having to wait for one in the heat of the midday sun is no joke. Probably the easiest way of getting around the lake is with a one- or two-day bus pass on Egged's Minus 200 Line which allows you to get on and off at 23 stops around the lake: you can get details from the bus station or the tourist information office in Tiberias. **Hitchhiking** during the day is a possibility, though taxis are a recommended if expensive option after sunset. To explore less-frequented areas, you really need your own transport. **Walking** around the lake, which can be completed in two or three days depending on your pace, is a popular alternative; another is to rent a **bicycle** from one of the hostels in Tiberias.

One place definitely worth a stop in order to find out what's happening around the Sea of Galilee is the helpful **information centre** at the southern end of the lake at Tzemah Junction, where Route 90 splits with Route 92 (March–Nov daily 9am–4pm; ☎06/675 2056, fax 670 9454). Situated in a shopping complex opposite Bet Gabriel (see p.215), the centre has details of accommodation, transport and activities throughout the area, and will provide discounts of around ten percent on such things as four-wheel-drive tours, with or without a guide.

Tiberias

*For two months in the year they gorge themselves on the fruits of the jujube bush which
grows wild and costs them nought. For two months they struggle with the numerous flies
that are rife there. For two months they go about naked because of the fierce heat. For
two months . . . they suck the sugar-cane . . . For two months they wallow in mud
. . . and for two months they dance in their beds because of the legion of fleas with which
they are infested. It was said "the king of the fleas holds his court in Tiberias".*

al-Muqaddasi, 985 AD

Despite its rather tawdry appearance, **TIBERIAS**, capital of the Galilee, is vaunted as
Israel's premier northern tourist resort, a reputation no doubt helped by its **climate**:
always at least a few degrees warmer than the surrounding areas, it's warm in winter,
very hot and humid in summer. The town itself has few notable historical or biblical
sights, but it is surrounded by glorious countryside and makes an ideal base for trips
to the Golan and the religious sites north of the town. Also, with the **Sea of Galilee**

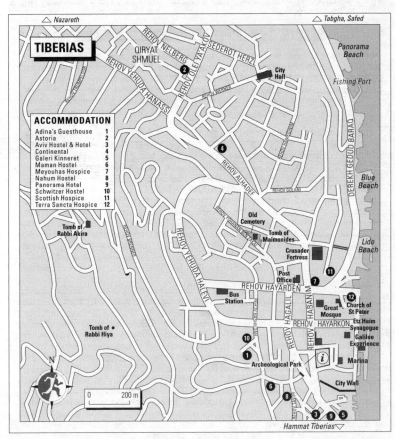

TIBERIAS TELEPHONE NUMBERS

Tiberias **telephone numbers** are now seven-digit; if you have an old six-digit number, try adding a six at the beginning.

(sometimes called Lake Tiberias) at its heart, the **mineral springs** just a mile to the south and the relative isolation of the eastern shore within easy reach, Tiberias is a good place to rest up and relax for a while.

The town is very much the centre of life in the area, crammed with visitors between June and September and with Israelis over every Jewish holiday; during the rest of the year, the atmosphere is more relaxed and hospitable. At any time, though, you will probably be surprised by the commerciality of it all; present-day attractions are for those with such hedonistic pursuits in mind as water sports, sunbathing, eating and pubbing.

But behind its rather brash exterior – at its most extreme on the waterfront – Tiberias hides a few traces of the place it was before the tourism industry descended on it – a mixed Arab-Jewish town bustling with merchants, and a holy Jewish city famed

JEWISH SCHOLARSHIP IN TIBERIAS

The growth of Tiberias was assured by the **revolt against Rome** in 132–35 AD, when the Jewish population of Jerusalem was expelled and many rabbis fled to the Galilee and to the relative peace and safety of the lakeside city. The rabbis cleansed Tiberias of its ritual impurity, enabling Jews to live there, and for several centuries it became one of the two leading centres of **Jewish learning** (the other being in Babylon – present-day Iraq). Tiberias was the seat of the Sanhedrin (Jewish High Court) and of the Nasi (head of the Jewish community).

Under the direction of **Rabbi Yehuda HaNassi** (c135–217 AD), Tiberias became a seat of studies that were to become central to Judaism. The *Mishnah* was codified around 200 AD, incorporating the Oral Law and the teachings of the rabbis during the first two centuries AD, teachings which were in danger of being lost with the destruction of Judea.

One of Rabbi HaNassi's disciples, **Rabbi Yohanan ben Nappaha**, founded the **Talmudic Academy** of Tiberias in 220 AD. The scholars of the academy set about providing an extensive commentary (the *Gemara*) on their predecessors' work (the *Mishnah*), which embraced the *Halakha* (religious law), as well as proverbs, parables, anecdotes, and historical and biographical tracts. Together, the *Mishnah* and *Gemara* are known as the **Talmud**, and the version compiled in Tiberias, and completed around 400 AD, is known as the "Palestinian Talmud" or (misleadingly) the "Jerusalem Talmud". It is about one-third the length of the more authoritative "Babylonian Talmud", compiled a century later in Babylon where Jews had lived continuously since at least the time of Nebuchadnezzar.

The Talmudic Academy saw a decline in the middle of the fifth century, but the Muslim defeat of the Byzantines in 636 AD brought the Jewish community relief from three centuries of Christian intolerance. Tiberias became the capital city of the Jordanian province, and winter palaces were built near Tiberias, at **Bet Yerah** (see p.213) and **Khirbet Minya** (see p.209). The Ummayad and Abbasid periods saw a spiritual renaissance among the Jews of Palestine, and again Tiberias was their religious centre.

The "Jerusalem Talmud" was already completed, but interpretations of biblical texts and of the *Halakha* continued and produced further texts based on the **Midrash**, a method of interpreting the Torah by looking for the spiritual meaning behind its words, a method developed largely by the authors of the Talmud. There was also a linguistic revival: a new, more efficient system of vowelling the text of the Hebrew bible (*Masora*) was compiled in 930 AD in Tiberias. By the ninth century, the religious authority of the Ga'on, or president of the Tiberias Academy, was recognized and accepted by Jews throughout the world, and the Jewish **calendar** for holy and other special days was set here.

for the learning of its rabbis. Several disused mosques lie tucked away and almost forgotten, while several **rabbis' tombs** have become venerated sites of Jewish pilgrimage. Remains of black basalt buildings adorned with balconies and wooden shutters also serve as a reminder of its former Arab community.

Some history

Tiberias was founded around 18 AD by **Herod Antipas**, one of the sons of Herod the Great. Although his town, named after the Roman emperor Tiberius, had baths, a main street, a magnificent synagogue and a gold-roofed palace, Herod is said to have had problems attracting the more devout Jews and Christians to live here, perhaps because it was built over an old burial ground. To encourage them, he exempted settlers from taxes – and, so the story goes, released petty criminals from his prisons and forced them to live here.

In 1099, Tiberias was taken by Norman Crusader leader **Tancred**, who declared it the regional capital and himself Prince of the Galilee; he erected a fortress in the north of the present-day city and several churches, including St Peter's (see p.201). Tiberias remained under Christian control until it was taken by **Saladin**, who routed the Crusader armies in 1187 at the nearby **Horns of Hittin** (see p.207). The city was all but destroyed in clashes between the Crusaders and the Muslims during the twelfth century, but revived under Turkish Ottoman rule, particularly during the reign of **Sultan Suleiman the Magnificent**. One of the many Jews who rose to high position at the Turkish court was a Portuguese banker and diplomat, **Joseph Nasi**. He became principal adviser to the Ottoman sultanate on European affairs, and his influential position enabled him to secure the rights to Tiberias in return for a minimal yearly remittance. Helped by his wealthy aunt, Donna Gracia, Nasi rebuilt the walls of the town, set up a silk industry and tried, unsuccessfully, to turn Tiberias into a Jewish enclave.

The eighteenth century saw the region flourish in general under the rule of the remarkable Bedouin leader of the Bani Zaidan tribe, **Daher al-Omar**. Daher was appointed governor of Tiberias by the Ottoman rulers, and invited Jews and Christians to settle in the city. He subsequently set out to force the Turks out of Galilee, and became the greatest of all local rulers who set themselves up – at different times and in different parts of the country – to challenge Ottoman hegemony. In 1740 he rebuilt the Crusader fortress in Tiberias and extended the city walls further north, using the large black basalt rocks that are still strewn around the town. Daher's regime – he was a legendarily just ruler – brought security from Bedouin raids, and his close friendship with **Rabbi Haim Abulafia** encouraged the latter to bring his community from Turkey. Daher provided houses in the city, a splendid synagogue, a bathhouse, market and a press for sesame oil.

Daher's growing power in the region presented a threat to the Ottoman rulers and, in an attempt to crush what was turning into an independent fiefdom, the Ottomans sent an army against him from Damascus in 1749, to no avail. In 1773, however, the Ottoman Turks renewed their offensive, and Daher was finally killed two years later. Tiberias returned to Ottoman rule under **Ahmed al-Jazzar**, whose 34-year regime brought relative peace and prosperity to the area and to the town's Jewish community.

An earthquake in 1837 flattened much of northern Galilee including Tiberias, and it was not until the **First Aliyah** (see Contexts, p.490) at the end of the nineteenth century that the city was resettled in any numbers. With the beginning of the **Zionist movement** and the founding of colonies in the region, the Jewish population of Tiberias once again increased. By 1918 and the start of the British Mandate, Tiberias had a mixed community of Arabs and Jews who enjoyed good relations with one another. However, increasing immigration of Jews into the country brought about Palestinian opposition and ultimately led to the **Palestinian Revolt** (see Contexts, p.492). In October 1938, Palestinian Arab rebels cut all phone lines from Tiberias before attacking British positions and entering the Jewish Quarter, where they set fire to homes and the synagogue, and killed nineteen people including ten children. A Christian missionary, Dr David Torrance, who came to the country at this period (and who founded the former Scottish Hospice, see below), described Tiberias at this time as a "cesspool of intolerance riddled with disease".

By March **1948**, Palestinian and Zionist forces were engaged in full-scale fighting for possession of the city. At the beginning of April, the Palmach besieged Tiberias and split the old town (where most Palestinians lived) in two. The Arabs asked the British to break the siege and put the town under British protection. The British commander in charge of Tiberias announced that he would continue to be responsible for the Arab population for only three days: most Arabs took this opportunity to leave the town in a convoy escorted by the British army. By April 18, Tiberias had become the first Palestinian town to come under Zionist control; the Star of David replaced the Union flag even before the official British withdrawal on May 15.

Immediately before the occupation of 1948, Tiberias had a population of around 6000 Jews and 5300 Arabs: in the main, the Palestinian-Arab community lived down by the lake, and the Jewish population up on the hill in the area of Qiryat Shmuel. Today Tiberias is an entirely Jewish city: those Palestinians you do meet in town are either working or passing through. A sizeable proportion of the present population is of Sephardi origin, many having come from Iraq and Morocco; in recent years, Jews from Ethiopia and the former Soviet Union have added to the number.

Arrival and information

Tiberias (Tiveria in Hebrew) is basically divided into two parts: the newer, upper city – **Tiveria Illit** or **Qiryat Shmuel** – is primarily residential but has seen the encroachment of some larger hotels; the **Old City,** down by the lake, contains all the action, antiquities, and atmosphere. This area is small, and getting around on foot presents little problem. Two main streets run east–west from the centre of town to the lakeside: **Rehov HaYarden** and **Rehov HaYarkon**, the east end of which is a *midrahov* or pedestrian walkway. These two are bisected by **Rehov HaGalil** and **Rehov HaBanim**, which join to run south along the coast, becoming Shderot Eliezer Kaplan (Route 90) on the outskirts of town. These four streets define the city centre, just a five-minute walk from the **Central Bus Station** on Rehov HaYarden, a couple of blocks west of HaGalil (☎06/679 1080).

The **tourist information office** is in the archeological park on Rehov HaBanim (Sun–Thurs 8.30am–3.30pm, Fri 8.30am–noon; ☎06/672 5666 or 2089).

Accommodation

For such a small town, Tiberias offers a wide range of **accommodation**, from four- and five-star hotels by the lakeside and up the hill in Qiryat Shmuel, to cheaper hotels and hostels in the city centre, as well as campsites and kibbutz holiday villages around the lakeshore. If you wish to base yourself along the lakeside, bear in mind that buses to and from Tiberias tend to stop early (around sunset), hitching at night is not recommended, and taxis (particularly specials) are expensive.

As you get off the bus at the Central Bus Station, you may be approached by people offering **rooms**. These are generally in the smaller hostels and often worth following up, particularly during a major Jewish holiday or high season, but check that they're not too far from the action. More reliable, long-established budget possibilities are listed below.

Plenty of **camping** opportunities exist around the lake: ask at the tourist information office in Tiberias or, if you are approaching from the south, at the Information Centre on Tzemah Junction (see p.194).

HOSTELS

Terra Sancta Hospice, on the wharf inside the Terra Sancta Church (☎06/672 0516). A quiet, characterful place popular with pilgrims. No meals. ①.

No-name Hostel, Rehov HaGalil (☎06/679 1613). Small, clean and pleasant. ①.

Nahum Hostel, Rehov Tavor (☎06/672 1505). Clean, friendly hostel with dorms and private rooms. A rooftop bar overlooking the lake serves good-value breakfast and snacks and has video shows. Bicycles for hire; tours to Upper Galilee and the Golan Heights. ①/②.

Aviv Hostel & Hotel, Rehov HaGalil (☎06/672 0007, fax 672 3510). Large, popular place with dorm beds and some 30 rooms (some with shower, a/c and fridge), plus a bar and verandah overlooking the lake. Bicycles to rent and daily tours to the Golan. ①/②.

Maman Hostel, Rehov Ha'Atzma'ut (☎06/679 2986, fax 672 6616). Offering dorms and private rooms, this is Tiberias's best hostel by some way, and the only one in town with a swimming pool. The atmosphere is secure and relaxed, and its seventeen rooms clean, comfortable and with a/c. There's a Moroccan restaurant on the verandah, and bicycles to rent. ①/③.

Mini Lon Hostel, 8 Ahva (☎06/679 0434, fax 672 3510). This new hostel, belonging to the same owner as the *Aviv*, is a bit run-down but very clean and very friendly. It has 22 a/c rooms with communal kitchen, toilets, television and cable. Bicycles to rent and tours available. ①/②.

Sea of Galilee Centre (The Scottish Hospice), corner of HaYarden and Gedud Barak towards Safed (☎06/672 3769, fax 679 0145). This magnificent establishment, founded as a pilgrims' hospice by Dr David Torrance 100 years ago and run by the Church of Scotland, is one of the best places to stay in town, with glorious buildings, tended gardens and a tranquil atmosphere. Guests in both the hostel and guesthouse (en-suite rooms with a/c) have use of the private garden, garden café and beach, plus there's a bookshop. The main gate closes at 7pm but guests have keys; if you want to check in after that time, ring the "emergency bell" outside, but it's best to reserve beforehand as the place is most often booked well in advance. ②/⑤.

Meyouhas Youth Hostel (HI) & Guest House, Rehov HaYarden (☎06/672 1775, fax 672 0372). Old stone building with modernized interior (a/c) containing both a thirty-room youth hostel (HI members get a discount) and a 24-room (en-suite) guesthouse. Prices include breakfast, (kosher) meals are served in the cavernous dining room, and snacks are available in the coffee shop. A strict 1–6.30am curfew is enforced, and you must be out between 9.30am and 1pm. The hostel often accommodates IDF soldiers, so can get a bit noisy. ②/③.

Schwitzer Hostel, 14 HaShiloah (☎06/672 1991). Set in lawn-covered grounds, with a choice of rather basic, stuffy two- and three-bed "bungalows" or double rooms with a/c. Communal showers and toilets, plus a kitchen, bar, and bicycles for hire. ②/③.

HOTELS

Adina's Guesthouse, 15 HaShiloah (☎06/672 2507). A clean, tidy, family-run establishment that's handy for the bus station. Kitchen and shower facilities available. ③.

Continental Hotel, Rehov Elhadeff (☎06/672 0018, fax 679 1870). Pleasantly old-fashioned with good food and friendly staff. ④.

Galei Kinneret, 1 Eliezer Kaplan (☎06/679 2331, fax 679 0260). Extremely elegant, old-fashioned hotel on the southeastern edge of town, part of the upmarket Israel Resort Hotels (IRH) group. Facilities include a French restaurant (see p.205), nightclub, pool and private beach. ⑥.

Panorama Hotel, 19 HaGalil (☎06/672 0963; fax 790146). Pleasant hotel with splendid views of the lake and town. All 47 rooms have private showers and a/c, and there's a cafeteria/restaurant upstairs. ⑤.

Peniel-By-Galilee, about 5km north of Tiberias (☎06/672 0675, fax 672 5943). A serene, eleven-room retreat operated by the Jerusalem International YMCA, with a private beach and beautiful garden; breakfast, lunch and dinner for guests and day visitors are served on a terrace overlooking the sea. ⑥.

The Town

Although the primary daytime focus for visitors is the clear blue waters of the **Sea of Galilee**, there are a number of Roman, Arab and Crusader remains scattered in and around the town. The main sites to visit include the **Crusader Fortress**, the hot springs at **Hammat Tiberias** and the **tombs of the rabbis**. Visitors to the tombs are required to dress modestly – no shorts or sleeveless tops.

THE PROMENADE

Fronting Tiberias is the **promenade**, running north–south along the shoreline. It's the sort of place you either love or hate: strolling up and down the waterfront promenade is where you can see and be seen by everybody in town, particularly on Thursday and Saturday nights when the place is chock-a-block with teenagers. Lined with endless open-air restaurants and bars mostly blaring pop music, it's a pleasant if not especially peaceful place to sit and look at the wonderful view over the Sea of Galilee.

At the southern end of the promenade is **al-Bahri Mosque** or **Sea Mosque**, a rather sad reminder of a vanished community. The mosque is now used as an archeological museum. Quite a different sort of attraction is located on the seaward side of the promenade in the shape of a **marina** – really a shopping complex with a bunch of cafés and shops. The best of this is the 27-projector, multi-image **Galilee Experience** (Sun–Thurs 9am–10pm, Fri 9am–4pm and Saturday evening; 18NIS), which claims to "bring Galilee alive through the lives of the personalities who moulded its history". Much of the show (hourly screenings in English) is devoted to an interesting mix of the life of Jesus and the creation of the Israeli state.

THE TOMB OF MAIMONIDES (RAMBAM)

In the northern part of town, the **ancient cemetery** of Tiberias contains the tomb of one of the most important figures in Jewish history – that of Maimonides, known and venerated by Jews as **Rambam**, an acronym of his Hebrew name (Rabbi Moshe ben Maimon). To reach the cemetery, go to the end of HaGalil, turn left onto HaYarden and right into Ben Zakkai; then follow the path on the right about 100m down, past the pitta bread factory. The white-topped tomb of Maimonides is in the centre of the cemetery; the fourteen black pillars lining the path leading to it symbolize the fourteen books of Rambam's seminal work, the *Mishnah Torah*.

Born in Córdoba, Spain, in 1135, Maimonides fled the persecution there and came to Cairo where he devoted himself to Talmudic study, completing his first major work, *Commentary on the Mishnah*, in 1168. He earned his living as physician and personal healer to Saladin. The written works of this remarkable scholar include the seminal text, the *Mishnah Torah*, completed in 1180, in which he set out to codify and rationalize the Halakha (Jewish Law), and *The Guide for the Perplexed*, completed a decade later and the last of his monumental studies (written in Arabic), which attempts to link reason and scripture, science and religion. His death on December 13, 1204, was marked by three days of public mourning in Cairo and a public fast in Jerusalem. The fact that his first name (Moshe) is the Hebrew name of the prophet Moses gave rise to a popular slogan: "From Moses to Moses there was none like Moses." According to legend, Maimonides instructed his students that when he died, his coffin should be loaded on a camel (or donkey) and that wherever it stopped would be his burial place. The animal walked from Egypt to this spot, now Rehov Ben Zakkai.

This street is named after the occupant of the tomb next to Rambam's, **Rabbi Yohanan ben Zakkai**, one of the most eminent sages at the time of Jerusalem's destruction by the Romans in 68 AD. It was ben Zakkai who founded the the Yavne Academy, established after negotiations with the Roman general Vespasian, which became influential in preserving Jewish religious life displaced from Jerusalem. The Bet Din (religious court) at Yavne came to be recognized by Rome as the supreme political, judicial and religious Jewish institution within the Roman Empire. Other tombs include those of **Rabbi Eliezer ben Hyrcanus**, a leading second-century scholar, and **Rabbi Avraham HaLevi Horowitz**, head of the Ashkenazi community in Jerusalem in 1621.

TOMB OF RABBI AKIVA

The white-domed tomb on the slopes of the hills to the west of the town, on Derekh HaGevura, is that of **Rabbi Akiva**, one of the most revered of Jewish scholars. To get to it from the ancient cemetery, follow Rehov Alhadef and continue along it as it becomes Yehuda HaNassi, then taking the fifth left (Rehov Trumpeldor) and from there the second left (Derekh HaGevura).

Born in 50 AD, Akiva married Rachel, the daughter of wealthy Jerusalemite Kalba Savua, who disinherited his daughter for marrying an illiterate shepherd but relented on seeing his son-in-law's perseverance at studying the Torah. Akiva rose to be a mystical leader teaching love, kindness and faith, compiled commentaries on the *Mishnah* and acclaimed Bar Kokhba, leader of the Second Revolt against Rome (132–35 AD), as the Messiah. He was finally imprisoned and publicly tortured to death by the Romans, during which he famously recited the Jewish prayer, the *Shema'* (see p.503) rather than forgo the Torah.

Buried next to Rabbi Akiva is **Rabbi Moses Luzzatto**, who died in 1746. Otherwise known as the Ramhal, this Italian scholar was a mystic who claimed to hear a divine voice. Despite the controversy and disapproval this provoked, his book, *The Path of the Just*, is regarded as an important work of Jewish ethics.

Another burial site, this one more suspect, is on Rehov HaShomer north of town, the **Tomb of the Matriarchs**. Here are buried, according to tradition, Moses's sister Miriam, his mother Zippora, his brother Aaron's wife Elisheva and, for good measure, Jacob's concubines Bilha and Zilpa, each traditionally held to be the mother of two of his sons, and thus the ancestor of two tribes of Israel.

THE CRUSADER FORTRESS

Tiberias's most significant ruin from the Crusader era is the **fortress** (daily 10am–1pm & 5–7pm; 8NIS), also known as the Citadel, built for Tancred and rebuilt for Daher al-Omar. It is along Rehov Donna Gracia, approached by a black basalt stairway across the road from Lido Beach. The steps are nineteenth-century but the grey, three-storey basalt castle to which they lead is the genuine article, restored by local artist Rivka Ganun, after whom the fortress is now widely known. Her restaurant and gallery form the fortress's main attractions.

THE GREAT MOSQUE, ETZ HAIM SYNAGOGUE AND CHURCH OF ST PETER

Three contrasting sites in Tiberias provide an indication of the mixed community that once lived in the town. Hidden away inside the modern commercial centre of Tiberias, between HaYarden, Elhadef and HaYarkon streets, is the **Great Mosque**, also known as the Omri Mosque after Daher al-Omar who built it in 1743. Swamped by surrounding cafés, shops and one of the biggest supermarkets in Tiberias, the mosque would make a great centrepiece to the square in which it stands were it not boarded up and in disrepair.

Within the block formed by HaYarden and HaBanim is an unassuming modern synagogue restored by the local community in 1950 but built over sixteenth-century foundations. The **Etz Haim** is named after the book of the same name – *The Tree of Life* – written by Rabbi Haim Abulafia, whose Turkish Jewish community populated Tiberias in 1740. Two earlier synagogues here were destroyed by earthquakes in 1759 and 1837, and a third by floods in 1934. It is from this synagogue (open for prayers on Shabbat) that the annual *hiloula* pilgrimage starts (see box on p.204).

Along HaYarden towards the shore, and opposite the Scottish Church of St Andrew, is another of the town's Crusader relics, the twelfth-century **Church of St Peter** or Terra Sancta (daily 8–11.45am & 2–5pm), whose apse is shaped like the prow of a boat to mark St Peter's profession. The Crusaders used old stones from the

Byzantine city in the church's construction; these can be seen on the outer walls. The relief above the entrance depicts Jesus handing over the keys of Heaven to Peter, while the walls are adorned with wooden effigies of apostles associated with the area. At one end of the courtyard, the statue of St Peter holding keys is a copy of the one in the Vatican, and at the other is a monument donated by a unit of the Polish Free Army that served with the British during World War II; among other symbols of Polish nationalism, it features an icon of the Virgin of Czestockowa. The church was used as a mosque (a mihrab is carved into the southern wall), later as a caravanserai, and even as a stable, before reverting to its original purpose in 1870; it is now run by the Franciscans.

Just to the west of this trio of religious buildings, on Rehov HaYarden, is a **memorial** to the event that irrevocably changed the town's demography: the 1948 War of Independence. The memorial takes the form of a plinth atop which stands one of the cannons used by the kibbutzniks at Gesher (see p.190) to hold off the Iraqi army.

SOUTH OF TOWN

About 100m south of the *Galei Kinneret* hotel, on Eliezer Kaplan (Route 90), is the **new cemetery** of Tiberias (modest dress), which contains the graves of several important rabbis. These include **Rabbi Haim Abulafia**, who founded the Etz Haim Synagogue (see above). Encouraged by Daher al-Omar, Abulafia brought his community from Turkey to Tiberias in 1740. When the Bedouin sheikh was attacked by the Ottoman army, their cannon fire missed Tiberias and landed in the Sea of Galilee – due, it is said, to the power of Abulafia's prayers. His grave, topped by a crown, is to the right of the cemetery. Other rabbis of importance, particularly to the Hasidic movement, are buried here. They include **Rabbi Nachman** (d.1780), one of the first Hasidim to migrate to Israel; **Rabbi Menachem Mendel** (d.1788), an early Hasidic leader; and **Rabbi Yisrael ben Shmuel** (d.1839), a messianic Hasid.

A few minutes further south along Route 90, a paved road on the right leads, via the town's sewage treatment plant, to a site that archeologists believe is the Bet Midrash or Study House of **Rabbi Yokhanan**, who lived here in the second century. Attractions are a mosaic floor of simple geometrical design, dating from the third century, and the remains of a *mikve* (ritual bath). Apart from his involvement in editing the Jerusalem Talmud, legends concerning Rabbi Yokhanan are of a decidedly sensual nature. According to the Talmud, he was known for his gracious physical attributes: "To envision the beauty of Rabbi Yokhanan, bring a new silver cup, fill it with red pomegranate seeds, put red roses along the rim, and place it between the sun and the shade. The resulting effect is similar to Rabbi Yokhanan's beauty." It is also said that the rabbi's looks led to him being accosted as a woman by the Jewish gladiator and bandit Resh Lakish. The rabbi responded by offering the rogue the hand of his sister – "even better-looking than me" – on condition that he give up his way of life and devote himself to study of the Torah, an offer he did not refuse.

More excavations on the southern edge of town, about 500m from the *Galei Kinneret* hotel, have revealed the remains of a **Roman bathhouse and cardo** (main street). The presence of the baths here indicates that, as at the spa at Hammat Tiberias further south, the curative powers of the area's mineral waters were known to antiquity. These Roman remains are thought to have been in use until the twelfth century; water was brought underground to the bathhouse building, which contained rooms for changing and relaxing. As usual, there was a mosaic floor, fragments of which have been saved: an array of animals and abstract designs are still visible. The site of the cardo is indicated by the stone pillars. Here there would have been shops and stalls – and there will be again if restoration plans go ahead.

HAMMAT TIBERIAS

Two kilometres south of town, on the coastal road, are perhaps the oldest known health baths in the world, created when a huge crack in the earth's crust carved out the Great Rift Valley. At **Hammat Tiberias** (Sun–Thurs 8am–5pm, Fri 8am–4pm), you'll find a museum, the remains of ancient baths and yet another mosaic synagogue floor, but its main attraction are the hot springs.

The curative powers of the **springs** have been noted by writers down the centuries and legends about them abound: one is that they date from the time of Noah and the Flood when the world was turned inside-out; another that King Solomon ordered demons to heat the water to cure his people; yet another that Jesus healed the sick here. Today, the waters have a well-established record in the treatment of arthritic and rheumatic ailments, and a less scientific reputation as a cure for infertility. The latter is an ancient tradition: it is said that by sitting on the stone lion in the Ibrahim Pasha pool, a woman will be granted her wish to conceive; if she can stand the heat of the water (60°C), she is probably strong enough to withstand childbearing.

The **Tiberias Hot Springs** complex (Sun, Mon & Wed 8am–8pm, Tues 8am–11pm, Thurs 8am–midnight, Fri 8am–start of Shabbat, Sat 8.30am–8pm; ☎06/679 1976, fax 672 1288) has a series of indoor and outdoor mineral and thermal baths, mud-pack treatment rooms and a large new swimming pool. It also has a staff of doctors, physiotherapists and masseuses. There are two centres: the health centre, housed in the distinctive Turkish building across the road from the lake, which offers treatment for skin and other ailments; and the resort centre, in a newer building on the lakeside, where you can relax, have a massage and choose from several restaurants. To **get to the springs** from Tiberias, either walk or catch bus #2 or #5 from the Central Bus Station or Rehov HaGalil.

The **Hammat National Park**, next door to the older spa (Sun–Thurs 8am–5pm, Fri 8am–3pm; 7NIS), contains the ruins of a sixth-century bathhouse, the remains of ancient synagogues, and the **Lehman Museum**. Housed in an eighteenth-century bathhouse, covering the geographical and historical importance of the hot springs and of Tiberias under Roman rule, the museum features a mural at the entrance depicting the legend of Rabbi Shimon Bar Yokhai, who, in the second century, purified the city which Herod Antipas had built over a cemetery, thereby making it ritually unclean for observant Jews. A copy of a *menora* found in the ruins of the second-century Hammat synagogue is also on display, while other exhibits include models of Roman and Turkish baths and scientific explanations of the water's healing properties.

However, the site's outstanding attraction is the exquisite fourth-century mosaic **synagogue floor**, the work of Greek artisans. This depicts the Ark of the Covenant and a zodiac reading from right to left; among the mythological characters portrayed are the Greek sun god, Helios, driving a chariot, and, in the corners, four female heads, each representing a season of the year. It is a beautiful piece of work, all the more interesting for the inclusion of "graven images" (and Greek ones at that) in a Jewish place of worship. According to Moshe Dothan, the site's leading archeologist, such figuration on a floor is acceptable because what is prohibited by the Torah is "a standing image" (Leviticus 26: 1) before which one could bow down.

TOMB OF RABBI MEIR

On the hill above Hammat Tiberias, two domes – one white, the other blue – mark the tomb of **Rabbi Meir** (Sun–Thurs 7am–8pm, Fri 7am–3pm; modest dress), known as the Baal HaNess or miracle-worker for rescuing his sister-in-law from captivity in a Roman brothel. It was Rabbi Meir who, with four other rabbis, continued to study the Torah despite such activities being banned by the Romans in the wake of the failed Second Revolt (132–35 AD). He also played an important part in the Talmudic Academy

---

PILGRIMAGE TO THE TOMB OF RABBI MEIR

In Tiberias, the festival of **Lag Ba'Omer** (the 33rd day after the beginning of Passover, and a one-day respite in a period without festivity, somewhat akin to Lent) is the occasion for the *hiloula* (festivity) commemorating the death of **Rabbi Meir Baal HaNess**. Accompanied by a police orchestra, a large procession sets out from Abulafia's synagogue, the Etz Haim, bearing the Scrolls of the Law (*Sifrei Torah*) to the rabbi's tomb near the Hammat Springs, south of Tiberias. The parade is led by pupils of the Bnei Akiva school in Tiberias, and attended by local dignitaries including the rabbi of Tiberias, resplendent in white robe and turban, who travels by horse and cart. Thousands come from all over Israel and abroad to take part in the celebrations, some of them spending two nights at the tomb. However, amidst the singing, dancing and lighting of bonfires, there is a serious purpose: people come to ask for favours and cures from the venerated "miracle worker".

---

and in codifying the *Mishnah*. One story attributed to him illustrates the rabbi's humility and humanity: a woman who returned home late on the eve of the Sabbath was locked out by her husband. He would let her in, he said, only after she had spat in the face of Rabbi Meir, whose classes were the cause of her delay. Hearing of this, the rabbi approached the woman in the market and, claiming to have something in his eye, asked her to get rid of it with her spit. His explanation for such an outrageous action was that any humility was permissible in order to reconcile a wife and husband.

The tomb is the site of annual **pilgrimage**. The white dome marks the building used by Sephardi Jews, while the blue one is that of Ashkenazim. Rabbi Meir's burial chamber is near a window on the right inside, where a curtain separates male and female worshippers.

TIBERIAS BEACHES

For a town claiming to be a prime resort, the **beaches** in and around Tiberias are disappointing; almost all of them are privately controlled, with restricted opening hours (roughly 8am–5pm) and charging a fee (12–60NIS) for access to a range of facilities including changing rooms, windsurfing, water-skiing, miniature golf, restaurants and discos. For a free swim you'll have to head south beyond the municipal beach or else cross the lake.

Of the places in town, **Lido Beach**, just north of the centre (12NIS), is about the best, with a reasonably priced restaurant and by far the largest swimming area. Further north are **Dekel Beach**, **Panorama Beach** and **Blue Beach**, which offer comparable facilities; **Hawaii Beach** holiday village is on the way to Majdal (see p.208). About fifteen minutes' walk south of town, there is the stony municipal **Ganim Beach** (7.50NIS); beyond it are places where there are no controls or lifeguards. Beaches on the east side of the lake are generally better, and are accessible with the Kinneret Sailing Company ferry (see p.206).

Eating and drinking

Naturally enough, the speciality of the Sea of Galilee is **fish** – particularly **St Peter's fish**, an ugly-looking character with marks beside its gills that were supposedly left by Peter's fingers. Nowadays, most of these come from the fish farms of nearby kibbutzim, but if you're camping and want to cook your own, it is possible to buy them fresh from the **market** on Rehov HaGalil (closed Sat), or direct from local fishermen. Gastronomically speaking, St Peter's fish is no great shakes – rather bony and tasteless – but worth trying while you're here. Most local restaurants serve it for prices upward of $10, particularly along the seafront promenade.

If you tire of fish and seafood, there's a wide range of more **exotic cuisine** to sample, from Indian and Chinese to Moroccan, Italian and French. **Vegetarians** are also well catered for. Most of the **restaurants** are grouped around the centre of town, plus you can eat out at all the big hotels and the holiday villages around the coast.

For **snacks**, there are falafel stalls on HaGalil and *shawarma* places on HaBanim, while a selection of places at Tzemah shopping centre serve grilled meat and chicken. Getting your own food together for a picnic is easy enough: there are a couple of **supermarkets** in the centre that stay open late and sell everything you need.

Au Bord du Lac, at the *Galei Kinneret* (☎06/679 2331). French cuisine with a bit of luxury. Daily 1–3pm & 7–9pm. Expensive.

Avi's Restaurant, Rehov HaKishon (☎06/679 1797). Typical Israeli food. Sun–Thurs 11am–midnight, Fri 11am–3pm, Sat nightfall–midnight. Moderate.

Blue Beach, Derekh Tzefat (☎06/672 0105). A fish restaurant worth checking out. Daily 8am–6pm. Moderate.

Casablanca, at the *Maman Hostel* on Rehov Ahva (☎06/679 2986). Moroccan restaurant on the hotel verandah. Sun–Thurs noon–midnight, Sat 8pm–midnight. Expensive.

El Gaucho, 9 HaBanim (☎06/672 4171). Argentinian grilled meat restaurant. Sun–Thurs 12.30pm–midnight, Fri 12.30–3pm, Sat nightfall–12.30am. Expensive.

Guy, Rehov HaGalil, near the *Panorama Hotel* (☎06/672 3036). Real home cooking (of Iraqi origin), such as vegetables stuffed with meat, dates stuffed with rice, and specialities such as lamb's brain, stomach and lungs. This was originally the Magen Avraham Synagogue – one of the first in Tiberias – whose *hazzan* (cantor) was the present owner's grandfather. The rabbinate of Tiberias granted permission for a restaurant on the site on the condition that it served kosher food, closed on Shabbat and Jewish holidays, and refused entry to anyone in a state of "undress". Inside, you can still see the original, 120-year-old walls and roof. Sun–Thurs noon–11pm, Fri noon–4pm, Sat nightfall–11pm. Moderate.

HaBayit, Derekh Gedud Baraq, opposite Lido Beach (☎06/679 2564). Excellent Thai and Chinese cooking with intimate eating and pleasant decor complete with fountain and waterfall. Outside peak season, it only works during Shabbat, leaving the rest of the week to its kosher sister restaurant, the *Pagoda*, just across the street. Between them, *HaBayit* and the *Pagoda* are open Sun–Fri 1–3pm & 6pm–midnight, Sat 1pm–midnight. Expensive.

Haltalkiya, Rehov HaGalil (☎06/672 3150). Italian restaurant with usual specialities plus fish and seafood. Daily noon–midnight. Moderate to expensive.

Karamba, at the north end of the seafront promenade (☎06/679 1546). A vegetarian restaurant – not the cheapest but it is one of the nicest, with birds singing in the trees above the tables and a great view out to sea. Daily noon–2am. Expensive.

Kohinoor, Moriah Plaza Hotel, Rehov HaBanim (☎06/672 4939). Fine North Indian Mughlai and tandoori food, with a lunchtime set menu available. Sun–Thurs noon–3pm & 6.30pm–midnight, Fri noon–3pm only, Sat nightfall–midnight. Moderate to expensive.

Lido, Lido Beach (☎06/672 1538). Another beachside fish restaurant worth checking out. Daily noon–3pm & 7pm–midnight. Expensive.

Little Tiberias, on Rehov HaKishon (☎06/679 2806). Good-value and very tasty Israeli and Continental food. Daily noon–1am. Moderate.

Maman, on HaGalil. One of the oldest and cheapest popular restaurants, serving typical Israeli food with such delicacies as lamb testicles and stuffed spleen. Sun–Thurs 11am–11pm. Cheap.

Marakesh, on HaGalil (☎06/672 6825). Mouthwatering Moroccan dishes including couscous, *tagine* and other typical North African specialities. Daily 10am–11pm. Moderate to expensive.

Nightlife and entertainment

Nightlife in Tiberias mainly consists of restaurants and bars around town or nightclubs in the big hotels. Among the travellers passing through, the most popular form of evening entertainment seems to be sitting around in the hostels, most of which have **bars** open to non-residents. Hostels such as *Nahum*, *Maman* and *Hotel Aviv* have par-

MOVING ON FROM TIBERIAS

There are regular services from the **bus station** to Acre (hourly; 2hr), Afula (hourly; 1hr), Bet She'an (2–3 per hour; 50min), Ein Gev (7 daily; 45min), Hadera (10 daily; 2hr), Haifa (1–2 per hour; 1hr 30min), Hammat Gader (al-Hamma; 2 daily; 30min), Jerusalem (roughly hourly; 3hr 30min), Megiddo Junction (2–3 per hour; 1hr 15min), Nazareth (every 30min; 45min), Qazrin (4 daily; 45min), Qiryat Shemona (hourly; 1hr 30min), Qiryat Tivon (for Bet She'arim; 30min), Safed (hourly; 45min), Tabgha (hourly; 25min), Tel Aviv (1–2 per hour; 2hr 30min). **Sheruts** from in front of the bus station serve Nazareth only.

Ferries operated by the Kinneret Sailing Company (☎06/672 1831) ply the lake, serving Ein Gev on the eastern shore three times daily (45min). The Lido Kinneret Sailing Company (☎06/672 1538) has sailings for Ginosar and Capernaum, depending on demand.

ticularly pleasant rooftop or verandah bars, some showing videos. Of the bars along the promenade, the current favourites with the young and trendy are *Big Ben* and *HaPirat* in the *midrahov*, and *Panchkook* near the Central Bus Station; others include *Amstel*, which belongs to the Hard Rock chain, and *Papaya*. None of the these comes cheap – expect to pay around 12NIS for a beer. For smarter surroundings (and smarter money), the larger hotels have bars, discos and nightclubs; these include the *Caesar*, *Jordan River* and *Galei Kinneret*, in the centre of town.

Impromptu barbecues and **beach parties** are a feature of Tiberias's nightlife during the summer, when there are also **open-air discos** on most of the beaches north of town: the most popular is at Blue Beach where you can cool off in the sea between dances. The Kinneret Sailing Company (☎06/672 1831) also runs "**disco cruises**" from Lido Beach nightly in summer.

Tiberias hosts a number of **music festivals**, which add a little cultural weight to an otherwise commercial nightlife. The largest, the Ein Gev Music Festival, takes place at the 5000-seat amphitheatre in Kibbutz Ein Gev on the eastern shore during Passover week, and features visiting international orchestras and performers as well as the Israeli Philharmonic. The other main event is the Kinneret Song Festival, held in May. This is primarily a folk festival, with music and dance from around the world. At other times a number of seafront folk and music events take place. The new centre at Bet Gabriel (see p.215), south of Tiberias, has films, theatre and shows, and a restaurant in which to spend the evening.

Listings

Banks and exchange Various banks are to be found on HaBanim, including Bank Leumi and the Mizrahi Bank, both with 24hr moneychanging machines. There's also a moneychanger on the second floor of the *midrahov* (Sun–Thurs 8am–7pm, Fri 8am–1pm).

Bicycle rental Bicycles can be rented by the hour or day from most Tiberias hostels (see p.199): if yours doesn't, try the *Aviv* or the *Schwitzer Hostel*.

Boat rental Ask at the harbour or at the Lido Beach (☎06/672 1538), or at the *Galei Kinneret* hotel (☎06/667 2888).

Books *Steimatzky*, 3 HaGalil.

Car rental Avis, Central Bus Station (☎06/672 2766); Budget, Rehov HaBanim (☎06/672 0864); Eldan, Rehov HaBanim (☎06/672 2831); Eurodollar, Rehov Yehuda HaLevi (☎06/679 0999); Europcar, Rehov Elhadif (☎672 2777); Hertz, *Jordan River Hotel* (☎06/672 1804).

Laundromats Akosevet, Kikar HaMisgad; Panorama, Rehov HaGalil opposite the petrol station south of HaKishon.

Medical services Magen David Adom's first-aid station is at the corner of HaBanim and HaKishon (☎06/679 0111). Poriya Hospital (☎06/673 8211 or 8311). There are a couple of pharmacies on Rehov HaGalil.

Police ☎06/679 2444 or ☎100.

Post office On the corner of HaYarden and HaBanim (Sun–Tues & Thurs 8am–12.30pm & 3.30–6pm, Wed 8am–1.30pm, Fri 8am–12.30pm).

Taxis HaGalil (☎06/672 0353); HaGolan (☎06/679 2888); Kinneret (☎06/672 2262).

Telecommunications The 24hr Solan Telecommunications Centre is in the *midrahov* (☎06/672 6470).

Tours Egged Tours (☎06/672 0474) runs trips from Tiberias to Upper Galilee and the Golan Heights every Tues, Thurs and Sat (around 45NIS); the SPNI (☎06/672 3972) runs three-day walking tours of the Galilee and Golan, and three-day cycling tours from the Jordan River to the Sea of Galilee.

North of Tiberias

The area north of Tiberias, packed with sites associated with the life of Jesus – particularly around the shore of the **Sea of Galilee** – attracts a huge number of Christian pilgrims and visitors. Quite apart from their religious significance, the **biblical sites** – including Majdal, Tabgha, the Mount of Beatitudes and Capernaum – are all beauty spots in their own right. West of Tiberias, on the way to Nazareth and Haifa, you pass the **Horns of Hittin**, where the Crusaders met their nemesis in the form of the great Saladin. Nearby are **Nabi Shu'eib**, revered by the Druze as the resting place of the prophet Jethro, and **Mount Arbel**, an important Jewish site dating from Talmudic times.

The Horns of Hittin

Inland, about 8km west of Tiberias, off Route 77 on Route 7717, the long, low double-peaked hill on the south side of the Arbel Valley is known as the **Horns of Hittin** (Qarnei Hittim). The hill – in fact an extinct volcano – was the scene of one of the most important battles in the country's history, when **Saladin** inflicted a decisive defeat on the Crusaders.

In 1187, Saladin's army of 12,000 archers were camped at the southern end of the Sea of Galilee and on the heights above Tiberias, enticing the Crusaders into battle. On July 3 the bait was taken, and a Crusader force of 1200 knights and 16,000 infantry set out from Sepphoris (see p.184) near Nazareth. Reaching the valley at the foot of the Horns of Hittin the following morning, the heavily armoured Crusaders found the spring there dry and, moving eastward, were caught with the sun in their eyes. There, parched, unequipped for the heat and weighed down by armour, they encountered the bows and lances of Saladin's forces, and were swiftly overwhelmed: by the end of the day vast numbers were captive, later to be sold into slavery, and the Crusaders' hold over Palestine had been destroyed.

Nabi Shu'eib

At the end of the Route 7717, overlooking the Horns of Hittin, lies the most sacred site for Druze in Israel, the grave of **Nabi Shu'eib** or the prophet Jethro, who was the father-in-law of Moses and is frequently referred to in the Koran as a messenger of Mohammed. The shrine is draped with the Druze flag, whose colours represent the five Druze *huddud* (founding fathers, see p.147); the stone beside the grave is believed to bear the imprint of Jethro's foot. Here members of the Druze community hold an annual spring pilgrimage and celebrations during which sheep are slaughtered, roasted and eaten.

Mount Arbel

North of the Horns of Hittin looms **Mount Arbel**, where Maccabean forces were defeated by the Seleucids in 160 BC. The mountain is best reached along Route 807 (off Route 90, 5km north of Tiberias), which passes through the canyon-like **Wadi al-Hammam**. According to one Jewish tradition derived from the Jerusalem Talmud, Mount Arbel is the place where a messiah, Menahem Ben-Amiel, will appear and meet up with the prophet Elijah and other noted sages. A second-century settlement is marked by a number of synagogues built on and around the summit, the remnants of which are still clearly visible. It is thought that the remains of Jacob's children are buried near the synagogue dating from the fourth century. The site has not been thoroughly excavated, but three rows of U-shaped pillars are visible among the swathes of yellow flowers that cover the place for much of spring and summer.

If you don't feel like making the arduous climb right to the top to catch the stupendous **view** (Safed to the north, Tiberias to the southeast), you can explore the **caves** honeycombed in the rocky cliffs, which served as hide-outs for rebels during the two Jewish revolts against the Romans; but take care – the tracks are very steep and rocky.

Majdal (Migdal)

Six kilometres north of Tiberias, to the left of Route 90, **MAJDAL** or Migdal was the village known in the New Testament as Magdala – birthplace of Mary Magdalene. The ancient village was named after the tower (*migdal* in Hebrew) that once defended it, and was important right through to the Crusader era. In antiquity the local weaving industry was well known, and the robes worn by Jesus at the time of his crucifixion are said to have been made here. But modern Majdal, founded in 1910, has little of interest beyond the beauty of its surroundings, an oasis of palm and eucalyptus trees, and a small, white-domed shrine, said to be on the site of the original *migdal*. On the coastal side of the road, *Hawaii Beach Holiday Village* (☎06/679 0202, fax 672 1624; ⑤) is a resort catering mainly for Israeli families. Loud music greets you at the entrance, where you can buy a ticket (20NIS) to use the **beach**.

Ginosar

Route 90 continues northward through the fertile **Valley of Ginosar** (Bik'at Ginosar), which marks the border between the Lower and Upper Galilee. This is the "Land of Gennesaret", which Jesus and his disciples frequently cross in the New Testament. **Kibbutz Ginosar** lies in the heart of the valley about 5km from Majdal. Founded in 1937, the kibbutz is famed for its out-of-season fruit and vegetables, but today its main economic base comes from tourism. On the side road leading to the kibbutz, the Kibbutz Camel Caravan Ltd offers guided **camel riding** trips (8am–1pm; 15NIS). Visitors are also treated to a guided tour of the kibbutz on tractors dedicated to the purpose.

Ginosar's main attraction, though, housed in a makeshift hut on the kibbutz complex, is the so-called **Jesus boat** (Sun–Thurs 8.30am–5pm, Fri 8am–1pm, Sat 9am–5pm; combined ticket for boat and video shown at the museum, 9NIS), whose 2000-year-old remains were found protruding from the sands during a period of particularly low water in 1986. As befits such a momentous event, the day of discovery saw a sudden downpour followed by a double rainbow, which was interpreted as "a sign". The boat, believed to date from between 100 BC and 100 AD, was preserved in near-pristine condition by the mud, and now lies in a tank, where you can observe a team of marine archeologists meticulously putting it through chemical preservation treatment. The boat must be typical of those used by disciples such as Simon, Andrew, James and John, who were fishing or mending their nets when Jesus told them, "Come ye after me and I will make you to become fishers of men." (Mark 1: 17) In the entrance of the Yigal Allon Museum, a fifteen-minute video show captures the excitement of the boat's discovery and removal to its current site (same ticket as boat).

In their rush to see the boat, many visitors miss out on the **Yigal Allon Memorial Museum** (Sun–Thurs 8.30am–5pm, Fri 8am–1pm, Sat 9am–5pm; 15NIS, including video and boat). You probably need around two hours to do justice to the place, which is set on three floors and divided into several interactive sections. These include: "Man in the Galilee", depicting life in a Jewish city in the Mishnaic and Talmudic periods; the "Arab Village", and the "March of Time", a chronology from the beginnings of history to the present. The most interesting section is entitled "Crossroads of War", where you can choose any of three computer programs (the Bar Kokhba Revolt, War of Independence or Six Day War) and determine the outcome based on your own choices and decisions.

The museum is dedicated to **Yigal Allon**, who lived on the kibbutz and died in 1980. Allon was commander of the Palmah (the strike force of the Haganah, see p.493), an army general in 1948, Foreign Minister under Golda Meir and Yitzhak Rabin, and responsible for a controversial plan envisaging Palestinian self-rule contained by strategic Jewish settlement on the West Bank. The memorial museum reflects his vision of combining a strong Israeli state with bridge-building between Israelis and Arabs. Opposite the museum is an upmarket **souvenir shop** staffed by the multi-lingual Ali Sabbah who has been working on the kibbutz for years and takes visitors to his home village of Tur'an about 15km west of Tiberias (see p.186).

Accommodation in the kibbutz is in the luxurious four-star *Nof Ginosar Hotel* (☎06/679 2161, fax 679 2170; ⑥) whose gardens have a small swimming pool and a private beach where you can hire kayaks, pedal boats and windsurfers, and a hostel (☎06/679 8762 or 3, fax 672 2991; ④) whose price includes a generous buffet breakfast at the *Nof Ginosar Hotel*, and access to Ginosar Beach, but not to the hotel's other facilities such as its swimming pool.

Nahal Amud

The **Nahal Amud nature reserve**, north of Ginosar on Route 8077 (signposted "Kibbutz Hukuk"), is a great place to **hike**. Around 2km into the reserve, the **Amud River** is particularly rich in wildlife during winter and spring; as well as wild flowers you may catch a glimpse of vultures and "rock rabbits", otherwise known as coneys or hyraxes. The upper part of this 25-kilometre-long river, near Moshav Amirim (see p.248), is called in Arabic Wadi Tufah (Valley of Apples) because of the surrounding orchards. It is the lower part which has acquired the name Nahal Amud (River of the Pillar) after the pillar that lies at its head about 500m along. **Caves** to explore in the valley include the Cave of the Skull, where the "Galilee skull" or Galilee Neanderthal (Paleantropus Palestinensis) was found in 1925, belonging to a man thought to have lived around 100,000 BC. The Amira Cave, a little further on, has also revealed important prehistoric flint tools.

Should you wish to **stay** nearby, *Hukuk Holiday Village* at Kibbutz Hukuk (☎06/679 9940, fax 679 9926; ⑤) has 38 bungalows set among lawns, ideal for families, with a nightclub and kibbutz restaurant used by guests.

Minya Palace

About 600m north of the junction with Route 8077 (to Hukuk), a sign points to *Karei Deshe-Yoram Hostel* (see p.210). A short way east of here, on the shores of the sea, are the ruins of the **Minya Palace** (Khirbet Minya in Arabic), one of the finest examples of Ummayad architecture in the country. Minya was so important that the Sea of Galilee was once known in Arabic as Bahr al-Minya – the Sea of Minya.

The palace was built for the great general Khalid Ibn al-Walid, whose forces had routed the Byzantine army on the banks of the Yarmuk River (which joins the Jordan just below the Sea of Galilee) at the start of the Muslim conquest in 636 AD. The large square structure has four round towers in the corner of each wall, some rising to 10m;

but the best of the place is inside, where there are remnants of a mosaic floor and, on the southern side, the oldest **mosque** in Israel, with a mihrab indicating the direction of Mecca. Sadly neglected, the area is overrun with weeds.

The giant Eshed Kinnarot pumping station, easily visible from the road, was built over **Khan Minya** – a caravanserai mentioned in writings of the seventeenth century. It is possible to swim nearby, although the sea here is often covered in a layer of petrol, making the stony beach distinctly slimy.

Tabgha

Just north of the Minya Palace, Route 87 splits off eastward towards the Golan Heights. A little way along is **TABGHA**, where Christian tradition has, since the fourth century, located the multiplication of the loaves and fishes (Mark 6: 35–44; John 6: 1–13), where Jesus made five loaves of barley bread and two small fish enough to feed five thousand people, and passed leadership to Peter (John 21: 15–17).

At Tabgha – the name is thought to be an Arabic contraction of the Greek *hepta pega* or seven springs – the main site is the **Church of the Multiplication of the Loaves and Fishes** (Mon–Sat 8.30am–5pm, Sun 9.45am–5pm). The original fourth-century church was built on the spot where the "feeding of the five thousand" is said to have taken place. Another church, erected over it a century later, is a unique example of early Palestinian church art: this cool, white stone structure with a wooden roof, contains exquisite **mosaic floors**, discovered in 1932. Many are simple geometric patterns (protected under the central carpeting), but between the columns of the nave is a startlingly exuberant riot of exotic birds, lotus flowers and even a snake. Before the altar (said to be the very stone on which the miracle happened) is that ubiquitous, beautifully simple image seen on postcards, ceramics and souvenirs – two fish either side of a basket of bread. To the left of the altar, part of the fourth-century foundations are visible under glass.

Set in verdant grounds, 500m east, on the shore of the lake, the black basalt **Church of the Primacy of St Peter** (daily 8am–noon & 2–5pm), was built by the Franciscans in 1933, again on the site of a fourth-century church. This very pretty old stone church with stained-glass windows encloses an altar – a flat rock said to be the table, the *Mensa Christi,* on which the resurrected Jesus offered a meal to his disciples: "As soon then as they were come to land, they saw a fire of coals there and fish laid thereon and bread" (John 21:9). It was here, too, that Jesus thrice conferred the primacy on Peter with the instruction, "Feed my sheep" (John 21: 17).

Beside the church is a rocky beach and steps from which Jesus called out instructions to the disciples casting their nets. Below the steps are six double, heart-shaped blocks, sometimes underwater, known as the **Thrones of the Apostles**. If you go for a swim, beware of the jagged rocks in the water.

Buses to Tiberias and Safed (both around 30min) run approximately hourly and stop on Route 90 by the turn-off for Tabgha and the turn-off for the Mount of Beatitudes. Nearby **accommodation** includes the HI-run *Karei Deshe-Yoram Hostel* by the shore of the lake between Ginosar and Tabgha (about 1km from the Tabgha turn-off on Route 90; ☎06/672 0601, fax 672 4818; ②/③), one of the best youth hostels in the country. Originally a cattle ranch, it is set in lush gardens (complete with peacocks), with its own private beach, a small campsite and kitchen facilities. It's advisable to ring or fax ahead: apart from the fact that the hostel is often full, you may find it no longer exists – the land on which it stands belongs to the German Church and promises have been made to return it.

The Mount of Beatitudes

Immediately behind Tabgha, set back from the lake, is the **Mount of Beatitudes**, traditionally held to be the site of the **Sermon on the Mount** (Matthew 5–7), a truly wonderful speech containing the most famous and fundamental of Jesus's teachings, beginning with the beatitudes, or blessings, and covering His attitude to the Torah ("Think not that I come to destroy the law, or the prophets; I am not come to destroy but to fulfil", 5: 17), to sin and judgement ("Judge not that ye be not judged," 7: 1; "Whoever shall smite thee on thy right cheek, turn to him the other also," 5: 39), to love ("Love thine enemies, bless them that curse you, and do good to them that hate you," 5: 44) and to prayer (the Lord's Prayer – "Our father which art in heaven . . ." – from 6: 9–13); the speech, which may actually be a compilation of Jesus's sayings from Matthew's main source, a lost "original" Gospel known to theologians as "Q", is a kind of Christian manifesto. Jesus leaves His audience astonished at the inspiration in his words, and the staunchest atheist would be hard-put to read a modern version of the sermon and remain unmoved by its genius, even if not accepting its divinity.

The octagonal **chapel** on the summit of the mount (daily 8am–noon & 2.30–5pm) was designed by the Italian architect Anton Barluzzi (who also built the Dominus Flevit on the Mount of Olives, see p.358) at the orders of Mussolini in 1937. Its eight sides are said to represent the eight Beatitudes (Matthew 5: 3–10), though verse eleven may be taken as a ninth. The best-known of them is the third ("Blessed are the meek: for they shall inherit the earth"), but of arguably greater relevance in this region is the seventh: "Blessed are the peacemakers: for they shall be called the children of God".

The seven virtues – justice, charity, prudence, faith, fortitude, hope and temperance – are represented in the pavement around the altar. The **Franciscan Church**, flanked by a pilgrims' hostel and an Italian convent set amidst grapefruit orchards, is one of the most peaceful sites in the country, despite its popularity. Sunset is a particularly good time to visit, when the yellow chapel walls reverberate to the chants of white-robed monks seated around the altar. And the **view** of the Sea of Galilee from the top of the hill is probably the best in the area.

The ruins of an earlier, fourth-century church commemorating the Sermon on the Mount lie below, off the road just beside Tabgha.

Capernaum

The scenery between the Mount of Beatitudes and **Capernaum** (daily 8.30am–4pm; 2NIS; "no shorts, no décolleté") is so gentle and beautiful that, if you have the time, you should try to walk; it's little more than 1km, although in midsummer heat even this can feel quite a trek. Capernaum – its name a Greek rendering of the Arabic Kufr Nahum (the Village of Nahum) – was adopted by Jesus as his "home town" after he was driven out of Nazareth and it later became the "headquarters" of his Galilean ministry, where he lived, preached and performed miracles. But, as in Nazareth, the local Jews thought little of the miracles, bringing down on themselves the curse: "And thou, Capernaum, which art exalted to heaven, shalt be brought down to hell." (Matthew 11: 23). There are two sites here: the ruins of a Byzantine synagogue, one of the largest in the country; and a nineteenth-century Franciscan church over St Peter's House.

The **synagogue**, believed to date from between the third and fourth century, was built over an earlier one which may be that in which Jesus preached: "And they went into Capernaum and straightway on the Sabbath day he entered into the synagogue and taught" (Mark 1: 21). The Franciscans bought the site in 1894, cleared the ruins and later restored the white limestone Byzantine synagogue. It consists of a prayer hall with a magnificent Roman facade and stone benches, with a column on the right inscribed in Greek. East of the main hall, on the side of the lake, is an annexe with a grand carved lintel at the main entrance. The stone carvings inside the synagogue represent Jewish symbols – a palm, star of David, candelabra – and other less obvious figures, such as a wagon, an urn, eagles and a curious legendary animal that is half horse, half fish. On the path towards the parking area are a huge, stone flour mill and an olive press, as well as carved stones and a pillar from the ancient synagogue.

Beside the modern concrete and glass octagonal Franciscan church stand the remains of a very early church (probably before 500 AD). A number of even earlier houses have been excavated from below the remains: one of these was identified as **St Peter's House** as early as the first century. Archeological evidence suggests that they were indeed fishermen's houses, mainly because of the number of fish hooks found on the premises.

Capernaum is a stopping place for **ferries** to the Lido Beach at Tiberias and across the lake to Ein Gev. The boat leaves Tiberias every morning for the round trip and heads back from here in the early afternoon. Check exact times at the pier.

Continuing eastward along Route 87 from Capernaum, you will notice a rather splendid red-domed building on the lakeside – this is a Greek Orthodox church, otherwise known as the **Church of the Seven Apostles** (daily 10am–4pm). The church was built in 1931 and is replete with icons and incense. You're unlikely to go inside, however, as it can only be approached by a rough track from the main road and its caretakers – two monks – do not encourage visitors.

For a place to **stay**, the *Paradise Kinneret Holiday Village* at Amnon Beach, about 2km northeast of Capernaum on Route 87 (☎06/693 4431, fax 693 4432; ⑤/⑥), has a real kibbutz feel, with 91 villas planted among lovely scented gardens, with a lakeside restaurant, plus a snack bar in the summer. Activities include kayaking, sailing, hang-gliding, jeep safaris and horseback riding, but the rooms are rather plain and somewhat claustrophobic.

Almagor and Korazim

East of Capernaum on Route 87, a signposted road to the north brings you to **Almagor**, the scene of twelve days' fighting between Israel and Syria in May 1951, where forty Israelis were killed and over seventy wounded in disputes over rights in the demilitarized zone between Israeli and Syrian lines (see opposite). The moshav here was established ten years later by soldiers of the Nahal Brigade, although it became a civilian settlement in 1965, surviving on the cultivation of exotic fruits.

Continuing north up the road from Almagor and taking a left at the fork (signposted in orange) brings you to the **National Park of Korazim** (Sun–Thurs 8am–5pm, Fri 8am–4pm; 8.50NIS) containing the remains of a Jewish town from the Byzantine period. Like Capernaum, the inhabitants of "Chorazin" were cursed by Jesus (Matthew 11: 21) for refusing to repent, and this was another Galilean town whose Jewish population swelled after the Roman expulsion of Jews from Jerusalem following the Second Revolt (132–35 AD). Although inhabited in the third century, the town was destroyed by an earthquake in the fourth; some of it has been reconstructed. Just inside the entrance is a *mikve* (ritual bath); a path from here to the right brings you to the remains of a black stone synagogue that once contained a chair thought to be one referred to by Jesus: ("the scribes and the Pharisees sit in Moses's seat", Matthew 23: 2). A signposted path leads from here to the southern part of town, where there is an oil press and restored houses. The town centre (follow the blue arrows) was where prayers for rain and other public activities took place.

A range of **accommodation** (guesthouse, campsite and well-equipped bungalows) is available nearby at *Vered HaGalil*, east of Korazim on Route 90, about 6km north of the Tabgha junction (☎06/693 5785, fax 693 4964; ④/⑤). They also have a restaurant and stables – take a ride up into the hills or down to the Sea of Galilee.

Jordan River Park and Bethsaida

Route 87 continues around the lake and crosses Arik Bridge over the upper part of the Jordan River. A left turn here onto Route 888 will take you to the **Jordan River Park**, which offers opportunities for **hiking** through unspoiled natural areas. Trails lead along the riverbanks, where you can see willows, tamarisks, eucalyptus and palms, as well as reeds, cypruses and other water plants in the river itself. It is also a particularly good spot for **bird-watching**, being on the migration path of many species. **Facilities** include a restaurant, picnic areas and bicycle rental; you can also rent a kayak or inner tube for an hour's exilarating float down the Jordan, from Abu Kayak (☎06/692 1078 for information and reservations).

The **flour mills** along the stream were in use by residents of the Bedouin village of Talawiya which once stood here. There are also the remains of the town of **Bethsaida**, which Jesus condemned along with Capernaum and Korazim for lack of faith (Matthew 11: 21). This is said to be the birthplace of Peter, Andrew and Philip; among the excavations still being carried out is a stone with a cross where Jesus healed the blind man (Mark 8: 22–25).

East of Bethsaida, Route 87 crosses the pre-1967 border into the Golan Heights. Just past the Arik Bridge, Route 92 branches off down the Sea of Galilee's eastern shore, past Kursi (p.477) to Ein Gev (p.216).

The southeastern shore

Somewhat more rural than the west shore, bordered by acres of banana groves and date palms, the **eastern shore** of the Sea of Galilee retains a sense of isolation despite the holiday villages springing up along the coast. Although the northern half of the shoreline is in theory part of Syria, the southern half was in Mandate Palestine from 1923 onward, and after 1948 found itself on one of the hottest borders in the world. The whole area was in a **demilitarized zone** (DMZ), established under the Israel-Syria armistice treaty (see map on p.463). Because the treaty was ambiguous, Israel claimed sovereignty over the DMZ, which Syria denied, and the result was that every time Israel attempted to do anything in the zone which was considered an assertion of sovereignty (such as road building), it attracted Syrian artillery fire from the Heights above. This ambiguity also led to several "incidents" involving Israeli and Syrian troops; throughout the 1950s and 1960s, vulnerable kibbutzim along the banks of the Galilee suffered bombardment from Syrian snipers, and Israel carried out attacks against Syrian military positions on the Golan Heights. One of the most serious events was the Syrian seizure of al-Hamma (see p.215).

In fact **al-Hamma (Hammat Gader)**, with its Roman spa, is chief among the area's attractions, but you can also see an ancient Canaanite city at **Bet Yerah**, Israel's first kibbutz at **Deganya**, an ostrich farm at **Ha'On**, and a fishing museum at **Ein Gev**. Most of the local kibbutzim provide accommodation of some sort, and there are a couple of famous restaurants in the area too. Transport is unfortunately sparse, consisting of a few buses from Tiberias to Hammat Gader, and a boat service across the lake to Ein Gev. In between, unless you have your own transport, you'll have to hitch or hike.

Bet Yerah

Immediately south of Tiberias, Route 90 passes a number of private **beaches**; complexes like Luna Beach, about 1km south of Tiberias, cost about $15 which allows you access to everything inside – such as large water slides.

After 9km, a gate on the landward side of the road leads to the site of a massive Canaanite city, **Bet Yerah** (House of the Moon). Despite its romantic name, there is little to see here, finds having been removed to museums such as Bet Gordon at Kibbutz Deganya (see p.214). Bet Yarah was a prosperous town between 3,500 and 1,500 BC but was apparently abandoned for a thousand years until it revived in the Second Temple period; a Byzantine bathhouse, synagogue and church have been excavated here. Under Arab rule there was a winter palace, but for reasons long lost in the mists of time the place was again abandoned.

Yardenit Baptismal Site

Less than 1km south of Bet Yerah, a road to the east leads 200m to the **Yardenit Baptismal Site** (Sun–Thurs 8am–6pm, Fri & Sat 8am–5pm). There are five different locations on the Jordan River where tradition places the baptism of Jesus (Mark 1: 9); this one is a modern and somewhat commercial site constructed as an alternative to those on the river bordering the West Bank. The fact that the Gospel is quite clear about John's baptisms being carried out in the Judean desert, not here, does not deter the pilgrims. There is a big car park to accommodate tour buses and the large groups of pilgrims they bring, souvenir shop, snack bar, changing rooms and toilets. The place often gets crowded; for those wanting a more spiritual experience, the baptismal site on the banks of the Jordan at the northern tip of the Sea of Galilee, by the Arik Bridge, offers a more unspoilt setting.

Kibbutz Deganya

To the south of Yardenit, just beyond the Jordan Bridge, is **Kibbutz Deganya**, the first kibbutz in Israel, and birthplace of Israeli general and Defence Minister, Moshe Dayan. Deganya was founded by Russian immigrants – ten men and two women – in 1909, becoming a collective the following year, after which its growth was rapid. Moshe Dayan's father Shmuel, an early recruit, later wrote that for him it meant the chance "to work in freedom"; a contrast to the "servitude" of working in a capitalist enterprise. "We are free employers and overseers," he said, "responsible to ourselves."

Now Deganya has grown so large that it has had to be divided into two sections: Deganya Aleph (A), the original part, is marked by a gutted **Syrian tank** at the gate, whose story is a reminder of the 1948 war, when the kibbutzniks found themselves on the front line facing a Syrian column of 200 armoured vehicles, including 45 tanks, pre-pared to invade as soon as the British pulled out. The only heavy artillery that Israel possessed at the time was four howitzers dating from the 1870s, of which two were rushed up to Deganya and hurriedly reassembled just in time to blow up the first Syrian tank as it entered the kibbutz. The Syrian army turned tail and fled, and the tank remains to this day. Deganya Bet (B), the newer extension of the kibbutz, holds nothing of special interest. Although set in beautiful, lush countryside, Deganya's economic base (like that of many kibbutzim) is nowadays industrial rather than agri-cultural – in this case, a diamond-tool factory.

Housed in **Bet Gordon** (Sun–Thurs 9.30am–4pm, Fri 8.30am–noon, Sat 9.30am–noon; 6NIS), in the grounds of Deganya Aleph, the **archeological museum** shows finds from the Jordan Rift Valley region, including animal and human remains and artefacts thought to be 1.5 million years old. They also have a copy of the mosaic synagogue floor from Hammat Gader (see p.215), dating from the Mishna and Talmudic period. The **natural history museum** on the upper floor is devoted to the flora and fauna of the area, displaying a rather macabre array of stuffed animals and even pickled human foetuses in old-fashioned wooden cases. A small observatory and telescope on the roof give great views of the surrounding countryside.

Bet Gordon is a memorial to **Aaron David Gordon**, a leading Zionist thinker who preached return to the soil and the honesty of physical labour. "Our people," he said, "can be rejuvenated only if each one of us recreates himself through labour and a life close to nature." Setting an example, Gordon worked on the kibbutz until he died at the age of 74, although he never actually became a member.

Next door to Bet Gordon, an **SPNI office** in the Kinnrot Field Study Centre (☎06/675 2340) can provide useful information on wildlife, camping and hiking around the lake. If you want to **stay**, Deganya Bet has air conditioned self-catering rooms and two-room apartments (☎06/675 5758, fax 675 5877; ⑤).

Tzemah

Route 92 meets the long, hot Jordan Valley Road (Route 90) at **Tzemah Junction**, at the lake's southern tip, 11km south of Tiberias. As well as the excellent **information centre** (see p.194) here, there's a large department store, Metav Massada (daily 8am–7pm) and a **restaurant**, *Bet Gabriel* (☎06/675 1175; Mon–Sat 10am–midnight; expensive) serving Italian fish, vegetable and dairy dishes.

Across the road from the information centre is **Bet Gabriel** (☎06/675 1175, fax 675 1187), a new cultural centre erected by Mrs Gitta Sherover (responsible for the land-scaped gardens on the Hill of Evil Counsel in Jerusalem) in memory of her son Gabi. Apparently, the former Mayor of Jerusalem, Teddy Kollek, refused permission for such a centre in Jerusalem, so Mrs Sherover built it here instead. The building is construct-ed of the yellow-white stone distinctive of Jerusalem rather than that found around the Galilee area. The centre holds music, drama, dance, art and cinema events. It also houses a bookshop and a splendid café.

Apart from being a sorely needed cultural oasis in this rather commercialized area, Bet Gabriel occupies a remarkable place in modern regional politics. It was here, in August 1995, that the late **Yitzhak Rabin** held his first (official) meeting in Israel with King Hussein of Jordan. And it is here, in a pyramid-shaped room, from where Israel, Jordan and Syria can all be seen, that any future peace accords between the three countries will be signed. The room is kept locked and unused until this momentous event takes place.

A real peace between Syria and Israel may also signal the re-opening of the **Turkish railway station** just north of the junction. This roofless, two-storey building stands on the track linking Damascus and Haifa, which was in use until 1948. Plans are now afoot to rebuild part of the railway as a tourist attraction.

Hammat Gader (al-Hamma)

Some 7km southeast of Tzemah on Route 98, the ancient spa of **HAMMAT GADER (al-Hamma)** (Mon–Thurs 7am–9.30pm, Fri 7am–11.30pm, Sat & Sun 7am–6.30pm; 27NIS), perched above the Yarmuk River, is one of the most compelling sites in the Galilee.

Politically, Hammat Gader is a curious anomaly: part of Palestine before 1948, it was placed in the demilitarized zone thereafter, but seized by Syria in May 1951 following twelve days of heavy fighting. Syria's occupation was confirmed by a UN ceasefire, but Israel retook the site in 1967 along with the Golan Heights. It is outside the Green Line, therefore, but does not form part of the Heights themselves (though Syria claims it), having the same status as the West Bank and Gaza Strip, and frequently referred to alongside them in PLO documents and declarations.

In Roman times, the spring here belonged to Gadara, modern Umm Qeis, just across the river in Jordan. Gadara was a member of the Decapolis (a federation of ten city states in Syria, Palestine and Jordan), and for a time the most important one. The spa was developed around 200 AD and became famous across the empire. Renovated under the Ummayads in the seventh century, it was destroyed by an earthquake in 749.

The ruins of the **Roman baths** are well-preserved and highly impressive. From the entrance hall in the northwest, you pass through a fourth-century doorway into the Hall of Pillars, originally the Tepidarium, where there was a deep warm-water pool. Beyond is the Hall of Inscriptions, where wealthy Greek patrons had their names inscribed to record their visits for posterity. Southeast of these halls is the oval Caldarium, the best-preserved part of the complex, whose pool was filled with hot water. Between this and the Hall of Pillars, you'll see a small tub, built specifically for the use of lepers, who hoped by using it to cure their condition. East of the Caldarium and just next to the spring itself was the hottest pool of all (51°C). The Hall of Fountains on the northeastern side of the complex held the cold-water pool, or Frigidarium, fed by thirty-two fountains.

To the northeast of the complex, you can see the beautiful minaret of a disused **mosque** from the pre-1967 Arab village, and, on a tel to the west, the not very extensive remains of a **fifth-century synagogue** and an observation point to view the site. North of the tel, in the **modern baths**, you can bathe in the smelly sulphurous water, stimulate your circulation with massage jets, or plaster yourself with brimstone-flavoured mud. To the east, near the main entrance, are the scant remains of a **Roman theatre**, and beyond them an **alligator farm**, where alligators originally brought in from Florida as a tourist attraction (though crocodiles were once native to Palestine) are now bred for export. To its south is a **mini zoo**.

There are all of two **buses** a day (none on Sat) to Hammat Gader from Tiberias (30min), returning at 1pm and 3pm in theory, though they may leave early. The only other way to get to or from the site is to hitch or hike.

Kibbutz Ha'On and Kibbutz Ma'agan

The attraction of **Kibbutz Ha'On**, on Route 92, 3km north of the junction with Route 98 for Hammat Gader (☎06/757555, fax 757557), is an **ostrich farm** (Sun–Thurs 9am–4pm, Fri 9am–1pm; 15NIS high season, 12NIS low season), whose residents, originally from South Africa, are occasionally slaughtered for meat but are basically a tourist attraction. Weird enough in this setting of date and banana plantations, the birds also have the unnerving habit of following you around, as if you are the spectacle and they the visitors!

Aside from the farm, the kibbutz offers a variety of **accommodation** (☎06/675 7556, fax 675 7557): a campsite with 100 camping places (②), lodging on the kibbutz in one of sixteen air-conditioned rooms (⑤), and a holiday village with 42 air-conditioned rooms (⑥). Other facilities include a bar and restaurant, disco and minimarket.

A couple of kilometres down the road, the *Holiday Village* in **Kibbutz Ma'agan** (☎06/675 3753, fax 675 3707; ⑥) has 100 family units and 24 spacious double rooms opening onto beautifully tended gardens. On site is a minimarket, cafeteria, restaurant, beach club where you can windsurf and rent pedal boats and kayaks. From here, there are spectacular views of the neighbouring kibbutzim, with the Golan Heights looming up behind. **Kibbutz Sha'ar HaGolan** (Gate of the Golan), 2km south of Ma'agan, provides **b&b** in the rather stately *El Mul Golan* (☎06/675 3544, fax 675 3545; ④).

Kibbutz Ein Gev

Kibbutz Ein Gev (☎06/675 8030, fax 675 8888), about 8km north of Kibbutz Ha'On, is on the shore directly opposite Tiberias. Founded in 1937, its first structures were an observation tower and wall since, until 1967, the kibbutz was isolated in the demilitarized zone, and directly in the line of fire from Syrian artillery on the Golan Heights. It certainly doesn't feel embattled now and is in fact pretty wealthy, owning just about everything in the area. Besides making a living from fishing, banana plantations, date groves and mango orchards, the kibbutz has a burgeoning tourism industry.

Chief among its attractions is the popular annual classical **music festival**, held in the amphitheatre during Passover. Throughout the year you can take the train tour of the grounds, with a commentary in various languages and a visit to the **Sea of Galilee Fishing Museum**. The kibbutz also boasts "the largest and oldest established sailing company working on the Kinneret" – the **Kinneret Sailing Company** (☎06/672 1831, fax 672 3743) – which runs regular crossings to and from Tiberias (3 daily; 45min), plus trips to various beach sites (including the "Jesus boat" at Ginosar, see p.208), and even "fun cruises" complete with disco and barbecues.

You can also **stay** here at the *Ein Gev Holiday Village* (☎06/675 2540; fax 751590) which caters mainly for families; its chalets hold up to six people, cost around $182 ($91 per person) and must be booked well in advance during the summer. For food, there's the renowned kibbutz **restaurant** on the lakeside (daily 10am–4pm, summer 10am–10pm; expensive; ☎06/675 8035), which specializes, naturally enough, in St Peter's fish.

North of Ein Gev, the lakeside road (Route 92) continues 5km north to Kursi (see p.477). Some 9km beyond that, it meets up with Route 87 just east of Bethsaida and the Jordan River Park (see p.212).

CHAPTER FOUR

UPPER GALILEE

The **Upper Galilee** is roughly the area north of Route 85, which runs east from Acre on the Mediterranean coast to the northern tip of the Sea of Galilee. The richly fertile soil of the coastal plain is tilled by numerous kibbutzim and Palestinian farmers, while inland, broad green **valleys** and sturdy peaks combine to create some of the most exciting scenery in Israel. The relatively high annual rainfall and moderate summer temperatures ensure an almost permanently green landscape, typically Mediterranean with its swathes of olive trees.

Most people come to visit the **coast**, whose standard-bearer, **Acre**, is among the most attractive of Israel's Mediterranean towns, certainly in terms of history; its fascinating Old City is a rich tapestry of architectural styles that bear witness to previous conquerors. Further north, **Nahariyya** is very much a resort, albeit a stylish and unusually elegant one, while from here to the Lebanese border, **Akhziv**, **Rosh Haniqra** and the surrounding area provide opportunities for days of idle wandering as well as some excellent **beaches**. The border itself is as strategic today as it has always been, the Crusader castles now replaced by a more recent line of defence in the form of numerous kibbutzim and moshavim.

Inland, the mountains and the Palestinian villages that hug their slopes are the main attraction, with the **Ammud** and **Keziv rivers** providing lush and diverse vegetation. **Mount Meron**, pilgrimage destination for Orthodox Jews during the festival of Lag Ba'Omer, offers hiking and magnificent views, but the jewel of the area is undoubtedly **Safed**, one of the four Jewish holy cities (the others being Jerusalem, Hebron and Tiberias) and a mountain-top place of antiquity, charm and Judaic revival.

In addition to its lush scenery, the relatively high Palestinian population and visible continuation of Arab traditions also helps to give the Upper Galilee a very different feel from the southern, more arid parts of Israel. However, here, as in the Lower Galilee, Jewish settlements now overlook almost every Palestinian town or village. As a visitor you will generally meet a warm reception in these villages (especially if you have a smattering of Arabic), but it is important to respect local sensibilities in terms of behaviour and dress.

In recent years, the Upper Galilee has seen a remarkable growth in **tourism**: almost every kibbutz, moshav or hilltop settlement now provides holiday **accommodation** of some sort, and this includes remote Arab villages keen for a slice of the action. For

ACCOMMODATION PRICE CODES

Throughout this guide, **hotel accommodation** is graded on a scale from ① to ⑥. The numbers represent the cost per night of the **cheapest double room in high season**, though remember that many of the cheap places will have more expensive rooms with en-suite facilities. For **hostels**, the code represents the price of **two dorm beds** and is followed by the code for a double room where applicable, ie ①/②. Hostels are listed in ascending price order.

① = less than $20	② = $20–40	③ = $40–60
④ = $60–80	⑤ = $80–100	⑥ = over $100

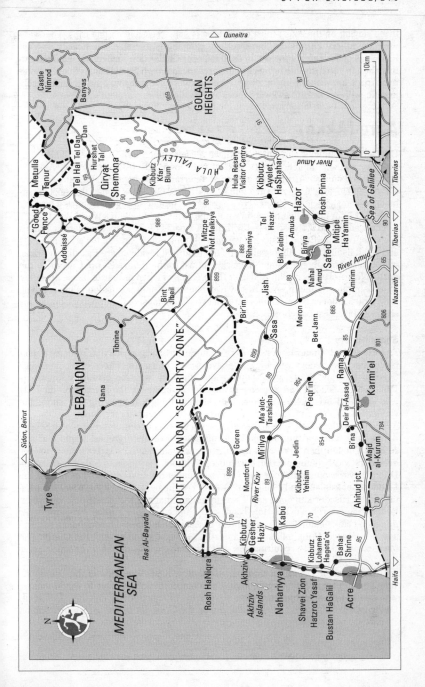

those staying on the coast, most of the area is still accessible on day trips. There are very few official **campsites**, but freelance camping is tolerated; the heavily wooded highlands of the **Tefen Plateau**, in central Upper Galilee, are particularly conducive to this, though you'll need to bring all your supplies. Although **buses** run frequently along main roads between the major towns, access to more out-of-the-way places can be problematic, with services at awkward times and tending to stop around dusk.

Acre (Akko)

Crusaders, Mamluks and Ottomans have all left their mark in Upper Galilee, but nowhere is their influence more evident than in **ACRE** (Akka in Arabic, Akko in Hebrew and on many roadsigns), whose Mediterranean ambience, refreshing summer climate and historical relics lend it infinite charm and character. Today, the most important surviving legacies are from Acre's days as a Crusader stronghold, and as a bustling Arab port from the sixteenth century until the British arrived after World War I.

The walled **Old City**, scattered with the remnants of previous conquerors, retains the essence of a Middle Eastern town with its souq, dusty streets, towering minarets and small fishing port. Almost all of the ten thousand residents are Palestinian Arabs, whose crumbling houses stand in stark contrast to the renovated **port area**. To the north, **New Acre** was established after the creation of Israel in 1948 to house the influx of Jewish immigrants; the now twenty-five-thousand-strong population inhabits a typically Israeli modern town, and it's here that you'll find most of the transport, numerous shops and the best **beaches**.

Some history

As early as the **Canaanite period**, Acre's natural harbour gave it a vital strategic importance that was recognized by successive waves of rulers: Phoenicians, Persians, Greeks, Ptolemy II of Egypt (after whom the city was for centuries known as Ptolemaïs), Seleucids and Romans. It was the Byzantines in the seventh century AD who presided over Acre's first economic boom, though it grew further under the Ummayad caliphs, who developed the port as a supply and storage depot.

The **Crusaders** took Acre in the early part of the twelfth century, renaming it St Jean d'Acre, and building the impressive fortifications and underground vaults that still remain. Though their first reign over the city was short-lived – in 1187 the Crusader defenders, vastly outnumbered, surrendered without a struggle to **Saladin** (Salah al-Din) – they recaptured the city four years later under the dual command of Richard the Lionheart of England and Philip II of France. For the next century, Acre was the capital of the Crusader kingdom, and it was from here that much of their spoil, in particular the religious relics of the Holy Land, were shipped back to Europe. From the other direction came notables such as **Francis of Assisi**, who passed through on a pilgrimage, and **Marco Polo**, followed by a host of merchants trading with the Orient. The town expanded rapidly, requiring new outer walls to enclose an area three times larger than today's Old City.

With the fall of Tripoli (in modern Lebanon) in 1289, Acre became the Crusaders' very last outpost in Palestine, though it succumbed two years later to the Mamluks, who sold its Christian inhabitants into slavery. In 1740 the Bedouin chieftain, **Daher al-Omar** (see p.487), constructed a new city on the Crusader ruins, adding fortification

---

Telephone numbers in Acre are now seven-digit; if you have an old six-digit number, try adding a nine at the beginning.

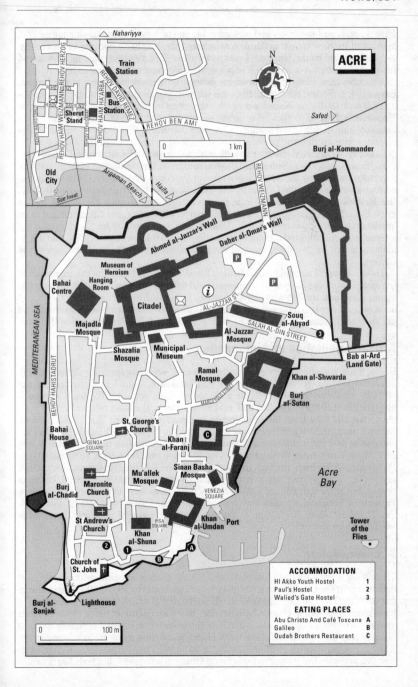

ACRE

△ *Nahariyya*

Train Station

Bus Station

Sherut Stand

REHOV HAIM WEIZMANN
REHOV HAIM HA'ABBA
REHOV HERZOG
REHOV DAVID REMEZ

N

Safed ▷

REHOV BEN AMI

0   1 km

Old City
See Inset

Argaman Beach △   Haifa △

Burj al-Kommander

REHOV WEIZMANN

Ahmed al-Jazzar's Wall   Daher al-Omar's Wall

MEDITERRANEAN SEA

Museum of Heroism

Bahai Centre

Hanging Room

Citadel

P

P

i

AL-JAZZAR'S

Majadla Mosque

Souq al-Abyad

SALAH AL-DIN STREET

3

Shazalia Mosque

Municipal Museum

Al-Jazzar Mosque

Bab al-Ard (Land Gate)

REHOV HAHISTADRUT

Ramal Mosque

Khan al-Shwarda

MARKOV KIKAR STREET

Burj al-Sutan

Bahai House

St. George's Church

GENOA SQUARE

Khan al-Faranj

C

Acre Bay

Burj al-Chadid

Maronite Church

Mu'allek Mosque

Sinan Basha Mosque

VENEZIA SQUARE

St Andrew's Church

PISA SQUARE

Khan al-Shuna

Khan al-Umdan

Port

Tower of the Flies

2

1

B

A

Church of St. John

Burj al-Sanjak   Lighthouse

0   100 m

ACCOMMODATION

HI Akko Youth Hostel   1
Paul's Hostel   2
Walied's Gate Hostel   3

EATING PLACES

Abu Christo And Café Toscana   A
Galileo   B
Oudah Brothers Restaurant   C

walls, hostels and mosques, and making it his capital before his assassination in 1775 by Ahmed Pasha – known as **Ahmed al-Jazzar** ("the butcher") because of his cruelty. He was installed by the Ottoman Turks as local overlord and continued rebuilding and restructuring the town, and much of his work still enhances the place today.

A combination of the city's awesome defences, the growing power of the **British Empire**, and disease emanating from the surrounding swamps saw off two attempts – in 1799 and 1801 – by **Napoleon** to take the city. On retreating, he left behind him **Napoleon's Hill**, an artificial rise on the eastern edge of town on which he placed his cannons, plus thousands of soldiers, who were eventually absorbed into the local population: some ascribe the prevalence of red-haired Palestinians in the Galilee to the genes of these defeated soldiers, though others claim it is a legacy of the Crusaders.

Al-Jazzar's successor, **Suleiman Pasha**, continued the rebuilding of Acre, until he was halted in 1832 by the advancing armies of Ibrahim Pasha of Egypt, himself defeated nine years later by the Ottomans who reinstated Turkish rule in the area. In 1917, **the British** took Palestine and from then on, Acre's significance declined as Haifa's grew, the latter becoming the British headquarters. However, the city continued to be important to the local economy of the Galilee, serving as a centre for the villages of the interior, as it still does today. Acre's last battle was in **1948**, when its Palestinian inhabitants held out for ten days; most of the inhabitants fled to the Arab villages of the Galilee.

Today, though Palestinians and Israelis live in an uneasy truce, the two mainstays of the local Palestinian economy – commerce and fishing – are under threat. Fishing has all but gone, and traders who rely on tourism for a living are struggling in the face of an organized day-trip industry that ferries visitors into a few selected restaurants and gift shops. It remains to be seen if the walls of Acre can defend the population this time.

Arrival, orientation and information

Buses, trains and sheruts leave you in the New City, well away from the sights and budget accommodation of the Old City. The **bus station** is around 1km northeast of the Old City, on Rehov HaArba, with the main sherut stand opposite. The **train station** is one block east of the bus station on David Remez Street, the main road to the north. To get to the Old City from the train station (a distance of around 2km), turn right up Rehov Remez, and left at the next junction ("Akko North Junction") into Rehov HaArba, continuing past the bus station and sherut stand, before turning right onto Rehov Ben Ami, New Acre's main thoroughfare. Two blocks down, turn right again into Haim Weizmann, which leads through the ancient walls and into the Old City car park. Once inside the walls, the only way to get around is on foot. The main sites are all well signposted, but it's worth getting hold of the pictorial **map** ($3) available from the Acre **Bureau of Tourism**, opposite the mosque in al-Jazzar Street (☎04/991 0251 or 1764, Sat–Thurs 9am–6pm, Fri 8.30am–2.30pm), to help you navigate your way through the winding alleyways.

Accommodation

There's not a great range of places to stay in Acre. Budget **accommodation** is almost exclusively in the Old City, with the more luxurious hotels located on the beach west of the Old City. The Old City has two main **hostels**, one of which is almost guaranteed to have room. If by some chance both are full, there are plenty of other private **rooms** available in the Old City to which either of the hostels can direct you. Easily the best place to stay in Acre, the *HI Akko Youth Hostel*, just across from the lighthouse in the Khan al-Umdan quarter (☎04/991 1982, fax 991 1982; closed 9am–5pm, 10.30pm curfew; ②), occupies the former palace of local Ottoman governors, but feels like a family-run hotel. It can get very hot in the summer, but the marble floors are adequate compensation. A popular, more basic option is *Paul's Hostel*, also near the Khan al-Umdan (☎04/991 2857; ①/②), which has mixed dorms and decent double rooms with shared washing and kitchen facilities; guests get their own keys to the main entrance. As a last resort there's *Walied's Gate Hostel* (☎04/991 0410, fax 991 0454; ①/③).

Of the **hotels**, *Argaman Hotel*, on Argaman Beach (☎04/991 6691, fax 991 6690; ④), is a modern building with access to the beach; while the *Palm Beach Hotel* next door (☎04/981 5815, fax 991 0434; ⑥), offers water-sports facilities, a tennis court, swimming pool and sauna.

The Old City

Walking around the **walls** – either on top or in the dry moat – is an excellent introduction to ancient Acre. The outer ramparts were built by al-Jazzar after Napoleon's retreat in 1801, while the inner walls were erected by Daher al-Omar and are still visible in the northeastern corner of the city. Five **towers** (*burj*) give strength to the walls and also provide good orientation points; the first, **Burj al-Kommander** (Commander's Tower), at the northeastern corner of the fortifications (to your left as you enter the Old City if coming down Rehov Weizmann), played a crucial role in al-Jazzar's defence of the city against Napoleon in 1799. The cannons on top of the fortress are known as Napoleon's Cannons, but although they are French they weren't actually made until 1857. Following the walls to the south, you come to **Bab al-Ard** (Land Gate), one of three entrances into the Old City (the others being Weizmann in the north, and Rehov HaHaganah in the northwestern corner).

Having found your bearings you can plunge into the winding streets of the Old City, stepping off the main streets occasionally to find quiet residential courtyards, surprisingly isolated from the activity around them. As you wander, you may be approached by local youths offering their services as **guides**. You'll be expected to pay, so it's as well to agree a price at the outset.

Al-Jazzar Mosque

Dominating the skyline of the Old City with its slender white, green-topped minaret, **al-Jazzar Mosque** (Sat–Thurs 8am–12.30pm & 1.15–4pm, Fri 8–11am & 2–4pm, 6pm in summer; 2NIS) is one of the finest surviving mosques in Israel. Built in 1781 by Ahmed al-Jazzar, it is the administrative centre of the local Waqf and a powerful focus for Acre's Palestinian community. A semicircular flight of stone stairs leads up to the **entrance** in al-Jazzar Street, where you hand over your entrance fee and have your dress inspected by the keeper.

Inside, there's a serene garden courtyard, and, surrounding the mosque, colonnaded **cloisters** built of marble from Caesarea and Ashqelon. The cloisters have served several functions over the years: as a hostel for pilgrims, a seminary for students of the Koran and offices for the Waqf. The beauty of the mosque lies in its perfectly proportioned interior, which can be admired from the marble entrance platform. Soft light filters in through the windows in the domed roof and reflects off walls inlaid with brown, grey and white marble, around which a fresco of verses from the Koran is highlighted in blue. In the far corner of the right gallery, a box behind a green grille contains a hair said to be from the head of the Prophet Mohammed.

A small building on the west side of the mosque by the base of the minaret houses two **tombs**: one belonging to Ahmed al-Jazzar; the other to Suleiman Pasha, his adopted son and successor. On the east side of the gallery, steps lead down into a vast **underground water cistern**, discovered recently: Crusader in origin, it served the town's population in times of siege.

The Subterranean Crusader City

Acre's Crusader past is revealed at its most impressive in the vast complex of buildings that have been excavated in the **Subterranean Crusader City** (☎04/991 1764 for guided tours; Sat–Thurs 9am–4.30pm, Fri 9am–12.30pm; 9NIS includes admission to the Municipal Museum, see p.225), opposite al-Jazzar Mosque. Originally built above ground, they were buried by the Mamluks after the Crusaders' defeat and later served as foundations for al-Jazzar's Citadel (see below). Archeologists have been severely limited in their explorations for fear of undermining the Citadel, so what you see today is just a fraction of the actual Crusader city, with the headquarters of the Knights of St John, or Knights Hospitallers, and hence of the Crusader armies, as a centrepiece.

The grand scale of the complex is apparent as soon as you enter the cathedral-like **entrance hall**, where three gigantic pillars indicate that the original floor level lay well below the current one. Just beyond the entrance are rooms thought to be part of the Hospitaller complex; the seven enormous halls in the northern section were each used by a different "Langue" – or national division – of the Crusader orders. The northern-most of these are the **Knights' Halls**, excavated in 1954 – a series of high-ceilinged chambers supported by pillars, forming well-preserved Crusader arches. The pictorial decorations on the pillars tend to be Crusader, while the more elaborate, abstract designs are Ottoman. The piece of concrete in the ceiling marks the spot where, in 1947, prisoners belonging to Jewish paramilitaries and held in the Citadel above (see below) made a hole while trying to escape by digging a tunnel.

Beyond the Knights' Halls, the **chamber of the Grand Maneir** was the seat of the Grand Master of the Order and his aides; from here a small passageway leads into the most impressive of all the halls. Generally known as the **Crypt**, because before its excavation you could look down into it from a window at street level, this magnificent chamber served as the knights' refectory and captures the very spirit of Crusader architecture. Note the heraldic fleur-de-lys cut into the stone of the supporting beams, along with the name Louis VII and the date, 1184. At the far end of the Crypt, a flight of stairs beside one of the columns leads down to an **underground passage**, which provided a secret escape route – perhaps to ensure that revellers were not set upon while weakened by too much food and drink. The seventy-metre-long tunnel gets smaller and smaller as you proceed, at times less than 1.5m high, and connects with another building – the **Post** – whose rooms were used as hospital wards and for assembling pilgrims.

During the autumn festival of Succot, these underground halls provide venues for the **Acre Theatre Festival**, the largest fringe event in Israel, featuring the best of Israeli and Palestinian theatre; details are available from the Bureau of Tourism. During the summer, you may catch a performance of *Time Tunnel*, a short play about Acre during the Crusader and early Ottoman period; informative and imaginatively presented through the medium of mime, it takes the audience on a tour of the complex and its roots.

The Citadel

The massive and intimidating structure of the **Citadel**, one of al-Jazaar's eighteenth-century improvements, takes as its foundations the Crusader buildings buried below (see above). It served as Acre's prison under both Turkish and British rule; one of its most famous inmates was the founder of the Bahai faith (see box on p.139), the Baha'ullah, imprisoned here by the Ottomans in 1868 and later transferred to what is now the Bahai Shrine, just outside Acre (see p.228).

Contained within the complex, the **Museum of Heroism** (Sat–Thurs 9am–5pm, Fri 9am–12.30pm; 5NIS) recalls those who were incarcerated here during the British Mandate, when the jail was one of the most important in the country. Among the Jews held here in the 1920s was Vladimir Jabotinsky, the founder of Zionist Revisionism (see p.492). The museum also remembers prisoners from his followers in the Irgun and the

Stern Gang (see box on p.85), who carried out attacks on British and Palestinian targets in the years preceding Israeli independence. The **gallows room**, chillingly austere and functional, lists the nine Jewish guerrillas hanged by the British; in the cells are the names of the inmates they once held, and display cabinets provide details about their lives. Much attention is given to the **escape** organized by the Irgun in 1947, which freed over 200 prisoners – an incident dramatized in the film *Exodus*, actually shot on location in the prison. Dressed in British uniforms, the raiders drove stolen British army trucks into the centre of the city and placed explosives against the Citadel wall adjacent to the prison exercise yard. Books on sale at the museum retell the tale. Just west of the Citadel, the sturdy **Burj Kuraijim** (Tower of the Vineyards) is an Ottoman addition to the Crusader defences.

The Municipal Museum

The **Municipal Museum** (Sat–Thurs 9am–4.30pm, Fri 9am–12.30pm; entrance included on Crusader City ticket), across al-Jazzar Street from the subterranean city, is housed in a former *hammam* (Turkish bath), another of al-Jazaar's legacies, which remained in use until 1947. Notable more for its splendid architecture than its contents, the building retains the pierced domed roof with delicate arches, and the steam rooms now contain archeological exhibits from Acre's Crusader and Arab past. Major finds have been taken to museums in Tel Aviv and Jerusalem, but don't let that deter you; the building alone is worth the visit. Also in the museum, a display of stuffed figures portrays a rather romanticized image of life in the region's Arab and Druze villages.

Souq al-Abyad

At the junction of al-Jazzar and Salah al-Din streets, **Souq al-Abyad** (White Market) is Acre's only surviving working covered market. Striking in its simplicity, it was built under Daher al-Omar in the eighteenth century, and restored by Suleiman Pasha in 1818 to include the small domes you see now. It's alive with activity from early in the morning and crammed with stalls overflowing with excellent fruit and vegetables – prices are fixed, so don't insist if traders refuse to bargain.

Heading south from the souq, you'll pass through **Parhi Square**, its name derived from that of Ahmed al-Jazzar's Jewish adviser, Haim Farhi. Once Acre's commercial centre, it's now lined with cheap restaurants. The far end of the square is taken up by one of Acre's four **khans**, or caravanserais – large inns, usually built around a central courtyard, for visiting merchants and their retinue. **Khan al-Shawarda**'s thirteenth-century tower, **Burj al-Sultan**, is still one of the town's great landmarks and from the top there's a fine view of Acre Bay, dotted with fishing boats. The symbols on the tower's walls were left by the original masons.

Standing to the right of Khan al-Shawarda, on Marco Polo Street, the **Ramal Mosque** (daily 4pm–6pm; free), was built in 1704–5, incorporating into its structure the foundations of a Crusader church; the original inscriptions are still visible on the southeast wall. One, written in Latin, reads: "Oh, men who pass along this street, in charity I beg you to pray for my soul – Master Ebuli Fazli, builder of the church." The mosque is now used as a Muslim scout hall.

Khan al-Franj and Venezia Square

Further down Marco Polo Street, past the bell tower of a large, eighteenth-century Franciscan church, is the **Khan al-Franj** or Khan of the Franks; the term "Franks" initially referred to the French but came to be used as a general term for any European. The oldest khan in Acre, it was established in 1600 to house a small group of French merchants who had been given trading concessions by the Mamluks in an effort to increase commerce between Palestine and Europe. Parts of the building incorporated a Clarissian nunnery – founded by Francis of Assisi – whose occupants committed suicide rather than surrender to the Mamluks when they captured the city in 1291.

Crusader remains can be seen in the foundations and columns of the building, but as most of the khan has fallen into ruin, these are hard to distinguish from other toppled masonry. Two main entrances lead into a central courtyard, where the overriding impression is one of neglect and decay.

From the southern end of the Khan al-Franj, head towards the large, Italianate tower to emerge in **Venezia Square**, a spacious cobbled area full of ice-cream sellers. The square's name is another legacy of the Crusader period, when each *Langue* (nationality) had its own quarter of town; this one belonged to the Venetians. All around are magnificent old facades, the most recent of which is the white-domed **Sinan Pasha Mosque**, to your left, which dates from the last century. Dominating the other side of Venezia Square is the **Khan al-Umdan** (Khan of the Pillars), the second largest and best preserved of Acre's khans. Erected under al-Jazzar in the eighteenth century on the site of a Dominican monastery, the building takes its name from the granite and porphyry pillars brought from Caesarea for its construction. The tall, square **clock tower** (now minus its clock) rising above the entrance was a later addition; built in 1906 for the Ottoman sultan Abd al-Hamid II, it is adorned with the Islamic symbols of crescent moon and star. As you pass into the central **courtyard**, it's immediately obvious how the khan got its name: the two-tiered quadrangle is a maze of colonnaded cloisters and blocked-off storerooms in a remarkable state of preservation. The lower level once consisted of storage areas and stalls where trade was carried out; the merchants' lodgings were on the upper level. The large trough (now used as a dustbin) at the centre was for the animals.

Of striking contrast is the ramshackle **Khan al-Shuna**, in a rundown area just west of Khan al-Umdan. Many of Acre's Arab residents live around here in houses built during the Crusader period, when this quarter belonged to natives of Pisa.

The port area

Acre's **port** is still perhaps the most attractive part of the Old City, where you can dine on freshly caught fish while watching the fishermen clean and repair their nets. **Boat trips** (20min; 10NIS) around the city walls leave from the end of the pier. From the port, the walls curve past the white stone **Church of St John**, dedicated to two British officers who fell at Acre in 1799 and 1940, to Acre's southernmost point, marked by a working **lighthouse**. The breach in the walls to the north of this was caused by an earthquake in 1837, as was the fall of the original lighthouse, whose remains, known as the **Tower of the Flies**, can be seen out in the bay to the east.

The beaches

The only things of interest in Acre outside the walls of its Old City are the **beaches**. HaHomot Beach, by Bab al-Ard, is closest to the Old City but it's not the nicest for swimming or sunbathing, though you can hire windsurfing gear here. The best beach is **Argaman ("purple") Beach**, 300m or so to its east, and so called because the Romans used to come here for the *murex* shellfish that provided their imperial purple dye. Views of the Old City from the beach are great, and on a clear day you can even see Haifa. If you fancy **diving**, The Diving Centre, by the port, offers courses and, for qualified divers, the chance to explore some of the wrecks just off-shore; they also rent masks, fins and snorkels by the day.

Eating, drinking and nightlife

When it comes to food, it's best to head for the **Old City**. The winding streets of the souq around the Khan al-Franj and Venezia Square harbour a number of good **cafés** serving falafel, hummus and snacks, while for delicious Arab coffee and mint tea, try the **qahwas**

Bethlehem: the Church of the Nativity

Bethlehem: the Chapel of the Manger – on the spot where Jesus was born

Tulul Abu al-'Alayiq, with Jericho in the background

Timna Valley: 'The Mushroom' rock formation

Jericho: the magnificent mosaic at Hisham's Palace

Hebron: the Haram al-Khalil (Tomb of the Patriarchs)

Eilat: diver and shoal of fish in the Red Sea

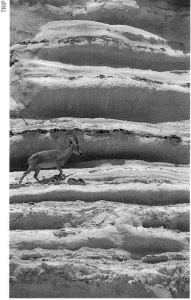
The Negev: ibex, Ein Avdat

Beersheba market

Masada: view from the fortress over the Roman camp

(coffee houses) just north of Khan al-Umdan, patronized by (almost exclusively male) locals relaxing over games of cards, chess and backgammon. The cheapest **restaurants** are mostly in the northern part of the Old City, along Saladin and al-Jazzar; they usually serve both Arab and European dishes for $2–6. For those not on a strict budget, the *Oudah Brothers Restaurant*, inside the Khan al-Franj (☎04/991 2013; daily 9am–midnight; moderate), is pricier than most Old City eateries, but excellent value, serving mezze, *shashlik* and other Middle Eastern favourites as well as great seafood. Equally good is the *Galileo* (☎04/991 4610; daily 9am–midnight; moderate), opposite the *Akko Youth Hostel*; its large helpings of Middle Eastern food will hit your hunger where it hurts.

Restaurants on the waterfront all serve fish plus regular Middle Eastern fare and have the added advantage of wonderful sea air and views (which may include wedding parties taking photos on the old walls). *Abu Christo*, right by the port (☎04/991 0065; daily 10am–midnight; moderate), is something of an institution, with a reputation as the home of some of the best seafood in the north of Israel. It's a huge place, with over 500 seats, and great views over the bay towards Haifa. *Ptolemais* opposite the marina (☎04/991 6112; daily summer 10am–midnight, winter 10am–8pm; moderate) is also good for Middle Eastern cuisine.

The *Abu Christo* is also a good place to go for a **drink** in the evening, as is the *Café Toscana* next door. These and the other bars around the port are the liveliest places inside the Old City.

Although **New Acre** has perhaps a wider choice of cuisine, it offers little of the atmosphere of the Old City. Its restaurants, cafés and bars, with a more European menu and higher prices than their Old City rivals, crowd on and around Ben Ami and Yehoshafat streets. The *Palm Beach* and *Argaman* hotels both have good restaurants and lay on night-time entertainment and discos.

Listings

Banks and exchange Most of the large banks are located on Ben Ami St, between the intersection of HaArba and Haim Weizmann. In the Old City, the Mercantile Discount Bank, al-Jazzar St, has an exchange bureau. If you get stuck for cash, the intersection of al-Jazzar and Haim Weizmann is the focus of a small black market.

Medical services There's a first-aid post at 2 Ben Ami, on the corner of HaHaganah (☎04/991 2333 or ☎101).

Police 2 Ben Ami, at the corner of HaHaganah (☎04/991 0244 or ☎100).

Post office Main office at 11 HaAtzma'ut St, off Haim Weizmann (Mon, Tues, Thurs 8am–12.30pm & 4pm–6pm; Mon, Wed & Fri 8am–12.30pm); it has an international telephone centre and poste restante facilities. There is also a small post office beside the underground Crusader City on al-Jazzar St (July & Aug Sun–Thurs 8am–2pm, Fri 8am–noon; Sept–June Sun, Tues & Thurs 8am–12.30pm & 3.30pm–6pm, Mon & Wed 8am–1pm).

Telecommunications International phones in the main post office.

MOVING ON FROM ACRE

Inter-city buses, sherut taxis and trains regularly connect Acre with most places in the country. Services from the **bus station** include Haifa (4 per hour; 30min), Karmiel (every 30min; 30min), Nahariyya (4 per hour; 30min), Safed (every 30min; 1hr) and Tiberias (hourly; 2hr). **Sheruts** leave from the main stand to Haifa, Nahariyya and Safed. Palestinian service taxis to the villages of central Galilee also stop around here. There are ten **trains** daily (except on Shabbat and festivals) to Nahariyya (12min), with fourteen heading south to Haifa (30–40min), Netanya (1hr 30min–1hr 45min) and Tel Aviv (1hr 45min–2hr), where one connects for Jerusalem, and two a week continue to Beersheba (4hr).

Acre to Nahariyya

The flat coastal land north of Acre, known simply as the **Plain of Acre**, stretches a little over 20km from the city to the Lebanese border. **Nahariyya**, just over halfway and linked to Acre by regular buses and trains, is one of Israel's best beach resorts. If you are planning a leisurely trip, preferably by car, there are a couple of places worth stopping at on your way to Nahariyya.

The Bahai Shrine and Gardens

Just 3km north of Acre, the **Bahai Shrine and Gardens** are a tranquil monument to the Bahai religion; the place where the Baha'Ullah (see box p.139) was placed under house arrest on his release from Acre prison, and where he died in 1892. His ornate tomb and the mansion in which he lived, now containing displays of religious artefacts, have become a shrine for members of the Bahai faith, though the **house** (Sun, Mon, Fri & Sat 9am–noon) will only really be of interest if you want to learn more about the religion. The **gardens** (daily 9am–4pm; free) are lush and peaceful, offering welcome shade.

Buses #271 and #251 from Acre (10min) run along the main Acre–Nahariyya road; look out for the sign "Shomrat". The entrance is a short distance down a side road to the right; only members of the faith can use the gilded gates just before the sign.

Kibbutz Lohamei HaGeta'ot

A couple of kilometres north of the Bahai tomb, to the east of the main coastal road, **Kibbutz Lohamei HaGeta'ot** (Fighters of the Ghetto) has one of the largest collections of material relating to the Holocaust in the country. Founded in 1948 by survivors of the concentration camps and ghettoes of Eastern Europe, the centrepiece of the kibbutz is its **museum** (☎04/995 8080; Sun–Thurs 9am–4pm, Fri 9am–1pm, Sat & Jewish holidays 10am–5pm; free but donation requested; guided tours by appointment only) focusing on the struggles of these Jewish communities against fascism and confronting the question as to why, in the main, the Jews failed to fight back, and citing instances

---

THE WARSAW GHETTO UPRISING

The Nazis opened the **Warsaw Ghetto** in October 1940, forcing all the region's Jews to move in and all non-Jewish residents to leave. No-one could enter or leave without a permit and very soon, with food and fuel scarce, conditions worsened and the ghetto's population shrank: by the time mass deportations to the death camps started in the summer of 1942, a fifth of the population had already died. Zionist and Communist cells, which had formed to defend the Jewish community against pogroms before the construction of the ghetto, now began to organize **resistance**. In early 1943, the Nazis moved in to seize deportees, street fighting broke out, and a permanent curfew was imposed. The resistance cells came together as the **ZOB** ("Jewish Fighting Organization") under **Mordekhai Ankiewitz**, and took to the streets on April 19 when the Nazis attempted further deportations. Fighting continued even after the Nazis took the ZOB's headquarters on May 8, killing Ankiewitz, and though resistance inside the ghetto had been wiped out by July, fifty Jewish fighters escaped and fled to the forest to continue the armed struggle alongside the Polish resistance. Ankiewitz is honoured in modern Israel both at Kibbutz Lohamei HaGeta'ot, and at Kibbutz Mordekhai, south of Ashqelon (see p.118), which is named after him.

where they did. A visit to the museum is, inevitably, a horrific but memorable experience; its collection, housed on four floors, includes photographic and documentary exhibits on life in East European Jewish communities before the Nazi occupation, and life, death and rebellion in the ghettoes – especially the 1943 **Warsaw Ghetto Uprising** (see box on p.228) – and the death camps. There is also a memorial to Janusz Korczak (see p.375) and one – Yad La-Yeled – dedicated to the 1.5 million children who perished during the Holocaust. An **art collection** includes works produced in the concentration camps and by survivors. The museum also contains an archive and library. Every year, on Yom HaShoah or **Holocaust Memorial Day**, the amphitheatre near the museum plays host to thousands of Israelis and visitors from abroad who come to participate in a sombre ceremony in remembrance of the Warsaw Ghetto Uprising.

The kibbutz itself, with fewer than 300 members and around thirty volunteers, survives on an agricultural base, supplementing its income by farming fish and running the museum. **Accommodation** is available (☎04/993 3271, fax 993 3218; ④); rooms have air-conditioning and TV, and facilities include a swimming pool, tennis and basketball courts.

Beside the kibbutz is the most easily accessible part of an Ottoman **aqueduct**, which runs from Acre to the Kabri Springs east of Nahariyya (see p.234). Built under al-Jazzar in 1789, the archways are extremely well preserved, despite being an obvious target for anyone attacking Acre – when Napoleon besieged the town, one of the first things he did was destroy part of it. After the defeat of the French, al-Jazzar's successor, Suleiman Pasha, built a replacement, which ran east of this one. Although much of this survives, too, it is harder to get to, with no access by road.

Nahariyya

Israel's northernmost beach resort, **NAHARIYYA**, is set on a rugged coastline with miles of glistening white sands and turquoise sea. It's an appealing place, retaining some old-fashioned charm and serenity (at least outside the height of summer), while its mixed Israeli and European population of 44,000, swelled by members of the UN peace-keeping forces serving in South Lebanon or the Golan, gives the place a marked cosmopolitan character.

Founded by German Jews in 1934, Nahariyya was originally conceived as a dairy and poultry centre, and today its main industries, apart from tourism, are the Strauss Dairy – famous throughout Israel for its ice cream – and a major meat-processing plant, which began as a German sausage-making factory. Locals joke that the town must be very kosher, since milk products made in the south of the city are separated from the meat stuffs produced in the north by the River Ga'aton in the centre. The latter, after which the town is named (river being *nahar* in Hebrew), flows down the main street, Sederot HaGa'aton, and waters the towering eucalyptus trees shading the central avenues. The trees, planted by the first settlers in an effort to dry up the mosquito-ridden swamps, have done their job well: you might still get bitten, but you won't catch malaria.

Modern Nahariyya has for years marketed itself as a **honeymoon** hideaway. On Lag Ba'Omer – the 33rd day after Passover, and the only day in the six-week period following that festival when Jewish couples are permitted to wed under Jewish law – you can see just how successful the campaign has been. The hotels are full of young couples and special activities are laid on by the municipality and local businesses.

Apart from its **beaches**, Nahariyya's proximity to several other resorts and sights makes it a good base for exploring the Upper Galilee; Acre is just 11km south, Akhziv 3km north, and Rosh HaNiqra 13km to the north.

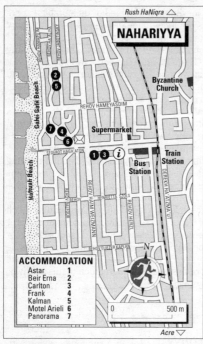

Rush HaNiqra △

NAHARIYYA

Galei Galil Beach

Byzantine Church

REHOV HAMEYASDIM

Supermarket

SEDEROT HAGA'ATON

Hattush Beach

Train Station

Bus Station

REHOV NAIM WEIZMANN

REHOV HERZL

DERKEKH HA'ATZMA'UT

REHOV ELIEZER KAPLAN

N

ACCOMMODATION
Astar	1
Beir Erna	2
Carlton	3
Frank	4
Kalman	5
Motel Arieli	6
Panorama	7

0   500 m

Acre ▽

Arrival and information

Arriving by **bus**, you will find your-self in the centre of Nahariyya on the main street, Sederot HaGa'aton; the **train** station is just to the east. The helpful municipal **tourist office** is a short distance towards the sea, on the ground floor of the Municipality Building in a little square on the south side of HaGa'aton (☎04/987 9800; Sun–Thurs 9am–1pm & 4–7pm, Fri 9am–4pm). Here you can get information about events in town and tours in the region, whether by bus or jeep or on horseback. A trio of **banks** can be found on HaGa'aton, as can the **post office** at no. 40. **Car rental** is available from Budget at 35 Lohamei HaGeta'ot (☎04/992 9252 or 3), Eurodollar at 66 Weizmann (☎04/992 1614), or Europcar at 63 Weizmann (☎04/982 6005).

Accommodation

Narahiyya offers a good range of **accommodation** in all price ranges. Be warned that rates rocket during the summer months and Jewish holidays, though at other times you should be able to bargain for the price. The budget **hostel**-type places crowd around Rehov Wolfson, which runs off HaGa'aton directly opposite the Egged Bus Tours office in the bus station. Of these, *Rehayim*, at no. 6 (☎04/992 0557; ①), is the best-value in town, with dorm beds for $4.50; it also rents out bicycles to res-idents and non-residents. The tourist office stocks a list of approved **zimmer** rooms, available in houses with "rooms to rent" signs outside. Many of these are very pleasant but can cost up to $50 in the summer (though here, too, you can try haggling out of sea-son). Several budget **hotels** can be found along Rehov Jabotinsky, parallel to the beach, with most of the upmarket options around HaGa'aton.

Sleeping on the beach is tolerated, though to avoid any hassle you need to walk a little way out of the town. If you have trouble finding accommodation in Nahariyya itself, alternatives are available at Akhziv, 4km to the north (see p.233).

Hotels

Astar, 27 HaGa'aton (☎04/992 3431, fax 992 3411). A pleasant, modest hotel whose visitors tend to return. Rooms have cable TV, a/c, telephone and baths, and prices include breakfast. However, its real strength is *Lachmi's Vegetarian Restaurant* in the grounds (see "Eating and drinking" on p.231). A ten percent discount is available for students or stays of more than three days. ④.

Beit Erna, 29 Jabotinsky (☎04/992 0170). Clean, bright and one of the better of several budget hotels along this road. ③.

Carlton, 23 HaGa'aton (☎04/922 2211, fax 982 3771). A former four-star establishment with a swim-ming pool, Jacuzzi and sauna. Its nightclub hosts occasional live shows on Thurs, Fri and Sat; entrance around NIS50. ⑥.

Frank, 4 HaAliya (☎04/992 0278, fax 992 5535). A rather sedate establishment, just a few steps from the beach, with a swimming pool, Jacuzzi and shaded garden. All rooms have TV, telephone and a/c. ⑤.

Kalman, 27 Jabotinsky (☎04/992 0355, fax 992 6539). Run by the HI but not really a hostel, this is one of the better Jabotinsky hotels with spotless, air-conditioned rooms. ③.

Motel Arieli, 1 Jabotinsky (☎04/992 1076). A reasonable budget establishment with bungalows as well as rooms in the main building. ③.

Panorama, 6 HaMa'pilim (☎04/992 0555, fax 992 5467). A pleasant, three-star equivalent right on the beach and boasting a roof with a view (hence the name). ⑥.

Sirtash House, 22 Jabotinsky (☎04/992 2586, fax 992 6539). Small but clean rooms with a/c, TV and bathrooms. ②.

The Town

During the day, there is little to do in Nahariyya but go to the **beach**. The most popular and central is **Galei Galil** – very clean and very crowded, with a full-time lifeguard and an Olympic-size outdoor pool. The admission fee (14.50NIS) includes use of the volleyball and basketball courts. South of Galei Galil, a *tayelet* (promenade) is being built which, when complete, will be lined with cafés, restaurants and pubs. Other free, more secluded, beaches lie south of the *tayelet*; these are not patrolled by lifeguards, so beware of the strong currents.

Culture is not the strong point of this resort town, but if you get bored with the beach, you could spend a couple of hours exploring Nahariyya's small **Municipal Museum** (Mon, Tues & Thurs 10am–12pm, Sun & Wed also 4pm–6pm; free). Housed in the Municipality Building on HaGa'aton, it offers a four-in-one deal: an art section with an exhibition of works by Israeli and foreign artists; an archeology section exhibiting finds from the area from prehistoric to Roman-Byzantine periods, including a human-shaped cover for a burial shrine and a limestone altar dedicated to the emperor Nero; a section devoted to the molluscs of the Mediterranean and the Red seas and a collection of seashells from around the world; and finally, a display on the history of Nahariyya from 1934 to the present.

The museum also arranges guided tours of **archeological sites** in the vicinity. One, a twenty-minute stroll north of Galei Galil, is a 4000-year-old **Canaanite temple**, discovered in 1947. Some say this was a shrine to Ashra, the goddess of seafarers, while others claim it was dedicated to the fertility goddess Asherah, which seems somehow appropriate to Nahariyya's image as a honeymoon hideaway.

Also worth a look are the recently reconstructed remains of a **Byzantine church** east of the town centre on Rehov Bielefeld (☎04/982 3070 for prearranged tours; 3NIS). Considered to be one of the largest and best of churches built in the Western Galilee between the fourth and seventh centuries, its main feature is a beautiful multicoloured mosaic floor.

Eating and drinking

Restaurants in Nahariyya are plentiful and central, particularly along HaGa'aton. One of the best is undoubtedly *Lachmi's Vegetarian Restaurant*, on the ground floor of the *Astar* hotel (see above). The choice of breakfasts – Israeli, Hungarian, Romanian, South American (25–30NIS) – is staggering, while at other times the menu features a vast array of reasonably priced light meals (11–25NIS), plus cakes, drinks and alcoholic ice-cream beverages. Another excellent place on HaGa'aton, especially for breakfasts, is the *Royal Café*.

MOVING ON FROM NAHARIYYA

From the **bus** station, there are services to Acre (every 15min; 20min), Akhziv (hourly; 15min), Haifa (every 15min; 45min), Jerusalem (3 daily; 4hr), Peqi'in (9 daily; 45 min); Rosh HaNiqra (6 daily; 30min), Tel Aviv (2 daily; 2hr 30min) and Yehiam (3 daily; 30min). There are ten daily departures by **train** to Acre (9min), Haifa (45min), Netanya (1hr 45min) and Tel Aviv (2hr 15min).

For more substantial but cheap food try the local branch of the *Pizzeria Capri* chain, in Kikar HaBanim just off HaGa'aton, or *The Pinguin* at 31 HaGa'aton (daily 8am–midnight; cheap), established since 1940 and serving good pasta dishes, blintzes, schnitzels and salads, with a café of the same name next door for a drink or a snack. If you want something more exotic, there's plenty to choose from: try the *Salaam Bombay* Indian restaurant, 17 Jabotinsky; the *Chinese Inn Restaurant*, 28 HaGa'aton; or the Romanian *Donnau Restaurant*. The *Singapore*, at the junction with Jabotinsky with HaMeyasdim (☎04/992 4952; daily noon–3pm & 7pm–midnight; moderate to expensive), is another good Chinese option also serving several Singaporean specialities. Finally, if you need a plain, nourishing meal and are short of cash, the Egged restaurant in the bus station is hard to beat. The best place to buy your own food is the large Supersol **supermarket**, at the intersection of HaGa'aton and Herzl streets.

At night everyone heads for the **bars** at the beach end of HaGa'aton, which is closed to traffic at weekends and given over to revelry. There are a couple of **nightclubs** behind the bus station and, during July and August, there's dancing in the amphitheatre at the mouth of the Ga'aton River.

Around Nahariyya

There are several interesting day trips north and east of Nahariyya, all of them accessible by public transport. Six kilometres to the north is the coastal site of **Akhziv National Park**, with the Lebanese border at **Rosh HaNiqra** a further 5km away. The campsite and picnic area at **Kabri Springs** lies 5km east along Route 89, with the Crusader fortresses of **Monfort Castle** to the north of the road, and **Jedin** at Yehiam National Park due south.

Akhziv National Park

The Kziv River flows out to the sea 5km north of Nahariyya in **Akhziv National Park** (Sat–Thurs 8am–5pm; Fri 8am–4pm; 10NIS), a stretch of manicured lawns and barbecue areas whose centrepiece is **Tel Akhziv**, the remains of a Phoenician port from the eighth century BC. There's also a sheltered sandy **beach** (daily 8am–5pm; 6NIS) with changing rooms, showers, snack bar and restaurant.

Outside the entrance to the National Park, the plaque reading "During the Talmudic period, Akhziv had a flourishing Jewish community... In later centuries it declined into a coastal village" refers to the Palestinian village of al-Zib, whose population numbered almost ten thousand until their departure in 1948. Most of the buildings inside the park are remnants of this village: beautiful white stone structures now transformed into restaurants and changing rooms. An account of the village's history is given in Nahariyya's Municipal Museum (see p.231). Near the entrance, the **Akhziv Diving Club** or Track Yam (☎04/982 3671, fax 928 0146) offers diving trips that include the beautiful undersea caves and crevices around the three small **Akhziv Islands**, 1500m offshore. You can also hire snorkelling equipment here or join sailing or jeep trips.

A few minutes' walk north of the National Park, **Akhzivland** was proclaimed an "Independent State" in 1952 by flamboyant eccentric Eli Avivi on land leased from the Israel Lands Authority. This incurred the wrath of the Israeli authorities, who spent the next fifteen years trying to oust him; on one occasion Avivi spent ten days in prison for relinquishing his Israeli citizenship and passport. Nowadays an effective truce has been declared, and Akhzivland has become a respectable tourist attraction – take your passport and get a colourful little Akhzivland entry stamp outlining Avivi's territory. There's a fascinating **museum** here, in part of a house that belonged to an al-Zib notable before 1948 (April–Sept 8am–5pm, Oct–March 8am–4pm; 7NIS). The exhibits, all collected locally, constitute a unique historical document of human settlement here, from Phoenician, Roman, Byzantine, Crusader and Arab artefacts to reminders of life in the Arab village.

ACCOMMODATION
Volunteers are always needed to excavate the area and maintain Akhzivland's extensive gardens. If you work for two hours you get to stay free at Avivi's **hostel** (no phone; ②) and while the accommodation is not palatial, staying in Akhzivland will never be anything less than entertaining. If that doesn't appeal you can pitch your own tent at Akhziv's **campsite** (☎04/982 5054; ①), just south of the National Park, or stay in one of the bamboo huts (up to 4 people per hut; ②). Facilities include communal toilets and showers, a swimming pool and a supermarket. Other alternatives are *Akhziv Holiday Village* (☎04/982 3602, fax 982 6030), to the north, which has a camping area (①) with shower and cooking areas, air-conditioned wood cabins (⑤), a pub with shows and dancing, and garden restaurant, or the *HI Yad LeYad Youth Hostel* (☎04/982 3345, fax 982 0632; ②) beyond. It's also possible to stay at the SPNI's field school, a couple of hundred metres further north (☎04/982 3762, fax 982 3015; ②); dorm rooms are available, with communal showers, toilets, and dining room, and a splendid rooftop overlooking the sea. You can join jeep, boat and snorkelling trips here.

For a little more comfort, **Kibbutz Gesher Haziv**, on a hill 1km off the coastal road inland from Akhziv National Park (☎04/982 5715, fax 982 5718; ⑤; breakfast included) is a clean and comfortable 26-room guesthouse with an excellent restaurant, nightclub and bar, sports facilities and a large, open-air swimming pool accessible to non-residents when not too crowded. Horse, jeep and tractor tours are also on offer. The kibbutz itself was founded to commemorate an incident that occurred during the **"Night of the Bridges"** (see p.493), on June 17, 1946, when fourteen Haganah members were killed as the explosives they were installing to blow up a bridge were ignited by a British soldier's flare.

Rosh HaNiqra
The most northerly point on Israel's Mediterranean coast, **Rosh HaNiqra** is a small border crossing between Israel and Lebanon with fabulous views and, surprisingly given its significance, a peaceful ambience. The main attractions here, however, are the craggy white chalk cliffs, riddled with an intricate maze of natural **caves** that form a reserve of unique flora and fauna. Rosh HaNiqra – a Hebraicized version of the Arabic *Ras Naqura* or "head of the grotto" – is topped by an **observation point** (Sun–Thurs: summer 8.30am–6pm, open till 11pm & Fri 8.30am–3pm during July & Aug; winter 8.30am–4pm), from where you can see Haifa on a clear day. Here, too, is the "Peace Train", an audiovisual show; and cable cars down into the caves (18NIS). A reasonable self-service **restaurant** (Sun–Thurs: winter 8.30am–4pm, summer 8.30am–6pm; Fri 8.30am–3pm) provides kosher fare and sea views.

The **Lebanese border** is closed to tourists, but in fact the Israeli presence in South Lebanon since 1982 means that the whole border area, stretching as far as 40km to the north, is effectively under Israeli control anyway. It is a sensitive military zone, so ask before taking photos of the fence or anything military. The *HI Rosh HaNiqra Youth Hostel* offers **accommodation** in pretty gardens at the foot of the cliffs (☎04/982 5169, fax 928 1330; ②/③). Facilities include sports equipment, swimming pool, snack bar and private beach. **Buses** #20 and #22 run three times daily between Rosh HaNiqra and Nahariyya, taking around half an hour.

Kabri Springs and Montfort Castle

Five kilometres east of Nahariyya, just off Route 89 to Ma'alot Tarshiha, the **Kabri Springs** provide a relaxing setting for a large, well-developed picnic area. The springs have provided cool, clear water for centuries: the Phoenicians were the first to build an aqueduct to divert it, and both Greeks and Romans followed suit. The Crusaders believed the water to have miraculous properties, and it was bottled and drunk throughout Palestine well into this century – one fifty-year-old guide book described it as "the only thing to drink in Palestine: don't be put off by something 'just as good' – it does not exist". Nowadays most bottled water comes from springs in the Golan, but you can still test its medicinal qualities, said to be especially good for digestive problems.

You can get to the springs on **bus** #43, which runs 18km inland from Nahariyya to the village of **MI'ILYA**, site of one of three Crusader fortresses built to protect Acre (the other two being Jedin, p.235, and Montfort, see below). All that remains of the **King's Castle** at Mi'ilya is a single hall on the eastern edge of the village facing neighbouring Tarshiha (see p.238). Mi'ilya is also a possible alighting point (the other is Goren, served several times daily by bus #25 from Nahariyya) for the famous Crusader castle of **Montfort** (Sat–Thurs 8am–5pm, Fri 8am–4pm; 5NIS), high on a hill overlooking a particularly lush valley, and built in the twelfth century on the remains of a Roman fortress. In 1228 the French Crusaders sold Montfort ("Strong Hill") to the Teutonic Order of Knights, supported by the German emperor Frederick II, who renamed it **Starkenburg** ("Strong Castle") and used it as their headquarters in the Holy Land. Although its strategic importance was small, the castle served as an administrative centre and useful source of income: taxes collected from the local peasantry in about fifty surrounding villages ensured its economic independence. Saladin captured and damaged the castle in 1187, but it was subsequently reconquered and rebuilt by the Crusaders. The Mamluk sultan Baybars unsuccessfully besieged the castle for months in 1266; five years later, however, his troops scaled the surrounding slopes and managed to tunnel a hole in the western wall. The Crusaders made a hasty retreat to Acre, and the castle was destroyed.

The five-kilometre **walk** from Mi'ilya up to the castle is as great an attraction as the ruins themselves, though the rough path requires sensible footwear. From Mi'ilya, follow the road towards the village of Hila; the road takes a sharp right and a little wooden sign points down a dusty track to Montfort. It's a further 1.5km from here to the castle along a trail marked with red and white posts. This is the most scenic part of the walk, winding through the wooded Wadi Qurein to arrive at the ruins. The **wall** to the left of the path up to the castle shows a breach thought to date from Baybars' siege. The original tower with high ceilings and balconies is directly opposite the entrance, while to the right are two vaulted chambers forming the foundations of a large meeting hall. Beside the tower lie a ruined chapel and a group of rooms that may have served as kitchens or armouries. At the far eastern side are the remains of the keep or citadel, overlooking a deep moat, with a great view of the Kziv River and the surrounding countryside.

If you want to **hike** the 12km back to Akhziv, you can descend from the keep and follow the marked trails along the banks of the River Kziv. Just below the castle, a rather unimposing two-storey building of Crusader origin, perhaps part of a farm, contains handsome arches on the second floor; there are rumours of a secret passageway from here up to the castle. Other sites along the river include the ruins of twelve ancient flour mills. The springs at the end of the Kziv River have large pools to bathe in, well worth the walk on a hot day.

Yehiam National Park

The third and best-preserved of the Crusader strongholds, **Jedin Fortress** (Sun–Thurs 8am–5pm, Fri 8am–4pm; 6NIS), lies 6km south of Montfort, high on the hills guarding the ancient road from Acre to Lebanon. Here, next to the forested **Nahal Yehiam Nature Reserve** with its popular hiking trail, the remains of Roman, Byzantine, Crusader, Ottoman and Bedouin settlements have been restored under the aegis of the National Parks Authority.

Together with Mi'ilya and Montfort, the fortress, thought to have been part of a fortified agricultural settlement (a prototype border kibbutz), passed over to the Teutonic Crusader order at the start of the thirteenth century and, like its neighbours, was destroyed with the Mamluk conquest under Sultan Baybars. However, it was thoroughly renovated in the eighteenth century under Daher al-Omar, who built "a large fortress with round towers and a moat hewn into the rocks". Though abandoned with the end of Daher's rule in Galilee in 1775, the remains are still impressive. The **burial caves** near the present entrance are Byzantine in origin, while a restored **bathhouse** within the complex dates from Roman times. However, the major constructions are the central **tower** and three-storey building, vaulted in typical Crusader style, and the defensive walls. Daher's reconstructed and fortified entrance gate to the fortress is true to the original style.

Jedin played a strategic role in more recent times when settlers of the HaShomer HaTza'ir movement established a kibbutz here in 1946 and turned the fortress into a military training camp. **Kibbutz Yehiam** was named after Yehiam Weitz, who was killed during the "Night of the Bridges" in June 1946 (see p.233). Defence posts on the ancient walls – still visible in positions around the fortress – enabled the settlers to hold out during the war of 1948, despite being cut off from other Jewish settlements. The Haganah lost a fleet of armoured trucks when it was ambushed at Kabri, 9km to the east, in March 1948, while trying to get through to Yehiam.

Three daily **buses** connect Yehiam to Nahariyya, and the fortress is well signposted from the kibbutz. If you're driving, take Route 89 from Nahariyya towards Ma'alot Tarshiha; turn right at Ga'aton Junction to Yehiam.

East of Acre: Routes 85 and 864

The main road **east of Acre** (Route 85) is one of the most picturesque in the country, encapsulating in a few kilometres all the beauty and ruggedness of the Galilee, from stunning mountain ranges to wide open plains. Leaving Acre, the route crosses the fertile coastal plain, passing a number of large kibbutzim, until it reaches the slopes of **Mount Gamal** at the staggered **Ahihud Junction**, about 10km east. Here, Route 70 branches off north, tracing the fringe of the highlands through Upper Galilee and all the way up to the Lebanese border, and south into the valleys of Lower Galilee, while Route 85 heads on into the Palestinian heartland of the Galilee, through the valley of **Bik'at Bet HaKerem**, crowded with olive groves – some of the trees here are estimated to be around 2000 years old and are said to have supplied oil for the Temple lamps in Jerusalem. At **Rama**, 25km east of Acre, Route 864 leads north through dramatic mountain scenery to **Ma'alot Tarshiha**; staying on Route 85 you come to the wooded mountains around Safed (see p.238).

The road is well served by frequent **buses** for Safed, Golan and Qiryat Shemona. It's easy enough to break your journey at any point and to continue by flagging down the next bus or one of the sherut taxis that also ply the route.

Majd al-Kurum and Deir al-Assad

On the far slope of **Mount Gamal**, the road descends amongst swathes of olive trees that were once the economic mainstay of local Palestinian villages Majd al-Kurum, Bi'na and Deir al-Assad. Many of the groves have been neglected since 1948 when Israeli authorities confiscated the land of Palestinians who had fled, but the remaining villagers, refused permission to cultivate the refugees' groves, continue to harvest their own around the end of September, using traditional methods; large cloths or nets are placed on the ground to collect the olives which are knocked or shaken from the trees with the aid of a long pole.

The first village you pass is **MAJD AL-KURUM**, approximately 16km east of Acre. Reputed to be the site of Bet Kerem, a Jewish settlement mentioned in the Talmud, today it has a Palestinian population of around six thousand; at its centre are an ancient well, a spring, a Roman tomb and remains from the Crusader period. You can linger a while in one of the cafés in the centre and soak up the atmosphere or even stay in locally owned accommodation; details are available from the new **information centre** (☎04/988 3750).

A couple of kilometres east of Majd al-Kurum, a small, winding road climbs north between a couple of villages situated high on slopes of the **Tefen Plateau**. Deir al-Assad, to the right, is Muslim, while Bi'na, on the left, is predominantly Christian, though distinctions have blurred in recent years as growing populations force each to straggle across the dividing line. As most buses continue along the main road, to visit the villages you'll either have to walk up the hill or stand at the junction and flag down a passing car.

According to local tradition, **DEIR AL-ASSAD** (Arabic for "Monastery of the Lion") was founded in the early sixteenth century. The story of the village's conception reads like a fairy tale: in 1516, so the legend goes, Sheikh Mohammed al-Assad set out from Safed on his donkey and, after many hours, stopped near a well to pray and fill his water-skin. While he was praying, a lion killed his donkey, whereupon he took the saddle from the dead beast's back, put it on the lion, and continued on his journey. As he approached Nahaf (a village a couple of kilometres east of Deir al-Assad), he met the troops of Ottoman general Sinan Pasha, travelling to Gaza and Egypt. After many of the pasha's horses had bolted in panic at the sight of the lion, Sinan turned to the sheikh and offered to grant him a wish. Sheikh al-Assad pointed to the nearby monastery of **St Georges de Labeyne** and asked for the deeds to the property. These he was granted and, having expelled the monks, he founded and developed the village of Deir al-Assad on the ruins of the monastery.

Events here in **1948** were of a much less story-book nature. Following the end of the second truce on October 29 (see p.495), the Arab Liberation Army (ALA) irregulars, who had been operating in the Galilee highlands, withdrew in the face of advancing Israeli forces, leaving the region's Arab villages undefended. The *mukhtars* (village leaders) of Deir al-Assad and Bi'na went to the Israeli command post in neighbouring al-Birwa and surrendered. Israeli troops arrived two days later, assembled all the villagers in the main square and commenced a search for ALA members. Villagers who asked to go to the nearby well to get water were allowed to go, but then mown down with automatic gunfire; of those remaining, some were taken prisoner, the rest ordered to disperse, though villagers who had not fled across the border to Lebanon were subsequently allowed to return.

Like many surviving Palestinian villages in the Galilee, present-day Deir al-Assad is a run-down place. But although its agricultural base is being whittled away, it is still famous for the quality of its **olive oil**, sold during harvest-time from the store that doubles as the village post office. The **mosque**, near the centre of the village, is a fine example of traditional local architecture, as indeed are the older parts of the village, east of the central square. Here, among remnants of early Arab and Crusader architecture, parts of the monastery of St Georges de Labeyne can still be seen; note the large circular rooms which remain cool in the long, hot summer months. If the heat is getting to you, retire to the **café** by the village square, which serves a selection of pastries and even cold beer during the summer months.

The walk to the top of the village provides some of the most breathtaking **views** in the country. To the south lies the Lower Galilee region, with the tower blocks of Jewish Karmiel in the foreground (see p.171); to the west you can see the Mediterranean shimmering in the distance. On the road leading north out of the village to the Tefen Plateau are rock-cut **caves and tombs** from the Byzantine period, now used by village herdsmen to pen goats and sheep.

Rama to Ma'alot Tarshiha

North of the Bik'at Bet HaKerem valley, the mountains rise to over 1200m, their upper slopes liberally sprinkled with Druze villages. Snaking from the junction at **Rama** to **Ma'alot Tarshiha**, Route 864 offers stunning views and is worth the climb if only to visit the picturesque village of **Peqi'in**. Note that some buses from Rama go only as far as the village of Bet Jann.

Rama and Bet Jann

Lying at the junction of Routes 85 and 864, the Druze village of **RAMA** has a large café-restaurant serving a variety of delicious traditional Arab dishes. For the fit and adventurous, the initial climb out of Rama, up punishing gradients to the Tefen Plateau makes a great hike – take plenty of water and leave early as there's nowhere to stay in any of the villages along the way.

A few kilometres north of Rama, a right-hand turning off Route 864 brings you to the first of these villages, **BET JANN**, perched high on the summit of Mount Meron and commanding magnificent vistas of wooded hills. There are numerous treks you can make from here to explore Mount Meron, and it's even possible to walk to Safed via the village of Meron on the far slope.

Peqi'in

Back on the main road to Tarshiha, tucked into the mountainside a few kilometres north of the Bet Jann junction, the village of **PEQI'IN** is well worth the climb. It's of particular interest for its mixed population of Druze, Christians and Muslims – the Muslim settlement of Peqi'in (al-Buqi'a in Arabic) dates from the eleventh century, Christians arrived during the Crusades and the Druze came in the eighteenth century. Although there has been a Jewish presence here since the destruction of the Second Temple in the second century AD, most of the community left during the Palestinian Revolt (1936–39) and did not return. Today, the village's one Jewish household announces itself with a large Star of David flag and is a few streets away from the modern village centre fronted by a functional municipal building.

The bus stops at the entrance to the village, where two café-restaurants serve Peqi'in's speciality – *khubz saaj*, a paper-thin **bread** baked on an inverted wok-shaped pot over an open fire, and eaten with *labaneh* or hummus. At *Kiosk Ra'aya*, on the left, you can sample the freshly baked bread while taking in breathtaking views from its verandah.

Getting lost in the maze of Peqi'in's streets is the best way to appreciate its rural ambience. The roadside map downhill from the café locates the various sites, but none is that impressive and they are best used as an excuse to wander around the village. Most crowd into a small sector that represents the oldest quarter, at the centre of which is Spring Square, where water from a spring trickles into a small pool by an ancient and venerated tree. Just off the square is the **synagogue**, a nineteenth-century structure incorporating the remains of a second-century one. Nearby are a Greek Catholic church and a couple of Druze *hilwe* (prayer halls), as well as an ancient oil press, flour mill and Jewish cemetery.

A winding road from the centre of the village leads up to the cave of **Rabbi Shimon Bar Yohai**, to which he is said to have fled from the Romans with his son Elazar following the Bar Kokhba revolt in the second century. According to tradition, they lived here for thirteen years, during which time the rabbi received daily visits from the prophet Elijah, who instructed him in the mysteries of the Torah. These discussions formed the basis of the *Zohar* (Book of Splendour), a seminal book in Jewish mysticism; his tomb, on Mount Meron near Safed, is the destination of thousands of Jewish pilgrims on Lag Ba'Omer (see p.247).

Ma'alot Tarshiha

The Arab township of **TARSHIHA**, 8km north of Peqi'in on Route 864, was the site of Christian-Muslim battles in Crusader times, and an ALA stronghold in 1948. Today its main attractions are a horseback riding ranch and a Saturday **flea market**. Adjoining it and under the same municipal council, the Jewish development town of **MA'ALOT** hit the headlines in May 1974 when three DFLP guerrillas penetrated the Lebanese border and captured the school, taking the teachers and children hostage, and demanding the release of 26 political prisoners. In the ensuing shootout, twenty children were killed along with the guerrillas. Today, Ma'alot is making its name with an artists' centre and sculpture-lined promenade, and a sculptors' symposium is held here every Passover (for information call ☎04/874 4890). Just north of Ma'alot Tarshiha is the village of Mi'ilya (see p.234).

Safed

The hilltop town of **SAFED** (variant spellings include Safad, Tzfat and Zefat) vies with Acre and Tiberias (see p.195) as Galilee's top tourist draw, boasting stunning views, fine ancient Islamic and Judaic architecture, and an air of tradition appropriate to its status as one of the four great Jewish holy towns. Indeed, it resembles a smaller, more intimate Jerusalem with its mix of secular and religious – the latter represented by the synagogues and Jewish study centres in the winding streets of the **Old City**, the former epitomized by the **Artists' Quarter**, where galleries sell prints of Orthodox Jews to coachloads of tourists.

As a bastion of Jewish orthodoxy, however, Safed has not allowed the outward changes to go too far: you won't find many bars or discos here, and in the secluded alleyways behind the prettified frontages, old traditions are staunchly maintained.

Some history

The hilltop position of Safed is a strategic one, with Lebanon to the north and the Sea of Galilee to the south, but its first real historical significance came in the first and second centuries AD when, like Tiberias, it became a haven for Jews after the failure of their two revolts against Roman rule. Most of what you actually see began to grow up almost a thousand years later, when the **Crusaders** conquered the town, ushering in a bloody

Safed's **telephone numbers** are all now seven-digit; if you have an old six-digit number, try adding a six at the beginning.

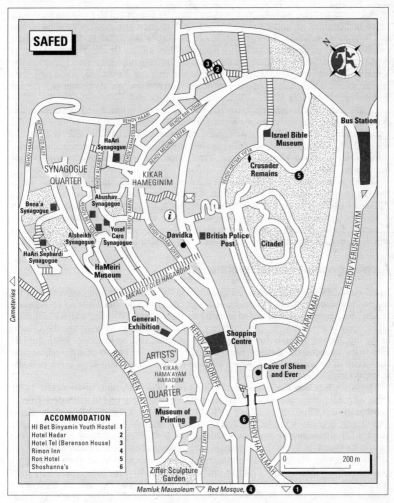

period that saw the Jewish community first decimated, then banished. When Saladin reconquered the region, ransacking the newly built Crusader fortress, Jews were briefly allowed back. But it was another century – until the Crusaders were finally driven from their kingdom based at Acre – before any sort of stability came to the town.

Under Mamluk control during the thirteenth century, Safed was a lively commercial centre, the capital of a province that included the Galilee and Lebanon. **Jewish immigration** began in earnest in 1492, when many of the thousands fleeing the Spanish Inquisition, often people of wealth and learning, ended up here. A letter sent from Safed in 1535 by an Italian Jewish merchant, David dei Rossi, describes how "improvements are being made and new settlements founded, while the population is increasing daily. ... He who saw Safed ten years ago, and observes it now, had the impression of a miracle. For more Jews are arriving here continually and the tailoring trade grows daily."

But it was not just business that was thriving: by the end of the sixteenth century, Safed had become an important centre of Jewish studies, attracting numerous scribes and holy men, including the foremost Kabbalist **Rabbi Isaac Luria**, and **Yosef Caro**, compiler of the authoritative code of Jewish law, the *Shulhan Arukh*. Many others were drawn to Safed for its proximity to the tomb of the Talmudic sage Rabbi Shimon ben Yohai at Meron (see p.247), whose writings inspired the Kabbalistic ideas of Jewish mysticism for which Safed became renowned. Today Safed stands alongside Tiberias, Hebron and Jerusalem as one of four cities holy to Judaism.

By the nineteenth century, however, the town's importance and population had declined considerably due to a combination of major earthquakes, famine and disease, and by 1948 the population of Safed consisted of 1500 mainly elderly Jews and over 10,000 Palestinian Arabs, the Jewish community having been considerably diminished following the 1929 ethnic riots, when 20 of them were murdered and many more fled.

British forces withdrew from Safed on April 16, 1948, leaving this vital strategic site to the Arabs. It was held by a force of Syrian mercenaries but Israeli troops under Yigal Allon captured it in house-to-house fighting on May 9, and its population fled, leaving only a hundred Arabs "with an average age of 80", who were rounded up and expelled to Lebanon. **Today**, Safed's population stands at just over twenty thousand, one quarter of which consists of recent Jewish immigrants from Eastern Europe, Russia and Ethiopia.

Arrival, orientation and information

Safed straddles three hills: atop the main one is the centre of town, containing all the major attractions, with the districts of South Safed and Mount Cana'an on adjacent peaks. The layout of **central Safed** is far from conventional. Winding stairwells make it all too easy to get lost, but it may help to visualise the town in three levels: the **Citadel** at the top; **Rehov Yerushalayim** girdling the middle; and, on the lower level, the **Old City** to the west and **the Artists' Quarter** in the south. The twenty-minute walk around the circuit of Jerusalem Street, which takes in the most important sites, is the best way to get yourself oriented.

The main **bus station** is in central Safed on Kikar HaAtzama'ut (☎06/692 1122), from where a ten-minute walk up Jerusalem Street will bring you to the **Safed Tourist Information Office**, at no. 50 (☎06/692 0961 or 2 or 3, fax 697 3666; Sun–Thurs 8am–4pm). Resources are limited, but the friendly staff do their best to be helpful and stock a list of private rooms in town. **Banks**, the post office and other businesses can mostly be found on Rehov Yerushalayim (see "Listings" on p.246 for more details).

For those with the time and inclination for some serious walking, Yisra'el Shalem's book *Safed, Six Self-Guided Tours in and around The Mystical City*, stocked by most bookshops in town, is invaluable. If you prefer a **guide** you can talk to, try Yisra'el Shalem (☎06/697 1870); Aviva Minoff (☎06/692 0901, fax 697 3116); Yisrael Ne'eman and Elliot Chodoff (☎06/674 1239); Yossi Reis (☎06/697 1803).

Accommodation

Much of the **accommodation** in Safed takes the form of private rooms or zimmerim. Demand is high during summer months, but you still shouldn't have too much difficulty finding something unless you plan to be here during the Kletzmer Music Festival (see p.245) when the town is packed, at which time it's best to book in advance. The simplest way to get a place to stay is to hang around the bus station until someone offers you a room, but check it out before accepting, and make sure that there are plenty of blankets – Safed can get cold at night. Prices are competitive and bargaining depends on season and availability.

Hostels and zimmerim

HI Bet Binyamin Youth Hostel, Lohamei HaGeta'ot, Hadar Quarter (☎06/692 1086). An HI hostel on the southern outskirts of town, with dorm beds and rooms. A 20min walk from the bus station or bus #6, #6a or #7. ②/③.

Ephraim Family, 27 Benei Betha (☎06/692 3221). Centrally located rooms with private bathroom, TV and radio. Book in advance. ⑤.

Rado Family, 55 Benei Betha (☎06/692 1276, not on Shabbat). Rooms in "villa" with bath, kitchenette and garden. Book in advance. ④.

Shoshana's, Rehov HaPalmah (☎06/697 3939 or ☎050/995623). Shoshana Briefer, somewhat of an institution in Safed, runs a couple of homely apartments that are hard to find, though she will probably find *you* at the Central Bus Station. Facilities are good, and if some of the rooms are small and dark, you can't complain for $7–12 a night (they may be closed in winter). ①.

Spiers Family, 92 Yod Bet, Artists' Quarter (☎06/697 4701, not on Shabbat). Run by an English-speaking Canadian family and offering rooms with kitchenette, garden and private bath. Book in advance. ③.

Hotels

Hadar, Rehov Yavetz (☎06/692 0068). Shulamit Reuven's 20-room establishment has an old-fashioned feel and a rooftop terrace brightened by deckchairs. ②.

Rimon Inn, Tel Zayin in the Artists' Quarter (☎06/692 0665, fax 692 0456). This is the best and most expensive hotel in town; four-star service in an Ottoman khan with swimming pool and gourmet dining room, as well as views of Mount Meron and the Galilee mountains. ⑥.

Ron Hotel Chativat Yiftach, on the edge of Citadel Park (☎06/697 2590). The nearest hotel to the bus station has a comfortable rural feel and is one of the few with a swimming pool. ⑥.

Tel Aviv, Rehov Ridbaz (☎06/697 2382, fax 697 2555). Otherwise known as Berenson House, this sparkling hotel in the heart of the Old City has 38 rooms with a/c and central heating, TV and private baths, as well as a fitness room, patio and pretty garden, with views of Mount Meron and the Old City. Fifteen percent service charge *may* be waived if you produce this book. ⑥.

The Citadel and around

Crowning the summit of Safed's main hill, a small park features the remains of the Crusader fortress, the **Citadel**, accessed by a stairway from Jerusalem Street. Only the odd foundation and wall survive, but the panoramas are gorgeous, and the park, shaded by tall trees, offers escape from the heat and crowds.

The fortress was originally constructed for Fulk of Anjou, Crusader king of Jerusalem, in 1140 and handed over to the Knights Templar by Amalric I in 1168. Twenty years later, following the Crusader defeat at the Horns of Hittin, the fortress was destroyed. Partially rebuilt when the Templars regained control of Safed in 1240, its ramparts were further restored under Mamluk rule and the outer wall extended. But in 1837, the Citadel was almost completely destroyed by an earthquake that hit much of the Galilee and today the most prominent structure here is a memorial to the Jewish soldiers who died fighting for Safed in 1948.

At the foot of the first flight of steps from the Citadel, the nineteenth-century mansion of Safed's last Turkish pasha is now home to the **Israel Bible Museum** (Sun–Thurs 10am–4pm, Fri 10am–1pm; free), whose elaborate arches and colonnades are complemented by the elaborate arches and colonnades. Its collection of art on biblical themes includes some fine works by local and international artists, of which those by American sculptor Phillip Ratner are particularly inspiring.

The Old City

Safed's **Old City**, a warren of alleyways, lies to the west of the Citadel and is approached by either of two steep stairways from Rehov Yerushalayim: the one opposite the post office leads to **Kikar HaMaginim** (Defenders' Square) in the centre of the

Old City, where a building on the north side was the Haganah's town command centre in 1948; the other, **Ma'alot Olei Hagardim**, was built by the British to divide the Arab and Jewish quarters in a straight line, down which they could shoot if necessary to keep the two sides apart. Between the two staircases, on Rehov Yerushalayim, is another memorial to the 1948 war, surmounted by a **Davidka**, a makeshift mortar used by the Haganah and named after its inventor, agronomist David Liebovitch. Also commemorated by a memorial in Jerusalem (see p.364), it was, at the beginning of the 1948 war, probably the most important weapon in Israel's armoury. What it lacked in range and accuracy, it made up for in noise – vital in persuading Safed's Arab defenders that the Israelis possessed some very heavy artillery indeed. Across the street is the bullet-pocked **British Police Post**.

For interesting background on aspects of Orthodox Jewish life, **Habad House** on Rehov Hatam Sofer between Ma'alot Olei Hagardim and Kikar HaMaginim (☎06/692 1414; Sun–Thurs 9am–4pm; free) offers a wealth of information in the form of free literature, books, paintings and audiovisual shows; it also has a good restaurant. Following Safed's great tradition of teaching and scholarship, Habad House is just one of several institutes in the town dedicated to Jewish studies, where Jewish people (and sometimes non-Jews too) with an interest in their religion can take short courses or attend lectures on Judaism (see "Listings" on p.246 for further details).

The third street down Ma'alot Olei Hagardim on the right, **Rehov Bet Yosef**, leads into the **Synagogue Quarter** (see below) but before exploring the synagogues there are a couple of sites of interest along Bet Yosef itself. The first building of note is **Bet Eshtam**, on the left side of the road almost immediately past Ma'alot Olei HaGardom. Built on this "frontier" to guard the entrance to the the Jewish Quarter, the bullet holes and memorial plaques on its walls testify to the confrontation that took place here in 1948. The street above Ben Yosef, Rehov Tarpat, is named after the 1929 riots ("Tarpat" being an acronym of the Hebrew year 5689). Just past Bet Eshtam, in the small **Ethiopian Folk Art Centre and Gallery** (Sun–Thurs 9am–6pm, Fri 9am–noon; free), you can buy fine examples of the traditional arts and crafts of Ethiopian Jews, including weaving and basketwork as well as pottery and sculpture. Many of the artists exhibiting here were secretly airlifted out of Ethiopia to Israel as part of the controversial Operation Moses (see p.498).

The Synagogue Quarter

The **Synagogue Quarter** (Qiryat Batei HaKnesset) is home to no fewer than 32 synagogues commemorating rabbis and scholars who were particularly influential on Jewish mysticism. Because of the religious nature of the area, modest dress is required. Along Rehov Bet Yosef from Ma'alot Olei HaGardom, 200m along on the left you come to a blue gate (just past the Ora Art Gallery), behind which is the **Josef Caro Synagogue**, one of the most important Jewish monuments in the quarter. Born in Spain in 1488, Caro and his family lived in Turkey and moved to Safed in 1536 where he served as a rabbi and head of a *yeshiva*. It took him 32 years to write his greatest work, the *Bet Yosef* ("House of Josef"), which was condensed into the *Shulhan Arukh* ("Set Table"), a detailed work on the application of Jewish law to everyday life. The synagogue itself was built in 1847 by an Italian Jew, Yitzhaq Guetta, who restored four of the synagogues after the 1837 earthquake. It overlooks the valley, providing a magnificent view of the setting sun, from which rabbis are believed to derive divine inspiration. Inside are a number of ornate scrolls and books, including some of the earliest known printed copies of the Torah.

On a lower road running parallel to Bet Yosef Street is the seventeenth-century **Alsheikh Synagogue**, named after Kabbalist Rabbi Moshe Alsheikh and not usually open to the public. Lying a little further along, the **Abuhav Synagogue** is one of the most splendid of the old synagogues. Designed along Kabbalistic principles by the famous fifteenth-century rabbi, Yitzhaq Abuhav, it is painted blue to evoke heaven and aid prayer, and has a majestic, domed roof – the ten windows represent the Ten Commandments and the crowns decorating it echo the messianic theme of Kabbalistic belief. A painting of the Dome of the Rock in Jerusalem provides a salutary reminder of the destruction of the Temple. There are three **arks** (cupboards containing Torah scrolls in the wall towards Jerusalem to indicate the direction of prayer): the one on the right contains a Torah written by Rabbi Abuhav and another by a student of Isaac Luria (see below); the central ark houses Torah scrolls from North Africa and India (ask the guardian to open it for you); and the left ark is used as a *geniza* – a "burial chamber" for disused holy books. Facing the central ark is Elijah's Chair; above it, a plaque commemorates the six million Jews who died in the Holocaust.

Just north of Kikar HaMaginim, the **HaAri Synagogue** and its rabbis proclaim the immortality of **Isaac Luria** – a young rabbi from Egypt who became the main exponent of the exiled mysticism that flourished in Safed. Luria arrived in Safed in 1570 and died two years later at the age of 32, but, in his short life, he managed to overturn accepted rabbinical teaching. His message was that God had exiled himself after the physical creation of the world; the creation itself had gone astray, and that it was up to the Jews to redeem this catastrophe through an understanding of law and the cosmos. Though in theory too young to fathom the mystical Kabbalah (whose study is traditionally confined to men over forty already well-versed in Torah and Talmud), Luria developed his own brand of Kabbalism, and it is largely thanks to him that Safed became its centre. The synagogue's name derives from the acronym of Adonainu Rabbi Yitzhaq (our master Rabbi Isaac), also meaning "Lion". A simple building, erected on the site where the Ari studied with his disciples, it is dominated by a large *bima* (platform) from which the Torah is read. Against the south wall is a beautiful **ark**, carved from a solid block of wood, which dates back to Luria's time. At the back of the synagogue, a small room contains Elijah's Chair which, it is believed, will bring a male child to couples who sit on it. For more information on Luria and his teachings, try latching on to one of the many tour groups, or ask any of the rabbis or attendants – though be prepared for a long lecture. Since the congregation here is mainly Ashkenazi, this synagogue is known as the HaAri Ashkenazi, as opposed to the HaAri Sephardi Synagogue (see below).

Near the HaAri Ashkenazi Synagogue, in Rehov Najara, the **Safed Candles factory** produces the beautiful beeswax candles for which the town is renowned. Usually multicoloured, they come in a variety of shapes and sizes – some for Shabbat, others for Hanukkah, with the speciality being plaited candles used for the ceremony to mark the end of the Sabbath. You can visit and participate in a fascinating tour to see the process of turning honeycomb into candles.

The **Hameiri Museum** (Sun–Thurs 9am–2pm, Fri 9am–1pm; 5NIS), housed in a sixteenth-century building on Rehov Keren HaYesod further down the hill, examines the various religious, cultural and historical aspects of Jewish settlement in Safed. Life over the last few centuries is illustrated with a mass of everyday artefacts and documents and, though many of the objects displayed are commonplace throughout the Middle East, the museum provides interesting background. Among the seven separate exhibitions are portrayals of local characters, illustrations inspired by Safed legends, a restored twentieth-century residence, and, in "Heroic Safed", historic events are retold in a room that was on the frontline in the war of 1948.

Stairs opposite the Hameiri Museum descend to Rehov HaAri, site of the other synagogue commemorating the Ari, supposedly where he studied with the prophet Elijah. Attended by a predominantly Sephardi congregation, the **HaAri Sephardi**

Synagogue is a rather simple but well-proportioned building, whose focus is a three-domed ark overlooked by a stained-glass window. Since the synagogue faced the Arab Quarter, it was requisitioned in the war of 1948, and a platform for a machine-gun installation erected. The nearby **Bena'a Synagogue** (not usually open to the public) houses the tomb of Rabbi Yossi Bena'a, known as HaTzadik HaLavan (the Snow White Sage).

To the west of the Ari Sephardi synagogue, further down the stairs to the left, is a **cemetery** containing the graves of many famous Kabbalist rabbis, including the Ari himself, Rabbi Yosef Caro, Rabbi Moshe Alsheikh, Rabbi Moshe Cordovero (the leading Kabbalist before the Ari), and Rabbi Shlomo Alkavetz (who wrote the popular Jewish hymn *Lekha Dodi*). The Kabbalists believed that burial in Safed enabled their souls to fly more swiftly to heaven. A short way down the hill is the site where **Hannah and her Seven Sons** are traditionally held to have been buried. Refusing to bow before Seleucid King Antiochus IV Epiphanes, who had declared himself a god, Hannah and her sons were put to death in 176 BC and have become a symbol of Jewish faith and resistance. A neighbouring cemetery houses the remains of members of the Jewish paramiltaries from the 1940s, including seven Irgun and Stern Gang members executed by the British at Acre prison. The *mikve*, or Jewish ritual bath, on the way to the cemetery from HaAri Sephardi Synagogue, is said to be that used by the Ari for cleansing himself.

The Artists' Quarter

To the south of the Old City, the **Artists' Quarter** (Qiryat HaZtayarim in Hebrew) is the most important surviving segment of the Arab town, its cobbled streets and pastel blue and white houses full of atmosphere despite the rather lifeless galleries that now occupy so many of them. There are artists from all over Israel here, many of them churning out standard landscapes or works on Jewish themes for the tourist market, but even if the art doesn't inspire you, the houses in which they live and work – high-ceilinged and often with a well in the middle of the main room – are reason enough for a visit.

Below Maalot Olei HaGardom, on Bet Yosef, the **General Exhibition** of the Safed Artists' Colony (Sun–Thurs 9am–6pm, Fri & Sat 9am–2pm; free), displays (and sells) the work of its members – there are pastiches of virtually any style here, as well as the occasional more original (and expensive) work. The exhibition is housed in one of two remaining mosques in Safed, built at the turn of the century on Mamluk foundations. Confiscated after 1948, it is still the subject of dispute between the present-day owners and the Islamic Waqf who want it restored as a place of worship. Next door, the **Immigrant Artists' Exhibition** (same hours; also free) exhibits the work of immigrant artists from Russia. If you like a particular artist's work in either exhibition, you can go and check out their studio in the quarter.

Nearby, in Tet Zayin Street, the imaginatively laid-out **Museum of Printing** (Sun–Thurs 10am–noon and 4–6pm, Fri & Sat 10am–noon; free) traces the history of book printing and binding in the Middle East. Safed was the centre of the industry during the sixteenth century – exhibits and text illustrate how, in 1578, the first Hebrew book was printed here on the press brought by Eliezer Ashkenazi from Lublin. Continuing south down Tet Zayin Street from here, you enter an area free of the tourist hordes. Towards the end of the road are the black-striped **Mamluk Mausoleum** (not open to the public) and the **Red Mosque**, two of the oldest buildings in Safed and both suffering from neglect. The former was constructed in the fourteenth century as the burial place of Musa Abu Haj Eroktai, a Mamluk ruler of the city. The mosque was built by the Mamluk leader Baybars, who took Safed from the Crusaders; the inscription over the mihrab (prayer niche) inside gives the date of construction as 1330. It's now used as a venue during the annual Kletzmer Music Festival. At the end of the street, opposite the junction with HaNassi, is a large park and a small children's zoo.

Finally, above the quarter on Rehov HaPalmah is the **Cave of Shem and Ever** where Noah's son Shem and grandson Ever lived and studied the Torah (the fact that they lived before the Torah was written does not seem to worry anyone). Later, the patriarch Jacob is said to have lived in the cave, and a Muslim tradition holds that it is the resting place of the messenger who came to tell him of the supposed death of his favourite son Joseph.

Eating and drinking

Safed's **restaurants**, uninspiring on the whole and serving kosher food, are mostly ranged along Jerusalem Street. For a range of meat and fish dishes, try *Pinati's* at no. 81 (☎06/692 0855), somewhat incongruously known as *The Elvis Inn*. Opposite the shopping centre at no. 75, *HaMifgash* (☎06/692 0510) has a similar menu, while on the third floor of shopping centre itself, *Rafi's Bar* (☎06/697 4032) is the only place in town open for food on Friday night. For a large, tasty pizza, *Palermo Pizza* at no. 47 (☎06/692 1217), is a good bet, or you can sate your desire for **falafel** at *Falafel Trito*, one of several of its kind in the area. More exotic cuisine can be had at *Metzuyan* (meaning "excellent"), at no. 51 (☎06/697 3245), whose Chinese food lives up to its name. **Vegetarians** can feast on a variety of pancakes, blintzes, omelettes and salads at the *Café Bagdad*, next door to the (closed) *Hotel Ya'ir*. From its wonderful terrace there are views over the Old City to the distant mountains.

Good views can also be enjoyed – along with traditional, reasonably priced Jewish food – from the open-air patio of *Habad House* on Rehov Hatam Sofer in the Old City.

If you want to get your own supplies, Safed's **market**, in front of the main post office (Tues & Wed), offers the best selection. There is also a large supermarket in the shopping centre on Jerusalem Street.

Nightlife and entertainment

Decent **nightlife** in Safed is scant. During the summer, the Artists' Quarter can be reasonably lively in the evenings, with various plays, musical recitals and dance displays organized by the municipality. Concerts are held in the Saraya, an eighteenth-century Ottoman khan and later government house, and plays, concerts and films are shown in the Yigal Allon Cultural Centre (see below); for details of these and other events, contact the tourist office.

If you are around during July and August, you may be lucky enough to catch the three- to five-day **Kletzmer Music Festival**. Kletzmer, originally played by itinerant Jewish musicians in central and eastern Europe (see p.53), is today seeing something of a revival in Israel, the contribution of Russian practitioners and the exposure to Sephardi rhythms adding new energy to somewhat emotional Yiddish refrains.

MOVING ON FROM SAFED

Buses run to Acre (every 30min; 1hr), Haifa (every 20–30min; 2hr), Jerusalem (1 daily; 2hr 30min), Meron (every 30min; 15min), Qiryat Shemona (every 30min; 1hr), Rihaniya (5 daily; 20 min), Rosh Pinna (every 30min; 15 min), Sasa (for Bir'im; 3 daily; 20min), Tel Aviv (1 daily; 3hr) and Tiberias (hourly; 45min).

Listings

Banks and exchange There are several on or around Rehov Yerushalayim above the Old City and the Artists' Quarter. Most open Sun, Tues & Thurs afternoons (4–6pm), except First International at 34 Yerushalayim, which opens 4–7pm Mon & Wed.

Jewish studies Ascent Institute of Tsfat, 2 HaAri (☎06/692 1346, fax 692 1942), the Lubavitch studies centre (also has a youth hostel for Jews), offering classes, tours, hikes and "Shabbat with the Mystics"; Livnot U'LeHibanot, Rehov Avritch (☎06/697 0311, fax 692 1848), three-week and three-month courses (for English-speakers aged 21–30) combine Jewish studies with hiking and community service in Jerusalem and Safed; Machon Alte, 33 Yerushalayim (☎06/697 4306 or 692 1300, fax 692 1412), courses for women wanting to (re)discover their Jewish roots; Pardes Rimonim Institute for Tsfat Heritage in Halakha and Kabbala (☎06/697 2946), programmes and lectures on Judaism and the town; Safed Regional College, 11 Yerushalayim (☎06/692 0055, fax 692 1068), an extension of Bar Ilan University, runs a variety of courses open to the general public.

Medical services Magen David Adom first-aid post by the bus station (☎06/692 0333) on Yerushalayim, east of the Citadel.

Police The police station is in the Canaan district, east of town (☎06/693 0444).

Post office The main office is on HaPalmah opposite the junction with Aliya Bet, below the Artists' Quarter (Sun–Tues & Thurs 8am–12.30pm & 3.30pm–6pm, Wed 8am–1.30pm, Fri 8am–noon). A more convenient branch office is at 37 Yerushalayim, above the Old City (same hours).

Taxis Edan Hasa'ot (☎06/698 9536); Kenaan (☎06/692 0444).

Around Safed

Safed's environs contain a number of interesting sites, most of which can be visited in a day. The fort of **Biriya**, just northeast of town, has both a biblical and a more recent past, while **Meron**, to the northwest, is of great importance to Orthodox Jews, who come to pay their respects to the rabbis buried here. For visitors more concerned with physical than spiritual rejuvenation there's the vegetarian moshav of **Amirim**, southwest of Safed, and the resort of **Mitzpe HaYamim**, southeastward, offering breathtaking views in addition to luxurious health facilities. Just northeast of Mitzpe HaYamim, the town of **Rosh Pinna** maintains an aura of the early days of the modern Israeli state. North of Safed, on the Lebanese border, are the remains of the disputed villages of **Bir'im** and **Iqrit**.

Biriya

One kilometre northeast of Safed, off Route 89, **BIRIYA** has a long association with the rabbis of the Galilee; it was here that Rabbi Yosef Caro wrote part of the *Shulhan Arukh* (see p.240). **Biriya Fort** (Metzudat Biriya), now used as a lookout by forest rangers, played a significant role in 1948 when, in defiance of the British authorities, members of the Palmah settled the place: a small room to the right of the entrance contains a cubby-hole in the floor where caches of arms were hidden, and a museum on site tells of the confrontation between the settlers and the British. The conquest by the Palmah of the Palestinian village of Biriya on May 1, 1948, like that of the neighbouring village of Ein al-Zeitoun (see p.247), was a serious blow to the morale of Safed's Arab population and greatly aided the city's capture by the Israelis.

To the left of the fort, the **Hula Observation Point** gives a spectacular view of the Hula Valley to the northeast. Follow the orange signs from here towards the village of Amuka, and you come after 1km to the recreation centre of **Bat Ya'ar** (☎06/692 11788, fax 692 1991), which offers a range of activities including horseback, walking and jeep tours in the area, and also has a steak-house where you can fill up afterwards. In Amuka itself is the grave of a student of Hillel the Elder, **Rabbi Yonatan ben Uziel**, whose Aramaic translation of the Torah is widely studied. Religious bachelors come here to pray for a spouse, a little odd given that the rabbi himself never married. Nevertheless, their prayers are said to be answered within a year – whether that's because it's a good place to meet other unmarrieds or a result of holy intervention is a matter for conjecture.

Safed to Meron

The ten-kilometre stretch of Route 89 from **Safed to Meron**, served by bus, contains several sights worth looking out for. The first is a couple of kilometres outside Safed, where two white domes to the left of the road mark the **tombs** of Rabbi Yehuda bar Ilai, an important figure in Jewish revival after the Bar Kokhba revolt, and Rabbi Yossi Saragossi, whose egalitarian teachings helped to establish Safed's religious status during Ottoman times. One kilometre further along, on the right, the stone buildings are the remains of the Palestinian village of **Ein al-Zeitoun**, whose capture by the Palmah in May 1948 was instrumental in prompting the flight of Safed's inhabitants; the turn-off (Route 886) nearby leads to **Ein Zeitim Park** which has picnic facilities.

A further 2km along Route 89, a dirt track to the left leads to the upper part of the Amud River, which runs down to the Sea of Galilee (see p.209). From here, a pleasant marked trail southward brings you after about thirty minutes to the **Nahal Amud Nature Reserve**, where an abundance of wild fruit grow; the valley is called Wadi Tufah (Apple Valley) in Arabic. The trail westward, another half-hour walk, brings you the tomb of Rabbi Shimon ben Yohai in Meron.

Meron

The best time to visit **MERON**, an Orthodox Jewish moshav on the eastern side of Mount Meron, is on **Lag Ba'Omer** (the 33rd day after Passover), when Sephardi Jews come here to commemorate the death of **Rabbi Shimon ben Yohai** (see p.238) – his **tomb** here is an important place of pilgrimage. The largest *hiloula* in Israel, it attracts over two hundred thousand pilgrims – an eighteenth-century account describes how "they have a tradition from ancient times, that on that day they have to make merry and hold big feasts with drums and dancing and everything possible." The celebration begins by bringing the Scrolls of the Law in a grand procession from Safed – though nowadays, instead of dancing all the way, participants dance to the bus station and get a ride the rest of the way. Bonfires are lit, sheep are slaughtered and traditional Jewish music provides entertainment, while vendors wander among the crowds with large trays of sweets, biscuits and sandwiches – you take what you want, with a glass of juice or *araq* to wash it down. Although all of this takes place in a party-like and joyous atmosphere, underlying it are deeply religious sentiments: as an onlooker, you are expected to dress and behave respectfully.

The tomb itself is a large, white multi-domed building with a number of wings, a yard and steps up to the roof. In the left wing are passages to prayer rooms and a library; standing out from the wall is part of the gravestone of Rabbi Shimon. People come here to pray, to light candles and to place notes asking for intercession. At the side, behind a lattice, is the grave itself. Also traditionally held to be here is the grave of another sage, **Hillel the Elder**, together with those of his wife and thirty students; turn right at Rabbi Shimon's tomb and walk down the path to his burial cave. Hillel, known for his humility and patience, was a head of the Sanhedrin (Jewish high court), which he and his students dominated for over 350 years. Another tomb, at Khirbet Shema' on a hilltop to the south, is held to be the grave of **Shammai**, a contemporary of Hillel. In contrast to the latter, Shammai was known for his inflexibility and impatience and their different approaches are illustrated in a story from the Talmud: "A gentile once came to Shammai asking 'Teach me all of the Torah while standing on one foot'. Shammai took a ruler and drove him away as a scoffer. The gentile then approached Hillel who replied, 'Do unto others as you would have others do unto you. That is the whole Torah; all the rest is commentary. Go and learn!' " The fact that Jesus used a paraphrase of this (Matthew 7: 12) has led some to believe he was a student of Hillel.

On the peak of a hill to the north overlooking Rabbi Shimon's tomb is an ancient **synagogue** dating back to Roman times: little remains apart from the outside walls, a couple of original doorways and a prominent gateway whose collapse, according to Jewish mystical belief, will herald the arrival of the Messiah. To the east of the parking lot, you can see the remains of the settlement of Meron of the third and fourth centuries, including a *mikve* (ritual bath).

PRACTICALITIES
Meron is served by **buses** running roughly every half-hour each way between Safed and Acre, with some through to Haifa. **Accommodation** (without breakfast) is available in private rooms at the moshav (⑤), which caters particularly, as you might expect, for Orthodox Jews. Alternatively, try the vegetarian moshav of **Amirim**, about 7km south of Meron Junction on Route 866, with a comfortable "vacation village" (☎06/698 8571, fax 698 0772; ⑤) and also private rooms. The moshav restaurant, *Amirei HaGalil* (☎06/698 7033), has an excellent reputation for wholesome and delicious vegetarian food.

Jish

More ancient **rabbinical tombs** can be seen four kilometres north of Meron at the Maronite village of **JISH**, formerly called Gush Halav (Milk Bloc), and renowned in Roman times for both its milk and its olive oil. It was also the home of Yohanan, one of the leaders of the 66 AD First Revolt. The tombs, in a small domed structure by Route 89 on the southern edge of the village, belong to Shemaia and Avtalion, who lived just before the First Revolt. Like Meron, Jish has remains of an ancient synagogue, this one from the third or fourth century AD, which lies a couple of kilometres east of the village, but the remains here are even sparser than those at Meron.

Bir'im and Rihaniya

Perched high in the mountains 1km northwest of Safed and a stone's throw from the border itself, **BIR'IM** (Baram) preserves ample reminders of both its distant and recent past. The village is an issue that frequently surfaces in the Israeli press, having been the subject of legal controversy since 1948 when the mainly Christian villagers (who were neutral during the war and even put up Israeli soldiers in the village) were ordered out by Israeli troops and prevented from returning. In 1951, they obtained an injunction from the Supreme Court giving them the right to return, but the military then declared the village an off-limits "security zone" and bombed it flat in 1953. Some of the land was taken over by Kibbutz Baram, part of the left-leaning Mapam movement, and much of what remained became Moshav Dovev in 1963. You can still walk around the old village, where many of the buildings are intact and the foundations of others clearly visible. Slogans (in English, Arabic and Hebrew) in support of the villagers' fight to return are prominent.

Amid the ruins of the village is the National Parks Authority site of **ancient Baram** (daily winter 8am–4pm, summer 8am–5pm; 9NIS) whose centrepiece is a large, highly decorative synagogue built in the third century when a Jewish community grew up here after the destruction of Jerusalem. What you see is basically just the facade, a massive structure of brick and pillars which served as a covered entrance for worshippers; an artist's impression of what the rest of the synagogue would have looked like is included in the leaflet. All around, the site is richly scattered with other remnants from this and later periods.

Bir'im can be reached from Safed by taking **bus** #43 (thrice daily) to the nearby kib-butz of Sasa. If you fancy **staying** right on the Lebanese border, you could try the guest-house at Mitzpe Nof Malkiya, about 15km east of Bir'im along the border road, Route 899 (☎06/946882, fax 959956). Situated on the summit of the Upper Galilee mountains, its 25 rooms command a spectacular view, and enjoy a range of facilities including a disco, bar and swimming pool. Guided tours are available, a well as horse riding and, for those really interested in the area, occasional lectures on local culture and politics.

A mere five kilometres east of Bir'im as the crow flies, but best reached from Safed (five buses daily) via Route 886, the village of **RIHANIYA** is home to members of one of Israel's smallest ethnic groups – the **Circassians**, who came to the region from their original homeland in the Caucasus after 1878, when Russia took it from the Ottomans. Many Circassian families loyal to the Ottoman regime emigrated, and the sultan gave them land in Palestine and elsewhere. There are only two communities of Circassians in Israel today, with little over a thousand members in total; Rihaniya is the larger, the other is at Kufr Kanna (see p.186). The Circassians find themselves in a position anal-ogous but opposite to that of the Druze: the latter are Arabs but not Muslims, whereas the Circassians are Muslim but not Arab. Politically, however, the effect has been the same, and the Circassian community has generally been loyal to the State of Israel, with members serving in the IDF since 1948. Visiting the village today, the most striking thing is the **mosque**, whose architecture with its red-brown walls and round minaret is strikingly different from that of Palestinian mosques. The Circassians have their own language, though they also speak Hebrew, Arabic, and usually English.

Mitzpe HaYamim

Southwest of Safed, off the road (Route 89) to Rosh Pinna and set in woodlands 570m above sea level, the health resort of **MITZPE HAYAMIM** (☎06/699 9666, fax 699 9555; toll-free in Israel ☎177/022-8338; ⑤) is a haven of luxury, with a hotel overlooking the Hula Valley, the Golan Heights, the Sea of Galilee and Mount Hermon. You can choose from a variety of health, diet and beauty treatments, enjoy the gastronomic feasts of vegetarian or fish and farm produce, and when you're ready for something more active, join a tour to the Dan and Hula reserves, or go skiing on Mount Hermon. The resort also has a studio-gallery that displays and sells the original artworks produced here.

Arkia Airlines operates regular 25-minute flights between Tel Aviv and Mahanayim Airport nearby (see below). If you have a reservation at Mitzpe HaYamim, a hotel lim-ousine will be waiting for you. Otherwise, buses from Rosh Pinna or Safed will get you there.

The Galilee Panhandle

The narrow northern strip of eastern Israel, known as the **Panhandle** or **Finger**, thrusts north from the Sea of Galilee up to the Lebanese border. Negotiating its fifty-kilometre length is Route 90, which passes through **Rosh Pinna**, the Canaanite city of **Tel Hazor** and the breathtaking **Hula Valley** before reaching the regional capital of **Qiryat Shemona**, in the far north. East of Rosh Pinna, **Mahanayim Airport** caters for domestic flights between Israel's major cities.

Rosh Pinna

You may find yourself at the town of **ROSH PINNA** when changing buses, with ser-vices north to Qiryat Shemona, west into Galilee and east to the Golan Heights. Located 1km east of Mitzpe HaYamim on Route 89, Rosh Pinna – meaning "cornerstone" – was founded by Romanian and Russian immigrants in 1882 and was the first settlement to use Hebrew as a spoken language. The settlers aimed to combine Torah studies with agricultural work and to be independent of public support, but the new venture ran into financial difficulties and had to be rescued by Baron Edmond de Rothschild. The place still has a rather small-town, olde worlde feel, reinforced by the presence of the Rosh Pinna Pioneer Settlement Site (☎06/693 6603), where some houses of the original settlement, a synagogue and garden have been renovated; a restaurant on site serves meals and snacks. There's also a **youth hostel** on Rehov HaHalutzim, in the town centre (☎06/693 7086; ②).

Hazor

A couple of kilometres north of Rosh Pinna, the modern town of **HAZOR** contains little of interest apart from the traditionally accepted **grave of Honi HaMa'agal** (the Circle-Maker). Honi is said to have brought rain to a drought-stricken area by drawing a circle in the dust, stepping into it and praying. The Talmud relates how when faced with the initial drizzle the Jews demanded more, Honi then prayed for the right amount, but when his request was granted, the Jews asked him to pray for it to stop. Honi expressed his exasperation to God saying, "The Jews cannot bear Your punishments, nor can they bear too much of Your bounty."

Five kilometres from Hazor, on the approach to the Hula Valley and clearly visible from the road, is the site of **Tel Hazor**. Like Megiddo (p.150), the city lay on the main route from Egypt to Mesopotamia and was an essential target for invaders from the north. It was inhabited from the Bronze Age (around 2500 BC) right through to the second century BC; evidence of at least 21 separate settlements has been discovered here. The **Canaanite city** was among the most important of its age (eighteenth and seventeenth centuries BC), mentioned in the Old Testament as the capital of many pre-Israelite kings and the site of one of Joshua's more bloodcurdling conquests, when he and the Israelites "turned back, and took Hazor, and smote the king thereof with the sword.... And they smote all the souls that were therein with the edge of the sword, utterly destroying them: there was not any left to breathe: and he burnt Hazor with fire." (Joshua 11: 10–11). By the tenth century BC, however, a substantial city had once again grown up, fortified by Solomon and then further strengthened by Ahab. Hazor was in turn destroyed by the Assyrians in the eighth century BC, and thereafter never regained its former importance.

What you see today, with so many superimposed levels, is complex but impressive – and big. Among the highlights are the **Canaanite Palace**, approached by a broad ceremonial stairway. Over it, a gatehouse and various defensive walls were constructed in the time of Solomon, and a large storehouse under the northern kingdom of Israel's ninth-century BC King Ahab. The Citadel, too, dates from the time of Ahab, as does the elaborate **water system**, designed (as in Jerusalem and Megiddo) to be accessible even if the spring outside the walls were cut off by attackers. Here, a shaft and tunnel system leads to an underground pool via restored steps descending into the ancient underground chamber. The **Temple**, again built over remains of earlier temples, is also worth seeing and dates from the time of the last Canaanite king, Jabin. It was destroyed when Joshua burnt the city.

The **Hazor Museum**, opposite (Sun–Thurs 8am–4pm, Fri 8am–1pm; 7NIS), displays a reconstruction of the ancient city plus finds from the site dating from the Bronze Age to the second century BC. The stone lions at the entrance of the museum originally stood guard at the Canaanite temple; they were found deliberately buried, presumably as symbols of idolatry.

The museum stands at the entrance to **Kibbutz Ayelet HaShahar**, whose large and rather splendid guesthouse is equivalent to an upmarket hotel (☎06/693 2611, fax 693 4777; ⑤). Facilities include a swimming pool, disco and restaurant, as well as jeep and camel tours around the area.

The Hula Valley

The **Hula Valley**, an area of lakes and swamps about 25km long and 6km wide, is part of the Syrian-African Rift, edged by the steep walls of the Naphtali Mountains to the west and the Golan Heights to the east. The entire Rift basin between the Hula and the Sea of Galilee, thought to have been formed about five million years ago, was once covered by a single lake until basalt movement and volcanic eruptions separated it into the Sea of Galilee and Lake Hula (the latter since drained). Situated at an important biogeographical junction, the Hula is the meeting point of flora and fauna from East Africa, the Persian Gulf and Europe, and also the most important stopover for waterfowl migrating between Europe and Africa, some of which can be seen at the Hula Nature Reserve (see below).

The valley was inhabited by **Bedouins** of the Ghawarna tribe – meaning those who live in a *ghor*, a depression or low place – until 1948. They lived in villages on the edge of the swamps and earned their living by raising water buffalo, growing crops, and weaving huts and mats from papyrus reeds that were much sought after by merchants. The first modern **Jewish settlement**, Yesud Hama'ala, was established in 1883 by settlers from Poland and Safed, who attempted to grow spices and farm silkworms. In the 1930s, immigrants from Germany moved into the area and founded **Kibbutz Hulata**, whose main industry was fishing, but the prevalence of **malaria** in the swampland made habitation extremely difficult; it's estimated that between sixty and eighty percent of adults were infected. The war on malaria began in 1940, with the draining of irrigation canals and kerosene treatment, though it was opposed by the Arab population who regarded the measures as disruption to their way of life and livelihood. Eight years later, the Arabs themselves became the focus of a clearance programme, when the Palmah set in motion **Operation Broom** (Meivzta Matate), designed to evict them from the Jordan Valley area south of Rosh Pinna.

Wholescale drainage of the Hula lake and swamps began in 1951, after the establishment of Israel, but was halted after opposition from environmentalists. In 1964, the valley was handed over to the Nature Reserves Authority, who began a rehabilitation of the area, flooding large sections and establishing seventeen **reserves** throughout the valley.

Hula Nature Reserve and Kibbutz Kfar Blum

The largest of the reserves is the thousand-acre **Hula Nature Reserve**, about halfway between Rosh Pinna and Qiryat Shemona (☎06/693 7069; daily 8am–4pm; 12NIS). Just inside the entrance are picnic tables, a cafeteria, and kiosks selling bird-watching brochures and renting out binoculars – worthwhile even for non-ornithologists. The **Visitors' Centre** provides an introduction to the natural history of the area, past and present: a fifteen-minute audiovisual presentation describes the landscape, photographs of the Hula Valley show it before and after draining, and, constituting the heart of the exhibition, are 56 stuffed animal specimens and models of plants; the "memorial wall" next to them lists species that disappeared with the drainage. Other exhibits include one on the lifestyle of the Ghawarna.

A partially shaded two-kilometre **walking trail** begins at the Visitors' Centre, arriving after the first bend at an observation point offering splendid views of the valley, the Golan Heights to the east, Mount Hermon to the north and the Naphtali Mountains to the east. In summer, you might get to see large yellow water-lilies, carnivorous climbing plants with heart-shaped leaves, fig and mulberry trees, and yellow irises. Further along, the "**Swamp Trail**" consists of a 600-metre-long wooden bridge that gives a grand view of the swamp and its dense groves of papyrus reeds, and, from its hidden lookout, the chance to observe the abundant birdlife including cormorants, herons and pelicans. The trail ends up at an **observation tower** – the highest point in the reserve – whose telescope affords occasional glimpses of water buffalo, wild boar and even jungle cats. Canals along the route back to the Visitors' Centre provide a home for turtle, catfish and otters.

Getting to the Hula Reserve is relatively simple: **buses** pass by on the Rosh Pinna–Qiryat Shemona road at least every hour, and it's easy enough to hitch (or walk) the 2.5km from the junction. At the southern edge of the Hula Reserve, **Dubrovin Farm** (☎06/693 7371; Sun–Thurs 9am–5pm, Fri 9am–3pm; 12NIS) has been renovated to show the lifestyles of early settlers in the area and features a cultural museum, sound and light show, ceramics studio, and restaurant.

About 12km north of the Hula Reserve, **Kibbutz Kfar Blum** (☎06/694 3666, fax 694 8555; ⑤) has a guesthouse with – among other facilities – an Olympic-size swimming pool, tennis courts and kayaks for rent. This predominantly Anglo-Saxon kibbutz is well known for its week-long classical **music festival**, which is held in April and features local and international musicians.

Qiryat Shemona and Tel Hai

Built in 1949 as a defensive settlement on the Lebanese-Israeli border, **QIRYAT SHEMONA** (Village of Eight), despite its status as border town and regional capital, is pretty unexciting – a collection of concrete blocks built with defence rather than aesthetics in mind. Named after the eight Zionist pioneers who were killed in the nearby settlement of Tel Hai in 1920 (see below), it's still dominated by the Arab-Israeli conflict, being a natural target for cross-border attacks, most famously in April 1974, when three PFLP(GC) guerrillas seized eighteen hostages in an apartment block and demanded the release of a hundred political prisoners. When the Israelis refused, and stormed the block, they killed themselves and their hostages, including eight children. Fatah and Hezbollah forces across the border in Lebanon have also regularly shelled the town, as Israelis will often point out when defending their army's invasion of Lebanon and occupation of the "South Lebanon Security Zone".

The only thing to recommend the place is that it's a useful point at which to pick up transport around the area and into the Golan. The **bus** station, a few hundred metres east of the main road, marks the centre of town, and has services to Banyas (2 daily; 20min), Jerusalem (6 daily; 5hr), Metulla (hourly; 20min), Qazrin (2 daily; 40min), Safed (every 30min; 1hr) and Tel Aviv (hourly; 3hr 30min). From the bus station shops, banks and anything else you might need are within a five-minute walk. If you do have **to stay** here, the *North Hotel*, opposite the bus station (☎06/694 4705; ④), offers reasonable accommodation.

In 1920, the village of Halsa (on which Qiryat Shemona was built) had been the launching point of an attack by Arab raiders on **TEL HAI**, 3km to the north, home of Zionist theorist and pioneer **Joseph Trumpeldor**, who was killed in the battle, along with seven comrades. First settled in 1905 on land bought by Baron de Rothschild, Tel Hai means "Hill of Life" and is a pun on Khirbet Talha, the name of the original village. It was taken over in 1918 by the socialist-Zionist HaShomer (guard) movement, the precursor to the Haganah. Trumpeldor was one of the first Zionists to take up arms, having formed a Jewish force which fought alongside the British in World War I, and when he died defending the settlement, he became the first great martyr and hero of the Zionist cause. His grave, in the settlement's **cemetery**, is a site of pilgrimage on the anniversary of March 1 for thousands of young Israeli conscripts. Marked by a statue of a lion, it is engraved with his supposed last words, "It is good to die for our country." The story of Trumpeldor's last stand is told in a small **museum** nearby (Sun–Thurs 8am–4pm, Fri 8am–1pm, Sat 9am–2pm; 6.50NIS).

Today, Tel Hai is part of **Kibbutz Kfar Giladi** (☎06/694 1414, fax 695 1248; ⑥), also founded by the HaShomer movement (in 1916), and temporarily abandoned after the Tel Hai incident. The kibbutz has a swimming pool, tennis courts and a three-star guesthouse. Less expensive accommodation is available at the Tel Hai **youth hostel**, just off the main Qiryat Shemona–Metulla road (☎06/694 0043; ②), where you can get a dorm bed with breakfast, and enjoy fine mountain views from many of the rooms; bus #20 or #23 from Qiryat Shemona serves the kibbutz.

Hurshat Tal and Dan

Another of the seventeen reserves in the Hula Valley, **Hurshat Tal**, 9km east of Qiryat Shemona in the foothills of the Golan (☎06/694 0400; Sat–Thurs 8am–5pm, Fri 8am–4pm; 8NIS), is an ancient **oak wood**, known in Arabic as Shajarat al-'Ashara (Tree of the Ten), after the legend that ten companions of the Prophet Mohammed stuck their staffs into the ground here to tie up their horses, and from these staffs the massive oak trees grew. The wood lies on the banks of the **Dan River**, one of the Jordan's three tributaries, here diverted into a large pool for swimming. Just north of the entrance to the park, the *Hurshat Tal* **campsite** (☎06/694 2360) offers excellent pitches for tents (①) and has bungalows for three to five people (②).

Kibbutz Dan, about 2km northeast of Hurshat Tal along Route 99, has a bird-watching centre in a small nature reserve noted for its lush vegetation and location on the River Dan – although swimming is not allowed here. For nature lovers keen to know more on the flora and fauna of the region, the **Bet Ussiskin Museum** (Sat–Thurs 8.30am–4.30pm, Fri 8.30am–3.30pm; 7.50NIS) offers audiovisual displays and illuminated tableaux of exactly that.

Another kilometre north, at the centre of the reserve, is the archeological site of **Tel Dan** or Tel al-Qadi (Sun–Thurs 8am–5pm, Fri 8am–4pm; 8NIS), northernmost outpost of the Israelites' biblical territory, which the Old Testament often describes as stretching "from Dan to Beersheba". Settled since the fifth millennium BC, and originally known as Leshem or Laish, it was a large city and local administrative centre in the 28th to 24th century BC, conquered in the twelfth by the eponymous Israelite tribe of Dan who, naturally, smote its inhabitants with the edge of the sword (Judges 18: 27). After Solomon's kingdom split on his death around 922 BC, the rebel northern king Jeroboam I (922–901 BC) "made two calves of gold" (I Kings 12: 28), one of which he set up in Dan for the people to worship. Nebuchadnezzar had the city destroyed, but it remained a cult centre and was settled again from the first century BC to the fourth AD. Excavations here include a Canaanite arched gateway and ruins from the Bronze and Iron Ages, including a ritual site, a magnificent tomb, city ramparts and gate. Artefacts from Tel Dan are on display at the Skirball Museum in Jerusalem (see p.368), along with an exhibition on the excavations. A guidebook to the site is available at the entrance to the nature reserve, where a kiosk serves refreshments.

Tel Dan is right on the border with the Golan Heights, a stone's throw from Banyas (p.467) and Castle Nimrod (p.469).

Metulla and the Lebanese border

The town of **METULLA**, at the northern tip of the Galilee Panhandle, is the archetypal border town. Founded by Russian immigrants on land bought by Baron de
Rothschild in 1896, its name is taken from the Arabic of the Druze village that stood
here, *al-Mutalla'* or lookout. Metulla was temporarily evacuated after the Tel Hai battle
in 1920 (see above), and at the end of the 1948 war found that most of its land in the
Iyun Valley (Marj 'Ayun) was stranded on the Lebanese side of the border.

Metulla's appeal lies in its dramatic setting, close to the Tanur waterfalls and
Lebanese border); the town itself – a collection of Swiss-style chalets – is pleasant
enough, but boredom can set in rapidly. Besides a couple of hotel bars and restaurants
in the town "centre", frequented by UN personnel and Lebanese day labourers, its
attractions are limited to the Metulla Sports Centre (☎06/695 0370; 10am–10pm;
32NIS), with the largest **ice-rink** in the country. There are also a number of rather
expensive **hotels** (⑤) should you want to stay, including *Hotel Arazim* (☎06/699 7143,
fax 699 7666) and *Sheleg HaLevanon* (Snows of Lebanon) (☎06/699 7111, fax 699 7118).
Bus #20 runs between Qiryat Shemona and Metulla every hour.

Around Metulla

According to the mayor of Metulla, it is possible to cross the border and go visiting in
South Lebanon; don't do so unless you have a powerful death wish, however. Safer
trips out of town include the **"Good Fence"**, a border crossing less than a kilometre to
the northwest of town. This was opened in 1977 for residents of neighbouring Lebanese
Christian villages to seek medical attention in Israel after fighting in the early Seventies.
Since then, there has been a flow of people from South Lebanon into Israel, and of
Israeli goods and military personnel into Lebanon. However, the Good Fence is only
good for some: Lebanese who want to cross must have a relative active in the Israeli-
backed South Lebanese Army (SLA). Every day, thousands of Lebanese cross the border to work as unskilled labourers in Israel and to earn wages that are meagre by Israeli
standards but go a long way in a country whose economy, after years of civil war and
foreign occupation, is still in tatters.

Looking out over the fence from the **observation point** (a snack bar sells cheap falafel
and hot dogs), the view of Lebanon is one of calm and normality. Yet you could be in
Beirut in a matter of hours, or in the Syrian-controlled Beqa'a Valley in less than thirty
minutes, were it not for the international strife that wracks the area. The Hezbollah bases
that Israel so regularly bombs are not far away either, mostly beyond the forty-kilometre
"South Lebanon Security Zone" occupied by Israel after the 1982 invasion of Lebanon.

Today, the "Security Zone" is flooded by Israeli goods, Israeli-funded militias and an estimated one thousand Israeli military personnel. The predominantly Shi'ite Muslim population of the south, who initially greeted the invading Israelis in 1982 as "liberators", are now
some of Israel's most implacable enemies. Since Israel's casualties during the 1982 invasion proved unacceptably high and it was forced to withdraw most of its forces, Israel's
proxy, the SLA, has found itself entrenched in a hopeless guerrilla war with the Shi'ites,
adding yet another explosive dimension to the country's splintered factionalism. On a hill
to the east of the crossing, **Beaufort Castle** was a major PLO stronghold until 1982, from
where the Palestinians bombarded Israeli border towns with Katyusha rockets.

Around 2km south of Metulla is the spectacular, eighteen-metre-high **Tanur
Waterfall**, at its peak in spring when the spray evaporates in the heat (*tanur* means
oven), creating a smoky mist. During the summer, even though the waterfall is reduced
to a trickle, the main pool usually holds enough water to allow a refreshing swim. About
3km south along the main road, there's a second, smaller waterfall in the **'Ayun
Nature Reserve** (Sat–Thurs 8am–4pm, Fri 8am–3pm; $5). Here you'll also find a
pleasant picnic area beside the 'Ayun River.

CHAPTER FIVE

THE NEGEV AND THE DEAD SEA

The south of Israel is more or less all desert. Put aside, however, images of endless rolling white sand dunes and solitary palm trees – this terrain is rugged and mountainous, with a feast of visual extremes. Sprawling for 350km from Beersheba in the north to Eilat on the Red Sea, the **Negev Desert** itself is stunning, particularly in the Central Highlands, where three giant craters pockmark the landscape. In the west, the arid highlands merge into the craggy mountains of the Sinai; while to the east, the land falls sharply to the Great Rift Valley – one of the longest gashes in the earth's crust – which borders Jordan and runs all the way from Turkey to the Zambesi River in southern Africa.

This great barren triangle of desert covers almost ten thousand square kilometres, more than half the area of the State of Israel, but contains less than ten percent of its population. The traditional inhabitants of the Negev are the **Bedouins**, but their semi-nomadic lifestyle has been all but destroyed by the enclosure of their land for other purposes, and while they still constitute the majority of the population, they are on the whole confined to arid "reserves" or soulless modern towns in the north, particularly around Beersheba.

The main **routes through the Negev**, Route 90 down the Jordan Valley from Jericho, and Route 40 from central Israel via Beersheba, are plied by buses serving Eilat, though these are not tremendously frequent and often nocturnal. The journey by car was once an awe-inspiring enough experience in itself – mysterious and dangerous if perhaps a little monotonous – but nowadays, romantic notions of exploring the wilderness lead many a modern tourist to venture further. If you have the time to get off the main road, you'll find a rich landscape, full of **hiking** possibilities. The government, having struggled long to develop and populate this barren land, has also cottoned on to the tourism potential; in 1988 they earmarked 25 million dollars for the Negev Tourism Development Agency and you'll come across many projects under construction, such as resorts and holiday villages, conceived to boost domestic and international tourism.

Your first port of call if coming down from Israel's Mediterranean coast, on the other hand, will probably be **Beersheba**, commercial capital of the Negev, and the fastest growing city in Israel. Further south in the central desert highlands and perched on the lip of the largest of five *makhteshim* – sea-eroded craters unique to this region – sandswept **Mitzpe Ramon**, little more than a village, is nevertheless the heart of desert tourism. Between Beersheba and Mitzpe Ramon, **Sede Boker** is the most celebrated kibbutz in the Negev, former home and now burial place of the first Israeli Prime Minister, **David Ben Gurion**. Today it's an important campus of the University of the Negev; scientists from around the world are working here to develop farming methods using brackish water – the main problem for agriculture in the region being not aridity, but the salinity of the soil and water table.

The desert tapers to a five-kilometre-wide tip at the popular holiday resort of **Eilat**, hedonist capital of Israel, if not the whole Middle East. Here, the underwater carnival

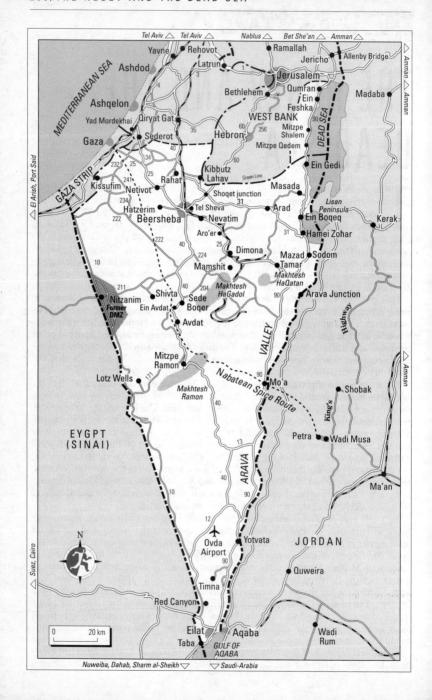

of the **Red Sea** combines with the beautiful location, set against a backdrop of pink hills in Jordan, to compensate amply for the unadulterated commercialism of the place. The town, served by its own international **airport** at Ovda some 50km inland, offers a different Israel, a world apart from the tensions in the north.

In the Judean desert, northeast of the Negev proper and shared between Israel, the West Bank and Jordan, the unique salt lake called the **Dead Sea** is an unmissable experience, where you can enjoy mud wraps, effortless floating and other weird sensations. Keen to develop their section of the lakeside with more hotel clusters and health facilities, the Israelis are promoting nearby **Arad**, famous for its clean air, as tourist capital of the region. Alternatively, you can stay down below normal sea level, by the spring and nature reserve at **Ein Gedi** or more upmarket **Ein Boqeq**, and pay a visit to the spectacular hilltop fortress of **Masada** and to **Qumran**, site of an ancient Essene community and where the **Dead Sea Scrolls** were discovered.

THE DEAD SEA

One of the natural wonders of the world, the **Dead Sea** is an extraordinary phenomenon, with its own unique ecosystem and sauna-like microclimate. As you descend from the Judean desert highlands, it appears in stunning glimpses between the rocks, a still-life trapped under a blanket of airless, motionless heat. The rose-coloured cliffs along the west shore contrast with blindingly white salt-flats, while across the water in Jordan the mountains of Moab and Edom shade through a full palette of purples and pinks as the sun crosses the sky. It's a landscape artist's dream, but the magic of the Dead Sea lies also in its silence: the solitude has long offered a refuge to zealots wanting to feel closer to their gods, kings escaping their fate, and more recently stressed or sick tourists.

This is a place of **superlatives**: the lowest point on the surface of the planet, it's also consistently one of the hottest; its water is the most saline on earth and its atmosphere the most oxygenated. No wonder then that it's also one of the deadest spots in the world; hence the name, coined by Christians who had wandered off the beaten pilgrimage track early this century. Now that life has been discovered here, however (see box on p.258), the Dead Sea's other titles – *Yam HaMelakh* (the Salt Sea) in Hebrew and *Bahr Lut* (the Sea of Lot) in Arabic – seem more fitting: the former for obvious reasons, the latter because the sea was the setting for the destruction of Sodom and Gomorrah, where Lot's wife was turned into a pillar of salt.

The Dead Sea's curative properties are world famous. It's a vast reservoir of chemicals, extracted in the processing plants at its southern end, while the **spas and health resorts** which dot the shoreline use the waters to cure a variety of ills, especially arthritis and skin diseases; Dead Sea mud, and soap made from it, are available all over Israel and increasingly abroad to treat skin ailments. Some European governments even send patients suffering from chronic skin and respiratory diseases here for treatment. Therapeutic care centres, rest houses, thermo-mineral bathing facilities and balneological services including immersion pools, mud packs, massage and solar irradiation by UV-filtered sunlight are all found here, while for those sufferering from little else than the extreme heat, the beaches, hotels and hostels provide ample relaxation and entertainment enjoyed by thousands of tourists every year.

Swimming is impossible owing to the salinity of the water (see p.258), which gives it a strange oily feel; instead you can bob about on your back, and, armed with a newspaper, pose for the inevitable snapshot, while the layers of salt crystallize on your skin. There are three public bathing **beaches** along the shore that have freshwater taps for rinsing off the sticky solution and, should the need arise, full-time **lifeguards**. If you swallow even a mouthful of the foul-tasting liquid, let someone know immediately (though you're more than likely to bring it straight back up again before you get the chance), as it can be dangerous. It can also sting terribly on cuts and grazes, and going in straight after shaving or during your period can also be quite painful.

Transport through the area is still limited to one road, albeit a fabulously scenic one, part of Route 90, starting in the West Bank at a junction not far from Jericho and sticking closely to the western shore all the way down from the northern tip to the southern extremity, with only one minor road turning off, at Masada. **Buses** run frequently along this road, to and from Jerusalem, and you should never have to wait more than an hour for the next to pass (though in the heat of summer, even an hour can seem an eternity). If you do get stuck, hitching is generally easy, perhaps because drivers appreciate the difficulties involved in travelling around here. If you are driving, ensure that you fill up with petrol before setting out, as there are few petrol stations in the region.

Climate-wise, the Dead Sea is in fact a desert region. The only rainfall is provided by thunderstorms from October to April, causing the occasional flash floods that are so dangerous throughout the Negev. Water pours down the Judean Hills from Jerusalem and the surrounding area, instantly transforming the landscape, washing away everything in its path, and occasionally closing the road along the shore. Pleasantly warm in winter when it is favoured by frozen Jerusalemites, the area becomes a steam bath during the summer, with temperatures regularly exceeding 40°C, exacerbated by exceptional humidity – you'll need to bring water, sunglasses and a hat for protection.

GEOGRAPHY, FLORA AND FAUNA

All three names – the **Dead Sea**, the Salt Sea and the Sea of Lot – by which this extraordinary body of water is known are wrong in one respect, for it is not a sea but a vast, enclosed **lake**, 295m below sea level, covering just over one thousand square kilometres, that gathers its waters from the Jordan River, floods and underground streams. With no exit from the southern end, the only escape for the water is for it to evaporate, which it does at an incredible rate, leaving behind bizarrely shaped **salt deposits**, and in summer frequently bathing the whole area in a sticky haze. The water that remains is so dense – twenty-five percent of it is solids – that it is practically impossible to swim in. Because it is a terminal lake, with no water flowing out, the Dead Sea is extremely sensitive to natural and man-made change. In fact, the **level** has fallen by seven metres this century; partly due to climate change, but accelerated by the increasing exploitation of the Jordan River. Already the sea is cut in half by the **Lisan Peninsula**, which juts out from Jordan (the southern half was always extremely shallow), and if the waters continue to recede at the present rate it is feared that it could disappear altogether in a few decades. The salt density in the southern part is extremely high and the water feels even more like oil. So far, it does not seem to be overly affected by the industrial areas at its southern end, over which, when there is no wind, clouds of **pollution** can be seen to hang.

Although the valley in which the sea lies forms part of the 6000-kilometre-long Afro-Syrian Rift that runs from Turkey to Mozambique, it is less susceptible to **earthquakes** than Turkey or the Red Sea, and fits into Seismic Zone 3 in the Uniform Building Codes – theoretically you're less likely to be shaken out of your bed in a huge hotel here than in Eilat.

The recent discovery by scientists of several species of micro-organisms has put paid to the myth that nothing can survive in the sea's mineral-rich waters. Around its shores too, the desert has subtle forms of **flora and fauna**; the area's one hundred species of plant life (mainly herbs and shrubs) struggle to life and bloom briefly after the spring rains. But the area is at its most lush in the oases along the western bank, where the establishment of nature reserves has also provided havens for wildlife, including leopards (see p.264). Twice a year the sky is clouded with millions of migrating birds en route to rest and refuelling at the land bridge where Israel, Egypt and Jordan meet around the Red Sea. Separated from the wider gene pool by its desert barrier, the plant and animal life of the Dead Sea area has evolved into a **microecology** of rare ecotypes, subspecies and even species unique to the area. Ein Feshka is home to an indigenous tropical river fish and the Ein Gedi asp (named after Ein Gedi – see p.263) seems to have speciated within the Rift Valley. Scientists have also recently identified algae unique to the area. The area is a **plant quarantine zone,** making it illegal to bring plants in or out.

Some history

Eight thousand years ago, human life flourished around the Dead Sea; the most famous traces have been excavated to the northeast, at **Teleilat el-Ghassul**, in Jordan, but cave remains have also been found in the Judean desert. In the south, too, huge cemeteries dating back to the Early Bronze Age have been excavated. But despite being the theatre for many biblical dramas, few biblical sites have yet been uncovered around the Dead Sea. However, peace between Jordan and Israel has brought frantic archeological activity on both sides of the border; the sites of Sodom and Gomorrah are now believed to be submerged in the shallow waters of the sea's southern end (see p.268). Both Israel and Jordan claim to have the pillar of salt into which Lot's wife was turned (see p.268), and **Lot's Cave**, discovered east of Safi town, just inside the Jordanian border, is an important Jewish site said to contain the remains of Lot, who survived the disaster that destroyed Sodom. In the desert beyond the Dead Sea, evidence of the solitary lives of the ascetic Christians, who came here from the Byzantine period onwards to escape life and practice the tradition of **hermetism**, is still being excavated.

The Dead Sea has had its fair share of economic and agricultural fortune. In the Greco-Roman period, in particular, palm growing, and the cultivation of spices and medicinal herbs were prevalent. Oasis farming remained typical until the Muslim conquest, and disappeared (with the exception of a brief period in the Middle Ages when sugar cane and indigo were grown) until the twentieth century. Extraction of the sea's vast reservoir of **chemicals and minerals** goes back a long way: in the Greco-Roman period, boats crossed the lake, possibly to collect floating bitumen, forging strong links around the shores, while commerical exploitation began in the fourth century AD when Nabatean merchants sold bitumen to the Egyptians who used it for embalming. In 1930, the Palestine Potash Company was set up by the British; potash is still extracted today for use as a fertilizer, and the mass of rather ugly plants that have burgeoned around the Sea's southern end testify to growth of industry based on the modern expoitation of the Sea's chemical resources.

With the arrival of peace in the border region between Jordan and Israel, the other main growth industry is **tourism**. Jordan, Israel and Palestine all have their own ideas: the PNA is now planning forty hotels along its 8km of shoreline at the northern end to compete with Israel and take advantage of pilgrim interest in the lower Jordan, in what is becoming known as "Monastery Country".

Arad

Sitting on the Judean plateau 1000m above the Dead Sea, the pleasant modern settlement town of **ARAD**, built in 1961, is now being groomed as a centre for tourism in the area; its blatant modernism succeeding, for some reason, where other planned towns have failed. In its favour, it has splendid sneak previews of the Dead Sea shimmering way down below, and its air (some say the best in Israel) is famously pure, pollen-free and blissful for asthmatics. Non-native plant cultivation is forbidden, as is industrial pollution (though most of the residents work in the far-from-pollution-free Dead Sea Works plants). All this makes Arad a sensible, cool **base** for anyone wanting to explore the Dead Sea, just 24km to the east. However, note that the road directly from Arad to Masada is a dead end; to reach the Dead Sea shores from Arad you need to take the southern road to Neve Zohar via Ein Boqeq.

The Town

The **town centre** is basically a rectangle marked by three parallel east–west streets, HaQanna'im, Ben Ya'ir and Yehuda, intersected by two shopping streets, Yerushalayim and the pedestrianized Hevron. Most of the things you will need are within this rec-

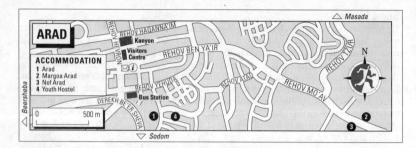

tangle or just off it, bar the two main hotels, which are a kilometre east on Rehov Moav. Opposite the bus station in the centre of town is a pedestrianized shopping centre and the indoor air-conditioned mall (*kanyon*), which is where you'll find most of the town's cafés and restaurants.

Although there is nothing much to see in Arad itself, there is a **tourist office** in the centre of town on Rehov Ben Ya'ir (☎07/995 8144; Sun–Tues & Thurs 8am–noon & 4–7pm, Wed 8am–4pm, Fri 8am–noon), and a **visitors' centre** run by the Nature Reserves Authority opposite at 28 Ben Ya'ir (☎07/995 4409; Sat–Thurs 9am–4pm, Fri 9am–2.30pm; 15NIS), with information on hiking and wildlife in the region. Staff will organize trips and help you understand the Hebrew topographical maps you'll need if you want to hike. The main attractions from Arad are **jeep rides** out into the Judean desert and trips to the Masada Sound and Light Show (see p.267). The visitors' centre shows educational videos about the desert, and also has a small **museum** of archeological finds from **Tel Arad** (see below).

Tel Arad National Park

Arad's only historical site lies within **Tel Arad National Park** (Sun–Thurs 8am–4pm, Fri 8am–3pm; 8NIS); take the turning to the right 8km west of the town on Route 31 towards Beersheba. There are really two archeological sites here: an Early Bronze Age city, probably dating from the third millennium BC; and, higher up the slope, a fortress probably built a couple of thousand years later, around the time of Solomon. Most of the original finds are now in the Israel Museum in Jerusalem (see p.373), and it's probably only worthwhile coming here for the great view of the surrounding desert or if you're particularly interested in seeing an early Israelite settlement. **Buses** between Arad and Beersheba will drop you at the junction on Route 31, a two-kilometre walk from the site, and there are also occasional buses from Arad direct to the site itself.

ACCOMMODATION PRICE CODES

Throughout this guide, **hotel accommodation** is graded on a scale from ① to ⑥. The numbers represent the cost per night of the **cheapest double room in high season**, though remember that many of the cheap places will have more expensive rooms with en-suite facilities. For **hostels**, the code represents the price of **two dorm beds** and is followed by the code for a double room where applicable, ie ①/②. Hostels are listed in ascending price order.

① = less than $20	② = $20–40	③ = $40–60
④ = $60–80	⑤ = $80–100	⑥ = over $100

MOVING ON FROM ARAD

The **bus station** (☎07/995 7393) is little more than a shelter in the centre of town at the junction of Yehuda with Yerushalayim. Arad lies off most Egged inter-city routes but local buses #384 and #388 will take you to Beersheba (1–2 per hour; 1hr), where you can pick up connections to Jerusalem and Eilat. There are direct buses from Arad to Tel Aviv (3 daily; 2hr), and to Masada (3 daily; 45min), Ein Boqeq (5 daily; 30min) and Ein Gedi (5 daily; 1hr).

Practicalities

A few **banks** can be found on Rehov Hevron, as can the **post office**, which is at the corner with Rehov Ben Ya'ir. **Car rental** is available from Europcar in the industrial zone (☎07/995 5365). B&B **accommodation** may be available in private homes (ask at the tourist office); in general, however, choice is limited. The only cheap option is the *HI Blau-Weiss Youth Hostel*, Rehov Atad at HaPalmah (☎07/995 7150, fax 995 5078; ②/③; ring ahead to check vacancies), basically a complex of six-bed huts, with a choice of dorm or private accommodation. Of the three hotels in or near Arad, the *Arad Hotel*, 6 HaPalmah (☎07/995 7040, fax 995 7272; ④), is the only one in the town centre; it's clean and comfy with a pleasant garden. The other two are 1km east of town on Rehov Moav: *Margoa Arad Hotel* (☎07/995 1222, fax 995 7778; ⑤) has great views of the desert, with a rooftop swimming pool and health club including sauna; *Nof Arad Hotel* (☎07/995 7056 to 8, fax 995 4053; ④), opposite, is more modest, though it too has a pool.

For **food**, there are **cafés** on Rehov Hevron and fast food in the *kanyon*. For something classier, *Apropo* in the *kanyon* (☎07/995 0766; expensive) and *Steiner's* on the Beersheba road west of town (☎07/995 3328; expensive) are your only choices. If you prefer a bit of self-catering, you can stock up on supplies at the two **supermarkets** in town: the Coop on Rehov Hevron near the bus station, and Supersol on HaQanna'im near the tourist office.

The Dead Sea shore

The first 25km of the Dead Sea's 85km of **shoreline** from the River Jordan southward is actually inside the West Bank (see p.391 for details on visiting the West Bank) and features the archeological site of **Qumran** and the beach at **Ein Feshka**. Although the Palestinians plan to develop a Dead Sea tourism to rival Israel's, the infrastructure is as yet not in place – in fact, there isn't even any public transport between Qumran and the nearest West Bank town, Jericho. Connections are much better southward along the shore to **Ein Gedi**, a rather more developed resort across the Green Line in Israel proper, from where it's a short bus ride to **Masada**.

Qumran

Though the **archeological site** (daily: winter 8am–5pm; summer 8am–6pm; 13NIS) of **Qumran** lies less than 100m from Route 90, and can be reached by bus from Jerusalem, 45km away, or Arad, you can get there from Jericho (some 25km away) only by "special" taxi. The story of the discovery here in 1947 of the **Dead Sea Scrolls** (see p.262) has a mythical quality to it: a young Bedouin shepherd out looking for a lost sheep came upon an ancient cave and on throwing a stone into it, heard it strike pottery. He investigated further and found fifty cylindrical jars containing the scrolls, now known to date from the first century BC. As they were written on animal hide, the scrolls were

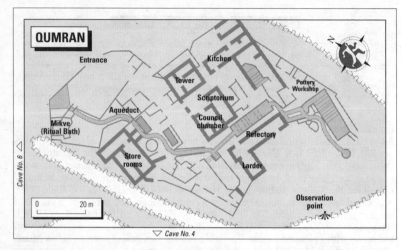

▽ Cave No. 4

first considered suitable for sandals, but news of the find finally reached Eliezar Sukenik, an Israeli archeologist at the Hebrew University, who was curious enough to cross the Green Line to buy them (against military advice since at that time the Line was a border between two countries still officially at war). The scrolls are now housed in the Israel Museum in Jerusalem in the specially designed Shrine of the Book (see p.373), depriving Qumran of the vital ingredient it needs to make it really worth a visit.

What you see on the site now is, in the main, the "**monastery**" in which **the Essenes**, authors of the scrolls, lived. Remains of a tower, kitchens, dining hall and

THE DEAD SEA SCROLLS

The **Dead Sea Scrolls** were written by an ultra-devout Jewish sect, **the Essenes** – rivals to the Pharisees and Sadducees – who first emerged around 150 BC. Reacting against what they saw as the wealth and corruption of the Temple at Jerusalem, the Essene sectarian movement aspired to an extremely simple life in strict accordance with biblical law. They believed in the imminent arrival of the Messiah, preparing for it by abstinence and purity – both in diet and lifestyle – in what must have proved a harsh environment in which to live. The spiritual, ascetic living has led scholars to believe that **John the Baptist** may have belonged to the Essenes. **Qumran** was their religious centre until 68 AD, when it was destroyed by the Romans after the Jewish Revolt; it was at this time that the community's library and other treasures were hidden in the **caves**.

The Dead Sea Scrolls were written mainly on cleaned and treated animal hides, although some also contain fragments of papyrus and thin copper plate. The ink used was a mixture of carbon and gum and the finished scrolls were then wrapped in linen and placed in **clay jars** of the distinctive Greco-Roman style of the period; the arid atmosphere of the desert contributed further to their excellent preservation. **Excavations** throughout the 1950s found documents in eleven caves, one of which yielded some 40,000 fragments of biblical text. These included a complete seven-metre scroll consisting of 66 chapters of ancient scriptures agreeing with Greek, Latin and present-day texts. Fragments of **Leviticus** dated to around 100 BC predate all other existing Hebrew manuscripts by over 1000 years. Except for the Book of Esther, there were parts of all the Old Testament books, as well as several Apocrypha works and documents relating to the daily life of the Essenes, including the description of a final battle – "The War of the Sons of Light Against the Sons of Darkness".

a "**scriptorium**", where supposedly the scrolls were written, can be seen, together with various cisterns, aqueducts and channels – evidence both of the importance of water in the desert, and of the role ritual bathing played in the life of the Essenes. At the far side of the site you can look out to the start of the gorge and the caves where the first scrolls were found. There are numerous possibilities for **walks** into the surrounding Judean hills, with well-marked routes taking you into the still and somewhat surreal desert. The site also has a small shop and cafeteria.

Any **bus** on the highway will stop if you signal it; there are nine daily to Jerusalem (1hr), and the other way to Ein Gedi (1hr). There is no direct public transport to Jericho so you'll either have to take a taxi or take a Jerusalem-bound bus to the junction of Route 90 and Route 1, and try to get a space in one of the service taxis heading north to Jericho from there – as they're often full, you'll probably end up walking or hitching the remaining 8km.

Ein Feshka

The reserve at **Ein Feshka** (daily: April–Oct 8am–5pm; Nov–March 8am–4pm; 25NIS), the first and perhaps the best of the Dead Sea **beaches**, lies just 3km south of Qumran, a pleasant walk if you're not too heavily laden, and is likewise served by buses between Jerusalem and Ein Gedi (9 daily). A freshwater **spring**, whose waters tumble down from the hills, provides a refreshing alternative to the heavy waters of the Dead Sea and brings life to the barren surroundings, creating pools of lush vegetation. It also attracts **wildlife** – ibex and hyrax – and if not as spectacularly verdant as Ein Gedi (see below), it's usually a great deal less crowded. A cafeteria sells the usual snacks and drinks at reasonable prices.

The road south meanders past more of these sudden bursts of life amid otherwise total desolation, each signifying the presence of a spring. At regular intervals, too, you'll see signs indicating apparently non-existent bridges (curiously named "Irish bridges") which mark the location of **floodwater channels**; flash floods in winter occasionally close the road.

Ein Gedi

It's no mystery why **Ein Gedi Nature Reserve** (☎07/658 4285; Sat–Thurs till 5pm summer, 4pm in winter; 8.50NIS), a true oasis of green and shade amid the surrounding brown barren desert, is so popular that it sometimes has to deny entry to tourists. The reserve, just inside the Green Line, is actually a complex of two valleys – **Nahal David** and **Nahal Arugot** – a youth hostel, and a public beach for mudbathing and floating. Blessed with two waterfalls and a **spring** (Ein Gedi means "Goats' Spring"), bountiful tropical vegetation and a host of wild animals, it's the best spot to base yourself for a few days of Dead Sea living. The spring has attracted people since the Late Stone Age and was well known in biblical times. Here David hid in a cave from Saul, who wanted him killed; while Saul took a break from the search to relieve himself, David snipped off a corner of the king's robe unnoticed, and showed it to him to demonstrate that he could have killed him, whereupon he was acknowledged by Saul as his successor (I Samuel 24). The area was also a base for rebels in the 132–35 AD Second Jewish Revolt against the Romans. Various excavations scattered through the reserve recall this history, but it is the natural attractions which make Ein Gedi a **hiking** paradise.

The hiking **routes** can be broadly divided into two areas – those which follow Nahal David and go as far as the large pool and the canyon (see p.264), and those which follow Nahal Arugot. They range from simple one-and-a-half hour walks to difficult five-hour hikes which should be attempted only if you're fit and properly kitted out. The simplest walk, along Nahal David (see overleaf) can be done by following the signs, but further information should be obtained for any of the lengthier ones. A set of **staggered times** for latest entry (the times depend on the route length) ensure that you complete your hike by closing time. Ask at reception for details, but whatever your plan, it really is best to get here as early as possible in the morning. Remember, too, that the delicate ecosystem means you shouldn't bring in any food (though you should of course bring lots of water), or touch any of the plants or animals. It is also advisable to **stick to the paths** since some independent-minded ramblers have been known almost to get themselves killed clambering down slippery scree slopes. **Information and maps** can be found at the SPNI-run **Field School**, near the youth hostel and the Nahal David entrance to the reserve.

The reserve

From the northern **Nahal David entrance**, you suddenly find yourself in a narrow wadi surrounded by lush vegetation. The combination of a hot climate and plentiful sweet water in an arid desert environment creates the conditions for a wide variety of vegetation ranging from sumptuous water plants to desert plants adapted to thrive in the harshest conditions. These in turn attract an interesting animal population – dozens of **hyraxes** (small grey animals which look rather like badgers but with strange, hoof-like toes) appear to stand to attention at the mouth of the wadi, and there are herds of ibex, too, which in spring come down with their young from the desert upland. There are also reputed to be thirteen **leopards** prowling around in the undergrowth – signs at regular intervals warn you about them and the danger of provoking them; advice you'd be wise to follow in the unlikely event that you come across one.

A memorable one-and-a-half-hour walk leads along the course of Nahal David (David's Stream) to the twenty-metre-high **Shulamit Falls**, whose waters crash over the rocks into a clear, cool pool where you can get down to some serious bathing. Twenty metres before this a path leads up to **Shulamit Spring** and **Dodim Cave**, to the south of which another trail leads to a **Chalcolithic Temple**, and down to the **spring of Ein Gedi** itself, before continuing on to the site of an ancient Israelite settlement at **Tel Goren**. From there, you can head west to the reserve's southern **Nahal Arugot entrance**, passing en route the excavations of a fourth-century synagogue.

Alternatively, you can strike out west from Tel Goren, following the wadi (Nahal Arugot) for an hour, until you reach the **Hidden Waterfall**. It is also possible to start at the Nahal Arugot entrance, and continue on from the Hidden Waterfall to the Upper Pools; to do this five-hour hike, you must make arrangements with a Nature Reserves Authority ranger at the entrance, and you'll need to get to the reserve as early in the morning as possible since you have to leave the Upper Pools by 2pm. Although more gruelling than the Nahal David hike, the effort is rewarded with more dramatic desert scenery and a greater sense of adventure.

The beach and spa

Behind the petrol station on the main road (Route 90), just south of the wadi of Nahal Arugot, is the entrance to the **public beach** where you'll also find a couple of snack places. The beach has a lifeguard and shower facilities. But, if you really want to do the Dead Sea experience in style, head 5km south to the **Ein Gedi Health Spa** (☎07/659 4813; daily: winter 7am–5pm; summer 7am–6pm), where, for just 45NIS, you can spend hours basking in heavenly, warm, indoor sulphur bathing pools, or wallow in the Dead Sea itself (hot showers, changing rooms and lockers available). There's also a snack bar and air-conditioned restaurant should you get peckish. Many organized tours stop here; with a licensed guide you get a reduction, greater for a group.

In the hills behind, and sadly all but inaccessible, are the remains of a **Roman Camp** above Nahal Hever. The camp was set up to besiege rebel forces loyal to Simon Bar

Kokhba in the Second Revolt, who were holed up in caves in the escarpment. A number of bones were found by archeologists working under Yigal Yadin in the 1960s, along with a cache of letters sent before the siege by Bar Kokhba himself. In one of them, he rebukes "the men of Ein Gedi" because they "sit in comfort, eat and drink from the property of the house of Israel, and care nothing for your brothers". Sadly, this situation did not last: the rebels were starved out by the Romans, and died of hunger and thirst.

Practicalities

There are four **bus stops** at Ein Gedi. Coming south from Jerusalem, the first is for the Nahal David entrance and the youth hostel; the second stop is by the public beach and "camping village"; the third is at the turn-off for the kibbutz; and the fourth is by the mineral bath resort.

Of **places to stay**, the *HI Beit Sara International Youth Hostel* near the Nahal David entrance (☎07/658 4165, fax 658 4445; ②/③) offers spotless, air-conditioned comfort in eight-bed dorms or double rooms; the only cheaper alternative is to pitch a tent at the *Ein Gedi Camping Village* by the public beach (☎07/658 4444, fax 658 4455; ①; double rooms ④). For something classier, with facilities including a swimming pool, go for the *Ein Gedi Guest House* at Kibbutz Ein Gedi, a couple of kilometres' walk to the south (☎07/659 4222, fax 658 4328; ⑤).

Moving on, there are buses to Qumran (7 daily; 1hr) and Jerusalem (10 daily; 1hr 30min), Arad (5 daily; 1hr) and Beersheba (5 daily; 2hr), Masada (3 daily; 30min) and Ein Boqeq (5 daily; 45min), and Eilat (4 daily; 4hr).

Masada

The single most visited archeological site in Israel, the hilltop fortress of **Masada** (Masada National Park ☎07/658 4207 or 8; daily dawn–sunset; 15NIS), 15km south of Ein Gedi as the crow flies, is famed for both its spectacular views and its tragic history. Visitors traditionally make the pilgrimage to watch dawn break from the summit, the dramatic landscapes of the Dead Sea, deserts and mountains providing ample tonic for tired eyes – and once your senses are fully warmed up, Masada's story cannot fail to impress.

The fortress was built for **Jonathan the Maccabee** in 150 BC but fortified under **Herod** the Great in 43 BC. For Herod, hated by his subjects and threatened by Cleopatra, Masada was above all a place of refuge, where he could sit out times of trouble behind impregnable defences. He built an elaborate system of dykes and channels which directed the rainfall, sparse in an area where rain sometimes does not fall for years, into twelve reservoirs hewn out of the mountainside. The reservoirs, which you can still see, have a combined capacity of 40,000 cubic metres and once provided enough water for public and private baths to ensure that Herod and his Roman backers could lead the life they were accustomed to. More importantly, the water supply allowed the defenders to withstand a siege for years if necessary.

However, the site is primarily known for its role in the final act of the Jewish War against the Romans, also known as the **First Revolt**. In 70 AD, when the Romans had regained control of Judea, Jerusalem had been sacked and the Second Temple destroyed, this remote mountain top became the last outpost of **Jewish resistance**, occupied by a group of Zealots, just under a thousand strong, who had fled to Masada and were determined to fight the Romans to the death. They managed to hold out for three years but eventually, with the siege unrelenting, the enemy laboriously scaling the steep cliff and capture imminent, they chose death over slavery, and carried out an elaborate **mass suicide pact**. First, each man executed his wife and family with a sword. Then ten men were selected to kill the other men and, finally, lots were drawn to determine the man who would complete the ritual slaughter, before falling on his own sword. Two women and five children, who had hidden themselves in a water

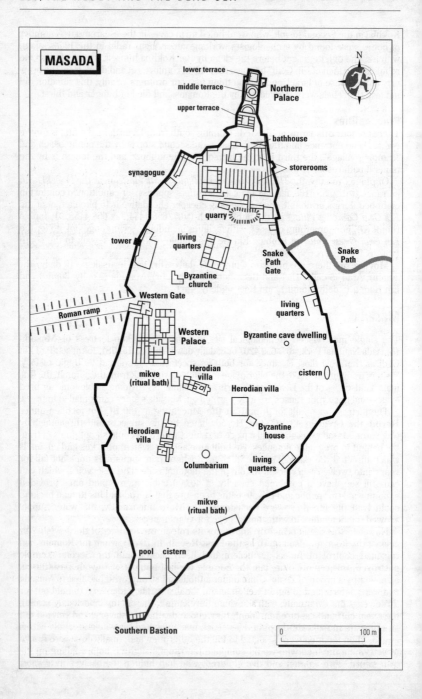

MASADA

lower terrace
middle terrace — Northern Palace
upper terrace

bathhouse

synagogue

storerooms

quarry

tower

living quarters

Byzantine church

Snake Path Gate

Snake Path

Western Gate

Roman ramp

living quarters

Western Palace

Byzantine cave dwelling

mikve (ritual bath)

Herodian villa

cistern

Herodian villa

Herodian villa

Byzantine house

Columbarium

living quarters

mikve (ritual bath)

pool   cistern

Southern Bastion

N

0   100 m

channel, lived to tell the tale to the Romans, who broke through the following morning to find 960 bodies. This heroism in the face of defeat has become a potent symbol in modern Israel: today, every Israeli schoolchild and army recruit is taken up to Masada to absorb the lesson, with the recruits taking an oath of allegiance that "Masada shall not fall again".

The site

The exposed stone **remains** at the site are magnificent in their rocky isolation. If you approach from the Dead Sea side, either by serpentine path or on the cable car (see below), you'll enter through the east gate, after passing some of the reservoirs on the way up. To your right are large **storehouses**, and beyond them, at the northern tip of the hill, Herod's fabulous **palace**. This exceptional construction clings to the cliff edge on three levels: at the top are the main living quarters with well-preserved baths and a semicircular terrace looking down over the lower levels; the central section, thought to have been Herod's summer residence, is enclosed by twin circular walls; at the bottom was a cloister-like open courtyard. From here, and indeed from vantage points all around the summit, the **Roman wall** surrounding the mountain, and some of the eight Roman army camps from which the siege was managed, are clearly visible. Heading back across the site from the palace, a **synagogue** built by the Zealots can be seen against the western wall, and there are a couple of ritual baths nearby. Further west, in the middle of the site, are Byzantine buildings and a church built when Masada was briefly occupied by a group of monks in the fifth century. Beyond these you come to the west palace and west gate (through which you'll enter if you come from Arad and up the Roman ramp), where you'll find some fine Roman **mosaics**, and Zealot living quarters.

Further remains (all well-labelled) of defences, baths and houses are liberally scattered around the mountain top. A comprehensive and inexpensive **booklet**, available at the site, describes all the ruins in detail. If you're wondering what the painted **black line** that adorns most buildings is, it's the dividing line between the excavated walls and sections that have been reconstructed.

Masada has its own **son et lumière** (nightly March–Oct), which attracts hordes of tourists. The show tells the story in Hebrew (simultaneous translation available) of the Jews' last stand against the Romans, and can be seen only from the western (Arad) side of the mountain, and round-trip tickets to Arad can be arranged from the tourist office there. Occasionally, big Israeli pop stars perform concerts here as well, but as the tickets are like gold dust, you'll have to keep your ears to the ground for news.

Practicalities

The easiest way to visit Masada if you are not particularly interested in the surrounding area is to take one of the **excursions** offered by hostels or travel agents in Jerusalem (see "Hostels", p.314, and "Travel agents", p.387). Otherwise, Masada is connected by **bus** to Eilat (4 daily; 3hr 45min), Jerusalem (8 daily; 2hr), Ein Gedi (3 daily; 30min), Ein Boqeq (5 daily; 30min) and Beersheba (3 daily; 2hr) via Arad (45min). It is also possible to get to Masada by **air**: *Arkia* flies three times weekly from Tel Aviv's Sede Dov Airport. **Cable cars** serve the summit approximately every fifteen minutes (Sat–Thurs summer 8am–5pm, winter 4pm; Fri summer 8am–3pm, winter 3pm).

Staying the night has the advantage of letting you see the site while it's still relatively cool and uncrowded. The *HI Isaac Taylor Youth Hostel* at the bottom of the mountain (☎07/658 4349, fax 658 4650; check-in 5–7pm; ②/③) is not especially recommended but it's the only accommodation for miles around, and as a result often full. If so, they may allow you to camp outside and use their showers and restaurant; the other cafés and restaurants nearby are expensive.

Ein Boqeq

Lying at the lowest point on land in the world at 394m below sea level, the southern part of the Dead Sea is the economic heart of the region: along its banks, the bright orange, yellow and red Meccano-kit constructions of the **Dead Sea Works** (processing plants for the minerals and chemicals) are an eyesore, but one that stands splendidly proud in a man-battling-against-nature kind of way.

At **EIN BOQEQ**, just south of the Lisan Peninsula, visitors are either staying in its luxury spa hotels or in the large clinic for sufferers of chronic skin and respiratory diseases, rheumatism and arthritis. The healing mineral properties of the water, mud and nearby sulphur springs are open to debate, but northern European governments pay for patients to come here nonetheless. Because the water is even denser at this end of the Sea, the resort offers one of the best floating experiences, and its public beach (with shower facilities), air-conditioned shopping centres and eating places are all worth planning into a trip. Moreover, if you're really missing your nightlife, it's the only place for miles where you'll find it, at the resort's hotel discos. That said, when visitor figures are down, the place is painfully dead. Overlooking the city are the remains of a Roman fort, **Mazad Boqeq**, built in the third century AD to guard the spring.

There is no budget **accommodation** in Ein Boqeq; luxury spa hotels include the *Hyatt Regency* (☎07/659 1200, fax 659 1235; ⑥) and the *Radisson Moriah* (☎07/658 4351, fax 658 4383; ⑥). **Buses** from Ein Boqeq serve Arad (5 daily; 30min), Beersheba (5 daily; 1hr 15min), Eilat (4 daily; 3hr 30min); Ein Gedi (5 daily; 45min), Jerusalem (4 daily; 3hr), Masada (5 daily; 30min) and Tel Aviv (1 daily; 3hr 15min).

Just 3km further south, the **Hamei Zohar Hot Springs** are the biggest and best-known of several mineral springs in the area which have been used therapeutically since antiquity. The smell of the sulphur can at times be overwhelming, and ruins the enjoyment of a meal at the excellent vegetarian restaurant next door. There are two hotels here, both deluxe "spa resort" affairs: the *Radisson Moriah* (☎07/658 4221, fax 658 4238; ⑥), and the *Nirvana* (☎07/658 4626, fax 658 4345; ⑥).

Sodom

The site of biblical **Sodom** (or, as road signs primly insist on calling it, "Sedom") is thought to lie beneath the waters of the southern part of the Dead Sea. Here Abraham's cousin Lot came to live, even though "the men of Sodom were wicked and sinners before the Lord exceedingly" (Genesis 13: 13). Despite Abraham's pleadings on their behalf, God decided to destroy Sodom and neighbouring Gomorrah, but first he sent three angels to go and fetch Lot. When the angels arrived at Lot's house, all the men of Sodom besieged it and demanded that Lot bring out the strangers, "that we may know them" (Genesis 19: 5), a statement from which it is supposed that Sodom was being punished for "sodomy" (ie, homosexuality) – though that interpretation is far from obvious to a modern reader. Either way, God wasted no time in dousing the place with fire and brimstone. The angels told Lot and his family to "escape for thy life [and] look not behind thee" (19: 17), but his wife disobeyed and was turned into a pillar of salt (19: 26). She can still be seen today, on **Mount Sodom**, a mountain made of rock salt, 7km south of the junction of Route 90 and Route 31 to Arad. There are a number of caves in the mountain, notably the **Flour Cave** (Me'arat Qemah) 6km further south, then 8km down a highly scenic track leading west off Route 90. The cave is so called because its inside is coated with fine white powder, as will you be if you go in.

THE NEGEV DESERT

Israel's southernmost third is taken up by the **Negev desert**. Flanked to the west by Egypt's Sinai desert, and to the east by the **'Arava Valley** and Jordanian border, it tapers to a tip at the Red Sea port and holidaymakers' playground of **Eilat**. The Negev is a desert of rocks, not sand, but its landscape is no less imposing for that, with crags and chasms, craters and rock formations, wadis and gorges, all every bit as dramatic as the great dunes of the Sahara, and with no shortage of possible **hikes** and **desert tours**. Here you'll find the **Makhtesh Ramon**, the world's largest natural crater, visited from the town of **Mitzpe Ramon** on its rim, and one of three such craters to be found in the Negev. Here, too, lie the ancient Nabatean cities of **Mamshit**, **Shivta** and **Avdat**, not to mention the reserve of **Ein Avdat** with its natural pools, a very welcome oasis. The Negev's main town is **Beersheba**, not the most exciting place in Israel, but a useful base, and as you head for the coral-fringed beaches of Eilat, there's also **Timna**, site of King Solomon's mines.

Given the proportion of desert in Israel, it's no wonder the modern state recognized immediately the need to "make the desert bloom", and, in the Negev's northern areas especially, great successes have been scored in **reafforestation**. In particular you'll see copses of fast-growing eucalyptus trees, planted in oval patterns to maximize the water run-off and prevent soil erosion. Israel's pioneering work in this field is recognized worldwide, and Israeli experts in desert reclamation and ecological management are much in demand. In fact modern Israel has taken a lead here from its ancient predecessors, the **Nabateans**, who first learned to make the desert bloom back in the first century AD (see below), and remain the inspiration for modern desert agriculture.

Agricultural development in the Negev nowadays centres on the scattered oases of kibbutzim and moshavim (of which there are 150 in all), many surviving only with the aid of state subsidies, and increasingly coming under threat from a government set on privatization and deregulation. The more you explore, however, the more you realize that far from being a wilderness, the desert is actually becoming rather crowded. Kibbutzim, development towns, nature reserves and holiday villages apart, the **Israel Defence Force** still controls sixty percent of the land. Be prepared to find yourself suddenly sharing space with troops on manoeuvres or tank exercises. For this reason, roads marked on maps are often closed.

But while conservationists are keen for the army to release areas into the hands of the **Nature Reserves Authority** so that they can get on with protecting the amazing birdlife, flora and geology of the region, the aim of the **Negev Tourist Development Administration** (NTDA; see also box on p.270) is to maximize the resources for tourism in the Negev; the increasing number of visitors will inevitably place a burden on natural resources that may, in the long run, take its toll on the area. So far the NTDA has poured money into developing the infrastructure, particularly along the main central axis of the desert between Mitzpe Ramon and Beersheba, which has in turn begun to attract private investors.

Some history

For thousands of years, the Negev has played host to a number of peoples and civilizations who have managed to adapt to desert life. Hundreds of sites dating back as far as 4000 BC are being discovered in the wadis around Beersheba, and their contents are on display in museums around the country. From around 2000 BC the Negev was inhabited by nomadic tribes – the **Amalekites** rose to prominence around 1300 BC, and according to the Torah (Exodus 18: 8–16), attacked the Israelites in the wilderness on their way back from Egypt. Later in the Bible (I Samuel 15: 2–3), God tells Saul through Samuel to wipe out the Amalekites, and Saul incurs divine displeasure by sparing their king. Nonetheless, the Israelites extended their dominion over the Negev, and it became part of the kingdom of David. His son, Solomon, built a series of defensive forts and developed the famous copper mines at Timna; his southern port at Etzion Geber is today's Eilat and there is growing evidence that the excavations on the border of Jordan and Israel are the remains of one of his forts.

After the kingdom of David split into Israel and Judah, the Negev was occupied by the kingdom of **Edom**. The Edomites, supposedly the descendants of Jacob's brother Esau (in other words a Semitic people closely related to the Israelites), had occupied the 'Arava Valley between the Dead Sea and Eilat since before the Exodus, but were in turn pushed out of the Negev by the **Nabateans**. Little is known about the exact origins of this most impressive of ancient civilizations who kept control of secret trade routes through the desert for over a thousand years. An Arab tribe, they considered themselves descendants of Nabath, son of Ismail (aka Ishmael), oldest son of Abraham by his concubine Hagar. Historians believe they were nomads who migrated north from Arabia, and whose civilization was well developed, with its own language and alphabet, and left thousands of rock inscriptions from Arabia to Italy. At the zenith of their power (100 BC to 100 AD), they ruled the desert from their mountain citadel, Petra, in Jordan and traces of their civilization can be seen in the impressive remains of their hilltop cities (among them Shivta, Avdat and Mamshit), each built one day's camel-ride apart, between Petra and Gaza.

Their power came from control of the burgeoning **spice route** between Africa, the Arabian Peninsula and the markets of the northern Mediterranean. In return for a cut, the Nabateans guaranteed safe passage for traders, whose cargoes of frankincense and myrrh were at this time more valuable even than gold, being not only the best spices

---

EXPLORING THE NEGEV

The Negev Tourism Development Administration, or **NTDA**, 1 Henrietta Szold, Beersheba (☎07/629 5546 or 7) and 7 Mendele, Tel Aviv (☎03/527 2444 or 5), can provide you with information about travelling in the Negev, and supply you with an excellent free touring map of the region. They can also put you in touch with organizations that provide tailor-made tours.

HIKING

You could get all the way from **Mamshit to Eilat on hiking trails**, a distance of 160km as the crow flies, though it's best to undertake any hiking in the Negev with an **organized tour**, such as those run by the SPNI (see below). These are run on an ad hoc basis – call their field schools for information. In fact, with the exception of a few managed routes (see below), **hiking alone** is inadvisable unless you are very experienced and well equipped. Even at the simplest sites you should wear proper walking boots and be prepared to encounter steep cliffs. If you are going to hike without a local guide, arm yourself with a topographical **map**, available from the visitors' centre at Mitzpe Ramon and from Negev Tourism Development Administration offices in Mitzpe Ramon, Tel Aviv and Beersheba. You must also let people know exactly where you're going before you set out, and inform them when you arrive at your destination.

The SPNI, the National Parks Authority and the Nature Reserves share the management of a growing number of **marked trails**, which use recognized symbols along the route to help you: three stripes with the relevant colour sandwiched between two white bands. Yellow signifies military land, which you must not attempt to enter; other colours indicate degrees of difficulty.

Whether hiking with or without a guide there are two major **dangers** to avoid. The first is **flash floods**, especially between December and April, when cloudbursts suddenly deluge the dry riverbeds. Avoid the valleys during or after rainy weather and if you see the river turn brown, head for higher ground. The other danger is **dehydration**, which can occur quickly and is heralded by headaches, drowsiness and even vomiting. It is advisable to carry at least a litre of water at all times, and to wear a hat to protect you from sunstroke. Midday temperatures in the desert can reach more than 45°C in the shade.

for preserving food, but an integral part of many religious ceremonies, and popular for personal adornment. After the decline of their trade routes in the first century AD, due partly to the Romans' diversion of trade from the Negev to Egypt, and partly to a decline in the use of frankincense and myrrh caused by the spread of Christianity, the Nabateans turned to farming and breeding livestock, adapting and developing highly sophisticated agricultural techniques to grow crops in the desert by channelling the run-off water from what rainfall there was. Their complicated **irrigation** systems are still being investigated and remain in use by Negev Bedouins. In fact Nabatean culture as a whole is very much in the forefront of archeological interest at the moment; peace between Jordan and Israel is likely to see the two countries cooperating to maximize this new source of tourist income. The Nabatean Empire finally came to an end in 106 AD, when the region was annexed by Rome, but parts of their ancient spice route can still be followed today (see pp.281 & 287).

From the Byzantine period, the Negev was inhabited primarily by **Bedouin** peoples, living as nomadic and semi-nomadic pastoralists and agriculturalists; in fact, during the period of Ottoman rule and under the British Mandate, the Bedouins were effectively the sole inhabitants. Many adopted increasingly sedentary modes of living, with rights to ancestral lands allocated among the 96 various tribes and sub-tribes. Today, the northern and central Negev desert is home to the majority of Bedouins in the State of

DRIVING

If **driving in the Negev**, the NTDA's Negev Touring Map is worth trying to get hold of from NTDA or IGTO offices. **Roads** in the Negev are generally good, and unless you depart from main routes, you sholuld encounter little difficulty. Things to bear in mind are the sparsity of **fuel stations**, and the very real danger of **flash floods** (see above), which are especially fierce on and off Route 90 in the 'Arava Valley: always seek advice if there has been rain, and especially if you intend to drive off the main roads. If the **army** is active in the area, signs will warn you to stay clear; obey these if you don't want to risk being hit by a stray bullet. You should also carry an ample supply of **water** in the car.

DESERT TOURS

If you can afford it, a **guide** in the desert acts like a magnifying glass, bringing to life the details that otherwise pass you by: every rock, animal and plant tells a story. The following are organizations specializing in trips into the Negev:

Camel Riders, at Shacharut, in the heart of the southern Negev (☎07/637 3218). From Beersheba or Eilat take bus #392 to Ovda Airport (20km) and ring ahead for someone to meet you. This experimental settlement was established in 1983 by an Israeli, Sefi Hanegbi, who lived with the Bedouins for two and a half years. Contact them about their archeological tours and two-day rides along the ancient Nabatean smugglers' route.

Desert Shade, down a track east off route 40, 300m north of petrol station in Mitzpe Ramon (information on ☎07/658 6229, reservations through their Tel Aviv office on ☎03/575 6885). Jeep, camel, hiking or mountain-bike trips into Makhtesh Ramon. They also provide accommodation (see p.285), and have a self-service vegetarian bar, *Dates*, open from 9pm.

Egged Tours, 59 Ben Yehuda, Tel Aviv (☎03/527 1212 to 5); 44a Jaffa Rd, Jerusalem (☎02/525 3453); Central Bus Station, Beersheba (☎07/623 2532). Reliable company offering four-day desert tours out of Tel Aviv or Beersheba, covering most of the region's major sights.

Galilee Tours, 3 Hillel, Jerusalem (☎02/625 8866). Memorable, if pricey, trips into the Negev.

Neot Hakikar, 36 Keren Hayesod, Jerusalem (☎02/669 9385), and Sederot HaTemarim, Etzion Hotel, Eilat (☎057/697 1329). Guided jeep and hiking tours, both in the Negev and Sinai deserts.

Society for the Protection of Nature in Israel (SPNI), 13 Helena HaMalka, Jerusalem (☎02/625 2357); 4 Hashfela, Tel Aviv (☎03/537 4884). Variety of trips offered by non-profit organization devoted to the preservation of Israel's natural resources, with four field centres in the south, at Eilat's Coral Beach (☎07/637 1127), Mitzpe Ramon (☎07/658 8615), Kibbutz Sede Boker (☎07/656 5828) and Hatzeva in the 'Arava Valley (☎07/658 1546).

Israel, who constitute a significant and distinctive segment of the Palestinian community. Of Bedouin populations elsewhere, the most notable are in the Galilee (see p.173).

On **Yom Kippur 1946**, in defiance of a British moratorium, Zionist pioneers set up eleven settlements in the northern Negev all in a single night. When hostilities broke out in **1948**, these found themselves isolated by Egyptian forces from the rest of Israel, and were relieved only by the capture of Faluja, in which they were instrumental (see p.119), following the breakdown of the second truce. Of the estimated 80,000 Bedouins living in the Negev before the war, more than two-thirds now fled, or were expelled, to Jordan or Gaza. The newly established State of Israel declared most of the Negev state land, and imposed military rule on those who remained; the early 1950s saw the Bedouins rounded up and moved to a closed **Reserve Area** in the northeastern Negev, ostensibly for security reasons. That triangle, between Beersheba, Arad and Dimona, is still the only region where Bedouins are allowed to farm and freely graze their herds. Many tribes were relocated – temporarily – from fertile lands to barren sites where, forty years later, they remain (see box on p.278).

Beersheba

Gateway to the desert, at the northern end of the Negev, **BEERSHEBA** is the administrative, legal and commercial capital of the region, with a burgeoning population of 165,000 made up largely of olim from Ethiopia and the former Soviet Union – a little Russian always comes in handy here. It's also a university town with a large student population. At present, Beersheba seems like one huge building site: the old city is being given a face-lift to exploit the tourist potential; civic buildings, three-lane ring roads and apartment blocks are all under construction; and new suburbs are pushing the frontier town even further into the desert. All this has given ample opportunity for some refreshing architectural experimentation. That said, there's really nothing amazing to see in Beersheba itself, except the weekly **Bedouin market**. Time your trip here for a Wednesday night or Thursday morning, and get up early enough to catch the best bargains – beaten copperware – bought in from out of town.

Some history
In the Old Testament, Beersheba is considered the southernmost limit of the Israelites' territory, which is described on numerous occasions (from Judges 20: 1 onward) as stretching "from Dan to Beersheba". The place is first mentioned as the region of wilderness into which **Abraham** casts his concubine Hagar and their son Ishmael following the birth of Abraham's second son Isaac (Genesis 21: 14). Later in the same chapter, Abraham makes a treaty with local ruler Abimelekh, who had let him live and graze his herds there, involving the right to sink a well too. Swearing an oath to deal fairly with his host, Abraham gives him seven ewe lambs, "wherefore he called that place Beersheba" (21: 31), which can mean both the "Well of the Oath" or "Well of the Seven". Two chapters on, the Bible gives a slightly different version of the same story in which Isaac is substituted for Abraham (Genesis 26: 26–33).

Of course history did not begin with the Israelites, and archeologists are currently investigating an even more ancient "Beersheba Culture" dating from the **Chalcolithic period**, around 4000–5000 BC. Its most distinct features are the underground caves and tunnels, which could have been used as dwellings or storage systems. Agriculture included cereals, fruit trees, cattle and pigs and some industry. Traces of ceramics and copper workshops suggest that the area was the centre for the copper industry in the Negev and finds of decorated stones and ivory figurines indicate that the inhabitants must have had strong trade routes with distant places. Most of the settlements were abandoned with no trace of destruction, but where the people went is as uncertain as where they came from in the first place.

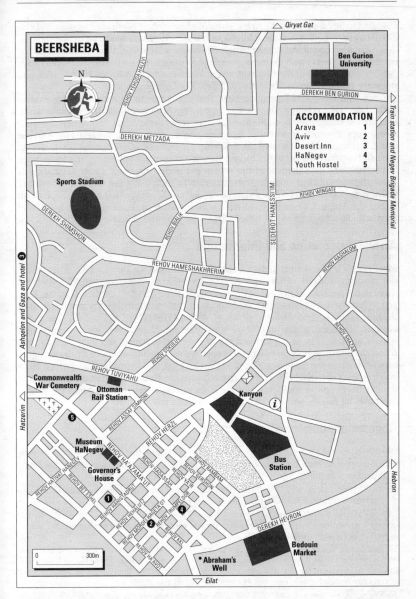

BEERSHEBA

N

ACCOMMODATION

Arava	1
Aviv	2
Desert Inn	3
HaNegev	4
Youth Hostel	5

Qiryat Gat

Ben Gurion University

DEREKH BEN GURION

Train station and Negev Brigade Memorial

REHOV YEHUDA HALEVI

DEREKH METZADA

Sports Stadium

DEREKH SHIMSHON

REHOV BIALIK

REHOV WINGATE

SEDEROT HANESSI'IM

REHOV HAMESHAKHRERIM

REHOV HASHALOM

REHOV SOKOLOV

REHOV SHAZAR

Ashqelon and Gaza and hotel

REHOV TUVIYAHU

Commonwealth War Cemetery

Ottoman Rail Station

Kanyon

i

Hatzerim

REHOV ASSAF SIMHONI

5

REHOV HERZL

REHOV RAMBAM

REHOV GERSHON

REHOV YAIR

Bus Station

Museum HaNegev

REHOV HA'AZMAUT

Governor's House

REHOV HATIVAT HANEGEV

REHOV BET ESHEL

REHOV HADASSAH

REHOV HAPALMAH

REHOV MORDE HAGETTA'OT

1

REHOV TRUMPELDOR

4

Hebron

REHOV KKL

2

REHOV HAAVOT

DEREKH HEVRON

Bedouin Market

• Abraham's Well

0   300m

Eilat

Until the beginning of this century, Beersheba and its environs were used by local **Bedouin** tribes as a trading centre and watering place; its wells remained its most important feature. In 1906, the **Ottomans** developed it as the district and administrative centre for the Negev to encourage the Bedouins to settle, with a new town – now the **old city** – planned and built by the Germans during World War I. It was the first town in

Palestine to be captured by the Allies under Allenby on their northward advance in 1917. The Australian Lighthorse were forced to make a charge on the town to preempt the destruction of Beersheba's wells by the Ottomans, which would have left them in the middle of the desert with no water; luckily they were successful. Witness to the heavy fighting can be seen in the Commonwealth War Cemetery on Rehov Ha'Atzma'ut, and the story is told in Simon Winger's 1987 film, *The Lighthorsemen*.

Under the UN's **1947** partition plan, Beersheba was to be part of the Palestinian Arab state, unsurprisingly since it was an entirely Arab town – its Jewish community, established here at the beginning of the twentieth century, had fled during the 1929 ethnic riots. The town was held by Egyptian forces as soon as they entered the war, but was taken by Israel on October 20, following the collapse of the second UN truce. As the administrative centre of the Negev, Beersheba became something of a boom town in the 1960s as development of the region got under way, with a new population of Jewish immigrants from mainly Arab countries. In 1963, it saw the first flex of Sephardi political muscle in Israel when a slate of council candidates fielded by local Sephardim forced the Mapai Labour Party to put up their own Mizrahi candidate, judge Eliahu Navi, who thus became one of Israel's first Sephardi council leaders.

Arrival, orientation and information

Most people arrive at Beersheba's **Central Bus Station**, on Derekh Eilat, from where the municipal **tourist office**, at 6 Ben-Zvi (Sun–Thurs 8am–4pm; ☎07/623 6001), is through the parking lot in front of the station and across a small garden. They can help you with accommodation and information about exploring the desert. From the front of the bus station, several services (#2, #3, #7, #8, #9, #11, #12, #18, #21 and #22) run to the **old city** (till 11pm), where most of the attractions are. Alternatively, it's an easy enough walk of around 500m or so: turn left out of the main entrance, and then right to walk round the futuristic HaNegev Kanyon shopping mall (open till 8pm). At the traffic lights turn left to cross the three-lane ring road Derekh Eilat, into Rehov HaHaluz, which leads into the heart of the old city. The old city is centred on **Rehov Ha'Atzma'ut**, which cuts the city northwest to southeast, and the **Rehov Keren Kayemet LeYisra'el**, or KKL (pronounced Kakal), part of which is a pedestrianized *midrahov*.

Accommodation

Beersheba doesn't offer a massive choice of hotel **rooms**, but if you don't mind paying a little more than rock-bottom, or missing out on five-star luxuries, however, what there is should be adequate.

Arava, 37 HaHistadrut (☎07/627 8792). Moderately priced town-centre hotel with basic facilities (a/c, private bathrooms) but not tremendously good value. ②.

Aviv, 40 Mordei HaGeta'ot, on the corner of Keren Kayemet LeYisra'el (☎07/627 8059). Slightly scruffy but warm and friendly with Bulgarian carpets everywhere; best of the town-centre hotels, especially in the winter months. ③.

HI Bet Yatziv Youth Hostel, 79 HaAztma'ut (☎07/627 1490, fax 627 5735) Clean and well-kept, with a range of rooms from dorm beds to spacious doubles. Book ahead if possible, as it's often in demand from school parties and businesspeople. The swimming pool opens in summer only (guests pay reduced rates). Take bus #13 from the bus station. ②/③.

HaNegev, 26 Ha'Atzma'ut (☎07/627 7026). Down-at-heel town-centre hotel with older, cheaper rooms in the annexe and better ones in the main building. ③.

Desert Inn (Neot Midbar), Sederot Tuviyahu (☎07/642 4922, fax 641 2772). A characterful 1960s-built place north of town, which for many years was Beersheba's only hotel. You'll need a taxi to get here if not driving. ④.

The Town

The **"old city"** (not so old really, dating from the beginning of the twentieth century) has a reasonably good local museum but few other specific attractions, and can be explored on foot in one afternoon. Out of the centre, a cemetery and a memorial testify to Beersheba's involvement in World War I and Israel's 1948 war of independence.

The old city

The most interesting thing to visit in town is the **Museum HaNegev** on Rehov Ha'Atzma'ut (☎07/628 2056; Sun–Thurs 10am–5pm, Fri & Sat 10am–1pm; 3NIS, guided tours 2NIS), temporarily housed in the Governor's House in the museum grounds while its usual home, the mosque, is being renovated. The Governor's House (which usually serves as an art museum) was built under the Ottomans in 1906. Inside, you'll find displays on the "Beersheba Culture" (see p.272), prehistoric finds from the tels of the northern Negev, several old maps and a Byzantine mosaic. There's no information in English, so it's worth phoning ahead to book a guided tour.

The **mosque** was built in 1901 by the Ottoman rulers to encourage the 5000-strong local Muslim population to settle in the town. It is well worth a look for its early twentieth-century Ottoman architecture, for the Ottoman sultan's medallion over the main door, and the elegance of its setting in small but beautiful grounds. Today, it is the subject of a legal battle between the Beersheba municipality and the local Bedouin community who, as part of a general campaign for their rights, want it restored to them as a place of worship. The Israeli authorities are unwilling to hand it over on security grounds, since the minaret overlooks an army camp across the street.

Passing southward through the city centre along the pedestrianized *midrahov*, you come at the other end of the "Kakal" (Rehov Keren Kayemet LeYisra'el) to **Abraham's Well** (Sun–Thurs 8.30am–4pm, Fri 8.30am–noon; free), somewhat misleadingly named since there's no evidence at all that this well had anything to do with Abraham; a far more likely site for the biblical settlement is Tel Beer Sheva, 5km out of town (see p.277).

The Bedouin Market (Souq al-Khamis)

The **Bedouin Market**, renowned throughout Israel, is held every Thursday in its newly refurbished home on the southern fringe of the old city, by the junction of Derekh Hevron and Derekh Eilat, and next to the wholesale market. The importance that this market once held for the pastoral Bedouin nomads of the surrounding region is evident in the size of the area set aside for livestock trading: camels, donkeys, sheep, goats and hens are still bought and sold here, though some of the prospective buyers now come from nearby kibbutzim and moshavim. Spices, incense and sweetmeats are also on offer and you can practise haggling over beaten copper coffeepots, Bedouin jewellery and carpets. Later in the morning, most of the traditional market is drowned out by Israeli stall-keepers selling everything from jeans to floor-mops, plastic jewellery to tape-recorders, and using megaphones to hawk their wares, but it remains fascinating nonetheless.

The market starts at 6am and goes on all day; it's best to get there as early as possible, however, not only to give yourself the chance to see all the goods available, but because the best buys go quickly.

North of town

Next door to the youth hostel on Rehov Ha'Atzma'ut, the **Commonwealth War Cemetery** is an incongruous and touching oasis immaculately maintained by the Commonwealth War Graves Commission. Pepper and cypress trees planted after World War I and more recent tropical eucalyptus trees cast shade on the graves of the

1239 soldiers who fell during World War I when the Allies captured Beersheba from the Turks. You can ask to see the "book" – a tatty register of those buried here; the visitors' book is also an interesting record of those who have paid their respects here and taken the time to pen their personal thoughts. From the cemetery you can see the **Ottoman train station** to its north in Rehov Tuviyahu, now being renovated for use as an art gallery.

Beyond the modern train station, northeast of town, is another **war memorial**, this one designed by artist Danny Caravan and dedicated to the Palmah's Negev Brigade, who took Beersheba in October 1948 ahead of a UN ceasefire proposed by the UK to forestall further Israeli gains. Also north of town, on the way to the train station on Derekh Ben Gurion, is the **Ben Gurion University of the Negev**, founded in 1969. Nearby at 50 Arlozorov, there's an **Ethiopian Jewish Handicraft Exhibition** (Mon, Wed & Thurs 9am–noon; free), with displays of tradional Ethiopian Jewish crafts including pottery, sculpture and gourd-engraving, which you can also buy.

Eating, drinking and nightlife

Eating and drinking centres around the *midrahov* on KKL and the *kanyon*, where you'll find a section of fast-food joints offering burgers, kebabs, falafel and hummus. *Bet HaFul*, at 15 HaHistadrut (Sun–Thurs 8.30am–12.30pm, Fri 8.30am–3pm, Sat 9.30pm–12.30pm midnight; cheap) is reputedly the best outlet in town for falafel and you can munch your sandwich in the neighbouring Gan HaNassi Park. Something of a Beersheba institution, the *Bulgarian Restaurant* (or *Bulgarit*), at 112 Keren Kayemet LeYisra'el (Sun–Thurs 9am–11pm, Sat 10.30am–7.30pm; moderate), has stood on the same spot, with the same owner, since 1940. It's certainly one of the more characterful places in town, serving hearty East European fare, and virtually the only place open on a Saturday (but closed Fri). Round the corner at 122 Herzl, *Pitput* (Sun–Thurs 8am–2am, Fri 8am–2pm, Sat 10pm–2am; moderate) serves home-made veg and dairy meals and snacks, including wonderful pastries and desserts. For chargrilled steaks or fish, try *Illie's* at 21 Herzl (☎07/627 8685; Sun–Thurs noon–midnight, Fri noon–3pm; expensive). There's a **supermarket**, Hypercol, on Derekh Ben Gurion.

Despite Beersheba's large student population, there isn't much in the way of **nightlife**. If you wander round the old city, however, you'll find a few **bars**, especially in the livelier area on Rehov Smilansky Street. *HaSimta* at 16 Trumpeldor is a good place for drinking and music; alternatives include *HaTrombon* at 18 HaAvot. There are a couple of bars in the newer part of the city, on Sederot HaNessi'im, which are more European in feel.

MOVING ON FROM BEERSHEBA

The Egged Central **Bus Station** (☎07/629 4311) is just east of the old city on Rehov Eilat. Destinations include: Jerusalem (roughly every 30min; 2hr); Tel Aviv (3–4 per hour; 2hr); Ashqelon (almost hourly; 1hr 30min); Ashdod (2 daily; 1hr 40min); Qiryat Gat (3–4 per hour; 1hr); Qiryat Arba (Jewish settlement by Hebron; 2 daily; 1hr); Dimona (2–3 per hour; 40min); Mitzpe Ramon (every 60–90min; 1hr 30min); and Eilat (every 90min, with additional seasonal services; 3hr).

Sheruts operated by Ya'el Daroma at 195 Keren Kayemet LeYisra'el serve Eilat and Tel Aviv, but not on Saturdays. There are also now, experimentally, two **trains** a week serving Qiryat Gat (40min), Lydda (1hr 15min), Tel Aviv (2hr), Netanya (2hr 30min), Haifa (3hr 30min), Acre (4hr) and Nahariyya (4hr 10min) from the station on Derekh Ben Gurion, east of the University (☎07/623 7245).

Listings

Banks Most are located in the centre of the old city. On the corner of Ha'Atzma'ut and HaHistradut, HaPoalim (Mon & Wed 8.30am–1pm; Sun, Tues & Thurs 8.30am–12.30pm & 4–6pm) specializes in foreign currency and is usually packed out: take a ticket and queue.

Car rental Avis, 11 HaNessi'im (☎07/627 1777); Budget, 8 Poalei Binyan (☎07/628 0755); Eldan, 100 Tuviyahu (☎07/643 0344); Europcar, 3 Hevron (☎07/627 5365); Hertz, 5a Ben-Zvi (☎07/627 2768); Thrifty, 47 Keren Kayemet LeYisra'el (☎07/628 2590).

Medical services Magen David Adom (first aid), 40 Bialik (☎07/667 8333). Soroka Hospital, Derekh HaNessi'im (☎07/640 0111). Pharmacies include SuperPharm in the *kanyon*, and PharmLin at 34 Herzl.

Police 30 Herzl at KKL (☎07/646 2744).

Post office Main office at HaNessi'im and Nordau (Sun–Thurs 8am–6pm, Fri 8am–2pm). There's also a branch in the old city at HaHistadrut with Hadassa.

Taxis *Taxi Sinai*, 48 HaHistadrut (☎07/627 7525); *Taxi Mezada*, 45 HaAzma'ut (☎07/627 5555); *Taxi Hazui*, Nordau (☎07/623 9333).

Travel agencies ISSTA, New Campus, Ben Gurion University (☎07/623 7255) is the best place for air tickets. Tours of Beersheba and the Negev are operated by Egged Tours at the bus station (☎07/623 2532).

Around Beersheba

Most of the routes north of Beersheba cross the triangle reserve where the majority of Negev Bedouins are now based (see box overleaf), living in new settlement villages or camping near main roads in their new-style huts with their Peugeots parked outside. **Tel Sheva**, **Laqiya** and **Rahat** are among Bedouin settlements that can be visited nearby, as well as a Museum of Bedouin Culture, not run by Bedouins, at **Kibbutz Lahav**, an Air Force Museum at **Hatzerim**, a community of Indian Jews at **Nevatim**, and an ancient archeological site at **Tel Beer Sheva**. Transport is sparse, but many of these sites can be reached by occasional bus; others are near enough to reach on foot. For the rest, you'll either need to have your own vehicle, or else hitch or charter a taxi.

Tel Beer Sheva

The most commonly accepted site for biblical Beersheba is the mound of **Tel Beer Sheva** (daily 9am–5pm; free), 6km northeast of its modern counterpart on the road to the settlement town of Tel Sheva. The earliest remains discovered here include pottery dating from around 3500 BC, after which time the tel was deserted until the arrival of the Israelites 2000 years later. Archeologists believe the forty-metre-deep **well** outside the city gates could be the real Abraham's Well (see p.272) – and that this is the first planned Israelite city to be uncovered so far. Excavations have revealed nine different layers of settlement since the first city walls were built during the reign of King David or Solomon. Sennacherib's forces burnt the city to the ground while putting down a rebellion against Assyrian rule by Egypt and Judah in 701 BC. Beersheba was rebuilt on its present site in the Greco-Roman period. Among remains to be seen are a tenth-century BC city gate at the southern end of the site, with a number of ancient storerooms to its north and, in the centre of the tel, the remains of a Roman fortress.

The **observation tower** erected on the tel gives good views of the desert plains around Beersheba, and there is a small **museum** on the site, focusing on the relationship between the desert environment and its human population, while the ubiquitous Bedouin hospitality tent has a restaurant with staged Bedouin "folklore" entertainment. Bus #55 (3 daily) from Beersheba will drop you at the turn-off to the site.

THE BEDOUIN TODAY

Today there are around 65,000 **Bedouins in the Negev**, one third of them living in five Israeli-built settlements near Beersheba. The new towns might have indoor plumbing, telephones and electricity, but they have little in the way of a modern economic base, either in industry or in agriculture, and risk becoming mere dormitories as people seek daily work on kibbutzim or in Israeli industry. Even the settlement of Rahat, north of Beersheba, the cultural capital of the Negev Bedouins, remains largely undeveloped. At the same time, although the courts have recognized traditional **land claims**, grazing land for sheep and goats has become increasingly scarce with the designation of large areas for military purposes or nature reserves and the spread of Jewish Israeli agricultural settlements.

Meanwhile, the Bedouins' requests for recognized agricultural settlements of their own is refused by Israeli officials, and Bedouin settlements in the Negev, no matter how large, are treated as illegal. Fruit, olive trees and crops planted by Bedouins in ancestral land are regularly uprooted, while goats and sheep grazing on "state land" are often confiscated by the notorious Green Patrol police, and can only be released from quarantine on payment of large fines. Houses built without legal permits (only granted within the new townships) are demolished. Because they are deemed illegal by the authorities, even larger Bedouin settlements are unable to obtain amenities such as electricity, roads or water supplies.

Despite the modern-day situation, the popular **image** of Bedouins in Israel remains that of a quaint nomadic people, a relic of the past, to whom the modern Israeli state has brought the benefits of civilization. At some point you'll probably be offered a visit to a Bedouin tent conveniently situated outside some tourist centre or other, to be shown how they live, to partake of traditional Bedouin tea or coffee or to encourage you to buy authentic Bedouin handicrafts. Or you may visit exhibitions on Bedouin culture, where an expert, invariably Israeli or Western, will interpret and explain away this people as though they were some exotic but extinct species. Occasionally, you may find a centre such as that at Rahat (see below), which is actually run by Bedouins themselves. On the whole, however, the Bedouin tents and hospitality centres of the Negev give a somewhat distorted picture of modern Bedouin life; those in the Galilee (see p.173) tend to be better.

One way to get beyond the sanitized image is to contact **the Association for Support and Defence of Bedouin Rights in Israel** (37 Hativat Hanegev, Beersheba; ☎07/623 1687), which attempts to raise public consciousness of the problems facing the Bedouins.

Tel Sheva (Tel al-Sab)

A little beyond Tel Beer Sheva and 5km east of Beersheba, **Tel Sheva** (Tel al-Sab in Arabic) is the first of the five townships built by the Israeli authorities in 1969 for the local Bedouins, and it's worth a glance after visiting the tel if you want an idea of how today's Bedouins really live. It's served by bus #55 from Beersheba three times daily. The village was designed with high-walled courtyards separating the houses to provide their inhabitants with a degree of privacy, a style which met with little success in a culture used to communal living; most residents have preferred to build their own houses. As in the other modern townships designed to encourage the Bedouins to settle, Tel Sheva has little in the way of industrial infrastructure or land for agricultural purposes. Wandering around it during the day is like being in a ghost town as most of the population leave to find unskilled work in nearby Jewish towns and settlements. By way of contrast, the affluent Jewish suburb of **Omer**, Beersheba's garden suburb, lies just 4km north. First established as a moshav in 1949 by a group of demobilized soldiers, it is today a prosperous town of around 3000 people.

Hatzerim Israeli Air Force Museum

The **Israeli Air Force Museum** at Hatzerim, 9km west of Beersheba (Sun–Thurs 8am–5pm, Fri 8am–2pm; 15NIS, guided tours available), will appeal to anyone with an interest in aeronautics, aviation or military history. You can see examples of planes used by the Israeli Air Force, and several planes captured by them from their Arab adversaries during the various Middle East wars, but the museum's most famous exhibit is the plane used in June 1976 to fly to freedom 103 hostages from Entebbe Airport in Uganda, where they had been taken aboard an Air France flight hijacked en route from Paris to Ben Gurion. Uganda's then dictator, Idi Amin, who had been helped into power by Britain and Israel, and subsequently turned on his one-time backers, welcomed the German hijackers (members of the Red Army Faction working on behalf of the PFLP). In what must rank as one of the most daring rescues ever performed Israel flew in commandos to disable Amin's fighters on the ground and snatch the hostages. Events were deemed dramatic enough to be the subject of no fewer than three feature films. The plane now contains a film about the IAF. Unfortunately, you can't get to the museum by public transport; a taxi from Beersheba costs about 35NIS. Hatzerim itself is one of the eleven settlements founded on Yom Kippur 1946 (see p.272)

Laqiya, Lahav and Rahat

Bedouins in the settlement of **LAQIYA**, on Route 31 northeast of Beersheba, have, in defiance of the common stereotype, long lived in stone houses, farming and tending flocks. In 1952 the inhabitants were moved to the region of Arad, where many worked on the construction of the town, and were allowed back to their original homes only in the late 1970s, by which time the land had been designated state property. The contrast between the well-irrigated kibbutz fields and Laqiya, across the road, is striking – only recently was the first water supply piped to the village.

The northern limit of Bedouin land is marked by **Kibbutz Lahav**, on the edge of the West Bank, roughly halfway between the Qiryat Gat and Hebron roads. Originally a border settlement, the kibbutz has one of the largest pig farms in Israel, with pigs kept on boards by rabbinical decree so as not to defile the soil of the Holy Land with their unkosher trotters (in fact, this was a compromise: originally the rabbis wanted them banned from Israel altogether). Incongruously, the kibbutzniks have built a **Museum of Bedouin Culture** in the kibbutz's Joe Alon Regional and Folklore Centre (07/996 1597; Sun–Thurs 9am–4pm, Fri 9am–2pm; 10NIS). Designed to resemble an encampment, the museum features various tableaux of daily life using models in traditional costume but, unsurprisingly, gives rather a romanticized view. One section displays Bedouin artefacts such as household utensils, traditional dress, jewellery and embroidery, while the archeological section exhibits finds of "Beersheba Culture" (see p.272) from the region. Guided tours are available on request or you could just attach yourself to a visiting group. You can also ask to be shown a video on desert life.

There are nine daily buses (except on Shabbat) from Beersheba to Kibbutz Lahav. If you arrive this way, walk 200m through the kibbutz towards the aerial on the hilltop (if the museum gate is closed, you'll need to shout or get a kibbutznik to ring through; the kibbutz is dead at lunchtime, but you may find someone to help you in the communal dining room). Hitching back to Beersheba with a tour bus or tourists shouldn't be a problem – ask the manager to help you if you get stuck.

If you've come by car, you could continue on to **RAHAT**, the first Bedouin city in Israel, 18km as the crow flies north of Beersheba (take Route 40 north and turn left at the Bet Qama junction and then sharp left again onto Route 264). The **Bedouin Heritage Museum** (Sun–Fri 8.30am–8pm, Sat 11.30am–5pm; 12NIS) here was set up by local people to tell their own story, though you will in fact see many of the same skills and handicrafts displayed as in Israeli Bedouin museums. You'll also have the chance to sample Bedouin food and caffeinous beverages. "Modest" dress should be worn if visiting Rahat.

Nevatim

Just 5km east of Beersheba on Route 25, a yellow sign indicates a turning to the **Nevatim** moshav's **Cochin community and heritage centre** (☎07/627 7277). This small desert settlement (one of the eleven originally set up on the night of Yom Kippur 1946, see p.272) is inhabited by Jews from Cochin in Kerala, Southern India. Until 1996, when the last family left – ending 2000 years of settlement – they formed the oldest Jewish community in the Commonwealth. The Cochinese Jews have kept many of their traditional customs and still wear Indian dress – their bright saris, worn especially during religious festivities, contrast sharply with the muted colours of the surrounding desert. They have also built a replica of Cochin's synagogue here. The continued existence of the village is ensured by its thriving flower-growing export business. Phone ahead to make an appointment to see the synagogue and museum. Buses between Beersheba and Dimona will stop here if you ask the driver.

Dimona and Mamshit

From Nevatim, Route 25 continues east to the develoment town of **Dimona** and the nearby archeological site at **Mamshit**, formerly one of the cities of the Nabatean spice route. From there it continues toward the 'Arava Valley, part of the Great Rift, which runs from the Dead Sea to the Red Sea, followed all the way by Route 90 and the Israel-Jordan border.

Coming from Nevatim on Route 25, you pass after 10km, southwest of the road shortly before the junction with Route 80, the scant remains of ancient **Aro'er**, whose inhabitants David rewarded for their support against the Amalekites (I Samuel 30: 28). Almost everything of any interest to the layperson from this site now resides in the Skirball Museum in Jerusalem (see p.368).

Dimona

About 20km beyond Aro'er, and 34km out of Beersheba on Route 25 towards Sodom, the development town of **DIMONA** was originally built in 1955 as a residential area for workers at the Dead Sea chemical works – mainly immigrants from Tunisia – and is a maze of half-empty blocks of flats, which give it rather a ghostlike atmosphere. Dimona also has the dubious honour of being the site of Israel's Atomic Research Station and the centre of Israel's nuclear weapons' industry, on which the whistle was blown by Mordekhai Vanunu, a former nuclear technician at the plant and Israel's most well-known political prisoner, who revealed all to the London *Sunday Times* in 1986. Vanunu was subsequently kidnapped by Mossad in Rome and remains in prison, the first eleven years of his 18-year sentence having been spent in solitary confinement.

Apart from this, there is nothing of interest in Dimona except for the chance to visit the **Hebrew Israelite community** (☎07/655 5400 for information). This virtually self-contained village, which houses 900 of the country's 1500-strong "Black Hebrew" community, is found near the central bus stand on Herzl Street. The Black Hebrews were founded by Ben-Ami Ben Israel (then known as Ben Carter) in Chicago in the 1960s after he had a vision telling him that black people were in fact the lost ten tribes of Israel. After a preparatory sojourn in the "wilderness" of Liberia, they began to return in 1969 to what they considered their homeland, claiming right of abode under the Law of Return (see p.496). The Israeli authorities refused to recognize their claim, and deported a number of them, prompting the Black Hebrews to respond with charges of racism. In 1990, however, negotiations to legalize their community began, and they are now Israeli citizens.

The Black Hebrews do not follow the Orthodox Jewish faith, and have their own communal rules; these include a strictly vegan diet, general abstemiousness, and the wearing of clothing made only from natural vegetable fibres. They are happy to receive visitors, though you should call to check before arriving. The community has shops where you can buy cotton clothes and shoes made from fibre, and a **restaurant** where you can eat delicious vegan food (Sun–Thurs 7.30am–4pm & 5–11pm, Fri 7.30am–4pm; cheap). There is also a small **guesthouse** (②; half-board). The community's bands give regular concerts, and in mid-August (not the coolest time of year to be in Dimona), they hold a two-day **music festival** attended by musicians from all over Israel (call for further information).

If the Black Hebrews' guesthouse is full, or you prefer to **stay** elsewhere, there's the *Drachim Guest House* at 1 HaNassi (☎07/655 6811; ②); clean, with a choice of dorms or private rooms run by an ex-SPNI wallah who can give useful advice on hiking or touring in the region. **Buses** from Dimona (☎07/655 2421 for information) serve Beersheba (2–3 per hour; 40min), Tel Aviv (12 daily; 2hr 40min) and Eilat (hourly; 3hr).

Mamshit (Kurnub)

Five kilometres east of Dimona on Route 25 is the site of the magnificently preserved Nabatean city of **Mamshit** (April–Sept: Sat–Thurs 8am–5pm, Fri 8am–4pm, closes one hour earlier Oct–March; 10NIS). The reconstructed spacious villas and elegant archways of this first-century AD town stand in a perfect setting overlooking the beautiful Makhtesh HaGadol. The Nabatean stone houses, some with balconies, are built around open courtyards; one of them still has its ancient wall paintings. The Romans took control of the town in 106 AD, and their presence is evident from the Latin inscriptions on the tombstones in the cemetery northeast of the site. Later the Byzantines also used the Nabatean buildings but, unlike the Romans, also added their own – two churches from the Byzantine period (324–640 AD), built on top of many Nabatean houses, are beautifully preserved with mosaic floors and baptismal fonts. The East Church is the oldest in the Negev. In Wadi Mamshit below the site, the remains of Nabatean stone dams and a watchtower to guard over precious water supplies are evidence of their ingenuity as water conservers. Mamshit was destroyed by the invading Muslim Arabs in the seventh entury AD and never rebuilt. **Buses** from Dimona to the Dead Sea and Eilat stop 1km from the site.

Beyond Mamshit

From Mamshit, Route 25 continues 30km east to the **'Arava Junction** near Sodom where it meets Route 90, which runs along the 'Arava Valley from the Dead Sea to Eilat. Ten kilometres before the junction it passes (north of the road) a small square Roman fort called **Mazad Tamar**, from where it begins the descent into the 'Arava, offering stunning views over the valley and the southern Dead Sea. A sign by the roadside marks the point where you reach sea level. North of the 'Arava junction, Route 90 takes you along the eastern side of the Dead Sea (see pp.261–265), up the Jordan Valley and eventually to the Galilee; southward it is pure desert, skirting the Jordanian frontier, with the next stop of any interest 30km south, where a turn-off to the west leads to the ancient Nabatean city of **Mo'a**. Not much is left of it today, apart from the remains of a first-century caravanserai, but for serious hikers, armed with the necessary advice and navigation aids from the SPNI (see box, p.271), it is possible to follow the ancient spice route from here all the way to Makhtesh Ramon (see p.284). Continuing south on Route 90, the next place of interest is 100km further at Yotvata (see p.302).

Beersheba to Mitzpe Ramon

The eighty-kilometre stretch of road (Route 40) from **Beersheba to Mitzpe Ramon** is packed with Negev highlights and easily negotiable by public transport. Local **bus** #60 travels the route every 60–90 minutes, and the infrequent #392 service (4 daily) between Beersheba and Eilat also stops at Mitzpe Ramon. Timetables are available at Beersheba Central Bus Station, and sometimes at the fuel station in Mitzpe Ramon.

Sede Boqer

An explosion of green 35km south of Beersheba marks the first major settlement – **Kibbutz Sede Boqer** – famous as the spiritual home and final resting place of the first Prime Minister of Israel, **David Ben Gurion**. Coming by bus, there are three stops; the westernmost is at the main entrance to the kibbutz, the next at Ben Gurion's house and the zoo, and the easternmost at Ben Gurion's tomb; ask the driver to let you off at your preferred stop.

Ben Gurion wanted to "make the desert bloom" and was keen to encourage Israeli settlement in the desert. The story goes that he came across the kibbutz while returning to Jerusalem from the south following his retirement as PM in 1953. It had been founded the previous year by a group of young people who had fought in the area during the 1948 war and were trying to settle the area as the original Israelites had done 2000 years before. The pioneering spirit of the kibbutz so impressed Ben Gurion that he decided to join it for a year: "That had been the ideal that had first attracted me to the Land," he later wrote, " . . . to begin all over by self labour." Though he returned to politics fourteen months later, becoming PM again in 1955, he returned to Sede Boqer after leaving office in 1963 and lived out his later years there. He died on the kibbutz at the age of 89 and was buried next to his wife on a hill overlooking the desert. Over the years, his home had become an example to others to take up the challenge of the desert.

You can visit the **Ben Gurion home** (Sun–Thurs 8.30am–3.30pm, Fri 8.30am–2pm, Sat 9am–2pm; free), which has been left exactly as it was when he died, as requested in his will. His bedroom is adorned with just one picture – of his spiritual hero Mahatma Gandhi – though there's no such minimalism in his extravagant library of 5000 books. To reach the home, take the second signposted turning off Route 40. Nearby there is a small **zoo** full of Negev deer, swans and flamingoes.

The third bus stop and turn-off from Route 40 is the entrance for the two simple **graves of the Ben Gurions**, in a small park commanding a stunning view of the Valley of Zin to the east and the spring of Ein Avdat to the south. Near the entrance to this park, through the cross barrier, is the Sede Boqer campus of the **Ben Gurion University of the Negev**, established in 1969 to encourage desert settlement. Following in the footsteps of the Nabateans, whose water-harvesting techniques are still being studied today, the Israelis are leading the way in desert research: scientists and development experts come from all over the world to study how to use water effectively, and how to cultivate using little irrigation. The university houses various desert research institutes, including a leading centre for solar power, which is now virtually standard in Israeli homes. Also on the campus is an **SPNI field school** (☎07/656 5016) where you can obtain information and advice about hiking and wildlife in the area, along with a few **shops** (including a supermarket and post office) and **cafeterias** open to the public. Should you need to stay here, the field school has a hostel (①/④), though it may be full, or there is the *Hamburg Guest House* next door (☎07/656 5902; ④).

Ein Avdat Nature Park

To come across an icy spring and tumbling waterfall cut into a shady canyon in the middle of the desert, is paradise, even if **Ein Avdat** (daily: winter 8am–4pm, summer 8am–5pm; 10NIS) has lost some of its wild desert charm since the Nature Reserve Authority took over its management. There are two entrances to the site. Coming from the north, the **northernmost (lower) entrance** is signposted just before the turning to Kibbutz Sede Boqer. There is a bus stop on the main road, and a place to park. From here you can take a pleasant, dusty walk, alongside warm brown rocks of varying shades and the dry riverbed, past two **pools** of ice-cold water lying at the bottom of a deep desert canyon. The second, larger pool is fed by a **waterfall** cascading from the rocks above. Up steps cut into the rock, you ascend to the top of the cascade, where there are breathtaking views over the canyon, before continuing on toward the **upper pools**. From here there is an even steeper climb to the clifftop, 50m up the sheer cliff face. Those who hate heights or clambering up ladders on a vertical cliff should turn back at the upper pools since you can't change your mind halfway up. Sometimes it is difficult to spot the next few steps but make sure you've identified them before pushing onward. Most have metal handles in the rocks to pull you up, and there are a couple of scary-looking but safe vertical metal ladders. If you can keep your head from spinning, the views from various points up the cliff face are breathtaking. It takes between two and three hours to walk the trail in its entirety.

Once you reach the top there's a Bedouin tent and coffee to revive you, a small Byzantine ruin and an **observation post**, where you can look out over the the the **Wilderness of Zin**, where the Children of Israel wandered, Moses's sister Miriam died (Numbers 20: 1), and Moses himself struck a rock at God's command to bring forth water (20: 11). You are now at the **southern (upper) entrance** of the reserve, on Route 40 some 7km south of the northern entrance. If you've left your car at the northern entrance you'll have to walk back along the main road (there's a Nabatean cistern east of the road about 2km south of the lower entrance), or wait for the next bus.

Avdat

A sculpture of a camel caravan 22km south of Sede Boqer marks the site of **Avdat** (April–Sept Sat–Thurs 8am–5pm, Fri 8am–4pm; Oct–March daily 8am–4pm; 12NIS), perhaps the best surviving testimony to the Nabatean civilization. Dominating its surroundings from a flat hilltop, Avdat was founded in the third century BC and, as a major staging post on the Nabateans' cross-desert trade routes, was a prosperous town until the first century AD. It is named after King Obodas II (30–9 BC), who was buried in the township and revered as a god; his name was then Arabized to Abdah and finally Hebraicized to Avdat. When the Romans conquered the Negev they built an army camp just to the northeast, and in the sixth century the town became a Byzantine monastic centre, seeing a second period of prosperity. At this time the population is estimated to have reached around three thousand. In 620 AD, Avdat fell to the invading Persians, and was finally abandoned after the Arab conquest in 634.

The sandstone **walls and columns** that remain almost seem designed to set off the deep desert blue of the sky, leaving you in awe of the ancient civilizations that managed to build a thriving city in such an apparently harsh environment. Though most of what you see is from the Byzantine era, there are also some impressive relics of the Nabatean trading centre, in particular a handsome **esplanade** (the open area in front of the fortress), which was turned into a covered portico during the Byzantine period. Other highlights include two Byzantine **churches**, the remains of a Byzantine monastery, bathhouses, a wine press, and an ancient spiral staircase. The rebuilt

Nabatean **pottery**, complete with an original kiln and potters' wheel, gives some idea as to the scope and sophistication of the Nabatean civilization. As well as the buildings, there's fascinating evidence of Nabatean agricultural methods; the complex system of **channels and dams** ensured that none of the area's sparse rainfall or night dew was wasted, enabling the cultivation of wheat, barley, grapes and other produce.

If travelling by bus, make sure you get off at Avdat archeological site rather than the Ein Avdat junction; driving, park in the car park at the top of the site, otherwise it's about an hour's walk uphill from the main road. At the entrance, there's a **snack bar** serving the best falafel in the area. The bar is also open in the evening and has a small buzzing social life that draws people from Mitzpe Ramon and around. The small restaurant at the site is expensive.

Shivta (Subeita) and Nitzanim

In contrast to Avdat, the Nabatean town of **Shivta**, 18km northwest, is unrestored, offering you the rare chance to discover for yourself some spectacular ruins. To get to Shivta by public transport, take bus #44 from Beersheba to Nitzanim and get off at the turn-off 8km from the site. By car, Shivta can be reached on Route 211, which branches west off Route 40 at Telalim, 14km north of Sede Boqer or 28km south of Beersheba. The site is not officially open to the public, so be careful when exploring and do not remove anything.

To survive in an area with an average annual rainfall of around 80mm, Shivta's Nabatean builders developed a unique town plan in the first century BC to capture every drop that fell. The reservoir on the northern edge of the city, still plainly visible, collected rain from the eastern slopes, while channels running either side of the streets directed more rainfall into the southern reservoir. The buildings themselves are Byzantine and later – Shivta was inhabited well into the seventh century – and, though the population could never have numbered more than a few thousand, they include three large **churches**. The South Church, near the entrance, had a mosque built alongside in the seventh century. From here you can walk northwards through the superbly preserved streets to the most impressive of the churches, the North Church, and near it the city cemetery, where ancient tombstones can be found.

Route 211 continues westward to **Nitzanim** on the Egyptian border, where there is another (but far less exciting) Nabatean site. The border post here is for freight only, and you will not be allowed to cross the frontier. At the end of the 1948 war, however, Israeli troops did just that, entering Egyptian territory for the first time and even threatening El Arish, the capital of Northern Sinai. They withdrew under the subsequent armistice agreement and the area around Nitzanim became a demilitarized zone.

Makhtesh Ramon and Mitzpe Ramon

The extraordinary **Makhtesh Ramon** – the largest natural crater in the world – is best visited from **MITZPE RAMON**. The town, perched on the rim of the crater, 900m above sea level, started life in 1956 as a camp for workers building the nearby highway and then became a support centre for a military outpost, armaments factory and developing tourist industry. In 1970, the construction of the newer, faster Route 90 through the desert diverted traffic away, leaving Mitzpe Ramon like a windy desert ghost town with a strange other-worldly feel. A few years ago, immigrants, many from the former Soviet Union, and Israelis from other parts of the country were being encouraged to buy property and settle here with incentives such as zero income tax and the promise of an eagerly anticipated desert tourism boom. However, as the population grows –

there is also a contingent of Black Hebrews (see p.280) in town – so does unemployment, and most Israelis, who spend at least some of their military service in the Negev, are sceptical of the town's tourist potential. Projected figures say that up to a million people will visit the crater, a national park, annually – and there's a new luxury *Isrotel* hotel under construction, perched right on the edge of the *makhtesh* – but at the moment, it's a party waiting for its guests to arrive.

Arrival, orientation and information

From Beersheba Route 40 runs along the western rim of the *makhtesh* before hitting the town. From the south, you actually travel through the *makhtesh* before winding your way up the steep cliff into town. **Buses** drop you on Route 40 at the petrol station in the centre of town, nearly opposite the beginning of Sederot Ben Gurion, Mitzpe's main drag.

The **visitors' centre** (see p.286), a circular bunker jutting out over the *makhtesh,* is the place to begin your visit and pick up information. The **Commercial Centre**, a small shopping arcade on Sederot Ben Gurion (closed Sat), has a supermarket, bank and post office and a handful of shops and a bar. There's also a small **market** on Tuesday morning selling clothes and fruit. If you need a dip (and we're not talking hummus here), there is also a municipal **swimming pool** on Sederot Ben Gurion, a couple of doors down from the Commercial Centre.

Moving on from Mitzpe Ramon, bus #60 goes to Beersheba (every 60–90min; 1hr 30min), #392 also goes to Beersheba, and the other way to Eilat (4 daily; 1hr 30min), while #391 heads for Tel Aviv (1 weekly; 3hr 30min).

Accommodation

Apart from the *Ramon Inn*, the only luxury **accommodation** in town, there are several options; some less conventional than others, such as a couple of desert campsites and an open-roofed *succah* as erected by religious Jews at the festival of Succot (Tabernacles). This tradition was intended to remind them of the nomadic desert life led by the Children of Israel in the wilderness, much of which was of course in this very region.

Be'erot Campground, in the *makhtesh*, 16km east of town, is the only place you can officially camp inside the crater. You can either pitch your own tent (the cheapest option), or sleep on a mattress in Bedouin-style tents (both ①). Electricity is provided. Enquire at the visitors' centre for details.

HI Bet Noam Youth Hostel, opposite the visitors' centre(☎07/658 8443, fax 658 8074). Situated right on the edge of the crater, this enjoys one of the best locations in town. No a/c, but doesn't seem to need it because of the wind. You can also book for an evening meal, not a bad option considering the scarcity of restaurants in town. It's a good idea to book in advance. ②/③.

Chez Alexis, 7 Ein Saharonim, (☎07/658 6122). A little out of the town centre, behind the *Puntak Ramon*. The former manager of the Youth Hostel offers clean rooms with kitchen facilities and a TV lounge. ②.

Desert Shade, off Route 40 just north of town (☎07/658 6229, fax 568 6208). Tour company (see p.271) with places to sleep in large tents with wooden panels separating the sleeping quarters. It looks quite romantic but can get extremely cold at night. ②.

Ramon Inn (Puntak Ramon), 1 Aqev, up on the hill just north of town (☎07/658 8882, from US ☎1-800/552 0140, from Canada ☎1-800/526 5343, fax 07/658 8151). Part of the *Isrotel* chain, with a great view of the *makhtesh*, this luxury hotel has apartments with tiny kitchens, for up to six people. If you are in a group, call ahead to see if you can negotiate, especially in winter. ⑥.

SPNI Field Centre Hostel, 2km west of town (☎ & fax 07/658 8615). The cheapest accommodation if you have a student card, but call first to check that there are vacancies as it's a bit of a schlep to get there. ①.

Succah in the Desert, 7km west of town on the road to the Alpaca farm (see below) (☎07/658 6280). Experience your own Feast of the Tabernacles (even when it isn't Succot) in the original biblical wilderness at Rachel Bat Adam's encampment of *succahs*. Placed 150m apart, the *succahs* are furnished with a blanket, mattress, jar of water, sheets and towels, solar-powered electricity and gas heating (there's a limit on how far this reminder of the ancient wilderness will go). There is a water supply, and the central *succah* has cooking facilities. Visitors tend to be meditating, or listening to the silence of the desert – a popular New Age activity – and the encampment is very environmentally conscious. Food, naturally, is vegetarian. It's a good idea to reserve in advance, or at least call to arrange for someone to pick you up from town. Dorm options available. ④/⑤.

The visitors' centre, BioRamon and SPNI Field School

Modelled on the shape of an ammonite fossil, the **visitors' centre**, on the western edge of town (Sun–Thurs 9am–5pm, Fri 9am–3pm, Sat 9am–4.30pm; 13NIS; combined ticket with BioRamon 14.40NIS), is an essential stop before venturing into the *makhtesh*. A 20-minute film details the history and geography of the area, and staff are on hand to help you plan your visit – with or without a guide. If you plan to hike alone, equip yourself with the 1:50,000 English-language topographical **map** (54NIS), and always leave details of your route with either the visitors' centre or the SPNI Field School (see below): if you're not back by sundown they'll send out the search party. The roof of the visitors' centre offers a breathtaking view of the crater, and the centre also has a café and restaurant.

In front of the visitors' centre, the open-air **BioRamon** (Sun–Thurs 8am–3pm, Fri 8am–1pm, Sat & holidays 9am–4pm; 5NIS; combined ticket with visitors' centre 14.40NIS), reconstructs the geology, flora and fauna of six desert habitats and brings you up close to some of the smaller inhabitants of the desert, such as insects, lizards and snakes. It's particularly popular with children.

If you are planning to go hiking in the *makhtesh*, or elsewhere in the Negev, it's a good idea to call in first at the **SPNI Field School** (☎07/658 8615 or 6), where you can get information or book nature hikes. The school is 2km west of town on the edge of the *makhtesh*.

Makhtesh Ramon

Some 40km long, 8km wide and over 300m deep **Makhtesh Ramon** covers 250,000 acres in total and is one of only five *makhteshim* in the world – three are in the Negev desert, and two in the Sinai. The other two Negev *makhteshim* are Makhtesh HaGadol ("the large *makhtesh*"), which straddles Route 225 some 10km south of Dimona, and the smaller Makhtesh HaQatan ("the small *makhtesh*"), south of Route 25 near Mezad Tamar, and reached by a track off the road between there and the 'Arava junction; neither is accessible by public transport.

Geologists are not sure how the *makhteshim* were formed, but the most popular theory at present claims that Makhtesh Ramon was formed half a million years ago. It was originally an assymetrical mountain whose summit was an island in a salty sea that stretched to Saudi Arabia. The sea came and retreated three times, and three times the mountain underwent deep tectonic movements. Whenever the land settled, the sea returned and the soft belly of the mountain was hollowed out by erosion, leaving the hard outer shell. When the sea finally retreated it left a valley surrounded by steep walls and drained by a single wadi that still floods following heavy rainfall. Inside the valley, wind, water, and heat erosion have created the most amazing sculptures.

Makhtesh Ramon's unique geology and desert habitat are a magnet for scientists and desert lovers. It is home to over 1200 species of vegetation, with rock strata dating back to the Mesozoic Era, the age of the dinosaurs. Here there are fossils, archeological relics including a Nabatean fort in the south, and a wealth of animal life – large predators, ibex and gazelles, wolves and foxes, desert snakes and insects; one of the most exciting discoveries has been the return of the desert leopard, though no one seems quite sure as to what enticed it back.

Even if you can't get down into the *makhtesh*, a bird's-eye view is stunning enough, and you can sit and gaze on it for hours without tiring of the patterns and colours – the effect is like looking down on a multicoloured mountain range. There will eventually be a hiking route that circumnavigates the whole of the *makhtesh* but for now you'll have to be content with the one or two short paths you can take without descending, from the visitors' centre. Southwest past the Youth Hostel, the path leads after 500m to the **Camel Observation Point**, a small mound with a lookout designed like a camel, with a rusty orientation map. In the other direction, you come after a similar distance to a **Desert Sculpture Park**, where you can check out some of the modern sculpture that is so popular (and so good) in Israel.

Exploring the makhtesh

For those who want to get to the heart of it, there is a range of options for **exploring the makhtesh** but for absorbing the still atmosphere and geological treats, you can't beat a simple hike with backpack, water and map. However, as elsewhere in the desert, don't underestimate the terrain nor the distances involved. There are a couple of simple **routes** you can follow, such as the **Carpenter's Workshop Trail**, a three-hour "novice's trail" that begins where the promenade along the cliff-edge ends southwest of town near a small amphitheatre – an orange sign points out the path down. The "Carpenter's Workshop" (HaMinsara) in question is in fact a bunch of rock formations that resemble sawn wood. From here the trail continues to the **Ammonite Wall**, where a rock face contains thousands of fossils of sea creatures called ammonites that were among the most common forms of life on earth for millions and millions of years, before all dying out at the end of the Permian Period 245 million years ago. Guides warn that for anything more complex than these short treks, it really is best to join a small group or hire a guide for the day. This might sound like a good sales pitch, but in the last few years overzealous holidaymakers, often desert debutants, have gained a reputation for needing rescuing. Apart from the expertise a guide can offer – most specialize in either geology or desert nature and are experienced rock climbers – they all carry mobile phones. Even if you are an experienced hiker, and armed with a topographical map (available in the visitors' centre), you will still need transport to get to the best trailheads inside the *makhtesh*.

If it's desert adventure and knowledge you want, a **camel or jeep tour** can reach the far corners of the *makhtesh*. In the eastern part, you can actually travel part of the **spice route**, a narrow winding camel path that cuts through high rocks; the jeeps just about manage to squeeze through. Most tours return to Mitzpe Ramon at sundown, as there's only one official place you're allowed to stay in the *makhtesh* after dark – the Be'erot camping ground (see "Accommodation" above). As Route 40 passes through the crater, the park does not actually close, but rangers will throw you out after dark if you don't have special permission to be there, and are not staying at the campsite. **Night jeep tours** are possible by special arrangement – they usually involve a quiet wait by a watering hole to see the animals come and drink, with leopard-spotting being the favourite pastime. *Desert Shade* (see p.285) is the best place to arrange jeep or camel tours. They also rent out mountain bikes.

Around Mitzpe Ramon

Out along the road past the SPNI Field School, the **Alpaca Farm** (☎07/658 8047; daily 9am–6pm; NIS13.50) is a bizarre experiment by a couple who, in 1987, decided on a whim to bring over a few llamas and alpacas from their native high Andes to the heat of the desert. That it has been a commercial success is a bit baffling – but the market for fine wool seems strong. Visitors can feed and pet these incredibly gentle animals, and even go out on a trek into the *makhtesh*, with a llama as pack-horse – or a mount for small children. Luckily, you get a trained llama handler as guide. Keen knitters can also buy skeins of natural alpaca wool for a souvenir woollie.

Eating and drinking

Mitzpe Ramon is not known as a centre for gourmets or even gourmands: **eating places** are sparse and most visitors either eat where they are staying or provide for themselves from the supermarket in the Commercial Centre (see p.285). Otherwise, choices include *Hanna's*, a good-value diner by the petrol station (Sun–Thurs 5.30am–8pm, Fri 5.30am–4pm; cheap to moderate), *HaTzukit*, serving the usual Israeli fare with a view over the crater (daily 8am–5pm; moderate), *HaMakhtesh* at 2 Nahal Tzihor with schnitzels and kebabs (Sun–Thurs 8am–11pm, Sat nightfall–11pm; cheap to moderate), or, for something more upmarket, the restaurant at the *Ramon Inn*, which offers international Jewish cuisine buffets (noon–2pm & 7–9pm; expensive).

For those in need of alcohol, *HaHaveet* at the Commercial Centre is a **bar** that also serves reasonable food. It is the liveliest place in town, and the nearest thing you'll get to nightlife (daily 7pm–2am).

Eilat

At the southern tip of Israel, the extreme desert conditions of the Negev meet the world's northernmost tropical seas at a point where four countries – Israel, Egypt, Jordan and Saudi Arabia – collide. Here, at the sun-mad holiday resort of **EILAT**, Israel dips a built-up 5km toe into the coral-rich waters of the **Gulf of Aqaba**, eastern finger of the Red Sea, featuring some of the best **scuba diving** and **snorkelling** in the world. The less than attractive sight of monolithic five-star hotels elbowing each other for space along the shore – the first thing you'll see on arrival – is more than made up for by the town's stunning **position**: set on hills overlooking the Gulf of Aqaba, the beaches stretch out east to the Jordanian border (the main hotel strip),while to the south and west there's the port and then more, less-developed, beaches, extending towards Egypt. The **views** are magnificent: you can clearly see Egypt, Jordan and Saudia Arabia, while the deep blue Red Sea contrasts sharply with the pinkish hills of Jordan and the more craggy heights behind the town, dominated by the eight-hundred-metre-high **Mount Solomon** (Jebel Masri). In a physical sense, if not a political one, you really feel yourself at the heart of the Middle East.

Given such amazing natural assets, it's no wonder that Israel is promoting tourism as a major industry with Eilat at its core. Israelis love the place for its complete contrast to life in the north, while foreign tourists flock here for the constant sunshine, water sports, the ever-expanding selection of desert adventure tours on offer, and the opportunity to do some serious hiking into the Negev, Sinai, or even Jordan. As the only landbridge between Africa, Asia and Europe, Eilat is also on the principal migratory route for vast numbers of **bird species**, from raptors to flamingoes (see p.290); in spring and autumn, the skies are filled with millions of migrating birds.

The need to balance tourism development in order to preserve vital natural habitats is a priority here. Unlike the eastern side of the Gulf of Aqaba in Jordan, Eilat is extremely poor in freshwater sources. In addition, the quality of **coral** has deteriorated drastically, partly because of pollution from the hotels, partly because of fish farming, but mostly because of the impact of huge number of divers. Israel, Egypt and Jordan realize that regional cooperation is essential to preserve the delicate biodiversity and,

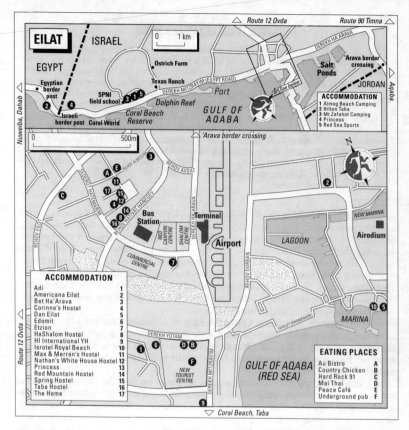

ACCOMMODATION
1 Almog Beach Camping
2 Hilton Taba
3 Mt Zefahot Camping
4 Princess
5 Red Sea Sports

ACCOMMODATION
Adi	1
Americana Eilat	2
Bet Ha'Arava	3
Corinne's Hostel	4
Dan Eilat	5
Edomit	6
Etzion	7
HaShalom Hostel	8
HI International YH	9
Isrotel Royal Beach	10
Max & Merran's Hostel	11
Nathan's White House Hostel	12
Princess	13
Red Mountain Hostel	14
Spring Hostel	15
Taba Hostel	16
The Home	17

EATING PLACES
Au Bistro	A
Country Chicken	B
Hard Rock 91	C
Mai Thai	D
Peace Café	E
Underground pub	F

indeed, aesthetic aura of the marine life. If anything, there is a sense of competition between the three over who can be seen to be the most "green".

Prices in Eilat are altogether rather on the high side, even by Israeli standards, and this despite the fact that it is a **duty-free port**, which means Israel's seventeen percent VAT is waived. In practice the only things whose prices it really affects are booze and car rental, which are both cheaper here than in the rest of the country.

Eilat's **climate** is markedly warmer than that of the rest of Israel, with year-round sun and a constant sea temperature of 20–26°C. July and August can be roasting hot, with midday temperatures well over 40°C. The only respite from the dry searing heat at this point is the wind which blows, almost daily throughout the year, from the north-north-east along the 'Arava Valley. Still known to local fishermen by its Arabic name, Aylat, this wind may well have given the town its name.

History

Eilat's apparent modernity – you could accurately suppose that almost everything you see has been built within the last thirty years – does in fact hide a considerable history. **King Solomon** built a port called Ezion Geber here (1 Kings 9: 26), which, after being destroyed in war, was rebuilt as the port of Judah (II Kings 14: 22) by King

BIRD-WATCHING

Eilat and the surrounding area is a **bird-watchers' paradise** almost as much as it is a marine biologist's one. Its location at the landbridge of three continents in the Afro-Syrian Rift Valley at the tip of the Gulf of Aqaba puts Eilat on one of the principal migration routes of European birds that winter in Africa. The main migratory periods are in spring and autumn – when ornithologists at times seem to outnumber beach bums – but there are thousands of birds here year round. The rarest siting has been **Didrix's Cuckoo**. The delicate relationship between the birds and tourists, as they have to learn to share their natural habitats, is being monitored at the moment by an international team of experts headed by Reuven Josef. Their campaigning efforts secured an old land-fill beyond the saltponds which volunteers helped to greenify. If you'd like to **volunteer** to help at the centre, contact the International Bird-watching Centre in the Commercial Centre on Sederot HaTemarim opposite the bus station (☎07/637 4276). They can provide food and an apartment.

Azariah (783–742 BC). In 735 BC it fell to Syrian forces, who passed it over to the sovereignty of Edom (II Kings 16: 6). In the internecine conflict which dogged the region over the following years, the port changed hands a number of times: it was renamed Berenice during the Hellenistic era, and then Aila by the Nabateans. During **Roman times** it became an important staging post when, in the third century, the Tenth Legion was moved here from Jerusalem, and, after the demise of the Roman Empire, the **Byzantine** rulers created a citadel near modern Eilat that became the focal point of their southern defence system. Remains of this are still visible, but nowadays they lie out of bounds on the Israel-Jordanian border.

In 1116, Baldwin I, then the **Crusader** king of Jerusalem, captured the port, and later the Arab presence was solidified with the erection of a fortress here under **Saladin**, to guarantee the safe passage of pilgrims on their way to Mecca. After 1588, however, Eilat was all but abandoned following the building of a new Turkish fortress east of Aqaba.

Not until the United Nations came to carve up Palestine did Eilat (Umm Rashrash as it was then called – really just a police post) regain some strategic and political importance. The Zionist lobby fiercely argued for its inclusion in the proposed Jewish state, since a Red Sea outlet giving direct access towards Asia was regarded as crucial to economic viability. Under the 1947 **UN Partition Plan**, it was awarded to the Jews; the Egyptian army moved in to claim it for the Arabs after the departure of the British on May 14, 1948, but by the end of the war it was unoccupied. On March 11, 1949, Israeli forces, in **Operation Uvda**, reached the Red Sea to claim it and hoisted a makeshift Israeli flag, hastily drawn in ink on cloth, presenting Jordan (which had hoped to claim it) with a *fait accompli* at the Rhodes armistice talks. At this time, Eilat was no more than a military outpost, but in the rush to consolidate such a strategically important location, the developers quickly began to build. The scramble for a firmer presence left little room for architectural and aesthetic considerations: the result was sturdy, but hardly pleasing to the eye. To complete the process of stabilization, and to encourage both Israeli settlement and foreign tourism, Eilat was declared a **tax-free zone** in 1985.

Arrival and orientation

Eilat Airport (used mainly for domestic flights) is built slap-bang in the centre of town at the end of HaTemarim. However, property developers are keen to get their hands on this prime site, so it may soon be relocated, or planes to Eilat may share Aqaba's airport, across the border in Jordan. International flights now use **Ovda International Airport**, 60km north of town. It's not particularly set up for individual tourists, and can be tricky to get to and from unless you're with a tour bus (charter companies may lay on transport for their passengers too). Egged bus #392 runs into town from the airport six times daily (last bus around 6pm), and also runs the other way to Beersheba; a taxi from the airport into Eilat costs around 150NIS. Most people arrive in Eilat at the **Central Bus Station**, a rather dilapidated, unmistakeably Israeli-designed building – functional, but certainly not beautiful. If you walk out of the bus station onto Sederot HaTemarim and look left down the hill, you should get your first glimpse of the Red Sea, peeking through between the buildings. Arriving **by land from Jordan or Egypt**, city buses from the border post will take you to the Central Bus Station.

Finding your way around Eilat isn't difficult, and a few days is quite enough to get to know it very well. Broadly speaking, the place can be split into three areas: the **town centre** built into the side of the hill; the ever-expanding **hotel zone** containing the plusher hotels on the seaward side of the airport and stretching out to the Jordanian border; and the area east of the town from the port to the Taba crossing, loosely referred to as **Coral Beach**. If you want to avoid the town and hotel area as much as possible, you can base your stay out along the Coral Beach area. The hills surrounding the town have conveniently limited the growth of the place and, wherever you are, provide an excellent reference point. **Sederot HaTemarim** is very much the main drag, lined with shops and cafés and with the great indoor air-conditioned shopping malls which characterize the town centre.

HaTemarim ends at Eilat Airport; to the left, Derekh Ha'Arava runs north out of town towards Beersheba, Tel Aviv and Jerusalem, while the road to the right (also known as Derekh Mitzrayim or the Egypt Road) runs south through the town past the ports and Coral Beach towards the Egyptian border crossing at Taba. The **IGTO tourist office** (Sun–Thurs 8am–8pm, Fri 8am–2pm, Sat 10am–2pm; ☎07/637 2111), located in a new building above Burger King on the corner of Ha'Arava and Yotam, will help with accommodation, and planning trips.

Accommodation

Eilat is popular year round, but during its two **high seasons** – winter for foreign tourists, end of June to September for Israelis – **accommodation** may be harder to find and prices higher than usual. It's also very busy at the major Jewish and Christian holidays (Rosh HaShannah, Passover, Christmas and Easter). If you are planning to visit during these periods, book in advance. On the other hand, if you arrive in Eilat in low season, you can shop around for good deals.

There are over one hundred places to stay in Eilat from campsites to luxury five-star hotels. **Budget accommodation** is plentiful: arrive in Eilat by bus and you're likely to be inundated by people offering hostel-type accommodation. Much of this is fine, but some hostels are overcrowded, overpriced, and pushed by aggressive hustlers; don't agree to anything until you've seen the place. Lists of the more expensive **hotels and private flats** can be obtained from the IGTO. Some of the better, and cheaper, options are listed below.

Sleeping on the beaches in Eilat has become commonplace over the years, and while it's officially illegal in town and westward, the police will normally turn a blind eye. The further out of the centre you go towards Taba, the better. On beaches east of town toward the Jordanian frontier, sleeping out is legal.

Budget travellers should be aware that **theft** is common in Eilat, especially on the beaches, but also in cheap hostels.

Hostels

In addition to those on the list below, there are plenty of **hostels** in the streets behind the bus station charging around $10 to $15 per night. Many of the diving clubs also have hostel accommodation for their customers, which can be a good deal if you stay with them while doing a course.

Red Mountain Hostel, Rehov HaTivat HaNegev (☎ & fax 07/637 4263). Good-value, clean a/c hostel near the bus station. ①.

Nathan's White House Hostel, 131 Retamim (☎07/637 6572). Small but homely and friendly with the usual facilities including a TV lounge and kitchen. ①.

Taba Hostel, Rehov HaTivat HaNegev (☎07/637 5982). A large place with rather cramped dorms, popular with long-stay travellers. ①.

The Home, Rehov Ofarim (☎07/637 2403). Neither spacious nor spotless, but cheap and cheerful with facilities such as a kitchen (free tea, coffee, bread and jam) and baggage store. ①.

Max and Merran's Hostel, 111 Agmonim (☎07/637 1333). A little cramped but friendly and popular with longer-stay travellers. Facilities include a TV lounge, daily videos, a baggage store, and a kitchen with free tea and coffee. No night curfew but closed 10am–1pm for cleaning. ①.

Bet Ha'Arava, 106 Almogim (☎07/637 4687). Friendly, with clean six-bed dorms (double rooms also available) and a great view. Lockers are available and there's a kitchen and TV lounge. ①/②.

HaShalom Hostel, Rehov HaTivat HaNegev (☎07/637 6544). This place was originally built as a hotel but failed to get a licence – hence the slightly upmarket entrance and building. Relaxed atmosphere (guitar-playing ex-hippies seem particularly welcome), nice patio and video bar. No curfew, but an "inconvenience" charge if you come in after midnight. Dorms and double rooms available. ①/②.

Spring Hostel, 126 Ofarim, opposite the Tnuva warehouse (☎07/637 4660). A hostel masquerading as a hotel and a decent place to spend a few days. Dorm beds, and private rooms sleeping up to four. There's a bar open until 10pm, and a fridge but no kitchen. They take Visa. ②/③.

Corinne's Hostel, 127 Retamim (☎07/637 1472). Private wooden huts and a few cramped, dank, and overpriced dorms. The owner likes to stress that there's no drunk and disorderliness on his premises. ②/③.

HI International Youth Hostel, Sederot Ha'Arava (☎07/637 2358, fax 637 5835). A cut above the cheap hostels and worth the higher price. Prices rise in June to September, when the place is overrun by school or army groups. Private rooms in any case are best booked. Check-in is after 2pm, and checkout 10am. Laundry, cafeteria, left luggage and TV room; no curfew. ②/②.

Hotels

There aren't a massive amount of mid-range options in Eilat, and hotels in all categories tend to be pricey for what you get, even by Israeli standards. Listed below is a selection of the better-value options. Many of the most expensive ones can be made more affordable if booked on a package tour.

Adi, behind New Tourist Centre, Derekh Yotam (☎07/637 6151 or 3, fax 637 6154). Small, quiet place handy for both town and beach ④.

Americana Eilat, Rehov Kamen (☎07/633 3777, fax 633 4174). One of the lower-priced North Beach hotels, with roughly three-star standards, and many of the trappings of its more expensive neighbours including a large pool, a nightclub and facilities for tennis and water sports. ⑤.

Dan Eilat, North Beach (☎07/635 2222, fax 636 2333). A typically classy *Dan*, and a cut above most of Eilat's beach hotels. Restaurants include Mexican, Polynesian and a carvery; there's also a jazz cellar, sauna, Jacuzzi and Turkish bath, a gym, a nightclub and squash courts. ⑥.

Edomit, New Tourist Centre, Derekh Yotam (☎07/637 9511, fax 637 9738). Good-value and quite homely town-centre hotel with a pool, five minutes from the beach. ⑤.

Etzion, Sederot HaTemarim (☎07/637 4131, fax 637 0002). Three-star hotel in the Commercial Centre: functional and slightly sterile, but boasts its own swimming pool and restaurant. Students get a ten per cent discount and low season prices can be negotiated. ③.

Hilton Taba, Taba, Egypt (☎07/637 9222, fax 637 9660). Across the border in Taba but before the Egyptian border post, so you don't need an Egyptian or Sinai visa to come or stay here, though you do need a passport and must complete Israeli border formalities every time you travel into Eilat. On the other hand, you get five-star service at Israeli four-star prices, plus a quieter beach and a casino. ⑥.

Isrotel Royal Beach, North Beach (☎07/636 8888, fax 636 8811). Swanky, five-star beach hotel trying to add a bit of chic to Eilat's beachfront. Stylish architecture, sea views, a variety of restaurants, and of course the full array of pools, keep-fit facilities, shops and services. ⑥.

Princess, Coral Beach (☎07/636 5555, fax 637 6333). Very stylish luxury hotel down towards the Egyptian border, and some way from all those frightfully vulgar places in town. Facilities include two pools, a spa and six restaurants serving a variety of international cuisine. ⑥.

Red Sea Sports Club Hotel, Coral Beach (☎07/637 3145 or 6, fax 637 4241). A hotel designed for divers, with the usual facilities (pool, restaurant, sauna), plus special facilities for divers (instructors, equipment, diving centre). ⑨.

Campsites

Almog Beach Camping Site (aka Caroline Camping), Coral Beach, just past the new port (☎07/637 9272). The cheapest official place in Eilat to pitch your own tent, this large campsite also rents out curiously designed semi-permanent tents. Demand is high, so call to check they have space available. A café on site sells soft drinks, alcohol and basics. ①.

Mt Zefahot Camping (formerly Mamshit Camping), Coral Beach, opposite Coral Beach Reserve (☎07/637 4411, fax 637 5206). Eilat's original campsite, set up when the Sinai was returned to Egypt. You can either pitch your own tent, rent a large tent that sleeps up to six, or stay in strange wooden cabins for up to six to eight people. Sheets and electricity are provided, but no breakfast is served, although there is a small kitchen. ①.

The beaches

There's sandy **beach** almost all the way around Eilat's shore, crowded close to town and around the hotel areas towards Aqaba, less so as you head south towards Taba. Most of the beaches are public, but you have to pay a couple of dollars to use a sun bed and umbrella. Outside *Red Rock Hotel* to the south of the town centre, the public beach seems a little quieter – although that could change when the new mall, HaAme HaShalom, opens. Here, Kisudski Sports hire out all the gear you need for snorkelling or you can take rides on "bananas" or jet-skis.

However, if staying in town it is definitely advisable to hop on a #15 or #16 bus heading south towards the Taba border, as the **beaches beyond the port** are much more conducive to a day's serious sunbathing. The Dolphin Reef (see below), 3km south of town on South Beach, is one of the nicest sandy settings (though the view of the port is less than romantic), but for the best snorkelling you should continue a kilometre or so further to Coral Beach Nature Reserve.

North Beach

The beach in town, wall-to-wall with sun-bronzed bodies, is definitely best left to those staying at the adjacent large hotels. Apart from the beach itself, the only attraction here is the **Airodium**, east of town between the New Marina and the *Sport Hotel*, a vertical wind tunnel where, for 90NIS, you can put on an inflatable suit and be suspended in a jet of air for ten minutes, thus simulating sky-diving without the inconvenience of having to jump out of an aeroplane.

Dolphin Reef

Apart from its pleasant beach – well worth the 20NIS entrance fee for the facilities – and cafés, **Dolphin Reef** (daily 9am–5pm) is where you go to mingle with dolphins. The trainers insist that they're not really trainers, they're merely communicating and interacting with the dolphins because they've struck up an equal relationship, though you won't see the trainers catching fish in their mouths. The notion that this quasi-open water reef is more dolphin-friendly than the usual dolphinarium is undeniable, but there's something a bit dubious about the set-up – after all, the dolphins are still in captivity. The buttonnose dolphins were brought from the Black Sea, where they were already in captivity; they are hugely friendly, and just looking at that permanent smile makes you feel happy. Dolphins have no natural enemies (except people and their marine pollution and fishing habits) and are extremely well-disposed towards humans; they have even been known to protect scuba divers in distress from sharks.

There are four sessions a day (at 10am, noon, 2pm and 4pm) when huge crowds gather to watch the entertaining spectacle of the family of dolphins, which has produced two babies in recent years, approach the "trainers" and perform. A whole range of other dolphin-based activities can also be enjoyed: scuba diving with dolphins and, for your companion-who-doesn't-dive, snorkelling or just plain swimming with dolphins (these activities cost 80NIS extra). There's also a research centre here for experimenting with the beneficial effects of interacting with dolphins on human depression; results indicate that the mammals can lift even severe cases. There are also sessions for people with physical disabilities to swim with the dolphins. You need to book for all activities except snorkelling (☎07/637 5935).

Coral Beach Nature Reserve

Coral Beach Nature Reserve (daily: winter 9am–5pm, summer 9am–6pm; 13NIS), whose entrance is opposite the SPNI Field School, doesn't have as charming a beach as

---

WATER SPORTS AND BOAT TRIPS

For many visitors, the main reason to come to Eilat is the water sports. These include **scuba diving**, for those who take these things seriously (and training courses in it for those who want to), or **snorkelling** for those who take them less seriously, but still want to ooh and aah at the coral and the fish. Above the waves, opportunities for **sailing and windsurfing** are plentiful. Windsurfing is from North Beach, although complaints abound that the more buildings go up, the fewer offshore breezes there are to pick up a tack.

Scuba diving

Eilat, and indeed the whole of the Gulf of Aqaba, has become one of Europe's favourite destinations for **scuba diving**. There are twelve schools in Eilat offering everything from guided introductory dives for US$40 to internationally recognized PADI certificates. Speciality dives include underwater photography, night dives, archeological and cave wreck dives, grotto and cave diving. To dive here in open water you must have a two-star licence, unless you intend to learn on the spot. The **Red Sea Sports Club** on Coral Beach is the largest diving club in Israel.

Snorkelling

If you've never snorkelled before, Eilat is one of the best places to learn. The coral reef lies only 6m offshore, and although a lot has already been destroyed through ignorance and neglect, everyone is trying to tighten up control to protect what's left. You can **rent equipment** from most of the beaches but if you're really in to snorkelling, note that this is one of the cheapest places to buy mask and fins; you can pick up a set for around $50. A good place to buy is the shop above the office of the Red Sea Sports Club on Coral Beach.

Snuba

Snuba is one of the new generations of diving techniques, where the tank is kept above water on a boat, and you dive to depths of about five metres with a long tube and an instructor. If you have any qualms about diving, or get phobic when faced with the strange breed of hi-tech meets lo-tech underwater breathing apparatus, try snuba. You

the one at Dolphin Reef, but it's the number-one place for serious snorkelling as the reef here is wonderful. This stretch of shoreline is owned by the Nature Reserve Authority and heavily patrolled by rangers out to catch – and incidentally fine heavily – anyone who infringes the laws. The idea is to protect the environment, not provide a pleasant beach for tourists – you really are privileged guests here. Although it is not a designated bathing beach and there are no lifeguards employed, **snorkelling** is allowed (a mask, snorkel and flippers can be rented at 20NIS a day) as long as you follow the etiquette: only enter the sea from the special jetties that take you out beyond the reef, never touch the coral, and especially never break it off – it is illegal (even though the souvenir shop down the road at Coral World is happy to sell imported coral from Thailand).

Emptier stretches of public beach can be found further south, towards the Egyptian border. In fact, for those who are serious about their snorkelling, diving, coral or beach-bumming, Eilat is just a rather expensive frontier post on the way down to the far superior beaches of the Sinai: Dahab and Tarabeen for the bush-blowing beach bungalow crew; Sharm el-Sheik and Ras Mohammed for the mask and flippers brigade. If you are going diving in Sinai or Jordan, it is better to go directly to a local dive school in those places, rather than booking one through an Israeli company here.

Visas valid for the southeast Sinai coast can be picked up at the border (see "Moving on" p.298).

---

don't get as in-depth instruction as with scuba, so if you do panic, make sure you keep the tube in your mouth – and let the instructor know. You can find a snuba-booking desk just inside the doors of the Coral Beach Nature Reserve. Typical costs are around $20 for an hour.

Boat trips
Organized boat trips range from the serene **glass-bottomed boats** to the less slick but perhaps more enjoyable **yachts** which operate from the Laguna in the hotel area. For around $20, you get a meal at sea and as much wine or beer as you can drink. One of the best firms is Jules Verne Explorer (see below), whose yachts are more like a hi-tech underwater observatory with transparent walls and bottom, and leave from the North Beach marina at 10am, 12.30pm, 3pm and 5pm; special night-time cruises go at 8.30pm on Mon, Wed and Fri. The price is 50NIS.

Water sports listings
Firms in Eilat organizing water sports, or providing facilities and renting out equipment for them, include: **AquaSport** (scuba diving) at Coral Beach (☎07/633 4404); **Coral Sea Divers** (scuba diving) at the *Carlton Hotel*, Dolphin Reef (☎07/637 0337); **Fantasia Cruises** (luxury diving and pleasure yacht) at Coral Beach Pier; **Galaxy** (glass-bottomed boat trips) at the Marina on the North Beach (☎177/022 3036 or ☎07/637 5189); **Israel Yam** (glass-bottomed boat trips) at the Marina on the North Beach (☎07/637 5528); **Menta** (windsurfing) (☎07/673 1456); **Divers Village** (scuba diving) at South Beach (☎07/637 2268); **Dolphin Reef** (scuba diving) at South Beach (☎07/637 5935); **Jules Verne Explorer** (glass-bottomed boat trips), Bridge House, North Beach (☎07/637 7702); **Lucky Divers Club** (scuba diving), 5 Bet Hagesher (☎07/633 5990); **Red Sea Sports Club** (boat rental of various sorts, waterskiing, scuba diving, snorkelling equipment rental) at Coral Beach (☎07/637 3145 or 637 9685) and Bridge House, North Beach (☎07/637 8363); **Sea World** (glass-bottomed boat trips) at Coral Beach (☎07/637 1659); **Siam Divers** (scuba diving) at the *Orchid Hotel* (☎07/637 0337); **Snuba Shallow Water Diving Tours** (snuba) at the Coral Beach Reserve (☎07/637 2722); **Windsurfing Centre** (windsurfing) at *Reef Hotel*, Coral Beach (☎07/637 1602); and **Yellow Submarine** (submarine dive, see p.296) at Coral Beach (☎07/637 6666).

CORAL CONSERVATION

Coral is a living colony of tiny animals called **polyps**, and every piece of it takes many years to build. Unfortunately, it is also very delicate and vulnerable to harm: even a touch can kill it. As a single diver or snorkeller, you obviously do far less damage than a boat dropping anchor on it, or a factory discharging waste into the sea, but you, too, can be inadvertently helping to destroy the unique ecosystem of the Red Sea's reefs if you do not take care.

You should always try to **swim** in as deep water as possible – at least a metre above the coral – as your flippers stir up detritus which damages this delicate living structure (sand landing on the coral can kill the polyps). Don't touch the coral, and never stand on it. If **diving**, make sure you can control your buoyancy sufficiently to avoid this, and beware of letting your equipment fall onto the coral too. No one who cares about the reef will leave litter, of course, and picking up other people's never does any harm.

Don't try to catch the **fish**, or even touch them – apart from being illegal, certain fish are also poisonous, notably the graceful lion fish, which packs a nasty sting, and the scorpion fish, which camouflages itself into the rock, as does the deadly stone fish, whose sting is invariably fatal. These fish are common throughout Eilat and the Red Sea. Trying to entice sea animals by offering them food can interfere with their feeding patterns, while touching them can cause them such stress that it, too, may interfere with feeding or breeding.

Coral World Underwater Observatory and Yellow Sumbarine

Beaches apart, the undoubted highlight of Eilat is **Coral World** on Coral Beach (☎07/637 6666; Sat–Thurs 8.30am–5pm, Fri 8.30am–3pm; 66NIS, with submarine ride 234NIS). Don't be put off by the hype – this place is nothing short of amazing, and well worth the price. Its chief attraction is the **underwater observatory** about 150m from the shore, and 6m below sea level. The observatory is built directly into the famous Red Sea Coral Reef, affording an unparalleled opportunity to view marine life in its natural environment without getting wet. Perhaps the most surprising thing, certainly for non-divers, is the sheer amount of marine life: brightly coloured shoals of exotic fish swim obliviously past the 360-degree observatory in a microcosm of tiered, multi-coloured coral – with the occasional human diver looking strangely awkward among them.

Even more thrilling if you can afford it, is to go down in the **Yellow Submarine** which submerges to 60m, a depth most divers never achieve. "Jacqueline" is the most technologically advanced and deepest diving passenger submarine in the world. For your one-hour underwater safari, you get a seat facing a large window, a set of headphones, and some atmospheric music. Your hostess does a microphone presentation for most of the trip and identifies some of the fish for you. Best of all, you get to cruise slowly past one of the most beautiful underwater sites in the Gulf of Aqaba – the Japanese Gardens, a mind-boggling cliff face of technicoloured coral and radiating fish, even at this depth. You can take photos, if possible with ASA400 film, making sure you place the lens against the window screen.

Back on dry land, and included in the Coral World ticket, the **Red Sea Reef Tank** is the home of a seemingly infinite variety of exotic fish, corals and sea life. Also in the complex are three concrete seashore pools, embedded into the rocks bordering the sea, which contain specimens too large to be kept in a regular aquarium – sharks, giant turtles, and a large collection of vicious-looking stingrays. The **Aquarium** and **Sea Museum** is fascinating, too, with a comprehensive collection of Red Sea life. Each of the small tanks contains a whole world in itself: once you've taken in the fish, you begin to notice that what you thought were rocks are really living, moving corals and sea anemones. The darkened display of luminous corals in the museum is particularly good.

The Coral World complex has a reasonably priced **cafeteria** and supermarket where snacks, drinks and gifts can be bought. Alongside there's a sandy **beach** dotted with palm trees and bordered by waterfalls which provides a place for relaxation and sunbathing, although you can't swim here.

The Ostrich Farm and Texas Ranch

On Coral Beach opposite the reserve, a **Texas Ranch** (Mon–Sat 7am–6pm) aims rather feebly to recreate the Old West. If such a place ever existed anyway, it probably didn't look like this, but there's desert and you can soothe a parched throat with a cold beer at the saloon. Horseback riding is also available (from 9am onward), as is camel-back riding (from 8.30am), despite the lower profile of that activity in 1880s Dodge City or Tombstone. Up the road beside the ranch, you'll find something even more incongruous, an **ostrich farm** (Sun–Thurs 9am–4pm; free), where you can meet the fastest bird on legs, along with other feathered and non-feathered members of the animal kingdom.

Eating

There are plenty of **restaurants** in Eilat but predictably most of them are poor-value tourist traps. Even a pitta-full of falafel is smaller and dearer here than anywhere else in the country – HaTemarim near the bus station is the main area for street food. The numerous **"eat all you can"** restaurants are worth trying; the going rate seems to be about 30NIS. There are also some good Moroccan restaurants, such as *Marhaba* in the Industrial Zone, and another on HaTemarim, at the corner of Sederot Hativat HaNegev, which offer a welcome relief from the array of soulless fast-food joints. For self-catering, you'll find **supermarkets** in the Shalom Centre and the Red Canyon Centre, and at the corner of HaTemarim and Elot. A good place for **bread**, cakes and savouries is the *Family Bakery* at 133 HaTemarim, open 24hr except Shabbat.

Au Bistro, 3 Elot (☎07/637 4333). If you need a plate of frogs' legs or pâté de foie gras, look no further: this is Eilat's top French restaurant, indeed Eilat's top restaurant of any variety, serving up haute cuisine with finesse, but open for dinner only. The seafood is especially good. Daily 5.30–11pm. Expensive.

Country Chicken, New Tourist Centre (☎07/637 1312). A good-value place for chicken (so no surprise there), but also for schnitzel, goulash and other meat dishes, and for fish too. Sun–Thurs 9am–midnight, Fri 9am–3pm, Sat nightfall–midnight. Moderate to expensive.

Fisherman's House, Coral Beach. One of the best "all you can eat" joints, with a selection of salads and fish, good atmosphere, and no pressure to move on. A full meal will cost you 30NIS, and you can buy alcohol here as well. Daily noon–midnight. Moderate.

Hard Rock 91, 179 Elot. Pasta, burgers and other basic gut-fillers, as well as beer, in a small dark dive bar. Daily 11am–2am. Cheap.

Mai Thai, Derekh Yotam by New Tourist Centre (☎07/637 0104). The best Thai food in town with a good-value set menu and oodles of noodles, and dishes spiced with fragrant combinations of coconut, ginger, lemon grass and green chilli. Daily 11.30am–3pm & 6–11.30pm. Expensive.

Mandy's, Coral Beach (☎07/637 2238). Last survivor of a chain of Chinese restaurants run by Mandy Rice-Davies (famous in Britain for her involvement in a 1960s sex scandal that brought down government minister John Profumo, but better-known in Israel as a restaurateur). The food is Cantonese and Szechuan with veg options available. Daily 1–4.30pm & 6–11.30pm. Expensive.

Underground Pub, New Tourist Centre. Travellers' hangout facing the sea, with a party atmosphere but no trouble tolerated. They serve filling grub of the "breakfast all day" variety, and they also have a TV showing international soccer matches, and a rotating menu where, before 7pm, dinner and a drink usually work out at around 30NIS, along with promotional deals such as the first fifty eat free. The small café next door, *Hollywood* – under the same management – does a *real* cappuccino. Daily 9am–5am. Cheap.

Nightlife and entertainment

The most important thing to get hold of in Eilat if you want a nightlife is news about the **beach parties** (try asking in places like the *Underground Pub* or the *Peace Café* for details). There are some venues such as the Dolphin Reef on a Tuesday and Thursday, as well as some impromptu events worth checking out. Don't bother turning up before midnight, and expect to pay a tourist entrance fee of about 10NIS which is waived for residents and hotel workers. The authorities are not thrilled about hosting beach parties, and it is possible they will be banned. Up at Wadi Shlomo (take a taxi for 10NIS), *Ya'eni* at the ostrich farm opens about midnight on Friday evenings for a sound and light show (10min) to the sound of Pink Floyd, followed by a disco of hip-hop and a mixture of Israeli/Euro sounds. *Club Shaka Zula* in the Arts Centre (Rehov HaNemalim, turning opposite the port behind the rows of imported cars) is open on Thursday and Friday nights and costs about 15NIS to get in (including a free drink). *The Roxy* on Sederot HaTemarim, which used to be a club, but now opens as a café bar, gets really packed late at night after the other parties wind down. In the Industrial Area, next to the Coca-Cola factory, *After Dark* plays acid jazz and techno.

Most tourists end up at some point having a **drink on the waterfont**. There are a few lively, cabaret-style bars, such as the *Yacht Club* or *Three Monkeys*, where Tina Turner lookalikes perform "I Will Survive" and get the audience up on their feet. The **dive bars** near Coral Beach seem by far the coolest places to hang out – the *Siam Divers Club*, the last before the Taba border, part of the swish *Orchid Hotel*, is a lively place for a drink.

MOVING ON FROM EILAT

The **bus station** is in the centre of town on Sederot HaTemarim (☎07/636 5111). Destinations served include Beersheba (every 90min; 3hr), Ein Boqeq (4 daily; 3hr 30min), Ein Gedi (4 daily; 4hr), Masada (4 daily; 3hr 45min); Tel Aviv (10 daily; 5hr), Jerusalem (4 daily; 5hr), Haifa (3 daily; 7hr) and Netanya (1 daily; 5hr 30min). **Sheruts** to Beersheba, run by Maxi Taxi (☎050/350169), should be booked in advance.

Arkia **flights** from Eilat's town centre airport (entrance on Derekh Ha'Arava opposite the junction with HaTemarim; ☎07/637 1185) serve Tel Aviv (approximately 12–15 daily; 1hr), Jerusalem (2–3 daily; 55min), Ben Gurion (17 weekly; 1hr), Haifa (3 daily; 1hr 10min) and Rosh Pinna (1 weekly; 1hr 35min). International flights almost all leave from Ovda Airport, 60km north of town (☎07/635 9442), which can be reached by Egged bus #392 (6 daily; 1hr) or taxi (around 150NIS).

To get **to Egypt**, take bus #15 or #16 to the border post at Taba (☎07/673 3110). To visit Taba only, you need a passport but no visa. For the Sinai coast as far as Sharm el-Sheikh and to St Catherine's Monastery, you can obtain a special visa at the border; this cannot be traded in for a full visa once you are inside Egypt, so if you might be going beyond the Sinai, pick up an Egyptian visa at the consulate first. If travelling beyond Taba, an Israeli exit tax of 56NIS (US$17) is payable, along with an Egyptian entry tax of E£24 (US$8). The border is open round the clock, but onward transport dries up around 3pm Egyptian time (Egypt is an hour behind Israel), and the last bus to Taba leaves Eilat around 9.30pm. On the other side, there are buses to Cairo (3 daily; 10hr), Suez (1 daily; 6hr 30min; taking this bus and then an onward service taxi is the cheapest way of getting to Cairo), Nuweiba (4 daily; 2hr), Dahab (2 daily; 3hr), Sharm el-Sheikh (2 daily; 3hr) and St Catherine's Monastery (1 daily; 4hr). You may also find service taxis down the coast, especially to Nuweiba and Dahab.

Travelling **to Jordan**, bus #16 runs three times hourly (the last around 4pm) to the border post at 'Arava, which is just 3km from town. The crossing (☎07/633 6815) is open Sun–Thurs 6.30am–10pm, Fri & Sat 8am–8pm. Exit tax is again 56NIS (US$17), and Jordanian visas can be obtained at the border. From the other side, a cab into Aqaba costs around JD3 (US$4.50).

For a more earthy experience, the *Underground* in the New Tourist Centre has your typical **pubs** abroad atmosphere. Affectionately promoted by the tourist office as Eilat's oldest pub, the *Tavern*, just round the corner, feels like a dive and attracts trouble. The *Peace Café*, at 13 Almogim, is almost as old as Eilat itself. This is the town's hippy hangout, as its name suggests, and the centre of what drugs trade there is in the town. It's also the place to come early in the morning if you're looking for casual work.

The only **cinema**, Red Canyon, shows the latest Hollywood blockbusters, usually subtitled in Hebrew. The **Phillip Murray Cultural Centre** on Sederot HaTemarim (☎07/667 2257; daily 5–11pm) puts on a variety of jazz, classical, rock and theatre performances (in Hebrew) and serves a nice cappuccino in the foyer restaurant. Games such as chess and backgammon are available at the cafeteria free of charge. The Municipal Conservatory puts on concerts; ask at the IGTO for details of this and other events. Two **festivals** take place in Eilat, too: in April it hosts a three-day rock festival, and in August a four-day jazz festival; details again from IGTO.

Listings

Airlines Arkia, Red Canyon Centre (☎07/637 6102); El Al, Khan Amiel Centre, Park Ophir (☎07/633 1515).

Banks and exchange Moneychangers can be found in the Commercial Centre opposite the bus station on Sederot HaTemarim. Should you need a bank, there's a Bank Leumi on Sederot HaTemarim opposite the bus station, a Bank HaPoalim on HaTivat HaNegev, also opposite the bus station, and a First International in the New Tourist Centre.

Books Steimatzky is at the bus station and in the Shalom Centre mall at the corner of HaTemarim and Ha'Arava. The municipal library, on Sederot HaTivat HaNegev, behind the Phillip Murray Cultural Centre, is worth joining if you're staying in Eilat for more than a few days. For a one-off membership fee of 55NIS you can take out one book at a time. There's a room full of English-language books, many of them by Israeli writers. Check our booklist (p.511) for recommendations.

Car and bike rental Avis, Eilat Airport (☎07/637 3164 or 5); Budget, Shalom Centre (☎07/637 4124 or 5); Eldan, Shalom Centre (☎07/637 4027); Eurodollar, Sederot HaTemarim (☎07/637 1813); Europcar, Shalom Centre (☎07/637 4014 or 5); Hertz, Sederot HaTemarim (☎07/637 6682); Thrifty, Shalom Centre (☎07/637 3511 or 2). ETI at the tourist information centre (☎177/022 0212 or ☎07/637 0380) rents out bicycles and scooters.

Consulates Egypt: 68 HaEfroni (☎07/637 6882), open for visa applications Sun–Thurs 9–11am, collect same day 1–2pm; UK: New Tourist Centre (☎07/637 2344).

Laundry Options include Gill Laundromat at HaTemarim and Elot and Mickey Mouse Laundromat at 99 Almogim.

Medical services Magen David Adom (first aid) on Sederot HaTemarim, 1km northwest of the town centre (☎07/637 2333). Yoseftal Hospital, Derekh Yotam (☎07/635 8011). Pharmacies include Avidgor in the New Tourist Centre, Michlin on HaTemarim, oposite the bus station, and Eilat at 25 Elot.

Police Rehov Avdat, at the northern end of HaTivat HaNegev (☎07/633 2444).

Post office Red Canyon Centre, Sederot HaTemarim (Sun, Mon, Tue & Thurs 8am–noon & 4–6.30pm, Wed 8am–2pm, Fri 8am–1pm).

Taxis 'Arava (☎07/637 4141); Sivan (☎07/633 0444); Taba (☎07/633 3339); King Solomon (☎07/633 2424).

Telecommunications Starcom in the New Tourist Centre, Express in the Shalom Centre and Phone Home on Rehov Almogim are among firms offering low-cost international calls and fax facilities.

Travel agents Egged Tours, Central Bus Station (☎07/636 5122); United Tours, New Tourist Centre (☎07/637 1720); ISSTA, c/o CETS Holidays, Neptune Hotel (☎07/631 6690). Among firms offering tours into Egypt and Jordan are Johnny Tours (☎07/637 6777) and Travel is Jordan at Bridge House, North Beach (☎07/633 6111).

Visa renewal Ministry of the Interior, City Hall complex, Sederot HaTemarim (☎07/637 6332). It's easier to pop across the border and back, so long as the border officials don't recognize you.

Work Bars and hostels may have some jobs going, or there may be construction work too. As usual, the cheap hostels are the places to ask, and the best places to stay if you are looking for this kind of employment. Otherwise turn up early mornings outside the *Peace Café* at 13 Almogim. Be aware, however, that the trick of not paying illegal casual labourers is especially common in Eilat.

Around Eilat

The region around Eilat is known, sometimes confusingly, as the **Eilot**. The **'Arava Valley** to the east, which runs all the way up to the Dead Sea, is where the Afro-Syrian Rift opens out into sandy desert, and into the Red Sea itself. The rift is still active, which accounts for the occasional tremors in the region. If you fly over this desert, you can see that the slightly higher water content has produced more fertile farming land; there are six kibbutzim grouped around Eilat, although as elsewhere in the desert, they are heavily subsidized.

To the west, wind and water erosion have created a wonderland of geological formations. These include the **Red Canyon**, 22km up Route 12 to the northwest of Eilat, where, if you can get to it (best done with your own transport), there's an interesting two-and-a-half-hour desert hike; and the **Timna Valley Park**, where traces of ancient human activity can be found, along with some of the world's oldest copper mines, used extensively by the Egyptian pharaohs.

As in other parts of the desert, renting a car can be a good option, though note that you cannot take an Israeli rental car into Egypt. The sites covered below are, however, accessible on tours or by regular buses from Eilat.

Timna Valley National Park

Some 28km north of Eilat, **Timna Valley National Park** (daily 7.30am–nightfall; 15NIS) is a vast geological playground where copper was mined continuously for almost six thousand years. Although Israel tried to revive the industry, the collapse of the copper market worldwide put an end to it for ever. Excavations began here around the turn of the century, and have uncovered traces from the Early Bronze Age and a particularly strong Egyptian presence from around 1400 BC.

At the entrance of the park have a look at the **video, maps and diagrams** explaining the geology and history of Timna, as well as the ancient techniques of copper mining and smelting – remarkably similar to many modern-day methods. If you want to do some hiking, ask for a route map. There are two **trails** – one takes about three hours, the other about seven.

Timna's most striking feature is the rugged rock face that hems in the large crater-like valley: an atmospheric, isolated vision that evokes vivid pictures of the conditions and lives of those early miners. The valley floor is arid and stained red and green by the rich mineral deposits, and the cliffs are etched with **rock carvings**. You can discern Caananite warriors on their ox-drawn chariots, and a multitude of ibex and oryx, animals which are now proliferating in the area after near-extinction.

The greatest of the natural wonders are **King Solomon's Pillars**, at the southern end of the park towards the artificial Timna Lake. Two great red pillars of rock, they protrude from the valley wall like the entrance to some vast prehistoric cathedral. Railed off nearby are the remains of the **Temple of Hathor**, an Egyptian shrine dating from the fourteenth century BC. If you climb high up the steps just to the side of this temple there is an engraving, visible from the temple, which is believed to be of Ramses III making an offering of a piece of copper in rock to the goddess Hathor, and receiving something from her in exchange.

Several companies run **tours to Timna Valley** from Eilat (try Egged or United in Eilat), or you can get Egged bus #397 or #444 (8 daily in all) from Eilat up the 'Arava Valley as far as the track leading to the park (*not* the modern mines), and hike 3km

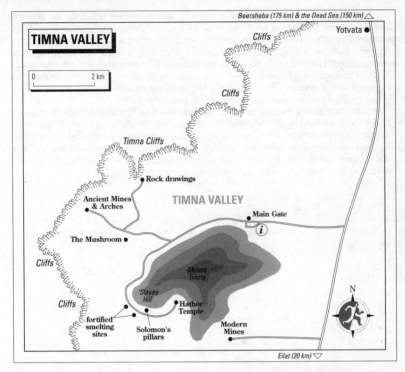

TIMNA VALLEY

0   2 km

Beersheba (175 km) & the Dead Sea (150 km) △
Yotvata ●

Cliffs

Cliffs

Timna Cliffs

● **Rock drawings**

Ancient Mines
& Arches ●

TIMNA VALLEY

Main Gate
ⓘ

The Mushroom ●

Cliffs

Cliffs

Mount
Timna

Slaves
Hill

● **Hathor**
Temple

fortified
smelting
sites

Solomon's
pillars

Modern
Mines

N

Eilat (20 km) ▽

from there to the entrance. Once inside, however, walking is not a particularly attractive prospect – the various attractions are widely scattered, and it's very hot. With a car you can drive between them, or you could consider renting a bike in Eilat and spending a few nights camping in the valley. A rough, free **campsite** by Timna Lake provides fresh drinking water and toilet facilities; it's crowded during the day when the tours roll in, but eerily quiet at night. A small snackbar sells the basics during the day, but if you intend to stay for a while, bring provisions with you to save money.

Hai Bar Biblical Wildlife Reserve and Kibbutz Yotvata

Some 40km north of Eilat, the **Hai Bar Biblical Wildlife Reserve** (Sun–Thurs 8.30am–5pm, Fri & Sat 8.30am–4pm; 15NIS per person, plus 5NIS per car) is a safari-park-style reserve with over 450 native animal species in their natural habitat. Some wander freely throughout the complex – ostriches, oryx, addax and other antelope-like animals – others, including large cats, wolves, hyenas and other predators, roam in spacious enclosures. Many of these animals are otherwise extinct or close to extinction in the Negev, where centuries of hunting has taken its toll. All of them are mentioned in the Bible, and the place gives some idea of the size of the animal population in biblical times, and perhaps goes some way to explaining how early human populations were able to survive here. The reserve is easy enough to reach by bus (#397 or #444 from Eilat, total 8 daily), which stops right by the main road, but you can only go round it in a vehicle; if you wait at the entrance, you may find someone with space who is prepared to take you. Guided tours by car (each vehicle gets a receiver to hear the guide, who is in the car at the front) start on the hour every hour between 10am and 2pm.

On the same site, the **predators' centre** (15NIS; combined ticket for the reserve and the centre 26NIS plus 5NIS per vehicle) features carnivores of both furred and feathered varieties, many of them rare species. By the road is a cafeteria belonging to **Kibbutz Yotvata**, where the kibbutz's famed dairy products are sold – any of the fourteen different kinds of yoghurts, milk drinks and ice creams are very refreshing and heartily recommended. Yotvata itself, little over 1km to the north, offers tours of its **regional dairy centre**, where again the highlight is sampling the end product. It's a popular kibbutz with volunteers, especially during the winter.

If you are planning to stay in the area, then **Ye'elim Holiday Village/Campsite** (200m from the road by the cafeteria) is your best bet. Owned by **Kibbutz Grofit**, 8km north of the site, *Ye'elim* offers caravan accommodation (②), and camping (①). The village has a dining room, clubhouse with bar and TV, a swimming pool with water slides, and at least makes a change from Eilat: at night especially, it is drowned in the stillness of the desert. From here, you can arrange to visit Kibbutz Grofit.

CHAPTER SIX

JERUSALEM

Ten measures of beauty gave God to the world: nine to Jerusalem and one to the remainder
Ten measures of sorrow gave God to the world: nine to Jerusalem and one to the remainder

The Talmud

E very visitor to Israel goes to **JERUSALEM** (Yerushalayim in Hebrew, Al-Quds in Arabic). Each brings with them their own image of the place, yet each is invariably surprised by what they find when they get there. Sacred to three religions and once considered to be the centre of the world itself, the Holy City is, for all its fame, an unexpectedly small place, provincial in many ways and conservative in outlook. Packed with museums, religious sites and ancient relics, it is home to three of the world's most venerated institutions: the **Church of the Holy Sepulchre**, held to be the location of the crucifixion, and the holiest site in Christendom; the **Western (Wailing) Wall**, last remnant of the Second Temple and most sacred Jewish relic in the world; and the **Dome of the Rock** – third most hallowed location in Islam as the spot from where the Prophet Mohammed made his ascent to heaven. But even without these monuments, and even to a non-believer, Jerusalem has much to offer – from the narrow alleys and vibrant **souqs** of the magnificent walled **Old City**, within which lies the **Via Dolorosa** (the path taken by Jesus to the cross), to the churches and tombs of the **Mount of Olives**, and the expensive shops and lively bars of downtown West Jerusalem. In fact, Arab East Jerusalem and Israeli West Jerusalem offer the visitor two worlds for the price of one: the tradition and relaxed pace of the Arab world and the cosmopolitan glitz of the West. And, in a city with an already diverse cultural mix, the Palestinian *fellahin* and Bedouin who meet their urban compatriots in the markets and shops of the East, and the Israeli farmers (from kibbutzim and moshavim in the foothills and the plain) who do much the same in the West, add further to the number of different people you encounter on the streets.

Perched high in the **Judean Hills**, the city's location is equally captivating. The view on approach is dramatic, with even the modern city providing a magnificent array of white high-rises that gleam in the sunlight – an architectural legacy of the first British governor who declared that all new buildings must be made from local limestone. To its west lie the fertile planted fields, olive groves and settled villages of the coastal plain and the Judean foothills, while to the east the harsh desert of the Jordan Valley stretches out to a horizon that, on a clear day, offers glimpses of the Dead Sea.

As far as the **Israel-Palestine question** is concerned, Jerusalem is at the heart of the matter. It may be one city, but it's definitely two countries, and if the pre-1967 border no longer exists in physical form, the political, legal and above all cultural divisions are still very tangible. The two halves live uneasily side by side; a tension heightened by the construction of new Jewish settlements that encroach upon Palestinian land. Though Israel has taken the position since 1967 that Jerusalem is the single indivisible capital of the Jewish state, it's a status recognized by few other countries, so while the Knesset is in Jerusalem, virtually all foreign embassies remain in Tel Aviv. Meanwhile, the Palestinians also consider Jerusalem their true capital – however unrealistic that may seem – and it remains the focus of their commerce, culture, political life and aspiration.

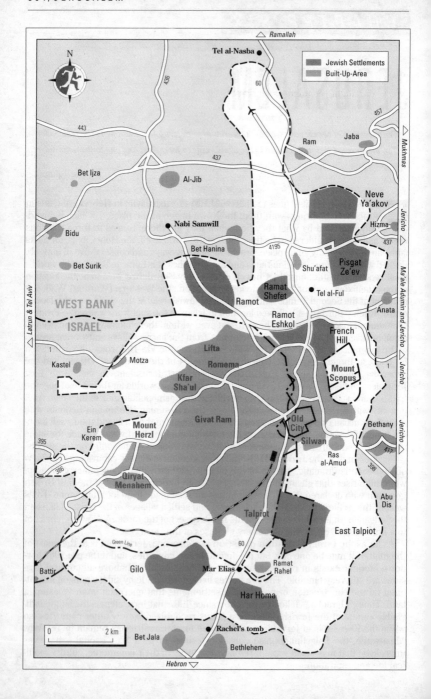

△ *Ramallah*

Tel al-Nasba ●

Jewish Settlements
Built-Up-Area

436

60

443

437

457

△ *Mukhmas*

Ram

Jaba

Bet Ijza

Al-Jib

△ *Jericho*

Neve Ya'akov

Bidu

Nabi Samwill ●

Hizma

437

Bet Hanina

4195

Ma'ale Adumim and Jericho

Bet Surik

Shu'afat

Pisgat Ze'ev

WEST BANK

Ramat Shefet

Tel al-Ful ●

Anata

Ramot

ISRAEL

Ramot Eshkol

△ *Latrun & Tel Aviv*

1

Lifta

French Hill

Kastel

Motza

Romema

Mount Scopus

1 △ *Jericho*

Kfar Sha'ul

Ein Kerem

Givat Ram

Bethany

△ *Jericho*

395

Mount Herzl

Old City

Silwan

417 △

386

Ras al-Amud

388

Qiryat Menahem

Abu Dis

Talpiot

East Talpiot

Green Line

Gilo

Mar Elias ●

Ramat Rahel

Battir ■

Har Homa

60

Rachel's tomb ●

0   2 km

Bet Jala

Bethlehem

Hebron ▽

Jerusalem then is a schizophrenic city, a frustrating and complex place that can seem overwhelming on a first visit. In fact such is the emotion that the city inspires in some visitors that it has its own mental disorder: some victims of **Jerusalem Syndrome** suffer the delusion that they are characters from the Bible – Jesus is the favourite of course, but others include Moses, King David, Elijah, John the Baptist and the Virgin Mary. You might see them wandering the streets, dressed in the robes of their adopted persona. Other sufferers commit bizarre acts in their certainty of the imminent Second Coming: in 1969, an Australian tourist tried to burn down the al-Aqsa Mosque in preparation for Jesus's arrival.

But despite its very real difficulties, Jerusalem is still a beautiful city, teeming and alive. It is a historical location without compare and the backdrop against which the mythologies of three religions were acted out. It was from here that Mohammed ascended to heaven on his night journey, from the same spot where God tested Abraham by asking him to sacrifice his son. It was the residents of this city who welcomed Jesus by spreading palm leaves on the ground before Him, along these streets that He dragged the cross, and here that He was executed upon it. Here, too, stood the capital of David and Solomon, home to the two Jewish Temples of antiquity; and this is the city for which the Jews through all their centuries of exile and persecution cried their ancient hope, "next year in Jerusalem". Little wonder that it inspires such dreams, such devotion, such love, such madness.

Jerusalem in history

Jerusalem's first mention in the Bible is as "Salem" (Genesis 14: 18). Later referred to as Jebus (Judges 19: 10), the first time it is called "Yerushalayim" (Jerusalem) is when David takes Goliath's head there in I Samuel 17: 54. The name may be a corruption of Ir Shalem ("City of Salem"), or it may come from **Ir Shalom**, ("City of Peace"), though the latter seems somewhat inappropriate given its violent history.

Whatever the origins of its name, the site has been settled since the early **Bronze Age**, around 2600 BC, but as it wasn't on a trade route its importance was always more strategic than commercial. Ancient Jerusalem receives its first documentation on "execration texts" (lists of Egypt's vassal states inscribed in hieroglyphics on bowls and figurines) dating from the nineteenth century BC, while among the **Armana letters** (see p.482), were six written by its Canaanite king Abdiheba to Pharaoh Akhenaton of Egypt, the last of which begs Egyptian help against the "Habiru" who are besieging it. The Egyptologist, David Rohl (see box on p.424), believes the Habiru referred to are David's forces, though most scholars date the Amarna letters to three centuries earlier. Either way, Jerusalem seems to have long been an **independent city state** whose people, the Jebusites, were regarded as a nation in their own right by the early Old Testament. Jebusite Jerusalem withstood the Israelite invasion under Joshua (around 1200 BC), and remained independent for the next two hundred years until its capture by **David** who made it his capital. Solomon, his son, built the **First Temple** here, but on his death the union of the twelve Israelite tribes split and Jerusalem became capital of the smaller, southern kingdom of Judah. In 586 BC, the **Babylonians** demolished the city, destroyed the Temple, and drove the population into exile in Babylon, but under Jerusalem's new Persian ruler, Cyrus, the citizens of Judah (now called Jews) were allowed to return in 538 BC, and went on to build the **Second Temple** in 515 BC.

Jerusalem surrendered to **Alexander the Great** in 332 BC. He was succeeded by his general, **Ptolemy**, whose dynasty then lost the city in 198 BC to their rivals, the **Seleucids** (descendants of another of Alexander's generals), under whom the Temple was Hellenized and dedicated to Zeus. The **Maccabees**, in revolt against such profanations, took the city and rededicated the Temple in 164 BC, an event celebrated by the Jewish winter festival of lights, Hanukkah (see p.50).

In 63 BC, Jerusalem fell to **Rome**. The Hasmoneans briefly gained control, but in 37 BC, after a five-month siege, the city was taken by the forces of Rome's appointed king, **Herod the Great**, whose massive programme of works here was crowned by his restoration and enlargement of the Temple. **Jesus** must have entered the city on the first Palm Sunday around 30 AD, to be crucified here a week later. The **Jewish War** of 66 AD saw the first revolt against Roman rule. Put down by Emperor Titus, under whose orders Jerusalem and the Temple were destroyed, it was followed by a **Second Revolt** in 132 AD, led by Simon Bar Kokhba, after which the city was flattened completely on the orders of Emperor Hadrian, who had **Aelia Capitolina** built on its ruins, and banned Jews from entering. The conversion of the Roman Empire to **Christianity** in 313 AD began a 300-year period of almost uninterrupted Christian hegemony over the city, brought to an end in 638 with the bloodless takeover by Caliph Omar Ibn al-Khattab (who came to accept its surrender in person), ushering in the first **Muslim Period**.

RELIGIOUS AND COMMUNAL DIFFERENCES

Jerusalem is a major centre of the three main monotheistic religions, **Judaism**, **Christianity** and **Islam**. Nowhere has worship of the same God provoked more conflict and nowhere is the dividing line between **theology and politics** more blurred, with religious quotations the stock-in-trade of reactionary and fundamentalist politicians of all three faiths. All have separate but, to an outsider, remarkably similar visions of the city as the centre of a theocracy in which there is no place for unbelievers. Nevertheless, the Israeli Tourist Board have chosen the golden cupola of the Dome of the Rock, a Muslim site, to advertise Jerusalem to largely Jewish and Christian tourists: the commercial worth of its overwhelming beauty for once overriding religious and political considerations.

Jerusalem's ethnic and religious divisions are more complex than they might at first appear: several communities do not fit into the two big ethnic groups of Jewish Israelis and Palestinian Arabs, and those two groups themselves contain a plethora of subdivisions. **Palestinians**, for example, are predominantly Sunni Muslim, but about a tenth of them are Christians, belonging to Syrian, Greek Catholic, Greek Orthodox, Coptic, Franciscan or Protestant denominations. **Jewish Israelis** may be ethnically Ashkenazi or Sephardi, and religiously Orthodox, Reform or secular, while among the ultra-orthodox *haredim*, there is a whole host of different sects, distinguishable by subtle differences of dress.

Of groups neither Jewish nor Palestinian, perhaps the most significant are the **Armenians**, traditionally concentrated in the Old City south of Jaffa Gate. The communities associated with the various monastic orders are also of long standing – those attached to **Ethiopian, Coptic** and **Greek Orthodox** churches can be easily identified by their flowing black robes, a common sight on the streets of the Old City. Meanwhile Jerusalem's **immigrant heritage** is reflected in the names of some of its neighbourhoods, such as the German Colony in West Jerusalem or the American Colony in the East, though these are now by and large heterogeneous. The multitude of tourists, religious pilgrims and other foreigners studying or working in the city all add to the mixture.

Overshadowed as they are by the central Israel-Palestine conflict, **disputes** between and within these communities are an enduring feature of Jerusalem life. Arguments between various Christian sects over the stewardship of sacred sites stretch back hundreds of years (especially within the Church of the Holy Sepulchre, see box on p.333), and fights between Orthodox and secular Jews can be just as bitter. Keen to impose strict religious observation on all Jews, the ultra-orthodox are willing to take to the streets to enforce their demands: those driving on the Sabbath run the risk of having their cars stoned in Orthodox neighbourhoods and, in recent years, more and more areas have been unilaterally declared no-go zones. They also try to stop Saturday filmshows, close non-kosher restaurants and cafés, and stop archeological digs that might disturb ancient cemeteries.

The city flourished under the **Ummayad** caliphs (660–750) and some of its most important buildings survive from this period, among them the al-Aqsa Mosque and the Dome of the Rock. During the subsequent period of **Abbasid** rule (750–969), Jerusalem was home to several prominent Muslim Sufi scholars and became a religious focal point for Christian and Jewish pilgrims. In fact it became so popular that at the beginning of the **Fatimid** period (969–1071), the first recorded complaint against the tourist trade was made, by a local historian, al-Muqqadasi, who wrote that Jerusalem was being overrun by pilgrims.

In 1099, the **Crusaders** – or "Franks", as they were known – put an end to the first period of Muslim rule, and heralded a Christian Kingdom of Jerusalem, under which the Jewish population were burned alive and its Muslims slaughtered or expelled. Such extremes of religious intolerance were dispelled in 1187 with the return of Muslim rule under the legendary **Saladin** (Salah al-Din al-Ayyubi), who allowed Christians to remain in the city (or to leave unharmed), and Jews to return. By the end of the **Ayyubid** period in 1248, Jerusalem, as part of a Syrian province with Damascus as its capital, was of minor political importance, a situation that didn't change under the **Mamluks** (1248–1517), when it became simply an outpost of an empire based this time in Egypt. The Mamluks refurbished the Old City but neglect during their later days led to its decline, not helped by earthquakes and an epidemic of the Black Death in the fifteenth century. At the end of 1516, Jerusalem was taken by the **Ottoman Empire**, the centre of power shifting to Turkey. **Suleiman the Magnificent** (1537–41) refortified the city and immediately embarked on a building programme, but for over three hundred relatively peaceful years Jerusalem remained a provincial outpost of a vast empire: Christian travellers in these years described the city as a ghost town, dusty and dilapidated.

By the **nineteenth century**, the Ottoman Empire had become so moribund that it could mount no serious resistance to the burgeoning economic and political strength of the northern and western European states. Foreign powers investing in the city vied with each other for a foothold as they waited for the "sick man of Europe" to die. New areas, with names like the Russian Compound and the German Colony, sprouted outside the city walls, while many of the educational and religious institutions which still exist today – Schmidt's Girls' School, the Alliance Française and St George's Anglican Cathedral – were founded at this time.

On December 11, 1917, British troops, under the command of General Allenby, dismounted and marched in through the Jaffa Gate on foot (out of respect for the city's venerable status), and Jerusalem became the capital of the **Mandate**. The city's expansion outside the walls continued under the British, as both Palestinian Arabs and new Jewish immigrants constructed new residential quarters.

Under the **United Nations Partition Plan** of 1947, Jerusalem was to be a *corpus separatum*, open to both the Jewish and Arab states. But even before the British pulled out in May **1948**, both sides were angling to control as much of the city as possible, and neighbourhoods that had long been mixed became polarized, with the losing community forced out. The Arabs tried to maintain a siege of Jewish West Jerusalem, but failed, though they did manage to force the Jews out of the Old City. By the end of the 1948 war, Jerusalem was **divided**, occupied by Israeli troops in the west and the Jordanian Arab Legion in the east, with an armistice line (now the Green Line) running through the city, and large UN-patrolled areas in the centre designated "no-man's-land". West Jerusalem remained the seat of Israel's government but Tel Aviv became the centre of economic and cultural life, while administrative power for East Jerusalem moved to Amman. The **Six Day War** of June 1967 saw the Israeli army take East Jerusalem and the Old City, unilaterally annexing them and declaring the city the "eternal, united capital of Israel".

Today, Jerusalem still awaits final resolution of the 1948 divisions. Most of the international community does not recognize Israel's jurisdiction over East Jerusalem, considering it to be a part of the West Bank, and many Western countries still maintain consulates in the east serving the Palestinian Territories. The Palestinians themselves see the city as the capital of a future independent state. Meanwhile, Israel has expanded the municipal boundaries as far as Bethlehem to the south and Ramallah to the north, and ringed East Jerusalem with three bands of settlements to forestall the Palestinian claim on the east – a process that has not been stopped by the Oslo Accord (see p.352), though each new settlement has been greeted by protests and resistance from the Palestinian side.

Arrival, orientation and information

In terms of getting around, it's easiest to view the city as two small towns: East and West Jerusalem. **East Jerusalem** is centred on the walled **Old City** – the focus of any visit. Beyond the walls, the commercial centre of East Jerusalem, in a time warp since investment and development stopped there in 1967, fans out northwards from the Damascus Gate along Nablus Road and Salah al-Din Street, where you'll find most of its money-changers, bookshops, travel agents, restaurants and hotels. Also part of East Jerusalem are the **Mount of Olives** to the east of the Old City, a hillside graveyard studded with churches, and the **City of David** to the south, whose rustic, village-like atmosphere is a world apart from the bustle of the commercial centre.

Downtown **West Jerusalem** can be approached from the Old City by walking west along **Jaffa Road**, its backbone. Shops, cafés, airline offices, banks, the visa office, cinemas and nightlife are all centred around its heart – the pedestrian precinct at **Ben Yehuda**. Tourist attractions in West Jerusalem tend to be scattered in the suburbs, so you'll need to make use of the buses; from Jaffa Road or **King George Street** there are services to sites such as Mount Herzl (see p.374), the Israel Museum (see p.373) and Yad VaShem (see p.375).

OPENING TIMES

Opening times can cause problems. On Friday afternoon and Saturday, for example, Jewish West Jerusalem closes up completely, while in East Jerusalem many Muslim-owned shops are closed on Fridays, and Christians generally take Sunday off. With three separate sets of religious holidays (see "Basics", pp.49–52) to take into account (not to mention the differences in calendar between eastern and western Christian churches), there's a good chance that something you don't want to miss will be closed for at least part of your stay.

Points of arrival

The local airport, **Atarot**, is 10km north of town, close to Ramallah. There are no Egged bus services into town, so you'll have to take a taxi, or walk to the main Jerusalem–Nablus Road (Route 60), and flag down a Ford Transit service taxi en route from Ramallah to the Damascus Gate, or Arab bus #18 on the same route. For details on how to get to Jerusalem from **Ben Gurion Airport** see the box on p.388.

Arriving by Egged **bus** from within Israel, you'll find yourself at the **Egged Central Bus Station** in West Jerusalem, between the Jaffa Road (upstairs) and Agrippas Street (downstairs). Numerous city buses run east along the Jaffa Road into town: #6, #13, #18, #20, #23 and #48 for downtown West Jerusalem; #6 to continue on to the Jaffa Gate;

and #27 for the Nablus Road terminal, near the Damascus Gate. Should you decide to walk, climb up to the Jaffa Road, turn right and you'll be in central West Jerusalem after a kilometre or so, and at the corner of the Old City after two. **Buses from the West Bank** drop you at one of the two bus stations in East Jerusalem, near the Damascus Gate. From here, bus #23 runs to West Jerusalem, or it's a twenty-minute walk – look for the walls of the Old City, turn right alongside them up Sultan Suleiman and Paratroopers Road until the wall ends, and then take a right up the Jaffa Road. Mazda Tours **buses from Cairo or Amman** arrive at their office on the corner of Koresh and King Solomon at the northwest corner of the Old City, near the New Gate and the Jaffa Road. **Sheruts** from Tel Aviv will bring you to HaRav Kook Street, off Jaffa Road in the centre of downtown West Jerusalem. Service taxis from Allenby Bridge or the West Bank will leave you in East Jerusalem by the Damascus Gate.

The **train** station is on David Remez, southwest of the Old City. It's a kilometre and a half walk along the Hebron Road to the Jaffa Gate (bus #30 or #38), or walk up David Remez and continue up King David and Shlomzion HaMalka to central West Jerusalem (bus #21 or #48).

Information and maps

The main **tourist information office** (Sun–Thurs 8.30am–4pm, Fri 8.30am–1pm; ☎02/625 8844), run by the city council, is in the City Hall complex at 17 Jaffa Road, 200m from the northwest corner of the Old City. There is also an information office just inside the Jaffa Gate, on the left, run by Solan Communications (Sun–Thurs 8am–5pm, Fri 8am–1pm; ☎02/628 0382). Both are friendly and informative enough, offering various leaflets and free publications, but can be less enthusiastic and informed in relation to all things Arab. For information about East Jerusalem and the rest of the West Bank, therefore, you're better off going to the **Christian Information Centre**, across Omar Ibn al-Khattab Square (Mon–Sat 8.30am–1pm; ☎02/627 2692, fax 628 6417; email: *cicbarat@netmedia.net.il*); the staff are extremely patient and helpful, and have lists of hospice accommodation, as well as various maps and other publications, mostly highlighting things of Christian interest.

A number of free **publications** provide information on what's going on in the city. The most useful is *The Traveller*, available at travellers' hostels, bars and eating places and listing the best bars and budget restaurants, together with a brief rundown of museums. Others include: *This Week in Jerusalem*, which provides information on museums and galleries; *Jerusalem's Handiest Tourist Guide*, handier indeed but harder to come by, giving a rundown of sights and events; and *Events in Jerusalem*, put out by the municipality and featuring details on classical concerts, sights and exhibitions. All are available from the Jaffa Road and Jaffa Gate tourist offices and the more upmarket hotels. *Your Jerusalem*, found in central West Jerusalem souvenir shops, lists exhibitions, concerts, talks and tours, though many of these will be of interest only to committed Zionists or religious Jews.

You're unlikely to get a free **map** from a tourist office, and although various maps of the Old City and Jerusalem as a whole exist, many of them are more souvenirs than aids to navigation. The map of the Old City given out by Stern's Jewellers, just inside the Jaffa Gate, fits that description but is at least free. For more detail, *MAP*'s (29NIS; also available as a book) is the best, though it gives anglicized versions of the Hebrew names for streets, including those in the Old City and East Jerusalem, rather than the English names used on street signs. Its closest rival is *Carta*'s (26NIS). Both can be purchased from Steimatzky's at 39 Jaffa Rd, 7 Ben Yehuda, and 9 King George St. A firm of Jewish Quarter residents called the "Jewish Quarter tourism administration Ltd" put out a detailed Old City map (available from tourist offices for 5NIS), based on an aerial photograph, which shows the Jewish Quarter extending most of the way up to the Damascus Gate.

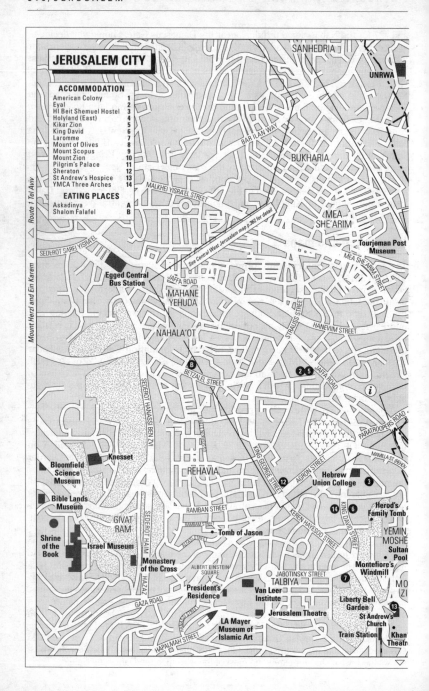

JERUSALEM CITY

ACCOMMODATION

American Colony	1
Eyal	2
HI Beit Shemuel Hostel	3
Holyland (East)	4
Kikar Zion	5
King David	6
Laromme	7
Mount of Olives	8
Mount Scopus	9
Mount Zion	10
Pilgrim's Palace	11
Sheraton	12
St Andrew's Hospice	13
YMCA Three Arches	14

EATING PLACES

Askadinya	A
Shalom Falafel	B

SANHEDRIA

UNRWA

BUKHARIA

BAR ILAN WAY

MALKHEI YISRA'EL STREET

Route 1 Tel Aviv

Mount Herzl and Ein Karem

MEA SHE'ARIM

Tourjeman Post Museum

SEDEROT SAREI YISRA'EL

MEA SHE'ARIM STREET

See Central West Jerusalem map p.382 for detail

Egged Central Bus Station

JAFFA ROAD

MAHANE YEHUDA

STRAUSS STREET

HANEVIIM STREET

NAHALA'OT

JAFFA ROAD

B

2 5

BETZALEL STREET

i

SEDEROT HANASSI BEN ZVI

PARATROOPERS ROAD

Knesset

AGRON STREET

MAMILLA ST (REHOV

Bloomfield Science Museum

REHAVIA

KING GEORGE STREET

12

Hebrew Union College

3

Bible Lands Museum

RAMBAN STREET

14 6

Herod's Family Tomb

GIVAT RAM

SEDEROT HAIM

Tomb of Jason

KEREN HAYESOD STREET

KING DAVID STREET

YEMIN MOSHE

Shrine of the Book

Israel Museum

HAZAZ

Monastery of the Cross

ALBERT EINSTEIN SQUARE

Sultan Pool

RAMBAN STREET

EITAN STREET

JABOTINSKY STREET

Montefiore's Windmill

MO ZI

GAZA ROAD

President's Residence

TALBIYA

Van Leer Institute

7

Liberty Bell Garden

13

HAPALMAH STREET

HANASSI STREET

LA Mayer Museum of Islamic Art

Jerusalem Theatre

St Andrew's Church

Train Station

Khan Theatre

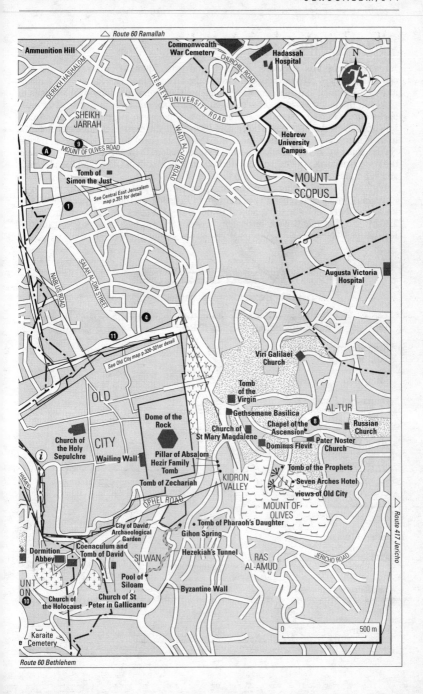

City transport

Jerusalem's city **bus services**, run by Egged (☎02/530 4704), are regular and efficient, though few and far between east of the Green Line. The flat fare of 4.10NIS makes them quite expensive for short hops but they come into their own for visits to places in the outer western suburbs, such as Yad VaShem and Ein Kerem. The most useful connections are shown in the box below. One or two independent **Palestinian bus operators** run services to outer East Jerusalem, the most useful of which are: #74 from Nablus Road bus station (near the Damascus Gate) to Bet Hanina; #71 from Nablus Road to Sheikh Jarrah; #36 from East Jerusalem Central Bus Station (also near the Damascus Gate) to Bethany and Abu Dis, via the Mount of Olives and Ras al-Amud; and #75 from the Central Bus Station to al-Tur.

It's best to avoid taking a **taxi** as you'll be overcharged whatever way you do it. Agreeing a price beforehand is preferable to insisting on the meter as at least you know you'll get there by the quickest route. Note that fares are higher from 9pm to 5.30am and that many West Jerusalem taxi drivers will balk at taking you to East Jerusalem.

BUS CONNECTIONS

(asterisk* denotes independent Palestinian bus co.)

From / To	Egged Central Bus Station	King George St/ Jaffa Rd	Jaffa Gate	Damascus Gate
King George St/ Jaffa Rd	6,7,13,18,20, 21,23,31,32,48	–	3,20,38	23
Jaffa Gate	6	3,20,38	–	1,2
Damascus Gate	27	23	1,2	–
Dung Gate	–	38	1,2,38	1,2
Mt of Olives	–	–	–	37,75*
Mt Scopus	–	4,23	–	23
Train stn	7,8,14,18,21,	48	7,8,21,48	30,38
Mea She'arim	11,27,34,35, 36,39,45	4,9,15,22	1,3	1,37
Israel Museum	17	9	–	–
Mt Herzl	13,17,18,20, 21,23,27,39	17,18, 20,21,23	20	23,27
Ein Kerem	17	17	–	–
Talpiot	7,21,48	7,21,48	30	–
Sanhedria	25,39,48	48	–	–

BUS TOURS AND WALKING TOURS

BUS #99
The easiest way to get a sense of the layout and size of Jerusalem is to take a round trip on the tour bus run by Egged – **bus #99**. Lasting about an hour and three quarters, the route takes in most areas of the city and many of the most important sights. From its starting point near the **Jaffa Gate**, it heads first into downtown West Jerusalem, where it passes the Hebrew Union College, King David Hotel and YMCA, before making a detour past the **President's Residence** and the Islamic Art Museum. Its route south then takes it almost as far as Bethlehem, past Liberty Bell Garden and St Andrew's Church, Talpiot and Mar Elias Monastery, before it turns north again for **Mount Herzl** and Yad VaShem. Passing the Israel Museum and the **Knesset** as it heads east back towards town, it then continues on to **Mount Scopus**. Its final approach into town brings it along the Nablus Road to the **Damascus Gate**, via the **American Colony** and the **Garden Tomb**, for its grand finale – a circuit around the perimeter of the **Old City** that gives you the chance to see Herod's Gate, the Rockefeller Museum, the Kidron Valley, the Dung Gate for the Wailing Wall and **Mount Zion**.

Buses depart on the hour (Fri 10am & noon, Sun–Thurs 10am–2pm & 4pm) from Mamilla Street (Rehov HaEmek), near the Jaffa Gate. You can buy **tickets** (1-day 20NIS; 2-day 30NIS) on board, but it's worth reserving in advance. Although it's a hop-on/hop-off tour, it's best not to break your journey as the buses are usually full and you may have a long wait till the next one. The driver provides a running commentary but if the majority of passengers are Israeli it will be in Hebrew, so check first that the commentary on your bus will be in English. For **information and reservations** call in at the Reservations Centre, 224 Jaffa Road (☎02/530 4422), *Egged Tours*, 44a Jaffa Road (☎02/625 3454), or the tourist information office at the Jaffa Gate (see p.309).

OTHER BUS TOURS
Guided tours are operated by Egged Tours and United Tours. Both run half-day options (77–80NIS) to the Old City, West Jerusalem (Egged also does a full-day tour) or Bethlehem, as well as a full-day tour taking in all three (155–195NIS). See "Listings" on p.387 for addresses.

WALKING TOURS
There is a large variety of **walking tours** available in English. The city council runs free tours every Saturday at 10am, leaving from the City Hall complex at 32 Jaffa Road. The section of the city covered changes from week to week but most tours last around three hours. If you're willing to pay, there's a greater variety on offer from Zion City Tours (☎02/628 7866; 35–70NIS), opposite the Citadel entrance inside the Jaffa Gate, with at least one departure every morning and afternoon bar Shabbat. Archaeological Walking Tours at 34 Habad in the Old City's Jewish Quarter (☎02/627 3515), has three-hour tours starting at 9.30am (Sun–Fri; 56NIS), but they cover only archeological sites of Jewish interest. Alternatively, several hostels in the Old City organize their own tours (see p.314 for details), or you could tag along on one of the specialized walking tours run for groups by freelance tour guides Khalil Toufagji and Sarah Kaminker (☎02/628 6045), and Abu Hassan (☎052/864205).

Accommodation

There are plenty of **hotels and hostels** in Jerusalem and you shouldn't have any problem finding somewhere to stay unless you're here for Christmas, Easter, Rosh HaShannah or one of the other big religious holidays. At these times the city is packed full and it's best to book in advance.

ACCOMMODATION PRICE CODES

Throughout this guide, **hotel accommodation** is graded on a scale from ① to ⑥. The numbers represent the cost per night of the **cheapest double room in high season**, though remember that many of the cheap places will have more expensive rooms with en-suite facilities. For **hostels**, the code represents the price of **two dorm beds** and is followed by the code for a double room where applicable, ie ①/②. Hostels are listed in ascending price order.

① = less than $20	② = $20–40	③ = $40–60
④ = $60–80	⑤ = $80–100	⑥ = over $100

For atmosphere and proximity to the sights, the **Old City** is unbeatable as a place to stay, and it's here that you'll find most of the best budget options, usually in characterful old buildings. However, the labyrinthine lanes and poor street lighting mean that some parts can be unnerving after dark, so make sure you know your way home before you go exploring. The rest of **East Jerusalem**, within walking distance of the Old City gates, isn't quite as atmospheric but offers more in the way of amenities and its hotels are extremely good value. There's comparatively little inexpensive accommodation in **West Jerusalem** and what it has can't touch the east side for character. Instead, the area has cornered the market in modern, mid-range to expensive hotels; this is the place to stay if you want fitted carpets, international cuisine or kosher food. For travellers in any budget category, West Jerusalem also offers far more in the way of nightlife.

The **Christian Information Centre** (see p.309 for details) has a list of Christian accommodation (also open to non-Christians) in Jerusalem, half of which is in the Old City or nearby. Most places are impeccably clean and quiet and some offer dorm accommodation (sometimes women only) as well as rooms. There's usually a curfew.

In addition to the places listed below, B&B or **zimmer** accommodation and self-catering apartments are also available, mostly some way out of town or in the settlements. For more details on these, get in touch with the Home Accommodation Owners association (☎02/581 9944, fax 532 2929), Good Morning Jerusalem (☎02/651 1270, fax 651 1272), or Jerusalem Inns (☎02/561 1745, fax 561 8541).

Hostels

The lowest-priced and best-value **hostels** are found in East Jerusalem, particularly the Old City. Not surprisingly, it's backpacker territory, with the old favourites tending to be the best. Most cheap backpacker hostels offer the choice of dorm beds, private rooms, or – the cheapest option and great in summer – a bed on the roof. Safe facilities are generally available (though you often have to pay), and curfews are the norm. They will probably have room if you just turn up, but it's advisable to book ahead if you want to stay in a particular hostel, especially at peak times of year such as Christmas or summer holidays.

Many of the hostels – particularly travellers' favourites such as the *Petra*, the *al-Arab*, the *Tabasco*, the *New Swedish* and *Cairo* – run **tours** (also available to non-residents), usually to Masada, but also walking tours of the Old City, and even visits to the Gaza Strip or refugee camps in the West Bank.

Old City near Damascus Gate

Al-Arab Hostel, Souq Khan al-Zeit (☎02/628 3537 or 7119). Popular travellers' hostel with kitchen, 24hr hot water, table tennis (beat the owner for a free night's stay, but 50 press-ups if you lose), message board, laundry service, safe, nightly video and 1.30am curfew. ①/①.

Al-Ahram Youth Hostel, Via Dolorosa, corner of al-Wad (☎02/628 0926). Friendly, popular hostel at the heart of things, offering dorm beds, rooftop mattresses, shared and private rooms. Midnight curfew. Facilities include a kitchen and hot showers. ①/①.

Tabasco Hostel and Tea Room, 8 Aqabat al-Taqiya off Souq Khan al-Zeit (☎02/628 3461). Another travellers' favourite with a full range of facilities, in a clean, quiet old building under renovation to expose the stone walls and arches. Dorms, private rooms (discount with ISIC card), or the roof. No curfew. ①/②.

Hashimi Hostel, 73 Souq Khan al-Zeit (☎02/628 4410, fax 628 4667). Family-owned hostel in a refurbished building with marble staircase and floors. Spacious, airy dorms and rooms. Kitchen, TV lounge, and splendid views of the Dome of the Rock. Curfew 3am. ①/②.

Armenian Guest House, Via Dolorosa (☎02/626 0880, fax 627 2123). Sedate hostel in a vast stone building belonging to the Armenian Patriarchate. Single-sex dorms (4–7 beds), and private rooms with central heating, showers, TV and phones. No curfew. ①/②.

Austrian Hospice of the Holy Family, 37 Via Dolorosa, corner of al-Wad (☎02/627 4636 or 1466, fax 627 1472). Imposing hostel with large dorms, and modern rooms with bathroom and phone. Gardens, roof terrace, Viennese coffee house and ornate chapel. Rates include breakfast. Doors close 10pm but key available to residents. ②/②.

Old City near Jaffa Gate

New Swedish Hostel, 29 David Street (☎02/626 4124 or 627 7855). Popular, central place, with helpful staff and a friendly atmosphere. Three dorms (one for women only), and three private rooms, plus kitchen, lockers, washing machine and dryer. Tours of the Old City and West Bank. 3am curfew. ①/①.

Petra Hostel, 1 David St (☎02/628 6618). Now a popular travellers' haunt, this was the oldest hotel in Jerusalem (it opened as the *Mediterranean Hotel* in the mid-nineteenth century), and claims Mark Twain, Herman Melville and Tsar Nicholas I among former guests. Big and roomy with three well-equipped kitchens, safe, laundry service and private rooms, though dorm balconies give great views of the citadel, or you can sleep on the roof, which has one of the best views in the city (non-residents can enjoy it for a small fee). No curfew. ①/②.

Citadel Hostel, 20 St Mark's Rd (☎ & fax 02/627 4375). In the basement of an old stone house near the heart of the souq. Three dorms (single-sex and mixed) of varying sizes and some private rooms. Kitchen, satellite TV lounge and a terrace with good views. Doors close midnight curfew but guests hold their own keys. ①/②.

Lutheran Hospice, St Mark's Rd (☎02/628 2120, fax 628 5107). A haven of tranquillity with a ravishing courtyard garden and beautifully restored Arab architecture. Mostly German clientele, single-sex dorms in a vaulted cellar, communal kitchen and small sitting room; there's also a guesthouse (see p.316). Strict 10.45pm curfew. ①.

Jaffa Gate Hostel, down an alley beside the Christian Information Centre (☎ & fax 02/627 6402). Old stone building with newly renovated jazzy interior, two kitchens, and pretty garden. Two single-sex windowless but clean dorms and nine double rooms with shower. Midnight curfew; alchohol and illegal drugs banned. ①/②.

HI Old City Youth Hostel, Ararat St in the Armenian Quarter (☎02/628 8611). The only HI hostel in the Old City, and usually full of groups. Although cleaner and better-equipped than the unofficial hostels, it's a lot less matey and more institutional (with single-sex dorms only), and pricier to boot. 11pm curfew and 9am–5pm lock-out. ③/④.

East Jerusalem

Palm Hostel, 6 HaNavi'im (☎02/627 3189). Travellers' haunt now run by Christian-American management. Dorms, slightly cheaper mattresses on the roof, and private rooms for up to four people. Midnight curfew. ①/②.

Faisal Hostel, 4 HaNavi'im (☎02/627 2492). Popular place with lively rooftop verandah offering a view of the Damascus Gate and all the action. Single-sex dorms, and private rooms holding up to four people. Kitchen, 24hr hot water, washing machine, dryer, safe and 1am curfew. ①/②.

Cairo Hostel, 21 Nablus Rd (☎02/627 7216). Characterful house that has seen better days, out of Old City bustle but near enough to be convenient. Helpful, friendly staff, dorms, two private rooms sleeping up to four, kitchen and safe. Tours to the West Bank, Gaza and refugee camps. ①/②.

West Jerusalem

Ben Yehuda (Jasmine), 1 Yoel Salomon (☎02/624 8021, fax 625 3032). Very central (on Zion Square) if you don't want to stagger back too far of a night, but with grubby dorms and a noisy location. 3am curfew except Thurs & Fri. ①.

My Home in Jerusalem, 15 King George St (☎02/623 2235 or 6). Clean and modern with four-bed dorms, some private rooms, and a discount for three or more nights. No curfew ②/②.

Jerusalem Inn Hostel, 6 HaHistadrut, (☎02/625 1294, fax 625 1297). Very popular but resting on its laurels somewhat and a little pricey for what you get. Basic but clean six-bed dorms or private rooms with discount for long-stay. Breakfast included. Doors close at midnight but keys available to residents. ②/②.

HI Beit Shmuel, 6 Shema'a (☎02/620 3466, fax 620 3446). Clean, bright and modern, with six-bed dorms, each with its own bathroom, and private rooms too. Run by the World Union for Progressive Judaism. No curfew. ③/④.

HI Beit Bernstein, 1 Keren HaYesod (☎02/625 8286). Usually full of groups, this place is clean and well-equipped but not especially friendly. Sexes are segregated by floor, and there is a midnight curfew and 9am checkout. ③.

HI HaDavidka, 67 HaNeviim (☎02/625 2706, fax 625 0676). Modern and well-maintained, if rather impersonal, with clean but spartan four- to six-bed dorms and double rooms, reasonably well-placed for West Jerusalem facilities and sights, and for the bus station. ③/④.

Mid-range hotels and guesthouses

Jerusalem has a wide variety of very interesting and often quite quirky **hotels and guesthouses**. As with hostels, the Old City and East Jerusalem tend to offer the best value for money, though there are some historic addresses and some home-from-homes to be found in West Jerusalem too. Many of the best places are run by religious institutions, and were originally opened for pilgrims; those listed here will take anybody, but they do ask guests to respect their religious nature.

Old City

Casa Nova, Custodia di Terra Santa, Casa Nova St between Jaffa Gate and New Gate (☎02/628 2791, fax 626 4370). Franciscan pilgrims' hospice, with bed and breakfast in austere but clean, safe surroundings in a grand 100-year-old building with a wonderful interior garden courtyard and rooftop terrace with panorama of the city. 11pm curfew. ③.

Christ Church Guest House, Omar Ibn al-Khattab Sq (☎02/627 7727, fax 627 7730). Clean and quiet evangelical Christian Guest House (for "Messianic believers in modern Israel") in a nineteenth-century church; unmarried couples cannot share rooms. ③.

Gloria Hotel, 33 Latin Patriarchate St, first left inside Jaffa Gate (☎02/628 2431, fax 628 2401). Unremarkable but clean and comfortable with central heating, a/c, bathrooms and phones. The rooftop terrace has a splendid view of the Old City. ⑥.

Lutheran Hospice, St Mark's Rd (☎02/628 2120, fax 628 5107). In the same building as the hostel (see p.315), a serene guesthouse with pleasant rooms, which should be booked in advance. Early (10.45pm) curfew. ④.

New Imperial Hotel, Omar Ibn al-Khattab Sq, just east of the Jaffa Gate(☎02/628 2261, fax 627 1530). Fifty-room grand old hotel in all its faded glory, with sweeping staircases and towering rooms. The balconied rooms at the front give stupendous views over the square and Citadel. ③.

East Jerusalem

Azzahra Hotel, 13 al-Zahra St, down a short alley (☎02/628 2447, fax 628 2415). Quiet jewel of a place in a beautifully restored, impeccably clean building. All rooms have central heating, bath, phones and TV. Wonderful garden and restaurant. ④.

Capitol Hotel, 17 Salah al-Din (☎02/628 2561, fax 626 4352). Rather upmarket hotel with all mod cons, and a nice balcony terrace set back from the street. ⑤.

Capitolina Hotel at the YMCA, 29 Nablus Rd next to the American Consulate (☎02/628 6888 or 627 6301). Imposing hotel, with spacious rooms, central heating and a/c. Has a range of facilities including pool, sauna and Jacuzzi. ⑤.

Christmas Hotel, Ali Ibn Abi Taleb St at Nablus Rd end of Salah al-Din (☎02/628 2588, fax 626 4418). Quiet location with clean, comfortable rooms. Has a lovely garden restaurant (for guests only) and bar. ④.

Jerusalem Hotel, off Nablus Rd, beside the bus station, (☎ & fax 02/628 3282). Best and most popular of the mid-range hotels (booking is essential). Comfortable, attractive rooms in a lovely old building restored to former grandeur. Delightful vine-covered garden, cosy cellar jazz bar and friendly, informative owner. ③.

Metropole Hotel, 6 Salah al-Din (☎02/628 2507, fax 628 5134). Unassuming hotel with plain rooms and rather thin carpets, but good value for the price; they may be prepared to give discounts, especially if you are staying a few days or longer. ④.

Mount of Olives Hotel, 53 Mount of Olives Rd, al-Tur (☎02/628 4877, fax 626 4427). On perhaps the best piece of real estate in the city offering the classic views, especially good in the mornings. ④.

Mount Scopus Hotel, 10 Sheikh Jarrah (☎02/582 8891, fax 582 8825). Modern hillside hotel with spacious balconied rooms, all with a/c, private bath, TV and phone, facing south across the Old City. ⑤.

National Palace, 4 al-Zahra St (☎02/627 3273, fax 628 2139). One of the grandest Palestinian hotels, with the oldest roof restaurant in Jerusalem. ⑤.

New Metropole, 8 Salah al-Din (☎02/628 3846, fax 627 7485). Slightly shabby with sombre but homely a/c rooms. The staff are friendly and may be prepared to give discounts for students or for those staying a few days or more. ④.

New Regent, 20 al-Zahra St (☎02/628 4540, fax 689 4023). Friendly hotel with spacious rooms and a vast, bright rooftop lounge/restaurant overlooking the Rockefeller Museum and the city to the mountains beyond. ④.

Ritz Hotel, Ibn Khaldoun St (☎02/627 3233, fax 628 6768). Grand hotel in a quiet part of town, with more than a hundred rooms, a large open lobby, restaurant and bar. ⑤.

St George's Cathedral Pilgrim Guest House, 20 Nablus Rd, behind the cathedral (☎02/628 3302, fax 628 2253). Peaceful cloistered retreat owned by the Anglican Church. Impeccable, comfortable rooms set around a courtyard garden, plus a dining room (open to non-residents) serving European and Middle Eastern food, lounge and gift shop. Sunday morning prayer services are followed by topical discussions. ④.

Victoria Hotel, 8 al-Masoudi St off al-Zahra (☎02/622 3870, fax 627 4171). Pleasant rooms with a/c, central heating, phones, and some balconies. There's a bar and dining room, and it has its own restaurant next door. ⑤.

West Jerusalem

Golden Jerusalem, 40 Jaffa Rd (☎02/623 3074, fax 623 3513). Friendly, central hotel with small but cosy a/c rooms. ④.

Jerusalem Inn Guest House, 7 Eliashar (☎02/625 2757, fax 625 1297). Just off Zion Square and run by the same firm as the hostel (see opposite), but more upmarket with merrily decorated rooms and jazz teas at five every afternoon. ④.

Mercaz Habira, 4 HaHavatzelet (☎02/625 5754, fax 623 3513). Quiet little place tucked away off Jaffa Road near Zion Square, with soft carpets and comfortable rooms, some with bathroom. ④.

Hotel Noga, 4 Betzalel St (☎02/625 4590). Small, family-run place in a quiet but reasonably central location and with big, airy rooms. It's best to call in advance as there isn't always someone around, and it's often full. ②.

Notre Dame Hospice, Paratroopers Rd (☎02/627 9111, fax 627 1995). An important strategic position in the 1948 war when it was an Israeli observation post, and now ideally positioned for the visitor, being handy for both East and West Jerusalem; the rooms are spotless with great views of the Old City walls. ⑤.

Palatin, 4 Agrippas (☎02/623 1141, fax 625 9323). Bright but poky rooms (the bed takes up most of the space) with TV and free email use. ③.

Ron Hotel, 44 Jaffa Rd (☎02/625 3471, fax 625 0707). Rather shabby and a bit noisy with small rooms, but retains a pleasantly old-fashioned feel and is conveniently central. From its balcony, Menahem Begin harangued the crowds generalissimo-like in his first official speech as Irgun leader after independence in 1948. ⑤.

St Andrew's Hospice, 1 David Remez (☎02/673 2401, fax 673 1711). Near the railway station and next to the British Consulate; look for the Scottish flag flying aloft. Friendly and homely with bright, airy rooms and small en-suite bathrooms, though the balconies are locked for security reasons. No curfew. ④.

Hotel Zefania, 4 Zefania Street (☎02/537 6384). If you feel like staying in the ultra-orthodox Mea She'arim district, this small (non-Orthodox) hotel, with large, bare, slightly grubby rooms, might fit the bill. ③.

Expensive hotels

West Jerusalem has the lion's share of the upper end of the market with plenty of downtown options and masses of mostly modern five-star hotels scattered around its suburbs. The older and more characterful hotels, however, tend to be closer to the centre, though you'll find few luxury options east of the Green Line. The places listed here either have a good location, or are a cut above the average in terms of character or value for money.

American Colony, Nablus Rd (☎02/627 9777, fax 627 9779). More of an institution than a hotel, and the meeting place for local and international diplomats, VIPs and journalists, with a wide range of accommodation to suit all their tastes (see also p.355).⑨.

Eyal, 21 Shamai (☎02/623 4161, fax 623 4167). Good-value option in the heart of downtown West Jerusalem with small but comfortable rooms. ⑥.

Holyland Hotel (East), 6 Rashid St, Herod's Gate (☎02/628 4841, fax 628 0265). Large hotel with spacious lobby, cosy bar, large dining hall (local and international cuisine) and attractive rooms in central East Jerusalem. The roof garden overlooks the Old City. ⑥.

Kikar Zion, 25 Shamai, off Zion Sq (☎02/624 4644, fax 624 4136). A tad more deluxe than the neighbouring *Eyal*, and run by the same management, with well-furnished rooms, a pool, sauna, Jacuzzi and fitness centre. ⑥.

King David, 23 King David St (☎02/620 8888, fax 620 8882). The swankiest and most famous hotel in the whole of Israel and the Palestinian Territories, now owned by the Dan hotel chain. For more on its history see p.369. The rooms are super deluxe, the service impeccable, and there's a full range of facilities. The price, of course, matches. ⑨.

Laromme Jerusalem, 3 Jabotinsky (☎02/675 6666, fax 675 6777). Well located, with good views of the Old City and Yemin Moshe from some rooms (ask for one), and a reputation for service with a smile. Bookable through El Al offices worldwide. ⑥.

Mount Zion, 17 Hebron Rd (☎02/568 9555, fax 673 1425). Built into the side of a hill facing Mount Zion, with the biggest hotel pool in Jerusalem, and full four-star facilities. Old wing built as a hospital early in twentieth century; new wing built in 1980s, both with large comfy rooms and great views. ⑥.

Pilgrim's Palace, Sultan Suleiman St, Damascus Gate (☎02/627 2135, fax 626 4658). Well located in the heart of East Jerusalem with friendly and efficient staff. The comfortable lounge has a panoramic view of the Old City walls. ⑥.

Sheraton, 47 King George St (☎02/629 8666, fax 623 1667). Standing tall on the edge of downtown West Jerusalem, but also handy for the Old City (over which some rooms have great views), essentially a business hotel, but known for its service and great dining, so popular with upmarket tourists too. ⑥.

YMCA Three Arches, King David Street (☎02/625 7111, fax 625 3438). Pronounced "imca" in Hebrew, a splendid and surprisingly upmarket hotel, with terrific views from its landmark tower, a cut above the usual "Y". Rooms are comfortable and tasteful though not massive, and guests have access to all sports facilities (see also p.369). ⑥.

The Old City

The **Old City** is the heart of Jerusalem, and contains almost everything that tourists come to see. Within its walls lie the **Dome of the Rock**, the **Wailing Wall** and the **Church of the Holy Sepulchre**, as well as two of the most well-trodden tourist paths: the **Via Dolorosa**, tracing the footsteps of Christ to the crucifixion, and the **Ramparts Walk**, which takes you most of the way around the city on the wall itself. There's also the bustling souqs of the Muslim and Christian quarters, the churches of the smaller Armenian Quarter, and the rebuilt Jewish Quarter, with its preserved and reconstructed Roman and Crusader sites in among expensive new housing. But the Old City's newest and most controversial attraction is the **Western Wall tunnel** which you can walk along on a tour, though you'll get little clue as to why its 1996 opening led to confrontations across the West Bank that left 29 dead. There are two main entrances to the Old City: at the **Jaffa Gate**, the big attraction is the Citadel, or "Tower of David", while the **Damascus Gate** is a sight in itself with a history to match.

Jerusalem's Old City is one of the best-preserved medieval **Islamic towns** in the world – its present shape dates mainly from the time of **Saladin**, who recaptured the city from the Crusaders in 1187 and initiated a building programme. The city's division into four quarters dates from around this time, too, though it was not a rigid system: members of all faiths and communities lived alongside each other throughout the city, and still do, with the exception of the Jewish Quarter, whose non-Jewish residents were expelled after 1967. Saladin's work was continued under the **Mamluks** (1248–1517), who constructed many mosques, Koranic schools, Sufi hostels, hospitals, bathhouses, public drinking fountains and pilgrims' hostels, but it was **Sultan Suleiman the Magnificent's** refortification (1537–41) that produced the walls you see today. He further improved the city's water system, installed the drinking fountains (*sabil*) still visible in many parts of the Old City, and lent his support to religious and teaching establishments. For the next three hundred years, the city remained inside Suleiman's walls until the appearance of the first suburbs to its north and west in the mid-nineteenth century.

The Old City changed little under the **British**, who preferred to build their administrative areas in West Jerusalem, but saw much upheaval in the **1948 war** when the Jewish Quarter was all but destroyed in the fighting and its religious community ejected by the Jordanians. The Old City remained under Jordanian rule until 1967, when it was taken by the Israelis, who immediately set about revitalizing the Jewish Quarter and also repaved most of the rest of the Old City. The biggest change under Israeli rule in the Muslim and Christian quarters, however, has been the growth of tourism, now by far the city's biggest industry.

The **people** of the Old City are a strange and not necessarily harmonious mixture. Groups of Jewish settlers have been taking over houses at the southern end of the Muslim Quarter, near the Wailing Wall, and there is some friction between them and the Muslim residents – you'll see *haredi* Jews scurrying heads-down through the quarter to avoid any trouble. In the Christian, and more particularly the Armenian Quarter, you'll encounter all manner of clergy, wearing habits and robes of many different styles. The other uniform you're likely to come across is that of Israeli conscript soldiers, uneasily patrolling the streets of the Muslim and Christian quarters and occasionally stopping people to demand ID. The Old City also has a Black community descended from African Muslims who came here during Jordanian rule. Centred around Ala al-Din Street, between al-Wad Road and the Temple Mount, they are part of the Palestinian community, and do not consider themselves to have anything in common with Black (Ethiopian) Israelis.

While some visitors will thrill to the crowds and the bustle of the Old City, others may find the lack of personal space intimidating. Tourist hustlers can be a problem, too, especially around the more popular tourist sights. Most of them just try to sell

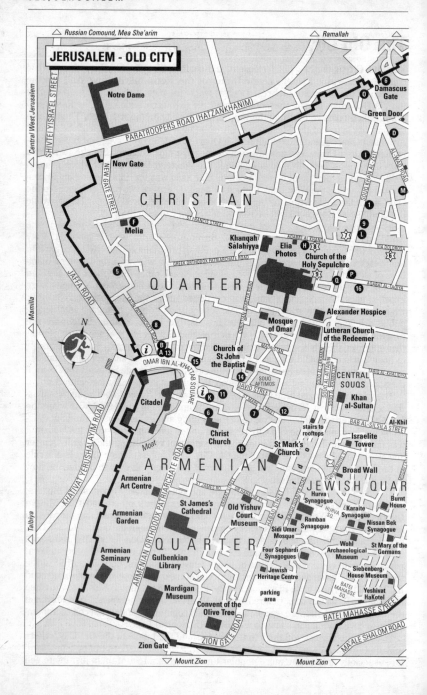

JERUSALEM - OLD CITY

Central West Jerusalem △

SHIVTEI YISRA'EL STREET

Notre Dame

PARATROOPERS ROAD (HATZANKHANIMI)

△ Damascus
Gate

Green Door

New Gate

NEW GATE STREET

C H R I S T I A N

JAFFA ROAD

△ Mamilla

Melia

ST FRANCIS STREET

Khanqah
Salahiyya

Elia
Photos

Church of the
Holy Sepulchre

GREEK ORTHODOX PATRIARCHATE ROAD

Q U A R T E R

Alexander Hospice

Mosque
of Omar

Lutheran Church
of the Redeemer

Church of
St John
the Baptist

CENTRAL
SOUQS

Khan
al-Sultan

Al-Khil

DAVID STREET

St MARY'S STREET

Israelite
Tower

stairs to
rooftops

BAB AL-SILSILA STREET

Citadel

Moat

Christ
Church

St Mark's
Church

Broad Wall

JEWISH QUAR

A R M E N I A N

Hurva
Synagogue

Burnt
House

KHATIVAT YERUSHALAYIM ROAD

△ Talbiya

Armenian
Art Centre

St James's
Cathedral

Old Yishuv
Court
Museum

Karaite
Synagogue

Nissan Bek
Synagogue

ARMENIAN ORTHODOX PATRIARCHATE ROAD

Q U A R T E R

Armenian
Garden

Sidi Umar
Mosque

Ramban
Synagogue

Wohl
Archaeological
Museum

St Mary of the
Germans

Gulbenkian
Library

Four Sephardi
Synagogues

Siebenberg
House Museum

Armenian
Seminary

Mardigan
Museum

Jewish
Heritage Centre

parking
area

BATEI
MAHASSE
SQ.

Yeshivat
HaKotel

Convent of the
Olive Tree

BATEI MAHASSE STREET

Zion Gate

ZION GATE ROAD

MA'ALE SHALOM ROAD

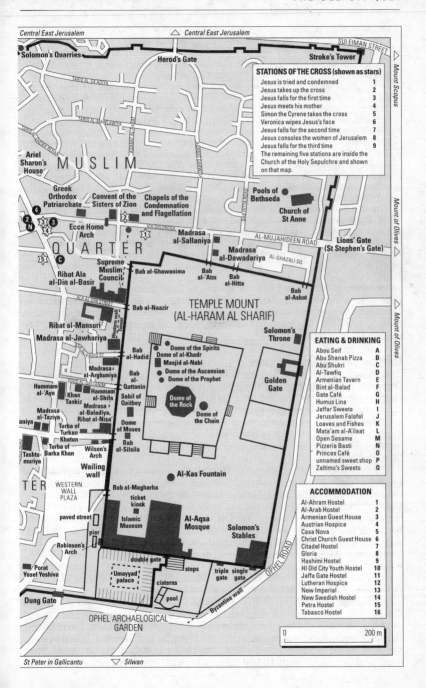

Central East Jerusalem △ Central East Jerusalem

SUI EIMAN STREET

Mount Scopus

Solomon's Quarries

Herod's Gate

Stroke's Tower

TARIQ AL-WAADIYA

STATIONS OF THE CROSS (shown as stars)

Jesus is tried and condemned	1
Jesus takes up the cross	2
Jesus falls for the first time	3
Jesus meets his mother	4
Simon the Cyrene takes the cross	5
Veronica wipes Jesus's face	6
Jesus falls for the second time	7
Jesus consoles the women of Jerusalem	8
Jesus falls for the third time	9

The remaining five stations are inside the Church of the Holy Sepulchre and shown on that map.

Ariel Sharon's House

M U S L I M

Greek Orthodox Patriarchate

Convent of the Sisters of Zion

Chapels of the Condemnation and Flagellation

Pools of Bethesda

Church of St Anne

Ecce Homo Arch

VIA DOLOROSA

Madrasa al-Sallaniya

AL-MUJAHIDEEN ROAD

Lions' Gate (St Stephen's Gate)

Q U A R T E R

Madrasa al-Dawadariya

AL-GHAZALI SQ.

Ribat Ala al-Din al-Basir

Supreme Muslim Council

Bab al-Ghawanima

Bab al-'Atm

Bab al-Hitta

Bab al-Asbat

Ribat al-Mansuri

Bab al-Naazir

TEMPLE MOUNT (AL-HARAM AL SHARIF)

Madrasa al-Jawhariya

Solomon's Throne

EATING & DRINKING

Abou Seif	A
Abu Shanab Pizza	B
Abu Shukri	C
Al-Tawfiq	D
Armenian Tavern	E
Bint al-Balad	F
Gate Café	G
Humus Lina	H
Jaffar Sweets	I
Jerusalem Falafel	J
Loaves and Fishes	K
Mata'am al-A'ilaat	L
Open Sesame	M
Pizzeria Basti	N
Princes Café	O
unnamed sweet shop	P
Zaltimo's Sweets	Q

Bab al-Hadid

Dome of the Spirits

Dome of al-Khadr

Masjid al-Nabi

Dome of the Ascension

Dome of the Prophet

Bab al-Qattanin

Sabil of Qaitbey

Dome of the Rock

Golden Gate

Madrasa al-Arghuniya

Hammam al-'Ayn

Khan Tankiz

Hammam al-Shifa

Madrasa al-Baladiya, Ribat al-Nisa'

Dome of the Chain

Madrasa al-Taziya

Dome of Moses

Turba of Turkan Khatun

Bab al-Silsila

Turba of Barka Khan

Wilson's Arch

Tashtumuriya

Al-Kas Fountain

Bab al-Magharba

Wailing wall

WESTERN WALL PLAZA

ticket kiosk

paved street

pier

Islamic Museum

Al-Aqsa Mosque

Solomon's Stables

Robinson's Arch

double gate

steps

triple single gate gate

OPHEL ROAD

ACCOMMODATION

Al-Ahram Hostel	1
Al-Arab Hostel	2
Armenian Guest House	3
Austrian Hospice	4
Casa Nova	5
Christ Church Guest House	6
Citadel Hostel	7
Gloria	8
Hashimi Hostel	9
HI Old City Youth Hostel	10
Jaffa Gate Hostel	11
Lutheran Hospice	12
New Imperial	13
New Swedish Hostel	14
Petra Hostel	15
Tabasco Hostel	16

Porat Yosef Yeshiva

Umayyad palace

cisterns

pool

Byzantine wall

Dung Gate

OPHEL ARCHAEOLOGICAL GARDEN

0   200 m

St Peter in Gallicantu ▽ Silwan

Mount of Olives

Mount of Olives

THE RAMPARTS WALK

An excellent way of getting an overview of the Old City before plunging in is to take the **Ramparts Walk** (daily 9am–4pm, Fri & eve of holidays 9am–2pm; 10.5NIS; ticket valid for two days) along the top of the city wall. Built for Sultan Suleiman the Magnificent between 1537 and 1540 AD, it runs for 4km around the city and you can walk along two sections: the northern section between the Jaffa Gate and the Lions' Gate, and the southern section between the Citadel and the Dung Gate. The section of the wall alongside the Temple Mount is not accessible to the public.

Although you can exit from the walk at any of the seven gates (an eighth – the Golden Gate on the eastern wall of Temple Mount – is closed until the appearance, or Second Coming, of the Messiah), you can enter only from the Damascus Gate (the entrance is inside the Roman Plaza below the gateway), and the Jaffa Gate, where there is an entrance at the northern side of the gate (by Stern's jeweller's) for the northern section, and one at the moat by the Citadel on the southern side for the southern section.

You can buy **tickets** for the Ramparts Walk at any of the three entrance points; alternatively, you can purchase a **combined ticket** (25NIS) which includes one-time entry to the Temple Mount Excavations (see p.340), the Roman Plaza at Damascus Gate (see p.324), Zedekiah's Cave (King Solomon's Quarries) just to the east of Damascus Gate (see p.353), and the City of David on the southeastern edge (see p.359).

you souvenirs, but one or two may want to be your "guide", with the express purpose of steering you into shops to get the commission on anything you are pressured into buying, and can get quite nasty if ignored or rejected. On the whole, though, you'll find the inhabitants friendly, open and generally willing to help you find your way around.

Orientation: quarters and gates

At first sight, the Old City appears to be an impossible maze of narrow streets and alleyways, but with a little time, these prove relatively easy to negotiate. In addition to the four quarters – the **Muslim Quarter** in the northeast, the **Christian Quarter** in the northwest, the **Armenian Quarter** in the southwest and the **Jewish Quarter** in the southeast – there is the enormous walled complex of **al-Haram al-Sharif**, or the **Temple Mount**, which takes up nearly a fifth of the Old City and hugs the eastern wall between the Muslim and Jewish quarters, overlooking the Kidron Valley opposite the Mount of Olives.

The main points of entry into the Old City are the **Damascus Gate** to the north and the **Jaffa Gate** to the west, serving East and West Jerusalem respectively. Of the remaining five gates, the **Dung Gate** gives best access to the Wailing Wall; the **Lions' Gate** (St Stephen's Gate) is the point of entry for the Via Dolorosa; the **Zion Gate** in the southeast offers access from the Old City to Mount Zion; the **New Gate** in the northwest is the quick way to get from West Jerusalem into the centre of the Old City; and **Herod's Gate**, in the northeast, is the quick way for Muslims to get from East Jerusalem to al-Haram, but the least useful gate for most tourists.

Entering via the Damascus Gate, the road ahead forks after fifty steep metres: to the left, **al-Wad Road** goes straight through the Muslim Quarter to the Wailing Wall; to the right, **Souq Khan al-Zeit** follows the course of the Cardo (the main street of Roman times), running south between the Muslim and Christian quarters into the **central souqs**, three parallel covered shopping streets that form the heart of the Old City and at whose southern end the four quarters meet. From the Jaffa Gate, **David Street** (Khutt Da'oud), directly ahead, separates the Christian and Armenian quarters on its way down to the central souqs, continuing thereafter as **Bab al-Silsila Street**. From the central souqs southward, **Habad Street** divides the Jewish and Armenian quarters, with **Jewish Quarter Road** running parallel to it a block over to the east; both follow the course of the Byzantine Cardo, whose excavations lie between them. Apart from David Street–Bab al-Silsila Street, the other main east–west route across the Old City largely follows the **Via Dolorosa**.

The Muslim Quarter

The **Muslim Quarter**, stretching down from Damascus Gate to al-Haram al-Sharif (Temple Mount), is the largest of the four, and the commercial and financial centre of the Old City. It is also the most classically Middle Eastern in feel, with its minarets, *qah-was*, and headscarf-clad inhabitants. The area is particularly rich in **Islamic architecture**. However, in contrast to European style, this means that many of the buildings' finest features are hidden inside and around internal courtyards, few of them open to the public, though some of the facades are splendid enough sights in themselves. You get a good impression of the varied styles and shapes on **Bab al-Silsila Street**, one of the Old City's chief thoroughfares, and on three smaller streets, off al-Wad Road and in the shadow of al-Haram: Ala al-Din Street, Bab al-Hadid Street, and Souq al-Qattanin. The most splendid and best-preserved exteriors date from the **Mamluk period** (see box below). Many buildings in Jerusalem, which elsewhere would merit special status as architectural or historic monuments, are now homes for local families, partly due to the housing shortage, but also because if left empty they run the risk of being taken over by Israeli settlers.

The most direct approach to the Muslim Quarter is from the north via the bustling Damascus Gate, which together with its excavations is itself one of the sights of the quarter. From the Lions' Gate, it's just a short walk to the start of the quarter's main attraction – the **Via Dolorosa**.

Damascus Gate

One of the best places to absorb the atmosphere of Jerusalem is on the steps leading down from Sultan Suleiman Street to the **Damascus Gate** (Bab al-'Amud in Arabic, Sha'ar Shekhem in Hebrew). Here the whole of the city's eastern half seems to converge in a melee of pilgrims, barrow boys, shoppers and tourists streaming in and out of the Old City past assorted beggars, street traders, *tamar hindi* vendors in their wine-red costumes, and country women selling fruit and veg. From stalls around the gate

---

MAMLUK ARCHITECTURE IN THE OLD CITY

At the start of the **Mamluk period** (1248–1517 AD), Jerusalem was part of the Syrian province whose capital was Damascus, but in 1376 its status was raised and its governor appointed directly from the Mamluk capital, Cairo. This increased importance was reflected in the construction of many beautiful buildings – colleges, hospices and mausoleums – all over the city and the restoration of existing ones. Mamluk buildings are noted for the lightness of their **design**, the distinctive arched entrances and the use of red, white and black striped masonry, known as *ablaq*. The Kufic lettering and geometric arabesques which are now familiar features of Muslim decoration were also developed by the Mamluks; other common artistic flourishes include elaborate bronze work on doors, carved wooden pulpits, beautiful mosaics and stained glass. During the Mamluks' 250-year reign, there were over fifty rulers, and prominent members of previous regimes were often exiled to Jerusalem when power changed hands, adding further to the number of fine Mamluk buildings in the city.

For further information, see the excellent (if rather pricey) *Mamluk Jerusalem* by Michael Burgoyne (1987; World of Islam Festival Trust, London).

you can get tasty snacks, local sweets and newspapers, while children hawk chocolate bars, Israeli cola briefly cooled on blocks of ice or anything else they can get their hands on. The place really buzzes on Fridays and Saturdays, or on Jewish and Muslim holidays when thousands of worshippers pass through on their way to pray at the Wailing Wall or the al-Aqsa Mosque, while during Ramadan the gateway is festooned with bright lights and the whole area is awake till late at night. It's also one of the best places to test the political temperature of the Old City, by observing the Israeli soldiers on patrol: if things are really hot, they, and their colleagues stationed on the ramparts, will be carrying gas canisters and riot sticks in addition to the usual assault rifles.

The largest, most elaborate and heavily fortified of the Old City's seven gates, it is also the only one to have been excavated, revealing several Roman ruins. Underneath the modern gate and pre-dating it by 1400 years, **Hadrian's Arch** (Sat–Thurs 9am–4pm, Fri 9am–2pm; 5NIS) is all that survives of a triple triumphal gateway built by Emperor Hadrian in 135 AD as part of his new town *Aelia Capitolina*. The arch leads through to the **Roman Plaza** – a pavement of huge irregular stones that formed the start of the Cardo (see p.322) – at the centre of which stood a column (shown today in a hologram), that originally bore Hadrian's statues and later, in Byzantine times, a cross. Both the gateway and column are clearly depicted on the Madaba Map (see p.343) and it was this column (*'Amud* in Arabic) that gave the gate its Arabic name – **Bab al-'Amud (Gate of the Column)**; the English version reflects the fact that it was from here that the road to Damascus was measured, while in Hebrew the gate is known as Sha'ar Shekhem (Nablus Gate) as it stands at the start of the ancient road heading north. From the Roman Plaza a corridor leads into a large room where steep stairs ascend through the centre of one of the towers flanking the gate. Climbing up is a little like a trip through history, emerging in the present day on top of the gateway. From here there's a **view** over the whole souq and the street leading into it, Souq Khan al-Zeit (the Market of Inn of the Oil), named after the **olive press** whose remains can be seen in a vaulted room below the gate.

Entering the Old City through the gate, whose angled entrance served to break the path of potential attackers, you'll find moneychangers and a number of cafés where you can sit and watch the comings and goings. Shops and stalls along the stepped street just beyond sell *ka'ak*, falafel, sweets and assorted snacks, while itinerant vendors proffer an array of goods you never knew you wanted. At the bottom of the stepped street, the road forks into two main thoroughfares through the Old City: to the right, Souq Khan al-Zeit, the main north–south artery, and to the left al-Wad Road leading through the heart of the Muslim Quarter to the Wailing Wall.

Souq Khan al-Zeit

The right fork after the Damascus Gate, **Souq Khan al-Zeit** separates the Muslim and Christian quarters and is the busiest shopping street in the Old City – exciting if you're just looking around, frustrating if you want to get somewhere. Boys pushing heavily loaded barrows (the main form of transportation in the souq) give you only one warning before running you down: if you hear a voice yelling "Alo, Alo, Alo", hit the wall. Even if you manage to avoid the barrows, you'll be hit by the bustling crowds, the noise from a thousand and one cassette players, and the smells of freshly ground coffee (with cardamom), spices and mint. Everything from nuts and fake Levis to electrical goods, tapes and videos, shoes, and pots and pans can be found here, and if the shop you're in doesn't have it, the owner's brother a few doors down probably will. Women from surrounding villages lay their produce – fruit and vegetables guaranteed to have been in the ground or on the tree that morning – out on the ground, facing running battles with the market authorities, who constantly try to move them elsewhere.

About halfway down, the street crosses the **Via Dolorosa** (see p.329) and the irresistible force of everyday chaos meets the immovable object of religious fervour – one way to get through the jam is to slipstream a boy with a suitably large barrow. Souq Khan al-Zeit continues past the Holy Sepulchre and down to the **central souqs** – a covered area of three parallel streets, which has been the centre of the Old City and its market since Byzantine times, when it formed part of the Cardo. **Souq al-Attarin**, straight ahead, originally a market for spices and perfumes, now sells mainly clothes, while **Souq al-Lahamin**, to its west, is the meat market, and definitely not for the squeamish: delights on offer include numerous varieties of offal, and whole sheep's heads complete with eyes.

Al-Wad Road

Al-Wad Road (Tariq al-Wad), to the left at the bottom of the stairs inside the Damascus Gate, is the chief route from East Jerusalem to al-Haram al-Sharif and the Wailing Wall, cutting across the Via Dolorosa (see p.329) on the way and marking the course of a valley (*al-Wad*) – the **Tyropoeon Valley** – which runs southeast right through the city. Immediately to the left, the small all-night bakery, known as the *Green Door*, was once something of an institution in Jerusalem as a provider of bread to the neighbourhood from open wood-burning ovens and the only place to get a snack in the small hours. Nowadays, you're better off going to one of the more hygienic 24-hour bakeries outside the Damascus Gate.

Al-Wad continues past a series of cafés, restaurants, souvenir shops and hostels on its way to the Wailing Wall. The further along you go, the greater the number of signs of Jewish expansion into the Muslim Quarter, with *yeshivot* and religious bookshops sprouting on every corner. Several buildings here have been taken over by Israelis; one of the more famous residents is Ariel Sharon, former defence minister and architect of the 1982 invasion of Lebanon. His house, above an archway spanning the street about 50m down from the junction with Souq Khan al-Zeit, is permanently guarded by Israeli soldiers; while the other occupied buildings have Israeli flags draped from windows, Sharon's hangs all the way down the side of his house. This gesture at the local Arab population is just that, however: Sharon doesn't actually live here.

About 100m further down on the left, at the corner of the Via Dolorosa, the **Austrian Hospice** (see "Accommodation", p.315) was the last hospital in the Old City until its closure in the mid-1980s. Beyond, on the final approach to al-Haram, the shops peter out and the street becomes quieter and darker. The streets running off to the left – Ala al-Din Street, Tariq Bab al-Hadid, and Souq al-Qattanin – each lead to separate entrance gates to the al-Haram compound (though not all of those can be used by non-Muslims, see p.347) and contain some particularly fine Islamic buildings. Al-Wad itself ends up at the heavily guarded entrance tunnel leading into the esplanade in front of the Wailing Wall.

Ala al-Din Street (the "African Quarter")

Left off al-Wad, **Ala al-Din Street** (also known as Bab al-Naazir Street, Inspector's Gate Street, Bab al-Habs Street or Prison Gate Street) leads to the Bab al-Naazir (Inspector's Gate) entrance of al-Haram. The street has been dubbed "the African Quarter" as a number of Palestinians who live here are descended from African Muslims who came to Jerusalem on pilgrimage when it was under Jordanian rule. A few of them live in the building on the right, **Ribat al-Mansuri**; its two finely decorated windows belong to a large main hall and the monumental entrance arch of distinctive red and cream stone opens into a large and impressive vaulted porch – the inscription states that it was built in 1282 by Sultan al-Mansur. Opposite, **Ribat Ala al-Din al-Basir** is one of the earliest Mamluk buildings in Jerusalem, dating from 1267. Founded as a pilgrims' hospice by the eminent Emir al-Basir (superintendent of both the Jerusalem and Hebron *harams*), it has an arched gateway with stone benches (*mastabas*) on either side. The cells around the inner courtyard were put to less religious use when the *ribats* were used as prisons by the Turks (al-Mansuri for those condemned to a sentence, al-Basir for those condemned to death) – a function they served until 1914, giving the street one of its alternative names, Bab al-Habs Street (Prison Gate Street). On the right of the courtyard, now full of shacks, is al-Basir's burial chamber.

The building with the columned entrance, to the left of the Bab al-Naazir itself, was constructed during British rule and now houses the administrative centre of the **Supreme Muslim Council**, the body responsible for community affairs in the Palestinian Territories.

Bab al-Hadid Street

Bab al-Hadid Street, which connects al-Wad to another of the Haram's entrances, Bab al-Hadid (the Iron Gate), boasts some of the finest Mamluk buildings in the city. **Ribat Kurt al-Mansuri**, on the north side of the street, is named after the governor of Tripoli who financed its construction in 1293, and is typical of the many small hospices that dotted the city in Mamluk times: its low square door is set in a shallow arched recess and flanked by stone benches, beyond which a long passage leads to an open courtyard where the rented rooms were grouped.

One of the street's several *madrasas* (schools of Islamic learning), the cruciform **Madrasa al-Arghuniya** (1358), stands opposite, behind a red and white stone arch. Around its inner vaulted courtyard are the tombs of Argun al-Kamili (the *madrasa*'s founder) and **Sharif Hussein bin Ali**, Sharif of Mecca and leader of the Arab Revolt against the Turks in World War I. The Sharif joined the Allies after being given assurances of support for the foundation of an independent Arab state – at much the same time as Britain and France were plotting to carve up the area between them.

A simple, cream-coloured arch, originally part of the Madrasa al-Arghuniya, now leads into its contemporary, the **Madrasa al-Khatuniya**, just to its east. The long vaulted passage opens into a courtyard enclosed by cells, an assembly hall and a domed chamber. On the other side of the archway is **Madrasa al-Muzhariya**, built in 1480 by Abu Bakr Ibn Muzhir – one-time head of the Chancery Bureau in Cairo – who left his mark all over the Arab world, financing two public fountains in Mecca, a *ribat* and *madrasa* in Medina and another in Cairo. Here, the tall entrance arch is decorated with black and white mosaics and, to the left of the doorway, a pair of identical iron-grilled windows are finely embellished with red and cream stone on grey marble. The inner courtyard is surrounded by rooms once used by students, but now family homes.

Opposite the Muzhariya, beside Ribat Kurt al-Mansuri and partly built over it, is the **Madrasa al-Jawhariya**. The Jawhariya was also a hospice and traditionally housed important visitors to Jerusalem – one of the two *qadis* sent from Cairo in 1475 to mediate in the dispute over a collapsed synagogue, received a delegation of the Jewish community at his lodgings here. It's now the administrative offices of the Waqf Department of Islamic Archeology, so you stand a better chance of getting a look inside than you do with the residential buildings.

Souq al-Qattanin

Next left off al-Wad, and linking it with Bab al-Qattanin in the western wall of al-Haram, **Souq al-Qattanin** (the Cotton Merchants' Market) was one of several new markets added to Jerusalem during the Mamluk period. Built in 1336–37, the covered souq was designed as a commercial centre for Sultan al-Nasir Mohammed and Emir Tankiz al-Nasiri, the celebrated Mamluk governor of Damascus (1312–40) noted for his public works and support for religious institutions. Monumental entrances graced each end, shops, with living quarters above, ran all the way along its length, and there were also two public bathhouses and a khan. By the nineteenth century, however, the market had fallen into decay and, although partly restored by the Waqf and re-opened in 1974, it is not yet completed: **Khan Tankiz**, behind heavy red gates a little way down on the south side of the market, is currently undergoing restoration and there are similar plans afoot for the **Hammam al-Shifa**, one of the original two bathhouses situated further down behind iron gates. **Khan al-Qattanin**, on the north side of the street, is a later construction, dating from the mid-fifteenth century.

In the meantime, if you can persuade the doorman to let you in, the other bathhouse, **Hammam al-'Ayn**, on the corner where Souq al-Qattanin meets al-Wad, is being restored and gives a clear picture of how public bathhouses operated. The entrance opens into spacious changing rooms from where bathers moved through cold and warm rooms to the hot room. The bathing rooms, which were heated from beneath, are domed and the shafts of daylight that penetrate the patterned perforations in the roofs create a beautifully soft and surreal light. Next to the Hammam al-'Ayn, you'll notice a decorated Ottoman drinking fountain, which dates from 1536.

Bab al-Silsila Street

South of Souq al-Qattanin, al-Wad goes into a tunnel under **Bab al-Silsila Street**, which runs from the centre of the Old City eastward to the principal gate of al-Haram – Bab al-Silsila (Chain Gate; open to non-Muslims). The street crosses al-Wad (connected to it by a stairway) on a wide bridge which dates from Herod's time but was rebuilt in the early Islamic period; the eastern part is known to westerners as Wilson's Arch (see p.342). The section of the street bordering the Wailing Wall piazza has become a focal point of conflict between Jewish settlers and Palestinians, as many of the buildings, particularly on the south side, have been seized and turned into either lookout posts or Jewish *yeshivot*.

Fine examples of **Mamluk architecture** can be seen all along Bab al-Silsila Street, though most, as usual, are not open to the public. At its eastern end, the twin, green-painted gates of **Bab al-Silsila** and **Bab al-Sikina** (Knife Gate) lead onto al-Haram from a vaulted porch that forms the western side of an open courtyard. The structure in front of the doors was a well. Set back from the street in the north wall, the small arched doorway is the entrance to the **Madrasa al-Baladiya**, built in 1380 as a mausoleum for Sayf al-Din al-Ahmadi, governor of Aleppo, and now housing the al-Aqsa Library. To the west of al-Baladiya, a simple but distinctive arched recess leads to the main entrance of the women's hospice, the **Ribat al-Nisa'**, just one of the many institutions founded by Emir Tankiz al-Nasiri (see opposite). One of his most impressive legacies, the three-storeyed **Madrasa al-Tankiziya**, lies opposite the women's hospice, on the south side of Bab al-Silsila Street. Its striking portal is decorated with black and white mosaics and an inscription dating it to 729 AH (1329 AD). The *madrasa* has had several different functions in its lifetime: tribunals were held here in the mid-fifteenth century, by 1483 it had become the seat of the town *qadi*, while from the nineteenth century until the British Mandate it was Jerusalem's law court, later becoming the residence of the Grand Mufti, Haj Amin al-Husseini. During their occupation, the Jordanians used the building as a secondary school; a large sign nailed to the mosaic lintel now proclaims it the "Western Wall Lookout of the IDF", with its own entrance into al-Haram for Israeli army access to the site.

Across Bab al-Silsila Street, where the street leaves the courtyard, **al-Sa'adiya** is the *turba* (tomb) of Sa'ad al-Din Mas'ud, a chamberlain in Damascus during the reign of Mohammed Ibn Qalaoun (who restored the dome and the mosaics of the Dome of the Rock). Built around 1311, its street facade has a doorway decorated with red and black arabesques and an unusual coloured marble frieze. A little further to the west, the **Turba of Turkan Khatun** is, according to one story, the grave of a Mongol princess who died in Jerusalem while on a pilgrimage to Mecca around 1352. The two windows overlooking the street facade are bordered by red and cream stone, surmounted by elaborately carved palms and stars.

On the same side of the road, a stepped street, Daraj al-'Ayn, leads down to al-Wad Road. Immediately west of the junction, over the valley below, you'll find **al-Jaliqiya**, the tomb chamber of Baybars al-Jaliq, one of Qalaoun's generals who drove the Mongols out of the country in 1281. The beautiful calligraphy above the iron grille that opens into the chamber is a funerary inscription. Almost directly opposite is the **Madrasa of Siraj al-Din al-Sallami**, identifiable by the archway blocked with large stones with a small stone window at its centre.

From here, as the street enters the market area, the buildings are increasingly difficult to identify as their facades are more often than not draped by clothes and hangings to attract tourists. However, look up and, jutting out at first-floor level over the north side of the street, you'll see a beautiful carved wooden *mashrabiya*, part of the **Madrasa al-Taziya**, built in 1362 for the Mamluk emir Sayf al-Din Taz. The emir rose from the position of cup-bearer to Sultan al-Malik Mohammed to become governor of Aleppo, but was arrested and imprisoned in Alexandria after a palace plot in 1358 – a fall from grace that left him with a relatively plain memorial, its only elaborate decoration a large grilled window with a dedicatory inscription on the lintel. The upper-storey window is typical of nineteenth-century Ottoman construction and is believed to have replaced an earlier Mamluk *mashrabiya*. The building, identified by the "Antiquities From Jericho Shop", is now a private home.

The splendid three-domed **al-Kilaniya** next door has been described as both a *turba* and a *madrasa*, and is thought to have been erected in 1352. Step back into the small street opposite (Aqabat Abu Madyan leading back down into the Wailing Wall esplanade) and you'll get a better view of the whole building; the central and eastern domes rest on octagonal drums, while the western one has a sixteen-sided drum. On either side of the domed and carved entrance are decorative grilled windows.

Opposite, on the corner of Aqabat Abu Madyan, the **Turba of Barka Khan** was built between 1265 and 1280 for Emir Barka Khan, commander of the Khwarizmians, a Tartar tribe that reached Gaza in 1244 but whose power was broken two years later in a battle at Homs (Syria), during which Barka Khan was killed. In 1900, the *turba* was converted into the **Khalidi Library**, containing some 12,000 books and manuscripts collected by Sheikh Raghib al-Khalidi.

On the western corner of the same junction, the **Tashtumuriya** is a particularly magnificent example of Mamluk architecture. Built in 1382, it houses the domed tomb of Emir Tashtumur and his son Ibrahim. Tashtumur was a noted Islamic scholar, First Secretary of State to Sultan Sha'ban until the latter's assassination, and governor of Safed from 1380 to 1382. The high arched entrance, up a flight of stairs, is decorated with black and white mosaics, while to the right, the square decorative windows of the mausoleum boast sills embellished with fine examples of marble mosaic work.

You are now approaching the heart of the central market: to the left is Jewish Quarter Road and to the right, Souq al-Khawajat. Just before this junction, an elegant vaulted passageway on the right leads into the Mamluk caravanserai known as **Khan al-Sultan**. Built in 1386 AD under Sultan Barquq (1382–99), it's a typical medieval urban khan where merchants stayed while they sold their goods to local retailers: the chambers on either side of the vaulted market hall were used to store merchandise, while the rooms on the upper floor were the merchants' lodgings. The great barrel-vaulted chambers at the end of the passageway on the west side of the main hall (or possibly the large courtyard at its northern end) were used to stable animals. The khan is currently being restored by the Waqf who plan to turn the rooms on the ground and first floors into workshops.

The Lions' Gate and around

In a city where everything seems to have at least two names, the **Lions' Gate**, on the eastern ramparts, actually boasts four: though commonly known as Lions' Gate, after the pair of stone lions on either side of the entrance, it is also called St Stephen's Gate after the eponymous saint said to have been martyred nearby, while in Arabic it is either **Bab al-Ghor** (Jordan Valley Gate) or **Bab Sittna Maryam** (Gate of Our Lady Mary), the latter stemming from the belief that the Virgin Mary was born in a house just inside. The gate is the way into the Old City if you're coming from the direction of the Mount of Olives, across the Kidron Valley, and leads into the Via Dolorosa (see below).

Inside the gateway, in a large walled compound to the right of **al-Mujahideen Road**, stands the **Church of St Anne** (Mon–Sat: summer 8am–noon & 2–6pm; winter 8am–noon & 2–5pm), named after the mother of Mary. One of the simplest and most beautiful Crusader buildings in the country, it was erected in 1140 on the ruins of a Byzantine church, itself constructed over an even older shrine. The inscription above the door shows that Saladin converted it into a *madrasa* in 1192; the building remained in Muslim hands until 1856, when the Ottoman rulers donated it to French Catholics in gratitude for support during the Crimean War. The fortress-like basilica has elements of French and Muslim styles, with beautiful frescoes on the walls. Inside, stairs lead into the ancient crypt which stands on the site of the house of Mary and her parents, Joachim and Anne, and contains remains of mosaics and columns dating from Byzantine times.

In the grounds to the northwest lie the ruins of the two great **Pools of Bethesda**, constructed around 200 BC to supply water to the Temple. The waters, believed to have medicinal qualities, were used by Jesus to cure a man who "had an infirmity thirty and eight years", according to the Gospel of St John (5: 1–13). Excavations show the remains of five porches referred to by the Gospel, with the small natural caves nearby adapted as baths for the thousands of sufferers. A detailed plan on the extensive site explains all. Objects found during excavations are held in a small museum which rarely seems to be open; the guardian, however, has the key.

A turn left on to Bab Hitta Road, the next street after St Anne's, brings you to **Bab Hitta** (Absolution Gate, closed to non-Muslims), to the left of which is the now-filled pool known as **Birket Bani Isra'il** (Pool of the Sons of Israel). Next left after Bab Hitta Road, King Feisal Road leads into the Haram compound at **Bab al-'Atm** (Gate of Darkness; closed to non-Muslims), and also contains two fine examples of Mamluk architecture: the **Madrasa al-Dawadarrya** with striking double vaulted gates; and **Madrasa al-Sallaniya**, noted for the decorations suspended above its coloured facade. Almost opposite King Feisal Road, Aqabat al-Darwish leads up to Herod's Gate, and thence East Jerusalem, while straight on along al-Mujahideen is the Via Dolorosa.

The Via Dolorosa

In Christian tradition, the **Via Dolorosa** ("Way of Sorrow" or "Way of the Cross") is the route taken by Jesus from Pilate's judgement hall to Golgotha, the site of the crucifixion – a path since followed by countless millions of pilgrims. Beginning at the Madrasa al-Omariya, 300m west of the Lions' Gate in the Muslim Quarter, and ending at the Church of the Holy Sepulchre in the Christian Quarter (see p.332), along its 500m length are the **fourteen Stations of the Cross** (see box on pp.330–331), each commemorating an event in the Gospel narrative, but in themselves a relatively recent innovation, some located only in the nineteenth century.

Today, the journey along the Via Dolorosa is more of an obstacle race than a spiritual odyssey – the busy street is lined with tourist-oriented snack bars and shops whose owners try their best to lure the pious from their prayers, taking the game every bit as seriously as their predecessors probably did at the time of the actual event. All the stations are marked by **plaques**, but they can be difficult to spot, particularly when the route enters the souq proper, so if you want to be sure to locate all fourteen, and expe-

ALONG THE VIA DOLOROSA: THE STATIONS OF THE CROSS

The **FIRST STATION**, at **Madrasa al-Omariya**, 300m west of the Lions' Gate, is held to be the site of the Antonia Fortress where Pontius Pilate condemned Jesus to death (Matthew 27: 11–24; Mark 15: 1–15; Luke 23: 1–25; John 18: 28–19: 16). Steps on the left lead up to the courtyard of the *madrasa*, which is still used as a school (7.30am–3.30pm; closed Fri, Sun & Muslim holidays), while from the top of the steps in the south, you can view the whole of the Temple Mount compound. Beneath the school, at street level, is the exit of the controversial Western Wall tunnel.

Jesus took up the cross at the **SECOND STATION**, across the road, next to the Franciscan monastery known as the **Sanctuary of the Flagellation and the Condemnation** (Mon–Sat: summer 8am–noon & 2–6pm; winter 1–5pm). The **Chapel of Judgement**, on the left, is where He was sentenced to crucifixion, and on the right, with a beautiful stained-glass window behind the altar, is the **Chapel of the Flagellation**, where He was beaten by Roman soldiers (Matthew 27: 27–30; Mark 15: 16–19; John 19: 1–3). The next turning on the left, Tariq Bab al-Ghawanimeh, leads to the northwestern gate of Temple Mount – Bab al-Ghawanima. Spanning the street just past this junction, the **Ecce Homo Arch** is where Pontius Pilate identified Jesus to the crowd, saying "*Ecce homo*" ("Behold the man", John 19:5). The arch, part of a gate dating from the time of Hadrian, was given its name in the sixteenth century; part of the original gate can still be seen behind the altar in the Convent of the Sisters of Zion, better known as the **Ecce Homo Church** (Mon–Sat: summer 8.30am–12.30pm & 2–5pm; winter 2–4.30pm; 3.50NIS). Below the church are large pieces of the **Pavement of Justice** (*Lithostratos*) where Jesus was tried: the grooves carved in its stone surface are variously explained as channels for rainwater (see the huge subterranean cistern below) or as a device to prevent horses slipping. What is agreed, however, is that the squares, triangles and other scratch marks on the slabs were made by game-playing Roman soldiers. Between here and the third station, on the north side of the road, the **Church of the Greek Orthodox Patriarchate of Jerusalem** (daily: summer 8am–noon & 3–6pm; winter 3–5pm) is supposed to be the prison of Jesus and Barabbas. The church itself is in the basement; an awesome and massive staircase leads up to a rooftop offering a splendid view of the street and the domed roofs of residential quarters.

rience the devotional flavour, join the main **Friday procession**, led by the Franciscans, which starts at 3pm from the **Pilgrims' Reception Centre**, about 300m inside the Lions' Gate. For information about alternative tours, ask at the Christian Information Centre (see p.309) or at tour agencies. Alternatively, you can go it alone, taking it at your own pace and browsing for souvenirs or snacks along the way.

The **route** itself has changed several times over the centuries. In Byzantine times, Christian pilgrims followed a similar path to the one today but didn't stop along the way. By the eighth century, the route had moved: beginning at the Garden of Gethsemane on the Mount of Olives, it headed south to Mount Zion and then doubled back around the Temple Mount to the Holy Sepulchre. A split in the Latin Church in the Middle Ages meant that for a period there were two rival routes: the group with churches to the west went westward, those with property to the east, eastward, while from the fourteenth to the sixteenth century, the route followed that of the Franciscans, starting at the Holy Sepulchre and comprising eight stations. However, in the meantime, a tradition of fourteen stations, marking the order of events in the Gospels, was developing in Europe and, so as not to disappoint European pilgrims, the difference was made up.

Whether the Via Dolorosa as now followed corresponds to historical reality still remains a matter of **controversy**. Many Anglicans believe Jesus would have been led north, towards the Garden Tomb; while Dominican Catholics set out from Herod's Palace at Jaffa Gate where Pontius Pilate usually stayed when he came from Caesarea

Lying at the junction with al-Wad Road, the **THIRD STATION**, marked by a relief sculpture above the door of a small Polish chapel, is where Jesus fell for the first time under the weight of the cross. The Armenian **Church of Our Lady of the Spasm** commemorates the **FOURTH STATION**, where Mary stood and watched her son go by. Inside, on the remarkable fifth-century mosaic floor, you can see the outline of a pair of sandals, said to be Mary's footprints.

The **FIFTH STATION** is on the corner where the Via Dolorosa turns right off al-Wad Road and becomes a narrow stepped street as it wends its way uphill. A "handprint" on the wall of the first house on the left is attributed to Jesus as he leant against it and it was here that Simon the Cyrenian, from Libya, was forced by Roman soldiers to help Jesus carry the cross (Matthew 27: 32; Mark 15: 21; Luke 23: 26). The Via Dolorosa climbs steeply to the **SIXTH STATION** where, according to accounts dating from the fourteenth century, **St Veronica** wiped Jesus's face, the image of which became imprinted on her handkerchief. The same cloth, known as the *Sudarium* or *Veronica* (the name Veronica may be a corruption of the Latin *vera icon* – true picture), is also said to have cured Emperor Tiberius of an illness; it is now kept in St Peter's in Rome. At the junction with Souq Khan al-Zeit, a Franciscan chapel marks the **SEVENTH STATION**, where Jesus fell for the second time. Across the market street, up the steps of Aqabat al-Khanqah, the **EIGHTH STATION** is found opposite the Station VIII Souvenir Bazaar. Here, a cross and the Greek inscription NIKA on the wall of the **Greek Monastery of St Charalambos** mark the spot where Jesus consoled the lamenting women of Jerusalem (Luke 23: 27–31).

From here, the Via Dolorosa seems to lose itself. Doubling back and turning north up Khan al-Zeit, the **NINTH STATION** is around 50m further along on the right, up a flight of 28 stone steps leading to the Coptic Patriarchate. A Roman pillar here marks Jesus's third fall. On the right is the **Queen Helena Church**, and beyond the steps is the **Ethiopian Compound** (see p.334) on the roof of the Chapel of St Helena in the Holy Sepulchre.

The **TENTH TO FOURTEENTH STATIONS** are inside the Church of the Holy Sepulchre (see p.334). To get to them, you have to go round to the main entrance of the church: go back onto Souq Khan al-Zeit, right into Souq al-Dabbagha and on to the end of the street.

to police the crowds on Jewish feasts. If he did condemn Jesus here, the path to the crucifixion would most likely have gone eastward along what is now David Street, north at the central souqs, and then west to the Holy Sepulchre. All this seems to matter little, however, to the crowds of pilgrims that walk the path, particularly during Easter Week.

The Christian Quarter

The **Church of the Holy Sepulchre** aside, the **Christian Quarter** is relatively thin (by Jerusalem's standards) on major sights, but it contains enough shops, cafés, hostels, churches and other buildings to make a wander through its streets worthwhile. Although the language is Arabic and its people very definitely Palestinian, the fact that it is largely Christian gives it a slightly more European feel, with a strong Greek influence. You'll also find alcohol on sale in the shops here.

Most tourists approach the Christian Quarter either along the Via Dolorosa (see above), or through the **Jaffa Gate** at the quarter's southwest corner (see p.336). Coming from West Jerusalem, the quickest way in is actually via the **New Gate** in the northwestern corner. Added in 1887 to provide access between the Christian Quarter within the city walls and new Christian properties outside them, it was last of the Old City's gates to be put in, and now leads into one of the quietest parts of the Old City. It's a short-cut few tourists use as it's off the main routes and away from most of the sights, but if you do come this way, take a stroll down Frères Street to **Melia**, a women's cooperative selling authentic Palestinian handicrafts.

The Church of the Holy Sepulchre

The holiest site in Christendom it may be, but the **Church of the Holy Sepulchre** (daily: summer 5am–7pm; winter 5.30am–8pm) lacks the dramatic impact of the Dome of the Rock or the Wailing Wall. Largely obscured from view in most parts of the city, its multiple domes are more easily spotted from the rooftops, or from outside the Old City altogether. The entrance to the church is located just north of the Mauristan; from the Jaffa Gate go straight ahead down David Street and take a left up Christian Quarter Road or Mauristan Road.

Traditionally ascribed as the site of **Christ's crucifixion**, **burial and resurrection**, it is the centre of Christian worship in Jerusalem and the most venerated Christian shrine in the world. Here, within the church, are the last five **Stations of the Cross** (see p.330): the tenth station, where Jesus was stripped of his clothes; the eleventh, where he was nailed to the cross; the twelfth, where he died on the cross; the thirteenth where his body was removed from the cross; and the fourteenth, his tomb. Each of the stations is marked with a decorated altar: the first four all on the **Hill of Calvary** enclosed inside the church and the fifth, the tomb, beneath it.

The earliest known Christian church on this site dates from before 66 AD, but the area was levelled by the Roman emperor Hadrian, who then raised a temple to Aphrodite here in 135 AD, following the Second Jewish Revolt. As it was standard practice to build temples on sites held sacred to other religions, especially subversive ones, the situating of Aphrodite's temple here led **Queen Helena** – who was visiting the country in search of traces of Jesus's ministry – to identify the site as the location of the crucifixion and burial, and to claim to have found the **True Cross** in an underground cave here. Her son, the Roman **emperor Constantine** built a church on the site which was completed in 348 AD. The authenticity of the claim that this is indeed Calvary,

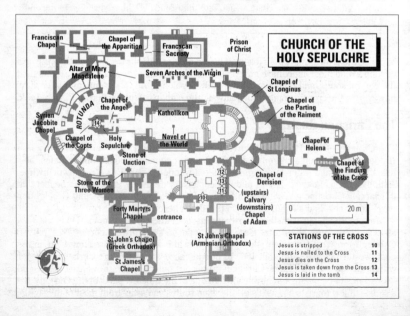

INTERDENOMINATIONAL WRANGLES

The Church of the Holy Sepulchre has long been the subject of **interdenominational wrangles** that leave its everyday operations and upkeep in something approaching a state of chaos. It is shared by six Christian communities – the Latins (Roman Catholics), Greek Orthodox, Armenian Orthodox, Syrian Orthodox (Jacobite), Ethiopians and Copts – who cohabit on an uneasy "cold war" footing, their activities controlled by a 1757 ruling on the **status quo** that regulates who can do what and when in the church. Each controls certain areas of the building and exercises the liturgy at different times of the day or night, while others are permitted only certain ceremonies on special occasions. **Repairs** are especially problematic under these circumstances. Restoration work following the 1927 earthquake wasn't completed until 1988, following thirty years of argument (finally resolved in a 1958 works agreement) and a further thirty years of construction. Even the smallest repairs can be a major source of contention, as those carrying them out can then lay claim to the area, while larger renovations require a degree of collaboration rarely forthcoming. Thus, in the restoration of three pillars in the Rotunda, the square pillar owned by the Greek Orthodox was renovated by them, while the other two Corinthian pillars were restored by their owners, the Armenians.

where Jesus was buried, depends on the assumption that in Roman times the site lay outside the city walls (challenged by some but probably correct, as confirmed by excavations under the Alexander Hospice, see p.335): Jewish burial grounds were traditionally located outside the walls, and St John's Gospel (19: 20) states that Golgotha, the site of the crucifixion, was "nigh to the city". The site's authenticity is not accepted by everyone, however: some believe that Jesus was buried in the Garden Tomb on Nablus Road outside the present-day city walls (see p.354).

Constantine's church was destroyed by the Persians in 614 AD and restored two years later by the Greeks. When he accepted the surrender of Jerusalem in 638 AD, the Muslim caliph **Omar Ibn al-Khattab** declined to pray in the church on the grounds that his doing so would encourage his Muslim followers to convert the building into a mosque. "Such generosity," notes Jerome Murphy-O'Connor, author of the *Archaeological Guide to the Holy Land* (see p.508), "had unfortunate consequences; had the church become a mosque it would not have been destroyed by the Fatimid caliph Hakim in 1009." With the permission of al-Hakim's son and successor, al-Zahir, the Byzantines rebuilt the church in 1048, but 51 years later it was the target of the invading European **Crusader** armies, who built the structure you see today. The church was again damaged by a fire in 1808, allegedly started by a drunken monk who then tried to douse it with *aquavit*. The main doorway of Constantine's 384 AD church still survives at the back of *Zaltimo's Sweets* at 162 Souq Khan al-Zeit, whose customers are normally allowed through to see it.

INSIDE THE CHURCH

The **interior** of the church is a vast and rambling arena of ponderous stone architecture and gloomy, smoke-blackened recesses. It's also very noisy, constantly permeated with the din of repairs and the hum of tourists and pilgrims, and filled at prayer times with a cacophony of rival chants from the various religious communities who none too happily share it as a place of worship (see box above) – if you're expecting an atmosphere of harmony and meditation you're more likely to find it in the market outside. The *baksheesh*-angling behaviour of some of its personnel doesn't do much to enhance the sanctity of the place either.

Immediately inside the entrance, the **Stone of Unction** (or Stone of Anointing) has itself been the subject of much interdenominational argument, for although the limestone slab beneath is held in common by the six denominations, each insists on hanging their own lamps over it, resulting in a somewhat uncomfortable clutter. According to the Greek tradition, the stone marks the spot where Christ was removed from the cross (the wall behind was purpose-built for Greek icons), while Roman Catholics believe that Jesus was anointed here before burial. To the left is the **Stone of the Three Women**, marking the spot where the Armenians believe Jesus's mother Mary, her sister and Mary Magdalene stood by the cross.

The site of the crucifixion – **Calvary** or **Golgotha**, the place of the skull – is to the right of the Stone of Unction, up a steep flight of stairs. Before ascending, take a look at the richly decorated Greek Orthodox **Chapel of Adam** – burial place of Crusader kings and, according to legend, where Adam's skull was discovered. At the top of the stairs is a room containing three altars: the Roman Catholic **Altar of the Crucifixion** containing the tenth and eleventh stations of the cross where Jesus was stripped and nailed to the wood; **Stabat Mater**, where, according to the Catholics (as opposed to the Armenians, who hold it to have been at the Stone of the Three Women mentioned above), Mary stood at the foot of the cross; and the glittery **Greek Orthodox Altar**, under which a silver-inlaid hole marks the spot where **Christ's cross** stood – the twelfth station of the cross. Two other discs indicate the placement of the thieves' crosses. Next to the twelfth station is the thirteenth, where Jesus's body was taken down from the cross and given to his mother.

Returning to the Stone of Unction, to the left you'll see the **Rotunda**, the only part of the church (apart from some of its foundations) that corresponds to Constantine's original structure. Its eighteen massive columns support a dome 11m above the ground, below which stands the **Holy Sepulchre** itself – a tomb monument built over the rock burial chamber after the fire of 1808 and set amidst a glittering jumble of 43 lamps provided by the various denominations. Entrance to the sepulchral chamber is through an anteroom, the **Chapel of the Angel**, which contains the stone on which the angel sat to tell of Christ's resurrection (Matthew 28: 1). The marble tomb room itself is tiny and able to hold only four people at a time, so be prepared to wait in line. Another part of the rock tomb can be seen in the **Chapel of the Copts**, behind the Holy Sepulchre. Opposite, in the fourth-century Constantinian walls, is the **Syrian Jacobite Chapel**: a low door behind it leads into a Jewish burial chamber dating from the first century.

Standing opposite the Rotunda, the main Crusader church or **Katholikon** now belongs to the Greek Orthodox Church – its principal feature is the marble basin under the dome, the *omphalos* or "Navel of the World". Beyond the Katholikon, at the eastern end of the church, the domed twelfth-century Armenian **Chapel of St Helena** is one of the most attractive places in the church, its rock walls covered with crosses scratched by medieval pilgrims. From here thirteen narrow steps (in the right-hand corner) lead down into the **Chapel of the Finding of the Cross**, the place where, with the assistance of a Jew named Judas, Queen Helena found the True Cross (nails and all), in a former cistern.

THE ETHIOPIAN VILLAGE

Situated on the rooftop directly above the Chapel of St Helena, the **Ethiopian Village** or **Deir al-Sultan** (Monastery of the Sultan) has been home to a community of Ethiopian monks since 1808, when "the big five" (Roman Catholics, Greek Orthodox, Armenian Orthodox, Syrian Orthodox and Copts) evicted them from the Church of the Holy Sepulchre following the loss of their documents in the fire.

There have been **Ethiopians** in the region since the fourth century, making them one of the oldest expatriate Christian communities anywhere; traditionally, they had a presence in five holy sites, including the Church of the Nativity in Bethlehem and the Grotto of David on Mount Zion. David, whose tribe was Judah, is the father of the Ethiopian church, which claims to have been founded by his grandson King Menelik, son of Solomon and the Queen of Sheba; both the Lion of Judah and the Star of David are embroidered in gold and silver on the monks' ceremonial robes. Some twenty monks now live in the "village" – basically a cluster of mud huts – but even this sanctuary is the subject of a legal wrangle, this time with the Egyptian Copts who claim title to this part of the roof: the Coptic Church of Egypt has ruled that no Egyptian pilgrims can visit Jerusalem until the conflict is settled.

Whatever the monks may feel about their present home, to an outsider they appear to be better off in the calm silence and beautiful surroundings of this veritable African village, than in the chaos downstairs. To visit them, head from the church into the souq, turn first left into Souq Khan al-Zeit and climb the stairs to the **Coptic Patriarchate** on the left. A small door at the end of the street opens onto the village.

The Mauristan

Immediately south of the Holy Sepulchre is the area known as the **Mauristan** – a group of unnamed little streets set around a square with an ornate (but graffiti-covered and dry) fountain, and several cafés and restaurants. The area was once crowded with lodging houses for pilgrims and travellers which is how it gets its name – "Mauristan" is Persian for hospital or hospice. Today you'll find a number of churches and other religious institutions here, and in the Greek bazaar known as **Souq Aftimos** to its south, shops crammed with tourist paraphernalia – leather goods in particular.

Charlemagne founded the enclave in the early ninth century, and although it was damaged in 1009 by the Fatimid "mad caliph" al-Hakim – known for his excesses as Egypt's Caligula but revered by the Druze (see box on p.147) as divine – many of the buildings were restored by a group of merchants from Amalfi in Italy (then an independent republic) in the eleventh century. **St John the Baptist**, clearly signposted off Christian Quarter Road in the southwest corner of the square, is the oldest church in Jerusalem, dating originally from the fifth century, and one of the buildings extensively rebuilt by the merchants, though the two small bell towers framing a striking blue-domed roof are later additions. The Crusader order of the Knights of St John of Jerusalem (also known as the Knights Hospitallers) was founded here, and will be familiar to British visitors in their modern form as the St John's Ambulance Brigade.

The imposing and rather austere-looking **Lutheran Church of the Redeemer** (Mon–Sat 9am–1pm & 1.30–5pm), in the northeast corner of the square, was commissioned by German Crown Prince Friedrich Wilhelm, who bought the site during a visit in 1869 and built over St Mary La Latine, a church erected by the Amalfi merchants that had fallen into a state of disrepair. Traces of the original church remain in the medieval northern gate, decorated with the signs of the Zodiac and the symbols of the months. If you climb to the top of the tower, you can decipher the outlines of the Constantinian Holy Sepulchre and see as far as the Mount of Olives and Mount Zion.

Opposite the Lutheran Church, the **Alexander Hospice** houses the church of Jerusalem's Russian Orthodox community – St Alexander's Russian Chapel (Mon–Fri 9am–1pm & 3–5pm). The **excavations** beneath it have revealed sections of the Herodian city's second northern wall, indicating that Calvary was indeed outside the city walls in Jesus's time, a fact disputed by those who doubt the authenticity of the Holy Sepulchre as the site of the crucifixion (see pp.332–333). There are also remnants of a triumphal arch from the time of Hadrian which may have led into the Forum of *Aelia Capitolina*.

On the west side of the square, overlooking the Mauristan Fountain, is **St John's Hospice**, occupied since April 1990 by Jewish settlers, and identifiable by the Israeli flag hanging from an upper window. In the northwest corner of the square, facing onto Souq Dabbagha, the real **Mosque of Omar** (the Dome of the Rock is sometimes mistakenly referred to by the same name) commemorates Caliph Omar's prayers in the courtyard of the Holy Sepulchre in 638 AD.

Just down Aqabat al-Khanqah, at no. 14, north of the Mauristan, **Elia Photo Service** is the best of Jerusalem's photo shops, with a unique and absolutely fascinating collection of photographs of the city and its people from original glass negatives dating back to the nineteenth century, collected (and often taken) by the owner's father, a refugee from Armenia. Prices are high but it's worth going in just for a look.

The Armenian Quarter

The **Armenian Quarter** in the southwest of the Old City is most easily reached via the **Jaffa Gate**, which opens up into Omar Ibn al-Khattab Square, flanked on its southern side by the imposing **Citadel**. Home to a dwindling two-thousand-member community which maintains a separate language, alphabet and culture, the quarter constitutes the heart of the Armenian diaspora – a city in miniature, with its own schools, churches and other institutions, mostly hidden behind high walls. Spreading along Armenian Orthodox Patriarchate Road, which leads south from the square, much of it is taken up by the **Armenian Compound**, home to most of the important institutions.

There have been **Armenians** in Jerusalem since before the Byzantine period – immigrants from ancient Armenia (corresponding now to eastern Turkey, modern Armenia, Azerbijan and Georgia), which, in 301 AD, became the first state to accept Christianity as its religion. Armenia fell to the Mamluks in 1375, and later came under the rule of the Seljuks and Ottomans, who actively suppressed Armenian culture and political aspirations. As the Ottoman Empire crumbled, Armenians became pawns in Europe-wide power struggles, and were victims of several **massacres** at the hands of the Turks, whose policy escalated from pogroms to genocide during World War I (when Armenians were suspected of having enemy sympathies), culminating in 1915 with the incarceration in concentration camps of most of the population and their subsequent murder. At the start of the war, there were two million ethnic Armenians living in Turkey; after the war, the figure was barely 100,000, with around half a million **refugees**, many of whom came to Jerusalem to join the already established religious community. Today, the former Soviet republic of Armenia is again an independent state but their holocaust casts a shadow over the community almost as great as that of the Nazi Holocaust over the Jews; you'll see posters detailing the massacre all over the quarter.

At the quarter's southern end, the **Zion Gate** provides access to neighbouring Mount Zion (see p.370).

Jaffa Gate (Bab al-Khalil) and around
The **Jaffa Gate** (Sha'ar Yafo or Bab al-Khalil) is the main western entrance to the Old City. As with so many places in Jerusalem, the gate's names reflect the differing viewpoints of its varied population: the English and Hebrew both refer to the ancient port of embarkation for immigrants, pilgrims and early tourists (see p.86), while the Arabic comes from the holy town of Hebron (al-Khalil; see p.407). This gate is accessible to cars, thanks to the touring kaiser, Wilhelm II, who had its portals destroyed in 1898 to provide access for his mounted entourage.

If you're coming from West Jerusalem (Egged bus #20 from Central Bus Station), you'll approach along the southern end of the Jaffa Road, which passes alongside the city wall. A concrete **plaza** now bridges the road, connecting the Jaffa Gate to the new Mamilla development. Once inside the gateway, the square of **Omar Ibn al-Khattab** meets you with shops, cafés, hostels and hustlers aimed purely at the tourist trade. Across the square, opposite the Citadel, the **Christ Church** was built in 1842 under the supervision of the first Anglican bishop of Jerusalem, Michael Solomon Alexander, a rabbi who converted to Christianity. The cool, airy interior reflects this Jewish influence, with a wooden screen inscribed with the Lord's Prayer in Hebrew as a centrepiece. Straight ahead from the square, the main Tariq Suweiqet Alloun, now called **David**

Street (Khutt Da'ud) runs east through the main market area into the heart of the Old City, separating the Armenian and Christian quarters. The route is often used by Israelis and Israeli-led tour groups wanting to avoid the Palestinian (Muslim and Christian) quarters of the Old City on their way to the main sights. To the right of the square, Armenian Orthodox Patriarchate Road leads into the Armenian Quarter.

The Citadel (Tower of David)

Beautifully excavated, with all the periods of its development clearly marked, the imposing **Citadel** next to the Jaffa Gate is well worth taking time to explore (April–Nov Sun–Thurs 9am–5pm, Fri & Sat 9am–2pm; Nov–March Sun–Thurs 10am–5pm, Fri & Sat 10am–2pm; 26NIS). Turned into the **Museum of the History of Jerusalem** by the Israelis in 1967, the complex combines the physical setting of the Citadel itself with archeological remains and findings from the site, together with displays on the history of the city. If you don't catch one of the free guided tours (Sun–Fri, English 11am, Hebrew 10.30am) from the entrance, the ticket office can supply you with a pamphlet outlining a **self-guided walk**, along with portable tape-recorders and cassette guides in English.

Surrounded by a now dry, litter-strewn **moat**, the Citadel occupies a strategic position on the western hill of the Old City, fortified by every ruler of Jerusalem since the second century BC. Herod strengthened the old Hasmonean walls by adding three new towers, and the historian Josephus tells us there was an adjoining **palace** "baffling all description", remains of which have been excavated in the Armenian garden to the south. This palace was the Jerusalem residence of the Roman Procurator (whose headquarters was in Caesarea) until it was burned down during the Jewish Revolt of 66–70 AD. When the city was razed in 70 AD, only one of Herod's three towers – Phasael – remained standing. During the Byzantine period the tower, and by extension the Citadel as a whole, acquired its alternative name – **Tower of David** – after the Byzantines, mistakenly identifying the hill as Mount Zion, presumed it to be David's Palace. The Citadel was gradually built up under Muslim and Crusader rule, acquiring the basis of its present shape in 1310 under the Mamluk sultan Malik al-Nasir. Suleiman the Magnificent later constructed a square with a monumental gateway in the east. The **minaret**, a prominent Jerusalem landmark, was added between 1635 and 1655, and took over the title of "Tower of David" in the nineteenth century, so that the term sometimes refers to the Citadel as a whole, and sometimes specifically to the minaret.

You'll need a good couple of hours to explore the remains, which include a **wall** from the Hasmonean period, a **Roman cistern**, and the ramparts of the **Ummayad citadel** which held out against the Crusaders in 1099. From the tower in the southeast corner there are good views over the excavations inside and the Old City outside, as well as into the distance south and west. Inside, specific historical periods are represented in eleven separate arched chambers, using reproductions, models, dioramas, holograms, computer graphics and animated video, while a fourteen-minute introductory film presents the history of Jerusalem in a novel way from the point of view of a Jerusalem stone, running from the Canaanite period through to the city's 1967 reunification. There's also a **Sound and Light Show** (April–Oct; English: Mon & Wed 9.30pm, Sat 10.30pm), which relates some of Jerusalem's history, and on Saturday nights (English, 9pm), you can be the judge in a historical whodunit at the **Murder Mystery** involving the demise of High Priest Aristobulus III.

The Armenian Compound

Running south from the Citadel, Armenian Orthodox Patriarchate Road narrows into a short tunnel, at the end of which a door on the left leads into the walled **Armenian Compound or Convent** (Deir al-Arman). Home to a religious community of five hundred and containing a number of buildings that provide an interesting snapshot of Armenian culture and history, it's a pleasant, quiet place to wander around.

St James's Cathedral (open for services only: Mon–Fri 6.30–7.15am, 2.45–3.30pm, Sat & Sun 2.30–3pm), dedicated to Jesus's brother (the first Bishop of Jerusalem), is one of the most attractive churches in Jerusalem – its rich carpets, carvings, paintings and countless golden lamps make it positively glow with light and colour. At the entrance are pieces of wood and bronze – *nakus* – which were used to announce prayer times from the ninth century when the ringing of church bells was prohibited by Palestine's Muslim rulers. There has been a church on the site since the fifth century, but the cathedral itself dates from the eleventh century and was expanded by the Crusaders.

In addition to the St Tarkmanchatz Armenian school and the **Armenian or Gulbenkian Library**, the peaceful, open courtyard of the compound also houses the **Mardigian Museum of Armenian Art and History** (Mon–Sat 10am–5pm; 7NIS). The rich collection is arranged in thirty rooms, formerly the living quarters of Armenian seminary students and set around an ochre stone courtyard dotted with cypress trees. The rooms at ground level provide the historical and cultural background, including the history of Jerusalem's Armenian community, and featuring Roman and Byzantine **mosaics** believed to have been made by Armenian artists. Upstairs, the most important and attractive exhibits are the jewel-encrusted, brilliantly coloured, **illuminated manuscripts**, some dating from the tenth century. Other highlights include the collection of eighteenth-century yellow, white and sky-blue tiles from northwest Turkey (together with the more familiar blue tiles which predominate in Jerusalem), intricate seventeenth-century filigree artefacts and ritual objects such as jewelled crosses, mitres and embroidery.

Still within the compound, the beautiful **Convent of the Olive Tree** (Deir al-Zeitouna), where Jesus is said to have been tied during the scourging before the crucifixion (Mark 15: 15; John 19: 1), is also known as the **House of Annas** after the father-in-law of Caiaphas, the high priest under whose authority Jesus was condemned. The small chapel was built around 1300; in one corner is a stone, allegedly the one which Jesus said (Luke 19: 40), "would immediately cry out" if the disciples had not praised Him as He entered Jerusalem on Palm Sunday; though this is unlikely, given that Jesus entered from the east through the Golden Gate.

The rest of the quarter

On the west side of Armenian Orthodox Patriarchate Road, just north of St James's Cathedral, Sandrouni's **Armenian Art Centre** (Mon–Sat 9am–7pm, Sun 2–6pm) sells some of the most spectacular and original **Armenian ceramics** in the Old City. The distinctive blue-green ceramic work is an ancient tradition, copied and reproduced and for sale in every second shop in the souq – those on sale here aren't cheap, but they're far superior. The road continues south towards the Zion Gate where, below the car park at al-Nabi Daoud Square, is a small area of unlabelled excavations of the old walls.

Alternatively, backtrack a little and follow St James's Road into the residential area. On the left, down Ararat Street, is the **Syrian Convent**, belonging to the Syrian Orthodox Church, also known as Jacobites after their founder Jacob Baradai. The Jacobites, who use the ancient language of Classical Syriac, are one of the smallest Christian sects in Jerusalem, established here since the end of the sixth century. They claim that **St Mark's Church** (9am–noon & 3.30–6pm; ask for the key), inside the convent, is on the site of St Peter's first church, where the Virgin Mary was baptized and the Last Supper eaten (a claim to rival the *Coenaculum* on Mount Zion, see p.371). At the bottom of Ararat Street, the souq is to the left, the Jewish Quarter to the right.

The Jewish Quarter

Situated in the southeast of the Old City, the wealthy, modernized **Jewish Quarter** is bounded by Bab al-Silsila Street to the north and Habad Street (Souq al-Husur) to the west, though it is beginning to encroach on the Armenian Quarter beyond. You can get here via the Jaffa Gate (see p.336) and straight ahead down David Street, from Damascus Gate (see p.323) via al-Wad Road, or through the Dung Gate (see below). The last two options lead to the quarter's main attraction and Judaism's holiest site – the **Western (Wailing) Wall** (see p.340). Security here is tight, with metal detectors and bag searches; at the Dung Gate entrance, there are separate checkpoints for men and women. To its south lies the fascinating area of excavations known as the **Ophel Garden**. Other highlights of the quarter include a section of the Roman and Byzantine main street, the **Cardo**, the Crusader **Church of St Mary of the Germans**, the controversial **Western Wall tunnel**, and a number of important **synagogues**.

In the time of King Hezekiah (c715–687 BC), this was one of the wealthiest parts of the city. Though expelled from Jerusalem by the Romans and then the Crusaders, the Jews were eventually allowed back in 1187 by Saladin, but it wasn't until 1267, with the arrival from Spain of the great **Rabbi Nahmanides** (Ramban), that the quarter became established as the centre of the city's small Jewish community. Ramban revitalized the community, established learning centres, and had a synagogue erected here (see p.344). The population received a further boost three centuries later with the arrival of more Spanish Jews, this time refugees from the Inquisition, and then again in 1700 with the arrival of the Ashkenazi community from Poland, though the latter were expelled twenty years later (see p.344), and banned from the city until 1820.

Severely damaged during the **1948 war**, and subsequently neglected under Jordanian rule, the quarter's fortunes improved considerably after Israeli occupation in 1967 and massive private and government funding has seen the area extensively excavated, restored and expanded. Consequently, the contrast with the other quarters is stark: its newly paved and lighted streets and renovated houses make this a chic and expensive area, but although the architects have tried to maintain the intrinsic dignity of the buildings, it all seems rather sterile, the craft boutiques, art galleries and studios replacing the atmosphere and life seen in the rest of the Old City. Its **residents** are, on the whole, rich, religious and extremely nationalistic; the quarter is dotted with *yeshivot*, whose students are predominantly North American "born-again" Jews. Palestinians are prevented by Israeli law from acquiring houses in the quarter following a notorious 1981 **Supreme Court decision** which prohibits non-Jews from buying property here.

The quarter is clearly signposted and most sites have explanatory notes and diagrams. It closes down on Friday afternoon, Shabbat and Jewish holidays, but these are good times for a quiet stroll around the area. A booklet entitled *Quartertour Jerusalem*, published by the Company for the Reconstruction and Development of the Jewish Quarter, presents the area and its history and is available in bookshops in West Jerusalem and in the quarter itself.

The Dung Gate (Bab Harat al-Magharba)

As the only city gate leading directly into the Jewish Quarter and the most direct approach to the Wailing Wall and Temple Mount (Egged bus #1 from the main bus station), the **Dung Gate** is the point at which most Israeli tours enter the Old City, with the result that the approach now resembles a giant car park. Its Arabic name, **Bab Harat al-Magharba** (Gate of the Moorish Quarter), derives from the fact that the area immediately inside it was traditionally inhabited by North Africans; the origin of its English name recalls less salubriously the time when Jerusalem's garbage was carted through here before being dumped into the Kidron Valley. In Hebrew it is known as **Sha'ar HaKotel** – (Western) Wall Gate.

The Ophel Archeological Garden

On the right just inside the Dung Gate and on the southern side of Mount Moriah, the huge and impressive maze of the **Ophel Archeological Garden** (Sun–Thurs 9am–5pm, Fri 9am–3pm; 8NIS; guided tours in English Sun, Tues, Fri 9am; 31.50NIS; including tour of Western Wall excavations) encompasses the whole of Jerusalem's turbulent history in one confined area. Here, you can see the remains of structures ranging from the tenth century BC, the time of Solomon, to the sixteenth-century reign of Sultan Suleiman the Magnificent; above all, the majestic hundred-metre-wide **flight of steps** that led pilgrims up to the **Hulda Gates** entrance of the Temple precincts. Other finds include the ruins of a vast public building from the First Temple period, sections of **Robinson's Arch** and a Byzantine residential quarter, including a two-storey house with mosaic floors. Muslim buildings have been excavated here, too: an administrative complex from the Ummayad period (661–749 AD) including the **caliph's palace**, and a tower built by the Fatimids (969–1071 AD) and repaired by the Crusaders, the Ayyubids and the Mamluks. Although Yigal Yadin, the archeologist leading the dig that unearthed them, wanted to "get rid of them and continue to the [Jewish] periods that interest us", he was thankfully prevented from doing so when the issue was leaked to the press.

The Wailing Wall

From the Dung Gate, you have a direct approach to the most sacred Jewish site in the world and one of the most impressive sites in the country: the **Western Wall** (HaKotel HaMa'aravi in Hebrew or simply the Kotel). The huge esplanade in front – usually packed with gawping onlookers – lends the Wall dramatic impact but for the best **view** of the whole go to one of the vantage points overlooking the esplanade from the other side, from where you will also see the spectacular Dome of the Rock rising above it.

Considered by Jews to be the only surviving remnant of the Second Temple, the Wall's significance for them cannot be overestimated: the chance to pray before it was a centuries-old dream realized again only relatively recently, while their lamentations here over the destruction of the Temple have given it the name by which it is more commonly known in English – the **"Wailing Wall"**. As part of al-Haram, the Wall is also sacred to Muslims who, in an effort to lay claim to it, identified it as the place where Mohammed tethered his winged mount, al-Burak, before ascending to heaven on his night journey, despite the fact that the al-Aqsa Mosque was the traditional site of this holy event. The Wall is technically Muslim property, belonging to the Waqf, who also own the synagogue area in front of it.

The Wall was never actually part of the Temple, but rather the retaining structure built to support the mount above – the massive stones of the lower section are typical of Herod the Great's building style and date from 20 BC, while the upper part of smaller stones was rebuilt during the Muslim period. However, this fact has never diminished its sacred status and prayer here is fervent. The **prayer area** directly in front of the Wall is treated as a **synagogue**; its permanent congregation consists of mainly Orthodox Jews in their black and white prayer shawls swaying back and forth with vigour. Congregations are largest on Friday evenings, Shabbat mornings (when scrolls of the Torah are read here), Jewish holidays, and for the fast of Tisha beAv (the ninth day of Av) commemorating the destruction of both Temples. The Wall itself is divided into two sections: the smaller part on the right reserved for women, the larger one for men. Ultra-orthodox Jews have long opposed women conducting prayer services at the Wall, claiming it as a male-only rite – a situation that has led to clashes,

THE RIGHT TO PRAY: CHANGING THE STATUS QUO

Historically, the **right of Jews to pray** at the Wall was guaranteed by the **status quo**, a set of agreements reached between the three faiths predominant in the city as far back as the Middle Ages and entrenched under the Mandate. Under the status quo, Muslims owned the Wall, but Jews had the right to stand on the pavement in front of it and pray. With the rise of Zionism, however, the religious significance of the Wall acquired a more political bent. When Jewish worshippers attempted to introduce a partition screen at the Wall in 1928, to divide male from female worshippers, Muslims objected that this breached the status quo. The Mandatory authorities agreed and ordered its removal. The Jews then complained that their freedom of worship had been violated, and the issue became an increasingly acrimonious bone of contention. Acting under directions from the Mufti's Supreme Muslim Council, Arab builders started construction work in the area around the Wall to disrupt Jewish prayers; an action which the British ordered to stop but which didn't prevent both sides from holding rival demonstrations at the Wall. Matters came to a head on August 23, 1929, after the death of a Jewish boy stabbed during a row with a group of Arab boys in a football field. Rival mobs gathered in the city, and the ensuing clashes left 29 Jews and 38 Arabs dead and scores wounded. The **rioting** lasted a week and spread throughout the country, forcing the British to bring in troops from Egypt to quell it, by which time 220 people had been killed. The worst incident in the rioting was the massacre of the Jewish community in Hebron (see p.410).

During **Jordanian occupation** (1948–1967), Israeli Jews were not allowed to pray at the Wall, but within a month of taking the Old City in 1967, the Israelis had bulldozed the Magharba quarter in front of it to make way for the massive esplanade you see today.

with Orthodox *yeshiva* students throwing excrement and other projectiles at Reform Jewish women trying to conduct a service.

Close up, the Wall resembles an enormous message board to God; every nook and cranny in its massive ancient stones is stuffed with **papers** bearing the personal prayers of the devout and the needy. All prayer notes are left long enough for God to peruse, then taken away and buried in a Jewish cemetery to make way for more. Ancient it may be, but the Wall is bang up-to-date with modern lines of communication: those who can't make it here themselves can fax their messages (☎02/561 2222), and have them placed there, and the Wall even has its own Web site (*www.virtual.co.il*).

The prayer area is separated by a metal railing from the vast, unshaded **esplanade** behind, which replaced the former Magharba Quarter (see box above) in 1967. Prior to that, only a narrow alley separated the Wall from the nearest houses; pre-1948 paintings, prints and photographs capture the intimacy of the devout at prayer, while around them non-Jews go about their daily business. Nowadays, Jewish people come from all over the world to hold Bar Mitzvah services for their sons in the esplanade, and it presents an especially impressive sight in the run-up to the New Year when packed with hundreds of young people who come here to sing hymns of praise throughout the night.

Note that the Wall is subject to the same rules of **behaviour** as a synagogue: modest dress is required, smoking and photography are forbidden on Shabbat or Jewish holidays, and men and married women must cover their heads when approaching.

ROBINSON'S ARCH AND WILSON'S ARCH

High on the southern end of the Western Wall are the remains of the fifteen-metre-high **Robinson's Arch**, thought to have been the first of the series of arches that formed a monumental bridge over the valley connecting the western part of the city with Temple Mount. Beneath it, archeologists have uncovered parts of a paved street containing cells which served as shops, as well as numerous artefacts including stoneware, weights, first-century coins and Herodian pottery. To the right of the Wall, a ramp leads up to the **Bab al-Magharba** (Moor's Gate) entry into Temple Mount, where a large sign warns observant Jews to keep out of the area (see p.346).

To the north of the Wall, **Wilson's Arch**, named after the archeologist Charles Wilson who discovered it in 1868, formed part of an ancient bridge carrying Bab al-Silsila Street (see p.327) from west to east, across the town's central Tyropoeon Valley, to the mount above. Below the arch, a series of **vaulted chambers** (Sun, Tues & Wed 8.30am–3pm, Mon & Tues 12.30–3pm, Fri 8.30am–noon) connect to the Western Wall tunnel (see below) and feature sections dating from the Second Temple period, the Ummayad period (seventh to eighth century) and from the fifteenth to sixteenth century. Two deep shafts in the floor of the prayer hall extend to the base of the Western Wall. Sections of the area are today used as synagogues, so dress must be appropriate.

The Western Wall tunnel

More of the Western Wall that runs along a south-north axis at the edge of the Muslim Quarter, together with other structures beneath it, have been excavated in the **Western Wall tunnel**, the opening of whose exit on al-Mujahideen Street/Via Dolorosa caused widespread protest in September 1996 (see box below). Given the politically sensitive nature of the excavations, it is not possible to enter them on your own but you can arrange to visit as part of a group guided tour (call the Western Wall Heritage Foundation ☎02/627 1333; 14NIS)

The tunnel starts under Wilson's Arch and reveals fourteenth-century "**secret passages**" from the Mamluk period where, inside the vault under a Herodian bridge that once spanned the city, food and water were held in reserve. A **plaque** in one of the vaulted rooms thanks all those who financed the dig, including Irving Moscovitz, a major sponsor of Jewish settlements in Palestinian neighbourhoods, whose activities have caused major controversy. From here, you descend two storeys back in time to the period of the Second Temple; stone bullets which may have been used by the Romans against the Jews in the revolt of 135 AD are on view here, as is a structure explained as a *mikve* or ritual bath. Further along, beside exposed parts of the **Wailing Wall**, is a **synagogue**, apparently dating from Ummayad times. It was located here because the site was thought to be close to the Foundation Stone (Even HaShivta), from which, according to the Babylonian Talmud, the world was created, and to the Holy of Holies, or inner sanctum of Solomon's Temple, above the other side of the Wall on the western part of Temple Mount. The arch in the synagogue is part of Warren's Gate, one of the four main gates to the Temple.

THE TUNNEL WAR

Called variously the Tunnel Intifada, the Tunnel War and, more prosaically, the September Clashes, the riots that followed the opening of the **Western Wall tunnel** in September 1996 left 80 Palestinians and 14 Israeli soldiers dead, and over 1200 wounded. The trouble arose out of the belief held by many Palestinians that the tunnel threatened the foundations of the al-Aqsa Mosque. In reality, their fears were unfounded: the tunnel lies to the west of al-Haram and never actually goes under it; moreover, the tunnels are ancient, and the only newly excavated part was the exit by the Via Dolorosa. Politically, however, the opening of the tunnel by the Israeli government without prior consultation with the Islamic Waqf or the PNA was perceived to be a declaration of sovereignty over East Jerusalem that many considered contrary to the spirit of Oslo. Excavations of the northern end had in fact been completed by 1995 but Rabin's Labour government decided not to open it "for political reasons". Netanyahu's government had equally political reasons for deciding the opposite in the following year.

Descending deeper still, you can actually see what Jerusalem looked like in the days of the Second Temple, in the form of a wonderfully detailed 3-D **model** complete with lights and moving parts. Past the **Hasmonean** cistern and colonnaded **Herodian** street, look up to see the foundations of a present-day house in the Muslim Quarter 12m above your head, apparently suspended in mid-air. The last part of the walk is perhaps the most impressive: a glass walkway leads over the narrow **Hasmonean Aqueduct**, bordered by towering slabs of green algae-stained rock, and on to a treacherous-looking staircase that descends from street level to the **Struthion Pool** – used for water storage in Roman times. The tour exits by the First Station of the Cross on the Via Dolorosa in the Muslim Quarter.

The Cardo

The most interesting of the quarter's archeological sites is the **Cardo Maximus** – the wide, colonnaded main street of Hadrian's *Aelia Capitolina* (132–135 AD) that later became the principal throughfare of the Byzantine city and the main market of the Crusaders. Lying at a lower level between the two modern roads that form the traditional western limit of the quarter – Habad Street, leading north from the Zion Gate to David Street, and Jewish Quarter Road (see overleaf), running parallel to the east – the street has been restored in a tasteful and atmospheric manner; as you walk along the Byzantine pavement between Byzantine colonnades, it isn't hard to imagine yourself back in its heyday.

At the open southern end of the excavated section, you can see **Hasmonean** city walls and remains of buildings of the **First Temple** period. The street then runs on underground to the north; diagrams and covered archeological exhibitions along the way describe the different historical periods, but the highlight is a reproduction of the famous sixth-century mosaic **Madaba Map**. Discovered on the floor of a church in Madaba in Jordan, the map depicts the country's towns and cities; Jerusalem is shown with the Cardo running from the Damascus Gate in the north to the southern Nea Gate of *Aelia Capitolina*. This part of it is in fact a Byzantine extension of the original Roman Cardo which began further north. The vaulted **northern end** of the Cardo (open and lit up at night) now contains expensive gift shops and (generally deserted) art galleries. Above one of the galleries you'll find the **One Last Day Museum** (Sun–Thurs 9am–5pm, Fri 9am–1pm; 4NIS), a small collection of photos by *Life* magazine photographer John Philips recording the Jewish Quarter's 1948 fall to Transjordan's Arab Legion.

Beyond here, at the northern end of Habad Street, you can get a different perspective on the central souqs by climbing the metal stairway that leads up onto the **rooftops** and peering down through the skylights. There's also a children's playground up here, and good views of the Lutheran Church and the roof of the Holy Sepulchre. This route is used by settlers in the Muslim Quarter to get to the Jewish Quarter without passing through the Arab streets below.

Pelugat HaKotel Street and Jewish Quarter Road

East of the Cardo's northern end, **Pelugat HaKotel Street** contains a couple of archeological remains, though you'd need to be an enthusiast of ancient walls to go out of your way to see them. The **Broad Wall** (Sun–Thurs 9am–4pm, Fri 9am–1pm; 9NIS) is a section of fortification erected under Hezekiah to protect the city from the invading Assyrians, while further north along the street, opposite the Yad Ben Zvi Institute, a flight of stairs leads down to the misleadingly named **Israelite Tower** (Sun–Thurs 9am–5pm, Fri 9am–1pm; 4NIS), which is in fact part of a gate dating from the seventh century BC. Babylonian arrowheads found here testify to the fact that it saw action in the Babylonian siege of Jerusalem in 586 BC. Next to it is part of the Hasmonean city wall whose continuation can be seen at the Cardo (see above).

A block south of Pelugat HaKotel Street on **Jewish Quarter Road** is the **minaret** of the fourteenth-century mosque of Sidi Umar, adjacent to which stand two synagogues built on the remains of a Crusader church. **The Ramban Synagogue**, the oldest in the quarter (open only for morning and evening prayers), was founded by the famous medieval scholar Nahmanides (aka Rabbi Moshe Ben Nahman – "Ramban" is an acronym of his name), who came to Jerusalem from Spain in 1267. The building was destroyed in medieval times (accounts as to why vary from collapse after heavy rain in 1474 to attacks by "Muslim fanatics") but was later rebuilt under the Mamluk governor Sultan Qaitbay. Little remains of the **Hurva (Ruins) Synagogue**, apart from an incongruously modern but impressive arch, erected in 1977, and spanning what used to be the central hall. Construction of the synagogue began in 1700 under Rabbi Judah the Hassid, a member of one of the first organized groups of Ashkenazi Jewish immigrants to Jerusalem, but was stopped on his death. Failure by the Ashkenazim to pay the debts incurred in its building led to the riots that resulted in their 1720 expulsion from the city. Restarted under Ibrahim Pasha in 1836, it was finally completed twenty years later, only to be destroyed by the Jordanian Arab Legion in 1948.

To the west of the synagogues at 6 Or HaHayim Street (strictly speaking in the Armenian Quarter), the **Old Yishuv Court Museum** (Sun–Thurs 9am–2pm; 6NIS), a restored complex set around an inner courtyard, has its rooms decked out in period decor and shows aspects of everyday life in the Jewish Quarter from the mid-nineteenth century to the end of Ottoman rule after World War I. The **Jewish Heritage Centre**, at 1 Jewish Quarter Road, is a more heavyweight offering, featuring a 35-minute multimedia history of the quarter (Sun–Thurs, English: 11am, 2 & 5pm) from biblical times to the present day. Emphasis is placed on the quarter's loss to the Arab Legion in 1948 and recapture in 1967.

HaKehuna Street: four Sephardi synagogues

Southeast of Jewish Quarter Road, in HaKehuna Street, the **Four Sephardi Synagogues** (Sun, Mon, Wed, Thurs 9.30am–4pm, Tues & Fri 9.30am–12.30pm; 2NIS) were built in the seventeenth century, deep below ground level in accordance with an Ottoman regulation that forbade synagogue roofs from being higher than those of surrounding buildings. Once the centre of Jewish community life, they remain the religious heart of Jerusalem's Sephardic community: it was here that the Jews of the Old City gathered and finally surrendered in 1948.

The **Rabbi Yohanan Ben Zakkai Synagogue** is named after the first-century sage who is said to have taught his pupils on the site and who, according to legend, was smuggled out of Jerusalem during the siege of 70 AD to meet the then general Vespasian and plead with him to spare the city of Yavne as a home for Jewish scholars. Note the synagogue's twin Arks, decorated with a bright blue and gold mural. The **Emtza'i (Central) Synagogue**, the smallest of the four, and the **Stambouli (Istanbul) Synagogue** – so called because many of its congregation came from Turkey – stand alongside each other. The latter has a gilded seventeenth-century Italian Ark and a four-columned *bima* (platform). **Eliyahu HaNavi** (Elijah the Prophet), the oldest of the four, gets its name from the belief that this was where the prophet prayed on Yom Kippur (the Day of Atonement). The chair at the entrance replaces the one on which he is said to have sat; inside there's a magnificent hand-carved wooden Ark, of sixteenth-century Italian craftsmanship.

Around Misgav Ladakh Road

To the east of Hurva Square, on HaKaraim Street, the **Kara'ite Synagogue** once served the city's community of Kara'ites, a sect that broke away from Judaism in the seventh century AD (see p.110). Originally built in the tenth century, the synagogue was destroyed by the Jordanians in the 1960s, and rebuilt after the Six Day War. In theory it is open to the public, with a small exhibition about the Karaite community inside; in practice, you'll be lucky to find it open.

East off Jewish Quarter Road, Tiferet Yisra'el Street leads past the facade, now topped by ugly grey cement, which is all that remains of the nineteenth-century Tiferet Yisra'el or **Nissan Bek Hassidic Synagogue**, destroyed in 1948. To its south, with its entrance at the southeast corner of Hurva Square, is the fascinating **Wohl Archeological Museum** (Sun–Thurs 9am–5pm, Fri 9am–noon; 6NIS includes entry to the Burnt House), where you can explore the remains, some very well-preserved and all well-presented, of six priests' mansions dating from Herodian times. At a time when Jerusalem as a whole was enjoying increased prosperity, this area of the city became one of the most sought-after locations in which to live; the remains alone give you a good idea of the opulence of the buildings in their heyday, and a general feel for the art, culture and everyday life of some of Jerusalem's wealthier citizens. Descending from street level, you enter the basement bathroom of the **Western Building**, complete with *mikve* (ritual bath; plural *mikvaot*), cisterns and mosaic floor. From here, a corridor leads to the **Middle Complex**, containing the remains of two houses and another fine mosaic, beyond which is the most important house on the site, the **Palatial Mansion**, a large house on two levels: the (formerly) ground floor built around a patio, and the basement containing a whole series of *mikvot*, more mosaics, and the remains of ancient frescoes. A scale model of the building shows what it would have looked like in its prime. Adjoining the Palatial Mansion are, to its north, a colonnaded court known as the **House of Columns** and, to its southeast, the large **Southern Building**, its rooms also built around a central patio. The exit from the Wohl Museum brings you out onto Misgav Ladakh Road, which leads north to Bab al-Silsila Street.

Just north of the museum exit, the **Burnt House** is one of the most intriguing sites in the Jewish Quarter (Sun–Thurs 9am–5pm, Fri 9am–1pm; 6NIS including entry to the Wohl Museum). The house, which would have been luxurious in its time, belonged to the priestly Kathros family and was torched during Titus's destruction of the city in 70 AD; the charred remains provide an eerie snapshot of domestic life at the moment the fire swept through. An entrance corridor, four rooms, kitchen and bathing pool can all be easily made out from the excavations, and among the more gruesome finds was the skeletal arm of a woman who apparently died struggling to escape the fire, the circumstances of which are vividly recreated in a 15-minute **audiovisual show** (English at 9.30am, 11.30am & 3.30pm). Next to the Burnt House are new excavations of the Herodian city.

Fifty metres south of the Burnt House, on Misgav Ladakh Street, stands a twelfth-century complex consisting of a hospital, hospice and the church of **St Mary's of the Germans** – a Crusader church built as a pilgrim centre and run by German members of the order of St John. These have survived despite objections from ultra-orthodox Jews as to the presence of a church on their doorstep. Roofless as it now is, though with most of its walls intact, the church is a peaceful spot to take a break from sightseeing. The broad stone steps next to the church lead past the newly rebuilt **Porat Yosef Yeshiva** (the largest in the quarter), designed by Israeli architect Moshe Safdie, down to the Wailing Wall piazza. Along the way you'll get great views of the Wall, the golden Dome of the Rock and the silver dome of al-Aqsa behind, with the Mount of Olives in the background, and, on a clear day, the Dead Sea beyond.

Yet another of the area's sprouting *yeshivot*, **Yeshivat HaKotel** (Western Wall *yeshiva*), can be found on Batei Mahasse Street, on the southern limits of the quarter. In its basement, a southern apse projecting outside the city walls is part of the huge basilica built by Justinian in 543 AD – the **Nea** or **New Church** clearly marked on the Madaba Map (see p.343). The carved columns and other masonry in the courtyard are thought to be part of a Hasmonean palace. Between the two *yeshivot*, at 35 Misgav Ladakh Street

(corner of Hagittit Street), is the **Siebenberg House archeological museum**
(☎02/628 2341; by appointment only), where excavations have uncovered a
Hasmonean cistern, sections of a water conduit which may be part of the lower aqueduct that once conveyed water from Solomon's Pools to the Temple and arrowheads
used to defend the city against the Babylonians in 586 AD.

Al-Haram al-Sharif/Temple Mount

> *At the dawn, when the light of the sun first strikes the dome and the drum catches the rays,*
> *then is this edifice a marvellous sight to behold, and one such that in all of Islam I have not*
> *seen the equal.*
>
> al-Muqaddasi, 985 AD

The vast paved esplanade of **al-Haram al-Sharif** (the Noble Sanctuary), known to Jews
as **Temple Mount**, takes up almost a fifth of the Old City and is a magnificent pedestal
for Jerusalem's greatest triumph of Islamic art – the spectacular **Dome of the Rock**,
the holiest Muslim site in Palestine, and third holiest in the world. The enclosed
expanse, shaded by greenery and dotted with shrines, is an oasis of calm in the heart
of Jerusalem's mayhem; you could easily spend a couple of hours just gazing at the
architectural wonders or relaxing away from the heat and crush outside while watching the goings-on – people preparing for prayer, strolling around, talking or reading in
the forecourt, kids playing and tourist groups wandering about. In addition to the
Dome of the Rock, the complex contains another important mosque: the smaller, silver-
domed **Mosque of al-Aqsa**. Scores of lesser Islamic monuments can also be found in
the sanctuary area – *mastabas* (raised platforms), mihrabs (prayer niches) and *sabils*
(fountains) – as well as the library of al-Aqsa and the **Islamic museum**. The compound has ten open **gates** and four closed ones – worth exploring in themselves, from
both outside and inside the walls of the enclosure.

The peace of al-Haram has on occasion been wrecked by angry confrontations and
attacks (see box on p.349) resulting from **religious disputes** between Muslims and
Jews, to whom the site is also holy as the site of the First and Second Temples, though
strictly speaking out of bounds according to Jewish law. One reason Jews are not permitted to enter the Temple precinct is that they might inadvertently stray onto the
Temple's Holy of Holies, forbidden to all but the high priest. The other reason is that
all Jews are nowadays ritually unclean since the extinction of the red heifer of biblical
times whose ashes, as specified by the Torah, conferred ritual purity (Numbers 19:
1–10). However, this has not deterred some nationalist religious Jews from coming to
pray here (see p.349), and recently one group even claimed to have bred the red heifer
with which, they say, they will be able to avoid the religious prohibition and enter
Temple Mount to found a Third Temple.

Some history
Mount Moriah, on which the complex stands, is the traditional site of the holy rock
where **Abraham** prepared to sacrifice his son (Isaac according to Judaism and
Christianity; his older brother Ismail according to Islam). Here, in 960 BC, Solomon is
believed to have erected the **First Temple** to house the Ark of the Covenant which his
father, David, had brought to Jerusalem. The temple was burned to the ground by the
Babylonians in 586 BC.

The **Second Temple** was consecrated in 515 BC, rebuilt by Herod in 20 BC and
destroyed by Titus in 70 AD following the First Jewish Revolt; few traces of it survive.
The Wailing Wall (see p.340) and Solomon's Stables (see p.349) under al-Aqsa Mosque
are thought to date from the time of Herod and, thanks to the comprehensive account

---

VISITING AL-HARAM/TEMPLE MOUNT

Admission to the Noble Sanctuary is free (Sun–Thurs 8am–3pm, Ramadan 7.30–10am, closed to non-Muslims on Fri & Muslim holidays) but for the Dome of Rock, al-Aqsa Mosque, and the Islamic Museum, you have to buy a **ticket** (26NIS) from the kiosk at Bab al-Magharba (the Moor's Gate). Note also that during prayer times (five times daily) the mosques and museum are open only to Muslims. There are ten **gates** leading into the compound, and although you can leave by any of them, non-Muslims are permitted to enter through only two, located along the Wailing Wall: **Bab al-Silsila** (Chain Gate) and **Bab al-Magharba** (Moor's Gate). As for all religious sites, dress must be modest; eating, drinking and smoking are not allowed, and shoes, bags and cameras must be left outside before entering the mosques.

Certain parts of the complex, mostly along the eastern wall, are **off limits to visitors**. Although no signs advise you of this, site officials will soon let you know if you've ventured into one of those areas.

---

of Josephus (*Antiquities* 15: 380–425) and the measurements detailed in the *Mishnah*, a model of how Herod's temple might have looked has been constructed and is on show in the *Holyland Hotel* (see p.376). After the Second Revolt in 135 AD, when Jerusalem was again razed to the ground, Hadrian erected a temple to Jupiter on this site.

The **Byzantine Christians** used the area as a dump and it was in this state that Caliph Omar Ibn al-Khattab found it when he accepted the surrender of Jerusalem in 638 AD. He ordered the place cleaned and built a small mosque at the southern end of the sanctuary. Omar's mosque, where al-Aqsa now stands, traditionally marks the spot where Mohammed tethered his winged horse, al-Burak, on reaching Jerusalem: according to Islamic tradition, **Mohammed** flew from here from Mecca in a single night on al-Burak, and, in the company of the Archangel Gabriel, prayed at the **Holy Rock of Abraham**, from where he ascended to heaven on a staircase of light, returning to Mecca before dawn. As the first *qibla* before Mecca became the main centre of the Islamic faith, it was towards Jerusalem that prayers were originally directed. Under the Ummayad caliphs (661–749 AD) the first great monuments were built: the Dome of the Rock in 691 AD and al-Aqsa Mosque in 705–715 AD.

The Dome of the Rock

With its landmark golden dome, dazzling mosaics and exquisite, mathematically perfect proportions, the octagonal **Dome of the Rock** (Qubbat al-Sakhra) is justifiably considered one of the wonders of the modern world and an enduring symbol of Jerusalem. Tradition has it that the **Caliph Abd al-Malik Ibn Marawan** built the mosque to put Islam on an equal footing with its predecessors, Judaism and Christianity, and to compete with the Church of the Holy Sepulchre – "lest that should dazzle the minds of the Muslims," as al-Muqaddasi puts it. Such was his devotion to his creation, that Ibn Marawan is said to have employed 52 official cleaners to wash the mosque with a mixture of saffron, musk and ambergris in rose water before prayer times.

The beauty and complexity of the exterior and interior decoration of the Dome of the Rock defy summary. There is no one point where you can stand and take in the whole and you find yourself drawn time and time again around the building, captivated by the intricacy of tiles and the play of light filtering through the stained-glass windows onto rings of Arabic calligraphy, arabesques and small arches. On the **exterior**, the walls are faced with marble slabs topped with glazed green and blue tiles; the outer face of the drum is similarly tiled. The present designs – a combination of Koranic inscription, geometrical shapes and vines and flowers – were originally commissioned by Suleiman the Magnificent in the sixteenth century and have been repeatedly renovated and repaired since. In the 1960s, the **dome** was covered with anodized aluminium, lighter than the lead covering that had been causing structural damage to the building, and cheaper than the gold which supposedly once kept out the elements before being melted down to pay the caliph's debts.

The atmosphere **inside** the mosque is tranquil and in the words of the Christian theologian, Alfred Guillaume, in his book *Islam* (Pelican, 1954):

> A Christian who, like the writer, goes from a visit to the Church of the Holy Sepulchre with its warring, noisy, competitive sects to the peace and devotion of the Great Mosque of Jerusalem cannot but be saddened and chastened to find in the one what he was looking for in the other.

The large barren **rock** at its centre, on which Abraham prepared to sacrifice his son, and from which Mohammed ascended to heaven, seems incongruous amid all the splendour. Vague impressions on the rock's underside are attributed to the **Prophet's footprint** and the imprint of the hand of the archangel Gabriel, who restrained the rock as it tried to follow the Prophet up to heaven. Hairs from the beard of the Prophet Mohammed are kept in a shrine next to it which is opened once a year – on the 27th day of Ramadan. Above, the drum and dome are decorated by bands of predominantly gold and green glass, mother-of-pearl and gold sheet mosaics, dating from the time of the original designers and featuring patterns mostly consisting of stylized vegetation. The ceilings of the ambulatories are patterned with abstract designs in gold, russet and green interspersed with octagons and circles. Around the rock, **the inner circle** is formed by twelve marble columns and four piers supporting the patterned golden dome, a soft greenish-gold light permeating through its sixteen stained-glass windows. The inner circle is surrounded by two octagons, the first formed by sixteen columns and eight piers, the second by the outer walls. A **cave** beneath the rock contains two small shrines to Ibrahim (Abraham) and al-Khader (Elijah and St George, see box p.468), underneath which, in the Bir al-Arwah (Well of Souls), spirits are said to await Judgement Day.

Al-Aqsa Mosque

> *Glory be to Him who carried His servant by night from the Holy Mosque to the Farthest Mosque the precincts of which We have blessed.*
>
> The Koran 17: 1

Simpler and less grandiose than the Dome of the Rock, the silver-domed **Masjid al-Aqsa** – the Farthest Mosque – is darker, cooler and less richly decorated within, its atmosphere more conducive to quiet meditation. Throughout its history the mosque has been constantly damaged by earthquakes and continually rebuilt; its relatively modern interior is a result of substantial restoration between 1938 and 1942. The original structure, erected around 715 AD by **Caliph al-Walid**, son of Caliph Abd al-Malik, was destroyed in 747 AD. Restored in 780 AD under the next caliph, Mohammed al-Mahdi, it had twenty aisles instead of the seven that exist today, a feature mentioned by al-Muqaddasi in 985 AD, when he described the mosque as having fifteen doorways in the north wall and eleven in the eastern wall, and an interior with 280 columns set in twenty rows. Damaged in the earthquake of 1016 AD, the mosque re-emerged with fewer gates, but with an enamelled pulpit and beautifully carved roof. The present structure is essentially that of Caliph al-Zaher who rebuilt it after yet another earthquake in 1033 AD.

In 1099, the **Crusader** leader Godfrey de Bouillon set up his headquarters here. On its west side he built his armoury – the beautiful arched buildings now used as the

Women's Mosque and the Islamic Museum (see below) – and the mosque became a church, its dome topped with a cross. The underground vaults, living up to their traditional name of Solomon's Stables, housed Crusader horses. The military order of the Knights Templar, founded in 1118, was named after the complex, known by the Crusaders simply as the Templum. **Saladin** removed the Templar constructions from the west side of the mosque, decorated the beautiful mihrab, and, from Aleppo, brought the famous cedar-wood *minbar* (pulpit), inlaid with ivory and mother-of-pearl, that was later destroyed in the fire of 1969 (see box below).

Entering al-Aqsa today, you pass through the impressive arched main doorway into the **central aisle**, the widest of the seven, which has a beautiful carved and painted roof supported by massive columns of pale marble. To the west of the *minbar* are two small prayer niches dedicated to Moses and Jesus. The exquisite green, gold and blue mosaic work of the **dome** was commissioned by Saladin in 1189, and the similarity of the motifs to those in the Dome of the Rock have led some to believe that the original artists were ordered to make copies. The dome is supported by four arches and inset with seven of the mosque's 121 stained-glass windows.

Outside the main northern entrance a flight of steps leads down into **Solomon's Stables**, a labyrinth of massive pillars and arches (usually closed to the public) where sacrificial animals in the days of the Second Temple may have been housed. A long vaulted passage leads from here to the closed Double Gate on the southern wall of the compound.

The Islamic Museum

To the west of al-Aqsa Mosque, the **Islamic Museum**, established in 1923, is the oldest museum in Jerusalem, housed in two historic buildings – one Ayyubid, the other Crusader – so much in harmony with the rest of the Noble Sanctuary that you barely realize that you're entering a secular building. Between the mosque and the museum

---

THREATS TO AL-HARAM

Since 1967, al-Haram has seen a number of incidents and attacks directed at its mosques by both extremist groups and individuals. Among the former are the ultra-nationalist **Ateret Cohanim** ("The Custodians of Temple Mount"), who have staged prayers and demonstrations around al-Haram, while probably the most famous of the latter was the Australian Christian who set fire to al-Aqsa in 1969, causing extensive damage. In 1981, a group of Israelis were detained outside Jerusalem with **explosives** and military equipment destined to destroy al-Aqsa and the Dome of the Rock in order to clear the way for a new Temple; other caches of explosives have been discovered closer to home in the religious seminaries of the Jewish Quarter. The Dome of the Rock itself was damaged in 1982 when an Israeli soldier opened fire on it and worshippers inside; an attack that saw several people killed when other soldiers fired on protesters. Further deaths occurred on the Mount in October 1990, when members of Ateret Cohanim attempted to place a Foundation Stone for a new Temple; in the riots that ensued as Israeli police went in to protect them from stone-throwing Palestinians, nineteen people died and three hundred were wounded. One bizarre outcome of this is the Israeli statute forbidding Jews to pray on the site, even individually and in silence.

The activities of **archeologists** burrowing around the edges of al-Haram have meanwhile caused concern for the structural integrity of buildings above. In one case, Waqf employees clearing out a basement came across a tunnel and followed it back to a building occupied by settlers. In the furore which followed, it was revealed that the settlers were carrying out their own search for evidence of the Temple and it was partly fears about this kind of activity that sparked off the riots over the opening of the Western Wall tunnel (see p.342), although the tunnel itself does not in fact go underneath the Haram.

there are dozens of column capitals from the numerous phases of the latter's history, beginning with those from a building erected in the early eighth century by the Ummayad caliph al-Walid.

It may have a secular exterior, but the museum itself is something of a shrine to all things Islamic, with **exhibits** ranging from tiny flasks for kohl eye make-up to giant architectural elements from mosques. The smaller objects are displayed in the **first building** (the Ayyubid construction) and include porcelain cups from the Far and Near East, inscribed brass mosque seals, glassware and filigree incense burners, among other things. Moving up in size, there are exquisite thirteenth-century gilded and enamelled mosque lamps from the Hebron area, a large jewel-encrusted Hand of Fatima, and a collection of decorated guns, swords and daggers from the seventeenth and eighteenth centuries. The **manuscript section** has some rare medieval and Ottoman copies of the Koran, including an eighth-century version ascribed to the Prophet's great-grandson.

The exhibits in the **second building** are much larger and include the burnt remains of the great cedarwood, ivory and mother-of-pearl **minbar** given to the al-Aqsa Mosque by Saladin in 1187. Here too are exceptionally rich religious vestments of silk and gold, fragments of al-Aqsa's seventeenth-century prayer-rug, and decorative cypress wood panels from the original eighth-century mosque. From the Dome of the Rock itself, there is the magnificent Crusader wrought-iron screen that surrounded the Holy Rock from the twelfth to the twentieth century, and remains of mosaic and ceramic walls. Also on display is the nineteenth-century cannon that was fired to mark the start of the fast during Ramadan, and huge copper kettles from the soup kitchen established by the wife of Suleiman the Magnificent.

Other structures

The gates to Temple Mount are worth checking out, in particular the **Golden Gate** in the east wall, originally Herodian, but replaced with a double gate under the Ummayads, and blocked off in the eighth century. This is the gate through which the Jewish Messiah is expected to enter the city, as Jesus did. To its north is **Kursi Suleiman** (Solomon's Throne), a small double-domed structure where the wise king is said to have died. The **arcades** in the north wall, originally built by the Crusaders, were restored in 1213; those along the west wall date from the fourteenth century, as does the minaret here.

Apart from the Dome of the Rock, a further nine domes can be seen within the complex, of which three deserve to be highlighted. Northwest of the Dome of the Rock, the **Dome of the Ascension** (Qubbat al-Miraj) was restored in 1200 AD, though its original date of construction is unknown. Between here and the Dome of the Rock, the **Dome of the Prophet** (Qubbat al-Nabi) was built on eight marble columns around 1845, while just east of the Dome of the Rock, at the exact centre of the compound, the **Dome of the Chain** (Qubbat al-Silsila) is an eleven-columned monument variously explained as a scale model for the Dome of the Rock or as the Treasury of Temple Mount; its name derives from a legend that, during Solomon's time, those who told a lie while holding onto a chain hung from the roof were struck dead.

Seven **fountains** can also be found in the compound, the most impressive of which is the **Sabil of Sultan Qaitbey**, west of the Dome of the Rock, in front of the al-Aqsa Library. Looking a little like a tomb, and topped with a typically Mamluk decorated dome, it is named after the sultan who restored it in 1482. Directly south of the Dome of the Rock and in line with al-Aqsa Mosque, the fountain known as **al-Kas** (The Cup) is used for washing before prayer; it originally drew its water supply from springs near Hebron. The approach is through one of the arches – the *minbar* of Judge Burhan al-Din, built in 1388 – at the top of the eight stairways leading to the platform of the Dome of the Rock.

East Jerusalem

The non-capital of a non-state, one hundred percent Arab **East Jerusalem** is where the PNA would really like to have its seat of government. Though not as ancient as the Old City, the area seems caught in more of a time warp, little changed since the days of Jordanian rule. There's a 1950s feel to its centre, reminiscent in some ways of Communist Eastern Europe: the shops are functional, aimed at local shoppers rather than tourists, with goods piled up rather than displayed in spotlit windows, and this side of town can seem rather drab in comparison to the more affluent west side. Nonetheless, for the tourist, East Jerusalem offers a character distinct from that of West Jerusalem, and one that's somewhat more Middle Eastern; its centre is a hive of activity crammed with buses and service taxis and bustling with local shoppers – all of which gives the place a slightly manic feel at times.

The area has no shortage of sights either. Highlights include the archeological collections of the **Rockefeller Museum**, the **Mount of Olives**, dotted with churches and overlooking the Old City from its most photogenic side, and the **Kidron Valley** and

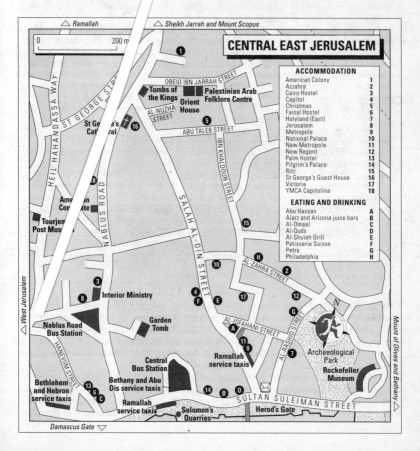

CENTRAL EAST JERUSALEM

△ Ramallah   △ Sheikh Jarrah and Mount Scopus

0   200 m

OBEID IBN JARRAH STREET

Tombs of the Kings   Palestinian Arab Folklore Centre
Orient House
AL-NUZHA STREET
ABU TALEB STREET

ST GEORGE STREET

St George's Cathedral

HEIL HAHANDASSA WAY

IBN KHALDOUN STREET

NABLUS ROAD

American Consulate

Tourjeman Post Museum

SALAH AL-DIN STREET

Interior Ministry

Garden Tomb

AL-ZAHRA STREET

AL-ISFAHANI STREET

HANEVI'IM STREET

West Jerusalem △

Nablus Road Bus Station

Central Bus Station

Ramallah service taxis

Bethany and Abu Dis service taxis

Bethlehem and Hebron service taxis

Ramallah service taxis

Solomon's Quarries

Herod's Gate

AL-RASHID STREET

Archaeological Park

Rockefeller Museum

SULTAN SULEIMAN STREET

△ Damascus Gate

Mount of Olives and Bethany ▷

ACCOMMODATION

American Colony	1
Azzahra	2
Cairo Hostel	3
Capitol	4
Christmas	5
Faisal Hostel	6
Holyland (East)	7
Jerusalem	8
Metropole	9
National Palace	10
New Metropole	11
New Regent	12
Palm Hostel	13
Pilgrim's Palace	14
Ritz	15
St George's Guest House	16
Victoria	17
YMCA Capitolina	18

EATING AND DRINKING

Abu Hassan	A
Alarz and Arizona juice bars	B
Al-Omaal	C
Al-Quds	D
Al-Shuleh Grill	E
Patisserie Suisse	F
Petra	G
Philadelphia	H

JEWISH SETTLEMENTS IN EAST JERUSALEM

The first flush of **Jewish settlements** east of the Green Line was underway a year after the Six Day War. Apart from the resettlement of the Old City's Jewish Quarter, they were placed on high ground around the city, at Gilo and East Talpiot to the south, and French Hill and Ramot Eshkol to the north, with the aim of surrounding East Jerusalem and thus backing Israel's case for sovereignty over the whole city. The settlements met opposition, not only from Palestinian residents, but also the UN Security Council, and even the United States. On the surface, they seem very attractive places to live: investment in the infrastructure has been massive and this is reflected in paved, tree-lined streets and community facilities. That said, they're lifeless places – quiet during the day (most of the inhabitants commute) and dead at night, and many of the apartments remain unoccupied.

The 1991 occupation of homes in **Silwan** (see p.361), south of the Old City, marked a more aggressive phase of settlement, carried out by Jewish individuals and organizations acting independently of the Israeli authorities. This time it involved not the creation of new areas of housing, but a takeover of homes previously occupied by Arab families, as had been done in the 1980s inside the Old City's Muslim and Christian quarters; forged documents were used to establish a spurious claim of Jewish ownership and enlist army support in evicting Palestinian residents.

The **Oslo Accords** have not put a stop to either type of settlement and have in fact increased Arab opposition – Palestinians having been under the impression that no more settlements would be built in the city after the agreement was signed; under this, the city's status is to be the last thing to be settled. To Israelis, on the the other hand, the opposite is true: that very provision allows them to continue building settlements until a final decision on Jerusalem's status is reached. In February 1997, the Israeli government gave the go-ahead for construction of a Jewish suburb at Abu Ghoneim, called in Hebrew **Har Homa** (Mountain of the Wall). Palestinians took serious umbrage and massive protests ensued. Their grievances are twofold: first, they object to the construction of new Jewish homes (though the Israeli authorities claim that the homes will be open to anyone) while they themselves are invariably refused planning permission to build new houses, and face demolition if they build without it; second, Har Homa completes the encirclement of East Jerusalem lying on the main Hebron–Nablus road, with the potential to cut off access to and from the rest of the West Bank.

While wrangles over Har Homa continued, attention shifted to the Arab suburb of **Ras al-Amud** where in September 1997 armed radical settlers broke into a bus company parking lot, raised the Israeli flag and evicted Palestinian staff at gunpoint. Israeli police then arrived to protect them. The lot, it seems, had been bought on their behalf by Jewish American millionaire Irving Moscowitz, although the Palestinian bus operator claims to be a protected tenant. Protests by Palestinians citywide have failed to budge the settlers, and both Har Homa and Ras al-Amud remain a source of friction. But, as Israel points out, there is nothing in the Oslo Accords to prevent the building of settlements in East Jerusalem, and it can therefore be expected to continue.

City of David, with their tombs, excavations and relics of biblical times, not least **Hezekiah's Tunnel**, whose construction is described in the Old Testament. Of the two chief commercial thoroughfares in its centre, **Nablus Road** has the offices and institutions, **Salah al-Din Street** the shops. **Al-Zahra Street**, further from the Old City and correspondingly less frenzied, has a couple of hotels and what few chic restaurants East Jerusalem has to offer.

Modern East Jerusalem grew up around the turn of the twentieth century, with its main arteries fanning out north and east from the Old City. At that time both East and West Jerusalem were part of the New City, but under Jordanian rule East Jerusalem became a town in its own right, administering the central part of the West

Bank and a base for many of the tourists who came here to see the holy sites of the Old City (which is strictly speaking part of it). Now surrounded by rings of Israeli **settlements** (see box opposite), East Jerusalem has become a small, isolated Palestinian community hugging the walls of the Old City. The dilapidated state of the buildings, roads and pavements here indicate the extent of municipal neglect: per capita spending by the city council here is only a sixth of what it is in West Jerusalem.

Although it is the heart and centre of the West Bank, East Jerusalem is cut off from its hinterland by periodic closure of the **Green Line**, and permanently cut off to most West Bank Palestinians, who need a permit to come here. To Israelis, it is, or ought to be, an integral part of their united eternal capital, but in practice most are scared to venture here. For most of the international community, however, East Jerusalem retains its status as the unofficial capital of Palestine, and a diplomatic colony has grown up around Orient House (the PNA's unofficial seat; see p.355) and the *American Colony Hotel* (see p.355).

King Solomon's Quarries and the Rockefeller Museum

Almost immediately outside the Old City walls, the entrance to **King Solomon's Quarries** is on Sultan Suleiman Street, between Damascus and Herod's gates (Sun–Thurs 9am–4pm, Fri 9am–2pm; 7NIS; also 5-sites combined ticket, see p.322. The well-lit, stepped descent plunges into a grotto 200m deep under the Old City, and if there's not that much to see in the cavernous stone interior, it's still an awesome experience, albeit one not for the claustrophobic. Although it's unlikely that King Solomon had stones quarried from here, material was being removed and used for important public buildings in Jerusalem right up to the beginning of the twentieth century. Jewish tradition holds that this was a tunnel used by Judah's last King Zedekiah (597–587 BC) as an escape route to Jericho when he fled from the Babylonians after their capture of Jerusalem – hence the grotto's other name, **Zedekiah's Cave**. Even if the legend is true, Zedekiah didn't get far: the Bible relates (II Kings 25: 5–7) how Nebuchadnezzar's forces captured him, killed his sons in front of him, then put out his eyes and carried him in chains to Babylon.

On the hill opposite Herod's Gate, the **Rockefeller Museum**, formerly the **Palestine Archeological Museum**, (☎02/628 2251, Sun–Thurs 10am–5pm, Fri & Sat 10am–2pm; 14NIS) is one of the richest and most fascinating museums in the country, boasting a remarkable collection of finds from the Stone Age to the present day. The building in which the museum is housed was constructed in 1927 under the British Mandate – a massive Neo-Gothic rectangular structure featuring a distinctive octagonal turret and built around a water-lilied courtyard pond. From its grand entrance, there are panoramic views of Mount Scopus and the Mount of Olives, with the northwest corner of the Old City wall at eye-level.

Inside, the museum itself is rather old-fashioned and a bit dry and dingy, but most of the exhibits are well labelled. The museum's most famous exhibits, the **Dead Sea Scrolls**, were removed after Israel's 1967 annexation of East Jerusalem, and are now in the Israel Museum on the west side of the city (see p.373), but plenty of highlights remain: Bronze Age skeletons and weapons, finds from Egypt and Mesopotamia, Roman sarcophagi and stunning jewellery, Romanesque sculptures from the Church of the Holy Sepulchre, fine examples of Greek and Byzantine pottery, and intricate eighteenth-century wood carvings from al-Aqsa Mosque. Also on display are chunks of the walls, ceilings, façades and plasterwork of **Hisham's Palace** in Jericho (see p.426), while the restored features of ten **skulls** (apparently associated with some kind of cult of the dead) show what Jericho's neolithic inhabitants may have looked like. However, the most intriguing of the exhibits are the so-called **Galilee Skull** dated to around

200,000 BC, and an eerily intact skeleton from about 10,000 BC. At times, the museum also presents **special displays**: these may be advertised in the free *What's On* booklets from the tourist office, or you can call the museum for details.

Nablus Road and Sheikh Jarrah

As its name indicates, **Nablus Road** was the main thoroughfare from Jerusalem to Nablus in the north of the West Bank until construction of the widened Hail HaHandassa Street, a block to the west, which marks the Green Line and was formerly the edge of no-man's-land between Israel and Jordan. At its Damascus Gate junction, the Nablus Road is narrow, dusty and congested with traffic pouring into the city, but once free of the crush it widens into calmer and cooler surroundings with a few sites of interest along its length.

The road passes the **Garden Tomb**, thought by some to be the true site of the crucifixion, **St George's Cathedral**, the Anglican seat in the Holy City, looking more like an English parish church than a cathedral, the **Tomb of the Kings**, in fact the tomb of a queen, and the **American Colony Hotel**, favourite Jerusalem haunt of diplomats and journalists, before reaching the district of **Sheikh Jarrah**, over which loom the military trenches of **Ammunition Hill**.

The Garden Tomb to St George's Cathedral

Two hundred metres up from the Damascus Gate, along a short alleyway to the east, is the **Garden Tomb** (Mon–Sat 8am–noon & 2–5.30pm; free), once regarded by Anglicans and some other Protestants as the site of Christ's burial. It was first noted by Charles George Gordon, the British general and sometime governor of Sudan ("Gordon of Khartoum"), on a visit to Jerusalem in 1883. Picturing Jerusalem as a skeleton, with the Dome of the Rock as the pelvis and Solomon's Quarries as the ribs, Gordon suggested that the hill to the north of the Damascus Gate was the Golgotha or "place of the skull" referred to in the Gospels – hence it was also known as "Gordon's Calvary". The tangible result of his hypothesis today is a beautiful **garden** of flowers and shrubs, pools and streams: a refreshingly tranquil spot. First laid out by a group of Anglicans in 1892, and now run by the Garden Tomb Association from London, it contains an unspectacular two-chambered **tomb** carved out of the stone and thought to date from the first to fifth centuries AD. It is now admitted that the site is unlikely to be that of Christ's tomb, but some would say the atmosphere is more conducive to prayer and meditation than that of the Holy Sepulchre, and in any case, as one Protestant minister put it, "We don't worship a place."

A little further along the road on the west side, the Israeli **Interior Ministry** is marked by crowds of Palestinians waiting in line at crash barriers trying to sort out such bureaucratic entanglements as ID cards and residency status. The latter is a particular bone of contention: under 1996 regulations, if East Jerusalemites live outside the city for more than three years, they have to prove that Jerusalem is their home and "centre of life" or their status as Jerusalem residents is revoked and they can return to the city only if they accept Israeli citizenship (and by implication, therefore, Israeli sovereignty). Palestinians argue that this is unfair as they are being forced to leave the city in the first instance owing to a housing shortage caused by refusal of planning permission for them to build homes. Whatever the situation, 1500 of them had lost their right of residence under these rules by May 1997, while 27,000 swallowed their pride and took Israeli citizenship. Outside the ministry, pavement typists offer their services to supplicants. More crash barriers and queues of hopefuls can be seen a little further up the street outside the **American Consulate**; opposite is the **Palestinian Pottery** at no. 14, where you can browse though a fine range of ceramics in a more hassle-free atmosphere than that in the souq.

A fine product of the British imperial/religious love affair with their former colonial possession stands a short distance further up Nablus Road. Part of a Crusader-like compound built in 1899, the British colonial **St George's Anglican Cathedral** is an attempt to build a piece of England's green and pleasant land in Jerusalem; all it lacks is the adjoining village green and game of cricket. The magazines of St George's School, next to the church, enshrine the pre-1948 cricket results of the sons of wealthy Palestinians: yet another monument to the failed attempt to give the "natives" the trappings of an English public school education while depriving them of the power for which their Anglo-Saxon counterparts were groomed. Dotted with wall-plaques in commemoration of British personnel who died during or since the Mandate period, the church is used by the Palestinian Anglican community as well as by English-speaking visitors. The compound also houses a **hostel** (see p.317) in an exquisite inner courtyard garden.

The Tombs of the Kings and the American Colony

Just beyond St George's Cathedral, at the corner where Nablus Road meets Salah al-Din Street, is the **Tomb of the Kings** (Mon–Sat 8am–noon & 2–5pm; 7NIS), so called because it was once thought to be the burial site of the kings of Judah. It is now believed to be the family vault of the royal family of Adiabene, an independent state within the Babylonian empire whose queen, Helena, along with her son Izates, converted to Judaism. On a pilgrimage in the first century, the queen decided to stay in Jerusalem and, according to the historian Josephus (*Antiquities* 20: 95), her son ordered her bones "buried at the pyramids which their mother had erected ...three furlongs from the city of Jerusalem". A wide flight of time-worn steps descends into a vast open courtyard in which a covered porch is carved into the rock. To the right of the porch, a tiny entrance, once closed and hidden by a rolling stone, leads into an underground labyrinth of **burial chambers** and passages – bring a flashlight if you want to explore.

Behind the Tombs of the Kings, Obeid Ibn Jarrah Street is home to **Orient House**, the Jerusalem office of the PNA, which, with its soldiers guarding the entrance and Palestinian flag flying, looks for all the world like a foreign embassy. It is unrecognized by Israel, whose government lodges protests whenever foreign dignitaries pay court here. Next door, Dar al-Tifl al-Arabi, the **Palestinian Arab Folklore Centre** (☎02/627 3477), is the nearest thing Palestinians have to a national museum: a small, five-room collection devoted to preserving the national culture and heritage. The thick-walled window arches of this 200-year-old house provide an appropriate setting for life-size mannequins displaying Palestinian dress and occupations, and there are also collections of jewellery, cloths, pottery and metal, all hand-labelled in English and Arabic. A detailed, coloured catalogue is available, and the centre is certainly worth a look, but the collection is privately owned, so call in advance to make an appointment.

If you've got this far along Nablus Road, another 50m will bring you the perfect reward. Just off to the right, the **American Colony Hotel** is an exquisite place to visit whether you can afford to stay there or not; a coffee or snack in its fragrant garden or in the mosaic-decorated lobby is well worth the extra dollars. It's a favourite with both the diplomatic community and the press corps and you may even get to rub shoulders with a celebrity or two (former guests include Allenby, Churchill, Chagall, Graham Greene, Lauren Bacall, Lawrence of Arabia and Peter O'Toole, who played him in David Lean's film). The hotel is the most important feature of the American Colony itself, a small suburb founded by the US evangelist Horatio Spafford in the late nineteenth century.

Just beyond the hotel, the small **Sheikh Jarrah Mosque**, housing the tomb of a twelfth-century saint, gives its name to the district that lies a five-minute walk further north. As you ascend into Sheikh Jarrah, a turning to the right onto Ibn Jubair Street, and immediately left onto Othman Ibn Affar Street, brings you to (on the left) the **Tomb of Simon the Just** (Shimon HaTzadik), a fourth-century BC high priest revered for his piety and devotion. The tomb, signposted in Hebrew and marked by Jewish graffiti, is closed to the public. Next to it is a small synagogue, whose ultra-orthodox *haredi* congregants look decidedly out of place in this completely Arab neighbourhood.

Sheikh Jarrah and Ammunition Hill

Overlooking the tomb is the more prosperous hillside Palestinian district of **SHEIKH JARRAH**. There's nothing of note to see here, but it was highly strategic in the **1948 war**, when it was the only connection between West Jerusalem and the Jewish enclave on Mount Scopus to the east. In April 1948, a ten-vehicle Haganah convoy, including two ambulances bringing medical personnel and wounded to the Hadassah Hospital on the Mount, was ambushed by local Arab irregulars on Mount of Olives Road not far from the *Shepherd Hotel*, after the convoy's schedule was leaked to the Arabs by a British officer. Two days after Deir Yassin (see p.378), Arab fighters were not inclined to be merciful to the Jews on the convoy, who were mostly unarmed. The British dragged their feet for hours before intervening, by which time 77 Jews had been killed. Even after 1948, however, Israeli convoys continued to ply the same route to supply Mount Scopus, which remained an enclave until the 1967 Six Day War gave them East Jerusalem.

Above Sheikh Jarrah, just to the south of Sederot Levi Eshkol, **Ammunition Hill** (Givat HaTahamoshet; bus #4, #9, #28 or #29), was the Jordanians' main defensive position in 1967. The successful assault on this position by Israeli forces in the **Six Day War** gave them control of East Jerusalem and it is now a monument to the event, with faithfully preserved **trenches** (Sun–Thurs 8am–6pm, Fri 8am–2pm, closing an hour earlier in winter) and a **museum** (Sun–Thurs 9am–5pm, Fri 9am–1pm; 8NIS) in the former Jordanian command post bunker. Its display of military insignia and names and photos of dead soldiers will really only be of interest to war buffs and Israeli patriots, though the triumphalist films on the battle shown in the auditorium are more exciting, and the trenches themselves, set in a grassy park with views over East Jerusalem, are a good place to get away from the bustle and fumes of the city below. Buses #9, #25, #26, #28, #28a, #45 and #48 run along Sederot Levi Eshkol to the north of the site. From Ammunition Hill it's 1km west to the tombs of the Sanhedrin (see p.367).

The Mount of Olives

The **MOUNT OF OLIVES** rises from the Kidron Valley, just east of the Old City. Green, fertile and nowadays dotted with more churches, shrines and cemeteries than olive trees, its summit affords a magnificent view over the whole of Jerusalem and, in the other direction, the Judean desert, the Jordan Valley and the Mountains of Moab beyond. The mountain itself is loaded with biblical significance: cited in the Old Testament as the place where David mourned the death of his recalcitrant son Absalom (II Samuel 15: 30), it is also closely associated with Jesus who used to walk over it from Bethany to Jerusalem – it was from its slopes that "He beheld the city and wept over it" (Luke 19: 41) and it was here, in the **Garden of Gethsemane**, that He was arrested (Matthew 26: 36–56, Mark 14: 32–51).

The best way to see the Mount of Olives is to start at the top and walk down – a distance of around 1km. Wear sensible footwear as the path is sometimes steep and time-worn, get here early – morning is the best time for photographs of the view – and allow the best part of a day for the visit (avoid Sunday when many of the sites are closed). Egged bus #37 runs from the junction of HaNeviim with Shavtei to the summit; alternatively bus #75 from the Damascus Gate bus station runs to the village of al-Tur, from where it's around 400m to the summit (service taxis from the Old City also make the trip). Finally, if you're fit, you can walk up from the Rockefeller Museum in East Jerusalem or from the Old City's Lions' Gate. Note that there have been several reports of pickpockets in the area and, following incidents of unpleasant harassment and even sexual assault on women tourists in the area, it is not advisable for women to visit the Mount of Olives alone.

The Chapel of the Ascension and nearby sites

From the bus stop in al-Tur, walk past the *Mount of Olives Hotel* to the minuscule **mosque** known as the **Chapel of the Ascension** (ring the bell for entry; 2.50NIS). It was from here that, as stated in some versions of St Luke's Gospel (24: 51), Jesus was "carried up into heaven" forty days after the resurrection – the rock inside the octagonal shrine is marked with the footprint Jesus left as he ascended. There has been a church on the site since 390 AD but this small and rather disappointing building was erected by the Crusaders, and converted into a mosque by Saladin in 1198, with a mihrab added in 1200. The presence of a mosque on the site is not as strange as it might seem, given that Islam recognizes Jesus as a prophet.

The small **burial crypt** next to the mosque has something for all three local religions: Jews believe it contains the grave of the seventh-century BC prophet **Huldah**, one of only seven women prophets mentioned in the Old Testament (II Kings 22: 14–20); Christians hold it to be the tomb of the fifth-century saint **Pelagia**; and Muslims maintain that **Rabi'a al-Adawiya**, an eighth-century holy woman, is buried here. Just to the east, the White (Tsarist) **Russian monastery and church** (closed to the public) is where the head of John the Baptist is said to have been found. Its six-storey bell tower crowning just about the highest point in Jerusalem has lent its name to the village, *al-Tur* meaning "tower" in Arabic.

Across the road from the Chapel of the Ascension, past a grove of ancient olive trees, **Pater Noster Church** (Mon–Sat 8.30am–noon & 3–5pm) is set in an enclosed garden and built over the cave in which Jesus preached on the ultimate conflict of good and evil leading to the end of the world (Matthew 24: 1–25). The original **Eleona Basilica** (Basilica of Olives), built under the direction of Queen Helena, was destroyed by the Persians in 614 AD. It was the Crusaders, believing this to be the place where Jesus taught his disciples the Lord's Prayer, who gave the church its present name – Pater Noster being Latin for "Our Father". However, the building that stands here today dates from 1894, when the site was under the care of Carmelite nuns. Inside, a short flight of stairs from the south side of the open courtyard leads to the **tomb of the Princesse de la Tour d'Auvergne** who bought the property in 1868 and had the Lord's Prayer inscribed in 62 languages on tiled panels in the entrance and cloister.

To the tomb of the prophets and the Jewish Cemetery

The road left along the crest of the hill brings you to the grand **Intercontinental** or **Seven Arches hotel**, built controversially by the Jordanians over Jewish graves and offering the view of the city that adorns so many postcards – you can snap it for yourself if you're able to elbow yourself some lens room among the busloads of tourists and their retinue of hustling young "tourist guides". Postcards, prayer beads and wooden camels are on offer here, or you could have your photo taken astride a real camel (agree the price before getting on).

Going downhill opposite the hotel, you come to the **Tomb of the Prophets** (Mon–Fri 9am–3.30pm) on the left, the traditionally ascribed resting place of the last three Old Testament prophets: Haggai, Zechariah and Malachi. The 100-metre-long semi-circular outer corridor contains fifty tombs belonging to first-century BC Jews and fourth-and fifth-century AD Christians, whilst the inner tunnel was used for prayers. The keys to this three-thousand-year-old catacomb have been held for generations by the Othman family who live next door; the present key-holder will gladly light your way (though you could also bring a flashlight if you have one) and give you a detailed guided tour of the tombs, for a small consideration, and may even invite you home for a cup of coffee. Ask at the house if all seems quiet.

Just below the tomb, to the right, lies the **common grave** of 48 soldiers who died in the 1948 war, and who were reinterred here shortly after the occupation. Beyond lies the vast **Jewish cemetery**, the biggest and oldest in the world, and a symbol of the belief that when the "day of the Lord" comes, as foretold by the prophet Zechariah (14: 1–9), "His feet will stand on the Mount of Olives", which "will be split in two from east to west", and all the Jews buried here will be resurrected. Later Jewish tradition associates the prophesied event with the arrival of a Christian-style Messiah, entering Jerusalem as did Jesus, through the **Golden Gate** opposite. Under Jordanian rule, many Jewish graves here were desecrated, some by simple vandalism, others by construction projects including the *Seven Arches* hotel (see p.357) and the widening of the Jericho Road in 1966. Among those awaiting Judgement Day here is the British press mogul Robert Maxwell. Problems being buried here, on the other hand, were faced by Russian immigrant and Jerusalem resident Grisha Pesahovic, victim of a fundamentalist suicide bomber in Ben Yehuda Street in 1997. Although Jewish enough to be murdered by the bomber, his mother was not Jewish by birth and the Rabbinate refused to allow his burial in a Jewish cemetery. The Russian Orthodox Church would not bury him without a Christian service, so he was finally interred in a small plot belonging to the Bahais.

Dominus Flevit, the Church of St Mary Magdalene and the Garden of Gethsemane

The path downhill leads to the Franciscan Church of **Dominus Flevit** (daily 8am–noon & 2.30–5pm), inside whose grounds, to the right, are the excavations of four burial chambers bearing Hebrew inscriptions and dating from 100 BC to 300 AD. The church itself, built over the remains of a fifth-century monastic chapel, was designed in 1955 by the Italian architect Antonio Barluzzi in the shape of the tear shed by Jesus (Dominus Flevit means "The Lord Wept") as he foresaw the fate of Jerusalem (Luke 19: 41). Its exquisitely simple outer form hides a more elaborate interior: above the altar, the arched wrought-iron grille window framing the golden Dome of the Rock in the distance is another popular postcard image.

Continuing down the steep path, the halfway point is marked by the White Russian **Church of St Mary Magdalene** (Tues & Thurs 10–11.30am), whose seven golden cupolas make it another of Jerusalem's most distinctive landmarks, though it's equally worth a visit for the delightful icons and wall paintings inside. Erected in 1885 by Tsar Alexander III in the old Russian style, the crypt holds the remains of his mother, the Grand Duchess Elizabeth, killed in the Russian Revolution of 1917. Also buried here is Princess Alice of Greece, Queen Elizabeth's mother-in-law, whose philanthropic actions included harbouring Jews during the Nazi occupation of Greece.

Further down on the left, the **Church of All Nations** (daily: summer 8am–noon & 2.30–6pm; winter 2.30–5pm) was so named because its construction in 1924 was financed by twelve different countries. Its other name – the **Gethsemane Basilica of the Agony** – derives from it being the place where Jesus came to pray with his disciples while awaiting Judas's kiss of betrayal (Matthew 26: 36–49, Mark 14: 32–45, Luke 22: 39–48); Jesus, unsurprisingly, being in a state of depression or "being in an agony", according to Luke. Another of Barluzzi's designs, the church is built over the ruins of two others: the Egeria dating from around 380 AD, and a Crusader basilica of around 1170. Above the entrance is a striking modern Byzantine-style mosaic arch while the rock in the nave is where Jesus is said to have prayed before being arrested. This, as well as parts of a mosaic floor, belongs to the fourth-century church. The basilica stands in the beautiful **Garden of Gethsemane** (the Church of St Mary Magdalene also claims that distinction), said to be two thousand years old, and full of flowers and ancient gnarled olive trees, one of which Judas may have hanged himself from. Before pressing on, you can take a break at the **Gethsemane Souvenir Shop**, to the right a little up the hill, and enjoy a cold drink at its outside tables. Nearby is the tomb of the Arab historian **Mujir al-Din al-Ulaymi**, who died in 1522 and whose detailed work is an invaluable source of information on the city of his time.

The Tomb of the Virgin and the Grotto of Gethsemane

Once you've made it to the bottom of the Mount of Olives, look to the right of the path for the **Tomb of the Virgin** (Mon–Sat 6–11.45am & 2.30–5pm), the supposed burial place of Mary. Writers of the late sixth century describe a church here but all the Crusaders found were ruins. The church was rebuilt in 1130 by Benedictines and taken over by Franciscans after the Crusaders left; since then Greeks, Armenians, Syrians, Copts, Abyssinians and Muslims have all had shares in it. To the right of the twelfth-century flight of marble steps is the **tomb of the Crusader Queen Melisande** who died in 1161; opposite it lies the vault of members of her son King Baldwin II's family and in the centre is a Byzantine crypt, partly cut out of the rock, which was once adorned with paintings. **Mary's stone tomb** lies to the right. The site is also venerated by Muslims since, on his night journey from Mecca to Jerusalem, the Prophet Mohammed is said to have spotted a light over Mary's tomb; the mihrab further along indicates the direction in which Mecca lies.

A short distance north of the tomb, the **Grotto of Gethsemane** (daily 8.30am–noon & 2.30–5pm) is a rival to the Church of All Nations (see opposite) as the spot where the disciples rested while Jesus prayed, and where Judas kissed him. The frequently restored cave contains traces of Byzantine mosaic floors, three new altars and frescoes. To walk to the Lions' Gate entrance to the Old City, turn right at the bottom of the hill along the Jericho Road and take the first left; buses and taxis from here will get you to central Jerusalem.

The Kidron Valley and the City of David

At the foot of the Mount of Olives, the **Kidron Valley** runs south past **Mount Ophel** and the excavations of the **City of David** to the west, and the Palestinian village of **Silwan** to the east, to join up with the Valley of Hinnom that skirts Mount Zion on the south side of the Old City. Three prominent monuments stand adjacent to each other beside the modern road that runs along the valley. Near to its junction with the Jericho Road at the foot of the Mount of Olives, the elaborate but curious bottle-shaped **Pillar of Absalom** dates from the first century AD, but is held to be the tomb of King David's rebellious son. Next to it is a tomb identified from its Hebrew inscription as that of the priestly **family of Hezir**, and next to that, with its pointed roof standing away from the rock, the **tomb of the prophet Zechariah**, whose image of the Day of the Lord inspired the Mount of Olives cemetery (see opposite). Bus #1 runs along the Ophel Road.

The City of David

Directly south of Mount Moriah, site of the Temple Mount, **Mount Ophel** is home to the **City of David** – the oldest part of Jerusalem, inhabited since the Early Canaanite period. Its biblical significance aside, the site is worth a visit for the extensive and important archeological excavations, some of which lie within the Dung Gate (see p.340), though the city that David made the capital of his kingdom of Judah occupies the upper slopes. Excavations began in the 1960s under the English archeologist Kathleen Kenyon; it was her discovery of Canaanite graves here that provided the earliest evidence of human habitation in the area – her books on the subject are still seminal works. The work of Israeli archeologists since 1978 has, over the years, been the subject of passionate protests by Orthodox Jews against what they regard as the desecration of ancient Jewish graves that may be in the area.

In all, no fewer than twenty-five strata of settlement have been revealed at the **City of David Archeological Garden** on Ophel Road (daily 9am–4pm; 5NIS), including the impressive remnants of Jerusalem's "Upper City", where the wealthy lived in luxury. A signposted path with explanatory signs and diagrams describing the significance of each structure takes you around the site. From the Upper City, you look over the massive stone walls of the base of the **eighteenth-century BC Canaanite Citadel** which served to defend the ancient Jebusite town against Joshua and was finally conquered some two hundred years later by King David, who brought the Ark of the Covenant into the city (II Samuel 6: 1–17) and made it his capital. There are remains, too, of the eighteen-metre-high stepped-stone foundations of **David's Fortress**, and of buildings destroyed in the Babylonian conquest of 586 BC, including the **burnt room**, and another which seems to have been a public archive – 53 clay seals (*bullae*) were found in it.

If you're exhausted after all this, the *David City Rest House* (subtitled *Under Green Trees*) is nearby, where under the shade of olive and lemon trees, you can sit and enjoy a mint tea, coffee or ice cream and look out over the neighbouring village of Silwan (see opposite) to the east.

SPRING OF GIHON, HEZEKIAH'S TUNNEL AND WARREN'S SHAFT

At the foot of Mount Ophel, 100m southeast of the City of David Archeological Garden, the gushing waters of the **Spring of Gihon** were the ancient lifeblood of Jerusalem and the most likely reason for the Jebusites building their city here in the first place. During the Assyrian siege in 701 BC, King Hezekiah took elaborate measures to protect the city's water supply and cut off that of its attackers', which involved blocking off the original spring and diverting its waters down to the west side of the City of David (II Chronicles 32: 30), and along a 512-metre-long underground tunnel beneath the wall of the city. **Hezekiah's Tunnel** (Sun–Thurs 8.30am–3pm, Fri 8.30pm–1pm) was carved out by two teams of rock hewers working simultaneously from both ends; they recorded their eventual meeting in the middle with the **Siloam Inscription** which tells how, "While there were still three cubits to go, the voice of a man [on the other side] calling to his workmates could be heard due to a cleft in the rock... and on the day the tunnel was driven through, the miners were working towards each other, pick against pick." The inscription was removed in Ottoman times, and is now in the Museum of the Ancient Orient in Istanbul, but you can still see where they met from the difference in levels of the roof and floor.

The non-claustrophobic can walk by candlelight or flashlight (bring your own), knee-deep in water, through the narrow, eerily impressive tunnel as it twists and turns through the hillside, to emerge blinking into daylight at the **Pool of Siloam** – the now reduced version of the pool where, as the Bible story goes, a blind man was cured after washing there on the instructions of Jesus (John 9: 8). Walled off from the tunnel a short way in at the sharp bend to the left, is the vertical shaft known as **Warren's Shaft** (Sun–Thurs 9am–5pm, Fri 9am–1pm; 7NIS). Named after its nineteenth-century discoverer Charles Warren, it is thought to have been driven through the rock by the Jebusites even earlier than Hezekiah's Tunnel, and may also have been used by David's emissary Joab to penetrate the city's defences (II Samuel 5: 8). You can enter this feat of aquatic engineering from the top, through an entrance in a renovated **Turkish building** at the foot of the City of David excavations. The building also houses a small **museum** where you can get a plan, maps and books to explain all, as well as taking a look at the small exhibit of pottery found at the site, a model of the Warren's Shaft water system, and colour photos of Captain Warren's expedition and the present excavations. A spiral stairway from the exhibition room leads to a stupendous rock-hewn tunnel descending to the mouth of the shaft – an incredibly deep well from where, if it's quiet enough, you can hear the distant gurgle of the running Gihon spring water.

Silwan

The village of **SILWAN**, whose name comes from biblical Siloam (Shiloah in Hebrew), has one monument of note: the **Tomb of Pharaoh's Daughter**. Easily mistaken for just another house, this five-metre-high cubic monolith is believed to date from the ninth to the seventh century BC and once had a pyramid-shaped roof. Silwan has recently been the scene of controversy involving Jewish settlers (see p.352).

Mount Scopus

Just beyond the Mount of Olives, **Mount Scopus** (reached through Wadi Joz on bus #4, #9 or #23 from West Jerusalem) with its marvellous views over Jerusalem and out across the Judean Desert, has been of vital strategic importance since Roman times. Forces under Cestius set up camp here at the beginning of the First Revolt in 66 AD before an abortive attack on Jerusalem, and four years later forces under Titus did the same when laying the siege that culminated in the final Roman victory over the city. The Crusaders camped here in 1099 before taking the city, as did the British after taking it in 1917. Although physically in East Jerusalem, Mount Scopus is spiritually – and in recent history – a part of the west. The northern part remained under Israeli control after the 1948 war, an isolated enclave maintained by fortnightly convoys under UN protection; the southern part was Jordanian, but the whole mount was a demilitarized zone, with a strip of no-man's-land between the two halves.

The mount is home to two important buildings: the fortress-like **Hebrew University**, which gives the impression that, should the need arise, it could disappear underground at the touch of a button, and **Hadassah Hospital** – a medical research and treatment centre of worldwide renown. Both moved out after 1948, but returned to much expanded grounds after 1967, and have since been joined by vast new government buildings. Nearby sites of more obvious interest to the visitor are the World War I **Commonwealth War Cemetery**, which lies near to the hospital, and, on the eastern edge of the university grounds, an **amphitheatre**, whose concerts and plays have magnificent **views** as far as the Mountains of Moab as a backdrop. It's also worth the extra climb to the top of the mount, to see the **biblical garden**. Founded in the 1920s, it contains samples of flora mentioned in the Bible such as saffron, sesame, figs and almonds and is tended today much as it would have been in biblical times, bar the unbiblical assistance of mechanical water sprinklers. On site is a reconstructed watchman's hut like those that stood on every farm in the area.

To the south, on what was Jordan's half of the Mount, the **Augusta Victoria Hospital** with its distinctive square tower is a landmark visible all over the city. Built in 1910, it was named after Kaiser Wilhelm's wife and was used as the residence of the British governor general after World War I. It now serves as the UNRWA hospital for the West Bank.

West Jerusalem

WEST JERUSALEM, the Israeli "New City", is indeed relatively new, its first inhabitants having moved out from the Old City less than a century and a half ago. But, in the ensuing years, and especially since 1967, it has grown tremendously, expanding with concentric rings of settlements. More prosperous and cosmopolitan than East Jerusalem, it's here you'll find most of the large shopping malls, the greatest range of shops and department stores, and most of what there is of the city's nightlife.

Mount Zion, adjoining the Old City, contains West Jerusalem's most venerable sites, including the Tomb of David and the reputed room of the Last Supper, but you'll have to venture further afield to the western suburbs to see the remainder of the highlights.

CENTRAL WEST JERUSALEM

ACCOMMODATION

Ben Yehuda (Jasmine) Hostel	1
Eyal	2
Faisal Hostel	3
Golden Jerusalem	4
HI Beit Bernstein Hostel	5
HI Davidka Hostel	6
Jerusalem Inn Guest House	7
Jerusalem Inn Hostel	8
Kikar Zion	9
Mercaz Habira	10
My Home	11
Noga	12
Notre Dame Hospice	13
Palatin	14
Palm Hostel	15
Ron	16
Sheraton	17
Zefania	18

EATING & DRINKING

7th Place	A
Al-Omaal	B
all-night bakery	C
all-night bakery	D
Alumah	E
Angelo's	F
Atara	G
Blue Hole	H
Bonkers Bagels	I
Cannabis	J
Cezanne (inside Artists' House)	K
Champs	L
Eucalyptus	M
Fink's	N
Galliano	O
HaTimani Falafel	P
Hen	Q
Ma'adan	R
Magic Fruit Juice	S
Marciano Baguette and Bali Baguette	T
Mike's	U
Misadonet	V
Mr Li's	W
Pampa Grill	X
Pepperoni's, Spaghettim and Aroma	Y
Pie Shop	Z
Pinnati	AA
Riff-Raff	BB
Secret Garden	CC
Strudel	DD
Tmol Shilshom	EE
Tutti-Frutti juice bar	FF
Underground	GG
Village Green	HH
Village Green	II
Yemenite Step	JJ
Zanzibar	KK

The hill of Givat Ram is home to the impressive **Israel Museum**, the **Bible Lands Museum**, and the **Knesset** – Israel's parliament, while further out on another hilltop location, **Yad VaShem** is Israel's moving tribute to the victims of the Holocaust.

Geographically, West Jerusalem falls into two sections: those parts of the city which developed as suburbs from the mid-nineteenth century until independence, and the new areas that have since grown up around them. Both have their points of interest, but the former are more aesthetically pleasing and fall into three basic types: traditional Jewish working-class zones like **Mahane Yehuda** and **Mea She'arim**; long-established and expensive Jewish enclaves like **Rehavia**; and former Arab areas such as **Talpiot**. All are easily accessible on regular buses from Jaffa Road or King George Street but while some are worth exploring in their own right, others can just be passed through on your way to the scattered sites of interest. Today, West Jerusalem is reeling under two connected pressures: exploding property prices and religion. Older neighbourhoods close to the centre of town are increasingly yuppified as prices take them beyond the reach of working people, a process fuelled by the influx of wealthy religious zealots from the US. Meanwhile, as the less wealthy, but even more religious *haredim*, faced with the biblical injunction, "go forth and multiply", move beyond their base in Mea Shearim, the more secular residents in those areas are opting to move out. The overall effect of all this is a West Jerusalem that is becoming ever more conservative and therefore increasingly polarized from the east.

Downtown West Jerusalem

The heart of West Jerusalem – the area around the Jaffa Road between the northwest corner of the Old City and its junction with King George Street – is where you'll find many of the big shops, most of the bars and restaurants, the **Jerusalem Municipal Tourist Office**, the main **post office**, buses to most suburbs, and sheruts to the coast. At night it may not exactly buzz, but there is definitely a gentle hum.

Forming its hub is the small plaza of **Zion Square**, 600m up the Jaffa Road from the corner of the Old City and dominated by the rather ugly *Kikar Zion* hotel, and the pedestrianized streets running off it. **Ben Yehuda Street** in particular is packed with cafés, restaurants and snack bars of every description. Once a rather old-fashioned shopping area, it has now become the haunt of buskers, jewellery artisans, flower and newspaper vendors, and, on occasion, raving latter-day prophets holding forth on the impending appearance of the messiah, the merits of expelling the Palestinians, and other such subjects, usually to general indifference. If you hang out here for a while, you might find yourself being asked the time by someone who is in fact a plain clothes police officer sizing you up – the area has been a favourite target for bombers since Abdel Khader al-Husseini's operatives (see p.126) planted a bomb here with the help of two British deserters in February 1948, which destroyed half the street and killed 54 people. Since 1971 there have been no fewer than twelve incidents, the worst of which, involving a bomb planted in a refrigerator in Zion Square, left fifteen people dead and 77 wounded.

Where Ben Yehuda meets **King George Street**, a distinctive and somewhat incongruous-looking clock arch and column northeast of the junction come from the Talitha Kumi Building, an orphanage and Arab girls' school that used to stand to its northwest. Parallel with King George Street to the west, **Shmuel HaNagid Street** has a few sites of interest. The **Artists' House** (Bet HaOmenim; Sun–Thur 10am–1pm & 4–7pm, Fri 10am–1pm, Sat 11am–2pm; free), owned by the Jerusalem Artists' Association, usually has exhibitions of work by local contemporary artists, as well as frequent concerts and lectures. Further south, the 1874 **Ratisbonne Monastery** was built in Italian style for Father Alphonse Ratisbonne, who founded the Fathers of Zion and Sisters of Zion orders of Roman Catholic monks and nuns. The **Yeshurun Synagogue** next door was built in 1936 as the central synagogue for West Jerusalem, and claims to be an example of the Bauhaus-inspired "International Style" of architecture (see p.82), although **Bet HaMa'alot**, an apartment building from the same era a little way back at the junction of King George Street with HaMa'alot Street, is a much better example of the school.

North to Mahane Yehuda and Nahla'ot

Heading northwest along the Jaffa Road from King George Street, you pass **Mashiah Borchoff House** at no. 64. Built in 1908 for a wealthy Uzbek merchant, it has a gateway topped by a pair of regal lions, and the portico is held up by Corinthian-style columns. Further on, at the corner of Jaffa Road and HaNeviim, is a monument notable only for its incorporation of a home-made "Davidka", a type of mortar that made up most of Israel's artillery at the beginning of the 1948 war (see p.242). **Mishkan Shmuel**, a little way north of here at 92 Jaffa Road, is a former immigrants' hostel and seminary set up in 1908 by American Rabbi Shmuel Levi; the sundial on the rather makeshift-looking facade serves to indicate the onset of Shabbat and religious festivals.

Across the Jaffa Road, the working-class district of **Mahane Yehuda** has a character of its own. Built to house Jewish immigrant workers, its chaotic maze of streets is crammed with minute houses of wildly differing character and little if any architectural integrity. The market here is famous both for the quality of its produce and the right-wing views of its stallholders. In July 1997, a bomb placed here by Islamic fundamentalists with even more right-wing views killed fifteen people. Just south of Mahane Yehuda, the **Nahla'ot** area is a predominantly Sephardi neighbourhood, increasingly populated by students and artists attracted by the cheap accommodation. Its narrow alleys are crowded and poor, but full of life and fascinating to wander around, while the contrast with the stolid respectability of nearby Rehavia is striking.

On and off Rehov HaNeviim

From the Davidka Monument at its junction with the Jaffa Road, **Rehov HaNeviim** (the Street of the Prophets), leads east across the Green Line to the Damascus Gate passing en route a number of impressive historic buildings whose history is recounted on blue plaques on their facades. One to look out for is the Rothschild hospital at the corner of HaRav Kook. When it opened in 1888 with money donated by Baron Rothschild, it became the first Jewish hospital outside the Old City.

HaRav Kook Street, running south off HaNeviim to the Jaffa Road, is named after the first Ashkenazi Chief Rabbi, who took up residence at no. 7 in 1902. Next to his former home, **Ticho House** (Sun, Mon, Wed & Thurs 10am–5pm, Tues 10am–10pm, Fri 10am–2pm; free) belonged to artist Anna Ticho and her husband, philanthropic eye-doctor Abraham Ticho. Ticho studied ophthalmology in Vienna before being sent to Jerusalem in 1912 by a German Zionist organization to open an eye clinic. His cousin, Anna, came too and they married the same year, buying the house in 1924 and running a clinic from it for rich and poor alike, until Abraham's death in 1960. The house contains many of Anna's paintings – mostly quite abstract watercolours of Jerusalem scenery – some of Abraham's correspondence, and his collection of lamps for the Jewish festival of lights, Hanukkah.

North off HaNeviim, at no. 11 Ethiopia Street, the former home of yet another famous local resident, Eliezar Ben Yehuda, the inventor of Modern Hebrew, stands opposite the small round **Ethiopian Church** (daily March–Sept 7am–6pm, Oct–Feb 8am–5pm; free), dating from 1874, and flying the red, green and gold banner of Ethiopia. Around it are the residences of monks and nuns of the church. It's worth a quick look inside the church to see the carpets, icons and Ethiopian-style furnishings and paintings. Back on HaNeviim, the **Ethiopian Consulate** at no. 38 has mosaics on its facade quoting in Ghees (classical Ethiopian) the words of Revelation 5: 5: "Behold the Lion of the tribe of Judah", and depicting said lion, symbol of the Ethiopian royal family, who claimed descent from King Solomon and the Queen of Sheba (hence the basis of Haile Selassie's Rastafarian status as messiah). As you approach Hail HaHandassa at the eastern end of HaNeviim, the road sign pointing north to Ramallah and south to Bethlehem (both on the West Bank) is the only pointer you'll get to the change that lies on the other side. As you cross the Green Line here, suddenly it's Arabic being spoken around you, the shop signs are in Arabic and the people are wearing *keffiyas* instead of *kippas*; while ahead is the very Islamic Dome of the Rock.

Just to the north, on the west side of Hail HaHandassa, the **Tourjeman Post Museum** at no. 4 (Sun–Thurs 9am–5pm, Fri 9am–1pm; 7NIS), commemorates Jerusalem's partition and reunification and is designed to show parties of Israeli schoolkids and soldiers "what a divided city looks like". The distinctive pink stone building was the private home of the Baramki family until their eviction in 1948 when the house became a frontier post separating Israeli and Jordanian forces and overlooking the former **Mandelbaum Gate** crosspoint, through which UN personnel, diplomats, pilgrims and convoys to the Israeli Hebrew University enclave on Mount Scopus were allowed to pass – you can still see the bullet holes it sustained during the fighting in 1967. Inside, there's a useful, building-by-building **model of Jerusalem** showing the borders as they were from 1948 until 1967, and an exhibition of photographs, maps and documents portraying the history of Jerusalem from Mandate times to the city's 1967 reunification, together with a four-minute film showing the Israeli view of the events of 1967. However, a few clues point to a city not as unified as the museum would like to make out: the labels are in Hebrew and English only.

The Russian Compound

Just north of the Jaffa Gate, in the area between the Jaffa Road and Shivtei Yisra'el Street, Jerusalem's new **City Hall** is part of a complex of much older buildings, some dating to the late nineteenth century, that now form part of the municipality offices. Within the complex, the building at 2 Safra Square used to house the Russian Consulate, while just to the north a turn west off Shivtei Yisra'el takes you into the **Russian Compound** proper, where you'll find some attractive Russian-built edifices from the late nineteenth century, a museum dedicated to the Jewish paramilitaries of the Mandate, and some of Jerusalem's more interesting drinking holes (see p.384). Its present name derives from its purchase in 1860 by Tsar Alexander II to provide services and accommodation for the twenty thousand or so Russian pilgrims who visited the city every year, virtually turning it into a walled city in its own right. Legend has it the Assyrian army camped on this site when preparing to attack Jerusalem in 701 BC, and that here too Titus planned to destroy the city.

During the Mandate, the whole area bounded by Shivtei Yisra'el, Heleni HaMalka and the Jaffa Road, with the Russian Compound at its heart, was a fortified administrative area containing the vital installations of British rule and nicknamed "Bevingrad" by Jews after the hated British Foreign Secretary Ernest Bevin. You get a hint of what Bevingrad was like by walking along Heleni HaMalka Street, still fenced off on its southern side with railings and barbed wire. When the British moved out, the Haganah, with the aid of sympathetic British and Jewish government employees managed to get hold of the exact timetable of withdrawal and move in to take this strategic area immediately on its vacation and ahead of the Arabs. On the right is the former Central Prison, originally a hostel for female Russian pilgrims and now an

Underground Prisoners Museum (Sun–Thurs 8am–4pm, Fri 10am–1pm; 8NIS), dedicated to Jewish paramilitary activity during the Mandate. Exhibits include original cells and a gallows; eight prisoners were executed by the British here, and two blew themselves up in 1947.

Around the corner, the road passes the 1863 **Duhovnia Russian Mission Building**, now a courthouse, on the way to the impressive green-domed **Russian Cathedral**, opened in 1872 (Mon–Fri 9am–1pm), and the notorious **"Al-Muscobiya" police station**, denounced as a torture centre in a 1977 exposé in the London *Sunday Times*. During the Intifada, most of those arrested in East Jerusalem were brought here and it still serves as an interrogation centre for Palestinian detainees – you'll often see groups of people waiting outside to be allowed to visit their relatives.

High on the hill just east of the City Hall complex, across Shivtei Yisra'el Street, the prominent landmark of the white stone **Notre Dame de France** (at its most impressive at night when floodlit) offers great views over the Old City and beyond from its terrace café. Built in 1887 by the Assumptionist Fathers, this massive building, with a central doorway topped by two towers, houses the offices of the papal representative to the city, a church, a monastery, an upmarket hotel (see "Accommodation", p.317) and Jerusalem's finest French restaurant, *La Rotisserie*, with Parisian prices to match (see "Restaurants", p.382). In the 1948 war, Notre Dame was on the front line, and an important Israeli observation post.

Mea She'arim and Bukharia

Founded in 1875 and lying 200m to the north of HaNeviim, the quarter of **Mea She'arim** is home to the ultra-orthodox *haredi* community and retains a curiously East European feel with backstreets that could have been lifted straight out of a pre-Holocaust *shtetl*. Many of its bearded and sidelocked male residents still dress in the Jewish fashion of sixteenth-century Poland, with a belt around the waist of their long black caftans to divide the holy upper half of the body from the profane lower half; on holy days, they replace their round felt hats with fur-trimmed ones (*shtreimals*). Different styles of dress and hair arrangement denote different sects and the women of the quarter wear long sleeves and either wigs or head scarves. You'll see synagogues and *yeshivot* everywhere (each sect has its own), shops selling religious items abound, and signs ask visitors to dress modestly – a request to be taken seriously (even long trousers on women are frowned on). Photography here can also cause offence, as can smoking on Shabbat, when the whole area is closed to traffic. Some of the inhabitants, particularly the members of the *Neturei Carta* movement, do not even acknowledge the State of Israel which, until the Messiah arrives, they regard as profane.

From Mea She'arim Street, the district's main thoroughfare, Strauss Street leads uphill into the district of **Bukharia**, founded at the end of the nineteenth century by Jewish immigrants from Uzbekistan. The area east of the main road (which becomes Yekhezkel Street as it goes over the hill) is full of synagogues dating from that period, some of them (such as the one at 24 Yoel) very tiny indeed. Although many have been taken over by the *haredim* spilling over from Mea She'arim, there are still some that practise the Uzbek rite. Look out, too, for the colourful little *shtetl*-style **market** at the end of Bukharim Street which resembles something out of *Fiddler on the Roof*. Most of the district's houses are small and quaint, but as many of the Uzbek immigrants were prosperous merchants, you'll find some larger residences across Yekhezkel, notably **Bet Sefer Shafitsar** (the "Palace"), at 19 Ezra. Used in the 1940s by the Haganah to train new recruits and as a base for actions against the British, it's now sadly neglected, but nonetheless magnificent in its palatial architecture. A couple of blocks downhill, the **Mokshell Centre** on David Hefez Square is another old mansion in much better shape, and now used by the city's social services department.

Yekhezkel Street leads onto Shmuel HaNavi with the village of Nabi Samwil (see p.429) on the skyline beyond. A couple of hundred metres up on the right, Sanhedrin Street (buses #10, 16 and 39) takes you past a public garden planted with fragrant pines and containing a number of first-and-second century rock-cut tombs, the last and most impressive of which is the **Tomb of the Sanhedrin**, the council of rabbis who consti-tuted the highest court of Jewish canon law. The tomb's imposing square doorway is topped by a lintel carved with reliefs of fruit and foliage. Inside, the catacombs extend to three levels, but are unfortunately closed to the public – the graffiti sprayed onto the rock is a good indication as to why. The tomb gave its name to the surrounding neigh-bourhood, **Sanhedria**.

Nahalat Shiv'a and Mamilla

The pedestrianized Yoel Salomon, branching off Zion Square, is the heart of **Nahalat Shiv'a**, one of the oldest districts of West Jerusalem, founded in 1869. The district's small houses were each built around a patio with a cistern for water storage, and set the pattern for subsequent houses in West Jerusalem. The cisterns proved their worth dur-ing the siege of 1948, when the Arabs had control of West Jerusalem's water supply and were able to shut it off: luckily, the local Haganah commander-in-chief, David Shaltiel, had the foresight to order all the new city's cisterns filled before the British pulled out, enabling West Jerusalem to hold out, albeit with strict water rationing. Since then, local residents have resisted all attempts by City Hall to knock down their quaint little hous-es and replace them with skyscrapers; in 1988, they finally won out when the council decided to restore the neighbourhood.

Near the southern end of Yoel Salomon, on its western side, a small side street, Bet HaKnesset, leads to the **Museum of Italian Jewish Art** (Sun–Tues 9am–2pm, Wed 9am–5pm, Thurs 9am–1pm; 10NIS), the highlight of which is an ornate eighteenth-century synagogue transported lock, stock and barrel from Congliano Veneto in northern Italy in 1952 along with its community, who still follow the ancient Italian rite of worship. The museum's other room contains some fine pieces of Judaica (see box on p.368), though enthusiasts may be better off saving themselves for the Wolfson Museum (see below). Bet HaKnesset Street leads onto Hillel Street, across which is **Independence Park**, the city's gay cruising ground, at whose eastern end, where the trees and undergrowth begin, lies the pre-1948 Muslim cemetery, **Mamilla**, a corruption of the Arabic *Ma'man Allah* (God's sanctuary). Among the graves, many of which have been desecrated or vandalized, is the domed cube of the **Zawiya Kubakiya**, the tomb of Mamluk Emir Aidughi Kubaki, governor of Safed and Aleppo before being exiled to Jerusalem and buried here on his death in 1289 AD. In the centre of the graveyard the now disused **Mamilla Pool** is typical of the cisterns excavated to supply water to the medieval city.

The **tax museum**, just across Agron Street to the south (Sun, Tues & Thurs 1–4pm, Mon & Wed 10am–noon; free), is as scintillating as it sounds, cluttered with tax stamps and knick-knacks often only tangentially related to the subject. But the building itself has a little history: as CID HQ under the Mandate, it was bombed by the Irgun in 1944, shortly after they ended their wartime truce with the British. Opposite, the Palace Hotel was built for the Grand Mufti's Supreme Muslim Council in 1929 as a luxury hotel, and now houses the Ministry of Industry and Trade. To the west, Agron Street meets King George Street, where the rather ugly **Great Synagogue** stands at no. 54. The main feature of interest here is the **Wolfson Museum of Judaica** (Sun–Thurs 9am–1pm; 3NIS) – a collection of Jewish religious items from communities worldwide (see box on p.368) that includes some beautiful pieces and rates as one of the best collections in Israel, and indeed the world.

JUDAICA

The practice of the Jewish religion involves the use of a number of ritual objects or "**Judaica**", whose design has become an art form in itself, somewhat akin to jewellery-making. Many of the items are made of silver, often decorated with inlay work, filigree, or even precious stones, and though their style varies from community to community and epoch to epoch, the range remains more or less constant. Many of these pieces of Judaica are used in every observant Jewish home, and widely sold in shops throughout Israel, but the most magnificent pieces are those used in the synagogue, in particular to decorate the scrolls of the Torah.

OBJECTS USED IN THE HOME

Mezuza A box containing passages from the Torah written out by hand on parchment and nailed to the doorposts of every Jewish home (see p.503).

Menora The seven- or nine-branched candelabra that has become a symbol of the Jewish faith. The nine-branched version (correctly called a *Hanukkiya*) is used to celebrate the festival of Hanukkah, when one candle is lit on the first day, two on the second and so on up to eight – the candle in the middle is used to light the others.

Sabbath candlesticks The woman of the house lights two candles just before nightfall on Friday to welcome in the Sabbath, and the same is done on the eve of festivals. Every Jewish home has a pair of candlesticks for the purpose.

Wine goblet Each Sabbath and festival is welcomed with a blessing over wine (*kiddush*), which is passed around the household for each member to take a sip, with one or more goblets kept especially for the purpose.

Havdala set The Sabbath is bid farewell with a ceremony called *havdala*, which requires another blessing over wine, the lighting and extinguishing of a plaited candle, and a spice shaker for the participants to smell.

Passover plate When the family celebrate the Passover feast, a dish is used which has places for all of the special foods used in the service, including green herbs, bitter herbs, a symbolic meat offering, a roasted egg, and an apple and nut confection called *haroset*.

OBJECTS USED IN THE SYNAGOGUE

Sefer Torah A parchment scroll containing the entire Torah written out by hand without errors or corrections. The scroll is held on two rollers and gradually rolled from one to the other as the Torah is read out in weekly instalments in the synagogue. Ashkenazim decorate the scroll with a velvet cover hung around with a silver plate and each roller surmounted with a silver cap usually hung with bells. Sephardim keep the scroll in a case surmounted with a silver crown. To read the Torah, a pointer called a *yad* ("hand") is used, which is indeed usually in the form of a pointing hand.

Talitt A white prayer shawl, bordered with black or blue, donned by men when praying in the synagogue.

Tefilin Boxes containing biblical passages on parchment (see p.503).

King David Street and Yemin Moshe

King David Street runs from Mamilla Street south toward Yemin Moshe, passing a number of sights worth checking out on the way, first of which is the Hebrew Union College. Inside the college (at the far end of the courtyard, on the right), the **Skirball Museum** (Sun–Thurs 10am–4pm, Sat 10am–2pm; free), is a small exhibition of artefacts from Tel Dan (see p.253), Gezer (see p.110) and Aro'er (see p.280), with explanations of their history and archeology, though it's probably of more interest if you've actually visited the sites. The museum is small but very well laid out, with photographs of the sites, accounts of their history and excavation, and finds including pots, figurines, an ancient dice and a ninth-century BC inscription that contains the earliest known extra-biblical reference to King David.

A little further down the street, two of the most impressive buildings in West Jerusalem face each other. With its imposing tower and cupolas, the **YMCA Three Arches Hotel** is a Jerusalem landmark. Built by the same company that constructed the Empire State building, its magnificent lobby, with vaulting reminiscent of Crusader constructions, is well worth visiting – you can also climb the ninety-metre bell tower (3NIS) for magnificent views of the city, but only in groups of two or more since one visitor threw himself from the top. The grandiose **King David Hotel** opposite (for details on staying here see "Accommodation", p.318), is the best in the land, built for the Jewish Egyptian Mosseri family in 1931. Former guests include Churchill, Sadat and Haile Selassie and other assorted royals, presidents and film stars. Its south wing was bombed by the Irgun in 1946, when it was the HQ of the British CID. Irgun leader Menahem Begin later claimed that a warning had been given by phone but British sources deny receiving one; whatever the truth, 91 people died in the attack. At the end of Abba Siqra Street, just south of the hotel, steps into a public garden lead down to what is supposed to be **King Herod's Family Tomb**. The beautifully constructed four-chambered tomb is empty, and it is not clear who was originally interred here, but it definitely dates from the correct period. While it may have housed his family, Herod himself is more widely believed to be buried at Herodion near Bethlehem (see p.405).

Two hundred metres south of the tomb, Mishkenot Shaananim (Dwellings of Tranquillity), was the first Jewish quarter to be built outside the Old City. The cloister-like living quarters, with a turret roof and Star of David over the entrance, were constructed in 1860 with money bequeathed by Judah Touro, a resident of New Orleans. Sir Moses Montefiore, the Jewish English philanthropist, was appointed executor of his will and subsequently bought the adjoining land, when the area became known as **Yemin Moshe** (Moshe being Hebrew for Moses). Its red-roofed town houses and cottages built of Jerusalem stone are some of the loveliest, and most expensive, houses in Jerusalem but the area's most striking building is the narrow stone **windmill** that Montefiore had built to provide flour for the settlement, although it was never actually used for this purpose. It served as an important Israeli observation post in 1948 and now houses a small **museum** (Sun–Thurs 9am–4pm, Fri 9am–1pm; admission free) dedicated to Montefiore's life and work. Born in Leghorn, Italy, but brought up in London, Montefiore was President of the Board of Deputies (the representative committee of Britain's Jewish community) most of the time between 1835 and 1884, and was knighted by Queen Victoria almost as soon as she ascended the throne. A prosperous businessman, he was always keen to help Jewish communities under threat abroad, often enlisting the support of the British government, and made seven visits to Palestine, donating generously to aid the development of its Jewish community.

Liberty Bell Garden, a large park across King David Street from Yemin Moshe, houses a replica of the original Philadelphia bell, the symbol of North American freedom. Across the valley from Yemin Moshe in the opposite direction is the Jaffa Gate, with a new plaza built outside it over the main road and, to its south, the modern "**artists' street**" – James Felt Lane. Beyond it lies the site of the **Sultan's Pool**; the sultan in question being Suleiman the Magnificent who repaired the 170m by 67m reservoir in the sixteenth century while rebuilding the Old City walls. It's now the **Merrill Hassenfeld Amphitheatre** and one of the biggest venues for outdoor concerts in the country. Suleiman also had a drinking fountain, called the **Sultan's Sabil**, installed just south of the pool on the Hebron Road, across from which is the rather more modern **Cinematheque**, Israel's premier film centre (see p.385).

The road continues to Bethlehem and Hebron, but a right at the next stoplight onto David Remez Street takes you past the **Khan Theatre**, housed in an early nineteenth-century caravanserai, and the **British Consulate**, looking rather like an outpost from the Khyber Pass. Sitting to your left all the way round, **St Andrew's Church** belongs to the Presbyterian Church of Scotland and proudly flies the Scottish flag, which is also of course the cross of Saint Andrew; it was built to commemorate Britain's victory over the Ottoman Turks in World War I. To its north, and heading back towards Yemin Moshe is an impressive modern **fountain**, featuring a fine pride of lions gushing water from their mouths.

Talbiya and around

West of the Liberty Bell Garden, Jabotinsky Street takes you into the **Talbiya** neighbourhood, with its beautiful houses and gardens dating from Mandate times, where both Jews and Palestinians lived side by side until the events of 1948. After 500m, Jabotinsky leads into HaNassi Street, with the **President's Residence** on the left. Continuing round onto Chopin Street, you pass the **LA Mayer Memorial Museum for Islamic Art** at 2 HaPalmah (Sun, Mon, Wed & Thurs 10am–5pm, Tues 4–8pm, Fri & Sat 10am–2pm; 12NIS), which contains an attractive and well laid-out collection of mainly seventeenth- and eighteenth-century pottery, glass, calligraphy, miniatures, woodwork, textiles, jewellery and ivory carving from as far afield as Egypt, Syria, Iraq, India and, above all, Iran (though Palestinian artefacts are conspicuous by their absence). Look out also for the fascinating collection of antique clocks and watches, mainly from eighteenth- and nineteenth-century Europe.

To the north of Talbiya, hidden away between nos. 10 and 12 Alfasi Street, the **Tomb of Jason** is a restored, pyramid-roofed, rock-cut tomb from the Hasmonean period. It belonged to the Sadducean high-priestly family of an Egyptian naval commander called Jason, who were expelled from Jerusalem by the Seleucids in 172 BC, but allowed back by the Hasmoneans under Alexander Jannaeus. The last burial here was in 30 AD. Unfortunately, you can't go inside, but the little garden above is a good spot to take a rest, with not another tourist in sight.

Mount Zion

> *They that trust in the Lord shall be as Mount Zion, which cannot be removed but abideth for ever.*
>
> Psalm 125: 1

Irremoveable it may be, but that didn't prevent **MOUNT ZION**, recognizable today by the distinctive conical roof of Dormition Abbey, from being separated on two occasions from the Old City adjoining it to the north. The Madaba Map (see p.343), shows the mount inside the city walls, but when Suleiman the Magnificent ordered the walls rebuilt in the mid-sixteenth century, his engineers somehow left Mount Zion outside – a mistake for which, it is said, they paid with their lives. This separation was enforced from 1948 to 1967 by the Israel-Jordan armistice line. Separate or not, however, Mount Zion, once synonymous with the city as a whole, and by extension with the whole country, lent its name to the Zionist movement; it was only two days before declaring independence that the Jewish state's founders finally settled on the name Israel rather than Zion.

The Mount is traditionally associated with **King David**, who is said to be buried here, and with events in the life of Jesus and the disciples, particularly the Last Supper. Though strictly speaking in West Jerusalem, the mount is most logically explored at the same time as Mount Ophel (see p.359), or the Old City's Armenian Quarter (see p.336).

The easiest approach is through the **Zion Gate** in the Old City's southwest corner, from where it's only 100m to Dormition Abbey, but it can also be reached via the Dung Gate, or from the Jaffa Gate, heading south on the Hebron Road and taking a left up the hill opposite the Sultan's Pool. Buses #1 and #2 go round Mount Zion on their way between the Jaffa Gate and the Dung Gate.

Dormition Abbey

Mount Zion's most prominent landmark is the black, conical roof of the **Dormition Abbey** (daily 8am–noon & 2–6pm) at the top of the hill. This attractive white stone building, erected in 1900, is traditionally believed to be on the site of Mary's death, an event marked by a mausoleum in the bright modern crypt, decorated with twelve columns. The church itself is round and uncluttered, giving a strong feeling of lightness and space. Its six round chapels are decorated in gold, and it also features an impressive mosaic floor, and, above the main altar, a delightful golden mosaic of the Madonna and Child. Remains of a mosaic floor from the Byzantine basilica that previously stood here are kept under a glass cover in the courtyard, though the reflection off the glass makes them impossible to see. There's a **cafeteria** serving light refreshments, and a bookshop with a selection of maps and (mostly religious) literature.

The Coenaculum and Tomb of David

Down the hill to the right and virtually in the shadow of the Abbey, the **Coenaculum** (from the Latin *Cenaca* meaning supper room; 8.30am–sunset, closed Friday afternoon; free), is reputedly the room in which the last supper took place. It is reached through a doorway with an Ottoman inscription above it and a red and white "Enter" sign next to it; inside, go up the stairs to the left. Somewhat smaller than the one depicted in Leonardo da Vinci's famous painting, the room also has pillars in the middle which might have made it difficult for Jesus and his disciples to have sat around a table. However, its authenticity is hardly an issue since, beautiful and peaceful as it is, and regardless of whether or not it stands on the site of the last supper, the room is actually a Crusader contruction, with characteristic Gothic arches. Part of a Franciscan monastery until 1552, it was then made into a mosque by the Ottomans, who added a mihrab and some beautiful coloured glass windows.

From the Coenaculum, turn right up the stairs by the minaret for the **roof**, from where there are views across the Kidron Valley to the Mount of Olives and beyond. Turn left and down the stairs for the **Tomb of David** (Sat–Thurs 8am–6pm, Fri 8am–2pm, closing one hour earlier in winter). According to the Old Testament (I Kings 2: 10), David was buried on the eastern hill of the city; this room, a bare chamber containing a simple cenotaph draped with green velvet, was declared his burial place in the tenth century AD. Its importance to Israelis increased between 1948 and 1967 when, with the Old City in Jordanian hands and the Western Wall out of bounds, the tomb became an alternative site of Jewish pilgrimage. Next to it and beneath the Coenaculum is the empty room where Jesus supposedly washed his disciples' feet after the last supper. In a room next to David's Tomb, the **King David Museum** (in theory Sun–Thurs 8am–6pm, Fri 8am–2pm; donation expected) is a curious Aladdin's Cave of a place, with a hotch-potch of archeological finds from Mount Zion, pieces of Judaica and other assorted artefacts.

Continuing through the medieval cloisters of the building housing David's Tomb and out the other side, you come to the memorial **Chamber of the Holocaust** (Sun–Thurs 8.30am–5pm, Fri 8.30am–3pm; 10NIS) – also easily reached from the Zion Gate by going straight ahead and bearing left at the Franciscan monastery. Its walls are covered with plaques commemorating over two thousand Jewish communities destroyed by the Nazis, and there is a chilling collection of Holocaust relics such as objects (including lampshades, bags and jackets) made from destroyed Bibles or human skin, and bars of soap made from human fat. The chamber also contains an exhibition on contemporary anti-Semitism, featuring anti-Semitic literature from around the world, and, in the main hall, a black stone memorial etched with the names of all the concentration and death camps.

Schindler's grave and St Peter in Gallicantu

Across the main road to the south of David's Tomb and the Holocaust Memorial, the Christian cemetery just below Mount Zion houses the **tomb of Oskar Schindler**, the Holocaust's most famous "righteous gentile", who managed to save hundreds of Jews from Hitler's death camps, and whose efforts were made into a film by Steven Spielberg – *Schindler's List* – based on Thomas Keneally's 1982 Booker Prize-winning novel, *Schindler's Ark*. Reduced to poverty after the war, Schindler was brought to Israel for burial through the efforts of some of those he had rescued.

A couple of hundred metres down the hill on the eastern slope of Mount Zion stands the rather pretty white stone **Church of Saint Peter in Gallicantu** (Mon–Sat 8.30am–noon & 2–5pm), built in 1931 on the former site of Byzantine and Crusader structures. Jesus is believed to have been imprisoned here by the High Priest Caiaphas; this is where Peter three times denied knowing Him, thus fulfilling the prophecy, "Before the cock crow, thou shalt deny me thrice" (Matthew 26: 75). At the entrance, the view from the terrace out over the City of David and the valleys of Jerusalem is another unforgettable one. As you enter the church, check the Byzantine **mosaics** to your right, discovered during restoration work in 1992, one of which was damaged in the eighth century by iconoclasts, who smashed all the pictures. The modern church is decorated in blue, with lovely mosaics and a beautiful stained-glass cross in the roof depicting God enthroned on high. Further sections of the original fifth-century church are preserved in the crypt, which leads out to the garden (from where steep Roman steps lead down to the Gihon Spring; see p.360), and further down to underground caves where some speculate that Peter and John were held (Acts 5: 19–42) for preaching at the Temple following the resurrection. Also here, the "Sacred Pit" is a dungeon excavated in 1889 where Jesus is said to have been held overnight while awaiting trial by Caiaphas and the Sanhedrin. Three Byzantine crosses are engraved on the walls of a hole from the ceiling of the pit to the floor of the crypt above.

Givat Ram

The hill of **Givat Ram**, reached by buses #9, #17 and #24, marks the western extent of the older parts of West Jerusalem. Here, solid urbanization gives way to grass and trees spreading up from HaNassi Ben and Haim Hazaz to create a green and pleasant area in which to relax in between checking out the attractions. These include a trio of museums, most importantly the massive **Israel Museum**, and also Israel's parliament, **the Knesset**.

Monastery of the Cross

In the valley below Givat Ram, the striking **Monastery of the Cross** (daily 10am–1.30pm) is a massive pink stone building topped by a dome and clock tower and founded in the eleventh century on the site where, according to legend, the tree from which Jesus's cross was made grew. The monastery has been Greek Orthodox since the seventeenth century, but the presence of Georgian inscriptions inside point to the nature of its earlier occupants. The courtyard, shaded by peach and lemon trees and vines, is overlooked by the wooden doors of 400 monks' cells, though the only resident nowadays is the Superior who will welcome you and show you around. A massive metal-plated, wooden door leads into the church, which is shaped like a Greek cross; its walls are covered with **frescoes** – many of them three or four hundred years old – showing events in the life of Christ, Old Testament figures and early Christian saints. Behind the altar screen separating the sanctuary from the main body of the church (as in all Orthodox churches), a small shrine marks the site of the tree from which the cross was cut.

Israel Museum

On the hill above the monastery, the prestigious **Israel Museum** (Sun, Mon, Wed & Thurs 10am–5pm, Tues 4–10pm but Shrine of the Book 10am–10pm, Fri 10am–2pm, Sat 10am–4pm, Sun closed; 26NIS, ticket also valid at Rockefeller Museum within a week) has collections ranging from ancient pottery to modern art, and is an absolute must for anyone with an interest in the country's archeological finds and the heritage of Jewish art. The museum is, in fact, five separate exhibitions all housed in a series of spacious, interconnecting modern buildings.

To the left of the main lobby, the **Samuel Bronfman Archaeological Museum** contains a well-arranged and fascinating collection of finds from the Canaanite to the biblical periods, including an extraordinary vase in the shape of a human head dating from the Middle Canaanite period (1750–1500 BC), the stone tablet from Caesarea bearing the name of Pontius Pilate (see p.163), and a city gate from Hazor. The material culture and folk art of the different ethnic groups living in Israel are displayed in the **Jewish Ethnography** section, next to which you'll find an exhibit of jewellery and costumes that extends further afield to include examples from Jewish communities around the world. Upstairs, the Jewish Ceremonial Art exhibit has a large collection of treasured pieces of Judaica from all over the world including Jewish costumes and a wealth of silver ornaments used to adorn scrolls of the Torah. At the end of the wing, there's even a reconstructed seventeenth-century synagogue from Italy, and a German *sukkah* (open-roofed structure for eating during the Festival of Tabernacles or Succot) that survived the Holocaust.

The **Bezalel National Museum** contains a permanent display of modern art which includes lesser-known but still impressive works by Cézanne, Gauguin, Picasso, van Gogh and of course Chagall (see box on p.377). The museum's children's section has an auditorium and workshops for six- to eighteen-year-olds to experiment with painting, modelling or photography. The artistic theme continues outside in the extensive **Billy Rose Sculpture Garden**, with works by sculptors such as Rodin, Picasso and Henry Moore; all of which are beautifully illuminated on Tuesday nights.

The showpiece of the museum, however, is the **Shrine of the Book**, built to house the **Dead Sea Scrolls** after their removal from the Palestine Archaeological Museum and featuring a distinctive white dome shaped like the lid of one of the jars in which they were discovered. Believed to have been written by the Essenes, a monastic sect who inhabited the area around Qumran where they were found (see p.261), the scrolls are some 2000 years old; the oldest of them, the complete **Book of Isaiah**, is a full thousand years older than any other biblical text in existence. Other ancient scripts, including letters and documents dating from the Second Revolt of 135 AD, are housed on the lower level, together with some interesting domestic finds, such as house keys, utensils and glassware, that provide an insight into the everyday life at the time of the revolt.

More museums

Across the street from the Israel Museum, and just as worthwhile, the **Bible Lands Museum** (Sun, Mon, Tues & Thurs 9.30am–5.30pm, Wed summer 9.30am–9.30pm, winter 1.30–9.30pm, Fri 9.30am–2pm, Sat 11am–3pm; 20NIS) concentrates on the ancient history of the Middle East and the Eastern Mediterranean. Its collection of archeological finds from different cultures of the region in biblical times is arranged in chronological order to give an overview of the whole region at each period, rather than treating each culture individually – an interesting and enlightening approach that helps to illustrate how the various cultures interconnected and influenced each other. The museum contains some stupendous objects, ranging from tiny seals and scarabs to massive sarcophagi and exquisite ivory carvings. One of the latest acquisitions (displayed in the "Israel in Egypt" gallery) is a collection of limestone **canopic jars** from an ancient Egyptian tomb, each designed to hold a different mummified organ, and topped with the head of a different Egyptian god.

For a change from history and archeology, continue on to the smaller and more hands-on **Bloomfield Science Museum** (Mon, Wed & Thurs 10am–6pm, Tues 10am–8pm, Fri 10am–1pm, Sat 10am–3pm; 20NIS), just up the road on Derekh Ruppin. In its airy, modern building you'll find lots of moving interactive exhibits – especially fun for kids.

The Knesset

Across Derekh Ruppin from the museums **the Knesset**, Israel's one-chamber parliament (enquiries ☎02/675 3333) occupies an understated cubic building whose simplicity and human scale avoid the pomposity or monolithic authoritarianism of so many seats of government. In front of the entrance stands the symbol of the State, the seven-branched *menorah* (this one donated by the British parliament) and a flame on a small monument, burning in remembrance of those fallen in battle. Prominent in the entrance hall is the image of the founder of political Zionism, Theodor Herzl, and **Chagall's triple tapestry and mosaics**. The tapestries, depicting God's creation of the world, the Exodus from Egypt, and Jerusalem are spectacularly colourful. Guided tours leave from the foyer on Sunday and Thursday regularly between 8.30am and 2.30pm, or, if you want to see the Knesset at work, you could sit in on one of the sessions which take place on Monday, Tuesday and Wednesday (in Hebrew of course); no fee, just join the queue. Note that for both the tours and sessions you will need to take your passport.

The 120-seat Knesset is elected on the purest form of **proportional representation** – the party list – in which voters choose a political party but not a candidate, and parties get seats in more or less exactly the proportion of the vote that they receive. This system has two main problems: first, no party ever has an overall majority, and coalition-building therefore involves handouts from the pork barrel (or kosher equivalent thereof), mainly to religious parties, who always seem to end up holding the balance of power; and second, Israelis do not have their own representative or MP, with Knesset members responsible only to their parties. To free the executive from some of the instability created by this system, the Prime Minister is now elected separately, while, on the positive side, PR does ensure representation to most political groups in the country, and to almost everyone who votes.

Adjacent to the Knesset, the **Wohl Rose Park** is filled with myriad varieties of the flower, worth stopping to admire even if you're not a connoisseur.

Mount Herzl and Yad VaShem

The **tomb of Theodor Herzl**, founder of Zionism, adorns a large pleasant park (daily: summer 8am–6.30pm, winter 8am–5pm) on **Mount Herzl**, 2km west of Givat Ram and reached by buses #13, #17, #18, #20, #21, #23 and #27. The road to the left leads to a small **museum** (summer Sun–Thurs 9am–6.30pm; winter 9am–4pm, Sun–Thurs 9am–6.30pm, Sat 9am–1pm; 5NIS) devoted to Herzl's life and work and containing, in addition to the usual documents, books and photographs, the **study** – transported piece by piece from Vienna and reconstructed here – in which he wrote his famous Zionist treatise, *Alt-Neuland* (Old-New Land). Also in the park is the tomb of the founder of Revisionist Zionism and mentor of the Irgun, Vladimir Jabotinsky, as well as the graves of Israeli Prime Ministers Golda Meir, Levi Eshkol, Menahem Begin and Yitzhak Rabin.

Adjacent to Mount Herzl, **Har HaZikkaron** – or Mount of Remembrance (buses #13, #17, #18, #20, #21, #23 and #27) – is the grassy hillside setting for **Yad VaShem** (Sun–Thurs 9am–4.45pm, Fri 9am–1pm; free; free tours in English Wed, Thurs, Fri & Sun 10am, Sun 2pm), Israel's most important memorial to the victims of **the Holocaust**, opened in 1953 and covering over eighty hectares. A visit here is an extremely moving and disturbing experience, but one that you may well feel duty-bound to make. Hitler's single-minded murder of over six million people, a million and a half of them children, simply for their race, is a crime of such enormity that it seems impossible to take in. Yad VaShem, meaning "a memorial and a name" (from Isaiah 56: 5), attempts to address this by giving us a glimpse of the individual victims – their names, faces, and suffering – while forcefully pushing home the point that these were ordinary people like ourselves whose lives were uprooted and extinguished with the collaboration (directly or indirectly) of other ordinary people, also just like ourselves. The site will leave you with a deep sorrow, but a feeling that it will never be sorrow enough: the testimony of Yad VaShem is enough to shake the deepest faith in human nature.

From the entrance, the path leads along the **Way of the Righteous**, which honours gentiles who helped the Jews despite the terrible danger to themselves in doing so, to **Ohel Yiskor**, the Hall of Remembrance. The stone floor of this sombre, tomb-like chamber is engraved with the names of 21 concentration camps, while an eternal flame burns above a casket of ashes from the cremation ovens. But it is the exhibition "Warning and Witness", tracing the rise of the Nazis and depicting the horrors of their regime with documents and photographs, that brings you face to face with the human cost of the Holocaust. One of the most famous of the photographs, in among depictions of piled-up corpses and emaciated camp inmates with blank stares of hopelessness, is that of a child in the Warsaw Ghetto, his hands raised in bewildered surrender. The inclusion of other images – most significantly Palestinian leader Haj Amin al-Husseini shaking hands with Himmler, and British soldiers sending illegal Jewish immigrants to internment camps in Cyprus – has led some to suggest that the association of these events with the Holocaust itself is unworthy of this powerful memorial.

The **art museum** displays paintings produced by inmates of the concentration camps and of survivors or artists using the Holocaust as their theme. Those inmates with artistic skills were given paper and drawing implements by the Nazis to try to get them to produce art forgeries or sanitized representations of the camps for propaganda purposes. One section is devoted entirely to works of art by children; their naive depictions of barbed-wire compounds and inhuman barracks are extremely moving. Next door, the **Hall of Names** records over two million of those Jews murdered during the Nazi regime, giving the names and biographical details of as many as possible, while survivors have added their own testimony. Searches can be made of the names on file to try to find out the fate of particular individuals. **Janusz Korczak Park** is named after the Jewish Polish author and teacher who set up an orphanage which he continued inside the Warsaw Ghetto, and who, in 1942, voluntarily went into the gas chamber at Treblinka with his students rather than desert them. Among the sculptures on the site is one depicting Korczak trying desperately to protect the children. Moving towards the end of the site, you pass a boxcar used to transport victims to the concentration camps by rail, beyond which the rocky **Valley of Destroyed Communities** commemorates every one of the whole communities wiped out by the Nazis in their occupation of Europe.

For Jews, the Holocaust is not just a lesson from history, or evidence of the horrific acts that people can commit against each other, it is also a massive trauma, the scars of which run deep in the Jewish psyche. Israel, for many Jews, is a place where they can be safe after two thousand years as victims, and when Arab leaders use the slogan, as several have since Kamal Irekat coined it in 1947, "We will sweep the Jews into the sea," the fact of the Holocaust may serve to cast light on the way that is taken by Israelis.

The southwestern suburbs

The sights **southwest of downtown Jerusalem** will appeal mainly to those staying a while in the city, or those who would like to escape it for a day. Among the highlights are the **model of ancient Jerusalem** at the *Holyland Hotel*, the Church of John the Baptist at **Ein Karem**, and the **Chagall Windows** at Hadassah Medical Centre. None of these sites is anything like walkable from the centre, but they're all accessible by bus (see accounts for details).

Malkha

Southwest of the centre in the suburb of **Malkha**, the gardens of the **Holyland Hotel** in Uziel Street, contain a detailed **model of the ancient city** (Sun–Thurs 8am–10pm, Fri & Sat 8am–6pm; 15NIS; buses #21 and #21a) – well worth a visit for the excellent impression it gives of what Jerusalem might have looked like in Herodian times. Made to a scale of 1:50 and measuring roughly 20m across, it was constructed with materials used at the time – marble, stone, copper, iron and wood – and to measurements derived from Josephus and the Talmud. You'll be able to see the Temple as it was, plus Herod's palace and the layout of the city's streets.

To the south, near Teddy Stadium off Agudat Sport Betar, **Ein Ya'el** (Sun–Thurs 10am–6pm, Fri 9am–2pm; 10NIS; bus #19 or #26) is an archeological site of little interest for its remains, though visiting groups can watch or even have a go at reconstructed ancient craft techniques. Just to the east, on the other side of Agudat Sport Beitar, is the **Kanyon Yerushalayim**, Israel's biggest and newest shopping centre. A kilometre to the west at the southern end of Derekh Gan HaHayot, the **Biblical Zoo** (summer Sun–Thurs 9am–7.30pm, Sat 10am–6.30pm; winter Sun–Thurs 9am–5pm, Fri 9am–3pm, Sat 10am–5pm; 28NIS; bus #26) featuring animals mentioned in the Old Testament, is pretty good as zoos go, with reasonably spacious enclosures but, because of its biblical limitations, no especially exotic or bizarre inmates.

Ein Karem

Two and a half kilometres northwest of Malkha, and 7km southwest of the Old City, **EIN KAREM** (bus #17 from Jaffa Road), is a quiet village surrounded by terraced hills dotted with olive and cypress trees – a refreshing change from the bustle of the city centre and ideal for a day trip or an overnight stay. Formerly a Palestinian village, it has now been repopulated by Jewish settlers; its beautiful old stone houses are mostly inhabited by Israeli artists and sculptors, and there are several art galleries and a variety of good restaurants. The village's name goes back to biblical Bet HaKerem, whose inhabitants rebuilt Jerusalem after the destruction of 70 BC, and it is traditionally held to be the birthplace of John the Baptist, the city of Judah mentioned by St Luke (1: 39–40) in which stood the house of Zachariah, John's father. In honour of its famous son, the **Church of Saint John the Baptist** (summer Mon–Fri 8.30am–noon & 2.30–6pm; winter Mon–Fri 8.30am–noon & 2.30–5pm, Sun 9am–noon & 2.30–5pm; free) was built on the site in 1674, though the building combines remnants of many periods: a statue of Venus in the courtyard shows that it was venerated in Roman times; mosaic fragments belong to a Byzantine floor; and there are also remains of a Crusader building. Inside, the church is decorated with seventeenth-century paintings, and the central aisle leads to a green wrought-iron gate behind which is the high altar of St John. To its right is the altar of John's mother, Elizabeth, and on the left steps lead into a natural cave, held to be the **Grotto of the Nativity of Saint John**.

On the slope of the hill south of Ein Karem, the **Church of the Visitation** (Sun–Fri: summer 8–11.45am & 2.30–6pm, winter 8–11.45am & 2.30–5pm; free), completed in 1955, is another of those designed by Antonio Barluzzi, this time commemorating Mary's visit

MARC CHAGALL

With his unmistakeable naive imagery and vibrant use of bright colours, **Marc Chagall** is by far the most important Jewish artist ever to have put paintbrush to canvas. Traditionally, Jewish people have eschewed the visual arts lest they should breach the commandment "Thou shalt not make unto thee any graven image, or any likeness of any thing" (Exodus 20: 4), yet in the images graven by Chagall, there is no mistaking the influence of his Jewish background: his paintings are full of rabbis and synagogues, religious occasions and *hassidim* with beards, though he himself was far from religious. Even his *Crucifixion* is a Jewish one, in which Jesus's modesty is preserved with a *tallit* prayer shawl, while his *Violinist* inspired the musical *Fiddler on the Roof*, depicting life in the peasant Jewish Russia from which he came.

He was born in 1887 in the village of Peskovatic, within the "pale" of Russia where Jews were permitted to live. His artistic talents led him to study in St Petersburg and in 1910 to Paris, where he became part of the **Cubist movement**, though he soon outgrew it. In 1941, escaping the persecutions of the Vichy regime, he reached New York, returning after the war to the south of France, where he lived until his death in 1985. Although he never lived in Israel, Chagall was a keen supporter of the Jewish State, and endowed it with many of his finest works of art.

Among Chagall's **works in Israel**, his stained-glass windows of the Hadassah Medical Centre in West Jerusalem (see below) are the most spectacular; others include the tapestries in the foyer of the Knesset (see p.374), his depiction of the Wailing Wall in the Tel Aviv Museum (see p.78), and *The Rabbi* in the Israel Museum in Jerusalem (see p.373).

to Elizabeth when she was pregnant. In it is a natural grotto, which once contained a small spring, in front of which are remnants of houses, some of which do indeed date back to Roman times. During the Byzantine period the grotto became a place of worship, and later the Crusaders built a large, two-storeyed church over it, with a smaller one in front – both collapsed after the Crusaders' left and in 1679 the area was bought by the Franciscans and restored. The lower church is adorned with large frescoes, the upper one has a painted ceiling in fourteenth-century Tuscan style. The courtyard is lined with ceramic tiles bearing the *Magnificat* (Mary's hymn of thanksgiving from Luke 1: 46–55) in 42 languages. At the bottom of the hill, a small mosque marks the site of the **Spring of the Virgin**. It is this spring from which Ein Karem took its name, which means "spring of the vineyard". Little water remains in the well today, most of it being used for vines and crops.

About 1km southwest of Ein Karem, the new **Hadassah Medical Centre**, founded in 1951 when the Mount Scopus site was abandoned, is famous for the twelve **Chagall windows** in its synagogue (Sun–Thurs 8am–1.15pm & 2–3.45pm, Fri 8am–12.45pm; 9NIS; bus #19 or #27). Designed by Russian-born Jew Marc Chagall (see box above) and presented to the hospital in 1982, each window is dominated by one main colour and depicts one of the twelve sons of Jacob and tribes of Israel. A guided tour in English (Sun–Fri 8.30am, 9.30am, 10.30am, 11.30am and 12.30pm) tells you all you'll ever want to know about the windows and also includes a film about the Hadassah.

The Hill of Evil Counsel

Southeast of the city, the **Hill of Evil Counsel** is so called because, in Christian tradition, it was here that the Sanhedrin decided to turn Jesus over to the Romans. Its Arabic name, Jabal al-Muqabbar (Mount of Proclamation), derives from the tradition that it was from here that Caliph Omar Ibn al-Khattab first caught sight of the holy city and proclaimed the greatness of Allah in 638 AD. Many found the hill's name appropriate when the British High Commissioner had his residence here during the Mandate – the palatial building, which stands on the top of the hill, surrounded by a garden complete with bandstand, is still known as **Government House** (Armon HaNatziv in Hebrew). After 1948 the area was a demilitarized zone and served as the HQ of UN observers; it was taken by the Jordanians on the first day of the 1967 war but captured by Israeli forces later the same day. Today it serves as the headquarters of the United Nations Emergency Force (UNEF) and United Nations Disengagement Observer Force (UNDOF). For those whose minds are on love rather than war, it is also the site of the **Haas Promenade**, whose view of the Old City rivals that from the Mount of Olives, and make it, together with the gardens below, a popular lovers' haunt.

A couple of kilometres to the south, **Kibbutz Ramat Rahel** (bus #7 from the Central Bus Station or King George Street) was founded in 1916 on the site where the pregnant Virgin Mary is said to have paused on her way to Bethlehem, and boasts fruit and vegetable farms, a vacation club, conference centre, swimming pool, and an elegant but expensive guesthouse. Though surrounded by Jerusalem, Ramat Rahel is not officially part of the city and is independent of Jerusalem's municipal authorities.

You won't really need to venture further north of Ramat Rahel to **Talpiot** unless you fancy joining the young Israelis out clubbing for the night; the area has some of the trendiest nightspots. Talpiot was a mixed-area pre-1948, with Jewish and Arab residents living side by side; neighbouring East Talpiot is a post-1967 settlement across the Green Line.

Northwest of the city: Deir Yassin

Five kilometres northwest of the city centre, on Katzanelbogen Street in the outer suburb of **Kfar Sha'ul** (bus #2, #11, #15 or #33), and surrounded by forest, is the Kfar Sha'ul Mental Health Centre, where patients suffering from "Jerusalem Syndrome" (see p.305) and other psychoses come to recover. Its grounds contain the remains of an Arab village, **DEIR YASSIN**, whose fate in the 1948 war is for Palestinians one of the most emotive symbols of their struggle.

At 4.30am on **April 10, 1948**, the village of nine hundred inhabitants, which had co-existed in relative harmony with its Jewish neighbours, was woken by a 132-man force of Irgun and Stern Gang irregulars as part of Plan Dalet (see p.494). Considering it an easy target, the Haganah had allocated Deir Yassin to the irregulars in the belief that its capture would be difficult to mess up. However, the villagers put up a stronger defence than expected, though by afternoon they had run out of ammunition and those with arms had fled, leaving the Jewish irregulars to go from house to house killing the inhabitants. "We were outside, open to fire," said Irgun deputy commander Yehuda Lapiot. "To stop the shooting from the buildings, we had to fire into them; but inside there were also women and children. That's how so many Arabs got killed." Haganah observer Meir Pa'el tells a different story, saying that after the fighting ended, the irregulars "went rushing from house to house, shooting, slaughtering, killing and looting," before driving the men to a nearby quarry, lining them up and shooting them.

A figure of 250 was originally given for the dead, but recent estimates suggest the number was much less, around 100. However, propagandists on both sides sought to profit by **exaggerating** the atrocities. Arab sources spread false stories of rape and butchery to discredit the Zionists, who in turn used the incident to strike terror into other Arabs and hasten their flight, even sending speaker vans ahead of assault forces to broadcast the message "Deir Yassin! Deir Yassin!" The tactic proved highly successful: Irgun leader Menahem Begin, who described accounts of the massacre as "lying propaganda", says in his book *The Revolt* that "the legend of Deir Yassin helped to carve the way to our decisive victories on the battlefield". Meanwhile, safe within the boundaries of the psychiatric hospital, the houses of Deir Yassin remain as they were in 1948, making this, ironically, one of the best-preserved ex-Arab villages in Israel.

Eating

You could spend weeks in Jerusalem **eating** well and healthily without ever going into a restaurant. Breads, cheeses and yoghurts, pickles, olives, fresh vegetables and fruit are freely available and cheap. Freshly pressed juices can be had on almost any street corner, especially in the east. Café and street stall foods such as hummus, falafel, corn on the cob, nuts and pulses and sweets are available everywhere. But the **restaurants** are good too – in the east for the excellent-value traditional Middle Eastern foods, in the west for their extraordinary variety, offering everything from Thai and Chinese to South African and South American.

Breakfast, snacks and sweets

Breakfast is generally provided in hotels, but if you're staying elsewhere you're probably best popping out for some bread and things like yoghurt, cheese or hummus-type salads. Otherwise, hummus bars – concentrated mainly around the Damascus Gate – are your best bet, opening early and serving good solid food to set you up for the day. The downside is that they don't usually serve tea or coffee. For a more Western-style breakfast, try *Riff-Raff* or the *Tabasco*.

Israel's best **bagels**, plain or filled, are at *Bonkers Bagels* on Zion Square and 10 King George Street. They are still – and this is why they do not match the real thing – steamed rather than boiled before baking, but they knock spots off the country's other attempts at a bagel. Alternatively, an increasing number of places sell filling **baguettes**, notably *Marciano Baguette* (open 24hr Sat night to Fri pm) and *Bali Baguette*, both at 31 Jaffa Road. For late-night/early-morning nibbles, there are a growing number of places staying open round the clock in central West Jerusalem (though most of them close Fri night & Sat to stay kosher), while in East Jerusalem, especially in HaNeviim Street outside the Damascus Gate, there are a number of **all-night bakeries**, many of which stock large falafel balls as well as assorted breads, and will give you a paper-twist of *za'atar* to dip them into.

Falafel is of course ubiquitous, but not always very good. On the east side, large falafels with an onion centre are available, but the small plain ones are usually better. Places known for good falafel are: *Shalom* in Bezalel Street, opposite the end of Ussishkin, *HaTimani* at 48 HaNeviim, opposite the end of Monbaz (sign in Hebrew only), and *Jerusalem Felafel* inside the Damascus Gate, on the right just before the road divides into Souq Khan al-Zeit and al-Wad Road (no sign at all – here it's best to just buy the balls rather than the whole shebang in a pitta). Mahane Yehuda is also a good place for falafel, and for mixed meats in a pitta (*meorav yerushalmi*): try *Sima* at 82 Agrippas for the latter. Junk food junkies in need of a fix will find *McDonald's* on Hillel Street in downtown West Jerusalem.

In East Jerusalem and the Old City, shops selling **sweets** usually have tables where you can sit down with the sticky confection of your choice. Souq Khan al-Zeit in the Old City is the best place to sample Palestinian sweetmeats: *Jaffar Sweets* at no. 42 is a good place for *kanafe*, *baklawa*, and excellent *burma*; a place on the corner of Aqabat al-Taqiya has a range of halva and other sweets cut off the block; and *Zaltimo* at no. 162, and backing onto the original entrance of the Holy Sepulchre, specializes in filled pancakes.

Snack bars and breakfast places

Abou Seif, Omar Ibn al Khattab Square. The first snack bar on the north side of the square, facing the Tower of David, and one of the oldest eateries in the area, with falafel sandwiches to eat in or take out; also a good place for breakfast. Mon–Sat 7.30am–6.30pm, Sun 9.30am–6.30pm. Cheap.

Abu Hassan, in the little alleyway between nos. 10 and 12 Salah al-Din. A perennially popular restaurant selling great hummus and delicious Palestinian home cooking. Daily 7am–noon. Cheap.

Abu Shukri, 63 al-Wad Rd. An Old City institution, famous for its hummus, and also offering a pretty mean *fuul*, as well as falafel, salad, tea and coffee: everything you need for a Middle Eastern worker's breakfast or light lunch. Daily 8am–4.30pm. Cheap.

Al-Omaal, 2 HaNeviim, on the corner with Sultan Suleiman (sign in Arabic only). The oldest and most reliable of the three snack bars outside the Damascus Gate and handy for a traditional breakfast of hummus, falafel and *fuul*. The *Ikermawi Restaurant*, next door, has similar food, while *Al-Ayed Restaurant*, next door to that, adds *shawarma* and kebabs to the list. The three share outdoor eating space in the little square adjoining. Daily 5am–6pm. Cheap.

The Gate Cafe, On the left as you enter Damascus Gate. A ringside seat overlooking the activity below, with good-value breakfast (eggs, bread, jam, orange juice, tea or coffee), sandwiches, falafel and freshly squeezed fruit juices. Daily 7.30am–7pm. Cheap.

Hummus Lina, 42 Aqabat al-Khanka. A traditional joint, serving tasty hummus with pitta, pickles, onions, hot peppers; also *fuul*, salad and cold drinks. Daily 8am–4pm. Cheap.

Open Sesame, 44 al-Wad Rd, opposite the Austrian Hospice. A good place for breakfast (jam, cheese, eggs, bread, tea or coffee), with naive art collages hand-painted by local artist Mohammed al-Usta. Also serves chicken, shnitzel, omelettes, hamburgers and kebabs, all with salad and chips. Daily 7.30am–9 or 11pm. Cheap.

Pinnati, 13 King George. Small, packed, unassuming but locally renowned hummus joint. Sun–Thurs 7.30am–8pm, Fri 7.30am–2pm. Cheap.

Princes Cafeteria (al-Omara'), Damascus Gate. To the right of the gate as you come in and tucked away in a quiet open-air plaza with sun-shaded tables, this place serves a variety of pizzas and baguettes plus desserts. Daily 24hr. Cheap.

Riff-Raff, 19 Hillel. Big sandwiches, juices and shakes and, best of all, bacon and egg breakfasts served round the clock. Daily 24hr. Cheap to moderate.

Restaurants

For information on places to eat, *Jerusalem's Restaurants* and *Jerusalem's Best Menus*, found in tourist offices and hotels, list restaurants and, in the case of the latter, even print the menus of the more popular ones, together with their address, phone number and opening times. Both are available free at hotels and tourist offices, and the restaurants covered range from Argentinian to Yemenite. For those on a budget, *The Traveller*, available free at an increasing number of locales (if all else fails, try *Michelle's Magazines* at 5 Havatzelet) lists places where you can eat for less than 25NIS (£4/$7).

The big food bargain as far as West Jerusalem is concerned is the **lunchtime business menu**, usually available from noon to 4pm, and offering a two- or three-course meal for around 37NIS (£6/$10). Most of the downtown restaurants offer such a menu, especially those around Yoel Salomon. Remember that in the Muslim Quarter and many places in East Jerusalem, you won't be able to drink alcohol with your meal.

The Old City

Abu Shanab Pizza, 35 Latin Patriarchate Road, first left past the Tourist Information Office inside Jaffa Gate. A great place with marvellous atmosphere and pizzas that, if they're not authentic Italian, at least try hard and certainly fill you up. During happy hour (6–7pm) you get two beers for the price of one. Daily 10am–11pm. Cheap to moderate.

Al-Tawfiq, 21 al-Wad Rd. Kebabs, *shashlik*, grilled chicken and a range of salads and dips served up amid bright blue and white decor. Daily 7am–10pm. Cheap.

Armenian Tavern, 79 Armenian Patriarchate Road. Basement restaurant with beautiful decor, trendy clientele, and delicious Armenian dishes such as *khaghoghi derev* (stuffed vine leaves), *soujuk* (spicy sausages) or *lahmajun* (Armenian "pizza"), and a special menu on Friday nights. Tues–Sun 11am–10.30pm. Moderate.

Mata'am al-A'ilaat (Families' Restaurant), 77 Souq Khan al-Zeit. A large, cool and clean establishment popular with Palestinians and specializing in shish kebab, *shawarma*, lamb chops, steaks, hamburgers and chicken, all served with chips, salad and bread. Also offers 18 different kinds of salad and freshly squeezed juices. Daily 8am–6 or 8pm. Cheap.

Pizzaria Basti, 70 al-Wad Rd, opposite the Third Station of the Cross. A 90-year-old family-run business offering pizzas, kebabs, hamburgers and shnitzel, all with chips and salad. Also does a good-value breakfast. Daily: summer 7am–11pm, winter 8am–9pm. Cheap.

Tabasco Tea Room, 8 Aqabat al-Taqiya, off Souq Khan al-Zeit. A travellers' favourite, popular and busy, where you can eat, drink and play backgammon; generous portions include cheese omelette, steak, cheeseburgers, spag bol and mouthwatering chocolate and banana pancakes. Daily 8am–midnight. Cheap.

East Jerusalem

Al-Quds, 23 Sultan Suleiman. Deservedly popular for roast chicken or kebabs with hummus and salad. Look for the spitted chickens broiling over charcoal out front. Daily 8am–10pm. Cheap.

Al-Shuleh Grill, 16 Salah al-Din, opposite *Capitol Hotel*. Popular among locals for its traditional snacks (hummus, falafel and salads) and roast meats (*shawarma*, kebabs and chicken). Daily 7am–8pm. Cheap.

Arabesque, *American Colony Hotel*, Nablus Rd (☎02/627 9777). The most upmarket restaurant in East Jerusalem, serving French and other European *haute cuisine*. The Saturday all-you-can-eat buffet lunch (noon–3pm) is popular, but pricey. The hotel also has a less expensive poolside restaurant with pasta and salad buffet nights (Sunday), a jasmine-scented garden restaurant for snacks and coffees, and a cellar bar for drinking. Daily noon–midnight. Expensive.

Askadinya, 11 Shimon HaTzadik, Sheikh Jarrah (☎02/532 4801). A new restaurant with a growing reputation for excellent French- and Italian-style food. Popular with the *American Colony* crowd. Daily 12.30pm–midnight. Expensive.

Azzahra, 13 al-Zahra St. Belonging to the hotel of the same name: classy indoor and delightful garden restaurant serving charcoal-grilled meats and kebabs. Daily noon–midnight. Moderate.

National Palace Restaurant, 4 al-Zahra Street (☎02/627 3273). Reputable and long-established rooftop restaurant at the hotel of the same name, which serves traditional Palestinian dishes. Daily noon–10pm. Expensive.

Petra Restaurant, 15 Rashid Street. Prettily done out, serving mezze, grilled meats, or fish such as sea bass in white wine or the ubiquitous St Peter's fish (see pp.42 & 204). Daily 11am–11.30pm. Moderate to expensive.

Philadelphia, 9 al-Zahra St (☎02/628 9770). This long-established place, which claims to be "the most popular restaurant in Palestine", has fed movie stars and US President Jimmy Carter. A lengthy menu including red mullet, stuffed pigeon, and meat with *tehina*, plus a 15-plate mezze and six kinds of stuffed vegetables to start, and an assortment of *baklawa* for afters. Daily noon–11pm. Expensive.

Victoria Restaurant, al-Masoudi St beside the *Victoria Hotel*. Small and spotless Middle Eastern restaurant whose menu features *shashlik*, kebab, *mansaf*, chicken or fish, plus alcoholic drinks. Daily 11am–8.30pm. Moderate.

West Jerusalem

Alumah, 8 Ya'avetz. Indoor and terrace wholefood vegetarian eating down a small alley off Jaffa Rd (by no. 40). Sun–Thurs 10am–11pm, Fri 10am–2pm. Moderate.

Angelo's, 9 Horkenos (☎02/623 6095). Great home-made pasta, Roman Jewish specialities, including *fettuccine al salmone* and *penne* in vodka sauce, not to mention proper pizzas. Fish and dairy products served, but no meat. Sun–Thurs noon–11pm, Sat nightfall–11pm. Expensive.

Cézanne, Bet HaOmenim (Artists' House), 12 Shmuel HaNagid. Stylish, French-style restaurant with good, inexpensive lunchtime business menu offering *broerwors* (South African sausage) as well as more European options. Daily noon–10pm. Expensive.

Eucalyptus, 7 Horkenos (☎02/624 4331). Renowned Jerusalem restaurant at the cutting edge of modern Israeli cuisine, serving the likes of Jerusalem artichoke soup, *za'atar* salad, and figs stuffed with chicken breast in tamarind sauce. Sun–Thurs noon–4pm & 6–11pm, Fri noon–2.30pm, Sat nightfall–11pm. Expensive.

Fink's, 2 HaHistadrut at the corner with King George (☎02/623 4523). Doubling as a bar, this place has been serving up goulash, schnitzel and other Jewish East European dishes since the days of the Mandate. Sat–Thurs 6pm–12.30am. Expensive.

Hen, 30 Jaffa Rd. Unassuming diner, handy for a lunch of grilled meat or stuffed vegetables, with Middle Eastern salads and dips or soup for starters. Sun–Thurs 8am–6pm, Fri 8am–3pm. Cheap to moderate.

Ma'adan, 35 Jaffa Rd. Low-price set menus, mostly involving *shashlik*, schnitzel or steak, available evenings as well as lunchtime. Sun–Thurs 10am–11pm, Fri 10am–3.30pm, Sat 6.30–11pm. Cheap to moderate.

Misadonet, in an alley by 12 Yoel Salomon. Home-style Kurdish cooking including stuffed meats such as *giri-giri* (lamb's heart stuffed with almonds and pine nuts) and *pishta mazo* (beef stuffed with rice), as well as a selection of *kubbeh* soups. Sun–Thurs 11am–11pm, Fri 11am–nightfall, Sat nightfall–11pm. Expensive.

Mr Li's, 12 Shamai. Classic Thai cuisine it isn't, but it does have wokfuls of filling food at low prices, and a "business meal" option that's valid all day with a choice of chicken or goose. Sun–Thurs 11am–1am, Fri 11am–3pm. Cheap.

Pampa Grill, 3 Rivlin. Argentinian meat rack with dishes based on a choice of steak, chicken or non-pork *chorizo*. Also takeaway sandwiches and *empanadas*. Sun–Thurs noon–midnight, Fri noon–4pm, Sat nightfall–midnight. Moderate.

Pepperoni's, 4 Rabbi Akiva (☎02/625 7829). Good home-style Italian cooking, including hors d'oeuvres, pasta, meat and sausage. Daily noon–midnight. Expensive.

The Pie Shop (Don't Pass Me By), in an alley beween 9 and 11 Yoel Salomon St. Legendary Jerusalem institution back after some years' absence, serving pies sweet and savoury, with salads to accompany the latter, and a great-value business lunch you'll be hard put to get through. Sun–Thurs 11am–2am, Fri 11am–3pm, Sat nightfall–2am. Moderate.

La Rotisserie, Notre Dame, Paratroopers Rd (☎02/627 9111). The best and poshest French restaurant in town, specializing in meat dishes. Daily 7–11pm. Expensive.

The 7th Place, Bet Agron, 37 Hillel. South Indian vegetable dishes, including veg *thali* and *masala dosa*, as well as vegetable pies, and kosher fish cooked to imitate prawns. Sun–Thurs 8.30am–midnight, Fri 8.30am–4pm, Sat nightfall–midnight. Moderate.

Spaghettim, 8 Rabbi Akiva (☎02/623 5547 or 8). Spaghetti with a choice of more than 50 different sauces served in a lovely grand old building off the road with an outside terrace. Daily noon–midnight. Moderate.

Village Green, 10 Ben Yehuda and 1 Bezalel. Vegetarian self-service with wholesome soups, generous veg pies, tofu bakes and salads. Sun–Thurs 11am–10pm. Moderate.

Yemenite Step, 10 Yoel Salomon. Yemeni restaurant specializing in *malawah* (filled flaky pastry) and spicy thick soups. Also does a good-value lunchtime business menu. Sun–Thurs noon–1am, Fri noon–4pm, Sat nightfall–1am. Moderate.

Drinking

Cafés are mostly to be found in West Jerusalem, though there are one or two in the East, including the Old City, too. In the west, they may serve alcohol as well as tea, coffee and soft drinks. There is a small but waning number of traditional **qahwas** (coffee houses; see box on p.43) in East Jerusalem and the Old City with real (as opposed to tea-bag) tea, strong Turkish coffee spiced with cardamom and sweetened to your taste, and hookah pipes of plain or flavoured tobacco; one such is to your left just after entering through the Damascus Gate, where they are used to the odd tourist dropping in; another is on Aqabat al-Saraya in the middle of the Old City by Souq al-Attarin. Bear in mind that they tend to be very male establishments, where a woman's presence will be considered somewhat strange (you won't see a Palestinian woman in one, though allowances are usually made for foreigners). They often serve hot **milk-based drinks**, too, such as *sahlab* spiced with cinnamon, coconut and pistachios – great during chilly

Jerusalem winters. Of the Old City tourist-trap cafés, the ones around the central fountain of the Mauristan near the Holy Sepulchre are quite pleasant; but the trio on the east
side of Omar Ibn al-Khattab Square opposite the Jaffa Gate and to the left of the
Christian Information Centre are best avoided.

Juice bars can be found on both sides of town but those in the west, such as *Tutti-
Frutti* at 23 Ben Yehuda and *Magic Fruit Juice* opposite, offer a wider choice. East of the
Green Line, the prices are lower, but you'll be confined largely to orange, grapefruit and
carrot, plus the traditional Palestinian drinks of almond milk (*'asir louz*) and tamarind
cordial (*tamar hindi*); the *Alarz* and *Arizona*, on Sultan Suleiman, a little to the east of
the *Pilgrim's Palace Hotel*, are two of the best addresses for sampling those. *Tamar hindi*
is also available from itinerant sellers, much in evidence just outside the Damascus Gate.

Alcoholic drinks are available in West Jerusalem, and in the Christian and Armenian
quarters of the Old City, but are not sold in the Muslim Quarter. Unsurprisingly, then,
most of the best drinking locales are west of the Green Line, though the best locally
produced beer, Taybeh, is hard to find there (Israelis may not make a point of boy-
cotting Palestinian products, but they certainly don't go out of their way to buy them).
Most bars in West Jerusalem, and certainly those patronized by travellers, have a
happy hour, which varies both in time and what's on offer from bar to bar; the usual
deal is two beers for the price of one, and this may extend to other drinks, but usually
only Israeli rather than imported spirits. Look in *The Traveller* magazine for the latest
on the happy-hour options.

The **music** played in most of the traveller bars is 1974-style American rock, though
the *Underground* has a back room playing dance music, and the others occasionally
experiment with indie-pop. In general, the bars in West Jerusalem will stay open until
the last person leaves, which may be 2am or so midweek in winter, and around 5 or 6am
on Friday nights in summer.

Cafés

Aroma, 18 Hillel. Popular espresso bar with good Italian-style coffees and a trendy clientele in the
heart of downtown West Jerusalem. Daily 24hr.

Atara, 7 Ben Yehuda. A popular place for terrace consumption of coffee and pastries amidst the hub-
bub of the Ben Yehuda Street pedestrian zone. Sun–Thurs 7am–midnight, Fri 7am–4pm, Sat
8pm–midnight.

Bint al-Balad, Freres Street, next door to Melia handicraft shop: lovely little pie and coffee house,
run by and for women. The Turkish coffee is good, but the espresso should be avoided. Also serves
savoury snacks like *za'atar* and cheese rolls, *sfiha* (Arabic "pizza"), *kubbeh*, tabbouleh, salads and
sandwiches, plus luscious cakes (orange, chocolate, fruit, banana and apple pie) using pottery that's
often on sale but rarely used. Mon–Sat 8am–4pm.

Loaves & Fishes, Omar Ibn al-Khattab Square (inside the Jaffa Gate, by the Christian Information
Centre). A clean and pleasant café staffed by active Christian evangelists with a Christian message
while you eat and drink. As well as tea and coffee, there are cakes, snacks and a salad bar. Mon–Sat
10am–6pm.

Patisserie Suisse, Salah-al-Din beside Capitol Hotel. A popular East Jerusalem hideaway, selling
the usual beer, tea and coffee. Snacks on offer include ham- and cheeseburgers, hot dogs, chicken
nuggets, roast beef and pastrami sandwiches, with ice cream for afters. Mon–Sat 9am–7pm.

Notre Dame Coffee House, Notre Dame, Paratroopers Road. Enjoy a tea, coffee, beer or soda
while admiring the views from the terrace. Also a good place for a snack: salads, dips, soups and
toasties. Daily 8am–1am.

The Secret Garden, 5 Havatzelet. At the back of a shop selling English-language magazines, a
quiet coffee bar with a secluded garden out back. Sun–Thurs 9am–8pm, Fri 9am–2pm.

Tmol Shilshom, 5 Yoel Salomon (rear entrance). Coffee and a variety of teas, not to mention a variety of seating in a popular downtown café that doubles as a second-hand bookshop. Sun–Thurs
8am–2am, Fri 8am–5pm, Sat 7pm–2am.

Bars

Arizona, 37 Jaffa Rd. Head downstairs for the live music dive bar with 32 beers including draught Taybeh. Daily 7.50pm–3am or later.

Blue Hole, 12 Yoel Salomon. A congenial drinking spot with an intimate atmosphere and free olives and pretzels with your beer. Daily 6pm–3am or later; happy hour 6–9.30pm.

Cannabis, 13 Monbaz, behind Strudel. Sign in Hebrew only, but the dope-leaf logo is of course international. Indian wall hangings and a big screen for music vids; popular among hip Israelis but, despite the name, no smoking of substances allowed. Daily 8pm–4am.

Cellar bar, *American Colony Hotel*, Nablus Road. East Jerusalem's only serious drinking venue, popular with expats and journos. Daily 6pm–3.30am.

Champs, 19 Jaffa Rd. Draught Guinness, a dartboard, and a stripper every other Tuesday are among the attractions at this rather seedy, beery dive. Daily 1pm–5am. Half-price happy hour 4–7pm.

Fink's, 2 HaHistadrut. A hub of Zionist subversion in the days of the Mandate, and still a Jerusalem institution, home to a strange mix of drinkers. Sat–Thurs 6pm–12.30am.

Galliano, 8 Horkanos. A spacious, pub-like bar complete with pool table, run by Brits in what looks from the inside rather like a tent, with a tree growing through it. Sat–Thurs 6pm–dawn, Fri 3pm–dawn. A long happy hour: opening time–9pm, with various special offers.

Mike's, Horkanos St. A poky little place with live rock and blues bands nightly (10.30pm), who just about squeeze in. Also claims to have the cheapest draught Guinness in Israel. Best in summer when it spreads onto the street. Daily 5pm–3am or later.

Strudel, 11 Monbaz. Jerusalem's first, and still best, Internet Bar, with Web and email access (*strudel@inter.net.il*), but also good food and drink. Mon–Fri noon–midnight, Sat 3pm–midnight; happy hour 7–9pm.

Tabasco Tea Room, 8 Aqabat al-Taqiya, off Souq Khan al-Zeit. The Old City's only real drinking den, popular with travellers, but closes early by West Jerusalem standards. On Friday night there's a Punch Party where you can drink as much as you like for a cover charge (around $3). Daily 8am–midnight. Happy hour 6.30–7.30pm & 9–10pm.

Underground, 1 Yoel Salomon, by Zion Sq. Two rooms of music, rock as you enter, dance in the back. At its best, this place is a heaving, sweaty den of iniquity, popular with travellers and Israelis alike, though it tends to go in and out of favour. Daily 8pm till the last person standing. Happy hour 8–9pm, and there is a "5NIS for as much as you can drink in 20 minutes" offer from 7.50–8.10pm nightly.

Zanzibar, 13 Shamai. Sophisticated yuppie bar, for the chic, and the chic-at-heart. Daily noon–3am.

Nightlife and entertainment

Jerusalem, East or West, is not the place for exciting **nightlife**. If it's pubs, clubs or discos you want, then Tel Aviv is the place to be and many Jerusalemites will take a sherut or drive to the coast for a night out. In general, and certainly in the centre of town, the bars listed above are your best bet. **Nightclubs** as such do exist, but most of them are to be found out in Talpiot to the south of town. They tend to be quite expensive to get into (reckon on paying around $15), and to operate dress codes. If that hasn't put you off try *Zoey* or the *Oman*.

East Jerusalem in particular is a virtual ghost town at night due to pressures from Islamists on the one hand and isolation by Israel from its West Bank hinterland on the other. As a tourist of course, you can pop over to the west, not so easily done by the local youth.

For up-to-date **listings** and information on events in Jerusalem, see *Your Jerusalem*, *This Week In Jerusalem*, the city council's monthly *Events in Jerusalem*, or the Friday supplement of the *Jerusalem Post*. The various tourist offices also have lists of events and entertainment in the Jerusalem region. The big problem with all of these is that they omit mention of anything in East Jerusalem, for which you will have to make your own enquiries: the *Nuzha* and *al-Qasaba* theatres in Obeid Ibn Jarrah Street are good places to start. **Tickets** for concerts and theatres in Jerusalem can be obtained from *Bimot* at 8 Shamai (☎02/625 0905), and *Klaim* at 12 Shamai (☎02/625 6869).

Film

Whatever your taste in film, you should be able to find one or two of Jerusalem's seventeen **cinemas** showing it each night and there'll always be something in English. Most of the cinemas are in West Jerusalem; the Old City doesn't have any and the few that exist in East Jerusalem show mainly Egyptian films. The *Jerusalem Post* Friday supplement has the fullest and most up-to-date listings. The comfortable **Cinemateque** (Hebron Road; ☎02/672 4131) shows three or four different, usually art-house, films daily, and is also a fashionable place to hang out. Art-house movies are also shown at the Israel Museum, Jerusalem Theatre (aka Jerusalem Centre for the Performing Arts, 20 David Marcus St; ☎02/561 7167) and Binyanei HaUma (the Jerusalem International Convention Centre, Jaffa Road near Herzl Boulevard; ☎02/655 8558). **French films** feature regularly at the Alliance Française (8 Agron; ☎02/622 7167).

Live music

There's a fair choice of **music** venues in Jerusalem, but even so the scene could hardly be described as exciting. In clubs and bars you'll hear predominantly folk (Israeli), jazz (sometimes excellent) and home-grown rock talent (usually mediocre). Of the bars and pubs mentioned opposite, *Mike's* has live **rock music** nightly at 10.30pm (arrive early if you want a seat), and the downstairs bar at *Arizona*, 37 Jaffa Road, also has live rock bands. There's live **jazz** on Tuesdays at the restaurant in Ticho House (see p.364; ☎02/624 4186), and a jazz jam session Friday afternoons 1.30–4.30pm at the Pargod Theatre (94 Betzalel; ☎02/623 1765). *Tmol Shilshom Bookstore Café* at 5 Yoel Salomon has live jazz Mondays from 11pm, and folk at the same time on Tuesdays, and **folk** musicians also sometimes perform at the AACI at 11 Pinsker in Talbiya. There are occasional pop concerts – both Israeli and foreign groups – at the Jerusalem Theatre at 20 David Marcus Street in Talbiya (☎02/561 7167).

   Classical music lovers are generally better served than pop music fans. Jerusalem's main concert hall is **Binyanei HaUma** (Jaffa Road near Herzl Boulevard; ☎02/655 8558) but concerts are also staged at the Jerusalem Theatre, 20 David Marcus Street in Talbiya (☎02/561 7167), the Targ Music Centre in Ein Kerem (☎02/641 4250), and occasionally at the YMCA in King David Street (☎02/625 7111). Other occasional venues are Dormition Abbey on Mount Zion (☎02/671 9927) for organ recitals, the Van Leer Institute on Albert Einstein Square (☎02/566 7141) for chamber music concerts, and the Church of the Redeemer in Mauristan Street (☎02/628 2543), which holds weekly concerts. The Jerusalem Centre at the Mormon University on Mount Scopus (☎02/627 3195) has classical concerts on Sundays at 8pm, and you can also catch recitals at the Israel Museum (☎02/670 8985) and the Rockefeller Museum (☎02/628 2251). **Open-air concerts**, classical and popular, are also held, particularly in summer, at the Sultan's Pool opposite Jaffa Gate.

Theatre and dance

Most **plays by Israeli authors** are, naturally enough, written and performed in Hebrew but there is some English language drama in Jerusalem, and if you have any understanding of Hebrew, it might be especially worth seeing works by such controversial playwrights as Yehoshua Sobol (*Ghetto*), Shmuel Hasafri (*The Last Secular Jew*) or Shmuel Amid (*Room-mates in Jerusalem*). The main venues are the Jerusalem Theatre (see above), the Khan Theatre at 2 David Remez near the station (☎02/671 8281) and the Pargod Theatre (see above). Dance performances are also frequently held at the Jerusalem Centre for the Performing Arts, at the Jerusalem Theatre (see above for address; ☎02/561 0011 for information on the dance programme), and Jewish and Arab **folk dancing** is performed (Mon, Thurs & Sat at 9pm) in the auditorium of the YMCA (see above). In Liberty Bell Park, the Train Theatre (☎02/561 8514) puts on **puppet shows** in an old rail car.

Palestinian theatre and dance can be seen at the Nuzha/al-Hakawati Theatre (al-Nuzha Street off Nablus Road, up an alleyway beside the Nuzha cinema; ☎02/628 8189), which became the first Palestinian arts centre in the country when it opened in 1984, and the al-Qasaba Theatre in Obeid Ibn Jarrah Street (☎02/628 0957). Plays are in Arabic, but English resumés are sometimes available. The Nuzha/al-Hakawati Theatre also puts on folklore evenings, exhibitions, conferences and other events. A lot of the plays are pretty political, and closure by Israeli military authorities, even detention of performers, is not unknown.

Talks

Public **talks and lectures** are a significant feature of Jerusalem life, and many of them are given in English. In general they're about issues only of relevance to practising Jews – some of them aimed at Jewish visitors with the intention of persuading them to "make *aliyah*" (immigrate), or to become more religious – but if you do practise or want to know more about the faith, they can be very interesting. Of talks of interest to a larger audience, many are about religion, but from a wider perspective ("Science and the Bible", "Christianity and Zionism"), while others deal with subjects such as history, politics, science, trade and business. The best listing of talks can be found in the free newssheet *Your Jerusalem* (see p.309).

Listings

Airlines Arkia, 97 Jaffa Rd (☎02/625 5888); British Airways, 33 Jaffa Rd (☎02/625 6111); El Al, 12 Hillel St (☎02/624 5725); KLM, 33 Jaffa Rd (☎02/625 1361); Olympic, 33 Jaffa Rd (☎02/623 4538); Tower Air, 14 Hillel St (☎02/625 5137); TWA, 34 Ben Yehuda St (☎02/624 7064).

Banks and exchange There are numerous moneychangers on Salah al-Din Street in East Jerusalem, and just inside the Damascus and Jaffa gates in the Old City, as well as on Jaffa Road and Ben Yehuda Street in West Jerusalem. All offer competitive rates, though it pays to shop around, and they do not generally charge commission on cash or travellers' cheques, but check first. Those in the west are closed for Shabbat. Money Net at 13 Ben Yehuda is open the latest (Sun–Thurs 10am–10pm, Fri 10am–3pm, Sat nightfall–10pm). Most banks are located around Zion Square on Jaffa Road, or Ben Yehuda, King George and Hillel streets.

Books Steimatzky has the largest collection of new books in English, and three downtown branches in West Jerusalem at 39 Jaffa Rd, 7 Ben Yehuda and 9 King George St. For second-hand books, the best selection is at Sefer VaSefel, upstairs at 2 Ya'avetz, just by 40 Jaffa Rd, which also has new books, and runs a café; *Tmol Shilshom* at 5 Yoel Salomon, by contrast, is a café that also sells a few second-hand books. Other shops with second-hand books in English include Moffet at 1 Alliance Israelite (off Jaffa Rd opposite the junction with HaNeviim), Gur Avieh at 8 Yoel Salomon, and The Bookshelf at the southern end of Jewish Quarter Rd in the Old City. The Educational Bookshop at 22 Salah al-Din in East Jerusalem stocks a number of publications by Palestinian and Human Rights groups on the political situation and other subjects related to the West Bank and Gaza. Franciscan Corner on St Francis Rd (near the corner with Casa Nova) in the Old City's Christian Quarter, open mornings only, has some interesting publications on archeology and religion.

Camping gear SPNI at 13 Heleni HaMalka St (☎02/625 2357) has the best selection of maps and information. Camping Lematayyil at 5 Yoel Salomon should have all the equipment you need.

Car rental Avis, 22 King David St (☎02/624 9001); Budget, 8 King David Street (☎02/624 8991 or 2); Eldan, 24 King David St (☎02/625 2151 or 2 or 3); Eurodollar, 8 King David St (☎02/623 5467); Europcar, 8 King David St (☎02/624 8464); Hertz, 18 King David St (☎02/623 1351); Orabi, opposite Dijani Hospital in Bet Hanina (☎02/585 3101 or 6) offers the choice of yellow number plates (for Israel) or blue (for the West Bank), see p.391 for explanation; Thrifty, 8 King David St (☎02/625 0833 or 4).

Consulates Many countries have two: one in West Jerusalem for Israel, and one in East Jerusalem for Palestine. As the USA now recognizes Jerusalem as Israel's "indivisible" capital, their West

Jerusalem consulate is due for an upgrade to embassy status, and their East Jerusalem one is likely to move elsewhere. UK, Tower House, HaRakevet St (☎02/582 8281) (West) and 19 Nashashibi Street, Sheikh Jarrah (☎02/582 8263) (East); USA, 18 Agron St (☎02/625 3288) (West) and 27 Nablus Road (☎02/628 2231) (East).

Cultural centres The British Council next door to the East Jerusalem YMCA (Nablus Road; ☎02/628 2545), a little bit of the Empire still unaware that the sun has definitely set, has a library and a reading room where you read British papers and magazines. The US Cultural Centre is at 19 Keren HaYesod (☎02/625 5755).

Emergencies Police ☎100, Ambulance (Magen David Adom, equivalent of Red Cross) ☎911, ☎101 or ☎02/652 3133; medical help for tourists ☎171/022 9110; fire ☎102; rape crisis line ☎02/651 4455 or ☎02/625 5558. See also "Medical services" below.

Human rights organizations Palestine Human Rights Information Centre, top floor, 12 Mas'udi (☎02/628 7076 or 7; email: *phric@baraka.org*); Citizens' Rights Centre, al-Ram, Mujahed Building, Qufr Aqab (☎02/574 7129); UNRWA, Karl Netter St, Sheikh Jarrah (☎02/589 0400).

Laundry The self-service laundromat at 12 Shamai behind Ben Yehuda Street in downtown West Jerusalem is the cheapest place, though many hotels and hostels have an in-house laundry service, either officially, or run by members of staff. In the Old City, there is al-Aswar at 68 al-Wad Rd opposite the Austrian Hospice.

Medical services Ambulance (Magen David Adom, equivalent of Red Cross) ☎911, ☎101 or ☎02/652 3133; emergency medical help for tourists ☎171/022 9110. Hospitals include the Hadassah on Mount Scopus (☎02/677 6040), and the Augusta Victoria, also on Mount Scopus (☎02/628 7122). For emergency dental treatment call ☎02/563 2303 8am–midnight. The *Jerusalem Post* prints a list of duty emergency pharmacies.

Newspapers and magazines The best newsstand in Jerusalem is at the bottom of Nablus Road, opposite Damascus Gate: it carries a comprehensive selection of local and foreign publications. In West Jerusalem, the best places for foreign newspapers are Steimatzky's bookshops. Michelle's Magazines at 5 Havatzelet near Zion Square has a large selection of foreign magazines.

Police Muscobiya, Russian Compound (☎02/539 1254); Omar Ibn al-Khattab Square, by the Citadel (☎02/627 3222).

Post offices The main office is on Jaffa Road in West Jerusalem (Sun–Thurs 7am–7pm, Fri 7am–noon) with poste restante and exchange facilities, and with a telegram office open round the clock; East Jerusalem's main office is at the corner of Salah al-Din and Sultan Suleiman (Sun–Thurs 8am–6pm, Fri 8am–noon, Sat 8am–2pm). Branch offices include one inside the Jaffa Gate opposite the Citadel entrance (Sun–Thurs 2.30–7.30pm, Fri and eve of holidays noon–8pm). Stamps can also be bought from stationers, souvenir shops, bookshops and large hotels. Unless otherwise specified, mail addressed to Poste Restante (general delivery) will be delivered to the Jaffa Road post office.

Taxis Companies include, in East Jerusalem: al-Ittihad ☎02/628 4641; al-Mattar ☎02/995 9312; Azzahra ☎02/628 4455; Mount of Olives ☎02/627 2711. In West Jerusalem: HaPalmah ☎02/679 2333; HaPisga ☎02/642 1111, 2222 or 3333; Rehavia ☎02/625 4444; Yisra'el ☎02/625 2333.

Telecommunications Solan Communications on AM Lunz St off King George St is open round the clock for international calls and faxes. They will also receive and hold faxes for a fee [2.50NIS per page] on ☎02/625 8879. The best place for email and Internet access is *Strudel* at 11 Monbaz (email: *strudel@inter.net.il*). Pricier alternatives are the *Internet Café* on AM Lunz St and *Tmol Shilshom* at 5 Yoel Salomon (open for emailing 11am–3pm; email: *online@tmol-shilshom.co.il*).

Travel agents ISSTA, 31 HaNeviim (☎02/625 7257), is the best place for student discounts and cheap flights. Mazada Tours, 9 Koresh, at the corner of Agron St (☎02/623 5777) runs buses to Egypt and Jordan, and can even arrange onward transport to Syria and Iraq if you have two passports with you! The *Petra Hostel* at 1 David St in the Old City (☎02/628 6618) can also supply *Mazada*'s Cairo bus tickets. Galilee Tours, also running transport to Egypt, is at 3 Hillel St (☎02/625 8866). Egged Tours is at 44a Jaffa Rd by Zion Square (☎02/525 3454), and United Tours is at the King David Hotel annexe, King David St (☎02/625 2187 or 8).

Visa extensions Ministry of the Interior, Binyan Klal, 1 Shlomzion HaMalka St (☎02/622 8211).

Work Jerusalem is not the best place to find work: less is available and wages are lower than in Tel Aviv or Eilat. Hostels often need casual staff who'll work for board and lodging, and prospective employers often come to them too (naturally, hostel guests get first refusal). The *Petra* and the *al-Arab* are good places to start looking.

MOVING ON FROM JERUSALEM

BUSES

Egged buses into Israel, and to the West Bank settlements, leave from the Egged Central Bus Station (☎02/530 4555). Destinations served from Jerusalem by Egged include Ashdod (roughly hourly; 1hr 20min), Ashqelon (roughly hourly; 1hr 15min), Beersheba (roughly every 30min; 2hr), Ben Gurion Airport (every 30–40min; 45min), Eilat (4 daily; 5hr 30min), Ein Gedi (10 daily; 1hr 30min), Haifa (every 30min; 3hr), Kfar Etzion (hourly; 20min), Latrun (3 per hour; 30min), Masada (8 daily; 2hr), Nahariyya (3 daily; 4hr), Netanya (every 20–30min; 1hr 45min), Qiryat Arba (Jewish settlement by Hebron; 2 daily; 1hr), Qiryat Shemona (11 daily; 5hr), Qumran (7 daily; 1hr), Ramle (every 20–30min; 1hr 30min), Safed (1 daily; 3hr), Tel Aviv (3 per hour; 1hr 15min), Tiberias (roughly hourly; 3hr 30min).

In general it is always faster, and no more expensive, to use service taxis (see below) for all West Bank destinations. However, **Arab buses** from East Jerusalem, **serving the West Bank**, leave from two terminals, both near the Damascus Gate. Nablus Road bus station, reached from West Jerusalem on Egged city bus #27, serves Ramallah (every 30min; 40min), Bet Hanina (every 30min; 20min) and Nabi Samwil (every 30min; 30min). East Jerusalem's Central Bus Station on Sultan Suleiman Street serves Bethany (every 30min; 20min) and Abu Dis (3 per hour; 20min). Through services from Hebron and Bethlehem to Ramallah also used to call here, but have been excluded from Jerusalem for some time and currently travel via Abu Dis and Bethany instead.

SHERUTS/SERVICE TAXIS

Sheruts for Tel Aviv operate around the clock from Harav Kook Street with Jaffa Road, near Zion Square in downtown West Jerusalem (☎02/625 4545), and occasionally from HaNeviim Street opposite the Damascus Gate in East Jerusalem. There is also a service to Ben Gurion Airport, operated by Nesher Taxis, 21 King George St (☎02/623 1231), and usually leaving in time to check in for certain flights: places should be booked a day in advance if possible, and they will pick you up from where you are staying (unless it's in the middle of the Old City and inaccessible to traffic). For a more orthodox sherut experience, there's also the Haredi express from Mea She'arim (Strauss with Hayei Adam) direct to Bene Beraq (no Sabbath service).

Service taxis for the West Bank, which usually have nothing to distinguish them from any other Ford Transit, gather around the Damascus Gate. As you come out of the gate, those for Bethlehem and Hebron are to your left, on the left-hand side of HaNeviim Street, while those for Ramallah are to your right along Sultan Suleiman Street (and also on Salah al-Din by the post office). Mercedes service taxis for Bethany and Abu Dis leave across Sultan Suleiman by the Central Bus Station, while those for Allenby Bridge, operated by Taxi Abdo (☎02/628 3281) are to be found on the corner of Sultan Suleiman and HaNeviim. There are no direct service taxis to Jericho or Nablus: change at Bethany and Ramallah respectively.

TRAIN

From Jerusalem's train station on David Remez, 1.5km south west of the Jaffa Gate (see p.312 for buses), there is just one train a day (except Saturday, of course), running to Tel Aviv (2hr) via Bet Shemesh (50min), Ramle (1hr 20min) and Lydda (1hr 30min). This is the scenic route, taking twice as long as the bus, and nearly three times longer than a sherut, but with pretty countryside, and the greater comfort of a train. It connects (very tightly on Fridays) for services southward at Lydda (Lod), and for services northward at Tel Aviv.

PLANE

For international flights from Ben Gurion Airport, take a bus or sherut (see above). Jerusalem also has its own airport at Atarot, 10km north of town (☎02/833440), which will probably take you as long to get to from central Jerusalem as it will to fly from it to anywhere in Israel. There are no direct buses, so either take a cab, or take a Ramallah-bound bus or service taxi from East Jerusalem to the turn-off on the main road, and walk to the terminal from there. Flights serve Eilat (Sun–Thurs 3 daily, 2 on Fri; 55min), Haifa (4 weekly; 30min) and Rosh Pinna (4 weekly; 30min).

CHAPTER SEVEN

THE WEST BANK

C reated in the 1948 war and covering almost six thousand square kilometres to the wexfst of the Jordan River, the **West Bank** is the heartland of Palestine and the setting for most Old Testament events. But for all its biblical significance, a visit here will tell you more about the 1990s AD than the 1990s BC; most of the West Bank's historic locations are now bustling Palestinian towns, somewhat less developed for tourism than their counterparts in Israel, but all the more interesting as a result, and with an unmistakeably Middle Eastern flavour. And while the West Bank may have its troubles, as a visitor you're unlikely to get embroiled.

Even those who prefer to stay firmly on the beaten track will be drawn by the region's ancient sites and biblical associations. Here, in the hills of Judea, lies David's royal city of **Bethlehem**, birthplace of Jesus and magnet for pilgrims, but also a friendly and charming little town in itself; while, to its south, **Hebron** is something of a hot spot in an already contentious area, partly due to the presence of the **Haram al-Khalil** (Tomb of the Patriarchs) – one of the most impressive and bitterly fought over ancient monuments in Israel and the Palestinian Territories. Here, too, nestling in the deep valley of the River Jordan, is **Jericho**, the oldest inhabited city on earth, where the walls tumbled to the sound of Joshua's trumpeters, Ummayad Caliph Hisham built his beautiful summer palace, and, more recently, the Palestinians gained their first taste of autonomy. In the desert around Jericho and Bethlehem are a number of ancient **monasteries**, while set among rather greener hills to the north is ancient **Samaria** (Sebastiya), capital of the biblical kingdom of Israel, and **Nablus**, with its labyrinthine Casbah – a little-known gem not to be missed. Just north of Jerusalem, the cool, upland retreat of **Ramallah** is famous for those rather un-Arab products, beer and the local spirit, *araq*, while Jerusalem itself lies geographically at the heart of the West Bank, and is linked to Israel by the "Jerusalem Corridor", gouged out of the middle of the territory. The West Bank is also home to around 120 Jewish settlements whose presence remains a sticking point in Israeli-Palestinian relations.

As far as **politics** go, the status and extent of the West Bank have been a matter of dispute since it was taken by Israel in the Six Day War in 1967. East Jerusalem and Latrun have been unilaterally annexed by Israel and it does not regard them as part of the territory, but although it does not claim sovereignty over the rest of the West Bank, it has so far officially refused to countenance a Palestinian state here. Legislation even forbids Israeli maps from showing the West Bank or the Green Line separating it from Israel. Israel now calls the territory "**Judea and Samaria**" – after the two post-Solomonic Israelite kingdoms (also called Judah and Israel) – implying that it is part of "Eretz Yisra'el", the land given by God to Abraham, Isaac, Jacob and their descendants in the Old Testament. Though the use of historical names is politically motivated the terms do have a genuine geographical meaning: the hill country around Jerusalem and

---

Due to transport and practical considerations, a few areas that are strictly speaking part of the West Bank are not dealt with in this chapter. They are: **East Jerusalem**, including the Old City, which is covered in the Jerusalem chapter (pp.319–361), **Latrun** on the Tel Aviv–Jerusalem highway, covered on pp.123–125, and the **Dead Sea area** including Qumran, covered on pp.261–263.

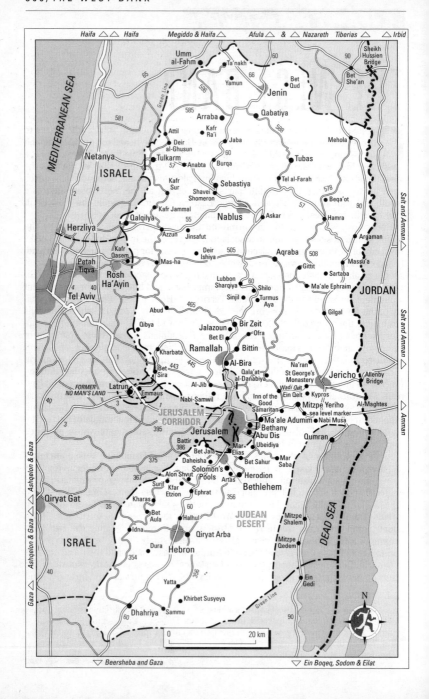

WEST BANK PRACTICALITIES

Transport to the West Bank is theoretically straightforward with **service taxis** being by far the quickest and easiest option. From Jerusalem, these run direct to Bethany, Abu Dis, Ramallah, Bethlehem and sometimes Hebron, but for destinations beyond (such as Nablus or Jericho), you will have to change. **Bus services** exist to most places (except Jericho), but are much slower and no cheaper. Buses from the northern part of the West Bank to the south cannot currently go through Jerusalem and so have to go around it via Bethany and Abu Dis. From Jerusalem, there are bus services to Ramallah and Bethany. Public transport invariably stops early (most buses at around dusk), so you'll need to check the time of the last return bus unless you plan to stay overnight. Note also that **closures of the Green Line** severely disrupt transport, cutting off Jerusalem and often isolating West Bank towns from each other. At such times, tourists can in theory go where they like (though anyone with an Arabic- or Muslim-sounding name may encounter problems), but there will be no service taxis or buses, except to Jewish settlements.

As for **driving**, you would be ill-advised in the current climate to take an Israeli-registered car to the West Bank. The **colour of the numberplate** is a dead giveaway as to its origin (yellow for vehicles registered in Israel or East Jerusalem) and stonings of such obvious targets may occur when tension is high; you definitely don't want to be driving one in the wrong place at the wrong time. Any cars with yellow numberplates that you do see on the West Bank will almost certainly either be owned by settlers or will originate from East Jerusalem. Vehicles registered in the rest of the West Bank have blue plates (or green for a public service vehicle) with a Hebrew letter on the left indicating the town, or, more recently, white number plates with red or green lettering, which are issued by the PNA. In general, you won't see blue or white plates in Israel. The car rental company **Orabi** supplies cars with blue plates for use in the West Bank and has offices in Jerusalem (see "Listings", p.386), Bet Sahur, Jericho (p.423), al-Bira (by Ramallah, p.432), Nablus and Allenby Bridge (p.428).

Accommodation on the West Bank is sparse and budget accommodation virtually non-existent, except for a couple of religious hospices in Bethlehem. On the other hand, if you are willing to pay $35–60 for a double room, you'll get a lot more for your money than you would in Israel. **Restaurants** are also better value here, in all price categories, but your choice of cuisines is almost entirely limited to Middle Eastern. If **sending mail** from the West Bank, remember that autonomous Palestine and Israel have separate postal systems (Israel runs post offices in Area C, the settlements for example, the PNA runs them in Areas A and B): Israeli stamps are valid only in Israeli post offices, and Palestinian stamps in Palestinian ones.

the desert to its southeast, including the southern part of the West Bank, has long been known as Judea; while "Samaria", though previously only used to refer to the biblical kingdom of Israel and its capital, has given the name "Samarian Hills" to the uplands of the northern West Bank.

Given the political situation, you may think it inappropriate to visit the sights, but local people are glad of tourism: it stimulates the economy for one thing, and also allows outsiders to see the real situation. The best way **to visit the West Bank** is with a local Palestinian resident, but it's no problem to go independently; most places are an easy day trip from Jerusalem. Israelis will generally advise that you visit only on Israeli-organized tours, but these naturally concentrate on sites of Jewish interest and will block any contact you might otherwise have with Palestinians. On the plus side, they take you to places you might not get to on your own, such as the Israeli settlements, or isolated religious sites.

As a foreigner you should be reasonably immune from the worst of the West Bank's **troubles** (see p.56 for advice on visiting the Palestinian Territories), but be aware that foreigners are sometimes mistaken for Israelis and, if so, may incur some aggravation.

ACCOMMODATION PRICE CODES

Throughout this guide, **hotel accommodation** is graded on a scale from ① to ⑥. The numbers represent the cost per night of the **cheapest double room in high season**, though remember that many of the cheap places will have more expensive rooms with en-suite facilities. For **hostels**, the code represents the price of **two dorm beds** and is followed by the code for a double room where applicable, ie ①/②. Hostels are listed in ascending price order.

① = less than $20	② = $20–40	③ = $40–60
④ = $60–80	⑤ = $80–100	⑥ = over $100

It's not usually an issue in much-visited places like Bethlehem or Jericho, but in somewhere like Jenin, where tourists are rare, it's a good idea to make it as clear as possible that you're a foreigner, and perhaps to wear a *keffiya* around your neck, or show some other symbol of solidarity. If necessary, seek advice from Palestinian or neutral sources (such as the Christian Information Centre in Jerusalem, see p.309) before setting out. You are particularly advised not to drive a car bearing yellow Israeli plates onto the West Bank (see box on p.391).

Today, some 400,000 of the West Bank's 1.2 million population (minus East Jerusalem and Latrun) are officially classified as refugees, while Israeli settlers number 110,000 or so. If the political situation is of particular interest to you, you could visit one of the **Palestinian refugee camps** or Jewish settlements. Whatever image the name might conjure up, the camps are not makeshift tent cities, but small towns in their own right, and while living conditions in them are hard, residents are pleased to see outsiders and be given the chance to tell their side of the story. It's best **to arrange a visit**, either through a hostel in Jerusalem (see p.314), or through the UNRWA in Jerusalem (see "Listings", p.387). Visiting the **Jewish settlements** is easier still as most are served (albeit infrequently) by Egged buses. Kfar Etzion (see p.407) is the most interesting, but Qiryat Arba (see p.413), next to Hebron, is probably the easiest, being connected by bus to Jerusalem and Beersheba, and accessible directly from Hebron via the Tomb of the Patriarchs.

Some history

The West Bank came into existence in **1948**, as the area which the Arab forces, especially the **Transjordanian Arab Legion**, succeeded in holding (helped by the region's mountainous landscape), with some adjustments following the Rhodes Armistice of 1949, including the handover of much of the Little Triangle (see p.152) to Israel. King Abdullah annexed the West Bank to Transjordan, renaming his kingdom Jordan, and dividing the West Bank (which held half of Jordan's population) into three administrative districts (Jerusalem, Hebron and Nablus) ruled from Amman; a set-up that continued under Abdullah's successor, King Hussein. The local economy was based on agriculture, with the East Bank (the rest of Jordan) its main market; all major industry was kept east of the river.

When Israel took the West Bank in **1967**, its population was 670,000, of which 120,000 were refugees from 1948. The same number fled before the IDF advance, although despite Absentee Property Regulations (see p.495), Israel did in fact let around a third of them return over the next three years. At first, Israeli rule was relatively light-handed; borders were left open, enabling West Bankers to export their produce freely (though the balance of trade moved swiftly in Israel's favour), and Israel also set up elected local government, with turnouts of over 80 percent at the first polls in 1972.

Nevertheless, there was **resistance** from the outset, with public sector strikes, walkouts of traders and students, and guerrilla activity. Israel responded with increasing military regulations, detentions, deportations, and collective punishments (including curfews and demolition of homes) of villages thought to be the source of guerrilla attacks.

Israeli settlement also began almost immediately, with Gush Etzion (see p.407), and the Nahal kibbutzim along the Jordan Valley, which provided a front line against invasion from the east. In 1970, the **Allon Plan** proposed Israeli settlements along the Jordan Valley and the Jerusalem–Jericho highway, leaving two Palestinian areas whose return could be negotiated with Jordan. But, the 1972 settlement at Qiryat Arba (see p.413), and 1974 establishment of **Gush Emunim** (see p.410), departed from the existing plan of establishing settlements only in places of strategic military importance (usually on sparsely populated non-agricultural land), and aimed instead to annexe land by settling it. This new type of politically motivated settler (often from the United States) gained government support when Likud came to power in 1977, with priority given to settling areas of high Palestinian population density. Major towns were ringed by Jewish settlements linked by a strategic road network but, despite massive state subsidies, financial incentives and funds from Zionist organizations abroad, few Israelis or immigrants moved in – even today many settlement homes remain unoccupied.

In the wake of the **1974 Yom Kippur War** there was an **upsurge of opposition** to Israeli rule. Solidarity was also expressed on an official level and the elections of 1976 returned PLO supporters as mayors in several West Bank towns. The 1978 Camp David agreement proposing Israeli withdrawal to "specified security locations" was opposed by both West Bank Palestinians and the growing number of militant Jewish settlers and led to disturbances across the territory, with an escalation of hostility between the two groups: in May 1980 there was a grenade attack on Jews in Hebron; on the same day the following month, Hebron market received a similar attack and the mayors of Nablus, Ramallah and al-Bira were victims of separate car bomb incidents – acts of revenge thought to have been perpetrated by settlers. Later that year, in an attempt to undermine the pro-PLO mayors, Defence Minister and Gush Emunim supporter Ariel Sharon set up a new **Civil Administration** of the West Bank and Gaza, under Menahem Milson, together with pro-Israeli "**Village Leagues**", but no reputable local politician would have anything to do with them and few local people would work for or cooperate with them.

Milson's next tactic, the dismissal of the mayors and councils of al-Bira, Ramallah and Nablus in spring 1982, led to **riots** across the West Bank. Though Sharon managed to quell the disturbances, they were a taster of things to come: in 1987, the **Intifada** broke out in Gaza (see p.450) and quickly spread to the West Bank, with Hebron, Nablus and Bir Zeit University the main centres of rebellion. The youth (*shabab*) took the lead, burning tyres to create a beacon of smoke visible from afar, then stoning and taunting Israeli troops when they arrived. Anti-Israeli graffiti appeared overnight in every West Bank town and the streets were littered with UNLU flyers ordering strikes and shutdowns, or giving news or propaganda on the latest situation.

With the **Oslo Accords**, Israel agreed a phased handover of the West Bank to a Palestinian National Authority, Jordan having given up its claim to the territory in 1988. Delays, naturally, slowed down the pull-out and a serious blow was dealt in February 1994 with the massacre by an Israeli settler at the Haram al-Khalil in Hebron (see p.410). Nonetheless, in May of that year, Israel handed over Jericho to the PNA along with Gaza, followed in November and December 1995 (behind schedule) by Jenin, Bethlehem, Nablus, Ramallah, Tulkarm and Qalqilya. Hebron remained a sticking point, but Israel substantially pulled out in January 1997, handing 80 percent of it over to the PNA.

The West Bank today is a patchwork of different areas of control: "Area A" (around six percent of the land), under PNA jurisdiction, comprises the main towns including most of Hebron, but not al-Bira; "Area B", includes a large number of Palestinian villages, with the PNA responsible for internal administration, Israel for security and policing; and "Area C", formed by the settlements and the roads linking them, is entirely under Israeli jurisdiction. For residents, things have worsened rather than improved since the Oslo Accords. Israel has now expropriated some 67 percent of the West Bank and, when the Green Line is closed, West Bank residents cannot cross into Israel or East Jerusalem, or even travel between the islands of Area A from one West Bank town to another. Even when the Line is open, West Bank Palestinians need a permit to cross it, which causes great difficulty as East Jerusalem is the West Bank's nucleus and transport hub, straddling the main route between its northern and southern halves. In the meantime, settlement continues, but Palestinians are rarely given permits to build in Area C, and their homes are regularly demolished for being built without permission. Unemployment remains high, imports and exports are restricted, and the PNA's record is increasingly suspect: alongside allegations of corruption, human rights abuses are commonplace, including arbitrary arrest, torture and press censorship, and, as public opinion is increasingly alienated from Oslo and the PNA, support for the radical fundamentalists of Hamas and Islamic Jihad grows, and real peace seems further away than ever.

SOUTH OF JERUSALEM

The road **south from Jerusalem** (Route 60, the Hebron Road), along the spine of the **Judean Hills**, may be faster now than it was for the ancient biblical figures, but it probably looks very similar: the vineyards, olive trees and rolling hills would all be familiar to Abraham, David or Jesus if they passed this way today. Heading out from the Old City's Jaffa Gate, the road crosses the 1967 border at the monastery of **Mar Elias**, before passing the **tomb of the biblical matriarch Rachel** on the edge of **Bethlehem**. Around Bethlehem and along and just off Route 60 as it continues on to **Hebron** are scores of sites reflecting the area's biblical and historical associations, among them the Shepherd's Field at **Bet Sahur**, Herod's fortress at **Herodion**, and **Solomon's Pools**. Along the way, you'll also see evidence of the region's more recent history in the form of numerous settlements and refugee camps. From Hebron, Route 60 continues south to Beersheba.

Mar Elias

Five kilometres south of Jerusalem, the white limestone building on the saddle of a hill giving a panoramic view of Bethlehem and Herodion is the Greek Orthodox monastery of **Mar Elias** (Mon–Sat 8–11am & 1–5pm), reached from Jerusalem on Egged bus #30 from Jaffa Road by City Hall or the Jaffa Gate. According to one tradition, the prophet Elijah slept here; another holds that a Greek bishop of Bethlehem, Elias, was buried here in 1345; while yet another version places the sepulchre of St Elias, an Egyptian monk who became Patriarch of Jerusalem in 494, on the site. Whatever its true origins (the original date is uncertain, but the buildings were restored by the Crusaders), the monastery did hold the tomb of a Bishop Elias up to the seventeenth century and was an agricultural community, its monks cultivating such crops as olives and grapes. Today, Mar Elias is believed to answer the prayers of barren women and ailing children and is also a popular site for pilgrimage. Before making their entry to Bethlehem on the **Christmas Day procession**, the Patriarchs traditionally pause here to be received by the notables of the area.

Close by, the **Field of Grey Peas**, covered with millions of small pebbles, gave rise to a parable on the consequences of telling lies. The story goes that a man was sowing chickpeas in the field when Mary (according to other versions it is Jesus) passed by and asked him: "What are you sowing there, my friend?" "Stones," the man answered. "Very well, you will reap stones," was the reply. When the sower came to gather his crops, he found nothing but petrified chickpeas. Opposite the field, the **Tantur Ecumenical Institute** was established in 1964 to promote understanding between the Churches. The building, originally a hospice built in 1876, houses a large and impressive library.

Rachel's Tomb

Next to Route 60 as it enters Bethlehem, 3km south of Mar Elias and 3km north of Manger Square, **Rachel's Tomb** (Sun–Thurs 7.30am–4pm, Fri 7.30am–1.30pm, though you may be allowed in outside those times depending on the mood of the soldiers guarding it; free) is traditionally held to be the burial place of the biblical matriarch, favourite wife of Jacob, and mother of two of his twelve sons, Joseph and Benjamin. According to Genesis 35: 19, "Rachel died and was buried in the way to Ephrath which is Bethlehem. And Jacob set a pillar upon her grave; that is the pillar of Rachel's grave unto this day." There has been a succession of synagogues on the site: the building which houses the tomb today was originally erected by the Ottoman Turks in the 1620s, although the dome over it was rebuilt for Sir Moses Montefiore (see p.369) in 1860. The all-new structure surrounding it was built in 1997.

Revered by Jews, the place is also holy to Muslims because of the cemetery of the Bedouin Ta'amre tribe that lies in its grounds. From 1948 to 1967, the site was under the protection of the Islamic Waqf and in theory open to Jewish worshippers, though not to Israelis, who were unable to enter Jordan. Today, barricaded off from the PNA territory in which it forms an enclave, it is under permanent guard by Israeli soldiers and open to all except Arabs. **Inside**, there's little to see: just a velvet-draped **tomb** inside a synagogue. Nevertheless, Jewish women come to pray here for children – a slightly dubious practice theologically, given that the concept of saintly intercession is frowned upon by Judaism, though of course the supplicants do not actually pray *to* Rachel, simply in her vicinity.

Bethlehem

Thou Bethlehem Ephrathah, though thou be little among the thousands of Judah, yet out of thee shall he come forth unto me that is to be ruler in Israel.

Micah 5: 2

BETHLEHEM, surrounded by gorges, fertile terraces and fields supplying grain, olives and grapes, straddles two plateaus just to the south of Jerusalem. As the birthplace of Christ, this small, rose-coloured city is known the world over, but don't expect too much holiness: modern Bethlehem is a major tourist attraction, with all the commercialism that this implies, and romantic as it sounds, **Manger Square** in the town centre is in fact a giant parking lot, struggling to cope with all the cars, taxis and tour buses.

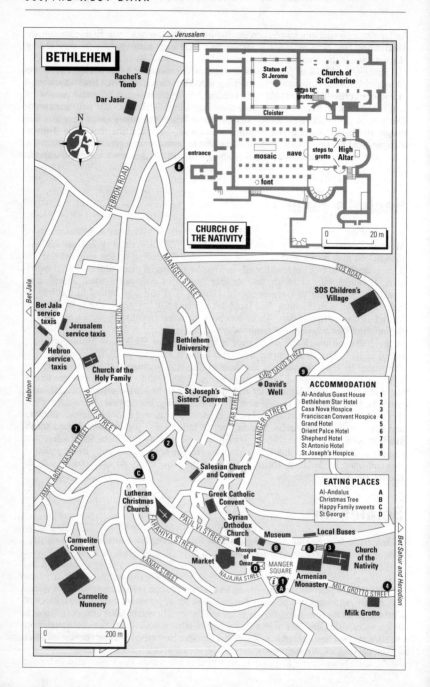

BETHLEHEM

△ Jerusalem

Rachel's Tomb

Dar Jasir

N

Bet Jala

HEBRON ROAD

Bet Jala service taxis

Jerusalem service taxis

Hebron service taxis

Church of the Holy Family

Hebron △

YOUTH STREET

MANGER STREET

SOS ROAD

SOS Children's Village

Bethlehem University

KING DAVID STREET

St Joseph's Sisters' Convent

David's Well

MANGER STREET

STAR STREET

9

PAUL VI STREET

JAMAL ABDEL NASSER STREET

7

2

5

C

Salesian Church and Convent

Greek Catholic Convent

Syrian Orthodox Church

Lutheran Christmas Church

PAUL VI STREET

FARAHIYA STREET

Carmelite Convent

KANAH STREET

Market

NAJAJRA STREET

Mosque of Omar

Museum

B

D

MANGER SQUARE

i

1

A

Local Buses

6

3

Church of the Nativity

Armenian Monastery

MILK GROTTO STREET

4

Carmelite Nunnery

Milk Grotto

△ Bet Sahur and Herodion

0   200 m

ACCOMMODATION

Al-Andalus Guest House	1
Bethlehem Star Hotel	2
Casa Nova Hospice	3
Franciscan Convent Hospice	4
Grand Hotel	5
Orient Palce Hotel	6
Shepherd Hotel	7
St Antonio Hotel	8
St Joseph's Hospice	9

EATING PLACES

Al-Andalus	A
Christmas Tree	B
Happy Family sweets	C
St George	D

Statue of St Jerome

Church of St Catherine

Cloister

steps to grotto

entrance

mosaic

nave

steps to grotto

High Altar

font

CHURCH OF THE NATIVITY

0   20 m

But away from the busloads of pilgrims, who rarely venture beyond Manger Square, Bethlehem is a charming little town, with quiet side streets, friendly people, and Christian monastics of various sects going about with a dignified air of quiet devotion. Its **souq** is a magic mixture of ancient and modern where you can find anything from hand-woven rugs to plastic kitchen utensils, and see students from Bethlehem University cross paths with priests, nuns and Bedouin traders. A wander around its shops turns up all manner of surprises: butchers advertise that rarity, "pork meat", and the local souvenir shops offer not only the anticipated kitsch nativity scenes and holy water, but more traditional items – religious objects carved from olive wood (with its unmistakeable odour, especially when being worked), mother-of-pearl and coral – the sale of which to tourists and pilgrims has brought the town much of its prosperity. Bethlehem is renowned for its beautifully delicate glassware, which you can see being made in the workshops around town; it also has a long tradition of skilled stonemasons who work the high-quality stone from surrounding quarries.

The plethora of chapels and religious institutions here represent every shade of Christianity: Egyptian Copts, Armenians, Syrian Jacobites, Greek Orthodox, Roman Catholics, Anglicans and Lutherans. Thus, **Christmas** is celebrated three times in Bethlehem: on December 25 by the Catholics and other Western churches; on January 6 by the Armenians who keep to the Eastern calendar; and on January 7 by the Greek Orthodox and other Eastern churches who follow the Julian calendar.

As you might expect, Bethlehem is banking on pulling in large numbers of visitors in the year 2000. The PNA has set up a **Bethlehem 2000** project under the popular Palestinian minister Hanan Ashrawi and, in conjunction with UNESCO, aims to reno-vate Manger Square, Star Street and the souq, as well as neighbouring sites at Bet Sahur, Bet Jala and Solomon's Pools. Top local and international artists and musicians will be performing here and celebrations are expected to last from the beginning of 1999 until the end of 2000, though it's uncertain as to how much of the work will be fin-ished on time. One of the major problems (as it was two thousand years ago) will be the lack of accommodation; a gap in the market that Israel is already making the most of by preparing suitable hotels just outside Jerusalem's city limits.

Bethlehem in history

Bethlehem, thought to have been inhabited since the Stone Age, occupies a place of some prominence in the **Old Testament**. Jacob's wife Rachel died and was buried here, and it was in Bethlehem that Boaz fell in love with the Moabite convert Ruth in the biblical book named after her; their great-grandson David was also born here and tended his flocks on the hills around until selected by the prophet Samuel to take over from Saul as king of Israel (I Samuel 16: 1–13). And, of course, it was to Bethlehem that **Mary and Joseph** came in response to a census ordered by Emperor Augustus. As St Luke tells it (Luke 2: 4–5), "Joseph also went up from Galilee, out of the city of Nazareth, into Judaea, unto the City of David which is called Bethlehem (because he was of the house and lineage of David) to be taxed with Mary his espoused wife, being great with child." Famously unable to find lodging for the night, the couple were forced to shelter in a stable (actually it was probably a cave in the back area of a house, as was typical of a Bethlehem home), and in such humble surrounds, the baby was born and laid in a manger to sleep. The "wise men from the east" (Matthew 2: 1) journeyed to Bethlehem to find Him, following the star which had stopped above His birthplace (Matthew 2: 9), and which remains today as the town's symbol.

Bethlehem gained the importance it holds for Christians today following the **Edict of Milan** of 313 AD, by which Emperor Constantine legalized Christianity. Only then were Christians able to emerge from their clandestine status. Constantine's mother, Queen Helena, embarked on a pilgrimage to the Holy Land in 326 AD to investigate three sites which had been revered since the early days of Christianity – the site of Jesus's burial at

Golgotha (see p.332), the Grotto of Gethsemane on the Mount of Olives (see p.359) and the **Grotto of the Nativity** in Bethlehem. The identification of this latter site is due in large measure to the Roman emperor Hadrian: in order to suppress any Jewish-inspired messianic movement following the Bar Kokhba Revolt (132–35 AD), Hadrian paganized all the main Judaeo-Christian holy places, including the Temple and the Holy Sepulchre in Jerusalem. Over the Grotto of the Nativity he planted the **Grove of Thammuz**, a shrine dedicated to Adonis. Far from deterring Christians from revering the site, it was thus affirmed as the birthplace of Christ. In 339 AD, Helena instigated the construction of a church, the **Basilica of the Nativity**, on the spot.

In **Byzantine** times, Bethlehem was a walled city with two towers, figuring both in the famous Mabada Map (see p.343) and in the accounts of early pilgrims. The city was damaged in the Samaritan Revolt of 529 AD, but the emperor Justinian (527–565) repaired its walls and buildings and ordered Helena's original church to be rebuilt "in such splendour, size and beauty that none even in the Holy City should surpass it". By 600 AD, many monasteries and churches had been erected in the now flourishing town and when, fourteen years later, the **Persian** invaders destroyed many of the sanctuaries in the land, the Basilica of the Nativity was one of the few saved; an event recorded in a letter from the Jerusalem Synod of 838, which states that, having reached Bethlehem, the Persians "were greatly surprised to discover a representation of the Magi from Persia. Out of reverence and respect for their ancestors they decided to honour these sages by sparing the church. And this is how it has survived until this day."

During the **Muslim period**, the sites revered by the two other "religions of the book", Judaism and Christianity, were protected. In 638, Omar Ibn al-Khattab prayed towards Mecca in the southern apse of the Church of the Nativity: the Mosque of Omar with its fine minaret opposite the church commemorates this gesture. With the **Crusader** invasion of 1099, Bethlehem was captured by Tancred and became the site for the crowning of Crusader kings, above all the great coronation of Baldwin I in 1100. Saladin's forces recaptured Bethlehem in 1187, but the Ayyubid sultan Malik al-Kamil returned Bethlehem to the Crusaders in 1229 and they held it until finally ousted from the country in 1291.

But for all its fame, Bethlehem remained an extremely small town. At the beginning of the twentieth century, the **population** numbered 8200 and by 1922 it had actually decreased to 6650. The fact that 30,000 people live here today is largely due to the influx of Palestinian refugees in 1948, who together with their descendants form some sixty per cent of the inhabitants.

Arrival, information and accommodation

Arriving by service taxi from Jerusalem or Hebron, you will be dropped on the Hebron Road at the corner of Paul VI street, which leads after a kilometre or so to Manger Square in the town centre. Bethlehem's **tourist information office**, run by the PNA tourist ministry (Mon–Sat 8am–2.30pm; ☎02/741581) is on the south side of Manger Square, up on the second floor, and has maps of Bethlehem and local information, but nothing on the rest of the West Bank. **Moneychangers** can be found on Paul VI Street, just off Manger Square, and there are three **banks** on the square itself. The **post office** is also on Manger Square, on the west side, next to the Municipality.

Accommodation

Bethlehem has a reasonable range of lodgings to suit all budgets, but it's very hard to find a room on spec around Christmas and Easter, when you're almost certainly better off visiting Bethlehem on a day trip from Jerusalem. Many hotels put their prices up at these peak times; in the summer, when business is slack, you may be able to bargain.

Al-Andalus Guest House, Manger Sq, south side (☎02/741348, fax 742280). Clean and central; all rooms have toilet and heating, and some have views over the square, which goes some way to compensating for the lino floor and chipboard furniture. ④.

Bethlehem Star Hotel, Freres St (☎02/743249, fax 741494). In a quiet location up a side street off Paul VI, with comfortable, centrally heated rooms and friendly staff, catering largely to Irish pilgrim groups. Some rooms have a view over the town centre, and if your room doesn't have a TV, you can ask for one. ④.

Casa Nova Hospice, Manger Sq, next to St Catherine's Church (☎02/743980 or 1, fax 743540). Run by the Franciscans with a central location and well-kept rooms, but often full with pilgrim groups. There's an 11pm curfew and 8am checkout. ③.

Franciscan Convent Hospice, Milk Grotto St, almost opposite the Milk Grotto (☎02/742441). Run by nine "White Sisters" – Les Soeurs Franciscaines de Marie – this is not strictly a hotel, but can offer a place to sleep (some rooms with shower) and is particularly welcoming to women (for whom there may also be dorm space). It's very quiet, and spotless, with a great view of the Judean desert. Curfew at 9pm, extended at Christmas time. ①/②.

Grand Hotel, Freres St, at the corner with Paul VI (☎02/741440, fax 741604). Bright, very spacious rooms, but rather impersonal. ④.

Orient Palace Hotel, Manger Sq, northeast corner (☎02/742798, fax 741562). Newly renovated, this is the plushest hotel in town with tasteful classical Arab decor and modern conveniences, including orthopedic mattresses on every bed. ⑥.

St Antonio Hotel, off Manger St (☎ & fax 02/647 0524). Homely and quiet if a little out of the way. You may be able to get bargain rates here out of season. ③.

St Joseph's Hospice, Manger St, north of Manger Sq (☎02/647 0155, fax 647 0334). Run by Syrian Catholics and often booked up by pilgrims and youth groups, but may have rooms available for others. ②.

Shepherd Hotel, Jamal Abdel Nasser St (☎02 740656). Fancy and comfortable, catering mainly for groups. ③.

The Town

The Bethlehem skyline is an amazing array of architectural forms, old and new, Arab and Western, towers and belfries, domes and spires. Most of its sights are within easy reach of Manger Square, where you'll find Bethlehem's number one draw, the **Church of the Nativity**, along with the neighbouring **St Catherine's Church** and **Armenian Monastery**. The **Milk Grotto**, **Market**, **Syrian Orthodox Church** and **Bethlehem Museum** are all within a stone's throw, though the Old Testament sites of **David's Well** and **Rachel's Tomb** (see p.395) are further afield.

The Church of the Nativity

Looking more like a fortress than a church, the **Church of the Nativity** (daily: Feb–April 5.30am–6pm; May–Oct 5.30am–6.30pm; Nov–Jan 5.30am–5pm), entered from Manger Square, holds pride of place in the town. Descriptions of the church by pilgrims through the centuries support the theory that the present structure is basically the original building established by Queen Helena at the time of Constantine, and enlarged and restored under Emperor Justinian in the sixth century, which makes it one of the oldest churches in the world. It was later expanded by the addition of several chapels and monasteries: on the south side, churches and monasteries belonging to the Armenian and Greek Orthodox churches adjoin the ancient basilica; at the northern end is the Franciscan hospice and monastery, and the Church of St Catherine. Inside, the different groups maintain a precarious coexistence through an intricate schedule of worship. Control of the church has more than once led to physical warfare, most significantly when Napoleon III, who considered himself successor to the French Crusader king Louis IX, declared the entire complex French property in 1852 – an act that brought him into conflict with Russia, which supported the rights of the Eastern Orthodox Church, and was one of the causes of the Crimean War.

The forbidding building has three **entrances**, two of them bricked up and the third small and out of scale with the importance of the interior. In fact this main door of Justinian's church was once grand (you can still see the shape of the original arch) but it was lowered by the Crusaders during the Middle Ages and further restricted during the Ottoman era to prevent mounted horsemen from entering the church. The vestibule behind the entrance leads directly into the main hall of the basilica, divided into a central **nave** and two aisles by golden-coloured columns of local stone; mosaics on the side walls and under the current floor (revealed under lifted-up wooden panels in the middle of the vestibule), show how splendid the original church must have been.

Often indicated by long queues, the stairs on the right of the altar lead down into the **Grotto of the Nativity**, supposed site of Jesus's birth; a fourteen-pointed silver star embedded in white marble marks the exact spot. The star was installed by the Catholics in 1717, removed by the Greeks in 1847 and replaced by the Turkish government in 1853, and bears the inscription, *Hic de Virgine Maria Jesus Christus natus est* – Here Jesus Christ was born to the Virgin Mary. Of the fifteen lamps burning around the recess, six belong to the Greeks, five to the Armenians and four to the Roman Catholics. In another corner of the grotto, down three steps opposite the Altar of the Nativity, is the **Chapel of the Manger** where Christ was laid. Behind the marble manger, in which a doll of the baby Jesus reposes on a bit of straw, is a painting of the nativity scene showing him in an altogether different type of manger. Facing this, is the **Altar of the Adoration of the Magi**. Other caves connected to the Grotto are usually closed off from it, and are accessed from the Church of St Catherine (see below).

The Church of Saint Catherine

A small door in the north wall of the basilica leads to the tranquil vaulted Crusader cloister, centred around the statue of St Jerome that stands in front of the Franciscan **Church of Saint Catherine** (daily: summer 5am–noon & 2–6pm, winter 5am–noon & 2–5pm). This church, where Christ is said to have appeared to St Catherine of Alexandria, was built in 1881, incorporating remains of Crusader buildings discovered during construction. A far lighter, airier space than the main basilica, it is from here that **Midnight Mass on Christmas Eve** is televised and beamed worldwide. If you want to be there, special buses usually run from Jerusalem (check with the Christian Information Centre inside Jerusalem's Jaffa Gate for details); the square is packed out and it gets pretty cold standing around, so take warm clothes. The daily procession of Franciscan Fathers from the church to the basilica (at noon, or 1pm during daylight saving) is also well worth watching – it's one of the few times when an air of solemnity descends on the bustle of Manger Square.

From the church, medieval stairs lead down into a complex of **caves and tombs** linked to the Grotto of the Nativity (although there's no public access from one to the other). The main altar in this impressive subterranean complex is devoted to **Saint Joseph**, the earthly father of Christ, and is said to be where he had the dream in which an angel warned him to flee to Egypt to safeguard the child Jesus from Herod's anger. Next to it, the **Chapel of the Innocents** commemorates the children who were slaughtered by Herod after the Holy Family had left (Matthew 3: 16). Also off St Joseph's chapel is the **Tomb of Saint Jerome**, a Dalmatian priest who arrived in Bethlehem from Rome in 386 AD, and adjoining it is the room where he secluded himself to study the Bible, and began a translation of the Old Testament from Hebrew to Latin which, as the **Vulgate**, was to become the official version of the Old Testament used by the Roman Catholic Church for the next 1500 years. Jerome died in 420 AD, and buried with him are two of his followers, St Paula and her daughter Eustochium, who founded a convent nearby. The cell where St Jerome executed his mammoth task is now a chapel.

The Armenian Monastery

To the south of the forecourt of the Church of the Nativity lies the **Armenian Monastery** (daily: Feb–April 5.30am–6pm; May–Oct 5.30am–6.30pm; Nov–Jan 5.30am–5pm), dating mainly from the Byzantine and Crusader periods. Once a major centre for Armenian hermits and later full of seventeenth-century scribes copying and illustrating Bibles, it's now home to only six monks and provides community services for Bethlehem's three hundred Armenians. The water of the well facing the arched entrance is believed by pilgrims to have curative properties.

The grand colonnaded **hall** in the arched vaults of the monastery – described by pilgrims as "St Jerome's University" – is thought to have been used by St Jerome as a lecture hall, and there are stables in the basement which housed the horses of the pilgrims and devotees who stayed at the monastery. The monastery church is adorned with magnificent blue Armenian tiles and three wood-sculptured altars; take a look, too, at the baptismal font and the eighteenth-century painting depicting the baptism of Christ. From the roof of the monastery you get a panoramic view of Bethlehem and its terraced surroundings.

Other sites around town

Five minutes' walk southeast of Manger Square, along Milk Grotto Street, you'll find the **Milk Grotto** itself (daily 8–11.45am & 2–5pm). In one version of the story, the Holy Family hid here during the Slaughter of the Innocents; in another, they made a hurried stop here during the flight to Egypt. Either way, in their haste Mary let a drop of her milk fall while nursing the baby Jesus, so turning the rock from red to chalky white. Ever since, Christians and Muslims alike have believed that the rock increases a nursing mother's milk and fertility; from the seventh century until the nineteenth, European pilgrims used to chip off tiny pieces of the rock to take home as souvenirs, and women hoping to conceive still come to pray in the chapel. The influence of Italian art on the facade of the church is evident, and can also be seen in many of the icons inside, mostly depicting a fair-skinned, light-haired Virgin. The cave-like interior, dominated by a golden statuette of Mary, has a blue-painted roof and is a wonderfully cool and serene escape from the summer heat outside.

West off Manger Square and up the stairs along Paul VI Street, you come to the impressive **Syrian Orthodox Church** with the small but atmospheric **souq** just beyond. Surprisingly untouched by the ravages of tourist commercialism, the goods on sale – clothes, household goods, meat, fruit and veg – are purely for local consumption, with not a souvenir or a bottle of holy water in sight. On the way, left off Paul VI before you reach the Syrian church, the **Bethlehem Museum** (Mon–Wed, Fri & Sat 8am–5pm, Thurs 8am–noon; 3NIS), is also well worth a visit. Established in 1971 by the Arab Women's Union with the aim of protecting a threatened Palestinian cultural heritage, the Union has collected popular household articles and displays them in a traditional house: there's a reconstructed *diwan* (living room) complete with carpets and *kanoon* (brass charcoal stove) and a kitchen with pottery, wood, brass and straw utensils. You can also see local embroidered clothing and traditional jewellery of coral, gold and silver, and lots of fascinating old photos of the town; one of them depicts the British High Commissioner on a visit, flanked by members of the politically rival Husseini and Nashashibi families. Free guided tours of the museum are given in English, and a small showroom upstairs sells exquisite examples of local hand-embroidered items, made by local women.

North of Manger Square in King David Street, **King David's Well** is the only monument in Bethlehem to the famous king who was born here. It marks the site where his soldiers broke through Philistine lines in order to fetch him drinking water from a well after he cried, "O that one would give me drink of the water of the well of Bethlehem which is by the gate!" (II Samuel 23: 15). David was so awed by this that he offered the hard-gotten water as a libation to God. The "well" is in fact three large cisterns.

MOVING ON FROM BETHLEHEM

Transport has been restricted by closures of the Green Line. If these are lifted, there should be **bus** services to Jerusalem (every 30min; 30min). In the meantime, buses run from the Hebron Road to Ramallah (every 30min; 1hr 30min), and Hebron (every 30min; 40min), while blue and white buses from Manger Street behind the police station serve local destinations such as Bet Jala (every 30min; 10min); Bet Sahur (every 30min; 10min), Solomon's Pools (every 30min; 30min), and the Israeli checkpoint at Tantura on the way to Jerusalem (every 30min; 15min). **Service taxis** from the Hebron Road at the junction with Paul VI Street reach Jerusalem, Hebron and Bet Jala. Bet Jala, Bet Sahur and even, at a pinch, Jerusalem, can also be reached on foot if you're fit and in the mood, but remember to take lots of water and sun protection. There is no public transport to Herodion.

Eating

For **food**, there are a number of places in Manger Square including the *Christmas Tree Restaurant* on the north side serving up falafel, *shawarma* and suchlike (daily 6.30am–5pm; cheap), and, in the square's southwestern corner, the *St George Restaurant* (daily 8am–6pm; expensive), offering a fine selection of grilled meat and poultry. The *Al-Andalus*, just off the square at its southeastern corner (daily 8am–5pm daily; moderate), caters mainly for tour groups, serving hamburgers and cheeseburgers in addition to more Middle Eastern fare. *Happy Family Sweets*, on Paul VI St near the Lutheran Church (daily 10am–10pm), offers the chance to sit down and get stuck in to its sticky confections.

Around Bethlehem

Within easy reach of Bethlehem there are a number of smaller sites worth exploring, most of them accessible on local buses, by service taxis (see box above for details) or on foot. First, and closest, is the Palestinian village of **Bet Sahur**, barely a kilometre east from the Church of the Nativity along Shepherds Street, but further to the east you'll find a couple of ancient **monasteries** and Herod's masterpiece – the fortress of **Herodion**. To the west are the villages of **Bet Jala** and **al-Khader**.

Bet Sahur and the Shepherds' Field

The village of **BET SAHUR**, set in an idyllic landscape of olive groves and cornfields 1.5km east of Bethlehem, has origins going back to the Bronze Age. Its modern economy is a mix of traditional and futuristic: in October and November every year – the **olive-picking** season – the population of around eight thousand is swelled by hundreds of people from surrounding villages who come to process their harvest at its oil presses (some modern, but most seemingly centuries old), but Bet Sahur has also established itself as a hi-tech manufacturing centre, the West Bank's answer to "silicon valley". If you don't want to walk here from Bethlehem, you can take the bus, which drops you in the centre.

There are some fine churches in the town and some beautiful villas but the reason most people come here is to visit the **Shepherds' Field**, ten minutes' walk away (take a left at the far end of the village). Since at least the seventh century, this has been identified as the place where the angel of the Lord visited the shepherds and told them of the imminent birth of the Saviour in Bethlehem (Luke 2: 12). Several rival sites claim

Nazareth: St Gabriel's Greek Orthodox Church

Safed: HaAri Ashkenazi Synagogue

Capernaum: the synagogue

Acre: Sinan Pasha Mosque

Sepphoris: view of the site from the Roman theatre

The Golan Heights: Castle Nimrod

Olive stall in Qiryat Shemona market

'Ayun Nature Reserve, near Metulla

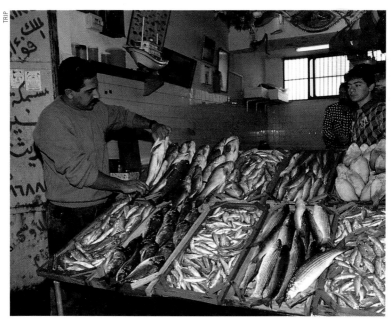

Gaza City fish market

Mount Hermon

Israeli war memorial, Golan Heights

to mark the exact spot, with the weight of tradition centring on two: **Der al-Ra'wat** (daily 8–11.30am & 2–5pm), operated by the Greek Orthodox Church, and **Siar al-Ghanem** (same hours), maintained by the Franciscans.

The 1989 **Greek Church** was erected near the traditional site of the Grotto of the Shepherds. Marking the scene of the apparition, the subterranean chapel here dates from the fourth century and contains frescoes and traces of a Byzantine mosaic pavement. The Franciscans' site has a similarly long history: excavations here revealed a vast monastic settlement, cisterns and grottoes, and there are remains of a Byzantine church from the fourth century. The modern, tent-shaped 1954 Franciscan **Church of the Angels**, designed by Antonio Barluzzi, is built over a cave in which the shepherds are supposed to have lived. Inside, the altar is decorated with fifteen panels depicting various scenes from the annunciation to the arrival of the Holy Family in Egypt. The figures are, as ever, fair-skinned and closer inspection of the sheep, particularly their tails, reveals a distinctly non-Middle Eastern breed of animal.

Nearby are the remains of a watchtower, the **Tower of Edar** or Tower of the Flocks, said to be a tower mentioned in the Torah (Genesis 35: 21) and yet another contender for the site of the angel's appearance to the shepherds. On a more romantic note, another field immediately to the north of the Greek Orthodox Church is identified as the **Field of Ruth**, were Boaz saw the biblical heroine gleaning in his field and fell in love with her (Ruth 2: 2–12). The couple subsequently married and became the great-grandparents of David and ancestors of all Judah's kings.

The Monastery of Saint Theodosius ·

On a rise to the left of the road, 8km east of Bethlehem and overlooking the village of Ubeidiya, lies the **Monastery of Saint Theodosius** (Mon–Sat 8am–11am; ring for admittance, though you may be refused). St Theodosius, a monk from Cappadocia, was staying in Jerusalem when he was directed by God to seek out a cave where the Three Wise Men from the east had rested after paying homage to Jesus in Bethlehem, having

---

MONASTICISM IN THE JUDEAN DESERT

The arid wilderness of the **Judean desert** rolls eastward from Bethlehem to the Jordan Rift Valley and the Dead Sea, a furnace of white light in the morning, iron red at sunset. Here, Jesus is said to have fought his greatest battle, led into the wilderness "to be tempted of the devil" (see p.425) after forty days and nights of fasting (Matthew 4: 1–2). However, monasticism in the Judean Desert actually predated Jesus: the prophet **Elijah**, called by some the first true monk, wandered in the desert for forty days and nights without food, while the Essenes of Jesus's own time chose desert isolation to seek God free from the distractions of the rat race. From the fifth century on, with the country in the hands of Christian rulers in Byzantium, the example set by Elijah and the Essenes began to be followed by **Christian monks**, mostly from Cappadocia in Central Turkey, Asia Minor and Armenia, who came in search of perfection and solitude. They lived at the limits of human endurance in the most remote desert gorges and caves, surviving on roots. The harsh climatic conditions were to them symbolic of the evil powers which threatened the human spirit and which had to be fought. Yet these ascetics were also active scholars and many stories of the saints and martyrs were recorded here. The **monastic settlements** that sprung from these beginnings played a leading role in the development of Christian liturgy and dogma, and monasticism in the West can also be seen as developing from these early desert institutions. On the eve of the Persian invasion in 614 AD, the Judean desert was a maze of monasteries, two of which – **St Theodosius** (see above) and **Mar Saba** (see overleaf) – still stand a few miles from Bethlehem.

been warned by God in a dream not to return the way they had come (Matthew 2: 12). Here, in 476 AD, Theodosius founded a monastery which at one time housed nearly seven hundred Greek, Georgian, Armenian and Slavic monks within a fortified compound with four churches but, along with virtually all monasteries in the region, was destroyed by the invading Persians in 614. The present building was constructed by the Greek Orthodox Church in the 1890s on the ruins of the Byzantine complex and incorporates the remains of an old Crusader building. Continuing the fifteenth-century tradition, it is inhabited by a dozen Greek monks. Inside, eighteen steps bring you down into the white-walled burial cave of St Theodosius himself, who died at the age of 105. In a cave recess is a cluster of skulls of monks with crosses between their eye-sockets.

Buses run from behind the police station in Bethlehem's Manger Square to Ubeidiya; the last return bus leaves at around 3.30pm.

Mar Saba

Some 6km east of the monastery of St Theodosius, along a bumpy but negotiable road, the spectacular Greek Orthodox monastery of **Mar Saba** (men only; daily 8am–5pm) represents a way of life unchanged since the time of Constantine. Built into the rock face of a gorge overlooking the Kidron River, the immense building, with its girdle of walls and towers, is a thrill when it suddenly comes into view amid the wilderness, the solitude and silence of which should give you some idea as to what brought the original hermits here.

The founder, **Saint Saba**, came from Cappadocia in the fifth century and originally settled in a cave in the Wadi al-Nar (Wadi of Fire) in the Kidron Valley, supplied with water and herbs by the local Bedouin. Many legends grew up around him. In one, St Saba entered his cave to find it occupied by a lion, but without batting an eyelid, the saint said his prayers and fell asleep. However, after the lion had twice dragged him out of the cave, the fearless saint assigned him a corner of the grotto and, apparently content with this compromise, the two lived happily ever after. Another, Androclean version of this legend has it that the saint pulled a splinter out of the foot of a limping lion who, out of gratitude, followed him faithfully for the rest of his life.

But it was not only lions that followed St Saba – so many disciples flocked to his side that the grottoes of the valley were soon overflowing and, to solve the housing problem, he founded the monastery in 482 AD, living there himself until the age of 94. The saint is said to have exerted great influence on the emperors of the time, including Justinian, and the monastery therefore enjoyed imperial patronage: in its heyday it is said to have housed five thousand monks and was the focal point for six smaller monasteries nearby. Although Mar Saba was twice destroyed and its monks slaughtered in the seventh century, it rapidly recovered and by the eighth century was home to many prominent scholars, among them the celebrated **Saint John of Damascus**, a Greek theologian known for his writings here in defence of the use of icons, under attack at the time by Emperor Leo II's iconoclasm.

The **monastery** has 110 cells, although today it houses only ten monks. You enter into a paved courtyard, centring on a green-domed octagonal **chapel**, the original resting place of St Saba. His remains, carried off to Venice in 1256 by the Crusaders and returned only in 1965 during a time of rapprochement between the Catholic and Orthodox churches, now lie beneath an elaborate canopy in the main church, whose incense-laden interior is one of the most beautiful in the Middle East. A profusion of rare icons, many of them said to possess miraculous properties, cover its high walls; above all a representation of the Day of Judgement, with the Deity enthroned amongst angels and a gigantic figure weighing souls beneath. On one side, the "minister of punishment" stands in flames whilst in the background the dead rise from their graves.

Another memorial to St Saba, this time in the form of a grotto, lies on the southern side of the monastery; next to it is the **Lion's Grotto**. In a chapel adjoining these early hermits' caves are the skulls of monks killed in the Persian invasion: the tomb of St John is here too, although his remains were removed to Russia when the Russian Church rebuilt the monastery in the early nineteenth century.

Although Mar Saba is reputed to have had a long tradition of hospitality to strangers, **women** have never been allowed to enter. This regulation persists today, so women visitors have to be content with a glimpse of the chapel and buildings from a nearby two-storey tower, the so-called **Women's Tower**. By way of doubtful compensation, there is a superb view of the gorge 180m below, dotted with hermits' cells and cave sepulchres.

The nearest you can get to the monastery on public transport is the village of Ubeidiya (accessible by bus from Bethlehem), from where it's a further 6km. A return trip in a taxi from Bethlehem should be possible to arrange, for around $15. Hitching, although possible, is difficult as traffic is sparse. Be sure to take drinking water to avoid dehydration in the desert air and to dress appropriately both for the monasteries and for the searing sun.

Herodion

Eleven kilometres southeast of Bethlehem, on the summit of an extraordinary flat-topped, cone-shaped hill, lie the remains of **HERODION** (Sat–Thurs 7.30am–6pm, Fri 7.30am–5pm; 11NIS), perhaps the most outstanding of all Herod's architectural achievements. Today, its fortified walls are long gone, and the structures remaining are sunk below the rim of the mound, making it look rather like a volcano with a crater. A strategic fortress 800m above sea level, it was built around 30 AD as a secure refuge from his enemies and is also thought to be his burial site. Josephus describes the elaborate funeral procession that brought his body here from Jericho, but archeological surveys have so far failed to discover his tomb. Following Herod's death, it was one of the last strongholds to fall to the Romans in the Jewish Revolt of 66–70 AD, conceding only after the destruction of Jerusalem; as at Masada (see p.265), its defenders took their lives before the Romans could. During the Second Revolt in 132–35 AD it was again a Jewish redoubt, with the labyrinth of underground water tunnels used as fortifications. The remains of three Byzantine chapels with rich decorative mosaic floors show that the site continued to be inhabited during the fifth and sixth centuries. Later, the Crusaders (or Franks) made their final stand here before being finally ousted from the Holy Land by the Muslims, giving the hill one of its alternative names – **The Mountain of the Franks**. To Arabs it is known as Jabal al-Faradis, the Mount of Paradise.

The curious **mound** on which the fortress and main palace were built is artificial: the top of the hill was flattened, and the resulting earth thrown up to form massive defensives. According to Josephus, the original ascent was from the north via "200 steps of the whitest marble", traces of which can still be seen. Today the way up is much less grand – a fifteen-minute climb from the southwest up a winding path. The glorious fortress and palaces which once stood on the summit are long gone, but **excavations** have uncovered a circular enclosing wall with four round watchtowers which once guarded Herod's living quarters, and the remains of a bathhouse, hot baths, arcades, synagogue, and an immense banqueting hall. Perhaps the most striking aspect once you're up here, however, is the view: Bethlehem and Jerusalem spread out to the north and in the other direction the bare expanse of the Judean desert, with the Dead Sea beyond. Back down below, at the base of the mound, excavations have revealed a pool built by Herod, once filled with water diverted here from Solomon's Pools. Surrounding it is a reconstructed parade of colonnades; a nearby amphitheatre and pleasure garden are currently being excavated.

Herodion cannot be reached from Bethlehem by public transport: Egged bus #166 from Jerusalem to the nearby Jewish settlement of Teqo'a passes the access road to Herodion, but services are sparse (6 daily, first at noon, last back at 7pm). A taxi should cost around $15 for a round trip including a reasonable waiting time; alternatively you could walk from Bethlehem or Bet Sahur.

Bet Jala

Two kilometres west of Bethlehem, **BET JALA** is famous for its apricots, for the distinctive brocaded dresses of its female inhabitants and for its expert stonemasons. Surrounded by greenery and raised on a hillside above the plain, the village has long been a popular summer excursion site among Palestinians but perhaps its greatest attraction is **Nahle Ka'aber's** restaurant near the municipal square, which specializes in barbecued chicken accompanied by exquisite garlic salad, sizzling chilli sauce, hummus, *baba ghanoush* (aubergines in *tehina*), Arab salad and charcoal-warmed pitta bread. Of the village's four **churches**, the most attractive is the Greek Orthodox church of St Nicholas with its square tower and glittering silver dome. **Accommodation** is available at the *Talitha Kumi Hospice* (☎02/741247; ②), but you should reserve rooms in advance; to get to it, continue through the village, past the churches some 700m to a crossroads, take a left towards Mount Gilo (the right goes to Cremisan), and the hospice is inside a yellow gate 500m down on your left.

If you pass right through Bet Jala to the top of the hill, you'll get a spectacular view from the summit, with the greater part of Jerusalem visible. From here, a road descends to the **Monastery of Cremisan**, renowned for the wine (which you can buy here) produced by its Salesian monks, who also run a farm. The monastery houses a high school and an impressive library. Three kilometres south of Bet Jala, on Route 3755, is the village of **AL-KHADER**, traditionally famous for its stone-quarries. The eighteenth-century **Church of Saint George** here was built over an earlier fifteenth century structure, and is a popular centre of pilgrimage, venerated by Muslims as well as Christians. The village takes its name from the church, al-Khader being the Muslim equivalent of St George (see box on p.468). The entrance to the village is marked by a distinctive stone arch.

Bethlehem to Hebron

South of Bethlehem, Route 60 continues 37km to Hebron, with several sites of ancient and modern interest along the way. One of the first things you'll notice along the route is a high, barbed-wire fence 5km south of Bethlehem, which surrounds the Palestinian refugee camp of **Daheisha**, established in 1949; its population of six thousand makes it one of the largest camps in the area. The road is also overlooked by the gleaming white buildings of the **Jewish settlements** on the hills above.

Solomon's Pools

About 4km south of Bethlehem, in a small valley surrounded by tall trees, are the three huge rectangular cisterns known as **Solomon's Pools**. Although tradition attributes these to King Solomon, they almost certainly date from the time of Herod, supplying his fortress and palace at Herodion, and may have been conceived by Pontius Pilate. Three great pools here made of rock and masonry hold about 160,000 cubic metres of water and are constructed in steps, each six metres above the next, to enable the water to be carried as far as Jerusalem by force of gravity. The system was in use as recently as 1947, and along much of the route from Bethlehem to Jerusalem original terracotta

piping can still be found lying around. Near the pools are the remains of a Crusader fortress, **Qal'at al-Burak** (Castle of the Pools), built to defend the water source and maintained throughout centuries of Arab rule.

Access to the pools is from a side road off the main highway. A little further on, the road descends Wadi Artas to the picturesque village of **ARTAS**, whose name derives from the Latin *hortus* (garden). In the village is the convent and church of the Sisters of Notre Dame du Jardin, and below it the **Monastery of Hortus Conclusus**, at the edge of huge gardens supposedly inspired by the biblical *Song of Songs* or *Song of Solomon* (4: 12): "A garden inclosed is my sister, my spouse, a spring shut up, a fountain sealed." The *hortus conclusus* is symbolic of virginity, and an emblem of the Virgin Mary.

Gush Etzion and Kfar Etzion

Some thirteen kilometres out of Bethlehem, the road passes the settlement area of **Gush Etzion**, now numbering seventeen settlements. The oldest settlement, **KFAR ETZION**, was established in 1935, abandoned the following year in the face of Arab hostility during the Palestinian revolt, and then revived in 1943, along with three others, to form a "bloc" (*gush*) of four. It was the last of the four settlements to fall to Arab Legion troops in 1948 (supported by local "irregular" volunteers), having been under siege for five months – most of those who surrendered were machine-gunned down by irregular troops in revenge for (or in imitation of) the previous month's massacre at Deir Yassin (see p.378). Re-established in 1967, it became the first Jewish settlement to be built on the West Bank after its occupation, and some of its members are children of original pre-1948 settlers. If you'd like to visit a settlement this is one of the more rewarding; its history is recounted in a **museum** (Sun–Thurs 9am–3.30pm, Fri 9am–12.30pm; 8NIS) – a little one-sided, but interesting nonetheless, with an audiovisual presentation on the events of 1948. Should you wish to stay, there is an HI **Youth Hostel** (☎02/993 5133 or 5233; ②/③). The massive white concrete buildings high on a hill, dominating the east side of Route 60, belong to **EPHRAT**, Gush Etzion's "showpiece".

On to Hebron: Halhul

As you continue on to Hebron, the beauty of the countryside testifies to the fertility and productivity of the soil here: abundant vineyards dot the area, producing the delicious and distinctive-tasting grapes for which the city is famous. Around 5km outside Hebron, on a hill to the left of the road, lies the Palestinian town of **HALHUL**. Just outside the town, the **Mosque of Nabi Yunus** is, according to Muslim tradition, built over the grave of the prophet Jonah. Later Jewish writers mention a tradition that Nathan the prophet and Gad the seer, mentioned in I Chronicles 29: 29 as authors of books now lost, are also buried here.

Hebron (al-Khalil) and around

All the country around Hebron is filled with villages and vineyards and grounds bearing grapes and apples . . . Its equal for beauty does not exist elsewhere, nor can any fruits be finer.

al-Muqaddasi, 985 AD

HEBRON (al-Khalil or Khalil al-Rahman in Arabic, Hevron or Qiryat Arba in Hebrew) is one of the oldest towns in Israel and the Palestinian Territories, and among the oldest continuously inhabited places in the world. Holy to Muslims, Jews and Christians alike as the burial place of the patriarch **Abraham**, it has become the arena for the

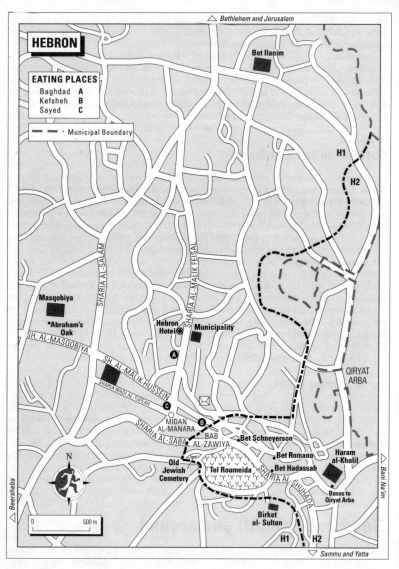

HEBRON

EATING PLACES
Baghdad **A**
Kefsheh **B**
Sayed **C**

– · – · Municipal Boundary

Bethlehem and Jerusalem

Bet Ilanim

H1

H2

Masqobiya

Abraham's Oak

SHARIA AL-SALAM

SHARIA AL-MALIK FEISAL

SH. AL-MASQOBIYA

Hebron Hotel

Municipality

SH. AL-MALIK HUSSEIN

QIRYAT ARBA

SHARIA WADI AL-TUFEAH

MIDAN AL-MANARA

SHARIA AL-SABA

BAB AL-ZAWIYA

Bet Schneyerson

Bet Romano

Haram al-Khalil

Old Jewish Cemetery

Tel Roumeida

Bet Hadassah

SHARIA AL-SHUHADA

Buses to Qiryat Arba

N

Beersheba

Bani Na'im

0   500 m

Birket al-Sultan

H1   H2

Sammu and Yatta

rather unholy sectarian bigotry that has unravelled between Jew and Muslim during the twentieth century and which has erupted into murder on several occasions.

Of all the West Bank towns, it is in Hebron that the Israeli **occupation** is at its most tangible. The Jewish settlement of Qiryat Arba is right next door, and a group of the most hardline settlers live slap-bang in the centre of town under the protection of the Israeli army, whose conscript soldiers seem about as happy to be here as Hebron's frequently militant Palestinian residents are to have them. In fact, the people of the region, called "Khalaila", have a popular reputation for hard-headed doggedness illustrated in their long history of rebelliousness: Ottomans, British and Jordanians have all had to watch their step here, and opposition to Israeli rule has been even stronger here than on the rest of the West Bank.

But, for all its troubles, Hebron is a fascinating place. With a population of around forty thousand, it is the chief town of the southern half of the West Bank and the largest industrial centre in the whole of the territory. Its souq is the commercial centre for traders from fifty or so surrounding villages, while the town itself produces jam and molasses, stone and marble (most of the facing on Jerusalem buildings comes from the area between Bethlehem and Hebron), pottery and leatherworks. Just to the north of town, on the road to Halhul (see p.407) **glass factories** produce the blue glassware for which the town is famous; the necessary skills are reputed to have been brought over in the fifteenth century by Spanish or Venetian Jews fleeing religious persecution. You can observe the process from beginning to end and choose from a variety of jars, vases, glasses, plates, baubles, bangles and beads at prices much lower than in the markets.

Politically, the town is divided into **two areas**: eighty percent is "**H1**", under PNA jurisdiction; the remaining twenty percent, including much of the market area in the middle of town, is "**H2**", under Israeli jurisdiction. It's not always obvious which area you are in, but the settler-occupied buildings, which are inside H2, are cordoned off, and guarded by soldiers, so you are unlikely to stray into them by accident. Do not wander around town without your passport, as you may well be required to show it, and as a last resort, you can wave it around to show that you are a foreigner and therefore neutral, though it's a good idea to make that as obvious as possible anyway. Don't let all this put you off from coming here but do be aware of the situation and think twice about visiting when tension is high. Bear in mind also that Hebron is a religious and traditional town, so you should dress and behave conservatively.

Some history

The Torah (Numbers 13: 22) states that Hebron was built seven years before Zoan in Egypt, which would date its foundation at 1720 BC. Excavations on Tel Rumeida, however, show that it was inhabited by the **Canaanites** as early as 2000 BC, while according to Muslim tradition it dates from the beginning of time: Adam and Eve lived out their days here after their expulsion from the Garden of Eden.

The Old Testament name for Hebron was Qiryat Arba, or the **Village of the Four**; the four in question, according to one legend, being giants who fell from heaven after a revolt against God. Another, more down-to-earth, explanation, is that the name derives from the four Canaanite tribes who lived in the town, while religious authorities say that it comes from the four biblical couples – Abraham and Sarah, Isaac and Rebecca, Jacob and Leah, Adam and Eve – said to be buried here. Whatever the facts, the city was certainly well established by the time **Abraham** and Sarah passed this way, pitching their tent by the oaks of Mamre (Genesis 13: 18). When Sarah died here, Abraham bought the Cave of Makhpela and the neighbouring field from the sons of Heth as a sepulchre for her and the rest of his family (Genesis 23); a purchase of modern significance too as, according to the town's Jewish settlers, it makes Hebron the perpetual property of the Jewish people, held to be the descendants of Abraham. The claim may not bear much logical scrutiny (Abraham's oldest son Ismail, aka Ishmael, is supposedly the ancestor of the Arabs for one thing) but for the settlers, it has become an item of faith.

As the gateway to the settled northern highlands from the sub-desert southern region, Hebron has always been strategically important. When, seven hundred years after Abraham, **Moses** led the Israelite tribes out of Egypt, it was to the area around Hebron that he sent his first reconnaissance mission. His scouts returned bearing, as proof of the land's fertility, a bunch of grapes so massive that it had to be borne between two on a staff (Numbers 13: 23) – an image used today as the emblem of the

Israeli Government Tourist Office. Hebron was then inhabited by people referred to by the Bible as "the children of Anak", and, according to Moses's spies, "the people be strong that dwell in the land, and the cities are walled and very great" (Numbers 13: 28), so it was left to Moses's successor Joshua to conquer Hebron and other areas of Canaan around 1200 BC.

After the death of King Saul, **David** ruled over Judah from Hebron for seven and a half years (II Samuel 5: 5) before subduing the northern tribes and moving the capital of his united kingdom to Jerusalem. Later, Hebron briefly became the headquarters of David's rebellious son Absalom (II Samuel 15: 10). The second book of Chronicles (11: 10) records Rehoboam as fortifying the city. Following the Babylonian exile, Hebron became part of **Idumaea**, and I Maccabees 5: 65 mentions a battle here between the forces of Judas Maccabeus and the Idumaeans, though it was Judas's nephew, the Hasmonean king John Hyrcanus, who finally took the city in 134 BC. **Herod** (himself an Idumaean) contributed to the city's prominence by building the basis of the massive Haram al-Khalil that houses the tombs of the biblical patriarchs and matriarchs. In 70 AD, following the Jewish Revolt, Hebron was destroyed, and Jews were banned from living in the rebuilt city. They were allowed legal residence with the start of **Muslim** rule in the seventh century, during which time Hebron grew into an important centre of commerce and pilgrimage and became known as Khalil al-Rahman (Beloved of the Merciful) – nowadays shortened to al-Khalil. The **Crusaders** conquered Hebron in 1100 AD and Jews were again banned from living there; a decision later reversed by the Mamluks (1248–1517 AD), who allowed them to return to the town, by then a district capital, though only Muslims were allowed access to the Haram.

Under the **Mandate**, Hebron, as the base of powerful traditional leaders, was naturally prominent in Palestinian opposition to British rule. Following clashes in Jerusalem in 1929 (see p.341), riots and murders took place across Palestine, but that in Hebron was by far the worst – 67 Jews were killed by a mob and the rest forced to leave the city, even though the two-thousand-strong Jewish community, mainly religious and non-Zionist, had lived in peace with their Arab neighbours for centuries.

Since 1967, "*tarpat*", an acronym of the Hebrew year 5689 AM in which the massacre occurred (numbers in Hebrew can be written as letters, Roman-numeral-style), has become the battle-cry of the town's **Jewish settlers** as they pursue access to sites they consider rightfully theirs, many of which belonged to the pre-1929 Jewish community. In 1968, religious right-winger Rabbi Moshe Levinger moved into a Hebron hotel and began a four-year sit-in that resulted in official recognition for his right to establish a settlement next to Hebron at Qiryat Arba (see p.413). This became the core of the **Gush Emunim** radical settlers' movement, started by militant members of Bnei Akiva, the youth wing of the National Religious Party, and led by Rabbi Levinger himself.

Tension in the city escalated following the 1978 Camp David agreement. In March 1979, Jewish settlers squatted in the Daboyah Building (see opposite) in the centre of town and gained permission to remain after a seven-month occupation, and in May 1980, following a grenade and firearm attack on Jewish worshippers at the Tomb of the Patriarchs in which six *yeshiva* students died, the Israelis deported the Palestinian mayor, Fahd Qawasma, along with the mayor of Halhul and the Hebron qadi. Qawasma's successor, Mustafa Natshe, was replaced by a junior Israeli army officer following the murder of another settler in July 1983.

By the beginning of 1994, Israel and the PLO were talking peace, but on February 25, a settler by the name of **Barukh Goldstein**, dressed in IDF uniform, opened fire on the congregation in the Haram during Ramadan dawn prayers, killing 29 people. Israeli troops, thinking the ensuing chaos was a riot, sealed off exits and shot at Palestinians fleeing the mosque. Israeli public opinion was horrified at the massacre, though some extreme right-wing settlers regard Goldstein (who was overpowered and beaten to death by members of the congregation) as a hero.

Many hoped that the most extreme of the settlers would be ousted from the town centre before its **handover to the PNA**, but Likud's 1996 election victory ended any chance of that: "There will be," said Israeli Prime Minister Binyamin Netanyahu, "no uprooting of the Jewish community in Hebron – not now, not tomorrow and not ever – in any shape or form." When Israeli troops were finally redeployed in January 1997, Hebron was partitioned into **PNA-controlled H1** and **Israeli-controlled H2**, the latter reaching right into the heart of town, with armed soldiers keeping the two communities apart. Unsurprisingly, tension remains high and incidents are common and if Palestinians are all in one mind about the Hebron settlers, Israelis are deeply divided. Many bitterly resent them, seeing them as extremists coming largely from abroad (America) to cause trouble and needlessly risk the lives of Israeli troops, at great cost to the Israeli taxpayer. Others see the settlers as guardians of Judaism's second most holy shrine, and their bumper-stickers can be seen on cars nationwide: "Hebron," they read, ". . . to our forefathers and to us." Hebron is a tinderbox that could go off at any time, and whose flames could spread far beyond its city limits.

The Town

Buses or service taxis will leave you right in the centre of town, at **Bab al-Zawiya** in the commercial district. From here, Sharia Ma'amun leads east into the heart of the **souq**, on the other side of which lies Hebron's main attraction, the **Haram al-Khalil**, housing the Tombs of the Patriarchs.

The souq and around

Hebron's **souq** is a warren of tunnel-like alleyways, twisting and turning under arched roofs. From its shops and stalls you can buy everything from pottery, olive wood and glass (including the local hand-blown blue glass) to spices, dried and fresh fruits (the grapes are still as sweet and fat as they were when Moses sent his spies to check out the land, and Hebron's peaches are delicious too), and trinkets of every description. It's also a good place to pick up local jewellery and metalware at bargain prices, though watch out for the difference in quality between traditional hand-made goods and the mass-produced items increasingly replacing them.

There are a couple of main routes through the market area; on either of them you'll come across buildings occupied by the Jewish settlers, easily recognizable by the Israeli flags fluttering from the rooftops. The first route, going east from Bab al-Zawiya along Sharia Ma'amun, takes you past **Bet Romano**; settlers have established a *yeshiva* on the top floor here, but Palestinian shopholders continue to trade below. Sharia Ma'amun continues to the left of this, but after another 100m, the market is suddenly dwarfed by the Daboyah Building – now named **Bet Hadassah**. The first in central Hebron to be occupied by settlers, it is a gleaming new compound, bristling with defences, guarded by armed soldiers and closed-circuit TV, and bears a large banner reading, "This market was built on Jewish property stolen by Arabs after the 1929 massacre". Its residents go about their daily business brandishing submachine guns. You may be able to persuade the soldiers to let you enter and see the settlers' **museum**, dedicated to the massacre, but that's liable to make any Palestinians who happens to see you going in suspicious of your motives for doing so. Around Bet Hadassah, the old **Jewish Quarter** is now being rebuilt under the watchful eye of the army. It's possible to visit the compound, along with other Jewish sites in Hebron, on a **tour of Jewish Hebron** (run by the settlers and used to subsidize their activities), which leaves from the lobby of the Jerusalem *Sheraton Plaza Hotel* at 9am on Mondays and Wednesdays, returning around 4pm, bookable in advance (☎02/996 2323; $45).

The other route runs also runs from Bab al-Zawiya to Bet Hadassah but this time around the southern side of the market along Sharia Da'oud (David Street). The area to its southwest is **Tel Roumeida**, the oldest part of the city and an as yet unexcavated mound, much of it covered by graveyards, including an ancient Jewish burial ground housing tombs said to be those of the biblical Ruth and her grandson, King David's father Jesse. South of Sharia Da'oud **Birket al-Sultan** is a large, disused reservoir, beside which David reputedly hanged the murderers of Saul's son Ishbosheth (II Samuel 4: 12). The place is now used as a rubbish tip.

The Haram al-Khalil (Tomb of the Patriarchs)

The **Haram al-Khalil**, **Abraham Mosque**, or **Tomb of the Patriarchs** (Sun–Thurs 8am–4pm, except during prayer times), just east of the souq, is the outstanding sight of Hebron – monolithic and austere, it dominates the city and, even without the heavily armed Israeli soldiers, looks more like a fortress than a tomb. Standing atop the **Cave of Makhpela**, reputed burial place of a host of biblical figures – the patriarchs (Abraham, Isaac and Jacob), the matriarchs (Sarah, Rebecca and Leah), Adam and Eve and, according to some, Joseph – it is, for Jews, second in holiness only to the Wailing Wall. For Muslims it is second in Palestine only to the Dome of the Rock, not just for its connection with Abraham and other Old Testament figures but because, according to Islamic tradition, it was also visited by the Prophet Mohammed on his night journey from Mecca to Jerusalem. Haram al-Khalil is also one of world's most disturbing religious sites, on a par with Ayodha in India, where prayer and piety go hand in hand with violence and sectarian hatred. Conflict between Jew and Muslim over the right to pray here is longstanding, the uneasy peace maintained by armed troops.

According to Arab legend, the massive stones of the **walls**, built without mortar, were laid by Solomon with the help of *jinn* or spirits. The construction of the walls and the pavement of the Haram, however, bear the unmistakeable stamp of Herod the Great with their huge but perfectly hewn stone blocks; the additional Crusader and Mamluk structures further add to its impressiveness. Until the **1994 massacre** (see p.410), Jews and Muslims shared the space, with prayers at different times. Since then, however, the shrine has been divided. If you want to go in, you will have to show your passport and state a religion. Jews are allowed only to enter the Jewish side, and Muslims may enter only the Muslim side; Christians and others may enter both, but you will have a hard time persuading the soldiers on guard that you are Christian or Buddhist if you have a Jewish or Muslim name. Visitors are asked to dress modestly and to "respect the sanctity of the place".

INSIDE THE HARAM

The basis of the building may be Herodian, but **inside** it's hard to work out what exactly is what, so many ages and religions have left their mark. A Byzantine church erected in 570 AD was converted into a mosque in the seventh century, adjacent to which a small synagogue was later built. The Crusaders replaced both with a church, which in turn was converted into a mosque by Saladin. Around 1318 the Mamluks added the adjoining Djaouliya Mosque (whose minarets tower above the walls), the Tomb of Joseph and a small mosque in the eastern corner of the complex.

Entrance to the **Muslim section** is up the Mamluk stairway on the northwestern wall of the edifice (from the thirteenth century onwards Jews were allowed only to the seventh step), which leads around the building to the **al-Is'haqiyya** or the **Great Mosque**. Inside, the remarkable stained-glass windows soften the light falling onto the geometric sheets of marble and the inscribed frieze that decorate the walls. Central to the mosque are the **cenotaphs of Isaac and Rebecca**, which in their present form date from 1332 and are supposed to lie directly above the tombs in the **Cave of Makhpela** (closed to the public, but written prayers can be dropped down into it). The cave's medieval entrance is a small opening in the floor to the right of the magnificent carved wood *minbar* – one of the finest examples of its kind in the world, made in 1091 for a mosque in Ashqelon and donated to the Haram by Saladin a century later. Beside it is the mihrab facing Mecca. The small **Mamluk mosque** in the western corner of the Haram is reserved for women. In one corner of it, a shrine holds a stone bearing the footprint Adam is said to have left on his way out of the Garden of Eden.

Entering the **Jewish section**, round the other side of the complex, you come into the calm interior of what was, until 1967, the Djaouliya Mosque, but is now the **synagogue**. To the right as you enter are the rooms containing the ninth-century **cenotaphs of Abraham and Sarah**, opposite which are those of **Jacob and Leah**, dating from the fourteenth century. To the southwest is what some Muslims believe to be the cenotaph of Joseph, although the Bible (Joshua 24: 32) clearly states that Joseph was buried at Shekhem (Nablus).

Mamre and Masqobiya

Three kilometres north of the town centre, a little to the east of the Jerusalem road, **Bet Ilanim** is one of the two sites purported to be the biblical **Mamre**, where Abraham offered hospitality to the three angels (Genesis 18: 1–8), who told him that he and Sarah – who was well past child-bearing age – would have a son, Isaac. A large oak tree marks the spot where they rested. Christians also identify this place as the site where the Holy Family rested on their way back from Egypt. The church built here in the seventh century was notable enough to have appeared on the famous mosaic map at Madaba (see p.343), but nowadays there's little to see beyond the overgrown lower walls of an undated enclosure and the foundations of a fourth-century Constantinian church at the eastern end of the site.

The other candidate for Mamre is **Masqobiya**, 2km west of the town centre, where a dead oak tree shored up by calipers claims to be the one where Abraham invited his angelic visitors to rest and eat. Russian monks have a small monastery here, built in 1871, behind which is a tower commanding a magnificent view extending to the sea. The convenient way in, a gate on Sharia al-Masqobiya, is usually closed, so you'll probably have to go round and enter the site from the west. Five kilometres east of town, at **Bani Na'im**, the tomb of Abraham's kinsman Lot, is marked by a mosque built on the foundations of a Byzantine church.

Qiryat Arba

Though not the most interesting, **QIRYAT ARBA**, bordering Hebron to the east, is the biggest and most accessible of the region's settlements (served by bus from Jerusalem and Beersheba), with a population of around five thousand, consisting mainly of American-born Jews. Apart from the one inside Hebron itself, it is also the most politically extreme, having been the headquarters of several far-right political movements. Given the biblical name for Hebron by its founders – the originators of Gush Emunim (see p.410) – it received massive funding from the government and World Zionist Organisation soon after its establishment in 1970, enabling it to expand throughout the surrounding neighbourhoods. Local resident Barukh Goldstein, perpetrator of the 1994 massacre, is buried here.

Hebron practicalities

Accommodation in Hebron is limited to the *Hebron Hotel* (☎ & fax 02/992 6760; ③), above the al-Amanah supermarket on Sharia al-Malik Feisal, almost opposite the town hall. It's new, clean and bright, with a manager who can tell you more about Hebron than any tourist office could.

MOVING ON FROM HEBRON

At present, **bus** services to or through Jerusalem are suspended, but there are buses roughly every 30 minutes to Ramallah (2hr, faster if running via Jerusalem) and Surif (30min). **Service taxis** are somewhat more convenient, running to Bethlehem, Bethany and Abu Dis, Ramallah, Sammu, Dhahriyya and sometimes direct to Jerusalem. From Qiryat Arba, you can pick up **Egged Israeli bus** services to Jerusalem (2 daily; 45min), Qiryat Gat (2 daily; 45min) and Beersheba (2 daily; 1hr).

For **snacks**, a number of stalls in the market and around Bab al-Zawiya sell falafel, *shawarma* and kebabs, but if you're after a **sit-down meal**, the *Kefesheh Restaurant* on Sharia Wadi al-Tufeah between Midan al-Manara and Bab al-Zawiya (daily 8am–8pm; cheap) serves tasty soup and good mezze to supplement the meats. Alternatively you can try one of several restaurants that serve chicken or *shawarma* with salads or dips, including the *Baghdad Restaurant* on Sharia al-Malik Feisal on the way from town to the town hall (daily 5am–midnight; moderate), and *Al-Sayed Restaurant* on Sharia al-Manara by Midan al-Manara (daily 8am–8pm; moderate).

Hebron is not very flush with **moneychangers** compared to other West Bank towns, but you'll find a couple on the south side of Bab al-Zawiya. The **post office** is on Sharia al-Malik Feisal, a little to the north. Public transport gathers at Bab al-Zawiya.

South of Hebron

Heading **south from Hebron**, the main road (Route 60) follows the spine of the Judean Highlands for some 30km before descending sharply to the drier Negev fringe and continuing on to Beersheba (see p.272). The annual rainfall decreases dramatically the further south you travel, which has a marked effect on both landscape and population density, with villages some way apart from each other.

Seventeen kilometres out of Hebron, a road to the east off Route 60 leads for a further 6km to the Palestinian village of **SAMMU** – site of biblical **Eshtemoa**, one of the villages with which David shared the spoils of a campaign against the Amalekites (I Samuel 30: 28). Next to the village mosque are the remains of a fourth-century **synagogue** which, according to local legend, contained David's treasure of silver and gold; excavations in 1968 did indeed unearth a cache of silver, but it wasn't old enough to date from David's time. The synagogue itself has a *bima* (raised platform) in the centre of the north wall, three niches believed to have held Torah scrolls and other ritual objects, and a mosaic floor. Sammu's other main attraction – its **carpets** – are of three types: wine-red with a thin white stripe; striped the colours of the Palestinian flag (green, red, white and black); and multicoloured. They're not cheap, being finely woven of pure wool, but they are good value; you can see them being made in the modern two-storey building 200m past the synagogue, which houses the Sammu Charitable Society and doubles as a carpet-making school in the mornings.

YATTA, 6km north of Sammu, has the remains of another synagogue, dating from the sixth century, but one almost identical to Sammu's, and in a much better state of preservation, can be seen in **KHIRBET SUSEYA**, at the end of a dirt track leading 4km east from the Yatta–Sammu road. Dating from the fifth century, it preserves, within walls several metres thick, an attractive and complete mosaic floor, with three distinct, geometrically patterned panels. The niche above the plastered benches was added as a mihrab in the time of Saladin, when the synagogue became a mosque. Sammu and sometimes Yatta are accessible by **service taxi** from Hebron, but for Khirbet Suseya, you'll probably have to charter a "special", or walk.

Back on Route 60, 20km south of Hebron, **DHAHRIYA** is the last village before Beersheba; the Wednesday morning **livestock market** here is still a genuine part of the economic lives of local Bedouin and villagers, and a fascinating slice of traditional life. Overlooking the marketplace is the former British Mandate police fort, which later became a Jordanian Legion post. Ten kilometres south of Dhahriya, Route 60 crosses the Green line, arriving 20km later at Beersheba.

EAST OF JERUSALEM

The forty-kilometre trip eastward from **Jerusalem to Jericho** on Routes 417, 1 and 90 is truly spectacular, though for those made of strong stuff there's also the option of hiking it along the **Wadi Qelt**. From its start 800m above sea level, the road winds down through the stark and dramatic limestone hills of the Judean sub-desert passing several biblical sites on the way to the oasis of Jericho – at 250m below sea level, the lowest city on earth. In summer, the landscape is generally bare, but after a winter storm the hills can burst briefly into a glorious display of flowers. On either side of the road lie small Bedouin encampments, some of black or brown goat's-hair tents, others mainly shacks of wood and corrugated iron – a reflection of the Palestinian Bedouin tradition of combining settled and nomadic lifestyles, depending on economic circumstance.

From Jericho, Route 449 runs east to the **Allenby Bridge** border crossing into Jordan.

Bethany (al-Azariya) and around

Leaving Jerusalem, Route 417 sets out through the Kidron Valley below the Mount of Olives, passes the village of Silwan, and then swings east to **Bethany**. Known in Arabic as **al-Azariya**, a form of the Greek Lazarion or place of Lazarus, it was here that Lazarus was resurrected (John 11: 1–44), that Jesus went with his disciples after the events of Palm Sunday (Mark 11: 11), and that He was anointed with precious ointment at the house of Simon the Leper before being betrayed by Judas (Mark 14: 3–9; Matthew 26: 6). Today you could easily drive through without noticing anything special about the place, but off the main road there are several churches worth a visit, while just beyond lies the Palestinian village of **Abu Dis**, and the site of **Bethphage** – from where Jesus began his entry into Jerusalem on Palm Sunday.

You can make the one- to two-hour **walk** to Bethany from Jerusalem via Ras al-Amud and the Jericho Road (Route 417), or over the Mount of Olives (see p.356) via Bethphage, but remember sun protection and drinking water, and bear in mind that the best views of Jerusalem from the Mount of Olives are in the morning. Alternatively, it's a fifteen- to twenty-minute journey by **bus** – #36 runs to Bethany from the Central Bus Station in East Jerusalem – or **service taxi**, which you can pick up outside the bus station for Bethany and Abu Dis.

Service taxis to Jericho leave from Bethany and Abu Dis, while both service taxis and buses from Hebron and Bethlehem to Ramallah or vice versa pass through on their way round Jerusalem.

Bethany: the churches and mosque

BETHANY stretches along either side of the main road. If you turn off by the souvenir shops on a sharp right-hand bend in the road, a lane leading up the eastern slope of the Mount of Olives brings you to several churches and a mosque. Built in 1954 and designed, like many in Jerusalem, by the Italian architect Antonio Barluzzi, the cruciform **Franciscan Church** marks the site of the **Tomb of Lazarus** (daily: summer 8–11.30am & 2–6pm; winter 8–11.30am & 2–5pm; 2NIS). The church may be modern but its grounds contain numerous earlier structures. On the left as you enter the courtyard and preserved under trapdoors are remnants of the mosaic floors of the earliest church at the site, built in the fourth century and destroyed by an earthquake. Adjacent to these are the walls of a fifth-century church, which was razed by the Persians in 614 AD and later rebuilt and reinforced under Crusader rule – note the stone buttresses as you descend from the street into the courtyard. To this, Melisande the wife of Fulk of Anjou, Crusader king of Jerusalem, added a large abbey complex in 1138, which, through its wheat and olive-oil production, became one of the wealthiest in the Crusader kingdom – a mill and oil press can be seen in one of the remaining rooms, accessible from the church courtyard. By the end of the fourteenth century, the chapel that Melisande had erected over the tomb of Lazarus had been supplanted by the **al-Ozir Mosque**, and it is here that the tomb is found today: from street level 22 rough stone steps lead into a dank cave with three rather uninspiring burial niches.

Further up the street, the attractive **Greek Orthodox Church** with its pale blue dome dates from 1965; you'll have to be content to look at the outside, however, as the gates are generally padlocked. To the left of the crossroads stands the ruined tower known as the **Castle of Lazarus**, once part of a nunnery founded in 1138 by Melisande, and thought to stand on the site of the House of Simon the Leper. East of here is the **House of Mary and Martha**, Lazarus's sisters, where Lazarus was famously raised from the dead. The two women had sent word to Jesus, apparently a friend of the family (see also below), because their brother was sick, but Jesus declared the sickness "for the glory of God, that the Son of God might be glorified thereby" (John 11: 4), and Lazarus died. He had been entombed for four days when Jesus arrived in Bethany, pronounced, "I am the resurrection and the life: he that believeth in me, though he were dead, yet shall he live," (John 11: 25), and ordered the stone covering the tomb to be rolled away, at which Lazarus, still in his shroud, emerged alive. A little further up the mountain are the excavations of ancient Bethany or **Bet Anania**, which have revealed evidence of habitation from the sixth century BC to the fourteenth century AD.

Bethphage

To the right at the crossroads by the Greek church, a track winds for around 700m to emerge beside the high-walled Franciscan monastery and chapel at **Bethphage**, from where you can look down into the wadi that was the ancient Bethany–Jericho road. Bethphage itself was the starting point for Jesus's triumphal entry into Jerusalem on Palm Sunday (Mark 11: 1–10), and is today the place from where the Franciscans' **Palm Sunday procession** begins. The chapel (daily: summer 8–11.30am & 2–5pm; winter 8–11.30am & 2–4.30pm) was built in 1883 on the remains of a medieval church commemorating Jesus's **meeting with Martha and Mary**, the sisters of Lazarus. Though the story of the meeting itself seems unremarkable – Jesus and the disciples visit the house (Luke 10: 38–42), and while Mary is "sat at Jesus's feet", Martha complains that she's been left with all the serving to do – it may have broader significance: St John (11: 2) tells us that this was the same Mary who anoints Jesus with ointment, a story told slightly differently in all four Gospels (Matthew 26: 6–13; Mark 14: 3–9; Luke 7 : 36–50; John 12: 1–9), but in St Luke's version, she is identified as "a sinner", and traditionally with Mary Magdalene (though this is not explicit in the Gospel). Some have deduced from a combination of these sources that this Mary was Jesus's wife, which would certainly explain Jesus's otherwise mysterious relationship with her and her family. Inside the chapel, beautiful medieval paintings on the stone depict scenes from Jesus's life. Look out, too, for the **Stone of Meeting**, which the Crusaders believed Jesus stepped on to mount his donkey when he set out for Jerusalem – they were apparently oblivious of the fact that little help is needed to mount indigenous Palestinian donkeys, which were considerably smaller than their own massive war horses.

From Bethphage, the road descends into the Wadi al-Hod (Valley of the Watering Place). **Hod al-Azariya**, known as the Apostles' Spring, is the only well between here and the Jordan Valley and is where the travelling apostles are believed to have stopped to drink.

Ma'ale Adumim and the Inn of the Good Samaritan

About 6km east of Jerusalem, the new Jerusalem ring road (Route 1) meets Route 417 from East Jerusalem, Bethany and Abu Dis near the Jewish settlement of **MA'ALE ADUMIM**, whose white apartment blocks overlook the road from their hilltop site. Established in 1978, it is the largest of the sixteen Jewish settlements in the Jerusalem area, with plans for a total population of thirty thousand, and for the whole settlement to be incorporated into metropolitan Jerusalem. Ma'ale Adumim was the centrepiece of the second phase of the Likud settlement campaign which set up suburban settlements within commuting distance of Jerusalem or Tel Aviv, providing super-cheap housing in places where more people were prepared to live; earlier settlements in the heart of the West Bank had been massively funded but were unpopular, attracting mostly right-wing political activists. Incongruously, there is an archeological site here, the remains of the fifth-century **Monastery of Martyrius** (Sun–Thurs 8am–4pm, Fri 8am–1pm), covering almost a hectare in the centre of the settlement, and featuring a church and a chapel with mosaic floors. Less impressive remains of another fifth-century monastery, that of St Euthymius, can be found 2km to the east in Ma'ale Adumim's industrial zone. Egged bus #174 serves Ma'ale Adumim from Jerusalem.

Four kilometres further east along Route 1, a sixteenth-century Turkish khan to the right of the road marks what is held to be the spot where the Good Samaritan took compassion on the injured traveller in Jesus's famous parable (Luke 10: 30–36). Known both as al-Khan al-Ahmar (Red Inn), because of the colour of the soil in the region, and as the **Inn of the Good Samaritan**, it was a lively meeting place in the days before modern transport, where travellers stopped to refresh themselves and their mounts. Nowadays, it's easily missed, but the tradition continues, with refreshments served in a Bedouin-style tent outside the khan, and the occasional tourist coach stopping by. The hill above the khan is the probable site of biblical Adummim (Joshua 15: 7), through which the border of the tribe of Judah ran; at the top stands the ruined Crusader castle of **Qala'at al-Dum** (Castle of Blood).

Beyond the khan, Route 1 begins its descent into the **Wadi al-Rummana** (Valley of the Pomegranates), with side roads to the left leading to the Monastery of St George and Wadi Qelt (see below). Eleven kilometres from Jerusalem, **sea level** is marked by a sign, showing that you have descended 800m (2600ft) so far – if travelling in a "special" or in your own vehicle, you can even stop off and have your photo taken here on a camel.

Wadi Qelt

The high, sheer rock walls of **Wadi Qelt** carve a deep and dramatic crevice in the hills for 35km between Jerusalem and Jericho. Formerly part of the main highway, the valley saw frequent use right up to the end of the Ottoman period; today the Wadi is a popular **hike**, either the whole way from Jerusalem to Jericho, or for just part of it (see box overleaf). Monks have inhabited this awesome place for 1600 years, initially in caves and rock-hollowed niches, later in monasteries and hermitages, their survival ensured by three perennial springs that also provided Jericho with fresh water. The monasteries flourished between the fourth and seventh centuries, the main period of desert monasticism (see box on p.403), but the only one to have survived is the **Monastery of Saint George of Koziba**.

Accessible only on foot, the easiest approach to the monastery is from the main Jerusalem–Jericho road (Route 1): a large orange signpost some 5km after the Inn of the Good Samaritan (see p.417) points the way. The fifteen-minute walk down is easy; coming back up, however, it can be quite a slog.

WALKING THE WADI TO THE MONASTERY OF SAINT GEORGE AND JERICHO

Hiking in Wadi Qelt should be approached seriously: make sure there are at least three in your party, let someone know where you're going and take lots of liquids with you to combat the heat (even in winter temperatures can reach the mid-twenties Celsius). Head-covering is also essential. The SPNI (see p.316) may be able to provide advice and information on hiking in the area; they also do guided hikes if you don't fancy doing it independently.

The easiest short walk (4hr) is to take the Egged bus from Jerusalem to the small Israeli agricultural settlement of **MIZPE YERIHO**, or ask to get off at Wadi Qelt on a Jericho-bound service taxi. Follow the track, signposted in orange from the main road, for some 700m until it forks. The right-hand fork is the Roman road to Jericho via the Herodian fortress of Kypros, but most hikers fork left, turning right after 100m along a dirt track which gives an awesome panoramic view of the limestone and chalk crags that wall the wadi. After a twenty- to thirty-minute walk, at the bottom of the track, you'll see the remains of a turn-of-the-century flour mill, which is still inhabited by a Bedouin family who are traditionally responsible for the upkeep of the aqueduct next to it. Around 1500m westward along the path of the aqueduct, you come to the perennial spring of **Ein Qelt**, an astonishing torrent of water gushing out of bare limestone rock. The spring is fed by the winter rains from around Jerusalem and Bethlehem which collect in huge aquifers (strata of porous rock below ground) and eventually pour out through a fault into the wadi. The wadi's other two springs, Ein Fara and Ein Fuwar, are above Ein Qelt in the upper Qelt canyon. The water of Ein Qelt is unsafe to drink, but people do swim in it – the pools are waist-deep, even in summer.

Retracing your steps toward the mill, a small ceramic plaque in the cliff sings the praises of the nineteenth-century builder of the aqueduct – only one in a succession of major water engineering projects here. To the right, the impressive arch of an eighth-century Ummayad aqueduct crosses a smaller wadi, and the surrounding hillsides are littered with traces of Hasmonean, Herodian and Roman **aqueducts** in which you can go for a paddle – but take care as the flow of water can be considerable. Just after passing some large caves on the far side of the wadi, the aqueduct traces a large horseshoe to the left. Here it is better to head down to the floor of the wadi and to follow the dry, rather rocky river bed for around 1500m or so until you reach the monastery.

Continuing **from the monastery to Jericho**, you can cross to the opposite cliff and take the road or stay on the north side of the wadi and follow a well-graded trail for forty minutes along the line of the Herodian aqueduct. The wadi emerges into the Jordan Valley at two hills that were once surmounted by the Hasmonean fortresses of **Taurus** and **Thrax**. Herod refortified the fortress of Taurus to provide himself with a safe retreat from his nearby winter palace and renamed it Kypros (see p.427) after his mother. This is thoroughly ruined, so you're probably better off saving your climbing energy for somewhere else – there are far better examples of Herodian architecture at Herodion (see p.405) and Masada (see p.265), for example. The course of the wadi continues past Herod's palaces (see p.427), whence a dirt road brings you to the main highway, a couple of kilometres further.

The Monastery of Saint George of Koziba

Carved out of the rock face and clinging to the canyon walls like a fairy-tale fortress, the magnificent Greek Orthodox **Monastery of Saint George of Koziba** (Mon–Fri: summer 9am–4pm, closes 3pm in winter; Sat 9am–noon; free but donation expected) lies above a beautiful garden of olive, palm and cypress trees. One of the oldest in the country, the monastery was originally a *laura* or spiritual centre for the hermits of the region who came here for divine liturgy. Towards the end of the fifth century it was converted into a monastery by John of Thebes, and in the following century it became known as St George (*Mar Jiryis* in Arabic), under the leadership of St George of Koziba. The prophet Elijah is said to have stayed at this place on his way to the Sinai, and here St Joachim was informed by an angel of the Virgin Mary's conception.

The present building was reconstructed between 1878 and 1901 to the design of a Crusader restoration of 1179. Until it was destroyed in the Persian invasion of 614 AD, the monastery housed scores of monks and was famed for its hospitality to travellers en route to such distant places as Damascus and Baghdad. Today, few monks remain and visits are mainly confined to two **chapels** within the monastery complex. The principal chapel is dedicated to the Virgin Mary; its interior, hung with a multitude of golden lamps and dominated by a double-headed Byzantine eagle in black, white and red mosaic, is so ornate that it feels more like being inside Aladdin's cave than a church – a feeling heightened by an exceptionally rich array of paintings and icons, most of which date from the 1901 restoration. The smaller of the two chapels, with a sixth-century mosaic floor that marks it as part of the oldest section of the monastery, is dedicated to Saints George and John. It has a delightful, domed, sky-blue roof and an altar dominated by glowing icons of the twelve Apostles. In one corner is a gruesome display of the skulls of fourteen monks, and the mummified remains of another, who were martyred in the Persian destruction.

From the **roof** of the monastery, a startling landscape is laid out before you: the lush green of the monastery garden and the natural vegetation of the wadi set against a backdrop of sheer, bleached rock is nothing short of incredible. The whole is enhanced by an awesome silence, broken only by the gurgle of spring water far below.

Nabi Musa

Twenty kilometres east of Jerusalem, as Route 1 approaches its final descent into the Jordan Valley, a signpost to the right points to **Nabi Musa**, where, according to Muslim tradition, Moses (Musa) – revered as a prophet in Islam – is buried. The complex of domes set against the rolling dunes of the desert is an example of Islamic architecture at its simple best, and definitely worth the two-kilometre detour.

The tomb has been a site of annual **pilgrimage** since the time of Saladin, although the main body of the present shrine was built by Mamluk Sultan Baybars in 1269. Later, rooms were added to house pilgrims and, in 1475, the hospice was extended to its present size. The Ottoman Turks further restored the building around 1820 and, to counterbalance the influx of Christian pilgrims to Jerusalem during the Holy Week at Easter, encouraged a week-long pilgrimage to the site to take place around the same time. Traditionally it was a time for celebration and relaxation: the procession set out from Jerusalem under the leadership of the Mufti and along the way the pilgrims sang, played drums, flutes and lutes and danced the traditional Palestinian *dabka*. The entertainment continued at the site itself with all sorts of activities and events ranging from traditional storytelling, shadow theatre, cards and backgammon, to horse racing and jousting. However, celebrations aside, the gathering of so many Palestinian Muslims from different parts of the country was always going to be an event of potential political significance and during the 1920s and 1930s, the power of this mass meeting was marshalled into demonstrations against Zionism. In 1930, the British army attempted in vain to quell tens of thousands of demonstrators gathered at the Nabi Musa pilgrimage, and in an effort to defuse such political resistance, the event was banned by the Mandate authorities in 1937. The pilgrimage was resumed only in April 1987, when it was attended by some fifty thousand Palestinians.

The site is cared for by a family who will gladly show you around; there's no entrance fee, but contributions are welcomed. Inside the beautifully simple and serene **mosque**, with its white-domed roof, is a glazed green mihrab and painted green wooden *minbar*. A small room to the right of the entrance houses the stone **mausoleum** of the prophet. Don't miss the view from the top of the minaret which displays the whole complex below, the desert hills beyond, the Jordan Valley and purple hills of Moab in the distance. The **cemetery** outside was used mainly for Muslims who died during the festival but Muslim legend identifies two of the tombs here as being those of Moses's shepherd, Hassan er-Ra'i, and the Prophet Mohammed's wife, Aisha.

A little beyond the turn-off for Nabi Musa lies the junction of Route 1 and Route 90; from here you turn left for Jericho, or go straight on for Qumran and the Dead Sea (see p.261).

Jericho

Claiming to be the oldest city on earth, **JERICHO**, the "City of Palms", lies low in the south Jordan Valley, 40km east of Jerusalem and 10km northwest of the Dead Sea. This sleepy, West Bank town (**Ariha** in Arabic), with a population of around 7500, is the archetypal desert oasis, a thriving agricultural settlement based on plentiful local springs. Rich in date palms (in autumn, dates are sold at roadside stalls around town), and tropical fruit and vegetables, Jericho is also famed for its medicinal plants and spices. At 250m below sea level, it's the lowest town on earth, which makes it extremely hot in summer, and warm in winter – a factor that has long made it a favourite resort.

Modern Jericho has little in the way of tourist attractions but within a radius of a few kilometres there are several fascinating historical sites: the ancient and archeologically important **Tel al-Sultan**; two ancient synagogues; the **Monastery of the Temptation** on the site where Christ was tempted by the devil; and **Hisham's Palace**, a unique Ummayad construction featuring one of the most outstanding mosaics in the world. Most people visit Jericho on a day trip from Jerusalem and the town's inhabitants are accustomed to and indulgent of the bus-loads of visitors who sweep in and out in the space of a few hours. However, you really need to spend longer to appreciate fully the history and absorb the town's laid-back and intimate atmosphere from its numerous outdoor cafés and excellent **park restaurants**. The best time of year to visit is in the warm winter months (Sept–April), as in summer the temperature often soars above 40°C.

Some history

Jericho's known history stretches back almost twelve thousand years; from the earliest times its perennial spring, Ein al-Sultan, would have enticed mesolithic nomadic hunters to camp by its abundant waters before resuming their trail. The oldest of some twenty successive **settlements** excavated here dates back to around 8000 BC, when a rectangular stone building was raised, probably a cult centre for the nomadic peoples. Over the next thousand years or so, a permanent settlement with a defensive wall became established, marking the change of its inhabitants from wandering hunter-gatherers to settled food-producers. As far as Kathleen Kenyon – the archeologist who

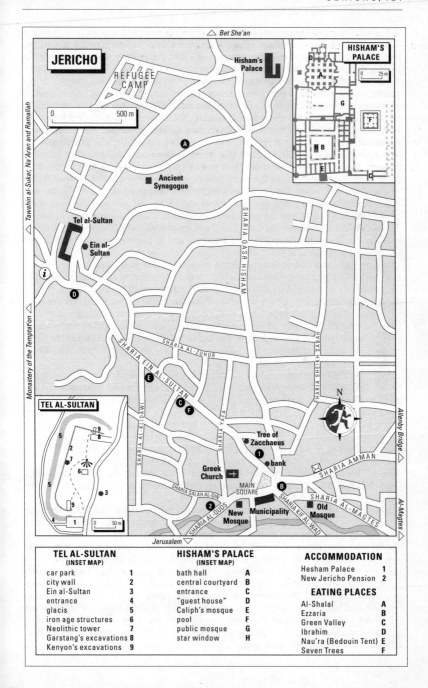

JERICHO

△ Bet She'an

REFUGEE CAMP

Hisham's Palace

0   500 m

Tel al-Sukar, Na'Aran and Ramallah ▷

Ancient Synagogue

Tel al-Sultan

Ein al-Sultan

i

D

Monastery of the Temptation ▷

SHARIA QASR HISHAM

SHARIA EIN AL-SULTAN

SHARIA AL-ZUHUR

E

C **F**

SHARIA AL-KIDAWI

SHARIA YAFA

SHARIA SHEIKH SABAH

SHARIA AMMAN

SHARIA AL-MAGTES

Allenby Bridge ▷

Al-Magtes ▷

N

Tree of Zacchaeus

1

bank

B

SHARIA AL-QUDS

Greek Church

SHARIA SALAH AL-DIN

MAIN SQUARE

2

New Mosque

Municipality

SHARIA KIF AL-WAD

Old Mosque

SHARIA AL-KIDAWI

Jerusalem ▽

HISHAM'S PALACE

D

A

G

H **B**

E

F

C

0   25 m

TEL AL-SULTAN

5
9
8
2
7
6
5
3
9
4
1

0   50 m

TEL AL-SULTAN (INSET MAP)		HISHAM'S PALACE (INSET MAP)		ACCOMMODATION	
car park	1	bath hall	A	Hesham Palace	1
city wall	2	central courtyard	B	New Jericho Pension	2
Ein al-Sultan	3	entrance	C		
entrance	4	"guest house"	D	**EATING PLACES**	
glacis	5	Caliph's mosque	E		
iron age structures	6	pool	F	Al-Shalal	A
Neolithic tower	7	public mosque	G	Ezzaria	B
Garstang's excavations	8	star window	H	Green Valley	C
Kenyon's excavations	9			Ibrahim	D
				Nau'ra (Bedouin Tent)	E
				Seven Trees	F

did much of the most important work at the site – is concerned, this effectively makes it the world's oldest civilization: village settlements known elsewhere are almost two thousand years younger, and the pyramids, the first major stone constructions in the Middle East, went up four thousand years later.

This city was eventually destroyed – whether by war or natural disaster is not known – and some time after 6000 BC was reinhabited by a different people, makers of pottery. After a brief move to a different site in the Wadi Qelt in the fifth millennium BC (perhaps because the water source moved), the city was re-established here, with a new city wall. This ancient site, today known as **Tel al-Sultan**, was a flourishing **Canaanite** centre as early as 3000 BC. But the event for which Jericho is perhaps most well known occurred around 1200 BC, when **Joshua** and the invading Israelites crossed the Jordan River, sounded their trumpets, and as the song tells it "the walls came tumbling down", or, as the more prosaic biblical version has it (Joshua 6: 20), "the wall fell down flat". The Israelites then "utterly destroyed all that was in the city, both man and woman, young and old, and ox and sheep and ass, with the edge of the sword" (Joshua 6: 21), and for good measure, Joshua then put a curse on it, saying: "Cursed be the man before the Lord that riseth up and buildeth this city of Jericho; he shall lay the foundation thereof in his firstborn, and in his youngest son shall he set the gates of it" (Joshua 6: 26).

Under Ahab, and in defiance of Joshua's curse, Hiel of Bethel reconstructed the city (I Kings 16: 34) and, later, Elisha purified the water of the spring after being lobbied by local residents who complained that it made the land barren (II Kings 2: 19–22). Jericho became an administrative centre under the **Persians** in 550 BC but thereafter declined, although under Alexander the Great (332 BC), an area to the south (again near Wadi Qelt) became a royal estate, its warm winter climate making it an ideal retreat from the cold of Jerusalem and the highlands. **Jesus** visited the town several times; here, he restored the sight of a blind beggar (Luke 18: 35–43) and on Jebel Quruntul, the Mount of Temptation, he spent forty days in meditation (Luke 4: 1–3).

In the Byzantine period, the centre of population shifted from Tel al-Sultan to the site of the present town. Alexander's estate continued in use in **Roman times** when it was given to Cleopatra by Mark Antony. Herod the Great is said to have initially leased the oasis from her but it was later given to him by Emperor Octavian and he subsequently laid out new aqueducts to irrigate the fields and supply his fabulous winter palace at Tulul Abu al-'Alayiq. Another magnificent palace was built here in 724 AD by the Ummayad sultan Hisham Ibn Abd al-Malik, whose hunting palace at Khirbet al-Mafjar is one of the most outstanding surviving examples of the Islamic architecture of the period. The conquering **Crusaders** introduced sugar production to Jericho, built a "New Jericho" at Tawahin al-Sukkar and erected a church in commemoration of the temptation of Christ on Jabal Quruntul.

In **modern times** the introduction of fruit production following World War I brought new wealth to Jericho, then a part of British Mandate Palestine. After the **1948 war**, it was held by Jordan as part of the West Bank and 185,000 Palestinian refugees from coastal territories captured by Israel flooded into the area. Three refugee camps were erected – 'Awawme, Ein al-Sultan and Aqabat Jaber – but, in the wake of the Israeli occupation in 1967, most of the refugees were again displaced. Today, 'Awawme stands empty whilst the population of the other two is much reduced. Under the **Oslo Accords** in May 1994, Jericho became the first West Bank town to be handed over to the PNA and business people from Western and Arab countries came here to look into the possibilities of investment. However, periodic closures of the Green Line since then and the cutting-off of connections to even the rest of the West Bank have hit both tourism and foreign investment hard.

Arrival, information and accommodation

Service taxis drop you off on the main square in the centre of town from where Sharia Ein al-Sultan leads up to Tel al-Sultan, and Sharia Qasr Hisham takes you to Hisham's Palace. There is a **PNA tourist office** up by Tel al-Sultan, but it's rarely open, so it's advisable to call first (☎02/992 2935). The town hall, police station, Cairo Amman Bank, and a couple of **moneychangers** are all on the main square. Just off it, on Sharia Amman, you'll find the **post office** and, on Sharia Salah al-Din, the **hospital**. **Car rental** is available from Orabi on Sharia al-Quds (☎02/992 3230 or 24hr on ☎050/405095). **Moving on**, there are service taxis from the main square to Bethany, Nablus, Ramallah and Allenby Bridge.

Accommodation

At present, Jericho has only three **places to stay**. The best option for budget travellers is the characterful and friendly *Hesham Palace Hotel* on Sharia Ein al-Sultan, just off the main square (☎02/992 2156; ①). In appearance, this rambling 1920s hotel with its creaking ceiling fans and peeling wallpaper is a shadow of its former self but it's still an atmospheric place, and you can easily imagine what it must have been like when it was a favourite gambling haunt of Jordan's King Hussein and his ministers. The hotel has recently re-opened after a ten-year closure and is gradually being renovated; the older rooms are paid for by the bed, usually four per room (though you'll probably be lucky and have a whole room to yourself), while the newer, brighter rooms have en-suite bathrooms. The *New Jericho Pension*, on Sharia al-Quds, the Jerusalem Road (☎02/992 2215; ②), isn't as good value; it's best to check out the motley collection of rooms before choosing. Again, you pay in principle for each bed rather than the room. The most upmarket accommodation in Jericho is offered by the *Jerusalem Hotel*, about 2km from the main square down Sharia Amman (☎02/992 1329, fax 992 3109; ③). Still unfinished in parts, it has bright, new air-conditioned rooms, some with nice balconies overlooking citrus groves, and a few less plush rooms downstairs where, again, you pay by the bed. At the time of writing new tourist hotels were under construction by the Tree of Zacchaeus just off Sharia Ein al-Sultan, and out by Hisham's Palace.

The Town and ancient sites

There's not much to do in the town itself except soak up the ambience, though the *qahwas* are worth popping into for a Turkish coffee or mint tea, and the inhabitants will probably stop you for a chat. The only sight actually in town is the **Tree of Zacchaeus** on Sharia Ein al-Sultan, a two-thousand-year-old tree which Zacchaeus, a rich tax collector, climbed to see Jesus en route to Jerusalem (Luke 19: 4). Spotting Zacchaeus, Jesus asked him for an invitation to his home, and, once there, so inspired him that he forthwith gave half his wealth to charity. Tour buses stop here for a quick snapshot before zipping off straight to the main attractions.

If you're **visiting the sites** independently, one of the best ways to do it is to **rent a bicycle**; try Zaki Bike Shop on the main square, or Mohammed Tawil's bike shop, just off it on Sharia al-Maghtas; expect to pay around 3–4NIS an hour, or 15NIS per day.

Tel al-Sultan (Tel Jericho)

Ancient Jericho is situated some 2km to the northwest of the modern town. From a distance, the **tel** (daily 8am–5pm; 8NIS) appears to be simply a huge mound of earth, but close up the excavations (most of which are below ground level, so you'll be looking down at them) reveal it to be the result of numerous settlements built upon the ruins of their predecessors; standing on it knowing that there are ten thousand years of civilization under your feet can be an awesome sensation, an experience further enhanced by the magnificent view from the observation point – oasis greens against a backdrop of parched, stark desert.

The first modern **excavations**, carried out in 1867, weren't a great success, missing an important stone tower by inches. Ever since, archeologists have been virtually queueing up to get their trowels into the ground and, today, the archeological importance of the site is unquestionable, largely due to the work of the late British archeologist Dame Kathleen Kenyon, who began the most extensive dig at the site in 1952 and discovered the remains of no fewer than 23 cities. With the discovery of the walls, she

JOSHUA AND JERICHO: TRUTH OR FICTION?

At the beginning of the twentieth century, **archeologists** hoped that excavations in Palestine would yield proof of events from the Bible and, with Joshua's conquest in mind, work began in earnest at Jericho. First off the block, in 1907, was Ernst Sellin, a respected German biblical scholar. He failed to find the required evidence, but the next investigation in 1930, led by John Garstang of Liverpool University, appeared to bear fruit, uncovering proof that the walls of Jericho had indeed collapsed at one stage in its history – the biblical story seemed vindicated. However, digs in the 1950s by **Kathleen Kenyon** showed that the timing was all wrong: the strata of material inside the tel indicated that the fallen walls dated from the Middle Bronze Age, putting them before 1550 BC, some three and a half centuries too early for the Israelite invasion. Moreover, at the time of Joshua's biblical conquest in the Late Bronze Age or Early Iron Age, Jericho was virtually abandoned, and no walled city existed. The Bible, it seemed, was pure fiction, or at best legend, and the archeologists' original idea that the early Old Testament could be taken as a reliable historical document was seriously discredited.

However, the idea has recently been revived, not by religious fundamentalists, but by a non-religious Egyptologist, **David Rohl**. In his book, *A Test of Time* (1995), Rohl argues that the conventionally accepted dates for strata such as the Middle and Late Bronze Ages in Palestine are wrong, because they are derived from a misdating of Egyptian history: unlike Egyptian remains, those from Palestine do not have hieroglyphs detailing who was on the throne or who built what, and archeologists rely on comparing pottery and other remains found here with contemporary pieces found in Egypt to give time frames to certain periods. So, it is known, for example, that the Middle Bronze Age in Palestine coincides with the 15th and 16th dynasties in Egypt, apparently around 1500 BC. Rohl believes, however, that the dates conventionally given for the classical period of Ancient Egypt are 350 years too early and proposes a **"New Chronology"** based on redating of later periods in Egyptian history, which therefore affects the dating of Palestinian history. Under this new chronology, the Middle Bronze Age city whose walls seem to have fallen down could well have been contemporary with the Israelite conquest and Joshua's curse and the city's abandonment would be consistent with the fact that there was no city here for the next three centuries.

Rohl's conclusions affect our interpretation of several sites in Israel and the Palestinian Territories other than Jericho: most notably Tel Balata in Nablus (see p.442), and Megiddo (see p.152). Rohl also challenges accepted correspondences between Egyptian history and the Bible, denying, for example, the accepted identification of the pharaoh of the Exodus with the great Ramses II, and instead identifying Ramses with Pharaoh Shishak who invaded Judah many years later in the reign of Rehoboam (I Kings 14: 25–26; II Chronicles 12: 2–9). Even more stunningly, Rohl asserts that Lebayu, one of the authors of the Amarna letters (see p.482), is in fact the biblical King Saul: if he is right, then the British Museum in London possesses correspondence sent by Israel's first king to a man thought to have pre-dated him by 350 years, Egypt's heretic Pharaoh Akhenaton. Rohl's theories remain controversial, but if he is right, Saul and Joshua are just two of the Old Testament characters who emerge out of legend and into history.

was also the first to claim that Jericho provided evidence of the transition from hunter to settled farmer. Her book, *Digging up Jericho* (Ernest Benn, 1957), contains fascinating photographs and is well worth trying to get hold of as her discoveries are now somewhat hard to distinguish among the piles of earth and ditches littered with rubble and empty Coke cans.

Narrowly missed by the 1867 excavations, the seven-metre-high **neolithic tower**, dating from around 7000 BC, is one of the site's major archeological discoveries. Its size and construction – with a central stairway – is unrivalled anywhere in the world for this period, and its position, just inside the walls, would have provided the city with an excellent defence against attackers. Just to the north of this lay the original shrine, the earliest structure at the site, though little remains of it today. The **city walls** that have been uncovered date from the Early Bronze Age (around 2600 BC). Centuries later, potential invaders would have been deterred by the sloping banks (*glacis*) of a fort built in the Middle Bronze Age (around 1600 BC, or perhaps 1250 BC). Although mud-brick walls from this period do appear to have "tumbled" down the *glacis*, the interpretation to be placed on that is controversial (see box opposite).

Sites around Tel al-Sultan

One reason for the original location of the ancient city of Jericho was its proximity to a constant source of water – **Ein al-Sultan**. The spring, opposite Tel al-Sultan, still provides a lifeline for Jericho, gushing water at the rate of 1000 gallons per minute, and distributed throughout the oasis by a complex system of gravity-flow irrigation. Early tradition identifies this spring with the one the prophet Elisha purified by throwing salt into it (II Kings 2: 19–22), giving it its other name: Elisha's Spring. Three hundred metres north from Ein al-Sultan, to the right of the road leading to Hisham's Palace, a sign points to an **ancient synagogue** dating from the fifth or sixth century (daily 8am–4pm; 5NIS). Here, in the basement of what is now a *yeshiva*, you can see the synagogue's beautiful mosaic floor. A rectangular building divided into three by two rows of columns, the floor is decorated with floral and geometric patterns. Beneath a *menora*, the Aramaic inscription reads "Peace Upon Israel" – somewhat appropriately the site is now run by the PNA and the Israeli National Parks Authority in collaboration.

On the road to Ramallah (Route 449), 300m northwest from Tel al-Sultan, **Tawahin al-Sukar** is the site of a Crusader sugar factory, featuring remains of mills, presses and a small mosque. The ruins aren't much to look at, but the site (free access) does offer good views over Tel al-Sultan and the town and desert beyond. A couple of kilometres further on are the remains of the Byzantine settlement of **Na'aran**, whose fifth-century BC synagogue, excavated in 1918, has an elaborate and well-preserved mosaic floor featuring commemorative inscriptions, geometrical designs containing flora and fauna, and a zodiac. Na'aran is situated by the springs of Ein Duyuk and Ein Nuwaiyyma. The route of the **aqueduct** that carried water to Hisham's Palace can still be traced; its most impressive remnant is the fine arch spanning the wadi close to the springs, which is still in use today.

The Monastery of the Temptation

Three kilometres northwest of the town, **Jabal Quruntul** is the mountain where Jesus fasted for forty days and was tempted by the devil with the words: "If thou be the Son of God, command that these stones be made bread" (Matthew 4: 3–4). Its Arabic name, Quruntul, derives from the Latin *Mons Quaranta*, or Mountain of the Forty, the name given to it by the Crusaders in commemoration of the fast.

The climb up the bare, rocky slopes to the Greek Orthodox **Monastery of the Temptation** (Mon–Sat: summer 9am–1pm & 3–5pm; winter 9am–1pm & 3–4pm) looks daunting, but in fact it's a trek of only fifteen to thirty minutes (depending on your fitness level), and well worth the effort. Perched on a rocky ledge about 350m above

Jericho, the monastery offers a bird's-eye view of the whole oasis and the Jordan Valley. The present building was constructed at the end of the last century around a crude cave **chapel** that marks the stone on which Jesus reputedly sat during the temptation – another of the holy sites said to have been identified by Queen Helena in her pilgrimage of 326 AD. Other sources, however, date the cave chapel only as far back as the twelfth century throwing into doubt the claim that some of the gold leaf **icons** in the chapel at the southern end of the building are Byzantine. The rest of the structure is taken up with monks' cells.

If the climb didn't tire you out, you may want to persuade the site custodian to let you continue along the path (barred by a gate) to the summit for an even higher view of the Jordan Valley and south towards the Dead Sea. The uncompleted walls here are the result of an unsuccessful attempt to build a church here in 1874. A fortress known as **Doq** originally stood on the summit. Built by the Seleucids, who conquered Palestine in 198 BC, it was taken by the Hasmoneans in 134 BC. Here Simon the Maccabee was murdered by his son-in-law Ptolemy in one of the internecine power struggles that were to dog the Hasmoneans, finally bringing down their dynasty and handing Palestine to the Romans.

Hisham's Palace (Khirbet al-Mafjar)

The splendid ruins of **Hisham's Palace** (daily 8am–5pm; 8NIS), around 2km from Jericho town centre and a similar distance northeast of Tel al-Sultan, are all that's left of one of the finest examples of Ummayad architecture in the country. The palace was built as one of a number of hunting lodges for the the Ummayad princes, and although named after Caliph Hisham Ibn Abd al-Malik, it was in fact designed by the caliph's high-living nephew and successor, al-Walid Ibn Yazid. Construction work began in 743 AD but stopped a year later when Yazid was assassinated. Three years later, the sumptuous palace was virtually levelled by an earthquake; stones from the ruins were used extensively in local building work as late as 1927 but excavation and recognition of the site in the 1930s have prevented any further destruction.

Entering through the imposing stone entrance to the left of the forecourt, you are immediately confronted by the amazing **star window**, made of stone and containing an intricately carved, geometrically rounded six-pointed star. The window has been placed in the **central courtyard** and surrounded by columns and the remains of what would have been the general living quarters. In the northeast and southwest corners of the courtyard, steps led to an upper storey that was reserved for the imperial residence. To the left of the star window is a small **mosque**, probably reserved for the caliph's personal use; behind the window, steps lead down to a small **bathhouse**, well-preserved with an arched ceiling and mosaic floor.

From the northwest corner of the courtyard, a paved path leads to the imposing remains of the massive **bath hall**, with its huge colonnade, sixteen quadrilobed pillars and twelve recesses. Its floor consists of thirty-six panels of pink and blue mosaic, only a few of which are on view: the rest are covered for their own protection. To the north of the hall, the building labelled "guest house" houses the palace's greatest treasure: a superb and undamaged **mosaic** forming part of the marble-edged dais in the *diwan* or reception hall; to see it you have to go round to the back of the guesthouse and climb the stairs. The mosaic depicts a lion and a group of gazelles in an allegory relevant to the function of the room: the two gazelles beneath the tree on the left are diplomats or guests that have good relations with the kingdom and are therefore welcome; the gazelle on the right, however, represents a visitor who wishes the ruler harm, and is therefore being savaged by the lion, representing revenge. Also in the scene is a huge pomegranate tree bearing fifteen fruits, each representing a country under the rule of Sultan Abd al-Malik. The pieces of the mosaic are so tiny that the whole has a marvellously detailed, woven effect. But apart from being arguably the finest in the region, it is also unique in that it follows no known contemporaneous school of design or influence – certainly not Islamic, as Islamic art usually eschews representations of animals as smacking of idolatry.

Next to the building with the mosaic, the bathhouse's hot room will be familiar to anyone who has used a *hammam baladi* (Turkish bath). To its north is the stove room where the water was heated – parts of the terracotta piping can still be seen in the walls. Heading back towards the exit, you pass the **public mosque**, of which really only the mihrab remains; while to your left lie the remains of an **ornamental pool**.

Tulul Abu al-'Alayiq

At the entrance to Wadi Qelt, about 2km southwest of Jericho along a dirt road, **Tulul Abu al-'Alayiq** (Tel Abu 'Alayiq) is the site of a winter palace built for the **Hasmoneans** and no fewer than three built for **Herod**. Partly as a result of squabbling with the Hasmonean side of his family and partly as a result of Cleopatra's territorial aspirations, Herod had to rent the estates of Jericho from the Egyptian queen, despite the fact that they formed part of his newly won kingdom. His mother-in-law, Alexandra, found favour with Cleopatra and consquently, in 35 BC, Herod was forced to replace his candidate for the high priesthood with Alexandra's son, his brother-in-law, Aristobulus, whom a year later he had brought to Jericho and drowned in a swimming pool. But by 34 BC, Mark Antony's military campaigns were failing, and with the demise of the alliance between him and his lover Cleopatra in 30 BC, the lands around Jericho reverted to Herod. At the beginning of his reign, Herod built a small residence where, according to the historian Josephus, he spent his final days in a state described as melancholy-mad. After Herod's death, his slave Simeon supposedly burnt the palace to the ground, though there is no archeological evidence to support either this or the reconstruction that Josephus attributed to Herod's son Archelaus.

Access to **the site** is not controlled, which means that it has suffered more than usual from the elements and from scavengers, and a shortage of paths and signs means making the best you can of a scramble over assorted mounds of earth. Adjacent to the road, and not particularly well-defined, is the outline of Herod's first palace, but the most interesting remains belong to the third palace, 100m further north. The depression here once enclosed an ornate sunken garden fronted by a grand facade with narrow colonnades at either end. To the right, a large open area is thought to have been an artificial **pool**, which served to keep the whole place cool. A bridge, small portions of which can be seen on the northern bank, crossed the wadi and led to the main living quarters, a reception hall and the obligatory **bathhouse** – the best-preserved part of the complex. Unfortunately, much of the construction was in mud brick, which doesn't weather the passage of time too well.

To the northwest are the remains of the **Hasmonean Palace** which Herod incorporated into his second palace. The Hasmonean foundations supported storerooms, a small villa and a *mikve* (ritual bath), all surrounding the swimming pool where Herod may have drowned his brother-in-law. The water supply from Ein Duyuk was here supplemented by two additional aqueducts from the perennial springs within Wadi Qelt.

Sites south of town

A short walk southwest of town along the ancient Jerusalem–Jericho road brings you to a strategic conical hill, **Tel al-Aqaba**, on the summit of which are the remains of another fortress built by Herod, which he named **Kypros** after his mother. He fortified the previous structure here and added the bathhouse which was supplied by cisterns from Ein Qelt. The fortress was used by the Zealots in the First Revolt against Rome (66 AD), but the square building you now see at the centre dates from the later Byzantine period.

Eating

Like all West Bank towns, Jericho has its share of small hummus, falafel and *shawarma* joints; you'll find plenty on and off the main square. What is special about Jericho, however, is the exceptional range and flavour of locally grown fresh vegetables and seasonal **fruit**, especially dates and pomelos (also known as shaddocks – like a grapefruit, but bigger), on sale at roadside stalls. For a sit-down meal, the *Ezzaria Restaurant* on the main square (daily 5am–10pm; cheap) does great-value chicken, kebabs and hummus, but the standard of hygiene is none too rigorous.

Jericho's best eating experience, however, is to be had in any of its famous outdoor *muntzaats* or **park restaurants**; people come to them from all over the West Bank both to eat (especially on Fridays) and to listen to some of the best musicians in the area. Most of them are strung out along Ein al-Sultan Street between the centre of town and Tel al-Sultan, and most serve alcohol. The best is the *Seven Trees,* which has a lovely shaded garden (daily 10am–midnight; moderate), and serves the likes of *shashlik,* chicken or fish, with of course a selection of mezze. Next door, the *Green Valley* (daily 11am–11pm; moderate), offers a very similar menu. The *Na'ura,* also called the *Bedouin Tent* (daily 8am–7pm; moderate), specializes in what they call Bedouin *shashlik* – skewered pieces of lamb served on flat, oven-baked bread and onions; they also offer set menus. Their garden is the most unusual, with an incongruous waterwheel among several children's amusements in a scruffy playground. You can also dine indoors in the "old house", though dating from the 1920s, it's not so old by Jericho standards. Almost at Tel al-Sultan, the *Ibrahim Restaurant* (daily 6am–10pm; moderate) offers slightly smarter indoor dining, catering mostly to tour groups, and features the usual combination of meat dishes, salads and dips.

Finally, if you feel like a swim before eating, the *Al-Shalal,* behind the synagogue near Ein Sultan (☎050/520932; daily 9am–5pm & 7pm–midnight), is a swimming pool with a moderately priced restaurant. Families make a day of it, swimming, then eating, and relaxing, smoking an *argila* or drinking a coffee.

Routes on from Jericho

The road east from Jericho (Route 449) leads 16km to the **Allenby Bridge** (or King Hussein Bridge to Jordanians) over the River Jordan. This very unimpressive wooden structure is the main border crossing between the Palestinian Territories and Jordan and can be reached easily by service taxi from Jerusalem, Jericho or Ramallah, and by bus or service taxi from Amman. Note that you cannot walk across the bridge so you'll need to take a shuttle bus (JD5).

Departing from the West Bank, you have to pay the Israeli authorities an exit tax of 100NIS (see box on p.19 for advice on avoiding Israeli and Jordanian stamps in your passport). On the Jordanian side, there are separate terminals for local and foreign passengers, and you must already have a visa to enter Jordan. From the foreigners' terminal, there are service taxis to Amman (JD5, but you may have to bargain). If you're on a really tight budget you can save yourself a few fils by walking to the local passengers' terminal and taking a bus from there: as well as Amman, buses run to Salt and Zerqa. Arriving from Jordan, there are service taxis to Jericho, Jerusalem and Ramallah, and Orabi car rental has an office at the border post (☎02/992 2505). For details of crossing from Jordan into the West Bank, see p.17.

A couple of kilometres south of the bridge is the supposed site where John the Baptist baptized Jesus in the Jordan River (Matthew 3: 13–17). Formerly popular with pilgrims who came at the Feast of Epiphany to immerse themselves in the water, the site of the **Baptism of Jesus**, known as **al-Maghtes**, is now usually closed to visitors for military reasons. Several alternative sites are now used, above all Yardenit, near to where the Jordan flows out of the Sea of Galilee (see p.214).

North from Jericho

Route 90 up the Jordan Valley from **Jericho** continues to the **Sea of Galilee** (see p.193) and **Tiberias** (see p.195). Running through bare hills laced with goat runs, where the only sign of life is the occasional Bedouin herder harrying the flocks, it's also the quieter of the two main routes to the northern part of the West Bank, with branches leading off to the towns of Ramallah (Route 449) and Nablus (Route 57).

Twenty-eight kilometres north of Jericho, a turn-off to the west leads to the scant remains of **Sartaba**, a castle built under the Hasmonean King Alexander Jannaeus, destroyed by the Romans, and rebuilt for Herod. There are great views of the Jordan Valley from here but the site can only be reached with your own transport or by chartering a "special" taxi.

NORTH OF JERUSALEM

Route 60 runs **north from Jerusalem** to the historically and politically important towns of **Ramallah** and **Nablus**, from where branches continue on to **Qalqilya**, **Tulkarm** and **Jenin**. It's a busy route; the bulk of the population of the West Bank live in the towns, camps and villages along the central highway, but between these are cultivated arable fields, beyond which olive trees clothe the stepped slopes of the hills.

Jerusalem to Ramallah

The road from Jerusalem to Ramallah is always busy with Palestinian traffic running to the villages of **Bet Hanina**, **Ram** and **Jaba**, and past the refugee camps of **Qalandia** and **Shu'afat**, and with Israeli traffic heading for the triple ring of settlements around the eastern side of Jerusalem, whose city limits have been expanded up to the edge of Ramallah. Along the way there are a number of sites of ancient and modern significance, well worth the effort of getting to if only to enjoy the countryside. Most are served by buses and service taxis from either Jerusalem or Ramallah; drivers will drop you on the main road at the entrance to the villages, from where you can walk or hitch the final leg. The only problem is getting back: you may have a long wait for the next available transport, so to avoid walking or hitching, leave in good time. (See the map on p.304 for locations of sites in this section.)

Nabi Samwil

Perched on a mountain top 890m above sea level, and clearly visible from West Jerusalem, 4km to its south, the village of **NABI SAMWIL** is traditionally held to house the tomb of the prophet Samuel who, according to the Old Testament (I Samuel 25: 1), was buried at a place called Rama. From the minaret (free access except during prayer times) of the village's large, turreted mosque you get a wonderful view over the hills of Jerusalem and Bethel, and, on a clear day, even the Mediterranean and the mountains of Jordan.

Samuel's cloth-covered **tomb**, lying in the darkened cellar of the mosque, has been the centre of pilgrimage and worship for Jews, Christians and Muslims alike from at least the sixth century. The Crusaders, approaching Jerusalem in 1099, caught their first glimpse of the holy city from this mountain and, to express their delight, named it *Mont de Joie* – **Mountjoy**. They built a church on the burial site in 1157, and its graceful, painted arches and buttressed walls were incorporated into the mosque when it was erected in 1911. Later is saw service as a Jordanian Arab Legion camp guarding access to Jerusalem, until it was taken by the Israelis in 1967.

The easiest way **to get to Nabi Samwil** is to take a #74 bus from the Nablus Road bus station in East Jerusalem to Bet Hanina and walk up from there. It can also be reached on foot from the Jewish settlement of Ramot, just to its south (Egged bus #36 from Jaffa Road and HaNeviim).

al-Jib (Giv'on)

A couple of kilometres to the north of Nabi Samwil lies the picturesque Palestinian village of **AL-JIB**, site of biblical Gibeon whose inhabitants tricked the leaders of the Israelites into making a peace treaty with them and taking an oath not to kill them (Joshua 9: 3–21). Five local kings, on hearing of the treaty, attacked the Gibeonites, who called on Joshua for help, and it was to prolong the battle against these five kings outside Gibeon that Joshua uttered his famous command: "Sun, stand thou still upon Gibeon; and thou, Moon, in the valley of Ayalon" (Joshua 10: 12). The city became prosperous through wine production in the seventh century BC, and was finally destroyed by the Babylonians in 587 BC.

Today, the main reason to visit Al-Jib is to see the excavations of Gibeon, the highlight of which is the excellently preserved **ancient water system**. Near the village cemetery is a great, rock-hewn **cistern**, over 11m in diameter and 10m deep, which, with the aid of a candle or flashlight, you can descend into from an opening at the back of the nearby tel. The worn, winding steps and polished sides show how frequently they were used, as do the smoke-darkened niches where oil-lamps once stood. The cistern's water would have sustained the Gibeonites through extended siege, aided by a tunnel which descended from inside the ancient city wall to the pool and denied water to attackers while making it available to the town's inhabitants. The original water system served al-Jib until very recently: another tunnel brought water from the spring in the centre of the hill to the pool, from where it was piped to a series of taps. Sixty-three **wine cellars** have also been discovered on the site (each capable of storing 42 large barrels of wine), along with wine and olive presses, and potsherds inscribed with the word "Gibeon".

To reach the site, take the Biddu road from the village and walk up the hill to the parking lot, from where a rough path leads to the excavations.

Tel al-Nasba

Tel al-Nasba, 3km south of Ramallah, was once a major Israelite town, known in the Bible as **Mizpeh**. It was here that Samuel assembled the Israelites to defeat the Philistines (I Samuel 7: 5–11), and here that the other tribes of Israel met to declare civil war against the tribe of Benjamin in revenge for a gang rape by the men of Gibeah (Judges 20: 1). The archeological site is not tremendously exciting, though a wall and a gate from the period of the kings of Judah has been excavated and you can also see a palace cellar complete with wine jars, a cloth-dyeing plant, temples and the ruins of a Crusader church.

Sites east of the Jerusalem road

Though there are a number of biblical sites **east of Route 60**, they're only really worth visiting if you have either a keen interest in Old Testament sites or a desire to get off the beaten track. Most of them are inaccessible on public transport, so you'll have to charter a "special" taxi, or walk from the main road.

TEL AL-FUL (Giv'at Shaul), 5km north of Jerusalem, overlooks the ancient Land of Benjamin, the Dead Sea and the Hills of Moab, and is thought by many archeologists to be the site of biblical Gibeah (but see below), an attack by whose men on travellers from the north of Israel (Judges 19) led to the civil war between Benjamin and the other Israelite tribes described at the end of the book of Judges. Gibeah later became Saul's capital, hence the Hebrew name, **Giv'at Sha'ul**, meaning "the Hill of Saul", also used (confusingly) by one of West Jerusalem's northern suburbs. Nowadays, all there is to see (apart from the views) is the remains of a fortress, thought to be Saul's, of which the base of one of the corner towers has been excavated. Also here is the half-finished palace of King Hussein of Jordan, untouched since its capture in 1967.

Two kilometres to the west, the Palestinian village of **ANATA**, birthplace of the prophet Jeremiah, is the site of Roman and Byzantine *Anatot*; the remains of a Byzantine church can still be seen here. Just over 2km north, **HIZMA**'s modest claim to fame is its prehistoric graves known to local people as *Qubur Beni Israel* – tombs of the tribe of Israel. **RAM**, some 6km from Ramallah near the airport, may have been the biblical **Rama** – home, birthplace and burial site of the prophet Samuel, though others think it might be Harama, where the biblical Judge Deborah (one of the Israelites' few female leaders) lived. East of Ram, a side road leads to the Palestinian village of **MUKHMAS**, dating from the Iron Age and probably the site of **Mikhmash** where Saul and his son Jonathan fought against the Philistines (I Samuel 14: 1–15) – remains of Roman and Byzantine settlements have been found here. Two kilometres southwest of Mukhmas, the village of **JABA** is the biblical **Geba**. In a sacred area by the village (on the western slope of the hill), sockets clearly bored into the rock may have supported standing stones, which may in turn support the view of archeologist J.M. Miller that this was the same place as Gibeah (usually identified with Tel al-Ful; see above), site of a Philistine garrison or perhaps a standing stone (the Hebrew word is ambiguous) according to I Samuel 13: 3. There the Hebrew text calls the place Geba and the Greek calls it Gibeah.

Ramallah

Sixteen kilometres north of Jerusalem and built across several hills some 900m above sea level, **RAMALLAH** (with the town of al-Bira on its doorstep) is famed for its pleasant, cool climate and pollution-free air. Pre-1967 it was a favourite summer resort for Arabs from Jordan, the Gulf region and Lebanon, its thriving hotels and restaurants renowned throughout the Middle East. Nowadays, it's frequented mainly by visiting expatriate Ramlawis and Palestinian honeymoon couples.

French Crusaders built a stronghold here during the twelfth century but **modern Ramallah** is thought to have first been settled around 1550 by Rashed Haddad and his older brother, both Christians fleeing from al-Karak in what is now Jordan. Many Ramlawis still claim descent from the Haddad family, and a large minority, concentrated in the town centre, are Christian. Though by no means the most militant of West Bank towns, Ramallah has put in its fair share of **resistance to Israeli occupation**; its mayor, Karim Khallaf, after surviving a car bomb attack in 1980, was dismissed from office by the Israelis in 1982 for refusing to cooperate with Menahem Milson's civil administration (see p.393), and for allegedly inciting the population to revolt. The town was transferred to PNA jurisdiction in December 1995, but it was here that disturbances first broke out in the "Tunnel War" following Israel's opening of the Western Wall tunnel in Jerusalem (see p.342).

The town itself has little to offer in the way of sights, but the temperate climate, proximity to Jerusalem and the relatively peaceful atmosphere still make it an ideal base for exploring the West Bank, with good transport connections to Jericho, Nablus and elsewhere. Situated on its doorstep, the working town of **AL-BIRA** has little of interest to the visitor other than a small **folklore museum** (to arrange a visit, call ☎02/995 2876), run by the Inash al-Usra Society (a women's self-help group) in a former church next to the main mosque.

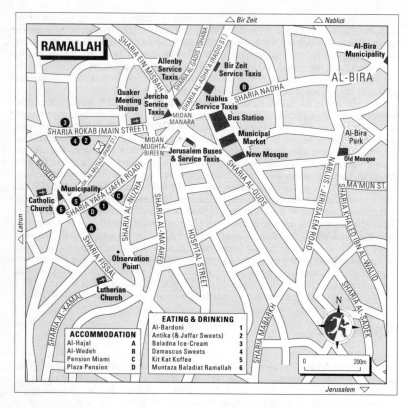

Arrival, information and accommodation

Buses almost all stop at the Central Bus Station right off Midan Manara (the round-about in the middle of town) between Sharia al-Quds (the Jerusalem Road) and Sharia Nadha. **Service taxis** will drop you at one of a variety of points, none more than a hundred metres from Midan Manara. **Moneychangers** can be found in the streets around the centre, with street changers nursing their wads on the corner of al-Adha'a (Radio Street) and Nadha, and on the corner of Yafa and al-Quds. The **post office** is on Sharia al-Mutaza (Park Street), with a mailbox outside for when it's closed. **Car rental** is available from Orabi on Sharia al Quds, south of town in al-Bira (☎02/995 3521).

The most convenient **accommodation** in Ramallah, and also the cheapest, is the *Al-Wedeh Hotel* on the third and fourth floors (no elevator) at 26 Sharia al-Nadha, near the bus station (☎ & fax 02/998 0412; ②). The alternatives are along Sharia Yafa (the Jaffa Road): *Pension Miami*, around 200m down from Midan Mughtabireen (☎02/995 6808; ②), is clean if sombre; while a little further on, opposite the Municipal Gardens, the *Plaza Pension* (☎02/995 6020; ③) is similar but slightly more expensive. Finally, the *Al-Hajal Hotel*, just around the corner on Sharia Feisal (☎02/998 6759; ④), is newer and brighter, if a little shoddily built, with friendly staff. All rates for the above include breakfast.

The Town

Ramallah is the easiest of places to get around; its seven main streets, busy with shoppers and traffic, all radiate out from **Midan Manara** and everything you need is within short walking distance of here. Just behind the bus station, you'll find the **municipal market**, piled high with fruit and veg, and fragrant with the scent of guavas, oranges, figs, or whatever's in season.

The remains of a Crusader tower, *al-Tira*, can still be seen in the old section of the city, northwest of the town centre, where there are also earlier remains from the Hellenic and Byzantine periods. The Crusaders also built a small church in Ramallah that was later converted into a mosque. The **New Mosque** on the site, which is next to the Jerusalem Road, was built in 1960.

Eating, drinking and entertainment

It's quite possible to survive on **falafel and shawarma**, available from several stands around Midan Manara, or from *Antika* in the alley between nos. 32 and 34 Sharia Rokab (Main Street), which stays open round the clock for low-priced, sit-down food in spotless surroundings. However, it is for its **muntazaat** – outdoor restaurant parks – that Ramallah is renowned. Most are found along Sharia Yafa and all offer excellent menus of typical Palestinian food served in beautiful surroundings, where you'll find yourself in the company of Palestinian families enjoying an afternoon or night out over mezze and a bottle of *araq* or a delicious full-course meal. First on your left coming from Midan Mughtabireen, *Al-Bardoni* (☎02/995 6141; daily 11am–midnight; expensive) offers a veritable feast of mezze in its pretty grass garden full of flowers and featuring two beautiful stone fountains. A little further along the road, at the smaller and marginally cheaper *Plaza Pension* (☎02/995 6020; daily 11am–midnight; expensive), you can feast on *musakhan*, kebab or *shashlik*, or sit in the white-pebbled courtyard and sip a whisky, beer or *araq*. Opposite, the splendid *Muntaza Baladiat Ramallah* (Ramallah Municipal Gardens; ☎02/995 6835; daily 9am–midnight; expensive) boasts a large jasmine-scented garden, shaded by ivy, vines and bougainvillea. The café-restaurant opposite in Sharia Rasheed, whose sign advertises *Kit Kat Koffee*, serves delicious fresh fish (daily 10am–11pm; expensive).

Sharia Rokab is the place for **sweets**, with several high-class, sit-down confectioners such as *Damascus* at no. 36 and *Jaffar* in the alley between nos. 32 and 34. *Baladna* at no. 29 is an **ice-cream** parlour whose pistachio flavour is unbeatable.

Grocers and supermarkets sell **alcohol** freely: if you're looking for a bottle of locally produced **araq**, the best brand is the Ramallah Distilleries Company's *Arak Extra Fine*, with a green and gold label, a make you'll be hard put to find inside the Green Line, or

---

MOVING ON FROM RAMALLAH

There are **buses** approximately every 30 minutes to Bir Zeit (30min), Nablus (1hr 30min) and Hebron (2hr, faster if running via Jerusalem) via Bethlehem (1hr 30min). Jerusalem buses stop on Sharia al-Quds, 50m from Midan Manara (every 30min; 40min). Much faster, and little if at all higher in price, are **service taxis**. For Jerusalem (minibuses with yellow plates), they leave from much the same place as Jerusalem buses; for Jericho, they leave from the taxi stand on Midan Manara between Rokab and Ein Misbah, with services for Allenby Bridge and Amman leaving opposite across Ein Misbah. Service taxis for Nablus and Jenin leave from a stand on al-Adha'a, 100m up from Midan Manara, on the right if coming from there; those for Bir Zeit (minibuses) leave a little further along the same street.

indeed the rest of the Palestinian Territories (though you can get it in Jerusalem's Christian Quarter). If smoking, rather than drinking, is your vice (and we're only talking tobacco here), the *Smoker's Shop* on Midan Mughtabireen has a wide selection of water pipes and different tobaccos to smoke in them (any *qahwa* will make you up an *argila* of your own tobacco on request).

Because of its high Christian population, Ramallah is largely free from the dictates of Islamic fundamentalists, and the main **cinema**, Al-Walid, remains open on Sharia Nadha, just off Midan Menara, specializing in Hollywood action movies and Bollywood masalas.

Ramallah to Nablus

The journey **from Ramallah to Nablus** is worth making if only for the views. The road climbs, dips and winds across spectacular landscapes of terraced hills planted with olive and fig trees. The rich browns and reds of the densely cultivated fields are at their best in spring and very early in the morning or, better still, in the red and purple glow of sunset. Here and there, they are broken up by the cooler tones of the white, blue and green houses of scattered hillside villages.

Most visitors travel the road to Nablus by **bus or service taxi** without stopping. But if you're in no hurry and prepared to wait for the next bus or *servees* to come along, there are a few stops along the way that may be of interest. Most villages will, at the very least, have somewhere where you can buy a cold drink.

Bittin (Bethel)

Just beyond Ramallah, Route 449 turns off east, towards Jericho, reaching the village of **BITTIN** a couple of kilometres further on. Set in a valley and surrounded by almond, fig, peach, apple and olive orchards, it's a picturesque village with houses painted blue and lavender and a mosque whose minaret, most unusually, has glass windows to keep out the wind.

The site is identified with the biblical **Bethel** and archeologists have uncovered strata from the earliest Canaanite period to that of the Second Temple (the time of Herod) and beyond. Abraham stopped here on his way south from Shekhem (Nablus) and "built an altar unto the Lord" (Genesis 12: 8), but it was his grandson Jacob who christened the place Bethel, meaning "House of God", following a dream he had on the hill (now named **Jacob's Ladder**) in which he saw angels ascending and descending a ladder up to heaven (Genesis 28: 10–19). Samuel held court here (I Samuel 7: 16) and it remained a cult centre until the establishment of the Temple at Jerusalem. When the kingdom divided on Solomon's death, Israel's King Jeroboam reinstated Bethel as a cult centre in place of Jerusalem, which remained in the southern kingdom of Judah (I Kings 12: 26–28). Later, after Israel's fall to Assyria, Judah's King Josiah pulled down Jeroboam's shrine in a crusade against idol-worship (II Kings 23: 15), and the prophet Jeremiah spoke of Israel's shame at having worshipped there (Jeremiah 48: 13). In the second century BC there was a fortified post here and later a Byzantine church and Crusader castle. A mosque was built over the remains of the church at the end of the nineteenth century.

Tel Bet El, site of the biblical cult centre, lies a few hundred metres southeast of the village, with some excavated remains of temple foundations that will be of interest only to enthusiasts. The remains of the Crusader castle (Borj Bittin) are nearby. If you're keen enough to have made it this far you might want to continue on to the tel of the biblical **Ai**, a kilometre to the southeast, and site of one of the earliest of Joshua's conquests when he overran Canaan. Remains have been found of enormous Bronze Age fortress walls and two early temples, as well as Iron Age buildings. A little further north along Route 60, in the Jewish settlement of **BET EL**, the luxury homes of Jerusalem commuters are contained within barbed-wire fences.

Bir Zeit and north

The town of **BIR ZEIT**, 20km north of Ramallah to the west of Route 60, is mainly of interest for its **University**, a hotbed of resistance to Israeli occupation since 1967, with a tradition of student militancy now almost dead in the West. Established first as a school in 1924, it acquired university status in 1975, and the Gulf-financed buildings of its new campus lie about 2km south of town (accessible on frequent transport from the old campus in the town centre). Students are likely to strike up conversation with visitors (if only to size you up, since Israeli intelligence has been known to send in plain-clothed infiltrators), and will no doubt be keen to express their views on the latest political situation. In the summer the university runs a series of **open classes** in Arabic and Palestinian sociology and history, and a couple of international **workcamps** (see p.63). Further information about the university and its courses can be found on its Web site at *www.birzeit.edu*.

East of the road, around 12km northeast of Bir Zeit, the village of **TURMUS AYA** lies 2km south of the site of biblical **Shiloh** (Seilun in Arabic), where the Ark of the Covenant was set up in the twelfth century BC (Joshua 18: 1), prior to its capture by the Philistines (I Samuel 4: 11), and where Samuel was summoned by God to become a prophet (1 Samuel 3: 4) Although it lost its religious status after the Philistine conquest, Shiloh was inhabited up to Roman times. Excavations from the biblical period can be seen on the tel, but more impressive are the remains of two sixth-century Byzantine churches at the southern end of the site, the **Pilgrim's Church** and the **Basilica** with surviving mosaic floors, next to two tomb complexes dating from the Roman period. Nearby, there are also two Muslim sanctuaries dating from Ummayad or Abbassid times: Jama'a al-Yetin and Jama'a al-Sittin, the latter of which may have originally been a synagogue.

As the road winds on towards Nablus it's worth stopping at the roadside café at the top of **Jabal Batin** to enjoy the breathtaking view down into the **Valley of Dotan**, dotted with ruined khans. As the road descends into the valley, it passes the village of **LUBBAN SHARQIYA**, famous for its incense and tobacco and a possible site of biblical **Lebonah**, before winding its way back up to the twin peak of **Jabal Rahwat** and on towards Nablus, a further 14km to the north.

Nablus

NABLUS, lying 63km north of Jerusalem between the historic mountains of **Gerizim** and **Ebal**, is the largest city on the West Bank outside Jerusalem – its population of 150,000 predominantly Muslim but also including a small community of some 400 Samaritans (see p.440). Situated right at the heart of Palestine, it forms the southern-most tip of the area called the Triangle (or Greater Triangle to distinguish it from the Little Triangle across the Green Line in Israel – see p.152), with Tulkarm to the north-west and Jenin directly north, and is surrounded by fertile fields mostly used for growing olives – the backbone of the regional economy. Although Israelis prefer to call Nablus by its biblical name of **Shekhem** (the ancient site of Shekhem lies 2km to the north of the town), the town which developed into present-day Nablus wasn't founded until 72 AD; ancient Shekhem lies to its east. In antiquity the two towns lay astride an important crossroads, where the main north–south trade route met a road from the coast to the Jordan Valley.

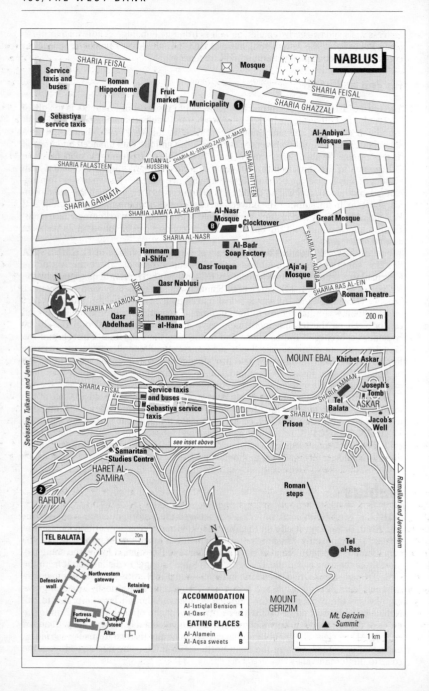

NABLUS

SHARIA FEISAL

Service taxis and buses

Roman Hippodrome

Fruit market

Mosque

Municipality 1

SHARIA FEISAL

SHARIA GHAZZALI

Sebastiya service taxis

Al-Anbiya' Mosque

SHARIA FALASTEEN

MIDAN AL-HUSSEIN

SHARIA AL-SHAHID ZAFIR AL-MASRI

SHARIA HITTEN

Ⓐ

SHARIA GARNATA

SHARIA JAMA'A AL-KABIR

Al-Nasr Mosque

Ⓑ Clocktower

Great Mosque

SHARIA AL-AQABA

SHARIA AL-NASR

Al-Badr Soap Factory

Hammam al-Shifa'

Qasr Touqan

Aja'aj Mosque

SHARIA RAS AL-EIN

Qasr Nablusi

JADE AL-YASMINA

JADE AL-QARION

SHARIA AL-QARION

Roman Theatre

N

Qasr Abdelhadi

Hammam al-Hana

0   200 m

Sebastiya, Tulkarm and Jenin

MOUNT EBAL   Khirbet Askar

SHARIA FEISAL

Service taxis and buses

Sebastiya service taxis

SHARIA AMMAN

Joseph's Tomb

Tel Balata

ASKAR

SHARIA FEISAL

Prison

Jacob's Well

see inset above

Samaritan Studies Centre

HARET AL-SAMIRA

Ramallah and Jerusalem

2

RAFIDIA

Roman steps

Tel al-Ras

TEL BALATA

0   20m

N

Defensive wall

Northwestern gateway

Retaining wall

Fortress Temple

Standing stone

Altar

MOUNT GERIZIM

ACCOMMODATION
Al-Istiqlal Bension   1
Al-Qasr   2

EATING PLACES
Al-Alamein   A
Al-Aqsa sweets   B

▲ Mt. Gerizim Summit

0   1 km

The extensive destruction of Nablus in an earthquake in 1927 means that much of what you see in the city now is relatively modern, traditional though it might be in style. However, of all the towns in Palestine, Nablus retains most the traditional Middle Eastern atmosphere. Its Casbah, or Old City, is a hive of narrow streets passing under stone archways and through covered souks, full of mosques, workshops and spit-and-sawdust *qahwas*, seemingly untouched by commercialism and Westernization. Nablus has a reputation for militancy and Israelis may warn you off coming here, but Nablusis – while obviously resentful of Israel – are warm and open to visitors, and it's one of the few places in the Holy Land where you can escape from the usual tourist fanfare. However, as the town's facilities for visitors are barely developed, the choice of accommodation is seriously limited – a pity, because you'll be hard put to see it all on a day trip. Nevertheless, don't miss out on Nablus: it could well be one of the highlights of your trip.

Some history

Scarcely anything remains above ground of the "New City" **Flavia Neapolis** in 72 AD, built by Titus in honour of his father Vespasian, though parts of it are revealed any time excavation is carried out, such as for construction of new buildings. In the early centuries of Christianity, Neapolis was the scene of constant strife between the local Samaritan and Christian populations, but in the wake of the **Samaritan revolt against Rome** in 529AD, which was put down with severity by Justinian, most of the Samaritans were expelled. In 636 the Arabs took the town, corrupting its name to Nablus, and it has been predominantly Muslim ever since, the only brief disturbance to Arab dominance coming under the **Crusaders** in 1099 AD when Tancred's army conquered the town. The Crusaders held the city until the arrival of Saladin in 1187 and during their occupation built a number of churches – many of them for Queen Melisande, widow of Crusader King Fulk of Anjou, who made it her base after her exclusion from Jerusalem by their son Baldwin III in 1152. With their keen eye for strategic positions, the Crusaders also built a fortress on the top of **Mount Gerizim**.

Nablus's modern reputation for commerce rests on the business acumen of its leading families, who have dominated the agricultural economy of the region for centuries, as well as controlling trade and manufacturing. During the eighteenth century, the inhabitants of Nablus were among the most prosperous in the country, depending for their wealth on wheat and olives: olive-oil **soap** has always been the one of the main products of Palestine and in addition to Nablus, there were once famous factories in Gaza, Ramle and Hebron.

Nablus is known for its history of militancy. Under the **British Mandate**, it was a centre of Palestinian resistance to Zionist immigration and it was here in 1936 that a National Committee was first set up; similar bodies were soon formed in all the towns and large villages of Palestine. The committee was crucial in rallying opposition and in calling for the General Strike of 1936. For a time after Israel's 1967 occupation, Palestinian President **Yasser Arafat** organized resistance networks from Nablus's Old City and the town maintains its radical reputation today; the former elected mayor, Bassam Shaka'a (who lost his legs in an assassination attempt by Israeli extremists in 1980, and was deposed by the Israelis the following year), lives here and continues to speak out against the peace process. In 1986, his successor Zafer al-Masri was murdered outside the Municipality Building, where a monument now marks the spot. The **al-Najah National University**, which overlooks the city, is the largest in the Palestinian Territories; a hotbed of rebellion, it was closed for much of the Intifada. Nablus is today surrounded by Israeli settlements.

Since 1967 Nablus has declined economically. Its exports are restricted, whether officially or unofficially, while subsidized products from Israel have flooded the market, closing its famous match factory and other small industries – an economic strangulation that has been only minimally relieved by the Oslo Accords.

Arrival, information and accommodation

Buses and service taxis arrive at the main transport stand 1km to the west of the town centre. Buses from here run south to Ramallah (every 30min; 1hr 30min), and there are service taxis to Ramallah, Tulkarm, Jenin and Jericho (for Sebastiya, they leave just to the north). The easiest way to reach the town centre from the transport stand is along **Sharia Feisal**, the main artery, though you could also take Sharia Falasteen to **Midan al-Hussein**, the square to the south of Sharia Feisal that marks the dead centre of town. Service taxis should let you off on Sharia Feisal on the way through. **Moneychangers** can be found throughout town, on Midan al-Hussein, on Sharia Feisal near the town hall, and in the Casbah on Sharia Jama'a al-Kabir by the Great Mosque, among other places. The **post office** is opposite the town hall.

Accommodation in Nablus is limited to two possibilities at opposite ends of the spectrum. The *Al-Istiqlal Bension* at 11 Sharia Hitteen (☎09/383618; ①), offers large, clean (but men only) dorm accommodation, while the new deluxe *Al-Qasr Hotel* on Sharia Omar Ibn al-Khattab, some 3km out of town (☎09/385444, fax 385944; ⑥, breakfast included), caters mainly to business clients with its tastefully decorated, comfortable and spacious rooms, fine restaurant with great views, and roof terrace.

The Town

To the south of Midan al-Hussein, the **Casbah** or Old City is traditional, untouristed and heady with enchanting smells: cardamom-spiced coffee being roasted and ground, bread being baked, kebabs being broiled over charcoal. Its centre is easy to navigate, based around two parallel streets – Sharia al-Nasr and Sharia al-Jama'a al-Kabir – which meet up at their eastern end and bear the names of the main mosques that stand on them. **Sharia al-Nasr**, the more interesting of the two, is lined with carpenters' workshops and stores selling loofahs, palm-frond brooms, perfumes and essential oils, spices (medicinal and culinary), and freshly baked bread. Its *qahwas* have *argilas* ranged along the shelves, sawdust on the floor, and coffee at a third of the price you pay in Jerusalem (but remember to say how much sugar you want or you'll get it *ziyada*, very sweet indeed: they aren't used to tourists here). Outside, traders push barrows loaded with fruit and veg, or bowls of rice pudding, and side streets disappear under arches and up staircases into the residential quarter on the slopes of Mount Gerizim. **Sharia Jama'a al-Kabir** is the more commercial street, running through a covered market devoted largely to clothes, cosmetics and accessories and full of bustle like the streets to its north that lead into the modern commercial centre of town.

The Great Mosque, at the junction of the two streets, was originally built in 1168 on the foundations of a Crusader church. Some sources have it that this was also once a Byzantine basilica, dedicated to **John the Baptist**, who baptized people by immersion in the nearby springs, while other sources claim it was built on the site of a **Samaritan synagogue** of similar age. The mosque is also said to stand on the spot where Joseph's brothers presented Jacob with the bloodstained coat of many colours to persuade him that his favourite son was dead (Genesis 37: 32).

Halfway along Sharia al-Nasr, Midan al-Manara with its clock tower marks the heart of the Casbah; adjacent to it, the green-domed **al-Nasr Mosque** is the most impressive mosque in the Casbah but is unfortunately closed to the public. Opposite, at 20 Sharia al-Nasr, the **al-Badr soap factory** is one of only five of the city's traditional soap factories to be still in operation and one of the most friendly and convenient to visit (you might even get a tour and spiel). Although traditional methods have now been modified Nablusi soap is still renowned for its purity and exported throughout the markets of the Middle East. It comes in two varieties: a gentle white soap made with virgin oil (which can also be used as shampoo), and a more acidic green one made from the second pressing. The factories belong to the city's most important families, whose mansions or palaces (*qsars*) are the grandest houses in town; some, such as Qsar Nablusi on Sharia al-Qarion, are impressive on the outside, but even better on the inside, though they are not open to the public.

A good place to try out the local soap is in the town's old **Turkish baths** (*hammam baladi*), two of which have been renovated and are now back in service after being closed for many years (both 8am–midnight, Mon & Wed–Sun men only; Tues women only). Hammam al-Shifa' lies up a small alley by 68 Sharia al-Nasr, and Hammam al-Hana, with its beautiful ceiling and light filtering in through small stained-glass windows, lies off Jadet al-Yasmina. A session costs around 10–12NIS, the same again for a massage, and you can relax afterwards with a tea or coffee, a cake and even a water-pipe.

On Sharia Ras al-Ein, above the Casbah to the south, a **Roman theatre** lies uncovered but unnoticed, proof that the abundance of Roman ruins in the town renders them unworthy of special treatment. To get to it, climb up the steep stairs of Sharia al-Aqaba, off Sharia al-Nasr opposite the Great Mosque, up to the Aja'aj Mosque on Sharia Ras al-Ein. The theatre is across the street through a gate by a metal workshop 20m to your left, usually locked, but you can see it from above by climbing the street 30m to the east. Part of a **Roman hippodrome** (chariot race track) has recently been unearthed in the modern centre of town, by Sharia Feisal and just off Midan al-Hussein; its future has yet to be decided.

Eating

Falafel and kebab stalls can be found in the Casbah and around Midan al-Hussein. Also on the square, the popular *Al-Alamein Restaurant* (Sat–Thurs 7am–10pm, Fri 7am–1pm; moderate) serves up the usual options of roast chicken, shawarma and mezze. Nablus is known for its **sweets**, particularly *kanafe*, a gooey delicacy consisting of a slightly crunchy orange topping on a white cheese base – at its best when served warm. *Al-Aqsa*, in a small street to the east of the al-Nasr Mosque in the Casbah, is renowned for its *kanafe*. Other sweet shops, serving the likes of *burma* and *baklava* as well as *kanafe*, can be found on Sharia al-Shahid Zafer al-Masri (formerly Sharia Merkaz Tijari, now renamed after the city's assassinated mayor).

Around Nablus

Close to Nablus, there are a number of sites worth making forays to: the Samaritan holy sites on **Mount Gerizim**, **Tel Balata** (ancient Shekhem), and, a little further afield, the picturesquely located remains of **Sebastiya** (ancient Samaria). Also in the immediate vicinity are four **refugee camps**: Balata, at the entrance to town on the Jerusalem road; Askar, on the main road out towards Amman; Fara'a, to the northeast of Nablus near Ein Fara'a; and Camp No. 1, to the west of Nablus on the Tulkarm road. Visits can be arranged through the Jerusalem office of UNRWA (see p.387).

Mount Gerizim and the Samaritans

Mount Gerizim and **Mount Ebal**, 881m and 940m respectively, dominate views of Nablus. From the top of Mount Gerizim you can see as far as the Mediterranean in the west and the Jordan Valley in the east, but the view from Mount Ebal is even more spectacular, with Safed and the peaks of Mount Hermon to the north, Jaffa, Ramle and the sea to the west. The striking difference in their appearance – Gerizim green and tree-covered, Ebal for the most part bare, grey rock – may have something to do with the Torah's order to the Israelites: "Behold, I set before you this day a blessing and a curse

THE SAMARITANS

The **Samaritans' history** dates from the fall in 721 BC of the northern kingdom of Israel (also called Samaria after its capital) to the Assyrians, who carried away the inhabitants, or at least the ruling class, and replaced them with people from other parts of their empire. These immigrants mixed with the remaining population, adopting their religion and considering themselves the heirs of the Israelites. When the descendants of the deportees from the southern kingdom of Judah returned from Babylon two hundred years later they found a mixed population (now known as the Samaritans) practising a religion that had diverged from their own. The Samaritans offered to help the returnees rebuild the Temple, but the Judeans (Jews) excluded them from the project (Ezra 4: 2–3) and the Samaritans eventually built their own temple on Mount Gerizim, the place to which they had been expelled by Alexander the Great (see p.444). Hasmonean king John Hyrcanus destroyed their temple and tried to impose Juadaism by force, but they were liberated from Jewish rule by the arrival of the Romans. Though the Samaritans can probably rightly claim to be the last remnant of the famous "lost ten tribes", the Old Testament denies them any descent from the Israelites (II Kings 17: 24–41).

The **animosity** that developed between the Samaritans and the Jews became so fierce that Jews on pilgrimage to Jerusalem from the Galilee would go the long way round, via Jericho, rather than pass through "pagan" Samaria. Hence the surprise of the Samaritan woman at being addressed by Jesus, a Jewish preacher, at Jacob's Well: "How is it that thou, being a Jew, askest drink of me, which am a woman of Samaria?" she asks, "for the Jews have no dealings with the Samaritans." (John 4: 9). Most Westerners of course know of the Samaritans through Jesus's parable of the Good Samaritan who rescued the robbed traveller (Luke 10: 30–36), but the story's significance lay in the fact that a Samaritan was the last person from whom a Jew would expect help.

The Samaritans took no part in the Jewish Revolt of 66 AD, but that didn't prevent Vespasian's general Cerealis from surrounding Mount Gerizim and slaughtering 11,600 of them. They didn't fare much better under Christian rule: following the **Samaritan revolt** in 486, the Byzantine emperor Zeno drove them off Mount Gerizim and built a church which the Samaritans then demolished. The Byzantines' attempt in 529 to suppress Samaritanism altogether sparked off yet another revolt, in which the Samaritans took over much of the country. After suppressing the revolt, the Byzantine emperor Justinian massacred large numbers of them, banned their religion and had the church on Mount Gerizim rebuilt. Though the mount was captured by the invading Arabs, the Samaritans finally got it back following the fall of the Abbassid caliphate to the Mongols in 1258; throughout the Middle Ages there were many flourishing Samaritan communities in Palestine and neighbouring countries.

Today, only two small groups of Samaritans remain: in Nablus and in Holon near Tel Aviv. Although they follow the Torah, they are at variance with modern Judaism on several points. One of the more important is their claim that Mount Gerizim, rather than Mount Moriah in Jerusalem, was the site of Abraham's sacrifice of Isaac. Another point of controversy is the site of Joshua's altar; the scriptures maintain the site to be Mount Ebal (Joshua 8: 30), but the Samaritans point to twelve rocks on Mount Gerizim as the true site. Their Bible is the Torah and the book of Joshua only (they reject all parts of the Bible written during and after the Babylonian exile), but the text differs slightly from that of the Jewish and Christian versions. They speak Arabic or Hebrew and their community is a hierarchical one, led by a hereditary high priest. The feasts of Passover, Pentecost and Tabernacles are celebrated in strict accordance with biblical injunctions.

Nablus's Samaritan community is concentrated in Haret al-Samira, the cramped **Samaritan Quarter** in the west of town. There's a *Samaritan Studies Centre* at 26 Sharia Omar Ibn al-Khattab.

... thou shalt put the blessing upon mount Gerizim, and the curse upon mount Ebal" (Deuteronomy 11: 26–29). Later, Joshua followed this injunction, and read out "the blessings and the cursings, according to all that is written in the book of the law" (Joshua 8: 34). A more prosaic explanation lies in the fact that Mount Gerizim faces north and has a great deal more shade than its south-facing sister.

Mount Gerizim is called *Har HaKedem* (The Early Mountain) by the **Samaritans** (see box opposite) as they believe it to be even older than the Garden of Eden. It is sacred to them because its peak remained above the Flood, and its mystique is further heightened by their belief that dust taken from here was used in the creation of Adam, and that it was here (rather than Mount Moriah in Jerusalem) that Abraham sacrificed his son Isaac – a point which differentiates the Samaritan faith from Judaism. The congregation spends the entire week of Passover on the summit, during which seven lambs are sacrificed on the altar (*mizbeah*), spitted, and then put into a pit (*tannur*) heated with twigs and branches, to be roasted as the Bible decrees. After the midnight meal, all the remains are burned in the altar depression. The sacrifice is now held on a plateau on the mountain, south of the tarmac road from Nablus; tourist buses from Jerusalem and Tel Aviv bring visitors to witness the ritual, or you can hire a taxi for around $10 or make the two-hour hike up the mountain.

Just beyond the plateau, a dirt track leads to the northern peak, **Tel al-Ras**, on which once stood the Samaritan temple constructed in the time of Alexander the Great, converted into a Greek temple by Seleucid ruler Antiochus IV Epiphanes, and later destroyed by the Hasmonean John Hyrcanus in 129 BC. Guided by the illustration on Roman coins minted in 159 AD of a temple on the summit, linked to the city by a long flight of steps, archeologists unearthed the large platform on which the temple once stood, as well as 65 steps cut into the rock of the mountain and following the precise line shown on the coins.

Jacob's Well and Joseph's Tomb

Jacob's Well, Bir Yakoub in Arabic (Mon–Sat 8am–noon & 2–5pm), is off the Jerusalem road 2km east of Nablus by the village of Askar (the turn-off is signposted "to Tamiumi"), and can be reached from town on foot or by local bus or service taxi along Sharia Feisal. The 35-metre-deep well stands on the land that Jacob bought from Hamor for a hundred pieces of silver (Genesis 33: 19) and it was here that Jesus, "being wearied with his journey", rested and asked the Samaritan woman to draw water from the well for him to drink (John 4: 9). It has since become an object of pilgrimage and its waters are believed to have miraculous properties.

Today it is hidden behind blue metal doors within the walled complex of a Greek Orthodox monastery. A church was built over the well as early as 380 AD, but was destroyed in the Samaritan revolt of 529. The Crusaders rebuilt it, but it fell into decay and, though work on it has started again, it remains uncomplete. For now, a beautiful small chapel shelters the well, its walls hung with icons and paintings of Jesus and the Samaritan woman. Ring the bell outside the gates to get in and be shown around. A small donation is expected.

A little to the north (out of Jacob's Well, turn right, take the first right after 50m, go down the hill, turn left at the end and right after another 50m), **Joseph's Tomb** is one of the three sites – the others being the Tomb of the Patriarchs in Hebron (see p.412) and Temple Mount in Jerusalem (see p.346) – to which claim is laid by extreme right-wing Zionists on the grounds that they were bought for "the Jewish people" by characters from the Bible, in this case by Jacob (see above). The cloth-covered **sarcophagus**, said to contain the bones of Joseph, is housed in a small, white-domed and entirely unspectacular building, surrounded by concrete and barbed wire, and guarded by

decidedly bored-looking Israeli soldiers and PNA police. In the September 1996 distur-
bances that occurred here following the opening of the Western Wall tunnel in
Jerusalem (see p.342), PNA police opened fire on Israeli soldiers shooting at
Palestinian rioters. Since then, the tomb has been closed to all but parties of religious
Jews wishing to pray there. Just to its northeast, **Khirbet Askar** is a grand recon-
structed Samaritan tomb dating from around 200 AD.

Tel Balata (Shekhem)

Opposite the turning for Joseph's tomb, a path leads up to **Tel Balata** (also accessible
from Sharia Amman to the north) – the remains of the ancient city of **Shekhem**, now
interspersed with fig and olive groves and freely accessible to the public.

The site was first settled by Chalcolithic people around 4000 BC; Shekhem itself
appears to have been founded in the nineteenth century BC and by the sixteenth century BC had become a powerful city state. Mentioned *passim* throughout the Old
Testament, it was already flourishing when **Abraham** built an altar here (Genesis
12: 7). His grandson **Jacob** did likewise, and the city's Canaanite ruler, also called
Shekhem, got into trouble with Jacob's sons when he slept with their sister Dinah,
thus defiling her honour (her opinion of the matter is not recorded). Shekhem asked
Jacob and his sons to let him marry her, to which they agreed if all the men of the town
were circumcised. The brothers then took advantage of the weakened state of the
men, still in pain from their operation, and killed them all before taking back their sister (Genesis 34).

After the Israelite invasion, **Joshua** gathered all the tribes of Israel to Shekhem
(Joshua 24: 1) to consolidate their faith and unity, and "took a great stone and set it up
there under an oak tree that was by the sanctuary of the Lord" (Joshua 24: 26); apparently his last act before his death. In the period of the judges, however, the men of the
city made **Abimelekh**, son of the judge Gideon their king (Judges 9: 6). Three years
later, they rebelled against him, at which he attacked the city, razed it and sowed it with
salt (Judges 9: 45); some citizens hid out in a temple to El Berith (God of the Covenant),
and Abimelekh had wood piled on top and burned them to death. Later, **Jeroboam I**
rebuilt Shekhem and made it the first capital of his breakaway northern kingdom of
Israel (I Kings 12: 25), though it was subsequently moved to Tirzah (see p.444) and
then Samaria. After Samaria was destroyed in the Assyrian invasion in 721 BC,
Shekhem regained some importance as the Samaritan capital until **John Hyrcanus**
destroyed it in 129 BC. The city was rebuilt, only to be destroyed again by **Vespasian**
in 67 AD. With the foundation of Flavia Neapolis (Nablus) in 72 AD, Shekhem faded
from the historical record, and was destroyed for the last time during the Samaritan
Revolt of 529 AD.

Excavations, under the direction of Ernst Sellin in 1913–14 and 1926–27,
unearthed a massive **defensive wall** (entered, if coming from Sharia Amman,
through its northwestern gateway) and the round-ended, land-filled platform on
which a massive Fortress Temple – identified as the Temple of El Berith mentioned
in the book of Judges – once stood. In front of it was a rounded projecting platform
which had been an altar. Sellin also found a standing stone, which he identified as
Joshua's, and re-erected in the middle of the altar. Later digs under American
George Ernest Wright discovered a filled-in sacred area with a retaining wall just to
its northeast, and determined that the El Berith Temple had been destroyed by fire.
This all seemed to fit with the Bible stories of Joshua and Abimelekh (the temple
then would be that of God of the Covenant, and the covenant referred to would be
Joshua's with the Israelites) barring one major problem: being Middle Bronze Age,
the remains were apparently far too early. In David Rohl's "New Chronology", however (see box on p.424), it all fits perfectly: the filled-in sacred area can be identified

as Jacob's altar, and the standing stone as Joshua's after all. The defensive wall, standing stone and Fortress Temple foundations can all clearly be seen today, and the land-filled platform has been reconstructed.

Sebastiya (Samaria)

In the Samarian Hills, 13km northwest of Nablus, the village of **SEBASTIYA** lies close to the impressive remains of the royal city of **Sebaste** or **Samaria** – the third capital of the ancient kingdom of Israel, which succeeded Shekhem and Tirzah (Tel al-Farah). The beauty of the rural setting is as much a draw as the history; the ruins are dotted amongst fig and olive groves and the site has a feeling of timeless tranquillity, although the lack of development makes navigating your way around a little more difficult given the worn paths and lack of clear signposting. The site is in Area C and, in theory, it is run by the Israeli National Parks Authority with set opening hours and an entrance fee; in practice, however, it is open and free, as there is no-one to sell tickets. This may change if the PNA takes it over, or if the NPA agrees to run it jointly with them.

Service taxis from Nablus leave you in the main square of the village, from which it's a five-minute walk up the road that leads directly to the main entrance of the site. There is also a western entrance at the other end of the site, which you may use if coming from the nearby Jewish settlement of Shavei Shomeron, 2km down the road at the junction of Routes 57 and 60 (accessible by infrequent Egged buses from Netanya). The village square itself is dominated by the huge buttressed walls of the **Mosque of Nabi Yaha** (John the Baptist), which stands on the site identified since Byzantine times as the place where John the Baptist's head was buried (and see overleaf). A church has existed on the spot since then. Superseded by a Crusader church in 1160, and later transformed by Saladin into a mosque, the building that stands here today is a nineteenth-century rebuilding of the mosque. Within the courtyard, a stairway in the small domed building leads down into a **cave**. Among the six burial niches here, one is said to be that of the prophet Elisha, who spent much of his life in Samaria, and one that of Obadiah – not the author of the Old Testament's shortest book, but Ahab's chief butler who, according to I Kings 18: 4, hid one hundred prophets here, feeding them on bread and water. From the mosque, there's a great view of the village and surroundings. For some pre-sightseeing refreshment, the open-air **café** in the middle of the square can supply you with tea or coffee.

Some history

King **Omri** (876 BC) bought the hill of Samaria from Shemer for two talents of silver (I Kings 16:24), and built a new city here; partly to make the most of a superior strategic situation, but perhaps also to eradicate the memory of the civil strife which had plagued the final years of the previous capital Tirzah (Tel al-Farah). The new capital stretched over some 25 acres, and its name was sometimes used by Judeans to refer to the northern kingdom, though local Palestinians are keen to explain that Samaria was founded by Canaanites long before Omri, and that it was therefore not originally a Jewish city at all. Be that as it may, Omri's son **Ahab** (871–852 BC) consolidated his father's work with extensive building, and expanded the kingdom through numerous military victories. His downfall is attributed to the influence of his Phoenician wife, the infamous Jezebel, whom the Bible regards as irredeemably wicked for acts such as building temples to the Phoenician gods Baal and Astarte, so incurring the wrath of the prophets Elijah and Elisha. From 743 BC onwards, the city and the kingdom came under increasing pressure from the Assyrians and, after a three-year siege, both finally fell in 721 BC. Thirty thousand people, about a third of the population, were deported and would become known as the "ten lost tribes". Those who remained became the **Samaritans** (see box on p.440).

Under the **Persians** (550 BC), Samaria became a provincial capital. Alexander the Great later populated the city with his Macedonian soldier-settlers and expelled the Samaritans to Shekhem after the assassination of one of his representatives. Samaria remained under Hellenic influence until its destruction by John Hyrcanus. In the latter part of the first century AD, Herod restored the city to much of its former glory in his usual grandiose style, renaming it **Sebaste** (Greek for Augustus) in tribute to his Roman patron, Caesar Augustus. Here he installed foreign mercenaries, celebrated his marriage to the doomed Mariamne and executed two of his sons. In the second century, Septimus Severus granted Sebaste the status and privileges of a Roman colony in an attempt to reduce the influence of Shekhem, whose population remained hostile to Roman rule.

The site
All periods of occupation are represented among the ruins, though the bulk of what you see dates from Septimus's reconstruction of the Herodian city. Coming from the village you arrive at the huge Roman **forum** which now doubles as a car park. The restaurant serves Middle Eastern food (daily 9am–4pm; moderate); next to it is a souvenir shop. The western end of the forum is littered with columns and capitals from a collapsed portico, beyond which was a raised **basilica**. From the northern end of the basilica, by the restaurant, a trail leads around to the stepped remains of the Roman **theatre** where the path divides: the trail straight ahead brings you eventually to the western gate, while a left turn goes up the side of the theatre and past the massive Hellenistic tower behind it, once considered the finest example in the region. Just above the tower, a viewing spot gives a panorama of the countryside. At the summit of the hill, stairs on your left lead to a podium – all that survives of Herod's **Temple of Augustus**, later restored by Septimus Severus. Sections of the Israelite palace walls, which provided the foundations for Herod's temple complex, have been excavated a few yards to the south and show the skill of the builders employed by Omri and Ahab; other finds here include a temple to Baal and a figure of Astarte, confirming the biblical accounts of Ahab's reign. The path that circles the temple is still strewn with pottery shards that play an important part in dating the various levels (see box on p.424).

South of the summit, the small Byzantine **Church of St John** stands on the site of the discovery of the head of John the Baptist and also, according to Christian tradition, the spot where Herod held the infamous party at which Salome danced and demanded the Baptist's head (Matthew 14: 8). The granite columns were introduced in the eleventh century to support a dome over the structure; later, in the twelfth century, the Greek Orthodox Church encased them in masonry and built a chapel over the crypt. Below, the road follows the course of a **colonnaded street** – some of its estimated six hundred columns still stand and, about halfway along, just down from the Byzantine church, the foundations of several one-room **shops** have been unearthed, suggesting that a bazaar took place here in Roman times. The road continues (to your right as you look down on it) past the **west gate**, Roman on Israelite foundations, and the Roman **city wall**, whose scale gives some idea of the former size of the city. The gateway is marked by the Hellenistic bases of two impressive watchtowers.

Tel al-Farah

Ten kilometres northeast of Nablus, on Route 588 toward Tubas, **Tel al-Farah** is the site of **Tirzah**, where Israel's king Baasha set up his capital (I Kings 14: 17). Settlement here dates back to the eighth millennium BC, though it was abandoned from around 2500 BC until around 1900 BC. Seven centuries later, Tirzah is mentioned as one of the cities conquered by the Israelites under Joshua (Joshua 12: 24). Sacked by the invading Assyrians in 723 BC, it was abandoned for good less than a century later.

Excavations have revealed extensive remains at the site which lies just to the west of Route 588, 4km north of its junction with Route 57, near the village of **Mukhalyam Farah**. The underground **sanctuary** at the northern end of the site was used for making sacrifices to the god of the underworld in the mid-second millennium BC, while, just to the south, an unfinished building from the ninth century BC was abandoned abruptly for reasons unknown, one of its stones left half-worked. West of the underground sanctuary, a well-preserved **city gate** breaches a Bronze-Age mud-brick wall which has been reinforced with stone.

Route 57, continuing down the **Tirzah Valley** to meet Route 90 some 24km southeast, makes a scenic drive through the arid Samarian mountains, but like Tel al-Farah, can only be reached in your own transport or a "special" taxi.

CHAPTER EIGHT

THE GAZA STRIP

Wedged between Israel and the Sinai, the **Gaza Strip** is an artificial entity born of the upheavals that accompanied the creation of the State of Israel – when the armistice lines were drawn between Israeli and Arab forces in 1949, it became (along with the West Bank) one of the two parts of Palestine still in Arab hands. Administered then by neighbouring Egypt, it was taken by Israeli forces in the Six Day War of 1967, and remained under Israeli occupation until the spring of 1994, when the Oslo Accord gave it autonomy under the Palestinian National Authority, along with the city of Jericho. Even so, a large chunk of the Strip, occupied by generally ultra-right-wing Jewish settlers, remains under Israeli administration.

Measuring 46km in length and only 10km at its widest point, its flat, generally arid landscape turns into desert proper at its southern end. After 1948, this small area of land was so crammed full of refugees that its population nearly equalled that of the much larger West Bank. It still does: massively overcrowded and under-serviced, the Gaza Strip is home to some 885,000 Palestinians, most of them officially refugees and many still living in the shantytown misery of the Strip's sprawling refugee camps.

The years of political tension and turmoil in the Strip have meant that there has never been a serious attempt to cater for outside visitors, or even to preserve sites and buildings of historic interest. Getting there is one of the main problems and, if you are on a budget, the lack of cheap accommodation. However, as an opportunity to see the Palestinian side of the Middle East conflict, a visit here can be a unique and memorable experience, certainly an enlightening one. **Gaza City** – capital of autonomous Palestine and the only real base for visitors – is a pleasant enough town with a long and turbulent history; its alleys, markets and mosque make for a couple of days of enjoyable exploration. To the south, the Strip's second city, **Khan Yunnis**, is another possible pit-stop – get here on a Wednesday and you'll see both its major attractions, the khan itself and the weekly market. And, while **refugee camps** and **Jewish settlements** may not be obvious tourist destinations, for anyone with a desire to get to grips with the complexities and realities of the political situation here, a visit to Gaza would be incomplete without a visit to one. The camps can be visited with UNRWA (see p.458), while the settlements are best seen from Israel on a separate trip from the rest of the Strip – needless to say, there is little love lost between the settlers and Gaza's Palestinian residents.

ACCOMMODATION PRICE CODES

Throughout this guide, **hotel accommodation** is graded on a scale from ① to ⑥. The numbers represent the cost per night of the **cheapest double room in high season**, though remember that many of the cheap places will have more expensive rooms with en-suite facilities. For **hostels**, the code represents the price of **two dorm beds** and is followed by the code for a double room where applicable, ie ①/②. Hostels are listed in ascending price order.

① = less than $20	② = $20–40	③ = $40–60
④ = $60–80	⑤ = $80–100	⑥ = over $100

Gaza's reputation for militancy might give you the impression that its residents will be hostile to Westerners, and that it is a dangerous place to visit. For many Israelis, this may be the case, but visitors from elsewhere will receive a warm and heartfelt welcome: Gaza Palestinians are incredibly friendly and hospitable. Nonetheless, there are a few things that you should bear in mind. First and foremost, keep your ear to the ground for **political developments**, and avoid a visit when tension is high. Second, remember that resentment of Israel is very strong here; although it will be obvious to most people that you're not Israeli, it might be worth establishing this fact fairly early on; if you do speak some Hebrew, Gaza is not the place to practise it. Kids may greet you with a Hebrew *shalom*, but as this is usually said with heavy irony, answer it with a forceful Arabic *marhaba*.

Visitors to Gaza City or the refugee camps are often surprised to find that most women do not wear the veil and most men do not have beards; nevertheless, Gaza is quite conservative, and traditional **Islamic values** are strong, more so than on the West Bank. You should dress modestly, ensuring your arms and legs are covered. Be aware, too, that **swimming** anywhere off Gaza can be hazardous: the beaches here are unpatrolled, and a vicious undertow along the coast claims a number of victims each year. Any woman venturing onto the beach will be an object of mass male curiosity. Finally, if **leaving Israel** by air (see box on p.3), remember that having visited Gaza will probably mean some heavy interrogation and possibly a strip search.

Some history

Under the **British Mandate** in Palestine, Gaza was a quiet backwater, dependent economically on its port (through which barley was exported to German breweries) and a handful of small industries. Lacking any real tradition of political activity, it was less affected than other parts of Palestine by the tensions arising from the growth of political Zionism, though Gaza City's Jewish community still had to be evacuated by the British when their Arab neighbours set upon them during ethnic rioting in 1929. Only one Jewish settlement, **Kfar Darom**, existed in what was to become the Gaza Strip at the end of the Mandate, one of the eleven Negev kibbutzim established on the night of Yom Kippur 1946 (see p.272).

Darom managed to hold out for three months in 1948 before being abandoned. Soon after, a quarter of a million **Palestinian refugees** from villages along the coastal plain streamed in, trebling the population of the area almost overnight, and putting enormous pressure on the **Egyptians**, who found themselves in control of the new Gaza Strip territory. Fearful of the instability so many dispossessed Palestinians might cause his fragile regime, Egypt's **King Farouk** kept Gaza under tight and repressive control. Despite Palestinian enthusiasm for the Egyptian Revolution of 1952, which toppled Farouk, there was little initial improvement in Gaza under Egypt's new leader, **Gamal Abd al-Nasser**, when members of the Muslim Brotherhood, Communists and other potential troublemakers were rounded up and detained in prison camps in the Sinai.

During the **Suez Crisis** of 1956, Gaza and Sinai were occupied by Israel for four months until American pressure forced a withdrawal. The conflict, however, marked a watershed in Egyptian policy towards Gaza and Nasser, impressed by unconditional Palestinian support for his anti-imperialist stance, began a liberalization programme for the Strip: attempts were made to revive the economy, Palestinians were placed in control of essential services and a Palestinian legislative body was created. He also introduced a Palestinian battalion to the Egyptian army and, after the creation of the **PLO** in 1964, its military wing, the **PLA**, was stationed in Gaza. Military training was also made compulsory for secondary school students. These measures, together with impassioned promises to liberate Palestine from Israeli rule, made Nasser enormously popular in Gaza, even among the hounded Communists.

Nasser's rhetoric, however, was no match for Israel's army, and Gaza was easily overrun during the Israeli rout of Arab forces in the 1967 **Six Day War**. For the first years of Israeli rule there was fierce armed resistance by the different factions of the PLO: this was effectively crushed in the early 1970s by a counter-insurgency campaign involving the destruction of homes and mass deportations of political activists. Throughout the 1970s and 1980s, the Israelis clamped down on political expression in Gaza and, to counterbalance the PLO, encouraged the Muslim Brotherhood, allowing them to open an Islamic Centre to run schools, mosques and medical facilities, and even to collect a religious tax, the *zakat*. This policy was to backfire badly. By 1984, a new group called **Islamic Jihad** had emerged in Gaza, uncompromisingly hostile to Israel, against which it declared a Crusade (*jihad*). The Israelis suddenly woke up to the Islamist threat and, though unable to lay its hands on the shadowy Islamic Jihad, arrested the Muslim Brotherhood leader, Sheikh Ahmed Yasin, for possession of arms. However, the movement was by now too large a genie to force back into the bottle.

On the economic front, meanwhile, land expropriation, heavy taxation and marketing restrictions led to the slow collapse of agriculture and industry in the Strip. Water resources for Palestinian agriculture were restricted, fruit trees uprooted and exports of any goods that might compete with Israeli produce curbed. Gaza now had to import from Israel goods in which it had previously been self-sufficient, while Gazan men, deprived of a living at home, had to take low-paid work across the Green Line.

In 1985, Israel stepped up its control of Gaza, a policy that was met by a growth in semi-clandestine political organizations and frequent **demonstrations**. Tension rose rapidly during 1987: the year opened with widespread protests, and in the summer, the assassination of a senior Israeli intelligence officer was followed by a spate of attacks on Israeli settlers and the killing of a number of Gazans in mysterious circumstances. By

GETTING TO THE GAZA STRIP

There are two main border checkpoints into Gaza: **from Israel**, the main point of entry is **Erez** in the north; **from Egypt**, it is **Rafah** in the south (see "Getting there from Egypt" on p.16 for a rundown of travel details from Egypt to Gaza). However, the ease with which you can get to Gaza is dependent on a political situation that can change from day to day. At present, the **autonomous area** of the Gaza Strip has no direct public transport links with either Israel, the West Bank or Egypt, although it is hoped that the services – buses to Gaza City from Ashqelon, and service taxis from Jaffa, Hebron and Jerusalem – that used to exist will be revived if the peace process gets back on track. Palestinians complain that preventing direct links with the West Bank violates the Oslo Accords, and are pressing for freer access – the option of arrival by air should also open soon with the new airport at Rafah (see p.457). In the meantime Palestinian Airways flies from Amman to El Arish, from where you can get a bus to Gaza (see p.17). Otherwise you'll have to travel to the border by whatever means available, and continue from there by taxi of one sort or another, which may have to be a "special" (a taxi to yourself) if no service taxis are available.

It may be possible, depending on regulations currently in force, **to bring a vehicle into Gaza**, but it would be extremely inadvisable to travel there in a car bearing Israeli yellow numberplates, even a rented car (in the highly unlikely event that a car rental firm would allow it). All vehicles entering and leaving the Gaza Strip at Erez (unless coming from the Jewish settlements) can expect long delays and very thorough searches.

Travelling **to the Jewish settlements** in Gaza is a different matter: some of them do have direct transport links with Israel (see p.460), and it is easy enough to reach them from Israel in a private or rented vehicle, but no transport connects them with the autonomous Palestinian parts of the Strip, and it would be unwise to travel directly between the two areas – certainly in an Israeli or Palestinian vehicle.

Israel to Erez
When the border is open for Palestinian workers to cross into Israel, you can join them for the afternoon return journey in buses and unofficial **service taxis from Jaffa and Ashqelon** to the border checkpoint at Erez. In Jaffa, they gather by Maccabi Yafo Stadium on Rehov Nes La Goyim near the junction of, appropriately enough, Derekh 'Azza (Gaza Road). Vehicles should be available between 11am and 4pm approximately. If you arrive and nobody is waiting around for a vehicle, the chances are that there are none that day, or that the venue has changed. Service taxis from Jaffa used to leave from the corner of Rehov Yefet and Rehov Dr Erlich, so you might also try there, or ask around; Arab residents of Jaffa should know what the latest situation is. Alternatively, **bus #37 from Ashqelon** to the Jewish settlement of Elei Sinai in the northern part of the Strip (3 daily; 30min) will drop you off at the border. You could also get a **bus to Yad Mordecai Junction**, 4km from the border, and walk or hitch from there. Buses stopping at the junction include #355, #362, #373, #374 and #379 **from Tel Aviv**, and #19, #36, #364, #365 and #366 **from Ashqelon**.

The border is like any international frontier, but with security rather than customs checks (though the latter are in theory possible). You have to show your passport and be entered into a ledger on both sides, and the Israelis may stamp your passport to show that you have been there. Note that if you are of Palestinian origin or have an Arab-sounding name, you will be the object of suspicion from the Israelis, and subject to serious questioning. They won't be thrilled if you're Jewish either.

Inside the Gaza Strip: south from Erez to Gaza City
Once **inside the Gaza Strip**, you will immediately be pounced on by taxi drivers wanting to take you to Gaza City as a "special" (30NIS). Depending on the time of day and the border situation, there may be no service taxis (fare 2NIS) available, and you may have no choice, unless you're willing to walk the 10km or wait for someone to share a taxi.

autumn, talk was of an impending eruption. When it did come, on December 8, its feroc-
ity and scale took both Palestinians and Israelis by surprise. Initial protests in Jabaliya
refugee camp at the deaths of four Palestinians in an accident at Erez (see opposite)
rapidly escalated into mass demonstrations as thousands of Gazans took to the streets
to erect barricades and trade stones for bullets with Israeli soldiers. Within a week, the
protests had spread to all areas of the Gaza Strip and the West Bank. Initially spontaneous, this **Intifada** (or "Uprising"; see p.498) quickly became organized and began to
take on new forms: strikes, boycotts and the resignation of government employees. As
the PLO began to assert its control through the United National Leadership of the
Uprising (**UNLU**), the Muslim Brotherhood set up a parallel organization, **Hamas**,
which gave out its own Intifada instructions and statements, with the ultimate aim of
turning the whole of Israel and the Palestinian Territories into an Islamic state.

The 1991 **Gulf War** worsened conditions in Gaza markedly. The PLO's support for
Saddam's occupation of Kuwait and his war against the United States and its allies,
proved a massive tactical error. Aid from Saudi Arabia stopped, and income sent by
Palestinians working in the Gulf dropped massively, especially from Kuwait, where
three-quarters of them had lived. The war also stopped Gaza's exports of fruit to the
Gulf, its main market. Worsening conditions, however, strengthened the Intifada, and by
1993 Gaza was pretty well ungovernable as far as the Israelis were concerned. In March,
newly elected PM **Yitzhak Rabin** closed the Green Line and prevented Gazans from
working in Israel. Meanwhile, Israel and the PLO held secret talks and, under the first
Oslo Accord in September 1993, recognized each other and agreed to the first transfer
of power. On May 17, 1994, following the signing of the Cairo Agreement, the **PNA** took
control of most of Gaza and made Gaza City its provisional capital. Israel, however, still
administered the Jewish settlements, and "lateral roads" leading to them, as well as military and perimeter areas – a total of forty percent of the Strip's land area. Support for
Hamas and Islamic Jihad peaked around this time, with roughly a third of Gazans claiming to support the militants (this subsequently declined to below one in five). In
November 1994, hostilities between fundamentalists and PNA police left sixteen dead
and two hundred wounded. Palestinian President **Yasser Arafat** responded by having
fundamentalist leaders rounded up and imprisoned. In the January 1996 **PNA elections**, Gaza saw an 86 percent turnout despite a poll boycott by Hamas and Islamic Jihad.

Unfortunately, in spite of autonomy, life **today** for most people in Gaza has in many
respects worsened. They are free to wave their flag, their homes are safe from unexpected visits by Israeli soldiers, services such as electricity, drainage and health have
been upgraded under the PNA, and some wealthy diaspora Palestinians have returned
to live here, but regular blockades by Israel have made it much more difficult for Gaza
Strip residents to work there, or to export their goods, and most people are in fact economically worse off than before. The PNA itself is also a fundamentally repressive
regime (see p.499) and most of Gaza's economy is now, as a result, in the hands of
Yasser Arafat or his associates. Few dare to speak out about the situation and those who
do face the possibility of arbitrary arrest and imprisonment. Resentment of Arafat's
rule, combined with pessimism in the face of the Israeli government's obstructive
approach to the peace process, has led to a revival in support for fundamentalism and
few are optimistic for the future.

Erez to Gaza City

The journey **south from Erez to Gaza City** is of interest only in as much as the transformation from the Israel you've left behind is so sudden and complete. Ordered fields
give way to scrubby sand dunes, Bedouin tents appear by the side of the road, and an
odd assortment of carts and battered cars jostle for position on the road south.

Just by the border, the Paz petrol station is the site where, on December 8, 1987, an Israeli army truck hit two vehicles carrying residents of Jabaliya refugee camp to work in Israel, killing four. Though it was an accident, the rumour spread that this was a deliberate act of retaliation for the previous day's murder of an Israeli in Gaza City, and it sparked off a riot in Jabaliya that marked the beginning of the Intifada (see p.498). To the east of the road a couple of kilometres south of Erez, the village of **BET HANOUN** was the scene of an incident in January 1995 when Israeli soldiers, fired on at the border post, chased their attackers into the village and opened fire on a group of PNA police, who they supposed to be the snipers. Four of the police officers were killed and another injured. Just beyond Bet Hanoun, a left fork leads to the Gaza bypass and the road to Egypt; Gaza City is straight on. If you keep a close lookout on your right you'll catch a glimpse of **JABALIYA**, the largest of the Strip's refugee camps.

Gaza City

One of the five cities of the Philistine Pentapolis (see p.482), cursed in several books of the Old Testament, **GAZA** is now the de facto capital of autonomous Palestine, home to its legislature, its ministries and its president. It is also the base for UN and other international organizations operating in the Strip, and, since this is really the only town in the Strip with accommodation, it will almost certainly be your base too. There isn't a great deal to do in Gaza – you can see the sights, such as they are, in half a day – but it's a friendly, easy-going town, and a pleasant enough place to spend a couple of days.

Some history

Gaza's position on the crossroads between Africa and Asia has ensured it a history as troubled as it is long. Since biblical times it has been fought over, invaded and occupied by nearly all the powers that have marched across the Middle East. The city rose to prominence as the chief port of the **Philistines**, and it was during Philistine rule that **Samson** met his end – legend has it that Gaza's Great Mosque is the site of the Temple of Dagon where the hirsute Hebrew pulled the temple down upon himself and his Philistine captors (Judges 18: 23–30). In 733 BC, Gaza fell to the resurgent **Assyrian** empire under Tiglath-Pileser III, despite strong opposition from Egypt, but with Assyria's fall, Gaza passed to the Babylonian empire, to be retaken by Pharaoh Necho in 608 BC. Gaza held out bravely against Persian Emperor Cambyses on his campaign to conquer Egypt eighty years later, but eventually fell after a long siege. Under the Persians, it became a major centre for the trade in frankincense and other spices and perfumes.

Alexander the Great captured Gaza in 332 BC and sold its 10,000 inhabitants into slavery. Over the next 300 years, the city developed into a cosmopolitan centre of Hellenistic civilization, despite constant wrangling for its control between the Ptolemies of Egypt and the Seleucids of Syria. In 96 BC, it fell to the Hasmoneans, and thirty years later to the **Romans**, who handed it over to **Herod the Great**. During the third and fourth centuries AD, Gaza was a religious battleground as its pagan majority struggled to maintain their faith against the devotees of the new Christian faith. Finally, in 395 AD, a Byzantine envoy, **St Porphyrus**, obtained a decree closing the temple of the Philistine god Marnas (who had taken over from Dagon as the main local deity). For a while Christianity was the official religion, and in 570 AD a Christian pilgrim to Gaza, Antonious Martyr, declared it a "splendid and beautiful city, its men most honest, liberal in every respect and friendly to pilgrims".

Gaza fell to the armies of **Islam** in 637 AD, early on in their conquests, having religious importance from its association with the Prophet's grandfather, who had died here. Although it suffered badly at the hands of the **Crusaders**, who took it in 1100,

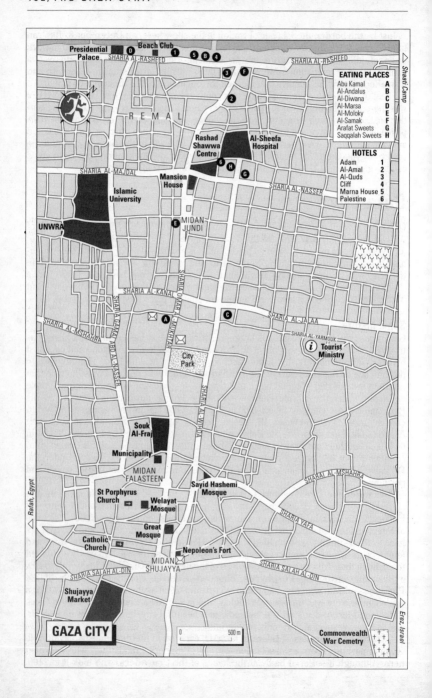

GAZA CITY

EATING PLACES
Abu Kamal	A
Al-Andalus	B
Al-Diwana	C
Al-Marsa	D
Al-Moloky	E
Al-Samak	F
Arafat Sweets	G
Saqqalah Sweets	H

HOTELS
Adam	1
Al-Amal	2
Al-Quds	3
Cliff	4
Marna House	5
Palestine	6

0   500 m

before they were booted out in 1187 by Saladin, it prospered under the **Mamluks**; traveller Felix Fabri, who visited in 1483, called it the main city of Palestine and noted that it was twice the size of Jerusalem. In 1516 Gaza passed to the **Ottomans**, whose 400-year rule of the city was interrupted only briefly by **Napoleon** in 1799 and by Mohammed Ali from 1831 to 1840 during his revolt against the Ottoman Empire.

During **World War I**, it was the scene of several major battles and suffered massive damage from British bombardment before General Allenby captured it from the Turks in 1917. The centuries of Jewish presence in Gaza ended in 1929 when the city's Arab population turned on their Jewish neighbours during nationwide **ethnic riots** (see p.341), causing the British authorities to evacuate the entire Jewish community. With the 1949 armistice, Gaza became the capital of the Strip and, in 1994, the seat of government for the whole of autonomous Palestine.

Arrival, information and city transport

Gaza's main street, **Sharia Omar al-Mukhtar** (named after a Libyan revolutionary) runs east to west from the town centre down to the sea. Coming by service taxi from Erez, odds are you'll be dropped off by Midan Shujayya, where Omar al-Mukhtar meets Sharia Salah al-Din, the main road in from Israel. Taxis from Rafah will take you to **Midan Falasteen** (Palestine Square), the bustling heart of the city, half a kilometre up Sharia Omar al-Mukhtar. The **Remal** district, where all the hotels are situated, is another 3km beyond that.

The PNA tourist ministry, off Sharia Tarek ben Ziad, doubles as a **tourist information** office (Sat–Thurs 8am–2.30pm; ☎07/829461 or 2); from Sharia al-Wihda, take the third right, turn down the first little street on the left and it's the second house, with a yard full of archeological artefacts. The staff are friendly but not exactly flush with information, though this may change as they become better organized. The city planning office at the Municipality on Sharia Omar al-Mukhtar, one block west of Midan Falasteen, has tourist **maps** in English.

There is no reliable **bus** service in Gaza City, but economic stagnation and underemployment have produced a wealth of **taxi** drivers, providing cheap and frequent transport. All you have to do is stand by the side of the road in the direction you want to go and stick out your arm (vehicles looking for punters drive along sounding their horns). Tell the driver your destination, and if he's going that way, jump in. There's a fixed **rate** of 1NIS for anywhere in town, which you should pay as soon as you get in. When you want to get out, tell the driver *aindak* or *hina minfadlak*. If you want a taxi all to yourself, ask for a "special" and negotiate the price before you get in; you shouldn't pay more than 10NIS for any trip within the city.

Accommodation

There are no budget options in Gaza City but six of the Strip's seven Palestinian-run **hotels** are here (the other is the *Nowras*, by the beach near Bet Lahiya to the north), all of them in the **Remal** district, all offering bed and breakfast, and most catering to Arab businessmen and aid agency employees. Payment is preferred in US dollars, though Israeli shekels and Jordanian dinars should be acceptable too, at least until autonomous Palestine has its own currency. Camping or sleeping rough on the beach here or elsewhere is not an option.

Adam, Sharia al-Rasheed (☎ & fax 07/866976). Comfortable enough, if slightly tatty, and the decor may be excessively kitsch for some tastes. ④.

Al-Amal, 33 Sharia Omar al-Mukhtar (☎ & fax 07/821798). Friendly establishment offering some of the cheapest rooms in Gaza, with shared bathrooms; en-suite rooms cost a bit more. ③.

Al-Quds International, 4 Sharia Omar al-Mukhtar (☎07/825177, fax 825181). Gaza City's newest and poshest hotel is also the best value in town. Plush and comfortable, its lower-priced rooms are cheaper than their equivalents elsewhere, and higher-priced ones have TV, balcony, fridge, bathtub and sea view. ③.

Cliff, Sharia al-Rasheed (☎07/861353, fax 820742). Despite the shoddy exterior, the rooms are large, clean and comfortable, with all mod cons. ⑤.

Marna House, 25 Ahmed Abd al-Aziz (☎ & fax 07/822624). Hang-out of journalists, aid workers and Red Cross personnel, but not tremendously good value compared to the other hotels, though the owner does keep a number of books on Gaza in English (some of them for sale), and a library of English books for her guests. ④.

Palestine, Sharia al-Rasheed (☎07/823355 or 6, fax 860056). A reasonable beachside hotel of a similar standard to the neighbouring *Adam*. ⑤.

The Town

In recent years, Gaza City has sprawled westwards towards the sea to the district of **Remal** ("Beach"), 3km from the centre. However, the historically interesting part of the city is remarkably compact, extending no further than a five-minute walk from the **Midan Falasteen** and containing almost all the sights, including Gaza's **Great Mosque**, and the city's oldest quarter, the largely Christian **Zeitoun**, where you'll find the charming fifth-century Greek Orthodox **Church of St Porphyrus**. Sadly for such an ancient city, there are few other historical sites worth searching out. It's more a town to wander around at leisure, exploring the alleyways and soaking up the sights and smells of the vibrant street life: one thing you won't find here are the souvenir sellers who have distorted much of the character of Jerusalem and Bethlehem. As tourists are something of a rarity, local people often want to strike up a conversation; though fewer speak English than in Israel or the West Bank, those who do are usually glad of the chance to practise it, and those who don't will do their best to be helpful.

Around the Great Mosque

A good place to start your wanderings is the **vegetable and spice market**, a narrow street running east from Midan Falasteen, parallel to Omar al-Mukhtar, and usually thronging with shoppers. Its stalls are laden with locally produced vegetables and sacks of multicoloured spices whose fragrances permeate the air.

At the end of the street, the **Great Mosque**, or Mosque of Omar (daily except Fri & during prayers), reputedly stands on the site of the ancient temple of Dagon, which was pulled down by Samson. Later a temple to Marnas was erected on the spot and then a Greek church, though the mosque itself is actually a conversion of a Norman church built by the Crusaders in the twelfth century, its round window and solid square walls Christian rather than Islamic in style. Much of the mosque was destroyed by British bombardment during World War I, and rebuilt in 1925. The interior is unremarkable but provides a wonderfully cool retreat from the midsummer heat – look out for the marble pillar engraved with a Jewish *menora*, which once excited speculation that there was a large synagogue here, though in fact it was probably imported from Alexandria or Caesarea.

Turning left out of the mosque, you come to a small, covered street on the left – Gaza's **gold market**, glittering with bangles and gold chains, and busy with merchants doing a brisk trade from tiny booths hollowed out of the massive walls. Many of the customers are mothers of prospective bridegrooms, buying jewellery for their future daughters-in-law. The gold market opens out onto Gaza's principal **money market**, where you'll get better exchange rates than in a bank; one of the moneychangers, on Sharia al-Karmelia (off Sharia Omar al-Mukhtar by no. 389, at the first corner on the left), has a window display of old Palestinian coins and banknotes (all for sale) dating from the Mandate. Further along, on the other side of Sharia al-Wihda, you'll see the imposing stone building known as **Napoleon's Fort**, where the great man spent a couple of nights on his way through town. It's now a girls' school, but if you bang on the gates on a Saturday or during the summer months, the caretaker might show you around. To the right of Napoleon's Fort, an Ottoman fountain known as **Abu al-Aazem** is said to be a monument to Samson.

A couple of hundred metres west along Sharia al-Wihda, to the right on Sharia Yafa, the unpretentious **Mosque of Sayid Hashemi**, with its octagonal minaret and white domed roof, was built in 1850 to commemorate the Prophet Mohammed's grandfather, a trader between Arabia and the Levant (Palestine, Lebanon and Syria), who died and was buried here. No-one should object to you looking round, except on Fridays or at prayer times.

Zeitoun and Shujayya

The fifth-century Greek Orthodox **Church of St Porphyrus** is definitely worth a visit. From Midan Falasteen head east along Sharia Omar al-Mukhtar, take the first turning on the right (after less than 100m) and, on your right again after 150m, just beyond the small Welayat Mosque (which dates to 1432), an open gate and modern stonework signal the entrance to a complex containing a courtyard, school, priest's house and the church itself. The church is charmingly small and quaint, but only its lower walls, built in 425 AD, are original; the upper walls and roof are twelfth-century additions. The interior is as dark and ornate as any Orthodox church. If it's locked, keys can be obtained from the priest who lives above the school opposite (up the stairs to the right of the school entrance); he speaks reasonable English and is usually happy to show people round.

Zeitoun, the area around the church, is Gaza's oldest quarter and a meander through its maze of tiny streets is a real treat. Home to many members of Gaza's small Christian community, it contains some fine old homes in various states of noble decay, many with impressive carved wooden doorways. Across Sharia Salah al-Din, the district of **Shujayya** boasts Gaza's largest **market**, specializing mostly in clothes and household goods. There are also two fourteenth-century **mosques** here, al-Zufurdimri and Ibn Uthman. Heading north along Sharia Salah al-Din, a turning on the right after 2km brings you to the **Commonwealth War Cemetery**, final resting place of troops, mostly Australian, who died here in World War I.

Remal

Leading westwards towards the sea, Sharia Omar al-Mukhtar contains little of interest. Just past Midan Falasteen on your right are a number of workshops selling cane furniture and basketwork, and on the left is Gaza's central food market, **Souq al-Fras**, though there's not much to detain you here unless you're on the lookout for cheap vegetables. Halfway towards the sea, you pass the massive white walls of the **central prison**, jokingly referred to as Gaza's first university, before entering, a little further along, the relatively prosperous district of **Remal**.

The road reaches the triangular **Midan Jundi** (Soldier Square) which gets its name from the unknown soldier buried here, a Palestinian *feda'i* (freedom fighter) from the 1948 war; the white plinth in the centre bore a statue pointing north towards the rest of Palestine, until it was pulled down by the Israelis in 1967. For a long time the square was just a scrappy patch of sand, but it has now been laid out as a public garden, where people come to hang out of an evening, some relaxing with a *shai* and *sheesha* (tea and water-pipe) in the café. At the western end of the square is the Mandate-built **Mansion House**, home to the Palestinian Legislative Council; the futuristic concrete fortress beyond it was built at enormous cost as a Cultural Centre by mayor **Rashad Shawwa**

– a wealthy Gaza notable and pro-Jordanian "moderate" appointed mayor by Israel in 1970. Heavily criticized for accepting the post, he resigned two years later, only to be reappointed in 1975 and deposed a few years later for his opposition to the Camp David Accords and for signing a statement supporting the PLO. Before moving on towards the beach, you might want to check out the souvenirs at the **flag shop** on Sharia al-Wihda, off Midan Jundi. Flags apart, there are umbrellas in the Palestinian colours and even inflatable Yasser Arafats, though, needless to say, the presence of any of these in your luggage won't go down too well with Israeli security should they decide to check your bags on leaving the country.

Omar al-Mukhtar comes to an abrupt end just before the sea. The **beach** itself is not particularly attractive at Gaza (the best are further south), but it's interesting in the early morning when the fishermen come in with the night's catch, and is also the location of Gaza's best **fish restaurants** (see below).

Eating and drinking

If hotel prices in Gaza come as a shock, you may find some consolation in the price of **eating** which, at the cheaper end of the scale at least, is rather lower than in Israel. Like the hotels, places to eat in Gaza tend to congregate in Remal, with upmarket **fish restaurants** down by the beach. In the old city, **street stalls** hawk beans and roasted sweet potatoes (red yams), as well as kebabs, falafel and hummus, especially on Midan Shujayya by the market (another group can be found at the top of Sharia al-Wihda, opposite the entrance to al-Sheefa Hospital). Several butchers grill kofta kebabs on small charcoal braziers outside their shops and some have tables inside.

Gazan men tend to hang out in the **qahwa** (see p.43) drinking tea or coffee and chugging on a *sheesha*. Coffee is Turkish; tea, alas, is usually made with a teabag, but one place you can be sure to get tea made with loose leaves is off Sharia Omar al-Mukhtar, by no. 120. As usual, a female presence in a *qahwa* will attract attention, as will that of any foreigner (UN personnel don't tend to frequent them either), though it's unlikely to be hostile.

Gaza's best **sweet shops** face each other across Sharia al-Wihda near al-Sheefa Hospital: *Saqqalah* at no. 4, and *Arafat* at no. 13, **Supermarkets** include Abu Samara, 17 Abdel Kader al-Husseini; El Kishari, 10 Falasteen; and the smaller Blue Bird, 19 Shuhada.

Some years ago the Muslim Brotherhood firebombed restaurants selling **alcohol** in Gaza, and it's now almost impossible to get hold of. You might strike it lucky with beer at the beach restaurants, but asking for booze anywhere else, apart from the UN Beach Club, will probably offend.

Abu Kamal, 154 Omar al-Mukhtar. Sign in both Arabic and Hebrew. A basic but good hummus and kebab joint, handy for a light lunch. Daily 6am–4pm. Cheap.

Al-Andalus, Sharia al-Rasheed. Grand seafront restaurant with massive interior and tip-top service. Daily 9am–midnight. Moderate.

Al-Diwania, 30 al-Jalaa. Orange and yellow sign in Arabic only. A great place for excellent Palestinian food in clean surroundings at low prices. Sat–Thurs 10am–midnight. Cheap.

Al-Ferdous, Sharia al-Rasheed. Renowned beachside fish restaurant. Moderate.

Al-Marsa, Sharia al-Rasheed opposite the end of Sharia Gamal Abd al-Nasser. Right by the fish market, for a freshly landed fish supper. Daily 10am–10pm. Moderate.

Al-Moloky, 1 Moustafa Hafez. *Shawarma* and Palestinian salads to eat in or take away. Daily 7am–11pm. Cheap.

Al-Sammak, Midan al-Mina. Excellent fish and seafood restaurant at the beach end of Sharia Omar al-Mukhtar. Daily 11am–midnight. Moderate.

MOVING ON FROM GAZA CITY

The **Gaza Bus Company** (☎07/822616) runs services to Khan Yunnis and Rafah town from Midan Falasteen, but they are very slow (every 30min; 1hr). Shared **service taxis** are the most convenient form of transport by far. For Khan Yunnis (3NIS), Rafah town (4NIS), and the refugee camps of Bureij, Nusseirat, Mughazi (all 2NIS) and Deir al-Balah (2.50NIS), they go from Midan Falasteen. For Jabaliya (1NIS) and Erez checkpoint (2NIS), they leave from Sharia Salah al-Din at Midan Shujayya. If direct services to Israel and the West Bank start again, they will also probably leave from there too. The only onward **bus** from Erez checkpoint is the #37 to Ashqelon (3 daily; 30min), but you could walk or **hitch** 4km to Yad Mordecai Junction, where there are more buses to Ashqelon and Tel Aviv, and better hitching possibilities.

There are no direct service taxis from Gaza City to Rafah border post – you have to go to Rafah town and take one from there (2NIS). See p.459 for details of onward travel into Egypt.

Gaza's **airport**, by the border post at Rafah, is not yet operational, but should open soon, depending on political developments. Palestine Airways hopes to have Fokker flights up and running to Cairo, Amman and Larnaca, supplemented by Egyptair, Royal Jordanian, and Cyprus Airways flights, with through tickets available beyond those destinations. In the meantime, they fly from El Arish with bus connections from Gaza City. For further details contact the National Tourist Office, Sharia al-Bosta (☎07/860616, fax 860682).

Listings

Airlines Egyptair, 170 al-Wihda (☎07/825180); Royal Jordanian, 171 Omar al-Mukhtar (☎07/825413); Palestine Airways, El Al, British Airways, TWA, Cyprus Airways, Olympic and several others, c/o National Tourist Office, al-Bosta (between al-Wihda and Omar al-Mukhtar opposite Napoleon's Fort; ☎07/860616).

Banks and exchange Moneychangers are concentrated between Sharia Omar al-Mukhtar and Sharia al-Wihda, just east of the Great Mosque, or outside the banks in Midan Falasteen. All will generally change between any hard currency and Israeli shekels, Egyptian pounds or Jordanian dinars, but do not usually accept travellers' cheques. For these you may have to resort to a bank (Sat–Thurs 8.30am–12.30pm); various branches of the Bank of Cairo and Amman take dollar cheques and issue cash on Visa cards, while the Bank of Jordan on Midan Falasteen and the Bank of Palestine, 343 Omar al-Mukhtar, takes travellers' cheques in sterling too.

Car rental Al-Ahly, 84 Omar al-Mukhtar (☎07/864007, fax 822350); Lathan, Lathan Building, Sharia al-Talatini (☎07/863956, fax 822628); Palestine, 49 Omar al-Mukhtar (☎ & fax 07/823841); Yafa, 29 Omar al-Mukhtar (☎07/865907).

Cultural centres British Council, Sharia al-Nasrah (Sun–Wed 11am–3.30pm, Thurs 11am–2pm; ☎07/820512).

Human rights organizations There are a couple of human rights groups with offices in the Gaza Strip. UNRWA (United Nations Relief and Works Agency) – the organization mandated by the UN to deal with the Palestinian refugee crisis – has a public information office (☎07/867044) at their headquarters on Sharia al-Talatini in Gaza City. They organize visits to the refugee camps and produce bulletins and information updates. The Palestinian Centre for Human Rights, at 29 Omar al-Mukhtar (☎ & fax 07/825893; email: *pchr@trendline.co.il*), issues critiques of PNA and Israeli actions, and regular bulletins about the latest situation.

Medical services The main hospital is al-Sheefa on Sharia Ez al-Deen al-Qassem at the western end of Sharia al-Wihda (☎07/865520, 860109 or 864009). Pharmacies are very common about town, including the comically but tragically named "Palestine Wounded Pharmacy" on Sharia al-Shuhada. Doctors include Dr Sameer Mohammed Murad (☎07/861606) and Dr Shams al-Din Samir Eddajanai (☎07/861162). The Red Crescent can be called on ☎07/860019.

THE REFUGEE CAMPS

It's arguable whether anyone could have devised a more ideal breeding ground for militancy and revolt than the vast **refugee camps** of the Gaza Strip. Established in the aftermath of the 1948 war by Quakers and the UNRWA, Gaza's camps still house an estimated 390,000 Palestinians, all classified as refugees although most were not yet born when their families fled their homes in 1948. Originally they were put up in tents, then mud-brick shelters, which were replaced by more permanent concrete houses in the 1960s.

The eight camps dot the length of the Strip and have developed into medium-size towns with their own schools, clinics and markets. However, conditions remain appalling, with extreme overcrowding (up to 64,000 people per square kilometre), sewage in the streets and a high incidence of disease the norm. Camp residents have also suffered the worst of Israeli repression, particularly in the clampdown of the 1970s and during the Intifada. For the Israelis, the camps were both a political embarrassment and a security headache, and to persuade refugees to move into resettlement projects established next to the camps, they denied them the right to improve or extend their homes. Most remained, however, refusing to give up their refugee status and with it the hope of returning to, or being compensated for, the homes they had lost.

Since the Israeli departure in 1994, people have been improving their homes as best they can, and a kind of refugee **camp architecture** has been born. With the way now open to expand upwards (the Israelis forbade buildings of more than two storeys for security reasons), one innovation has been the appearance of an unwalled "missing storey" held up by pillars in the middle of a building, and taking the place of the traditional patio around which, if space permitted, the house would be built.

The most straightforward way to visit the camps is through **UNRWA** (see "Human Rights Organisations" on p.457 for details); call or visit their Public Information Office at least a day before you want to go. There is no charge for the trip, but you should be prepared to make a donation – the organization is having to cut back on services because of budget deficits and is working under tremendous pressure. UNRWA tours concentrate on visits to their own institutions in the camps – kindergartens, clinics and feeding centres – and should give you protection from encounters with anyone (especially children) who may be suspicious of non-Palestinian outsiders. Yet it's no substitute for a tour with a Palestinian resident: if you get an offer don't hesitate to accept. Those camps most easily visited (and those to which UNRWA organizes trips) are the ones nearest to Gaza City: **BEACH (SHAATI)**, with a population of 65,000, adjacent to the coast and an easy walking distance from Gaza City, which encloses it, and **JABALIYA**, just north of the city, which is the largest (population 85,000) and most militant of all the camps. Jabaliya residents will be keen to point out where the first protest that began the Intifada took place. The other camp of particular interest is **RAFAH**, by the Egyptian border (see p.460).

Post office The main post office is by the Municipal Park on Sharia Omar al-Mukhtar, with smaller ones on Sharia al-Wihda near Midan Shujayya, and on Sharia al-Qadissia just off Omar al-Mukhtar. Opening hours are Sat–Thurs 8am–2pm. Note that the PNA issues its own stamps: Israeli ones are not valid here.

Taxis Vehicles circle the streets continually, but if you need to order one, try Azhar (☎07/868858), Central (☎07/861744) or Midan Falasteen (☎07/865242).

Telecommunications You can call from your room in any of the city's hotels, but it is cheaper to call from the main post office (see above) or from a firm like El Baz, at 173 Omar al-Mukhtar (daily 8am–10pm), where you can also send and receive faxes (fax 07/821910).

South of Gaza City

Though scenically dull, lined with fields and orange groves for much of the way, the road **south from Gaza** to the Egyptian border at Rafah is reasonably good and there is a perceptible change from the Mediterranean vegetation around Gaza City to the near desert scrub south of **Khan Yunnis**, complete with a smattering of camels and date palms.

Unless you have an invite, there no particular reason to visit the refugee camps of **Bureij**, **Nusseirat** or **Mughazi**, situated just off the main road 8–10km south of Gaza. A little further, the village of **Deir al-Balah** has a Commonwealth war cemetery and a small fourth-century chapel dedicated to St Hilarion, a hermit who lived, died and was buried here. Beyond the village, on the coast, is **Deir al-Balah** refugee camp.

The easiest way to get from Gaza City to points south is by service taxi from Midan Falasteen; bus services are much slower (see box on p.457 for full details).

Khan Yunnis

KHAN YUNNIS, the second city of the Strip, is 25km south of Gaza and about 4km from the sea. A market town for agricultural produce from the surrounding villages, it is hemmed in on the west by a large refugee camp and cut off from the sea by a massive zone of Jewish settlements stretching from the Egyptian border for some 12km up the coast. Architecturally, the town has little to offer: its warren of narrow streets and the crumbling facades of nondescript buildings give it the look and feel of a poor Cairene suburb. For many years a stronghold of the Muslim Brotherhood, Khan Yunnis is so conservative that it makes Gaza City seem positively cosmopolitan: only rarely do you see women here who are not completely shrouded in black. There is no hotel in the town and only a handful of cafés around the town centre where you can sit down to eat.

However, Khan Yunnis is not without its saving graces. The **town square** (the drop-off point for taxis) is bordered by an impressive **khan** or fortress built in the thirteenth century by an obscure Mamluk official called Yunnis (hence the town's name), as a garrison for soldiers guarding pilgrims on their way to Jerusalem and Mecca. Though pretty solidly built, time, earthquakes and neglect have taken their toll, and one side of the building has now fallen away. Nevertheless it still dominates the town. There's no tourist guide or literature but inevitably someone will be at hand to show you round and practise their English. If you arrive here on a Wednesday morning, spend a couple of hours strolling about or observing the weekly **market** on the left-hand side of the khan: a riot of colour and smells, selling everything from fish to camels.

Rafah

RAFAH (Rafiah in Hebrew), the border town with Egypt, can be reached easily from Gaza or Khan Yunnis. When you take a taxi, however, be careful to specify whether you want the **town** (Rafah *balad*) or the **border crossing** (*Masr*, ie Egypt) – the two are a few kilometres apart.

MOVING ON FROM RAFAH

Rafah town is connected with Gaza City by **bus** (every 30min; 1hr) and **service taxi** (much faster). The border post has direct bus connections into Israel with Tel Aviv (1 daily; 2hr) via Ashqelon (1hr), and with Beersheba (1 daily; 2hr 20min). It is also the site of Gaza's airport, hub-to-be of the newly established Palestine Airways.

To get to the **border post** by service taxi, you will almost certainly have to go via the town. Border **taxes** are levied leaving Gaza or Israel (90NIS), and entering Egypt (E£7), but not coming the other way. Across the border in Egypt, there are service taxis to El Arish (30min), Qantara (2hr 30min) and usually direct to Cairo (5hr; if not, change at El Arish or Qantara).

Rafah has nestled against the Egypt-Palestine border since the boundaries were drawn in 1906. A sleepy dust bowl of a place, its wide main street and ramshackle single-storey buildings could well double as the setting for a B-movie western. There are no hotels in Rafah and only a few kebab or hummus stalls, and though the beach is something of an unspoilt beauty spot, it's currently in the hands of settlers. The only thing that really makes this one-horse town worthy of a visit is the **border**. Just east of town, towards the border post, **Dekhel Avshalom** is the site of a palm tree said to have grown from a date in the pocket of Avshalom Feinberg, a spy from the NILI ring (see p.166) working for the British in World War I. He was ambushed, killed and buried here by Ottoman forces in 1917, but his remains were not positively identified until 1968.

Rafah's **refugee camp**, which merges with the town, was the largest of the camps when it was set up in 1949. During the Israeli occupation of Sinai, the camp was extended over the border, but when Israel gave Sinai back to Egypt under the Camp David peace treaty, the new border cut off this extension, leaving 5000 refugees in Egypt; fam-

THE SETTLEMENTS

After 1967, Israel confiscated a third of the Strip's land area and handed much of it over, in contravention of international law and despite Gaza's extreme overcrowding, to Israeli settlers, who have now established eighteen **settlements**. Some of these, perched crazily on top of sand dunes, resemble a cross between a prison camp and a caravan park, but the more established sites have all the trappings of middle-class suburbia – along with ample helpings of razor wire. These have remained under Israeli jurisdiction since the Oslo Accords, connected to Israel by special "**lateral roads**", which are under Israeli control and guarded by Israeli soldiers. Today's **settlers** number 3000, down from a peak of 4500 at the time of the Oslo Accords, with a population density of 38 people per square kilometre, compared to 2500 for the Strip as a whole, and 64,000 in the refugee camps. Almost all are politically motivated and hold extreme right-wing views, though that doesn't necessarily mean that they are unfriendly, especially if you are Jewish: some of them are as aggressively nationalistic as you might expect, but others do seem motivated more by religious fervour than by hatred.

There are two main groups of settlements: one up against the Green Line by Erez in the north, containing three settlements, and **GUSH QATIF** in the south of the Strip, a large chunk of coastline (the Israelis control a huge proportion of the Gaza coast, to the chagrin of Palestinian fishermen) containing fourteen settlements, joined by lateral roads to the Israeli villages of Sufa and Kissufim. The northernmost part of Qatif is **Kfar Darom**, a revival of the kibbutz that resisted the Egyptian army in 1948 (see p.448). Between these two groups, the single settlement of **NETZARIM**, joined by a lateral road to the Israeli village of Alumim, is the most contentious of them all, seen by Gazans as cutting the Strip into two, and described by the PNA as "a bone stuck in our throat". The target of regular blockades by Palestinians at the junction of Route 4 with the lateral road, it has also been attacked violently on occasion, for example in November 1994 when a member of Islamic Jihad blew himself up, taking three Israeli soldiers with him.

The settlers see the Gaza coast as "the Hawaii of Israel" and aim to develop its tourist potential. In the first wave of this, the settlers at **HOF TEMMARIM** in Gush Qatif have opened the **Palm Beach Hotel** (☎08/647 6160, fax 646 2834; ③). The beach here is a fine one, but it is bizarre, after having to negotiate checkpoints, barbed wire, armed soldiers, watchtowers, lateral protected roads and international semi-frontiers, to come upon a hotel, advertising itself as "a real vacation for the kids" (complete with playground rides and a carting track), and acting for all the world as if it were a normal holiday resort. Guests tend to be Israelis showing their solidarity for the settlers or in search of an empty beach.

Around 300m away, there's an officially recognized **youth hostel** (☎08/684 7596 or 7; ①/②), with compulsory full board at weekends. Hof Temmarim is connected by one bus a day each to Ashqelon and Beersheba (a #36 and a #38 respectively).

ilies were divided, and houses cut in two. Two decades later, nearly half of them are still there, despite promises to reincorporate them. Every morning little dramas are acted out along the barbed-wire border between the two halves of Rafah as messages are shouted across to family and friends on the other side. The area over the border is called "**Canada**" after a contingent of Canadian UN troops based here after the 1956 Suez Crisis.

As well as Canada, there is also a **Swedish village**, to the west of town, constructed for refugee fishermen by the Swedish government in the 1950s, and nudging right up against the border. Only 100m from the sea, it is cut off from the rest of Rafah by the Jewish settlements and Israeli military posts. Nearby, **Tel al-Sultan** was originally a refugee resettlement project sponsored by the Israelis, which now houses some 3000 people repatriated from "Canada" under agreements reached between Israel and Egypt.

CHAPTER NINE

THE GOLAN HEIGHTS

The basalt plateau known as the **Golan Heights** rises to the north and east of the Sea of Galilee, between the River Jordan to its west and the River Yarmouk, which forms the Jordanian frontier, to its south. Yet another territory created and defined by the Arab-Israeli conflicts that have wracked the Middle East since 1948, the Golan Heights is, strictly speaking, part of Syria, though it was annexed by the Israeli government in 1981, and is considered by them to be part of Israel. As a result, where the Golan meets Israel and the rest of Syria the map shows a mess of no-man's-land, demilitarized zones, theoretical frontiers, and present or former ceasefire lines variously coloured green or purple according to the conventions of the UN. One thing Golan does not claim to be, however, is part of Palestine.

One look at the plateau's massive presence is enough to understand the **strategic importance** of this beautiful yet desolate place: overlooking four lands, it brings a military and psychological advantage to whoever commands it. Venturing onto it is an awe-inspiring experience, not just for the panoramas of Syria, Lebanon, Israel and Jordan, but for the emptiness, the clean, dry air, and the sheer natural beauty of the place. From wherever you are, **Mount Hermon**, in the northeastern corner on the border with Lebanon and the highest peak in the region, is a permanently snow-capped landmark. It's skiable in winter – though at a price – and although the piste is nothing to write home about, the view of the Galilee on a clear day, and the climatic changes experienced during the two-hour trip from the Jordan Valley, below sea level, to the peak certainly are. Apart from its position, the Golan offers something else of vital and increasingly political importance in the region – an abundance of **water**, supplying about a third of Israel's current resources and helping to make this excellent farmland that produces some of Israel's best **wine**. It's perfect **hiking** territory, too, boasting four nature reserves, among them the **Banyas** reserve in the northern part of the region and **Gamla Nature Reserve** in the south; in both, beautiful waterfalls and rivers have cut steep valleys into the hard basalt rock. A visit to the Golan repays at any time of year, but it's in **spring** that it really comes into its own, with a glorious flower show of poppies, rape and apple blossom attracting a multitude of butterflies.

Its natural assets aside, the area is also rich in history. Just east of Banyas lies the Crusader and Arab castle of **Nimrod**, one of the most impressive Crusader fortresses that can be visited from Israel, while excavations in the area continue to reveal traces of ancient Jewish settlement. One of the most stunning of these is the Talmudic synagogue with intricate mosaics at **Qazrin** – the territory's main town and administrative centre, otherwise notable only for its winery. Nearby, **Gamla**, with its dolmens, waterfall, and excavations of another venerably ancient synagogue, is thought to be the site, described by Josephus in *The Jewish War*, of a Jewish stronghold in the first revolt

---

MINES: A WARNING

Do not ignore the barbed-wire fences or red and yellow warnings of **minefields**. Fenced-off, abandoned fields may also contain mines, even if there are no signs. When hiking, therefore, it's best to assume that only the main roads and marked trails are safe. Take care even inside nature reserves, and keep to approved paths.

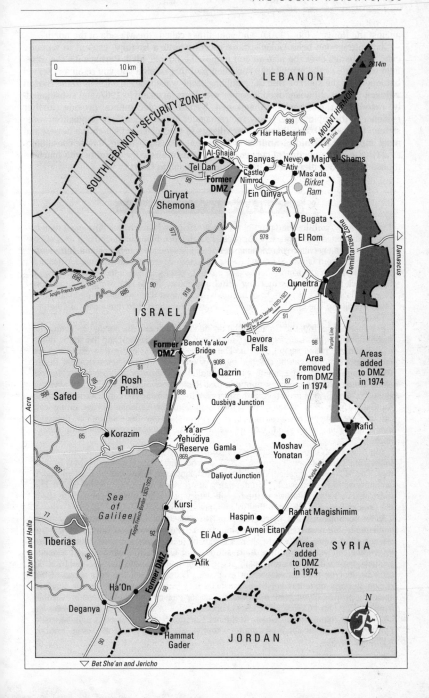

0   10 km

LEBANON

▲ 2814m

SOUTH LEBANON "SECURITY ZONE"

MOUNT HERMON

Purple Line

999

Har HaBetarim

98

Al-Ghajar

Banyas   Neve
          Ativ   Majd al-Shams

Tel Dan

Castle/   Mas'ada
Nimrod   Birket
Former   Ram
DMZ

99   Ein Qinya

Qiryat
Shemona   Bugata

978   El Rom

976

959

886

918   Quneitra

Anglo-French border 1920-1923

90

886

ISRAEL   Damascus

Anglo-French border 1920-1923

91

Former   Benot Ya'akov   Devora
DMZ   Bridge   Falls

91   9088
                      Qazrin   Area
88   removed   Areas
998   from DMZ   added
Rosh   888   in 1974   to DMZ
Pinna   in 1974
                      Qusbiya Junction
Safed   87
                                      98
85   Korazim
                      Ya'ar   Rafid
          87   Yehudiya
                      Reserve   Gamla
807   869   Moshav
                                      Yonatan
                      Daliyot Junction

                                      Purple Line
Sea
of   92   Kursi
Galilee
                      Haspin   Ramat Magishimim
77   Anglo-French border 1920-1923
                      Eli Ad   Avnei Eitan
Tiberias   Area
                      Afik   added   SYRIA
90   to DMZ
          Former   in 1974
          DMZ
Ha'On
          98

Deganya
          90

                      Hammat   JORDAN
                      Gader

▽ Bet She'an and Jericho

Demilitarized Zone

Purple Line

Acre ▷

Nazareth and Haifa ▷

N

against the Romans (66–70 AD), and sometimes called "the Masada of the north".

Such attractions belie Golan's more recent war-torn **history**, evident in an eerie calm that hangs over the plateau and haunts the bucolic idyll. Perhaps it's the mine-field warnings or the army tanks rumbling past that remind you you're on a deserted battlefield, or the spider's web of crumbling stone walls bearing witness to the **Syrian villages** (139 in all) abandoned together with their farmland in 1967, and subsequent-ly razed by the Israelis. Abandoned Syrian emplacements provide further evidence of the rapid flight. Today, the remainder of the Syrian Arab population, some sixteen thousand **Druze** living in four villages in the north – of which the largest and most important is **Majd al-Shams** – and the one-thousand-strong Alawite community at al-Ghajar in the northwest corner of the territory, share the Heights with fourteen thousand Israeli settlers, living in 32 settlements and in Qazrin.

GOLAN PRACTICALITIES

Unfortunately, **public transport** in the Golan Heights is much less developed than in Israel proper and does not particularly cater for independent tourists; relying on it effec-tively cuts out any chance of reaching sites away from the areas of population. Infrequent **buses** leave from Qiryat Shemona (see p.522) and sometimes Rosh Pinna for destina-tions in the north and from Tiberias (see p.206) to places in the south, but often the only buses back are in the early morning. **Hitching** is slow due to lack of traffic, and in any case tourists in recent years have been advised against it, especially at night and cer-tainly not alone. The best way to explore the area, therefore, is to rent a **car** (in Tiberias, for example).

For ease of **touring**, the Golan can be divided in two areas: the north, containing the most popular sights (Banyas, Castle Nimrod and Mount Hermon); and the south, home of the administrative capital, Qazrin. The north, where the plateau swells to a more mountainous region, can be reached by car or bus from Qiryat Shemona along **Route 99**. From the south, you can either travel parallel to the border with the Golan Heights along **Route 90**, which turns right just past Rosh Pinna on to Route 91 and over the Benot Ya'akov Bridge up in the northern area of the Golan, or you can drive north round the Galilee from Tiberias and up on to the Golan along the Jordanian border. Either way, the tiny area can be easily navigated in a whistlestop, one-day tour by car, though a longer stay would allow you to explore further what is one of the greenest wildernesses in the area.

You might also consider joining an **organized tour**. Egged and United run one-day tours from Tiberias (see "Listings", p.207), or from Haifa (see "Listings", p.144) in sum-mer. The SPNI runs excellent three-day English-language **hikes** that include transport, accommodation and a wealth of interesting information about the natural world. The tours also include a rundown of the recent history of conflict and an open debate about the pros and cons of giving up the Golan in favour of peace.

As for **accommodation**, there are bed and breakfast places in Qazrin and many of the settlements, but if you're planning on skiing, you'll probably want to base yourself at the ski resort of Neve Ativ, where there's a glut of (expensive) accommodation. Nature lovers are catered for by three **field schools** (at Qazrin, Kibbutz Snir and Moshav Keshet), which, though aimed mostly at the Israeli market, particularly school trips, do offer hostel-type accommodation for everyone. They also sell the best **maps** of the region (though none has yet been translated into English), and can provide English-speaking **guides** if you book in advance. Further information about these is available from the SPNI on ☎03/638 8688. Lists of accommodation, including phone numbers for b&b, can be found on the Golan Residents Committee (see box on p.466) Web site (*www.golan.org.il*), or obtained from their tourist information centre in Qazrin (toll-free ☎177/022 7595).

ACCOMMODATION PRICE CODES

Throughout this guide, **hotel accommodation** is graded on a scale from ① to ⑥. The numbers represent the cost per night of the **cheapest double room in high season**, though remember that many of the cheap places will have more expensive rooms with en-suite facilities. For **hostels**, the code represents the price of **two dorm beds** and is followed by the code for a double room where applicable, ie ①/②. Hostels are listed in ascending price order.

| ① = less than $20 | ② = $20–40 | ③ = $40–60 |
| ④ = $60–80 | ⑤ = $80–100 | ⑥ = over $100 |

Some history

When the Ottoman Empire finally fragmented at the end of World War I, the Golan Heights became entangled in emerging superpower plots. The **Mandate** system placed the Golan Heights under French control, despite pressure from both the Zionist lobby and Britain, who didn't want the Golan's water supply separated from the Mandate of Palestine. Nonetheless, the British gave over their part of the area to French control in 1923, in exchange for al-Hamma (Hammat Gader), the southeastern shore of the Galilee around Ein Gev, and a strip of northern Palestine along the Lebanese border. The sticking point in the agreement was the **Banyas Spring**, whose sovereignty was never satisfactorily decided. In 1940 the French Mandate collapsed and the Golan Heights came under Syrian control.

During the 1948 war, the Syrian army took land west of its border with Palestine and, under the armistice agreement that followed, this became a demilitarized zone, though its sovereignty was disputed (see p.213). In April 1967, the Israeli government announced its intention to cultivate all areas of the demilitarized zone, but as soon as they began working Arab-owned land, the Syrians commenced heavy bombardment. Israel responded by sending in seventy jet fighters with napalm and explosives; six Syrian planes were shot down, most of their fortified positions were hit, and many died. The following month, Yitzhak Rabin, then General of the Armed Forces, added to the general sabre-rattling of the time by declaring on Israel Radio that "The moment is coming when we will march on Damascus to overthrow the Syrian government." On the Arab side, Egypt's President Nasser sent forces into the Sinai, ordering the UN to withdraw from the Israeli-Egyptian frontier, blockading Eilat, and threatening to "totally exterminate Israel for all time". All sides mobilized, and on June 5, the **Six Day War** began. Israel made huge advances on all fronts, taking the West Bank, Gaza and Sinai within three days, and forcing Egypt and Jordan to accept a humiliating ceasefire. But the situation remained unsure with Syria, which continued to shell the northern settlements. Rabin's account in his book *Pinkas Sherut* states that a delegation of Jews from the Galilee insisted the Israeli government remove the threat. "If the state of Israel can't protect us, we have a right to know that. They should tell us that we aren't part of the country and we aren't entitled to have the IDF defend us like the other parts of the country. They should tell us that we should leave our homes and flee this nightmare."

On June 9, Moshe Dayan, hitherto loath to attack the Syrian positions, apparently changed his mind, though he was unable to get hold of Rabin to inform him. Israeli forces of the elite Golani Brigade under General David Elazar attacked in the north by Banyas, the most heavily fortified area of the front, but one which offered fast access to the Quneitra road, and the Syrians' rear. The Syrians, incredulous at this assault on their strongest positions, defended to the last, but had lost by that

ISRAELI SETTLEMENT: THE GOLAN RESIDENTS COMMITTEE

Despite huge incentives offered by the Israeli government, only the most pioneering **settlers** have been lured to the Golan. Of the present 14,000-strong Israeli population, 5200 live in the main town, Qazrin, with the remainder in 32 communities scattered throughout the territory. Since Binyamin Netanyahu came to power, however, house prices have doubled in the Golan, some indication that stability is expected and, in the last five years, the residents, represented by the powerful **Golan Residents Committee** (GRC), which likes to claim victory for Israel's 1981 decision to annex the Heights, have started a more aggressive campaign to convince both the government and the public that the Golan should remain firmly under Israeli control; their blue and white "Golan with Peace" banners and car bumper stickers reading "The Nation with the Golan" can be seen all over Israel proper. In the meantime, the GRC's **Golan 2000** plan has been approved by the Prime Minister, paving the way for over $2 million dollars' worth of investment in public infrastructure in the area in an attempt to almost double the Israeli population by the year 2000. This would finally give Israelis a majority over the remaining Syrian Arab villages.

In the population statistics game, though, it's difficult to know exactly how many people actually live on the Golan Heights: in times of tension, with Katyusha rockets being lobbed over the Lebanese border on nearby Qiryat Shemona, or fears of Syrian troops manoeuvring over the border, people leave. Whereas the settlers were once made up of left-wing Israelis looking for a better quality of life away from it all, recent arrivals have come mostly from the new wave of former Soviet Union immigrants, who may not have such a commitment to the area. If you surf the GRC Web site (*www.golan.org.il*), you will often find postings asking for volunteers to join a moshav or kibbutz.

evening, and ordered a ceasefire as demanded by the UN. Israel claimed to have ordered one, too, but in fact Israeli troops were heading for Quneitra, aiming to take the whole of the Golan plateau and neutralize it as a threat to the Galilee. They were within sight of Damascus, and had the Syrians ready to evacuate their capital, when the ceasefire finally came into effect on June 10. The next day, however, keen to secure the slopes of Mount Hermon, and under the advice of deputy chief of staff Ezer Weizman, the Israelis sent out a plane to fly over the mountain; it was forced to land when it ran out of fuel, and its crew raised an Israeli flag where it landed, marking the limit of Israel's gains.

During the war, over 100,000 Syrians fled the Golan Heights, to join Palestinian refugees in camps near Damascus, but the Druze (and one community of Alawites) were allowed to remain. Of over a hundred villages in the region, only five are left, the rest having been demolished and their lands handed over to Israeli settlers. Now, flattened slabs of concrete and old houses' roofs are all that remain of the villages. The Arab population was reduced to 12,000 (now 17,000), mostly Druze, whose opposition to Israeli occupation has put a certain amount of strain on the traditionally strong support of Druze in Israel for the Jewish state (see p.147).

In the **Yom Kippur War** of 1973, Syrian forces briefly reoccupied the Golan Heights, until the Israeli army recovered and advanced even further east than the 1967 border lines, reaching Deir al-Adas, 36km from Damascus, which they were then able to bombard. Under the May 1974 **Separation of Forces Agreement**, a section of the Golan including Quneitra was returned to Syria and a slightly wider UN buffer zone established between Israeli and Syrian forces. In December 1981, without any fighting but with strong opposition from its Druze residents, the Golan was unilaterally annexed by Israel, in contravention of UN resolutions. It remains, however, an occupied territory under international law.

Northern Golan

Almost all of the Golan's unmissable sights are located in the **northern part**. One of the most popular routes is the trip up Route 99 to the summit of Mount Hermon, or Jabal al-Sheikh. Heading northeast from Qiryat Shemona, the road crosses the 1967 border about 1km past Kibbutz Dan, passing the ancient village of **Banyas**, and nearby **Nimrod Castle**, before reaching the Route 989 turn-off, which heads north through the moshav and ski-resort of **Neve Ativ** and the Syrian **Druze villages** in the shadow of the mountains.

Banyas (Nahal Hermon Reserve)

A dramatic waterfall in a beautiful landscape, an important spring feeding the River Jordan, archeological gems from all ages and great hiking opportunities make the **Nahal Harmon Reserve** on Route 99, 10km northeast of Qiryat Shemona (Sat–Thurs 8am–5pm in winter, 8am–6pm in summer, Fri 8am–4pm; visitors may enter up to one hour before closing time; 11NIS; ☎06/695 0272), the most popular nature park in the Golan. The complex is better known as **Banyas**, the Arabic rendering of Paneas, "place of Pan", the god of country matters to whom the ancient Greeks built a temple next to the spring, also carving niches to Echo, the mountain nymph, and Diopan, god of music.

Around 200 BC, the Seleucid king Antiochus III won a decisive victory here over the army of Egypt's child king Ptolemy V Epiphanes, giving the **Seleucids** control of southern Syria and the whole of Palestine. Since then, nature and its bounty have attracted a whole host of worthy visitors: **Herod** dedicated a marble temple to the emperor Augustus "hard by the fountains of Jordan", according to Josephus; and Herod's son Philip built the town of Caesarea Philippi here. **Jesus**, too, was drawn to this pagan heartland with his disciples, asking them (Matthew 16: 15): "Whom say ye that I am?"

"SWEET" WATER

Present control of the Golan affords Israel an additional supply of fresh – or sweet – **water**. One third of the country's water comes from the Sea of Galilee, which in turn receives nearly all its water from within the Golan region: the various sources of the Jordan River, thought to be the Hatsbani (which rises in Lebanon), the Dan and the Banyas rivers, as well as streams and wadis that drain into the Jordan. If the Golan Heights is returned to Syrian sovereignty, an agreement will need to be reached over supply, though opinions differ as to whether this would be such a huge sticking point as Israel and Jordan managed to come to an agreement over water distribution while at war with each other.

The Golan source is especially precious given the problems surrounding the other water basins used by Israel: **Mountain Aquifer** is an underground reservoir of high-quality water that runs down the mountain backbone of the West Bank, but, because of the political situation, the Israelis have not invested money in the infrastructure, claiming they don't want to become dependent on a supply likely to dry up. The other source, which currently provides around half of Israel's water, is the **Coastal Aquifer**, but the state's dependence on it has resulted in over-pumping, which in turn causes seawater to seep in and salinity to rise until the water can no longer be used for drinking or irrigation. Already evident on the Gaza Strip, this now threatens to occur all along the coastal plain and also in the Sea of Galilee. The Coastal Aquifer also faces a deterioration in quality due to human, industrial and agricultural pollution from the two-million-strong population crowded on to the coastal plain. Nitrate levels in Israel's drinking water are double those accepted in the British Isles or North America.

When Simon replied, "Thou art the Christ, the son of the living God," Jesus blessed him and changed his name to Peter (from the Greek *petros*, meaning "rock") saying: "Thou art Peter and upon this rock I will build my church." Christian pilgrims still come to the source of the Banyas to see the site of that famous declaration. A few years later, to celebrate the capture of Jerusalem in 70 AD, Titus is said to have staged games here in which Jewish prisoners were thrown to wild beasts or forced to fight each other to the death. The **Crusaders** took Banyas in 1129, but it was retaken by Nur al-Din in 1164, and remained under Arab rule until the Six Day War. Remains from all these periods are visible inside the reserve, including the pre-1967 Arab village of Banyas.

There are two **entrances** to the reserve (both served by buses along Route 99). From the direction of Qiryat Shemona, the first is marked "Banyas Waterfall", and the second, 5km on, is marked "Banyas" – close to the spring and temple to Pan. By far the best way to explore the reserve is on foot, following one of two **hiking trails**: the first, taking about two hours, is circular, beginning and ending at the car park at the spring and temple entrance, while the second trail (about one hour) takes you from one entrance to the other.

Ask at the entrances for the excellent English leaflet and **map** of the reserve, which compensates for the signs along the way being mostly in Hebrew. A word of **warning**: make sure you stick to the trails to avoid unexploded mines.

The spring and waterfall

At the **spring** just north of the eastern ("Banyas") entrance to the reserve, water gushes forth right at the point where the limestone Mount Hermon meets the hard basalt rock of the Golan plateau. The large **cave** here probably used to house the spring, but a landslide rearranged the rocks and the water now emerges outside it. Relishing the abundance of water, spring **flowers** and plants bloom from January to April, making this by far the most colourful time of year to visit.

ELIJAH, ST GEORGE AND AL-KHADER

In some books you'll see the shrine of Weli al-Khader at Banyas attributed to St George, while others say it honours the Old Testament prophet Elijah. In fact all of them are partly right, for to Muslims St George and Elijah are one and the same; human manifestations of a spirit known as **al-Khader**, "the Green One". This immortal being, eternally young, wanders the world invisible to humans, but appears from time to time in human form to rescue the righteous from danger or, it would seem, to preach righteousness to the ungodly. Al-Khader can circle the earth in seconds and is said to pray each Friday at all of the world's five most holy Islamic sites.

The **legend of al-Khader**, Babylonian (and pagan) in origin, was adopted early on by Islam and, by the tenth century or before, he had become identified with the ever-peripatetic Elijah who, like the Green One, would pop up when least expected, and who did not die but ascended to heaven in a chariot of fire (II Kings 2: 11). The identification of al-Khader with St George occurred later and the reasoning behind it remains obscure, though it may derive from the fact that both were horsemen and popular figures in local mythology, and that St George's famous rescue of the damsel from the dragon was very much in the style of al-Khader. But whatever the reasons, across modern Palestine, Israel, Lebanon, Syria and Jordan, places associated by Jews with Elijah and churches dedicated by Christians to St George are often revered by Muslims as holy to al-Khader.

Apart from the shrine at Banyas, **sites** associated with al-Khader include Elijah's cave at Haifa (p.140), the Church of St George at Lydda (p.106), a ruined Byzantine church on a hill just east of Taibe in the Little Triangle, a shrine in the village of al-Khader (see p.406) just southwest of Bethlehem, and one at the northwest corner of the platform where the Dome of the Rock stands in Jerusalem (see p.348). The Siloam Pool in Jerusalem (p.360) is al-Khader's preferred bathing place.

Above the cave is the white-domed shrine, **Weli al-Khader**, revered by Muslims and Druze as sacred to St George and the prophet Elijah (see box opposite). The church that once marked the spot was turned into a mosque – one of the few intact remnants of the Arab village and of particular religious importance to members of the Muslim Alawite sect. Apart from the mosque and "Herod's Palace" beyond (which may in fact have been a place of worship, though it dates to the time of Herod), the most visible remains are of the Syrian Arab village. Other ruins scattered around are those of the first-century Roman city, **Caesarea Philippi**; in 1994, excavations found an exercise area and health spa of that period under the car park. If you're up for a rather strenuous and unshaded two-hour hike, a path leading up from the car park takes you to the observation point and Nimrod Castle.

Whichever trail you take, you'll pass the only surviving water-powered **flour mill** in Israel and the Territories, where the power of cascading headwater was long harnessed to generate power for grinding flour. Heading south from here towards the western ("Banyas Waterfall") entrance, a fork to the left before you reach the riverbank leads to the **Breikhat Haketzinim** (Officers' Pool), a pool built around a spring for Syrian officers. The wall was deliberately smashed and the water dispersed after some visitors drowned, although there are plans to restore and use it. Just before you reach the pool there's often a small Druze kiosk open serving pitta and *labaneh*.

As you approach the **waterfall** site and begin to descend through the dank, densely packed foliage of carob and plane trees, the noise of the water begins to tantalize. Eventually, you reach the lower pools and, further round the rocks, the ten-metre cascade of water. Although it isn't a huge waterfall, in such a dry region the attraction is almost spiritual. Swimming here is forbidden, but if you can't resist you'll probably find yourself sharing the pool with a gang of Israeli soldiers on a day trip. In summer, the waterfall may be no more than a trickle, but in spring it gushes with water from the melting snows of Mount Hermon, and the mountainsides are swathed in lush vegetation.

Practicalities

The nearest **accommodation** to Banyas is the SPNI's *Hermon Field School* at Kibbutz Snir (☎06/694 1091; ④), which can also provide maps and information about hiking in the Golan. Banyas is served by **bus** #55 to Qiryat Shemona, Neve Ativ and Qazrin (twice daily each way). If you miss the last bus to Qiryat Shemona, which leaves around midday, Kibbutz Dan is a five-kilometre walk away, and has bus services running until early evening.

A turn-off to the south off Route 99 at Banyas leads to **Mitzpe Golani**, where you can visit former Syrian gun emplacements and see for yourself how commanding a view they had over the Hula Valley below. A Syrian tank still stands on the spot where it was abandoned in 1967.

Castle Nimrod

Perched like an eagle's nest 3km northeast of Banyas, **Castle Nimrod** (Sat–Thurs 8am–5pm, Fri 8am–4pm; 12NIS), known in Arabic as Subeiba after a medieval hamlet, offers breathtaking views for anyone who can manage the hour's steep climb. If you're driving, as you leave Banyas on Route 99, take the first left turning (Route 989) that winds its way north.

According to legend, the castle was originally built by "Nimrod the mighty hunter", listed in Genesis 10: 8 as a great-grandson of Noah, and apparently ancestor of the Assyrians, who built it high so as to be able to shoot his arrows at God. The present structure was clearly built by medieval architects more concerned with earthly defence, but historians argue over whether what you now see is a Crusader or Arabic design, or both. As the Crusader kingdom advanced east from the Mediterranean, the Muslims reinforced their positions in anticipation, and began to

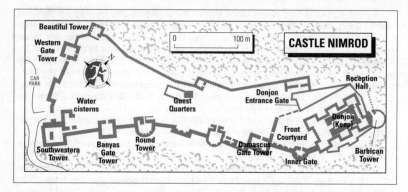

build a fortress here. Like Banyas, however, in 1129 the keys to the fortress were handed peacefully to the army of Jerusalem's Crusader King Baldwin II by the Isma'ili sect known as the **Hashishin**; a Shi'ite splinter group, they preferred the Christians being in power to their arch enemies, the Sunni Muslim Abbasid caliphs. The Hashishin were named after their founder, Hassan (or Hashin) I Sabah, the "Old Man of the Mountain", and known for their daring exploits of infiltration and assassination (our word assassin derives from Hashishin). To prepare them for a mission, Hassan allegedly – and this story comes only from Christian sources, not Muslim ones — gave them a massive dose of hashish (also named after him, though whether it was the same as what we call hashish today is a different matter) to convince them that they were in heaven. On their return, he promised them another dose, with a permanent home in heaven should they die in the attempt, rendering them fearless.

Three years after the Crusaders' 35-year residency began, the fortress proper was started. It was taken by the emir of Damascus in 1132, and then by the Seljuk ruler Zangi in 1137, but an alliance of Damascenes and Crusaders wrested it from him three years later. In 1154, Zangi's son (and Saladin's uncle) Nur al-Din took Damascus, and the Knights Hospitallers were charged with the defence of Nimrod, which they enlarged to its present size. Despite their efforts, it fell to Nur al-Din in 1164, and the Crusaders never regained it, though they tried twice. It was restored under the Ayyubids in the 1220s, and later used by the Mamluks as a prison. In the sixteenth century, the castle was abandoned, but it was used as an observation post by the Syrians in the Six Day War.

Today, all that remains are nine **defensive towers** and a large section of the outer walls. The square towers along the eastern wall belong to the original Crusader structure, and are interspaced with round towers added by the Muslims after 1164 (the westernmost has some fine Arabic fan vaulting). To the north is a **moat** and a rectangular **keep**, on the walls of which early Muslim paintings, now rather faded, were discovered. The area around the keep is the oldest part of the castle, constructed before the Hospitallers took it over.

Bus #55 (twice daily each way) from Qiryat Shemona to Qazrin stops right at the bottom of the steep climb. There are also sometimes **sheruts** from Qiryat Shemona. Alternatively, you can reach the castle by a path leaving from the Banyas car park.

Mount Hermon (Jabal al-Sheikh)

The climatic contrast between the plains of the Galilee and the perpetually snowcapped peaks of **Mount Hermon** is extreme – half an hour after skiing on the summit, you could be swimming in the warm waters of the Sea of Galilee down below. Hermon's Arabic name, **Jabal al-Sheikh**, the "Mountain of the Old Man", may be a reference to

Hassan I Sabah, the founder of the Hashishin (see opposite), or to local chieftain Rashid al-Din al-Sinan, who led the Hashishin in Syria virtually independently of their main base at Alamut in Iran.

The tallest mountain in the area, its highest peak, away to the northeast in land added to the demilitarized zone from Syria in 1974, is 2814m above sea level and the awesome summit is a mesh of international borders, military no-go areas and serious-looking forward battalions – another place where the political turmoil of the Middle East is painfully tangible. In summer, hikers can enter the nature reserve on the mountain (free) and join in free guided tours organized by the Nature Reserves Authority. It's possible to enter the area classified as a military zone – ask your guide.

Also on the slopes of Mount Hermon, at **Har Kahal**, ancient lead mines have been discovered, which are believed to be the source of raw material for making lead sulphide kohl eye-liner (kohl can also be made from antimony, which is a lot less poisonous). Another site of interest is **Har HaBetarim**, by the Lebanese border on Route 999, where, according to rabbinical tradition, God promised Abraham that He would give the land to his descendants (Genesis 15).

Neve Ativ

Perched on the slopes of Mount Hermon, **Neve Ativ**, with its wooden chalets and flower-dotted meadows, is more like Switzerland than the Middle East. It's the region's only **ski resort**, with a season running from the end of December through to around mid-April – a day's skiing here will set you back around $90 all-in (a lift pass costs 110NIS, and equipment rental is 90NIS), and it's best to get an early start, especially at weekends when it gets quite crowded. Details of snow conditions and facilities can be obtained from the **Ski Information Centre** (☎06/698 1337 in winter, ☎03/565 6040 in summer). For those who just want to check out the scenery, and summer is the best time to do that, the chair lifts run all year.

The resort is run by the Neve Ativ **moshav**, originally established in 1969 as a *moshav shitufi* (with common production but separate family units, see box on p.62). It was disbanded and replaced by the present moshav in 1971. The name Ativ is made from the initials of four Israeli soldiers who died in the Golan. Besides a swimming pool, tennis court and restaurants, the moshav offers the only **accommodation** within reach of the slopes. Prices are sky-high from December to April, though off-season, when the place resembles a ghost town, you may be able to bargain them down. The hotels are generally small and comfortable, with good breakfasts included. Options include: the *Hotel Harimi*, whose facilities include a swimming pool (☎06/698 1345; ⑥); the *Holiday Village* with luxury bungalow accommodation (☎06/694 1744; ⑤); the *Hunter's Lodge* (☎06/698 1686; ⑤); and the *Hermon Ski Motel* (☎06/698 1531; ⑥), which is rather cheaper out of season. Call the main office of the moshav (☎06/698 1333, fax 698 4280) for **information** on accommodation, and a guide to take you up the mountain, whatever season you arrive.

The moshav is accessed from Route 98, with a turn-off to the left winding its way up into the mountains a couple of kilometres past Majd al-Shams if heading north from Banyas or Mas'ada. The gates of the moshav are usually closed in the evening, although someone will open them for you. Barbed-wire fences along the way and the yellow and red signs warn that the land to your left and right is mined. Neve Ativ is connected by **bus** #55 (2 daily each way) to Qiryat Shemona via Banyas, and to Qazrin.

The Druze villages

There are four **Druze villages** lying in the shadow of Mount Hermon, all far less commercialized than their counterparts on Mount Carmel (see p.146) and worth visiting for the unique culture that they represent. Remember to respect their traditions and dress

THE GOLANI DRUZE

Before the 1967 war, the Golan Heights was administered as the Syrian Province of Quneitra, with an Arab population of 147,000. After the war, when Israel occupied about seventy percent of the region, the vast majority either fled or were expelled, and struggled in vain to return. Today, the Syrian Arab population numbers about 17,000, almost all of whom belong to the **Druze** faith, which broke away from Islam in the eleventh century (see p.147), and have since lived predominantly in isolated mountainous regions.

Their close-knit, intensely loyal community has made the Druze a formidable force in the Golan. Unlike the Druze within the 1948 borders of Israel, Golani Druze refuse to serve in the army and have as little to do with the Israeli state as possible. On December 14, 1981, when the Knesset voted to **annex the Golan Heights**, the Golan residents became Israeli citizens subject to Israeli law – a status similar to that of Palestinians in East Jerusalem. However, in January 1982, the authorities' attempt to issue Israeli identity cards to the Golanis was met by a mass act of **civil disobedience** and the ID cards were ceremoniously burnt. The Golanis held a sustained and unanimous general strike and withdrew their labour in Israel.

The protest turned into a long and drawn-out battle of wits and stamina. The communities soon began to look after their own interests and food was shared amongst all the villages, with solidarity expressed by Palestinians. **Demonstrations** erupted frequently, and bloody scenes of the army opening fire on unarmed crowds became a familiar sight. As the weeks dragged into months, the Israeli authorities concluded that the best way to break the strike would be to cordon off and isolate each of the four villages. No one was allowed in or out, and even food parcels sent by Israeli peace activists were turned back. After almost nine months, the invasion of Lebanon took centre stage and the authorities backed down and agreed not to classify the Golanis as Israelis on their ID cards. Their **citizenship** was – and still is – "Undefined".

The spirit of the strike is still very much alive in the villages, and demonstrations against Israeli occupation are commonplace. Most disputes arise around issues of land; recently the Israel Land Authority has refused to grant building permits and even retracted permits issued under previous governments. In 1992, the inhabitants of the Golan villages under Israeli rule reconfirmed their opposition by signing a **declaration** that they would not convey land to the Israeli Land Authority (ILA) or anybody whose origin is not Syrian from the Golan Heights.

accordingly. Druze men are traditionally distinguished by their impressive moustaches, white head-dresses, and baggy trousers called *shirwaal*; the moustaches were adopted as a sign for other Druze in the face of constant oppression by Muslim rulers.

By far the best way **to visit** the villages is in the company of people who know, and are known in, the area. Any of the alternative sources of **information** (see p.28) can point you in the right direction; the Alternative Information Centre in Jerusalem will also be able to put you in touch with the Druze Initiative Committee, which is active inside Israel supporting Druze draft resisters.

Majd al-Shams

The main Druze village, **MAJD AL-SHAMS** (meaning "Tower of the Sun"), lies 1150m above sea level on the Syrian-Israeli Disengagement of Forces line. Route 98 to the Hermon ski-slopes runs through the village, which itself is surrounded by snowcapped mountains. The village is strung out along one main street, ever more congested with no land available for expansion. Many of the houses and shops are decorated with ornate French-style metalwork, betraying the influence of Syria's former colonial master – the Syrian Eagle is a common sight around the village, indicating where even present-day loyalties lie. In the main square is a monument erected in 1987 in memory of the struggle against the Israeli authorities.

The six thousand residents of Majd al-Shams live primarily from income derived from the **apple orchards** in the valley below, most of which, in keeping with the originally socialist Ba'ath policies of the Syrian state, are cultivated collectively. Under Israeli legislation, farmers are prohibited from planting new orchards without a permit, and often come into conflict with the Israel Land Authority, which continually tries to restrict the villagers. The farmers built large water containers in the fields to collect rainwater, giving them a degree of independence from Israeli-controlled water supplies which are diverted to Israeli agricultural settlements. However, even these have now been taxed, and farmers required to measure their usage.

The nearest you, or indeed the villagers, can get to the Syrian side of the Purple Line is at the **shouting fence** just south of the village. As in Rafah in the Gaza Strip (see p.461), this is the only place the Druze of the Golan can keep in direct touch with their relatives and friends in Syria. With the aid of megaphones, the separated communities try to bridge the gap by shouting greetings and messages across the fence. From time to time, the Israeli military forbids even this minimum contact.

If you arrive in the village without any contacts, ask anyone to point you in the direction of the Arab Association for Development (☎06/698 4149), where someone will fill you in on what's happening and provide a guide.

PRACTICALITIES

With no **accommodation** in the vicinity, it's only really possible to visit the village on a day trip. However, there are a few good **cafés** near the centre of town where you can watch the world go by and strike up conversations with the residents, and at the southern end of the village, just before the left hairpin bend that goes on up Mount Hermon, there are a couple of places to **eat**; the Hebrew-only signs outside indicate the source of their main custom.

Public **transport** to and from Majd al-Shams is sparse. Bus #55 to Qiryat Shemona runs through twice in the morning, and twice daily the other way to Qazrin. Failing that, your best bet would be to walk to Mas'ada and hope for a sherut, or walk on to Ein Qinya (see below) and put up in the guesthouse.

Ein Qinya

About 3km northwest of the Mas'ada junction (see below) is the tiny hamlet of **EIN QINYA**, where a tel reveals habitation from the early Bronze Age and the Roman-Byzantine period. It also contains a tomb believed to belong to the sister of al-Nabi Shu'eib (Moses's father-in-law, Jethro, revered by the Druze as a prophet). Across the stream south of the village is a bridge built by the Israelis to replace one destroyed by retreating Syrian forces during the war of 1967. It's called the **Bridge of Friendship**, though how much friendship the 1200 villagers feel towards their occupiers is a moot point.

Organized tours often include a visit to Ein Qinya, whose **guesthouse** (☎06/698 3638) offers just about the only option for staying in Arab accommodation in the Druze villages. This doubles up as the **House of Druze Heritage**, where visitors are shown a fairly low-key slide show with the emphasis on the non-political aspects of the Druze, their religion and culture.

Mas'ada, Birket Ram and Buqata

South of Ein Qinya, the Druze village of **MAS'ADA** is set on relatively flat land at the foot of Jabal al-Sheikh, on the important road junction of Quneitra–Banyas–Majd al-Shams. The two thousand residents are predominantly farmers working the mountain valley and ridges. The village has the Golan's central high school and a delightful village mosque.

A couple of kilometres east of Mas'ada, the perfectly round lake of **Birket Ram** is where Herod's son Philip conducted an experiment to determine the true source of the River Jordan. Josephus described the attempt: "To outward appearance the source of the Jordan is near Banyas, but in fact it issues from a pool known as the bowl, from where it follows to Banyas by an underground route . . . Formerly no one knew that the Jordan issues from the pool until Philip discovered it by practical experiment: he scattered chaff upon the water, and found that the chaff was brought down to Banyas, where it floated on the water." In fact, the chaff is said to have conveniently appeared in Banyas thanks to a diplomatic courtier. Source of the Jordan or not, the lake is a great area for a picnic or summer swim.

Beside the lake is the only decent **restaurant** in the area, *Birket Ram* (daily 8.30am to 6.30pm; moderate), usually packed with American and Israeli tourists. A stall in the car park also sells Druze snacks such as *labaneh* with *za'atar* and large Druze pittas. It also rents out rowing boats (14.50NIS an hour) and sailboards (21.50NIS for half an hour). From an **observation point** nearby you can see the village mosque and surrounding area. There are two daily **buses** to Qiryat Shemona, and two the other way to Qazrin. Sheruts run to Qiryat Shemona, usually in the afternoons.

The fourth Druze village, **BUQATA**, lies 4km south of Mas'ada on Route 98, and is somewhat larger, with a population of over three thousand. Also south of Mas'ada, on Route 978, is **Moshav Odem**, where **accommodation** is available in the form of four- and six-person apartments complete with bathroom and kitchenette (☎06/698 3585, fax 698 1542; ④).

Kibbutzim

Thirteen kibbutzim have been set up in the Golan Heights since the Israeli takeover. **Kibbutz El Rom**, on Route 98 5km south of Buqata (☎06/698 1204), has the largest **film studio** in Israel and the Territories, which is open for guided tours; they prefer groups, but independent travellers may be able to join in by ringing ahead. You can also view films produced here, in particular promotional videos about the region – about the Golan's water sources, for example – with English translation.

Just south is **Merom Golan**, the first ever kibbutz to be established in the area. You can stop for **food** – the steaks are good – at the *Ranch Restaurant* (daily noon–midnight; expensive; ☎06/696 0206), complete with Wild West decor emphasizing the pioneering frontier spirit needed to establish the kibbutz in 1968. The kibbutz has guest **rooms** and a hostel. Accommodation is also available at **Kibbutz Ortal** off Route 91, 6km south (☎06/696 0702, fax 696 0800).

Quneitra

On Route 98, just south of the turn-off for Kibbutz Merom Golan, Mitzpe Quneitra offers views over **QUNEITRA**, the former Syrian capital of the Golan – before 1967, it had a population of 30,000, but now it is practically a ghost town (though there's a museum and restaurant for the occasional tourist). The town was returned to the Syrians in 1974 in an uninhabitable state – graffiti left by retreating Israeli soldiers reads: "If you want Quneitra you can have it in ruins." Despite Syrian efforts to repopulate the town, only a few former residents have returned, reluctant, presumably, to put themselves once again in the firing-line: though now under Syrian jurisdiction, Quneitra is within the UN "Disengagement Zone" between Israeli and Syrian lines. With a pair of binoculars or a telephoto lens, you can see the Syrian flag flying on the edge of town alongside the blue flag of the United Nations. As you peer through the binoculars you'll probably see a tourist on the other side of the fence staring at you, just 500m away. A few Golanis are admitted through the UN buffer zone with permission to study in Damascus and rumours abound of local residents and kibbutz volunteers being able to bribe soldiers to take them through, but officially the line is, of course, well and truly closed. If and when the wall finally comes down, Damascus, the ancient seat of civilization, awaits the tourist only 50km away.

Southern Golan

The flatter southern part of the Golan Heights is home to the administrative capital, **Qazrin**, surrounded by the beautiful hiking territory of the **Yehudiya and Gamla reserves**, as well as lookout points down on to the rest of Syria, the Galilee and Jordan, laid out map-like below.

Qazrin (Katzrin)

A soulless collection of modern houses, **QAZRIN** (or Katzrin) was founded as an Israeli settlement in 1974, and its inhabitants began to move in three years later. It retained the name of the Arab village that once stood on the site, which in turn was built on one of the oldest Jewish settlements in the Golan, dating from the third century AD. The centre of town is the shopping mall where the town's main street, Rehov Daliyot, meets Derekh HaHermon (Route 9088) and, parallel with that a block to the south, Rehov Tziyon.

The **Golan Archeological Museum**, on Rehov Tziyon (Sun–Thurs 8am–5pm, Fri 8am–3pm, Sat 10am–4pm; 9NIS), houses a collection of archeological artefacts from the region including arrowheads and ballista stone "bullets". One of the highlights is a film about Gamla (overleaf), covering its part in the Jewish War of 66–70 AD and its 1970 rediscovery. Almost next door, the unusual **Doll Museum** (Sun–Thurs 8am–5pm, Fri & Sat 8am–2pm; 10NIS) recreates eighty scenes from Jewish history and legend using clay dolls in little tableaux.

Excavations at the the **Ancient Katzrin Park**, south of town on the way to the industrial zone (same ticket and opening times as Archeological Museum), have uncovered remains of a synagogue dating from the third century, complete with ornate door lintel, vaulted rooms, water cistern, columns and pedestals engraved with Aramaic inscriptions and Jewish religious symbols. Clustered in the courtyard are everyday work tools collected during excavations of the site.

For a pick-me-up, head into the industrial area a little further south, where you'll find the **Golan Winery**, established in 1981 by Californians keen to return viniculture to the area after centuries of Muslim rule had neglected the tradition. Now owned by four kibbutzim and four moshavs, it produces some of the best wine available in Israel; tastings are included in the **guided tours** (Sun–Thurs 9am–5pm, closing two hours later in summer; Fri & holiday eves 9am–2pm; 10NIS; ☎06/696 2001). Teetotallers may prefer the **Mei Edan mineral water plant**, also in the industrial zone (visits by appointment Sun–Thurs 9am–4pm; ☎06/696 1050), where you can watch a video about the water, followed by a tasting session.

Practicalities

Accommodation in Qazrin is available at the SPNI's *Golan Field School*, on Rehov Zavitan, off Rehov Daliot at the southern end of town (☎06/696 1234, fax 696 1233; ②), which has dorm beds and can provide information on the Golan's only **campsite**, a five-minute walk east along Zavitan; it may even help locate homestay accommodation in the Golan. The school also sells hiking maps.

The handful of cafés and fast-food joints in the central shopping arcade are your best bet for **eating**. In the industial zone, near the winery, is the Golan's only all-night bakery, run by a Moroccan Jewish family.

There's an **information centre** (Sun–Thurs 8.30am–4pm, Fri 8.30–12.30pm; ☎06/696 2885), **supermarket** and **post office** in the central shopping mall, with a branch of Bank Leumi close at hand, and a **swimming pool** near the Archeological Museum (Sun–Fri 9am–5pm, Sat 8am–4pm; ☎06/696 1655).

From Qazrin, **buses** run to Rosh Pinna (4 daily; 35min), Tiberias (4 daily; 45min), and Qiryat Shemona (2 daily, mornings only; 45min), via Mas'ada, and Banyas.

Gamla and Ya'ar Yehudiya

Route 9088 south of Qazrin meets Route 87 at **Qusbiya** or **Qazrin Junction**. To the right, Route 87 passes through the peaceful **Ya'ar Yehudiya Nature Reserve** and on down to the Sea of Galilee; to the left, it leads to the ancient ruins of **Gamla**, 20km southeast of Qazrin, and the spectacular **Gamla Waterfall** nearby.

Ya'ar Yehudiya Nature Reserve

The **Ya'ar Yehudiya Nature Reserve**, the perimeter of which can easily be reached on foot from Qazrin, spreads along both sides of Route 87 and offers optimum hiking terrain – the countryside is magnificent, its rolling hills and streams set in an uncompromising calm. Maps are available at the park entrance to the reserve. As in Israel proper, trails are marked clearly, though sometimes only in Hebrew. Don't be fooled by the cooler climate here: you'll still need to maintain your water intake and wear a hat.

From the entrance on Route 87, the most interesting trail (taking around 6hr) leads west 3km from the car park through the former Arab village of Khirbet Sheikh Hussein to the amazing **Hexagon Pools** (Brekhat HaMeshushim), enclosed by six-sided basalt pillars formed by the slow cooling of flowing lava after volcanic action. Other, less impressive, pools of this type lie along a trail that branches off to the right and heads northeast along the edge of the Nahal Zavitan gorge (the "Black Canyon", so treacherous that access into it is prohibited) to a 25-metre waterfall, and then back to the reserve entrance. On the eastern side of the main road are the remains of **Yehudiya** itself (also called Sogane), a Jewish settlement of the Roman-Byzantine period. These include a synagogue with adjoining rooms, columns and capitals. There is a **campsite** at the reserve (call ☎06/696 2817 for further details). Four daily **buses** pass the reserve entrance each way between Qazrin and Tiberias, but buses from Tiberias do not arrive early enough for you to do the full trail.

Gamla

The ruins, dolmens and natural attractions around the ancient hilltop fort of **GAMLA** are rewarding but difficult to get to without your own transport. If you take Route 87 east of the Qusbiya junction, you'll come after about 1km to a turning on the right (Route 808) signposted to Ramat Magshimim. Follow this road until you pass a road to Moshav Yonatan on the left and take the next turning right at Daliyot Junction. With no bus service to the site, you have to be either driving, or prepared to walk or hitch the 10km or so from Ramat Magshimim to the south (reached by five daily buses from Tiberias and one from Qazrin), or Ma'ale Gamla to the west (reached by bus #22 from Tiberias).

Gamla is so called because, according to **Josephus**, "Sloping down from a towering peak is a spur like a long shaggy neck, behind which rises a symmetrical hump, so that the outline resembles that of a camel [*gamal*]; hence the name". Overlooking the Daliyot River, and protected by deep ravines on two sides, it is known as "the Masada of the North". Like the Dead Sea fortress, the occupants were besieged for thirty days by Vespasian's Roman soldiers during the First Revolt of 66–70 AD and, in the same spirit, chose **suicide** rather than surrender. Josephus, who was the rebel commander here, states that four thousand were killed in battle with the Romans and five thousand committed suicide by throwing themselves off the cliff. Only two women survived to tell the tale. Although the story of Gamla is indisputable, some would argue that the layout of this particular site does not match Josephus's description, which fits better with that of Tel al-Dra near the village of Jamle in Syria, just over the Purple Line. Certainly, however, this site was a Jewish fortress town; and that it was involved in battle is testified by the ballista stone "bullets" found in the region. Excavations so far have revealed one of the oldest **synagogue**s in the country, two dykes, a city wall and watchtowers.

Even today, it's extremely difficult to reach the actual fortress. Instead, as you wander the trails of the nature reserve, you can read descriptions from Josphus's account (*The Jewish War* 4: 4–8 and 55–83). Scattered around the grasslands northeast of the fortress are hundreds of "**dolmens**", prehistoric graves made from the basalt rocks which form small altars for each cadaver. North of here, you can watch vultures and other birds of prey from a couple of viewpoints on the edge of the ravine.

Heading southeast from the fortress and the main area of dolmens, a trail marked in red and white leads to the truly spectacular **Gamla Waterfall**, at 52m the highest in the Golan Heights. The sight of the spring waters gushing down the slopes of the Golan plateau is worth the two-hour hike here, particularly in the summer, when the pool is a delight to swim in (though beware of the jagged rocks).

Avnei Eitan

Nahal El Al, a river running just west of Haspin, becomes a canyon to the southwest between the moshavim of **Avnei Eitan** and **Eli Ad**: here you'll find two waterfalls, the White Waterfall, whose water falls onto limestone, and the Black Waterfall, where it is basalt. Should you find yourself **camping** in the region, be on the lookout for snakes and scorpion spiders, especially the dangerous black ones. A campsite exists at Moshav Avnei Eitan (☎06/676 2151, fax 676 2044; ①), with donkey rides to the falls available, and teepees available for those without their own tent, as well as wooden cabins (⓪).

A particularly scenic route out of the Golan is the road that runs south along the Syrian border, on the slopes of the valley leading down to the Yarmuk River, through peaceful countryside strewn with relics from the 1967 war.

Kursi

A recent addition to the Christian pilgrimage trail around the Sea of Galilee, **Kursi** is unfortunately only accessible by private car. lying off Route 92, just south of the turning towards Afik (Route 789), 6km south of its junction with Route 87 from Qazrin and Ya'ar Yehudiya.

Kursi is traditionally held to be the site of the "miracle of the swine", when Jesus exorcized the devils possessing, according to St Matthew (8: 28–32) two men or, according to Mark (5: 1–20) and Luke (8: 27–33), one man by the name of Legion. On being expelled, the spirits entered the bodies of a herd of swine which then "ran violently down a steep place into the sea, and perished in the waters" (Matthew 8: 32). In the pilgrimage heyday of the fifth century, the Byzantines built a **church** and **monastery** to mark the site of the miracle. These have been partly restored, and the site is now a National Park (Sun–Thurs 8am–4pm, Fri 8am–3pm, closing an hour later in summer; 8NIS).

Heading south from here, Route 92 takes you after 7km to Ein Gev (see p.216). Southeast on Route 789, you meet Route 98 from Ramat Magshimim and Haspin to Hammat Gader (al-Hamma) (see p.215).

THE

CONTEXTS

HISTORY

The area currently occupied by Israel and the Palestinian Territories has always been the crossroads of the Middle East, of vital strategic importance since ancient times. It is the western arm of the "Fertile Crescent", an arc of crop-bearing land still often referred to as "the cradle of civilization", that sweeps around the northern edge of the Arabian desert from the Persian Gulf through Mesopotamia (the alluvial plain of the Tigris and Euphrates rivers, in modern Iraq), across Syria, and down the Mediterranean coast towards Egypt. Under the pharaohs, Egypt was a powerful empire with strong military influence and wide trading links. Mesopotamia, to the northeast, was home to numerous empires including, at various times, Sumeria, Akkadia, Assyria and Babylon. To the north, Asia Minor was the centre of the Hittite Empire from the eighteenth to the twelfth century BC.

The link between Africa, Asia and Europe, Canaan – as Palestine was first known – was a key crossroads that lay uneasily between these great empires, and carried most of the trade between them. Not surprisingly, all of them aimed to control it and, in their time, most of them did.

THE CANAANITE PERIOD

Human habitation in Canaan stretches back about 50,000 years. For the first 30,000 years or so, the inhabitants lived in the open during the warm, dry summers and in caves during the cold, wet winters. The **Canaanites** who lived here were on the whole Semitic tribes who had migrated up from Arabia or across from Mesopotamia. They had begun to settle as farmers around 20,000 BC, and to build houses with beautifully painted and polished floors, mostly near water sources. The discovery of copper around 4000 BC transformed their culture and, over the next thousand years, they learned to combine it with tin to make **bronze** for hard and durable tools and weapons. In the early Bronze Age they built massive walls to encircle and protect their towns, such as Beisan, Jericho, Jebus and Megiddo, and were trading with Egypt and Mesopotamia. One of the most important Canaanite peoples were the **Amorites**, who arrived around the eighteenth century BC; their name means "westerners", which is what the Akkadians of northern Mesopotamia called them. Other groups took their names from the places where they settled – the **Jebusites**, for example, from Jebus (Jerusalem). Those who remained nomadic were known as the Apiru or **Habiru**, from whose name comes our word "Hebrew". The biblical patriarch **Abraham** was apparently a Habiru whose family had originated in Ur, southern Mesopotamia, and who had himself migrated from Haran in northwestern Mesopotamia, perhaps around 1800 BC.

THE EGYPTIANS (C2800–1200 BC)

The earliest recorded foreign rulers of Canaan were the powerful **pharaohs** of the first and second Egyptian dynasties who had made the country a colonial possession around 2800 BC. Although the pharaohs continued to claim Canaan as part of their empire, they were gradually ousted by the northern, nomadic **Hyksos**, whose empire lasted from the eighteenth to the twentieth century BC, and whose inscribed seals have been found all over the region in their thousands.

Probably around 1550 BC (these years are disputed by some Egyptologists, who date the classical pharaohs around 350 years later, giving rather different correspondences between Egyptian and Palestinian history before 664 BC; see p.424), the Egyptians drove the Hyksos out and held onto Canaan for the next 130 years, despite a **rebellion** under eighteenth-dynasty Queen Hatshepsut, put down by her successor Thutmose III in the 1450s BC. The following century, the heretical **pharaoh Akhenaton** and his Queen, Nefertiti, instituted a revolution, overthrowing the power of the priesthood to bring in a monotheistic regime. The cost was great, however: so concerned was Akhenaton to bring in this revolution at home that he virtually lost his grip on Egypt's empire outside. This is demonstrated clearly in the **Amarna letters**, an amazing cache of correspondence to Akhenaton from rulers all over the empire and beyond, written in cuneiform on clay tablets and discovered by a peasant woman at Akhenaton's capital, Tel al-Amarna, in 1887. The letters show how the weak and divided city-kings of Canaan were unable to impose independent control, and begged the pharaoh for support, which never came. Instead the **Hittites** moved in from Asia Minor with a new war weapon, iron. They took control of Syria, then Canaan. Egypt under **Ramses II** reoccupied the southern part of the Canaanite corridor about 1290 BC. Ninety years later, the Hittite empire was wiped out, its cities burned by invaders referred to in Egyptian records as "Sea Peoples", who came from the Aegean.

The biblical Exodus probably took place around this time (though redating the pharaohs puts it much earlier in Egyptian history). The **Israelites** apparently entered Canaan from the west around 1250 BC, taking control of the hill country of central and southern Canaan, then striking northward to overrun Galilee, but avoiding the main fortified cities such as Jerusalem, Gezer and Megiddo, and unable to take the coastal plain which was occupied by one of the "Sea Peoples", the Philistines.

THE PHILISTINES (C1200–1000 BC)

The **Philistines** arrived by sea soon after 1200 BC and set up a Pentapolis (federation of five city states – Gaza, Gath, Ekron, Ashqelon and Ashdod) on the coastal plain. Their iron technology gave them the edge over their adversaries, chief among them the Israelites, with whom they seem never to have been at peace. At the battle of Eben-Ezer, they managed to capture the Israelites' most holy object, the Ark of the Covenant, and enslaved them, according to Judges 13: 1, for forty years. In the face of Philistine military success, the Israelites, who had been led by a series of charismatic chieftains known as the "judges", gave up their nomadic-style tribal confederation around

1020 BC in favour of a monarchy under **Saul**, but even this brought them limited success: at the battle of Gilboa, Saul and his son Jonathan were slain and the Israelites routed (I Samuel: 31).

Despite the meaning of the term "philistine" in modern English, the real Philistines were in fact highly cultured, with both artistic and technological accomplishments markedly superior to those of their neighbours, including the Israelites. They used iron, not only for chariots, shields and swords but also for making iron-tipped ploughs, which the Israelites had to buy from them (I Samuel 19: 19–22), while Philistine ships and camel caravans maintained commercial links with the rest of the Mediterranean and the Fertile Crescent. One lasting mark they left on the country was their name; it ceased to be known as Canaan and became Philistia (Palestine), a term referring at first only to the area of the Pentapolis, but coming eventually to refer to the whole country between the Mediterranean and the Jordan, and sometimes beyond.

DAVID AND SOLOMON (C1000–922 BC)

On Saul's death, the Israelites split, with the northern tribes supporting his son Ishbaal, while the tribe of Judah supported **David**, who had been a national hero after killing Goliath, was later a Philistine protégé, and now set himself up as king of Hebron. After defeating Ishbaal and uniting the Israelites under his rule, he turned on the Philistines, beat them back onto the coastal plain, and went on to conquer the neighbouring kingdoms of Moab, Ammon, Edom and Syria across the Jordan, setting up a sizeable empire; he was able to do this because, at this time, Egypt and the empires of Mesopotamia were all in decline, and there was no one to stop him. Taking the formerly independent city state of Jerusalem, he made it capital of a now united Israel. David's empire was inherited by his son **Solomon**, whose rule was Israel's golden age, sustained by an alliance with neighbouring Phoenicia, and maritime trade on the Red Sea and the Mediterranean. In Jerusalem, Solomon ordered the construction of the **First Temple**, built between 957 and 950 BC. But his heavy taxation and forced labour alienated the northern tribes, who had already tried to secede under David, and on Solomon's death around 922 BC they rebelled again.

THE DIVIDED KINGDOM (922–597 BC)

The northern ten tribes, under the rebel leader Jeroboam, set up the **kingdom of Israel**, apparently with Egyptian backing, while the tribes of Judah (David's tribe) and Benjamin (Saul's tribe) remained loyal to Solomon's son Rehoboam, and formed the smaller southern **kingdom of Judah** or Judea, forced to pay tribute to the resurgent power of Egypt under the 23rd dynasty. For the next half-century, Israel and Judah were at war. That ended after Judah formed an alliance against Israel with Syria, and the Syrian king Benhadad invaded the Galilee around 878 BC, precipitating a coup d'état by Israel's army chief **Omri**. Omri then formed an alliance with Judah, evicted the Syrians, and began building a new capital at Samaria. His successor **Ahab** married Phoenician princess Jezebel, importing much of Phoenicia's culture and religion, to the chagrin of Old Testament prophets such as Elijah and Elisha, and also allied himself with Judah's king **Jehosaphat** against the Syrians. On Ahab's death, Israel and Syria joined forces to oppose a new rising power to the northeast, that of Assyria in northern Mesopotamia, with its capital at Nineveh near Mosul in modern Iraq.

In the mid-ninth century BC, Moab's king Mesha rebelled against Israel under Jehoram, as described in the Bible (II Kings 3: 4) and on the Moabite Stone, set up by Mesha to record his victory (the stone can now be found in the Louvre in Paris). Then, around 842 BC, Elisha backed a bloody coup against Jehoram's successor Ahaziah, led by army commander **Jehu**, who killed not only the entire royal family of Israel, ending Omri's line, but also Judah's king Jehoram. This sparked off a coup in Judah led by the king's mother Athaliah, who was also Ahab and Jezebel's daughter, and nearly succeeded in anihilating the Davidic dynasty. She was stopped by an alliance of priests and landowners, who assassinated her, put the infant Joash on the throne, and set Israel and Judah at loggerheads again. A victory by Israel at Beth Shemesh made Judah its vassal, but Israel was soon itself reduced to vassalage by Assyria under Tiglath-Pileser III, who ascended the throne in 742 BC and introduced a policy of transmigration: forced exile of conquered peoples. In Israel, a coup brought to power **Pekah**, who formed an anti-Assyrian alliance with Syria and in 735 BC attacked Judah to replace its hostile king **Ahaz**. Ahaz appealed for help to Assyria, which invaded Syria and Israel, occupied the Galilee and forced payment of tribute, but on Tiglath-Pileser's death Israel rebelled. Assyria's Shalmaneser V died fighting to subdue it, but his successor Sargon II besieged and took Samaria in 722 BC, ending the northern kingdom, deporting over 27,000 Israelites (the "lost ten tribes") and importing exiles from elsewhere to replace them. The non-deportees mixed with the new immigrants to become the **Samaritans**.

On Sargon's death in 705 BC, Babylon in southern Mesopotamia revolted against Assyria with Egyptian support, Judah under **Hezekiah** joining in. The Assyrians under Sennacherib put down the rebellion, defeating Egypt at Ekron, and besieging Jerusalem in 701 BC; luckily for Judah, a new Babylonian uprising forced the Assyrians to lift the siege and head back east. In 626 BC, Babylon under Nabopolassar finally broke free from Assyria, whose empire began to crumble, Nineveh falling to Babylonian forces fourteen years later. Judah under **Josiah** stopped paying tribute and formed an alliance with Egypt's pharaoh Necho against Babylon, aiming to take over the former kingdom of Israel, but was stopped from doing so after Babylon's victory against him at Megiddo in 609 BC. Necho set up a puppet king in Judah, Jehoaikim, but was unable to prevent Babylon's eventual occupation: Nebuchadnezzar invaded in 597 BC, exiling the ruling class and putting his own puppet, Zedekiah, on the throne and, when Judah again joined Egypt against him nine years later, besieged and took Jerusalem, destroyed the Temple and exiled Judah's inhabitants to Babylon. Much of Judah's territory was then occupied by the kingdom of **Idumea**, successor to ancient Edom, whose people had been pushed northward by the invasion from the southeast of an Arabic people, the **Nabateans** (see p.270).

THE PERSIANS (539–333 BC)

Israel and Judah were unlucky to be defeated by two of the only empires to operate the harsh policy of exiling conquered populations. But Babylon's empire was no more immortal than any other and in 539 BC, it was defeated at the Battle of Opris by the forces of Persia under **Cyrus the Great**. An unusually enlightened ruler for his time, Cyrus believed in cultural diversity in his empire and reversed the Assyrian/Babylonian policy of enforced exile, allowing the Judeans, or Jews as they were now known, to return home under the Davidic heir Zerubbabel. Only a minority chose to leave, as they were by now well-established in Babylon, with their own commercial, political and religious institutions. The 50,000-strong community in Jerusalem, under the leadership of the prophets Haggai and Zechariah, built a smaller and more austere **Second Temple**, completed in 515 BC. The new Judean state was very small, the area to its north coming under the Persian province of Samaria, and to its south under the kingdom of Idumea, but Jewish life in Judea was revitalized in the middle of the following century by the Persian-appointed Jewish governor, **Nehemiah**, and by the migration there of the Babylonian Jewish leader, **Ezra**, around 400 BC. The **Samaritans** (see p.440), who were excluded from the new Judea, resented the empire's favouritism of the returned exiles, and emnity between the two peoples set in. In other respects, however, Persian rule heralded an era of peace for Palestine.

THE GREEKS AND THE HASMONEANS (332–63 BC)

Next to invade was **Alexander the Great**, who led a Greek army through the Middle East and conquered Persia, taking Palestine in 332 BC. The rich civilization of the Greeks provided sculptors, architects, scientists, mathematicians, poets and philosophers. Their influence in Palestine was considerable: young and eager Jews learned new ideas which departed from tradition, infuriating their elders.

When Alexander died in 323 BC, his Middle East empire was divided between two of his generals: Ptolemy, who acquired Egypt, and Seleucus, who got Syria. Initially ruled by the **Ptolemies**, Palestine fell to the **Seleucids** in 198 BC. This division brought weakness and, between 167 BC and 141 BC, the Jews of Palestine, led by the **Maccabees** (see p.107), revolted against the now enforced Hellenization of their culture. Their victory over the Seleucids, with help from the up-and-coming republic of Rome, enabled them to set up an independent state ruled by the **Hasmonean** family (descendants of Simon the Maccabee). In 129 BC, under John Hyrcanus, they subdued Idumea and

forcibly converted the Idumeans to Judaism. The Hasmoneans fell prey in their later years to internecine struggles and corruption, but they maintained their independence for over a century, and their victory over the Seleucids is still celebrated by Jewish people today at the festival of Hanukkah.

THE ROMANS (63BC–395 AD)

When the Hasmonean king Aristobulus II took the throne in 67 BC, his brother Hyrcanus, supported by the Idumean leader Antipater, tried to wrest it from him. Hyrcanus also sought support from Aretas of Nabatea, and when that was denied, turned to the might of **Rome**, whose general Pompey took Jerusalem in 63 BC, installing Hyrcanus as a puppet king. When his successor Antigonus tried to ally with Rome's enemy Parthia 26 years later, however, the Romans deposed him and installed Antipater's son **Herod the Great**. The hated Herod levied taxes, impressed labour and commissioned enormous and expensive public works, including rebuilding and refurbishing the Temple in Jerusalem.

Although Herod was an astute politician, he is renowned for his cruelty toward rebels and rivals (he murdered his Hasmonean second wife Mariamme and their two sons). Before his death in 4 BC, he split his kingdom between his four sons, but Judea, which covered most of Palestine, was brought under direct rule in 6 AD, and the whole country was united under direct Roman rule in 44 AD. Herod and the Romans were far from popular and there were numerous uprisings, but lack of unity prevented their success. The Jewish population was split into two main political factions: the **Sadducees**, a conservative, priestly and privileged class who held onto their position by obedience to Rome, and the **Pharisees**, who believed in strict adherence to the Jewish law, and in the coming of a Davidic heir or "messiah" who would rescue them from Roman rule. In addition to these, the **Essenes** cut themselves off and set up isolated communities in the desert, while the **Zealots** refused to accept Roman rule and began a guerrilla war against it. This was the time of **Jesus**, who is traditionally held to have lived from 1 BC to 40 AD, though His birth has also been dated at 6 BC (it would have to be before 4 BC to be within the reign of Herod the Great), and 6 AD (when the census of

Cyrenius, mentioned in Luke 2:1, probably took place). The Herod of the New Testament could be Archelaus, son of Herod the Great. Of Jesus as a historical personage, little is known other than what is written in the Gospels. These appear to pit him against the Pharisaic party, but His teachings seem very much in line with theirs, and He may also have been a claimant to the throne, since He was apparently descended from David and Solomon (Matthew 1: 6–16). To begin with at any rate, His followers remained within the Jewish community.

Meanwhile, the Jews fought two bloody but unsuccessful revolts against the Romans. The **First Revolt** or Jewish War, in 66 AD, culminated in the destruction of Herod's Temple in 70 AD by Titus, son of the Roman emperor Vespasian. Bands of Zealots, however, continued to hold out against the Romans in their fortresses, above all at **Masada** (see p.265), which was the last to fall, in 73 AD. Six decades after the fall of the Temple, there was a **Second Revolt** (132–35 AD), led by **Simon Bar Kokhba** (Simeon ben Kosiba, see p.127). This time Jerusalem was completely razed by Hadrian who built a Roman city, Aelia Capitolina, over its ruins and banned Jews from living in or even entering the city. Official Jewish connection with Jerusalem thus came to an end in 135 AD, although pockets of Jewish culture survived elsewhere, above all in the Galilee.

THE BYZANTINE ERA (330–637)

In 330 AD Emperor **Constantine** succeeded in reunifying the Roman Empire after a period of division, and moved its capital to the Greek city of Byzantium (Constantinople), ushering in Byzantine rule in Palestine. **Christianity** became the official state religion, and many sites associated with Jesus were identified and consecrated for the first time, with the building of churches and monasteries and an influx of pilgrims into the country. Much of the local population converted to Christianity at this time, but restrictions placed on Jews and Samaritans led to **Samaritan revolts** in 486, when the Samaritans tried to set up their own state, and again in 529. In 614, the Persians under Khosrow II attacked from the east, with much support from the Jewish and Samaritan communities. They went on a spree of destruction, massacring Christians and desecrating Christian sites, before being driven out again by the

Byzantines in 628. But Byzantine rule was to last less than a decade more.

THE EARLY ARAB PERIOD (636–1095)

The Arabian peninsula had long been inhabited by largely nomadic Semitic tribes, the **Arabs**, speaking a single language, Arabic, and regarded by the Jews as "cousins" (still a euphemism for Arabs in modern Israel), being descended from Abraham's older son, Ismail (the Old Testament's Ishmael). From time to time, Arab tribes moved into the more fertile lands north of Arabia, and even established empires: the Nabateans (see p.270) were Arabs.

In 611 AD, the **Prophet Mohammed** began to preach the new faith of Islam in Mecca, near the Red Sea in central Arabia, a major centre of Arabic culture, and from the time of the Hegira in 622 (see p.504), started a campaign of conquest that had united the entire peninsula under Islamic rule by the time of his death ten years later.

Mohammed's successor as leader of Islam, the first caliph **Abu Bakr**, continued the Prophet's miltary campaigns to bring all Arabs into the Islamic fold, expanding his battleground from Arabia into Syria and Palestine. Around 634, Abu Bakr dispatched four armies into the region, including one under Amar Ibn al-'As to southern Palestine to secure the allegiance of local Arab tribes, including the **Nabateans** who had run the region's spice trade from their capital at Petra in modern Jordan since the third century BC. On Abu Bakr's death, his successor **Omar** continued with a military campaign against Byzantine forces, culminating in victory at the **River Yarmuk**, which gave the armies of Islam control of the region by 637. Omar himself came to accept the surrender of the Byzantine patriarch of Jerusalem (already revered by Muslims as their third holiest city), and commissioned the al-Aqsa Mosque. Administratively, Palestine became a province (*jund*) of the Islamic empire, with Jerusalem its capital, though the north fell under the *jund* of Jordan, based at Tiberias. Of Palestine's cities, only Caesarea, supplied by sea, put up any serious resistance.

The new Muslim rulers interfered very little with the internal life of the Christian, Jewish and Samaritan communities, whose members had freedom of movement and worship, and were able to occupy quite high administrative and economic positions. For this reason, there was no major rebellion against them. Conversion to Islam was a gradual process, but Arabic soon became the dominant language. The **Ummayads** took power after the assassination of the fourth caliph, Mohammed's cousin and son-in-law Ali, in 661, and ruled the Arab empire from Damascus until 750. They were succeeded by the **Abbassids**, who moved the capital to Baghdad. In 969 Egypt, and with it Palestine, fell into the hands of the **Fatimids**, Isma'ili Shi'ites who claimed to be heirs of the murdered Ali. Meanwhile, Muslim Turkic tribes under the leadership of the **Seljuk** family were sweeping across Central Asia. In 1055, they took Baghdad, and Palestine fell to them in 1071.

THE CRUSADES (1095–1291)

Of the eight or more expeditions between 1095 and 1270 that are known as the Crusades, it was the first three that really affected Palestine.

As the Seljuks advanced on the heartland of the Byzantine empire in the 1080s and 1090s, Emperor Alexius Comnenus called on the West for help. In 1095 at the Council of Clermont, Pope Urban II called for an expedition to aid Eastern Christendom and to take control of Jerusalem, a prime centre for the pilgrimages which had become extremely popular among European Christians. Thus began the **First Crusade**, largely led by French nobles. The Crusaders, who mainly spoke French, came to be known as Franks. They took Jerusalem in July 1099, and murdered all the city's Muslim and Jewish inhabitants, setting up a **Kingdom of Jerusalem** under Godfrey of Bouillon, Duke of Lorraine, who had led the assault on the city, succeeded on his death the following year by his brother Baldwin I. Three other Crusader kingdoms were set up further north, but Jerusalem encompassed by 1112 the whole of Palestine from what is now Eilat up as far north as Beirut, controlling the entire coastline except Ashqelon (which held out until 1153). The Crusader kingdoms were known in Europe as "Outremer".

In 1144 **Zangi**, the Seljuk governor of Mosul (Northern Iraq), took the northernmost Crusader kingdom, Edessa. Pope Eugenius III responded by calling a **Second Crusade**, but the Crusaders were hampered by infighting, lack of communication, and a serious defeat in Northern Turkey en route. For reasons unknown,

they decided to besiege Damascus, whose Muslim emir had sought an alliance with Jerusalem's king, Fulk of Anjou, against Zangi's Seljuks. Now, however, he called for help from Zangi's son and successor, **Nur al-Din** (Nureddin), before whose approach the Crusaders were forced into a humiliating retreat.

Manoeuvring by the Seljuks and King Amalric of Jerusalem in 1164 to control the teetering Fatimid caliphate in Egypt led first to a standoff, and then to its takeover in 1171 by Nur al-Din's nephew, Salah al-Din al-Ayyubi, known in English as **Saladin**. Saladin's defeat of the Crusaders at the Horns of Hittin on July 4, 1187 opened the whole of Palestine to him. When his forces took Jerusalem in October, Pope Gregory VIII responded by calling a **Third Crusade**, led by Phillip II of France and **Richard the Lionheart** of England. By now, much of the Crusader army was made up of members of the two orders of monk soldiers, the Knights of St John of Jerusalem or **Knights Hospitallers**, originally set up to provide hospitals for pilgrims, and the Poor Knights of Christ and the Temple of Solomon, or **Knights Templar**, originally set up to protect pilgrims. Saladin had taken virtually the whole kingdom of Jerusalem, bar Tyre in Lebanon and the fort of Belvoir (see p.189), but Crusader forces were besieging Acre, which fell in July 1191 following Richard the Lionheart's arrival. Richard went on to take Jaffa and restore the kingdom of Jerusalem along the coast between there and Beirut, with its capital at Acre but, despite its name, this "Second Kingdom" did not actually include Jerusalem, which remained in the control of Saladin's dynasty, the **Ayyubids**, until ceded to the Christians by diplomatic agreement along with Bethlehem and Nazareth in 1229.

In 1244 Jerusalem fell to the Khwarizmians, a Turkish tribe moving west before the advance of the apparently unstoppable Mongol empire. The **Mongols** under Hulagu Khan, grandson of Genghis Khan, took Baghdad in 1258, ending the last vestiges of the Abbassid caliphate, and moved into Palestine. They were stopped by Egypt's new rulers, the Mamluks.

THE MAMLUKS (1250–1516)

The Ayyubids depended on an army of slaves called **Mamluks** (also spelt Mamelukes). The last Ayyubid sultan, Ayyub, had married a slave girl, Shagar al-Dur, who took power on his death but was assassinated and succeeded in 1250 by her commander, Baybars the Crossbowman, and most of his Mamluk successors took power the same way. Another Baybars, a general known as **Baybars the Great**, managed to inflict the first defeat on the Mongols, at Ein Jalut near Nazareth in 1260, following a historic treaty with the Crusaders. The same year, he murdered the previous ruler and took the throne, conquering most of Palestine by the time of his death in 1277, and destroying the seaports to prevent landings by European Christian forces, who still had naval superiority. Buildings of his reign such as the Lions' Gate in Jerusalem often bear his symbol, a pair of lions.

Qalaoun (1277–94) saw off Baybars's sons and went on to found the **Bahri dynasty** of Turkish Mamluks that ruled until 1382. In 1281, he defeated the Mongols at the Battle of Homs in alliance with the Crusaders, and went on to take Palestine's last Crusader outpost, Acre, ten years later. The Bahris were succeeded by the **Burgi dynasty** of Mamluks from Circassia in the Caucusus, who ruled Egypt until 1517. Despite their brutal politics of assassination and poisoning, the Mamluks were great patrons of the arts who sponsored many buildings, constructed in the distinctive style of their era, and set up a network of khans (caravanserais, where trading caravans could stop and lodge) linked by a network of roads and bridges. Jerusalem under their rule became a centre of Muslim pilgrimage and learning.

THE OTTOMANS (1516–1917)

In 1516, the **Ottoman Turks** under Selim I (the Grim) defeated Mamluk forces at Aleppo (Syria) and took control of Palestine, conquering Egypt and finally ending Mamluk rule the following year (though the Mamluks continued to exercise influence in the army and the state). Selim's son, **Suleiman I** al-Qanuni, also known as Suleiman the Magnificent, instituted a massive programme of public works including rebulding Jerusalem's walls and generally improving the infrastructure.

After Suleiman's death, the empire became very fragmented and local governors, called **pashas**, had effective power with little interference from Turkey, so long as the taxes kept coming in. Palestine was officially governed from Damascus until 1830. A renewed Jewish presence as refugees came in from Spain in the

sixteenth century to escape the Inquisition (see p.489) led to a revival of Jewish culture in the Galilee, in particular the Kabbalist movement in Safed (see p.240). In fact, Safed was on the southern edge of a Druze fiefdom in Lebanon and the Galilee established by Qurqmaz ibn Yunis al-Ma'ni, which was largely independent of the Ottomans. This Ma'nid state reached its height under **Fakr al-Din II** (1590–1633), and brought an influx of Druze from Lebanon to the Galilee. Fakr al-Din also had Acre rebuilt, but Ottoman sultan Murad IV refused to accept Ma'nid autonomy, and sent in his troops to end it, capturing Fakr al-Din in 1633 and taking him to Constantinople, where he was executed.

In 1730, however, a Bedouin chieftain, **Daher al-Omar** of the Beni Zaidan tribe, made Acre the capital of another Galilean fiefdom that, by the time of his death in 1775, covered most of Palestine. He was killed and succeeded by a Bosnian-born pasha, **Ahmed al-Jazzar** ("the butcher"), known for his cruelty, but also for repelling an assault on Acre by the French emperor Napoleon's forces in 1799. Napoleon went on to attack Jaffa and Egypt, but was finally repulsed in 1801 with the help of the British under Nelson.

In 1831, Egypt's pasha **Mohammed Ali** made himself effectively independent of Turkey, and took control of Palestine and Syria, holding it until pressure from Britain and the European powers forced him to leave in 1840. Back in control, the Ottomans reorganized the administration, finally in 1888 splitting it into provinces based at Acre and Nablus but governed from Beirut, and an autonomous province based at Jerusalem. Meanwhile, liberalization of land ownership and development in the 1850s boosted the cultivation of crops for export, which became the country's economic mainstay.

THE JEWS IN EXILE (135 AD–1896)

All this time, the Jews, expelled from Jerusalem in 135 AD, had lived in exile, maintaining their identity as a distinct religion and ethnic group, and reaffirming yearly at the Passover feast their hope that they might celebrate it "next year in Jerusalem". Jews had lived abroad in the **diaspora** since Solomonic times, when communities were established in Egypt, and probably that far back too in Yemen and Ethiopia. Jewish communities also remained from the Babylonian exile, in Iraq and across the Persian empire. In general they lived in peace, though there was a tradition of hostility between Jews and Greeks that originated in Maccabean times and occasionally blew up into ethnic strife. Following the Second Revolt in 135, Jewish refugees from Palestine streamed into Syria, Asia Minor and North Africa, as far west as Morocco and Spain, but Babylon became their biggest centre. Most Jewish communities abroad maintained contact with Babylon and Palestine, though some became cut off from their co-religionists for extended periods, notably the community in Ethiopia which only re-established contact in the nineteenth century. Even by 135, the Jews had spread far: their community in Kerala (South India), for example, probably dates from that period.

The first serious persecution came with the **rise of Christianity**, originally a Jewish sect. Taking over the Roman empire in 312 AD, Constantine guaranteed religious freedom for all, but the first anti-Jewish decrees, banning Jews from trying to convert Christians, were introduced only three years later. In 325, the Council of Nicosia moved Easter from its coincidence with Passover, completing the separation of the two religions, and the idea of the Jews as "murderers of Christ" began to gain currency. Christian Roman emperors were invariably worse for the Jews than pagan ones – Theodosius II (379–95), who finally made Christianity the religion of the empire, banned the building of synagogues, a ban renewed twice in the next fifty years, and Jews were soon banned from imperial public office too. Meanwhile in the Sassanian empire of Persia, the Zoroastrian clergy began attacks on Jews and Christians, while the same century saw the first anti-Semitism in **Babylon** under the regime of Peroz (457–484), though this did not prevent Babylon's Jews from their completion of the Talmud.

Heretical Christians were less inclined than orthodox Catholics to persecute the Jews, and Rome's 489 fall to the Ostragoths, who followed the Arian heresy, gave European Jews a breather. By that time, Jewish communities existed across the Roman Empire, throughout France and Italy, and north as far as Belgium. By far the most important community in the west, however, was in **Spain**, whose Visigothic kings, also Arians, left them largely in peace. In Byzantium, by contrast, Jews faced ever-increasing restrictions on their religion and employment. In the fifth and sixth centuries,

conversion of Arian monarchs to Catholicism (Spain's Reccard I in 587, for instance) led to further persecution of Jews, who often ended up moving around Europe to avoid it. But the largest Jewish population in Europe was about to be liberated: in 711, the **Muslims** under Tariq ibn Ziad crossed the Straits of Gibraltar and within five years the whole of Spain was theirs, a fact due in no small measure to the support of Jews, who constituted around a third of the country's population. Jews already lived throughout the Arab empire and, though Mohammed's attitude toward them had been mixed, their religious rights were generally respected and they lived in peace. The leader of the Babylonian community, the **Exiliarch**, supposedly descended from David and Solomon, was the political leader of Jews in Muslim lands, regarded by the caliphs as the equivalent of a vassal king; the Jewish religious leader, also based in Babylon, was the **Gaon**, in effect a chief rabbi.

The early victories of Islam in Spain and Asia Minor virtually isolated Christian Europe, cutting it off for example from Indian spices, Chinese silk and West African gold. But Jewish merchants known as **Radanites** set up a trading network based on communities far and wide, connecting Europe, North Africa, Arabia, India and China (Jews arrived in China with Tamurlaine in the ninth century, setting up communities in Kaifeng and Canton). They were also perfectly placed to bridge the gap between Christianity and Islam: a German Jew, Isaac of Aachen, went as interpreter for the French emperor Charlemagne to the court of Abbasid caliph Haroun al-Rachid, for example. In the Caucasus and the Ukraine, meanwhile, the rulers of a Turkic tribe, the **Khazars**, converted to Judaism and set up a Jewish kingdom that lasted from 740 AD until the end of the tenth century. But the centre of Jewish intellectual life by now was Spain, the most liberal part of the Arab empire. Spain's most famous Jewish son was **Maimonides** (1135–1204), the great religious philosopher from Córdoba who was also Saladin's doctor (see p.200).

Although the papacy continued to promote restrictions on Jews (forbidding them to farm and barring them from ever more professions), the 1179 **Third Lateran Council** inadvertently gave them a niche that was to make some Jews very powerful: by banning the lending of money for interest by Christians, already forbidden to

Muslims, it gave Jews an effective monopoly in Europe on banking, whose importance to the economy was then ill-understood by heads of church and state. It was also a role that made Jews rather unpopular, a fact that proved very handy for monarchs who found themselves in debt to their Jewish bankers, and often saw to their Jewish creditors by sponsoring anti-Semitic riots and massacres.

The Crusades brought the Jews more misery, with attacks on them by mobs across Europe, but it was **England** that initiated two of the most serious forms of persecution. In Norwich in 1144, the first case of "**blood libel**" arose when the city's Jewish community was blamed and massacred for the kidnap and murder of a Christian boy, supposedly for religious rituals, and in 1290 England set another trend when King Edward I expelled all Jews from the country. As blood libels and expulsions swept the Jews across Europe, the 1348 Black Death was widely blamed on Jews poisoning wells, and over 350 whole commmunities were slaughtered in revenge; in fact, attacks on and massacres of whole Jewish communities were by now commonplace throughout Europe, and any Jewish community would expect an attack from its neighbours every few years. Through the fifteenth century, **expulsions** in Germany drove the Jews east into Poland, Bohemia and Austria, but the biggest expulsion was yet to come.

Following the 1212 Battle of Las Navas de Tolosa, the Christian *reconquista* had wiped out most of Muslim Spain. By 1248 only the kingdom of Granada remained. In 1474, the crowns of Aragon and Castile joined in the kingdom of Spain, and in 1480 the first tribunal of the **Inquisition** opened in Seville. In the face of increasing persecution many Jews had converted officially to Christianity, but continued to practise Judaism on the quiet. The Inquisition was determined to expose these "**Marranos**" and promptly arrested 15,000 of them, burning 300 at the stake in its first nine months alone. With Granada's 1492 fall, all Jews were expelled from Spain and soon from Portugal too. Many Marranos remained, but persecution, prosecution, torture and execution increasingly their lot. The rest of the Iberian peninsula's Jewish population spread north into Europe, south into North Africa, and east across the Mediterranean: these were the **Sephardim** (from *Sefarad*, Hebrew for Spain), whose name

came to refer to everyone in the Jewish communities they joined. Jews of German origin were the **Ashkenazim**.

Jews had high hopes from the Reformation, but Luther's pamphlet *On the Jews and their Lies* repeated all the old anti-Semitic myths of blood rituals and well-poisoning. Meanwhile in 1555, Pope Paul IV obliged Jews in Rome and all cities under papal rule to live in separate walled enclosures called "**ghettos**" and to be in them by nightfall. Soon most cities in Italy had ghettos, and the trend spread north into Germany and eastern Europe. In the seventeenth century, the expanding Russian empire brought in a wave of Cossack-led **pogroms** in the Ukraine, Belarus and Lithuania, starting a trend that was to last three centuries, and complementing the increasing persecution in neighbouring Poland. Belatedly, however, the Reformation was about to bring some relief.

In 1579, the Protestant **Netherlands** declared independence from Spain and promised religious freedom to all. Marranos fleeing the torture chambers of the Inquisition found refuge there and sent word to their co-religionists. In 1624, the Netherlands took control of Brazil and many Jews moved in, heading for North America when Portugal regained Brazil twenty years later. With the fall of **Britain**'s monarchy to Cromwell in 1648, Jewish leaders asked to be readmitted to England. Unofficially, Cromwell said yes, and because it was unofficial, the restored monarchy did nothing to reverse it. Thus the Jews with their trading networks and banking expertise moved north, and so did Europe's economy: within a century, its centre had shifted from the Iberian peninsula to Britain and the Netherlands. Elsewhere, monarchs who expelled the Jews found that it caused severe economic damage, and some were forced to invite them back. The **United States** was the first country to give Jews full rights as citizens, which it did from its foundation, but as the wind of liberalism blew across the West, Jews obtained citizenship and full religious freedom in Britain and much of Western Europe too. For the first time, their rights in Christian countries were greater than in the Muslim world. However, anti-Semitism lived on, becoming a *cause célèbre* in France in 1896 when Jewish army captain **Alfred Dreyfus** was framed as a spy for largely racist motives. Meanwhile, southern Europe was slow to follow the West's lead in Jewish emancipation, as was Eastern Europe, where most Jews were poor peasants living in Jewish villages and ghettos, called **shtetls**. In Russia anti-Semitism remained government policy until the 1917 revolution, sending waves of Jewish emigrants to countries such as Britain and the US, and also to Palestine. In Germany, the massive Jewish community had religious freedom from 1871, but for them of course the worst still lay ahead.

THE RISE OF ZIONISM

In Palestine there had always been a religious Jewish community, known as the *Yishuv*, living primarily in the holy cities of Jerusalem, Hebron, Safed and Tiberias. **Moses Montefiore**, who later became the acknowledged leader of Britain's Jewish community, made his first visit to Palestine in 1827, and later gave money to found a Jewish suburb, Yemin Moshe, in West Jerusalem (see p.369). As the century wore on, Jews seeking refuge from anti-Semitism in eastern Europe and Russia obtained the permission of the Ottoman rulers to immigrate to Palestine, making what they called "*Aliya*" (literally, "going up"). Their first colony, Petah Tiqva, was established in 1878, and a surge of immigration, known as the **First Aliya**, took place in 1881 following a wave of officially inspired anti-Semitic pogroms across the Russian Empire. One group of Jewish emigrants, an association called **Bilu**, aimed at self-supporting Jewish communities in Palestine, and one Bilu group in Constantinople mooted the idea of a Jewish homeland there. Meanwhile, further pogroms in 1904 led to the **Second Aliya**.

The idea of a Jewish state in Palestine emerged slowly. It was first suggested by a German Jewish journalist named **Moses Hess** in an 1862 essay, *Rome and Jerusalem*, combining the liberal nationalist ideas of Italy's founding father Giuseppe Mazzini with the long-time Orthodox Jewish dream of a "return to Zion". In Russia, state-sponsored anti-Semitism, especially the May Laws of 1882, which forced Jews off the land in the "Pale of Settlement" where they were allowed to live, led to the growth of Jewish nationalist societies called *Hovevei Tziyon* (Lovers of Zion), which spread into Romania, Austria-Hungary and Germany in the 1890s. In 1882, a Ukrainian

Jew called **Leo Pinsker** promoted the view that the Jews needed their own state, in an essay called *Selbstemanzipation* (Auto-emancipation). The idea even had a name, **Zionism**, first coined in 1893 by Nathan Birnbaum.

Zionism really took off in 1896, when Austro-Hungarian Jewish playwright and essayist **Theodor Herzl** published his seminal work *Der Judenstaat* (The Jew-State) which called for the establishment of a Jewish state, not necessarily in Palestine. Suddenly the movement found inspiration: as the non-Jewish central European press panned the book, Jews worldwide got in touch with Herzl, who proposed a Zionist congress. In August 1897 this opened in Basel, Switzerland, and declared its aim "to create for the Jewish people a home in Palestine", setting up a World Zionist Organization, with Herzl as its president. At its fifth annual congress in Basel in 1901, the Jewish National Fund (JNF) was set up to finance the purchase of land for Jews in Palestine. Tel Aviv, aiming to be the world's first all-Jewish city, was founded in 1909, as was the first **kibbutz** at Deganya. Aiming for socialist self-sufficiency and eschewing any exploitation of Arab labour, the kibbutzniks refused to employ Palestinian Arabs, apparently oblivious of the implications of this policy. The Arabs, however, took this as nothing more than racism. Indeed, coming as they did from Europe, many of the settlers, consciously or not, could hardly avoid suffering the racist assumptions of colonialism; with exceptions (notably Haim Arlosoroff and Ahad Ha'Am, who attempted to educate their brethren), they saw Arabs as "primitive". The first part of the Zionist slogan, "A land without people for a people without land", shows how they ignored the Arabs, failing to understand that they too had an ancient culture and aspirations to self-rule. For their part, many Palestinian Arabs had come to resent the settlers and their idea of a Jewish homeland in Palestine: in 1908, an anti-Zionist journal called *al-Karmil* was set up in Haifa, and 1911 saw the foundation in Jaffa of the first Arab association against Zionism.

THE END OF THE OTTOMAN EMPIRE

During **World War I** Turkey sided with Germany against Britain, France and Russia; so did most Jews, mainly from hatred of Russia's Tsarist regime. Arab subjects of the Ottoman

Empire, by now seeking independence, joined with the Allies to fight their Turkish rulers. In return, the British undertook to recognize and support their independence in the Arabian Peninsula and the Levant. But behind the scenes, Britain signed a secret deal with France in 1916 (the **Sykes-Picot Agreement**), under which the two countries agreed to divide the defunct Ottoman Empire between them, with Palestine under "international administration". At the same time, the Ottomans were suspicious of the Jews whom they treated as enemy aliens, driving out large numbers (10,000 Palestinian Jews ended up as refugees in Alexandria) and turning the Jewish community against them.

Meanwhile, Zionist leaders were pressing Britain to support a Jewish homeland in Palestine, stressing the strategic advantages of an ally in the Middle East to be, in Herzl's words, "a portion of the rampart of Europe against Asia, an outpost of civilization as opposed to barbarism". **Haim Weizmann** had taken over as Zionism's leading voice following Herzl's death in 1904, became a British citizen in 1910, and succeeded in obtaining support from both of Britain's main political parties. Foreign Secretary Arthur Balfour originally declared support for a Jewish home in the whole of Palestine with internal autonomy and unrestricted Jewish immigration, but watered this down following advice (much of it from anti-Zionist Jewish politicians in Britain) to the **Balfour Declaration** of November 2, 1917, in the form of a letter to Lord Rothschild, son of Britain's first Jewish MP. The letter stated that "His Majesty's Government view with favour the establishment in Palestine of a national home for the Jewish people, it being clearly understood that nothing shall be done which may prejudice the civil and religious rights of the existing non-Jewish communities in Palestine, or the rights and political status enjoyed by Jews in any other country." At that time, there were only around 60,000 Jews in Palestine out of a total population of some 600,000, but the Arabs, as yet ill-organized, had failed to make their opposition felt. To reassure them, an Anglo-French declaration issued a year later promised "the complete and definite emancipation of the Arab peoples...and the establishment of national governments and administrations deriving their authority from the initiative and free choice of the indigenous populations", but Britain's true atttitude is better gauged from a secret 1919 memorandum from Balfour to his fellow Cabinet members, in which he wrote: "In Palestine, we do not propose even to go through the form of consulting the wishes of the present inhabitants of the country."

THE BRITISH MANDATE (1917–1948)

After the defeat of Germany and its Turkish ally, the Ottoman Empire was dismembered. The earlier agreement for the internationalization of Palestine was nullified and in April 1920 Britain was **mandated** by the newly formed League of Nations to control Palestine and Transjordan (made into a separate kingdom, today's Jordan, in 1921). The British reiterated the Balfour Declaration, stressing the second part of it in an attempt to appease Palestinian Arab opinion, which by now regarded Zionism as a major political issue.

The reaction to Bolshevism (blamed on the Jews) led to a wave of anti-Semitic pogroms in Eastern Europe and a **Third Aliya** in the early 1920s; and dispossession of the Jewish middle class by an anti-Semitic government in Poland caused a Fourth Aliya later that decade. Despite growing opposition in most of the Arab community, the **Jewish Agency**, set up by the World Zionist Organization in 1922 to represent the Jewish community in Palestine, continued to buy real estate from (usually absentee) Arab landlords, and by 1929 Jews owned 4 percent of Palestine's land area and 14 percent of all cultivable land (though a fair amount of this had been reclaimed by them from swamp or desert). The settlers' policy of employing only Jewish labour meant eviction and unemployment for those who had worked it, and the Arabs more clearly saw the expanding *Yishuv* (now 17 percent of the population) as a threat to their own hopes of independence, not least when the British used the Jews to "divide and rule".

The Arab response, however, was ill-organized, finding expression in waves of **rioting** and attacks on Jews, the first in 1920, with subsequent waves in 1921, 1929 and 1933. The worst of these was in 1929, when 133 Jews were murdered and several Jewish communities, notably those of Hebron and Gaza, both ancient, disappeared completely. Each wave of rioting was followed by a commission of enquiry, but no real action from the British, who did however set up a post of **Grand Mufti of Jerusalem** – a Muslim equivalent of the Jewish Chief Rabbi. In 1921, the British High Commissioner, Herbert Samuel (himself Jewish), helped to fix the election to the post of **Haj Amin al-Husseini**, a virulent anti-Zionist who had been involved in the 1920 riots. This was a serious mistake: vain, authoritarian and racist, al-Husseini opposed any compromise with the Jews, and objected to any organization that was not under his personal control. He kept the Arab community from participating in the structures of the Mandate, but allowed it no serious political structure of its own to act as an alternative. His main opponents were the **Nashishibi** family, landowners and long-time rivals of Haj Amin's family. Although the Nashishibi interest from 1935 was promoted by a political party, the **National Defence Party**, rivalry was based on clan and personal loyalty rather than policy, and infighting between the Mufti, the Nashishibis and their smaller rivals weakened the Arabs politically still further.

The Jewish community, on the other hand, had been organizing itself, led by the Jewish Agency, a virtual government, to the extent of even having elections and political parties. A labour federation called the **Histadrut** was formed in 1920 for "all workers who live by their own labour", and to which most kibbutzniks and moshavniks belonged. The Histadrut marketed kibbutz and moshav products and ran services for its members such as schools and hospitals. Also in 1920, a militia called the **Haganah** was formed from the units of watchmen used by the settlers to protect their property from raiders. Officially under the Mandate, civilians were not allowed to carry arms so the Haganah was illegal, but the British turned a blind eye, a policy that was soon to prove useful. The group was left in orientation and run by Histadrut, but an agreement with the World Zionist Organization (who were unwilling to vote it funds while it was entirely in the hands of the left) gave equal representation to non-union members. At this time, Zionism's right-wing tendency was increasingly dominated by **Revisionism**, a movement founded by **Ze'ev Jabotinsky**, a Russian Jew who had joined the Zionist movement in 1902; he rejected the socialism of the Zionist mainstream and argued that, since

Jewish and Arab nationalism were incompatible, only superior force could create a Jewish homeland. The Revisionists split off from the Haganah in 1931 to form a rival paramiltary, the **Irgun**, which rejected the Haganah's purely defensive function and started attacking Arabs rather than wait for them to attack Jews first. Meanwhile, the rise of Nazism in Germany and anti-Semitic governments across Eastern Europe led to further waves of Jewish immigration (sometimes called the "Fifth Aliya"). By 1936, the Jewish population of Palestine stood at 29 percent.

That year a full-scale **Palestinian Revolt** broke out. A series of strikes brought the country to a standstill; roads, railways, telegraph and telephone lines, oil pipelines and other government property were sabotaged. The revolt began at street level, but an **Arab Higher Committee** was set up under the Grand Mufti in April 1936 to coordinate it. At the height of the revolt, the rebels ran most of the country, with their own courts and taxes, and British rule more fiction than reality. It was at this time that the *keffiya* headdress of the rural *fellahin* became the symbol of Palestinian resistance. The British banned the Arab Higher Committee and arrested hundreds of Arab "notables", though not the Mufti, who escaped to Lebanon. 20,000 British troops were brought in to reconquer Palestine, which they did with some brutality, and with the help of Jewish auxiliary police, who doubled as Haganah members and would later put their training to good use against the Arabs.

The Palestinian Revolt made the British realize that their rule could not last. The **Peel Commission** in 1937 concluded that "the situation in Palestine has reached a deadlock. We cannot...both concede the Arab claim to self-government and secure the establishment of a Jewish National Home." Its solution, ending the Mandate and partitioning the country, was accepted by the Jews but rejected by the Arabs.

By 1939, the British had regained control of Palestine (helped by a breakdown of Arab solidarity stemming from the Mufti's campaign of assassination against members of the National Defence Party), but with the approach of war, they realized that they needed Arab support again, and so began to back-pedal on partition and on the Balfour Declaration. A 1939 **White Paper** proposed a unified state with both Jews and Palestinian Arabs sharing in government. It also tried to put a cap on Jewish immigration. Jewish organizations rejected the White Paper and began a campaign of armed resistance and illegal immigration.

World War II itself did not reach Palestine, give or take the odd Italian bombing raid, but it threatened to. The Jewish paramilitaries, the Haganah and the Irgun, made a truce with the British to work against the common Nazi enemy (only the Stern Gang, an Irgun splinter, refused – see p.85). Certain Arab leaders, however, notably the Mufti, saw Hitler as a potential ally against both the British and the Jews. The Mufti spent most of the war in Berlin trying to recruit a pro-Axis Arab legion, and broadcasting propaganda to the Middle East. Meanwhile, the Haganah set up a special strike force called the **Palmah**, intended to carry out acts of sabotage and protect the Jewish community should Axis forces take Palestine (which seemed very likely as they swept across North Africa before being halted at El Alamein). But within the Zionist movement, Revisionism was growing stronger. Jabotinsky died in 1940 but his mantle was taken by Irgun leader Menahem Begin. The 1942 World Zionist Congress at Biltmore meanwhile demanded unlimited Jewish immigration into Palestine and the establishment of a Jewish state, and announced plans for organising a Jewish army to confront the British policy of a unified Palestine. Their campaign began in earnest when the war ended in 1945.

When the scale of the **Holocaust** became clear, worldwide horror crystallized into general sympathy for the Jewish people. Of the Nazis' eleven to twelve million victims, over six (and possibly nearer seven) million were Jewish, most of them systematically murdered in death camps as part of Hitler's "final solution". The Allies knew about the slaughter by August 1942 but, despite pleas from Jewish organizations, refused to bomb the death camps – such an action would show the Germans that the Allies knew where they were, which in turn would reveal that the Allies had broken German military ciphers – or to grant safe passage to Jews fleeing Nazi-occupied Europe. In the end, a third of the world's Jewish population perished in the worst act of genocide ever, with hundreds of Jewish communities wiped completely off the map. Of those who survived, hundreds of thousands were refugees; with countries worldwide

closing their doors, few had anywhere to go. Though immigration was still illegal, many made their way to Palestine.

The British were discreetly allowing far more than the legal quota of immigrants to enter the country: some 18,000 a year (still nowhere near enough as far as the Zionists were concerned), and behind the scenes they were working with the Haganah for a peaceful settlement, but they increasingly saw the Arab states of Egypt, Transjordan and Iraq as a potential bulwark against Soviet ambitions in the Middle East, and postwar British Foreign Secretary **Ernest Bevin** alienated Jewish public opinion with his attempts to keep the Arabs on side by rejecting partition and putting a lid on Jewish immigration. The Irgun under Menahem Begin ended their wartime truce and took up the tactics of the extremist Stern Gang, including bombings of targets both civilian and military, most famously the **King David Hotel** in July 1946 (see p.369). The Haganah concentrated on running in illegal immigrants, and acts of sabotage such as the "**Night of the Bridges**" on June 17, 1946, when they destroyed eleven bridges on the country's borders. The British reacted by cordoning off the whole of Tel Aviv and West Jerusalem in a four-day "**Great Curfew**", trying largely in vain to root out the paramilitaries and their arms supplies. Meanwhile, the Arab Higher Committee was revived, still under the Mufti, who had escaped to Egypt after the war, and continued to hold out against partition and any kind of compromise with the Jews. Sectarian murders by both sides rose by the month, and by 1947 the British decided that the country was ungovernable. Commissions of enquiry, conferences and negotiations having proved futile, they concluded that "the only course now open to us is to submit the problem to the judgement of the United Nations".

PARTITION AND WAR (1947–48)

Palestine was a land of violent strife when the question was taken up by the **United Nations** in February 1947. The United Nations Special Committee on Palestine (UNSCOP) agreed on the termination of the Mandate and independence for Palestine, and also asked the UN to deal with the plight of European Jewry.

The proposal put forward was to **divide Palestine** into two states joined in an economic confederation: the plan allocated the

BORDERS SINCE 1918

LEBANON

1967 "Purple Line" moved slightly in 1974

Mt. Hermon

South Lebanon "Security Zone"

Acre

Haifa

Mediterranean Sea

SYRIA

1920-23 Anglo-French borders

TEL AVIV
Jaffa

Ashdod

Green Line

Gaza

Jerusalem

Bethlehem

Beersheba

N

JORDAN
(united with Palestine under British Mandate 1918-1921)

1947 PARTITION PLAN

Proposed Jewish State

Proposed Palestinian State

Proposed International Zone

SINAI
(occupied by Israel 1956, & 1967-1982)

Eilat

Taba
(Israeli occupied until 1989)

Aqaba

0   50 km

they organized their forces (some 30,000 Haganah and Palmah troops, 32,000 reserves and around 4000 Irgun and Stern Gang "irregulars"). From April, under **Plan Dalet**, they started to move on Arab-held territory. Most importantly, they moved to hold the Tel Aviv–Jerusalem corridor. It was as part of this operation that the infamous massacre of **Deir Yassin** (see p.378) took place.

Palestinian Arab forces under the Mufti's Arab Higher Committee had some 2400 riflemen, who lacked the training received by their Jewish opponents in the British army. These were supplemented by 3800 volunteers from around the Arab world (about a thousand were Palestinian) in the **Arab Liberation Army** (ALA) put together by Arab nationalist leader Fawzi al-Kaukji. Rivalry between the two forces didn't help matters, though they eventually agreed to split areas of operation geographically. Arab villages supported them on an ad hoc basis, and put up local resistance to Jewish forces in their vicinity. Arab states, most importantly Egypt and Transjordan, agreed to send help, but not until the British left on May 15. In the end, the help that they sent proved inadequate.

As the British left, the last vestiges of government disappeared. The Jews already had their own organizations in place to replace them, and declared the **State of Israel** on May 14, 1948. In principle, this declaration only included the land given to them under the partition plan; in practice they moved to take control of as much of Palestine as they could. Israel's first Prime Minister was Labour Party leader **David Ben Gurion**, its President was veteran Zionist Haim Weizmann. Henceforth, the Jews were no longer "Palestinian", and the term came clearly to refer to the country's Arab population only, though Israel refused to use it for many years on the grounds that the Palestinians did not constitute a "nation". Meanwhile, the Palestinians' only real political structure, the Arab Higher Committee, was largely dedicated to fighting the Zionists and keeping the Mufti in power: to replace the structures of the Mandate, they had nothing.

Hostilities began in earnest well before the British left. The Haganah took Haifa on April 21 and Safed on May 10. Jaffa fell as soon as the British pulled out. Meanwhile, the ALA, supported by local villagers, tried to maintain a **siege on West Jerusalem** by blocking access on the main road from Tel Aviv, the Jews' only

Palestinian Arabs (some seventy percent of the population) just under half of the country, with a Jewish state getting 53 percent, including most of the fertile land. After intense negotiations the General Assembly approved partition (**Resolution 181**) on November 29, 1947. The Zionists accepted the plan, but the Palestinians, perhaps not surprisingly, rejected it. Meanwhile, as violence escalated towards war, with an estimated 2000 people killed or injured between November 1947 and January 1948. Britain announced it would withdraw all its forces and terminate the Mandate on May 15, 1948, leaving the Jews and the Arabs to get on with it.

The Zionists were somewhat better prepared for the coming war than the Palestinian Arabs. Under **Plan Gimel**, in operation until April 1,

route for supplies to the city, and ambushing any Jewish convoys that tried to get through. On May 15, armies of five Arab nations entered Palestine, some 30,000 troops, but most of them were ineffectual. Syrian and Lebanese forces virtually stopped at the border, the Syrians after being held off at Deganya (see p.214). Iraq held the hill country in the north of what is now the West Bank, while Transjordan's Arab Legion managed to hold the vital post at Latrun on the Tel Aviv–Jerusalem road (see p.123), and the Old City of Jerusalem including the Jewish Quarter, though they failed to take the city's western half. But the most effective Arab army was that of Egypt, which advanced up the coast and across the Negev, holding Beersheba and Bethlehem, and threatening Tel Aviv. On June 11, the UN mediator, Swedish count Folk Bernadotte, managed to negotiate a **first truce**, during which (and in violation of its conditions), the Israelis were able to build up their arms stocks.

With the collapse of the truce on July 8, the Israelis, previously at a disadvantage armswise, now well outgunned their Arab adversaries. They easily beat the ALA out of the Galilee, and in the centre of the country took the main Palestinian towns of Lydda, with its airport, and Ramle. Infighting on the Israeli side, however, led to the **Altalena incident** when a ship full of arms bought by the Irgun was fired on and sunk off the coast by Haganah troops because Ben Gurion feared it would enable the Revisionists to launch a coup against his government.

Bernadotte managed to arrange a **second truce** on July 18, aiming for a permanent settlement, but he was murdered two months later by members of the Stern Gang, and war was renewed in October as the Israelis made a final push against Egyptian forces at Faluja (see p.119), taking Beersheba and the road to Eilat, and even crossing the Egyptian border to threaten El Arish. Transjordan finally agreed a ceasefire with Israel on December 1, and the **Rhodes peace talks**, beginning in January 1949, resulted in separate armistices between Israel and each of its Arab neighbours. The big losers were the Palestinians.

THE STATE OF ISRAEL (1948–THE PRESENT)

By the time the Armistice Agreements were signed in 1949 almost eighty percent of Palestine was in Israeli hands. Of the rest, the **West Bank** of the Jordan River (including the eastern half of Jerusalem), was annexed by the now renamed Hashemite Kingdom of Jordan – King Abdullah had in any case long accepted partition privately, and took the Old City of Jerusalem as partial compensation for his family's loss of Mecca and Medina to the rival Saudis earlier in the century. Egypt administered the **Gaza Strip**, setting up an "All Palestine Government", nominally under the Mufti, though they deported him as soon as he set foot there. The United Nations armistice line along the battlefront dermarcating Israel from Jordan and Egypt became known as the "**Green Line**".

The 750,000 Palestinians who had lived in what was now Israel found themselves **refugees**, exiles in the diaspora as the Jews had been before them. Why they had fled remains controversial: Israelis point to the decision of Haifa's Arab leaders to evacuate despite a plea by the city's Jewish community asking their Arab neighbours to remain, while Palestinians counter that Zionist troops forced people out of their homes, and dynamited them, spread rumours that Palestinians would be killed (actually, the Palestinians themselves were equally guilty of this), and sent in loudspeaker vans telling them to leave (or simply broadcasting the chilling message, "Deir Yassin, Deir Yassin", the name of the massacred village – see p.378). Most people, however, didn't need telling: as the battlefront approached they left. Some went to neighbouring Arab countries, most to nearby peaceful areas of Palestine, intending to return after the war, but were then prevented from doing so by the Israeli military. The Israelis destroyed 250 Arab villages, and in 1950 passed the **Absentee Property Act**, under which land belonging to anyone who had left during the war, whether abroad or to parts of Palestine outside Israeli control, became state property. This included land belonging to the Waqf (Islamic Trust), a sixth of the country before 1948 – "so God is an absentee too!" commented Palestinians sarcastically. On Israel's Independence, Jews had still only owned 6.6 percent of Palestine's land area: it was the Absentee Property Act which gave them the balance. Development of the land was funded through the JNF by massive donations from wealthy Jewish communities abroad, especially in the United States, and also by reparations for the Holocaust paid to Israel by West Germany.

Another controversial Act passed in 1950 was the **Law of Return**, giving every Jew the right to settle in Israel. Orthodox Jews have tried to restrict this right to exclude converted members of the non-orthodox Conservative, Reform and Liberal synagogues, and the debate about "who is a Jew" continues to this day (see p.503). The first wave of immigrants to take advantage of the new law were mainly Sephardim from Arab countries where, having lived peacefully for centuries, they now became the object of hostility, violence and persecution. Ashkenazi Jews of European origin tended to see these new immigrants as "backward", and the Sephardim faced a certain amount of discrimination which remains a problem and a source of friction in Israeli society, even leading to rioting on one occasion (see p.134).

The first **elections** for Israel's Knesset (parliament) were held in January 1949, and set the pattern for the next twenty-eight years, with Ben Gurion's "Labour Alignment" of the two main left-wing parties (Mapai and Mapam) dominant, but needing support from the religious parties, which meant accepting laws to impose religious observance, and giving special privileges to the ultra-orthodox Haredi community, including exemption from military service for religious scholars attending *yeshiva*.

In 1952, **Gamal Abd al-Nasser** launched a coup against Egypt's King Farouk, ousting the British from Egypt. Ben Gurion retired as PM in November and his place was unexpectedly taken by dovish Foreign Minister, Moshe Sharett, who opened up a line of communication to Nasser and started moving tentatively toward a permanent peace. But Ben Gurion used his protégés in the cabinet, in particular Defence Minister Pinhas Lavon, to undermine Sharett's position, ending communication with Nasser. At the 1955 election, Ben Gurion led the left and returned as Prime Minister. Egypt was now getting weapons from the Soviet Union, and Ben Gurion wanted a war before the Egyptian army could be trained to use them. In 1956, Nasser gave him the perfect opportunity when he precipitated the **Suez Crisis** by nationalizing the Suez Canal. Ben Gurion agreed with Britain and France to invade Sinai and give them a pretext to intervene. Israel's end of the deal would be a buffer zone in the Sinai, and control over Gaza's

restive Palestinians. On October 26, 1956, Israeli forces entered and occupied Gaza and Sinai; British and French troops landed at Port Said in response, but the USA refused to support them and the threat of UN sanctions forced all three invaders to withdraw. But UN troops were stationed on the Egyptian border, providing some defence from any attempt at invasion.

In 1963, Ben Gurion retired and was succeeded by **Levi Eshkol**. Meanwhile, a new element was added to the region in the form of an organized Palestinian resistance movement. Small bands of assassins had already been infiltrating the Green Line and killing Israeli kibbutzniks, but the nearest thing to a Palestinian anti-Zionist organization thus far had been **George Habash**'s Arab National Movement (ANM), which was Pan-Arab rather than Palestinian. In 1964, The Palestine Liberation Organization (**PLO**), was established in Jerusalem under the leadership of Ahmed Shuqairy. On January 1, 1965, the first military operation against Israel was launched by **Fatah**, not yet within the PLO, but eventually to become its main constituent group: this failed attempt to blow up the National Water Carrier, Israel's main water supply channel, made Fatah known throughout the Arab world. Fatah's leader was **Yasser Arafat**, who had founded it with Palestinian friends in Kuwait in 1961 as the Palestine Liberation Movement, inspired by the success of the Algerian FLN.

In the 1960s, Israel became increasingly an ally of the US, while Egypt relied more and more on Soviet support. In 1967, hoping to benefit strategically from a war, the Soviets falsely informed Egypt that Israel was amassing troops on the Syrian border. This set off a round of confrontation and sabre-rattling which led that June to the **Six Day War**, as Nasser formed an alliance with Jordan and Syria, ordered UN peacekeepers out of Gaza and Sinai, and blockaded the Gulf of Aqaba against Israeli shipping. Israel responded by destroying its adversaries' airfields and invading all three simultaneously, occupying in six days the whole of Gaza, Sinai, the West Bank and the Golan Heights. More Palestinian villages were destroyed and a further 380,000 Palestinians crossed the Jordan river to become refugees, some for the second time. The UN passed **Resolution 242**, calling for "a just and lasting peace" with Israel's withdrawal to pre-1967 boundaries in return for its acceptance by the Arabs "with secure and recognized boundaries", free navigation in international waterways and "a just settlement of the refugee problem". But Israel refused to withdraw on the grounds that its pre-1967 boundaries were not secure and unilaterally annexed East Jerusalem. The Arab countries, for their part, refused to recognize Israel. Guerrilla activity against Israel continued, often followed by Israeli reprisals. When Israeli forces attacked the Fatah base at **Karama** in Jordan on March 18, 1968, Fatah scored their first real success by repelling the IDF with help from the Jordanian army. In July 1968, at the fourth congress of the PLO's ruling council, Fatah and a number of other guerrilla groups joined it, and henceforth it became an umbrella organization of which they were constituent parts.

Levi Eshkol died in 1969 and was replaced as Prime Minister by **Golda Meir**, while Nasser was succeeded on his death the following year by Anwar Sadat, eager for a rapprochement with the United States. The West Bank (apart from East Jerusalem), the Gaza Strip and the Golan Heights were under military administration, with elected mayors who were seen by the PLO as collaborators. Defence Minister Moshe Dayan proposed that Israel should, as he put it, "**create facts on the ground**" in the Palestinian Territories by building Jewish settlements to establish a reason for not returning land. Some 42 were established by 1973, with 35 more on the drawing board, and the start of Soviet Jewish immigration in 1971 provided new immigrants who could be housed in them. The controversial **Allon Plan**, suggested by Deputy PM Yigal Allon, proposed Israeli settlement and annexation of strategically important areas in the West Bank and Gaza, while returning the main population centres to Jordan and Egypt respectively. Meanwhile, agriculture and industry in the Territories declined, making them dependent on the Israeli economy and producing a pool of cheap labour.

In October 1973 (the October, Ramadan or **Yom Kippur War**), Egypt and Syria attacked Israel simultaneously during the Jewish fast of Yom Kippur, taking the IDF by surprise (even though Jordan's King Hussein had flown secretly to Israel to warn Golda Meir in person). The Egyptians retook the east bank of the Suez Canal. Israel managed to turn the war around, and chased the Syrians halfway to Damascus, but the war brought about negotiations between Israel and Egypt, with Israel agreeing to a partial withdrawal from the Sinai. Golda Meir resigned in response to a report criticizing her government's unpreparedness for the 1973 war, and was succeeded by **Yitzhak Rabin**. Rabin was replaced as Labour leader during the 1977 election campaign by Shimon Peres; the election was won for the first time by the right-wing Likud party under former Irgun leader **Menahem Begin**, who formed a coalition with three religious parties. One factor behind the Likud victory was a commitment to the rights of Sephardim, the majority of Israeli Jews since 1965.

Following Sadat's visit to Israel in 1977, the **Camp David Accord** was signed by Israel, Egypt and the US. The peace treaty led to the staged withdrawal of Israeli forces from Sinai, mostly completed in 1982, although wrangling over the last town, Taba, continued until 1989. Proposals in the Accord for "Palestinian Autonomy" came to nought, and Likud stepped up settlement-building in the West Bank and Gaza, a policy particularly associated with the hardline Agriculture Minister, Ariel Sharon, while in 1981 Israel unilaterally annexed the Golan Heights. Israeli troops, however, forcibly evicted Jewish settlers from Sinai ahead of its return to Egypt.

In June 1982, responding to the PLO's control of South Lebanon as a result of that country's civil war, Israel invaded Lebanon in what was named "**Operation Peace for Galilee**". Opposition in Israel to the invasion was led by **Peace Now**, a pacifist movement originally set up in 1978 to hasten the Israel-Egypt peace talks. Israeli forces advanced as far as Beirut, and took effective control of it, but massacres of Palestinians in the Sabra and Shatilla refugee camps by far-right Christian Phalangist militias, which could not have been carried out without an Israeli blind eye, turned public opinion at home against the operation, and Israel agreed to withdraw to the Awali River, south of Beirut.

In 1983, Begin was replaced as Prime Minister by Stern Gang veteran **Yitzhak Shamir**, whose biggest problem was the **hyper-inflation** that the country was sliding into following its espousal of unfettered free-market economics under Likud. Inflation rose from 190 percent in 1983 to 445 percent in 1984, and led, along with the war in Lebanon, to an inconclusive result in the 1984 election and a

Labour-Likud **government of national unity** with Peres and Shamir alternating as Prime Minister. Israeli troops withdrew from most of Southern Lebanon, leaving a "security zone" 11–20km wide along the Israeli border, which was controlled by Israel's Christian allies in the South Lebanon Army, aided by Israeli military "advisers". Austerity measures at home led to a wave of strikes, but eventually brought inflation under control. In the Territories, there was a new wave of **settlement-building**; by the end of 1987, over half the West Bank's land area was covered with settlements.

One wave of **new immigrants** in the Eighties came from the Soviet Union, where *glasnost* allowed members of that country's massive Jewish community to emigrate. Soviet Jewish immigration peaked in the early 1990s, raising Israel's population by over 20 percent. The other main wave was from Ethiopia, where a secret airlift via Sudan began in 1980, suffered a major glitch when the Sudanese government's role was publicized in 1985, and was then continued on the quiet by the USA. Israel's rabbis insisted on symbolically converting Ethiopia's Jews on arrival in case they were not pukka Jews, but without telling them what they were doing, until Ethiopian rabbis protested vehemently. This and other unintentional slights have led to accusations that Israel has repeated with the Ethiopians the same errors of discrimination that were made with the Sephardi immigrants of the 1950s.

THE INTIFADA AND OSLO

Palestinian opposition to military occupation of the West Bank and Gaza grew steadily in the Seventies and Eighties. Bomb attacks by guerrillas belonging to Fatah, the PFLP and other PLO member groups were regular events in world news, but mostly ordered and carried out by Palestinians in exile. In December 1987, however, the vanguard of resistance shifted to the streets of the Palestinian Territories when the accidental killing of four Gaza Palestinians by Israeli troops (see p.450) led to riots in the refugee camp where they lived, spreading in days across the Territories to become the **Intifada**.

At first the Intifada was spontaneous and unorganized, though local activists soon started to organize strikes and protests. The PLO, based in Tunis, were taken completely by surprise, but gradually took the reins, setting up a **United National Leadership of the Uprising (UNLU)** that coordinated action, called strikes and orchestrated the campaign. Israel, too, was taken by surprise and found itself at a loss to deal with unarmed civil disobedience by the civilian population. Rather than order the use of arms, Defence Minister Rabin ordered his troops to use physical force (it was alleged that he gave an order to "break bones"; he always denied uttering those words, but he certainly ordered the army to beat demonstrators rather than shoot at them). Many Israeli conscripts, however, balked at the use of force against unarmed civilians, and repression of the Intifada became highly unpopular among much of Israeli public opinion, notably in the growing Peace Now movement. Meanwhile, in July 1988, Jordan relinquished its claim to the West Bank and, in November, the Palestinian National Council in Tunis declared a State of Palestine, while endorsing UN Resolution 242, and thus implicitly accepting Israel's right to exist for the first time. The following month, Yasser Arafat explicitly backed a **two-state solution** to the Israel-Palestine question, proposing both "a Palestinian state and a Jewish state, Israel." Also in November, an Israeli general election produced another hung Knesset and another Likud-Labour government of national unity, but growing Labour support for and Likud opposition to peace with the PLO caused its rapid disintegration and the formation of a Likud government under Shamir the following year. Among the Palestinians, a new force, Islamic fundamentalism in the shape of Islamic Jihad and Hamas, was making itself felt, especially in Gaza; along with left-wing PLO factions such as the PFLP and the DFLP, the fundamentalists refused to accept Israel's right to exist and continued to aim for its destruction.

Israeli repression of the Intifada alienated public opinion worldwide – film of IDF soldiers breaking the arms of demonstrators with rocks caused international protest – and split it in Israel, but the Palestinians also shot themselves in the foot by backing Saddam Hussein's 1990 **invasion of Kuwait**. When the USA and its Western and Arab allies attacked Iraq, Israel stayed out of it despite Scud missile attacks from Iraq on Israeli cities, earning political credit for their restraint. Palestinians, meanwhile, were expelled from the Gulf States, especially

Kuwait, bringing a massive loss of earnings, and their miscalculation severely weakened them diplomatically. The Intifada had deprived Israel's economy of cheap labour, but this was now being replaced by "**guest workers**" from Eastern Europe, Southeast Asia and West Africa, under a controversial system where foreigners are allowed to work in the country but have no citizenship rights nor right of abode. This turned the tables on the Palestinians whose strikes became in effect lockouts with the Green Line closed for days and weeks at a time, seriously hitting the economies of the West Bank and Gaza.

In July 1991, following its rapprochement with the United States, Syria agreed to direct negotiations with Israel. This paved the way for a series of four-way **peace conferences** between Israel, Syria, Lebanon and a joint Jordanian-Palestinian delegation to try for a permanent Middle East settlement. Unfortunately, little was achieved despite a general election in 1992, won by Labour, now again led by Yitzhak Rabin. Following the murder of an Israeli police officer by Hamas in December, Israel arrested and deported 400 alleged Hamasniks to Lebanon, where they were trapped in a no-man's-land between the Israeli "security zone" and government-controlled Lebanon. Matters were aggravated further by a July 1993 Israeli attack on Hezbollah targets in Lebanon that caused many civilian casualties, and the February 1994 massacre of 29 people in the Haram al-Khalil at Hebron by a right-wing Jewish settler (see p.410).

In spite of this, behind-the-scenes Norwegian diplomacy secured a major breakthrough in September 1993, when Israel and the PLO signed a Declaration of Principles that set the basis for what are usually termed the **Oslo Accords**. The Declaration proposed a phased withdrawal by Israel from the Palestinian Territories, the establishment of a **Palestinian National Authority** to run the areas vacated by Israel, and a final Israel-PLO settlement by the end of 1998, in which the status of Jerusalem would be the last question to settle. Opposition to the Accord came from hardliners on both sides including Likud and Hamas. Rabin and Arafat met in October 1993 in Cairo and, despite delays and disagreements, the peace process moved forward. In May 1994, Israeli forces withdrew from Jericho and the

Gaza Strip, which became the first areas under the jurisdiction of the newly formed PNA, with Yasser Arafat as its President and some trappings of statehood. Several Arab states recognized Israel and gradually more areas of the West Bank were turned over to the PNA. However, there has been criticism of this approach, some have even compared it to apartheid South Africa's policy of "independent" bantustans, while the PNA's suppression of fundamentalist groups has led to accusations by Hamas, Islamic Jihad, the PFLP and various human rights groups, of it being an Israeli stooge. In Israel, bomb attacks on civilians by Hamas and Islamic Jihad succeeded in turning Jewish public opinion against the peace process, while the Israeli government's response – closing the Green Line – did not endear it to Palestinian public opinion in the Territories. Even at this early stage, moreover, **abuses of human rights** by the PNA were being reported by human rights groups. A proliferation of shady security forces responsible only to Arafat in person, and press and party political restrictions brought in by the PNA, run largely by Arafat's colleagues from Tunis, led many to doubt his democratic intentions for the new Palestine, and tended to strengthen the hand of fundamentalists and other opponents of the peace deal.

In November 1994, **Rabin was assassinated** by a right-wing Jewish law student (see p.78) and for a time Israeli public opinion moved back behind the peace process so closely associated with him. Over the next year, Israeli forces withdrew from Jenin, Bethlehem, Nablus, Ramallah, Tulkarm and Qalqilya. The only major town in the West Bank still under Israeli jurisdiction was Hebron. In January 1996, elections on the West Bank and Gaza resulted in a massive victory for Arafat's Fatah, with a massive turnout despite a boycott by left-wing and fundamentalist parties. In April, the PNC finally got rid of all the articles in its covenant calling for the destruction of Israel.

In May 1996, Israel went to the polls. The result was a surprise victory for Likud under **Binyamin Netanyahu**, committed to slowing down the peace process and preventing the establishment of a State of Palestine. Although the new government agreed to meet commitments already made, and Netanyahu eventually met with Arafat in September 1996, despite an earlier promise not to, a policy of expanding settlements and building new ones has not gone down well among Palestinians. Violent confrontations in Hebron accompanied the Israeli government's agreement to turn part of the city over to the PNA while continuing to occupy the city centre with a settlement of ultra-orthodox right-wingers whose presence causes almost daily confrontation. Jerusalem has also become a major bone of contention with Israeli attempts to assert sovereignty over the eastern half of the city leading to violent demonstrations when, in September 1996 and without consultation, Israel opened to the public a tunnel under Temple Mount that some Palestinians claimed would undermine the al-Aqsa Mosque (see p.342), and when in February 1997 Israel began building a new settlement at Har Homa that East Jerusalem's Palestinians saw as a ploy to cut them off from the rest of the West Bank. In June 1998, Netanyahu's government proposed a further extension of Jerusalem's municipal boundaries, and the extension of its jurisdiction over certain services to Israeli settlements on the West Bank, a move widely seen as a step towards further annexation of West Bank territory.

To many, the peace process that held so much hope at its inception seems now to have ground to a halt. Whether it will be revived or disintegrate into yet another war remains to be seen. If Israel and Palestine are like Siamese twins who hate each other, the operation to separate them has hit complications, and whether either or both will survive is by no means certain. Outside interests have a part to play: following the Gulf War, many in the United States favour a Middle East realignment, with a group of pro-American states, that would include both Israel and Palestine as well as all their immediate neighbours, forming a common front against anti-American "terrorist states" such as Iran, Iraq, Sudan and Libya. But Israel is America's main protégé in the region, and the Clinton administration, the most pro-Israeli so far, is loath to push it too hard. Even when the peace process does get going, between fits and starts, Palestinian rejectionists are able to halt it with ease by murdering Israeli civilians and strengthening the hand of rejectionists on the Israeli side, while intransigence by Israel combined with the manifest failings of the PNA strengthen rejectionists on the Palestinian side. A peace of sorts there is, but a final settlement seems as far away as ever.

RELIGION IN THE HOLY LAND

The "Holy Land" is home to some of the most revered sites of the three great monotheistic religions, and as in many other parts of the world, religious fundamentalism – Jewish, Christian and Muslim alike – is on the increase. Almost everywhere you go, and particularly somewhere like Jerusalem, you'll be struck by the sheer number of berobed representatives of the three main religions. All have their own holy sites, and many of the most important are sacred to all three, often sources of contention among them and among factions within them.

For Jews, the principal place of prayer is the Western or **Wailing Wall** of the Temple Mount in Jerusalem; for Christians, the **Church of the Holy Sepulchre** in Jerusalem and the **Church of the Nativity** in Bethlehem; for Muslims, **al-Aqsa Mosque** and the **Dome of the Rock** in Jerusalem. As well as the "big three", there are other religious groupings – the **Druze** (see p.147), **Bahais** (see p.139), **Samaritans** (see p.440) and **Kara'ites** (see p.110). Each religion has its own laws, rituals, times and ways of worship, dress and holidays. In practice this means that opening times at the various sites will vary, that some place you wanted to visit may be closed for a festivity or fast, that what you are required to wear will be different. The best advice is to be prepared for all eventualities.

JUDAISM

The fundamental tenet of **Judaism** is belief in a single God; its most sacred text is the **Torah**, Pentateuch, or five books of Moses (Genesis, Exodus, Leviticus, Numbers and Deuteronomy), given by God to Moses on Mount Sinai. According to tradition, the Torah is both historical record and divine law, and a complete guide to human life. It forms the first part of the Hebrew **Bible** or *Tenakh*, whose books are the same as (though in a slightly different order from) those of the Christian Old Testament. The other two parts of the *Tenakh* are the books of the Prophets (*Nevi'im*), and the Sacred Writings, or "Hagiography" (*Ketuvim*).

According to the Old Testament, **Abraham** (originally named Abram) founded Judaism when he rejected the "idolatrous" religion of his father and migrated from Mesopotamia to Canaan. God rewarded him for his faith by promising the land to his descendants who would be a people special to God. This promise was renewed to Abraham's son Isaac and grandson Jacob (later renamed Israel). Together, the three are known as the **patriarchs** or forefathers of Judaism. It was **Moses**, though, who was the lawgiver, and to him that the Ten Commandments and the rest of the Torah, as well as the unwritten "oral law", were given on Mount Sinai after the Exodus from Egypt.

Many of the characteristic ideas and institutions of Judaism emerged during the **Babylonian exile** after the destruction of Solomon's Temple by Babylonian King Nebuchadnezzar in 586 BC, and following the **return** of the Judeans – now called **Jews** – under Cyrus the Great some 48 years later. The Babylonian exile marked the beginning of the Jewish **diaspora** or dispersion, since many Jews remained in Babylon which, in late antiquity and the Middle Ages, had one of the largest and most important Jewish communities in the world. In Babylon, much of the Hebrew Bible was rewritten, codified, annotated and completed; the ancient Hebrew alphabet – which the Samaritans still use – was replaced by the Aramaic one in which Hebrew is written today.

After the destruction of the Second Temple in 70 AD and the razing of Jerusalem after the Second Revolt in 132–35 AD, the centre of Judaism moved to the Galilee and Mesopotamia. The **rabbis** (Jewish sages and religious authorities) codified and elaborated the "oral law"; two such compilations – the **Talmud** – emerged. The vast Babylonian Talmud was compiled between 200 and 500 AD in the rabbinic academies of Babylon where Jews had lived continuously at least since Nebuchadnezzar's time; the second version, less complete and authoritative and often misleadingly called the Jerusalem Talmud, was compiled predominantly in Caesarea, Tiberias and Sepphoris. Both have the same starting point, an older part called the **Mishnah**, which was codified in Galilee around 200 AD, and a development and commentary on that called the **Gemara**.

The main internal crisis in Judaism came with the Karaite schism in the mid-eighth century (see p.110), but divisions also emerged in Eastern Europe in the eighteenth and nineteenth centuries with the **Hassidic** movement, which placed the emphasis on piety and prayer as opposed to the scholasticism of the Talmudic academies. The Hassidim maintained their identity, and still do, by their dress – black hats, long coats, sidelocks (*pey'ot*) and beards – while the less orthodox were more in favour of integrating into the societies in which they lived. A more recent split, mostly now centred in the United States and to a lesser extent Britain, was brought about by the rise of **Reform Judaism**, which began in Germany in the early nineteenth century, and which attempts to adapt traditional Judaism to the modern world. It has two modern branches: Conservative Judaism (confusingly known in Britain as Reform), which is more restrained in its reinterpretation, and Reform Judaism (known in Britain as Liberal or Progressive), which goes further. The reforms include many of the ritual laws, acceptance of modern biblical criticism, services in languages other than Hebrew, and full equality for women, even women rabbis. The divisions between Reform and Orthodox Judaism have recently put great strains on the religion (see opposite).

JUDAISM IN PRACTICE

The most obvious features of Judaism, apart from belief in the oneness of God, and the total eschewing of any representation of God as an image (shared by Islam and by much of Protestant Christianity), are observance of the Sabbath (*Shabbat*), and the dietary laws (*kashrut*).

The **Sabbath**, lasting from Friday night until Saturday night, since the Jewish day is measured from nightfall to nightfall, is not merely a holy day and a day of general rest, but a day on which no work whatsoever may be performed. What constitutes work is very clearly defined. It includes lighting or extinguishing a fire, which also means turning on or off a motor, or anything electrical. A fire may be *left* on throughout the Sabbath (hence the traditional Sabbath dish, *cholent*, cooked on a low light over twelve hours in an oven ignited on Friday evening and put out on Saturday evening), and setting a time switch to turn things on and off during the

Sabbath is also permissible. Other work prohibited during the Sabbath involves carrying anything outside the home, though a walled area called an *eruv* (such as a ghetto or walled Jewish city) is considered home for this purpose, and carrying something is distinguished from *wearing* it. This kind of legalistic definition creates a few loopholes, but not many.

Similar rules apply to Jewish **holy days**. Chief among these are **New Year** (*Rosh HaShannah*), a solemn religious occasion, and, even more solemn, **Yom Kippur** (the Day of Atonement) ten days later. This is a fast day, during which nothing may be eaten, and which is observed by many Jews who keep nothing else religious. **Succot** (Tabernacles) is a harvest festival commemorating the Israelites' nomadic existence in the wilderness following the Exodus, when Orthodox Jews build, and even live in, temporary structures attached to their homes for eight days. Next comes **Passover** (*Pesah*), a spring festival celebrating the Exodus from Egypt, when the fleeing Israelites had no time to leaven their bread and on which the consumption of anything that might be construed as leavened grain, or even to have come into contact with it (food has to be specially certified as leaven-free), is prohibited for eight days; **Shavuot** (Pentecost), celebrating the giving of the Torah to Moses on Mount Sinai, is seven weeks after Passover, the intervening period being the **Omer**, when celebration and festivity are avoided, as in the Christian Lent (**Lag Ba'Omer**, on the 33rd day, is a brief respite). Other Jewish festivals, without religious strictures, are **Hanukkah**, a winter solstice festival of lights to recall the Maccabees' rededication of the Temple after taking Jerusalem from the Seleucids (see p.107), and **Purim**, in memory of Persian Queen Esther's victory over anti-Semitic Prime Minister Haman in the biblical book named after her.

The dietary laws of **kashrut** revolve mainly around restrictions on the eating of meat. The Torah (Leviticus 11) specifies that of all animals, only cloven-hooved ruminants and scaly true fish may be eaten. That means that rodents such as rabbit, non-scaly fish such as eels or shark, and all invertebrates such as shellfish are prohibited (the Torah allows certain locusts and grasshoppers, but their exact identity is now uncertain, so sky prawns are also off the menu). The eating of pork is specifically condemned; it is, according to the Torah, "an abomination".

THE SHEMA'

Three times daily, practising Jews recite a prayer, **the Shema'**, consisting of three biblical passages. The first, from Deuteronomy 6: 4–9, translated into modern English, reads:

"Listen to Jehovah your God, Israel: Jehovah is One. Love Jehovah your God with all your heart, your soul and your might, and take these words that I am commanding you today to heart: instil them in your children and talk about them when you are sitting at home and when you are walking down the street, when you go to bed and when you get up. Tie them as a sign on your arm and tie them round between your eyes; write them on the doorposts of your house and on your gates."

The phrase "Jehovah is One" is a basic declaration of monotheism, implying that not only are there no other gods besides Jehovah, but that God is indivisible and cannot be seen as a multiple entity as in the Christian trinity or the Hindu pantheon. As commanded by the passage, observant Jewish men do tie these words to their arm and between their eyes, as you will see if you go down to the

Wailing Wall of a morning: those boxes strapped to their arm and head, called **tefilin** in Hebrew (phylacteries, if you want the correct English term), contain a scroll of parchment bearing the passages written out by hand. Likewise, the little box (**mezuza**) nailed to the right-hand doorpost of a Jewish home, and of each room bar the bathroom, contains a scroll bearing the same words.

The tassels that hang out from the clothing of Orthodox Jewish men are explained by the third passage in the same prayer, which is from Numbers 15: 37–41, and instructs Jews to put a fringe on the four corners of their garments with a sky-blue thread in it to look on and think of the sky and therefore God wherever they are. For that reason observant Jewish men wear a four-cornered garment under their shirts, with a tassel on each corner that they let hang out. The blue thread is missing because the exact dye to be used is no longer certain and the rabbis have decided that it is better to use none at all than to use the wrong one.

But *kashrut* does not end there: certain parts of an animal are out of bounds too, notably kidneys, and land animals must be killed in a specified manner – their throat slit and their carcass hung to drain the blood (some animal activists have condemned this as cruel, though Jewish religious authorities point out that the method is specifically defined to minimize suffering by the animal). Even then, blood must be extracted from all meat using salt before that meat can be eaten. Finally, following the biblical command "thou shalt not seethe a kid in his mother's milk" (Exodus 23: 19), meat and dairy products may not be eaten at the same sitting, nor is the same cutlery used for them. Thus all kosher restaurants are classified as either meat, dairy, or *parev* (neither).

If some of these strictures seem extreme compared to the original commandment, that is because observant Jews wish to avoid even the remotest possibility of breaking God's commands, and build "a wall around the law" to make sure of this.

JUDAISM IN ISRAEL

Israel's Jewish inhabitants are subject to the jurisdiction of the Chief Rabbinate, with separate **Chief Rabbis** for the Ashkenazi and Sephardi communities, in matters concerning *kashrut* (dietary laws), opening hours on Shabbat and other holidays, and marriage and divorce. Since a rabbi will perform a wedding only if both parties are Jewish, and there is no civil marriage and divorce in Israel, members of different faiths cannot marry there, and this includes marriages where one partner is Jewish through a paternal line only (the result is a booming trade in trips to Cyprus for a municipal wedding).

Under the **Law of Return** (see p.496), all Jews have a right to settle in Israel. This law has raised the question of "Who is a Jew?" According to a strict interpretation of the law, only those born to a Jewish mother or who have converted to Judaism according to the *halakha* (religious law) are Jewish. **Conversion** into the faith, though at one time commonplace, is nowadays very arduous (to discourage all but the most sincere), and puts off many who would convert largely for the purpose of marriage. Moreover, Israel's Orthodox rabbis do not recognize conversion by Reform synagogues (known in Britain as "Liberal" or "Progressive") or Conservative synagogues (known in Britain as "Reform"), which encompass a sizeable body of world Jewry including the vast majority of US Jews, and they reject out of hand the Reform synagogues' acceptance of those who are Jewish through a paternal rather than maternal line. When **Ethiopian Jews** arrived in Israel prior to 1985, Orthodox rabbis tried to insist on their symbolic reconversion to Judaism, and even tried to do it without telling the new arrivals what they were up to, until Ethiopian rabbis kicked up such a stink that they were forced to abandon this and reluctantly accept the Ethiopians as fully-fledged Jews without reconversion. One group whose status as Jews remains controversial are the **Black Hebrews**, a group of African Americans who believe themselves to be descendants of the ten lost tribes and have a community at Dimona in the Negev (see p.280).

The Orthodox lobby in Israel is influential: fundamentalist groups such as Shas, Agudat Yisra'el and the National Religious Party hold the balance of power in the Knesset, and other religious groupings, such as Gush Emunim and the Faithful of the Temple Mount, are at the forefront of the settler movement. The Chief Rabbis have declared that the *halakha* forbids the giving up of any part of the land of Israel to non-Jews, even if it means overruling the supreme law that the saving of life takes precedence. However, some ultra-orthodox Jews oppose the State of Israel altogether, believing that it is blasphemous, and that there cannot be a truly Jewish state until all Jews practise the **mitzvot** (religious duties) and thereby bring about the coming of the Messiah prophesied by Isaiah (7: 14, 9: 2–7 and chapters 11 and 12).

ISLAM

Islam, which in Arabic means submission (to God), originated in the early seventh century in Mecca, now in Saudi Arabia. The essential creed of Islam is that there is one God, Allah, and that Mohammed is his prophet. The basis of Islamic belief and practice, and the source of its legal and social system, is the **Koran**, the literal word of God dictated through the Archangel Gabriel to the **Prophet Mohammed**, who received it over a number of years beginning around 610 AD (the first verse that he received was almost certainly 96: 1: "Recite in the name of your Lord who creates: creates man from a clot of blood"). The Koran consists of 114 **suras** or chapters, arranged according to length and written in Classical

Arabic. One of the suras (number 17) describes Mohammed's **night journey** from Mecca to **Jerusalem** in the company of the Archangel Gabriel, where he prayed and then ascended to heaven. It was towards Jerusalem that Muslims first directed their prayers, and although this later changed, Jerusalem has remained the third holy site of Islam, after Mecca and Medina, and has long been a place of Muslim pilgrimage. The revelation which prompted the change of the **qibla** (direction of prayer) is set out in the second sura of the Koran, which established the **Ka'aba** in Mecca (Saudi Arabia) as the religious centre to which all Muslims have turned in prayer ever since. Mohammed claimed **Abraham** and his son Ismail (Ishmael in Hebrew) as founders of the Ka'aba and of Arabian monotheism, thus predating and independent of both Judaism and Christianity.

Mohammed was born in 571 AD in Mecca and worked for a merchant for whom he travelled along trade routes as far north as Damascus. He became disillusioned with the multiple idolatries of Arabia, with the exclusiveness of the Jews, and with the ritual and doctrine of the Christians. But the new monotheistic faith that Mohammed introduced into his native city of **Mecca** met with opposition and persecution so that, in 622 AD, he and his followers were forced to flee to **Medina**. It is from this event – the **Hegira** – that Islam is dated. Seven years after the Hegira, the new code of social justice had gained such influence that Mohammed was able to return to Mecca as a powerful political leader. After the Prophet's death in 632 AD he was succeeded by four **caliphs** (successors). It was under the third caliph, Uthman, that the revelations which had been preserved by Mohammed's followers were collected.

Not long after Mohammed's death, the spiritual leadership of Islam became a source of contention. The first three caliphs were all related to Mohammed by marriage, but the fourth, Ali, was not only the Prophet's son-in-law but also his cousin. A substantial minority – the **Shi'ites** – supported Ali (Shi'at Ali) and broke away from the mainstream **Sunni** Muslims. The Shi'ites believe that the Islamic community should be ruled only by a direct descendant of Mohammed (and therefore of Ali), called the **Imam**, a divinely appointed ruler who possesses superhuman qualities; the

Sunnis, on the other hand, supported the Ummayads, descended from Mohammed's uncle Ummaya, and later the Abbasids who deposed them in 749, as **caliphs**, responsible for the administration of justice through the **shari'a** (Islamic law) and for the defence of the realm of Islam. One of the offshoots of Shi'ite Islam is the **Isma'ilis**, who broke away from the mainstream of Shi'ite Islam over the question of succession on the death of the sixth Imam; the Fatimids, who ruled Egypt and Palestine in the eleventh century, were Isma'ilis. Non-Isma'ili Shi'ites recognize twelve Imams, the last of whom, Mohammed al-Muntazar, disappeared around 873, and is considered to still be living – the Hidden Immam, who will one day reappear and be known as the **Mahdi**.

In the seventh and eighth centuries, Islam extended through the Middle East and North Africa, later spreading to sub-Saharan Africa, India, China, Southeast Asia, parts of Russia and the Balkans and Spain. Islam was brought to Palestine in 638 AD under the third caliph, Omar Ibn al-Khattab, and the land lay under Muslim rule for the next 1300 years, interrupted only by around eighty years of Crusader dominance (1099–1187).

Islam shares a number of beliefs with Judaism and Christianity, accepting the Torah, Psalms and Gospel as divine in origin, but regarding them as corrupted texts which are superseded by the Koran (the Koran, being in perfect verse, is safe from alteration). There is no formally organized church or priesthood, but there are five fundamental duties, known as the **five pillars of Islam**, which a Muslim must perform: the **declaration of faith** (*shahada*) that there is no God but Allah, and Mohammed is His prophet; **prayer** (*salah*) recited five times daily at set times facing Mecca; the observance of **Ramadan**, the holy month when no food or drink must be taken from sunrise to sunset (those with specific difficulties are excused or may postpone the fast); the **giving of alms** (*zakah*); and the **pilgrimage** (*haj*) to Mecca, which should be undertaken at least once in a lifetime. Islamic fundamentalists often stress, too, the duty to fight a **jihad** (Crusade) to expand the faith or to defend it when under threat. Friday is not for Muslims a Sabbath as Saturday is for Jews or Sunday for Christians, but a day when Muslims should all pray communally if they can. As in Judaism, meat must be slaughtered by cutting the throat and draining the blood to be **halal** (permitted). Pork is forbidden (**haram**), as is alcohol (though arguably, it is not alcohol per se which the Koran forbids, so much as drunkenness).

PALESTINIAN MUSLIMS

The Muslims of Palestine are predominantly Sunni, with their own religious institutions. The **Supreme Muslim Council** consists of a president (Ra'is al-'Ulema) and four members, two representing the district of Jerusalem, one Nablus and one Acre, who are elected by an electoral college for a period of four years. The council, based in Jerusalem, has authority over all Muslim **Waqf** (plural: Awqaf) property and shari'a courts. The Awqaf are Muslim religious endowments, whose property is dedicated to charitable uses; the Waqf Committee in Jerusalem has authority over all Awqaf in Palestine. The **shari'a** courts, each of which is presided over by a **qadi** or judge, have exclusive jurisdiction in matters such as marriage, divorce and inheritance and can adjudicate in matters concerning Waqf properties.

The Waqf administers the Muslim holy sites of the Dome of the Rock, al-Aqsa Mosque and other Islamic institutions in Jerusalem, and often finds itself in dispute with the Israeli authorities about jurisdiction over the properties, notably over rights appertaining to Jerusalem's Temple Mount, and to adjacent properties such as the Western Wall tunnel (see p.342) and Solomon's Stables (see p.349). Even the Wailing Wall is in theory Waqf property (see p.340).

With the rise of Islamic fervour in Shi'ite Iran, and especially with the success of the Shi'ite population of South Lebanon in making life for the Israeli army there unbearable, the Muslim lobby in Palestine has grown. Fundamentalist groupings have been elected onto student unions at Palestinian universities, and the influence of Islam in the politics of already conservative areas, such as the Gaza Strip, is on the increase. One reason why fundamentalism tends to be stronger in Islam than in Judaism, Christianity or Hinduism, is that the Koran itself specifies legal and political norms, and the idea that a government should defend the faith goes back to the very roots of Islam itself: Mohammed, after all, was a political as much as religious leader.

One group whose claim to being Muslim is disputed are the Ahmadis, who have a small community in Haifa (see p.141). The Druze, originally a breakaway group from Isma'ili Shi'a Islam, have always been a separate religion (see p.147).

CHRISTIANITY

Christianity is based on the teachings of Jesus, which had their origins in Judaism. Central to Christianity is the belief in the **Trinity** (triple nature of God as Father, Son and Holy Spirit), and the divinity of Jesus as **Christ**, God the Son and also the Messiah prophesied by the Old Testament (Isaiah chapters 7, 11 and 12, and Micah chapter 5). According to the New Testament, Jesus is the only conduit between humanity and God. Jesus was a Jew, born in Bethlehem and resident in Nazareth. He taught in synagogues in the Galilee, gathering around Him twelve **Disciples** or **Apostles** who accompanied Him to Jerusalem, which He entered in triumph on Plam Sunday, but a week later He was arrested, tried and **crucified**. According to Christian belief, He was **resurrected** three days later (Matthew 28, Mark 16, Luke 24, John 20). By suffering and dying on the cross, Jesus atoned for the sins of humanity, thus offering salvation to all who accept Him.

Despite persecution under Nero and later emperors, Christianity spread rapidly through the Roman Empire. The belief was first taught orally by the Apostles but was later written down in the four **Gospels** of Matthew, Mark, Luke and John. The Gospels, together with the Acts of the Apostles, the Epistles and the Book of Revelation, constitute the **New Testament**, which covers a period from the birth of Jesus to the spread of Christianity and was written between 80 and 120 AD. Five patriarchates were established – in Antioch, Alexandria, Constantinople, Rome and Jerusalem – whose leaders (patriarchs) claimed that their line from the Apostles gave them the authority to disseminate correct doctrine.

In the early centuries of Christianity, Palestine was a hive of activity as hermits came to the desert to follow in Jesus's footsteps. At first living in isolated caves, they soon attracted followers and disciples, and founded desert hermitages that were the precursors of the **monastic** movement in Europe and elsewhere. The desert monasteries became important centres of study, and in them biblical texts were translated, copied and annotated.

In the fourth century AD, Emperor **Constantine** legitimized Christianity and declared it the state religion of the Roman Empire. Constantine's establishment of his new capital, Constantinople, led to a growing polarization between the **Eastern Orthodox Church** and the **Roman Catholic Church**. In the fifth century AD, the Syrian and Egyptian Churches, which were under Byzantine occupation, broke away from the Eastern Church to form **Oriental Orthodoxy**.

Despite the collapse of the Western Empire, Western Christianity spread vigorously, but the Orthodox Church became increasingly isolated until finally, in 1054, a formal separation from the Roman Catholic Church took place. A second major schism took place in the sixteenth century when the **Protestant** churches broke away from Rome, a movement basically against the wealth and simony of the established church towards a simpler form of worship, but with political roots too in the growing power of the northern European nations.

Thus there are four major branches of Christianity: **Eastern** and **Oriental Orthodoxy** in the East, and **Catholicism** and **Protestantism** in the West. Eastern Orthodoxy is composed of the Greek, Russian, Serbian and Bulgarian Orthodox churches; each has its own patriarch but all recognize the seniority of the Ecumenical Patriarch of Constantinople. Oriental Orthodoxy comprises the Armenian, Coptic (Egyptian), Ethiopian and Syrian Orthodox Churches, which do not follow Constantinople. Catholicism is primarily the Roman Catholic (Latin) Church but includes Eastern Catholics, such as the Maronite and Melkite Churches (see below) which keep their own liturgies but come under the jurisdiction of Rome. The Protestant churches embrace a multitude of varied and subdivided denominations.

Under Muslim rule from the seventh century AD, the Christians of Palestine, many of whom had converted under Byzantine rule, were free to practise their faith, most remaining Christian until around the eleventh century when conversion to Islam increased. In the twelfth century, the Western European **Crusaders** invaded Palestine, temporarily ousted the Orthodox Primate from Jerusalem and installed a Latin bishop. With the defeat of the Crusaders, the

Orthodox Church regained its place but Catholicism had established a foothold in the country. Later Catholic missionaries encouraged local Christians to detach themselves from the indigenous Orthodox Churches and to come under the patronage of the Papacy. Two Catholic Churches developed: the **Roman Catholic (Latin)** and the **Greek Catholic (Melkite)** (with Greek rites but under Rome).

CHRISTIANITY IN ISRAEL AND PALESTINE

From the fourteenth century until the establishment of Israel in 1948, some ten percent of Palestinian Arabs were Christian, but due to the exodus of Palestinians, the number has dropped to below three per cent. There is now a higher percentage of **Palestinian Christians** outside the country than in.

The vast majority of them are members of the three major churches: the Greek Catholic or Melkite, the Greek Orthodox and the Roman Catholic. The Greek Catholics live mostly in the Galilee area and come under the jurisdiction of the Melkite archbishops; the Greek Orthodox, mainly in the Jerusalem area, are under the Greek Orthodox patriarch who claims direct descent from St James, the first bishop of Jerusalem.

Whilst the patriarchs and bishops of the Melkite Church are entirely indigenous Palestinians, the hierarchies of the Greek Orthodox and Roman Catholic Churches have traditionally been dominated by Greeks and Italians. The European influence can be clearly seen in icons and paintings in Palestinian churches, almost all of which depict Jesus and the Virgin Mary as blonde and blue-eyed, even though they were both indigenous Semites. The Via Dolorosa in Jerusalem (see p.329), among other sites, is also largely a figment of European imagination. This century, however, there have been moves to bring Christianity back home: in January 1988, a Palestinian Arab, Michel Sabbah, was appointed Latin Patriarch of Jerusalem.

On top of these major divisions, there are a plethora of denominations from all over the world. In addition to the 2000-strong **Armenian** community (Catholics and Orthodox) in Jerusalem, there are also smaller congregations of Maronites, Copts, Ethiopian and Russian Orthodox, Syrian Catholics and Syrian Orthodox. Many newer churches also claim rights to the holy sites; these include Anglicans, Presbyterians (primarily the Church of Scotland), Seventh Day Adventists, Quakers, Mennonites, Mormons and Jehovah's Witnesses. A more recent phenomenon is the arrival of fundamentalist, **born-again Christians**, mostly North American, who believe that the State of Israel is the fulfilment of biblical prophecy. These Christian Zionists now have a "Christian Embassy" in Jerusalem to spread the message – one of their main aims is the conversion of Jews.

BOOKS

There are possibly more books written about Israel and Palestine than about anywhere else in the world, and certainly too many to list here. They range from early travel writings to ancient and modern histories, religion and archeology, the whole spectrum of politics, and some fiction in translation.

The selection that follows includes all the classics, and our own favourites, as well as a number of books on history or politics. Many of the latter are quite blatantly partisan, one way or the other, but we have tried to list those that are informative or interesting rather than just plain propaganda.

GENERAL BACKGROUND

The Bible The obvious book to read on the Holy Land, whether you regard it as a work of fiction or not. Parts of the Bible of particular interest to a traveller are: Genesis 12–50 dealing with the patriarchs; the "historical" books of the Old Testament (Joshua, Judges, I and II Samuel, I and II Kings, I and II Chronicles, Ezra, and Nehemiah), the Gospels, and the Acts of the Apostles. The King James (Authorized) Version is best-loved for the beauty of its language, but a modern English translation such as the Good News Bible is easier to read and understand.

George Antonius *The Arab Awakening*. One of the best historical accounts, considered a classic, of the origins and development of the Arab national movement from the nineteenth century to World War I, covering Ottoman rule, through the Arab Revolt and British involvement in it (Lawrence of Arabia), ending with the British and French mandates in the Middle East.

Abba Eban *Heritage: Civilization and the Jews*. British-educated Israeli statesman, diplomat and scholar, Abba Eban charts the history of the Jews from the time of Abraham to the establishment of the modern state of Israel, examining the Jewish influence on civilization throughout the ages. Illustrated with objects from museums around the world.

Isidore Epstein *Judaism*. A good all-round introduction, wide-ranging but concise, covering the Torah, the prophets, the Talmud and the Kabbalah, as well as Jewish philosophy and history, in accessible (and affordable) paperback form.

Werner Keller *Diaspora*. A comprehensive history of the Jewish people from Roman times to the foundation of Israel. Translated from the original German by Richard and Clara Winston.

Peter Mansfield *The Arabs*. A clear, perceptive and wide-ranging introduction to the Arab world, starting from the beginning of Islam and ending in the 1970s, with sections on individual countries.

Edward Said *Orientalism*. This heavyweight but extremely important book, written by Palestinian-born Professor of English and Comparative Literature at Columbia University in the US, sets out to show how the West discovered, invented and sought to control the East. The wide-ranging study covers nineteenth-century Western authors, travellers, politicians, linguists and archeologists who were caught in the trap of racism and colonialism, and shows how the myths and prejudices they created have lasted until today.

ARCHEOLOGY

Kathleen Kenyon *The Bible and Recent Archeology*. One of the foremost modern Palestinian archeologists, especially noted for her excavations at Jerusalem and Jericho, summarizes the changes in the interpretation of the Bible over the last forty years, based on the results of archeological discoveries. Illustrated by drawings and black-and-white photographs of excavation sites, this is one for the more serious student of archeology.

Jerome Murphy-O'Connor *The Holy Land: an Archeological Guide from Earliest Times to 1700*. A clearly written, detailed but accessible layperson's guide by a New Testament professor and Jerusalem priest, covering all the country's main archeological sites in alphabetical order, with historical and archeological accounts and site plans.

David Rohl *A Test of Time.* Readable and lavishly illustrated TV spin-off in which Rohl expounds his controversial theory that by redating the pharaohs we can see archeological evidence of characters and events from the Old Testament, and cast new light on sites in Israel and Palestine (see p.424).

Yigael Yadin (ed) *Jerusalem Revealed: Archeology in the Holy City 1968–1974* (Israel Exploration Society). A collection of articles by eminent Israeli archeologists, covering excavations undertaken at several locations in Jerusalem's Old City to show how they add to our knowledge of its Jewish, Christian and Muslim history.

HISTORY

Meron Benvenisti *City of Stone: the Hidden History of Jerusalem.* Balanced account of Jerusalem's history by former deputy mayor of the city.

Larry Collins and Dominique Lapierre *O Jerusalem!* Well-written and researched account of the 1948 struggle for Jerusalem seen through the eyes of participants, mainly from the Israeli point of view. A good, easy read.

David Hirst *The Gun and the Olive Branch: the Roots of Violence in the Middle East.* A critical survey of the Palestinian-Israeli conflict, written by a London *Guardian* journalist from a pro-Palestinian viewpoint. Clear, detailed and well-researched.

Flavius Josephus *The Jewish War.* An account of the 66 AD Jewish Revolt against the Romans by a rebel-turned-collaborator who was there. Josephus's *Antiquities*, a history of the Jews until his day, contains information obtained from the access the Romans gave him to the Temple archives.

Amin Maalouf *The Crusades Through Arab Eyes*, translated from French by Jon Rothschild (Al-Saqi). Account of the Crusades by a Lebanese journalist based on Arab chroniclers of the time, giving a completely different angle on a period normally seen only from a European point of view.

Howard M. Sachar *A History of Israel.* Thorough account of Israel's history since the beginnings of the Zionist movement, with which the author clearly sympathizes though he is not afraid to confront its failings or refute its myths.

Mark Tessler *A History of the Israeli–Palestinian Conflict.* The best recent history of the conflict based on fresh research, with no axe to grind for either side but a real feeling for the ordinary people involved.

PERSONAL TESTIMONY

Fawzi al-Asmar *To be an Arab in Israel.* Lively personal account, by journalist, poet and political activist, born in Haifa in 1937, of life in Palestine from the establishment of the Israeli state to his release from prison in 1970.

Yoram Binur *My Enemy, My Self.* A Jewish Israeli journalist disguises himself as an Arab to see life from the other side of the fence. His insights do little more than confirm what you (and he) probably suspected, but confirm it they do, and his anecdotes make interesting reading.

Elias Chacour *Blood Brothers* (Chosen Books). Chacour is pastor of the Melkite Church in the village of Ibilin, and studied the Bible and Talmud at the Hebrew University. Born in Bir'im, a border village from which the population was expelled, Chacour urges reconciliation between Arabs and Jews.

David Grossman *The Yellow Wind*, translated from Hebrew by Haim Watzman. The account of this Israeli novelist's journey into the West Bank in 1987 caused a sensation when it was published, and was described as "the most valuable contribution of all the millions of words produced by Israel to mark the anniversary of the Six Day War". Grossman talks with both Palestinians and Jewish settlers, and exposes his own moral dilemmas.

Beata Lipman *Israel: the Embattled Land. Jewish and Palestinian Women Talk About Their Lives.* A "journey of discovery" focused on Palestinian and Israeli women of all ages and viewpoints, throwing light on the changing situation of women and their experience of the conflict.

Amos Oz *In the Land of Israel.* One of Israel's foremost novelists interviews a cross-section of Israelis and Palestinians to record their views on the conflict, giving space to some very disparate viewpoints indeed.

Raja Shehadeh *The Third Way: a Journal of Life in the West Bank*. The author, a Palestinian lawyer and founder of al-Haq human rights organization, charts his personal experience of daily life in the West Bank.

David Shipler *Arab and Jew: Wounded Spirits in a Promised Land*. Shipler, correspondent for the *New York Times*, interviews a cross-section of Palestinians and Israelis across the spectrum of religious and political convictions.

BIOGRAPHY AND AUTOBIOGRAPHY

Menahem Begin *The Revolt*. Like him or loathe him, Begin cast a giant shadow over Israel's history. In this account of his role in Israel's independence, he attempts to justify his right-wing nationalist stance and his actions against the British and the Palestinian Arabs.

Michael Bar-Zohar *Ben Gurion*. A biography of Israel's first leader, based on his papers and on interviews with him. Readable and often insightful, but also rather fawning.

Alan Hart *Arafat: Terrorist or Peacemaker?* A biography of Arafat and history of the PLO based on interviews by a BBC foreign correspondent.

Golda Meir *My Life*. Meir, regarded in the West as a lovable Yiddische momma, is more harshly judged by Palestinians (for acts of oppression) and Israelis (for her government's errors and corruption). Her autobiography, though obviously avoiding such issues, makes an easy and relatively light read, and gives an interesting inside view of Israel's early political leaders and their thinking.

Robert Slater *Rabin of Israel, Warrior for Peace*. Thorough if less than critical biography of Yitzhak Rabin, a key figure in Israel's history since independence, and a man who always put himself at the heart of events.

CONTEMPORARY POLITICS

Henry Cattan *The Palestine Question*. The background and history of the Palestinian question, with a study of the various peace solutions by a Jerusalem-born international jurist, who was a lecturer at the Jerusalem Law School and represented the Palestinian Arabs at UN debates in 1947 and 1948.

Noam Chomsky *The Fateful Triangle*. The distinguished American linguist and libertarian intellectual deals with American policy towards and involvement in Israel.

Uri Davis *Israel: an Apartheid State*. In-depth study by a prominent anti-Zionist Israeli academic, examining the structures of the Israeli state to show how ninety percent of the country's land is reserved for Jews only.

Jonathan Dimbleby *The Palestinians*. Though now three decades old, this book by a much-respected British journalist, with great photos by Donald McCullin, remains a worthy testament to the Palestinian people, whose cause it did much to promote.

Amos Elon *The Israelis: Founders and Sons*. A prominent Israeli journalist quotes, compares and examines the ideals and attitudes of two generations of Israelis.

Simha Flapan *The Birth of Israel: Myths and Realities*. Fascinating and eye-opening book by an Israeli writer, publisher and peace activist, which sets out to debunk widely accepted myths about the foundation of Israel.

Robert I. Friedman *Zealots for Zion*. An examination of the West Bank settler movement, covering their history and their beliefs, and showing how they aim to take over the West Bank, and particularly relevant to Jerusalem and Hebron.

David Gilmour *Dispossessed: the Ordeal of the Palestinians*. A book in three sections: the first looks at Palestinian society before 1948, the second deals with the new diaspora, and the last section deals with resistance, the PLO, Lebanon and relations between the international community and Palestine.

Sarah Graham-Brown *Palestinians and their Society 1880–1946*. Beautifully produced photo-essay documenting the social and economic life of Palestinians through Ottoman and British rule.

Dilip Hiro *Sharing the Promised Land*. Excellent and incisive post-Intifada exploration of the history and politics of the Israel/Palestine question, which seems to leave no stone unturned in its examination of the issues.

Beverley Milton-Edwards *Islamic Politics in Palestine*. A comprehensive and well-researched, if rather academic, account of the rise of Islamic fundamentalism in Palestine, looking in particular at Hamas and its agenda.

Benny Morris *The Birth of the Palestinian Refugee Problem*. A revealing study based on Israeli, British and American documents, tracing the 1947–49 Palestinian exodus from Israel, examining its causes, along with Israel's decision to prevent the refugees' return, and the fate of their abandoned villages.

Michael Palumbo *The Palestinian Catastrophe*. Palumbo uses archive material from the US, Europe and Israel, as well as the testimonies of Jewish veterans, to argue that Ben Gurion always planned to "expel the Arabs and take their place".

Edward Said *The Question of Palestine*. One of the best historical accounts of Palestinian-Israeli conflicts, written from the Palestinian point of view. In *After the Last Sky*, Said combines his eloquence with the photos of Jean Mohr. *The Politics of Dispossession* is a collection of essays on the Palestinian question and related issues, written between 1969 and 1994.

Rosemary Sayigh *Palestinians: From Peasants to Revolutionaries*. A "people's history" recorded from interviews with camp Palestinians in Lebanon, from the period of the British Mandate, through the uprooting and the new reality of living as refugees, to the growth of the Palestinian resistance movement.

Shlomo Swirski *Israel: the Oriental Majority*, translated from Hebrew by Barbara Swirski. Dr Swirski's study of the history and present role of Sephardi Jews as Israel's underclass is an important contribution to a little-publicized aspect of Israeli society.

POETRY AND FICTION

Yehuda Amichai *Selected Poems*. English translations of some of the best works of perhaps the best contemporary Israeli poet. Well worth a look.

Soraya Antonius *The Lord* and *Where the Jinn Consult*. Two blockbuster novels set in Palestine at the end of the British Mandate, packed with characters and fast-moving action against a backdrop of struggle.

T. Carmi (ed) *The Penguin Book of Hebrew Verse*. The first anthology of Hebrew verse, covering all periods from classical to modern, with the Hebrew original alongside the English prose translation.

Orly Castel-Bloom *Dolly City*. Irreverent, Kafkaesque, surrealist novel by a young Tel Avivian novelist who has won several top writing awards in Israel.

Mahmoud Darwish *Selected Poems*, introduced and translated by Ian Wedde and Fawwaz Tuqan. Selections of excellent poetry by Darwish, a Haifa-born Palestinian member of the PNC, including such classics as *Identity Card*, *Letter from Home* and *To My Mother*. *Memory for Forgetfulness* is another collection by the same author.

Mahmoud Darwish, Samih al-Qasim and Adonis *Victims of a Map* (Al-Saqi). A bilingual anthology of new poetry by Darwish, al-Qasim, a Druze from the Galilee, and Adonis, a Syrian poet.

Risa Domb (ed) *New Women's Writing from Israel*. An anthology of short stories by Israeli women writers including well-known names such as Shulamith Hareven and Orly Castel-Bloom.

N. and A. Elmessiri (eds) *The Palestinian Wedding*. A bilingual anthology of some of the best contemporary Palestinian resistance poetry. The authors include Mahmoud Darwish, Samih al-Qasim, Tawfiq Zayyad, Rashid Hussein and Fadwa Tuqan. *A Land of Stone and Thyme*, by the same editors, is a collection of short stories by Palestinian writers from within the Palestinian Territories and beyond.

Michael Gluzman and Naomi Seidman (eds) *Israel: a Traveller's Literary Companion*. A modern, varied and very refreshing collection of Israeli short stories for the traveller, exploring different places, different styles and different attitudes.

Batya Gur *The Saturday Morning Murder; Literary Murder; Murder on the Kibbutz*. Israeli whodunnits by an accomplished writer giving an insight into Israeli life as well as being a jolly good read.

Emile Habibi *The Secret Life of Saeed, The Pessoptimist*, translated from Arabic by Salma Jayyusi and Trevor LeGassick. Emile Habibi, editor of the Haifa-based Arabic daily, *al-Ittihad*, is also a superb novelist and satirist. Saeed, the hero (or anti-hero) of this wonderfully funny and painful book, is a Candide-type character, gullible and wise at the same time, who somehow manages to walk the tightrope of contradictions of being a Palestinian citizen of Israel.

Amos Kenan *The Road to Ein Harod* (Al-Saqi). A political thriller by a peacenik and former

Stern Gang member, set after a military coup in Israel, when an Israeli opposition member making his way to Kibbutz Ein Harod, the centre of resistance, meets an Arab "going beyond Ein Harod", and the two travel together through a landscape of violence and impending doom.

Salma Khadra Jayyusi (ed) *Modern Palestinian Literature*. A massive collection, a definitive one indeed, of prose and poetry by contemporary Palestinian writers from both Palestine and the diaspora.

Simon Louvish *The Therapy of Avraham Blok, City of Blok, The Death of Moishe-Ganef*. In the first two books, Louvish, a film-maker who spent his youth in Israel and is now living in London, portrays the surreal chaos of Israel, and specifically Jerusalem. His myriad characters rush, tumble and collide with resurrected figures from the past in a wonderfully funny, and often tragic, confusion of madness. The third novel, set in London and Jerusalem, is a hilarious "whodunit" satire, with innocents caught up in Mossad murders, plots and intrigues in the country and abroad.

James Michener *The Source*. Michener's usual treatment of a country's history applied to Israel and Palestine in a well-researched, rather schmaltzy, but unputdownable account of the country's history through fictional accounts of its inhabitants' lives.

Amos Oz *My Michael, The Hill of Evil Counsel, The Black Box, Elsewhere Perhaps*. Amos Oz has gained some acclaim as one of Israel's finest prose writers. The first novel, set in Jerusalem of the 1950s, tells the story of a marriage that goes wrong; the second is a group of three stories that take place in Jerusalem during the British Mandate. Although his characters seem at times a little flat, the books do offer an insight into Jewish concerns and aspirations in the early days of the Israeli state.

Anton Shammas *Arabesques*. Shammas is a Palestinian from within the pre-1967 borders of Israel who made the headlines by writing in Hebrew. This is a translation of his first novel.

Michal Snunit *The Soul Bird*. This cult children's book, now a worldwide bestseller, but rather over-sentimental for some tastes, is a description rather than a story, of a bird which represents the human soul.

Leon Uris *Exodus*. Melodramatic account of the struggle for Israeli Independence based around the voyage of the famous immigrant ship whose Holocaust survivor passengers were barred from Palestine by the British and eventually sent back to Germany. The book looks at both where they came from, and where they were headed to.

A. B. Yehoshua *Continuing Silence of a Poet*: collected short stories, *Five Seasons, Late Divorce*. An Israeli novelist deals with the contradictions and tensions of Israeli society, particularly within the Jewish community.

GUIDES: ANCIENT AND MODERN

FIELD GUIDES

Bemert and Ormond *Red Sea Coral Reefs* (Routledge). All you ever wanted to know about the Red Sea reefs – and more.

Dave Gosney *Finding Birds in Israel* (Gostours). A handy bird-watchers' booklet published by a small British firm in Sheffield.

Hollom, Porter, Christensen and Willis *Birds of the Middle East and North Africa* (Poyser). The best published for this region.

Polunin and Huxley *Flowers of the Mediterranean* (Hogarth). Not specific to Israel, but the best field guide you'll find.

Hadoram Shirtai and Ofer Bahat *Birdwatching in the Deserts of Israel* (Israel Ornithological Centre). A field guide to Israeli desert birdlife which has the advantage of being available inside the country itself.

GUIDES TO PALESTINE

Baedeker *Palestine*. The guide no early twentieth-century traveller would be seen without. Originals are available – though early ones are valuable – and there's also an American abridged reprint, *Baedeker's Historical Palestine*.

Cook's Travellers Handbook *Palestine and Syria* (London, 1929). One of the best of the early travel guides, packed full of quirky tips and sometimes bizarre information.

Canon J. E. Hanauer *The Folklore of the Holy Land* (London, 1907), *Walks about Jerusalem* (London, 1907). Both are readable, enjoyable and surprisingly relevant.

Thomas Hodgkin *Letters from Palestine*. Reprinted letters of a colonial civil servant travelling in Palestine between 1932 and 1936.

Luke and Roach *The Handbook of Palestine and Syria* (Macmillan, 1930). The official government issue handbook for Mandate officials. Good on history and archeology, and full of arcane information such as the number of goats in Safed.

Fr B. Meistermann *Guide to the Holy Land.* (OFM, 1923). One of many from this prolific writer on the Middle East, with some perceptive description.

LANGUAGE

Although both Hebrew and Arabic are official languages, who speaks what, when, where and to whom can be a minefield as bewildering to an outsider as other more directly political issues.

Within Israel, **Hebrew** is the dominant language, though the Palestinian minority, including the Druze, speak Arabic, and many Israelis, especially Sephardim, are able to speak it (but may not like to do so). Arabic is the language of the West Bank, the Gaza Strip and the Golan Heights, spoken by all bar the Israeli settlers. Again, most Palestinians are able to speak some Hebrew, but may be loath to do so: on the whole, it is better to address them in English, which is widely spoken by Jew and Arab alike, on both sides of the Green Line.

Many **Israelis** speak languages other than Hebrew, determined by their or their parents' country of origin. Thus, many Ashkenazi Jews may know languages such as English, French, German or Russian. Some, especially the ultra-orthodox (many of whom regard it as sacrilegious to have ordinary conversations in Hebrew, a holy language of prayer), may speak **Yiddish**, a language based on German mixed with Hebrew and Polish, that has given us words like nosh, spiel, schlep and schmooze; anyone who speaks German should be able to understand a lot of Yiddish and vice versa. Sephardi Jews may well know languages such as Arabic, Farsi or Turkish, or they may speak **Ladino**, a dialect of medieval Spanish, which speakers of modern Spanish should be able to understand reasonably well. Note that, despite their origins, Yiddish and Ladino are written with the same alphabet as Hebrew.

Palestinians from inside the Green Line will know Hebrew, and most speak and read it fluently. It is usually important in their jobs and many will follow the Hebrew-language press and media. But Arabic is the mother-tongue which Palestinians on both sides of the Green Line speak at home and among friends.

NUMBERS

	HEBREW	ARABIC			HEBREW	ARABIC	
1	ekhad	wahid	١	18	shmona esray	tamantaash	١٨
2	shtayim	itneen	٢	19	tsha esray	tisataash	١٩
3	shalosh	talata	٣	20	esrim	ashreen	٢٠
4	arba	arba	٤	21	esrim ve-ekhad	wahid w-ashreen	٢١
5	khamaysh	khamsa	٥	22	esrim ve-shtayim	itneen w-ashreen	٢٢
6	shaysh	sitta	٦	30	shloshim	talateen	٣٠
7	sheva	sabaa	٧	40	arbaim	arbaeen	٤٠
8	shmoneh	tmaniya	٨	50	khamishim	khamseen	٥٠
9	taysha	tisaa	٩	60	shishim	sitteen	٦٠
10	eser	ashara	١٠	70	shivim	sabaaeen	٧٠
11	ekhad esray	hidaash	١١	80	shmonim	tamaneen	٨٠
12	shtaym esray	itnaash	١٢	90	tishim	tiseen	٩٠
13	shalosh esray	talataash	١٣	100	maiya	meeya	١٠٠
14	arba esray	arbataash	١٤	200	matayim	meetain	٢٠٠
15	khamaysh esray	khamastaash	١٥	300	shalosh maiyot	talata meeya	٣٠٠
16	shaysh esray	sittaash	١٦	400	arba maiyot	arba meeya	٤٠٠
17	sheva esray	sabataash	١٧	1000	elef	alf	١٠٠٠

In the West Bank and Gaza, many people speak and understand Hebrew, particularly the young, and especially those who have found themselves on the Israeli employment market. But for them it is the language of occupation and visitors to these areas are advised not to practise their Hebrew there. Palestinians, however, are always delighted when foreigners try to speak Arabic, however falteringly, and any attempt to speak it will be greeted with enthusiasm. In the Golan Heights, many of those who you meet will be Israeli, though the Druze speak Arabic, as do their co-religionists in Israel itself.

The big problem with Arabic, especially for those who have learnt it elsewhere, is that local spoken versions of the language are very different and often mutually incomprehensible. Palestinian Arabic is not the same as Syrian, Egyptian or Gulf Arabic, let alone the dialects of Morocco or Tunisia. Most Arabic speakers will try, when speaking to a foreigner or to an Arab from elsewhere, to tone their speech towards Classical Arabic (the language of the Koran) or Modern Standard Arabic (the modern written language). Of colloquial Arabic, Egyptian is most likely, apart from Palestinian, to be understood, because of Egypt's cultural weight in the Arab world, and especially its prolific film industry.

In the **phonetic system** in the following boxes, kh is always pronounced as the ch in loch; gh as a guttural g.

HEBREW

Yes/No	ken/lo	. . .the post office	. . .ha-do'ar
Please	bevakasha	. . .the toilet	. . .ha-bait shimush
Thank you	toda raba	Left/right/straight on	smol/yemin/yashar
You're welcome (response)	al lo davar	Near/far	karov/rakhok
		Here/there	po/sham
Hello	shalom	When . . . ?	matai . . . ?
How are you?	ma shlomkha (m)/shlomekh (f)?	. . .is the bus	. . . ha-autobus
		First/last/next	ha-rishon/ha-akharon/ha-shaini
Fine, thank you	beseder		
Goodbye	shalom	Today	ha-yom
See you	lehitra-ot	Tomorrow	makhar
Good morning	boker tov	Yesterday	etmol
Good evening	erev tov	What time is it?	ma ha-sha'a?
Goodnight	laila tov	How much is that?	kama zeh?
Sorry, excuse me	slikha	It's too much	zeh yoter midai
Never mind	ain davar	I want something . . .	ani rotzeh (m)/rotzah (f) mashehu
What's your name?	aikh korim lakha (m)/lakh (f)?		
My name's . . .	korim li . . .	. . .cheaper	. . .yoter zol
Do you speak Hebrew?	ata medaber Ivrit?	. . .better	. . .yoter tov
A little . . .	ktsat . . .	. . .bigger/smaller	. . .yoter gadol/katan
What's that in Hebrew?	ma zeh be-Ivrit?	Do you have (anything) . . .	yesh lekha (mashehu) . . .
How do you say . . . ?	aikh omrim . . .?		
Where is . . . ?	eifo yesh . . . ?	There is/is there? . . .	yesh/yesh? . . .
. . .a clean hotel	. . .malon naki	There isn't . . .	ain . . .
. . .a restaurant	. . .misada	I don't want . . .	ani lo rotzeh (m)/rotzah (f)
. . .the bus station	. . .eifo takhanat ha-autobus	I don't understand	ani lo meveen(m)/meveena (f)
. . .the taxi to . . .	. . .ha-sherut li . . .		

HEBREW (cont.)

I'm tired	ani ayaif (m)/ ayaifa (f)	kilo	kilo
		half	khetzi
...hungry	ani re'ayv (m)/ re'ayva (f)	quarter	reva
...thirsty	ani tsamay (m)/ tsmaya (f)	Saturday	shabbat
		Sunday	yom rishon
		Monday	yom shaini
Everything's OK	ha-kol beseder	Tuesday	yom shlishi
		Wednesday	yom revi'i
Let's go	yalla	Thursday	yom khamishi
		Friday	yom shishi

Hebrew phrasebooks and courses

Modern Hebrew is a language created by Eliezar Ben Yehuda at the beginning of the twentieth century from biblical Hebrew, with the addition of words from European languages. Since it was necessary to teach a standard language to successive waves of immigrants into the new country, there is no shortage of phrasebooks, course books or *ulpanim* – Hebrew language schools, mainly aimed at new immigrants. Good **phrasebooks** include *Say it in Hebrew* and *Berlitz Hebrew for Travellers*, both widely available. The standard **course book** is *Elef Milim* which provides you with a basic 1000 words. Many kibbutzim run *ulpan* courses, offering half-day studies and half-day work. There are also Hebrew **classes** in town-based *ulpanim*, such as Ulpan Akiva (PO Box 6086, Netanya 42160; %09/835 2312 or 3, fax 865 2919) which runs a variety of residential courses ranging from 24 days to twenty weeks, with prices starting at just under $2000, and not specifically immigrant-oriented. For information on other *ulpanim*, contact the Ulpan Office at 11 Bet Ha'Am, Bezalel Street, Jerusalem 94591.

ARABIC

Arabic phrasebooks and courses

While it is different from the Modern Standard Arabic found in most English-Arabic phrasebooks, Palestinian Arabic does bear some similarities to it. There are no **phrasebooks** specifically geared to Palestinian Arabic, but if you scour the bookshops, particularly in East Jerusalem, you may be lucky enough to come across a large green book, simply called *Lessons in Spoken Arabic*, by Y. Elihai – and even luckier to find the cassettes that go with it – or *Let's Speak Arabic*, a beginner's course by Omar Othman. Both of these are course books rather than phrasebooks, but are highly recommended. Others, rather more Egyptian-based, are *Getting By In Arabic* by Salah el-Ghobashy and Hilary Wise, which comes with two cassettes and has a useful quick reference word list; *Colloquial Arabic of Egypt, Syria, Iraq and Saudi Arabia*, by DeLacy O'Leary, shows its outdated, Orientalist bent in such phrases as "Boy, do not beat your donkey"! *Berlitz Arabic for Travellers* is as good as any of the standard phrasebooks.

If you're serious about learning and have the time, both Bir Zeit University and the Hebrew University run summer courses. Bir Zeit's covers either Modern Standard Arabic or Palestinian Colloquial Arabic, and there are courses at all levels. For further information contact Bir Zeit University, Bir Zeit, near Ramallah, West Bank, or in Britain, Friends of Bir Zeit University, 21 Collingham Rd, London SW5 0NU (☎0171/383 8414).

ARABIC

Yes/No	aiwa/la shukran	Here/there	hoon/hoonak
Please	min fadlak (m)/fadlik (f)	When . . . ?	imta . . . ?
Thank you	shukran	. . .is the bus to	. . .el-bus ila
You're welcome (response)	afwan	First/last/next	el-awal/el-akhir/et-tani
Thank you (for food)	sallim idaik (m)/ idaiki (f)	Today	el-yom
		Tomorrow	bukra
(after eating)	ammar	God willing	insha Allah
Hello	marhabah	Thank God	el hamdu lil-lah
Hello (response)	marhabtain	What time is it?	ad-eesh es-sa'a?
Hello (formal)	assalamu aleikum	How much is that?	ad-eesh hada?
How are you?	keef halak?/ shu akhbarak? (m)	It's too much/ expensive	hada ktir/ghali
	keef halik?/ shu akhbarik? (f)	I want something . . .	bidi aishay . . .
		. . .cheaper	. . .arkhas
Fine, thank you	mabsut/mnih (m) mabsuta/mniha (f	. . .better	. . .ahsan
		. . .bigger/smaller	. . .akbar/asghar
Goodbye (leaving)	bi-khatrak (m)/ khatrik (f)	Do you have (anything) . . .	fi 'andak (aishay) . . .
Goodbye (response)	maa salameh	There is/is there . . .?	fi/fi . . .?
Good morning	sabah el-kheer	There isn't . . .	ma feesh . . .
Good morning (response)	sabah en-nur	I don't want . . .	bideesh . . .
		I don't understand	ana mush fahim (m)/ fahmeh (f)
Good evening	masa el-kheer		
Good evening (response)	masa en-nur	I'm tired/unwell	ana taaban (m)/ taabaneh (f)
Goodnight	sayeedeh	. . .hungry	. . .jawaan (m)/ jawaaneh (f)
Sorry	aasif (m)/aasifa (f)	. . .thirsty	. . .atshaan (m)/ atshaaneh (f)
Never mind	maalesh/baseeta		
What's your name?	shu ismak (m)/ismik (f)?	Everything's OK	kulshay tamaam
My name's . . .	ismi . . .	Let's go	yalla
Do you speak Arabic?	btehki Arabi?		
A little . . .	shwaiyeh . . .	kilo	kilo
What's that in Arabic?	shu hada bil-Arabi?	half	nus
How do you say . . . ?	keef bitool . . .	quarter	rub'
Where is . . . ?	wain fi . . . ?		
. . .a good hotel	. . . otel mnih	Saturday	yom es-sabt
. . .a restaurant	. . . mataam	Sunday	yom el-ahad
Where is the bus station?	wain mahatat el-bus?	Monday	yom el-itneen
		Tuesday	yom et-talaata
. . .the service to . . .	. . .es-service ila . . .	Wednesday	yom el-arba
. . .the post office	. . .el-bareed	Thursday	yom el-khamees
. . .the toilet	. . .el-hamam	Friday	yom el-juma'
Left/right/straight on	shimaal/yemin/dughri		
Near/far	areeb/bayeed		

GLOSSARY

In the following list of words, Ar = Arabic, Heb = Hebrew, Tur = Turkish, and Yid = Yiddish.

ABBASIDS Dynasty of caliphs who ruled the Arab empire from Baghdad 749–1258

ABU (Ar) Father, often used as part of a name or nickname

AID (Ar) Muslim festival

AIN (Ar/Heb) Spring

AL-/EL- Arabic definite article ("the")

ALA Arab Liberation Army, volunteer force set up by Fawzi al-Kaukji to fight for Arab Palestine in 1948 (see p.494)

ALIYA (Heb; literally "going up") Immigration of Jews to Palestine/Israel (First Aliya 1881–1903; Second Aliya 1904–18; Third Aliya 1919–23; Fourth Aliya 1924–28)

ANM Arab National Movement, a pan-Arabist, anti-Zionist organization founded by George Habash in Beirut, 1952

ARGILA (Ar) Hookah pipe

ARIANISM Early Christian heresy based on an attempt to reconcile Christianity with Germanic pagan religions

ARK The place where the Torah scrolls are kept in a synagogue, basically a cupboard in the wall that you look towards if facing Jerusalem and which indicates the direction of prayer

ASHKENAZI (Heb) Jews of European or Western origin (from *Ashkenaz*, meaning the Rhineland)

ASSIMMON (Heb; pl. Assimmonim) Old telephone tokens

ATZMA'UT (Heb) Independence

AVODA (Heb; literally "work") Labour Party

AYYUBIDS Dynasty of sultans founded by Saladin who ruled Egypt and Palestine 1171–1250

BIR (Ar) Well

BIRKAT (Ar) Pool

BAB (Ar) Door or gate

BALADIYA (Ar) Municipality or town hall

BCE Before the Common, Current or Christian era; a "non-Christian" version of BC, often used by Jewish historians

BEIT (Heb) House

BET (Ar/Heb – sometimes transcribed as Beth or Beit) House

BETH (Heb) House

BET KNESSET (Heb) Synagogue

BIMA (Heb) Raised platform in the centre of a synagogue, from which the Torah is read to the congregation

BORJ/BURJ (Ar) Tower or fort

CALIPH (Ar) Muslim ruler, successor to the Prophet Mohammed as leader of the Muslim community

CARAVANSERAI Inn for travellers and traders

CE Of the Common, Current or Christian era; a "non-Christian" version of AD, often used by Jewish historians. See also BCE

CHUTZPAH (Yid – the "ch" pronounced as in "loch") Barefaced cheek, and then some

CONDITORY Café and patisserie

DAR (Ar) House

DEIR (Ar) Convent

DEREKH (Heb) Way or major road

DFLP Democratic Front for the Liberation of Palestine, a PFLP splinter group under Nayef Hawatama, also called the PDFLP

DIASPORA The world outside Israel where the Jews lived in exile, and now more widely used for any peoples in exile

DOS (Heb slang – pl. Dossim) Derogatory term for ultra-orthodox Jews, imitating the Yiddish pronunciation of *dat* meaning "religious"

DUNAM/DUNNUM (Ar/Heb) A thousand square metres, or a tenth of a hectare; roughly a quarter of an acre

EID (Ar) Muslim festival

EIN (Ar/Heb) Spring

EMIR (Ar) Prince or commander

ERETZ YISRA'EL (Heb) Literally, the Land of Israel, but often a euphemism for "Greater Israel"

ETZEL (Heb acronym) The Irgun, a right-wing pre-independence Jewish paramilitary (see p.492)

FALASHA Originally a derogatory term for Ethiopian Jews used by their non-Jewish neighbours in Ethiopia and for a time by Western journalists, but never by Ethiopian Jews themselves

FATAH (Ar acronym meaning "Palestine Liberation Movement") The main faction of the PLO (see p.496)

FATIMIDS Dynasty of Isma'ili caliphs who ruled Egypt 961–1171

FEDA'I (Ar – pl. Feda'iin) Freedom fighters or guerrillas

FELLAH (Ar – pl. Fellahin) Farmers, agricultural workers

GALUT (Heb) The Jewish diaspora

GAN (Heb) Garden or park

GEMARA (Heb) Expansion of the Mishnah to form the Talmud (see p.501)

GLACIS Sloping fortification

GREEN LINE The 1949 armistice line between Israel and the rest of Mandate Palestine: Israel proper is "inside" the Green Line; the West Bank and the Gaza Strip are "outside" it (though Israel regards the Golan, East Jerusalem and Latrun as inside the Green Line)

GUSH (Heb) Bloc, as in Gush Emunim (Bloc of Believers), Gush Etzion (Etzion Bloc)

HA- (Heb) Definite article ("the")

HAGANAH (Heb) Underground Jewish defence force established in 1920. See p.492

HAJ (Ar) Pilgrimage to Mecca; one who has made the pilgrimage

HALAKHA (Heb) Jewish religious law

HALAL (Ar) Permitted by Islamic law

HAMAS (Ar acronym meaning "Islamic Resistance Movement") Islamic fundamentalist movement founded in 1987; see p.450

HAMMA (Ar – pl. Hammat) Hot spring

HAMMAM (Ar) Bath

HARA (Ar) Area or quarter of a town or village

HARAM (Ar – literally, forbidden) Holy sanctuary or precinct, but also anything which is not halal

HAREDI (Heb – pl. Haredim) Ultra-orthodox Jew

HASSID (Heb – pl. Hassidim) Member of the main movement of ultra-orthodox Jews

HATTA (Ar) Keffiya (see below)

HERUT (Heb) Right-wing Israeli political party, precursor to Likud (see below)

HIJRA (Ar) Mohammed's 622 AD flight from Mecca to Medina, from which Islamic years are dated

HISTADRUT (Heb) Zionist labour federation

HOF (Heb) Beach

HURVA (Heb) Ruin

IDF Israel Defence Force, the Israeli army

INTIFADA (Ar) Palestinian uprising in the Palestinian Territories 1987–93 (see p.498)

IRGUN (Irgun Zvi Le'umi) Pre-1948 Revisionist Zionist paramilitary led by Menahem Begin (see p.492)

IRIYA (Heb) Town hall or municipality

ISLAMIC JIHAD Radical Islamist paramilitary

JAMA'A (Ar) Mosque

JEBEL/JABAL (Ar) Mountain

JUDEA AND SAMARIA The West Bank (with the implication that it is part of "Eretz Yisra'el")

KABBALA (Heb) Jewish mysticism (see p.243)

KAKH (Heb acronym) Extreme right-wing (and illegal) political party advocating expulsion of Palestinians

KALA'A (Ar – Kala'at when followed by a name) Fort

KANYON (Heb) Shopping mall

KEFFIYA (Ar) Men's headdress, symbol of Palestinian resistance: a black and white one indicates support for Fatah, red and white for left-wing factions such as the PFLP

KFAR (Heb) Village

KHAN (Ar) Caravanserai or inn for travellers and traders

KHANQAH (Ar) Sufi hostel or hospice

KHIRBE (Ar) Ruins

KIBBUTZ (Heb – pl. Kibbutzim) Communal settlement based mainly on agriculture (see p.62)

KIKAR (Heb) Square

KIPPA (Heb) Jewish skullcap

KIRYA (Heb) see QIRYA

KNESSET (Heb) Israeli Parliament

KORAN (Ar) Muslim holy scriptures

KOSHER (Heb) In accordance with Jewish religious law, especially food

KUFR (Ar) Village or hamlet

LEHI (Heb acronym meaning "Fighters for the Freedom of Israel") The Stern Gang, a right-wing pre-independence Jewish paramilitary (see p.85)

LEVANT (adjective: Levantine) Geographical area encompassing Israel, Palestine, Lebanon, Syria and Jordan

LIKUD (Heb; literally "light") Main right-wing Israeli political party

MA'ABARA (Heb) Absorption camp for new Jewish immigrants

MA'NIDS Dynasty of Druze emirs who ruled Lebanon and the Galilee 1516–1633 (see p.487)

MADRASA (Ar) School – originally only for religious studies, but often now with a wider remit

MAGEN DAVID (Heb) Star (literally, shield) of David – the hexagram star apparently used by David on his shield, the symbol of Judaism, used in the Israeli flag

MAGEN DAVID ADOM (Heb) "Red Star of David", the equivalent of the Red Cross or Crescent

MAJDAL (Ar) Tower

MALON (Heb) Hotel

MAMLUKS/MAMELUKES Slave-descended professional soldiers who ran the army under Ayyubid and Ottoman rule, and themselves provided Egypt and Palestine's rulers 1250–1516 (see p.486)

MAPAI (Heb acronym) Israeli Labour Party founded in 1930, merged with two other parties to form Avoda in 1968

MAPAM (Heb acronym) Left-wing Israeli political party, now merged with Meretz

MASHRABIYA (Ar) Lattice-work window, usually of wood

MASTABA (Ar) Stone bench

MENORA (Heb) Seven-branched candelabra, a Jewish and Israeli state symbol; a nine-branch version is used for the festival of Hanukkah

MERETZ (Heb acronym) Left-wing Israeli political party, now merged with Mapam

MIDAN (Ar) Square

MIDRAHOV (Heb) Pedestrianized street

MIGDAL (Heb) Tower

MIHRAB (Ar) Niche in the Qibla wall of a mosque indicating direction of prayer

MIKVE (Heb – pl. Mikvaot) Jewish ritual bath

MINBAR (Ar) Pulpit for sermons in a mosque

MISHNAH (Heb) Legal codification of Jewish oral law, core of the Talmud (see p.501)

MITZPE (Heb) Hilltop settlement

MITZVA (Heb; literally "commandment") Jewish religious obligation

MIZRAHI (Heb; literally "Eastern") Sephardi (see below)

MOSHAV (Heb) Cooperative village combining collective and private farming (see p.62)

MOSHAV SHITUFI (Heb) Cooperative village with private housing but collective farming (see p.62)

MUEZZIN (Ar) The one who calls Muslims to prayer from the minaret of a mosque

MUFTI (Ar) Expounder of Islamic law, leader, but particularly the Grand Mufti of Jerusalem, Haj Amin al-Husseini (see p.492)

MUKHTAR (Ar) Village leader

NABI (Ar) Prophet

NAHAL (Heb) River or agricultural/military settlement operated by army unit

NARGILE (Ar) Hookah, water-pipe

NEVE (Heb) Oasis

-NIK (Yiddish suffix) Person, as in "Kibbutznik", "Peacenik", "Likudnik", "No-goodnik"

OLIM (Heb) New immigrants

OMMAYADS see UMMAYADS

PA Palestinian Authority, same as the PNA

PALMAH (Heb – guttural final "h", like the "ch" in "loch") Haganah commando strike force

PASHA (Tur) local representative of the Ottoman sultan, in practice often a largely independent local chieftain

PDFLP Popular Democratic Front for the Liberation of Palestine, same as the DFLP

PEACE NOW (Shalom Akhshav) Israeli peace movement founded in 1978

PFLP Popular Front for the Liberation of Palestine, radical left-wing PLO faction

PFLP(GC) Popular Front for the Liberation of Palestine (General Command), a PFLP splinter group

PLF Palestine Liberation Front, a name used by two separate guerrilla groups: one established in the mid-1960s, and a splinter from the PFLP(GC) active in the late 1970s

PLO Palestine Liberation Organization, umbrella group for Palestinian resistance organizations

PNA Palestinian National Authority, ruling body of autonomous Palestine

PNC Palestine National Council, ruling body of the PLO

PURPLE LINE Demarcation line between the Golan Heights and the rest of Syria

QADI (Ar) Muslim judge

QAL'A (Ar) Fort

QASR (Ar) Palace

QIBLA (Ar) Direction of prayer for Muslims, ie towards Mecca

QIRYA/KIRYA (Heb – Qiryat before another word) Town or suburb

QUR'AN (Ar) Muslim holy scriptures (a variant spelling of "Koran")

RAMADAN Muslim month of fasting

RAS (Ar; literally "head") Summit or headland

REHOV (Heb) Street

REVISIONISM Right-wing Zionist tendency (see p.492)

RIBAT (Ar) Pilgrims' hostels

SABIL/SEBIL (Ar) Drinking fountain

SABRA (Heb; literally "prickly pear") Native-born Israeli

SANHEDRIN (Heb) Jewish religious council of rabbis

SEDERA (Heb – pl., or when followed by name, Sederot) Boulevard

SEPHARDI (Heb; literally "Spanish") Jews of non-Western, especially Arab, origin

SERVICE TAXI Seven-seater communal taxi (see p.32)

SHAB/SHEB (Ar – pl. Shabab) Youth

SHALOM AKHSHAV (Heb) Peace Now protest movement (see p.497)

SHARIA' (Ar) Street or road

SHARIY'A (Ar) Muslim law

SHAS (Heb) Sephardi Orthodox political party

SHEESHA (Ar) Hookah, water-pipe

SHEIKH (Ar) Term of respect for learned, or old, man (Sheikha, for a woman); often local (ex-) squire, or Sufi holy man

SHERUT (Heb) Service taxi (see p.32)

SHESH BESH (Tur; literally "double six") Backgammon

SHI'A, SHI'ITES Minority faction of Islam, originally supporters of Mohammed's son-in-law, fourth caliph Ali, against the Ummayads

SHIKUN (Heb) Housing estate

SHTETL (Yid) Jewish village or ghetto in pre-Holocaust Eastern Europe

SHUQ (Heb) Market

SOUQ (Ar) Market, often covered

SPECIAL Privately hired (as opposed to "service") taxi

STERN GANG Splinter of the Irgun (see p.85)

SUFI (Ar) Muslim mystic

SULTAN (Ar) King, ruler

SUNNI (Ar) Orthodox Muslim, follower of the Ummayad and Abbasid caliphs

SURA (Ar) Chapter of the Koran

TALA'A (Ar) Ascent

TALMUD (Heb) The Mishnah and Gemara; the oral law of Moses as codified by rabbis in the second to sixth century AD (see p.501)

TARIQ (Ar) Way or path, small city street

TAWLA (Ar) Backgammon

TAYELET (Heb) Promenade

TEL (Ar/Heb) Mound created by layers of ancient settlements

TORAH (Heb; literally "law") The Pentateuch or Five Books of Moses, the first five books of the Old Testament (see p.501)

TZAHAL (Heb acronym meaning "Israel Defence Force") The army

TURBA (Ar) Tomb or graveyard

ULPAN (Heb) Intensive Hebrew school for new immigrants

UMMAYADS Dynasty of caliphs who ruled the Arab empire from Damascus 661–749 (see p.505)

UNLU (United National Leadership of the Uprising) Committee to coordinate the Intifada (see p.498)

WADI (Ar) River or creek

WAQF (Ar – pl. Awqaf) Trust or endowment set aside for charitable or religious purposes; organization administering such property (see p.505)

YA'AR (Heb) Forest

YAD (Heb) Memorial

YARMULKE (Yid) Jewish skullcap

YESH GVUL (Heb; literally "There's a Limit") Movement against conscription in the Palestinian Territories

YESHIVA (Heb – pl. Yeshivot) Jewish religious seminary

YISHUV (Heb) Jewish community in Palestine prior to establishment of Israel

YOM-TOV (Heb; literally "good day") Jewish religious festival

ZAWIYYA (Ar) Living quarters for Muslim holy men

ZIMMER (Heb) Room available for bed and breakfast

ZIONISM Jewish nationalism, belief in a Jewish state in some or all of pre-1948 Palestine, or simply support for the State of Israel (see p.490)

INDEX

Stay in touch with us!

ROUGHNEWS** is Rough Guides' free newsletter.
In three issues a year we give you news, travel
issues, music reviews, readers' letters and the
latest dispatches from authors on the road.

I would like to receive ROUGH*NEWS*: please put me on your free mailing list.

NAME . . . .

ADDRESS . . . .

Please clip or photocopy and send to: Rough Guides, 1 Mercer Street, London WC2H 9QJ, England
or Rough Guides, 375 Hudson Street, New York, NY 10014, USA.

direct orders from

Amsterdam	1-85828-218-7	UK£8.99	US$14.95	CAN$19.99
Andalucia	1-85828-219-5	9.99	16.95	22.99
Antigua Mini Guide	1-85828-346-9	5.99	9.95	12.99
Australia	1-85828-220-9	13.99	21.95	29.99
Austria	1-85828-325-6	10.99	17.95	23.99
Bali & Lombok	1-85828-134-2	8.99	14.95	19.99
Bangkok Mini Guide	1-85828-345-0	5.99	9.95	12.99
Barcelona	1-85828-221-7	8.99	14.95	19.99
Belgium & Luxembourg	1-85828-222-5	10.99	17.95	23.99
Belize	1-85828-351-5	9.99	16.95	22.99
Berlin	1-85828-327-2	9.99	16.95	22.99
Boston Mini Guide	1-85828-321-3	5.99	9.95	12.99
Brazil	1-85828-223-3	13.99	21.95	29.99
Britain	1-85828-312-4	14.99	23.95	31.99
Brittany & Normandy	1-85828-224-1	9.99	16.95	22.99
Bulgaria	1-85828-183-0	9.99	16.95	22.99
California	1-85828-330-2	11.99	18.95	24.99
Canada	1-85828-311-6	12.99	19.95	25.99
Central America	1-85828-335-3	14.99	23.95	31.99
China	1-85828-225-X	15.99	24.95	32.99
Corfu & the Ionian Islands	1-85828-226-8	8.99	14.95	19.99
Corsica	1-85828-227-6	9.99	16.95	22.99
Costa Rica	1-85828-136-9	9.99	15.95	21.99
Crete	1-85828-316-7	9.99	16.95	22.99
Cyprus	1-85828-182-2	9.99	16.95	22.99
Czech & Slovak Republics	1-85828-317-5	11.99	18.95	24.99
Dublin Mini Guide	1-85828-294-2	5.99	9.95	12.99
Edinburgh Mini Guide	1-85828-295-0	5.99	9.95	12.99
Egypt	1-85828-188-1	10.99	17.95	23.99
Europe 1998	1-85828-289-6	14.99	19.95	25.99
England	1-85828-301-9	12.99	19.95	25.99
First Time Asia	1-85828-332-9	7.99	9.95	12.99
First Time Europe	1-85828-270-5	7.99	9.95	12.99
Florida	1-85828-184-4	10.99	16.95	22.99
France	1-85828-228-4	12.99	19.95	25.99
Germany	1-85828-309-4	14.99	23.95	31.99
Goa	1-85828-275-6	8.99	14.95	19.99
Greece	1-85828-300-0	12.99	19.95	25.99
Greek Islands	1-85828-310-8	10.99	17.95	23.99
Guatemala	1-85828-323-X	9.99	16.95	22.99
Hawaii: Big Island	1-85828-158-X	8.99	12.95	16.99
Hawaii	1-85828-206-3	10.99	16.95	22.99
Holland	1-85828-229-2	10.99	17.95	23.99
Hong Kong & Macau	1-85828-187-3	8.99	14.95	19.99
Hotels & Restos de France 1998	1-85828-306-X	12.99	19.95	25.99
Hungary	1-85828-123-7	8.99	14.95	19.99
India	1-85828-200-4	14.99	23.95	31.99
Ireland	1-85828-179-2	10.99	17.95	23.99
Israel & the Palestinian Territories	1-85828-248-9	12.99	19.95	25.99
Italy	1-85828-167-9	12.99	19.95	25.99
Jamaica	1-85828-230-6	9.99	16.95	22.99
Japan	1-85828-340-X	14.99	23.95	31.99
Jordan	1-85828-350-7	10.99	17.95	23.99
Kenya	1-85828-192-X	11.99	18.95	24.99
Lisbon Mini Guide	1-85828-297-7	5.99	9.95	12.99
London	1-85828-231-4	9.99	15.95	21.99
Madrid Mini Guide	1-85828-353-1	5.99	9.95	12.99
Mallorca & Menorca	1-85828-165-2	8.99	14.95	19.99
Malaysia, Singapore & Brunei	1-85828-232-2	11.99	18.95	24.99
Mexico	1-85828-044-3	10.99	16.95	22.99
Morocco	1-85828-169-5	11.99	18.95	24.99
Moscow	1-85828-322-1	9.99	16.95	22.99
Nepal	1-85828-190-3	10.99	17.95	23.99
New York	1-85828-296-9	9.99	15.95	21.99
New Zealand	1-85828-233-0	12.99	19.95	25.99
Norway	1-85828-234-9	10.99	17.95	23.99

UK orders: 0181 899 4036

around the world

Pacific Northwest	1-85828-326-4	UK£12.99	US$19.95	CAN$25.99
Paris	1-85828-235-7	8.99	14.95	19.99
Peru	1-85828-142-3	10.99	17.95	23.99
Poland	1-85828-168-7	10.99	17.95	23.99
Portugal	1-85828-313-2	10.99	17.95	23.99
Prague	1-85828-318-3	8.99	14.95	19.99
Provence & the Cote d'Azur	1-85828-127-X	9.99	16.95	22.99
The Pyrenees	1-85828-308-6	10.99	17.95	23.99
Rhodes & the Dodecanese	1-85828-120-2	8.99	14.95	19.99
Romania	1-85828-305-1	10.99	17.95	23.99
San Francisco	1-85828-299-3	8.99	14.95	19.99
Scandinavia	1-85828-236-5	12.99	20.95	27.99
Scotland	1-85828-302-7	9.99	16.95	22.99
Seattle Mini Guide	1-85828-324-8	5.99	9.95	12.99
Sicily	1-85828-178-4	9.99	16.95	22.99
Singapore	1-85828-237-3	8.99	14.95	19.99
South Africa	1-85828-238-1	12.99	19.95	25.99
Southwest USA	1-85828-239-X	10.99	16.95	22.99
Spain	1-85828-240-3	11.99	18.95	24.99
St Petersburg	1-85828-298-5	9.99	16.95	22.99
Sweden	1-85828-241-1	10.99	17.95	23.99
Syria	1-85828-331-0	11.99	18.95	24.99
Thailand	1-85828-140-7	10.99	17.95	24.99
Tunisia	1-85828-139-3	10.99	17.95	24.99
Turkey	1-85828-242-X	12.99	19.95	25.99
Tuscany & Umbria	1-85828-243-8	10.99	17.95	23.99
USA	1-85828-307-8	14.99	19.95	25.99
Venice	1-85828-170-9	8.99	14.95	19.99
Vienna	1-85828-244-6	8.99	14.95	19.99
Vietnam	1-85828-191-1	9.99	15.95	21.99
Wales	1-85828-245-4	10.99	17.95	23.99
Washington DC	1-85828-246-2	8.99	14.95	19.99
West Africa	1-85828-101-6	15.99	24.95	34.99
Zimbabwe & Botswana	1-85828-186-5	11.99	18.95	24.99
Phrasebooks				
Czech	1-85828-148-2	3.50	5.00	7.00
Egyptian Arabic	1-85828-319-1	4.00	6.00	8.00
French	1-85828-144-X	3.50	5.00	7.00
German	1-85828-146-6	3.50	5.00	7.00
Greek	1-85828-145-8	3.50	5.00	7.00
Hindi & Urdu	1-85828-252-7	4.00	6.00	8.00
Hungarian	1-85828-304-3	4.00	6.00	8.00
Indonesian	1-85828-250-0	4.00	6.00	8.00
Italian	1-85828-143-1	3.50	5.00	7.00
Japanese	1-85828-303-5	4.00	6.00	8.00
Mandarin Chinese	1-85828-249-7	4.00	6.00	8.00
Mexican Spanish	1-85828-176-8	3.50	5.00	7.00
Portuguese	1-85828-175-X	3.50	5.00	7.00
Polish	1-85828-174-1	3.50	5.00	7.00
Russian	1-85828-251-9	4.00	6.00	8.00
Spanish	1-85828-147-4	3.50	5.00	7.00
Swahili	1-85828-320-5	4.00	6.00	8.00
Thai	1-85828-177-6	3.50	5.00	7.00
Turkish	1-85828-173-3	3.50	5.00	7.00
Vietnamese	1-85828-172-5	3.50	5.00	7.00
Reference				
Classical Music	1-85828-113-X	12.99	19.95	25.99
European Football	1-85828-256-X	14.99	23.95	31.99
Internet	1-85828-288-8	5.00	8.00	10.00
Jazz	1-85828-137-7	16.99	24.95	34.99
Millennium	1-85828-314-0	5.00	8.95	11.99
More Women Travel	1-85828-098-2	10.99	16.95	22.99
Opera	1-85828-138-5	16.99	24.95	34.99
Reggae	1-85828-247-0	12.99	19.95	25.99
Rock	1-85828-201-2	17.99	26.95	35.00
World Music	1-85828-017-6	16.99	22.95	29.99

US/International orders: 1-800-253-6476